21293

D1121480

Library
Oakland S.U.M.

Library
Oakland S.U.M.

THE WORKS OF
THOMAS GOODWIN

The Works of
THOMAS GOODWIN

Volume VIII
The Object and Acts of Justifying Faith

THE BANNER OF TRUTH TRUST

THE BANNER OF TRUTH TRUST
3 Murrayfield Road, Edinburgh EH12 6EL
P.O. Box 621, Carlisle, Pennsylvania 17013, U.S.A.

*

Reprinted from Volume Eight of the
Works of Thomas Goodwin, published by James Nichol in 1863

First Banner of Truth Trust edition 1985

ISBN 0 85151 447 2

*

Printed in Great Britain at
The Camelot Press Ltd, Southampton

THE WORKS

OF

THOMAS GOODWIN, D.D.,

SOMETIME PRESIDENT OF MAGDALENE COLLEGE, OXFORD.

𝔚𝔦𝔱𝔥 𝔊𝔢𝔫𝔢𝔯𝔞𝔩 𝔓𝔯𝔢𝔣𝔞𝔠𝔢

BY JOHN C. MILLER, D.D.,

LINCOLN COLLEGE ; HONORARY CANON OF WORCESTER ; RECTOR OF ST MARTIN'S, BIRMINGHAM.

𝔄𝔫𝔡 𝔐𝔢𝔪𝔬𝔦𝔯

BY ROBERT HALLEY, D.D.,

PRINCIPAL OF THE INDEPENDENT NEW COLLEGE, LONDON.

VOL. VIII.

CONTAINING :

THE OBJECT AND ACTS OF JUSTIFYING FAITH.

EDINBURGH : JAMES NICHOL.

LONDON: JAMES NISBET AND CO.   DUBLIN: W. ROBERTSON.

M.DCCC.LXIV.

EDINBURGH
PRINTED BY JOHN GREIG AND SON
OLD PHYSIC GARDENS.

CONTENTS.

A PREFACE TO THE READER.*

As in this fourth volume of the author's works, which by the generous encouragement of some few worthy gentlemen, who in a noble zeal to promote the doctrines of the gospel, engaged to take off the whole impression, there are great and important truths discoursed with the same life and spirit which shined in the former, so I doubt not but it will find the same grateful acceptance. After the discourse of the person and mediation of our blessed Lord Jesus, which you had in the third volume, it naturally follows in order to have the knowledge of the genuine nature of that faith which looks to the Mediator, and comes to him from an interest in his person, sacrifice, blood, and righteousness. You have first the infinite mercies of God's nature displayed as far as man's thoughts and words can reach them, proposed as the great object which a believer regards, as the spring of all those acts of grace exerted in saving a sinner, and in which he trusts and hopes. You have then the promises, which are nothing but the mercies of the divine nature, and his gracious purposes proclaimed to us, and so are absolute as they themselves are, proposed as another object which the soul considers in believing. You have then Jesus Christ set forth as the great object of faith in his person God-man; and it is indeed a sufficient argument to prove his divinity, that we are commanded to believe on him; nor could we have a certain and undoubted faith in him if he were not God: for what assured confidence and hope could we have in a creature, whose goodness, wisdom, and power, in the highest excellence of them, are imperfect and defective ? The author therefore insists on it, that the true believer who heartily comes to Christ for life and salvation, regards him as the Son of God, and looks to and considers the spiritual excellencies of his person. He is the object of faith, too, in respect of what he hath done and suffered for our salvation, and of what he at present doth. He is the object of faith proposed to us in his death, resurrection, and intercession : and therefore I once had thoughts to have drawn into this discourse of the object and acts of faith, as into their proper place, those

---

* As the greater portion of this preface relates to the treatise contained in this volume, it is inserted here.—ED.

treatises of the triumph of faith in Christ's death, resurrection, and intercession, which were many years ago printed in quarto by my dear father
himself. But when I considered that that excellent book is in so many
hands, and perhaps the most of them who will have this volume have that
already, I apprehended it would look like a wrong, and an imposing upon
them, to reprint it again, to make them pay for what they had already.
Therefore the reader is to take notice, that the latter end of the title of the
second book in this first part of the object of faith, directs him to those
discourses of the triumph of faith which are in the quarto volume.

The second part of this treatise is concerning the acts of faith, in which
that chapter about joy in the Holy Ghost was his *Concio ad Clerum*, which
the author made when he commenced Bachelor of Divinity in Cambridge,
but finding in his papers that he designed it to be a part of this discourse,
and not finding that he had done it into English himself, I translated it,
that it might be suitable to the other parts, though my English doth not
reach the eloquence of his Latin.

The third part treats of the properties of faith, and in it you have discouragements removed, and the Arminian objections answered. They
reproach us, that by depriving men unregenerate of power to believe, and
by ascribing the work of faith entirely to grace, we make men's endeavours
to believe impossible, and all their attempts of this nature frivolous and
vain. The author, with great strength of thought and clearness of expression, baffles these unreasonable cavils, and shews how the prevailing and
always victorious grace of God and our endeavours may very well be consistent together.

In the discourse of the order and government of the churches of Christ,*
though the author hath drawn down those forms which have been erected
by men, and fashioned to suit with the political regiment of kingdoms, and
hath in the room of it asserted that order which is of Christ's own institution, which, though it doth not dazzle and take men's vain minds with any
appearance of greatness and state, yet sufficiently recommends itself by its
own plain native beauty. Though it is not pompous, yet it is handsome ;
though it is not framed according to the admired rules of human policy,
yet it is orderly, and so perfectly suited by the wisdom of the Great King
of saints to the cases, circumstances, and necessities of them his subjects
in all ages, so fitted to prevent corruption both of doctrine and manners, to
promote holiness, and to attain all the ends of religion, that as there never
hath been any need, so there never will be, to add anything to his orders.
It is this institution of Christ which the author asserts, but maintains it
with that candour as well as strength of mind, that they who differ from
him in judgment cannot be angry. Here is no pride nor arrogance, which
is insufferable in any man, much more in a minister of the gospel. Here
are no reproaches, no base and sly insinuations, no invidious reflections
with which controversies are usually managed ; but here are sober thoughts,

* To be given in a subsequent volume of this series.—ED.

calm reasonings, and the truth shewing itself in such a mild and lovely aspect as may create inclinations to it in the souls of all persons whom passion or interest hath not too much prejudiced.

Thus I have endeavoured to set before thee at one view the general design of this book ; and that thou mayest see that thou hast all the MSS. which I promised printed in it, I have annexed a catalogue* of them, directing in what part of the book thou mayest find any of them.

I am,

Thy hearty servant,

In our Lord Jesus,

THO. GOODWIN.

* This catalogue it has not been thought necessary to insert.—ED.

OF THE OBJECT AND ACTS OF JUSTIFYING FAITH.

PART I.

Of the object of faith.

BOOK I.

The mercies in God's nature the object, and support, and encouragement of faith.—How we are to act faith thereon.

CHAPTER I.

The words of the text opened.—That the mercies in God's heart and nature are a fundamental object and support of faith.—Presumption thereon beaten off.

Let Israel hope in the Lord: for with the Lord there is mercy, and with him is plenteous redemption.—PSALM CXXX. 7.

THE ' work of faith,' John vi. 29, whereby a sinner's heart is first won, then strengthened and supported to trust and stay itself on God for its eternal salvation, is in general experience found to be a matter of greatest difficulty, exercise, and conflict. There is need therefore of all sorts of encouragements and suggests that can possibly be raised out of the holy Scriptures, with the largest dilatings on them, which may either serve to bring humbled and broken hearts and God together at first, or afterwards to hearten them to ' hold fast the beginning of their confidence firm and stedfast to the end,' Heb. iii. 6, 14, and all little enough ; such, and so great, and so manifold are the discouragements which unbelief within us doth foment, and which Satan doth indiscernibly cast in. Now above all other inducers and supporters unto faith, the consideration of the mercies in God's heart and nature is the strongest, the most winning and obliging. Unto thoroughly humbled and broken hearts it is I write this. As for others, who were never heavy laden with sin, look as sin sits light upon their hearts, so they set as light by the mercies of God, and a confused slight apprehension that God is merciful (which yet is their common plea) serves their turn, and is a salve sufficient for their sore ; which indeed is but proportionable unto that like confused apprehension of their sinfulness, which in like manner they use to wrap up, that we are all sinners. Ay, but take a soul that hath been unhinged from off the opinion of his being in a good estate, which is so natural to us, and our souls do turn themselves upon, and who also is made thoroughly sensible of the abounding ' sinfulness of sin,' as sin, the least ; and then hath taken in the dismal prospect of the heinous guilt of his bold presumptions and crying rebellions against knowledge, and especially hath been amazed with that numberless account of the innumerable multitude and variety of sinnings which he is to give unto God the judge of all men ; and together herewith hath been struck as with lightning and a thunderbolt, with the dreadfulness of that wrath of the great God that is due thereunto (all which apprehensions do yet prepare men's souls for faith justifying, and dispose them the more readily to attend to, and take in these encouragements unto faith that follow); and to work some apprehensions of these, and to set forth these, hath been the drift of those the subjects of the foregoing treatises. Unto such a soul (I say), filled with the apprehensions of these things, the most enlarged, full discovery that can any way be made of the riches of the mercies that are in the heart and nature of God, and of the fulness of merit that is in Christ's righteousness and redemption, do all prove little enough effective, either to beget a sound and saving faith, when upon this conviction it is anew to be wrought in such a soul, or when some beginnings of that faith are in some degree raised to keep it up, nourish and sustain it in a comfortable rest and confidence unto the end ; which difficulty doth not arise from any want or scantiness in the objects themselves, which are so overrich and superabundant for the pardon of sinners, but from the deep incredulity, and vast fears, jealousies, and misgivings which our souls (when the hideous apparitions of sin and wrath are raised up once in men's consciences) do create and harbour in themselves in matters of so infinite moment, as salvation and damnation appear then to be at such times. The truth of these things, besides daily experience, we may readily perceive by the pulse of his heart that penned this psalm, and the beatings thereof therein ; who being sunk into the greatest depths—' Out of the depths have I cried,' &c.—which depths (when we fathom them) we find to be his sins, both in the multitude and heinousness of them, as the following verse, ver. 3, tells us : ' If thou, Lord, shouldst mark iniquities' (therein lay the bottom of his distress), ' O Lord, who shall stand ? ' In which conflict and sad condition, what hath his faith its next and immediate recourse unto of all other things, which the word of God (for that, as the 5th verse says, he consulted) did afford, and which he commends unto all the Israel of God, ver. 7, as the mainest prop and support unto his and their faith? Even this : ' With the Lord there is mercy, and with him there is plenteous redemption,' ver. 7 ; and then again, ' With thee there is forgiveness,' verse 4, as the fruit both of mercy and redemption ; and therefore it is that ' my soul doth wait for the Lord,' ver. 7. And therefore ' let Israel hope in the Lord.' And ' he shall redeem Israel from all his iniquities,' ver. 7 and 8. This is the summary effect of this psalm. Nor yet herein do we find this poor humbled soul to pitch his hope and confidence upon any gracious works had been wrought, or were in or with himself; he is altogether silent as to any mention of such, but wholly and absolutely his affiance is upon what was with God, and in God : ' Mercy is with him,' &c., says he.   And this is it was the foundation and bottom of his hope ; this was all he had now to say ; and yet opposeth this alone unto all the sins and iniquities which came up before his view, whether in their greatness or multitude.   There is mercy with God, enough to pardon them, yea, and more than enough : ' *plenteous* redemption,' overflowing redemption, and of mercies together with it.   Again, whether all these mercies were as yet his own in particular or no, he speaks not that neither; not whether God were the God of his mercies (as David, when established in assurance, elsewhere speaks, Ps. lxxxix. 24), but only utters this for the present (and that he was sure of) that ' mercy was with God,' and in God : ' Forgiveness was with him ;' there it was to be had for such sinners as he was, and for the Israel of God, and therefore he personally puts in for a share in them ; that was all his hope.   Yea, and thereupon he quietly ' waits,' as he there professeth to do, till the Lord should give forth some farther special word of comfort to his doleful and desolate soul.

I. Three things are here said to be with God, which phrase, *with God*, he again and again chooseth to express the grounds of his hope in God by. He applies it: 1. To mercy, the original and womb of all: ' Mercy is with him.'   When a quality is in one as a disposition, or his nature, we find it said, that it is *with* him : of Nabal, ' Folly is *with him ;* as is his name, so is he,' 1 Sam. xxv. 25.   2. To redemption, which I understand to be the mediation and satisfaction of the Messiah (which was in those times in the psalmist and other believers' eyes) the procuring cause of all.   3. To forgiveness, as the fruit and effect of both : ' Forgiveness also is with thee.'

Yet, II., these three are said to be with him in a differing sense or respect.

1. Mercy is with God ; that is, it is in him as his nature, and is all one as if he had said, He is of himself, and of his own inclination, a most gracious and merciful God, mercifully disposed to forgive ; ' ready to forgive,' as the 86th Psalm expresseth it.   It is his name, it is his nature ; and in this sense it is said to be with him.   It is also in his purposes and resolutions of his will ; yea, it is the ' delight' of his soul.

2. Redemption is in that sense said to be with God, as his treasures are elsewhere said to be with him, that is, laid up with him or by him, Deut. xxxii. 34.   And thus Christ's redemption or righteousness was then with him, in the virtue of Christ's bond and covenant given to God to perform it ; and as truly with God then as since that Christ hath actually paid it, Christ being ' the Lamb slain from the beginning of the world.'   And God did accordingly then under the Old Testament pardon sinners upon the intuition and security thereof, as Rom. iii. 25, 26 shews ; which place plainly speaks forth this truth, as also Acts xv. 11 the same.   In Job, you have a term equivalent unto the psalmist's word ' redemption:' Job xxxiii. 24, ' Deliver him' (saith God of an humbled sinner); ' I have found a ransom,' or atonement.

III. In the virtue and intuition of these two it is that David says, ' Forgiveness is also with him ;' that is, it is laid up ready by him on purpose to be had from him ; as money coined lies ready by a rich man, as a rich man lays up ready money designed for such a special use, so is forgiveness laid up as on purpose.   He is ' ready to forgive,' Ps. lxxxvi. 5.   And God hath minted his mercies forth from out of his purposes into promises, where they lie exposed, and to be given forth to every one that will come in for grace, and take them from mercy's hands, even ' redemption from all iniquity,' whereof there is this undoubted evidence given in the psalm, that God would have the sons of men thereupon, and for that cause to ' fear' him; that is, to worship him and come to him, which if forgiveness were not *with him*, and to be had from him, for him, they would never do. You find moreover a special encomium of *plenteous* given to one of those three, in saying 'plenteous redemption,' which is placed in the midst of the three, on purpose to shew that the glory of this epithet is to be trans-fused to both those other; and so what is given to that one is in like manner to be attributed to the other two, but especially unto the first, viz., mercy, which hath in other scriptures eminently the glory of riches or plenteousness ascribed unto it, that being the original both of redemp-tion and forgiveness, and they but derivatives from it. And so it is all one as if he had plainly said, that '*plenteous* mercy' also is with him. And indeed elsewhere David gives the very same attribute unto mercy: Ps. ciii. 8, 'The Lord is plenteous in mercy.' And for that other of for-giveness (the effect of both), it is impliedly all one as if he had said of that also, that 'plenteous forgiveness is with him,' which very style God himself doth in terms equivalent elsewhere use of it: Isa. lv. 7, ' I will abundantly pardon.' So then plenteousness and riches were intended, and are to be attributed to them all, but above all unto mercy, of which you so often read the same to be spoken of; as ' abundant mercy,' 1 Peter i. 3; ' the exceeding riches of his grace,' Eph. ii. 7.

The heart and drift of the psalmist being thus laid open, I begin with the MERCIES of God, these being the original, the matrix, the *primo primum*, the first causes of our salvation, and that other of Christ's right-eousness (or redemption) but a *primo ortum*, or that which sprang or rose up from thence. This therefore of the mercies in God's heart ought to have the priority, as having deservedly the pre-eminence in the thing itself, and as being most fundamental, and accordingly procreative of faith.

Obs. The observation for our practice which comes forth and meets us out of the whole is, that it is a most behoveful and advantageous way for humbled sinners, in their treaties with God for forgiveness, to take the most ample view of the infinite mercies that are in the heart and nature of God, together with promises of forgiveness indefinitely delivered, and so to plead them unto God; which to do will prove the greatest support and strength to their souls for believing. This I confess to be in view so plain a point, and so obvious in the very proposal of it unto every common understanding in Christianity, that it will perhaps be wondered at that I should so largely insist upon it; yet this I will aforehand say, that the true and real spiritual exercise and practice of it, as it is not commonly enough and experimentally understood, but very greatly disused, so the use and benefit that follows thereupon is exceeding great, and not suffi-ciently known. And unto souls humbled and broken as aforesaid, that this course should be taken by them, is so remote from strengthening presumption in them, that on the contrary, through the efficacy of the same mercy, it proves most operative to make the soul holy and obedient unto God, according unto that true, ancient, and frequent character given of saints under the Old Testament, where we find these two joined, as impossible to be ever separated (when they are in truth either of them), ' one that feareth God' (whereby his obedience is expressed), and ' that hopes in his mercy' (whereby his faith is expressed); as Ps. xxxiii. 18,

' Behold, the eye of the Lord is upon them that fear him, upon them that hope in his mercy;' and Ps. cxlvii. 11, ' The Lord taketh pleasure in them that fear him, in those that hope in his mercy.' And as you find these two distinctly thus mentioned, and these two alone mentioned, to speak the whole sum of all true practical religion, so of the two you find the special indigitation to be set over and put on that latter of these characters in both places, ' *upon them* that hope in his mercy.' Those, and those especially, that are eminent in that grace it is that ' his eyes are upon,' and whom he hath pleasure in. And let this be sufficient once for all to strike off the presumptuousness of impenitent sinners, that resolve to go on in sin, from laying on impure hands upon these ' holy mercies' (as the mercies of Christ are styled by the apostle, Acts xiii. 34, out of Isa. lv. 3, see the margin of your Bibles). And finally, to roll the fatal stone upon the sepulchre of such sinners as shall thus presume on mercy, take but that one scripture, Deut. xxix. 18–20, ' If any man or woman hearing the words of this curse' (which is there pronounced upon one's turning away from the Lord after the tender of the covenant of grace, published in that and the following chapter, as Rom. x. shews), ' shall bless himself in his heart, saying, I shall have peace, though I walk in the imagination of mine heart: the anger of the Lord shall smoke against that man, and all the curses that are written in this book shall lie upon him, and the Lord shall blot out his name from under heaven.' And this, to be sure, is load enough to press down such sinners above any other to the very bottom of hell, who, bearing themselves upon that grace made known and tendered them, shall wilfully go on in sin without repentance and turning unto God.

CHAPTER II.

An explication how this assertion is to be understood: 1. On the negative. Not as if alone considered, the mercies in God (as they are abstractly in God's nature) were a sole foundation for faith, but as being joined with an indefinite declaration of his good will to us men; and in that conjuncture all the mercies that are in God do flow in to support our faith. This negative part of this explication confirmed from the instance of the devils, and of our first parents, until God's revelation of his good will to mankind made to them. 2. The positive ground of faith laid open, and the reason why a declaration of his will is necessary.—Two premissory cautions more added, for the understanding the assertion.

Ere I come to the proof of the assertion, it is necessary to state and explain it, to prevent mistakes.

And first, on the negative; it is not as if the knowledge of the mercies in God's nature were alone a single adequate ground of faith, though we could attain unto never so enlarged apprehensions thereof. This negative is evident,

1. Because where and whom God hath absolutely and peremptorily, and for ever, by a special bar and proviso, declared, and excepted from mercy and pardon, there and unto those all the mercies that are in God's nature, though known by them, can no way be drawn in, or ever become an object or ground for their faith, such as shall anyway benefit those persons

declared against. This is the case of the devils, who are shut out from mercy : and this not only by that single bolt of the law, ' Cursed be every one that continues not,' &c. ; for that doth alike shut us men up, until faith, that is, the gospel, be revealed; but they have that, and a farther and stronger bolt and bar, never to be shot back, or rather (as the apostle meta-phors it), ' everlasting chains,' of God's making, never to be broken or knocked off, that hold them fast under darkness. Which chains are super-added to that single sentence or curse, which merely the law pronounceth against them, for that alone might have been annulled through a grace of pardon, as well as to us men it is ; but God did further declare, irreco-verably against them, and each of them, personally, on the negative, that he will never be merciful to them : ' He spared them not,' says the apostle, ' but cast them down to hell, and delivered them into chains of darkness, to be reserved unto judgment ;' he gave them no quarter. And thereupon some divines have said (which I will not dispute) that despair of mercy, taken abstractly for this single apprehension in their understand-ings, that God will have no mercy on them ; and that apprehension also, as it is accompanied simply with no hope of mercy, that this alone would be no sin in them, seeing it is but conformed unto what is the truth, which God hath revealed to them concerning themselves ; only the consequences hereof in them are the sins, as blasphemy and the like.

2. But however, secondly, I may more safely assert, whatsoever the devils do believe, or may be supposed to believe, of the mercies that are in God's nature, that yet, however, their faith thereof doth no way capacitate them to lay hold upon them for pardon, but cause them the more to tremble at the thoughts that they are for ever utterly excluded, whilst they revolve within themselves that such riches of mercy are in God, but in nowise do concern them, and withal to think (which hath the sting in it) that all those mercies should be ' kept,' and entirely ' reserved' (as God's expression in the second commandment is) for the sinners of the sons of men, while themselves, on the contrary, are ' kept' and reserved under those ' chains unto judgment,' as the words of two apostles are, 2 Pet. ii. 4, Jude 6. But, that these apprehensions should enrage and provoke them unto that resolved and obstinate malice and revenge, which they bear against God, these all, I am sure (without any debate), are sins, yea, the highest kinds of sinnings, and yet are but the consequents of that despair fore-mentioned, which in itself alone would be no sin.

3. Nor yet, thirdly, would the single knowledge of all the mercies that are in the nature of God have been a full and sole ground of actual posi-tive faith, unto us sinners of the sons of men, had not God after the fall first unbosomed himself, and declared his purposes of mercy towards us in his Messiah. Our first parents, during that doleful space of *interim* (sus-pension shall I call it) between their fall and that ever-to-be-blessed decla-ration let fall by God, of his good will to men, in the promise of the blessed ' seed of the woman,' &c., until then, I say, although they were not utterly debarred upon their sinning, as the devils were upon theirs, yet they had not any ground or footing for a positive act of faith, for forgive-ness : notwithstanding we should or might suppose them to have known, and (after their fall) to have retained, and continued to have known or remembered that infinite goodness, which is the spring of mercies in God, to have been in the divine nature, as well as any other divine perfections ; and that possibly that goodness might be dissolved and melted into mercy and forgiveness unto sinners, such as now themselves were become. But

yet still the curse of the law, ' Thou shalt die the death,' standing in full force and full butt (as we say) against them ; and that being the whole of the mind and will of God, which at that present was revealed to them ; therefore they had no ' door of faith' and hope in any way open before them, but were, as to their own apprehension, utterly shut up, unless some ' word of faith' should be further made known to them. God had not let fall the least intimation of mercy, neither by proclaiming his nature to be merciful, nor as yet had he said, ' I will be gracious to whom I will be gracious ;' nor was there any instance or example of any one of the sons of men (for, alas ! there were but those two extant) whom he had *de facto* pardoned, which might give them any encouragement or dawn of hope.

But notwithstanding, perhaps it might be proposed as a question that would require a just debate, whether an utter despair (such as we speak of to be in the devils), singly considered, and cut off from the cursed consequents fore-mentioned, had not yet in them been properly a sin during that interval, which in the devils simply and alone it is not. And the ground of the demur is this apparent difference between the devils' condition and theirs, during that space, that God had not negatively pronounced of them, I will never be merciful, as of the devils he had from the first of their sinning. Yet still this must be said, that they had not the smallest twig for a positive act of faith to ' set foot upon' (I allude to that in Noah's flood) : but in that condition of theirs, nothing in sight did appear, but an overflowing deluge of wrath, which did environ and overspread them, and their posterity in and with them, through the first curse, not as yet taken off, nor mitigated by any new declaration of God. This for the negative state of the assertion.

II. For the positive ground of faith. Blessed, yea, for ever blessed be our God, who hath not only by that promise to them, but with millions of other promises and declarations since made to us, thrown open all the windows of heaven, and freely exposed all the mercies in his heart and nature unto us the sinful sons of men, ' Peace on earth, good will towards men,' &c., not in hell, nor to the devils : and withal hath given an invitation, nay, a command, to hope in them ; and hath taught us to know him by this of his mercy, above all his perfections ; yea, and pronounced of our knowledge and faith thereon, that he esteems it to be our glory, yea, his own greatest glory, that we should ' know him to be a God that exerciseth loving-kindness, righteousness, and judgment in the earth' (on earth still, not in hell) ; and ' that therein he doth delight,' Jer. ix. 24. Moreover, in that he hath not, by any express proviso or exception, declared against any sort of sinners, or any individual person of the sons of men ; so as to say of any such, or such, I will never be merciful to, nor pardon them (as against the devils he did), that sort only excepted that sin against the Holy Ghost ; thereby it comes to pass, that not any one can say, I am debarred or excluded. And hence a wide door for hope and faith stands open, for any one to come in at. Nay, he further ' commands every man everywhere to repent,' upon the hopes of mercy, through the indefinite promulgation of it ; adding withal, ' whosoever believeth and repenteth, he shall be saved,' laying at the gage for the performance thereof, all the mercies in his nature, by which we, through these declarations, have free access unto, and full liberty to plead them all afore him, and urge him with them. The product or issue of all which is, that the revelation of the mercies of his nature, thus joined with the declarations of his gracious willingness to shew mercy to us men, is now become a just and meet ground and object for a sinner's faith : whereas otherwise, like as breasts never so full, if there were not a teat, and a vent fitted to the child's mouth, they would never afford any succour to a perishing infant, so here in this case. And it is not an allusion foreign to the Scriptures, to compare God's mercies and promises unto ' breasts of consolation.' And the reason of this conclusion is, because God's shewing or his actual exercising of mercy dependeth upon an act of his will, and is not a mere, sole, single effect of his nature. For if it were solely an act of his nature, it would have been, and would still be necessary for him to shew mercy on the devils : and therefore look as God's actual shewing mercy dependeth upon an act of his will,—' I will be merciful to whom I will,' &c.—so some revelation or manifestation of his good will (at least indefinite to mankind) is necessary for our faith, and not merely the knowledge of the mercy in his nature ; and as both concur to the effecting the thing, so also the apprehension of both should do unto our believing. And otherwise, ' Who hath known the mind of the Lord, or who hath been his counsellor ?' Rom. xi. 34. And it is notorious that the apostle utters that maxim upon this very point of God's will, in shewing mercy, for which compare ver. 30–32.

I add unto these things concerning the stating of this assertion, these two premises more, for the practical understanding of it.

1. I must not be understood, as if that every time the soul doth exercise an act of faith, he must of absolute necessity take into his thoughts such an ample review of these mercies ; and that otherwise it were not faith. No : for it often falls out, that in the exercise of believing, such things as are most fundamental to faith, and were at first explicitly taken in and considered by believers, are afterwards but as things taken for granted and supposed. And yet, notwithstanding, all those subsequent after-acts of faith are put forth in the strength of them. We may know that general principles of knowledge in any kind being once inlaid and preconceived, do yet virtually work, and the force of them conduces to the making of every conclusion, when yet we do not explicitly think of those principles. And in like manner it comes to pass, that our souls do many times really act true faith upon particular promises of forgiveness, or the like promises, when yet we did not aforehand, or together therewith, revolve in our minds at large the thoughts of these mercies, which yet are to be always supposed the bottom of those promises, and fundamental to our faith. And notwithstanding this, yet the belief of them doth secretly and really work and accompany such a faith : even as principles of knowledge, innate and taken for granted, are wont to do our improvements of knowledge from them, whilst those principles lie dormant as to our thinking, and yet those improvements grow up in the virtue and strength of them. We may see this in that one most fundamental principle of faith of all other, that there is a God ; which being inlaid in the bottom of the heart of every believer, works in all particular acts of faith whatever ; and they are all founded and borne up upon the strength and weight thereof, when itself, in the way of a formed proposition, is not discerned, nor brought forth into an explicit act or thought. And thus it falls out in the faith of forgiveness, it is always put forth in the force of the belief of those mercies, when yet the conceptions thereof lay hidden deep in the soul. Which to be so, may appear by this experiment : that all our faith for forgiveness may at any time be readily and finally resolved into the mercies of God, as the *ultimum objectum in quod*, as the ultimate object or foundation. This will be found if the heart will at any time call for the bottom-ground of its faith, or of its

recourse unto God for forgiveness, and but ask of itself the reason why it so believes, Yet,

2. It still stands good (and is even sufficiently inferred from that which was last said) that the more ample diffused prospect, view, and contemplation of these mercies, which upon all great occasions (especially in conflicts of believing) we can possibly make or attain to, is the most conducible expedite way to give an abundant evidence unto faith, and doth wonderfully hearten a broken-hearted sinner to lay hold upon any particular promise, especially of forgiveness; which otherwise comes but barely clad, in comparison of what it appears to be, when the riches of mercy (being apprehended with it) do environ and array it, which superadd wonderful allurements to our faith. And this assertion, as I said, is inferred even from what was spoken afore, viz., that if the tacit hidden belief of fundamental principles (such this is) do virtually, yet strongly, influence all subsequent acts of faith, then much more if there be an extensive revolving of them in our thoughts, they will come to have, according to the proportion of that enlargement (through the Spirit's accompanying of them), answerable effects, in an enlargement and increase of faith in us.

CHAPTER III.

The proofs of this assertion: 1, by Scripture, and afterwards by reasons.—One Scripture above all other singled forth, and that alone, Exod. xxxiv. 6, 7.— This made a new text for the subsequent discourse.—The grand assertion resolved into two heads, both of them distinctly drawn out, and proposed to be proved out of the text.—The eminency of this one Scripture is commended thereby to all our faiths.—Old Testament faith, and New, one and the same.

I come to the confirmation of the assertion, as thus stated and explained, which proceeds,

1. By Scripture.

2. By the true and innate reasons thereof, drawn from the nature of faith, and the wonderful suitedness that the mercies in God's heart hold, by way of object, with and unto that principle of faith in our hearts, so as to attract and draw forth faith in all the acts of it.

1. By Scripture. I single out only that renowned original God himself immediately published unto Moses concerning his pardoning mercies to him and us all; for unto him it was, though on our behalf also, that they were proclaimed, Exod. xxxiv. Two grand deeds there were, which Old Testament faith held all upon. The first, of the promised Messiah, given to Eve and Adam at first by God himself, the immediate revealer, and after renewed to Abraham, David, and so on. The second, this glorious display of pardoning mercies, which was as immediately, but far more solemnly proclaimed, *regio more*, by God himself. And these two were as the two pillars, Boaz and Jachim, in the house of God, and are in Ps. cxxx. set out as two known 'cities of refuge' for broken hearts to fly unto. I shall make the latter of these the stage or *substratum* of all throughout this treatise, the grace and mercy in God being the *originale originans*, the womb or original even of the promise of Christ himself, and bears up an answerable pre-eminence of order and stress in the foundation of our faith. And this scripture, Exod. xxxiv. 6, 7, holds forth the amplest and largest display of mercy any other affords. And therefore I have most deservedly

made choice of this one, to sustain henceforth the whole weight of all that
follows, and shall accordingly found all upon it as upon a new text.

*And the Lord passed before him, and proclaimed, The Lord, the Lord God,
merciful and gracious, long-suffering, and abundant in goodness and truth,
keeping mercy for thousands, forgiving iniquity, transgression, and sin, and
that will by no means clear the guilty ; visiting the iniquity of the fathers
upon the children, and upon the children's children, unto the third and to
the fourth generation.*—EXOD. XXXIV. 6, 7.

I shall not yet handle it in such an orderly and continued way as is usual
to complete the exposition of a text, but do reserve that when I come to
the merits of it afterwards.   In the mean while, I shall only make observation of such things about and out of it, as do directly tend to prove that
general subject I affixed as the title to the whole discourse in the front,
upon the entrance unto it; the substance of which is resolved into two
propositions and heads.   1. That the mercies in God's heart and nature
are a prime object and support of faith, as it hath been stated.   2. That
mercy and grace in God are truly and properly properties of the divine
nature and being; or, that God is of a merciful nature, and that his heart
and purposes are to shew mercy, as the effects of that mercy in his nature ;
which two will make the demonstration complete.   And my design is to
allege the heads of no other proofs for either than what these words, and
the coherence of them, and circumstances about them, or citations of them
elsewhere, do afford ground for ; and shall call in no other scriptures, but
reductive only, for aid, and but such as of themselves will come about
this, to back and confirm those proofs first, so grounded on the words.
The grounds for the first head are two : 1*st,* Some special observations
made upon this proclamation itself of mercy, which contains the occasion,
circumstances, end, and purpose of it, and the issue and use made of it by
Moses at that instant time.   All which, as they do wonderfully enhance
the grace and mercy of God proclaimed in it, so do mightily also commend
these words unto our faith.   2*dly,* That these very words (as to before the
substance of them) were ever after made use of as the common refuge and
asylum (and therefore the object) of the faith of the saints of the Old Testament, as to which they ordinarily had recourse for their support in point
of forgiveness, and upon other occasions in which they stood in need of
mercy ; the evidence of both which, when they shall be spread before us,
and punctually exemplified in so many instances of the best and greatest of
saints, and their practice, this rich parcel of Scripture will come concredited
and recommended to our faith, with a mighty testimonial, under the hands
of so many renowned witnesses that lived and died in the faith ; as the
apostle speaks of those saints, Heb. xi., throughout that chapter, and in
chapter xii. ; and as the apostle there exhorts those Hebrews of the New
Testament to live by faith, from the instances of such a cloud of witnesses
under the Old Testament, of whom he gives the catalogue, so may I, upon
as just a ground, invite all believers heedfully to attend this scripture, as
being also the spring of all other scriptures about God's mercies that after
followed, which are but as lesser streams from a fountain.   And I may
withal invite them to study the mercies of God as they are set forth
therein, and to have it much in their meditations, treaties, and pleadings
with God, and in all their exercises of believing ; because in this small
compass of words God hath met with, and by it supported so many of his

precious ones of old. And we that are believers under the New Testament, ' we having the same spirit of faith; according as it is written, I believed, and therefore have I spoken, we also believe, and therefore speak,' 2 Cor. iv. 13, as the great apostle, citing David's Old Testament faith to express his own New Testament faith by ; and we professing with all the apostles and primitive saints to ' believe that we shall be saved by the same grace of Christ' and mercy of God that they, under the Old Testament, were saved by (which great maxim is expressly uttered in the name of the apostles, and of all the Christians of the New, Acts xv. 11), may well be induced to make a like improvement and valuation of this Old Testament carkanet,* bestudded with so many jewels.

CHAPTER IV.

That the mercies of God's heart and nature are the prime object of faith.—The first proof drawn from some special observations upon this proclamation of mercy, Exod. xxxiv. 6, 7; and upon the story, occasion, occurrences, circumstances, end, and purpose of it by God.—The issue and effect of it, and the use Moses made of it; which, as they exceedingly exalt the grace and mercy proclaimed, so do greatly commend it to our faith, for the support of it.

That this proclamation of grace was fully intended by God for a foundation to our faith, and that it tendeth directly to prove the assertion, the following observations will, I hope, when taken along and put together, sufficiently possess us of. It is true that these observations themselves are but about circumstantials of the proclaiming it, in comparison unto the gracious matter and merits themselves contained in the proclamation itself; and these concern but the occasion, season, &c., which God took for this first publishing of it; yet such they are as the consideration of them doth greatly tend to the exalting of God's grace, which is proclaimed therein; and the two last of them will end in a punctual proof of this first head.

Obs. 1. That it was God himself who immediately published this. Wise princes, if matters of extraordinary grace be to be declared or manifested, choose to do it themselves, and not by others, though favourites. And if ever there were words of grace spoken, then are these such. They are *suavissima concio* (as one† styles them), the sweetest sermon that ever was preached. And God himself was the preacher, and for the reason forementioned would be the proclaimer of them.

The vulgar translation, and the Romanists addicted thereunto, do put the honour of proclaiming it upon Moses (forsooth), and that it should be he who said, ' Jehovah, merciful,' &c., to the great obscuring of the greatness, yea, majesty, of God, given demonstration of herein.

It is true those words in verse 5, translated ' he proclaimed the name of Jehovah,' are elsewhere rendered ' called on the name of Jehovah.' And indeed the very same words, in the Hebrew, are used of Jacob:‡ Gen. xii. 8, that he ' called upon the name of the Lord.' And so if the coherence here had not apparently contradicted it, it might have been so understood here, and attributed to Moses. But, to be sure, those words, verse 6, ' And the Lord passed by before him, and proclaimed, The Lord,

* A collar or necklace.—Ed.   † Osiander.   ‡ ' Abraham.'—Ed.

merciful,' &c., this must necessarily be referred to God himself, not to Moses. For,

1. He that passed by was he that proclaimed this, and that was God.

2. We find God himself, in chap. xxxiii., to have given it out to Moses, and to have beforehand promised that himself would be the proclaimer: 'I will proclaim the name of the Lord' (saith he), and so not dictate it only for Moses to proclaim it. And accordingly we see that here in chap. xxxiv. he performs it: ver. 5, 6, 'The Lord descended in the cloud, and stood with him there, and proclaimed the name of the Lord. And the Lord passed by before him, and proclaimed, The Lord, The Lord God, merciful,' &c.

3. Moses's true time and first beginning to speak was but at the 8th and 10th verses: 'And Moses made haste, and bowed his head, and worshipped. And he said,' &c., namely, after that God had done speaking. And thereupon it was that he began to speak in all great haste, and to urge what God himself had said. So as indeed it is plain that both speeches, both that in verse 5 as well as that in verse 6, are to be understood not of invocating the name of the Lord, but of proclaiming the Lord, as our translators have rendered them both, and both alike to be wholly referred to God as the proclaimer. And that it should be twice said he proclaimed, was to put a notoriety upon it, and to shew of what moment it was for us to know that the great God proclaimed thus his own name and glory. And the stream of the Hebrew text runs thus, verse 5, 'And the Lord descended in the cloud, and stood with him there, and proclaimed the name of the Lord.' He that descended and stood with Moses, he it was that proclaimed it; and that, to be sure, was God.

But we find Moses, in Num. xiv., expressly urging these words as God's own words upon him, so to put the more force into his plea: ver. 17, 'And now, I beseech thee, let the power of my Lord be great, according as thou hast spoken, saying' (*quemadmodum pronunciasti dicendo,** even as thou hast pronounced, O God, in saying), 'The Lord is long-suffering,' &c.

Obs. 2. It is further said, that 'God descended to proclaim this,' in verse 5, which still speaks the more grace. I know it is historically meant of God's visible descending in the cloud; yet give me leave from that shadow or type thereof, to decipher the impresses of grace signified thereby. For,

1st, That God should shew mercy to sinners, hath the greatest condescension in it, but much more to come down and proclaim it: 'He humbled himself to behold things in heaven' (even to behold his angels that never sinned), Ps. cxiii. 6; but for him not only to behold, but withal to deign to cast an eye of grace and mercy upon sinners, the things on earth, yea, and himself to descend unto earth to proclaim it, this is condescending indeed in 'the high and lofty One.' And further,

2dly, For the great God to shut up the emblazoning his incomprehensible simple nature into the narrow compass of a few words and form of speech, and those words importing several distinct things, and so, as it were, to pourtray forth himself by piecemeals and brokenly, by an imperfect delineation (for such these epithets are) to the end to bring himself down to our low capacities and conceits, this was a farther condescending indeed; it is a speaking to us of himself in the image of our own puerile understandings. But,

* Junius and Tremel.

3dly, This his visible descending in the view of all the people, to pro-claim this grace by words, was a most certain pledge given that he who was the Jehovah, God blessed for ever, would one day break the heavens, and come down and take our nature, and dwell among us, and put this proclamation into full force and virtue, which in the mean while, until he should do this, had yet its efficacy upon the saints of the Old Testament; and upon that descending, to be sure, we shall have cause to say, as in the same chapter, that ' the law came by Moses, but grace and truth by Jesus Christ;' which are the great materials of this great proclamation, and of which the second person, the Son of God, was indeed the proclaimer.

Obs. 3. The subject-matter of this proclamation consists chiefly of grace and mercy. It is true matter of justice comes in and hath a place in it, but how ? Afterwards; but mercy excels, exceeds, and is the prevailing argument.

1. In the number of the particulars here recited. There are thirteen titles (say the Jewish writers) given to God here; others reckon fewer, some but eleven (that is the least), whereof the three first are counted by them to be the proper names of God: Jehovah, Jevohah El, translated the Lord, the Lord God; all which three do yet suit with and impliedly intend mercy. The other nine (which are attributes) even seven of them speak altogether God's gracious affections towards repentant and believing sinners, as is evident in the very reading and counting of them.

2. If all the first three be taken for the proper names of God, yet of those attributes that follow, mercy, &c., have the first place and rank ; yea, and all the seven (the whole set for mercy) are placed together first, and so claim to have the chief place in point of order and precedence before all.

3. In God's own foreshewn declaration of what his mind was to be therein (chap. xxxiii. 19, which explains this), where, when he promiseth, ' I will proclaim the name of the Lord before thee,' he adds, ' I will be gracious to whom I will be gracious, and I will shew mercy to whom I will shew mercy.' Why are these latter so nearly and immediately subjoined to his proclaiming his name, but that his great name, which he then and here intended to proclaim, consisted most in his being merciful and gracious,* &c. Himself beforehand professeth it ; yea, and the other, the first words before these in the same verse refer most properly thereunto. ' I will cause all my goodness to pass before thee;' and goodness is the *genus* that comprehends mercy, grace, long-suffering, kindness, truth, &c., in it, as branches from that as the root.

4. The quotations that David so often, and the prophets, make of the words, do confirm this, they rehearsing no other but only those that belong to mercy :† Ps. lxxxvi. 15 ; Ps. ciii. 8 ; Ps. cxlv. 8.

The two latter, indeed: 1. ' That will not clearing clear the guilty ;' 2. ' Visiting the iniquities of the fathers upon the children, to the third and fourth generations ;' these two are commonly referred to punitive justice, as importing acts and resolutions in God thereof, the first being rendered, that will by no means clear the impenitent. And yet,

1st. About this meaning there is a very great controversy among inter-preters, some very judicious casting this very clause in among God's mercies, in chastising, but not destroying ; in taking vengeance on their

---

* Quod potissimùm in misericordià consistit.—*Oleaster.*

† Non est pars ultima gratiæ quòd nos ad se talibus blanditiis allicit Deus.—*Cal. in* Ps. cxlv. 8.

inventions, and yet forgiving them, as in Ps. xcix. 8, of which interpretation afterwards. And if so, then justice hath but one left, and mercy may challenge eight of the nine to belong to it; but however mercy may triumph and say, if justice be avenged twofold, mercy is gracious sevenfold, it carries it clear.

2dly. This rehearsal of his mercy and grace doth come in directly and absolutely and for themselves, and the current of them hath its spring purely from the heart of God, and runs with a straight, direct, natural stream; but these of justice mentioned come in but accidentally, and indeed but as occasioned by God's having gone so far in declaring so much mercy, and having poured forth so much grace from his whole heart, to the view of sinners of all sorts and sizes. Because he knew how much and how deeply this root of bitterness was seated in men's hearts, to say in their hearts, 'I shall have peace though I walk in the imagination of my heart,' &c., Deut. xxix. 19; and how apt are they to 'turn all this grace into wantonness;' therefore it is that at last, and but at last, he brings this high threatening in, 'that will by no means clear the impenitent.' And so, as the apostle says of the law, that it was 'added because of transgression,' so is this a mere occasioned additional (though most necessary by reason of man's corruption), because of obstinate sinners continuing in sin against light, and indeed but to vindicate and turn the glory of his mercy, which he is pleased to account his highest glory, from impure claim and profane hands of presumptuous sinners laying hold thereon when resolved to continue in their sins. And look, as mercy itself in him is from and of itself, not moved by anything in the creature, but [on the contrary, justice (though it is as essential to him as mercy) yet makes and puts forth itself but only upon man's sin, just so doth the mention of it come in but in relation and for the prevention of man's sin, and abusing of his mercy.

3dly. Again, unto those acts of justice specified there are bounds and limits set, 'visiting the iniquities, &c., to the fourth generation,' and further; and after that is passed and gone, leaving the door for mercy wide open; and it is for them that hate him, which is the second commandment's addition; and those that hate him love death. Yea, in that very decalogue, the law (which, if any part of Scripture, was designed to speak justice and wrath), the comparison between the shewing mercy exceeds by thousands, so as it is not the proportion of one thousand to three or four, but of thousands; * and to how many thousands he limits not that neither, but leaves room for to set down millions of millions of thousands, and yet this is in the law. But here in this gospel declaration he plainly sets no number either of thousands or millions of thousands, none at all; for of his mercy there is no end.† And at this very time, whilst God renewed that law and those words in it with his own hands, he utters with his own mouth this proclamation of grace so far excelling, professing to pardon all sorts of iniquities, transgressions, and sins, which he knew and foresaw the sons of men would commit against that law.

Obs. 4. The season which God was pleased to take the advantage of is most observable. It was this: this people had immediately before committed that greatly heightened sin in all manner of circumstances of it, of making and worshipping the golden calf; the story of this you find to be

---

* Quia Dei clementia judicium exsuperat.—*Calvin. in verba.*

† Notandum est Deum iræ suæ terminum ponere, misericordiæ nullum.—*Rivetus in verba.*

the subject of, chap. xxxii. throughout, by which high transgression they had utterly, on their parts, broken the covenant, as Moses his breaking the tables of stone did shew; the sense of the high heinousness of which sin the Jews bear upon their spirits unto this day, it being usual with them when any eminent punishment befalls their nation, to say that an ounce of the golden calf is in it. In which chapter you also have the deep resentment which God took thereat, and a most eager zeal to have been avenged was breaking forth: 'Let me alone,' says he to Moses, that was about to intercede for them, 'that my wrath may wax hot against them to consume hem,' ver. 10, which, though in sound of words seems to express an high indignation conceived, and to check Moses, as it were, for praying for them, yet in reality did tacitly insinuate an inclinableness to mercy upon Moses's farther entreaty; and indeed, to invite him the more earnestly to put himself forth in interceding for them, importing that he was not absolutely or wholly resolved, but overcomeable by entreaties, which Moses took the advantage of, and followed his suit, and upon the assault God began to relent of the severity he had threatened;* and yet still God did not reveal this to Moses, but kept it to himself, for, ver. 30, Moses, as it were, speaks of it uncertainly to the people: ' Peradventure I shall make an atonement for your sins.' But God carried it still to him, as if it still stuck with him, so as to be avenged, as by the hard conflict Moses had with God, carried dialogue-wise between them, and God's quick reply unto his prayer, ver. 31 to the end of the chapter, appears. And again, chap. xxxiii. to ver. 4, the tidings hereof the people hearing, though they mourned and humbled themselves, ver. 4, yet still God carries it reservedly and aloof off to them, as unto what he would do with them (as those words shew, 'that I may know what to do unto thee,' ver. 5), whether pardon or destroy them. But Moses thereupon farther speaking with God, the Lord was so familiar with him above all times ever before, either with himself or ever with any other man, that Moses was bold to plead for farther favour to that people, and for a special high privilege to himself: ' Shew me thy glory;' all which transactions were the most lively representations and types of Christ's intercession and prevalency for us, in and by whom God was to manifest all his glory, specially of grace and mercy, to his chosen children; John i. 17 and 18 compared. And hereupon God sets him a time, which was the next day early; and at his time set comes down to him (which was in view of all the people), and then comes off like the great God himself, proclaiming all those his mercies to him of 'pardoning iniquity, transgression, and sin.' And though this was done in his hearing alone, yet for the people's sake, and on their behalf, for whom he had so vehemently interceded, whose concernment this was as well as his own, as that clause, ' keeping mercy for thousands,' shews. And having done this, he restores and estates them into the same favour they were in before, he renews his covenant with them which they had broke: ver. 10, ' Behold, I make a covenant; before all thy people I will do marvels, such as have not been done in all the earth, nor in any nation; and all the people amongst which thou art shall see the work of the Lord.'

Obs. 5. Observe the haste God made to do this. After that this treatment between himself and Moses was come to its full issue, he makes no delay, his heart was so full of it: ver. 2, 'Be ready,' says God to Moses, ' in the morning.' And it could be appointed no sooner; for the solemnity which the Lord was pleased to make and observe in the doing it, which

* Diodati.

was to have all the people forewarned, ver. 3, put in expectation, &c., and then himself to descend in their view, ver. 5. And according to God's command, 'Moses rose up early in the morning,' and, it is added, 'as the Lord had commanded him' (so that God had appointed the very earliest of the morning too), and all speed was used that could be, and God made him not stay for a moment. After Moses was come, 'the Lord descended in the cloud and stood with him there;' and then 'the Lord passed by before him, and proclaimed,' &c. And what he performed to Moses and the people in this respect he also doth to us; for how often do you read of his hearing us in the morning; as in Ps. v. 3, and of his 'causing us to hear of his loving-kindness in the morning;' as Ps. cxliii. 7, 8, 'Hear me speedily, O Lord! Cause me to hear thy loving-kindness in the morning.' And Ps. xc. 14, 'O satisfy us early with thy mercy.' Look, as Moses hasted, ver.'8 (as is said), to put up his suit and petition upon it, and that we are bidden to seek God early, so God was as early with him, which was intended for a precedent for us that shall for ever need this grace and mercy which he here proclaims. Nay, sometimes God prevents us before we call, but is always ready to forgive' (as the Psalmist's word is), and, to be sure, comes down to 'help in time of need,' Heb. iv. 16. Oh the riches of his grace! and the depth of the 'riches of the wisdom and knowledge of God,' Rom. xi. 33, that thus contrived and took the fairest season and opportunity for advantage for his expressing his grace and heart to us, magnifying thereby his mercy and goodness to the utmost. I said there were two grand pillars in the Old Testament: one, God's promise of Christ; and the other, this *manifesto* of God's gracious nature : and lo, the advantage God took for both, upon the commission of the most heinous sins ; the one upon occasion of the first and greatest sin, and of the largest extent of mischief in the consequence that ever was committed, viz., our first parents' fall, by which all mankind were undone ; and it was upon that occasion he let fall that promise of Christ, which was the first foundation of Old Testament faith, and continues such to the end : and now again upon the first greatest sin this people did commit after their having received the law, and heard God's voice, it was that he publisheth this other. And he pardoned each of these their sins whilst he was a-speaking and uttering of these promises ; and this latter of his mercy was the original of that other of the Messiah himself, considered as he is our Saviour, and the overcomer of Satan for us. We may well, therefore, hereupon glorifying him say, as that the Lord is 'gracious and full of bowels' (with the apostle James), so in respect to the opportunity God took, that he 'waiteth to be gracious' (with the prophet Isaiah), that is, to manifest it in the fittest season ; for he is a God of judgment, Isa. xxx. 18. What heart guilty of the most heinous sins, that is now humbled for them, should not this move and encourage to come in unto such a God !*

Obs. 6. Moses having heard what God had spoken, God then speaks anew inwardly to Moses's heart, and Moses instantly puts it into practice and suit. Now, as this shews most effectually what God's intention had been in uttering his meaning, Isa. lv. 10, 11, so it doth most exemplarily instruct us what use this publication of mercy is to be put out unto by us; that we should lay hold on it by faith, and turn, and put it into prayer, but especially in the case of pardon of sins. For so of Moses it is said, ver. 8, that when God had done speaking, and was passing apace by him, 'Moses made haste, and bowed his head towards the earth, and worshipped;'

* Talibus blanditiis allicit ad se nos Deus.—*Calvin.*

even as one that is an humble suppliant to a king, as he passeth by him, follows him, and humbly presents his petition in haste, lest he should be gone out of sight; so here.

If it be said, might he not at leisure have, at any time afterwards, put up the same petition upon the same ground? the answer is, that when God is near, and greatly present to the soul (as he was here to Moses), that is the most acceptable time of praying for all or anything a believing soul desires. Let them take that opportunity, and though such a special nearness should not fall out till towards the end of one's prayer, yet let them then take the advantage of that time and tide to pray over again afresh, and put in all they desire to pray for, or would have God do for them, for God is with them.

Now, what was Moses's petition? It follows, ver. 9, ' And he said, Now if I have found grace in thy sight, O Lord, let my Lord, I pray thee, go amongst us, for it is a stiff-necked people, and pardon our iniquities and our sin, and take us for thine inheritance.' In which, as I said, he puts into use and practice (laying hold on the words now spoken by God) himself to speak a good word from thence for that people. The effect of which prayer is, that although they were indeed a stiff-necked people, as any in the world (this he first confessed), that yet God, for this his name's sake, would not leave them, but pardon their iniquities, and mine own too, Lord, says he, for the expression is, ' pardon *our* iniquities.' Which for God to do was the plain intent of his declaring it. And it is implied that God would do this not for the present only, but to continue to do it. He prays for the future as well as for the present when he says, ' Pardon our iniquities,' &c. This the words foregoing, 'for it is a stiff-necked people,' *i. e.*, they will ever and anon be sinning against thee, and also the words that follow, do shew, ' Take us for thine inheritance,' says Moses, which words Calvin renders *ut possideas nos*, that thou mayest possess us for thine inheritance. As if he had said, says he, God cannot come to enjoy and possess his chosen as his inheritance, otherwise than by pardoning their sins continually; for man's frailty is such that they would, after his receiving pardon, fall from that grace, if they be not continually reconciled to him ; which concerns us Gentiles as well as them then. God must not only take us to be his, but keep us to be his, and continue to be merciful to us, according to this his great name, or we shall be utterly lost and undone.

CHAPTER V.

That the mercies of God's nature, as they are proclaimed in Exodus xxxiv., are a prime object and support of faith.—That this name of God, Exodus xxxiv. 6, 7, was an asylum or strong tower, unto which the faith of the most eminent saints of the Old Testament had recourse, especially for forgiveness ; and the evidence hereof carried through the times of the Old Testament, from Moses, by a cloud of witnesses, as Moses, David, Nehemiah, and the prophets.

This proclamation of grace being a *magna charta* of the Old Testament, was so highly valued by the prophets and saints of those times, that ever after it had been proclaimed to Moses, they had, throughout all ages,* frequent recourse thereto; and their wont was to make rehearsals of it upon several occasions, as either when particular mercies were to be obtained, or exhortations made to bring men in to God, or thanksgiving and praise offered. Their manner was upon such occasions to rehearse these words, but especially in the point of forgiveness. Besides that use that Moses made of it instantly upon the place, when God had done proclaiming it, he putting it presently in suit in all haste in the behalf of that people, the same Moses, in more cool blood, makes the same improvement of it in after times. And the occasion was another most heinous sin of murmuring committed by this people, and then he again urgeth God with these his own words for a forgiveness of them: Num. xiv. 17, 18, 19, ' And now, I beseech thee, let the power of my Lord be great, according as thou hast spoken, saying, The Lord is long-suffering, and of great mercy, forgiving iniquity and transgression, and by no means clearing the impenitent,'— or perhaps, rather as others, ' clearing I will not clear;' that is, although he forgive, yet he will chastise, and not altogether leave unpunished,— ' visiting the iniquities of the fathers upon the children, unto the third and fourth generation.'

Next comes David, who, although he had, over and above this proclamation of mercy, common to him with all the saints, a personal covenant of sure mercies particularly made and renewed to himself, yet, however, he had an usual recourse unto this more general refuge ; of such use and valuation was it with him, and ought to be with us. Thus in Ps. lxxxvi., twice, in ver. 5 and 15, by way of prayer, ' Thou, O Lord, art a God full of compassion, long-suffering, plenteous in mercy and truth ; O have mercy upon me, and save me,' ver. 16. And then again, in another psalm, viz., cxlv., he brings in all the saints, with their hearts and mouths full of it, pouring forth in a way of praise (for in that channel the stream of that psalm runs) the very same words; having first said, ver. 7, ' They utter the memory of thy great goodness, and sing of thy righteousness.' Then in the next follows, as being their universal joint outcry, and the burden of their singing, ' The Lord is gracious, full of compassion, slow to anger, and of great mercy.' So as this was the general vogue of the saints of those times to cry this scripture up.

In Psalm ciii. we have a reference to these words, yea, an express quotation of them. David repeats these very words of Moses in ver. 8, ' The Lord is merciful and gracious, slow to anger, and plenteous in mercy.' In which rehearsal there is not only a *videtur alludere ad illud Mosis*, an allusion, &c. (as Calvin), but a plain citing or quoting of the words, as·having been spoken to Moses by name, and as punctually alleging them out of him in such a manner as we use to quote Jeremiah, Isaiah, or any other of the prophets' writings when we have occasion; for in the very words before, ver. 7, he says, ' He made known his ways unto Moses, his acts unto the children of Israel.'

The coherence of which words, ver. 7, interpreters have wholly drawn

---

* Nec mirum est Davidem sumpsisse hæc Elogia ex celebri illo Mosis loco, Exod. xxxiv. 6, quum prophetis visionem, quæ illic refertur, summo in pretio fuisse : quia, nusquam clarius, vel familiarius, exprimitur Dei natura.—*Calvin in Ps.* cxlv. *ver.* 8.

Mollerus, upon the 86th Psalm (where this description of mercy is twice rehearsed), hath these words: ' Sumptus est hic versus ex Mose, et quia tanquam insignis quædam gemma inter cæteras promissiones elucet, crebrò repetitur in scriptura.'—*Mollerus in ver.* 15. *Ps.* lxxxvi.

up, and exhale into ver. 6, as if these words, ' He made known his ways to Moses,' were intended only for a particular instance of God's delivering the oppressed, as he had done the Israelites ; because, in the verse before (ver. 5) say they, he had spoken of God's vindication of such as were oppressed. But some later critics have, to a more ample scope, drawn those words of ver. 7, down to a coherence with the next, ver. 8, ' The Lord is merciful,' &c., the very words of God to Moses ; and to justify this coherence rather than the former, those writers do pertinently compare the words which Moses had first spoken to God, chap. xxxiii. 13, with these of God's unto Moses in this chap. xxxiv., which (say they) were spoken by God, as in answer unto what Moses had there said.   Now, in the foregoing chapter, Exod. xxxiii. 13, Moses had said, ' I pray thee, if I have found grace in thy sight, I pray thee shew me thy way' (or thy ways, as Junius, and Drusius, and others render it), ' that I may know thee' ; that is, say they, know thee by what thy inclination and disposition is, and dealings shall be towards this people ; for, in the following words, he had presented before him the case of this people : ' Consider,' says he, ' that this nation is thy people' ; and thereupon was further bold to ask, ' Shew me thy glory.' Upon which request on Moses's part it was, that God promiseth there to proclaim his name.   Now, the Jewish writers* usually understand by *thy ways*, the properties of God, his inclination and disposition ; by which, or from which, being inwardly in his nature moved, he outwardly goeth forth to dispense unto his people ; and so by *ways*, in this speech of Moses, are complexly understood both the attributes of God's nature, as the root and the principles in his heart, or the original cause, and his dealings, proceeding from thence, as the effects ; and to know what these ways were, was that thing which Moses desired of God, that he would fully reveal to him, that so he might know him, both for his own comfort, but especially in reference to what was, or how his mind stood, towards this people.   And God in answer hereto did punctually, according to these two requests, first promise to do this for him : chap. xxxiii. 19, ' I will cause my goodness to pass before thee : and I will proclaim the name of the Lord before thee' ; and then did perform it, in the words of my text : chap. xxxiv. 6, ' Proclaiming the name of the Lord, the Lord God, merciful,' &c.   Hereupon these interpreters, comparing all these things together, are bold (and that rightly) to understand this passage in Ps. ciii., ' He made known his ways to Moses,' to be meant both of that his name and properties proclaimed by God in Exodus unto Moses.   What ways ? (says Drusius on Exod. xxxiii. 13) or what properties ?   He is passionate for this explication of Moses ; and that by *ways* God's purposes, innate dispositions, *mores* or *ingenium* should be meant.   And before him Genebrard, out of the Jewish writers, doth the like on Ps. ciii.   Dr Hammond, on Ps. ciii. 7, 8, vehemently contends for the same coherence : The place (says he) evidently refers to Exod. xxxiii., where Moses petitions God : ' Shew me thy way' ; then, ver. 18, ' Shew me thy glory.'   By his way and glory, meaning his nature, and his ways of dealing with men.   'And God said, I will make all my goodness pass before thee, and proclaim the name of the Lord ;' by which his nature is signified ; and what that name is, is set down by the enumerations of his attributes, chap. xxxiv. 6.   He proclaimed the Lord

---

* *Vias suas*, hoc est, qualiter se gerat erga suos.—*Muis.*   Apud Hebræos plerunque via significat rationem, et institutum vitæ, mores, negotia, &c., et Scire viam tuam, id est, rationem agendi quâ uteris erga tuos, vel simpliciter quomodo cum piis agas. —*Mollerus in Ps.* lxxxvi. 11.

merciful, gracious, &c., just as here (says he) in the Psalm, in the next verse, the Lord is merciful, &c. Only Dr Hammond differs from the other in this, that he interprets by *ways* made known to Moses, God's manner of his dealings, or his actions, to be meant; and the following words, his *acts*, to the children of Israel, the word translated his *acts* he would have to import his nature and attributes that follow, according to his understanding the Hebrew phrase, &c.; but he and they all agree in that scope I allege this place for. And indeed the psalmist teacheth us that God's ways mean his inward dispositions, Ps. ciii., for after he had said, ' He made his ways known to Moses,' he subjoins, ' The Lord is merciful and gracious, slow to anger, and plenteous in mercy,' God thereby declaring at once to Moses that these were the dispositions in his nature, and that according unto these they should find his proceedings should be, not with this people only, but with all his children for ever in the world, as also with wicked men impenitent; so as Moses might certainly know him thereby, as he requested, and know where to have him, as we use to say, which was the main intent of what he had desired to know. And accordingly the rest of the psalm that follows is a verification in so many experiments of what God's ways in mercy had been to that people from Moses's time downwards, drawn into maxims or propositions, according unto what he had here declared to Moses so long before.

And that his *ways* should more particularly and eminently note out his mercies in pardoning sins, &c. (which is one of David's applications and interpretations of Moses here), that passage in Isa. lv. confirms. For speaking of God's ' having mercy,' and ' abundantly pardoning,' ver. 7, he adds, ver. 8, 9, ' For my thoughts are not your thoughts, neither are your ways, *my ways*, saith the Lord : for as the heavens are higher than the earth, so are *my ways* higher than your ways, and my thoughts than your thoughts.' The like many other scriptures express. I conclude, What is all this other than that David, in this famous psalm of mercy, as in which he makes a celebration of the mercies of God to himself, from ver. 1 to 7, and from thence towards others of his children, in sundry particulars, doth first professedly take these words of Moses for his text, even as we are wont to do some portion of scripture, and make a sermon upon it; that is, that part of them that concerned mercy, and then plainly writes a comment upon it in the rehearsal of sundry particular gracious dealings? All which are but explanations, confirmed from experience, of these several properties of grace, mercy, long-suffering, &c., more briefly summed up by God himself, in Moses. And this might, though not in the same order, be exactly shewn, if prolixity here forbade it not.

But we meet not with these words only in David, upon these occasions specified, but as frequently also, at least with some pieces of them, in the prophets, unto the same or other like purposes. As Jeremiah, in that solemn prayer for the church, in the condition it was in his times, Jer. xxxii. 18. Then again, in the prophet Joel, he lays it as a foundation and corner-stone of faith and hope, to persuade the people to come in, and turn to God: Joel ii. 12, 13, ' Turn ye to me,' says God himself by him, ' with all your heart, with fasting, and weeping, &c., and turn unto the Lord your God, for he is gracious, and merciful, slow to anger, and of great kindness,' &c. These are still God's words in Moses anew repeated.

Yea, Jonah points as plainly unto these words, as those the remembrance whereof moved God to be merciful in pardoning the Ninevites, upon their serious and solemn repentance. He attributes that his sparing them, unto the substance of these words which Jonah had learned from Moses, as the cause of God's pardoning them ; and was certainly led to do it by the Holy Ghost that penned that prophecy; although he uttered it whilst he was expostulating the matter with God for his having spared them, that when he had sent him with so precise a message to foretell them of their utter destruction within so many days : ' I knew,' says he, ' that thou art a gracious God, and merciful, slow to anger, and of great kindness, and repentest of the evil,' Jonah iv. 2.   And his saying, ' *I knew*,' prompts evidently that the knowledge he had of God, had been taken from these words in Moses, as that which from his writings was the familiar, wonted, and common notion ; which both he and that people that knew the law were nourished up in.   And that when matter of threatening judgment was apprehended (which excited to repentance), the thoughts of this scripture was at hand, and rose up in their minds, as here it did in his, although to a worse purpose, as in his thought.   Yea, and Jonah tells God there plainly that, from the knowledge of that very declaration of mercy, and God's wont in pardoning, he had suspected that this might or would prove to be the issue ; and that the remembrance of mercy, as he had declared it to Moses, would overcome him, and prevail with him haply to give repentance to those Ninevites, and thereupon to save them, even against the peremptory message of their destruction, wherein God shewed he loved the glory of his mercy more than of his justice, or his own declared threatening, and his own prophet's credit.

And which is yet more to be wondered at, and God to be adored in it, is, that although the prophet knew this aforehand from this scripture in Moses, yet the poor Ninevites knew not thereof, having not seen as then Moses's writings, nor had ever heard one tittle of this proclamation of mercy ; nor can we think that Jonah had revealed it to them, for a denunciation of destruction was precisely all of his commission; but it was God's own Holy Spirit who alone prompted these poor ignorant souls with this suggestion, to ' cry mightily unto God ; and to turn every one from his evil way, who can tell if God will repent, and turn away from his fierce anger, that we perish not ?' chap. iii. 8, 9.   And they had to do with God, who to be sure knew and was privy to himself, what he had set forth himself by, as that which was in his heart and nature; and he ' could not deny himself,' and his own declaration of it, though these poor souls could not have challenged him by it.

I only add this comfortable observation (comfortable indeed to us Gentiles) from Jonah's allegation of these words, even that ' Jehovah, gracious and merciful,' &c., as in Moses it was proclaimed, that this proclamation concerned not only the Jews, or was a measure for God to go by towards that people, but was intended by God, even at the first delivery, for us Gentiles also.   For he proceeded according to the tenor of it with those Ninevites, who were an handsel of the Gentiles' conversion to come. And therefore let us Gentiles, from the apostle's instruction, Rom. xv. 9–11, adore and glorify God for his mercy, and exercise our faith much upon these blessed words, ' Jehovah, gracious, merciful, long-suffering, abundant in kindness and truth,' as having been proclaimed and written that we might have as much hope as the Jews had therein, and so turn to the Lord, as these Ninevites did.   This for Jonah.

Next the prophet Micah brings in a piece of it, chap. vii. 18, by way of wonderment at such and so gracious a God : ' Jehovah, Jehovah God, pardoning iniquity and sin.'   Thus God speaks to Moses : ' Who is a God like unto thee, that pardoneth iniquity, and passeth by the transgression of the remnant of his heritage ? ' So the prophet there. ;

Hezekiah also, that holy king, writing to his brethren of the ten tribes, inviting them to return to God from forth of that long and great apostasy and revolt from God and his worship which they had made, assuring them that God would notwithstanding pardon and receive them again upon their repentance. He assures and he persuades them of it by God's own words, the words of this proclamation, so commonly known amongst all Israel : 2 Chron. xxx. 9, ' For the Lord your God is gracious and merciful, and therefore will not turn away his face from you if you return unto him.'

Lastly, good Nehemiah, almost a thousand years after Moses, doth make mention of these words : Neh. ix. 17, ' Thou art a God ready to pardon, gracious and merciful, slow to anger, and of great kindness, and forsookest them not.' Mark the whole drift of that which follows in that chapter, and you will find it to be : *first*, to ascribe all the mercies and forgivenesses of that people, both in the wilderness, and in after ages that followed, upon and after most grievous backslidings, which he there all along reciteth, unto that declaration of mercies first uttered to Moses, as the cause of all, and as that which had been verified over and over in so many experiments, through so many ages ; and, *secondly*, his scope was to put force into his present prayer and plea for mercy and restoration for the future to this then so sinful and broken a people, which he pursues as his main drift in that chapter, concluding his prayer thus : ' Thou art a merciful and a gracious God.' Ver. 13, ' Now *therefore* our God, the great, the mighty, and the terrible God, who keepest covenant and mercy.' &c. Now that word of his *therefore* draws unto this his conclusive prayer the strength of all he had alleged, both of that proclamation recited, ver. 17, and of all God's merciful dealings with that people in former ages, according to the tenor thereof ; and that, *therefore*, God would please to manifest and magnify, and put forth the same grace now to them. Yea, and to that end he repeats and revives again the memorial of the same words (for it is a blessed memorial to all generations), as our translators have observed, in referring us unto Exod. xxxiv. 6, 7.

And Nehemiah's times being with the last of those (I do not say the last) wherewith Scripture records of the Old Testament do end, and he in that 9th chapter having gone over all times that had been past from Moses's time, and having devolved all God's merciful dispensations during all those times into the mercy of God then published, as the well-head of them all, and he still continuing to plead the same for the whole time to come, from those times of his, from hence I may well conclude that this publication of mercy was accounted the basis or foundation of Old Testament mercies on God's part, and faith on theirs, in all the after ages of it.

You see I have traversed this from Moses to the last of Scripture records. And though a thousand other promises had been given between, yet still this is above all rehearsed, as the original of all other. So as I may well conclude it to have been a main article of the Old Testament creed.

CHAPTER VI.

What is imported by the name Jehovah *made use of in this proclamation of mercy, Exod.* xxxiv. 6, 7.—*That as it signifies God's infinite essence, it denotes the subject of all those mercies which are in him.—That this name of God, Jehovah, doth best suit, and is most fitly joined with those epithets* merciful *and* gracious.—*What supports of faith may be derived from these two, Jehovah and* merciful, *joined together.*

Having thus shewed that the mercies of God's nature, as proclaimed in Exod. xxxiv., are the great object and support of faith, I now come to the description itself in this his proclamation, and which is God's picture drawn by his own pencil, as far as words could render it; the smaller models whereof David and the prophets drew, as I have shewn, and wore next their hearts, as men wear precious medals of their friends upon their breasts.

It is *suavissima concio*, as one* styles it, the sweetest sermon that ever was preached, and preached by God himself, upon the highest subject, and therefore the richest text the whole Bible affords. It is *maxime insignis naturæ Dei descriptio,†* the most renowned and signal description of the nature of God.

Dr Preston‡ hath singularly displayed the glory of God set out in this delineation, as altogether most lovely, but his scope was to win the souls of men to *love* him (which the reader may consult as he thinks meet), but my design in this explication which follows is to consider it as it is a ground for and support of *faith,* to draw men to believe, which was God's original and primary purpose in this his first delivery of it, though it as fully conduceth to that other end also.

And we have example for disposing it to either of these purposes, the prophet David having penned two Psalms, more eminently appropriated by him to himself as his own: the one enstyled *David's prayer,* though many other psalms are prayers—it is Psalm lxxxvi.; the other, *David's praise,* Ps. cxlv., no psalms else in their titles bearing these ensigns of honour but these two, the first his *tephilla,* the latter his *tehilla ;* in each of these he makes a solemn rehearsal of these very words in Moses. In the first, Ps. lxxxvi., he brings them in as they were a support unto his faith in his distresses from sins and miseries, to which use he puts them, ver. 3, 4, 6, and 7. And again, ver. 16. 17, he makes a plea of these words by way of prayer (which is exercising faith) in that distressed condition. In the second, Ps. cxlv., he brings them in as they are an *elogium* or celebration of the glorious nature and excellencies of God, to excite the sons of men to love and praise him. And upon the like design he doth again resume them in a rehearsal, in Ps. ciii. Now as that worthy man fore-mentioned made this latter his design, so I shall take the first for mine. And yet as David, in those places specified, culls out and takes only what of God's words concerned his mercies, leaving out the threatening part, as that of ' visiting the iniquities of the fathers on their children,' so shall I insist only on the mercies of God therein promulged, that being the sole subject of my pursuance.

The materials of this description I reduce to two parts, which of themselves the words fall into.

* Osiander.   † Calvin in Psalm lxxxvi.   ‡ In his sermon of *Love,* from p. 35 to 44.

1. *Quis sit,* who he is, and what proper name or names of his it is, of which and under which he makes this proclamation of himself. It is *Jehovah, Jehovah,* twice repeated, translated ' the Lord, the Lord;' to which is added *El,* ' the strong God.'

2. *Qualis est,* what a God he is. This is expressed in those several perfections that follow, attributed to him, which we usually call properties and attributes; as that he is strong, merciful, and gracious, &c. Or if you will,

1st, That name *Jehovah* notes his infinite essence, as the *substratum* of those attributes.

2dly, The other that follow set out those perfections of that essence, as merciful, &c.

I. Who ? *Jehovah.*

There are of those proper names of God which signify (and we so translate them) God or Lord, three that are most eminent, and all three revealed to Moses.

1. *Ehije,* I am : first mentioned, Exod. iii. 14.

2. *Jehovah,* Exod. vi. 3.

3. The abridgment of Jehovah, *Jah :* Exod. xv. 2, ' *Jah* is my strength,' first there used.

And these are the chiefest names of God, and for substance signified one and the same thing. 1. And all of them, *Jehovah* especially, are the chiefest names, proper to God alone, and never given, or to be given (as other names are) to any creature : Ps. lxxxiii. 18, ' That men may know, that thou whose name alone is *Jehovah,* art the Most High over all the earth.' And of *Jah* it is said, it is that name by which God will especially be exalted : Ps. lxviii. 4, ' Sing unto God, sing praises to his name ; extol him that rideth upon the heavens by his name *Jah.*'* 2. They all three of them signify that God is *being,* being fulness of being, the original of all being. They all speak absolute essence and existence alone, and of himself.

Jehovah, therefore, is of all other names placed here designedly, as the seat and subject of these attributes that follow ; for as this name speaks him to be the whole of being, so these attributes speak the excellencies and perfections of that divine being, and are but particular explications and decipherings of what a God he is that entitleth himself *Jehovah,* or *I am.*

But, 2 (which is more to my purpose), the first revelation of it with God's own comment made upon it, was to betoken, and be a sign of mercy, and in a more especial design. And *primum* being *mensura reliquorum,* the first, the pattern or measure of what follows it, therefore *Jehovah,* of all other names, doth best suit and join with *merciful* and *gracious.* Now that it was first given and revealed as a token and signal of grace and mercy, is evident thus.

When God first appeared to Moses in the burning bush, Exod. iii., and had thus told him, ver. 7–11, ' And the Lord said, I have surely seen the affliction of my people which are in Egypt, and have heard their cry by reason of their task-masters ; for I know their sorrows ; and I am come down to deliver them out of the hand of the Egyptians, and to bring them up out of that land unto a good land and a large, unto a land flowing with milk and honey ; and to the place of the Canaanites, and the Hittites, and the Amorites, and the Perizzites, and the Hivites, and the Jebusites. Now therefore, behold, the cry of the children of Israel is come unto me :

* From הוה.

and I have also seen the oppression wherewith the Egyptians oppress them. Come now therefore, I will send thee unto Pharaoh, that thou mayest bring forth my people the children of Israel out of Egypt.' Moses thereupon, to obtain a farther information and confirmation from God of his intentions of grace to that people, particularly desires to know by what name he should represent him unto them, ver. 13–15: ' And Moses said unto God, Behold, when I come unto the children of Israel, and shall say unto them, The God of our fathers hath sent me unto you; and they shall say to me, What is his name? what shall I say unto them? And God said unto Moses, I am that I am: and he said, Thus shalt thou say unto the children of Israel, I am hath sent me unto you. And God said moreover unto Moses, Thus shalt thou say unto the children of Israel, The Lord God of our fathers, the God of Abraham, the God of Isaac, and the God of Jacob, hath sent me unto you: this is my name for ever, and this is my memorial unto all generations.' Ainsworth, penetrating into the mystery of this question and petition, conceives Moses's drift therein to be to draw forth from God more fully and explicitly, whether he sent him upon a message of mercy (pure mercy), or for judgment (as in the issue it might prove); and that he would signify so much by some special name he would please to assume, to testify so much thereby. And in answer unto Moses, God first there tells him his name was *Ehijeh*, &c., ' I am that I am,' ver. 14. And this was his first answer unto Moses's request. Now this *Ehijeh* is in signification for substance the same with this of Jehovah.

Therefore, again, when a second time God was pleased to renew his instructions to this his ambassador (the most extraordinary of any other until Christ came) in Exod. vi., still in further answer thereunto, God says, ver. 1–7, ' And Jehovah said unto Moses, Now shalt thou see what I will do unto Pharaoh; for by a strong hand shall he send them away, and by a strong hand shall he drive them out of his land. And God spake unto Moses, and said unto him, I am Jehovah. And I appeared unto Abraham, unto Isaac, and unto Jacob, by the name of God Almighty; but by my name Jehovah was I not known to them. And also I established my covenant with them, to give unto them the land of Canaan, the land of their sojournings, in the which they sojourned. And also I have heard the groaning of the sons of Israel, whom the Egyptians keep in servitude, and I have remembered my covenant. Therefore say thou unto the sons of Israel, I am Jehovah, and I will bring you out from under the burdens of the Egyptians, and I will rid you out of your servitude: and I will redeem you with a stretched-out arm, and with great judgments; and I will take you to me for a people, and I will be to you a God, and ye shall know that I am Jehovah your God, which bringeth you out from under the burdens of the Egyptians.' God in this declaration puts over the whole of that covenant, and these mercies thereof, and his purposes therein, unto the import and memorial of his name Jehovah, to signify so much to them, and doth farther lay that as his gage, to inform them thus at the close of all, ver. 8: ' And I will bring you in unto the land which I did lift up my hand to give it to Abraham, to Isaac, and to Jacob; and I will give it to you for an heritage: I am Jehovah.' This last clause, ' I am Jehovah,' I look upon to be put in at last, as one useth to do his name and seal unto a covenant or deed (such as this is) for performance; so God he subscribes unto all, ' I am Jehovah;' all hath this seal, as the apostle elsewhere speaks.

Now the ground upon which Ainsworth affixeth this meaning upon that question of Moses, chap. iii. 13 (besides that God himself, in the 7th verse of that chapter hath solemnly assured us, that he did electively give, and designed himself this name unto these graceful ends and purposes), his ground I say is this (as in his note on the 13th verse of the 3d chapter he declares), that Moses understood that God by names might, or was wont to manifest his works. So the Hebrews teach upon this place (says he), that when God judgeth his creatures, he is called *Elohim* (God), *Sabaoth* (Lord of Hosts); when he doth mercy unto the world he is called *Jehovah*, as in Exod. xxxiv. 6, ' Jehovah, Jehovah, God merciful and gracious.'

You see the sense which the Jews themselves do put upon it, and how that they refer us to this very text, ' Jehovah, merciful, gracious,' &c. And surely if God himself did so expressly assume this name as a sign and seal of his gracious covenant, and the mercies thereof, &c., then that in this new proclamation of grace and gospel-mercies he should to a greater emphasis double it, ' Jehovah, Jehovah, gracious,' &c., surely it was electively and designedly done, to shew that this name (of all other) should bear the flag and colours of mercy.

And let us farther join to all these this one remark, that in that deliverance specified in those chapters, Exod. iii. and vi., their redemption out of Egypt (which was the occasion of God's first revelation and application of that name to the mercy of that deliverance, put afterwards into the command-ments), God had therein an higher aim unto that mercy promised their fathers to be performed by Christ, of whom as Moses was the type, so this deliverance was of that redemption performed by Christ, Luke i. 72. And I am Jehovah, is the gage to the performance of both, the latter as well as the former. We may see reason, then, why that when God cometh to proclaim his gospel-mercies more illustriously (as here he doth, if any-where in the Old Testament, yea, in the whole Scripture), he should make his proclamation of them under his great and chiefest name Jehovah, as the great standard-bearer of those transcendent mercies.

2. And what if in the New Testament you find (conform to what is here) this his name *Jehovah* expressly assigned as the fountain of the whole of his grace, as the spring likewise of peace, which is the whole of spiritual, yea, all, blessings? And yet thus we do expressly find it; and in the last book of the New Testament, which puts the farther weight upon this notion. ' Grace and peace' had been often wished in other Epistles of the New Testament from God, as ' the Father of our Lord Jesus Christ,' &c.; but in Rev. i. 4, ' grace and peace' is prayed for ' from him who is, and which was, and which is to come.' This directly points us unto these very places in Exodus, 3d and 6th chapters, where the name Jehovah is used, and which we have explained as the most judicious interpreters do gene-rally observe, and our worthy translators have in their marginal citations referred us.* And as his name *Jah* is the brief of *Jehovah*, so he that *is*, he that *was*, and he that is *to come*, is, in words at length, the un-deciphering of the same name *Jehovah*, of which afterwards. Now, from God as such, that is, as Jehovah, is the whole of gospel grace at once wished and prayed for, this name being the ground and original of the gospel itself, and of all the mercies of it.

Use. And ere we go any farther, let us here stand and wonder at the

---

* And otherwise this is strange and uncouth language to Grecian ears to say, ἀπὸ τοῦ ὁ ὤν, and so of the rest, and not ἀπὸ τοῦ ὄντος, &c. But the reason is this, his great name *Jehovah* stands as inflexible and indeclinable as his nature is immutable. It keeps its state, and will not be subject to the laws and rules of grammar, as in other languages.

thought that this name, of all other names, this ' great and terrible name, by which he chooseth to be exalted, Ps. lxviii. 4, that this great name, as Jer. xliv. 26, which is so terrible and so holy (as, Ps. xcix. 3, he meaneth this name there, for it is that name which was made known to Moses and Aaron, as it follows there, verse 6, whereby we are referred to those very passages in Exodus, 3d and 6th chapters), that name so terrible to the Jews for these many hundreds of years, that they have not dared to pronounce it, and is called his ' dreadful name among the heathens,' * Mal. i. 14, that this should be made the basis, the subject, the signal of so much grace; this must needs (in the very entrance) afford us strong consolation, in that out of the strong should come forth sweetness, Judges xiv. 14. And the reason hereof doth hold forth this, that God accounts mercy to be his greatest attribute (at least in the name Jah), as Jehovah his greatest name, which he hath chosen to be the special subject of mercy and grace as the predicate.

The inquiry next will be, what special particular affinities there are between this great name *Jehovah* and the *mercies of God*, or rather (as being more close to our purpose) what special supports of faith (the aim of my subject) may be fetched from the blessed and intimate conjunction of these two, *Jehovah* and *merciful*, put together ? I answer, much every way. I shall instance but in some few, leaving it to others to enlarge unto more on this argument.

1. This great name wholly and abstractly speaks *being* itself: ' I am Jehovah;' that is, I have fulness of being, I am an immense sea of being, and am all, and in whole, very being itself. That then God should put *Jehovah*, and *merciful*, and *gracious* together, what is the result hereof ? and what would God have us to understand thereby, but that his mercies have being itself for their root and foundation, not only that mercies are with him, but that they have a very being itself to rely upon, whilst we rely upon them ? So as look what Wisdom, or Christ (who is Jehovah), in the Proverbs says of himself—Prov. viii. 21, ' I cause those that love me to inherit substance,'—the same (God thus inviting us to believe on Jehovah, merciful) may we as confidently say, that we believe upon what is substance, upon substantial mercies. And hence it is that even our faith, when pitched on God, is alone dignified (and no other kind of knowledge is so) with the title of ὑπόστασις, subsistence or reality, Heb. xi. 1, and said to be our rest. For why, God himself is the ultimate object of it, 1 Peter i. 22, and basis of its reliance ; as also his Son Christ, they being subsistence and reality. And to this purpose you find these his names, *Jah, Jehovah* (which is indeed Jehovah doubled or repeated twice as here), to be put under the feet of our faith as a firm rock of being to stand upon: Isa. xxvi. 4, ' Trust in the Lord for ever: for in *Jah Jehovah* is the rock of ages.' So in the original; and the translators have here signally, on set purpose, put JEHOVAH in capital letters. They might have done so by *Jah* also, which they translate ' the Lord;' for it is not singly *Jehovah*, but accompanied with *Jah*, which is *being*, and *being itself*. And he fetcheth this out of these two names, that he is therefore a rock, and a ' rock of ages,' whom we may therefore perfectly trust on; for in the relation he speaks this in the verse before, ' Thou wilt keep him in perfect

* That the heathens knew him to be the God of the Jews under this name *Jah*, or Iαῶ, as the Grecians wrote it, and that they called their chief god Jove, is well known. See *Aug. de Consens. Religionis*, c. 22; *Diodor. Siculus*, lib. ii. c. 5; *Macrobius*, lib. i.; *Saturni*, c. 18; and *Grotius* his *Animadvers. de Verit. Relig.*

peace, whose mind is stayed on thee;' unto which perfectly answers that
of the apostle, 1 Peter i. 13, 'Trust perfectly on the grace revealed' (so
in the margin also). And why? Because in trusting on that grace you
have being itself for the foundation, *Jehovah*, gracious, who is the first
being, and therefore the lowest foundation, on which all that is built stands
firm.

2. *Jehovah* imports that God only *is*, or alone hath true being in him.
For why else doth he appropriate this name *Jehovah* to himself alone as
incommunicable unto creatures, since all his creatures are but *æquivocè
entia*, shadows or pictures of being, not true being itself; as a man's picture is called a man equivocally, and not in a true sense. And as their
being is but a shadow of being, such are all the mercies in them but
equivocally mercies, in comparison unto the mercies that are in God, who
is Jehovah, merciful, in whom his mercies have being, or rather are himself. So that it must be said that God alone is 'merciful and gracious,'
as truly as Christ says that God alone is good, for mercy is but a branch
of goodness. That Jehovah is merciful as God, not as creatures, I shall
have occasion afterwards to pursue this more fully.

If therefore we at any time think we may have any degree of confidence
upon the mercies and pities that are in creatures, even such as are in nearest
and dearest relation to us, as fathers, &c., of whom Christ says, 'Though
evil, they yet know how to give good things to their children,' and so likewise to pity them, then how much more may we be encouraged to rely on
God, who is a heavenly Father to us, the only true and loving Father, as
he only is the true and living God, and is withal styled 'the Father of
mercies,' 2 Cor. i. 3. And his mercies are true and living mercies, as
himself is. That passage in Ps. lxxxvi. 10, 'Thou art God alone,' will be
found eminently to be spoken as a magnifying of him, in relation to his
mercy (if the 5th and 15th verses be compared with it); and indeed it is
the main current of that whole psalm, of which hereafter; so as we may
say he is merciful alone. And if sins come to be pardoned, there God's
mercies solely and alone can stand us in any stead, not only because that
God alone can pardon sins committed against himself, the great sovereign
Being, nor can any creature have any influence thereinto—'none can
forgive sins but God,' Luke v. 21—but besides, for this, that he alone
hath mercy great enough in him to do it. The creatures have not mercy
sufficient enough in them, great sins they could not find in their hearts
to pardon; so great an iniquity, if to themselves, as sin is against God,
they cannot forgive: 'Who is a God like unto our God, pardoning
iniquity?' &c.

The inference and direction to our faith from hence is, as to trust perfectly on him (as before), so only and alone upon him: 'My soul, wait
thou *only* upon God; for my expectation is from him. He *only* is my
rock,' Ps. lxii. 5, 6; all one as to say, he only hath firmness of being,
whom my soul can build upon; and therefore he is my salvation. If any
creature had all the goodness and clemency, mercy and grace, that is diffused throughout the whole of intelligent natures, angels and men, it were
not to be relied upon, but being laid in the balance with God, he were
'altogether lighter than vanity,' as it follows there, ver. 9. And the
reason is correspondent, if in their being they are vanity—Isa. xl. 17,
'All nations before him are as nothing; and they are counted to him less
than nothing, and vanity,'—then in their goodness much more. And as
God only is being, so only to be relied on as merciful. Yea, if your own

graces, that are in your own hearts, though wrought by God's Spirit, even that mercy and kindness which you have for yourselves, whom you love so much, yet are no way to be trusted in, but are as to such a purpose lighter than vanity, and would fail but for his mercy, the maintainer of them, then much more all that is in all creatures else whatever.

I shall after have occasion to shew, that the ground for all this exhortation, thus only to trust in God, is, in the latter end of this very psalm, centred upon, and referred to the words of this proclamation, my text, in verses 11, 12.

3. *Jehovah* imports that his being is of himself, ἀυτοῶν, ἀυτοφυης, and such is Jehovah as merciful, or his saving mercies; and indeed all his mercies whatsoever, they flow and proceed wholly from himself, having no motive but from what is in himself, either as to the persons to whom, or as to the things and mercies bestowed. For although to be merciful is his nature, yet the dispensation or giving forth of mercy is from his will; and that which his will is guided by is the good pleasure of his will, Eph. i. 5, and according as he is pleased to 'purpose within himself, verse 9, you may observe is this, 'I will be merciful to whom I will be merciful.' This is the royal preface and effort unto this proclamation of his nature,* in which he speaks but himself to be Jehovah, merciful, or the possessor of all being. And that looking as Jehovah, he is Lord of being itself, so the Lord of all his mercies themselves; and that as his being is of himself, so that his shewing mercy is from himself. And all reason is there for it; for his mercies, whence these acts of mercy flow, are himself; and also where and to whom his saving mercies go, himself goes with them. He bestows his whole self on whomsoever he bestoweth them. This you expressly find, Isa. xliii. 25, '*I*, even *I*, am he that blotteth out thy transgressions for mine own sake, and will not remember thy sins;' *i.e., I* that am what *I am*, Jehovah, am he that doth it, and I do it of myself. He resolves it wholly into himself, and as moved by nothing but himself, so as he assumes this thing to himself, and takes it wholly on himself. The prophet Ezekiel, chap. xxxvi. ver. 22, thus expresseth it, ' I do not this for your sakes, but for my own holy name's sake.' And again, lest they should not take in the weight of this sufficiently at once saying, he repeats it, and withal leaves a smart and round *memento* behind him for them to think on, why they should consider it: ver. 32, not for your sakes do I this, ' be it known to you.' And this there spoken of was the cleansing them from their sins, ver. 25; and giving them a new heart and saving repentance, ver. 26, 31; mercies to salvation all of them. And that clause at the close of all, its being known to them, rounds them in with a witness. And by a good token of the clean contrary in yourselves do you remember (says he): ver. 31, ' Then shall ye remember your own evil ways, and your doings that were not good, and shall loathe yourselves in your own sight, for your iniquities, and for your abominations.' Thus mercy comes over them with a triumph, as sinners confounded even with their being pardoned; as elsewhere it is said, that ' mercy rejoiceth against judgment.'

4. Jehovah imports him in general to be the fountain of all being to all things else that have being, and him to be the original Being, other things but derivative; so the best and noblest, highest sort or rank of beings, do derive their original, and hold their dependence entirely upon Jehovah, as he is gracious and merciful. And therefore *Jehovah, merciful* are well

* Compare Exod. xxxiii. and xxxiv.

joined together, seeing it is grace and mercy that gives being to the most transcendent works of God.

Those of our redemption, the first sort of beings, that hold their copies of him, are the works of his first creation, of which himself thus speaks, Isa. lxvi. 1, 2, 'All these things have my hands made,' pointing to heaven and earth, this visible world, and all therein. And all 'those things have been' (says he); that is, by this same hand of mine all these things exist and have a being, as you also have it Acts xvii. 25, 28; or all these things 'continue in being,' as elsewhere the word is used. And this is *dictum Jehovæ*, the saying of Jehovah; and it is as if he had said, You all that have being and existence hold of me *in capite*, as I am Jehovah. But there is another, an higher rank of beings, that holds of him as he is Jehovah, gracious and merciful. And such a superior kind of beings God himself there intimates in saying, with difference from those other makes or beings, 'To him will I look' (or 'but to those will I look') 'that is of poor and contrite spirit, and trembles at my word;' that is, who hath a gracious heart, of which, and all that belong to it, Jehovah as merciful is the founder. And the dilating on this being full and pertinent to the notion in hand, and tending so much to the glory of our Jehovah, and the mercy of him, I shall enlarge upon this division of these two ranks, as taking up and dividing between them the whole breadth of beings, as both the Scriptures and the schoolmen abundantly shew.

1st, The schoolmen reduced all things derivative from God as the fountain unto two orders. The first is *ordo naturæ*, the order of things in nature, which are those by the first creation, which are continued in existence by common providence, whereof God in the prophet there first speaks. Secondly, *ordo gratiæ*, the order of things in grace, which are wholly supernatural, which also the prophet there insinuates, with distinction of one from the other.

2dly, The Scripture also itself speaks the difference of their productions, as when it speaks of some things 'not made with hands, and not of this building,' Heb. ix. 11; that is, not of this ordinary make, by the first creation or common providence, of which God also so slightly and undervaluingly had spoken in that of Isaiah, 'These things my hands have made; but,' &c.

(1.) For the proof of this I will instance in the highest of that rank, in the order of grace, and things supernatural, the head of them all, viz., Christ's human nature, in its advancement by personal union with the Son of God; ay, and Christ's body too, as having been conceived by the Holy Ghost, Heb. ix. 11, where it is said that hereby he became an high priest 'by a greater and more perfect tabernacle, not made with hands, that is to say, not of this building.' Also as to the work of grace wrought by a new creation in the heart of a sinner (which is the image of Christ with difference from that of Adam), as it is said to be 'a new creature,' so the way of producing it is said to be a new creation 'made without hands,' Col. ii. 11. And this new creature, with the whole system of things belonging to it, is called another new world, or beings of another kind. And,

(2.) All those things appertaining to this order of grace have the name and nature of being as truly as those other: 'of him' (that is, of God) 'you are in Christ Jesus,' 1 Cor. i. 30; *i.e.*, you have another being founded in Christ *de novo*, anew. You have your existence in him; God declares himself there the founder of a new creation, and Christ to be the head of it. And these things that are by this new creation, he sets in

opposition to all else of the old creation, and that are the highest perfections of them, in saying he brings to nought things that are by things that
are not, which he nameth anew to be of him.

(3.) And these things of the new creation are an higher and more transcendent kind of beings (not only a differing being), and are so in God's
esteem; for in that place of Isaiah he speaks of the greatest things of the
first creation, pointing to them undervaluingly, ' All these things have my
hand made;' but ' unto him will I look,' and have respect, and my eye is
upon, that is of my new creation.   And of Christ's human nature (in that
Heb. ix. 11), though it be made of the same stuff we are all made of, yet
because it was brought forth by this new way of creation, he terms it ' a
greater and more perfect tabernacle, not made with hands.'

(4.) All things of the new creation hold their existence of Jehovah upon
this title of *Jehovah, gracious.* ' Of him ye are in Christ Jesus,' says the
apostle; but of him as Jehovah, gracious and merciful, says the prophet;
for the apostle refers us for the proof of this unto Jer. ix. 23, 24, ' Thus
saith Jehovah, Let not the wise man glory in his wisdom,' &c.: ' but let
him that glories glory in this, that he understandeth and knoweth me, that
I am Jehovah which exercise loving-kindness, and judgment, and righteousness, in the earth: for in these things I delight, says Jehovah.'   To
this place the apostle refers us, as appears by his next verse: ver. 31,
' That according as it is written,' says he, ' He that glories, let him glory
in the Lord.'   He hath Jehovah and Jehovah over and again, and him as
exercising loving-kindness, and so as merciful (in which he delights), as
the foundation of this new being in Christ: ' Of him ye are in Christ
Jesus,' whereof this he brings as the proof.

And this is the account given why he assumes the name *Jehovah*, as if
he had never been known by that name before ; though we find it in Moses
from the very 2nd of Genesis, and so on, often used, yet our most judicious
commentators say that it was to signify he came to give being to his promises.   He had made promises before, made a covenant, promised that
good land, which he had done under other names; but now, says he, I
come to shew myself *Jehovah*, in giving being to those promises and that
covenant, to give existence to them.   Which is all founded on this, that
his name *Jehovah* is not only to shew that he hath being in himself, but
to give being to all things else, but especially to his covenant of mercy and
grace, whereof those things were the types.

In the New Testament, this is the founder of this new rank of beings in
grace, as ' Jehovah merciful' is set out by that blessed title, more suitable
to the expression of the New Testament, of his being ' the Father of mercies;' that is, the *conditor* or *author novi ordinis:* 2 Cor. i. 3, ' Blessed be
God, even the Father of our Lord Jesus Christ, the Father of mercies, the
God of all comforts.'   His being Father of all gospel mercies is set next to
his being the Father of Christ, because of him we are in Christ Jesus
what we are in grace.   This his title of ' Father of mercies' bears two
senses :

1. That he is a merciful Father, it being an Hebraism, say some, as
when he is called the ' Father of glory,' &c.; that is, a glorious Father.
And in that he says of mercies in the plural, this intends or augments the
emphasis of it.   It is as if he had said, he is *summè misericors*, he is a most
merciful Father in the highest degree.   Thus Beza, Grotius, and others.

2. He becomes the author and original of all gospel mercies that are
founded in Christ, having taken on him first the relation of a father to us

in Christ, *mercies* being here taken for the effects of mercy, as often in Scripture the word mercies is used for merciful effects or benefits. And the word διχτιϱμῶν, in Latin *miserationes*, doth properly signify the gracious effects flowing from mercy in God, which are called his mercies, and so do differ from ἔλεος, which signify the mercy that is seated in the heart of God himself.* And mercies being thus understood, when it is said he is the Father of mercies, it implies he is a Father that gives being to those mercies, as a father doth to his child. And they are the mercies of the gospel, and all the mercies of the gospel in Christ, which here he especially and apart intends; for he speaks of such mercies, which he bestows as he is the Father of Christ, as well as he is the Father of mercies, as the words following imply, ' the God of all comfort,' and therefore likewise the Father of all mercies.

Now of these mercies or benefits of this new rank of beings which God, as Jehovah merciful, is the Father of, there are two sorts:

1*st*, Such as impress something on us, work some real new being in us, which we call a physical change.

2*dly*, There are privileges granted us, which work a mighty change in us in our state and condition before the Lord. The first are such as when he makes us holy, and the like, and such were most of the benefits of the first creation, when we were framed and formed first out of nothing. But the greatest benefits in grace do impress nothing upon us, make no physical change (though such a change is the consequent of them), and yet are things of the greatest make, and have the greatest reality in them, and the title of creation given to them. The first sort are like unto that, that he will at the resurrection ' change our vile bodies into the likeness of his glorious body,' in Phil. iii. 21, which is done ' according to the working whereby he is able even to subdue all things to himself.' But the latter are ἐξουσίαι, they are privileges; as in John i. it is said, he gave us ἐξουσίαν, power, or right, or privilege (as it is in the margin) to become the sons of God. And answerably (to explicate this), there is a twofold power in God. *First*, That which we call *potentia*, whereby he is the author of all those works which flow from mere power and force, whereby he made the world. But, *secondly*, there is *potestas*, dominion or sovereignty; and the acts of this kind of power, or sovereignty, by which he makes things that are not, to be, of the two are the greater, far greater than the other. The greatest works in the order of grace are of sovereignty's make; you may see it by that in kings, who have no more physical power than other men; by their own hands they can work no more than another man, yet they can do strange acts of another kind, which flow from their sovereignty: they can make knights, create noblemen, set up favourites, which are called their creatures; which actings of theirs are not by any internal workings *on* the person, but by external works as *to* the person, that resides in their own breast, and then expressed and put forth: and yet they are as real effects in their kind as any other.

You may see these two different works in that, 1 Cor. i. 30, where Christ is said to be made righteousness to us, and sanctification to us. Righteousness of justification is a work of God *upon* us, but sanctification is a working holiness *in* us; and yet each of these have the title of being given to them, ' Of him ye *are* in Christ Jesus, who is made both these to you.' I shall only enlarge upon the latter of these two, namely, that these out-

---

* Vid. Drusium in 2 Cor. i. 3.

ward privileges have yet the most real being in them; which will also appear by the consequents that follow.

Thus, in Scripture phrase, God's advancing to an office or dignity is said to be a making or constituting: thus Ex. vii. 1, ' The Lord said to Moses, See I have made thee a god to Pharaoh, and Aaron thy brother shall be thy prophet.' And 1 Sam. xii. 6, ' The Lord advanced ' (that is, made) ' Moses and Aaron,' and set them up in those offices, furnishing them with gifts suitable. Thus, Mark iii. 14, it is said, ' Christ ordained twelve,' apostles namely; the word is ' made ' them. He prefers them to that office out of grace; for in Rom. i. 5 it is called ' grace and apostleship.' These were acts of grace, making of them, or constituting of them in an outward office, the consequence whereof was enabling them with such and such gifts; but the office was but an external privilege with authority. Now, there are many of the greatest blessings or benefits we receive in Christ that are an external preferring us unto a dignity, an high privilege, in which the benefit mainly consists, but hath for its concomitant and its consequence the most real effects of any other. And the privilege itself hath a transcendent being in itself, and they are bestowed upon us by way of a creation, or God's making or calling us so to be, according to what is said, Rom. iv. 17, ' God calls those things that are not as though they were,' and gives them being. From this general I give particular instances.

First, That we should be the people of God. His calling us to be so is his making us so by way of privilege, from the contrary state wherein we were, of not being his people till he is pleased to call us so; and this is answerable unto a new creation of mercy: 1 Pet. ii. 10, ' Who in times past were not a people, but are now the people of God, which had not obtained mercy, but now have obtained mercy.' This was done by calling, ver. 9. Here is a change wrought in our state and condition, analogous to that political change which a king makes in a man when he prefers him; and this wholly the effect of mercy, ' who have obtained mercy;' and hereof the Scripture uses the same phrase of making us his people, as truly as it is used of the old creation: Ps. c. 3, ' Know ye that the Lord he is God; it is he that made us, and not we ourselves, his people;' that is, made us his people. He speaks in distinction from the first make, and it is founded on this, that he gives us this new being as he is Jehovah, as he is God, and this is done by way of preferment or exaltation. That in Deut. xxxii. 6, ' Is not God thy Father? hath he not made thee, and established thee?' in Acts xiii. 17 is thus expressed, ' The God of his people Israel chose our fathers, and exalted the people.'

Secondly, He hath called us to be the sons of God: it is but a title and privilege in itself, as out of John i. 12 I shewed. He gave them ἐξουσίαν to become the sons of God, as a privilege by patent; as also to be heirs and co-heirs with Christ, as in Rom. viii. 17. But this in the consequents of it appears to have the greatest being to follow upon it; it hath so in itself; but I say it doth appear, it will appear one day to have so: 1 John iii. 1, ' Behold what manner of love the Father hath bestowed upon us, that we should be called the sons of God. Beloved, now we are the sons of God, and it does not yet appear what we shall be.' What will be the consequent of it? ' But we know that when he shall appear, we shall be like him, for we shall see him as he is.' And it is but the Father's calling us to be his sons. What is that? It is but giving us that relation upon his own saying, we shall be so. It is calling us what we were not to be now what we are; and his saying we shall be his sons, it is but an act external upon us; and yet this hath the greatest reality of being flowing from it, and contained in it.

Thirdly, It is thus also in justification. It is but calling us from what we are not, yea, from the contrary, to be righteous in his righteousness, by the power and dominion of him that is Jehovah, the fountain of being, who says to an ungodly person, 'Thou art righteous,' and in saying it makes him such : Rom. v. 19, 'By the obedience of one many shall be made (or constituted) righteous.' This is a matter of the greatest reality, and hath the firmest being in it, and yet is but an act external upon us ; the soul in itself hath no being as to this righteousness, for God justifies it as ungodly; it hath no such being, but God gives it, and gives it by an act that is external to us, answering to that forensical act of pronouncing a man innocent at the bar.

The second sort of beings or blessings of grace are such as do impress something upon us, and their beings consist wholly in such an impression. As when God comes to a soul that is nothing but sin, and gives it a new heart, and a new spirit, and it becomes a workmanship created to good works, this he does by working this new creature in it, by internal changing our corrupt hearts, as one day he will do our vile bodies. These, and all such effects, are but the fruits of Jehovah merciful.

3dly, There is a third sort of this rank of mercies which are imminent* in the heart of God, which are called his thoughts of peace and mercy, Isa. lv. 7, 8, which in Ps. xl. 5, Christ says, are infinite for multitude towards us, being continued, fixed in him from everlasting : Jer. xxix. 11, ' I know the thoughts that I think towards you.' And these I call imminent* in himself, according to that Eph. i. 9, 11, ' which he purposed in himself.'

There are also a middle between his purposes in himself, and the execution of them upon us, all which are called mercies. There are also promises which are his promises of mercy, a middle between both, and unto all these he gives a being as he is Jehovah merciful : ' All the promises of God are yea and amen,' 2 Cor. i. 20. And that these in Christ are said to be *amen*, it imports they have a real being and existence ; for what is *amen* but ' so be it ;' so that he sets to his promises answerably, ' Let it be so' (which was the word at the first creation, and it was so), and so shall these promises one day be.

But what do I, treating of these little makes of grace, mercy in and upon, and towards us, that shew Jehovah gracious and merciful, in giving a being to them all, while I am to give instances of a far greater make and being that flow from Jehovah gracious to be sure ? for it is the grace of union we now speak of.

1. What say you to Jesus Christ, that new thing ? Jer. xxxi. 22, Jehovah ' created a new thing in the earth, a woman shall compass a man ;' that man of men, that strong man Jesus, conceived in the womb of that virgin in Nazareth, a city of the ten tribes, whom therefore he exhorts to return. Now take Jesus Christ as God-man and mediator, and all of him from top to toe, and all he was made of, it is all of God, out of grace, I will not say of mercy. That the Son of God should take that flesh was a new thing, which I need not insist on.

2. As his person, so all his offices were all made things by Jehovah gracious : Acts ii. 36, ' That all the house of Israel may assuredly know, that he hath made that same Jesus Lord and Christ.' He made him a

* Qu. ' immanent ' ?—ED.

king : Ps. lxxxix. 27, ' I will make my first-born, higher than the kings of the earth.' He was made a surety and mediator : Heb. vii. 22, ' He was made a priest after,' &c. ' By so much was Jesus made a surety of a better testament ; ' ' made an high priest,' Heb. iii. 2, so the margin hath it ; all out of grace and prerogative. Thus in himself.

3. To be sure, whatever he is made to us to be, that is of Jehovah merciful to us : 1 Cor. i. 30, ' Of him are ye in Christ Jesus, who of God is made to us wisdom, righteousness, sanctification, and redemption.'

4. Then how was he made these to us ?

He ' made him sin,' 2 Cor. v. 21, as strange a work for God to make his Son to be, as any of the former. ' He made him sin, that knew no sin.' Will you have it further ? ' He made him a curse,' Gal. iii. 13. And these were real makings, for his soul felt the effects of them, though in themselves they were but external imputations. But he felt the effects of them as we do the benefits of his being made such. And thus as to his person and offices, and what he is made to us all, are new beings of Jehovah gracious to him, and merciful to us.

3dly, He is Jehovah merciful ; he is the Father of all the mercies that are in the heart of Christ himself, through whose heart all God's mercies run and flow to us. Jehovah merciful gave being to them, God commanded him to love us, and put into his heart, as a man, that ' love which passeth knowledge,' Eph. iii. 19. All those sure mercies of David, that is, of Christ (Acts xiii. 34, and Isa. lv. 3), that are either in his heart towards us, or are the benefits he purchased and bestows upon us, Jehovah merciful is the Father of them all ; that he is ' a merciful high priest,' Heb. ii. 17 ; that he does pity us according to the measure of our needs, Heb. v. 2 ; that he hath mercies in his soul wherewith to do it : all this is what God bestows upon his heart to make him such. As God gave him a body fitted, he gave him a heart fitted : Ps. lxxxix. 24, speaking of Christ under the type of David, says he, ' My faithfulness and my mercy shall be with him,' and he speaks it as in relation unto his government and dispensation of things to us, even as of David in the type it is there spoken in relation to his government. My mercy shall be with him (says God) to execute all for me, and to dispense all the mercies out of mercifulness in himself, which I myself would dispense, God having given up all into his hand, God's mercies and faithfulness are with him in the execution.

Lastly, It would be too poor a thing for me now to tell you that Jehovah merciful gives being to all the mercies in the hearts of fathers, mothers, friends, or whomever you know to be pitiful. Read over all stories, and put all the mercies you can read of or hear of into one heart, if a father had all the mercies that a father ever had, how pitiful would he be. But who is the Father of these, and gives being to them ? It is Jehovah merciful ; and shall not he that made the eye see, and shall not he that put these mercies into all the hearts of all the creatures, yea, into the hearts of them that are evil (for such are parents, both fathers and mothers), be himself merciful ? And shall it be said, ' How can a mother forget her child ? ' And shall not this, in a more infinite transcendent manner, be attributed to God ? I have told you he is the Father of Christ, and of all the mercies in Christ, and that is beyond all. Remember that he is Jehovah merciful, that gives being to all in whom your souls do trust.

5. The name Jehovah, by which God makes himself known in this proclamation of mercy, Exod. xxxiv. 6, imports him also to be the first and last in being, and so his giving being to all things from the first unto the

last, and that they all wholly and all along depend upon him for being; which is in a great part the mind of that speech, Isa. xliv. 6, ' I am the first, and I am the last.' And in another place of the same prophet, chap. xli. 4, ' Who hath wrought and done it, calling the generations from the beginning? I the Lord, the first, and with the last, I am he.' He speaks it in relation unto all created beings, from the first creation throughout all generations. Wherein observe how he is absolutely in both places said to be the first, but not with the last, which is only in the latter text, for time was when there was no creature with him from all eternity, and then he was first only and alone. But in this second text he is said to be with the last, and yet nevertheless he is said to be the last in that other. The reasons of which I take up thus, that for time to come God hath ordained some sort of creatures to exist to eternity, like as himself doth, and so in that respect he is said to be with the last, even of them; but yet take in this with it, that nevertheless he is also the last, as truly as the first, chap. xliv. 6, as also Rev. i. 11. This is to be understood in respect (say I) of their total, and absolute, and continual dependency upon him; and it is all one as if he had said, although they do continue to eternity, yet it is through me and from me, for I am the last however, because it is I uphold them in being so to do; for I only have immortality of being, 1 Tim. vi. 16, and they but by participation from me, and so in truth and *de jure*, of right, ' I am the last.'

Now what the prophet speaks, as in respect to those first beings of the creation, the apostle in his Revelation applies unto grace and salvation, the things of the second sort of beings. For in respect thereto it is the apostle utters the same saying, as by comparing Rev. i. 4th and 8th verses appears. In the 4th verse he wisheth ' grace and peace from him which is, and which was, and which is to come.' And from Jesus Christ, ver. 5, who, ver. 8, says of himself, ' I am Alpha and Omega, the beginning and the ending, saith the Lord, which is, and which was, and which is to come, the Almighty.' And this his title, ' I am the beginning and the ending,' is spoken in relation unto grace and salvation; for upon this title it is that grace is wished from him as well as from the Father; and also they are the very benefits of salvation which he had there spoken of, ver. 5, 6. Thus then in grace he is the first and the last, as well as in the prophet he is said to be so in relation unto the beings of the first creation.

And his being the first and the last notes forth not only the two extremes of grace and salvation, that is, of the first beginning and last ending or accomplishment of our salvation, as if he were the author only of these; but this expression of his being the first and last encloseth and taketh in the whole line and series of benefits of grace and salvation whatsoever, continued all along between that first and last. Even as in respect of natural beings (as life and motion), his being the first and last takes in all, whatsoever of them, from first to last.

Only I observe, that his being ' Alpha and Omega' in this respect is resolved into his being Jehovah, for both in ver. 4 and 8 it runs thus, ' From him that was, and is, and is to come,' which is the deciphering of Jehovah; and thereby he is apparently made and is declared the fountain of all and every whit of grace, both past, present, and to come; and not only at first, or at the last alone, but all along in the intervals of time between. 1. ' From him that was;' and so he is the eternal spring of that grace which was from everlasting, and is shewn at conversion. 2. Which is;' that is, he at present continues to dispense all grace to us.

3. ' Who is to come;' so he is the author of all grace, for everlasting, unto the last.

And yet I will not restrain these his titles only unto matters of grace and salvation, for they comprehensively relate unto all other works which Christ doth for his church, or towards others, or that are prophesied of in this book, as by the repetition of them, chap. xxii. 13, at the end of this book, and as after all the works of his kingdom perfected, it appears. ' I am Alpha and Omega, the beginning and the end, the first and the last;' yet still so as here at the beginning of the book, wherein grace and peace is wished, it must be allowed to have a special relation to grace and the works thereof. Thus God is the immediate forger of every link of that golden chain, whereof the first is rivetted in his own heart, and the last ends in him also. Thus it is in his loving us, and thus it is in his saving us; he is the first and last in both.

1. In loving us (which is the foundation of all grace to us, for love is the ground of all mercy, Eph. ii. 4, and so of all benefits of salvation) he is the first. So it is said expressly, 1 John iv. 19, ' We love him because he first loved us,' and not we him, ver. 10. And he is the last in loving also; ' whom he loved he loved to the end,' John xiii. 1 ; and we should not love him to the end, if he did not continue to love us to the end. Thus it is in the foundation of mercy.

2. In the works of salvation he is the first and the last, Heb. xii. 2. He is the ' author of our faith,' and so the first, and ' the finisher,' and so the last. Thus he is at death too, when we ' receive the end of our faith, the salvation of our souls,' 1 Pet. i. 9. And after that, he is thus to us at the day of judgment: 2 Tim. i. 18, ' The Lord grant he may find mercy at that day.' It is then we have need of mercy, and he is the giver of it. And as at the first and last, so all along between, he is thus the fountain of all mercy and grace to us. ' It is by the grace of God I am that I am,' says the apostle, 1 Cor. xv. 10; ' and it is not I, but the grace of God that is with me;' i. e., which is all along with me in every act and step. We are therefore continually to look for, and depend upon the mercy of our Lord Jesus Christ even all along unto eternal life, Jude 21.

It is not as the Papists say, who acknowledge God to be the first in the benefits of salvation, as that at the first mercy doth all in justification (and they call it therefore the first justification), which they ascribe to God's grace wholly; but then they feign a second justification, as that which saves us, and makes us heirs of eternal life through the merits of works. Oh, but Jehovah merciful and gracious is the first and the last, and all and everything of grace depends upon him, and it is wholly grace and mercy from first to last.

Yea, and he is Jehovah gracious with the last (as you heard the prophet Isaiah speak, chap. xli. 4), for eternal glory is as much from his grace as conversion itself at first. ' It is the gift of God,' Rom. vi. 23, and ' grace reigns' even in heaven to eternity, Rom. v. 21, as much as ever it did in this life, and more, and it is grace then that entertains us in heaven: Eph. ii. 5–7, ' Who hath quickened us and saved us' (so in this life, as he had said in the verses before), ' that he in ages to come might shew the exceeding riches of his grace in his kindness towards us through Christ Jesus.' This is to be done in heaven. We have grace here but by driblets, and but imperfect holiness, and a defective communion with God, &c.; there it is he profusely spends and pours forth his riches reserved to that time, and then the vessels of mercy possess the whole of ' the riches of glory,' Rom. ix. 23, the well-head whereof is mercy, as there is expressed.

6. This name of God *Jehovah* imports also his being ' from everlasting to everlasting;' and as his name *El* that follows, translated *God*, notes forth his power, so *Jehovah* and *Ehije* his eternity, as Calvin and others observe. But we have a surer word of prophecy that the import of it is eternity, from the before-cited apostle's own paraphrase upon it: Rev. i. 4 (which many of our divines upon that place have observed), ' Him which is, which was, and which is to come,' which is the unciphering of the very name *Jehovah*, and the true reason why he saith not ἀπὸ τοῦ ὄντος, but ἀπὸ τοῦ ὁ ὤν, was (as Calvin and Beza have observed), to point as with the finger unto this very name *Jehovah*, I am, Exod. 3d and 6th chapters. Yea, the form of the Hebrew word *Jehovah*, says Ainsworth, implies so much, *Je* being a sign of the time to come, and so *Jehovah*, he will be; *Ho*, of the time present, *Hovah*, he that is, and *Vah*, of the time past; *Havah*, he was. And again elsewhere the same author observes,* that *Jehovah* cometh of *Havah*, he was, and by the first letter, *J*, it signifies he will be, and by *Ho*, it signifies he is;† and this the Hebrew doctors, says he, acknowledge, in saying that the three times, past, present, and to come, are comprehended in this proper name *Jehovah*, as it is known to all, say they. Thus Ainsworth on Gen. ii. 4 out of them.

Now, as his being, so these his mercies are from everlasting; for both Jehovah and merciful are still correspondent: Ps. xxv. 6, ' Remember, O Lord, thy tender mercies, and thy loving-kindnesses, which have been ever of old.' They are mercies as to time past, which the word ' remember ' insinuates; and they are his special mercies to his elect, which with difference he styleth his ' tender mercies;' and they are his ' loving-kindnesses,' which word imports his entirest love, as Ps. xviii. 2. The same word signifies to love heartily in the midst of the bowels. And these have been ' ever of old,' and that not only as of a time of an old date, and so the word is elsewhere used, but these have been for ever of old; it is that oldness of eternity. They are as old as Jehovah himself, the ' Ancient of days,' is. And why? Because they are the mercies of him that is Jehovah. And thus we find his everlasting love stated in difference from what is of old: Jer. xxxi. 3, the Lord hath ' appeared to me of old.' This the church says, that is, in ancient times, in former times; ah, but appears not now to me. In answer thereto says God, Dost thou speak of times of old? Yea, ' I have loved thee with an everlasting love,' &c., and so of an elder date than that old time thou speakest of, in which I should have appeared to thee. And thus here our translators have emphatically translated the words ' for ever of old.'

But what, are they everlasting only from time past? No; but as Jehovah imports his being to everlasting also, so his mercies are: Ps. c. 5, ' The Lord is good, his mercy is everlasting, and his truth endureth to all generations.' And the eternity in this place is that part of it for time to come, for it is from generation to generation. And as we find the everlastingness of them either way thus singly and apart set out in these Psalms mentioned, so we find them in Psalm ciii. 17 to be conjoined, ' The mercy of the Lord

---

* Ainsworth on Ps. lxxxiii. 18, which is, with a special observation, cited by Dr Jackson, of the divine essence and attributes.

† Phrasis est quæ occurrit apud Judæos, quâ Deum significare volunt, et æternitatem παραφραστικῶς exprimi.—*Capellus in Apoc.* chap. i. ver. 4.

is from everlasting to everlasting upon them that fear him.' So, then, Jehovah that was, that is, and that is to come, is merciful and gracious.

And this speaks more than what is in the former assertion; for by this he is not simply the first in grace, and so in mercy to us: that might have been, though he had begun to have loved but then when he first wrought on us, or as having purposed it from some very ancient date; but this imports his having ever loved us since he was God, and had being, or shall have being, both his own nature inclining him, together with his purposes of mercy taken up by his own will towards us. For he would have his mercies unto his children to bear the resemblance of his very being Jehovah, and so answer to his name in being as eternal as himself: Isa. liv. 7, 8, 10, ' For a small moment have I forsaken thee; but with great mercies will I gather thee. In a little wrath I hid my face from thee for a moment; but with everlasting kindness will I have mercy on thee, saith the Lord thy Redeemer. For the mountains shall depart, and the hills be removed; but my kindness shall not depart from thee, neither shall the covenant of my peace be removed, saith the Lord that hath mercy on thee.'

Use. The use of which is this, to trust on him at all times and seasons. You heard before, out of Ps. lxii., you should trust in Jehovah solely, and alone, so ver. 5; but ver. 8 you have that added, ' Trust in him at all times;' for he that was, is, and is to come, is your Jehovah merciful. The worst times are those when you have sinned against him, yet come to him with faith at such time. You are not to imagine that indeed when we have walked holily, and only then, we may come with expectation of mercy and pardon from him: no, but trust in him ' at all times,' only come humbling yourselves, and turning unto him; draw near to him and he will draw near to you. God is not as man, to be merciful by fits, when the good humour comes on him; but consider, he is merciful as Jehovah, and therefore with a constancy, and continually, which in express words you have, Ps. lxxi. 3, ' Be thou my strong habitation whereunto I may continually resort: thou hast given commandment to save me; for thou art my rock and my fortress.' Ver. 14, ' But I will hope continually, and will yet praise thee more and more.'

7. The name *Jehovah* also imports immutability, unchangeableness of being: Mal. iii. 6, ' I am Jehovah, I change not;' so in the original. It is as if he should say, My name *Jehovah* speaks my being to be unchangeable. His name, *I am*, in short, imports, that he is always one and the same in being; which Christ, as being God, assumes when he said, ' Before Abraham was, I am,' John viii. 58. And the apostle says also of him, Christ, ' the same to-day, yesterday, and for ever,' Heb. xiii. 8. And therein also you have interpreted what is spoken of Christ, Rev. i. 8, ' He that was, that is, and is to come' (the paraphrase of *Jehovah*), to be meant of unchangeableness; *semper idem*, always one and the same. And as God is thus in his being unchangeable, so in his mercies; the mercies of this David are ' sure mercies,' Isa. lv. 3; Acts. xiii. 34. These his special mercies to his chosen have the similitude of his being. It is Jehovah that is merciful; and as Jehovah signifies firmitude of being, and is therefore compared to a rock, &c., so these his mercies are likened to things of longest duration, to those things which to us men are such in our account. Thus he compares them to the mountains, which cannot be removed; yea, mountains of brass, Zech. vi. 1: Isa. liv. 10, ' For the mountains shall depart, and the hills be removed; but my kindness shall not depart from thee, neither shall the covenant of my peace be removed, saith the Lord that

hath mercy on thee.' Also, in Ps. lxxxix., the perpetuity of mercy is one eminent piece of this psalm ; for with that he begins, ver. 2, ' For I have said, Mercy shall be built up for ever : thy faithfulness shalt thou establish in the very heaven.' And they are the sure mercies of our spiritual David (Christ), he means. Now, to set forth the perpetuity hereof, he first useth words that express firmitude, as ' established,' ' built up for ever,' ver. 2, 4. Then he uses such similitudes as are taken from things which are held most firm and inviolable amongst men, as ver. 4, *fœdus incidi*, I have cut or engraven my covenant (so in the Hebrew), alluding to what was then in use, when covenants were mutually to be made, such as they intended to be inviolate, and never to be broken ; to signify so much, they did engrave and cut them into the most durable lasting matter, as marble, or brass, or the like. You may see this to have been the way of writing in use, as what was to last for ever : as Job xix. 24, ' Oh that my words were graven with an iron pen and lead, in the rock for ever !' And what is that rock or marble here ? No other than the heart itself of our gracious and most merciful Jehovah, and his most unalterable and immoveable purposes, truth and faithfulness.* This is that foundation in the heavens, whereon mercy is built up for ever ; as ver. 2, which (as the apostle says) ' remains for ever ;' and so they become ' the sure mercies of David,' Isa. lv. 3. Again, solemn oaths amongst men serve to ratify and make things sworn to perpetual. This also is there specified as having been taken by God, ' Once have I sworn by my holiness,' &c., and sworn by him that cannot lie, and sworn to that end, ' to shew the immutability of his counsel,' Heb. vi. 17. And not only is the immutability of his mercy illustrated by these things taken from what is firm on earth, but he ascends up to the heavens, and first into the very highest heavens : ver. 2, ' For I have said, Mercy shall be built up for ever : thy faithfulness shalt thou establish in the very heaven :' comparing them to an house built not on earth, or upon a foundation of earth, which thieves break through, and violence destroys, but in heaven, whither they cannot reach. And there is good reason for it, for these mercies have a ' sure foundation' laid in God's heart, ' The Lord knows who are his.' And then they are founded also on that ' cornerstone, elect and precious,' Christ ; and which having been begun to be laid in the heart once of every one that is regenerate (though but the other day converted), yet will never cease to be built up even to eternity. We are apt to think, How little of mercy have I yet shewn forth upon me ! Consider, God hath but begun with thee ; he laid in thy heart at conversion a small spark and seed of grace ; and therewith, as the foundation, the pardon of all thy sins, which, as to all that is to follow, is but as a foundation buried under ground. But mercy hath not done with thee ; for it is in infinite glorious works that follow, to be ' built up for ever,' continually to be added unto, both in grace and glory. For God's dispensations in heaven are but a continuation of mercy to eternity, and a laying forth riches of grace and kindness on this structure, Eph. ii. 7. The prophet adds in that verse, ' Thy faithfulness shalt thou establish in the very heavens.' Some say, *cum cœlis*, with the heavens ; that is, it is a mercy as stable as heaven itself, meaning the visible ones. But I take it to be a supernatural supercreation phrase, to express a grace and mercy above all that is or was earthly in our first creation-condition, and above all comparisons to be made therewith, consisting altogether of blessings heavenly ; yea, supercelestial, as the word is in Eph. i. 4. And thus much the expression ' in

* Marmor hic nihil aliud est quam immotissima Dei fides, veritas, &c.—*Musculus.*

the heavens' doth import: as in Luke x. 20, ' Rejoice that your names are written in heaven.'   And Heb. xii. 23, ' The first-born whose names are written in heaven.'   And in saying here that these mercies are ' established in the heavens,' I understand them to be such super-celestial mercies spoken of.   The heavens is the place they came from, and where they are established and fixed, and unto which they tend, rising up to their original, and where they are finished and completed.   They are established in the heavens, in the highest heavens, where the angels and saints are,* ver. 2, 5, 6, 7, compared. And therefore they are as sure and safe as treasure there laid up is, as Christ says.   This house of mercy is as eternal and unde-molishable as that our house in those highest heavens is, 2 Cor. v. 1.

And because we see not those highest heavens (but only by faith) he farther points us to the heavens we see: ver. 28, 29, ' My mercy will I keep for him for evermore, and my covenant shall stand fast with him. His seed also will I make to endure for ever, and his throne as the days of heaven ;' which in ver. 36, 37, is more punctually amplified : ' His seed shall endure for ever, and his throne as the sun before me : it shall be established for ever, as the moon ; and as a faithful witness in heaven. Selah.'   And he introduceth these not as examples only, to which his mercies for their unchangeableness may be likened, but he proposeth them as God's faithful witnesses thereof.†   As the rainbow is set forth as a wit-ness that God will destroy the world with waters no more, thus the conti-nuation of the heavens, and of the sun and moon, are proposed as wit-nesses of the perpetuity and unchangeableness of these mercies ; and this not for duration only, but immoveableness and fixedness.   For though the sun sets, and leaves darkness behind him for half the time of his course, yet this Father of lights is without so much as ' shadow of turning' in his mercies towards us, as the apostle's comparison is, James i. 17, and else-where.   He hath pawned the covenant of day and night : Jer. xxxi. 35, 36, ' Thus saith the Lord, which giveth the sun for a light by day, and the ordi-nances of the moon and of the stars for a light by night, which divideth the sea when the waves thereof roar ; The Lord of hosts is his name : If those ordinances depart from before me, saith the Lord, then the seed of Israel also shall cease from being a nation before me for ever.'   The like is in Jer. xxxiii. 20, ' Thus saith the Lord, If you can break my covenant of the day, and my covenant of the night, and that there should not be day and night in their season ; then may also my covenant be broken,' &c.   Yea, and that covenant of the waters of Noah (we spake of) to which the rainbow is appointed as a faithful witness, is also appealed unto, and called in by God as a wit-ness of this his mercy's covenant : Isa. liv. 9, 10, ' For this is as the waters of Noah unto me : for as I have sworn that the waters of Noah should no more go over the earth ; so have I sworn that I would not be wroth with thee, nor rebuke thee.   For the mountains shall depart, and the hills be removed, but my kindness shall not depart from thee, neither shall the covenant of my peace be removed, saith the Lord that hath mercy on thee.'

Now this unchangeableness of mercy is put upon the account of his being Jehovah, as was observed out of Mal. iii. 6, ' I Jehovah change not ; therefore you sons of Jacob are not consumed.'   Unto which bring that of Lam. iii. 22, and then you have what it is in Jehovah which is the cause that we are not consumed : ' It is the Lord's mercy we are not consumed,'

* Cœli non visibiles, sed qui mundi architecturam superant.—*Calvin.*

† Non solum proponit ea ut exempla, sed ut testes : Quarum rerum ? Earum scili-cet quas Davidi promisit.

which is all one as to say, It is of the Lord's mercy, as the cause why we are not consumed. So then the evident inference or conclusion from both is, you are not consumed, because my mercies, who am Jehovah, change not, which the words that follow do more expressly shew to be the cause or reason of this, ' because his compassions fail not ; ' which still carries this before them, that we are not consumed, because his mercies consume not, because God, that is, Jehovah, consumes not, fails not, changeth not. Job xiv. 11, ' The waters fail from the sea, and the flood decayeth and drieth up,' but these his special mercies fail not, nor are ever drawn dry, because Jehovah, or inexhaustible being, is the inexhaustible fountain of those mercies.

I have given the reason why the name Jehovah merciful is used ; but farther, the duplication of it here is to be considered : Exod. xxxiv. 6, ' Jehovah, Jehovah.' The reason hereof, which interpreters ordinarily give, riseth but to this, that it was to stir up Moses his and our attention the more unto the matter that follows. I should rather and further say,

1. It is to shew an infinite vehemency and heartiness of affection to have been in the heart of God when he uttered this, and it manifests how much his soul was in what his voice proclaimed. Such duplications have (as it were) a double strength in them, to heighten and enforce those things they are prefixed unto, according to the nature of the matter unto which they are prefixed. Thus if the matter be an affirmation, the reiteration affixed intends and makes it an asseveration far the stronger. Thus when the two tribes and a half made an appeal to God in the case of their altar, to the intent to express the truth and sincerity of their souls therein, in the highest manner, say they, ' The God of gods, Jehovah, the God of gods, Jehovah, he knoweth,' &c., Josh. xxii. 22. In this appeal to God as a witness (for such it is), they rehearse no less than three names of God (say some), *El, Elohim, Jehovah ;* or, as others interpret it, ' God of gods, Jehovah.' But whatever meaning we take, it is certain that they are repeated twice over, which must needs have the greatest emphasis that could be given, and all was to give the greatest confirmation to the matter affirmed by them. Again, if it be set unto matter of prayer or praise, the repetition of ' Lord, Lord,' Ps. lxxii. 18, or of ' Jehovah' (as of the person invocated or praised) or the doubling the matter petitioned for, as ' be merciful, be merciful,' Ps. lvii. 1, likewise when the seal to either is put at the close of either, as of ' Amen and amen,' Ps. lxxii. 19, such doubled rehearsements do manifest a redoubled vehemency and intention in the invocators. Now according to this general rule,

2. In this duplication of the name of Jehovah here must be allowed the like intended emphaticalness, according to the kind of the matter it is prefixed unto. Now that which it is prefixed unto is a description of God, or a lively character of him, even as when we would notify the character given of a man to be most proper, genuine, and expressive of what the man is, we use before or after it to make a double indigitation of his name, which carries this import or signification : ' This is the man, this is he.' To the same purpose is it that God's name is doubled here. And it is as if in words he had more plainly said, ' This is your God, this am I ; ' or if you would know what a God I am, look upon this description of me, upon this my portraiture drawn to life : ' Such a God am I, Jehovah, Jehovah merciful.'

When the watchmen in the Canticles saw the spouse keep such ado, Cant. v. 9, 10, and to make so anxious an inquisition after her beloved :

' What is thy beloved,' said they, ' more than another beloved ? '   ' What ' ?
says she.   She then describes him in all his beauties from head to foot ;
and at the close, having said, ' he is altogether lovely,' she adds, ' This is
my beloved, and this is my friend.'   She doubles it there, and with the
same efficacy doth God in his setting forth himself double this his name
here : ' Jehovah, Jehovah,' &c., as if he should say, ' This, this am I.'

Nay, yet further here in this proclamation in my text there is not a
duplication only, but a triplication of the subject ; that is, the name of
God is not only twice repeated, but thrice, אֵל יְהוָה יְהוָה, translated ' The
Lord, Lord, God.'   And what is or can be the mind or intent hereof other
than this, that God, the whole that is in God, is merciful and gracious ? &c.

CHAPTER VII.

*The other name of God, אֵל, El, used in this proclamation of mercy, Exod.
xxxiv. 6, 7.—This name imports that all the three persons are merciful,
which is particularly proved concerning the Holy Ghost.—This name El
also imports an attribute in God, his strength and power, and that it is in
conjunction with mercy.—How much this hath an influence to make mercy
effectually prevailing, and to conquer all difficulties which lie in the way of
its acting.*

I have considered the first name of God, *Jehovah*, implied in this proclamation of mercy, Exod. xxxiv. 6, 7, and have evinced that mercy is an
essential property of his nature ; what remains next to be considered is
what the other name of God, אֵל, *El*, here made use of, imports.

There are two significations of this name of God.   It is sometimes put
for an essential name proper to God, as our translators have rendered it in
this text, and it is sometimes put for a special attribute of God, ' strong,
powerful,' noting greatness and dominion, and both here intended, for it
signifies both ; and truly Junius always translates the word *El* wherever he
finds it *Deus fortis*, the strong God, and so puts both together.

Now if we translate it as our translators have done it, ' God, Jehovah,
Jehovah,' *El*, God (he repeats the name of God three times), the import
of that is, that the three persons are herein proclaimed to be merciful and
gracious.   There must be some great mystery in the thrice repeating it.
If the thrice repeating an attribute, ' Holy, holy, holy,' if the thrice repeating, ' The Lord, the Lord, the Lord,' Num. vi. 23–26, hath the mystery
of all three persons, then the repetition of the name of God, fixed to mercy
and gracious, hath the like.   So Ainsworth and others have improved it.
So that from this it is evident that all three persons incline to be merciful
and gracious, God the Father, God the Son, and God the Holy Ghost ;
and what is this other than what we have, 2 Cor. xiii. 14, ' The grace of
the Lord Jesus Christ, and the love of God, and the communion of the
Holy Ghost, be with you all.   Amen.'   The Holy Ghost is therefore both
gracious and loving, as well as the Father and Son, for it is he communicates
the love and grace of both those persons.   I find not (I confess) a scripture
where the Holy Ghost is called merciful, but I find scripture where he is
called good, which is the root of mercy : Ps. cxliii. 10, ' Thy Spirit is good.'
Neh. ix. 20, ' Thou gavest them thy good Spirit.'   I find also that love is
ascribed to him, Rom. xv. 13.   Now what is mercy ?   It is but love and
goodness extended to creatures in misery.   I find also that grace and

mercy are the fountain of all blessings both spiritual and temporal, Eph. i. 2, 3. And I find grace, and mercy, and peace is wished as from God the Father, and God the Son, so from God the Holy Ghost, Rev. i. 3, 4. So then he is the fountain of grace. I will not open that controversy between papists and us about seven spirits; it is but one Spirit, 1 Cor. xii. 4. But what I will insist on is, an answer to that question, Why the Holy Ghost should bear the name of אל, *El*, ' strong,' ' the strong God,' for it signifies both an attribute as well as a person; Jehovah the Father is called, and Jehovah the Son is called, and the Holy Ghost is called so too; but why is this name *El* here, ' the strong God,' given unto him rather than Jehovah?

The answer is, he hath the execution of all the mercy that God doth dispense to us; it is committed to him. The Father had the decreeing part of all mercy, the Son the purchasing part, and the Holy Ghost the operative part, which requires power and strength; and therefore you find so often the Holy Ghost to be expressed as ' the power of God,' as Christ's person in the Proverbs is called ' the Wisdom of God.' The Holy Ghost is called ' the power of God:' Luke i. 35, ' The Holy Ghost shall come upon thee, and the power of the Highest shall overshadow thee.' And in Luke xxiv. 49, he is called ' the promise of the Father.' Who is that promise? Compare it with Acts i. 4, and you will find it is the Holy Ghost. What is the Holy Ghost called in that place of the Acts? ' Christ being assembled together with them, commanded them that they should not depart from Jerusalem, but wait for the promise of the Father.' Where was that promise? The 5th verse tells us, ' You shall be baptized with the Holy Ghost.' How is the meaning of that expressed? ' You shall receive power, after that the Holy Ghost is come upon you,' ver. 8. And in Scripture these things are often joined: ' The gospel came not in word only, but in the Holy Ghost, and power,' 1 Thes. i. 5.

The Holy Ghost then is he that shews mercy, he is ὁ ἐλεῶν. There are five offices which the Holy Ghost exerciseth in the churches, mentioned in Rom. xii. 8, and the last is called ὁ ἐλεῶν, a shewer or executor of mercy, to supply all needs and necessities to the sick, &c.: ' Let him that is the shewer of mercy do it with cheerfulness;' *i.e.*, whose office is to be merciful. There are many particular mercies which the Holy Ghost hath the office to distribute, as he is the dispenser of mercy. For example,

1. Begin with regeneration; that is mercy: ' According to his abundant mercy he hath begotten us,' 1 Peter i. 3. Who begets? The Holy Ghost.

2. Who brings home all the sure mercies of David, all that the Father hath decreed, or the Son purchased? John xvi. 14, 15. He will not leave us as orphans unprovided for. Therefore,

3. Is it not mercy to take care of orphans, children that are fatherless and motherless, that else would be destitute? John xiv. 17, 18. The Holy Ghost says, ' I will not leave you orphans;' the word is so in the original. Is it not mercy to tend the sick? Alas! how doth the Holy Ghost attend thy soul all the time of thy infirmities and sicknesses; and to ease thee he bears them, Rom. viii. 26.

4. Who is the advocate to plead for thee, and undertakes all thy suits for thee, and to obtain all good? It is the Holy Ghost? Who makes all thy prayers, Rom. viii. 26, draws all the petitions thou puttest up? He indites them. Who does bear with the noisomeness that is in thee? It is the Holy Ghost. And is it not that mercy, as it is in a nurse or mother, to bear the noisomeness of a poor child? And though he be grieved, yet

he continues his love and care, so as no mother nor nurse doth the like. Is not this mercy? Who mourns with thee in misery like a dove (as he is called), who keeps thee company, and brings thee cordials? It is he who is the author of all comfort, Acts ix. 31. Who fills thee with all joy and peace in believing? It is the Holy Ghost, Rom. xv. 13. To conclude, who strengthens thee in all temptations, and upholds thy feeble knees and weak hands? It is the Holy Ghost. And is not that mercy? Eph. iii. 16, 'That you might be strengthened with might, by his Spirit in the inner man.' I have done with this word אֵל, *El*, as it signifies a person, and imports the mercy of the Holy Ghost. I come now to אֵל, *El*, as it is an attribute (and the most of translators so render it; Junius calls it *Deus fortis*, 'the strong God'), and so the word signifies strength, strengthening, strong in might. We call it *vis* in Latin, 'that power that subdues all things to itself,' Philip. iii. 21. And so God is 'mighty in strength,' Job ix. 4. Now I am to handle it as an attribute, I join greatness with it, for so they are joined, and both with mercy; as in Jer. xxxii. 17–19, where he joins 'great,' and 'mighty,' and 'merciful' all together: *magnus ille, potens ille*, as Piscator renders it. I confess I wonder at it, to find it up and down when they make prayers in Scripture, as Jeremiah does here, that they should put 'merciful' and 'mighty,' 'terrible' and 'great,' all together; you shall find it so, Neh. i. 5, 'O Lord God of heaven, the great and terrible God, that keepest covenant and mercy,' &c. Here they are joined together. And so when he made his solemn prayer, Neh. ix. 32, 'Our God,' says he, 'the great, the mighty, and the terrible God, who keepest covenant and mercy,' &c.; which is plainly the same that Moses expresseth it in Exodus. You have it also in Dan. ix. 4, in his solemn prayer, 'O Lord,' says he, 'the great and dreadful God, keeping the covenant and mercy,' &c. Thus mercy, and great, and terrible are joined all together, and all refer to this passage in Moses, as the margin of your Bible shews. Now, when he says 'the terrible God,' truly it imports two things:

1st, His being glorious and illustrious, and that he is to be reverenced.

2dly, It imports a dreadfulness: he is 'terrible in praises,' Exod. xv. 11. What doth that imply? That he is magnified, illustrious, great, and glorious in praises, not only doing things that are dreadful, though so he is said to be terrible in doing to the sons of men, and yet he speaks not of judgment, Ps. lxvi. 5, but wonderful works of mercy.

That which I am to give account of is, that power and mercy should be joined together, God the strong and God the merciful. Take in greatness (if you will) and take in terribleness. In Ps. lxii. 11, 12, says he, 'God hath spoken once; twice have I heard this, that power belongeth unto God. Also to thee, O Lord, belongeth mercy, for thou renderest to every man according to his works.' I confess it is alleged, I heard it once, and twice, that is, God set it on upon me as a special ground of comfort. You have the phrase so used in Job xxxiii. 14, 'For God speaketh once, yea, twice, yet man perceiveth it not.' I confess I was suspicious it might refer to this passage of Moses. I found, first, the English annotators say, that it was a plausible interpretation to refer it to what God had said upon mount Sinai, where there are two things (say they) said: first, that God was a jealous God; secondly, shewing mercy, Exod. xx. 5, 6. I consulted Hammond, and he in his paraphrase refers us to what God had spoken in mount Sinai, but he speaks it indefinitely; but the others refer it to the second commandment. I stick at this, that jealousy is mentioned in the commandment, but power is not; but here he says, 'Power belongs to thee, O Lord God, and mercy.' I thought therefore I might go further, and take a step further upon mount Sinai, where the law and this declaration was given, as it is expressed, Exod. xxxiv. The psalmist says, 'he heard it twice;' he heard it from God's mouth, 'that power belongs to God,' and he heard it that mercy belongs to God; and he heard the same from Moses, Num. xiv. 15, 16, 'Let the power of my Lord be great, according as thou hast spoken, saying,' &c. In Psalm ciii. he expressly quotes God's saying to Moses, 'The Lord, gracious and merciful;' and in Psalm lxii. he says he heard it once and twice, again and again, both from God and Moses, that power belongs to him, and mercy belongs to him.

I come now to that which is the main thing which I shall endeavour to make use of, which is this, why these two are joined together, power and mercy, by Moses, Num. xiv., by Daniel, Nehemiah, and Jeremiah. I will not give you the heathen account; you know Tully says, Jupiter is called *optimus maximus;* he reduceth it to this very thing; he is called *optimus,* the most good god, the most good, or thrice good god (says he), he is for his benefits; *propter vim vero et potentiam maximus;* for his force and power he is called the great God; he knew God to be good, but knew not God to be merciful. But let us follow Scripture.

The inquisition is this, why he joins strength, and greatness, and dreadfulness with mercy. 1. Say I, to set mercy out the more, to exalt mercy the more. Certainly it is prefaced to that purpose, Neh. ix. 32, 'Our God, the great, the mighty, and the terrible God, who keepest covenant and mercy,' &c. It was well he could say first 'our God,' before he says 'the great and terrible God,' that so they might be sure that should import no hurt to them. But the preface is to set forth and aggrandise mercy the more, that a God so great, so dreadful, should yet be merciful. The lion in Christ commends the lamb that is in him, as Rev. v. 5, 6, that he that is so great, and strong, and terrible, should be a lamb. It is because 'the name of God is in him' that he is strong, and he is merciful too. Look, as the unworthiness and sinfulness of us, whom God loves and shews mercy to, commends his love, as you have it in Rom. v. 8, so the greatness and terribleness of the person that loves doth advance and magnify his goodness and mercy, that he that is so great and terrible, and hath such power, should yet be so merciful, Psalm lxxxix. It is a Psalm which professeth to sing and set forth the mercies of God, and the sure mercies of David; 'I will sing of the mercies of the Lord for ever,' and 'mercy shall be built up for ever,' ver. 5. 'The heavens shall praise thy wonder,' thy miracle. He calls mercy the greatest miracle that ever was. Wherein lieth it? He tells us in these words, 'Who in the heavens can be compared to the Lord? God is greatly to be feared in the assembly of the saints, and to be had in reverence of all that are round about him: Who is a strong Lord like unto thee?' &c. So that mercy in the first verse meets in this God, that in the seventh and eighth verses is so great a God, so fearful to all that are round about him; and they that are nearest him know him best; they say so of him, that this God should be a God of mercy. This begets a stupor, an amazement, that he that is able to rebuke all, and destroy all with a nod, should yet have so much love and mercy. This exalts and sets out his mercy, and makes it a wonder. 2. This greatness and power in God conduce to make him—we must not use that word *make* but after the manner of men—to be merciful and gracious. The multiplying grace issues from Jehovah as he is almighty. This is the difference between God and man. In man, weakness is the foundation of mercy very much; those that are weakest for age, as children, will cry bitterly if they see any one in misery ; those that are weakest in sex, as women, are most pitiful ; those that are of softest tempers amongst men, are more merciful, which ariseth from weakness; but in God mercy flows from strength, and power, and greatness : ' The Lord God, strong, merciful.' You find in scripture God is merciful, not after the manner of men : 2 Sam. vii. 19, ' Is this the manner of man, O Lord God ?' Thus he spake when he considered the greatness of the mercy bestowed, as when it is said, ' My thoughts are not your thoughts; but as the heavens exceed the earth, so,' &c., Isa. lv. 8, 9. It is also true, God is merciful not after the manner of men for kind of mercies : ' I am God, and not man,' therefore you are not consumed, Hos. xi, 9 ; *i. e.*, because I am merciful as God. His mercy then proceeds from his greatness and his strength. From his greatness, as is plain from 2 Sam. vii. 19, when he had said, ' Is this the manner of men, O Lord God ?' says he ; ' according to thine own heart hast thou done all these great things : wherefore thou art great, O Lord God : for there is none like unto thee, neither is there any God besides thee.' God did it out of his own heart, as having a great heart. The mercies he declares to David there, proceed from strength, as he is ' the Lord God, strong and merciful.' So it is also Num. xiv. 17, ' Let the power of my Lord be great, as thou hast spoken.'

I would make it plain that God's mercy proceeds from strength; or that, because he is a strong God, able to do all things, because he is almighty, therefore he is merciful. 1*st*, It fits him to be merciful; his strength doth so qualify him, as we may speak after the manner of men. He hath all that qualifies a person for the reality of mercy. He is free from all misery, hath no subjection to any kind of misery whatsoever; hath no subjection to potentiality, as the schoolmen speak in this point. Why? Because he is a strong God, he is a powerful God, and an almighty God, and that keeps him off from all misery, and exempts him from all the dints and impressions of misery.

There is, I say, a blasphemous question that hath been traversed up and down by corrupt divines, Whether God hath mercy truly in him, and be of a merciful disposition ? And what reason do they give for it but this? Say they, Mercy arises from sense of misery, that one lays to heart others' misery, as that which may be one's own, which we cannot suppose to be in God.

Say I, to answer it, Here lies the question, What it is that is truly mercy, whether it be that one out of weakness is condoling you or pitying you, that is unable to help, whether that be truly mercy or no? Or whether a readiness of will and a propenseness of affection, joined with ability to succour effectually and irresistibly, whether this be not mercy rather? since the first proceeds from weakness, but this from strength. I say here lies the question, whether yea or no, one that out of weakness and passion condoles with you, and hath from that ground pity in him, that affection of pity, of suffering with you, and is sorry you are in misery, and troubled you are so, but yet is unable to help, whether this be mercy truly or no? Or whether one that hath readiness of will, his soul is inclined to help, and he joins ability to help, which of these two is mercy? Say I, the last, and that is in God, and it is demonstrable thus:

1. If he that is merciful be himself liable to misery, he is not in that sense merciful. Why? Because he is so far weak and unable to help.

That same king in the famine could not shew mercy, because he could not help: 2 Kings vi. 26, 27, ' O lord my king, help,' says the poor woman. If anybody help, a king could; but, says he, ' if the Lord helps thee not, I cannot.'   I am a poor weak creature, in plain words.   Should I help thee out of the barn, to give thee bread; or winepress, to give thee drink ? I can do neither, saith he.   What was the reason he was thus unable to grant an aid ?   He was weak and ready to die, as well as other men. That is mercy which in the issue and event will prove itself so; that is mercy indeed and truly.

2. If he be not able to help you efficaciously, he does but increase your misery, as you see in the case of this poor woman and the king.   Poor woman, what ailed she ?   He told her he could not help her.   The woman was extremely disturbed that she came to the king, and the king could not help her.   ' What aileth you ?' says he, 2 Kings vi. 28.   Says she, I come not to you for mercy, but for justice; here is a woman ate my child yesterday, and I should have ate her son, but she hath hid him.   So she came to the king for justice.   Directly he could not help her in that neither; he could not order the child to be killed, it had been murder, but he increased her misery by all this.   So that now, say I, that which fits for mercy is, that one is free from all misery, impotency, and weakness, and hath a fulness of ability to succour, and this is from strength. Now,

2dly, To pardon sin (which is our case) is in itself an act of the greatest strength in God, and therefore strength fits him for being merciful.   The Pharisees said, ' No man is able to forgive sins but God,' Mark ii. 7. Says Christ, I will shew you I am able to forgive sins.   Why ?   To the man sick of the palsy, says he, ' Take up thy bed, and walk.'   He did this to shew that he who had power and strength to heal such a disease, had power alike to be merciful; and had he not been the almighty God, he could not have said, ' Thy sins are forgiven thee.'

3dly, For a man to contain his anger, it is from strength: Prov. xvi. 32, ' He that is slow to anger is better than the mighty: and he that ruleth his spirit than he that taketh a city.'   Thus it is the strength of a man to overcome his passion: ' Let the power of my Lord be great, according as thou hast said, The Lord is long-suffering,' Num. xiv. 17-19, There is a good saying in one of the Collects in the Common Prayer Book: ' O Lord, that shewest thy omnipotency chiefly in shewing mercy,' in forgiving sins; wherein it is accounted an high act of omnipotency to forgive sins.

But you will say, Though here is an ability to succour, and out of strength to shew mercy, yet where is the affection of mercy, and whence ariseth that ?

Ans. The seat of mercy is the will, as appears by that speech, ' I will be merciful to whom I will be merciful,' Exod. xxxiii, 19.   Now the will of God hath affections in it; for there is hatred of sin, which is an affection that is natural; and love, an affection of the will, that is natural. Though these affections in God are but various postures of his will to various objects, what then is mercy in his will ?   Not a mere act, but a propensity, an inward inclination, from out of his goodness of will, to shew mercy to them that are in misery: Ps. lxxxvi. 5, he is ready to forgive: ' The Lord is good and ready to forgive, and plenteous in mercy.'   These are not metaphors (as bowels and the like, used of mercy); Ps. xxxiv. 18, but ' the Lord is nigh unto them that are of a broken heart;' not in respect of omnipotency merely, so he is to all, but in readiness of disposition and inclination, he is ready and quick to be merciful so soon as he sees their hearts. If any say that God willeth mercy, and it is his will to shew mercy, let them but add and acknowledge that there is a propenseness in his will thereunto unto such merciful acts; and then they must say too, that mercy (as to the affection of it) is a property in God.

But doth his power and strength move and stir that affection in him, and render his will propense unto mercy?

Ans. Yes. And to prove that it moves, I take that of Moses for my ground, Num. xiv. 17–19; when pleading for forgiveness, he says, ' Let the power of my Lord be great. Pardon, I beseech thee, this people, as thou hast forgiven them hitherto.' He woos God with that very consideration, and presents it to him. Now it is a sure maxim, that what Moses was taught by God to move God with, that God himself is certainly moved withal.

If you say unto me, But in what manner is he moved with it thereunto?

Ans. Because he hath power lying by him to ' help in time of need,' and he can put it forth as easily and readily as we think a thought, or speak a word.

There is a saying in 1 John iii. 17, ' If a man hath this world's goods, and seeth his brother hath need, and shutteth up his bowels of compassion from him, how dwelleth the love of God in him?' Truly God hath love dwelling in him, yea, ' God is love,' 1 John iv. 16, and he hath power to help them whom he loves, and he sets himself to love his children. Why then, thinks he with himself, have I power to help them I love, and do I see them in misery, and shall my power lie by, and not shew itself? I may say that if he thus sees them whom he loves to abide in misery, and yet shut up his affection of mercy towards them, how doth love dwell in God? how is he love to such? So that this is my conclusion. Mercy implies in itself a non-subjection to misery, and also an ability and fulness of strength to help; and a will which, though it hath not passions in it, yet hath love and propenseness to goodness. There is a readiness to forgive, there is an affection which is the foundation of shewing mercy; so that he only is truly merciful. It is a bastard-mercy that is in creatures, for that is true mercy that is able to help, with a propenseness to do so, which alone is in God, who is ' the Lord God strong, and the Lord God merciful.' It is then but a bastardly, spurious mercy that is in creatures, and only God is merciful upon this respect, that God only is God.'

Use 1. Is God's power and strength joined with mercy? Is it that which fits him for mercy? Oh bless him that you find so dreadful an attribute as power joined with mercy. Why, you find them divided elsewhere, when they are to be exercised on others than the elect: Rom. ix. 22, ' What if God, willing to shew his wrath, and make his power known, endured with much long-suffering the vessels of wrath fitted for destruction?' There is power joined with wrath; let us therefore adore this God, that hath in this proclamation of mercy, Exod. xxxiv., put the God strong and merciful together.

Use 2. Do we find mercy and power joined together and paired elsewhere, as in Ps. lxii. 11, 12? Then, as it is n that psalm, go, trust him in all times; for upon these two grounds he b ds us, ver. 8, to ' trust in him at all times.' But there are some times in your lives that you are in such a case and condition that you have no kind of hope, or possibility of thought, that such a thing should come to pass; but ' trust in him at all times.' Why?

Because power belongeth to him, and mercy; these two put together will effect anything. What is too difficult for God the strong, and God merciful? Now I draw this use out of Jer. xxxii. 17, 18 (which I cited before), 'I prayed unto the Lord, saying, Ah, Lord God, behold thou hast made the heaven and the earth by thy great power, and stretched-out arm; and there is nothing too hard for thee: thou shewest loving-kindness unto thousands, and recompensest the iniquity of the fathers into the bosom of their children after them: the great, the mighty God, the Lord of hosts is his name.' The case stood thus: The prophet Jeremiah was bid to buy a purchase of land, as you read in the fore-part of the chapter; it was at a time when the city was destroyed by the sword, famine, and pestilence, as at ver. 24, and the city given into the hands of the Chaldeans, and they were by prophecy to be seventy years. The thing that was signified by this was, as God told him: 'Thus saith the Lord of hosts, houses and fields shall be possessed again in this land.' The poor man's spirit was extremely exercised about it, not for the loss of his money, but strangeness of the thing (as you will see it a strange thing, but he saw more), and it was the strangest thing could fall out, and the greatest mercy to the people of God that could fall out. Because the manner of conquerors was to remove all the people; as when they conquered Judea they took all the people and removed them, and planted them in other countries, and brought people out of those countries and planted them in Judea. They did so with the ten tribes; they took the ten tribes out of their own land, and carried them into Media, and planted in the room of them the natives of those countries where themselves were planted. The land of Judea was a fruitful place; and that there should be brought into that land strangers to possess it, and that there should be seventy years' time before they should return, this was the greatest wonder in the world they should return; yet, notwithstanding, the Lord intended that the land should not be inhabited but by a company of poor Jews that were left. But the land was made desolate; 2 Chron. xxxvi. 21, it is said, the land enjoyed its Sabbaths. There was a law, that the land, every seventh year, should not be digged, and accordingly God says, 2 Chron. xxxvi. 21, 'Your land shall enjoy its Sabbaths, it shall be desolate.' But all this tended to make good that which was so strange a thing to be done. There was the Babylonian monarchy to be destroyed. Of them it is said, 'The children of Israel and the children of Judah were oppressed together, and all that took them captives held them fast, they refused to let them go: but their Redeemer is strong, the Lord of hosts is his name,' Jer. l. 33. When they were destroyed, that they should possess every one their own land again, what a wonderful thing is this! The Turk does not thus, yet they were as barbarous as the Turks, Neh. v. 12. Nay, the priests were free from taxations upon their land; Jeremiah's land stood free, Ezra vii. 24, 25. Was not that a strange word, that there should be buying and selling of land again? It was not done for any nation else; that in Ps. cxxvi. 2, the heathens among themselves said, 'The Lord hath done great things for them.' Now Jeremiah received the revelation of this in ver. 15, that there should be houses, and fields, and vineyards possessed again in the land. He goes to God to strengthen his faith therein: ver. 17, 'Thou art the great and potent God, thou shewest loving-kindness unto thousands.' He urges these two attributes upon God—you may see what it is to urge two such attributes upon God, and have faith to do it.—When he had urged these (I shall shew you the issue of it), directly God makes this gracious promise upon this prayer of his, to restore them to their own land, and restore him not only his money, but land too. Read what God did in answer, from the 36th verse, to the end of the chapter. This good prayer of his, urging in this difficult case these two great things : the power and mercy of God; you see what it drew out from God, and what great things God did for his mercy's sake, and by his power, for these poor people. Therefore let us, in all straits and difficulties, make use of it, and remember to do likewise. God is the strong and merciful. ' Is anything too hard for me ?' says God, in the same chapter. No ; mercy sets God on work, and causes him to exert his power, which effects everything.

Use 3. Let us glorify him according to the greatness of this mercy and greatness joined together. Men, the more great they are, do degenerate into rigour, and severity, and cruelty. Your great kings have but the name of gracious, says Christ, by a reflection on them : Luke xxii. 25, ' The kings of the Gentiles exercise lordship over them, and they that exercise authority upon them are called benefactors.' I take his meaning to be this: You call them benefactors ; you are fain to call them so gracious, and so clement, and just and gracious, and you call them benefactors for all their greatness and exercise of lordship over you, though they rule you according to their lusts. But our God, that is, the strong God, is the merciful God ; and he that is the great King, whose name is terrible, Mal. i. 14, is also a good God, a merciful God, a gracious God. He is so merciful a God as all the angels adore him, and worship him, while they consider the miracles and wonders of his mercy. Let us therefore adore him, since the angels do it. Consider Ps. lxxxix., where the sure mercies of David are set out, and the angels celebrate the miracles of his mercy, those angels to whom he is so dreadful and fearful in their assemblies, ver. 6–8. Oh, how much more, if they magnify the conjunction of power and mercy in God, should we, whom God shews mercy to, who are the objects of mercy, and subjects of mercy, which the angels are not !

Use 4. Is mercy thus joined with power and greatness ? See, poor wretch, what need thou hast of his power and mercy every day, need of his strength, need of all mercies to thy soul. As for sanctification, and holiness, and faith, and helping us to believe, they are from strength, and depend upon the strength of God : Ps. lxxxvi. 15, 16, ' But thou, O Lord God, art a God full of compassion, and gracious, long-suffering, and plenteous in mercy and truth.' Thou, O Lord, *Adonai*, art a God; *El*, the strong God, full of compassion ; the same words as Moses useth. Instead of *Jehovah*, *Adonai* is used, O Lord ; but then *El*, strong God, is the same word. The meaning is, let all the strength and power thou the strong God hast in thee be for my advantage. Now, is it not a bold request to say, Lord, wilt thou give me all thy strength to help me ? A very bold request indeed ; but his mercy moves him to grant it. Thus then petition him : Thou art a God merciful and gracious, give thy strength to me ! Thou, O God, givest all thy attributes up to thy children, to serve their advantage, as well as to serve thy own glory ; give me thy strength ! Dost not thou need strength, poor wretch ? How oft is thy heart apt to sink, and thou canst not believe but so long as God helps thee to do it. How apt to swoon in thy despondencies and doubts. Dost thou find strength come in to help thee to believe ? It is the strong God helps thee : Ps. cxxxviii. 3, ' He strengthened me with strength in my soul,' says he, when my soul is sinking. Thou hast a heart weak to duty, feeble hands, weak knees ; who strengthens thee in the inner man ? He does it according to the riches of his glory, that is, of his mercy, which is eminently called his glory; he strengthens us in the inward man, Eph. iii. 16. Lastly, Is God strong and merciful? Ps. xxxi. 24, 'Be of good courage, all you that hope in the Lord, and he shall strengthen your heart;' for he is your strong God, and he is your merciful God., Indeed, if we had faith and hearts to improve and put together these two things, what might we not obtain from the hands of God? Where there is power to enable, and mercy to make willing, what cannot be done? Jeremiah putting together these two things, Jer. xxxii. 17, 18, says God, in answer to Jeremiah's prayer, 'There is nothing too hard for me;' I have power to do it, and heart to do it. Improve all to the good of your own souls. Go and say unto God, O thou God, plenteous in mercy, and full of compassion, give me thy strength, I am a poor weak creature! A little cordial, you see what strength it gives; so a little of the strength of God, how doth it strengthen the soul! Make use of his strength, 'he is the God of your strength,' Ps. lxxxix. 16.

Use 5. If power be thus joined to mercy, then make use of it for pardon of sin. Though sins be great, yet in such cases, let the soul go to God with these words, 'Let the power of the Lord be great to pardon' and to forgive, as you see Moses pleads it. That strength that concurs to do all things else, it doth conduce to pardon sin. 'Is it easier to say, Take up thy bed and walk, or to say, Thy sins are forgiven thee?' saith our Saviour Christ. It is twice said in Jer. xxxii., 'Nothing is too hard for me;'' God speaks it once at ver. 27, and Jeremiah says it at ver. 17. He speaks it of matters of providence; apply it to sin: there is no sin too hard for him, for merciful power, or powerful mercy to pardon. God is as strong in forgiving sin, and in the power that forgives, as he is in his providential working power; and as God's power is good at making worlds, nay, at making his heavens wherein he dwells, the high and holy place, so his power is as good at pardoning sins; and the one is as great a work as the other. In such cases, let thy faith bring it to this, God is able to pardon thee; and do but think with thyself, He that was able to make a world is able to pardon me; he can find that in his heart as is sufficient to pardon me. It is a great step of faith when men see and are convinced of their sinfulness, to go to God and say, Thou art able to make me clean, thou art able to pardon my sin.

Use 6. Doth power thus yoke with mercy; nay, is it the RATIO of mercy? (I mean of that phrase) then take God's counsel to lay hold on his strength. Isa. xxvii. 4, 'Fury is not in me.' He speaks as to his vineyard, his church; fury is not in me against my church, I can do that no hurt; but my fury is against briars and thorns: as ver. 4, 'Who would set the briars and thorns against God in battle? He would go through them, and would burn them together.' Well, is there no remedy if they be briars and thorns? Yes; even for them there is a remedy. What is that? Ver. 5, 'Let them take hold on my strength.' Of my strength; what is that? It is an allusion to Jacob's story, that had power with God, Gen. xxxii. 28. The meaning is, humble yourselves. Suppose a child or servant should see one coming to strike him, they fall down in the humblest manner, and lay hold upon their hands. Lay hold, says God, upon my mercy, and strength joined with mercy, and I am charmed, you may rule me; mercy says it twice before power's face, you may make peace with me, and you shall make peace with me.

CHAPTER VIII.

The next word in this proclamation of Exod. xxxiv. 6, 7, *explained;* merciful,
—from whence mercy ariseth in God.

I come now to the next attribute expressed in this proclamation, *merciful:*
' The Lord, the Lord God, strong, gracious, merciful, abundant in goodness and truth, keeping mercy for thousands, forgiving iniquity, transgression, and sin,' Exod. xxxiv. 6, 7. Things attributed to God here are of
three sorts :

1. The inward disposition or inclination, or aptitude and readiness to
mercy, that is in the four first attributes, merciful, gracious, long-suffering,
much in goodness, and truth is added.

2. There are his purposes and resolutions of mercy, keeping mercy for
thousands; and they are immanent acts in God, kept and laid up in God's
own breast.

3. There are extrinsecal acts of mercy issuing from both: ' pardoning
iniquity, transgression, and sin.'

The meaning plainly is, first, God is merciful as he is Jehovah ; that is
his nature.   Secondly, he fully resolves to shew mercy ; there is his heart.
Thirdly, he hath done it, and doth it every day, in pardoning sin ; there is
his wont and practice.   So that God is every way merciful : in his nature,
in his purposes, and in his deeds and performances.   These four, merciful,
gracious, long-suffering, much in goodness, are all of mercy's kindred and
alliance ; and it is very observable, that when, in Ps. ciii. 8, the psalmist
doth quote Moses's words, he only quotes these four attributes, and leaves
out *truth*, for it was not akin to mercy; it was not congenial to it, and was
not recited there.   Though it fell in with mercy, yet it is not of mercy's
pedigree.   These four are therefore attributes of pure mercy, which yet
have their distinguishment, which I shall after shew.

Obs. That which I observe is, that to describe the merciful designs of
mercy, and grace, and long-suffering, is to define the nature of God.   Of
which I shall say two things :

1. That all God's being merciful, it is resolved into God's nature of
being merciful, because if being merciful be the cause of merciful effects,
then mercy must have an existence before; and where but in him?
Merciful effects suppose his being merciful as the root and principle in
himself; so that merciful effects, and pardoning sin, &c., are attributed to
him as the cause : Ps. lxxviii. 38, ' But he being full of compassion, forgave their iniquity, and destroyed them not.'   It is plain forgiving their
iniquity is resolved into this, his being full of mercy, as the cause.   Saith
Calvin, the cause is ascribed to mercy, which is naturally in him.   In
Ps. lxxxvi. he implores merciful gracious effects towards himself; ver. 1-4,
' Bow down thine ear, O Lord, hear me ; for I am poor and needy.
Preserve my soul, for I am holy : O thou my God, save thy servant that
trusteth in thee.   Be merciful unto me, O Lord : for I cry unto thee
daily.   Rejoice the soul of thy servant : for unto thee, O Lord, do I lift
up my soul.'   These mercies he implores in these verses upon this ground,
because God himself is merciful; it is his nature.   And so, too, Neh.
ix. 31, ' Thou didst not utterly consume them, nor forsake them : for thou
art a gracious and merciful God.'   Here these merciful effects of not consuming them is ascribed to mercy as the cause.   Jer. iii. 12, ' Return, and

I will not cause mine anger to fall upon you: for I am merciful, saith the Lord.' Still it runs in the causal particle; therefore they are infinitely out that say, he is said to be merciful because he does merciful effects, whereas the Scripture says he does merciful effects, *for* he is merciful.

2. The second thing I would say to shew he is merciful is, that he says, ' Jehovah, Jehovah, God,' and then 'merciful, gracious, long-suffering.' This thrice repeating the substantial name of God hath not only a mystery in it of the Trinity, but refers also to those attributes that follows to signify what Jehovah is; he gives him his substantial names, and then his other properties four times, which declare in reality that *Jehovah, Jehovah*, God, are one and the same with *merciful* and *long-suffering*, as I have shewed you largely before. And to this end too the name of God is joined with faithfulness: Deut. vii. 9, ' Know therefore that the Lord thy God, he is God, the faithful God, which keepeth covenant and mercy with them that love him, and keep his commandments, to a thousand generations.' Here is, first, a vehement indigitation of God's being God : ' Know ye therefore,' says he, ' know that the Lord thy God he is God.' And to the end they may thus know him, he adds, that he was ' the faithful God.' Faithfulness is his truth. That he insists thus on the name of God first, and then the faithfulness of God, it is to bring over the Godhead into faithfulness, that so they might trust to his faithfulness as his Godhead. And indeed you find it expressly called himself: 2 Tim. ii. 13, ' He abideth faithful; he cannot deny himself.' Faithfulness is himself: Titus i. 2, ' God that cannot lie.' Why? Because he is God; it is his Godhead to be true and faithful. Wherever he hath engaged his word, there his Godhead is engaged to make it good, for he is the faithful God; and wherever his mercy is engaged, there is his Godhead engaged, and laid at stake to eternity, to shew mercy to that soul. Now read over that Deut. vii. 9 once more: ' Know therefore that the Lord thy God, he is God, the faithful God, which keepeth covenant and mercy with them that love him, and keep his commandments, to a thousand generations.' Then read these words in the text of Exod. xxxiv., ' Jehovah, Jehovah, God merciful, gracious.' What *faithful* is there, *merciful* is here.

Let us now consider why *merciful* is in order placed first; the truth is, in order of nature, grace is before mercy, and I could give many scriptures where grace is first named ; but the reason why he here puts merciful first is, because he is to speak to sinners. He presents himself to sinners; and if to them he had said at first dash, God is good, or God is gracious, or God is love, sinners would have said, This speaks short to us, and why ? Because he is good to all his creatures that never sinned; he is gracious to angels that never sinned ; ay, but merciful, with that proper effect, ' pardoning iniquity, transgression, and sin,' that is a welcome saying to sinners, and speaks home to their case.

I shall now consider what is the rise of mercy, which doth involve the Godhead itself ; that one attribute should be *ratio alterius*, as to our apprehension, is allowed by them that did most exquisitely argue about God and his attributes. Now then I shall shew you what it is makes him merciful (it will help our faith to consider it), not how all attributes fall in, as holiness, &c., do, but what is the special genealogy and descent of mercy (we speak after the manner of men, and yet the Scripture speaks the same), what is the *ratio misericordiæ*. Mercy fetcheth its pedigree,—

1. From his blessedness. God comes to be merciful by descent, from his having all fulness of perfection completely in him, and being happy in him-

self, and having no need of any thing, Acts xvii. 25. He is the blessed God, and all-sufficient God, and so all-sufficient, that he is above all misery, that misery cannot reach him; and this makes and inclines him to be merciful. God having all within himself transcendently and completely, that he need not any thing that is out of himself, he is therefore able and hath power to make others blessed; and being merciful, therefore, he can pardon, though sinners sin against him. For why? Their sins do not hurt him, he is full of all enjoyments, and is equally happy, whether the creatures be or not be; and as equally happy, whether the creature sin or not sin against him, for they no-way reach to hurt his enjoyment: Job xxxv. 6, 7, ' If thou sinnest, what dost thou against him? or if thy transgressions be multiplied, what dost thou unto him? If thou be righteous, what givest thou to him, or what receiveth he of thine hand?' Neither the one nor the other can any-way hurt him, or benefit him; he is not benefitted by the righteousness of any creature. Nay, Christ himself says, Ps. xvi. 2, ' My righteousness extends not to thee;' thou art never the better by it, thou art so perfect a God. Nor is he hurt by sin; therefore he can easily pardon. All are not alike to him as to his external glory; but as to his inward essential happiness, they are all alike as to any prejudice they can do it.

What made Paul that he could forgive injuries? It was that he got good by them; he was not injured at all, Gal. iv. 12. And so the blessedness of God, and his being above all so high, and above the reach of all, is a ground of his being merciful. I observe in Luke i. 72, that mercy is there said to be promised; ' To perform the mercy promised to our fathers, and to remember his holy covenant.' Among these it was to Abraham God made himself known by name, and it was to strengthen his faith in the promise of mercy. And the first name by which he manifests himself is this: ' I am,' says he, ' God all-sufficient,' Gen. xvii. 1, and the word signifies, I am full of paps, I am all-sufficient of myself, and therefore I am a God that can afford what is in me unto others; I have a breast full for others, as well as happiness in myself. And thus, ' God of comfort,' and ' Father of mercies,' are well joined together, 2 Cor. i. 3, that is, he that is so blessed in himself is merciful in himself. Abraham, to whom God thus proclaimed himself all-sufficient, is the standard instance of being justified, and the father of the faithful; and that maxim is drawn from his example, Rom. iv. 5. Now it was all-sufficiency that Abraham heard of, which encouraged him to believe.

There was also another name of God, and that was אֵל עֶלְיוֹן, El Helyon, ' God most high,' brought up by Melchisedek, when he came to Abraham, Gen. xiv. 19. It is four times used there, and that is the first use of it upon Abraham's occasion. What is the meaning of this ' the most high God'? It is, that he is above all, out of the reach of all. Now you find the Scripture calls it, ' the mercy of the Most High,' Ps. xxi. 7. Nay, it is observable, that ὁ ἐλεῶν in Greek, and in the Hebrew ho eleon, is the word for merciful. The most high and the merciful God, are well then joined together. The schoolmen ordinarily say, true mercy is only in God. Why? Because he only is above all misery, and therefore able to help his people out of it. The Scripture says, it is the mercy of the Most High: Luke vi. 34, 35, ' Be ye merciful, as your heavenly Father is merciful.' That is the exhortation, imitate your Father; and, says he, ' you shall be the children of the highest.' You shall be like him that is highest; therefore ' be merciful, as your heavenly Father is merciful.'

2. Mercy is in God *ad modum virtutis*, as a perfection, which you know

is after the way of being a virtue. All perfections are in God, and there are these three sorts of perfections in him : *First,* Such as we call metaphysical transcendent excellencies in himself, as majesty, glory, unchangeableness, infiniteness, eternity. *Secondly,* We say there are perfections of faculties, of understanding (which the Scripture says is infinite), and of his will. But, *thirdly,* there is also in him *perfectiones morales,* moral perfections. We are forced, and God himself is forced, to speak of himself in this manner, that we may understand. It is a good saying of the schoolmen, It becomes God to be most perfect, not only in his absolute being, and the excellencies thereof, but also in virtue. If you would have Scripture, see 1 Peter ii. 9, ' Shew forth the praises of him who hath called you.' We translate it ' praises,' but in the margin it is ' virtues.' Whom doth he speak of? Not of Christ only, but of God the Father : ' Now you are the people of God,' ver. 10. ' As he which hath called you is holy' (there is one virtue) ; ' so be ye holy in all manner of conversation,' 1 Pet. i. 15. And answerably hereto, ' shew forth the virtues of him which hath called you.' Now mercy is one virtue eminently intended in Peter ; for it followeth, ' which in time past were not a people, but are now the people of God ; which had not obtained mercy, but now have obtained mercy,' from God, by calling you ; and therefore shew forth that virtue. Now holiness is a virtue we all acknowledge : ' As he which hath called you is holy, so be ye holy in all manner of conversation.' And what ? Is not this parallel to that Scripture, ' Be you merciful, as your heavenly Father is merciful,' Luke vi. 35. As holiness, then, is a virtue in him, so mercifulness is a virtue in him. If you yet doubt of it, consider further what is said, ' Be you perfect, as your heavenly Father is perfect,' Mat. v. 48. He speaks it of mercy, for it refers to verses 44, 45 : ' Love your enemies, bless them that curse you, do good to them that hate you, and pray for them that despitefully use you and persecute you ; that ye may be the children of your Father which is in heaven.' Now, then, that mercy whereby God is perfect, must needs be himself, his essence, nothing can perfect God but himself ; he should otherwise be beholden to an accident, and quality, and creature, if anything perfect him but himself. Now to shew the descent of mercy for strengthening our faith, consider,

1. The blessedness of God is the rise of goodness in him (still we speak after the manner of men). Now there is his goodness of being, entity of goodness ; and there is his goodness by which he communicates himself, and that is an attribute, which is all one with his being, only it inclines him to communicate : Ps. cxix. 68, ' Thou art good, and dost good.' The nature of goodness is to communicate itself, and to be sure goodness in God is his nature. But how doth it rise from blessedness ? says our Saviour Christ (there is but one saying of his that is not in the Evangelists), Acts xx. 35, ' It is more blessed to give than to receive.' Is he a blessed God ? He will give then, he will communicate himself. In Exod. xxxiii. 19, which is the preface to this text, Exod. xxxiv. 6, 7, says God to Moses, ' I will cause all my goodness to pass before thee, and I will proclaim the name of the Lord before thee ; and will be gracious to whom I will be gracious, and will shew mercy on whom I will shew mercy.' Doth God proclaim all his goodness here ? No ; there be many attributes he doth not proclaim. The best interpretation I have is, that which is his goodness communicative for us (as for his essential goodness, it is himself), such as mercy, and grace, and truth, these are those he proclaims, so that his goodness is the ground of his being merciful and gracious ; Ps. xxv. 6, 7,

David there praying earnestly for forgiveness, 'Remember,' says he, 'O Lord, thy tender mercies and thy loving-kindnesses; for they have been ever of old. Remember not the sins of my youth, nor my transgressions: according to thy mercy remember thou me for thy goodness' sake, O Lord.' He enters upon this, that God was good, and goodness itself, because he knew that mercy centred in goodness : Ps. lxxxvi. 5, 'Thou, Lord, art good,' that is the first; then 'ready to forgive, and plenteous in mercy.' And this is the first burden of many psalms, 'The Lord is good, and his mercy endures for ever.' And it was that they sung in the temple, as you may read in the Chronicles. You see, then, there is blessedness first, and goodness ariseth from blessedness.

2. The next thing in God is love, and that ariseth from goodness. The goodness that is in God inclines him to love, and to be the most profuse lover. You read in 1 John iv. 7, 8, 'God is love.' The question is, whether this speech doth not import, that he is love in himself, as well as that he shews love. There are these reasons why it imports what he is in himself, when he says, God is love. Says he, ver. 7, 'Every one that loveth is born of God, and knoweth God,' that is the affirmative; and ver. 8. 'He that loveth not knoweth not God, for God is love'; that is, he knows not God in what is most proper to him, as to what doth most abound in him, for God is love. We ordinarily say of a man that is of such a disposition, I know him, he is so and so ; so the believer knows God to be love. Thus the apostle says positively, 'He that is born of God knows God, for God is love.' I take the meaning thus : When a man hath tasted that the Lord is gracious, the truth is, it is not only an act of love that he tastes, but he tastes God, he sucks *in dietatem*, he sucks in this, that there is a principle in God to maintain his love to eternity. And so God being love, he knows him to be so. Again, he says, 'All love is of God, for God is love.' What is the meaning of that ? That if God be the author of all love, then certainly there is love in him ; 'He that made the eye, shall not he see ?' But that which most convinceth me is, that he saith, ver. 12, 'No man hath seen God at any time.' He speaks it of his love, which none sees but as manifest by effects; but God is love essentially. Says Aquinas, Whoever hath a will, hath a proneness to love. Says Musculus, As every one is in goodness, so in love. If God then hath a will inclined to anything, it is to love ; he hath hatred in him to sin, he hath the opposite: he hath a love also to something, only it is guided by his will towards creatures.

3. Love and grace are the roots of mercy. Where he sets his love, if there be misery, there love is drawn out to pity and mercy. The schoolmen say, it is but *extensio amoris*, but an extending of love to the creature when in misery. And indeed the Hebrew word for mercy, חֶסֶד, signifies also love or good will. Our translators oft render it, 'merciful loving-kindness :' Ps. cxvii. 2, 'His merciful kindness is great towards us.' And it is mercy he speaks of, for it is quoted in Rom. xv. 9, 'The Gentiles shall glorify God for his mercy.' And Ps. cxix. 76, 'Let thy merciful loving-kindness be for my comfort ;' or thy loving-kindness be stretched out into mercy where there is need. Where there is love, there is a design of good to the party loved ; then desires follow. Where there is love, there is a rejoicing over the person : when he prospers, then there is joy ; if he be in misery, there is a drawing out that love into pity. If you say, 'The Lord is gracious,' you go not beyond merciful, for that is grace and love drawn out to the full length, as far as grace and love can reach. What phrase

the schoolmen expresses it by, the Scripture doth the like ; Ps. xxxvi. 10,
' Oh continue thy loving-kindness :' draw out at length thy loving-kindness
(so in the margin). And it speaks of mercy, for he magnifies mercy : ver.
5, ' Thy mercy, O Lord, is in the heavens.' In that scripture too which is
famous amongst us, Jer. xxxi. 3, ' I have loved thee with an everlasting
love, therefore with loving-kindness have I drawn thee,' that last clause
hath two significations (it is varied in the margin) : I have extended loving-
kindness to thee, I have stretched out loving-kindness to thee; so Piscator
reads it. Now hence it comes to pass, that in shewing mercy God makes
the foundation of it to be love : Ephes. ii. 4, 5, ' But God, who is rich in
mercy, for his great love wherewith he loved us.' Rom. v. 8, ' God commendeth his love towards us, in that while we were yet sinners, Christ
died for us.' Mercy is there called love ; and it is indeed but a commending
or extending of love towards sinners ; ' when we were sinners, Christ died.'
Tit. iii. 4, ' The kindness and love of God our Saviour towards man appeared, not by works of righteousness which we have done, but according
to his mercy he saved us.' When the kindness and love of God appears,
mercy follows ; according to his mercy (being sinners) he saveth us.

Use 1. Is mercy the nature of God, and is he mercy himself ? Then
consider, look how great God is, so great is his mercy. Our translation reads it, As is his greatness, so is his mercy. Why ? Because
it is God's. Where he pitcheth mercy by his will, there the whole Godhead is engaged, Jehovah, Jehovah, God gracious and merciful ; he brings
over all the whole Godhead when he will be merciful.

Use 2. We do not treat with the will of God every day. He that is a
believer treats with the will of God, that he would but be merciful to him.
Now those that treat with the will of God, either in a way of assurance, or
in throwing themselves upon him, and hoping in his mercy, what have they
to plead ? All the mercies in the nature of God, to be a ground of plea
before him, to tell him what a God he is in mercy. Oh that we would but
inure our hearts to this practice ; it would be a mighty advantage ! In Num.
xiv., Moses having first urged the mercies that were in God himself, that he
is a God long-suffering, great in mercy, then he prays, ' According to thy
great mercy do thou pardon.' What mercy ? The mercy he mentioned
which is in God himself : ' Deal,' says he, ' according to this mercy in thee
which thou hast spoken of.' As if one were to supplicate a merciful man,
he implores the mercy and ingenuity of his nature, which upon all occasions
he had shewn. Moses was the first that brought up this happy expression,
' According to thy mercy' (I know not where it is used by any other man),
that is, according to the infinite mercy in thy heart and nature. David did
next use it, Ps. xxv. ; and in the great case of his sin of adultery, Ps.
li. 1, ' that he would be merciful to him according to the multitude of his
mercies.' And as he needed all the mercies in God, so he confessed the
sin of his nature, and hath recourse to the mercies in God's nature. But
it is Ps. xxv. 7 I pitch on ; there he doth not content himself only with
this expression, ' According to thy mercy,' but he adds another phrase,
' For thy mercy's sake', and ' goodness' sake.' Muis observes in this coherence, ' Good and upright is the Lord,' that he centres in his nature.
Thou hast a merciful nature ; deal with me according to that, and for the
sake of that, according to thy mercy, for thy goodness' sake. The meditation of that attribute was the foundation of his faith and prayer herein.
When he hath done, he referreth himself to Moses : ver. 11, ' For thy name's
sake, O Lord, pardon my iniquity, for it is great.' He refers to that name

proclaimed before Moses, Exod. xxxiv. 6, 7. But you will say, How do these expressions, 'for thy name's sake,' 'for thy goodness' sake,' 'for thy mercy's sake,' imply the same as ' for himself,' 'for his own sake'? how do they involve the Godhead ? Look to Isa. xliii. 25, 'I, even I, am he that blotteth out thy transgressions for mine own sake,' that is, for my self: Isa. xlviii. 2, 'For mine own sake, even for mine own sake, will I do it.' You have it twice in one verse ; and that which is ' for mercy's sake' in one place, is 'for mine own sake' in another : and behold it is I, I am he, as I am God, who doth it. What is this but ' Jehovah, Jehovah, God merciful'? We may learn from Old Testament phrases that which we do not so much consider. They have taught us in their prayers from Moses's example, how to pray and urge the mercies of God ; Dan. ix. 18, 19, he has said ' For thy mercy's sake do this ;' and at ver. 19, ' For thine own sake do this ;' he puts them both together. To me this is a great thing, that when we go to pray, we have the liberty to urge God to shew his mercy for his own sake ; that although it is we who have the benefit of the mercies, yet we may urge him, Thou shalt have the glory of it, thou shalt have the glory of thy grace by it, and the glory of thy mercy by it. It is yet again a greater advantage in praying, that we have all the mercies in God before us to spread before him; mercies in his word might be limited, but in his nature they cannot. What may we not obtain at the hand of God, if we could improve this notion, to go to God to be merciful to us as God, and according to the mercies that are in his nature, and for the sake of them!

CHAPTER IX.

The other part of the proclamation of the mercies of God's nature in Exod. xxxiv. *explained.—The meaning of those words,* Jehovah, *pardoning iniquity, transgression, and sin, shewed by the explication of another text, Ps. lxxx. 30 to 37.—That the covenant of grace in Christ is the substantial scope and design of the psalm.—That the promises of God's pardoning mercies do concern, and are made unto Christ's spiritual seed.—That there is such an amplification of grace in them as to extend to the worst cases they can possibly be supposed to be in.—That they are strengthened by the firmest engagements.*

*If his children forsake my law, and walk not in my judgments ; if they break my statutes, and keep not my commandments ; then will I visit their transgression with the rod, and their iniquity with stripes. Nevertheless my loving-kindness will I not utterly take from him, nor suffer my faithfulness to fail. My covenant will I not break, nor alter the thing that is gone out of my lips. Once have I sworn by my holiness, that I will not lie unto David. His seed shall endure for ever, and his throne as the sun before me. It shall be established for ever as the moon, and as a faithful witness in heaven. Selah.—*Psalm LXXXIX. 30–37.

I shall centre in the 89th Psalm for the illustrating that great attribute of Jehovah merciful, Exod. xxxiv., ' Pardoning iniquity, transgression, and sin,' &c. ; although, first, I must necessarily premise some few things concerning the main drift of the psalm.

I shall first remark the occasion of making this psalm. It is certain the penman of it lived in such times wherein great and sad disasters did befall the house and throne of David, as appears by what so bitterly he complains of, from ver. 38 to the end. But the question lies, what times this should belong unto, which ariseth from hence, that Ethan the Ezraite is the author of it, of whom we read, 1 Kings iv. 31, that he lived in Solomon's time, and therefore most interpreters assign this calamity unto the times of Rehoboam's reign, until when that this Ethan should live is no wonder ; for Rehoboam succeeded Solomon, and it was in the beginning of his reign that the ten tribes were deplorably cut off from David's house, and given to Jeroboam, and never did return again.

Now Piscator and others object, that in ver. 40 it is said, ' Thou hast broken down all his hedges, thou hast brought his strongholds to ruin,' which cannot (says he) belong to any other times but those of the captivity. The answer given by some is, that within the first five years of Rehoboam's reign, Sishak king of Egypt took also the cities of Judah, and the strongholds, 2 Chron. xii. 4, yea, he came to Jerusalem itself, and spoiled the temple, 1 Kings xiv. 25, by all which David's throne lost its virgin primitive glory ; as likewise by this Rehoboam himself, the king and his kingdom, servants, &c., were made tributaries to Egypt, 2 Chron. xii. 2. This event those interpreters judge a full and sufficient ground for the prophet to utter his fore-mentioned complaint upon. And indeed it may be said, that in this great change there was an initial performance then, and a beginning of those final disasters upon David's throne and family, though it had a more full accomplishment in the captivity of Babylon, unto which Piscator and others do rather refer this psalm. But there is this difficulty attends that interpretation of theirs, that there must have been another Ethan, and he an Ezraite too, living at the captivity ; which though it possibly might fall out, those of the same kindred giving to their posterity the same names of their famed ancestors, yet this not being extant, I should, to compound all, rather think that this Ethan of Solomon's time, seeing that this dismal calamity began in Rehoboam's time, did further, by the spirit of prophecy, foresee how an after total eclipse would in the issue fall out from this unhappy beginning, it foreboding that final ruin which followed, this being a laying the axe to the root of the tree, and so he wraps up both in one. But be it either the one or the other, however, he that wrote it did upon these fatal events begin deeply to consider what that covenant made with David should mean and intend, especially as touching that clause of the perpetuity thereof; the promise being, that it was established for ever, as at the first promulgation of it was declared, 2 Sam. vii. 13, whenas this prophet by these occurrences foresaw that David's successive outward kingdom would one day cease. And that at the captivity it had a fatal period, Ezekiel did pronounce: chap. xxi. 25–27, ' And thou, profane wicked prince of Israel, whose day is come, when iniquity shall have an end; thus saith the Lord God, Remove the diadem, and take off the crown: this shall not be the same : exalt him that is low, and abase him that is high.' With which compare this Ps. lxxxix. 39, ' Thou hast profaned his crown by casting it to the ground.' And as he had begun, so he threatens to go on : ' I will overturn, overturn, overturn it: and it shall be no more, until he come whose right it is ; and I will give it him;' that is, until the true David shall come, who was intended by the type of David's temporary kingdom. And by the consideration of these things our psalmist was by the Spirit led into the clear understanding of the mystery of the covenant of grace, founded on Christ the spiritual David, to set forth which is the intimate scope of the psalm. And by this it was that he comforts and relieves himself (as he well might) against those sad overthrows that fell upon that external successive kingdom and shadowy covenant of David's house over Israel, which was temporary. And those words (which I understand to be the prophet's own), ver. 23, ' I have said, Mercy shall be built up for ever, thy faithfulness shalt thou establish in the very heaven ; for I have made a covenant with my chosen, I have sworn unto David, my servant,' do express so much. And it is as if he had said, I have, notwithstanding the wreck I have seen hath and shall fall out to David's family, set down with myself as a fixed conclusion, that there are sure, stable mercies of David signified, that shall be built up for ever. And this he was resolved and assured of (and his words at last do argue as much), that notwithstanding those doleful miseries befallen David's family, and the Jews, related from ver. 39, &c., that he should yet be in the faith and confidence of those spiritual mercies. And accordingly he concludes the last verse, ' Blessed be the Lord for evermore. Amen, and amen.'

This he according to this scope proposeth at the beginning : ver. 1, ' I will sing of the mercies of the Lord for ever: with my mouth will I make known thy faithfulness to all generations.' And these mercies (as was said) are those of the covenant of grace (which afterwards are in this psalm set forth), and summarily they are the mercies promised unto Christ and his seed, whom David typified, as they are formed up into a covenant of grace ; of which he professeth to sing throughout this psalm; and therefore the most particulars therein are to be understood to relate thereunto. This summary or breviate of all he declares in the 3d and 4th verses expressly, as the words of God himself, whom he introduceth to speak in the midst of his own discourse in these words : ' I have made a covenant with my chosen ; I have sworn unto David my servant, Thy seed will I establish for ever ; and build up thy throne to all generations. Selah.'

That the covenant of grace in Christ is the substantial scope of this psalm, all Christian interpreters * do agree, and the arguments are invincible which Musculus and Calvin have urged to persuade this, as not only that our Saviour hath the very name of David their king given him by the prophets, Jer. xxx. 9, Ezek. xxxiv. 23, Amos ix. 11, and by the apostle, Acts xiii. 34, as in relation to these sure mercies, who is therefore intended as the substance of this shadow, but because the promises in this psalm are not fulfilled if not in him. For not only David's seed, but his kingdom and throne, are said to continue for ever. And if the fleshly seed of David can be supposed to continue still on earth, yet to be sure his kingdom hath not, whereas the promise is of his kingdom's continuance for ever, as well as of his seed. And if God hath failed in point of his successive kingdom, who will believe that other of his seed, unless as both were accomplished in our Jesus ? And this the angels at his conception do expressly assert : Luke i. 32, 33, ' He shall be great, and shall be called the Son of the Highest ; and the Lord shall give unto him the throne of his father David : and he shall reign over the house of Jacob for ever ; and of his kingdom there shall be no end.' Which was taken from Isa. ix. 6, ' For unto us a Child is born, unto us a Son is given : and the government shall be upon his shoulder: his name shall be called Wonderful, Counsellor, The mighty God, The everlasting Father, The Prince of peace.'

Christ's kindgom is said to be the throne of David, because shadowed

* Regnum Christi vocatur regnum Davidis, quia adumbratum fuit regno Davidis, &c. Sic Theophilactus inter Græcos, Bernardus inter Latinos.—*Lucas Brugensis in locum.*

out by that of David; * himself professeth that his ' kingdom was not of this world,' John xviii. 36, which David's kingdom was, after the mode and splendour of other earthly kings, which hitherto Christ's hath no way been. And in this psalm those great promises of pardon of sin, from ver. 30, appertain to that spiritual kingdom which Christ did found. And answerably, the seed of this David are a spiritual seed, which by his word and Spirit he begets, who are therefore named Israel, even the very Gentiles, Isa. xliv. 5 (who are the surrogate Israel), and their conversion (as well as of the Jews) the apostle expressly terms ' the building again the tabernacle of David :' Acts xv. 16, 17, ' After this I will return, and will build again the tabernacle of David, which is fallen down ; and I will build again the ruins thereof, and I will set it up : that the residue of men might seek after the Lord, and all the Gentiles, upon whom my name is called, saith the Lord, who doth all these things.' In which speech is also confirmed, that David's outward successive kingdom was utterly brought to ruin (as to be sure in Herod's time, wherein Christ was born, it was), and that now it was wholly to be raised up anew by Christ in a spiritual kingdom, then begun over both Jew and Gentile, they becoming one fold, and David their king becoming one shepherd over them, as the prophet hath it, Ezek. xxxiv. 23.

These covenant mercies then being the declared *ditto* of his song, and the most eminent mercies in that covenant being God's ' pardoning mercies ' to those under this covenant, he therefore particularly singles forth those, and they have a special and large room in this psalm, from ver. 30, &c. But before I come to discourse of the greatness of these mercies in pardoning sin, I cannot pass over that praise and celebration which the psalmist breaks forth into, of our great God who is the Father and Founder of this mercy and covenant, in the 5th verse, which is as a preludium to his song : ' And the heavens shall praise thy wonders, O Lord ; thy faithfulness also in the congregation of thy saints.'

Herein to provoke us men to sing and set forth these mercies, he sets before us the example of the glorious angels in heaven, who though never having sinned, and so never needed the pardoning mercies of this covenant, do yet praise God for it, and on our behalf; then how much more are we obliged !

' The heavens do praise thy wonders, O Lord.' These wonders are those wonderful mercies last mentioned (for he continues to speak punctually to this his subject he had thus proposed to sing and celebrate), and so they are not chiefly to be understood of God's wonders at large, though that is a truth also, that the angels celebrate God for them.

That the angels are expressed by the heavens,† sundry places do shew : Job xv. 15 : ' Behold, he putteth no trust in his saints ; yea, the heavens are not clean in his sight ;' compared with chap. iv. 18, ' Behold, he puts no trust in his servants ; his angels he charged with folly.' See also Ps. l. 4, 6. And that the angels are meant in this place by the psalmist, all interpreters, from the force of the coherence before and after, do agree. For it follows immediately in the same 5th verse, ' Thy faithfulness also in the congregation of thy saints ;' that is, is also praised among them ; which being a continuation of the same sentence and matter, must be understood of the same kind of praise, though indeed by another order of

---

* Dicitur Messiæ imperium Davidis solium, quod Davidis solio adumbrabatur. Et sic locum, 2 Sam. vii. 13, explicat Isaac Ben. Arama.—*Grotius in locum.*
† The Eastern translations, Syriac, &c., do concur with this.

praises.* That it is not meant of the material heavens is clear, it being the praise of the wonders of his mercy and faithfulness, as was said. And such praises are subjects of that super-celestial nature, which the material heavens are not capable to set forth the praise of. Nay, they have not the least material impress or stamp upon them to hold them forth unto us men. They declare indeed the glory of God in his works of creation, providence, &c., but not those of grace. And if anywhere it be applied thereto, it is but merely allusively, as out of Ps. xix. The apostle doth, in Rom. x., apply the psalmist's word of the heavens, Ps. xix. 1 ; and, indeed, but as by way of parallel type, shadowing forth the apostle's preaching throughout the earth. And besides, would he set (think we) and join the material heavens, inanimate creatures, and the congregation of the saints, in one choir together, in their praising God ; as in like manner in singing forth these like praises of covenant-mercies and faithfulness, especially when the heavens spoken of are brought in as the precentors, or chief and first singers in this sacred concert ? The heavens therefore here are the inhabitants of heaven, as earth is often put for the inhabitants of the earth ; you have both in one place, Ps. l. 4.

His wonders. The word in the original is the singular number : *mirabile tuum*, ' thy wonder,' the eminent wonder above all wonders, the sum of wonders, which are the contents of the covenant of grace. The contrivements and dispensations of it are all wonders, nothing but wonder, both in the whole of it, and every the least part of it, and all make up but one wonder of wonders, above and beyond all wonders ; and therefore by way of transcendent eminency it is thus styled. The head of this covenant also, Christ, our spiritual David, his ' name is Wonderful,' Isa. ix. 6. Again, God's pardoning iniquity, transgression, and sin (to celebrate which so many verses in this psalm are spent), is a wonder of wonders: ' Who is a God like unto thee, that pardonest iniquity ? ' &c., Micah vii. 18.

It follows in the psalmist, in the same verse, ' Thy faithfulness also in the congregation of the saints' ; namely, of the saints on earth, who have the most reason to magnify God for his mercy in it, as Rom. xv. And from whom also it is, by what is published in their assemblies, that the angels do learn much of these wonders, as that scripture shews (which is a place greatly parallel to this here), Eph. iii. 10, ' To the intent that now unto the principalities and powers in heavenly places, might be known by the church the manifold wisdom of God.' I say, parallel to this, for as there the angels and the church (on earth), so here the heavens and the congregations of the saints on earth, are joined in their adoration of these mysteries.

I only shall observe, that the angels' principal part in this celebration is distinct from that of us men ; it is to praise the wonders of this covenant ; or as it is a wonder, so it is most proper to them to admire and adore God for it. Well, but the mercy itself, and the faithfulness of God therein, that you see is ascribed and allotted to the congregations of the saints, or men on earth, as their theme, and to praise, that is our part. For why ? That is an interest peculiar and proper to us, the top and height of our joy and comfort lies herein. But the angels they fall down chiefly to the wonders and excellencies of wisdom and glory that are discovered in it, which they are therefore (as out of curiosity) said to pry into, 1 Pet. i. 12. And it is upon the account hereof they worship: Rev. vii. 11, 12, ' And all the angels stood round the throne, and about the elders and the four

* Qu. ' praisers '?—Ed.

beasts, and fell before the throne on their faces, and worshipped God, saying, Amen : Blessing, and glory, and wisdom, and thanksgiving, and honour, and power, and might, be unto our God for ever and ever. Amen.' Which place, though at first it shews that they heartily rejoice in what concerns the salvation of us men contained therein, in that they first say *Amen* unto a song which the sons of men had in praise of God begun before them to sing, ver. 10, ' Salvation' (that is, the glory of our salvation) ' be unto God, and the Lamb ;' and unto this the angels say *Amen* first, ere they begin their own, of blessing him for his glory, wisdom, &c. The salvation then, and so the mercy and faithfulness of God therein, is the eminent argument of our song. But the wisdom and power shewn therein, though we chant forth the glory of them also, is principally the matter of theirs.

The grand mercies and faithfulness promised unto Christ our David (the subject of this song), I reduce unto three heads, according to what we find summarily put together in ver. 3, 4, where you have,

1. The promise of a throne and kingdom to be established.

2. The choice and designation of the person (Christ), the true David, under the type and shadow of king David.

3. The promise of mercy to the seed of Christ under the same type. As for the perpetuity of these mercies, it runs along through the whole of all.

1. As touching the throne promised, you have a magnific description of a kingdom, which begins at the 7th verse, and reaches to the 15th, which kingdom, indeed (as there described), is that which God the Father promiseth unto his Son Christ, our David. And it is a matter worthy our inquiry, why the kingdom which God the Father did hold and visibly execute in the Old Testament, should be set out here, when he promiseth his Son a throne, &c. The true mystery and resolve of which is, that it is the same throne and kingdom for substance and economy which himself held, which he promiseth to his Son, and that therefore he sets forth his own herein ; for indeed it is all one. We know how Christ himself says, that God the Father had ' committed all judgment' to him, because he was the Son of man, John v. 22–27 ; and that the Father visibly judgeth no man, but hath given up all to his Son ; and this to that end, ' that all men might honour the Son as they honour the Father,' ver. 23 ; and therefore it is he is said to ' come in the glory of the Father,' and to ' sit on the Father's throne,' Rev. iii. 21, yea, and it is called ' the throne of God and of the Lamb,' Rev. xxii. 3. Hence therefore it is that the prophet being to declare what a throne it was which God here intended and promiseth to give to him, makes so ample a description of God's own kingdom (although much in the Old Testament language) as that which he meant to estate this his Son into, who yet because he was to come of David in the flesh, and David was his type, this kingdom is styled the throne of David in the shadow, but in reality and in the substance is indeed the kingdom of God the Father. And this, to be the true air or scope of those verses, seems to me most genuine and accommodate, and the best account that perhaps will be given of those verses. This for the kingdom, expressed in the first part of the psalm.

There is inserted between this and the other parts that follow a most comfortable application, directed (as in the midst of this discourse) to those that are under this covenant, and are the blessed objects of this grace and mercy of so great a God their King, who either live under the continual sound thereof, and have their hearts stirred and awakened with the sound thereof, so as by faith to pursue after the enjoyment of it, or especially those that have arrived unto a solid assurance of their share and interest therein. Or, if you will, the following words are a congratulation of their infinite happiness, as elsewhere it is expressed, 'Blessed are the people whose God is the Lord,' Ps. xxxiii. 12. The blessedness of the people instated in this covenant is displayed in this Psalm lxxxix., 15–18, 'Blessed is the people that know the joyful sound: they shall walk, O Lord, in the light of thy countenance. In thy name shall they rejoice all the day; and in thy righteousness shall they be exalted. For thou art the glory of their strength; and in thy favour our horn shall be exalted. For the Lord is our defence; and the Holy One of Israel is our King.'

2. The choice, and advancement, and dignity of the person who was to be estated in this throne, even of Christ, is described under the shadow of David. This Christ he dignifies with the highest titles of honour ; 'his holy One,' 'his mighty One,' upon whom God laid help for us all; 'his chosen, his exalted One,' ver. 19, 'his Servant,' his Christ and Messiah, with God's own holy oil anointed by God himself, ver. 20, in whom should rest all the power of God (which before in ver. 8, 10, 13, you heard of), to establish and strengthen this his Christ, and beat down his enemies, and wherewith to overrule all, ver. 21–23. And compare but the expressions in ver. 8, 13, with these ver. 21–23, likewise ver. 9 and ver. 25; in like manner ver. 10 with ver. 22–24, in which latter he says, their* mercy also and faithfulness (which the prophet had said did support God's throne, and did go before him to execute all the administrations of his kingdom, ver. 8 and 14) is promised unto this his King: ver. 24, 'My mercy and my faithfulness,' says God, 'shall be with him;' that is, in the whole of his government towards my church, to perform all with as much mercy and faithfulness as I myself would. If you will farther have it, God committed all the mercies that ever he had promised, or meant to bestow upon any or all his children, into the hands of his Christ, to give forth to them, and constituted him to be his own executor, and hath given him an heart of mercy of equal largeness thereunto, and faithfulness to perform it unto every tittle, as himself hath; so as he that shall compare all those descriptions of God's kingdom in the foregoing verses with the expressions of Christ's kingdom here, will readily acknowledge that God's Spirit in this psalmist did on purpose set forth the former representation of God's kingdom to the end, to shew that the like glory, yea, the same kingdom for substance, he hath devolved upon his Son, and put into his hands; which was the genuine drift and scope of so large a description of God's kingdom therein made. In the conclusion he proclaims, among other of the royal titles which God bestows upon his Christ, that of being God's Son: He shall cry unto me, 'Thou art my Father, my God, and the Rock of my salvation.' Which in how transcendent a manner it is true of Christ, you may read, Eph. i. 3, 1 Pet. i. 3 ; and of all sons, his first-born is 'higher than the kings of the earth,' ver. 26, 27 of this 89th Psalm, with which comports that of Rev. i. 5, 'The Prince of the kings of the earth.' These titles of Christ you find from ver. 19 to 28.

3. The other part of Psalm lxxxix. is that which I have chosen as my text, from ver. 28 to 37, and this part principally concerns the seed, the spiritual seed of Christ, as the former does his kingdom and personal dignities. You may remember how it was said that the mercies of this covenant were prophesied by the Psalmist as the eminent subject of his song:

* Qu. 'his'?—Ed.

' I will sing,' says he, ' of the mercies of the Lord for ever,' &c.; that is,
' which are for ever.' And in this special part of the song we find mercy's
voice elevated to the highest note, or to the highest *ela*,* which can be
supposed it should reach unto. For as the height and top of mercy's glory
is put forth and seen in pardoning of sins—that is the most proper seat
or subject wherein and whereupon the mercies of God are manifested and
spent—so in this paragraph, if anywhere in all the Scriptures, pardoning
mercies are ascendant, and in their supremest elevation.

Two things are to be farther cleared towards a foundation unto that
setting forth the greatness of God's pardoning mercies to his children, as
here they are held forth. The first, that by David's children here the
spiritual seed of Christ are intended, as by David Christ himself is (as hath
been shewn), and so the parallel runs thus: 1. David's person is the
shadow of Christ's person. 2. David's temporal throne of Christ's throne,
who was his eminent seed after the flesh. 3. That as David had other
children after the flesh in a succession, so Christ a spiritual seed in their
several generations. And of this spiritual seed, or children of Christ, and
of God's pardoning mercies unto them, is this paragraph to be understood.
1. That Christ hath a spiritual seed, unto whom he is the father, as David
was a father to his other successive seed; and that David bore the shadow
thereof, there are many passages in this and other scriptures which do confirm it. It is observable that in the 9th of Isaiah, before cited, when the
promise of the throne of David is again more expressly than here repeated,
that withal, ver. 6, one eminent title amongst those other is, of his being
' the everlasting Father,' which title doth necessarily relate to a seed, unto
whom he that is said to sit upon David's throne is also a Father. And
answerably, we see both the promise of Christ's throne and these promises
to his seed and children to be nearly conjoined in several passages in this
Psalm, as being inseparably riveted and involved both of them in this one
and the same covenant, and as the alike substantial parts thereof, and involved in the same oath. Thus ver. 28–30, ' My mercy will I keep for
him for evermore, and my covenant shall stand fast with him. His seed
also will I make to endure for ever; and his throne as the days of heaven.
If his children forsake my law, and walk not in my judgments,' &c. At
the entrance of my text, and again at the conclusion, ver. 35, 36, ' Once
have I sworn by my holiness, that I will not lie unto David. His seed
shall endure for ever, and his throne as the sun before me.' For he possesseth his throne upon such terms as that his children also should be
effectually saved. And what reason there should be that any should sever
these two, which God hath so closely joined together, I understand not.
We cannot conceive that the promise of the throne, which is unto Christ's
person, should be the sole and alone subject of the oath, but the promise
concerning the other seed and children should be without oath, and limited
to David's other fleshly children in their successions as unto temporal
respects, and not to take in the spiritual seed of Christ, or those of David's
seed who were such, especially seeing in other scriptures true believers on
Christ, whether Jews or Gentiles, are so frequently termed the seed and
children of Christ (our David), ' Lo here am I, and the children which thou
hast given me,' Heb. ii. 13. And in Psalm xxii., which so lively sets forth
Christ as he was hanging on the very cross, the issue and product of his
crucifying is in the close said to be, that ' a seed should serve him, and it
shall be counted to the Lord for a generation.' Parallel unto which is that

---

* The highest note in the musical scale, according to the notation then in use.—ED.

Isaiah liii., in which Christ Jesus is as evidently also held forth as crucified; the fruit whereof is there declared to be, that ' he shall see his seed,' and ' see the travail of his soul, and be satisfied in them,' and their effectual salvation by him, ver. 10, 11, for nothing else will satisfy Christ about them.

And to this purpose it may be farther observed, that in these promises in my text, made in David's name, as in behalf of his children, there is this strange difference apparently made between David the father and his children, that the Holy Ghost says not on his part, ' If he forsake my law, I will visit him with rods,' &c., but only if his children do, ver. 30, 31, whenas yet we all know, take David personally, he did foully forsake God's law, yea, despise the commandment, as the prophet Nathan challenged him, and was sharply visited with rods. Yet there is no mention of any of his sins, nor so much as of an *if* about any such matter, but all of him is passed over in silence. And to what other mystical purpose should this be, but that as Melchisedec's genealogy is omitted to make up a likeness to the Son of God, to the like intent there is omitted the mention of David's sins in this place, that David hereby might bear the type and shadow of Christ's person, and withal be a perfect type of him in his relation unto his children, who was in his own person not only without sin, but above the least supposition of it ? But if his children should sin, and some of them might be left unto great sins, yet for the mercy promised him they should be pardoned. And under this representation David comes to personate Christ, as he was to bear the relation of father unto his spiritual children, as for whose sake those promises were made. And in this manner, upon Christ as such a father and our David, and those promises to his seed, did that oath rest, as well as for the throne. If we also take the succession of David's fleshly seed, good and bad, the mercies and forbearance of God towards them (taking the circumstances of their sinnings, &c.) were greater towards them than unto any other succession of men that have been on earth. And we find it often in the story of the Kings and Chronicles put literally upon this reason, that is, ' for David my servant's sake.' And these dispensations of temporal mercies to those his children were but the shadows of those sure mercies, of pardoning mercies, promised to the spiritual seed of Christ. And for a farther confirmation of this, the spiritual children or seed of Christ are also termed David's seed and children here in the text, by the same just reason that the faithful are termed the sons of Abraham. For the foundation of Abraham's title to his being the father of all the faithful stood thus, that because a covenant and oath was promulged personally and particularly unto him, how that in Christ, who was to be his seed after the flesh, all the nations of the earth should be blessed; and that seed out of all nations being Christ's seed first, therefore he had the honour to be styled ' the father of all the faithful,' whether Jews or Gentiles, and the representer of Christ therein. Yea, and that oath and covenant involved the spiritual seed, as made unto them as well as unto himself, who laid hold upon it by faith, or as unto Christ, or rather with Christ for them, for so it is expressly interpreted to be: Heb. vi. 16, 17, ' For men verily swear by the greater; and an oath for confirmation is to them an end of all strife. Wherein God, willing to shew unto the heirs of promise the immutability of his counsel, confirmed it by an oath.' Now, the very same covenant and oath being in more ample and plain terms renewed unto David, the analogy holds between David and Abraham, and this psalm is an evidence of it. If then Christ and the spiritual seed in Abraham's case are not to be separated, then not in the case of David, wherein both are more distinctly and expressly mentioned, and included in one and the same covenant, than in Abraham's they were. Only David being a king set up so immediately by God, therefore the promise of the throne unto Christ his successor is more eminently indeed spoken of, yet not so as that it should be the sole object of that oath, but that God's faithfulness unto the children of Christ, or heirs of salvation, is taken in, as in Abraham's case it was, though far more obscurely.

And that the spiritual seed of Christ are reckoned as David's house and children, that place alone may perhaps be sufficient to prove, in which the conversion of the Gentiles is termed 'the building up the tabernacle of David:' Acts xv. 15–17, 'Unto this agree the words of the prophets; as it is written, After this I will return, and will build again the tabernacle of David, which is fallen down; and I will build again the ruins thereof, and I will set it up: that the residue of men might seek after the Lord, and all the Gentiles upon whom my name is called, saith the Lord, who doth all these things.' Among the Hebrews* a tabernacle was put for one's house; and that house signifies children is well known: Luke i. 33, 'He shall reign over the house of Jacob for ever;' by which is meant the spiritual seed, whether of Jew or Gentile, as before opened.

Having thus cleared and evinced it, that by David's children here in this Psalm lxxxix. 30 is intended the spiritual seed of Christ, I come now to shew how in verses 30–37, the glories of Jehovah, pardoning iniquity, transgression, and sin, are most signally displayed in this 89th Psalm, from verse 30 to verse 38, 'If his children forsake my law, and walk not in my judgments; if they break my statutes, and keep not my commandments; then will I visit their transgression with the rod, and their iniquity with stripes. Nevertheless my loving-kindness will I not utterly take from him, nor suffer my faithfulness to fail. My covenant will I not break, nor alter the thing that is gone out of my lips. Once have I sworn by my holiness, that I will not lie unto David. His seed shall endure for ever, and his throne as the sun before me. It shall be established for ever as the moon, and as a faithful witness in heaven. Selah. But thou hast cast off and abhorred, thou hast been wroth with thine anointed.' That God will pardon your sins of ordinary infirmities that you commit, that you think easily the covenant of grace doth reach and extend to; ay, but here is a proviso (you call them so in acts and wills) which is an ampliation of the covenant of grace upon the supposition of the worst of cases, of the worst of those who are under the covenant of grace: 'If his children forsake my law, and walk not in my judgments,' &c. You see the amplitude of the covenant of grace (what hath God to do to run out to this?), and you shall see the largeness of the covenant of grace, how far it extends.

1. I begin with the word *if:* it implies, that it is a case may fall out, God hath not said *temere*, rashly, or used all these words in vain. It is a case may sometimes fall out.

2. What is the reason of this *if*, if they shall do so and so? It is not so much, as Musculus says, to shew what man will do, but it is to shew what God will do. If men do so and so (and make a supposition to the utmost), if they do so and so, yet I will do so and so (says God), as far,

---

* Hebræis omne habitaculum σκηνὴ dicitur, quia ea habitatio vetustissima.— *Grotius in locum.*

nay, beyond what the imagination of man can reach, as Christ is a Saviour to the utmost.

3. He useth the word *if*, not that what is supposed does oft fall out, for there are millions of saints go to heaven, and not come within the compass of this place, and therefore it is what seldom happens.   Ay, but sometimes it does, for God would not in vain use so many words.   It is hard to. say what sins God pardons after regeneration; in some God exalts his justifying grace more, in some his sanctifying.   If one of ninety-nine be gone, he leaves all the other for those few's sake; he hath made provisoes in this covenant of grace, he hath put this *if* in.

4. He repeats it, and indigitates it over and over; for, as Calvin says, it is the hardest thing in the world to believe it, and whoever lives in great sins, it is the hardest thing in the world to believe that God will pardon him.

But doth he speak of the members of Christ, is it of those that are actual members of Christ that he speaks this?   Is it not of their sins before conversion rather?   Nay, but it is after: ' If his sons forsake my law,' says the 30th verse.   Those that are his sons and children are actually in the state of grace.   At the day of judgment, says he, Heb. ii. 13, ' Lo I and the children which God hath given me;' and he is called an ' everlasting Father,' Isa. ix. 6.

Another observation is concerning his seed, that the greatest of their sins may come under this *if*, under this proviso; so Calvin and Musculus observe.   David did not commit a sin of infirmity when he despised the commandment of the Lord, but his sin extended to the most heinous guilt.   And he speaks of such sins as may not be called mere infirmities.   Observe how he sets out their sins supposable.

1. He reckons up all sorts of laws broken: ver. 30, 31, there is my laws, judgments, statutes, and commandments; and interpreters fetch out all the judicial laws in rites and statutes, and moral laws in commandments.

2. Then observe how he expresseth it, for the act: ver. 30, ' If they forsake my law, and walk not in my judgment;' ver. 31, ' If they break my statutes, and keep not my commandments;' here is a worse than all, ' If they profane my statutes.'   It is translated, ' If they break my statutes;' but in the Hebrew, and so in the margin, it is ' If they profane my statutes.'   Now, for a saint to be a profane person, as Esau was, Heb. xii., how heinous is the guilt !

3. Take the title of their sins ; he calls them ' transgressions' and ' iniquities,' ver. 32 ; ' pardoning iniquity, transgression, and sin.'   One of the words signify falseness, treachery of sin.   Thus he sets out the greatness of those sins which it is supposed saints may fall into, after they are children.

4. Here are sins of omission and commission.   Of omission : ' if they walk not in my judgments,' ver. 30.   Of commission : ' if they forsake my law, and break my statutes, or profane them,' ver. 31.   I will not say that it is not to be said how far men may sin ; as it cannot be said how far men may go and not be sincere, so neither how far a man may sin.   Though it is certain there was a seed of God remained, yet that person that was excommunicated is called ' the wicked person.'   And you know the story of the apostle John's young thief, recorded by Eusebius, which was an amazing instance of a man's falling into sin.   Water may be so heated, that any body that puts his hand into it may say, Here is no cold in it ; but yet, though it scalds, let it stand a while and all the heat will be gone.   Let

men in a state of grace be inflamed with lusts, that one would think there is nothing of grace, yet there is a principle of grace which will reduce them at last. Thus much for the greatness of sin.

5. God promiseth chastisements in such cases. He does not bring great chastisements for ordinary infirmities, but for such sins as these are, that they may not be judged of the world: 1 Peter i. 17, ' If ye call on the Father, who without respect of persons judgeth according to every man's work, pass the time of your sojourning here in fear.' Though he be a Father, yet therefore be afraid of him. It is not for men to say, Let men live as they list, they shall be saved; no, says God, I will put a stop to you by chastising you. See what these chastisements are in these cases, and how he speaks of them: you may see the covenant of grace to shine in all still. First he says, he will ' visit them with rods and with stripes.' He calls them rods, 2 Sam. vii. 14, when the promise was first made to David (this very promise), ' I will be his Father, and he shall be my son. If he commit iniquity, I will chasten him with the rod of men, and with the stripes of the children of men.' It is a moderation of the correction, I will not whip him so hard as to kill him, says God, but as you whip men: I will not chasten with soreness of my displeasure, but deal with them as men. The truth is, God whips with rushes, in comparison to his vengeance in the other world: it is with the rod of men, which men may bear. He hath a sweet word, ' I will visit their transgressions with rods.' He says not, I will strike; no, it is a fatherly word, I will visit them as you do sick folks, to help them: it is a word full of tenderness. Again, he says, ' I will visit their iniquities:' it is a sweet word; he does not say, I will visit them; no, I love them, I have no anger at them, and wrath for them, but I have at their transgressions, Isa. xx. This is all the fruit of my chastising, to take away sin.

6. Consider the promises he makes to this case (the promises of chastisements you heard), but consider the other part of the promises that are here mentioned, and it will extremely affect your hearts.

1st, Says he, I will be kind for all this, I will not make my kindness void: so it is in the Hebrew, ver. 33, ' Nevertheless, my loving-kindness will I not utterly take from him, nor suffer my faithfulness to fail.' My kindness shall never fail in pardoning iniquity, transgression, and sin; I will ever be abundant in kindness and truth, Exod. xxxiv. 7. Well, go then, count the number of promises he makes of this kind; they are just the number of what he says of their sins. He had said four things of their sins: ' If his children forsake my law, and walk not in my judgments: if they break my statutes, and keep not my commandments;' and there are four several expressions which relate to his pardoning them. ' Notwithstanding my loving-kindness will I not make void, nor suffer my faithfulness to lie: my covenant will I not profane, nor alter the things gone out of my lips.' So that here is four to four.

2dly, Consider how he suits these expressions in correspondency to their sins.

1st, ' If they keep not my commandments,' ver. 31; ' My mercy will I keep for him for evermore,' ver. 28.

2dly, ' If they forsake my law,' ver. 30; ' I will not alter the thing gone out of my lips,' ver. 34.

3dly, ' If they profane my statutes,' ver. 31; ' I will not profane my covenant,' ver. 34. It is a mighty speech; as if God had said, I should run into profaneness, and be as profane as you, if I should break covenant:

as if God were in danger of this, if he failed Christ's seed in this case, of being a profane God, and an unholy God, and a lying God to David, which can never be.

7. He binds all this with an oath; ' Once have I sworn by my holiness, that I will not lie unto David.' I have sworn absolutely. Now consider:

1st, An oath is the highest confirmation of all other, Heb. vi. 6.

2dly, He tells you it is an oath but once taken. Why but once? To shew that all is irrevocable, both oath and thing sworn to.

3dly, Though it be sworn but once, to shew it is irrevocable, yet notwithstanding we hear of it twice in this psalm: ver. 3, ' I have sworn unto David my servant;' and again, ver. 35, he took the oath but once, but we hear of it twice. He took an oath to his Son, that he would make him a king, and set up his throne ; that the 3d verse shews ; and he takes an oath for his seed, and his seed in this case of sinning, and it is as sacred to him concerning his children, as it is to Christ, to oblige himself to give him a throne and kingdom.

4thly, Consider what he swears by. Of all things else this amazeth me, he swears by his holiness : ' Once have I sworn by my holiness.' Now bring all your consciences to God, and what is it you do dread in God? His holiness. What is it provokes him? It is laid in the foundation of justice and wrath ; and because he is a God so pure that his eyes can endure no iniquity. Now then that his holiness, which is the most against sin, should be brought in to be sworn to pardon sin, what can you have more? Calvin says, to swear by his holiness, is more than to swear by himself ; for he swears by that thing which is like to be your greatest enemy, to condemn and destroy you.

5thly, Lastly, He swears by that which is most eminent in his holiness, and must be profane and lie, if he doth not perform.

8. Consider that all this is founded upon Christ, though the mercies are in the heart of God. It is a mighty expression when he says, ' If his children forsake my law, I will visit their transgressions.' He speaks to them, If they do so and so ; but when he comes to make his promise, ' notwithstanding my loving-kindness shall not be void from him.' *From him*, ver. 28, *i. e.*, from Christ. What, does Jesus Christ need any mercy? Ay, it is well for us he doth not for himself. But thus, as he is the head of all saints, and he and they make one body, the covenant of grace and mercy was made with him, and so they are called ' the sure mercies of David,' Isa. lv. 3. All the mercies God bestows are for his sake ; and it is well now that God hath sworn, that he will not take his mercies from Christ in relation to us ; and that Jesus Christ can go to God and plead, Lord, I have no need of mercy ; but thou hast given me all thy mercies for those who are mine ; Lord, fulfil them to them. There is one use which Calvin makes, Live upon the covenant of grace, you need no more ; and if you be guilty of great sins, you had need live upon it. But let me commend one use, which David makes in the midst of the psalm, ver. 15–18, ' Blessed is the people that know the joyful sound,' &c. He speaks in relation to the covenant of grace, to all them that are under it. He sets it in the midst as an use of application to the persons under it. But what kind of persons are they that are under it? They ' know the joyful sound.' All interpreters acknowledge it is an allusion to the sounding the trumpets, which you read of, Num. x. 4, 10 ; Lev. xxiii. 23. This I find by Ainsworth and others, that ' joyful sound' here imports (what was typified by the

sounding their trumpets and cornets) the spiritual joy the people of God should have in the favour of God, and meeting with God, and communion with God, in his covenant of grace. This is plainly the meaning, for (says he) ' they shall walk in the light of thy countenance.' When did they sound trumpets ? They sounded trumpets for war, for feasts, upon extraordinary occasions of great joy, as at the dedication of the temple, Ezra iii. 11, 12 ; when the people returned from captivity, 2 Chron. v. 12, 13 ; when the foundation of the temple was laid, Ezek. iii. 10 ; and at its dedication, Neh. xii. 35 ; and every new year they had trumpets and cornets sounded ; the one was made of rams' horns, which they called a cornet, the other of silver ; the one had a loud sound, the other a shrill, Ps. xcviii. 6. There is both trumpets and sound of cornets ; with these they made a joyful noise. Now what is the meaning of this, but to tell us, Oh blessed are those people into whose ears God blows joy, and peace, and salvation ? Says the apostle, ' If the trumpet gives an uncertain sound,' who knows what is meant ? 1 Cor. xiv. 7, 8. But when God comes and speaks to a man's soul all this that I have said of the covenant of grace, and tells him, that he is his salvation, and blows this with his own immediate voice, ' Oh blessed is that man that hears this joyful sound :' this man may ' walk in the light of God's countenance.' Consider what he says of it : ' They shall walk in the light of thy countenance, and in thy name shall they rejoice, and in thy faithfulness shall they be exalted : thou art the glory of their strength,' &c. Such as have had this trumpet sounding in their souls, are enabled to walk triumphingly, and are prepared for war. They sounded the trumpet for war : we are in war ' more than conquerors ;' ' O grave, where is thy victory ?' Oh seek to the Lord that he would blow and make this blessed sound in your souls, that you may have God to rejoice in, and God himself alone. The angels may wonder at the wonders of the covenant, but you rejoice in them as yours, and you may do it all the day long ; and in doing so you will be taken off from all that is in yourselves. ' In thy name shall they rejoice :' ' They glory in this, that they know thee that exerciseth loving-kindness in the earth,' and ' their joy shall none take from them,' Ps. lxxxix. 6.

CHAPTER X.

Of the mercies of God's heart and nature.—That mercy and grace are true essential properties in the divine being.—That there are some that deny this. —This head discoursed in three branches: 1. An explication ; 2. The proofs out of the text ♦ 3. Answers to the principal objections.—1. The explanation : 1st, How it is to be understood that mercy, or any other attribute, is the nature of God ; 2dly, Of the difference between those mere similitudinary attributes borrowed from man, as sorrow, repenting, &c., and those substantial attributes in God, the likeness whereof are communicated to man, and so attributed both to God and also to man, such as holiness, goodness, mercy.—The state I put the question into, for the proofs of the assertion.

It may be greatly wondered at, that it should ever so much as have entered into the thoughts of any of the sons of men,* sinful men, who there-

* It need not stumble any that such an opinion is vented by the same persons that speak at the same rate of the sacrifice which Christ made by offering up him-

fore need an infinity of mercy from the great God, to save and pardon them, to affirm that all the mercy which God himself so magnifies in this scripture, and for which other scriptures do so highly extol him, should be ascribed to God only *è similitudine effectûs ;** that is, because he doth and exerciseth loving-kindness; and only because that his outward dispensations are such as men who are mercifully disposed use to exercise, out of a pitiful nature. But God, say they, without any inherent disposition or affections which should properly have the name of mercy, or which, as such, should be the root and inward principle of such merciful acts, doth exert them. They answerably affirm mercy to be an attribute of that rank which are usually termed after the manner of man : as when God is said to grieve and repent, which are merely ascribed to him, because he doth such things towards us, as we men are wont to do when we grieve and repent; but God doth them without any inward principle of grief or repentance: and it is so here in the case of mercy, say they. But their questioning this great truth is not the occasion of my speaking to this point in this place ; but my method and subject necessarily lead me to it; without the demonstration of which added to the former, my grand assertion, which bears the title of my subject, would be imperfect, and' of less power and force upon believers' minds : and being thereby obliged to prove it out of the text, I saw some necessity first to premise that general explication that follows, to prevent mistakes out of vulgar apprehensions.

I offer then an explication, how it is to be understood that any of God's attributes are of the nature of God, or may be said to be the nature of God.

This explication of this I shall absolve by these two explanatory propositions : 1st, The Scriptures say, that he is God by nature, Gal. iv. 8, in difference from those that are but called gods ; and so we may affirm that what God is, he is by nature, that is, by his being himself God ; and so the perfections of his being are himself, and termed his Godhead, Col. ii. 9.

1. These *divina nomina* (as the ancients call them), that is, these names attributed to God, such as wise, powerful, holy, good, merciful, are said to be his nature, because there is that in his divine nature or Godhead which truly answers to what is intended to be signified by these names, and he is by nature that which these attributes do express him to be.

2. It were absurd to think or understand that any attributes whatsoever, as they are words and outward characters or expressions, should be the nature of God ; but yet these things signified by these outward words and characters are truly and inwardly in the nature of God, and he is such a God by nature ; and that these outward words and names do *proprio et primario significatu*, as the schools speak of them, in their primary and proper signification, convey to our minds what is really in God's nature.

3. Nor yet are those glorious inward conceptions and apprehensions that are conveyed to, and begotten in, our minds by these significant characters,

---

self for the sins of us men ; denying that also to be a price or ransom properly to redeem us, and would make it to be but metaphorical. And truly, when these two grand pillars of faith are thus enervated, and made weak, by taking from them what gives the strength and substance unto them, what remains there of solidity sufficient for the heart of a sinner, loaden with that infinite weight of his sins, to sustain and bear it up, and him to stay himself upon ?

* Quoad actus secundos; non quoad actus primos : quoad effectum, non affectum : objectivè ; shewing mercy to us ; not *subjectivè*, as from mercy in himself : χατ' ἀνθρωποπαθειαν.

begotten by the Spirit in us; nor are these the nature of God, although they be the inward bright rays and shinings thereof. Both which is evident from that speech, 2 Cor. iv. 6, 'God, that commanded' (by creation namely) 'light to shine out of darkness, hath shined in our hearts, to give the light of the knowledge of the glory of God, in the face of Jesus Christ;' where, first, it is the glory of God himself that is said to be known; and yet, secondly, the most illustrious light that was in the minds of the apostles themselves, whereby they knew him, was but a created resemblance of that glory of God made in and through the face and person of Jesus Christ, who is a far more glorious representation of the Godhead than what those attributed names can any way render to us.

4. It remains to be proved, that yet the things themselves conceived of by us, and expressed by these names, are substantially and by nature in God; or that there are those perfections in his nature and Godhead as do really answer to what these outward significant characters of attributes, and those inward beams of himself in our conceptions, do represent his nature to be. And the evidence for this may be drawn from the lesser to the greater, from that lower representation of God and his Godhead, made to the heathens by the works of God's providence and creation. And surely, look what those representations or manifestations of God made to them are termed, or what is spoken of them, we are warranted to speak the same, yea, much more, of these attributes of God's own choice to set forth himself by. Now, it is expressly said, Rom. i. 20, that 'the invisible things of him from the creation of the world are clearly seen, being understood by the things that are made, even his eternal power and Godhead;' where, 1st, 'those invisible things of God' are his properties, such as are essential to him, and particularly power and eternity are there instanced in; which, 2dly, are invisible in themselves to us, as his Godhead is, and but known of us, as God is pleased to make show of them unto us, as ver. 19, 'Because that which may be known of God is manifest in them, for God hath shewed it unto them.' And, thirdly, that those invisible things or properties of God are essentially and by nature in him; there is this evidence in that text, that what of them is manifested is said to have been in God himself before he made, yea, although he had never made the world (which is the manifestation of them there specified), or had any of these names given him; and he gives for instance those two essential attributes, eternity and power. And in that he says *eternal*, he proclaims the reality of that attribute which we call power, to have been substantially in him from eternity, like as eternity itself also, before ever these attributed names were given him, or before any such works or effects of his were extant, by which these are made manifest. The things were in him before.

Yea, he riseth up higher, and expressly styles that which was signified and represented by these works, &c., to be his Godhead, in adding his eternal power and Godhead, which let critics interpret how they please, either to his divinity, as Beza, or Godhead, as our translators, yet either both do and must centre in this conclusion, that it is styled either of these, because there is that in his Godhead and divine being which in an excess of fulness doth in truth answer unto that manifestation of him. And so the argument becomes strong and prevalent for the point before me, that if those ruder and obscurer impresses made of himself by the works of creation, ver. 20, and those imperfect medals of himself stamped upon the souls of those heathens thereby, of which, ver. 19, he speaks ('for God hath shewed it to them'), be called his Godhead, then how much more do these names or attributes which God in his word, by his own institution, hath appointed, and in infinite wisdom himself invented and revealed, being accompanied and brought home by the power, supernatural light, and blessing of his Spirit to the souls of his saints, through his word (as out of 2 Cor. iv. 6 was observed); how much more, I say, shall these be styled his Godhead in the sense and for the reason above said, even because they do, in their proper, direct, and absolute signification, shew what his Godhead is ! And there is that in God that corresponds to, and to an infinity doth make good what is spoken of him by these, as we call the representation of a man's face in water the man's face which it represents, because, as Solomon says, it answers ' as face to face ; ' and so it is here. And the representations by these are but as those of a man's face or whole person in broken pieces of a looking-glass severed one from the other, whereby it comes to pass that not the whole in any is entirely seen, but one lineament or cast of the countenance is represented in one ; another part, as an eye, in another piece of that glass, and so of the rest. And therefore in the plural it is here said, ' The invisible *things* of God are clearly seen,' &c., in relation unto our multiplied conceptions of them in and by his works or attributes severally. For whilst by one act we take into our conception that he is wise, we then do not so much as think of his power or goodness. We see an eye in a distinct attribute severed as it were from the rest, but actually see not an hand at that instant, and so of the rest. God hath cast the apprehensions of himself into lesser moulds, to fit the narrow bore of our understandings. And if any man, apprehending some one or more, as those in the text, should say, there are no more, he should greatly derogate from the Godhead. But notwithstanding the multiplicity of the representations of these attributes, or of our conceptions thereby, yet still there are all those perfections in the Godhead, which do *in omnimodá et unitissimá simplicitate*, in an undivided unity and simplicity in the Godhead, answer unto all these. And look as we call the broken, scattered, diffused beams of the sun upon disturbed or surging waters, the sun, although they represent it but by piecemeal, this beam in one wave in one part, and that beam in another wave another piece of it, because though it be thus scatteredly and brokenly done, yet there is that in the light and body of the sun that answereth unto all these, so it is here. And were it not thus, we could not be said to ' know him that is the true God,' as John xvii. 3, nor to know the truth of God as it is in God ; and so the heathen had not been ' without excuse, in that when they knew God they glorified him not as God.'* Only we are to correct these our imperfect conceptions by this rule, that whilst we make a composition of all these, to the end that thereby we might come to understand what God in the whole is (which is but a multiplicity in our imperfect contemplations of him), that yet still in the close of all we sit down with the faith of this, that in him all these perfections are inseparably one indivisible being, and all of them himself, and withal comforting and relieving ourselves against that present deficiency, that God hath reserved a time in the other world, in which with one intuitive act of knowledge or

---

* I leave it to the schools to dispute : the Scotists on the one side, other schoolmen on the other ; *Quid sit fundamentum distinctionis attributorum in Deo, num in re an in ratione ratiocinante.* This I am sure of, that what of the things of God are multiplied in our conceptions, are but one in God, and one God. *Sicut si quæratur an potentia sensitiva coloris et odoris sint idem, an distinguantur ? Respondendum, in sensibus externis quidem distingui, in sensu interno esse realitèr idem.*—(Raphael Aversa de Sanseverino in Part. prima, Quæst. 3. Sect. 4).

entire view at once, we shall see all those perfections of his to be but one simple nature and fulness of the Godhead, which is a seeing God face to face.   And then we shall find also that these attributes in this life did yet truly and really represent what was really and truly in himself.

And thus much for the first explaining narrative or account (as I call it, because it consists of so many branches), which though it contains but what is common to other attributes, yet was necessary to be premised both for the better understanding of the proofs, and for the preventing mistakes perhaps in some vulgar understandings, as also conducing to the bringing forth something towards the state of this question, as it particularly concerneth mercy, viz., this,

That this attribute of merciful is said to be natural to God, or the nature of God, because it directly signifies what is in God's nature, truly answerable thereunto; and that God's intent in proclaiming himself merciful, &c., is to declare what properly himself is, and his Godhead is.

II. The second explanatory proposition is, that there are two ranks of these attributes, as our divines, and the attributes themselves, as in the Scriptures they are related, speak them to be.

1. The first is of such as are utterly incommunicable unto us creatures, nor have they any respect unto the creatures; such are God's infinity, simplicity, immensity.

2. There are those that are communicable to us, that is, in the shadow and likeness of them, as wisdom, holiness, truth, goodness, mercy ; and such as have a respect unto the creature, as power, which is seen in creating and governing the creatures; and goodness likewise, which respects a communication of good unto the creature, whereof grace and mercy are eminent branches, and to be sure do respect the creature only, for God is not merciful to himself.   ' The Lord is good, and his mercy endureth for ever,' was the solemn set song in the temple wherewith to praise the Lord.   And this communicableness of some that are God's essential properties is evinced by that speech, ' He makes us partakers of his holiness,' Heb. xii. 10.   And in like manner it holds of his wisdom, truth, goodness, mercy, kindness, long-suffering, &c., in that these are styled the image of God, that is, of what is in God, as the original pattern, πρωτότυπον.   Now because the attributes of this latter rank are in a shadow communicable to the creature, and have a respect unto the creature, &c., therefore these men do confound these kind of attributes, at least some of them (as they please to except), with those that are but metaphorically attributed to God, and are apparently but borrowed from what is really in the creatures, and attributed unto God.   And they do utterly deny these are first really and essentially in God, but only the image and shadow of them communicated to us, as hath been said, whilst yet they acknowledge those of the first rank to be essentially in God.   But for the confirmation that the second rank communicated, &c., are no less essentially his divine nature than the first, I shall allege but two arguments.

1st. The first is out of 2 Pet. i. 4, where we are said to be ' partakers of the divine nature;' whereby either, 1, the divine nature or Godhead itself is intended: and so we are said to be partakers of it in this just sense, by way of communion with the Godhead in the three persons, who, becoming our God, gives up himself, and all the perfections that are in him, unto us, to be enjoyed by us; and so either here or hereafter we are to be ' filled with all the fulness of God,' Eph. iii. 19; not bodily (or by personal union, as Christ, Col. ii. 9), but in the objective communications thereof, for our eternal happiness. And if this be understood, as many do understand it, we have his Godhead directly and immediately termed his divine nature, which yields an additional confirmation to what was affirmed in the former explication. Or, 2, by divine nature there is meant that *Dei formitas*, as the ancients called it; that is, the image of God, or a conformity unto God in us, which is the more common opinion; and so understood, it falls in to be a proof of the assertion of this second explication; for therein three things are necessarily imported: 1, that there are in God such perfections, as whereof we, in the likeness of them, are participants; and so that that whole set and sort of communicable perfections in God are intended, and are expressly termed the divine nature, because they are first and originally in him, and then in us. Again, 2, the image of those perfections are styled the divine nature in us, as being the imitation of his; and that not only in respect of the resemblance or likeness which the graces communicated have to his perfections, as those we have inherent in us bear the semblance of those in him. But further, 3, in respect that they become a new and divine nature in us, in our kind, even as his perfections (thus communicated) are a nature in him, even a blessed and divine nature. And for their resemblance unto him in that very respect, they are in common called a divine nature in both him and us; being first true of him, and then in us, as the apostle John, in case of love, speaks of Christ and us, 1 John ii. And for that they are a nature in him as well as in us, therefore the conclusion is, that these communicable attributes are truly his divine nature, as well as the incommunicable. But, 4, there is this difference betwixt these perfections in God and those communicated to us, that in us they are but inherent qualities, which are termed a nature, because they become as natural in us as any inbred and innate qualities can be said to be; whereas in God, look as he himself is ' the most high God,' Gen. xiv. 22, and elsewhere, ' God most high,' so these perfections are accordingly in him after a most high and transcendently supreme surpassing manner, incomprehensible by us; whereof the following argument is an invincible evidence.

Arg. 2. These communicable attributes of wisdom, holiness, truth, goodness, power, &c., are so attributed to him, as such as are in him *alone;* notwithstanding that we men do partake of these, and the angels also do far excel us men in all these; thus, ' as wise as an angel of God' is the expression, 2 Sam. xiv. 17, and they are styled ' the holy angels,' and ' that excel in strength,' Ps. ciii. 20, far above us men in this life. Yet God alone retains and challenges the honour of being ' only wise,' Rom. xvi. 27, ' only holy,' Rev. xv. 4, ' only good,' Mat. xix. 17, ' the only true God,' Rom. iii. 4. Which attributions with an *only* must and do necessarily import, 1, that this wisdom, holiness, goodness, truth, and strength, are in God as God, and that they are of his divine essence and nature, which we creatures are in no wise capable of. Our souls are one thing, namely, substances; our graces another, namely, accidents; but the essence of God, and his divine properties, are but one and the same; of which more afterwards. And hence it is that although these are communicated to us, yet indeed are but *equivocè* attributed to the creatures, and are in them but in a semblance, even as the picture of a man is called a man. And though because men assumed and imposed these names first, and applied them to men, and seeing such and such qualities in them, they thereupon gave them the names of wise and merciful, to signify those things in a man which, according to man, is wisdom and mercy; and it was they that gave these denominations to men like themselves, because men are next and first in our view; yet in truth and reality the sole honour and glory of these names, thus invented by men, and applied to men, are due to God alone, for the true reality and substance of these in the creature is in God, and men had the gifts and qualifications of them derived from God. And men having given such and such several names unto those excellencies that are in men and angels, calling man, for that little wisdom in him, wise; for holiness, holy; yet these falling out to be the likeness and resemblance of what is in God substantially, therefore God, in speaking of himself unto men, useth the same terms and style, to set out those glories in himself; and this account the schoolmen* have wisely given. Seeing, then, that these attributes that are communicated to the creatures are as they are in God his nature, as well as the incommunicable, there are these consectaries from thence.

The *first* is to shew the apparent and yet infinitely vast difference that is between those attributes which are said to be ascribed to God after the manner of man, which have been specified again and again, and those we call communicable to men, and are in common ascribed to us and to God. The difference is manifest; that those after the manner of man (as when God is said to grieve, Gen. vi., be troubled, Jer. xxxi. 20, his repentings, Hos. xi. 8, &c., of which sort those men would persuade us the mercies in God to be, and would reduce and bring mercy in God thereto) are such as are truly, and properly, and originally in the creature first, and then borrowed from the creature by way of similitude only, God condescending in that language to speak of himself after our manner, and weaknesses, and passions, so to make a smart and sensible impression upon our dull souls. But, on the clean contrary, these communicable attributes, whereof mercy is one, are first and originally in God, and derived from his fulness, which God vouchsafes to express to us by those names which we men give to the semblance of them in us men, as hath been explained.

Hence, 2, we may likewise discern how easily men may err from the right in this matter; because mercy in us men, in the sound of it, speaks weakness and an affectionate passion as the conjunct of it; and when spoken of God, is expressed by the sounding of bowels, &c., and by God's being troubled for us, which is acknowledged to be indeed spoken of him; but it is to be understood after the manner of men, because he doth that which merciful men are wont to do when their bowels yearn within them. But yet still mercy itself, that is the root of all as it is in God, is another thing. We must cut off all such imperfections, whilst yet we are helped by them, as we are men, to conceive how tender his mercies are towards us. We poor creatures are apt to drench our conceptions in what mercy in the creature is, and through the tincture and apprehension we have thereof, taken from the creature, do we look upon the mercies in God, and so conceive of them as if God had borrowed the denomination of them from us, to express himself to us by; and so we are apt to think mercy to be a mere metaphorical 'attribute in God. We grant mercy in us to be analogous to what is in God, but that mercy in God to be the original idea, and not metaphorical or similitudinary.

Hence, 3, let us, in our thoughts about these mercies in God, form and cast our conceptions in the mould of this rule, that though they be in God,

---

* Ista nomina per prius dicuntur de Deo, quam de creaturis: sed quantum ad impositionem per prius à natis imponuntur creaturis (quas prius cognoscimus).— *Aquinas,* 1 parte, Quæst. 13, articulo 6, in fine.

yet after an unconceivable manner to us ; and that they are in God for the kind and being of them, with an infinite difference,—as being in God as God, and in the creature but as a creature ; and therefore, that as far as God's essence and being transcends ours for kind of being, so far doth holiness and mercy in him exceed the mercies that are in us, even for kind also, as Christ in the very point of mercy informs us, in saying, ' So shall you be the children of the Most High,' Luke vi. 35, 36. And so much higher in mercy is God than we, for our comfort, ' as the heavens are higher than the earth ;' as God himself speaks of himself, Isaiah lv. 9.

These things forelaid, the true measure of the decision of this question (if any will dare to make a question of it) is,

Whether that these attributes, merciful and gracious, &c., although in common attributed unto man, do not yet serve, and be not intended by God, as really and fully to express and set out to our faith what a God he is in himself, and what his very nature and inward disposition, and inclinations of soul are, and affections of heart, a root and principle of merciful effects ; as when he is said to be holy, good, wise, true, strong, powerful, or the like ; which are all communicated to man, and yet not ascribed to God after the manner of men only ; as when he is said to be grieved, and pricked at the heart.

And if any will deny these, and such-like, to be essential attributes, or expressive of the true nature of God, they must affirm that no attributes, whereof men partake the name, are at all such, and that all do serve to express but outward effects merely, and no way inward dispositions, as the principle of those effects in him. And thus proposed, I shall make this one main argument of the assertion, viz., that mercy is a parallel attribute with those other. None dare say that he is holy in his works, or in respect he doth holy works, but that he is holy in his being, as he is God. The like is to be understood of his being good, wise, merciful, &c.

CHAPTER XI.

That mercy and grace in God are properties of his divine being and glory.—
No other proof alleged but from the text, Exod. xxxiv. 6, 7.

I come now to the farther proofs of this assertion, that mercy and grace are properties of the divine nature. And I profess to allege no other (that I may shew this text to be a complete abundary of all God's mercies) than what the text, either in the words themselves, or the aspect of them upon what went before, do afford the heads of, and foundations for ; and I shall then call in the help but of such other scriptures, which as volunteers willingly offer themselves to assist in this cause, and verify and confirm each hereof, when first extracted out of the word.

The point to be proved is, that mercy and grace are glorious properties of the divine being or nature.

Arg. 1. The first argument is drawn from the true reference and strict correspondency this proclamation of God, merciful, &c., holds with the foregone transactions in the chapter before, Exod. xxxiii., which lead on to it, which were Moses's request, God's answer and promise unto his request ; and here in my text, God's performance according to his promise. These three are correspondent, one to the other. Observe we then, 1st, what it was Moses desired of God ; and, 2dly, what God promised to gratify him in; and, 3dly, the thing which God did punctually perform. And, in my beginning with this first, I shall but keep to that method generally observed for the opening of a text, in discovering its occasion, coherence; and yet withal prove my assertion at once. In the 33d chapter, Moses had desired of God that he would shew him his face and glory; that is, his divine essence immediately, or his essential glory as it is in himself. This Moses aspired unto, ver. 18, 'I beseech thee, shew me thy glory;' but God tells him that this seeing his face, or the immediate vision of his essence or being, none is capable of, and live, ver. 20, which yet leaves a room for hope that the frailties of this life being removed, a man may see God's face in that other life. But yet, in lieu thereof, God, to gratify him, professes his gracious resolution to grant the privilege, as far as was possible for any mere man to partake of it and live; and to manifest his foresaid face and glory, and his being God, as far as was expressible, and might be represented unto man, and he live, in these words : ver. 19, 'And he said, I will make all my goodness pass before thee, and I will proclaim the name of the Lord before thee, and will be gracious to whom I will be gracious, and will shew mercy on whom I will shew mercy.' And the best interpretation of this is that which I find in Oleaster,* who paraphrasing those words of God's, ' all my good,' that is, myself, says he, in whom is all that is good or excellent, or a perfection, shall pass before thee, and be made known by voice signifying it, ' I will proclaim my name,' &c., or by a vision of his, ver. 23, 'Thou shalt see my back parts,' representing it. And you heard how the names or attributes of God do signify truly and properly what is really the nature of God. So then God's essential divine perfections are intended and promised by God, to be seen and proclaimed by such characters of words; or a name and attributes, as far as was possible, those perfections in himself to be by words expressed; yet so as still these words should be such as should represent what was in himself, or the divine nature, in truth and reality answering thereunto, as in my explication premised, chap. vi., I have shewn.

From whence I argue, that if these first and chief attributes proclaimed, viz., Jehovah, merciful, gracious, long-suffering, much in goodness and truth, had not served to signify that essential goodness which was in himself; or if there had not been that glory essentially in himself which these names were intended to signify, then God had neither gratified Moses to the utmost he was capacitated for, nor answered his desire to see his glory, as far as he was capable to see it, and live. For that there are some such other names and attributes of his in Scripture which do express his nature and essence, all do, and must acknowledge, as wisdom, holiness, &c., which are not here expressed; and therefore, if he doth it not in these here, professedly by himself proclaimed, and proclaimed as professedly to that very end and purpose, make his essence known; then nowhere else should he be thought or judged to do it; nay, he had done it in none, for he had professed beforehand he would do it in these, that he would proclaim his goodness and glory. And whereas there are (as was said) other attributes and epithets that would have set forth his divine being and glory, that he should name none of those, but, in lieu thereof, choose and single forth *merciful, gracious*, above all others, to express his glory by, argues that mercy is not only his nature, but the glory of it; at least, it must be

---

* Ego transire faciam omne meum bonum, id est, meipsum; in quo sunt omnia bona quæ coram te explicabuntur voce: Clamabo nomen Domini.—*Oleaster in verba.*

acknowledged such as do signify what his nature is, as really and as properly as any other denomination whatsoever can do, or ever will do. Yea, he would, since he professeth to proclaim that name which should express his glory, rather have made choice of those other names that are essential, if those had not been such as much as any. And this first argument is but as the porch or portal to the whole building.

Arg. 2. My second argument is from the very order and division which the words (as to the point of mercy) do naturally fall into ; and this may well be taken for one proof of this assertion, a preliminary one, for I yet make but an entry to the text. For three things may be easily discerned distinct in this proclamation, and succeeding one the other in an orderly dependence one upon the other.

1. An inward, merciful, and gracious disposition to shew mercy, which is the root or spring, placed therefore in order the first : 'Jehovah, Jehovah, God merciful and gracious, long-suffering, much in goodness and truth.'

2. His blessed purposes and resolutions to bestow it, in these words : ' keeping mercy for thousands ;' that is, reserving it in his intendments to bestow it, which are immanent acts in God, flowing from the former, kept and laid up in his own breast, and now uttered.

3. Extrinsecal, or outward works of mercy issuing from both : as ' pardoning iniquity, transgression, and sin,' that being given as one instance (the most eminent), for all other of that sort, external mercies.

Whereof the sum is, 1st, he *is* merciful and gracious : that is his nature as he is Jehovah, Jehovah ; 2dly, he fully *resolveth* to shew mercy : there is his heart ; 3dly, he hath *done* it, and doth it, in pardoning every day : there is his wont and practice, as Moses upon it says : Numb. xiv., ' Pardon as thou hast pardoned, from Egypt until now.' And by these three God sets himself out to be every way, and all sorts of ways, merciful.

And this general may serve instead of a more exact division of the words which others would give, and doth give some light to prove this head, if there were no other to follow ; but this is but as the threshold or first entrance to the whole.

Arg. 3. Merciful effects are ascribed unto the mercy of God as the proper cause of them, and therefore the mercy attributed to God must be properly an inward principle in God, whence those effects do proceed. It is an approved maxim, and will approve itself, and carry itself thorugh the whole Scriptures, that as in the general all God's works are ascribed to God as God, Ps. lxxxvi. 8, 10 ; so in particular every genuine attribute hath, for the glory of it, proper work attributed in a special eminency unto it as the special cause of that work. As the creation of the world is attributed to power, Rom. i., and to wisdom, Ps. cxl. 24, yea, and the greatness of his work is attributed to the greatness that is in himself, Ps. lxxxvi, 10, and Ps. cxlv. 3–6, as in like manner the goodness of them to the goodness that resides in him ; and thus the performance of his promises is attributed to that essential truth that is in him, and are styled truth ; the like must be allowed unto mercy, whilst we find the Scriptures attributing such and such works unto mercy in God as the proper cause of them. Furthermore, the distinction of one essential attribute from another is, to our understanding, fetched from that special and proper relation they have in Scripture given them unto their several objects and effects. Justice refers to a sinner as to be punished, mercy to a sinner to be forgiven, and are thereby distinguished as to us, who cannot conceive of their simple oneness

as it is in God's divine being.* There is that really in God which answers
to each and every one as so distinguished.

Now, that merciful effects are ascribed to the mercy of God, as the proper
cause of them, as truly and as roundly as any other effects are to any other
attributes whatever, is evident out of this text, to which, as for the groundwork of my proofs, I have limited myself; as also from other scriptures
which confirm the same.

I. Out of this text.

1. It appears from God's own method. First, ' Jehovah, merciful,' &c.,
absolutely simply such is proclaimed; and then, ' a God that pardons
iniquity.' The first is placed before as the principle or cause, the latter as
the effect thereof.

2. It is evident by Moses his gloss upon the interpretation of it, Num.
xiv., where he first allegeth, as the foundation of his request, the two chief
of these first five absolute abstract attributes, power and mercy, as the
summary of the other: ' Let the power of my Lord be great, according as
thou hast said, saying, The Lord is long-suffering and of great mercy.'
Thus as they are in God himself; and then he mentions those that speak
the effects thereof, ' forgiving iniquity and transgression.' Which having
premised, his petition is framed accordingly, verse 19, which he indites
thus, ' Pardon, I beseech thee, the iniquity of this people, according to the
greatness of thy mercy, and as thou hast forgiven this people from Egypt
even until now.' Now, compare we the one and the other together, and
look as the words he cites of God's speech have two parts or clauses—1,
the Lord, long-suffering and of great mercy, which are the abstract attributes;
2, pardoning iniquity, &c., that speak the effects—accordingly his application of them in his petition hath two parts or clauses manifestly answering
to and expounding those other two: 1, that phrase, ' according to his great
mercy,' answereth and expoundeth these words, ' the Lord, long-suffering,
great in mercy,' &c., as strongly pleading that according to that mercy he
had thereby declared to be in himself and gracious nature as a principle of
pardoning, he would please to pardon them; 2, his adding, ' As thou hast
forgiven them all along from Egypt until now,' denoting matter of fact
done and put forth by mercy, doth as pertinently expound that clause in
God's own words cited by him, ' forgiving iniquity and transgression,'
which in like manner also denoteth matter of fact as the effect of mercy.
And put both together, and they fall into this true and genuine sense and
meaning; as if he had said, According to that infinite mercy abounding in
thy divine nature, who art Jehovah, God, merciful and long-suffering, &c.,
out of which, and according to which, thou hast *de facto* pardoned them
hitherto, pardon them again now; which that it is the scope of God's
words in my text, is the thing I am a-proving. So then in these words,
' the Lord, long-suffering, and of great mercy,' there is the cause first
specified, or principle in God moving him, and which therefore Moses in
the first place premiseth as his foundation to move God withal. Then in
the other words, ' pardoning iniquity,' there is the effect promised, with
this declaration of his nature, which flows from that inward blessed disposition or principle of mercifulness, which he sues unto, and implores
that God would accordingly put forth in an actual pardoning of them.

* We must not say, Formalitèr, quod Deus quatenus misericors punit, nec quatenus puniens est misericors : non dicitur per misericordiam punire, aut per justitiam
vindicatricem misereri, sicut non dicitur, per intellectum vult, et per voluntatem
intelligit.—*Sanseverinus*, Part 1, Quæst. 21, Sect. 1.

The first speaks mercy to be an attribute of his nature, for he clearly parallels it with his power, as an essential attribute: 'Let the power of my Lord be great, according as thou hast spoken, the Lord God of great mercy.' The second, of pardoning iniquity, speaks that effect flowing from that nature as an act of his will yet put forth, according to his nature, which those words of Moses, 'according to the greatness of thy mercy,' do sufficiently import. And it was Moses that first brought up this so happy expression in praying, 'according to thy mercy,' upon this occasion, and as extracted from those words, 'the Lord, long-suffering, merciful,' which was afterwards often used by David and the prophets as a ground of their seeking of pardon and mercy, and that unto this very purpose and meaning in which I have now expounded it. For this of Moses was the original of it, and is the highest and utmost motive that can be used to God, to put forth all the mercies of his nature to succour us in all our distresses, and that according thereunto he would deal with us; which is enough and enough (as we say) for us to ask, or to support our faith in asking. And all these are at once seconded by Nehemiah, chap. ix. 31, 'Nevertheless for thy great mercies' sake thou didst not utterly consume them, nor forsake them; for thou art a gracious and merciful God.' 1. There is the root or δύναμις of mercifulness in God himself, the efficient cause: 'for thou art a gracious and merciful God;' 2, there is the effects of that mercy: 'thou therefore forsookest them not;' and 3, there is the same mercy in his nature, and set out as the final cause moving him thereunto: 'for thy great mercy's sake.'

By David's application of the words of my text, I shewed in the foregoing chapter how David, rehearsing first these four attributes appertaining to mercy word for word, hath likewise by name cited Moses, as out of whose writings he had them. And his method there is accordingly the same with this we have shewn was that of Moses. First, abstractly to recite those attributes as the principles in him and the cause: Ps. ciii. 8, 'The Lord is merciful and gracious, slow to anger, and plenteous in mercy.' And then to bring in many of the outward effects of that mercy: ver. 9, 10, 'He will not always chide; neither will he keep his anger for ever. He hath not dealt with us after our sins, nor rewarded us according to our iniquities.' And amongst others he introduceth that of pardoning iniquity, &c.: ver. 12, 'As far as the east is from the west, so far hath he removed our transgressions from us.'

Elsewhere and in other scriptures we find the same; and indeed other scriptures that speak about the mercies of God, speak but according to God's intent in these words, they being derivatives all from this. Now, when in Psalm lxxviii. 38 it is said, 'He, being full of compassion, forgave their iniquities,' he plainly assigns the mercifulness in God to have been the cause* of his forgiving them, and therefore mercy is most properly ascribed to God, and is in God. And this speech of his there is but explicatory of these words here in the text. In like manner, in Psalm lxxxvi., after he had so earnestly sought for mercy at God's hands (as 'preserve my soul, save thy servant,' ver. 2; 'be merciful to me,' ver. 3), he foundeth all his petitions on this, 'For thou art good, and ready to forgive; plenteous in mercy unto all them that call upon thee.' He supplicates his good and merciful nature to move himself to put forth these acts of mercy towards him. Likewise Nehemiah, chap. ix. 31, giving an account of God's gracious dealings with that people notwithstanding their

---

* Causa attribuitur ejus misericordiæ, quæ naturalitèr in ipso est.—*Cal. in verba.*

sins, 'Nevertheless,' saith he, 'thou didst not forsake them, for thou art a gracious and merciful God.' That particle *for*, in this and those other places, doth undeniably testify that God being himself truly and properly merciful, from thence and according thereunto it is that he acteth graciously and compassionately towards us, as moved by and from a true principle and disposition in himself. Oh how perfectly contrary are these professed dictates of the Holy Ghost unto what some would elevate and dilute this attribute unto, viz., that he is only said to be gracious and merciful, &c., for or because he doth merciful things; whereas the Scripture style all along you see is, he doth merciful works *for* he is gracious and merciful.

Yea, further, to confirm this, it is so remote that God should be styled merciful in relation to his works of mercy, that his works of mercy have their denomination or name of mercies * (as frequently they have in the Scriptures, and in common use of speech) given them from that proper special relation they owe and bear unto the mercy that is in God, from whence they do proceed. And so they are not styled mercies because they respect us or our needs, the objects of them, but in respect to the merciful God, who is the original subject in whom mercy is, and he the Father and fountain of them. And as the effect ordinarily bears the name of its proper cause, as the child of the father, so those mercies bear their name of and from his mercy, who is more eminently styled the Father of them than of any other his works wrought by other attributes. And that which confirms this notion is, that in the case of other attributes, their proper works or effects have their denomination from that attribute which is their cause, wherefore so in this. Thus Psalm cxix. 137, 138, ' Righteous art thou, O Lord, and upright are thy judgments. Thy testimonies that thou hast commanded are righteous and very faithful.' There they are termed righteous and faithful judgments, as proceeding from his being a righteous and faithful God, and as from whose righteousness they proceed. In like manner also the works of his grace in us are termed grace, grace freely given, being the free impressions and fruits of the grace that is in himself. And indeed, in that elogium of him that he is the ' Father of mercies,' 2 Cor. i. 3, look as the word *of mercies*, οἰκτιρμῶν, doth import mercies bestowed,† so Father of those mercies is spoken of God to a like purpose; as when the sun is said to be the father of lights (for unto the sun is that allusion of God in the apostle, James i. 17), the meaning is, that the sun hath first all light originally seated in itself, and so communicates all those lights and glory with which the moon, stars, and air are enlightened. Looking-glasses are arrayed and do borrow from that sun, and yet themselves are called lights. But how? Only by participation from it, the original light. And in the same respect is God the Father of mercies, as he is also entitled the ' Father of glory' in Eph. i. 17. Which in like manner notes, 1st, that he is a glorious God in himself—' the God of glory,' Acts vii.2—having an essential glory abiding in him, as light doth in the sun. And then, 2dly, that he disperseth glory to his saints and angels, as the Father of all their glory. And in and for the same reason he is magnified to be the ' fountain of life,' Ps. xxxvi. 9: 1, because he is the living God, and hath life in himself, as a fountain

* As in that speech (to name but one instance), ' I am less,' says Jacob, ' than the least of all thy mercies;' less in worth than this staff, or any other mercy bestowed.

† See Drusius *in locum*.

hath water first in itself; and, 2, that from thence he derives life to others in lesser streams. And answerably in the words of the apostle Paul, 2 Cor. i. 3, he is styled merciful, and the Father of mercies. These being the offspring of his mercy, do bear the name of mercy from God the Father of them.

It hath been sufficiently by all those foregoing passages of Scripture proved, that all outward effects of mercy are ascribed unto mercy, an attribute of God, as their cause and principle. I shall shut up this argument with a further proof of this inference, that therefore there is an inward principle of mercy in God himself, which is that cause.

1. First, in reason. If the mercies of God be the cause, they must have a real being and existence afore all outward effects of mercy, and a greater than the effects, for it produceth them; and in whom or in what can that mercy have an existence or being, but in God himself, whose mercy alone, and greatness of mercy too, it is said to be? It is the mercy of God to which those effects are attributed, and therefore it is in God. And certainly did those merciful effects proceed from other principles in God more eminently than mercy, he would never give the honour away from them, and cry up his mercy so much as the principal cause; he would not give the honour to it if it were but a made attribute, and not real and genuine. And if that which I before laid at the entrance be true (as it is), viz., that genuine attributes have their proper effects attributed to them, in relation to which they are distinguished one from another as to our conceptions of them, it must then hold, that if all merciful effects are set over by the Scriptures unto the mercy of God as their proper cause (as hath been shewed), then mercy itself also is and must be as genuine and essential an attribute as any of the other. I hope the same plea for other attributes in this cause will be admitted and allowed in mercy's behalf; as, for instance, when it is said, 'the Lord is good, and doth good,' Ps. cxix. 68, here *doing good*, being the effect of his *being good*, and attributed thereunto as its proper cause, doth invincibly argue his being good to be an essential attribute in him, &c. Thus, in like manner, when it is said, 'God being merciful forgave their iniquities' (which is the highest act of mercy), and divers others like to this that have been alleged, doth it not as aloud speak that God being first merciful in himself, doth out of that merciful disposition pardon and forgive sins? Again, when it is said, 'The righteous Lord loveth righteousness,' Ps. xi. 17, hereby is imported that God first is himself righteous, which righteousness in this place is that integrity, rectitude, and uprightness of his nature, whereby he is wholly addicted, and disposed, and inclined unto holiness and righteousness, and then thence a suitable affection flows, he loveth righteousness. Then surely on this other hand, when it is said God is merciful, and delighteth in mercy, that affection of delight ought to be interpreted to arise from an innate propitiousness unto merciful acts, as proceeding from a merciful inclination and disposition of heart, unto which to shew mercy is so naturally agreeable, as he delights in it; and therefore it is said, that above all he is known by it; that is, known how merciful in himself he is, even as when it is said he is known to be a just God by the judgments that he executes, Ps. ix. 16.

And indeed, those and such like speeches up and down the Scriptures— 'Shew us thy mercy, O Lord,' Ps. lxxxv. 7; thy mercy, that is, which is in thee, in thy heart and nature, lying of itself hid and latent there, unless and until thou puttest it forth in mercies towards us; and in Ps. xvii. 7, 'Shew thy wonderful loving-kindness,' or, as others read it, *Mirifica misericordiam tuam,* 'make wonderful thy mercy ; thy mercy,' which is so wonderful in itself, and as it is in thee, therefore shew it and give demonstration of it by wonderful effects ; to which corresponds that of Ps. cxi. 3, 5, ' His work is honourable and glorious ; and his righteousness endureth for ever.   He hath made his wonderful works to be remembered : the Lord is gracious and full of compassion ; ' as also that in Eph. ii. 7, to ' shew outwardly the exceeding riches of his grace' (namely, within himself),—and many the like phrases, I say, do evidence the point in hand. For so in the case of other attributes it is acknowledged, that to prove them to be essential such expressions do serve ; as when of God's truth and uprightness it is said, Ps. xcii. 15, ' To shew the Lord is upright, and there is no unrighteousness in him.'   So of his power, ' to make his power known,' Rom. ix. 22.   ' To shew himself strong,' 2 Chron. xvi. 9.   And this for the third argument, fetched from the relation of mercy in God as the cause, and mercies as the effect.

Arg. 4.   That which gives a farther addition of strength unto the foregoing argument, and will withal grow up to a new one, is, that God hath placed and ranked this of merciful amongst other attributes, which must be acknowledged to be of his essence, and to express what his nature is. And *merciful* being seated on this royal throne together with them, without any character or difference from them, yea, with the first of them, and with an height of greater eminency in some respects, how shall we otherwise understand it than that it is an attribute of the same kind, of equal rank and dignity, and of as high an alliance to the divine nature as they are of ?

Here are in the text two attributes especially, or indeed four, which God hath seated on this high bench, and hath set MERCIFUL in equal royal state with them, next himself, Jehovah, God.   *First,* the two ; the one sitting on the right hand, the other on the left, of *merciful* placed in the midst, as on the throne between them.   1. *Strength,* or power to assist and strengthen the hands of it ; **אל**, *El,* indifferently signifies either *strong* or *God* (as is well known) ; I take both, as Junius throughout the whole Old Testament doth, everywhere translating it the ' strong God.'   2. There is on the left GRACE, to quicken mercy in all its actings ; so read the words thus, ' God, the strong, merciful, gracious.'   3. Unto which two are added *goodness* or *kindness.** And 4. *Truth.*   I might reckon in *long-suffering* as a fifth ; but it is so apparently a sprig of mercy, or rather indeed but mercy itself stretched out at length, or continued (as waiting is but faith continued), that therefore I shut up that into mercy, and mention it not here as distinct.

But I do take in the other two, ' abundant in goodness and truth,' as distinct, and as importing inherent principles in God of goodness and truth, in which his nature doth abound ; and although in our English the word abundant would seem to carry the sound or report more toward actual kindness, and to God's performance of truth, yet the original word itself, and as it is by others translated, signifies as well much, ample, large, plenteous in goodness and truth, and is by our own translators, in Ps. ciii. 9, rendered ' plenteous in mercy' ; and these words much, plenteous, &c., do in their connotation strike deeper, and reach unto the bottom, and express the mind and treasury in God's heart and nature, as it is stored with a plenteousness in all goodness and truth, and how out of that infinite riches it is that in the outward dispensation he so abounds in goodness and truth.   And that it is thus intended is undeniable ; for, as the Lord is first

* Note, that some translate that word goodness, others kindness.

good in himself, and out of that goodness doth good, as in Ps. cxix. 68, and like as he is essential truth first, who ' cannot lie,' Titus i. 2 ; *i.e.*, his nature is truth ;* and then from out of that nature it is that having spoken once the word, he performeth truth, so for the same reason the ground why he is so much and so abundant in goodness and truth, dispensatorily or in actual execution, must be, that he is much in goodness and truth first in himself essentially. That such exceeding abundance in the one is from the superabundancy of the other ; and the reason is, because the degrees of much kindness and goodness in outward effects do as much depend and hold on the plenteousness of each of them in his nature, as simply his doing good in the least degree doth upon his being good, or no good at all would be done. The abounding therefore of goodness and truth in his nature must fundamentally be here understood as the spring, the overflowing of which causeth those high floods of each in his actings and dispensations. And goodness and kindness in any one who is such do most genuinely express nature in him, and what is natural to him, since by way of eminency we give such dispositions the style of ' good nature.' And so, seeing goodness and kindness are thus attributed to God, they speak nature in him also, or if you will, the goodness of his nature (as with reverence I may speak), the most of any attributes.

Upon these fore-mentioned accounts I may justly reckon upon four compeers which mercy here hath, and is every way equal with them, and with each of which I might vie on mercy's side, and plead it to be as natural as any of them. I reason from them now as they are placed altogether as fixed stars, all of them in this glorious constellation, declaring the glory of God, Ps. xix., and of the like brightness and equal magnitude ; they are all merciful, and all alike formed up and cast in one and the same mould, that is, one and the same uniform kind of speech, and under that attributed alike to God, viz., such a form as was in the foregone argument, said to be, denoting inward, innate, inherent dispositions, which the four here for certain do, under such a form, denote, and are all four in themselves such. And it is very hard to think and judge, that one alone of *merciful*, uttered in the same tenor, should be otherwise, that that alone should be adventitious. God is said to be good, and true, and the strong God, from that innate strength, goodness, and truth that is in himself, and not only from his doing good, &c. And why ought we not as well conceive him to be merciful (as it is here placed amongst these other) from an inherent inward merciful disposition in himself, and not in relation only to the merciful effects he doth, and every day brings forth ? And God himself, who best knows himself, and how to speak of himself, having put no character of difference, who shall dare to make a difference ? so vast a difference, as to affirm that merciful is but a made, artificial attribute, raised up merely from his outward works of mercy, as his style of being the Creator is from the works of his creation, without which he had not had the actual glory of that title ; whenas those other that sit round about it here have the honour (*de jure*, and of right) to be acknowledged absolutely, and *de se*, to be and to have been in him, whether he had ever acted according to them, yea or not.

And further, there may be added unto this that which I inserted, that *merciful* holds this its rank and place amongst them with so great an eminency. Search this and other scriptures ; first, here in this it is placed

* Verus in naturâ, verax in sermone ; so, in respect of strength, he is ἰσχυρὸς οὐσιωδῶς, καὶ ἐνεργετικῶς.

with the first, and by Moses made the great dominator, together with power, which two he alone supplicates whilst he allegeth these words, Num. xiv. 17–19, they two being as eminently set up in the words ; and, second, elsewhere the Scripture gives and bes.ows a richer and larger coat of arms upon mercy, than on any other attribute that is not akin to this. One word usually serves to express any other attribute; but what a multiplication and heaping up of words frequently is there to emblazon the glory of this ! In the text here, there is ' merciful, gracious, long-suffering, plenteous in goodness,' which are in a manner all but various characters of mercy, and are much the same with mercy. However (as we say), they are of nearest kindred to it, and are therefore singled out and severed from all the rest of the words that follow in the text, by the psalmist, Ps. ciii. 9.

Lastly, The Scripture loads mercy in God with titles of honour, and supperadded epithets of greatness, riches, glory, plenteousness, fulness, abundance, multitude, variety, manifold, eternity, everlastingness, unchangeableness, and what not. The like super-attributions might be observed given to the outward effects of it, above what to the effects of other attributes. It would be therefore yet more strange, and beyond a possibility of imagination, that this so magnified an attribute, extolled (as we say) to the heavens, yea, above the heavens, yea, great above, and so far above the heavens, Ps. cviii. 4, should in the end be but a similitudinary metaphorical attribute, *ex similitudine effectûs*, and after the manner of men only, and so to have in comparison but the shadow of an attribute, but in reality and truth infinitely below all other.

But there is in other scriptures that which brings in yet new and farther confirmation to this fourth argument, in that we find mercy not only naturally growing up in one bunch or cluster thus with these four (as in this one place), but that traversing the large garden of the Scriptures, we may besides frequently meet with each of those and mercy apart, and yet sometimes joined and sprouting forth as two flowers growing upon one sprig ; that is, you may up and down espy mercy and power, and they two alone joined together in one stalk, then grace and mercy singly and alone on another. The like may be observed of mercy and goodness, as also of mercy and truth in other scriptures, and thus mercy and they are Σύμφυτοι; so that if we acknowledge any of these four, especially if we own all of them to be natural attributes in the Godhead, we cannot but own mercy to be so too ; for we find both altogether with mercy (as here), and each (elsewhere) to grow alike as a natural branch together with another, which to be sure is natural, that it must be too hard to think that in so multiplied a variation, mercy should still be but as an ingrafture by art, and should not naturally grow out of one and the same stock of the divine nature.

In this argument it holds that both *juncta et singula juvant;* we have argued in general from the conjunction of all together, and now we shall argue particularly from the singular and apart constellation of each with mercy. And as the conjunction of all, so the singular constellation of each with mercy so often will evidence it to be a fixed star indeed in this firmament.

1. Mercy and power (the two first in the text) are singly paired by Moses, when he hath occasion to allege these, God's own words, Num. xiv., ' Let the power of my Lord be great,' ver. 17; and pardon joined with it also, ' The Lord great in mercy, pardon according to the greatness of thy mercy.' He pairs these two and that for greatness alike equally; then are they pairs in kind and eminency, which is the particular we are arguing. Yea,

and of the two he greatens mercy, for mercy hath the epithet *great* twice given it; the ' Lord of great mercy,' ver. 18; and again, ' According to the greatness of thy mercy,' ver. 19; and greatness in the latter is in the abstract given, but to power this title is given but once.   The prophet David also sets these two alone together as most eminent in God: Ps. lxii. 11, 12, ' Power belongs to God: also unto thee, O God, belongeth mercy.' Look how power is God's (as some read it), or belongs to him, and is with him; so and in like respects mercy is God's, and is with him.   There is no difference at all put, and that is enough, for power is God's in that transcendent manner that it essentially belongs to him.   And whereas power to be such in him might discourage, he therefore, for his own comfort, and of God's people, adds, 'To thee *also* mercy belongeth,' so to poise and balance it; which, if mercy were not every way equal to it, it would no ways poise his power, and so not have relieved souls that tremble at the power of ' the great and mighty dreadful God,' as Nehem. ix, where merciful is also joined.   And this is not the first time they have been thus paired as by David; for David himself adds, ' For God hath spoken once, and twice have I heard this.'   It is David's preface to those former words. And what will you say if this citation of his refers us and brings us back again to those very words, first, of God to Moses in my text, and then of Moses to God in this Num. xiv., as that which from both he had heard of twice ?   Sure I am I find no reference to any other, or any sense given by interpreters more probable or so proper.   Now, that power is an essential attribute of the divine Being, there was none that ever yet denied it, it being so expressly entitled his ' eternal power and Godhead,' Rom. i. 20, and therefore no less must its compeer mercy be.

A second pair is mercy and grace, here placed next to merciful, gracious. You find these two alone singled out, and paired, as the two great letters of his name are, though many more are in it.   First, when God promised to Moses to proclaim this his name, he specifies but these two only: Ex. xxxiii. 19, ' I will proclaim the name of the Lord before thee; and will be gracious to whom I will be gracious, and will shew mercy on whom I will shew mercy.'   And how often elsewhere do you meet with these two in like single couples?   I need not abound in instances, they are so many: Ps. cxlv. 8, ' The Lord is gracious, and great in mercy;' moreover, Ps. cxvi. 5, before cited.   Likewise Neh. ix. 31, ' Nevertheless for thy great mercy's sake, thou didst not utterly consume them, nor forsake them; for thou art a gracious and merciful God.'

Now, besides that as to the things themselves, grace and mercy are substantially one (for grace, considered in its distinction from mercy, what is it but love or favour simply considered, with a connotation of freeness in God, as not being obliged by any worth in the creature why he should be gracious?)   The very definition of grace given by God himself is a love that is free, and that loveth freely.   Thus, Hos. xiv., ' Receive us graciously,' prays the church, ver. 2 (and it was God that put those words into her mouth, as in the same verse), and God answers, ' I will love them freely,' ver. 4, so explaining it.   And that love in God is the root and ground of mercy, and mercy but love ampliated, or stretched out and enlarged to those he loves when they be in misery, I shall have a fairer occasion to demonstrate; and therefore, that if love and grace be an essential principle in God, then mercy must needs be also.   Besides this way of proof (which I now waive), I insist only upon this at present, as that which is proper to what is now afore me, viz., that grace and mercy are compeers and equals in every respect; and that, therefore, if *gracious* be an essential attribute, then *merciful*. Now, that grace is such, I urge this one argument, that God accounts his being gracious as the height and top of his glory, yea, and his being merciful to be so too. Give me leave to put a weight upon this. When, in general, it is said of God (as often) that he is a glorious God, that which this carries to every understanding is, that an infinity of surpassing glory is in himself, and proper to him as God, and essential to him, which glory it is required of us to glorify. In like manner, when, in particular, it is said of any attribute that it is his glory, and which we are also called upon to glorify him for, in the manifestation of it to us, there is necessarily, withal, imported therein an essential glory, which is the root whence that manifestation proceedeth, and which is therefore to be glorified by us, the proper glory of that particular attribute being the end of that manifestation. As when either in special it is said of grace, as Eph. i. 6, ' To the praise of the glory of his grace,' it is no less nor no other than when in general it is said, ' that we should be to the praise of his glory.' Surely as in the latter speech, ver. 12, ' To the praise of his glory,' by his glory to be praised is meant all the attributes, as power, wisdom, &c., the result and crown of all which is his glory, that are the causes of, and are manifested in our salvation, all which, both the attributes and this glory of them, must be acknowledged to be essential, and that answerably there is an essential glory of them in himself, which was and had been in him although he had never made any outward manifestation at all thereof. So in the former speech, ver. 6, his particular instance, the glory of his grace, must necessarily be understood, that his grace is glorious with the same kind of essential glory proper to it as the other, and to import this it is styled the glory of his grace. Some would have it, that by the glory of his grace to be praised should immediately and directly be meant the glorious manifestations of his grace, yet still there must be imported therewith and thereby an essential glory that is the glory manifested ; and it must needs be so, for all manifestation is but of what is and hath being as the object of that manifestation, so as still we must resolve all into an essential glory that is at the bottom, and is the foundation ; yea, and that intrinsecal glory of any attribute is that which is the ultimate object of our praise when we are called upon to glorify it, the farthest mark, the *terminus* which we transmit our glorying of God in that respect unto, as that which we aim to praise and glorify, as indeed it is expressed, ' to the praise of the glory of his grace.' The aspirements and holy aims and reachings of godly souls in their giving glory to God, rest not in praising or in giving glory to the manifestation of his glory, although that be never so glorious, but by means and upon occasion thereof are carried out to and terminate in his essential glory itself, as that which is in their aims to give glory to. And indeed thereby only it is fulfilled, that ' he that glorieth, glorieth in the Lord,' as the apostle and prophet calls us to do, whilst both speak of mercy manifested, 1 Cor. i. 31, Jer. ix. 24. And indeed either none of those attributes of wisdom, power, &c., shewn in our salvation, that wear and have the title of his glory stamped upon them, are essential to him, or this of grace also must be so, which is styled his glory, κατ' ἐξοχήν, by way of eminency and singularity. The truth of these things that one place, Rom. ix. 23, declares, ' that he might make known the riches of his glory on the vessels of mercy.' Here is at first a manifestation of glory, in those words *make known*, and withal *a riches* of his glory which is manifest, whereby it is evident that glory must needs be understood to be different from that manifestation, be it never so glorious; for it is the thing that is manifested, and what can that be other than those riches of glory which he possesseth in himself, and makes known by communications and manifestations thereof on his saints, as it follows there; like as in that speech in the verse afore, verse 22, which in coherence is parallel to and yokes with this, ' God willing to make his power known;' that is, his power being an intrinsecal, essential attribute in himself, he manifests it, and makes it known; the like holds of his glory spoken of here. And the close of this is, that those riches of glory there do prove to be the glory of his grace and mercy in a special manner intended, and so bear the name of glory by way of eminency. This Æstius and others have observed; and my ground why specially mercy is intended is, because the saints, who are the vessels, or receptacles, or subjects unto whom these riches, &c., are to be communicated and manifested in them, are in respect unto this styled ' vessels of mercy.' The riches of the glory of mercy, then, are those which are the principal contributors, although the glory of all other attributes do likewise empty their streams into the same vessels, to fill them with glory. So then mercy stands every way equal with grace (an essential attribute), and that in glory, yea, in riches of glory, and therefore is of as high an alliance to God as that is. They are every way rated alike in God's books, the Scriptures; and God, who is an equal prizer and valuer, doth not set a deeper estimation or value than the real worth doth bear. As then I shewed afore, mercy and power were paired as equal for greatness, so mercy and grace we find to be equals. These two are for estate and riches equal, and are as peers for glory and honour too, and they are both alike God's riches and glory, by the valuation of which God shews what a rich and glorious God he is in himself. I conclude this, as I did the former, who then shall dare to say to rich mercy, to mercy which God accounts his glory (when withal he shall see it placed by God himself immediately, and bidden to sit there by him on the same throne with equal royalty with other so high-born essential attributes of mine), who then shall bid and say, Thou rich, and great, and glorious mercy, come off the seat thou sittest on, as too high for thee, and sit thou at the footstool of all these other ?

For those other two attributes, goodness and truth, so much having been said of the former two, it is not necessary to enlarge on these; yet, to complete this confirmation, I shall add some things as to both.

A third pair is mercy and goodness. ' Merciful, and much or plenteous in goodness,' says the text; where, whether goodness imports (as in the general notion of it) a communicativeness of good things—' The Lord is good, and doth good,' Ps. cxix. 68, it being the innate property of goodness to be communicative—or whether more specially kindness, bounty, benignity be intended, as many translate the word here and elsewhere; however it be taken, it is singly paired with mercy.

1. As to goodness, how many psalms do begin with, and some also do begin and end with, ' The Lord is good, his mercy endures for ever.' I instance only in Ps. cxviii., whereof both the first and last verses have those words. It was the usual form of praising the Lord, to sing: ' The Lord is good, his mercy endures for ever,' Jer. xxxiii. 11, and had been prescribed unto the Levites, 1 Chron. xvi. 41. And though he is good to all his creatures, Ps. cxlv., yet here it is that goodness that extends itself to his Israel, as Ps. lxxiii. 1, which draws forth the goodness in his nature in the communications of it to its full length; and that is specially intended

in this text, for it is that goodness which brings forth pardon of sins, saving mercies which the text speaks of, which two the psalmist puts together : Ps. lxxxvi. 5, 'For thou, Lord, art good, and ready to forgive ; and plenteous in mercy to all that call upon thee.'

2. And as his goodness and mercy are paired, so kindness ($\chi\rho\eta\sigma\tau\acute{o}\tau\eta\varsigma$) and mercy : Titus iii. 4, 'After that the kindness and love of God our Saviour toward man appeared.' And mercy is not far off them : for ver. 5, ' According to his mercy hath he saved us,' for indeed they are all but one. And again, Luke vi. 35, 36, 'He is kind unto the unthankful, and to the evil. Be ye therefore merciful, as your Father also is merciful.' And to shut up this, you have both kindness and goodness joined and paired with mercy in Ps. xxv. 6, 7, ' Remember, O Lord, thy tender mercies, and thy loving-kindnesses ; for they have been ever of old. Remember not the sins of my youth, nor my transgressions : according to thy mercy remember thou me for thy goodness' sake, O Lord.' These two import not barely his affording outward favours, which we call kindness, nor barely a doing kindness, as we use to say, or God's being good to us in benefits communicated ; but they connotate withal a root that is in God's nature, from whence these outward kindnesses proceed. The Lord is first good in himself, and thence and therefore doth good ; and in like manner he is of a kind heart and nature in himself first, and thence and therefore is kind to others, even to the evil and unthankful, as Luke vi. 35, and the abundancy of his goodness and kindness in effects is from the amplitude and largeness of the goodness and kindness in his own heart and nature, as I shewed in the beginning of this second confirmation, and as is evident from the 8th verse of that 25th Psalm now cited, it immediately following, ' the Lord is good and upright ;' which as an essential principle in God, and the root of that mercy and kindness which he sued for, he resolveth ultimately his faith into, as Muis hath observed. And among men we use, by way of eminency, to express goodness in a person by good nature ; and one that is kind in his outward deportment, we term him one of a kind heart and nature. And indeed kindness denotes an inward kind disposition more principally, and in the first place ; even as when the Scripture denominates a man ' a liberal man,' it doth it principally from that noble, free, and large disposition of liberality in his spirit, whence liberal actions proceed, as Isa. xxxii. 8, ' A liberal man' (such in himself) ' deviseth liberal things :' thus it is in kindness also. And in God, to whom these are thus attributed, it holds much more ; goodness is so essential to him, as he alone is to be called good, as also that ' he alone is holy,' Rev. xv. 4, which evidently imports he as God hath such and such an holiness and goodness in him as is proper to him alone, and transcendeth that goodness that is in creatures, and theirs is no goodness in comparison. And as he was essential holiness, and should have been so for ever, although he never had produced a work (who yet is holy in all his works he doth produce), so he was and had been essentially good, although he never had communicated a good thing to any creature. And if it be the nature of goodness to communicate itself, then it is the common voice of all mankind, as the common voice of the Scriptures too, that goodness is the nature of God. Now mercy is not only paired therewith, but it is indeed essentially all one with it. Mercy is but *bonitas summè extensa*, as the school speaks, it is but goodness extendible, an aptness or readiness in his goodness to extend itself to sinners, as well as to communicate good things to others that had not, nor have not sinned, which by creation God did. Mercy is but a promptitude to communicate so much

further, viz., to sinners. Mercy is but goodness with a *nevertheless*, that is, though they are sinners, as Neh. ix. 31. And, indeed, as in the schoolmen's right apprehensions, they are but one and the same in God, so in the sense of the Scriptures also. Thus his mercy to sinners is expressly styled his goodness: Rom. xi. 22, 'towards thee goodness,' &c., which along after in the chapter doth bear the name of mercy, ver. 30–32, and chap. xii. 1. And again, his mercy to sinners is in like manner termed kindness, as expressly, Luke vi. 35, ' He is kind to the evil and unthankful.' Ver. 36, ' Be ye therefore merciful, as your Father also is merciful.' To conclude this, mercy, goodness, kindness, are so near akin, and of one stock, that if one be essential to God, then must the other be also.

The last pair are truth and mercy : these two are alone thus yoked, one under the names either of truth or of faithfulness, the other of mercy or loving-kindness. And thus you meet with them so frequently in so many psalms as I scarce need particularise any, but might refer it either to the reader's remembrance, or adventure upon his advertency thereof, at his but turning over a few leaves, soon to find enough. I will instance but in one or two : Is God to be praised ? The height of praises is for his ' mercy and truth :' Ps. cviii. 3–5, ' I will praise thee, O Lord, among the people : and I will sing praises unto thee among the nations. For thy mercy is great above the heavens : and thy truth reacheth unto the clouds. Be thou exalted, O God, above the heavens : and thy glory above all the earth.' And you have these words over and over in two several psalms, Ps. lvii. 9–11. In Ps. cviii. his mercy is magnified not only to the heavens, but as great ' above the heavens ;' that is, to an infinity, as that which the heaven of heavens do not, cannot contain, as they do not God himself. And so it is an extolling of mercy by this, that it is an infinite, as God himself, in whom it is. And that which is translated ' the clouds,' which his truth is said to be exalted unto, are indeed the heavens, as two learned critics* have with vehemency contended for. And the 138th Psalm hath not only joined them together for praise† (ver. 2, ' I will praise thy name for thy loving-kindness and thy truth'), but adds, ' for thou hast magnified thy word' (namely, as it sets forth those two attributes) ' above all thy name.' The greatest part of his word is taken up either with promises which loving-kindness or mercy made, or of the performance of them which truth effecteth ; so then these two are to be magnified above all his other properties whatever ; which two to celebrate all nations are specially called upon to praise him for, Ps. cxvii. 1, 2, which is interpreted to mean both Jews and Gentiles when converted ; as the summary of the gospel, Rom. xv. 8, 9, imports, and as Christ's ministry in the 40th Psalm (a psalm made up for Christ, if any other, see ver. 6–8) was foretold : ver. 10, ' I have not concealed thy loving-kindness, and thy truth, from the great congregation.' Or is God to be prayed unto for any kind of saving mercies, and the continuance of them ? it follows, ver. 11 of that psalm, ' Withhold not thou thy tender mercies from me, O Lord : let thy loving-kindness and thy truth continually preserve me.' I need mention no more ; paired we see they are equally : and of the two, if either be greater, it is his mercy,

---

* See Piscator on Ps. lvii. ver. 11, and on Ps. xxxvi. 6, and Dr Hammond on Ps. lvii. 10.

† See Dr Hammond, Annot. on the 2d verse of the 138th Psalm. His word being here annexed to loving-kindness and truth, must needs be that part of his word to which these two are applicable: 1. His promise; the matter whereof is loving-kindness. 2. In the performance of which is truth and fidelity.

as to whomever, that will attentively consult those scriptures, it will appear.

Now that his truth is an essential attribute, none can deny that will read that scripture, 2 Tim. ii. 13, 'He is faithful, and cannot deny himself.' It is himself; he is true in such a transcendent manner as no creatures can ever come to be partakers of. Which difference between him and them, in respect of truth, I take to be the adequate meaning of that Rom. iii. 4, 'Let God be true, and every man a liar.' It is a vehement asseveration on God's behalf, as if he should say, Although all men should be liars, yet God is truth, that is, there is a possibility for the most faithful plain-hearted man that ever was yet, to become a liar (Adam and the angels that fell were created true and holy, but 'abode not in the truth'); but of God it is pronounced, that he is true in such unchangeable a manner, that it is 'impossible for him to lie,' Heb. vi. 18, for his truth is his Godhead, and himself, and so is mercy.

Arg. 5. It is a common professed maxim among divines, that whatever is in God, is God himself. *Quicquid est in Deo Deus est.* This in the utmost latitude of it I argue not now, for all internal acts are not God's.* But when we speak of such as are attributes abstractly given him, whereby to describe him; that these should express his being God, yea, his very Godhead, this is generally, and must be adhered unto by us. And how this is to be understood and cautioned, I hope to shew afterward.

That this should hold true of mercy, long-suffering, &c., in a more eminent way of evidence, that which I shall now further observe out of this text, may, I hope, for the present serve to evince, which, if gained, doth afford a fifth strong argument, and meet to be brought the last for the shutting up of all.

I have so much considered and dilated within myself what should be the mystery of so vehement a triple or thrice recital of the substantial names of God, by themselves alone first, as 'Jehovah, Jehovah, God,' before these four or five attributed abstract names, 'merciful, gracious,' &c., which then do as entirely by themselves follow, I cannot but apprehend that some more than ordinary mystery must be in it, the like not being ordinary that I know of.

I know that it is put over to the importing the mystery of the three persons, Father, Son, and Holy Ghost, to shew they are all merciful, long-suffering, &c., and equally or alike such. And that is a great mystery indeed, and greatly for our faith and comfort. But then withal reflecting that these merciful three do possess and subsist in that one Godhead and simple divine essence, and that the attributes they have in common are the attributes of the Godhead, or of God himself as God, and so are theirs, because each of them is God, I came to this farther inquiry, Why should not this triple rehearsal of the names of God be intended to declare that God, as God, is merciful, long-suffering, &c., or that merciful, &c., are himself in the same, and in as true a sense as any other attribute is said to be in Scripture. In the substantial names 'Jehovah,' &c., he proclaims *who*, in the attributed names or properties he declares *what* that Jehovah is, as in which his Godhead and his being Jehovah consisteth, namely, in 'merciful, gracious,' &c., so as *Jehovah, Jehovah*, is these attributes, and reciprocally these attributes are *Jehovah, Jehovah*. In those his substantial names he speaks himself as at once by the great; in these attributed names or properties he unfolds himself, and explicates himself by parcels,

* Qu. 'God?'—ED.

for the letting in of himself into our understandings, the bore of which is not large enough to take in the whole at once. Thus elsewhere we also find such conjoined to the being of God, though not with this triple mention of his name : ' O Lord, the great and terrible God, that keepeth covenant and mercy,' &c., Neh. i. 5. And Solomon before him thus speaks, ' Lord God, there is no God like thee, who keepest covenant and mercy,' 1 Kings viii. 23. And so for pardoning : ' Who is a God like unto thee, that pardoneth iniquity ?' &c., Micah vii. 18. And though these, being acts, are not God or God himself, yet you see they are attributed as proper and peculiar to him as he is God, and do argue him to be God alone, and are such as, if he were not God, could not be acted by him; concerning which this rule is to be held, that therefore they necessarily proceed from the Godhead itself; and farther, must be ascribed unto those properties of the Godhead of the first sort, which in the Scriptures are held forth as the proper causes of such acts or effects, and so *reductivè* (as we say), must be resolved unto those attributes in God, their causes, which are the very Godhead. And in this sense here Jehovah keeping mercy, and pardoning iniquity, as acts proper to Jehovah, are to be ascribed to Jehovah (as here), Jehovah merciful and gracious (that goes before), as divine properties in him, that are causes thereof, and as those that do immediately express his Godhead, and are himself, as this triplication of the name of God prefixed imports. And thus considered and stated, both sorts do indeed come all to one. So, then, we may call them essential attributes, that imports his being God, and without which he were not God.

Nor need it here to stumble any, that ' pardoning sin,' &c., ' keeping mercy for thousands,' are also here attributed to him ; but of them it must not be said that they are God ; if he shall withal consider that there is this vast difference between those first abstract attributes immediately coming next to ' Jehovah, Jehovah,' and those other that follow, they being apparently acts in God, and from God, as his wonts and practices, whereof those five of the first rank are the causes, as was at large shewn in the argument. And yet even those acts speak him to be God too in this respect, that they do necessarily suppose and involve his being God as God, as proper to him above,* as he is God, or they would never proceed from him.

I begin with the first, that ' merciful,' &c., are one with Jehovah. And now I must call in the help of other parallel scriptures, both to confirm the thing itself, viz., that as other true and real attributes are one with Jehovah himself, or are himself, so mercy is, and that upon the same grounds ; as also, by way of parallel, to justify that construction and collection I have made of this thrice repetition, and which I make the rise of this argument out of the text.

1. One attribute which is undeniably evident to be essential to and with Jehovah is truth and faithfulness, which is his Godhead and himself : Tit. i. 2, ' God that cannot lie ;' that is, because he is God, or that truth is his Godhead, and his Godhead is truth. He were not God else ; and he must cease, if otherwise, to be God : whereof the one can no more be than the other. Yea, and *in terminis* it is styled himself : 2 Tim. ii. 13, ' If we believe not, yet he abideth faithful : He cannot deny himself.' Why ? For faithfulness is himself.

Now let us bring a parallel scripture speaking this very thing of God's being faithful as God, and expressing this in the like, yea, well-nigh the

* Qu. ' alone' ?—Ed.

same equipage of language with this in Exodus xxxiv., proclaiming Jehovah God, merciful God. And the language being the same, and that being the intent of it there, it must be the same here. That scripture is Deut. vii. 9, ' Know that the Lord thy God he is God, the faithful God, which keepeth covenant and mercy with them that love him.' Here is first a vehement indigitation of his being God, ' the Lord thy God he is God,' to the end that they might know that he was the faithful God, as God. He that is God, the Lord thy God, is faithful; that is, faithfulness is essential with his Godhead, that therefore they might surely build upon it as upon his Godhead itself. For why? Faithfulness was he himself, and it is to the intent they might know him. Now, do we not hear God proclaiming himself in a like strain, Jehovah, Jehovah, God merciful, &c., and this to the same intent, that they might know him, and know what a God he is, in and by these; yea, and truth or faithfulness being one of those very attributes that follow, ' much in truth,' as you have heard? This place, then, in Deut. vii. 9, must refer unto that uttered before it in Exod. xxxiv., and therefore may well serve to illustrate it, which this also confirms, that ' keeping mercy for thousands' here in Exodus very well accords with ' he keepeth mercy,' &c., in Deuteronomy. Now, then, after you have read over once more a second time that passage in Deuteronomy, ' Know that the Lord,' &c., and then that preface joined to ' the faithful God,' to shew that he is faithful as he is God, with those other said places pre-confirmed, then bring this of Exodus to it, ' Jehovah, Jehovah, God merciful,' and the same construction and purpose will arise up out of it, that this God, as God, is a merciful, gracious God, in the same sense and intendment that ' the faithful God' comes in in Deuteronomy, and after comes in here, ' much in truth;' and thus uttered to the same full intent and purpose, that we might know what a God God is.

And if the parallel of these two be not sufficient to evince the same, then take another passage in Psalm lxxxvi. 15, ' But thou, O Lord, art a God full of compassion, and gracious; long-suffering, and plenteous in mercy and truth.' He says not simply, Thou, Lord, art full of compassion, but manageth it with this reduplication, ' Thou, Lord, *art a God* full of compassion;' and so speaks no less than that, as he is God, so he is merciful, &c., and that his Godhead is the substantial root and subject of his mercy. And that which adds farther confirmation is, that ' plenteous in truth' comes in, and is coupled with mercy. They are pairs, then, and pairs alike in this, that they are his being, and God himself both. This for the first, which at once gives strength to our argument and illustration to this place.

2. Holiness is argued to be God himself. And why? Because whereas in one place it is said ' he swore by himself, having no greater to swear by,' Heb. vi. 13 (God will swear by no less than himself never), in another place it is, ' He swore by his holiness,' Ps. lxxxix. 35. And these two oaths were, as to the matter of them, of a kind, being set as seals to the covenant of grace and mercy both. The first was given to Abraham, ' to perform the mercy promised,' Luke i. 72, 73; the second to David, and in his name and type, unto Christ, to ascertain ' the sure mercies' given him. And the like instance of the same forms of swearing is given in the case of verifying God's threatenings: Amos iv. 2, ' The Lord sware by his holiness. And in chap. vi. 8, ' The Lord hath sworn by himself.' So, then, his holiness is the Lord himself. And we may add this reason, because he can swear by nothing less than himself, as the apostle affirms; and there-

fore swearing by his holiness, his holiness must be himself. The evidence on mercy's side, that it is himself, is equivalent; for whereas in some places it is said, 'Remember not the sins of my youth, according to thy mercies, and for thy goodness' sake,' Ps. xxv. 7; and Neh. ix. 31, 'Nevertheless, for thy great mercy's sake, thou didst not consume them,' &c.; when God speaking the same in·Isaiah xliii. 25, 'I, even I, am he' (that is, that Jehovah merciful) 'that blotteth out thy transgressions for mine own sake, and will not remember thy sins.' What in the one is 'for his goodness' sake,' and 'for thy great mercy's sake,' is 'for his own sake' in the other. So, then, goodness (as all must confess), yea, and mercy, are himself. You have it again in Daniel's prayer, chapter ix., and there both these conjoined are brought in together as explicatory the one of the other. In ver. 18, 19, 'We do not present our supplications before thee for our righteousness, but *for thy great mercies*. O Lord, hear, O Lord, forgive, *for thine own sake*, O my God!' What in the very words before is 'for thy great mercies,' which is plainly 'for thy mercy's sake,' is in the next petition 'for thine own sake;' and you have these two picked out as scattered, one in one place, the other in another, and so brought together, and argued from.

I come now to a third proof. It is certain when we hear such and such effects as involve his being God, and which could not be done unless he were God, and do argue him God alone, that then those effects must proceed from the Godhead itself. And farther, unto what in the Godhead can we ascribe them, but such properties in the Godhead as in the Scriptures are held forth as proper to produce such or such effects? And whilst we say such or such a property in God did effect such or such a thing, we may warrantably also say that his Godhead did it. The creation of the world is a mighty product of the Godhead, and argues him God alone : as Isaiah xliv. 24, 'I am the Lord that maketh all things.' And we must say that the Godhead did effect it, for 'he made them by himself.' Yet further, we find the making of them attributed peculiarly unto power and wisdom, as proper causes of such effects; and withal, that power of his to be styled his Godhead, Rom. i. 20. So his wisdom also we find to be styled infinite, Ps. cxlvii. 5, which is equivalent as to say it is his Godhead, for that alone is infinite and without bounds. Now, in correspondency unto these, we find the effects of pardoning sin, &c., to involve his being God, as that which could never be done if he were not God : Micah vii. 18, 'Who is a God like unto thee, that pardoneth iniquity, &c.? because he delighteth in mercy.' That speech, 'Who is a God like unto thee?' is still used to snew he is God alone, and that, as the great God, he doth such and such works,* which, if he were not God, he could not do: Ps. lxxxvi. 8, 'Among the gods there is none like unto thee, O Lord ; neither are there any works like unto thy works;' and ver. 10, 'For thou art great, and dost wondrous things, thou art God alone.' Now, pardon of sin is a work of such wonder and greatness, as none ever more. And you see in that prophet how they stand aghast and wondering at him, as a God so great, as God alone, none like him, in that he can pardon sin. And if he were not so infinite a God, he could not do it; for sin and sins are infinite. It is his Godhead pardons sins, as well as his Godhead made the world. It is a truth, though ill intended by those that spake it: Mark ii. 7, 'Who can forgive sins but God?' And had not Christ been God as well as man, he could not have done it then. Now, as other works of God have some special attribute in God as

* Ps. xxxv. 10, as in Micah in pardoning, so there in delivering.

their more proper cause, and unto which those works are ascribed for the honour of that attribute; and from thence we rightly argue that they are his Godhead (as all those 'invisible things of God' the apostle terms his 'Godhead,' Rom. i. 20), so as the Godhead pardons sins; so read the Scriptures, and you find pardon attributed specially to mercy in God as its proper cause. I need cite no places. And this is done for the glory of his mercy and grace. And certainly he would not instruct us to give this honour due to his Godhead, and in which he, as God, is so highly concerned, if mercy were not his Godhead, as well as any other attribute is. He will not give his glory to what is not himself. We may as warrantably then say his mercy and Godhead, as the apostle doth his power and Godhead. And this as intending to make both one and the same; yea, and add his eternal mercy too, for that epithet is given to it, Ps. xxv.

And when it is pleaded to God that he would pardon sins for his mercies' sake, Neh. ix. 31, the plain meaning and resolution is this, for thy great mercies' sake, which are thyself, or which are in thyself. And there is this farther reason to back this, and as strong as that before mentioned was for the former, that for his mercy's sake, or for the glorifying of thy mercy. This denotes God's utmost and most proper end for which he pardons and shews mercy, and withal, the highest motive by which he is moved to forgive, &c. And it is urged by these in their petitions as the most prevailing plea they could move God withal. Now that can be no less than himself, whose highest and supremest end is himself; and he is moved to acts of grace and pardon by nothing but what he is moved with in and from himself. And therefore, in that 43d of Isaiah, he holds up himself to their view, and himself alone: 'I, even I, am he that blots out thy transgression for mine own sake;' and we are sure it is mercy for which and by which he only is moved thereto within himself, and is himself. And truly doth not his thrice repeating there *I, I, he,* answer to his thrice repeating *Jehovah, Jehovah, God merciful?* &c., Exod. xxxiv. 6.

Arg. 6. The four first attributes we meet with at the entrance in this divine proclamation, Exod. xxxiv. 6, do, in what is common to them all, prompt us with a sixth argument, that mercy and grace are essential properties of the divine nature.

1. The four attributes are, 'merciful, gracious, long-suffering, abundant in goodness and truth.' But I reckon not that of *truth* in this enumeration, as likewise the psalmist doth not in his rehearsal of the words of this proclamation, Ps. ciii. 9, which is word for word the same as to these first four. They are in the original in both places, though our translators have varied their translations of them there from what is here, yet without any material difference; for what there they have rendered 'plenteous in mercy' (which they have varied too in the margin, 'great in mercy,' according to the Hebrew), here they render 'abundant in goodness.' But the psalmist omitteth the mention of 'and in truth.' And the reason of that omission may be the same that mine is in stopping there, namely, because he takes those attributes that purely concern mercy, and are branches of it; whereas truth or faithfulness comes in here, not as being any way a branch of mercy, but as mercy's supervisor, or mercy's remembrancer, to see to it, that mercy does perform what God out of grace hath promised and declared; according to that *memorandum* of old Zacharias, deduced out of the three names of himself, his son John, and Elizabeth: Luke i. 72, 'To perform the *mercy* promised, and to remember his holy *covenant*, the *oath*,' &c.

2. That which I call common to all these four, from which I would

deduce my argument, are two things. First, that the form of speech they are attributed to God in is nouns, not participles, which denotes them to be inherent dispositions, or properties in God, which set him forth *ab intra*, or by what are in him, the inwards of himself. The second is, that for the special kind of them, they are of those which divines style the virtues of the divine nature.

3. The argument from these, or either of them, riseth thus: 1st, That inherent dispositions in God are to be accounted his nature. 2dly, And specially virtuous dispositions are so to be esteemed; and such mercy and grace are, and therefore are truly his nature.

There are two things then to be performed by me in handling this argument, which consists of two branches. (1.) To establish the proof of this one proposition, that these four names are attributed in such a form of speech as denotes them to be inherent dispositions, intrinsecal properties, that are truly in him. (2.) That for the special kind of them, they are among the virtues, or virtuous dispositions of the divine nature of God. This proposition hath, as you see, two branches.

2dly. The second thing to be proved is the consequence inferred from them, viz., 1. That if they be inherent properties that then they are in and of the divine nature. 2. That if they be properly to be reckoned among the virtues of God, and so to be esteemed, that then much more they are in and of his divine nature. But all these being in their order joined and put together will make the argument complete.

My method shall be to handle the two branches of the proposition and the proof of them first, and then the two consequences and the proofs of them, whereof the first is a step to the proof of the latter, and both centre in one and the same reason of either.

1. As for the first branch of the proposition or hypothesis, it is the animadversion of that learned critic and literal expositor Genebrard, commenting upon the 8th or 9th verse of Ps. ciii., which I even now cited, to shew that these four first attributes that set forth mercy are word for word in the original, the same with these four here. He beginning to expound this first word *merciful*, speaks on this wise of it, and the like of the rest. It is a noun, says he, not a participle, as also those that follow; because thereby is declared not the *acts* of God, but, as it were, an *immoveable quality*, or that which is perpetual in God. And then of the other three that follow, for the same reason he pronounceth the same of them: for these are properties, says he, that are innate in God; nor are they assumed by him contingently, according as circumstances are and give occasion. Thus he. Wherein his argument lies not simply in this, that for the form or manner of speech they are nouns, which are not qualities, as great, immense, but taken conjunctly therewith, that the matter of the things attributed are qualities. And whereas Genebrard says that *merciful* denotes, as it were, an immoveable quality in God, his *quasi* is but to allay and qualify our apprehensions, that we should conceive of them with an infinite disproportion, as they are in God, and in us men. In us they are mere qualities, differing from the essence of us, as accidents are from the subject they are in, but in the divine nature there are no accidents; and yet he is fain to make use of an assimilation to these of qualities, to convey their inherency, as of qualities, to our apprehensions, as the nearest notion to do it by; and that however they are immoveable principles in the divine nature, as inherent qualities use to be. This he absolutely affirms to be signified thereby; and so that mercy is and was permanently in his nature,

whether he had ever purposed or shewn any act of mercy, yea or no, and not contingently attributed for that he acteth mercifully. And this diffè-rence he observed to be between such attributes that are expressed of God by way of nouns and quality-wise, which these are; and such as denote acts, by participles.

And this being thus explained, the foundation of the argument proceeds from the common use of speech, that when qualities are simply and absolutely attributed unto a person in the form of nouns, as that he is liberal, holy, devout, courageous, bold, and the like, that then, in the wonted acception of speech, men commonly understand, and readily con-ceive and apprehend, that he is a person of a liberal spirit, an holy and devotional soul, and so addicted inwardly, so or so disposed, inclined, and affected within himself; of such a temper, frame, and constitution of spirit, or a man of such inherent principles of heart inwardly moving him, sway-ing him to liberal and holy actions, and that these are his *indoles, ingenium,* his spirit, as the Scripture word is. And in like manner, God's intention, who makes use of our wonted language to make himself known unto us by, as in other his attributes is apparent, here analogously should be to describe himself in such attributions of speech as we use when we would set forth a person, who and what he is, and paint him forth by such qualities and dispositions as we know are in him. Thus God here, thereby signifying what properties are truly and really in himself, as far as possibly they are by words expressible to us. And as we when we have set out a man of such qualities, good or evil, we use to say, That is the man; so we may say, This is our God. And indeed, God himself here doth say *in terminis,* fully as much as this of himself thrice over, ' *Jehovah, Jehovah, El,* God, God, God, merciful, gracious,' &c., as if he had said, This is your God. And as for those other attributions given to God, purely after the manner of man, which the opposers would choke this truth with, they are expressed by words that denote acts only, and those but occasionally expressed: as that ' it grieved him,' ' it repented him,' and the like, as it is obvious to observe in these scriptures where they are used. But these are solemn names and denominations, whereby God purposely makes a description of himself what a God he is; and accordingly they do fully answer to this question, whenever it be demanded, *Qualis deus sit, ac quis?* who and what a God is he? as plainly, and directly, and absolutely, and in the like strain of speech, as any other of their fellow-attributes do; as when it is said, he is wise, and good, and almighty, these words are justly judged and acknow-ledged to signify what a God he is in his essence; and in like manner, these here to be a description of his nature, and that even such a God he is, set out by such characters as are given him *ab intra,* as our divines speak; that is, such as do declare what a God he is inwardly, that shew his very inwards to us. And those characters do express in reality that to be in his divine being which answers to all these (as I have opened it in the explication I premitted), it being a commonly received maxim among divines of all sorts: *Deus dicitur quis, ac qualis est, ab eo quod natura est.*

And for the close of this point we may affirm, that this his title of mer-ciful, gracious, doth as roundly give and return an absolute answer to any such inquiry, What a God is he? as any other attribute whatsoever: Ps. cxvi. 5, ' Gracious is the Lord, and righteous; yea, our God is merciful.' This is the saints' vogue and saying of him, as here he speaks these of himself; and it is formed up so as it may serve to be an answer (as the apostle's word is), an account in readiness to be given to any stranger to religion who knows not God. If an heathen, suppose such as were in those times, or are now, should be inquisitive, and demand, What a God is your God? say this to him, Our God is merciful; yea, our God is merciful, with an emphasis. And it is as if they had said, If any would know what our God is, let him know him by this, that if he have any internal perfection (who is all perfections, good, holy, wise, gracious), he is as perfectly merciful as any of these. And (say I) if any such an one be not satisfied with the saints' plain verdict, given in upon their own knowledge, let them then hear and attend to what God himself says of himself, and take from his own mouth what he is: 'Jehovah, Jehovah, God merciful and gracious.' He multiplies his substantial name thrice, as well as his attribute of mercy four times. And why, but because if God, as God, be to be known by anything, it is by these. The psalmist seems to vie with all other attributes whatsoever, yea, as it were outvies all other, with this of his being merciful, whilst he so vehemently speaks it, 'yea, our God is merciful.' He sets the crown upon the head thereof.

There was an additional branch in the supposition, that these attributes are the characters of virtues in the divine nature, or virtuous dispositions in God, which superadds unto the former, and is a farther step towards the proof of the consequences therefrom, which are to follow, viz., that therefore they are in and of his divine nature.

All perfections are in God, in all kinds of perfections whatsoever. The attributes of God are usually reduced by schoolmen, as well as our divines, to three heads.

1. Such as are utterly incommunicable to us creatures, as unchangeableness, infinity, eternity, ubiquity, or to be everywhere, and his divine glory. These are the absolute and metaphysical excellencies (as I may call them) of his divine entity.

2. There are also all super-excelling habilities that belong to and are found in intelligent creatures; as faculties of understanding, which the psalmist says is infinite, knowing all things, &c. So of a sovereign will, which doth whatever he pleaseth in the earth, and in the heavens.

3. All sorts of virtues belonging to either of these, *perfectiones morales*, all such as are not founded upon imperfection (as humility, self-denial, &c., are), and when I call them virtues, I mean all the excellencies of goodness, such as are holiness, righteousness, and mercy, and grace there; and truth also, which is mentioned here. God ought to be every way most perfect, say the schoolmen, not only in the perfections of entity, or of natural being, but in the eminency of goodness and virtue, in that kind of being also. Hence his royal titles among the heathens were *Deus optimus maximus*, a God that is most great in power and the absoluteness of being, and a God most good. And the goodness therein meant was that virtuous goodness we speak of, whereby he is inwardly, and of himself, ready to do good to his creatures, according to that of the psalmist, 'The Lord is good, and doth good;' of which goodness, mercy and grace are the eminent branches, according to that of the psalmist, 'The Lord is good, and his mercy endureth for ever.' And therefore I rightly said that the virtuousness of mercy in Scripture language is the excellency of his goodness.

And let no man boggle at the word *virtue*, or deem it as a lowering of the Godhead to say he excels in virtues; for the Scriptures ascribe this to him *in terminis*, 1 Peter ii. 9, where the apostle exhorts 'to shew forth the virtues' (so in the original) 'of him that called you.' Observe, they are the virtues of him that calleth us, not our virtues that are in us that are called.

And by him that called us is meant not Christ only, and his virtues as man, but God the Father chiefly,* to whom our calling is there ascribed; as also in chap. i. 15, it had been by the same apostle, with the like exhortation, for there he says, 'As he that hath called you is holy, so be you holy,' &c., as children of your Father. Thus in like manner, though in other phrase but in substance the same, he entered his exhortation to all sorts of goodness, wherein we are to imitate him and be like him, shew forth the virtues of him that hath called you; that is, says Gerard, those attributes of God which in calling you he shewed forth. And particularly and to be sure the most eminent is that which the apostle specially instanceth in, and in this, and in no other else; so in the following verse, 'which have now obtained mercy.' So as in effect this exhortation is all one with 'Be ye merciful,' because your God that called you is merciful; even as in the former exhortation he had said, 'Be holy, for I am holy;' holiness in God being the foundation of all those virtues in God, as well as in us, which the comparing of those verses shews; and the apostle also there enforceth from this, that we must be like our Father.

These virtues are to us poor creatures the especial attributes we praise God for, insomuch as the Holy Ghost records it for the title and name of praises, the word ἀρετὰς there used signifying at once both *virtues* and *praises*, as it is there translated; or else let those that boggle at the word virtues say of them, that in God they are the patterns, and samples, or ideas of what are called virtues in us;† and it is enough to my purpose. And the reason why that is to be acknowledged is, that there is not, nor can be, any perfection which the creature partaketh of a likeness to God in, but it is and must be found after an infinitely more excelling manner in God, and the nature of God, than it is in the creature. Only take this in, that they are found in God after the manner of God, in us creatures after the mode or manner of creatures, with an infinite difference.

Observe how in the forming this argument I put in this limitation, there is no perfection in man, *in which he partaketh of a likeness to God*, but the perfection thereof is in God. And the reason of this my limitation is, because there are two sorts of gracious perfections in us, whereof some indeed are not in God, though in Christ they are found; as humility, lowliness of heart, submission of our wills. These are not by way of likeness to the like which correspond in God, but by way of applyings of the soul unto God, or by way of subjection of the creature to such other attributes in God as are incommunicable; as his sovereignty, greatness, absolute will, &c. And in that respect it is they are reckoned parts of the divine nature, because they give the greatest glory to the divine nature, in the way now specified. But as for such perfections as are said to bear a likeness with what is like unto what is attributed unto God, of them all we may and must say, that there is no perfection of such in the creature but it is much more in God, which is the *major* or first proposition. And this doth in a more special manner hold true in such virtues or spiritual graces, in which we are said to be like him, and wherein he is expressly made our pattern in the Scriptures. And of those it must be acknowledged, that if they be properly in the creature, then they are more properly in God; of

---

* See Gerard *in locum.*

† Non tam virtutes quam ideæ virtutum in Deo sunt.—*Kekerman, Syst. Theol.,* c. 4.

all which the holiness and purity of God's nature is the root, as being in himself first, and so becomes the first rule and measure of such virtues in us.

And that this is particularly true of this virtue of mercy (the thing in hand), those speeches of Christ, who came out of the bosom of the Father, and hath declared him both in his nature and in his will, do uncontrollably evince: Luke vi. 27, 28, 'Love your enemies, do good to them that hate you;' and verse 35, 'Love your enemies, and ye shall be the children of the Highest: for he is kind to the evil and the unthankful.' And in the close of all, verse 36, 'Be ye therefore merciful, as your Father also is merciful:' *as*, that is, after the image of God, as Col. iii. 10, 'Put on the new man, after the image of him that created him;' whereof mercy and love are in the 12th verse following mentioned to be an eminent piece: 'Put on therefore, as the elect of God, holy and beloved, bowels of mercies, kindness, humbleness of mind, meekness, long-suffering.' And then add those other speeches of our Lord in Mat. v., which correspond with those recited out of Luke vi.: Mat. v. 48, 'Be you perfect, even as your Father which is in heaven is perfect.' He speaks of the perfection of virtues, and specially of that of mercy; for unto works of mercy unto enemies, &c., he had particularly exhorted: ver. 44, 'But I say unto you, Love your enemies, bless them that curse you, do good to them that hate you, and pray for them which despitefully use you, and persecute you.' And this he exhorts to by the instance of God's mercy to the worst sinners: ver. 45, 'That ye may be the children of your Father which is in heaven: for he maketh his sun to rise on the evil and on the good, and sendeth rain on the just and on the unjust.' And thereupon exhorts us to be perfect in that grace, upon this very ground, because it is a perfection in God first, and originally in him, and that we have thereby the likeness of the perfection of our Father. This for the proof of the two branches of the proposition.

2. I come to the proof of the consequence in the second place proposed, from both, viz., that if these attributes do denote inherent dispositions, properties, or permanent qualities, and not acts only, especially such qualities as are virtues in God, that then they are of the divine nature itself. I put both into one, because the reason of either centres much in one, although the reason of the latter greatly adds force to the other.

And that reason will at once serve both for a proof of the consequence and also for a caution in this case, that whilst we are forced to use the term of qualities to express them by, to relieve our apprehensions of them (whereas indeed they are not such qualities as are in the creature, and yet denoting inherency and permanency of like properties in God, and not of acts only), they can be no other but his divine nature.

And the reason is founded on this, that in God there are no accidents (and such those in us creatures are) inherent or permanent in him; and therefore these attributes denoting properties, like to qualities in us that are inherent and permanent, they therefore can be no other than the divine nature itself; which is confirmed by the infinite difference that is and must be acknowledged to be between the creatures and God blessed for ever in this respect, that the inherent qualities in us men or angels, be they never so excellent, yet they differ from the substance or being of the persons in whom they are, as accidents do from their subject; and they are said to be added to perfect and adorn the subjects in which they reside. And although the most eminent of creature qualifications do vastly differ from the substances or essences they are in, yet there are some of them that so immediately flow from their substances, and are so proper and specifically peculiar to them, that if we should suppose they could be separate from that subject or person, the very nature and proper being of that subject would withal cease to be what it was. It is an assured maxim, *Proprietatum negatio est naturarum deletio;* as to deny the faculty of reason itself to be in one of mankind is to degrade a man as a man, and blot him quite out of the catalogue or roll of men, and to set him down a brute; of which it is said, Ps. xxxii., ' They want understanding.' So that commonly we allow the term of *natural* unto such properties, and call them essential, or belonging to the essence, although not the essence itself; but yet they rise to no higher dignities than of faculties and qualifying abilities, which are at best but accidents, though of another kind than ordinary accidents are of, and therefore called natural, because they are inbred, inlaid, and blended with the inward constitution and temper of the substance itself. But, on the contrary, when we speak of God, and say, that mercy is a property, and of his nature; our intentions, and God's also in so speaking, reach infinitely higher, and intend thereby that it is his very divine nature, as far as it is by words expressed to us; even as eternity and power are said to be his Godhead, Rom. i. 20. And the reason thereof is, because God, and the essential nature of God, is perfected by nothing but himself, and so not by anything differing from his own being; for then his Godhead, as he is God, should be imperfect, and needed something besides himself to add perfection and hability unto it, which the Scripture utterly denies of him: Acts xvii., ' that he needeth not anything.' And therefore all such attributes, and this of *merciful,* being in tenor of speech given to him, after the manner of the attribution of inherent qualities, for our conception's sake, are to be understood to be his divine nature, in a transcendent manner, inconceivable by us.

Moreover, take in this for a second caution also, that when we call both these, or any like qualities in men or angels, as also these attributes in God, *natural* or *nature* in either, the word nature or natural must be taken and understood with an infinitely vast differing respect in the one and in the other; for these qualifications, thus said to be natural to us angels and men, are but at the best the shadow of what is substantially natural in God; and accordingly, that mercifulness which is in man is but the imperfect shim* of that essential mercy which is in the divine being. And hence it is so far remote from God's being called merciful, righteous, after the manner of man (as those other attributes, the opposite instances, which are styled but *ad similitudinem effectus*), that to the contrary, these inherent qualities in man (take them in their perfection) are said to be ' after God,' Eph. iii. 24. And therefore they are *propriissimè,* most properly in God first; yea, and in truth only in God (as goodness is said to be), and but similitudinarily, and by way of semblance, in man. And this by way of caution also.

But, 2dly, I urge this reason further, upon and from the account of that additional, viz., that mercy and grace are to be reckoned among the highest virtues that are in God. Now, true and perfect virtues are inherent in that person that deserves the style of virtuous, and if they be true, they are permanent, and constantly abiding in him; yea, and the perfection of them lies in the inward disposition and addictment of the mind as the root of the actings, or performing virtuous things, though they, as being the fruits

* That is, ' shimmer '?—ED.

thereof, have the name of mercy, and their due valuation; but still that inward principle of those actings much more and above all, so far as they have been inbred, and by nature found in any person, that is the height of their perfection. And therefore in God, if they be true and perfect virtues indeed, as they must be supposed to be, they must be all these, both inward dispositions, strong inclinations, propensions unto merciful acts, and seated in his nature, and to be his nature. And to be sure, God is not perfected (as man), or grows up in virtue by acquisition, or by the increase of habits that use to be acquired by use, practice, and exercise; this were to lower him infinitely yet more, so to affirm. And therefore, if virtues be at all in him, and these virtues (as we have proved them to be), then they must be acknowledged his divine nature, and his perfections by nature.

I shall cast in a *coronis* to all, and which will without contradiction confirm all that I have hitherto said in this third argument: it is those words which our Lord hath made the conclusion of his exhortation unto us to be merciful, in that 5th of Matthew, last verse, 'Be ye therefore perfect, even as your Father which is in heaven is perfect.'

1. You see here is a perfection attributed to God, which man is exhorted to imitate, 'Be ye perfect, as your Father in heaven is perfect.' God's perfection is the original pattern, and man's imitation that is to be the copy to that pattern; and God's perfection is to be understood after the manner wherein God is or ought to be understood to be perfect, as a God; or as the evangelist Luke upon that occasion entitles him 'the Highest,' and men, as men in their kind, as 'children of the Highest;' so in ver. 35. And he therefore speaks it of such a perfection in God as is of the highest kind of perfection proper and essential unto God. And to be sure, there are some attributes of his that are the essential perfections of his divine nature, and then this spoken of by Christ's own arguing is among them that are of the highest rank.

And, 2, it proves to be this so rich and precious attribute of mercy which Christ intended here, as appears both by the interpretation, that by comparing Christ's discourse about this of our being merciful in those two evangelists is apparently given of it. For whereas the one says, Mat. v. 48, 'Be ye perfect, as your Father in heaven is perfect,' the other says, Luke vi. 36, 'Be ye merciful, as your heavenly Father is merciful.' And each come in as the last close and conclusion of Christ's exhortation unto mercy in either place. So then mercy is one of the highest perfections that perfect him that is 'the Highest,' or the most perfect in all perfections.

3. This perfection of mercy must necessarily be understood to be intrinsecal to him, and so his nature. For nothing extrinsecal or outward to God can add any perfection to him. His own works, be they of mercy and never so excelling, add nothing to him; he was as perfect a God before he made the worlds as since. And what is it can be his perfection but what is and was then in himself and of himself? who of himself is the fulness of all being; and if anything added the least perfection to him, he must be said to be of himself and in himself imperfect. And mercy being so plainly, expressly, in particular thus styled his perfection, it must be a property in himself and of himself, and without which he would not be so perfect as he is said to be; yea, we may upon this ground further say, that without it he were not God. Let the opposites bring all their deductions and wonted pleas to make void this so great a truth, and you will see them all melt before this speech, as wax when it comes unto the fire, and be confuted in every part thereof.

1st, They distinguish and say, God is merciful *quoad effectus*, in and for his doing works of mercy, and not because he is of a merciful nature and inward disposition of mercy.

(1.) Consider that man is here exhorted to be merciful, as God is ; and though he in his exhortation mainly instanceth in works of mercy which man should perform, yet I demand, doth not the exhortation chiefly intend that men should be moved by an inward principle of mercy (compared therefore to bowels, which are called the inwards), that should move the heart to works of mercy ? Col. iii. 12, 'Put on therefore, as the elect of God, holy and beloved, bowels of mercies, kindness, humbleness of mind, meekness, long-suffering.' And when Christ pronounceth that blessing upon their souls, Mat. v., 'Blessed are the merciful,' &c., doth not the word ἐλεήμονες import inward mercy and pity more than outward ? as Spanheim hath observed upon it. And if God were not in like manner filled with merciful dispositions moving thereto in his shewing mercy, why is his mercy set before them as the excellent pattern, when yet, according to them, it reacheth not to this, to be a pattern of inward mercy ?

(2.) If God were not thus merciful *ab intra*, his inwards moving him thereto, do not they that affirm this make man more merciful than they would have God to be, seeing man is merciful with an inward affection of bowels, besides his works of mercy; but God should be merciful only *quoad effectus*, only because he doth acts of mercy without the affection or inward principle of mercy ?

And, 2dly, whereas they say, Mercy is spoken of God after the manner of man, or in like sense only as that God is said to grieve, repent, &c. But, 1, here in Christ's exhortation, on the contrary, man is called upon to be merciful after the manner of God, 'Be ye merciful, as your Father is merciful.' And, 2, if it were otherwise, according to that opinion they have of God, man should only be exhorted here to exercise and put forth outward acts and effects of mercy, for God, say they, doth only so. Again, 3, that mercy which is there exhorted to is that which is the perfection of mercy ; and certainly to be merciful inwardly, and of a merciful nature, is that which is the life, the height, the perfection of mercy.

I finally close up all with this summary argument, that grace and virtue, that in man is a perfection and a piece of the divine nature in him, and likeness to what is in God (he being created after the image of God in truth, as the apostle's words are), and which same is likewise attributed to God as a perfection of him, and a pattern to us of the same ; that must be acknowledged to be in God as his divine nature and being. But such this grace or virtue of mercy is ; it is in man a piece of his divine nature, created after the image of God in truth ; and it is ascribed unto God as a perfection of his Godhead, and made the pattern of our perfection ; therefore, as it is attributed to God, it must be his divine nature.

CHAPTER XII.

Some of the principal objections why mercy should not be a natural attribute of the Divine nature, answered out of the proofs and parallels in the foregone chapter.

The proofs in the foregone chapters, especially the paralleling of power with mercy, and then of those other attributes, grace, &c., as they confirm the thing, so they will most amply serve to answer the greatest objections that are alleged against it.

Obj. 1. The first objection lies thus, that is not natural* wherein God is arbitrary and free in working any effects thereof, or in the using of it, and puttings of it forth. But such is mercy, as even in these very passages unto Moses which are alleged; ' I will be merciful to whom I will be merciful,' which is adjoined to this proclamation. Compare Exod. xxxiii. 19, ' I will proclaim the name of the Lord before thee, and will be gracious to whom I will be gracious, and will shew mercy on whom I will shew mercy.' In brief, that they say is not natural, the working and operation of which depends upon God's free will.

Ans. The answer is ready, and clear, and home, as it may be taken from the instance of God's power; for, according to this rule and measure, power itself in God should not be a natural attribute; for ' all things ' which he worketh by his power, ' he worketh after the counsel of his own will,' Eph. i. 11 (and therefore it is he doth not all he can do, Mat. iii. 9 ; chap. xxvi. 53), which is the same with the exercise of his mercy, of which it is in like manner said they are ' according to the good pleasure of his will ' again and again, Eph. i. 5. His will keeps the operations both of mercy and power, as it were, under lock and key, and lets them out as God himself pleaseth. Yea, and further, you have both of these at once put together; and, as you have heard mercy and power in themselves paralleled, they are so in their operations too, as being like instances of this very thing, as appears in the apostle's allegation, and putting into one those two speeches of God: Rom. ix. 17, 18, ' For this same purpose have I raised thee up, that I might shew my *power* in thee, and that my name might be declared throughout the e. rth : Therefore hath he *mercy* on whom he will have mercy, and whom he will he hardeneth.' So, then, both are said to depend, and to be guided in their actings by his will alike. Again, look, that although the acting and effect of power is but voluntary, yet still that effect proceeds from that *vis*, force, strength, or power, that is natural to God, and which in God is infinite ; which power sets itself to the effecting everything, only his will still orders that putting forth of it where, and when, and the measure of it. And therefore it is all one to say, ' Who hath resisted his will?' as the apostle, as to say, ' Who hath hardened himself against his power?' as in Job ix. 4, for his natural power immediately is that in him which exerts itself in every such act of his will, and without that nothing would be done or hath been done. And in parallel unto this, the manifestation of mercy in all the works of our salvation depends upon his good pleasure, and yet in and unto the effecting or endowing us with any and every benefit or saving work thereof, the whole of the riches of his grace that is intrinsecal to him doth immediately put forth themselves; and without a mercy so infinite and natural to God, none of them would be bestowed or effected. Moreover, look, as if you should deny power to be in God essentially, because it is put forth by his will and pleasure, and affirm it to be but a metaphorical attribute, you should thereby make him no God at all; for a weak God is no God. So, if you take mercy from him, denying it, in the reality and principle of it, to be in him, you despoil and rob him of his greatest riches, and make but a poor God of him to all that shall call upon him, and so, in effect, no God at all, either to be feared or worshipped.

The mistake of the argument proceeds on this, that because acts or

* Deus non utitur naturalibus, say they.

shewing of mercy do hold of his will, therefore his very being merciful, the principle of those acts, must do so too. We grant his *acting* graciously to be arbitrary in him, and from his will, but not his *being* merciful and gracious; that depends not on his will, though with his will; that depends not upon an act of his will, though it be with will.

But the true resolve of all is, that indeed his will (take it for the power of willing, or that whereby he willeth) is the very immediate subject of mercy, which mercy, as it is in his will, is but a propenseness, a strong and ready inclination in his will, that moves and sways him to those merciful actings, which is not from an act, but an inherent disposition in his will, and natural to it, that it should be readily so disposed.

Obj. 2. A second objection is, that mercy imports and ariseth from the weakness and deficiency in man's nature,* as from an apprehension that men themselves, being subject to the like miseries, shew mercy to the miserable, and so mercy is always joined with a passion (which we call compassion), trouble, or grief, in the heart of a man that is merciful; all which infirmities and passions man only, not God, is said to be subject to, with difference from God, Acts xiv. 15.

Ans. This is utterly an heathenish imagination, and had its original from them. Aristotle says, that † it is an uncouth, not agreeing to, or becoming the being of God, to say he loves. He thought it stood not with his greatness, nor was compatible with it. And Epicurus before him said, the divine nature was not penetrable by mercy or pity, because these find no entrance into the hearts of men, but through some defect or want. I may say of them in this point (as Christ of the Sadducees' denying the resurrection), ' They erred, not knowing the Scriptures, nor the power of God.' For whereas they would that mercy and pity should spring out of weakness and deficiency, as in man since his fall, or at least is always accompanied with it; such as grief and trouble, and the like passions; on the perfect contrary in God it ariseth from and is accompanied with his infinite power, all-sufficiency, and blessedness. And by how much he is above all and utterly incapable of any defect, the more able he is to succour and relieve us in misery, and also by so much the more his glorious will is the more disposed and propense to mercy. Kings who live in an higher region, and are not subjicible to the common gusts of innumerable miseries, which their subjects in the lower regions are, yet out of the greatness and generosity of their spirits are oftentimes mercifully disposed, and forbearing unto those that apply themselves to them under such miseries which themselves never had, and of which they have not the least apprehension that they shall fall under them. The lion's strength and courage makes him sometimes to spare a poor lamb's life that lies prostrate at his feet; which holds a semblance of what is in kings, and in God more transcendently, though both these indeed are but imperfect shims and glimmerings of what to an infinity is super-eminently in God. I betake myself, for the proof of this, to Moses his unfolding the mystery of God's joining power and mercy : ' Let the power of my Lord be great, as thou hast spoken, The Lord is long-suffering and of great mercy, forgiving iniquity and transgression : forgive, I beseech thee, this people ;' which is as to say, Let thy mercy, which is thy power, or which proceeds

---

* Misericordia est compassio super alienâ miseriâ, et in tantum miseretur in quantum dolet.—*Aquinas* 22, q. 30, Art. 2d.

† ἄτοπον γὰρ ἄυ εἴη εἴ τις φαίη φιλεῖν τον Δία.—Aristot. Mag. Moral, lib. 2, cap. 11, Tom. 3, oper. Edit. Du Val, Paris, 1639.

from and is strengthened by the almighty power that is in thee, be shewn in pardoning; or, Thou, O God, which declarest thy almighty power chiefly in shewing mercy and pity, forgive thy people.

But be it so, that want, and weakness, and passion, as in man, are furtherances unto and companions of, yea, and the very rise of mercy in man; yet that the same must hold in God, so as he cannot be inwardly in his soul merciful, unless he be merciful from the same principle that man is, must be denied. How oft is it said, that God is not merciful as man is, but is infinitely beyond all that the thoughts and apprehensions of man can reach to, either in his own mercies he thinks himself to shew, yea, or that he is not able to think what mercy is, or what it should be in God, they are of such an infinite extent beyond his possible imaginations, ' as heaven is above the earth'! Shall, then, man's mercies, or the imperfections and passions of them, be made the measure of what mercy itself is in God? God forbid. Man loveth not without a passion, and therefore shall not God, who is love (because he loves not as man doth), be said properly to love his creatures out of a pure and perfect principle of love in himself, as truly as to love himself or his Son? It is said, ' the weakness of God is stronger than man;' and shall the weakness of man be the measure to him that is the God and strength of Israel, which in 1 Sam. xv. 29 is so highly protested against? ' The strength of Israel is not as man,' &c. O that ever the weakness of the creature should have been thought to have been a rule for the strength of Israel!

Again, in what doth the true substance and reality of mercy lie and consist? Not in an apprehension of one's own self to be subject or exposed to the like distresses, or in being troubled and grieved as the consequents of that apprehension, especially if he cannot help. These are but accidental unto mercy, and but as it is in such or such a subject that is subjected unto infirmities, as in a man it is, who alone is capable of those fore-mentioned passions; for mercy, and that more truly, is in Christ glorified, yea, in the angels and ' spirits of just men made perfect;' and therefore perfect in this virtue, but without any of these passions and disturbances as requisites to move them to be merciful. In what doth the substance, yea, the height of mercy lie or consist, but in a readiness and promptness of affection in the will of God to relieve and succour those that are in misery, whom he loves, joined with fulness of power to relieve them? Which latter clause, *with fulness of power*, doth especially render him most truly and highly merciful.

I shall further proceed to shew how the parallel of those other attributes, grace, goodness, and truth, as well as with mercy, will abundantly put to silence another objection.

Obj. 3. How can that, say they, be an essential attribute in God's nature, which if man had never been miserable had not been in God? For mercy speaks a relation unto sin and misery, and if it depend on such a condition of ours, or the creatures' being first miserable, then it must be in God but contingently and occasionally, and not naturally.

Ans. The answer is from what the parallel of these four attributes afford, as likewise many other attributes which might be instanced in.

1. Power or might in God relateth unto external effects, as unto the creation of this frame of heaven and earth, &c., Rom. i. 20. Now before God ever made any of them, or suppose he never had made any, shall we say he had not essential power inherent in him, whereby he was able to make them, and in respect thereunto was truly a God almighty?

2. Again, his power relates unto all he is still able to make or effect, and not to be confined unto what he hath done.   There are an infinity of things possible to be done by him, which his power will never produce, but shall remain in a state of mere possibility; and yet his being styled almighty includes a power to be in him in respect to those, as when it is said, ' God is able to raise up out of these stones children to Abraham,' Mat. xxiv. 53, Luke xix. 40, Mark xiv. 36.   His divine ability is expressly said to extend to these, and shall we affirm he had no such radical power in respect to these, because he will never put it forth in bringing them to existence ?   Nay, it must be said, that things thus possible are only and merely called such in respect of the power of his nature, but things which he causeth actually do respect his will and good pleasure joining with the power of his nature : Ps. cxv. 3, ' But our God is in the heavens, he hath done whatsoever he pleased.'

3. In like manner the parallel of grace and goodness evinceth the same. Had not God been good (who is goodness itself, both as he is God, and in respect of a communicative disposition in himself, who is the fountain of goodness), although yet he had never made a creature to communicate any good things to.   Surely yes.   Then likewise he is gracious, though his pleasure had been never to have had one angel or man existed whom he would be gracious unto.   The root of this matter had been in him, though never no effect or fruit of it had appeared above ground.   His grace must be acknowledged to respect the creature only, for he is no way gracious to himself; and would he not thus have been, though no creature had been ? Must he of necessity have made creatures, if he would be truly gracious ? A man is to be acknowledged one of a liberal disposition, who is so in his natural temper, though he lives alone in a desolate wilderness uninhabited, where there are no poor, nor any one person to bestow his alms, or communicate his riches to.   The great element of fire is fire, and ready to burn, though it never yet had any fuel to prey upon.   The like is to be said of truth, ' God cannot lie,' Titus i. 2 : and it is impossible, Heb. vi. 8, it is contrary to his nature ; and therefore truth (the contrary thereto) is his nature ; and this had been so eternally, although he had never given forth one word or promise, of threatening, or the like, for the performance of which he might have been styled true.   Now yet it is apparent it was purely at his will and pleasure whether to have given forth any such word or not.   And thus God also was truly and really merciful, and ready to forgive, although he never had pardoned one sin, nor ever had promised pardon to any one sinner.   What need we say more ?

Obj. 4. If any further object that word *merciful* (רחם, *Racham*) here used is a metaphor taken from bowels ; but God hath no bowels, and therefore it is but a metaphorical attribute ; I answer,

Ans. 1. That some, as Polanus, render the word רחם, *Racham, diligere,* to love, to be at the root of it ; and to be sure love in God is no metaphorical attribute.

Ans. 2. According to the measure of this argument, because this almighty power or strength in God is expressed by an arm, as Ps. lxxxix. 13, Luke i. 51, or that his all-seeing knowledge is set forth by an eye, and eyes that ' run through the earth,' 2 Chron. xvi. 9 ; that ' behold the nations,' Ps. lxvi. 7 ; yea, ' behold all things in heaven and earth,' Ps. cxiii. 6 ; doth this put any prejudice that power and knowledge in him signified thereby should not be essential ?   No more doth the ascribing bowels to him exclude mercy from being such.   God speaks to us hereby in our own *puerilis*, in our own childish language, so to affect us the more, yet so as there is substantial reality in his heart answering to, yea, transcending what metaphors can express. And should he speak these heavenly things in their own language, we could not receive them, as Christ tells us, John iii. 12.

And certainly the psalmist's argument is so convincing, that as himself prefaceth of it, none of the most brutish among the heathens should be able to gainsay it, Ps. xciv. 9, namely, why God as God must have an omnisciency, or an all-knowing power, within himself, which the Scripture expresses by an ear or an eye : ' He that planted the ear, shall not he hear ? He that framed the eye, shall not he see ? He that teacheth man knowledge, shall not he understand ?' This as certainly holds undeniable in this point of mercy ; shall not he that planted the inwards of us men, and bowels of mercy and pity in them, a natural *storge** in parents to their children, and hath taught us to love, 1 Thes. iv. 9, and be good, and kind, and merciful to one another after his own example : Col. iii. 12, 13, ' Put on, as the elect of God, bowels of mercies, kindness, humbleness of mind, meekness, long-suffering ; forbearing one another, and forgiving one another,' &c. Shall not he have eminently and transcendently the perfections of all these towards them he intends to love and make his children ? ' Like as a father pitieth his children, so doth the Lord them that fear him,' Ps. ciii. 13. The foundation of the psalmist's reasoning lies in this, that it is impossible any excellency should be in the creature, of which God is and must be the author, but the same must be virtually and in an higher reality in God himself. It is true indeed, that God hath neither eyes nor bowels of flesh, as Job says of him, and to him : ' Hast thou eyes of flesh ? or seest thou as man sees ?' that is, by the means of such organs or instruments of that sense, Job x. 4. So say I, Hath he bowels of flesh ? that is, such dolorous painful pangs of grief and trouble as we frail men clothed with flesh use to have, when moved with pity ? or is he merciful only as man is ? Woe were then to us. ' I am God, and not man,' says he, Hos. xi. 9, and he speaks it upon occasion of his being moved to mercy, as ver. 8, and yet he professeth himself moved to mercy as God, though not as man ; and yet as infinitely beyond us as the Godhead ; from whence he argues his transcending mercy exceedeth what is in man, as that speech insinuates. So as whilst in ver. 8 he speaks of himself after the manner of men, as of his heart and ' bowels being turned within him,' yet there, in the 9th, he avoweth of himself, that he is moved hereunto as God, and not as man is ; in so high sublime a way as is proper to him alone as God, and yet with a mercy, represented by bowels and heart, which is as infinite as his Godhead is, yea, it is his very Godhead. For so that speech that he assumes to himself, and this which I have brought forth by way of answer to an objection, I might have improved into two strong arguments for the thing in hand, that mercy is substantially and properly in him.

Ans. 3. That bowels, though a metaphor, yet in its analogy is peculiarly fitted and adapted singularly to express what the inward natural disposition of any one is. For,

1st, It imports a natural affection, for it is put to express that which we call *storge*,† or the natural affection that is in parents.

And, 2dly, with all the most inwardness and depth of that affection.

* *i. e.,* στοργη.—Ed.

† Rahum, quasi visceratus, misericordiâ, στοργῇ, naturali amore et affectu prosequens.—*Genebrard* upon the word in Ps. ciii. 13.

The eye that served to express God's omiscience, the arm, his omnipotence, these are outward parts ; but the bowels are of all most inward, and therefore of all other speak what is most inward in God himself, and imports a principle of being mercifully moved from within himself.

CHAPTER XIII.

That in every object there is some special attractive to affect the faculties and principles in man's heart, to excite them to act on it.—That this general maxim holds true, as to all the main acts of faith, for forgiveness : and that the mercies of God have the most proper influence into the faith of forgiveness of sins, of all other attributes of God.—This assertion carried through, and made good, in all the eminent acts of faith.

We all know and acknowledge, that, in the nature of the thing, the whole being and subsistence of all sorts of mercies vouchsafed to us, hold of those mercies that are in God ; so as were it not that mercy is with him, our faith would be in vain, and we should have no such things or subject-matter at all for us to believe. But that which I endeavour to demonstrate is, that take all sorts of mercies, with the particular promises made of them, as they come to be made objects of our faith, and in that respect the original mercies in God's nature are the great fundamental which doth give and contribute an *esse credibile*, a credibility, or a believableness unto all the promises of mercies,* and a hopefulness to obtain them, so as not only an apprehension that God, who is faithful in his nature, hath made such promises, and useth to bestow such mercies, but the thought that there are such riches of mercy in his heart and nature plentifully and naturally to afford them, wonderfully addeth to the credibility and believableness (as I call it) of those promises and particular mercies, to be derived from that fountain, which we need or desire. For as all particular mercies promised have their dependence upon the mercies of God's nature, *in esse rei*, in the nature of the thing (for they have their being thence, as from the Father of them), so further, our knowledge and apprehensions that such a treasure of grace is in his nature, mightily strengtheneth, and encourageth, and enhanceth faith in us. There is that in all other objects, whether of sense or knowledge, which philosophers term *motivum objectum*, viz., that thing or consideration in the object proposed or apprehended, which is apt and fitted most properly to move, affect, and make impression upon that faculty, principle, or habit, that God hath made for it and suited to it ; as that beautiful colour should affect the sight or fancy. The like by analogy holds in the objects of divine faith. And what those naturalists term the objective motive, or that which the object moveth, that in divine objects proposed to faith, the Holy Ghost (as we shall see), using the same language, styles *persuasivum fidei*, the persuasives of faith. There are some special things in these objects that chiefly persuade the soul unto believing them, or bringing the heart over to believe, and so to embrace them accordingly. We find in Scripture the great act of believing to be from our being first ' persuaded ;' as Heb. xi. 13, ' Having seen the promises afar off' (there is the object), ' they were persuaded,' it is said, ' and embraced them.' And again, the same word is used of Abraham's faith ; ' being

* Quod constituit objecta divina in esse credibile : nam credibile, ut credibile, est ratio objectiva.—*Suarez de fide.*

persuaded,' &c., Rom. iv. 21.   The schoolmen do therefore accurately inquire, what in divine objects principally it is that constitutes them *in esse credibile*, or that gives their being of credibility to them.

To bring this down to our purpose.   From hence it follows, that what thing or things in divine objects revealed are found to be the most fit and powerful in the way of object, to make a persuasion in the heart to a believing or embracement of them when they are proposed to us, that thing or those things we must acknowledge to give unto them their *esse credibile*, or their being of believableness.   Let us therefore now consider if that the view of the sight and light of the mercies in God's nature let into the soul, and shining upon the promises of mercy, like as the light upon colours, do not superadd a lustre and life upon them, and impregnate them, as the sun doth the plants, and all things below that have either life, spirit, or virtue in them.   Let us try if the thoughts of these mercies in God will not put life into and quicken the soul of him that views them together with those promises, yea, and contribute so much to persuade to the faith of them, although the promises be but indefinite promises or declarations of God's will touching the forgiveness of sins, although these promises be indefinite, I say, as to persons, not naming who, nor excluding any ; yet let us [see] if the thoughts of God's mercies do not contribute and bring with the consideration of them the most of what is or may be supposed *motivum*, or *persuasivum fidei*, that which may persuade or draw out a faith on such promises.   The truth of this will best appear by a survey made of what are the most eminent acts of faith.   There are three more eminent acts of faith for forgiveness and all other spiritual blessings.

1. There is a sight of the things promised, or to be believed ; but then that sight must be such a sight as hath an ὑπόστασις or subsistence of the things promised, made, and given to the heart of a believer, together with the proposal of them.

2. There is a discerning of a goodness in them, to allure the will and affections to embrace them, and cleave to them.

3. There is a trusting on God, and a relying on him for the performance of them.

I need not quote scriptures that these are the acts of faith.   Two of them, viz., sight and embracing them, you have seen in the fore-mentioned Heb. xi. 13.   The other of trusting you meet with everywhere almost where faith is spoken of.   I shall carry the reasons of the present assertion through each of these three acts, and shew how it holds good in each of them.

1st. The first act of faith is a sight of the things believed, with a real subsistence given to them in the soul until the time of performance.   Now the mercies in God apprehended, do give the most real subsistence unto forgiveness, and all other benefits whatsoever.

The nature of faith requires that its object be presented to it, not with bare knowledge thereof only, but with a subsistence and reality given to it in the heart of a believer: for faith is defined to be the ὑπόστασις, ' the substance,' or subsistence, ' of things hoped for,' Heb. xi. 1, and likewise ' the evidence,' or sight, ' of things though not seen.'   For which compare Heb. xi. 1, 19, 27.   God in the mean while, during the space and time that comes between the promise and the performance itself, is pleased to vouchsafe an aforehand image and substantial impress or ὑπόστασις, to the end to support the heart.   Look, as the Son of God, the second person, being at last actually to be made flesh, it was meet and proper for him in the mean time, while he was but in the promise, that he above any other of the persons should be the person who should vouchsafe these precursory forehand apparitions unto the fathers of the Old Testament, which gave an ὑπόστασις unto their faith, until the great promise of his coming in the flesh, personally united, should be performed, so in some analogy it is in the matter before us. I have alleged this but by way of illustration only of God's gracious dispensation to his people in respect of a subsistence vouchsafed to their sense, which bears some resemblance unto this subsistence vouchsafed to faith inwardly, whereby the things as yet remaining in the promise are set before the soul; which things therefore, when believed, must be some way made real and subsistent; otherwise, indeed, it is not a true sight or spiritual faith, but vanisheth with its object proposed into an empty notion and speculation. It is therefore that thing in God, the revelation of which gives a subsistence to the object of faith, that doth put it into an *esse credibile*, a being of believableness.

I now proceed then to demonstrate that our first real believing the mercies in God do give a subsistence unto forgiveness in the promises.

The subsistence that any divine object hath, is from a real and true knowledge of God himself made subsistent, first to the soul, and then explicitly or implicitly it concurreth to every true act of faith of any other particular object. Our Saviour therefore, instructing them in particular acts of faith, Mark xi. 23, 24, first proposeth this general rule to them requisite to all true faith : ver. 22., ' Have faith in God,' or have the faith of God, because into that faith of him, or something in him (as his power or truth, &c.), is the subsistence of every particular thing promised resolved. ' He that comes to God must believe that he is,' &c., Heb. xi. 6. This is general to all true faith, but more particularly that attribute or relation in God which is the most proper and direct cause of the thing promised, *in esse rei*, in the being thereof; that very same attribute being viewed by faith, together with the promise, is of all other fitted most properly to give this subsistence to our faith. Thus when Abraham found that his body was dead, and Sarah's womb dead as to procreation, Rom. iv. 19, and that yet God had promised him a son; that attribute in God, on which this thing promised did most directly and proximately depend, that attribute accordingly was with the promise presented to Abraham's faith, and ' he was persuaded that what he had promised, he was able to perform, and so became strong in faith, giving glory to God,' Rom. iv. 20, 21. Where we see that persuasion the apostle speaks of, the most proper *ratio credendi*, or ultimate ground of believing, and persuasive of his faith in that very particular thing, was that special attribute that in God was the most proper cause of the thing promised ; and the same was it which gave the subsistence to the thing and to his faith.

Now therefore, to come home to the thing in hand. It is hence to be observed by this general rule or maxim, that whensoever the heart of a sinner shall attempt to believe the forgiveness of sin, there is nothing can be supposed to be in God, or concerning God, revealed, that should give a greater reality, and subsistence, and certainty of the promises in and to the heart of a believer, than the consideration of those mercies in God, which are the most eminent cause of that forgiveness, which is the thing promised. When the soul considers, that he who is so great a God, and so greatly merciful and gracious, is the same God who hath promised it, and hath means in him to make it good, what other thing (I say) can be so great a persuasive to believe as the light hereof? And the greater the light thereof is, which is brought down into such a promise, and with the promise shines into the heart, the more, and in the greatest degree, doth the light of the true subsistence of forgiveness shine with it, and becomes realized to the soul, and appears clothed with such an evidence and subsistence as will efficaciously strike, move, and draw out real faith, that being the principle which is properly and specially suited to that object. And seeing it is the light of God himself shining in some attribute or other, either habitually or actually, implicitly or explicitly, immediately or remotely, that must be the bottom of faith, and accompany faith always, and in every promise give that subsistence spoken of unto faith (whether it be his truth, faithfulness, goodness, or the like) ; then certainly that which of all other must needs be most effectual and genuine, in this case of forgiveness, is this light and faith into God's mercies ; for they are those which move God most to forgive, and therefore move us most to believe in God for it.

And the reason of this further is, that although all benefits whatever are the effects of mercy, and so styled (as the call of the Gentiles is, Rom. xv. 9, and the ' Gentiles glorify God for his mercy,' and the splendour of the whole of their salvation from conversion downwards, as a people ' that had not obtained mercy, but now have obtained mercy,' 1 Pet. ii. 10), yet forgiveness of sins doth of all other most purely, immediately, and directly, depend upon mercies. Forgiveness is a pure act of and from grace ; as old Zacharias speaks in his song : Luke i. 77, 78. ' To give the knowledge of salvation by the remission of sins, through the tender mercies (or bowels) of our God.' To give other things, or to do for us in another kind, may require the calling in the help of some other attribute immediately to effect it ; as the resurrection of our bodies and glorifying of us, which (though it be a work of infinite mercy), requires the aid of power to effect it, even that ' power whereby he is able to subdue all things to himself,' Philip. iii. 21. But forgiveness and pardon of sin peculiarly and immediately hold of mercy, and own and adore mercy for their immediate founder and benefactor. Pardon and forgiveness are a pure emanation from grace, and issue in the glory thereof, above all other in God : Eph. i. 7, in Christ we have ' the forgiveness of sins, according to the riches of his grace ; ' Exod. xxxiv. 7, ' The Lord God, gracious and merciful' ; and then, ' pardoning iniquity, transgression, and sin.' This is a stream that springs and flows out immediately from that fountain : Ps. lxxxvi. 5, ' The Lord is good, and ready to forgive ; plenteous in mercy.' His being ready to forgive, flows gushing forth from his goodness, and his being plenteous in mercy. God is ' the Father of mercies,' all mercies bestowed being the most natural and immediate children of mercy in himself, and he thereout giving existence and being to them, as a father doth to his children. And from hence the heart of a humble sinner, when it is to seek any mercies at the hand of God, or hath received any, may and will readily know and acknowledge mere mercy, infinite mercy, to be the father of them. But above all other, pardon (when either we come to seek it, or to be thankful for it, this forgiveness of sins being the first-born of benefits in our calling) will own and know its Father, the Father of mercies, and cause the heart to fall upon its knees, and ask blessings for it.

The truth of that general maxim holds in any other attribute, as touching that particular dependency which its proper effects have upon it : as when God is styled ' the Father of lights,' in relation unto wisdom to be asked and given ; and when he is called ' the Lord of hope,' when joy and peace in believing are spoken of; and the ' God of all comforts' and ' Father of glory,' when comfort and glory are to be bestowed. But there is a farther reason why this or that attribute in God, that gives the subsistence to the performance, should, above all other, most properly conduce to give the subsistence to the faith of a believer (although the subsistence of the performance is differing from the subsistence given to faith in the mean time), because that hereby faith doth see all along, even until the performance of the promised blessings, the existence of them in what are their native roots and direct immediate causes. Thus it is said, Heb. xi. 13, ' They saw the promises afar off, and were persuaded.' That phrase, *afar off*, refers not, wholly or altogether, to an importing the distance of time to come ere performed (though take that in also), but also to the words that went before, ' they saw them afar off,' that is, though the mercies were at a distance as to their individual existence, which was afar off, and remote out of sight, yet however this act of their faith was a sight, for they saw them really subsisting, or else their faith had not been worthy the name of sight. So then they were presented as if really subsisting afar off. Now, wherein or whereby should it be that they saw them thus subsisting aforehand, when the things had not any actual existence? There certainly was a seeing them in God, and in God by viewing those attributes especially that were to be the most direct and native causes of them. The knowledge of philosophy holds some resemblance, or like kind of existence, with this. Philosophy instructs us that though roses in winter have no existence, and though tulips have no flower nor stalks above ground for the greatest part of the year, and so they have not an actual existence for so long time, yet that in a true sense they may be said to have a real being and existence in nature, the mother and womb of all things. If vulgar apprehensions might be judges of this, they will say, Where is it? they are not, for we see no such things extant. But a philosopher or a wise gardener will tell you that they have a being in their roots; yea, and that each and every kind of those flowers have a several being in their several roots proper to their kind, in which, as in their causes, they have a latent hidden existence and being, which reason assures them to be true. And therefore a gardener doth, before summer comes, put a high value upon such roots as those that will bring forth such flowers. He sees them afar off in those roots, as their causes, many months before, and expects their growing up in their seasons. Even thus, and more satisfyingly, doth faith see in God a subsistence of the promises, whilst it views them in those attributes which are the proper originals of them, according to their kind.

I shall now consider the second act of faith, which is, ' embrace the promise'; and I shall demonstrate that an enlarged consideration of the mercies of God's nature do wonderfully persuade the heart to embrace the promises of forgiveness. The promises do thus persuade, by mercy's super-adding a real taste of transcendent goodness and sweetness, an overcoming sweetness, unto this grand benefit of forgiveness, and the promises thereof, by which the will and affections are demulced, and effectually drawn to embrace them. That these benefits of salvation are in themselves good, and must needs be most welcome, or, as the apostle expresseth it, 1 Tim. i. 15, ' worthy of all acceptation,' by a sinner sensible of his own sinful misery, we may very well and readily conceive, for they are suited unto all self-love in such a soul. But farther, that unto a truly broken, humbled sinner, the mercies that are in God, out of which he pardons, should have, as needs they must, infinitely more of goodness and sweetness in them than pardon, or all things else that are in the promises, or apprehended with them, is that which a soul that hath tasted how good the Lord is will instantly acknowledge. A promise of life to a condemned man is sweet, for life is sweet, as we say; but 'thy loving-kindness,' said David, who had tasted how good the Lord is, 'is better than life,' and infinitely sweeter, Ps. lxiii. 3. And again says David, 'Because thy mercy is good, deliver thou me,' Ps. cix. 21. Deliverance was good; yea, but the mercy in God apprehended therewith was infinitely more good to him, which was the greatest inducement to him to seek deliverance. And indeed God's mercy doth eminently bear the style of goodness. Thus God himself says to Moses (Exod. xxxiii. 18, 19 compared), 'I will make all my goodness pass before thee ; I will be gracious to whom I will be gracious.' And David in this psalm first laid hold on the goodness that is in the mercy of God, and then prays and pleads, Deliver me. The same again you have Psalm lxix. 16, 'Hear me, for thy loving-kindness is good;' that is, it is sweet, it is pleasant.* And when the thing sought for comes to be granted and obtained, a believer rejoiceth more in the mercy and loving-kindness he finds to be in God's heart towards him, than in the benefit vouchsafed, and that is it which takes his heart: Ps. xxxi. 7, 'I will be glad and rejoice in thy mercy: for thou hast considered my trouble; thou hast known my soul in adversities.' That God's mercy and kindness should own his soul at such a time, was more than the deliverance. And as the mercy of God stirs up the soul thus to a rejoicing at the performance, so it pleasantly allures and obligeth the soul to trust on the promise in hope of performance; as those words, 1 Peter ii. 3, imply, 'If so be you have tasted that the Lord is gracious.' As we find them in the apostle, they do refer unto the psalmist's speech—Ps. xxxiv. 8, 'O taste and see that the Lord is good!'—for his grace and mercy are his goodness: for so the apostle renders it, 'If you have tasted that the Lord is gracious.' The vulgar translation, whenever the psalmist says ' God is good,' do still render it *Suavis est Dominus*, 'the Lord is sweet;' and his mercies indeed are the *primum dulce*, the original sweetness of all other, which diffuse deliciousness both into the promises and the benefits vouchsafed, and make them to be as honey to the taste; and it is that taste of his graciousness which causeth us joyfully to receive and embrace them, and then to trust in him (which is the next act), for it follows in the next words of that verse of that psalm, 'Blessed is the man that trusteth in him.' The apostle in that place mentioned instanceth in those that were and are but new-born babes in Christianity; of whom yet he says, 'If so be you have tasted that the Lord is gracious.' What is it especially that Christians, whilst babes, do from the first of their faith seek out in the first and chief place for ? It is the forgiveness of their sins; and that benefit it is which God first vouchsafes them as to their sense. And therefore most suitably to that state of theirs the apostle speaks thus to them, with difference from others grown up, ' I write unto you babes, because your sins are forgiven you,' 1 John ii. 12. He writes it as the most welcome news to them, and as that which whilst babes they are in the most eager pursuance of, and thence they seek out in the word for promises that speak forgiveness, and those they suck and lie tugging at, even as infants use to do the breast for the milk that is in it, and this from the first of their birth, next after crying. And if they could come at variety of breasts, they would and do affect the sweetest milk; and hereto they are led by a taste of that sweet-

* Piscator *in locum.*

ness. And the apostle's allusion is unto this, whilst he exhorts us 'as new-born babes, to desire the sincere milk of the word,' and subjoins, 'if so be you have tasted that the Lord is gracious,' namely, in his having forgiven you all your trespasses, which so earnestly you then sought. And he joins these two together; for whilst we are seeking or sucking of forgiveness out of particular promises of forgiveness, we find God come at last, and his mercy and grace that forgive we meet with therein, and feel them to flow in with the promise, for they are the fountain of forgiveness, and of the promises also. It is God, you see, who is said to be tasted, and the sweetness of his mercies. It is not said so much that the sweetness of pardon, or that salvation, or the promise, are tasted; but over and above all it is God's grace that is tasted in and with them all, and that is it which makes us so greedy and desirous to suck comfort out of those breasts of consolation. For that desire, the apostle says, flows from taste, and this our sucking and tasting are through faith, and in the exercise of that we taste the grace that is in God's and Christ's heart towards us, whereof that grace in God's nature is the spring, or ocean rather, and we find that to be the most delicious of all other. My advice therefore to those that seek to believe is, to put in all of this sugar they can gather and grasp out of the original cane itself, as in the Scriptures they find it sprouting up, and therewith to sweeten all the promises they do or would lay hold on, as that which will most overcomingly persuade their wills to embrace them.

We will now consider the third act of faith, which is trust in God, and will prove that the view and intuition of the mercies in God doth mightily strengthen the heart to trust and stay itself upon God for forgiveness. And I shall shew how this is done, by persuading the heart even of the very truth and faithfulness of God in the promises, and of the assured performance of them, and how they give the most real evidence: 1st, of God's real intention; and, 2dly, of ability in the event to fulfil them; which two are the main causes of trust on the truth of any promise. And God's mercies do sufficiently alone assure us of all these, though we had no other evidence thereof.

It is needless to insist that trust is an act of faith, and an eminent act thereof, and how a saint is characterised to be one that 'hopes in God's mercy,' Ps. xxxiii. 18, Ps. cxlvii. 11; and one that 'trusteth in his mercy,' Ps. xiii. 5; and Ps. lii. 8, 'I trust in the mercy of God for ever and ever.' That which is specially incumbent on me is to give demonstration that the ample meditation of God's mercies will prove most effective to cause (as David's word is, Ps. cxix. 49) the heart to trust in God, over and above the consideration of the promises alone.

It may be thought that God having once given forth promises of forgiveness in his word, we should need the consideration of his mercies no more; for out of mercy it is that the promises are given, and of mercy it is they speak, and carry it in the mouth of them. Of what use then can it be to have a distinct view of these mercies whereof we treat, in order to draw forth trust on them, since the ground of that is the truth of God? If therefore our faith needed an establishment in those promises, it may have recourse rather unto the truth of God, or unto the assurance that God is true in his word and faithful in his promises; and as for mercy, that is sufficiently supposed in his promises themselves.

I acknowledge that these other attributes of truth and faithfulness have their share, and a great share too, in influencing the support of our faith.

We cannot want the knowledge of any of his attributes, but our faith will be the weaker for it.   We cannot be without the knowledge of truth especially, which is therefore so frequently mentioned with mercy.   But yet still our hearts being too 'slow to believe' (as Christ hath told us), when deeply humbled once, do foment and harbour so many jealousies of God, and are as full of dark cells of fears, doubts, suspicions of God, as full of unbelief, carnal reasonings against itself, as the earth is of damps, stifling vapours contained in vast caverns within the womb of it.   Our hearts, I say, do therefore stand in need of the most spiritual cordials (as those that dig in mines, and work in the earth's caverns, are wont ever and anon to take); which cordials, the most sovereign to such a fainting soul apt to sinkings, are the rich mercies in the heart of God, which like to a box of the most costly ointment, do, when opened, fill the whole house (the heart) with the savour thereof; a savour (if any) of 'life unto life,' as the apostle speaks, 2 Cor. ii. 16.   But over and above what spirit of life and consolation God's mercies in themselves immediately afford, my undertaking further is to shew, that an ample view of these infinite mercies entertained by us doth by inference or consequence wonderfully conduce to our very belief of the truth, and faithfulness, and willingness of God manifested in those promises to forgive and pardon us upon that account. And I shall also still continue the prosecution of my begun exhortation, to press and urge this practice and course upon the spirits of believers, or souls endeavouring to believe, viz., to fill and possess their souls with the most comprehensive apprehensions of the mercies of God, as to the drawing forth of trust or affiance on the promises of forgiveness, to be the most behoveful of all other.   It is certain that in all trust and confidence upon another, whether in human matters on man, or divine on God, the knowledge of the person whom we trust, and the inward qualifications, and dispositions, and habilities that are in that person, are a greater basis and ground for trust than all or any sorts of declarations of that person, or any obligations by promises, oaths, &c., can be supposed to be: 2 Tim. i. 12, 'I know whom I have believed,' or 'trusted,' as it is varied in the margin. His perfect knowledge of the person, viz., of God, did weigh above all with him, unto which fully accordeth that of the psalmist: Ps. ix. 10, 'They that know thy name will trust in thee.'   And though promises are the means by which we believe, yet it is the promiser that is the basis or the foundation on whom our hearts ultimately and quietly rest for the performance.   All our confidence is therefore resolved into the person, and what he is.   Indeed, the greatness of the sum or thing promised, and the security given (whether it be by bond or the like), do greatly conduce to cheer the heart of one that trusts; but still all these are in the virtue of what we apprehend the promiser to be in his inward and innate disposition and habilities.

There are two things especially that give the real truth to any promise made, and chiefly beget the adherence thereto in the soul of any that confide thereon.

1. The honesty of the promiser, in respect of a real intention in him when he made the promise, and still continuing in him to perform it.

2. That in the event it will assuredly de facto be performed.

The reason why I add the latter to the first, and join both together, is, that the truth of a promise notes a respect and relation unto an actual performance, as that without which the promise cannot be said to be, or at least will not prove true in the reality of the thing, though it should be never so faithfully intended by him that promised. Hence then he that doth believe the truth of the promises of forgiveness, must necessarily be assured of the latter as well as the first, and indeed of both these two things fore-mentioned.

I shall speak to each particularly, and shew how much our faith on these two is confirmed, even by our belief of this, that so great and infinite mercies are in the heart and nature of God.

1. As to the truth and faithfulness of God's intention in these promises, that (say I) is as abundantly if not more confirmed to us by our firm belief of the mercies in God, than by any other arguments whatsoever; for it was mercy in God that wholly made those promises, and was the founder of them; and God had no other motive to make them than his mercies, and could have no other or greater design in the making, but firmly to resolve to perform them to the glorifying of his mercy, which is the Alpha and Omega, the beginning and ending, of all therein. And therefore the belief of his mercies must needs have as great an influence into our belief of the truth of the promises as any other thing whatever.

1st, Mercy, pure mercy, tenderness of mercy, made the promises, and caused him first thus to declare of himself, ‘I will be merciful,’ as Rom. ix., Exod. xxxiii. Yea, and his mercy was utterly free in his doing this. The grace we are saved by is the freest principle in God's nature. He might have chosen whether ever or no he would have let fall a word of mercy to any of mankind, and yet to choose he did it. And it was mercy, pure mercy, that was the head of and leader on of all the rest of the attributes to concur in this design.

Nor, secondly, had he any other end to attain upon the sons of men which he should have aimed at, or would obtain by his giving and uttering those promises, but that truly and really he should forgive, must be all and the whole of his intent, and utmost of the design. Forgiveness of our sins is wholly ascribed unto mercy, as being from ‘the riches of his grace,’ Eph. i. 7.

Nor, indeed, 3dly, could he have any other design but this; it could not be to gain or bring us unto himself under the pretensions of offers of mercy, and the overtures thereof; for himself knew and foreknew that we all were and would be such wretched reckless creatures in ourselves, that all the promulgations and offers that should or could be made would not stir or move our hearts a jot unto the least attempt of nearer access unto God, unless himself first moved us thereunto. Mercy itself must work with the promises, or we should sit still and move not: Eph. ii. 4, 5, ‘But God, who is rich in mercy, for his great love wherewith he loved us, even when we were dead in sins, hath quickened us together with Christ (by grace ye are saved), and hath raised us up together,’ &c. And faith, it is ‘the gift of God, and not of ourselves,’ as there it follows. And therefore it had been in vain to have made pretensions of promises, in hopes or expectation of our being willing, or of our coming in, if God himself were not really resolved. No; the apostle hath resolved us it must be God himself must shew us that mercy to cause us to will and run, Rom. ix. 16. Therefore, as mercy was the first and sole mover, so it must itself be the performer, or all is in vain.

4thly. Besides this, let us weigh that our great God did, long before he put forth those promises, both know and perfectly consider with himself what riches of grace and mercy lay by him, whereby he found his own sufficiency over and over abundantly to perform such promises, which to perform is more easy for him than for us to think or speak a word. 'I say unto thee' (says Christ, ὁ λόγος, *the Word*), 'thy sins are forgiven thee,' Mat. ix. 2. It was but a word of his mouth. The all-sufficiency of his own heart told him how merciful he could for ever find in his heart to be (as our phrase is of ourselves), and he first reckoned with himself, and told over what his ' riches in mercy ' were, and to what an infinite sum they arose, and found, by the largeness of his heart therein, that he could never be disenabled or impoverished in the expense of them, nor his heart grow narrower or scantier in process of time afterwards, when men should have acted and perpetrated their sins, than now it was when he made the promise before they had sinned. ' I know my thoughts towards you, thoughts of peace,' &c., Jer. xxix. 11. And thereupon and withal there declares how in the end and event, as I have phrased it, the thing will assuredly be fulfilled which he had promised; so it follows, ' to give you an expected end.' For ' I know my thoughts towards you,' says he; I have summed and cast up all. I know what I have resolved I am able to do, and therefore wait you, and expect the issue. And likewise he found in himself that he had for ever the absolute and full power of his own will. And upon this and such forethoughts within himself it was that he both took up those purposes of forgiveness, and issued out from thence those promises adequate thereunto.* When the covenant of grace and mercy, the sure mercies, were given forth to David under the type of him and his house, but signifying his seed Christ, and those that were to be of him, David, *in totum*, and in the whole, resolveth all those promises into God's own greatness and all-sufficiency within himself, as that from which alone, together with the consideration of his Christ, he was moved to make those promises : 2 Sam. vii. 21, ' For thy Word's sake' (which I would interpret of Christ, ὁ λόγος, *the Word*†), and according to thine own heart hast thou done all these great things.' And the great things he speaks of as done by God were his uttering those promises by Nathan, ver. 11–16, which David indigitates, ver. 19, ' But thou hast spoken,' &c., all which was in the reality intended of Christ, and those children whom God gives him (as the apostle calls them), so Ps. lxxxix. 28, 29 ; Isaiah lv. And the consideration that God made these promises so freely, and out of his own heart, was that great foundation which confirmed David's heart in the faith of those promises, and may abundantly strengthen ours. Yea, the promises themselves that were made being so high and illustriously great, this became an invincible argument to David's faith, that God that made them was the true God, and he alone : so ver. 22, ' Wherefore thou art great, O Lord God : for there is none like thee, neither is there any God besides thee.' For he considered with himself that it could not enter into the hearts of men, or of any mere creature, to make such promises, of so large and ample extent, of such and so great mercies and forgiveness : ' Is this the manner of men, O Lord God ?' ver. 19. And therefore, if there were no other evidence, this alone sufficiently testified to him the greatness of God, 'Thou art God alone ;' and his heart being thus filled and enlarged with the mercies of God, and the greatness of God in them, he thereupon readily gave up his faith to the belief of the truth of them. And no wonder if we find in that first proclamation, Exod. xxxiv. 7, ' The Lord God, gracious, merciful, abundant in goodness or kindness,' set first, and then to follow ' abundant in truth' also ; for the abun-

---

* Compare with it Psalm lxxxix, 28, 29 ; Isaiah lv.

† Compare Dan. ix. 17, ' For the Lord's sake ;' that is, for Christ's ; and ver. 19, ' For thine own sake,'

dancy and overflowing of that kindness and mercy that God in those declarations professeth to be in himself, is that which assures us of the truth and reality of God's heart in the whole of it, as also of those promises which next do follow, of 'pardoning iniquity, transgression, and sin.' His truth in his promises doth spring, and hath its rise, from that fountain, his super-abundancy of mercy. And as the promises are said to be 'true in Christ,' 2 Cor. i. 18, 20, because he purchased them, so upon the like ground they may also be said to be true in God, because mercy is the founder and maintainer of them. And from hence it follows, that as God's own knowing his own heart, and riches, and all-sufficiency to perform what he should promise, caused him to engage his truth at first in making these promises, so answerably it is operative in the soul of a believer, the more it comes to believe the truth of those promises, as there is a good reason it should do so. For this is a sure and undeniable rule, that what most moves God's heart to do a thing, that, when declared and revealed by God, must needs be most efficacious to cause the heart of a sinner to believe that he will do it.

The second thing I proposed, as that which goes to make up the truth of a promise, is the assured reality of the performance of it in the event, or, as the prophet speaks, that 'though it tarry, wait for it, because it will surely come, it will not tarry,' Hab. ii. 3; that is, that it will certainly in the issue be fulfilled, for otherwise the promise is not *re ipsa* true as to the thing itself, and so not such as he that is to confide in it may build upon it. And the reason of this is, not only that the substantialness and essentiality of a promise relates to the actual execution of it, but farther, likewise, because often it falls out that the person promising may have honestly and faithfully intended it, and promised it, and yet in the issue prove unable to perform, as we see amongst men it often falls out; and then in that case and respect the promise doth in reality fall short of its eventual truth. Hence, therefore, to constitute a promise true, there must be added unto the sincerity of the intention of the promiser the reality of making the promise good; and that as necessarily doth farther depend upon a full and sufficient ability in the promiser to perform it, as it doth upon the honesty of his intention. Hence, therefore, in like manner it must be acknowledged that in and to the full confidence of faith of him that depends upon the promise of another, there must necessarily also be a persuasion of the full and perfect ability of the promiser in the issue certainly to perform it, so that on his part it shall not nor can any way be hindered. And this belief of the ability of the promiser to accomplish, is as great an ingredient into trust as any. This we may see in the apostle's faith: 2 Tim. i. 12, 'I know whom I have trusted, that he is able,' &c. Thus that wherein God's greatest sufficiency and ability, *de facto*, or actually to forgive our sins, doth lie, the apprehension and belief thereof must needs be judged the strongest inducer of us to trust on God for the forgiveness. Now it is evident that his all-sufficiency and ability to forgive doth properly and peculiarly consist in his being merciful. Not to cite many scriptures, this 34th of Exodus may suffice, 'The Lord strong, merciful and gracious, pardoning iniquity, transgression, and sin.' Likewise Ps. lxxxvi. 5 (which is an extract from this), 'For thou, Lord, art good, and ready to forgive, and plenteous in mercy, unto all them that call upon thee.' You see here that his readiness to forgive flows from his goodness, and his being 'plenteous in mercy.' And in analogous reason this may be seen in its shadow, the mercy that is in man. What is it that enables a man to forgive?

Merely the goodness and mercy that is in him, so as a weak woman, or the poorest and otherwise most impotent man (if they abound in bowels of mercy, and be of tender hearts and natures), are able to forgive an injury, when yet they are utterly unable to do any other good thing, especially not any great thing, for the party whom they forgive. But the mercy that is in them alone sufficiently empowereth them unto forgiveness, when to nothing else. So, then, if a firm belief of the ability of the person be the strongest persuasive unto trust and confidence, joined with that of his honest intention, further to confirm us of the certain real performance itself, then although from other topics we may come to believe that God is true in those his promises of forgiveness, yet more abundantly, as the apostle says in a like case, this belief springs from the intuition of the abundancy of the mercies that are in God, than from any other whatsoever; and the firm belief of the ability to perform is that which most of all causeth trust. Thus it was in the faith of Abraham, that he staggered not at the truth of the promise as to the real performance, because he chiefly believed God's all-sufficiency to make it good: Rom. iv. 20, 21, ' He staggered not at the promise of God through unbelief, but was strong in faith, giving glory to God, and being fully persuaded that what he had promised he was able to perform;' and so was assured thereby that the event would be accordingly. If a great person that had promised to give such or so vast a sum of money as is necessary to furnish a private man's house with household stuff and utensils, wares and provisions of all kinds, and to stock the man's ground, and had given his word and truth for the performance of all these, but, together therewith, had led that poor indigent person into all his treasures, and shewn him his riches, and where it was that all those kinds of such furniture do lie, and then had carried him into his fields, barns, and warehouses, where he should also see stock for cattle, corn, and wares of all sorts lie piled up, how would this hearten that man, or any of you, to believe that great person, the promiser, in his word and promise given. So it is here. Now consider those great riches of God which the Scriptures predicate so much, and out of which he pardons; they properly consist in his mercies. These are they that are his substance, and give him ability to forgive: He is ' plenteous in mercy, and ready to forgive,' Ps. lxxxvi. 5. It is mercy that is even the principal obligee in the promise or bond, and truth and other attributes come in but secondarily as to this business of forgiveness, and rather but as witnesses to confirm what mercy had declared and signed before them.

CHAPTER XIV.

The uses of the doctrine.—That the thoughts of the mercies in God's nature should encourage us to come to him for salvation and life.—That the consideration of them should cause any soul to hope that God will pardon him in particular.

Use 1. Let the thoughts of these treasures of mercies, which have been described and demonstrated to be in God's nature, encourage us to come to him. Let us consider that there is no other use of all these riches of mercy in God, but to be given all forth unto sinners for his glory : whereas all his other attributes are to himself, and for himself. Thus his wisdom is the perfection of his own being: his love is that whereby he loves himself: his all-sufficience is that which makes himself blessed; but his mercies redound not in this manner unto or upon himself (for he is not merciful unto himself, or for himself), but the sole improvement and glory of them consists in extending them to others, so as otherwise they would lie useless by him. Now then, as a man's having a great estate lying by him, is the greatest provocation that can be to him to make him willing to lay it forth unto an improvement; so these vast treasures of mercies which God possesseth, are a motive unto him to expend them upon sinners. Full breasts love to be sucked and drawn, their fulness otherwise becomes a pain. It is the greatest vanity to have riches, and not to know on whom to bestow them. Do but possess thy heart then with the thoughts that there is this fulness of grace, these great riches of mercy in God, and it will make thy soul easy of belief, that there is a willingness in God to bestow them, and that he is resolved to give them out to thee whenever thou comest to him, especially since himself hath set them forth, and proclaimed them on purpose to us; as we find in the Scriptures, that where God doth set himself to persuade sinners to come to him, he thinks it sufficient to give them promises of mercy and pardon.

When convinced sinners come to have the prospect of their hearts, and of their lives past, and of their sins therein, in the great aggravations of them, set in order before them; when the account of their ten thousand talents comes in; then, unless the superabounding mercies in God, which should pardon them, arise up to their faith, and are *in solido* told out before their eyes, and their faith prevails to assure them in good earnest that there are such infinite mercies in God, they cannot entertain a thought of hope or comfort. Till they see how the mercies of God are superaboundingly able to forgive all these their heinous and aggravated sins, and to remove those heaps upon heaps of them, they will not be brought to believe; but as Jacob's heart fainted, and he believed not till he saw the waggons which Joseph had sent to carry him, and then his spirit revived, Gen. xlv. 26, 27, so neither will these sinners believe till they see the mercies which God hath sent forth to carry them to heaven. Till then they are apt to cry out (as Cain did, Gen. iv. 13), ' My sin is greater than I can bear:' or as those in Jer. xviii., who, when God had invited them to turn from their evil ways, say at the 12th verse, ' there is no hope,' or our case is desperate. And so they forsook their own mercies (as Jonah expresseth it), and left the everlasting and never-failing spring thereof, ver. 14, and forgot the Lord, ver. 15, and betook themselves to lying vanities to give them comfort and ease. And other souls who are preserved from despair, yet think within themselves, and say, Oh, where are the mercies to be found that should pardon all those sins? Is it possible that God should find in his heart to do it? Is it possible that God should find in his heart mercy and grace enough to pardon such, and so great a sum of sins committed against grace itself? And in this lies the stop and obstruction of faith, as it did in like manner with them in the wilderness, who said, ' Can God furnish a table in the wilderness?' Ps. lxxviii. 19. Their doubt (when matters came to a stress) was more of his power and ability, than of his will. The question is, *Can God?* They do not say God will not. And truly there is as much unbelief in men's hearts about his mercy, when it comes to a pinch, as about his power; though men ordinarily say that they question neither, and indeed till they are put to a distress, they question neither, but take them in an overly way for granted. But still there is the same reason of men's questioning the all-sufficiency of God's mercy, as there was in those Jews, and is in us upon any the like occasion, of questioning his power.   Accordingly, we find these two in like manner expressly joined as parallel, and as points of like difficulty to be believed, Ps. lxii. 8, 11, 12 ; and indeed in doubting one we question the other, especially when we hear that God's ability to forgive lieth in his mercy ; for then to limit his power is as to this particular all one as to limit his mercy. And when men's consciences are throughly awakened to see their sins, then unbelief, on the other hand, awakens thoughts in them to limit God's mercies, which is another phrase used, Ps. lxxviii. 41.   For men's narrow spirits, if not enlarged by faith, do much measure God's heart by their own, and so think God to be like themselves, Ps. l. 21.   They cannot imagine how a person so high, so great, and so grievously provoked, should be able to forgive, and therefore apprehend that he cannot be willing ; and hence a thousand jealousies of God do arise in men's souls, which are as full of dark cells of unbelief as the earth is of vast caverns within the womb of it. We may judge that the disease lies here, by the remedy and application the Scriptures make, which, to satisfy men's souls in these very scruples, do set forth God in the greatness and prerogative power of his mercies, as the mercies of so great a God, and proportionable to his greatness.   As men's hearts rise not up to glorify God as God, Rom. i. 21, so nor to believe mercies to be in him as a God so great and infinite, proportionable to his greatness.   God hath therefore in the Scriptures taken several ways, and at sundry times hath set forth his mercies to persuade men.   Sometimes they are set out by way of admiration and wonderment : Micah vii. 18, 19, ' Who is a God like our God, pardoning iniquity, and passing by the transgression of the remnant of his inheritance, and that delighteth in mercy ?' Sometimes they are displayed by comparing his thoughts and heart in pardoning, with what may be supposed to be in the thoughts of the largest and most tender-hearted parent, father or mother, and with the bowels which all men put together may be supposed to have in them ; and God's heart is declared to exceed them all in mercies and thoughts of forgiveness, as much as the heaven exceeds the earth : Isa. lv. 7, ' Let the wicked forsake his way, and the unrighteous man his thoughts ; and return unto the Lord, and he will abundantly pardon.'   Yea, but the sinner will say, My thoughts of sinning have for time past already been infinite, ' only evil, and continually' evil from my infancy, and my ways have been continually perverse and froward, ungracious and opposite to God and his mercies, that should pardon me.   Humbled sinners' thoughts will go on so far in a belief that God may pardon them, though they have gone out so far in sinning, as to think that if they had only at such a time of their lives sinned so and so against him, and been false to him, and not continued to sin out of the presumption of that grace that now should pardon them, then they might have hope of mercy.   But they think that because they have so long provoked him, that now he may have sworn against them in his wrath, and that he cannot find in his heart to forgive such a wretch, though he may otherwise pardon as much as all men and angels putting their stock of mercies together, and making up one great purse of mercy, as would be sufficient to extend to forgive and discharge great debts.   Oh but, says God, measure not my thoughts in pardoning either by the evil in your thoughts, or by your ways in sinning ; nor yet measure them by what the thoughts and ways of yourselves, men or angels, have or can have to forgive withal !   ' For my thoughts are not your thoughts, neither are my ways your ways, saith the Lord.   As the heavens be higher than the earth, so are my ways higher than your ways.' My ways of mercy are both above your ways of sinning, and they also exceed all the thoughts of mercy which the best natured of you can have in pardoning others. My ways and designs that I have upon you, and dealings I purpose towards you, transcend them all in opposite goodness, graciousness, and forgiveness, as much as the heavens do the earth. And also says God, 'My thoughts are not as your thoughts.' He speaks all this of his exceeding them all in pardoning. Nay, further, it rises higher, to this, meaning that the mercies of God do not only exceed men's thoughts in what any, or all of them, could find in their hearts in their proportion to pardon, but that also if you extend the compasses of your thoughts, that you or any believers have had of what mercies of God, and what thoughts of grace, have been exercised in pardoning themselves or other sinners; yet the merciful thoughts of God in reality do exceed, and are above all such apprehensions that you or any can take up, as much as the heavens are above the earth, and are still higher also, since 'his mercies are above the heavens.' For lo! 'these are but parts of his ways, but how little a portion is heard of him,' or apprehended by us men, or that can be spoken by himself, unto what is in himself! Job xxvi. 14.

I have enlarged upon these reasons, not so much for conviction, which in so plain a point needed not, as to stir up believers to the frequent exercise of this so useful an experiment, wherein when faith is versed it will find an abundant entrance into every promise that belongeth unto mercy in any kind, as well as in the point of forgiveness; and yet this practice is neglected by Christians, for the want of which their faith continues weak and narrow, and their joy and comfort in believing kept low and small, and God himself bereft of much of the glory would arise unto his mercy, if, together with the promises laid hold on, they would have recourse unto the spring and fountain, the mercies of God. But the narrowness of their spirits in believing causeth them to content themselves with a single and bare view of the things promised, and of the promises of them under the notion of being the word of God; but they enlarge not in considering the rich mercies of God, that moved him to make those promises. They have the consideration of the truth of God in them to perform, but expatiate not to the mercies that both gave the promises, and is the cause of all the causes of the performance.

My advice to believers is, to meditate much upon, and to study the infinite riches of God's mercies, as the Scriptures so frequently (and therefore call for the like frequency of thoughts upon them in our hearts) have set them forth unto us. Let us still join them all together upon any great and solemn occasion of exercising faith on promises; and as, in the point of thanksgiving after mercies received, we have many precedents of saints recounting 'the loving-kindnesses of the Lord, according to all he hath bestowed on them, according to his mercies, and according to the multitude of his loving-kindnesses,' Isa. lxiii. 7, so in like manner our faith should, in its pursuit to obtain mercies, collect and make the like catalogue, as we have been even now abundantly instructed; for hereby we shall greatly honour God, and strengthen our own hearts.

1. We shall honour God greatly (to give glory unto whom in the most ample manner is the most proper use of faith, Rom. iv. 20), for thereby we acknowledge and do homage to his mercies as the universal cause of all; for this is an undoubted maxim, that what is first in any kind is the universal cause of all that kind. Consider then in God all that is mercy in any

kind, and he being originally and only merciful as well as only good, all else of mercy must hold its tenor of that mercy that is in him.   This I understand to be the full of that title given him by the apostle, 2 Cor. i. 3, ' The father of mercies;' *i. e.*, he being a fulness of mercy in himself first, he became the Father of all mercies, of what kind soever.   He is the first in that kind; mercy itself is his nature, and all mercies purposed, promised, performed, held forth, or applied to faith, are all his immediate children, and not one of them have any existence but from him, and that considered as he is merciful too.   Thus in another respect he is styled ' the Father of lights,' James i. 17, in respect of heavenly gifts from above, they holding in chief of him as such in that kind of effects; like as the sun (to which the allusion manifestly there is) may be called the father, or first original of all heavenly light that comes down upon the world from itself, or from stars that have their light from it.

2. And also this course of meditating on the riches of God's mercies will prove most comfortable to us; for, 2 Cor. i. 3, now cited, where he propounds him to our faith as the Father of mercies, he adds this other immediately, ' the God of all comforts;' for in exercising our faith on him as a Father of mercies, we shall find him to be a God of comfort to us, whilst we are but expectants and waiters on him by faith all along until the performance.

3. And by virtue of his mercies being the universal, supreme, and sovereign cause of all mercies, promises, &c., it holds good that our faith may have a free, ample, and immediate recourse unto them in all cases, or occasions whatsoever.   For the law or privilege that accompanies his being the first cause in other kind of effects, doth by analogy hold in this.   Take him as he is *primus motor*, the first and universal cause of all being and motion, and it is a maxim universally consented to by all divines, that although there be a chain of second causes subordinate one to another, that have a power each to bring forth their proper effects (as the sun brings forth light, and that light heat and warmth, and that warmth quickens and enlivens the seeds and roots in the earth, and they bring forth herbs, which herbs and flowers have divers colours and qualities they are adorned withal), yet God, who is the first and universal cause, hath an immediate influence and concurrence into all and each, as immediately into the very last as into the first; and that a far greater than they have all or severally into their effects; so as God not only works by them, but with them, and he as immediately causeth the light to quicken plants as to send out light, and as immediately he causeth the plants to bring forth flowers, yea, and that last effect too, those orient colours with which the lilies (that are our tulips) are arrayed above Solomon in all his royalty; yet these particulars are immediately attributed unto God more than unto their second causes : ' If God,' says our Saviour, ' so clothe the grass of the field,' Mat. vi. 28, 30, Luke xii. 17, 28 ; and indeed he works ' all in all,' 1 Cor. xii. 6.   I need not insist on it further, being it is but for illustration; be you only exhorted to hold this golden chain and descent of mercies let down to your faith to lay hold upon ; see his thoughts and purposes to have mercy immediately flowing from the essential mercies of his nature, and then regard his promises of bestowing such and [such] mercies as another link let down from his purposes.   And though the faith of a believer lays hold on these promises as on what are next it, yet those first and essential mercies (so celebrated in his word) do immediately touch, influence, and reach unto all and each of these, unto the last as well as the first, to give subsistence to them, and

to make all good to the faith of a sinner. And hence the faith of believers, whilst it clasps itself into the promise of forgiveness, or any other promise in the word, may not only remotely depend on God's mercies (as a man that hangs his whole weight upon the lowest link of a chain, may be said to hang also upon the uppermost, to which all are in subordination fastened), but he may in and with the promise have an immediate recourse to the top and supreme mercies themselves, for they are ready and present with the declaration of his word to make them good and real to the faith of a sinner, for whose sake and comfort they are and were written. He may bring down the consideration of all these mercies into every such promise, &c., to strengthen his heart in believing, and in treating with God for forgiveness, for they are the original cause of those promises, and all promises of mercy are immediately conjunct unto, and dependent on, the mercies in God's nature, even as all particular rivers depend upon the universal ocean, from which they all come, and into which they run, as Solomon tells us, Eccles. i. 7, and each of them have the whole sea to maintain and feed them. And as they flow also into the sea, and every vessel, small or great, that floats in any of those particular rivers hath an open passage into the main, keeping to the course of that river, so is it here between the mercies of God, the ocean, and the current of promises of salvation, and the faith of a believer. And in this case there is that privilege which often falls not out in such as we have alluded to, viz., that the smallest rivulet of salvation running in the promises may bear up a vessel of mercy, and may be for his supply, if he thinks or finds he wants water, and sticks in the deeps of mire and quicksand. The believer's faith hath the freedom and liberty to suck and draw in the ocean of God's mercies, to draw (if it were possible) the whole of the sea itself to make a full stream for its support, and to help it off aground, and to help its being borne aloft above all mire of temptations. Nor are there any stints set how much or how little it may let in ; and to confirm this, why should not faith as well have this immediate recourse, in and with the promises whilst yet unperformed, unto these essential mercies aforehand, to bestow and give forth the things promised, as well as after in thanksgiving, when we have received the mercies as performed unto us, we bless God for them, and we celebrate all those essential mercies in God as the original and immediate causes of them ? Thus Nehemiah did, Neh. ix. 17–20, &c. The great return which the Gentiles, and all the nations in the world, are said to bring unto God (when converted by the gospel), as the richest present of thankfulness, is set out by this, ' to glorify God for his mercy,' Rom. xv. 9. Now there is the same reason for one as for the other, and we shall find that, in the exercise hereof, and treating with God thereby, there will flow in upon our souls an abundance of strength and consolation, even spring-tides of them, to fill the channels of the promises, and also of our hearts, that give themselves up to them.

Use 2. I shall yet farther, by way of use and application, enlarge this head, by adding, that this comprehension or intuition of the mercies in God's nature will also prove a great persuasive and encouragement to a bringing on an hope in men's souls, an hope of God's willingness to pardon themselves in particular. And this is a matter of great moment, it being found, in ordinary and common experience, that whilst humbled souls are helped so far on in their way of believing as to acknowledge the truth of God's intentions in the promises of forgiveness, and the reality of the performance to some or other, yet still they stick or waver whether God be willing to pardon them in particular. Now, whatever other encouragements unto such a soul others will allege, whereof there may be many, yet I shall insist on this one, and that alone, it lying in my way, and being suitable to the design of my discourse; that if God but possesses and fill thy soul with an ample and enlarged apprehension of the mercies that are in himself, this will create withal an encouragement to thee that he intends good to thy soul in particular. As the flood, when it rose higher and higher, did lift up together with itself the ark, so an inuring thy soul to those comprehensions will insensibly elevate and raise up thy soul to a confidence that God doth intend all good to thee. Look, as if one that is timorous, and unused to travel in great waters, should be set in never so safe a vessel in the midst of the sea, or great overflow, where he saw himself environed about with nothing but waves, he would fear his being drowned and cast away; so, on the contrary, if you set the most weak and fearful soul in the full view and prospect of God's mercies, and the vast ocean thereof, that he sees neither shore nor bottom, this poor but otherwise tumbled soul will soon take heart and courage to itself. For,

1. The full and clear revelation of any divine truth in a way of subsistence to a man's soul, doth leave some application of itself to a man's soul. And if a discovery be made of good things, the manifestation thereof doth usually leave an encouragement in the heart that they belong and appertain unto one's-self. The very manifestation that God makes of them (when God makes it) carries so much engraven in it. As this is found true in experience, so that definition of faith, Heb. xi. 1, 2, confirms it, even that the main of faith lies in a conviction of the substance of the things themselves, which, when it is made in the abundancy of the object revealed, the very sight and presence thereof is that which mainly draws in the heart to apply it, and cleave and adhere unto it for its ease in particular. The truth of this might be abundantly made out, and it holds good in the particular point before me in a more especial manner, by how much the infinite sweetness of God's mercy hath a magnetic or a loadstone virtue in it, by alluring (as Hosea's phrase is, chap. ii. 14) to attract and draw in the heart unto them, and cause men to think that they may come to have a part and portion in them. Whilst they deeply consider that there is such an height and depth of mercy, a bottomless gulf in God's heart, it induceth the soul to cast anchor within the veil, as mariners do their anchors in the bottom of the sea blindfold; which anchor is an hope of mercy for a man's self, upon what he clearly as yet sees not to belong unto him.

2. For the confirmation hereof (besides this general ground) I observe, that when God himself doth set himself to draw men unto him, to turn to him, and so to believe and lay hold on his mercy, and would persuade them thereunto, the most efficacious course he takes is, in the most ample manner that may be in the first and chief place, to possess the hearts of those he addresseth his invitations unto of those infinite riches of grace that are in his heart and nature only in a general declaration of them only, whilst yet, in applying of them and of the promises to the persons, he is pleased to give but imperfect intimations and suspensive discourses of what he will do for them in particular. That one instance in Joel ii. 13, 14, may sufficiently serve for many others; for the thing he there instantly exhorts unto is this, ' Therefore also now, saith the Lord, turn unto me with all your heart,' &c. But what are the encouragements or invitations by which he would induce them to it? What grounds doth he propose unto their faith? They are two. The first and great one is, the royal declaration of the mercies that are in the nature of God barely proposed, and it is the same

in the very words with that of his old and first proclamation, so often repeated throughout all ages (which he will for ever abide by), Exod. xxxiv., for so he begins, ' For he is gracious and merciful, slow to anger, and of great kindness, and repenteth him of the evil.' 2. There are and use to be in the word more particular promises, wherein he far more utters what his will and resolution is for shewing mercy unto those whom he speaks to. Now, indeed, you will find that some promises are also annexed hereunto in this his exhortation, and both intended to provoke them to believe and turn to God; but I beseech you to observe the vast and strange difference; that is, the manner of his declaring the first and the latter.

The first, viz., magnific description of his nature, he utters in the fullest and most enlarged, absolute, assertory way that possibly might be. He proclaims that with open mouth, and speaks plainly without reservation or hesitation. That magnific description of himself he utters with open mouth in the fullest and amplest manner that possible might be; but the second, viz., the promise made to the persons, and the things promised, he is pleased but to mutter (as I may so speak), and concerning this he says no more but, ' Who knows if God will repent and leave a blessing behind him?' He is sparing and reserved, you see, in this way of the declaration of his will: yea, and elsewhere, the hope he gives as to this part is yet more slender; for but to an ' It may be,' Amos v. 15; Zeph. ii. 3; yea, but to an ' If there may be hope,' Lament. iii. 29. To say that ' there is hope,' gives us a sight but afar off; but to say, ' If there may be hope,' gives a far more uncertain sound. Yet this is what God doth in this sort of declaration concerning what his will in promises to these persons lets fall to them.

By all which we may clearly see that it is the certain and clear conviction and evidence of the grace in God, though joined but with such promises that speak but indefinitely, and contain but imperfect obscure hints and intimations, and that give but a slender hope (as one would give of good will to a man in his particular) that it is this conviction which hath the strength and attractive influence in it, and is sufficient, with those promises, to draw in the soul to cast itself upon God, and to hope in his mercy. And this inference from that fore-mentioned passage in Joel is strong and clear; for it must not be denied that God, in those treaties and proposals to men, did apply himself to work faith in them, and accordingly gave forth what was most effective, at least sufficient, to beget faith in men's hearts, and to bring them in to him. And further, it must be owned that the great God (the proposer here), knowing our frame, and what it is wherein the unbelief in men's hearts doth mostly lie, did therefore apply himself, and frame his exhortations up of such things as would be most effective of faith in us, and best able to remove the contrary obstruction of unbelief. Now, we plainly see that in these passages he spreads the plaster thickest and deepest with that medicinal salve, viz., of the display of the mercies of God's nature, and but thinly with that other of suspensive intimations of his good will to the persons in the promises annexed. And therefore that which is the most hardened core of unbelief in us, must be understood to consist chiefly in the doubting of the plenteousness and fulness of mercies that are in him to pardon us. This is the great and deep ' sore of men's hearts,' if men would but know it in themselves, as Solomon speaks, 1 Kings viii.; and the virtue and influence of this sovereign plaster mentioned is it which doth dissolve that core and work of the devil; and in our believing of these things of our God it is that the main stress of faith doth lie (though men discover it not), and in that point their faith needs most to be strengthened and relieved, rather than in the other. And this one thing apprehended once, though but with slender half promises of that mercy to us, which are but intimations rather than promises, will yet be abundantly effective to persuade the heart, and beget in it a good hope through grace of mercy for itself, and thereupon to come in and turn unto God, who thereupon will reveal himself in other promises more fully to his soul.

CHAPTER XV.

That God, considered as justifying the ungodly, is the object of faith.—How we may be said to be justified from eternity.—In what sense it is to be understood that we were justified upon the resurrection of Christ.—How we are said to be justified when we believe.

Who shall lay anything to the charge of God's elect?   It is God that justifieth.—Rom. VIII. 33.

In seeking justification, our faith must have recourse to God, as justifying also. Thus in the words of the text it is expressed, 'It is God that justifies.' And upon this the apostle builds his confidence, as well as upon that, that Christ died. Therefore we find, that as Christ dying, so God as justifying is made the object of faith; Rom. iv. 5, 'That believeth on him that justifieth the ungodly' *i. e.*, who believeth on God the Father, imputing Christ's righteousness to persons ungodly. And therefore you shall find that the righteousness we are justified by is called as often 'the righteousness of God,' as of Christ: thus Rom. i. 17, 'The righteousness of God is revealed from faith to faith;' for as faith looks at this righteousness as purchased by Christ, so appointed by God, and bestowed by him, and imputed by him : 2 Cor. v. 21, 'For he hath made him to be sin for us, who knew no sin, that we might be made the righteousness of God in him.' We see Christ there to be the meritorious cause of that righteousness, for his soul paid for it. But his Father was the original cause of all, for he made him sin for us, and he makes his righteousness ours. It is called 'the righteousness of Christ,' as he is the worker of it; but 'the righteousness of God,' as he is the appointer and imputer of it. So Rom. iii. 25, 26, it is called 'the righteousness of God' for a double reason; because God sent forth and appointed Christ, ver. 25, and because he is the justifier by it, ver. 26. It is called 'the righteousness of faith,' as the apprehender of it, Rom. iv. 13. It is called 'man's righteousness' (Job xxxiii. 26, 'He will render to man his righteousness'), because it was extended to him, and paid for him. Yea, let me add this farther, that God justifying is the main and ultimate object of your faith. Christ, though he is the first and next to you, yet God is the ultimate, in whom faith rests. Therefore believers, 1 Pet. i. 21, are said 'by him to believe in God, that their faith and hope might be in God.' Thus, as the promise brings you to Christ, so Christ brings you to God.

The reason of this is, because God hath as great a hand in justifying you as Christ; yea, he is the principal in it: 2 Cor. v. 18, 'And all things are of God, who hath reconciled us to himself by Jesus Christ, and hath given to us the ministry of reconciliation.' Therefore in the matter of justification, Isaiah liii. 11, God calls him his servant; ' My servant shall justify many.' It was God against whom principally our sins are committed, and unto whom the satisfaction of Christ was paid, and by whom it was ordained, and by virtue of whose decree it hath power to justify. As the value of it to justify us depends on the worth that is in Christ, so the acceptation of it for us depends upon God's will; ' By which will ye are sanctified through the offering of the body of Jesus,' Heb. x. 10. It is the will of God, spoken of before, which Christ came to accomplish. It was God that appointed the persons for whom Christ died, and Christ, as Mediator, put not in a man, but whom his Father gave him; and then the great blessing of pardon comes to be bestowed. God guides, and directs, and orders the bestowing of it, and sets his hand to the act of grace, ere pardon comes down. Christ's merits have their efficacy to justify us *ex compacto*, from agreement between the Father and the Son; for though the merits are in themselves superabundant, ὑπερεπλεόνασε, 1 Tim. i. 14, the apostle therefore shewing how the righteousness of Christ is more to us than Adam's sin, tells us also that free grace must put in before it can be accepted for us, Rom. v. 17.

There are two things in justification.

1. The righteousness imputed; and that is Christ's, and to him we go for it.

2. The act of imputation, the accounting it mine or thine; and that is the act of God primarily.

Justification is attributed as much to free grace as to Christ's righteousness, for both are joined: Rom. iii. 24, 25, ' Being justified freely by his grace, through the redemption that is in Jesus Christ: whom God hath set forth to be a propitiation, through faith in his blood, to declare his righteousness for the remission of sins that are past, through the forbearance of God.' Therefore faith looks as much to free grace ordaining and imputing, as to Christ performing. In a word, God's free grace is the original, Christ's righteousness is instrumental to the manifestation of free grace, and faith is the instrument of apprehending all; and yet God still is in all, 2 Cor. v. 18; and Christ is ' all in all,' Col. iii. 11. And faith, as it is our act, is nothing at all in our justification, but only as it apprehends all.

Now, for a direction concerning God justifying as the object of your faith, you are to consider all the acts and ways of God justifying, and to direct you to a right conceiving of God as justifying, you must know that there are *tria momenta*, or three stages of motion in this way. I do not say that there are three parts of justification itself, which, as it is applied to us, is *actus individuus*, an individual act; but three several steps, three paces and progresses of God, as I may call them; though, in respect of the materials which justification consisteth of, it is *actus totalis*, an entire act, a complete discharge from all sin, and a perfect investiture with the whole righteousness of Christ. God pardons not the debt by halves, nor bestows Christ's righteousness by parcels, but entitles us to the whole in every of those moments of justification: yet, in regard of our investiture into this, there are several pauses, or several iterations of this act; as in passing over an estate in land, when the deeds are drawn, written, and sealed, there is a title or interest given into the whole estate; and then again, when possession is further given, it is not an interest into any new parcel, but both convey the whole estate; yet they may be called several acts of conveyance, and of title and admission into it: and such several acts of investiture of us into this whole grace of justification were performed towards us by God, which go to the accomplishment of it. This also answers to the distinct works of the three persons, who, as they have a distinct hand in the whole work of redemption, so also in this main point of our justification.

1. The first progress or step was at the first covenant-making and striking of the bargain from all eternity. We may say of all spiritual blessings in Christ what is said of Christ, that their ' goings forth are from everlasting.' Justified then we were when first elected, though not in our own persons, yet in our Head, as he had our persons then given him, and we came to have a being and interest in him. ' You are in Christ,' saith the apostle, and so we had the promise made of all spiritual blessings in him, and he took all the deeds of all in our name ; so that in Christ we were ' blessed with all spiritual blessings,' Eph. i. 3 ; as we are blessed with all other, so with this also, that we were justified then in Christ. To this purpose is that place, Rom. viii. 30, where he speaks of all those blessings which are applied to us after redemption, as calling, justification, glorification, as of things already past and done, even then when he did predestinate us : ' Whom he hath predestinated, them he hath called, them he hath justified, them he hath glorified.' He speaks it as in the time past. Neither speaks he thus of these blessings as past simply in regard of that presence, in which all things stand before him from eternity, all things both past, present, and to come, being to him as present. Nor doth he speak it only in regard of a resolution or purpose taken up to call and justify, he ' calling things that are not as if they were,' Rom. iv. 17. For thus it may be said of all his other works towards the creatures in common, that he hath created and preserved them from everlasting. But in a more special relation are these blessings decreed said to have been bestowed, because, though they existed not in themselves, yet they existed really in a Head that represented them and us, who was by to answer for them, and to undertake for them, which other creatures could not do ; and there was an actual donation and receiving of all these for us (as truly as a feoffee in trust may take lands for one unborn), by virtue of a covenant made with Christ, whereby Christ had all our sins imputed unto him, and so taken off from us, Christ having then covenanted to take all our sins upon him when he took our persons to be his ; and God having covenanted not to impute sin unto us, but to look at him for the payment of all, and at us as discharged. Of this seems that place, 2 Cor. v. 19, evidently to speak, as importing that everlasting transaction, as I have shewn,* ' God was in Christ reconciling the world unto himself, not imputing their trespasses unto them ' ; i. e., not imputing them then, when he was reconciling us unto himself in Christ. So as then God told Christ, as it were, (for it was a real covenant), that he would look for his debt and satisfaction of him, and that he did let the sinners go free ; and so they are in this respect justified from all eternity. And indeed, if the promise of life was then given us (as the apostle Paul speaks, Titus i. 2), then also justification of life, without which we could not come to life. Yet this is but the inchoation, though it be an estating us into the whole tenure of life.

2. There is a farther act of justifying us, which passeth from God towards us in Christ, upon the payment and performance by Christ at his resurrection : for Jesus Christ (who as he was one with us by stipulation

---

* In his discourse of Christ the Mediator, Book i. chap. i. in vol. iii. of his works·
[Vol. V. of this edition.—Ed.]

before, so then by representation), at the time, the fulness of the time of payment appointed (which the apostle therefore calls the ' due time,' Rom. v. 6), came into the world as our surety, and as representing our persons, as Adam once did ; and at several payments, for three and thirty years and upwards, at last finished all at his death, and laid down the last payment when he laid down his life and his body in the grave, sin and the curse all the while holding him in bands as a debtor : but at that instant when he arose, God then performed a farther act of justification towards him, and us in him, admitting him as our advocate, into the actual possession of justification of life, acquitting him from all those sins which he had charged upon him.   Therefore we read, that as Christ was made sin in his life and death, so that he was justified also, 1 Tim. iii. 16.   After he had said, that he was ' manifested in the flesh,' *i. e.*, the likeness of sinful flesh, he says, he was ' justified in the Spirit,' when by the power of that eternal Spirit he was quickened, and so declared to be that righteous one with power ; at which time, as he vindicated himself before men, of all those imputations laid on him by men, as being an impostor (which, when he was under the curse, he lay under, but now was justified to all the world), so also before and by his Father he was discharged, and justified also from all those debts he had before charged him with, as now having fully paid the utmost farthing, and so received him up into glory, as it follows in that text.   I say then, in the same sense that God made him sin, in the same sense he is said to have justified him ; and therefore, Heb. ix. 28, it is said, he shall at the latter day ' appear without sin ;' implying, that when he appeared here, he appeared with sin : therefore there was a time when these sins were taken off, and the first moment of it was when he rose from under that state of humiliation (whereof the last part was his lying in the grave), and when he began to enter upon a glorified state, which was at his resurrection.   And that he should be thus justified, is not spoken of him abstractly considered in himself, but as he hath us conjoined in him, and as he connotates us ; this new title to life, and of being righteous, he entered not upon for himself alone, but he was an attorney, took possession, and was admitted for us, and we by him as our advocate ; which I take to be the meaning of that place, Rom. iv. 25, ' He died for our sins, and rose again for our justification.'   When he died, then he paid our debts, and God received from him the price, and therefore the matter of justification is indeed the merit of his obedience and death ; but at his rising, then the formal act and deed of discharge was delivered to him by God, and that for our justification : ' He rose for our justification.'   And our justification is attributed to his resurrection, not only because he rose again to apply it, but principally in this respect, because at his rising he received it for us, for he being justified then, we were justified in him : and therefore, as justification in respect of the matter imputed is attributed to his death and blood (we were justified by his blood) so the formal imputation of it to us ; may be ascribed to his resurrection, when the discharge of all was reckoned to Christ.   And in this respect, when the apostle would shew them the benefit and necessity of Christ's resurrection in respect of themselves, he says, 1 Cor. xv. 17, ' If Christ be not risen, your faith is in vain, ye are yet in your sins,' *i. e.*, that although Christ died for your sins, and you had faith in that his death to be justified from your sins, yet this faith would be in vain, and neither it nor Christ's death would justify you ; and your title to justification were nothing worth, if Christ be not risen : for though you did believe, and could say the money was paid for you, if

Christ had not risen to take delivery and seisin of the estate in your names, your plea would have been made void, the formality of justification being wanting. Now all this argues that our justification hath a farther dependence upon his resurrection than merely as to working faith, and that he rose not only to give us faith, but that supposing we could have faith in his death, yet without his resurrection it had been in vain. For indeed this present state of our justification by faith depends upon that fore-passed justification of his in our stead then ; and as when he ascended we ascended with him (and therefore we are said now to ' sit together with him in heavenly places,' Eph. ii. 6), so when he was justified we were justified also in him ; and as it may be said, Adam condemned us all, and corrupted us all, when he fell, so did then Christ perfect us all, and God justified us all, when he died and rose again.

3. But these two acts of justification are wholly out of us, immanent acts in God ; and though they concern us, and are *towards us*, yet are not acts of God *upon us*, they being performed towards us, not as actually existing in ourselves, but only as existing in our Head, who covenanted for us, and represented us : so as though by these acts we are estated into a right title to justification, yet the benefit and the possession of that estate we have not without a farther act to be passed upon us, whereby we have not as existing in our head only, as a feoffee in trust for us, as children under age, this excellent grace given us, but are to be in our own persons, though still through Christ, possessed of it, and to have all the deeds and evidences committed to the custody and apprehension of our faith. We are in our own persons made true owners and enjoyers of it, which is then done at that instant when we first believe ; which act is the completion and accomplishment of the former, and is that great and famous justification by faith which the Scripture so much inculcates, and almost only mentioneth ; yea, and so speaks of it, as if we were not justified at all till then : so 1 Cor. vi. 11, ' Such were some of you ; but now ye are sanctified, now ye are justified :' which before they were not ; and therefore the apostle speaks of a *now* of justification, being ' now justified,' Rom. v. 9, that is, ' now we believe,' ver. 1 ; and so ver. 11, ' By whom we have now received the atonement,' because though it was given in Christ afore for us, yet then only we receive it ; and therefore before faith the Scripture pronounceth the very elect, even those whom Christ died for, ' children of wrath as well as others,' till they believe, Eph. ii. 3. So as when we are said to be justified by faith, it is not only because then faith apprehends that justification that was in God's breast before, and that then we are justified merely *foro conscientiæ*, though before we were so *in foro Dei*, as much as ever (as some express it) ; but further it must be said, that even *in foro Dei*, in God's court, and according to the judgment of that open court which God hath set up in his word, and according to the proceedings of his word (which is the rule he professeth to judge men by, and therein he keeps to the rules of his word, as Christ says, ' I judge no man, but the word I speak shall judge you,' John xii. 47, 48), God doth judge, and pronounceth his elect ungodly and unjustified, till they believe ; yea, and by the Spirit of bondage he testifies to their consciences, that before faith they are ungodly, unjustified, and children of wrath. If it were not a real truth, the Spirit of truth would not evidence this to them : so, therefore, when we are said to be justified by faith, it implies more than a justification in our consciences, and causing us to apprehend our justification ; for upon believing there is an act passeth from God which makes a real change

in our estates, from a state of ungodliness to an estate of justification; which is a real moral change, as truly and as really as sanctification is a physical change, and that not only in our apprehension and judging of ourselves, but in the course of God's proceedings of judgment upon us; that whereas before, he, by the rules of his word, which he keeps to, would and must have proceeded with us as persons ungodly, out of Christ, now according to those rules he doth pronounce us just, and we come actually to have a real claim, title, and interest, according to course of law, as we say, in justification, which till now we were debarred of.

But the question may be put, How could they be said to be justified afore, both from eternity and in Christ, if they may be truly said even in God's judgment to be justified but now, and that they were till now unjustified?

The answer is, That these seeming contradictions, in divers respects, are both true.

1. That before God, according to the rules of his word, which are the rules of his proceedings before men, being God's revealed will, they are as yet unjustified; but according to those secret passages of his secret will transacted with Christ, and to which he is privy, they are justified persons before him.

2. Though the person abstractly considered is always justified before God, yet the person concretely taken, as invested with, and remaining in an estate of unbelief, is in relation to that estate, according to the rules of his word, unjustified; so as the change is first and primarily in regard of the state of the person from unbelief to faith, and then it looks towards the person himself.

3. Their justification before faith, *coram Deo*, in the sight of God, is of them not as actually existing in themselves, but only as they were represented in their head; for their persons, as considered as represented in Christ, did in him, as their head, receive justification, and all blessings else, but not in themselves do they receive them actually as existing until faith; as we are said then to be condemned and corrupted in the first Adam, when he sinned, as representing us, but we are in our own persons not actually corrupted till we exist and are born from him. So as to conclude this, they are said before faith to be justified in Christ by representation only, and not as in themselves. They are said to be in themselves actually justified through Christ after faith, but they cannot be said to be justified of themselves without Christ, neither before nor after faith. At the closure of these three advancements and passings forth of our justification, take these two observations concerning them all.

Obs. 1. That each of these being in and through Jesus Christ, who is our righteousness, and so they all depend upon him, therefore these three progresses of God going on to justify us, depend upon three several acts of Jesus Christ, which as he puts forth, so doth God also answerably put forth a new step in this work.

(1.) When Christ did but undertake for us, and took by covenant our sins off from us, and indented with and entered into bond to God for our debts, God then discharged us in his secret purpose; and knowing Christ able and faithful, expected all from him.

(2.) When in the fulness of time he had performed what he undertook, as Christ did a new act, so did God also therein justify both him and us.

(3.) When Christ by his Spirit knits us to him, and works faith in us, to look towards that satisfaction and justification wrought for us, then doth God put forth another act (and it is the last act, and the accomplishment of all), and pronounceth us righteous in ourselves through him.

Obs. 2. All these acts of justification, as they depend upon Christ, so upon our being one with Christ; and look what kind of union there is, answerable is the act of justification passed forthwith. From all eternity we were one with Christ by stipulation, he by a secret covenant undertaking for us; and answerably that act of God's justifying us was but as we were considered in his undertaking. When Christ died and rose again, we were in him by representation, as performing it for us, and no otherwise; but as so considered we were justified. But now when we come in our persons, by our own consent, to be made one with him actually, then we come in our persons through him to be personally and in ourselves justified, and receive the atonement by faith.

BOOK II.

The second object of faith, Jesus Christ.—Of our being drawn to him by the
Father, and our treating with him for an interest in his person and salva-
tion by him.—That Christ as God-man in one person is the object of our
faith.—That as a spiritual Messiah and Saviour he is propounded to our
faith.—That not only Christ in his person, but in all that he hath done
and suffered for our salvation, and now doth for us in heaven, is the object
of our faith.

CHAPTER I.

That the mercies in God's nature are not the object of our faith, but as they
are considered together with Christ.—That God's mercies and Jesus Christ
are accordingly propounded jointly to our faith.

THERE are two grand objects our faith doth act upon, God the Father and
Jesus Christ; the Holy Spirit being the person who anoints us, generally
teaching us all things.   Our Saviour Christ therefore, John xvii. 3, having
spoken of giving eternal life to them that believe, superadds, ' This is eternal
life, to know thee' (the Father), ' the only true God, and Jesus Christ, whom
thou hast sent;' thereby setting forth them two as the objects which our
faith and knowledge are carried out unto for eternal life; which eternal life
is begun in this world by the knowledge of faith, and perfected by the knowledge of sight in the world to come.

That which in the Father our faith doth specially act upon, are the riches
of his grace; and free grace is indeed, and in reality, but the love of God
in election, though uttered in absolute promises and declarations, yet expressed indefinitely as to persons.   God indeed absolutely declareth in the
promises and covenant of grace what his heart was and is unto an elect
company, but conceals the persons (which promises I therefore term
indefinite), thereby ascertaining us that there are some of mankind he so
loves resolvedly and unchangeably, whom he intends therein; which promises shall infallibly take hold on them.   And that covenant and those
promises I call absolute, because they promise to give the very conditions
required to salvation in that covenant.

The other object of our faith is Jesus Christ, both in his person and his
suffering, death, resurrection, intercession; and likewise the benefits that
are the fruits of all these.   And our faith is to aim at the having fellowship with him in all these, as the object of faith, as well as the free grace
of God the Father.   In all which benefits which our faith seeks from these
two, I might quote many scriptures, wherein Christ and the free grace of
the Father are still joined, and go hand in hand.   I instance particularly

in justification for all the rest, in which there is both the grace of the Father and the righteousness of the Son, that concur both thereunto; and our faith is distinctly to exercise itself upon both these, for obtaining justification. This conjunction you see in Rom. iii. 24, 'Being justified freely by his grace, through the redemption that is in Christ Jesus.' You have it also in Rom. v. 15, 'The grace of God,' that is, of God the Father, and 'the gift by grace' (the gift of righteousness and justification thereby) 'which is by one man Jesus Christ, hath abounded unto many.' And again he says at verse 17, 'They which receive abundance of grace, and of the gift of righteousness,' &c.—a righteousness by which we are made righteous, ver. 19. There is both the grace of God in the heart of the Father, and there is the gift of righteousness by grace, 'which is by one man Jesus Christ,' as by whose righteousness we are made righteous; and these concur to our 'justification of life,' as it is termed in verse 18. Now, there being these two grand objects of the faith of all believers for the first benefit they are brought to seek at first, all converts under the gospel are therefore brought to a distinct communion and fellowship (through faith) both with the Father and also with the Son, to obtain both grace and righteousness from both, and afterwards in the course of their lives they enjoy a distinct fellowship with both Father and Son: 1 John i. 3, 'These things I write to you, that you may have fellowship with us: and truly our fellowship is with the Father, and with his Son Jesus Christ;' with these two objectively is our fellowship transacted. The Holy Ghost is he who, 1 John ii. 20, is styled the 'anointing' of us and our eyes, to converse with these, and by whom we 'know all things;' but our fellowship is objectively with the Father, and with his Son.

In the old covenant there were two grand utensils placed at the uppermost end of the holy of holies (which the believing Jews had their eyes upon whilst they looked towards the holy temple), the ark and the mercy-seat. The ark was the type of Christ's person; the mercy-seat, as the apostle denominates it, Heb. vii., was the type of God's grace joined with Christ's person, as atoned and made propitious by Jesus Christ; for the word in the Hebrew signifies expiation, which alone was made by Christ, but imports therewith pardoning mercy through his expiation; and so it respected at once both the grace in God atoned, and also Christ; who is therefore, Rom. iii. 25, styled 'the propitiation for our sins.' And yet withal that propitiatory hath the name of mercy-seat given it by the apostle himself, Heb. ix. 5, by which name our translators have therefore, in Exodus xxv. 17, rendered the Hebrew. Thus it was in the type; and the thing signified thereby is that throne of grace whereat Christ officiates, as the same apostle in substance styles it, Heb. iv. I cite it to shew that these two, ark and mercy-seat, were immediately and inseparably conjoined together, and the one set upon the other; as if you should set two plain chests one on the top of the other immediately, and nothing between. The mercy-seat was uppermost on the top of the ark, as you read Exodus xxv. 21; this being imported thereby, that all the grace in God's heart flowing to us is through Christ, and as supported by Christ, and his mediation and expiation, so as it is God's grace and mercy as in Christ. And unto these two the eyes of the believing Jews were cast, and had their expectation fixed for grace and mercy, as appears by the instance of that humbled publican—'Lord, be merciful to me a sinner'—whose coming to the temple to worship, as it doth shew him to be a Jew or Jewish proselyte, so the word wherein Christ forms that his petition is Old Testament language, as of one who, looking towards the propitiatory or mercy-seat, prays to God to this effect, 'Lord, be mercifully propitious to me from thy mercy-seat;' which in gospel language is 'from thy throne of grace.' And furthermore observe, that these two were both of a like size and proportion, as long, as broad, as deep, the one as the other (Exod. xxv. 10, 17 compared), to shew that however the essential grace and mercy in God's nature is essentially infinite, yet his dispensatory mercy and grace laid up for us, and intended towards us sinners of the sons of men, are of the same extent and commensuration with Christ, and his merits and righteousness, &c., because all that grace which God hath intended to bestow upon us, for the matter, manner, or measure, is but commensurable, and of like extent, with all that Christ purchased and procured, and is no more nor no less. As also because that these two must never be separated; for God hath conjoined them thus closely and immediately one to the other, only God's grace is uppermost, and the fountain of us, and Christ, and all; and the glory of it is the supreme end of all, Eph. i. 5, 6. Some converts indeed more distinctly, and withal amply and abundantly, have their hearts run out sometimes to God the Father, and pursue after the attainment of his love and grace, and have their hearts drawn and set more largely to treat with the Father, and his grace, and to seek the obtaining more frequently the manifestations of his grace, and have their hearts more intent upon what his work for their salvation in his heart is. They consider that it was he who first decreed Christ, and our salvation through him, and called Christ to die for us, and gave us to Christ, &c., and with a peremptory and unchangeable love ordained the salvation of some through faith and holiness ; and accordingly they desire to have the manifestations of his grace made forth upon their souls. But others have the Lord Jesus Christ in their eye, and treat with him through his death, redemption, and the works which he performed towards it, in a more large and abundant manner. But though his heart goes out thus more amply to Jesus Christ, and hath communion with him and his righteousness, yet he believeth also on God the Father, that ordained and sent his Son out of his grace, and believes on him as the pardoner of his sin. And, *è contra*, he that hath communion with God the Father in seeking his love, he doth it in Christ impliedly, as through whose mediation he hath access unto the Father. But still the eyes of either may be more setly and wistly set, and fixed upon one of them, as on Christ, or the Father, more explicitly than on the other. It is what the apostle intimates, 1 John ii. 13 (I cite it to this very purpose, to shew that sometimes the heart of one Christian runs out more to the Father, and at other times more to the Son), 'I write unto you, fathers, because you have known him that is from the beginning.' Who is that? Jesus Christ; chap. i. 1, 'That which was from the beginning, which we have heard, which we have seen with our eyes, which we have looked upon, and our hands have handled of the word of life:' that is apparently Jesus Christ. Then again, says he, 'I write unto you, little children, because ye have known the Father.' Here the spirits of the one run out at differing seasons, sometimes more to God, sometimes more to Jesus Christ. I will not stand to explain whom he means by fathers, and whom by babes, nor need I do it as to my purpose ; it is enough for the present that it is ascribed to the same sort of persons at different times, that when they were babes, they knew the Father ; when fathers, they knew Christ more intently. The reason of which different intentions of our spirits is, that our souls are narrow vessels, and use not to be intent on two so eminent objects at once, which therefore take their turns in our hearts, that we take in sometimes the one, and sometimes the other.

There must also be allowed a great variety of God's method herein. The apostles, though living under Christ's ministry, yet their faith had acted a long while on God, far more than unto Christ, of whom then they had but the Old Testament notions and conceptions, though they believed he was *he*, the Messiah already come : John xiv. 1, ' Ye believe on God, believe also on me.'   And so it is now with many Christians, who at first have recourse to Old Testament promises, which speak of grace and mercy in God for pardon of sin, through a promised Messiah, and so treat with God for their salvation ; and though they do it with an intermingled knowledge of Christ, yet not so much applying themselves to him.   And the reason is, because it is God in whose name the arraignment for the guilt of all our sins is in Scripture drawn.   And therefore the nature of the thing, when we are convinced of sin, calls for it, and we apply ourselves to him, whose grace and mercy is to forgive us : and repentance being that grace, which in a special manner is called for towards God, Acts xx. 21, hence, therefore (though with imperfect actings of faith, and hopes of mercy from God), it is taken for granted, that it is in and through Christ, in whom God alone is merciful.   Though, according unto John the Baptist's ministry (who directed to believe on Christ, in the close and issue of it), we come to Christ at last, yet at first we attend far more unto repentance towards God ; but God leaving us unto a failure of comfort from the evidences thereof (as to our discerning them), the Father sets our hearts agoing unto Jesus Christ amain, as sensible how much we had neglected him, and his interest in our salvation ; and he sets us a-work to seek and look for justi-fication from him with might and main ; and then to come to God himself again for mercy.   But there are others who at first dash do believe and fasten on Christ at the work of humiliation ; as the jailor (in Acts xvi. 31, where his first conversion is recorded) comes to Paul trembling, being struck with a sight of, and terror for sin, and cries out, ' What shall I do to be saved ?'   The apostle puts him upon Jesus Christ at very first : ' Believe,' says he, ' on the Lord Jesus, and thou shalt be saved.'   The apostle took the shortest course with him ; and thereupon his heart entertained the Lord Jesus.   But then read on the story at verse 34, and you will find that his believing on Christ brought him to God ; for it is said, ' He rejoiced, believing in God, with all his house :' whereby was answerably fulfilled that of 1 Pet. i. 21, ' Who by him,' namely Christ, ' do believe in God, who raised him up from the dead, and gave him glory, that your faith and hope might be in God.'   And Rom. v., shewing the fruits of faith, how that ' being justified by faith, we have peace with God, through our Lord Jesus Christ,' ver. 1.   And going on to other effects of faith, the last fruit he mentions is in ver. 11, ' Not only so,' says he, ' but we also joy in God, through our Lord Jesus Christ.'

CHAPTER II.

That when we come to Christ, and believe on him, there is a concurrence and consent of all the three persons in the Godhead unto that great work.

No man can come to me, except the Father, which hath sent me, draw him; and I will raise him up at the last day.
And he said, Therefore said I unto you, that no man can come unto me, except it were given unto him of my Father.—JOHN VI., 44th and 65th verses compared.

I design to prove from these words, that as Christ is the object of faith, so, when any soul is converted, and drawn to believe on him, there is the concurrence of all the three persons in the Trinity to that work, and that they all put forth conjointly a renewed act of agreement in it. I confess in this text there is mention only of the Father, and his consent in it, for indeed it is hard for me to take a text that will hold forth all three persons together; but in this chapter you have all three. You have the Father's consent here in these words, ' No man can come to me, except the Father, which hath sent me, draw him.' You have the Son's consent, ver. 37, ' Him that cometh to me, I will in no wise cast out.' And you have (as some interpret it) the Holy Ghost's also at the 63d verse, ' It is the Spirit that quickeneth, the flesh profiteth nothing; the words that I speak unto you they are spirit, and they are life,' though I think by spirit is there rather meant the Godhead quickening the human nature of Christ. This is a subject of great and weighty moment, and will be of use to you many ways to quicken your hearts. I will first open and prove it to you, and then make use of it.

When God doth convert and draw our souls on to believe, we use to look upon the work itself as a great work wrought in ourselves; and it is true, as I shall after shew. But there is more done for us in heaven than is done in our hearts at that time. At that great union which is made between Christ and the soul, and the drawing on of the heart to close with Christ, there is a special council called; there is a concurrence, a consent, a joint meeting of all three persons to this great work, and that in a special manner. Though they concur in all works, yet where a council of them all is professedly called, there is a plain note and character of a more special and remarkable concurrence. Thus, at the making of man especially, they are all named: as you read in Gen. i. 26, that when God made man, he called a council: ' Let *us* make man,' saith he, and all the three persons did concur and join in that great work. Now, at the making of the new man there is the like council held; there is the Father, Son, and Holy Ghost. The Father draweth, the Son accepteth, and the Holy Ghost is the instrument of both, and quickeneth and enliveneth the heart. Such a great conjunction is a matter of infinite wonder. If you look into the heavens, you shall not see great conjunctions of planets every day. There hath been but seven since the creation itself, and the creation itself began with one of them. But here is a greater conjunction in the heaven of heavens, when there is an influence of all the three persons into a soul at its first turning to God.

There are four great conjunctions (as I may so speak) of these three persons.

1. The one was from everlasting, at our election, in which both Father, Son, and Holy Ghost had a hand.

2. The other was at our redemption, when Jesus Christ himself was sealed up to be the son of God; and at his baptism the Father from heaven appears and owns him, and the Holy Ghost descendeth like a dove and lighteth upon him. And there was the Son of God, the second person, dwelling in the human nature. Thus did all these three meet together at that time. And upon the cross likewise they did the like, for the Father's hand bruised him; therefore he cries out to him, 'My God, my God,' &c., but all that while the Holy Ghost supported and upheld him, and he was filled with the Spirit beyond measure for strength to stand under the weight of the Father's wrath, for no created strength could have done it. And he himself also, through the eternal Spirit, the Godhead dwelling in him, offered up himself as a sacrifice to his Father, Heb. ix. 14.

3. The third conjunction of them is, when faith is wrought, when the sinner is called to Christ, which I am now to speak of.

4. The last conjunction is in heaven, when God and all the three persons shall be all in all for evermore, which is the great conjunction indeed, and to which all the rest tend, and where they all centre.

I remember, in Acts xiv. 27, faith is called 'the door of faith.' Truly there are three keys to open this door, and they are severally in the hands of these three persons of the Trinity, and they all concur and bring their keys with them when the heart is opened and the soul is drawn to Christ.

Though I dare not say that faith on our part is always explicitly a marriage act, or that the soul did at first take Christ under the nature and consideration of a husband explicitly so considered, yet the thing in itself, in the nature of it, is a marriage, and it is the solemnisation of the greatest marriage that ever was but one, and that was when the human nature and the Son of God were married together, whereby that man Christ Jesus became the natural Son of God. Now at this marriage all the Trinity are present; and although Christ is offered to the soul at other times in the preaching of the word, yet now he is actually given and bestowed. The souls of all believers were given to Jesus Christ from everlasting, John xvii. 6, and Jesus Christ was given for thee upon the cross; but when thou comest to believe, and God cometh to reveal Christ in thee and for thee, then he is actually given to thee even by the Father.

That I may express it to you, and tell you what great things are done in heaven for you when your hearts are drawn to believe, and then make it out when I have done,

1. Let me tell you, that when your souls are first turned to God, and when you believe, though perhaps you know neither the time nor the thing I now speak of, yet notwithstanding even at that time, first God the Father riseth up in heaven (as I may so express it), and as Jesus Christ said to his mother when he hung upon the cross, ' Woman, behold thy Son,' so saith God the Father, ' Son, yonder is a soul which I gave thee from everlasting, which thou diedst for upon the cross, and now is the fulness of time come for to have mercy upon that soul, go take him and own him for thine, and actually now possess him.' This you have here in John vi. 37, ' All that the Father gives me shall come to me.' Here is, you see, a giving before our coming, and it is a giving *de præsenti*, at present, to distinguish it from that of everlasting; a deed of gift made, and that by the Father; an actual delivery and seizin, whereby the soul is put into the hands of Jesus Christ. And the Father likewise, he whispers to the heart

of the sinner, woos the soul to come to Christ; and therefore the 43d verse
saith here, that 'they shall be all taught of God,' that is, the Father; and
that 'no man can come unto Christ except the Father draw him,' ver. 44.
It may be thou art at church, or in the assembly of the saints, and there
thou hearest the word preached, and perhaps standest in the crowd mingled
among many others; or it may be thou art at home, and there art weeping
and bewailing thy lost condition; saith God the Father unto Jesus Christ,
'Son, behold thy spouse; behold yonder soul that stands in such a place,
I will marry you two before such time as this soul stirs out of this place.'
It is as if a king, when his son comes into an assembly, should rise up
from his royal throne, having spied out a beggar all in rags standing in the
midst of the crowd, and should say, Son, yonder is your wife, go and take her
and marry her here presently before me. So it is here; for there is none
comes to Christ but those to whom he is thus given. And then Jesus
Christ is glad that the hour is come; This is the joyful day (saith he), that
I have long expected; and so he goes and embraces that soul, though perhaps the soul knows not this.

2. Our Lord and Saviour Christ knows all his by name, John x. 14, 15,
which place indeed is very emphatical; for he saith, that look as the
Father knows him, and as he knows the Father, so he knows his sheep,
and is known of them (for known of them he shall be in the end), and he
knows them all by name. And when the Father hath thus commended
and actually given a soul unto him, Jesus Christ looks upon that soul, and
thinketh with himself, Yonder soul I should know; that is the soul that
my Father presented unto me in all that beauty from everlasting, which I
now am to be the author of, and must bestow upon it. Ay, but doth
Christ know the soul in all her sins? Yes; and by a good token (saith he),
I should know that soul though in her sins, for I remember she was brought
to me in all her sins, when I hung upon the cross to die for her; and together
with her was the catalogue of these very sins presented to me when I was
in the garden, and when I hung upon the tree. And what doth Christ now
do? He apprehends this soul (as the apostle saith, Phil. iii. 12), takes it,
and takes it as commended unto him actually by the Father: 'That I may
apprehend,' saith Paul there, 'that for which I am apprehended of Christ
Jesus.' He had spoken before of a race which he was to run; now, saith
he, Jesus Christ took me by the hand when I entered into this race. It
may have an allusion to that, or it may allude to the mother's apprehending the child in the womb, which she doth, though the child apprehends
not her. However, this is certain, that he speaks of conversion and
entrance into the race of Christianity; and that before we apprehend Jesus
Christ, he apprehends us, and takes us upon the gift of his Father as his;
even as we love God because he loved us first, so we apprehend Christ
because he apprehends us first. And Jesus Christ doth this with the
greatest gladness that can be; for as he longed to die for all our souls
('Now is my soul troubled,' saith he, John xii. 27, and 'for this cause
came I unto this hour'), so when the fulness of time is come that the
Father hath appointed for him to receive a soul, how glad is he of that
hour! If he sits in heaven expecting when his enemies shall be made his
footstool, how much more doth he expect when a soul which he hath loved
and paid so dear for shall be brought unto him.

3. And then when the Son hath thus owned and acknowledged this soul
anew, the Holy Ghost, who is the third person, and who is privy to God's
election, and to the heart of Jesus Christ when he died, and knows for whom

he died, and had a hand in all, he is sent down from heaven by Jesus Christ: Gal. iv. 6, ' Because you are sons' (sons by election), ' God hath sent forth the Spirit of his Son into your hearts, crying, Abba, Father.' And as there was a fulness of time, and when that fulness of time was come (as it is verse the fourth), ' God sent forth his Son, made of a woman, made under the law;' and as the Holy Ghost did come and overshadow the Virgin Mary (as you have it in Luke), and did unite that man, that beginning of an infant (how shall I express it ? for Christ was in the womb as we are, as small and as little as we are), as there was a fulness of time in which that nature was formed by the Holy Ghost, and was united to the Son of God, so there is a fulness of time whenas the Holy Ghost, thus sent by Jesus Christ, having taken and apprehended the soul, cometh down into the heart. In Isa. liii. 1, the Holy Ghost is called ' the arm of the Lord;' and why is he called so ? but because he is the arm of the Son of God by whom he takes hold of the soul. Now this Spirit, when he comes down thus into the heart, works eyes, and feet, and hands, and all for to look upon Christ, and to come to Christ, and to lay hold upon Christ ; for faith is expressed by all these: by seeing of him, and coming to him, and receiving him, and laying hold of him. And faith is eyes, and hands, and feet, yea, and mouth, and stomach, and all ; for we eat his flesh and drink his blood by faith. It is compared to all the members, for the new man is originally nothing but faith. Thus now, as Jesus Christ takes hold of us, so by the work of the Holy Ghost we come to take hold of him ; and we embrace him, as the phrase is in Heb. xi., and we embrace him gladly, as it is in Acts ii. 41.

And all three persons having thus severally and apart agreed together in it between themselves, the Father beginning the business in commending us to the Son, and the Son sending the Spirit into the soul, and the Holy Ghost working grace in us, he leads us from one person to the other back again. And therefore in our coming unto God, you have all the three persons mentioned together : Eph. ii. 18, ' Through him we have access by one Spirit unto the Father.' Here is Christ, Father, Spirit. The word there which we translate *access*, in the original it is a conduct, a leading us by the hand, προσαγωγὴν ; for as Jesus Christ took us, and took us by the hand as it were, and led us into that race, and took hold of us by his Spirit, so what doth the Spirit do ? He leads us by Christ to the Father, for we come to God by and through Christ, being led in the hand of the Spirit. Thus the soul comes to have communion with all the three persons, fellowship with the Father, and with the Son, and with the Holy Ghost, till this fellowship is perfected in heaven. And though you see not these things, though you see not what the blessed Trinity do for you then at that time when you believe, as that the Father thus gives you to Christ, and that Christ himself apprehends you, and that the Holy Ghost is sent down into your hearts, and takes you by the hand thus, and carries you back again through Christ to the Father, yet all these things are done, and they are done for you ; and when God causeth your souls to close with the Lord Jesus, they are thus transacted in heaven for you.

I will give you some instances of this in the conversions of men in the New Testament, and I will take Paul's first ; and although his story has this extraordinary in it (which indeed is all the privilege he had in this above us), that Jesus Christ appeared visibly from heaven unto him, and the Holy Ghost likewise in a visible manner fell down upon him ; and the story tells us distinctly, that Christ and the Holy Ghost did thus and thus appear in

it, and in that I say the story is extraordinary ; yet notwithstanding whatsoever was done at his conversion by God the Father, and by Jesus Christ,
and by the Holy Ghost visibly, the like is done by the three persons between themselves invisibly at the conversion of every soul that is drawn to
believe in Christ.   For in matter of redemption, and of salvation, and of
conversion, and of faith, and the like, the apostles themselves had no privilege which we have not.   Now we see how all three persons met at his conversion.   First, in Gal. i. 15, you have the Father ; he had appointed a time
when he meant to give Paul to Christ, and to reveal Christ unto Paul.
Mark the phrase, ' When it pleased God' (that is, when the time was come),
' who separated me from my mother's womb, and called me by his grace,
to reveal his Son in me.'   When it pleased God, saith he, *i. e.*, God the
Father, for he saith, it pleased God to reveal his Son in him, so that it
was he who appointed the time, and who at that time began anew to act
for him.   And though God had Paul in his eye from his mother's womb,
yet there was a time appointed to call Paul in, and until then (saith he in
the verses before), I lived as other Jews ; but then when it pleased God,
namely, God the Father, to reveal his Son in me, then it was thus and thus
with me.   Here now is God the Father.   You shall see likewise the second
person, Jesus Christ, coming in.   When Paul was journeying towards
Damascus, Acts ix. 6, Christ from heaven appears to him, and thus speaks
to him, 'I am Jesus whom thou persecutest; arise, and go into the city,
and it shall be told thee what thou must do.'   And as Jesus Christ himself
speaks to Paul, so likewise Christ goes and speaks to Ananias : verse 11,
' The Lord said unto him in a vision, Ananias, arise, and go into the street
which is called Straight, and inquire for one called Saul of Tarsus.'   You
see both that Christ knew Paul fully, and took notice of him, and knew
him by name ; and so he doth every soul that is turned to him.   And he
names the house too, he vouchsafeth to do so ; ' Go,' saith he, ' and inquire
at the house of Judas.'   This was to shew what notice he takes of all
circumstances when a soul is converted to him.   And he tells Ananias likewise what Paul is doing : ' Behold,' saith he, ' he prayeth,' he is mourning
and bewailing his condition.   And he takes notice too of his election, and
under that notion sends Ananias to him : ' He is,' saith he, verse 15, ' a
chosen vessel unto me.'   You see how withal he orders every circumstance.
Thus now you have, first, the Father appointing the time, and at that time
putting forth his act,—' When it pleased the Father to reveal his Son in
me,'—and you have the Son likewise appearing from heaven to Paul, telling
him that he would send Ananias to him (so verse 12), and appearing to
Ananias likewise, and telling him that he must go to Paul.   Now, at the
17th verse, you have the Holy Ghost, the third person, for he in a visible
manner falls upon Paul when Ananias came to him, and had laid his hands
on him.   Here then, in this instance of Paul's, you have all three persons
concurring in this great work.   Now that which was thus acted in this
extraordinary and visible manner towards Paul in his conversion (I mean
visibly by the Son, and by the Holy Ghost), the like is done invisibly, that
is, undiscernibly to thee.   Paul's conversion had a pattern in it, and it is
a pattern of the extraordinary conversion of the Jews his countrymen, who,
it is thought, shall be called after the same manner, and it is most likely
they shall be so.   But yet, notwithstanding, if you take that in this conversion of Paul's, which is the privilege of all believers, namely, to have
then the joint consent of Father, Son, and Holy Ghost, so far his conversion
is a pattern of all conversions, and of the work of faith in all God's people

to the end of the world. And do but mark it, that which was done here visibly, in the conversion of Paul, and by express direction from heaven, is in effect oftentimes done as plainly in ordinary conversions here below. You shall find a soul guided by a secret providence to go to such a church to hear such a man. Though it is true indeed he is not directed by an extraordinary revelation, as Paul was to Ananias, yet moved and guided he is to go to such a place, and there he goes, he knows not why ; and when he is there, God directs the minister to speak that to the soul which shall most nearly concern it, even as in a vision he directed Ananias to speak to Paul what concerned him. Now when he hath brought the heart and the word thus together, by his providence (for what he did then visibly, he doth now by his providence) the Holy Ghost falls upon the heart, and draws it to Jesus Christ.

You shall find the like in the story of Cornelius, Acts x., which likewise is an instance of the same thing. While Peter was speaking those words, namely, preaching of Christ to him, for, saith he, verse 43, ' To him give all the prophets witness, that, through his name, whosoever believeth in him shall receive remission of sins.' While Peter yet spake these words,' saith the text, ' the Holy Ghost fell on all them which heard the word.' And you have the same story repeated again by Peter himself, Acts xi. 15. ' As I began to speak,' saith he, ' the Holy Ghost fell on them.' And as the Spirit fell on them thus in their hearing the word, so Christ himself bade Peter go, for he had a vision from heaven, and the Lord spake to him to that purpose. Here now is both the Son and the Holy Ghost visibly concurring in the working of faith, yea, of that distinct degree of faith which Cornelius had to believe evangelically, though he had a faith before in the Messias to come. Now look what extraordinarily the three persons did thus in heaven, and from heaven by revelation then, the same thing, though in an ordinary and in a secret invisible way, doth the Holy Ghost, and the Son, and God the Father, now do for all souls that are turned to Christ. They do by a secret providence guide thee, and cast thee to live in such a family, and there thou receivest this and that instruction ; or they guide thee to such a ministry, or to such a passage of Scripture, and then the Holy Ghost falls on thee. Jesus Christ hath as much hand in this, and the Holy Ghost as strong a hand, and it is as great and strong a fruit of the eternal decree of God, as it was to Paul and to Ananias.* Though many do not know the time of their conversion, yet by the story of it you shall have as strange and as extraordinary providences of God, in bringing them to the means of comfort, and the means of comfort to them, and in bringing them to the means of faith, and setting it on upon their hearts ; and you shall herein have as strong a providence as this was of speaking visibly from heaven to Paul and Ananias. And the reason of it is plain ; for what is our calling and believing ? It is but the acting, or rather fulfilling, of election ; and accordingly it hath the name of election given to it oftentimes in the Scripture. Now what the three persons did at thy election, the same is done when thy soul is called and believeth ; though perhaps thou hast not the knowledge of the time when, much less of the thing, yet all this is done for thee, and that in heaven, when God doth draw thy heart first to believe.

* Qu. ' Cornelius' ?—Ed.

CHAPTER III.

The uses of the doctrine.—We should consider faith on the Lord Jesus as a matter of the greatest importance, since all the persons of the Godhead concern themselves in it.—We should not neglect this great business of believing.—We should glorify all the three persons for the great things which they do for us at the time of our believing.

The doctrine which I have explained and proved in the former chapter, affords us these great and useful inferences.

1. You see that salvation is no slight thing, and that believing and turning to God is no slight matter, when all the three persons do thus concur in it. The converting and drawing of a soul to believe is a business of infinite moment; and why? Because all heaven, and all hell, and oftentimes earth, or much on earth, are stirred about it, even as they use to be at great transactions. What a stir there is in the spirits of men when a great transaction falls out in state affairs! There is much more in this. All in heaven are stirred, for you have seen that the three persons move in it; and Christ tells us there is joy in heaven even amongst the angels when a soul is turned to God. And all in hell are stirred about it too, for all the devils rage and come forth, and are all in arms. The strong man, when he is bound and cast out, is in a rage, and therefore pours forth all the floods of persecutions, and disgraces, and temptations, and violence upon the soul. And earth is stirred about it too, for you shall have carnal friends and companions, and this world, stand amazed at it, and think it strange, as the apostle saith. Herein the soul is conformed to the image of Christ himself. When Christ was born, they were all stirred at it. Heaven was stirred at it, for the Father sent the Holy Ghost down; and the angels came and sung the news of it, and the shepherds come and bring the news of it; and 'Herod was troubled, and all Jerusalem with him,' Mat. ii. 3, Luke ii. It is a great business, and God gives evidence of it that it is a great business; for all heaven (I say), and earth, and hell are stirred when God doth thus bring a soul home to Christ.

2. We therefore should not neglect the great business of salvation, nor the time of God's stirring of us. Though God offers Christ at all times in the ministry of the word, yet you never come actually to believe till all three persons thus concur in it, and till they join in a special concurrence together for your turning and conversion. Consider with yourselves, you that think you can believe and repent when you will, can you call this great council together in heaven? Can you appoint God the time when it shall be done? No. 'It pleased the Father,' saith the apostle, 'to reveal his Son in me.' It is the Father draweth, and it is the Son that must take hold of you, and it is the Holy Ghost that must come down into your hearts. And it is not in man's power to call this great assembly together, thus to join votes together. Is it in the power of subjects to call the three estates, of king, and both the other estates when they please? No. So neither is it in the power of any creature to call together this great council of heaven. You may as well order the conjunction of the stars, and call the planets together when you will, which is impossible, Job xxxviii. 31. He speaks under the very allusion that I now mention it for: 'Canst thou bring forth Mazzaroth in his season? or canst thou guide Arcturus with his sons?' He meaneth stars, which have these several names given them.

'Knowest thou the ordinances of heaven? Canst thou set the dominion thereof in the earth?' that is, canst thou appoint when the stars shall meet, and by their conjunction have great influences upon men? can you go and set that clock? No, saith he, you must wait upon God at his time to do it. When therefore the Spirit of God moves you, then think, Now I will follow, and now it may be is the time that God will reveal his Son to me; and because thou knowest not the time, therefore, I say, wait upon God at all times. Though God in the ministry of the word offers at all times, and stands ready to bestow (if thou couldst come) faith upon thee, and to draw thy heart, and actually to bestow Christ upon thee, yet for this there is a fulness of time, a special time, which thou must wait for, even as the world waited for the fulness of time when God should send his Son in the flesh. This conjunction is not towards the elect at all times, it is but then when the fulness of time comes in which God means to turn them. And this is the reason why the elect, though they are moved often beforehand, and have many motions in their hearts, yet there is not an effectual faith wrought till such a time appointed by the Father. And this should make no man neglect, but stir him up rather, because salvation is so great a business, and the time is not in our own hands. Canst thou move God to give his Son to thee actually when thou wilt? Or canst thou move Jesus Christ to come and take possession of thee when thou wilt? Or canst thou move the Spirit of God to come and give thee faith when thou wilt? No; all these are in the gift of the three persons; and no man receiveth anything except it be given him from above, John iii. 27. Therefore you should wait upon the Lord, and observe his time, and that with fear and trembling (if I may so express it by the contrary). They that serve the devil, as conjurors and witches, wait for the falling of fern seed, as they call it, night after night, when it is told them it is in the possession of such and such angels; which, when they have got, they think they can do great wonders by it. Are they in this dependence upon their head, Satan, that damneth and undoeth them? How should we then wait upon God for the droppings and influences of heaven, and for the sending of the Holy Ghost into us to work faith in us?

3. Thou that art a believer, do but look back upon the work in thy conversion and turning to God; though perhaps thou canst not tell the time when it was done, yet it may be thou canst tell when it was not done. Do but think with thyself (I say) what great matters were done for thee in heaven, when thou wast first brought to Jesus Christ, which it may be thou never takest notice of. Perhaps thou hast been searching into the work of God within thee, and thou hast done well so to do; and it may be thou hast seen and took notice of the great difficulty of that work, and what a great many lifts were put to thy heart, and a great many knocks, before such time as it was driven home to the Lord Jesus. But hast thou withal considered that there was as great things actually done for thee then in heaven as when thou wast first chosen, or as when Jesus Christ hung upon the cross? The Father, Son, and Holy Ghost were all set on work to make up the marriage between thy soul and Christ; and they all set providences on work to that purpose. If a condemned man were not to have a pardon till three kings met, and there were no more but three kings in the world, and these must all concur together for the sealing and signing of it, how would he value that pardon! Thou lookest, it may be, on the difficulty of the work in thine own heart only, and how thou wentest from one ordinance to another, and what rubs there were in the way, and thou hast

considerations what was done upon earth in thy own heart; but look up higher, and consider what was done in heaven as the original of all, and let that be the thing for which thou praisest and blessest God. Go home, and down upon thy knees, and thank these three persons that have done all this for thee, though thou sawest it not, when thy heart was first drawn to Christ. For God doth give thee assurance, that all the three persons concur, 1 John v. 7, 8. There is the Father from heaven, and the Son, and the Holy Ghost, and all these give a testimony; and the truth is, a testimony is to be had distinctly from all these apart, for the apostle would never have mentioned them there unless the witness both of the Father, Son, and Holy Ghost was to be given apart; even as water, and spirit, and blood are distinct, though they all concur, so are the witness of all these three persons in giving assurance.

I have known them who, when they have been turned to God, have looked back upon the greatness of the work to be such, as that for ten hundred thousand worlds they would not have it to be done again. Why? For fear it should not be wrought. I would not have you to do so, for that God who did work it out of his eternal love, he repents not, and therefore he would do it again if it were not done, or if it were to do again, so well he loveth you. Only in this imitate them, to set an high price and value on it, and consider that ere this match was made, the Father said *Amen* in heaven, and the Son said *Amen*, and the Holy Ghost said *Amen*, before ever thy heart said *Amen*. And withal consider that all the three persons are likewise engaged, and will everlastingly carry on this work.

4. You see the reason why, though the gospel is preached, and sets forth Christ the great object of faith, yet all do not believe. Our Saviour resolves it even into this, that the three persons do not concur in the doing of it, as you may observe it here in John vi., ver. 36, 37, ' I said unto you,' saith he, ' that ye also have seen me, and believe.' What is the reason? Look the next words, ' All that the Father giveth me shall come unto me;' and the reason why you do not come is, because my Father hath not bestowed you upon me. And therefore he goes on in like manner, ver. 44, ' No man can come to me, except the Father draw him;' which he brings in to answer the murmuring of the Jews (for, ver. 41, it is said they murmured amongst themselves), and to shew the reason why they did not believe; ' No man can come to me,' saith he, ' except the Father draw him.' And so likewise afterward, ver. 64, he gives the reason why, when he had twelve disciples, yet one of them believed not: ' For Jesus knew from the beginning who they were that believed not, and he said, Therefore said I unto you, that no man can come unto me, except it were given unto him of my Father.' You shall see it evident, saith he, amongst yourselves, all among yourselves do not believe. Why? Because those only believe that are drawn by the Father, and are given to me by the Father, and to whom the Father doth give power to believe.

5. Therefore by this also magnify the free grace of God in calling you, and in working faith in your hearts. Do not only consider that you had the three persons thus concurring, but likewise that they have called you out, and not others; and that though the same gospel is preached to others that is preached to you, who come and hear the same sermons which you do, yea, and it may be their hearts are mightily moved by the Holy Ghost, yet thou hast faith wrought effectually in thee, which is not in them. What is the reason? Because that was done in heaven for thee by all three persons, which was not done for them; and they were not given to

Jesus Christ by the Father, and therefore he did not give his Spirit effectually to dwell in their hearts. By this consideration also magnify the free grace of God.

CHAPTER IV.

Of a believer's being drawn unto Christ by the Father.—The reasons why it is the proper work of the Father to draw the soul unto Christ.

No man can come unto me, except the Father, which hath sent me, draw him : and I will raise him up at the last day.—John VI. 44.

The subject I have next afore me is, a believer's being drawn to Christ, and that by the Father, and the soul's treating with Christ for its salvation. My assertion is, that Christians are to make it one great exercise of their faith distinctly to treat with the person of Christ for their salvation, as well as with God the Father through Christ : and this, as at their first conversion to obtain salvation, so afterwards all along in their lives, to maintain fellowship both with the Father and the Son. But I shall first discourse how it is the Father who teacheth us to know Christ, and draws us to him; and also shall shew how the Father teacheth.

1. I speak not of the working the principles and habits of faith, the hearing ear, and the understanding heart; but of the actings of faith, which the Father draws out in the soul towards Christ.

2. I limit it not unto the actings of faith at first conversion, but I mean those which are continued all a man's life long, which are all ascribed to the Father, as well as those at one's first conversion, as in Mat. xi. 25–27 you find it, where all that is revealed of the Son is ascribed unto the Father. And indeed, at our first conversion, our treating with Christ is eminently for pardon of sin, and justification, which are the usual inducements of our first coming to him. But that is too narrow, for Christ, in the whole latitude of him, in his person, and in whatever belongs to him, is that which the Father goeth on to teach us all our lives long.

3. I yet limit it to the attainments by faith of recumbence (a sort of faith which is common to all Christians), and my reason is, because in the text it is that faith whereof he speaks, which all shall be taught. And so in Isaiah liv. 13, and in Jer. xxxi. 34 (which two are the prophets which our Saviour here refers to, speaking in the plural), the promise runs, ' They shall be all taught, from the least to the greatest.' I shall not therefore speak of that faith which only some particular Christians arrive to, as faith of personal assurance, accompanied with joy unspeakable and full of glory, for that is the Spirit's work, as he is the Comforter ; but I shall discourse of that faith which is common to all the children, as in Isaiah liv. 13 they are called ; and as salvation is called the ' common salvation,' Jude 1, so that act of faith is the act that is common to all Christians in all states, whereby the soul casts itself on Christ to be saved and justified ; and such is the apostle's faith said at first to have been, Gal. ii. 16. It is a believing in Christ, that we may be justified : ' We believed in Christ,' says he, ' that we might be justified.' So they began thus to treat with Christ, to have salvation from him. This is the faith which I intend, whereby I come to Christ (though I know not I am the person designed by him in his dying), my heart being drawn from its being taken with what it

knows of Christ in order to its salvation ; all which I plead to move him to receive me, and to plead which my heart is strengthened, trusting on him to obtain it.

4. I animadvert here about this faith of recumbency, that there may be many attainments in the course of this sort of faith, which every such believer arrives not at : so as my meaning is not that unless all and every one hath experimented in themselves all and every such actings, that they should not have a true faith of recumbence ; but my intent is to mention no other acts than what such a state and elevation of believing is capable of, and so may be attained by all, though their faith for their salvation rises not up to personal assurance, which much tends to the comfort of such believers, and serves to provoke them to seek those attainments.

5. I animadvert that I aim not to set down in a method these workings and actings of faith on Christ in such an order as to say this is first wrought, then follows that, and so a third; for God himself in his workings doth not always use one and the same method, but according to his good pleasure. God's ways of wooing us to his Son, and Christ's winning of our hearts to himself, are as the way of a man with a maid (as Solomon speaks of their wooings), various ; and as occasions lead on to their discovery, temptations being diverse, the discoveries which answer them are various. So as what I for my method's sake may handle first, God may have wrought last in thy soul; and what I shall mention last, or in the middle of this discourse, God may have wrought first in thee. But first and last such dealings of his as follow use to be transacted with us, and in us, in the way of believing.

6. When I limit it thus to faith of recumbency upon Christ, where may fall out many experiments I shall mention, which every particular person hath not yet attained to, who yet is a true believer ; for they are the experiments of a man's whole life in this way of treaty which I aim at ; yet some or other of these experiments will suit the lowest of all in that lower form. But however, though a man should continue all his days but a recumbent, he is yet capable of them at one time or another.

7. Into this drawing of our souls to Christ by the Father I shall not draw in the handling of the preparatory works ; as the work of humiliation for sin, contrition, self-emptiness, regeneration, and the like, which yet the Father, in drawing us unto Christ, maketh use of; but the work itself is properly the Spirit's, to whom our first regeneration is attributed : ' That which is born of the Spirit is spirit,' John iii. 6. This is also the effect of John Baptist's ministry, who baptized with the Spirit as with water, which Spirit did regenerate : Luke i. 16, ' Many of the children of Israel shall he turn to the Lord their God.' And in Isaiah xl. (in which chapter his ministry is prophesied of), the effects of it on men's hearts are expressly attributed to the Spirit : ver. 7, ' The Spirit of the Lord blows upon it;' blasting, through the sight of sin, all the excellencies that men glory in. And this ministry, as preparative to the actings of faith, must last to the end of the world ; for as Christ himself preached it, Mark i. 15, ' to repent,' in order to receiving the gospel, so, when he sent his apostles out, he gave this commission, that ' repentance and remission of sins should be preached in his name among all nations,' Luke xxiv. 47 ; that is, repentance in order to receiving remission of sins by faith. But the working the acts of believing, and to teach and instruct souls to come to Christ, this is the work of God the Father, and is my subject.

Obs. That to teach and instruct souls to come to Christ, and to draw them to Christ, is the Father's work; even as to make known the Father in his love and grace, so as to draw us to believe on him, is the work of Christ the Son. It is the honour our Saviour Christ hath given his Father in this text, John vi. 44, interpreting that great promise made to the church of the New Testament (Isa. liv. 13, that 'they shall be all taught of God') to mean, that it is God the Father who teacheth, and causeth souls to come to Christ himself; and he repeats it again, ver. 65 of this chapter, that none do come, 'unless it be given them of the Father.' We all know that all three persons do concur in every outward work, but yet so as some one work is more eminently attributed to one person, and another to another. And this of revealing Christ, and drawing to Christ, is more properly attributed to the Father; as to reveal the Father is attributed to the Son; and to reveal both Father and Son in the way of personal assurance, is attributed to the Spirit, who is therefore called 'the Comforter.' I shall give a scripture or two to prove it: Mat. xi. 27, 'All things are delivered unto me of my Father: and no man knoweth the Son but the Father; neither knoweth any man the Father, save the Son, and he to whomsoever the Son will reveal him.' And whereas you may object, that it is not there affirmed, 'none knows the Son but the Father, and he to whom the Father shall reveal him,' and that this last clause is not added in Christ's speech, the answer is, that there being that addition concerning the Son's knowing the Father, that 'none knows the Father but to whom the Son reveals him,' it doth by the law of parallels imply, that the like is also to be added to that of the Father's knowing the Son. But the second answer is, it is expressly affirmed before, and was the occasion of this his speech; for he had said, 'Father, I thank thee that thou hast revealed these things to babes.' And the things revealed were himself, and faith to lay hold upon himself; for he doth upbraid the city, that they had not entertained his ministry in his preaching the gospel; the substance of which was his preaching himself, and to believe on him, which those babes had received. And the apostle ascribes it expressly to the Father that had revealed it to him: Gal. i. 15, 16, 'When it pleased God, who separated me from my mother's womb, and called me by his grace, to reveal his Son in me, that I might preach him among the heathen.' He speaks eminently of God the Father's revealing his Son at his first call, which also the Father continued to do, and went on further and further to do all his life long; for it was to this end, that he might preach him among the Gentiles, which the apostle went on to do, and accordingly grew in knowledge, and in the revelation of Christ all his life long, that he might so preach him. You have the same, 1 Cor. i. 9, where the calling of us to fellowship with his Son is eminently attributed to the Father: 'God is faithful, by whom we were called into the fellowship of his Son Jesus Christ our Lord.' And his calling there is not only by commission, as when a man is called to an office, but operatively; and it is unto the whole fellowship of Christ, from first to last, that we enjoy. And it is the Father who is meant in both places, for he calls Christ his Son.

There is a great harmony in theological reason, why this working of faith in the soul to Christ, why this wooing work should belong to the Father.

1. The Father was he that chose our persons for his Son: 'Thine they were, and thou gavest them me,' says Christ, John xvii. 6. It was the Father that commended us to his Son at first, and presented us to his Son in all the glory of which Jesus Christ, if he would but take us and own us

to be his, should be the author. He did it to allure him, he did speak to his heart to die for us, as you have it, Ps. xl. 6–8, which is quoted in Heb. x. 7 : ' Lo, I come to do thy will, O God.' It is added in the psalm, ' Thy law is in my heart.' It was God the Father commanded him ; also it was he moved him to it, and drew him to it, to speak in the words of the text, and did write the very law of it in his heart, for the law written in his heart hath reference to his dying for us, and being mediator for us. He wooed him, and told him he would love him, if he would die for us : John x. 17, ' Therefore doth my Father love me, because I lay down my life.' Now then, who so fit a person as the Father to woo us, when we are to be won, and our hearts to be brought to Christ ? and to whom is it more proper to woo for his Son than the same Father that commends his Son to us ? And who is fitter also than the Father to move the matter to us, to teach us and instruct us, and commend his Son to us, and to draw us to take him, and to write this law in our hearts, as the greatest obedience we can per- form to him ? I speak not of the ministry of humiliation in that work going before, but of the wooing part, which is proper to God the Father.

2. Our believing is a receiving Christ ; it is a giving ourselves up to him as to our lord and husband, and it is proper for the Father to woo for him, because all other fathers have the power of bestowing their sons or daugh- ters, and therefore God hath it much more. Hagar, though but a woman, yet had a right, and exercised the power of getting a wife for her son. To give in marriage is oft spoken of in Scripture to be by parents, and thus it is here in Ps. xlv., where Christ is represented as the husband, and the church his wife. Who is it that speaks to the church, to love her hus- band, to worship her husband, and to forsake all for him ? It is God the Father : ver. 10, ' Hearken, O daughter, and consider, and incline thine ear,' &c. This is God the Father speaking of Christ unto his church. But you will say, This is not found amongst other fathers, that they should con- descend to woo the wife for their sons, but it is enough for them to give their consents, and leave it to their sons to gain the heart themselves. Thus it is amongst men, and the reasons for it amongst men are plain, which will not hold as to God.

1st, Fathers are strangers to the person whom the son is to woo, and so leave it to his liking ; it is enough for him to give his consent and leave to get the person's heart. But the case here is otherwise, for every elect soul is the daughter of God, even in election, before conversion ; and as he knows his Son, so he knows the soul, he knows his daughter too, not only as made his daughter by marriage to his Son, but as originally chosen by him. As Eve is said to be the daughter of God by creation, as Adam was the son of God by creation, Luke iii. 38, so it is here. Therefore he leaves it not to his Son only to speak for himself, and gain her, but he out of the same fatherly interest which he hath in the soul, as well as in his Son (though he hath interest in her as his daughter, which is a lower inte- rest than what he hath in his Son), wooes her.

2dly, Marriages amongst men stand upon equal terms, and persons of a like rank use to marry together ; and the father will not condescend in that case to woo for the son ; no, it were uncouth if he should, and not proper. But the church, and every poor soul, is the unworthiest creature to be matched so gloriously to Christ that ever was. Nay, it was an enemy before, an utter enemy, utterly averse ; so that it becomes a matter not only of love, but of grace and mercy, for to have this soul gained and brought in to Christ. And it is fulness of mercy and grace to woo such a soul, and an infinite condescension so to do, and none greater but that of God's giving his Son to die. And since it thus belongs to grace, the Father will have the honour of it as well as the Son, for you read of ' the grace of the Lord Jesus, and of the Father,' and sometimes both put together, 2 Thes. i. 12. Is it a matter of infinite grace, the person being so low and unworthy ? In that case, saith the Father, I will be your spokesman, for it is matter of grace. It is not matter of pure affection, as a husband hath to a wife, but it is a matter of grace which I have to such a soul ; I will therefore shew it in this my wooing such a soul. Oh this infinite condescension in the great God !

3dly, The Father doth engage to woo us to come to Christ, because he promised his Son when he wooed him to die for us, and gave us to him ; and he promised that when we came to be converted, he would give us, and would draw us to his Son : John vi. 37, ' All that the Father giveth me shall come to me ; and him that cometh to me, I will in no wise cast out.' Our Saviour Christ doth not speak like a wooer there, for all he saith is, I will not refuse them if they come. He hath indeed an hand in drawing the soul : ' When I am lifted up,' says he, ' I will draw all men after me,' John xii. 32, but he doth it secretly, and those thou hast given. But what is the meaning of those words, John vi. 37 ? It is resolved into this, that his Father, in giving them, promised they should come to him, and there-fore the Father draws them : and it is therefore the work of the Father. In Ps. cx., the Father speaks to Christ, and he promiseth there, that they shall be a willing people to him : ver. 1, ' The Lord said unto my Lord' (i. e., God the Father said to his Son, the great God Jehovah said to his Son), ' Sit thou at my right hand until I make thine enemies thy footstool ;' and I will destroy thine enemies for thee. And ver. 3, God the Father makes this promise to him, ' Thy people shall be willing in the day of thy power.' It is the Father's promise ; I will bring the will and heart of thy people off to thee, and thy people shall be willing in the day of thy power, when the gospel comes.

Use 1. Let us then encourage ourselves in the hope that the match is like to go on, if God the Father thus strikes in, and God the Son also. Hath God begun with thy soul to represent Christ to thee, to take thy heart ? Dost thou set thyself to seek him, to have him ? Thou hast not only thy husband Christ to draw thee, but thou hast his Father to draw thee ; and he is thy Father too ; and that match will thrive and must go on.

Use 2. Wouldst thou see and know who it is that is at work in thy heart ? (thou poor soul that lay at God day and night to give thee Christ, and have thy heart inflamed towards the Lord Jesus) dost thou know who it is that is at work in thy heart all this while ? Who ? It is the Father of our Lord Jesus Christ. Perhaps we have had little knowledge of this, to return the thanks to our God and Father of our Lord Jesus Christ, whereas indeed it is he does it. Thou hast not one degree of fellowship with the Son, but God the Father draws thee to it. ' Not that any man,' saith Christ, John vi. 46, ' hath seen the Father.' None seeth the Father while he is doing of it, for he doth it secretly, and doth not tell you, I the Father am drawing of you. No ; but still he holds up Christ to you, and Christ will come and tell you of his love afterwards. The Father does not come in to me here as an object of faith in his work. When he works, he doth not say, I am he that works it. He doth not come with authority and tell thee, I thy Father draw thee, but he is the efficient that draws, though he propose not himself objectively nor authoritatively. As Christ said to Peter when he washed his feet, 'What I do to thee, thou shalt know hereafter.' So God the Father comforts himself (if I may so speak) with this, or reserves this glory to himself, that we shall know one day what he is doing. 'In that day,' says Christ, John xvi. 25, 'I will shew you plainly of the Father.' The Father had wrought all this while, but secretly, and had not discovered himself; and though Jesus Christ in his doctrine had taught the apostles, and instructed them about the Father, yet, alas, poor creatures, they did not understand it! they did not take it in; it was but as a speaking to them in proverbs : 'But in that day' (after his ascension) 'I shall shew you,' says he, 'plainly of the Father,' ver. 25. What do I quote this for? To shew that though these poor disciples had heard say, it was the Father that drew them to believe, and they found the work upon them to be powerful and effectual, yet it was obscure to them that it was he that did it; but he tells them that the time cometh (which time must be after his ascension) when he would tell them plainly it was the Father did it. It was the Father, though now unseen, and spoken of in parables and proverbs, that drew thy soul in morning by morning; and thou wilt give all the glory to the Father one day : 'Oh what manner of love is it' (viz., of the Father), 'that we should be called the sons of God!' 1 John iii. 1. Oh what manner of love is it that the Father should woo us to be his children, and to receive his Son, and so to be his sons; for herein he 'gives us power to become the sons of God,' John i. 12. It is enough for other fathers to give consent, and leave it to their sons; but here in this case, as Jesus Christ came down from heaven to redeem and purchase his church and spouse, so God the Father comes down into the hearts of men, and draws them, and does it immediately. I do not say he doth it by his Spirit, as if himself did it not. It is true, the Spirit doth join in it, and so doth the Son, but the Father does this himself immediately. Is it not a mighty thing that the Father should teach us to woo his Son, and become a tutor to us and an instructor of us. What condescension would it be in kings to tutor their children. Poor creatures! we are no more able to woo Jesus Christ than the meanest country creature, one that walks up and down the streets in all rags and poverty, is able to woo a king; but the Father comes and teaches us to woo Jesus Christ, and makes representations of Christ to us. He made the match with Adam and Eve; and as Adam was his son, and Eve his daughter, he wooed her heart for him. And he who created her body and soul, and made her a woman, and gave Adam her heart, gives the heart of every Christian to his Son. You then that know the Lord Jesus, magnify the Father for ever, that hath called us to fellowship with his Son.

CHAPTER V.

That the Father teacheth us to know Christ as the great object of our faith.— That he instructs us that eternal life is to be found and obtained only in Christ his Son.—That he teacheth us to seek this life only in him.—That he teacheth us to look to the person of Christ, and to seek and desire an interest in himself, as well as salvation by him.—How God the Father teacheth us to know Christ his Son, and what are the effects which his instructions have upon us.

I come to the other part of my subject. As I told you it was the Father drew you to Christ, so the other part of the subject is this, That the Father teacheth us to know Christ, as the matter of his teaching, and instructs us in what concerns him that may woo us, and teach us to come to Christ. As he draws us, so he useth variety of cords, or motives, or persuasions, to draw.

I shall first shew what it is materially that the Father teacheth us, and then I shall shew you the manner how he teacheth. It were infinite to run over all the particulars concerning Christ that the Father teacheth. There is a great variety herein, and something takes hold on one man's heart, and something on another, as they are scattered up and down. All the doctrines which Christ delivered, that we read of in the gospel of John, and which persuade to come to himself, are all of them the words of the Father. ' The word which you hear is not mine, but the Father's which sent me,' John xiv. 24. And those words doth the Father himself speak inwardly to the soul of a man. It is a large field, to shew you what he teacheth concerning his Son Christ. I think it therefore the best way to give you what is said in one scripture, which expressly sets down what is the Father's record: 1 John v. 11, 12, ' This is the record, that God hath given us eternal life ; and this life is in his Son. He that hath the Son hath life : and he that hath not the Son of God hath not life.' This is the great record of God the Father concerning his Son ; and he that believes not the record God gives of his Son, makes God a liar. Here is the great doctrinal record summed up to you, and it is short and brief. But you may ask me, Was this record given to draw men to believe ? Is it so intended ? I answer, that though it intends assurance, yet it intends also the matter which God hath recorded to cause faith, and to bring men on to believe. This is plain from ver. 13, ' These things have I written to you that believe on the name of the Son of God, that ye may know that ye have eternal life, and that ye may believe on the name of the Son of God.' There is assurance : but suppose you want assurance, yet there is what may draw you to believe, ' that you may believe on the name of his Son.' It is to bring men on to believe ; and therefore in the words before he saith, ' He that believes not makes God a liar, because he believeth not the record God gave of his Son.' That which causeth them that believe further to believe, causeth one that doth not believe to come in to believe. It is not designed for them that have assurance. How is that proved ? Because the apostle saith, ' He that hath not the Son hath not life ;' and therefore what he speaks is to draw men on to believe. Let us see what things they are God hath recorded of his Son for to believe concerning him, that we who do believe may believe further.

1. The first record is, that ' the Father hath given us eternal life.' By us here is not meant only us that believe already, but it is as well intended to induce others to believe. He hath given us, i. e., us men ; he hath given amongst us (give me leave to express it) eternal life. As if a man goes to a college, they of the college tell him such a founder hath given us such a fellowship or exhibition, though every one is not capable of that fellowship or exhibition, but yet it is given to the college, and they all can say, it is given to us, i. e., to that body amongst us for such uses. Thus to give is taken plainly, John vi. 32, ' My Father giveth you the true bread from heaven.' He speaks to them that never did believe; yet, saith he, my Father gives to you eternal life; to you the sons of men, that grace, that mercy is given ' before the world began,' 2 Tim. i. 9. It is made known to all the sons of men to whom the gospel is preached, as that which is given amongst them ; and there are those among them which

hear this grace of the gospel to whom it shall be given effectually, and therefore it may well be indefinitely expressed, that God intends eternal life to the sons of men. This is a great thing in the heart of God, which God the Father doth reveal to a poor soul, that his whole purpose, intention, and resolution, which he will never be frustrated of, is to give eternal life unto the sons of men. This is his heart, his whole heart, and thus much of his heart he doth reveal of himself, that his purpose is in and through Jesus Christ to give eternal life, John. iii. 16. He hath given eternal life with the most serious purposes and unchangeable resolutions to the sons of men. Though he doth not tell you the names of the persons, and so declare who they are, yet he declares that he gives it to them that believe; therefore, you that hear it, believe and come in.

2. He says, I have given eternal life, but how must you have it? This life is conveyed to men in my Son (saith God), and by my Son, and there is no means else whereby you may have eternal life. Jesus Christ is the common receptacle of life eternal, for God hath made Jesus Christ his Son to be the fountain of life, to be the bread of God that should give life to the world : John vi. 33, ' I am the bread of life, that came down from heaven, and giveth life unto the world.' This life is only to be had in his Son ; and if you will have life you must go to him, for it is in him. God the Father did never vocally preach the gospel in the New Testament but once or twice, and then he spake from heaven himself, and not his Spirit ; and what said he? Mat. xvii. 5, ' This is my beloved Son, hear him,' i. e., take him, receive him, go to him. Well, though God doth not speak vocally now with an outward voice, but secretly in the souls of poor sinners, yet he says, This life is in my Son, there I have laid it; you cannot have it from me, but him ; he gives his flesh for the life of the world, and there is not anything else in heaven or earth will give you life ; nay, I can give you life no other way (i. e., according to his own appointment in the New Testament), but by having my Son. The soul sees it is not having grace, as humiliation, contrition, but it must have the Son if it have life. I have sometimes thought that if I had the life of grace in me, I had the Son; but it is contrary here, you must have the Son if you have life. You must not go to God for the righteousness of Christ only, and not go to the Son himself. You must do more, you must go to Christ for life : ' This life is in my Son,' says God. You must not go to God for Christ's sake only, but you must go to Christ. I do not say that you have no grace else, for you may have gone to him for his Son's righteouness, and for his favour; but yet you must take his person in too : John vi. 53, ' Except ye eat the flesh of the Son of man, and drink his blood, ye have no life in you.' The Father causeth souls to see a necessity of coming to his Son at last. If you could suppose you could give your body to be burnt, and had all faith, and knew all mysteries, all would be in vain ; if you have not the Son you have not life : ' Except you eat my flesh,' says Christ, ' you have no life in you.' The Father puts souls upon a necessity of going to Christ.

3. I observe, that the Father doth allow in his record that a man should out of love to himself seek life in Christ and salvation in Christ. He allows thee to go to him to be saved, for it is what God bids thee do, and prompts thee to it. His record doth declare it to thee ; nay, it is the first thing he mentions ; for before he tells you life is in my Son, he tells you, eternal life is given amongst you, and bids you seek it. The aim of going to Christ for salvation is an allowed aim by God the Father in the record

concerning his Son ; nay, he threatens you, that you shall not have life if you do not go to him : ' You will not come to me,' says Christ to the Pharisees, ' that ye might have life,' John v. 40.   Every soul that comes to Jesus Christ comes at first for life : ' We believed in Jesus Christ,' says the apostle, Gal. ii. 16, ' that we might be justified ;' it was a self-aim in them, you will not come to me to be saved ; this the Father sets on in a conviction to the heart, and he puts men on a necessity to come to Christ, and allows self-love in coming.   The argument is invincible, God in ordaining your salvation did ordain it chiefly for his own glory, and yet he had infinite love to you.   And doth this love of God to you stand with God's glory ?' Then certainly your aiming out of self-love at your own salvation stands with the glory of God in saving of you, and this is in order to believing.   But withal he tells men this, ' This life is in my Son.'   If you ask, Where doth it lie ?   It lies in my Son (says God), and in having him you have life, for eternal life lies not in anything out of the Son of God ; no, it lies in himself.   Therefore there is no danger in any man's seeking Jesus Christ for his own salvation, for he seeks it in Christ himself ; for if thou seekest happiness in the Son of God, and life in him, thou mayest make self-love thy aim as much as thou wilt, he is your life, Col. iii. 2, 3, and Christ lives in you, Gal. ii. 20.   People desire heaven ; do you know what heaven is ?   It is to live in God and with God for ever, and you place in God glorified above yourselves that happiness you seek.

4. He puts you upon seeking his Son, and puts you on coming for his Son, as that which above all concerns yourselves.   How is that proved ?   ' He that hath the Son,' saith he.   It is a powerful phrase, it is a marriage phrase.   To have him, to enjoy his person (says a poor virgin that truly loves him), is more than all.   I desire to have him to save me, to have him that I may have eternal life, but I principally desire to have himself. This is the record which God the Father gives concerning his Son, to draw men on to believe.

5. God the Father directs us to seek to have Christ as the Son of God, as well as [as] a Saviour.   ' He that hath the Son,' saith he, ' hath life ;' we must then come to him as the Son, and give up ourselves to him as the Son, as well as regard him as the author of life and means of salvation to us : it is not having the Redeemer only, but it is having the Son ; as he lives by the Father, so we live by him ; and as Christ says, ' My Father is mine, and I am his,' so the soul comes to be Christ's, and Christ becomes its salvation and life. Observe what the apostle says, Gal. ii. 20, ' The life I lead in the flesh it is by faith,' of two things, or of Christ considered in two notions, as Son of God, and as Redeemer, ' who loved me, and gave himself for me.'   If you rightly examine the story of the disciples' believing in Christ, recorded in the 1st, 2d, and 3d chapters of John, you will find that sometimes they say, they had found the Saviour of the world, sometimes they would say they had found the Son of God, and sometimes the Son and Saviour ; you are therefore to have him as Son of God, and to believe in him, and to love him as God loves him.   What doth God love him for ?   What, only because he died for you ?   No ; he loves him above all, because he is his Son.   Now you are to have the image of God's heart in your hearts ; you must have an heart after God's heart toward the Lord Jesus.   You love him because you come to him to be saved by him ; but if you love him as God doth, you must come to him as the Son, and love him as the Son, the glory of whose person is infinite.   This is the record God gives of him, that you must not only look at Christ as an ordinance to save you, but as

the Son. I do not say all this is done for a poor soul at first conversion, but this is the record God teaches you and will bring you to, viz., not only to seek his redemption, but to have his Son, and to have your hearts flaming in love after his Son.

Secondly, I come now to shew how God doth teach these things concerning his Son. Will you know how the Father teacheth, and when it is his teaching ? His teaching is not to teach you the doctrinals of salvation and of the Son, for he leaves that to ministers and to the Bible, to teach you the doctrinals only in a doctrinal way. But God the Father's teaching,

1. Is to bring the knowledge you have of Christ home to your souls, to say to your souls, Ps. xxxv. 3 ; to speak to your hearts, Hosea ii. 14. They all heard Christ's sermons, but ' those come to me,' says he, ' that have heard and learned of the Father,' John vi. 45. The Father doth not speak to us of his Son vocally, as I told you he spake of his Son to Adam (the giving of the ten commandments was by the ministration of angels), but he teacheth your hearts. What is the meaning of that ? Among all the notions which you have of Christ as the object of faith, if there is but one notion of Christ set home upon the soul (I call it an intuitive beam of light of the knowledge of Christ), that is the notion the Father teaches ; and all the knowledge thou hast otherwise is not the teaching of the Father, nor will save thee. No ; it is what he teaches thy soul, what he opens thy heart to receive, that is saving. If you would go to Christ with all the knowledge that notionally you have, and spread it before him, and woo him, it would not take effect ; but if thou feel such a light brought into thy soul concerning Christ that comes to thy heart, go to Jesus Christ with that one notion, and he knows his Father's voice in thy heart, and he accepts thee, and listens to thee. When a man comes to die that hath a great deal of knowledge, it is one little promise, one beam of light that comforts him, and he hath that instruction sealed to him : Isa. l. 4, ' He wakeneth morning by morning; he wakeneth my ear to hear as the learned.' It is a prophecy how God the Father taught Jesus Christ ; he did not know everything at once, but morning by morning he knew something still of himself. Thus the Father comes and awakens thine ear, and causeth thy soul to be attentive, and brings home something to thy soul ; thou mayest read the Bible all the day afterward, and not understand so much as to have it brought thus home, and thy heart awakened.

2. A second thing he teacheth : he doth take thy heart with what he saith thus to thee, by an intuitive beam. I compare this to the beams of the sun in a burning glass; as they burn the thing they fall upon, so this beam from God takes and inflames the heart. The poor disciples (Luke xxiv. 32) talked with Christ, and knew not that it was Christ, till ' he opened their understandings,' ver. 45, and then (say they) ' Did not our hearts burn within us ?' &c. There is an inflammation of the spirit, a taking of the heart, that accompanieth such teachings as the Father teacheth. A father's teaching imports affection, which doth draw : 1 Cor. viii. 3, ' If any man love God, the same is known of him ;' *i. e.,* is made to know God (so Beza and Austin read it), whom God hath made to know ; so that still when God teacheth, there goeth affection with it. As there he speaks of love, I speak of believing ; when the Father comes and teacheth, and brings in the light of Christ, then the affections, the will, the whole heart follow, there is longing, thirsting, eager desires.

3. The manner of his teaching is expressed, Eph. iv. 20, 21, ' If so be

that ye have heard him, and have been taught by him, as the truth is in Jesus.' He speaks of such a teaching as all Christians have, for he speaks it of such a teaching as makes them holy. It is spoken of Christ himself, of Christ properly, therefore he saith, ' as the truth is in Jesus.' The words are a plain distinction of a double knowledge. There is a knowledge which is not as the truth is in Jesus; but if you have been taught the truth as it is in Jesus, that is the Father's teaching, and that is his Son's teaching. Truly, if the gospel of John had been written before Paul writ this epistle, I would have said Paul had alluded to those words of John, for he hath all three words, *heard, read, learned of the Father.*

But you will say, is it a false knowledge which carnal men have of Christ, who are not taught of the Father? Truly, I say, it is not a true knowledge, it is false in regard it is not as the truth is in Jesus; it is not a fantastical knowledge, but it is a phantasmatical knowledge. Now what is it to be taught Christ as the truth is in Jesus? It is a real knowledge: 1 John v. 20, ' He hath given us an understanding to know him that is true :' he speaks it of the Father, but it follows of Christ too, to know the true Christ. There is a parhelion of Christ, you call it a false sun, but the true sun always outshines it, and the other is but a shadow; but this is to know Jesus Christ in the substance of himself. If you see the picture of a man, it is a knowing the man, but it is not a knowing the true man indeed whose person it represents. As God the Father did beget his own Son from eternity, so he begets that real idea of the Lord Jesus Christ in a poor believer, that never entered into the heart of any other man: so that the believer can say, I have been with Christ to-day, as one said, Jesus Christ and I have been together this day; I saw him this morning. He who sees the Son, and believes on him, hath life, John vi. 40; it is a real, solid, substantial sight, so that we have an understanding given anew to know the true Christ. It is not the *phantasma*, but it is something let in from the person himself, that begets that idea that is taken from the person himself. Though it is hard to express it, yet our ordinary comparison illustrates it. When a man is asleep, we call them phantasms which in a dream represent images of fathers and mothers, and persons that are dead; but if you see the person himself, you say, Man, I am sure that this is he; this is not a dream; as the poor blind man said, ' Behold, I see ;' therefore this is put in by Christ and his apostles themselves, ' We know assuredly thou art the Son of God,' and that thou camest from God. Thus the Father's teaching shews you the true Christ, whom the apostles have seen, heard, and felt, 1 John i. 1, 2. When Christ rose again, said he to his disciples, ' Feel, here is flesh and bones, a spirit hath them not ;' a *spectrum* hath them not. When Christ is represented to the soul by the Father, the soul is not deceived, though it hath not assurance personal of its own interest : his presence is real, and it is called the real presence of the Lord Jesus; and this is to teach the truth as the truth is in Jesus.

4. It is so to teach you, as to persuade you that all you know of him is for his glory, that all tends to the glorifying of him. Look what particulars the Father teacheth you concerning Christ, there goes along with and accompanies that light, that which tends to glorify the Son; and if you cannot believe that he is yours, there will be secret veins and strains of holy affections accompanying your glorifying him in your hearts : 2 Thes. i. 12, ' That the name of our Lord Jesus Christ may be glorified in you, and ye in him, according to the grace of our God, and the Lord Jesus Christ.' Therefore, if the Father teach you any thing about his Son, his

person, sufferings, justification, or the like, there is something in the heart doth rise up to the glorifying this Jesus : 2 Cor. iii. 18, ' We behold the glory of the Lord,' which is meant of Christ.   Thus when Thomas would not believe, John xx., our Saviour, as a means to make him believe, shews him his hands and his feet ; his heart falls down, though his knees did not, and he cries out, ' My Lord, and my God.'   You read in the evangelists of many that received cure from him, came to him and worshipped him with their bodies and souls too, as it is commanded, Ps. xlv. 11, ' He is thy Lord, worship thou him,' says the Father to his church. Oh, when there comes in but a beam of the excellency of Christ's person, that makes the believer to glorify him : Oh how precious is this Lord Jesus ! And the soul doth sanctify him in his heart, in his will and affections, and the soul comes to him for his blood, and the Father hath taught it so to do. Oh how precious is that blood, saith the poor soul, if I might have a part in it, that can make sinners righteous, that can bring in everlasting righteousness, that sin shall never undo me, that can justify all my sins in a moment !   Perhaps the soul cannot say, I have a portion in it, but yet it can say, I come to him to have it so, 1 Pet. ii. 7.   No cordial so precious as this blood of Christ to justify the soul ; and though the soul cannot say, I have part in this righteousness, yet it doth say, if I had all the righteousness of men and angels, I would account it dog's-meat, fling it away that I might have his righteousness.   The soul falls down aghast at this righteousness in an admiration, Oh how glorious is this righteousness !   So that although the soul knows not its interest in it, but remains in doubts, yet it hath the highest value of it, and stands adoring, as John did, when he said, ' Behold the Lamb of God, that taketh away the sins of the world,' John i. 29.   In seeing this Jesus that hath sufficiency to take away sin, the soul stands aghast, and worships him ; and though it doth not fall down on its knees, yet it adores him in its heart.   These are the teachings of the Father, which have such effects, and thus you have seen how he teacheth. He brings home the light of the knowledge of God and Jesus Christ to the soul, he induceth a special light, he wakens the soul morning by morning, affects the heart, takes the soul, represents all in the truth, in the reality, as the truth is in Jesus, and teacheth the soul so to know Christ, as to give glory to him.   For when Christ is represented as he is a Jesus, there is a glory that accompanies that representation, a glory which so raiseth the soul above itself, that it stands amazed at him, and falls down before him, and glorifies him.

CHAPTER VI.

Christ our Saviour typified by Noah's ark.—As Noah was instructed by God to enter into the ark for his safety, so God in the covenant of grace teacheth us to know Christ, and to come to him for salvation.—That our faith looks both to the free grace of God bringing us to Christ, as well as to Christ.— Without Christ the grace of God doth not, nor can, save us; and therefore it is necessary that we explicitly act faith on him for salvation.

For this is as the waters of Noah unto me: for as I have sworn that the waters of Noah should no more go over the earth; so have I sworn that I would not be wroth with thee, nor rebuke thee.   For the mountains shall depart, and the hills be removed; but my kindness shall not depart from thee, neither shall the covenant of my peace be removed, saith the Lord that hath mercy on thee. O thou afflicted, tossed with tempest, and not comforted! behold, I will lay thy stones with fair colours, and lay thy foundations with sapphires. And I will make thy windows of agates, and thy gates of carbuncles, and all thy borders of pleasant stones. And all thy children shall be taught of the Lord, and great shall be the peace of thy children.—ISAIAH LIV. 9–13.

I have, in a discourse* on this scripture, shewed the parallel betwixt Noah's covenant, about his entrance into the ark to be saved from the flood, and the covenant of grace. I came to an use, which hath been this, that the example of Noah in his entrance into the ark, and making of the ark, and the like, was a figure of the saving work that God effects upon the hearts of his people, in bringing them under the covenant of grace, and within the safe bounds of it. I shall accordingly consider the work of faith wrought in Noah, he being made heir of the righteousness of faith. Noah was instructed by God in two things as objects of his faith. The first was the grace of God: ' Thou hast found grace in my sight.' The other was the necessity of his entrance into the ark, which was to him the type of Christ; hence correspondently to answer the type we have what is said in verse 13, ' They shall be all taught of God.' The covenant of grace did undertake, Jer. xxxi. 34, that God would teach them to know him, and that they should not need any other to teach them. The grace under the covenant of the gospel teaches us to know two things. The first is, to know God in his grace: Jer. ix. 24, ' Let him that glorieth glory in this, that he understandeth and knoweth me.' As to what? It follows, ' That I am the Lord that exerciseth loving-kindness, judgment, and righteousness, in the earth: for in these things do I delight.' To know God in his loving-kindness, this is what God doth instruct his people in, and teacheth them to exercise faith about it. The second thing which the covenant of grace teaches us is, to know Christ who is our ark: John vi. 45, ' It is written in the prophets, And they shall be all taught of God. Every man therefore that hath heard, and hath learned of the Father, cometh unto me.' So then these two things before me are naturally deduced from the text, and example of Noah. God teaches his people to know him in his free grace, and he teaches them to know him in his Christ, and instructs them in the nature of faith in him. From God's instructing Noah to enter into the ark, we may infer that God doth also, in the covenant of grace, which this is a prophecy of, instruct us to know his Son Christ, and to come unto him. When the ark was prepared, God invites Noah into the ark: Gen. vii. 1, ' And the Lord said unto Noah, Come thou, and all thy house, into the ark;' which words I shall by and by translate into pure gospel, and I will shew you that the very same language is used concerning our believing in Christ only. I must first shew you this thing, that the ark was the type of Christ, for that is the first thing I must turn into gospel, the ark into Christ. The ancient writers of the church, the fathers (as they call them), say, that by ark is meant the church. Now, it is true that one and the same type often signifieth two or three things; as, for example, the temple signified the body of Christ—' Destroy this temple,' saith Christ—it signified the church universal, the body of Christ mystical; it signifieth every particular soul: ' Ye are the temple of the Holy Ghost,' 1 Cor. vi. 19. But this let me say, when you shall find a parallel made between the thing and the thing signified, and in particular applied to one

* In vol. ii. of his works.

thing, you must only understand it so, and there you must not understand
it as a type of the other. In 1 Peter i. 21 you have Noah's ark made a
type of Christ, as he is administered to us in baptism: 'The like figure
whereunto' (having spoken of the ark) 'wherein few, that is, eight persons
were saved through water.' The like figure is baptism, whereby we are
saved; but here baptism, signified by the ark, bears not the figure of the
church, and that plainly for this reason, because the ark is the figure of
that wherein we are saved ('wherein few were saved, eight persons').
Now, the eight were the persons saved, and saved in the ark, and they
bare the resemblance of the church in being saved; but it is the ark that
bears the resemblance of that wherein we are saved, who is Jesus Christ,
the Saviour of the world, signified and applied to us in baptism. You will
say it is baptism that saves us; but how doth it so? Because we are baptized into Christ, Rom. vi. 3; and it is said to be therefore by the resurrection of Christ that he saves; although he mentions the resurrection as
signified in baptism, he means his death too, for he puts that part, the
resurrection, for the whole. Baptism unto the person baptized under the
water (whether by pouring it upon it, or dipping under it, it is all one, for
baptism is called sprinkling) implies a covering under the water and rising
again. How doth Christ save? 'He died for our sins, and rose again
for our justification,' Rom. iv. 25; and we are said to be 'baptized into
his death' as well as into Christ and his resurrection, Rom. vi. 3. It is
the most lively example that ever was; we are baptized into Christ, and
into his death, and into his resurrection, as ye have it there expressed.
This baptism thus representing Christ is said to be figured out by the ark.
As for the ark, Ainsworth, that holy man, well observes concerning it:
Every Christian (saith he) is baptized with Christ; and as Noah was in
the ark, so we were all in Christ representatively, when he hung on the
cross, and when he rose. And so we were in the ark: when that was
under water, we were under water; when the ark got up, we rose up upon
the water. It was impossible for the ark to be overwhelmed, because
God took care of it; so it was with Christ, God upheld him; and death,
although he was laid in the grave, could not have dominion over him. It
was impossible for death to hold him. The ark too kept Noah and the
church, the ark bare off all (I need not stand to enlarge upon it); there is
no example or figure (as I know) so lively. Moses being baptized in the
cloud and the Red Sea of baptism (because it was the figure of it), is nothing so lively as this. Now, the ark being thus proved to be a type of
Christ, wherein we are saved, we shall next consider God's invitation of
Noah to come into the ark: Gen. vii. 1, 'Come thou, enter into the ark.'
I shall decipher this out into gospel language, and give you plain words
for every tittle of it: 'Come thou, and thy house, and enter into the ark.'
Here is,

1. An invitation to come into the ark, like to Christ's inviting sinners to
come to him: Mat. xi. 28, 29, 'Come to me,' saith Christ, 'all ye that
are weary and heavy laden;' and Rev. xxii. 17, 'The bride saith, Come,
and the Spirit saith, Come, and take of the water of life freely.'

2. What is this coming? It is that which is applied to Christ: John
vi. 33, 'He that comes to me shall never thirst.' Coming is believing, for
to believe is to come to Christ to be saved: 'You will not come to me,'
saith Christ, 'that you may have life,' John v. 40.

3. The words of God's invitation to Noah are, 'Come, and enter.' The
expression is answerable concerning faith: Heb. xi. 3, 'Through faith we

understand that the worlds were framed by the word of God; so that things which are seen were not made of things which do appear.' This it is likewise expressed, Mat. xi. 28, ' Come unto me, all ye that labour and are heavy laden, and I will give you rest.' By coming to Christ, and believing on him, we enter both into him and also into rest.

4. We are said to enter into Christ only by coming and believing, whereas we were out of Christ before : ' He was,' saith the apostle, Rom. xvi. 7, ' in Christ before me.' When he did believe, he entered into Christ, he came to be in Christ, as Noah was in the ark, and so was saved. Suitable hereunto is also that text in Rom. viii. 1, ' There is no condemnation to them that are in Christ,' no more than there was destruction unto them that were in the ark, for they were brought safe to land. As we thus enter into Christ by faith, so we dwell in Christ, and continue in Christ, 1 John ii. 23, 24.

5. Yet it falls well, as God invited Noah to come into the ark, so he invited his family too : ' Come thou and thy house.' The gospel invitation runs thus in these very words, Acts xvi. 11, when the poor jailor came, and knows not what to do to be saved ; ' Believe thou on the Lord Jesus,' says the apostle. Do but come into the ark, and ' thou shalt be saved, and thy house.' Thus the gospel was preached, as might apparently be shewed at large ; so that I have demonstrated unto you that Gen. vii. 1 is plain gospel, and the word about believing answers it. Christ is your ark, and faith is your coming, and by faith you enter into Christ, and continue in him (answerably as Noah did in the ark), till thou arrivest safe to land, thou and thy house. Thus you see that still the parallel holds on about Noah in his covenant and the work of faith. I shall now proceed to shew in some proportion that God teaches us to believe upon Christ as he taught Noah to enter into the ark.

1st. I shall first answer a case or two. I told you that Christ is the object of your faith, distinct from free grace, or that we are to believe on Christ, and treat with him, as well as with God's free grace. Now the case to be resolved is this : Many souls (some such souls I am sure I have known) have been mightily carried out to treat with God the Father and his free grace, and they have found an open door, if they will go in at that room. If they will go to the Father, they find all the love in his heart in giving men to Christ, and commanding him to die for them ; and they find all this love to be free and unchangeable, and they find the thoughts of it to be a support of faith ; and although they have not found assurance, yet they are so much assured of the will of God, as to know that he is resolved to save sinners, and they know that salvation must flow from it, and that makes them seek God, and apply themselves to free grace ; and they can turn all other considerations of Christ into motives and pleas, and so lay themselves at the feet of God. Yet, while they do this, they take it for granted that all God's love is through Christ, and that he was God in Christ reconciling the world to himself, or that he had never done it else. And so, though Jesus Christ is implicitly honoured by them apart and distinctly, yet they do not explicitly apply themselves in a distinct manner to the Lord Jesus. They do not make use of Christ so distinctly, although they go to God through Christ. The answer to this case is useful and profitable.

1. I say that here are two objects of faith, and they are equal objects of faith at least, and equally necessary ; but I say, too, that where the Father is, there is the Son : John xiv. 10, 11, ' I am in the Father, and the Father

in me, and I in you ;' and you shall know this one day ; and ' my Father and I are one,' and we ' agree in one, John x. 30. Their hearts are not divided ; so that if thou canst find the heart of God open to thee, and that there is a full door open, and that thy heart is strengthened to go in at it, then for certain thou hast also a sense of the love of Christ, and thou takest it for granted that all that thou hast is through Christ, and is from the heart of Christ; and so far thou givest him the honour of it. Thou mayest be sure of it by this token, that Christ himself hath to do with his Father in saving us, more than with himself. He eyes his will, and regards what he hath said to him about our salvation, and the undertaking of it, and the carrying of it through : John vi. 37, 'I came down from above, not to do my own will, but the will of him that sent me ;' thus saith Jesus Christ himself ; ' And this is my Father's will, that he hath sent me, and that of all that he hath given me I should lose none.' Now, canst thou go unto the heart of the Father, and regard him as the fountain of all that Christ hath done, and look on him as giving to Christ them that he would have saved ? Dost thou see that Christ hath undertaken to him for thee, and that he hath such and such a love in his heart to save thee, and that thou hast a declaration of it, and the indefinite promise of it in the gospel ? And do these thoughts take thy heart, and dost thou thus treat with the Father, and his will, and free grace for salvation ? Thou herein honourest Christ, for it is no question but Christ, that came to do his Father's will, agrees to it, and hath it always in his view. He tells us that he doth his Father's will as to the persons who are to be saved : John vi. 37, ' All that the Father giveth me shall come to me ; and him that cometh to me I will not cast out, for I came not to do my will, but the will of him that sent me,' i. e., to save the persons that God the Father gave me. Dost thou go to God, although he doth not tell thee immediately that he loves thee ? This is the will of the Father, and Christ came to do the will of the Father unto persons, and therefore to those persons whose hearts are taken with his grace. And this is a sign Jesus Christ hath satisfied for thee, and makes application to the Father for thee : John v. 24, ' Verily, verily, I say unto you, he that heareth my word, and believeth on him that sent me, hath everlasting life, and shall not come into condemnation ; but is passed from death to life.' You must know this, that one great end of Christ's preaching was to discover the Father, and to shew how much the Father's heart was engaged in saving man by him, and in sending him into the world. Now suppose that in his preaching a good soul had been taken with this love of God the Father that gave his Son, and that this soul was drawn out upon that to apply itself to the Father, it herein heard Christ, and applied itself to him also. ' He that heareth my words,' saith Christ, while he is magnifying God the Father, John v. 24, and understandeth, ' and believeth on him that sent me' (i. e., believes upon him as having sent me), that man, saith he, ' hath everlasting life ;' although eminently thus his heart is carried unto the Father that sent him.

2. The soul of man is apt to be intent upon one object, and so to be more flat in another : this is undeniable matter of experience. Oh that I were humbled ! says the soul sometimes, when the heart goes out to be abased for sin. At another time the heart is as much drawn out for Christ and for his grace ; and while it is drawn out that way, a zealous love for holiness comes in, and then it runs out to that. We cannot be intent upon many objects with intenseness of thought, through a narrowness of mind. Sometimes all about the Father and his free grace takes up our

thoughts, and the soul runs out that way; and sometimes the Son, and sometimes the Spirit, employ all our thoughts, as indeed we must adore every person in his office. Sometimes we are carried to communion with the Father, and sometimes to enjoy it with the Son, and sometimes to have it with the Holy Ghost. Now all this ariseth from the narrowness of our minds, and therefore Father, Son, and Holy Ghost are fain to take their turns, and to be entertained by vicissitudes.

3. Is the Father discovered to thee in his free grace to draw thy heart into communion, while Christ is not so free to thee when thou attemptest to go to him? Know this for a truth, that whatever is discovered of the Father's heart, it is done by Christ; and whatever is discovered of the Son's heart in dying and rising, it is done by the Father; therefore thou mayest be sure that the Father is with thee when thy heart is drawn to Christ, for that drawing is from the Father; and if thou hast thy heart drawn to the Father, it is effected by Christ, Mat. xi. 27. How is it that thy heart is drawn unto the Son, and thy heart is all set upon Christ? It is the Father that doth it, and he doth it secretly in the word he doth teach thee; yet no man hath seen him; he doth it, and doth it secretly; and so likewise no man cometh to the Father but by Christ. Thou art no sooner with Christ, and hath put forth a few acts of faith, but he sends thee to the Father, or thou couldst not come to him, as thou couldst not come to Christ but by the Father, and as the Father discovers him. And therefore be assured that he who hath the Father hath the Son, and he that hath the Son hath him by the Father.

4. It is best to have the heart both drawn out to the free grace that is in the Father's heart, and to have the heart drawn out to Jesus Christ and his fulness. It is best for thee to have thy heart from the beginning (as some have had) to know both the Father and the Son, and to continue thy addresses to either. Oh that is best! I will give you a great many scriptures for it. Thus it was with Paul from his first conversion: 1 Tim. i. 14, ' The grace of our Lord was abundant, with faith, and love, which is in Jesus Christ.' By *our Lord* there is meant the Father, for he is made distinct from Jesus Christ in the next words. Paul had an abundant entrance both to God the Father in his free grace at his conversion, and he had abundant entrance unto Jesus Christ with faith and love drawn out unto him. To the same purpose is 1 John ii. 13, ' I write unto you, fathers, because ye have known him that is from the beginning. I write unto you, young men, because you have overcome the wicked one. I write unto you, little children, because ye have known the Father.' Let that therefore abide in you which you have heard from the beginning, let it remain in you, and you shall continue in the Son and in the Father. You knew the Father at first, and believed on him and Christ, and if you will cleave unto your first works, to what you have heard and had from the beginning, to what you have known of God the Father, and of the Son, you will continue in both, and there lies your comfort; and if you cast it off, as those heretics did (who knew the Father, but not the Son), thou hast not the Father nor the Son. Thy case, indeed, may be such, that though thou knowest both, yet thy heart is not so taken with the one as the other; but yet, while thou goest unto Christ, it is because the Father hath sent him, and it is his will that thou believe on him. If thou dost go unto the Father, it is because Jesus Christ hath died, and they both agree in one. It is best to join both: Rom. iii. 24, ' Being justified freely by his grace, through the redemption that is in Jesus Christ' It is best to join

the grace of God, and faith on the blood of Christ, and to have our hearts equally carried to the one and the other, although the Father must have the pre-eminence. This is the truest and rightest frame of a Christian.

But you will say, Is not the knowledge of the Father and his grace alone sufficient, although I have not the other? Is not the saving knowledge of the mercy and grace of God sufficient, although I do not know Christ nor believe on him? And so on the contrary.

1. I answer, No; grace alone would not save you without a Christ, for he is to satisfy the justice of God, that so grace may save thee, and that God might be just, and the justifier of those that believe. I will not enter into that discourse, that through the whole Old Testament there was a glimmering of Christ, that it began in Adam (that Christ should destroy the works of the devil), and in Enoch's ministry, and in Noah's ministry, who as he was ' heir of righteousness by faith,' so he was the preacher of it, and is said to preach Jesus Christ in his day. Peter, speaking of the Jews, how they were saved, saith, Acts xv. 11, ' There was a yoke that neither we nor our fathers could bear; yet if we believe on the Lord Jesus, we shall be saved, as they were;' and how? By the grace of Christ, and by believing on him, and having an eye to Christ. They knew not the way how Christ would save them; they did not dream it should be by dying, but they had an eye to him, as shewed in the type. There was the temple, and they looked towards it and the mercy-seat, &c. The ark was Christ, and the mercy-seat was the favour of God, and the mercy-seat and the ark were equal. Thus look what purpose of grace he hath to save, the ark, which is Jesus Christ, is as large. You have the mercy-seat, the favour of God; and the purchase of Christ, who is the ark, is equal to it.

2. The necessity of coming to Christ was more clearly insisted on after the time of Christ's ascension, and the publication of the gospel to all nations. They are required to believe on Christ distinctly, and to treat with him distinctly, as well as with the Father; and sooner or later the elect shall do it, and have some glances to Christ. Christ answerably prays, John xvii., ' I pray not for these only, but for all that shall believe on me through their word;' we all believe through their word to this day. How doth Jesus Christ characterise his church that was to come? He doth it by this mark, that they should believe on him, and (saith he) ' I pray not for the world.' Can you think then that any man since should have knowledge to grow up to salvation, from a principle of nature, without Jesus Christ? No; they are left out in Jesus Christ's prayer. Thus likewise Christ saith, John viii. 24, ' If you do not believe that I am he; if you do not come to me that ye may have life, that ye may be saved, you will die in your sins.' There must be an absolute treating with Jesus Christ, a flashy faith is not sufficient; nor is it enough that you have purposed such an act, but you must come to Christ, and treat with him, and continue to do so to the end. In Noah's covenant (for I follow the figure, and I have shewed in another discourse how it was a type of the covenant of grace unto the church in the New Testament) it was necessary for Noah and his family to come and enter into the ark if he would be saved; and so it is as necessary for us to come and enter into Christ by faith to be saved: as Noah entered into that ark to be saved from the waters, so we into this ark to be saved from the wrath of God. All that grace which Noah found in God would not have saved him by way of his ordination, but in and by the ark. I have saved you and you. Though he was acknowledged by God to be a righteous man, and though he had been a preacher

of righteousness, yet all this righteousness, and all the good sermons which he had made, would not save him from these waters, but he must have drowned with the rest had he not entered into the ark. Thus though thou wert as righteous as Noah, yet if thou art saved, it must be by coming into the ark. Say what you will of yourselves, being puffed up with vain hopes, you must be saved by Jesus Christ alone. And therefore it is said that Noah and his house entered into the ark. If you take the church in general, there is no salvation out of the church (so some have applied this figure of the ark); ay, but I say, ‘there is no other name by which we can be saved, but that of Jesus,’ and no other benefit but faith, *nulla salus extra Christum*, no salvation out of Christ. If thou art without God and without Christ, thou art in a desperate case.

My design is to shew the necessity of faith on Christ, by going over the story of the progress of the gospel from the first and earliest beginning of it, when the gospel began. When John the Baptist began it before Christ preached, his point was to point and direct men to believe on Christ. You find that the gospel began with John: Luke xvi. 16, ‘The law and the prophets were until John;’ when he baptized men, he said to the people, I baptize you, but, saith he, believe on Christ. John verily baptized men with the baptism of repentance and humiliation; though he taught them repentance, he yet enjoins them to believe on Christ, Acts xix. 4, he did join faith with repentance: he pointed men to Christ, and told the Pharisees there was such a one among them, whose shoe-latchet he was not worthy to unloose, and sets forth the fame of Christ's ministry. He baptized, to make Christ manifest unto the people of Israel, John i. 38–41, and his disciples, Simon and Andrew, fell to Christ. It is also set down in the very beginning of the gospel, that faith on Christ is the only way of life: John iii. 36, ‘He that believeth on the Son hath everlasting life: and he that believeth not the Son shall not see life; but the wrath of God abideth on him.’ When the gospel began, this was still put into it, that we must believe on Christ. It is evidenced also by the care that our Lord and Saviour is at to make himself known to poor souls, that they may believe on him, although he preach the Father's love too. The poor blind man had his eyesight given him, but he knew not who did it, yet there was something within him that did defend Christ against the Pharisees; and Jesus Christ takes occasion to meet him again, and though even then he did not know him, yet afterwards he did make himself manifest. There were some that did know him, as Nathanael, but they did not believe distinctly on him; but Christ takes care that this poor blind man should. There is a poor woman also, John iv. 26, to whom Christ reveals himself: ‘I am he,’ I am the Christ that speaks to thee, saith he. And then there were others too who did believe on him, as ye read there. He would go out of the nation of the Jews, to a place where an elect woman was, on purpose to reveal himself to her. When the time was come for the Canaanitish woman to believe on him, he went out to the coasts of Tyre and Sidon; and so he never went out but once to the coasts of the Gadarenes. And then he came to that poor woman* to discover himself to her; and yet how averse was she at first, but at last she followed him, and found that he was the Messiah, and Christ did approve and own her faith. The eunuch, Acts viii. 37, came to Jerusalem to worship, and

---

* The author seems here to go back to the case of the woman of Samaria. There is no woman mentioned as having been brought to follow him while he was in the country of the Gadarenes.—Ed.

believed on Christ to come, but did not know that he was come; yet what care doth Christ take that he should know him! He was devoutly reading in the Scriptures in his chariot (he employs his time well), and he reads that full text of the Old Testament concerning Christ. Providence so orders it that Philip is going the same way, and is commanded to join himself to him to do that work of instructing him, and he preacheth Christ to him, and the eunuch's heart is taken, and straightway he believeth. As Christ calls poor fishermen, and they straightway left their nets and followed him, so this man straightway believed on Jesus Christ, and goes home, and rejoiceth.

What is the reason that after Christ's suffering, and after the gospel was thus preached, God would have us, in order to salvation, to know Christ, and come to him?

1. It is ' that all may honour the Son, as they honour the Father,' John v. 23. In honouring Christ, they honour the Father and his grace. In looking to the grace of God that was in his heart to save, they honoured the Father, they believed on him, and so honoured him; but you must believe also on the Son and honour him, and how is that but by believing? John v. 23. Christ having spoken of believing, brings the other in; God will have all men to honour the Son, by believing on him, as well as on the Father. Salvation runs on in the knowledge of God the Father and the Son, John xvii. 2, 3; 2 Pet. i. 2.

2. Another reason is, because now God had fully manifested his Son unto the apostles who preached him; whoever therefore upon their preaching did not believe on Christ, it was a sign that the god of this world had blinded their minds. For God had now sent his Son : ' He hath in these last days spoken to us by his Son,' Heb. i. 1, immediately after his taking flesh, and therefore he would have the knowledge of his Son to take place. John vi. 37, Christ speaks to the same purpose, ' Him that comes to me, I will not cast out; and all that the Father hath given me shall come to me, for my Father sent me.' And he sent Christ on purpose that he might be known and manifest unto all the world. He therefore that doth not now believe on the Son, doth frustrate the end of God's sending him, for he did it with an intention that those souls that are saved should believe on him.

3. It is the ordination cf God, it is the will of God that it should be so, John vi. 36-38, our Saviour Christ doth use a very sweet argument and parallel. The reason (saith he) that I must receive all that come unto me is, because the Father sent me, and gave me them before I came into the world, and I was sent to do his will answerably. That you should come to me, this is the Father's will, because he hath sent me on purpose to be made known to all that shall be saved : John vi. 40, ' All that the Father hath given me shall come to me.' The text doth plainly shew this, that God himself, that gave his Son, doth not save men unless they come to his Son; and therefore if he will have them, whom he did give unto Christ to be saved, he is fain to draw them to come to him. In marriage you have the father usually to give the daughter unto the husband; but if she doth not give her consent, it is not the father's giving that makes it a marriage. Thus it is not our Father's gift, but our consent unto Christ, that makes a match with our souls. All the Scriptures, and all in the Scriptures, will not save you, if you have not faith in Jesus Christ. If you should suppose that you had all the Scripture in your mind and heart, it would not save you, 2 Tim. iii. 15. Though thou art a Timothy, brought up from a child

to read the Scriptures as he did, and knowest them, yet they are able to make thee wise unto salvation only through faith which is in Jesus Christ. If thou hast not faith in Jesus Christ, all that wisdom in the Scriptures will not save thee, nor have power to save thee. If they save thee, it is through faith on Christ revealed in them. ' Search the Scriptures' (says Christ, John v. 39), ' for ye think therein ye have salvation;' but search them, for they speak of me more than of anything else, and ye ought to know me, or ye shall die in your sins. But you will say, May not a man have love to God the Father upon the thoughts of his free grace alone, and may he not then repent for sin ? I say, no ; you cannot repent unless you believe on his Son Christ, Rom. i. 5. Love to God, and turning to God, will not save you, if you swerve from the means of grace and the way of faith. What says Christ ? John v. 42, 43, ' But I know you, that ye have not the love of God in you. I am come in my Father's name, and ye receive me not : if another shall come in his own name, him ye will receive.' I know that you have not the love of God in you ; why ? Because you want faith in me. Love to God springs from faith in Christ, and therefore never talk of love to God, if you have not treated concerning salvation by faith in Jesus Christ. Acts xxvi. 17–19, what saith Christ himself from heaven, when he gave Paul his commission ? ' I send thee,' saith he, ' to open the eyes of the Gentiles, to turn them from darkness to light, and from the power of Satan unto God, that they may receive forgiveness of sin, and an inheritance among them that are sanctified.' Will not all this do ? Will not turning unto God from self-love, and loving God, and being sanctified, serve to save us under the gospel ? No ; read the next words : it must all be, says Christ, ' through faith that is in me.' Christ saith it from heaven, this is his commission, and he declares it, that, under the gospel, remission of sins and turning to God, forgiveness of sin and sanctification, were all through faith in him. Be convinced then, that if ever you be saved, there is a necessity that God teach you to come to the Son. You think it is an easy thing to come to Christ, and to look to him and to his name for pardon, and to go to him for forgiveness and sanctification : but let this be preached to you, and inculcated to you, to go to Christ : let it all be urged upon you, yet you will not come to Christ that you may have life, and you will die in your sins, unless God the Father draws you to him. Our Lord Jesus Christ gives a great instance of this : John vi. 63, 64, ' It is the Spirit that quickeneth ; the flesh profiteth nothing : the words that I speak unto you, they are spirit, they are life. But there are some of you that believe not. For Jesus knew from the beginning who they were that believed not, and who should betray him.' He doth give the greatest instance in the world, that let men live under the highest preaching of the gospel, and the powerfullest ministry that ever spake, even the preaching of Christ himself, yet a man will not come to Christ. Whom doth Christ pitch upon for an instance but upon Judas, that had been with him from the beginning, and had heard him preach all his sermons, and heard his parables ? and yet he is a devil for all this. ' For he knew from the beginning who they were that believed not, and who should betray him. Therefore I said,' says he, ' that no man can come to me, except it were given unto him of the Father,' ver. 65. Therefore there must be a teaching from God, and none but those that are taught by a secret work, beyond what any powerful minister in the world can make, will believe. A man otherwise will never do it, he will never give up himself to God and Christ, but there will be ' a heart departing from the living God,' Heb. iii. 12, that is, from Christ, as the coherence of the words shew. So that it is a plain case, that those who live in gospel-times, must all of them be taught of God, if they ever come to Christ. They that live under never so powerful means, if God doth not touch their hearts, they will never come. Oh bless the Lord, that hath taught you to know his free grace, and to believe on his Son, which is the great work of God, as Christ calls it, John vi. 29. It is instead of all else to believe on God, and him whom he hath sent. To him to whom the gathering must be, to him you must come, as members to a head, and as lost creatures to a Saviour. Do not come to this and that sign, and think you have none of Christ, because you cannot find them; but come to him, and dwell with him, and remain with him, day and night.

CHAPTER VII.

That Jesus is proposed to our faith as a spiritual Christ and Saviour.—That unless he was the Son of God, he could not be a quickening Spirit to us.

In the 6th chapter of John our Lord makes it the set subject of his discourse, to draw his hearers unto a true spiritual faith upon himself; and to that end proposeth himself altogether (as indeed he was) a spiritual Messiah, and inculcates it over and over. The occasion which he took was the falling short of this spiritual faith, in that faith which those of Capernaum had of him. They acknowledged him indeed upon the miracle of the loaves,—ver. 14, ' This is of a truth that prophet that should come into the world,'—a prophet, and a far greater prophet than Moses, who had given their fathers bread from heaven in the wilderness, ver. 31. But Christ speaking of a living bread which his Father would give, and which himself would give, vers. 27 and 32, and that it was the ' true bread ' typified by Moses his manna, and which endured to eternal life, they had upon that speech a further advance of faith concerning him, viz., That he was able, by his interest in God his Father, to procure a bread whereby their bodies might live for ever, as Adam's should have done by eating of the tree of life : ver. 34, ' Then said they, Lord, evermore give us this bread.' Thus far they went in believing on him. But when they heard him say that he himself was that living bread that came down from heaven, and that he who eateth that bread should live for ever; yea, and that it was his flesh, as he was Son of man, which they must eat, and that which he would give for the life of the world ; there they stopped and left him, and were offended (vers. 61 and 66) at his sayings, which were too hard to bear, ver. 60. That glorious sermon wherein he makes this very argument his subject, you may read from ver. 27 to the very end of that chapter. At ver. 63 he opens and unriddles all, and discovers the mystery to them to lie in this : ' It is the Spirit that quickeneth, the flesh profiteth nothing. The words that I speak unto you, they are spirit, and they are life,' thereby explaining how and whence it was that he was living bread, and what made his very flesh or human nature to be eternal life, and gives a perfect reason why those who do eat it, and receive it, and himself therewith, in that manner as he and his Father intended in the giving of it, and agreeably to the nature of it, should live. The words are the key to all that sermon foregoing, and unto what follows after ; and it is as if he had said, You must all know that my very person, whom you do not yet truly understand and fully believe in as you ought; for you see and behold me but as a man who works these wonders (as ver. 36, 'Ye have also seen me, and believe not'); you must yet know, that this my person consists of more than a mere man consisting of body and soul, which you only look at, and whom you suppose God is present with, more than ever with any man that hath been in the world; but know I am God in my person as well as man, and it is that Spirit or Godhead which is that which gives the life that I speak of, 'it is the Spirit that quickens,' which elevates and advanceth my flesh or humanity to that high state of life, as to give life to men, in that I who am God united unto that flesh in one person, and giving and offering it as a sacrifice to my Father 'for the life of the world' (they being sinners)—as his words are, ver. 51, 'And the bread that I will give is my flesh, which I will give for the life of the world'—I who am God have sublimated and spirited this sacrificed flesh (by reason of this union) to be a spiritual food to your spirits and souls, which flesh alone, if it had been separated from, and not thus united to this Spirit, would have profited nothing as to giving that life I have been speaking of; and therefore you must understand all my former words I have been speaking about eating my flesh, &c., spiritually, and of a spiritual eating, for so the nature of the thing requires; for I am a spiritual Christ, and a spiritual Saviour, and not a fleshly. And hence it is that 'my words' which I have uttered 'are spirit and life,' and do become such to any of you that hear and understand me aright; and there were some present who at that time, and in that manner understood those words, and found him and these his words to be spiritual life unto them, as ver. 67, 68 shews. And as my flesh is by virtue hereof the procurer of life unto you as sinners, so my person, consisting of God-man, is eternal life in itself to them who as sinners do eat my flesh by faith. And they have not only eternal life from me, but I am in my person eternal life unto them in their communion with me.

This passage, as thus interpreted of his Godhead and human nature, is the centre into which all the lines of that sermon do run, and will approve itself to be the true and genuine meaning, as wherein he doth at once not simply give an explanation of what his scope and meaning was, namely, that the eating his flesh, &c., was in a spiritual way to be understood by faith, and not of a carnal eating (which his last words of that verse do import, 'My words they are spirit and life'), but chiefly beyond that, it is to give the account and ground why it was so in those first words: 'It is the Spirit that quickens,' &c., which putting life into the human nature, and offering it up to God to give us life, made his flesh and himself to be altogether a spiritual food (though the most real of foods, 'meat indeed,' as ver. 55) unto the souls of men; and also, because thereby he answers all their cavils, queries, and exceptions they had before made. And the view of all these have confirmed me in the foresaid interpretation of his Godhead to be meant by spirit, and by flesh his human nature, which was the sense of the ancients. And I have wondered that the most of our latest interpreters have diverted from it, and betaken themselves wholly to expound this scripture to design the manner of eating to be spiritual (as Beza, and after him divers), and have rested solely in that sense as full and adequate; whereas this other interpretation I have given not only takes in that of theirs, but beyond it gives the reason of it, why it can be no other than a spiritual eating, for the life the Godhead gives cannot be corporeally eaten. And then the concurrence of other scriptures, using the same words to express the Godhead's dwelling in his human nature personally, doth further confirm me in it. And lastly, the disciples' words which they return in answer to this discourse of Christ's (which shews how they understood it), doth put me out of all doubt that this was indeed his meaning ; and I am more confirmed in it by the concurrence of other scriptures.

1. We have the concurrence of Rom. i. 3, 4, ' Concerning his Son Jesus Christ our Lord, who was made the seed of David *according to the flesh;* and declared to be the Son of God with power, *according to the Spirit of holiness*, by the resurrection from the dead.' Where, as his ' flesh' is his humanity, so that ' Spirit of holiness' is the Godhead of him, as he is the Son of God, and termed here the ' Spirit of holiness ;' as Heb. ix. 14, it is called the ' eternal Spirit,' the Son of God being the fulness of the Godhead dwelling in that flesh, which (as he adds) he was declared to be, by the resurrection from the dead, that Spirit or Godhead of his raising him up again by his own power. For which cause he is also said to be ' quickened in the Spirit,' or by the Spirit ' having been put to death in the flesh,' 1 Peter iii. 18, and likewise ' justified in the Spirit,' 1 Tim. iii. 16, namely, to be God as well as man, as himself had declared himself to be. But would you have this of the first chapter to the Romans more plainly deciphered ? The same apostle doth it in plainer words in the same Epistle. That parallel in the same Epistle, Rom. ix. 5, relates to what hath been said, ' Whose are the fathers, and of whom, as concerning the flesh, Christ came, who is God over all, blessed for ever. Amen.' As in that first chapter he had distinguished about his person, saying, *as concerning the flesh*, that is, his human nature received from David his forefather, as his seed, so in this chap. ix. he useth the same again, ' Of whom' (viz., the fathers), ' as concerning the flesh, Christ came.' And in his so cautious distinguishing in both places *as concerning the flesh*, doth evidently import he had somewhat else, some other thing or nature besides which his person (the Christ) consisted of. And what that other nature should be, required a farther declaration, and might be expected he should say it, which the apostle doth with the highest solemnity and adoration of him, when he addeth, ' who is God, blessed for ever. Amen,' which Godhead acknowledged in the 9th chapter he had styled ' Spirit' in chap. i., and which you find also in John vi., in Christ's speech : ' It is the Spirit that quickens, the flesh profiteth nothing,' that is, of itself alone. And this Spirit or Godhead, thus united into one person, is said to ' be made a quickening Spirit' to us, 1 Cor. xv. 45, 46, in similitude to Adam his being a living soul ; that is, a person consisting of a reasonable soul, united to a body which it dwelleth in and inspireth, and then by generation propagateth us the like unto him therein ; so here in Christ typified by him, his Godhead or Spirit dwelleth bodily in his flesh or human nature, and thereby doth first quicken and spirit that flesh even by the spiritualness and heavenliness, above all that is communicated to mere creatures ; and therefore he is himself there styled a spiritual and heavenly man, who in the virtue hereof is then made, by a regeneration both of our souls and bodies, ' a quickening Spirit' to us. And though this there spoken of him (as to us) is particularly in relation to his quickening and raising our bodies, yet his so doing must first and more specially be understood, that he is a quickening Spirit to the souls of those in this life, whose bodies he raiseth at the resurrection, as Eph. ii. 1 the phrase is used.

2. This interpretation doth alone solve all the riddles and quarrels which had been raised before by the Capernaites ; and this sense therefore, containing a sufficient answer unto all and each of them, must needs have been

intended and directed as an answer to them, whereas that other narrowed sense mentioned falls short of this scope. They murmured, ver. 41, 42, because he said, ' I am the bread which came down from heaven. And they said, Is not this Jesus, the son of Joseph, whose father and mother we know? how is it then that he saith, I came down from heaven?' Now this one speech of his, ' It is the Spirit that quickeneth,' is a sufficient account how both might stand. I am God, says he, the Son of God, and the Godhead (which he calls Spirit, and is the Spirit of that Son) is in me, and it was *that* which came down from heaven; but my flesh, my human nature, that indeed I had from my mother, whom you knew; and yet let me withal further tell you, says he, that this Son of man, whom you think only to be a mere earthly man, should, by the right of natural inheritance had from his being united into one person with the Godhead and Son of God, have been in heaven at the first instant of that union, and by due never have lived upon earth in frail flesh, but only to that end to redeem you by giving his life for the world, ver. 51, and this Christ tells them in the very words before : ver. 61, 62, ' When Jesus knew they murmured at it, he said unto them, Doth this also offend you? What and if ye shall see the Son of man ascend up where he was before ?' *i. e.*, in his due right. And accordingly, in 1 Cor. xv., it is from this very ground of his union with that Spirit, the quickening Spirit, his Godhead, ver. 45, that he, the man, is said to be the Lord from heaven ; ver. 47, ' The first man is of the earth, earthly; the second man is the Lord from heaven;' and an heavenly man, ver. 48, for in the right of that union he was to have been ' in heaven;' and in that respect he is said to be ' from heaven' here in John vi., as also in this to the Corinthians, 1 Cor. xv., because that his due was to have been there before ever he came on earth. They had also quarrelled with him how he, being but a mere man, could be the living bread that came down from heaven, as he had said, ver. 41 and 52, and that ' he that eateth of that bread shall live for ever,' ver. 58. Now this word *quickening spirit* resolves the difficulty, for it was his Godhead, united to that flesh, that was the principle of that eternal life which we partake of from him ; therefore ' he that eateth me,' saith he, ' even he shall live by me,' ver. 57, and yet so as it was that his manhood and flesh, as it was united to the Godhead, which made him to become bread and food to us, without which his Godhead alone simply would not have been fit meat either for soul or body; nor would his flesh alone, if it had been separated from the Godhead, have profited anything. And thus the personal union between both natures is not only asserted, but made the ground of all he had spoken of himself.

3. Again, that question, ver. 52, ' How can this man give us his flesh to eat?' is by this mystery unfolded, even that he is in his person Spirit united to flesh. And it is the Spirit that gives the life; and therefore it was that his flesh must be understood to be a spiritual food, made to be such by the Spirit in him. And this also shews his speeches to have been so intended, that thence and therefore answerably their eating must be a spiritual eating of the soul or spirit by faith ; and that any one hearing and understanding those his words which he had uttered concerning it, and receiving them by faith, their souls should find them to be spirit and life to them, by conveying himself (who is eternal life) to them through faith on him, who, as a quickening Spirit, is their life : and thus their cavil (how can this be?) is solved ; for thus it might and could well be, according to spiritual principles, rationally suited to and corresponding one with another.

And, moreover, it further appears that he meant it not at all of a corporeal eating, as our bodies do our ordinary food, by that saying he subjoineth, ver. 56, ' He that eateth my flesh, and drinketh my blood, dwelleth in me, and I in him ;' for no man is said to dwell in his meat, though for a while, till concocted, his meat may be said to be in his body; but, says he, ' He that eateth my flesh dwells in me, and lives in and by me, even as I live in the living Father,' as it follows, ver. 57.   Thus this interpretation answers all their exceptions.

4. That confession which his disciples hereupon made, which is the last part of the chapter, is indeed but a short sum of all this, even a brief exposition and confirmation of Christ's whole sermon, but especially of this, ver. 63.   The print and impression on their souls who had savingly believed punctually answered to this his doctrine; for when our Saviour saw that his new disciples of Capernaum had so soon left him (ver. 66, ' From that time many of his disciples went back, and walked no more with him '), he turneth himself to his old disciples, Peter, and the rest of them that had stood by, and heard all the discourse ; thus speaking to them, ver. 67, ' Then said Jesus to the twelve, Will ye also go away?'   And now hear them speak according to their experimental sense : ver. 58, 59, ' Then Simon Peter,' in the name of the rest, ' answered him, Lord, to whom shall we go?   Thou hast the words of eternal life; and we believe, and are sure, that thou art that Christ, the Son of the living God.'   They had by blessed experience found him to be a fountain of spiritual life to their souls, because he was God's Son.   They had found, they had felt him to be their life, because that flesh, that is, that man, whom they saw with their eyes, whom they had conversed with, and had heard so many words and sermons from, and this among the rest, was indeed in his person the Son of God, and united to the Son of God personally, and that the Spirit or Godhead in him the Son had quickened their souls full many a time ; for they had found that his words he had spoken concerning himself, in declaring that he was the Son of God, and God, had been eternal life to them.   They therefore cry out as men that should be undone if they should ever come once to leave him ; ' Whither shall we go?' say they ; ' thou hast the words of eternal life.'   And this life he had in his very person, and in his being God's Son, which, therefore, Simon, ver. 69, superadds, ' And we believe, and are sure, that thou art that Christ, the Son of the living God.' If, therefore, there should be a parting of us and thee, farewell eternal life, and let go our souls, and all, for thou art the soul of our souls, the life of our lives ; which life he withal affirms to be conveyed to them, and maintained in them, by and through their believing on him as the Son of God.

And now observe the full and express correspondency which the words of this their confession holds in reference unto Christ's words, specially those in ver. 63.   Our Lord had, in the 57th verse, ascended higher in setting open the fountain and original source or cause of his own blessed and eternal life, to the end that, carrying their thoughts to the well-head of all life, they might know to whom ultimately to attribute the glory of this life together with himself, and might discern the blessedness of that life itself derived to them, and the descent and derivation of it.   His words are, ' As the living Father hath sent me, and I live by the Father, so he that eateth me shall live by me.'   It is as if he had said, The Father is the *primum vivens*, the original principle of all spiritual life ; being a Spirit (as John iv. 24), the fountain of that life which is in me, and from me let

down to you; whence it is that the life with which I quicken you and other
believers is a communication of the life that is in my Father himself
through me; and the foundation of my own life in myself, and of being
life unto you, or any believers, lies in this, that I am his Son, the Son of
God; having the same, the very same life essentially in me who am God
that is in my Father, so as there is the same Spirit and Godhead in both.
I am the living Son of this living God, who, as such, is my Father, and
have life in myself, though from him; and he sent me who am this life
down from heaven in this flesh, which you behold with your bodily eyes,
to give life to the world; and therefore I am able, through and by means
of this my flesh, who is one person with me, to derive and let down this
life to you, and the life which my Father himself hath, even eternal life;
for he is the eternal God, and therefore I am eternal life also; and therefore it is that the life I can and do communicate from him to you is eternal
life likewise.   And again, as my Father is a Spirit (as John iv. 24), so am
I, and therefore it is a spiritual life which I make souls partakers of, which
is conveyed to those souls by a spiritual means, wrought on purpose by
my Father in their hearts, unto whom he hath appointed to give this life;
which means is believing on me with their whole hearts, and by that faith
entertaining my words which I speak of myself, who am life to them.

Now let us come to their short and summary confession fore-mentioned:
ver. 69, ' We believe and are sure thou art that Christ, the Son of the
living God.'   This they allege as the ground and reason why they found
that he was eternal life to them; concerning which confession I note three
things, answering to what had gone afore in Christ's speeches.

(1.) That he is God; which is evident they acknowledge, by saying the
Son of the living God, the natural Son of the living Father, as he had said
before, ver. 57.   Creatures that are living themselves, animals, as we call
them, do beget living creatures too, endowed with a life like their own,
and they beget in their kind, as a lion begets a lion, and a man begets a
man.   Thus God begetting this Son (and he is his only begotten Son), he
begets him like himself, a God; and therefore to say he is the Son of the
living God, imports that he is God, and that living God.

(2.) Observe (which in substance is the very same), he had said of himself in ver. 63, ' It is the Spirit,' or the Godhead in me, ' that quickeneth.'

(3.) Observe that it was by faith on him and his word that they had life
eternal derived unto their souls from him.   ' We believe,' say they; which
is in return unto all that Christ had spoken of believing, and eating his
flesh, to be that spiritual eating by faith throughout that sermon, from
ver. 14.

(4.) And let me cast in this to this confession of theirs.   One of those
apostles that then stood by (the apostle John, who survived, and wrote his
first Epistle after all the rest of them were dead), reviveth this very same
confession of theirs, here made, in his own name, and in the names of
them all (as Peter here), though dead, and allegeth that their general sense
and experience they had of the same of which they here spoke.   Thus in
1 John i. 1, 2, ' That which was from the beginning, which we have heard,
which we have seen with our eyes, which we have looked upon, and our
hands have handled, of the Word of life; for the life was manifested, and
we have seen it, and bear witness, and shew unto you that eternal life,
which was with the Father, and was manifested unto us.'   *We*, by which
he means these his fellow-apostles that had been, not himself only, nor
other fellow-Christians then alive, for he speaks of those who had seen,

heard, and handled of the Word of life, viz., the true Christ; and how they had all found that he was that Word of life, and eternal life that was with the Father afore the world was; whom after often in that Epistle he styles his Son, and God, and concludes the Epistle with the same, even as he had begun—'This is the true God, and eternal life.'

Thus we have seen the truth of all this justified by wisdom's children, and sealed to by their experience.

Now, in the last place, take notice (and it is to our purpose) that in the midst of this sermon it is that Christ lets fall the words of my grand text, for a part of this sermon it is; and that for this cause, and on this occasion it was, that because he is so spiritual a Messias, that therefore it is necessary that every one that believes in Christ, so as to have life, must be 'taught,' and have 'learned from the Father,' that grand teacher of his Son; and that all this is put upon this very ground, because they are to know and receive him spiritually,—spiritually, I say, in both those respects fore-mentioned at the entrance; for he is a spiritual Christ, who is the object, and the faith he is to be received withal, in the subject, must be spiritual, suited unto the true spiritualness that is in this object; his person, as God-man, or a quickening Spirit in flesh, and as he is a Saviour, giving his flesh for the life of the world (both which he treats of in that sermon) in the real savoury eating whereof, and in whom eternal life consists, and is derived, neither of which no man can do unless first taught by the Father to know him, and then drawn by God to him as to a spiritual Saviour. And for confirmation of this you may again observe, how that presently after he had uttered these words, ver. 63, from the doctrine thereof he infers, ver. 65, 'Therefore said I unto you, that no man can come unto me, except it were given to him of my Father.' Which speech and particle *therefore* plainly refers unto the words of ver. 63 we have been upon, and is as if he had said, Because I am to be believed on as a Spirit, or God dwelling in this flesh, to be the quickener of all that believe, *therefore*, or for that reason it is, that no man can come to me for life unless taught by the Father spiritually; for to believe on me in a suitable manner, that is, spiritually, suitable unto what I am in my person, and also in my salvation and life, that I do give to others, and in both which I am a Spirit quickening; and correspondently, to believe on me, and on the Godhead dwelling in my flesh personally, this is above the reach of nature, or of flesh and blood, and therefore this must be given by my Father, who seeks such professors and disciples of me as believe on me in spirit and truth.

From all which we may conclude, that to know Christ spiritually, both in himself: 1, as he is a spiritual Christ; and, 2, a Saviour in the true spiritualness of him; and, 3, in a spiritual manner to understand him in both, and come to him under the true representation thereof, is that teaching of the Father meant as the truth is in Jesus, and for want of which, or falling short of which, it is that men perish. This therefore must be accounted a point of greatest moment to us to know, and to be searched into.

CHAPTER VIII.

That Christ represented as a quickening Spirit is a proper object of our faith.

My next work therefore shall be to shew that Christ, as represented a quickening Spirit, in that latitude of sense which the Scriptures in that notion of him intended, and revealed by the Father as the truth thereof is in him, and taken in and understood by us accordingly, doth become and prove as proper and full an object for our faith to exercise itself upon, as any other notion whatsoever wherein he is represented.

I have in this large title comprehended the main materials that follow, and in laying open the spiritualness of our Christ (the object, which in Scripture is expressed by Spirit that quickens), the spiritualness of the faith and heart of a true believer, with difference from common faith in a carnal heart, will all along appear, and appear by this, that when the spiritualness that is in the object is spiritually discovered, if the actings of the soul be really and in verity conformable, and answerable thereto, then it is spiritual faith in us also. For it is a certain rule, that the spiritualness of the subject, viz., the soul, lieth in a suitableness unto, and closing with the spirituality of its objects as represented in their bare and naked true spiritualness, abstracting from other respects, for then they attinge and affect that object as it is in itself. So here in this case, when the true spiritualness of Christ is presented, and apprehended as the truth is in Jesus, the spiritualness or fleshliness of the heart will be discovered thereby, as the heart shall be found to fall in with or bear off from what is in that object purely spiritual. I shall not then need to discourse any more than to discover to you what a Christ you have, and how spiritual, and then do you lay your hearts to the naked apprehension thereof, and see how your hearts agree with him, and are affected accordingly towards him, and what it is in him causeth you to ' desire him,' as the prophet speaks, as such a Christ, comparing spiritual hearts with spiritual Christ, see how they agree and like each other.

Other ways and modes out of scriptures are and have been taken by others unto a great success in their discoveries of Christ, and the truth of saving faith thereby, and for substance they are the same with this of mine that follows. But I chose this as that which my Saviour's sermon in this sixth chapter of John hath led me to, and which hath fallen into my own heart, and hath animated my pursuances after Christ in a more special manner than any other apprehensions of him whatsoever. I limit myself unto what this notion, viz., ' a quickening Spirit,' will afford herein. For it is made a kind of definition of him (if I may so speak), or the most proper description, whether in his person or what he is made to us, in two words, ' a quickening Spirit,' 1 Cor. xv. 45. Christ's speech, ' God is a Spirit,' John iv. 24, is as proper a definition of God as can be given (for he passeth our logic), it expressing the kind of his being, as his name Jehovah, that he is fulness of being. And this definition of Christ is like it; given first by Christ himself in this 6th of John, and then by the apostle : ' The Lord is that Spirit,' 2 Cor. iii. 17; and again, ' a quickening Spirit,' 1 Cor. xv. 45, and I call it a definition of him, or rather the exactest description of him, because it is used to illustrate both his person and his work as a Saviour : 1 Cor. xv. 45 to 50, ' The first man Adam was made a living soul ; the last Adam was made a quickening Spirit. Howbeit that was not first which is spiritual, but that which is natural ; and afterwards that which is spiritual. The first man is of the earth, earthy : the second man is the Lord from heaven.' I think I may, without the hazard of being confuted, undertake to say, that this is a more perfect definition, or at least an exacter character of Adam the first man, given him by God himself, from and upon his very creation, than ever any philosopher gave of man, whilst they went about to make a definition of him ; and I may answerably affirm the like of this definition of Christ, that he is a quickening Spirit. It denotes his person to be God, ' the Lord from heaven,' and withal a man in one person with God, ' the second man.' That the word *spirit* in the New Testament is often set to express his Godhead as his humanity flesh, is so well known (Rom. i. 3, 1 Tim. iii. 16, 1 Peter iii. 18, 19, Heb. ix. 14), as it needs not be insisted on. The parallel then between our Christ and the first Adam, by way of super-eminent comparative on Christ's part, will run thus: Look, as Adam the first man was in his own person first and originally made a living soul, having that animal rational soul, ' the breath of lives' infused by God into a body organised for that soul to act and enliven, as our souls do our bodies, and so make up one person with it; so the Godhead of the second person, united into one person, was thereby made a quickening Spirit unto that flesh of his assumed. Only we must here abate of the parallel (for it is but a type, and so holds not in all things), that the Godhead in Christ is not the soul of his body, for he hath a soul which makes up with his body an entire human nature ; but his Godhead is that which makes up one person with that human nature, and infinitely enliveneth and spiriteth it above what our souls do, or can do our bodies. And he useth the word *quickening* to express that super-celestial life by; not that Christ's human nature was dead before, but that it was called up to and raised from* what it was not (and God's calling things that are not as if they were, the apostle parallels with a resurrection, Rom. iv.), nor never would have been, if he had been but a mere man, though made by a new creation, bestowing never so excelling a soul and body, above the soul and body which the first man, Adam, consisted of. But here the Spirit or Godhead elevated that soul and body of Christ's human nature into a state of life, of an higher kind and rank, infinitely surpassing the life which any soul or body, if but mere creatures, could have been capable of, or than even God's power (without making a personal union thereof with the Godhead) could have raised such a mere creature unto. It is a divine and super-celestial life, above all that of angels in heaven, peculiar to him through that union by inheritance, as being now become by inheritance the Lord of heaven, and in taking flesh the Lord from heaven, which to have been was his right at the first instant that he was man. The apostle therefore, being to express that life which by the Godhead the second Adam was raised unto, doth it by a term of super-excellency, in a way of comparison unto the first man's being but ' a living soul;' but calls this and gives it an higher term of ' quickening,' denoting this high and transcending elevation of it above what by mere creation could have been communicated. And he useth the word *spirit* in the way of super-eminency unto that of *soul;* that look, as the Godhead in Christ's person excels the soul or spirit in man, so proportionably doth that life, flowing from that spirit or Godhead in Christ, excel the life that was in Adam by creation, or that could have been in any mere creature. And because it is a raising it up unto a life (that was not, nor never would have been, in any mere creature, but is wholly a super-creation life), he therefore deservedly calls it a quickening even of the human nature of Christ. And whereas it is said, he was ' made a quickening spirit,' the meaning is not, nor can be, that the Spirit or Godhead itself in him was made. No; far be it from me so to interpret it; but the meaning is, that by that union of the Godhead with the human nature, the Godhead was made a quickening Spirit thereunto. And so the

* Qu. ' to' ?—ED.

parallel, as to Christ's person, runs no further than to this, that as Adam's soul breathed into his body, and becoming one person with it, did inspire and impregnate it, and he became a living soul, so the Godhead inspirited this his human nature with a divine life, suitable to the glory of that Godhead which dwelt in him. And the reason why this parallel, as in respect to Christ's own person, is intended to extend no further, is, because this of Adam's state is alleged but as a type and shadow, and therefore not in all things holding a likeness unto the substance typified out thereby. Thus it is true first of the person of Christ, that his person as God-man is constituted or made up of a quickening spirit; and certainly as the first man Adam is in his person intended first in this of being a living soul, so Christ's person in that of a quickening spirit.

But, 2, as Adam is said to be made a living soul also in respect of conveying a like life and image unto us men his sons, as the next verses do plainly express the scope to be, so the parallel of Christ's being made a quickening spirit, aims to signify also what he is made (by virtue of that his personal union) to be unto us, of which there can be no doubt. From this notion of his being a quickening spirit (as it hath been explained), the spiritualness of this our great Christ, as he is made and set forth the spiritual object of our faith, and accordingly taught by the Father, as the truth is in Jesus, to all believers, hath these two branches in it, in the handling of which distinctly I shall accomplish this task I have undertaken.

1. You have the spiritualness that is in the person, as 'the Word was made flesh;' or what he is in himself, Son of God, and God dwelling in our nature personally, and quickening thereof.

2. The spiritualness of him as a Saviour, or in what he is and hath done for us as sinners, that were dead in sins and trespasses. And although the particular occasion of the apostle's introducing these words, was what he is to us in the resurrection of our bodies, yet it in general reacheth to all that he is to our souls, for our eternal salvation. I divide this argument into these two heads; for these two were the two eminent titles or descriptions given him, as he was the Christ, by those disciples that first believed on him from the beginning of his manifestation to Israel. John the Baptist (from whom Christ's other disciples learned him to be the Messias or Christ), in a sermon to his disciples, recorded by the evangelist John, chap. i., first represents him to their faith as a Saviour for sinners: 'Behold,' says he, 'the Lamb of God, that takes away the sins of the world!' So at the beginning of it, ver. 29; but in the close of it, ver. 34, 'And I saw, and bare record, that this is the Son of God.' And the Son of God consisting of two natures: as a man, he was conceived after the Baptist himself (as by the story, Luke i., appears); but he had another nature, in respect of which he says he was 'afore him,' that is, as God, and Son of God. Thus verse 30, 'This is he of whom I said, After me cometh a man which is preferred before me; for he was before me.' So then Christ as God-man, the Son of God, and Saviour from sin, is set forth to a believer's faith, and this from the first, by John.

And sometimes some of those first disciples utter their faith on him as Son of God, sometimes others speak their faith on him as Saviour of the world. Some express their faith on him as Son of God. So Nathanael upon his very first seeing and hearing of him: John i. 49, 'Nathanael answered and said unto him, Rabbi, thou art the Son of God, thou art the King of Israel.' The faith of the Samaritan disciples, chap. iv., is thus expressed: John iv. 42, 'Now we believe, for we have heard him ourselves, and know that this is indeed the Christ, the Saviour of the world.' And Peter, in the name of the disciples, expresseth the same: Mat. xvi. 16, 'Thou art Christ, the Son of the living God;' just as here in John vi. 69 you find. And the revelation of this, in that spiritual manner that you have heard, was that which caused them to cleave to him and say, 'Whither shall we go?' &c. And it was from the Father teaching: Mat. xvi. 17, 'Blessed art thou, Simon: for flesh and blood hath not revealed it unto thee, but my Father which is in heaven.' It was the Father had taught him so to believe on his own Son; 'and upon this rock,' saith Christ, ver. 18, 'I will build my church;' for all the saints of the New Testament did all 'come to the unity of faith, and knowledge of the Son of God,' Eph. iv. 13. And in their so believing he was the Son of God, they believed that he was such a Son of God as was God, or that Son of God who was God, which their confessing him the Son of the living God imported, as was observed. And therefore Christ, in his arguing with the Jews (who quarrelled with him, that he being a man should make himself God), makes the conclusion of an argument, wherein he proves he was God, to run thus: John x. 33–36, 'The Jews answered him, saying, For a good work we stone thee not, but for blasphemy; and because that thou, being a man, makest thyself God. Jesus answered them, Is it not written in your law, I said, Ye are gods? If he called them gods unto whom the word of God came, and the scripture cannot be broken; say ye of him whom the Father hath sanctified, and sent into the world, Thou blasphemest; because I said, I am the Son of God,' that is, such a Son as was true God; for the thing wherein they had said he blasphemed, verse 32, was, that he said he was God, yet he concludes that he was the Son of God ; so that to believe he was the Son of God, was all one as to believe he was God. And hence it also was that in other scriptures to believe on him as God, and on him as Saviour, are also joined in the apostles' confession by the same Peter: 2 Peter i. 1, 'Simon Peter, a servant and an apostle of Jesus Christ, to them that have obtained like precious faith with us, through the righteousness of God and our Saviour Jesus Christ.' And they are also by Paul joined together: Titus ii. 13, 'The great God, and our Saviour Jesus Christ.'

CHAPTER IX.

That Christ's person, as Son of God, in one person with the man Jesus, is the prime object of faith, and taught by the Father, as the truth is in Jesus.

To evidence that Christ's person, as the Son of God in one person with the man Jesus, is the great object of our faith, two things are to be considered :

1. That the spirits of the first believers on Christ were generally taught by God, and carried out to him, to receive, obtain, close with him as such ; that is, under the apprehension of his person, Son of God, and God-man (which properly is called his person), not God simply in his divine nature singly considered, but God manifest in flesh, or the Son of God made flesh. You heard before the Baptist's confession, who was the leader on unto this distinct faith on him in this particular, as also the confession of the apostles, even long before Christ's ascension.

Other particular instances may be given ; as you find this to have been at the bottom of Martha's faith, when Christ himself ransacked and searched into it : John xi., Christ puts her faith to it by way of question, ver. 25, 26, ' Jesus said unto her, I am the resurrection and the life : he that believeth in me, though he were dead, yet shall he live.   And whosoever liveth and believeth in me, shall never die.   Believest thou this ?'   But she answers not *in terminis* and directly : ver. 27, ' She saith unto him, Yea, Lord : I I believe that thou art the Christ, the Son of God, which should come into the world.'   She brings forth the very bottom of her faith, and ground of all, the chief, the primary thing which she believed about him, which carried all the rest.   She utters what lay most near her heart.   Thus also unbelieving Thomas, when his faith had obtained a resurrection, upon occasion of Christ's being risen from the dead (whereby he was declared to be the Son of God, and God, Rom. i. 3, 4), whither runs his faith thereupon ? ' My Lord, and my God,' John xx. 28.   The eunuch heard Philip expound to him the 53d chapter of Isaiah, which treats of Christ's being a Saviour, and bearing our sins : Acts viii. 32, 33, ' The place of Scripture which he read was this, He was led as a sheep to the slaughter ; and like a lamb dumb before his shearer, so opened he not his mouth.   In his humiliation his judgment was taken away ; and who shall declare his generation ? for his life is taken from the earth.'   This text must needs lead Philip to preach Jesus to him as a Saviour for sinners ; but he beginning (as it is there said) but with that scripture, proceeded to add many more : ver. 35, ' Then Philip opened his mouth, and began at the same scripture, and preached unto him Jesus.'   And whereas there was but one passage in that which he read that gave occasion to preach him to be the Son of God, viz., ' Who shall declare his generation ?' or whose Son he was ; yet that necessarily fell in, and deciphered who the person was that was to be the Saviour. Now observe how the eunuch's faith took hold of that above all other ; for when Philip told him, ver. 37, ' If thou believest with all thine heart, thou mayest be baptized, the eunuch's heart tells us what it was above all other which his whole soul closed in with ; and that was, ' I believe that Jesus Christ is the Son of God.'   And yet we may well suppose that Philip's discourse had run mainly upon his being a Saviour, and his bearing our sin, for it was the main argument of the text, which the eunuch gave him to expound, and sure he kept to it : ' He was led as a sheep to the slaughter, and as a lamb dumb before the shearer ;' which the Baptist referred to in his ' Behold the Lamb of God, that takes away the sins of the world,' John i. 29.   But the Spirit of God did (we see) set that other character of his person, which the Baptist also gave him, ' Jesus Christ, the Son of God.'

But to give over the pursuit of any more single instances, let us see the universal effect of this doctrine, both in the Baptist's ministry, and of the apostles', upon the whole lump, body, and generality of believers.   What the effect of John Baptist's ministry was, is prophesied of Isa. xl. 3, ' The voice of him that crieth in the wilderness, Prepare ye the way of the Lord, make straight in the desert a highway for our God ;' which is undeniably applied by three evangelists to mean, that that Lord and God, to make way for whom in men's hearts that preparation was, is evidently our Lord Christ, as appears in the same evangelists.   And what was the issue and consequent of it, that Christ coming and preaching after John ? ' The glory of the Lord' (Christ) ' was revealed ; and all flesh' (that is, believing flesh, whose eyes Satan had not blinded) ' saw it together ;' that is, they all entertained him by faith, as their Lord and their God (as Thomas professed him), when he began to manifest his glory, John ii. 11.

Then again, what was the effect of the apostles' ministry, who, after Christ's ascension, were sent forth to preach him ? It follows in the same prophecy, Isa. xl. 9 : ' O Zion, that bringest good tidings, get thee up into the high mountain ; O Jerusalem, that bringest good tidings, lift up thy voice with strength : lift it up, be not afraid : say unto the cities of Judah, Behold your God.' This gospel message was, ' Behold your God !' that is, your Christ, who is your God, Son of God in his person, the ruler, the rewarder, in whom is eternal life, and the shepherd of his people : ver. 10, 11, ' Behold, the Lord God will come with strong hand, and his arm shall rule for him ; behold, his reward is with him, and his work before him. He shall feed his flock like a shepherd ; he shall gather the lambs with his arm, and carry them in his bosom, and shall gently lead those that are with young.' The voice of the crier, the Baptist, had cried him up, ' Behold the Lamb of God !' the Son of God ; and the eminentest message which the apostles delivered, was, ' Behold your God !' that is, we preach a Saviour unto you, who is God. So they preached, and so they believed that heard them : 2 Cor. iv. 5, 6, ' For we preach not ourselves, but Christ Jesus the Lord ; and ourselves your servants for Jesus' sake. For God who commanded the light to shine out of darkness, hath shined in our hearts, to give the light of the knowledge of the glory of God, in the face of Jesus Christ.' In the *face*, that is, in the *person* of Jesus Christ, who is God, and the image of God, ver. 4. And when the veil was taken off from all nations, and specially when it shall be taken off from the few* (which in the 3d chapter, ver. 15, 16, afore, he had applied the prophecy of Isaiah unto), Oh, how will they stand astonished at the faith and revelation of this very thing, that the person of their Messiah, they so long waited for, proves to be their God, Isa. xxv. 7. When the veil shall be taken off from all nations, &c., then, ver. 9, ' It shall be said in that day, Lo, this is our God, we have waited for him.' Oh, wonderful (will they say), this Messiah we waited so for, is our God ; he is so in his person, he will save us ; he is our Saviour also, and his name is Jesus, that saves his people from their sins ; this is the Lord, and he will save us. God and Saviour, you see again, Son of God and Saviour joined ; and this is the faith of believers, this is he they believe upon, and this universally. What one saint is there distrusting it, or questioning it ? For it found the most general acceptation in the hearts of believers, when he wrote to Timothy : 1 Tim. iii. 16, ' And without controversy,' saith he, or with one consent, ' great is the mystery of godliness : God was manifest in the flesh,' or made flesh ; ' justified in the Spirit :' *i. e.*, his Godhead manifested in the resurrection ; ' preached to the Gentiles, and believed on in the world.' This last is that which proves that Christ is God-man, Son of God in the flesh, and was, as such, the prime grand object of all the believers' faith that were in that age of the world ; and he is the great mystery and foundation of all Christian religion ; and therefore under that notion and apprehension of him, made lively and real to our souls, it is that we must come to him. I have not alleged these places singly to prove that Christ is God, though they serve for it, but that as such he is the primary foundation of a believer's faith.

2. The second thing is (which I carry with me still along), that to teach and reveal to souls, that Christ is the Son of God, is the work of the

* Qu. ' Jews' ?—Ed.

Father, which he doth in such a manner, as no human understanding doth
arrive at, nor can attain unto, without his teaching: this is express and
recognised by our Saviour, as his seal of approbation, set to that confession
of Peter's, ' Thou art Christ, the Son of the living God,' Mat. xvi. 16.
' And Jesus answered,' ver. 17, ' and said unto him, Blessed art thou, Simon
Bar-jona : for flesh and blood hath not revealed it unto thee, but my Father
which is in heaven.' It was a revelation which made him blessed, and
such as was peculiar to them that are saved, and which all that are saved
were to have ; and it had not been taught him by man, and by education
alone, &c., nor from his own natural understanding (by which men that
live under the knowledge of divine truths come to profess them, but without
the special revelation of the Father they cannot attain to the blessedness of
true faith), but wholly it was to be ascribed to the Father's revelation,
which is there opposed to flesh, or fleshly ways, of discovery. And lastly,
it is the Father of Christ, his Son : ' My Father,' saith Christ, ' hath
revealed this to thee,' to whom principally this belongs, to reveal this point
of all other, that I am his Son ; for he begat me, and he discovers me to
them whom he means to bless. ' He is thy Lord, worship thou him,' Ps.
xlv. 11. The point the Father instructs her in is, that Christ is her Lord,
and means her God withal (' My Lord and my God,' says Thomas, instructed
by the same hand), as the following words, ' worship thou him,' evince ;
for it is God alone whom we are to worship.

CHAPTER X.

*The uses of the foregoing doctrine.—How we are to exercise faith on the
person of Christ, God-man.*

Use 1. One end of mine in enlarging upon this head is to direct your
faith in your approaches and addresses to Christ, viz., to pitch your souls
upon his person of being God-man, and under the notion and apprehension
thereof, taken in and formed in your minds, still to act all the other several
exercises of your faith upon him. I do not say you have no true faith
unless you have explicit thoughts hereof in all such actings; for foundations
(as this is one) firmly laid in the soul do implicitly work when they are
not *in actu exercito*, or explicitly thought upon, but an habitual apprehension thereof carried along in the soul may have a true and real efficacy
in it ; yet the more you have of explicit, enlarged conceptions thereof, and
reflections thereupon, and the oftener they are renewed, you will find them
the more powerful and working ; for it being so great a truth, that in the
reality of the thing itself, his person in being God and God-man, is that
which gives the ground and foundation, influence and virtue, into all we
believe upon him for; then the explicit acting of faith hereon, and through
the faith of it, upon all else he doth for us, must needs have a proportionable
effect in all. You all know and profess, as touching his person, that he is
God, Son of God, &c., and volant or flying thoughts thereof run through your
minds at times, but do your hearts dwell upon the meditation of it as that
which puts life into your hearts in all you believe concerning him ? For
this his person is not only eternal life (taken abstractedly, as it shall be
possessed in heaven) in the sequel alone, but it is the life of your faith
exercised on his death for forgiveness of sins, for saving from wrath. Many
in their judgments think that the doctrine of the Trinity, and the doctrine

that Christ is God, is but a matter of speculation and contemplation ; and though it is a truth, yet it is such as one might let lie by him, as that which will do them no hurt nor good.   And most men in the practice of their faith make little more use of it than this comes to, whereas it is such a truth as thy life lies in it, even eternal life.   And such the apostles and those believers accounted it, and did cleave to Christ accordingly through the faith of it, and of him under the contemplation of it.   Christ having said he was 'the bread of life that came down from heaven,' and it was his Godhead made him to be that living bread, John vi. 56, useth this phrase, 'He that eateth my flesh, &c., dwelleth in me, and I in him.'   As a man first chews with delight, and then takes down his meat, and by its abiding, its dwelling in him, and his digesting it, it turns into his own body, and so gives life and strength to him, so must it be with our knowledge of Christ ; he must dwell in us by faith, and we in him, and this will quicken you to purpose.   Hath the Father thus taught and instructed thee to live upon him, and to come to him for life as such ?   It is his participation of life from the Father, and so his being Son of the living God, that gives him life, and so through him thou comest to have that life of the Father in thee, by dwelling in him, as the next verse, ver. 57, shews, 'As the living Father hath sent me, and I live by the Father ; so he that eateth me, shall live by me.'

Use 2. The next use is for information of the right state of this assertion I have been upon, that the person of Christ as God-man is the principal object of faith.   You will ask me, Do all that truly believe on him come to him under that apprehension, simply for his person's sake, as moved thereunto by the consideration simply of his person ?   This is a spiritual pitch indeed ; but do all believers at first come to him under this apprehension, and cleave to him for it ?

I answer, that there are two scopes or purposes that I drive at in my having pressed this, that Christ's person is the object of faith.

1st. That the faith on his person as God-man is the foundation of all else we believe upon him for as he is our Saviour ; and as that is it which makes him able to take sins away, and to give us a righteousness to justify us, and which puts that power in force which his death hath to kill sin, and which himself hath to quicken us, so all that we have to deal with him for, and all that our faith is carried out to him, and to God through him for, is all in the virtue and force of this faith first begotten in you, that he is God-man, the Son of God : 1 John v. 5, 'Who is he that overcometh the world, but he that believeth that Jesus is the Son of God ?'   And so in the force, and virtue, and strength of this, that Jesus is the Son of God, it is that we have victory over the world.   It is remarkable, that when Christ had uttered these faithful sayings about himself, John xi. 25, 26, unto Martha, 'I am the resurrection and the life : he that believeth on me, though he were dead, yet shall he live ; and whosoever liveth and believeth on me shall never die.   Believest thou this?'   He then puts her faith strictly to it to answer to these particulars (as one puts a catechist to answer catechetical questions).   Now we see that she doth not answer as one would have thought she should, directly and distinctly unto these particular points of faith in question put unto her, but seems to divert unto another head, unto the great article of faith.   She saith unto him, ver. 27, 'Yea, Lord : I believe that thou art the Christ, the Son of God, which should come into the world.'   This answer she utters in full, and upon the whole matter, unto the question he had put, and though it was [not] in express terms, not *in terminis*, nor in the particulars, but yet fundamentally it was a comprehensive answer, and most direct; for therein she shews she believed that that was the foundation of all these particulars, and of many more things that she believed of him, and indeed of whatever else that Christ might ask her. ' I believe,' says she, ' that thou art the Son of God ;' and this she conceived, and most rightly, to be a full answer unto these particulars; for she saith, Yea, Lord, I believe them all, I believe all that thou hast asked me, by believing this one thing of thee, that thou art the Christ, the Son of God, and so art the cause of all these, and of whatever else is attributed unto him that is the Christ, in the prophecies of him, that he should come into the world. In the virtue and strength of this she believed he was the resurrection of souls dead in sins and trespasses, and of souls that had begun to believe on him ; and then of their bodies at the resurrection, and that he was eternal life, so as they that believe on him shall never perish, and their souls shall never die, whatever their bodies for a while did. And she believed all in the strength of this, that he was the Son of God; so that the believing of this is fundamentally necessary for every Christian to know.

Only I add this, that foundations, though they bear up the whole building, yet oftentimes lie hid under ground after they have been first laid ; and so it is in our faith of principles and foundations, though they remain in the heart, and bear up all of our faith else about what we do believe, yet they are not always drawn out in our thoughts into formed-up propositions, though at first they were inlaid as such. They bear the weight of all, and to have the faith of them is common to all believers, and is universally assented to as a foundation : 1 Tim. iii. 16, ' This is the great mystery of godliness' (that is, the great ground of all godliness, the pith of it) ' God manifested in the flesh, believed on in the world.' And Eph. iv. 13, they ' all come to the unity of the faith,' that shall be saved through all ages ; all that either are now converted, saith the apostle, or that are to be converted (take the lowest Christian) and have these things in their faith about Christ's person, that he is God, and the Son of God.

So that, 1, in coming to him for that which will save them, they come to his person in so doing. They would not have his righteousness and blood, and the fruits of either, pardon of sin, &c., without having himself also; and so it is his person they believe on for their salvation.

Yet, 2, they may be at present moved rather with that in his person which will save them, than with his person himself.

And yet withal, 3, even that also, to come to his person for itself, as the principal motive wherewith to close, is *in radice, in semine*, in the bud, but not in the blossom. There is that in the heart (if drawn out) which is prepared to it, disposed to it, and suited to it.

2dly, A second end and purpose for which God first inlays in the heart the knowledge of Christ's person, and the fulness of the Godhead dwelling personally in our nature, and for which end also I have pressed it, is, that first or last it should become the greatest motive and inducement of our coming to Christ, and to close with him, and cleave to him as such, rather than as a Saviour; that the thought of it should be above that of Saviour, yea, and abstracted in the consideration of it from that of Saviour; and this explicitly, the heart being drawn to him upon that account, and accompanied with affection answerable.

Those that will urge that either this is the first inducement, or the more common inducement, to come to him, principally to have his person, considered in itself and for itself, do press too hard upon weak believers, and urge that to be at first which they are growing up to all their days, and perhaps attain it not in this life. Alas! at first our hearts are taken up with the thoughts of sin, and with Christ as the remedy and Saviour from sin. John's ministry began there in the hearts of his disciples, and he called upon them to 'behold the Lamb of God, that took away the sins of the world.' And the great apostle pronounceth this to be the most 'faithful saying, and worthy of all acceptation, that Christ came into the world to save sinners.' And I am induced to think that in his proposing of it in that place, where he speaks of his own conversion, he had an intent to insinuate that himself had that sentence in his eye at his first conversion chiefly or mainly. Dr Preston's similitude is the best to express this by (I mention him, for I think he was the first that used it of any other), that as when a marriage is proposed unto a woman, that which may move her at first to listen to it may be the hearsay of an estate, and paying her debts with which she is encumbered; these may persuade her to view and see the person, and to entertain a visit from him, and to acquaint herself with him; but after some long converse, her heart is so taken with his person, that if he had nothing, she could beg with him all the world over, for she is satisfied with his person alone. And thus it is between our souls and Christ: we come to Christ at first, as the Lamb of God that takes away our sins, that will save us from wrath, and pay our debts (and the truth is, we must always come so to him, to cleanse us from sin every day). But through 'acquainting ourselves' with him (as the phrase in Job is), there often appears that to us in his person which takes our hearts more than his being a Saviour to us: *est aliquid in Christo formosius Salvatore*, there is something in Christ more beautiful than a Saviour, and our hearts in time may rise up to this. The best composition of this matter is that in the prophet Isaiah, which takes in both, which speaks the hearts of converts from whom the veil was taken off, chap. xxv. 7, who thereupon (in that verse 9) are brought in saying and uttering the bottom of their hearts, 'Lo, this is our God, we have waited for him, and he will save us.' They looked at Christ, and received him both as God and as their Saviour (for of Christ it is spoken, compare 2 Cor. iii. 16–18); and it follows, 'We will rejoice in his salvation.' God allows us we should aim at, and hope for, and rejoice in our salvation by Christ, and come to him upon that account, as well as on the account of his being our God, and Son of God. God and Christ love us so well, as they love we should love ourselves in coming to the Son, and therefore would have us come to him as a Saviour as well as for his person; yea, and to be glad, and rejoice in his salvation. And truly there is good reason that we should do so, both on our part and on his also, for it cost Christ's person something to save us; for he humbled his person, and gave away himself, for he gave away the present glory of his person due to him, that he might save and redeem us, and no less would have done it. And he hath no reason to have his love herein lost or forgotten, or swallowed up only in his person.

Nay, further, led me add, you, being sinners, cannot come to rejoice in his person, or to think with yourselves what a husband you have of him in himself, till you believe on him for pardon of your sins and the salvation of your souls (and therefore faith for justification is in that Epistle to the Romans pressed first); and after you have seen yourselves lost by reason of sin, then you are directed to come to Christ as a propitiation for sin. This he doth discourse in chap. iii., from ver. 21, and in chap. iv., and we must have peace with God as sinners, being justified by faith, Rom. v. 1, ere we can rejoice in God. But then to rejoice in God is made a further attainment and fruit of this faith in the issue in these words, ver. 11, ' But we joy in God through our Lord Jesus Christ.' Yet still take this along with you, that if you come to him as to a Saviour, you may and must come to him as God, and the Son of God, and believe on him as the person who, as such, is your Saviour, and is the foundation of your whole faith on him for your salvation. Yea, and though you come as moved chiefly because he is Saviour, as that for which you come at first, and, in doing so, are accepted of God, and justified and pardoned, yet, let me tell you, you will be more accepted by God after your faith riseth up to take his person as in itself, and as moved to love him from what you see in his person alone, or chiefly considered. God the Father loves it more that you should love the person of Christ in and for himself: John xvi. 27, ' The Father loveth you, because ye have loved me, and have believed that I came out from God;' which is all one as to say, You have believed on and loved me, because I am his dearly and only beloved Son ; than which nothing can endear you more unto him, nor be a higher exercise of faith in you. Some strains of such thoughts and affections as these, though but in the bud, have, as was said, some puttings forth intermingled in weaker believers, that are drawn to him by the faith and hopes of his being their Saviour. Such spirits may run in the veins of your hearts, whilst yet you are most eager to seek salvation; but then they are but as in the bud, they are not fully blossomed. A soul may find he hath some such things offering to rise, and mix themselves with his faith and hopes for salvation ; and this will make your prayers accepted wonderfully, as the words before speak in that John xvi. 26, 27, ' At that day ye shall ask in my name ; and I say not unto you, that I will pray the Father for you ; for the Father himself loveth you, because you have loved me.' And this will more obtain with God, than your faith that your sins are pardoned, and that Christ died for you : yea, far above it. I use to say Christ's love in suffering is more to be valued by you than his suffering, or the fruits of it ; but his person more than all of them. You must know that it is his person you must ultimately abide by ; for in the enjoyment of him in his person will be the top and height of your eternal life, and so, consequently, you have to do with him for evermore; and therefore to have him so revealed to you as to have your hearts taken therewith at present in some lesser tastes and glimpses, is the most spiritual teaching by the Father of all other. And this is attainable in this life, for it is in grace as in the root, and will be drawn out and ripened by the Father. And surely the disciples had the seeds of such dispositions in their hearts, that did look forth sometimes into actual exercises, as appears in that speech that Christ useth of them, ' The Father loveth you, because you have loved me.' And sure some such thing was in Peter's heart when he said, ' Lord, thou knowest that I love thee ;' and that because he was the Son of God ; for that is the main thing they expressed why they cleaved to him, as was said before. And the imperfection of this, and that it abounded no more in them, made Christ complain that they should mourn for themselves, because of his departure from them to heaven; whereas, says he, ' if you had loved me ' (that is, my person itself, as the next words shew), ' you would rejoice, because I go to my Father.' I put this gloss upon that text; for it is all one as if he had said, If you loved my person for itself, you would love my personal good and happiness more than your own, and so have rejoiced more for this than have mourned for your own supposed loss and want of present comfort in me. And many of those primitive Christians had such goings forth of spirit towards the person of Christ as those had whom Peter wrote to: 1 Pet. i. 8, ' On whom believing, though you see him not, ye rejoice with joy unspeakable, and full of glory.' This must be chiefly in and for his person; for his person it is whom we shall one day see, and rejoice in glory with him; and it is faith in the mean time rising to such a pitch as supplies the room of the sight of him with a joy springing from something which is answerable to that sight. And sure Paul had it, who, above all, and in the first place, expresseth his desires to be to win Christ, that is, Christ himself, his person, and to be found in him, and then to have his righteousness, and the power of his death, &c. And I have been induced to think that some such strain of heart was somewhat more prevalent in that eunuch, Acts viii. The man was truly godly before, and therefore he came to worship; and you read his devout employing of himself whilst he was a-travelling. He had the 53d of Isaiah preached over to him by Philip, for the words of the chapter he gave Philip for his text to preach on. And in that chapter we read how that God ' laid upon Christ the iniquity of us all, and made his soul an offering for sin;' and that ' he was led as a sheep to the slaughter,' to take our sins away, as the Baptist had interpreted it. And so Philip preaching to him Jesus, as the text hath it, it lay in his way principally to set out Jesus Christ as a sacrifice for sins; and surely Philip did keep to his text. There is but one passage in the chapter, and in the words which the eunuch read, that gave occasion to him to preach his person to be the Son of God, and that is those words, ' Who shall declare his generation?' Yet we read that when he desired to be baptized, and Philip said to him, ' If thou believest with thy whole heart,' &c. (as if he had said, What is there in thy heart, which thy heart most closeth with, concerning this Christ that I preached to thee?), the eunuch says, ' I believe that Jesus is the Son of God,' so as he pitcheth upon that as that which his heart was most on. And though he closeth with him as a Saviour, according to Philip's preaching, yet *that* is not mentioned by him, but *this*, that he was the Son of God; and so it is said he went away rejoicing, being baptized into Jesus Christ, upon that account.

But though this is attainable, yet Christians are a-growing up to it ordinarily, but by degrees; for, poor creatures as we are, we learn Christ by piece and piece, as when we look upon the moon through a telescope, it appears so big, and vastly great, beyond what we can take in at once, that we must travel over it with our eyes, first taking a view of one part, and then removing the glass to another, and see, perhaps, but a quarter of it at once. And thus it is with our knowing Christ; that is, with such a knowledge as affects us and draws our hearts to him; with such a knowledge we know one thing of him in one year, and another in another. For one stage of our lives our hearts run after him for his blood to wash away our sins, and for his righteousness to cover us in the presence of God. In another stage we pursue after holiness to be had from him, for the subduing corruption through the power of his death, and quickening our hearts with his life; and, in another way* we pursue after him for the loveliness of his person; and it is that we should make the top of our desires, why we should desire him (as the prophet Isaiah speaks unto believers), we are perhaps a-growing up to this all our life long, and attain it not till we come to the being of a more perfect man, and to the fulness of our stature in Christ,

* Qu. ' stage '? —ED.

which we shall have in this life in the knowledge of him as the Son of God; whereof the apostle there speaks, Eph. iv. 13. Yet this let me add, that faith of recumbence may be capable of this, and yet remain in the course of a faith of recumbence; that is, want settled assurance that sins are pardoned; and they may remain such to whom Christ hath not yet said, 'Your sins are forgiven,' and thou art the person that I died for: and so they have not an assurance that he is their Saviour, though they continually exercise faith on him, to be saved through his death; yet their souls in this posture or dispensation are capable of being raised up under this faith, to cleave to him, and follow after him for his person more than as a Saviour. And the reason is, not only because God often works one way, and discovers one thing more to take the heart than he doth another, according to his good pleasure, and so he may give a beam of the knowledge of Christ in his promise, 2 Cor. iv. 6, more bright to inflame their hearts towards him than the apprehension that he is a Saviour. There is not only this reason of it, but God also deals thus with them, that such may be assured, with a clear and certain light, that his person is thus amiable, and glorious, and lovely in himself, which causeth them to cleave to him so as they would not part with him, no, not with his person, for ten thousand worlds; when yet, whether he died for their sins, or will pardon them, is doubtful to them. But the other truth they may have no doubt of, but a discovery of it, and the notion of it lieth more open to such a spirit than the attainment of the assurance of the pardon of his sins.

BOOK III.

The free grace of God, as declared and proposed in the covenant, is the object of faith.—Of the soul's applying itself unto the free grace of God, and treating with it for its salvation.—That the absolute declarations of this free grace, or the absolute promises of the gospel, are the object of faith of recumbence, or adherence.—That election-grace, and the immutability of God's counsel, as indefinitely proposed in the promises, are also the object of faith.—How the believing soul may consider and regard God's absolute decree of election.

CHAPTER I.

How the soul may for its salvation treat with the free grace of God as declared in the covenant.

I SHALL first discourse of a soul's treating with the free grace of God as it is proposed to us in the covenant of grace, before I consider what kind of promises they are which are the object of our faith.   There is a great crying up of free grace, as that which, in the way of believing, men's souls rely upon; but they who have traversed the paths of it, so as to arrive at a free and familiar intercourse therewith, find it exceedingly difficult, until God guides them into it by a straight and direct line.   And there are many dangerous mistakes in the application of our souls unto it in the seeking of it.   I shall therefore treat of it in a way of giving directions about it. (1.) We must lay hold on free grace according as it is set forth in the covenant of grace.   The covenant you have at large in Jer. xxxi., and in Ezek. xxxvi., cited in Heb. viii.   Now the covenant of grace is but the pure resolutions of grace in the heart of God, put into written promises. It is a translating of the pure grace in the heart of God, and purposes thereof, into promises, into indefinite promises, not naming the persons to whom they are designed : they are expressions of purposes as they lay in his heart.   Men think it an easy thing to deal with the grace of God for salvation, and that they need no directions and teachings, for God, say they, is merciful in his nature; he is a merciful God, and it is but going to him for mercy, &c.   But the free grace of the purposes of God, as it is set forth in the covenant, is a further thing than a declaration that God is merciful in his nature; and a man needs teaching how to treat with free grace, as it is in God's heart, set forth in the promises, in the immediate and absolute promises : 2 Thes. iii. 5, ' The Lord direct your hearts into the love of God.'   He speaks of that love which is in the heart of God himself towards us : rightly to go to, and close with, and lay hold on that grace, needs direction, and that from God.   ' The Lord,' says he, ' direct your hearts into the love of God !'   He speaks to those that already had been in some measure acquainted with that love.   All of you whom God saves, one piece of the indenture of his covenant is, that he will teach you to know him.   To know him in what ?   To know him in the pardon of your sins, and how to obtain it at his hands ; for so it follows, ' I will forgive their sins, and their iniquities will I remember no more.'   And to know how to deal with the grace of God for pardon of sin upon grace's own terms, for this men's souls need direction in.   ' The Lord direct your hearts into the love of God !'

I shall shew you some of God's teachings.   ' You shall be all,' says he, ' taught of God ;' taught of God in his free grace.   When free grace comes to teach the heart to treat with grace, it teacheth it,

1. To renounce all self, or else free grace will have nothing to do with you.   From the very first purpose free grace had to save man, it laid that for a foundation, that the salvation should not be of works, but according to the purpose of his grace given us before the world was, 2 Tim. i. 9. There you have it purely set down as it was in God's heart.   And the holy apostle, when he speaks of grace, and of our being saved by grace, he still puts in this negative, ' not of works,' as the opposite of grace, Rom. xi. 5–7.   And whereas faith is required wherewith to close with that grace,— Eph. ii. 8, ' By faith you are saved, through grace, it is the gift of God,'— a man must renounce all power in himself to believe, and all helps to believe, but what are drawn from the pure grace of God : Hosea xiv. 2. See there God's instructions : ' Take with you words,' says he, ' and turn to the Lord, and say to him, Take away all iniquity, and receive us graciously,' &c.   Here you have free grace (as free grace) instructing and teaching men that would turn to God, how to apply themselves unto it.   It is a treaty of free grace's here that is recorded, ' Receive us graciously.'

' I will love them,' says he, ' freely.' ver. 5.   Now he teacheth you upon his own terms how you must deal with his grace.   And that it is upon his own terms, it is clear by this ; for he bids them take these words in their mouth.   So that it is a sure way to know how to treat with the free grace of God.   It must be done with a renunciation of all that is opposite to it, and which will spoil the treaty, and enervate and make it void.   Accordingly they say, ' Asshur shall not save us, we will not ride upon horses,' &c. Asshur *shall not save us.*   He expresseth it in Old Testament language under the figure of a temporal deliverance.   We will not (say they) call in the help of Asshur, nor think to ride upon horses.   You must be helpless, you must not think to deal with free grace on horseback, for you shall not prevail so ; no, nor on foot neither, for ' it is not in him that willeth, or that runneth, but in God that sheweth mercy,' Rom. ix. 16.   And so the close is here, It is not our hands in which we trust ; we will not say, the work of our hands shall save us ; but how then ?   ' With thee the fatherless find mercy :' as if he had said, The strengthless, the helpless, the utterly desolate of all helps by means, but only the free grace of God and Christ, the fatherless, shall find mercy.   For the soul to give up itself to the graciousness of grace to accept it, to receive it graciously, to give up itself to the efficacy and power of free grace to work what it will, with renunciation of all else, this is the first lesson free grace teacheth, when a man will come to have salvation by it.   I will not meddle with you else, says God ; lay that for the foundation of your treaty, or my grace shall not treat with you at all.   What is free grace ?   God tells you in these words, ' I will love them freely.'   What is grace ?   It is love : ' I will love them freely,' says God ; and all their backslidings shall be no discouragement to me.   Now you see God bids you take words; he hath put the substance and efficacy of those words into your mouths, and they are his own terms.   I have oft said, If a soul would but go and take the very words (understanding them) as they are recorded where the covenant of grace was penned (Jer. xxxi. 33, 34, and the like in Ezek. xxxvi., ' I will give a new heart :' and in Jer. xxxii. 40, ' I will put my fear into your hearts, and you shall not depart from me ;' this is pure absolute grace).   If a man should take these words that God hath put into his mouth, and use them, or the effect of them, to God, saying, Lord, I present them to thee, and beseech thee to make them good to my poor soul, and should seek God day and night, the Lord would own and accept that poor soul.

2. God teacheth the soul to treat with the grace of God in the free sovereignty of it.   There is the grace of God's nature, which you read of in Exod. xxxiv., ' The Lord God, gracious and merciful,' &c.   The 33d chapter was a preface unto what follows in the 34th chapter concerning the proclaiming his name; and, saith God, ' I will proclaim my name before thee ; and I will be merciful to whom I will be merciful, and I will be gracious to whom I will be gracious.'   This is a plain declaration that that grace of salvation he would not shew to anybody.   It is a limitation : ' I will be gracious to whom I will be gracious, I will be merciful,' &c. ; I will have freedom, and exercise dominion in doing of it.   Are you to treat with grace ?   You are to treat with this same declaration—' I will be gracious,' &c., ' and I will be merciful to,' &c.—and you are to apply yourselves to the sovereignty of it.   This is to treat free grace upon its own terms.   When a poor soul sees itself lost, and comes to God, to the free grace of God, he doth not come on horseback, nor on foot neither, but he falls flat down at the throne and sovereignty of God: ' He will be gracious to whom he will be gracious,' &c.   He hath to do with this same will of the great God, and the soul acknowledgeth that he is absolutely free, and that he may choose whether to do it to me or any such poor unworthy wretch as I am; he may if he please not shew me any mercy: ' Whom he will he hardens,' as the apostle saith, Rom. ix.   And I am a poor creature, says he, and I lay down myself at thy feet; if thou wilt be merciful, here I am; I throw myself upon thee, thou mayest give me up to hardness.   If souls come thus nakedly to him, he then hath a dominion, to cast them off, as fully as to accept them.   If thou comest thus nakedly to him, thou hast nothing to ingratiate his grace but his own grace, which he shews to whom he will; and that *will* hath a will: ' I *will* be gracious because I *will* be gracious.'   Because mercy pleaseth him, and mercy and grace hath taken thy heart, poor creature, thou comest to him to cast it that way.   The absolute freeness and dominion of grace is the glory of it, and God will have our hearts brought to seek it, as it lies in his heart. God loves to have it acknowledged, at one time or other, by every soul he saves.   Though I dare not say that there is an absolute necessity of such a disposition of soul, yet to be sure when the soul thus applies itself in treating with grace, there is true faith and dependence on God.   There is not only an acknowledging that God may refuse me if he please, but the soul says, If thou hast no pleasure in me, here I am; my will is made subject as well as my understanding, it must be thine own pleasure purely must cast it on me; this is faith of submission.   And yet withal thinks the soul, Who knows but he may be merciful, and merciful to me ?   And that keeps it at the throne of grace, and will not let it go away.

3. Free grace loves to be treated according to the fulness of its own free-

ness, and the extent of its own freeness. The meaning is, it is absolutely as free to God to save any sort of sinner, one as another, it is as indifferent to him to save out of any condition. So that put what case you will, put what condition you will, free grace hath a freedom to extend itself to it. It is not only said, ' I will be merciful to whom I will be merciful' as for the person, but there is a nobleness of liberality, so that there is no sort of sin (the sin against the Holy Ghost excepted) but may be pardoned, no sort of condition—be it poor, weak, contemptible, what you will—but a man may be saved in it. Now, when the soul sees this, he honours free grace mightily; he comes not to be accepted because he hath fewer sins, that were to derogate from grace, nor is he discouraged because of the abundance of sin; no, for there is an amplitude in this grace, Rom. iii. 22–24. As to the point of being saved by grace, grace knows no differ- ence; so for thy outward condition, be it what it will, there is no condition any one is in but one or other have been in it and saved; for God is no accepter of persons, but is rich to all that call upon him. Now, to have a soul possessed with the thoughts of the freeness of his grace, and to treat with God accordingly, this honours his grace, and this God loves, and this he delights in.

4. We must treat with this grace as that which is absolute, unchange- able, irreversible, where it is once pitched. If I in seeking God can find this grace of God to own me and embrace me while I seek it, then what do I come to ? To a state of irreversible grace, of grace that will carry on the work, that will undertake all for me, that is faithful, and will do it. What says God ? Ps. lxxxix. 32, 33, ' Though they break my laws, I will visit their transgressions with the rod, and their iniquities with stripes. Nevertheless my loving-kindness will I not utterly take from him, nor suffer my faithfulness to fail.' You have it also in Isaiah liv. 10, ' With ever- lasting kindness will I have mercy on thee. The mountains shall depart, and the hills be removed; but my kindness shall not depart from thee.' Noah's waters may as soon overflow to cover the earth, as thy sins over- flow thy heart. When the soul shall thus have the amplitude of grace, of grace past, present, and to come before it, and turns itself round about, and sees no end, Oh, says the soul, that my heart may be the subject of this grace ! that I may come under the dominion and protection of this grace ! For this grace will do the business, it will do it thoroughly; it answers all my objections, makes provisos for them; it satisfies all the desires that I have or can have. Now, suppose that God yet carries it concealed towards thee, yet thou art happy if he fires thy heart with this grace, and causeth thy soul to seek after it, and teacheth thy heart to come to God, and to spread all these properties of his grace before him, whereby he saves men, and thy heart is strengthened to plead that God would cast them upon thyself, and thou canst by the hour relate between him and thee how by this grace thou desirest to be saved, and by no other. Though thou hearest of other ways, of free-will grace, where God moves but leaves thee to will, yet if thou hadst ten thousand souls thou wouldst not venture one that way. Dost thou heartily say to God, Lord, I had rather go upon this way of free grace than upon that way of free-will grace, though offered to all ? Oh save me this way ! Lord, I have no- thing to return, but I shall ' render the calves of my lips;' I shall adore thee and bless thee. Oh that there should be such purposes of grace, and that they should thus take my heart; I am resolved to be saved no way if not saved this way, and by this grace. To be thus taught and instructed,

you had need have the Lord 'direct your hearts,' 2 Thes. iii. 5. In the original it is to direct by a right line; it is an emphatical expression to signify such a direction as that they shall not go about, but go straight and immediately unto the heart of God and love of God.

What do men do? They come with their conditions to ingratiate themselves with God when they come to treat with grace, which is to bring to grace what should ingratiate their souls to it. We use to say, God's grace is a preventing grace, preventing what is in man; but by this way men would prevent the grace of God, and be aforehand with it. Do not go round about, but go by a right line, and venture thyself, though thou knowest not whether thou beest the person or no, and lie at God's feet. To bring conditions whereby thy faith should be raised to free grace is not agreeable to the mind of grace. The truth is, you will find free grace will say to your souls, I will not be thus dealt withal.

Obj. Would you have us use no endeavours, means? &c.

Ans. This I said is so remote from it, as nothing is more. In Noah's instance, though God said to him, 'Thou hast found grace in my sight,' yet 'he prepared an ark.' And in Philip. ii. 12, 13, we are commanded to 'work out our salvation; for it is God that worketh,' &c. But how work out our own salvation? We are to use those endeavours which we have power to use, in subordination to the grace of God, that works the will and deed, and we are to wait in the use of means, renouncing all we do as to any purpose of ingratiating ourselves with God, yet we are to use these means in subordination to God, that works the will and the deed.

Obj. But would you have a man treat free grace thus, and leave out holiness?

Ans. God forbid; for if you seek the grace of God in truth, and as it is in itself, and in the heart of God, then if your heart know the grace of God in truth, it will teach you to be holy, and to make gracious returns to God again: Titus ii. 11, 12, 'The grace of God hath appeared, &c., teaching us to deny all ungodliness,' &c. It is spoken of the gospel and doctrine of it which thus teacheth you. But if God the Father do instruct your heart, and make known to you his free grace as it is in his heart and draws you to depend upon it, wholly upon it, if so be you have learnt from the Father what it is for God to be gracious, and how he is gracious to a poor soul (or as it is in John vi. 45, if you have 'learnt of the Father'), you will be taught to be holy, yea, it is part of your indenture when you come to plead the covenant of grace. The grace of God is the greatest teacher of holiness that ever was: says God in that covenant of grace, Jer. xxxi., 'I will write my law in their heart.' Of all laws else he will write the supreme law which free grace hath to write. What is that? To have the grace in God answered with grace in you; to have your hearts ingenuously wrought upon to comply with his grace, and not to abuse it: Col. i, 6, 'If you have known the grace of God in truth,' &c. There is a true knowledge of the grace of God, and there is a counterfeit one; but if it be true, it teacheth all holiness, it stamps a frame of heart upon you, it teacheth you how to apply yourselves to grace in its kind, and therefore to return grace for grace and love for love. It is the law of the thing, it is the law of nature to love those that love you, and on whose love you depend. It is the law of pure nature, and it is the pure law of grace: 1 John ii. 4, 'He that saith, I know him, and keepeth not his commandments, is a liar;' that is, doth not know God. Not know him! In what? Do not know him in his love, ver. 13, 15. For it is the love of the Father he speaks of. I tell you, no man seeks grace in this manner I speak of, but he professeth to God and his own soul that he would not be saved by that grace unless it wrought holiness in him. It is part of the indenture he draws with God. I acknowledge that to be made holy simply upon the sight of the pure grace of God, it is a high and spiritual thing, and our hearts are carnal. The law is holy and spiritual, the terms of free grace are holy and spiritual, and we poor wretches are carnal and sold under sin, and cannot come off to the motives thereof, to be acted by it continually. It is true, but yet when the soul lay at God's feet to obtain it, and humbled itself, that soul thereby kept on a plea for holiness as well as for grace, and doth obtain it, and hath it wrought in his soul. He that hath the love of this world, hath not the Father's, 1 John ii. 15. A man whose heart is taken with the grace of God to be saved by it, if he loves the world inordinately, or more than God, the love of the Father is not in him, he knows it not; but of a gracious soul the apostle saith, Rom. vi. 14, ' Sin shall not have dominion,' for grace shall break the dominion of sin. Those cursed men, Jude 4, turned the grace of God into wantonness (they were Simon Magus's followers, and the devil was his master), and what did they profess? That a man was saved wholly by grace, do what he would, and that was the grace of the Father. Oh how doth the apostle fly out against these men, and follow them with all the curses that God brought upon wicked men in the Old Testament, and upon the angels that fell ! Men that have nothing but self-righteousness in them to be wrought upon, they wonder to hear that the grace of God should work a man above himself, to love God above himself, that a man should be taken with free grace, and not abuse it; for the nature of self-love is to run away with free grace, and be unthankful. But what is the grace we speak of, as it is in the heart of a Christian? If self-love only, it were the worst direction ever was given to teach self-love to serve its turn, and to run away with salvation, and let self do as it pleaseth. But the doctrine of free grace which we profess to salvation, is a principle of love to God above a man's self; there is that at the bottom. If it be so, then the more pure and clear you can bring this grace in the heart of God towards a poor soul, you move that man so much the more, you boil up grace to a height. If there be love and grace in the soul, and that grace be prevailing, it will work answerably, it will make the grace of God its greatest interest, because it is God's. We profess this is the principle of grace, and therefore to teach men thus to follow the grace of God is to teach them that principle that must be put into them by the Holy Ghost.

CHAPTER II.

What high regards the faith of the apostle Paul had to the free grace of God the Father as the object of it.—How he magnifies and celebrates this free grace discovered to his apprehensions and thoughts.

*I obtained mercy, because I did it ignorantly in unbelief. And the grace of our Lord was exceeding abundant with faith and love which is in Christ Jesus.—*1 TIMOTHY I. 13, 14.

The Holy Ghost hath declared Paul ' a pattern' in his conversion ' to those that are after to believe,' 1 Tim. i. 16, and as a pattern of encouragement and hopes to the greatest of sinners that were to come after him, to believe. And so likewise in the very work of conversion he is proposed as an example also unto them, although he indeed at first attained unto that perfection therein which other converts are growing up unto in their whole lives. But yet the seeds of the whole being sown, and foundations laid in their first work, they are springing up to a full growth throughout their whole lives. As every child that comes into the world by ordinary generation hath the same parts essential to mankind, both of the inwards of bowels and ventricles of the head, in a less size and proportion than Adam had, who was made a man of full stature by an extraordinary way of creation, and therefore had all in the full proportions of a man grown up to perfection, and also each part acting in their full vigour and activity from the first; so is it here, every convert receives all the same principles of faith and love at first, only the actings and increase thereof do in many things grow up into an actual energy, and yet so as at the first those principles do necessarily so far act in all converts as is requisite to put them into a state of life and salvation. And this, in the point of the actings of faith upon God and Christ for justification and salvation, is in a special manner seen; some men's spirits being more intensely carried out unto God the Father for grace and mercy, others more unto Christ Jesus for his righteousness, although whilst they act faith more upon the one or the other, they yet implicitly take in the other, whilst they look more on God's grace and mercy, yet so as they regard it in and through Christ, and è contra.

But our great convert here, in this narration of his conversion, is propounded unto us as an high example of faith drawn forth in an intense manner unto each, both the grace of God and Christ, in the most abounding workings of it. In the book of the Acts, we find an historical relation of the outward circumstances and manner of his conversion, twice related by himself. In this Epistle to Timothy, he acquaints us with the most intimate working, impressions, and sentiments of his spirit, and what principally his heart was taken up about at the time thereof, the sense whereof he retained unto that day; and these especially he utters in ver. 14 : 'And the grace of our Lord was exceeding abundant with faith and love which is in Christ Jesus.' He had begun to give solemn thanks to Christ (the great donor and endower of all gifts unto men, Eph. iv.), ver. 12, for putting him into that office and dignity of the apostleship, and this from the time of his conversion. 'And I thank Christ Jesus our Lord,' says he, 'who hath enabled me, for that he counted me faithful, putting me into the ministry,' which blessing he greateneth from the consideration of his having formerly been so great a blasphemer of Christ, and a persecutor of his new created Christian church, and professors of him : ver. 13, 'Who,' says he, 'was before a blasphemer, a persecutor, and injurious.' But then, in the middle of that ver. 14, he proceeds more particularly to magnify the mercy and grace of his conversion for the salvation of his own soul, without which, though the grace of apostleship might have saved others, yet himself had proved a castaway, as was the case of Judas; that therefore is the great mercy which he centres in the following verses, and therein first (as I take it, and humbly submit it, together with this my analysis of the whole paragraph to ver. 18) he predicates the grace and mercy of God the Father shewn to him in and through Jesus Christ; 'But I was bemercied,' says he, or was 'endowed with mercy, because I did it ignorantly in unbelief.' And the grace of our

Lord was exceeding abundant with faith and love which is in Christ Jesus.'
Then, secondly, he magnifieth Jesus Christ for his mercy also in coming
into the world to save him, the chief of sinners ; ver. 15, 16, ' This is a
faithful saying, and worthy of all acceptation, that Christ Jesus came into
the world to save sinners ; of whom I am chief.   Howbeit for this cause I
obtained mercy, that in me first Jesus Christ might shew forth all long-suffering, for a pattern to them which should hereafter believe on him to life
everlasting.'   And then, lastly, he shuts up the whole with this solemn
doxology, or giving glory to God the Father : ver. 17, ' Now, unto the
King eternal, immortal, invisible, the only wise God, be honour and glory
for ever and ever.   Amen.'

And when he enters upon this narrative of his conversion, he at first
useth a word somewhat uncouth, whereby to express the mercy of it, a
word whereof in the English tongue we cannot give the full and proper
force in one word (which the Greek itself is), I was ' bemercied' (if we
may so speak), *misericordia donatus*,* endowed with mercy, encompassed
with mercy.   It is a like word unto that spoken to to the blessed virgin,
Luke i. 28, κεχαριτωμένη, ' gracioused,' or one whom God's singular grace
owned, embraced ; and so here says the apostle, I was 'mercified,' ' endowed
with mercy,' I had nothing but mercy, and was all over mercy.   There was
not only nothing of merit, but no fitness or any disposition in me towards
it to make way for it, but the contrary ; only there was a capacity, a possibility left of having mercy bestowed upon me (that was all), ' because I did
it ignorantly,' says he, ' and in unbelief ; ' which imports that if he had
pursued those injuriousnesses, and persecuted Christ and his saints, having
first had a conviction of sight that accompany those actings, they had been
that unpardonable sin, and would have rendered him incapable of all grace
and mercy.   And he useth this word this first time (for it is after also) in
relation to God the Father's mercy then vouchsafed in calling him by
grace (as he elsewhere says, Gal. i. 17, speaking of the Father), which
proceeded from his electing love, grace, and mercy towards him, which
there, Gal. i., you have also expressed in those words, ' When it pleased
God, who had separated me from the womb' ; (that that is an election-
phrase, see Æstius on the words, and others).   And this separation of him
had ordered all things all along from the womb about him, and in his
course of life before his conversion had taken care to keep and prevent
from falling into that unpardonable sin, upon the very brink of the pit
whereof he had at last walked.   And then ' called me by his grace,' says
he there ; the wonderful mercy of which he here also, narrating his conversion, celebrates ; and indeed our first calling, as it is the breaking forth
of election-grace and mercy, so it bears the image and pattern of it.   I was
then bemercied (says he), drenched, and covered all over with the abundant
mercies thereof.   It was poured forth upon my soul by wholesale, and
on the sudden, and at once.   This was the execution of election ; and
this first mention of this word I in my interpretation refer to God the
Father's grace, to whom both calling and election are everywhere peculiarly
attributed.

Now, observe how he again repeats the same word (for he useth it twice
on this occasion and in this place, for he delighted in it and in the very
thinking of it), and inserts it when Christ's part at his conversion comes to
be related ; ver. 15, 16, ' This is a faithful saying, and worthy of all acceptation, that Christ Jesus came into the world to save sinners ; of whom I

* See Beza's reason against the ordinary translation.

am chief. Howbeit for this cause I obtained mercy, that in me first Jesus Christ might shew forth all long-suffering, for a pattern to them which should hereafter believe on him to life everlasting.'

Now in this verse 14 he proceeds to magnify this grace of God the Father, discovered at and in his conversion, with the highest elogy and epithets that could be given it—'and the grace of our Lord,' says he, ' was super-abundant,'—and together therewith to acquaint us with the principal inward workings of his heart, and most intimate exercises and actings of his own spirit towards that superabundant grace that shined on him at his first conversion; and to declare with what entertainment or acceptation (as his word is, ver. 15) he received that, and took in that grace then discovered, he adds these words, ' With faith and love, which is in Jesus Christ,' which are the two graces that answer, by way of return and reception, unto the grace of God when discovered, and are exercised about, and act thereupon. He speaks not here of the work of his first humiliation for sin, which is the first work in all true conversions (though he hints that he had deep and thorough impressions that way, in saying, ver. 15, ' me, the chiefest of sinners'), but here he omits it, and mentions only the work of faith and love, the principal object directly acted upon being the free grace of God. And to set forth these actings of his soul thereupon I take to be his principal scope in this verse. The chiefest question about this interpretation is my referring those words, ' and the grace of our Lord,' unto God the Father, because the title *our Lord* is more frequently given to Christ, in distinction from the Father, and is given unto Christ in ver. 12 afore, and also Christ is only mentioned in ver. 15, 16 afterward. I find some interpreters, as Calvin and others,* on this 14th verse call it ' the grace of God,' without the mention of Christ here ; and some others say *gratia Dei in Christo*, the grace of God in Christ, which still denotes the grace of God, though in and through Christ. And many of those that carry the words to Christ, yet ever and anon put in also ' the grace of God,' and, as it were, could not forbear but to do it. But the reasons of my interpretation, which will also serve to solve the objection, are,—

1. Because grace is most frequently ascribed to the Father in the point of justification and salvation (which is the thing he speaks of here, as ver. 15 shews), and that in distinction from Christ, as out of Rom. v. and chap. iii. may be observed ; though also it is sometimes given to Christ, yet most usually, I say, unto the Father ; even as the title of *our Lord* is sometimes given the Father, though more commonly to Christ, which solveth part of the objection. But besides, to speak more close to the point, those other places wherein Paul gives the account of his conversion, which I call parallels to this, and therefore argue from them as such, he still entitleth the grace thereof unto the Father. Thus Gal. i. 15, 16, ' But when it pleased God, who separated me from my mother's womb, and called me by his grace, to reveal his Son in me, that I might preach him among the heathen.' And the very same you find, 1 Cor. xv. 9, 10, ' For I am the least of the apostles, that am not meet to be called an apostle, because I persecuted the church of God. But by the grace of God I am what I am: and his grace which was bestowed upon me was not in vain; but I laboured more abundantly than they all : yet not I, but the grace of God which was with me.'

2. There did always rise up to me, in the reading of this scripture, a distinction, implied in the verse itself, of Jesus Christ from him whom he

* Calvin, Dickson, Illyricus.

calls our Lord, to whom the grace is ascribed. 'The grace of our Lord,' says he, 'was exceeding abundant with faith and love which is in Christ Jesus.' That last clause, 'and love which is in Jesus Christ,' speaks of Christ as of another person from *our Lord* spoken of afore. He says not, 'and love *unto* Jesus Christ,' but *in* Jesus Christ, noting that love of his to have been borne to some other person in and through Christ. And if so, then unto whom more properly than unto that person of whom he had immediately before spoken, and whose grace, he says, had been so abounding to him? Which person must be the Father, if a person distinct from Christ; and so he speaks of a love returned unto him in and through Christ, for his grace shewn him in Christ, as all the Father's grace is said to be, who hath chosen us in Christ.

3. Though he from thence runs the rest of his discourse upon Jesus Christ in the two following verses, 15, 16, magnifying him for his hand and mercy shewn in his conversion, yet in the conclusion he issues all in giving glory to God the Father, ver. 17, and as one not having words to set forth that grace any further, he chooseth to break off, and falls to adoring God the Father: 'Now unto the King eternal, immortal, invisible, the only wise God, be honour and glory for ever and ever. Amen.' Wherein he speaks in the usual style of doxologies given to God the Father upon such solemn occasions. Thus in the same Epistle we have it, chap. vi. 15, 16, 'Who is the blessed and only potentate, the King of kings, and Lord of lords; who only hath immortality, dwelling in the light which no man can approach unto, whom no man hath seen, or can see: to whom be honour and power everlasting. Amen.' Wherein this honour and praise is given to God the Father distinct from Christ, as by the comparing the last words of the verse afore it appears. Now this glory, thus solemnly given in this first chapter, all acknowledge to refer to the grace of his conversion before related, and so to signify him to have been the person whose infinitely abounding grace had done all this for him. He had begun to thank Jesus Christ, ver. 12, but he ends with glory to the Father; and in reason, that being the grand and solemn conclusion of this his narrative, it may well be thought that an express mention of the Father his grace therein should be found somewhere in the premises; and where else if not in these words of ver. 14? for all the rest did run wholly upon Christ. Yea, and if it be not there, then that of the mercy of God the Father is wholly left out, unless argued by way of inference, in this narrative of the greatest conversion that ever was in the world; and also that when he sets himself to celebrate the grace towards him shewn therein in words so high, as superabundant, &c., the like to which are not anywhere else to be found, unless in that Rom. v. 20, ὑπερεπερίσσευσεν ἡ χάρις, and there it is apparently spoken of the grace of the Father, in distinction from, though in conjunction with, Christ and his righteousness, as verse the last and those afore shew. 'The grace of our Lord was exceeding abundant,' ὑπερεπλεόνασε, it flowed over, or issued forth with an abundancy, yea, overplus; so in Rom. v.; it overfilled Paul, and ran over and over, as more than enough. He compares himself to a vessel (and we are styled vessels of mercy and grace, Rom. ix.), into which, on a sudden, were poured forth from above spouts and floods by wholesale, that not only filled it brimful, but to a running over on every side. Yea, he speaks as if the windows of heaven, the flood-gates thereof, even of the heart of God, filled with that infinite treasury of love and grace towards him, had been set open, and had poured down the streams thereof into his soul.

The next inquiry may be, in what manner it is he intends that this grace of God had so superabounded, whether in the way of effects, that is, in so stupendous a work of converting so prodigious a sinner unto God, in implanting in his soul the principles of faith and love, and of the whole new creature, in one so confirmed and hardened in unbelief, and so resolute in such a violent fury against Christ and his saints; so that the abundance of that grace was demonstrated in so mighty and wonderful effects (which is all, or the main that interpreters here take notice of, as wherein this superabounding grace was seen), or whether withal he intends not to speak *apprehensivè*, that is, in respect of the discovery of that grace itself, as it was and had been borne towards him in the heart of God, and now broke forth upon his soul in and to his own apprehensions. To this query I answer,

1st, That it is true that the superabundancy of God's grace must needs have been discovered to him in so great and wonderful a change and work wrought upon him, for it was unparalleled grace to work it, and there was a just ground for him to adore it as he doth. Yet,

2dly, In the knowledge of it barely by such effects, the cause itself remains hidden, and might still not have been known in itself, no otherwise than in what is different from itself, for so the effects are from their causes; and such a knowledge is but secondary. And,

3dly, It would not have been said that the grace of the Lord had been over-full, or more than enough, in respect of the works of faith and love, for the works thereof themselves were yet imperfect in him; but we may say of the grace as it is in God's heart, and as it is apprehended and laid hold on by us, by immediate faith, that so indeed it superabounds, both as to what it hath wrought, and in all which it hath undertaken to work for us; and this is infinite, and stretcheth itself, and extendeth to all eternity. And this grace, thus taken in as it was by Paul (that chosen vessel, Acts ix.), might well be deemed to be infinitely more than he could take in, and so to overflow, as hath been said.

But further, we may know that there is a flowing of the grace and love that is in God himself to men's souls in manifestation made by itself, and of itself, which the apostle calls a ' shedding abroad the love of God into the heart by the Spirit,' Rom. v., and it is one after-fruit of faith which many attain to. There is a taste of the pure unmixed sweetness in and of the grace of God, as it comes from out of his own heart, and is immediately conveyed through those breasts of consolation, the absolute promises whereof even new-born babes do oft partake : 1 Pet. ii. 3, ' As new-born babes desire the sincere milk, &c., if so be you have tasted that the Lord is gracious.' Which surely this our apostle (if ever any) had at this his very infancy of regeneration ; and that was it, and the experience thereof was it that drew him here to declare that the grace of our Lord was superabundant; not *re ipsa* only, as it resides in God's heart unknown to us, nor as demonstrated only by those gracious effects it had wrought in him, but *apprehensivè*, or in his own apprehensions and sentiments of it ; and in that sense it is he especially utters this here. He saw and laid hold of, and took in, that fulness of the grace of God borne towards him, and as it now was, and had been, from everlasting ; a grace which was over-full, as his word is, that is, as to his own thoughts and comprehensions. What he prayed for the Ephesians, that they might ' comprehend with all saints, the height, the breadth, length, and depth of God's grace towards them, and know the love of Christ which passeth knowledge,' the same himself found in his measure, in the glorious sight, sense, and taste of this superabounding grace, which he found was not only ' sufficient' (as 2 Cor. xii. 9), but more than enough for his turn ; and, to be sure, more than enough for his soul to take in.   It came upon his spirit as a mighty sea, which had neither shore nor bottom.   He saw there was an infinity of it, which he was no more able to take in into his comprehension, no more than a narrow vessel is able to take into itself the main ocean; and in this respect it is he terms it such abundant grace.   To conclude ; in a word, it is *objectivè* spoken, as to the grace itself, as it was presented unto him for the object of his faith, but *apprehensivè* as to his soul, and not *efficienter* only, that is, as an efficient cause of that work of faith God had wrought upon his heart, unto which most would needs narrow it.   It was not a mere reflection upon the operation of the grace of faith and love, as in his heart, but a far more enlarged contemplation and admiration of the height and depth of the grace itself as it was in God's heart, now manifesting itself unto him, how superabundantly and how greatly he was beloved (as the angel says of Daniel), or how abundantly he was graciously accepted by God in his beloved, as in Eph, i. 6.   And the grace in God himself was its own reporter of it.   Paul first had seen how sin had abounded in himself, the chiefest of sinners (ver. 15), and then that that grace borne in God's heart to pardon, love, and accept him, had abounded much more for the pardon of it ; and grace, as justifying him without anything in himself, was the object his heart was now taken up withal at his conversion.

CHAPTER III.

That absolute declarations about God and Christ, and absolute promises of salvation, are the most proper and only objects of that act of application of faith we call faith of recumbency or adherence.

By absolute declarations, &c., I mean such as are not made unto conditions or qualifications, which first should be viewed by the soul to be in itself as a ground to believe upon God and Christ for justification.

Gerard, in his controversy* with Bellarmine, puts this meaning upon the terms absolute promises and conditional.   The promises (says he, speaking of the gospel-promises) may be called absolute as in opposition unto our works and merit, and yet conditional in that God requireth faith, and so no works being required to justification, they are in that respect not conditional.   But granting, as well as he, that faith is requisite, and faith alone, I do withal affirm that there are promises that are absolute, holding forth no condition, as they are the object of faith.   And faith, viewing merely what is in those promises, which specify no condition of faith itself, lays hold on God's grace, and Christ as therein manifested.   And thus absolute promises stand in a full opposition unto all conditional promises, as those absolute promises may be supposed, and objected first unto faith's view, and as they are the raisers up of it thereupon, so as upon the sight thereof the soul is brought to apply the salvation made known in such promises.   Now the promises are such as these : Jer. xxxi. 33, ' This shall be the covenant that I will make with the house of Israel; after those days, saith the Lord, I will put my law in their inward parts, and I will write it in their hearts ; and I will be their God, and they shall be my people.'

* Ger. de Justif., sect. 134.

Which being immediately made to the elect, and being an absolute undertaking on God's part, to perform the conditions themselves, I therefore call them most absolute. That declaration also is absolute in John vi. 37, ' All that the Father hath given me shall come to me.' Likewise, Heb. iv. 6, ' some must enter in,' whereunto God hath bound himself with an oath (as there) to perform it. Now as for the persons concerning whom these promises are made, they are only known to God : ' The Lord knoweth who are his,' 2 Tim. ii. 19. Some detract from the absoluteness of these promises, in saying they are made upon other fore-supposed lower and subordinate prerequisite conditions to be performed first by men, as to improve natural helps well, &c. But this were to embase the covenant of grace by subjecting it to the covenant of works, as that which must take its rise from former actings of ours, predisposing to the gifts of grace. From all which works in that very place in Jeremiah, the prophet distinguisheth those promises of that covenant of grace.

Thus absolute promises in the controversies with the remonstrants are on all sides understood ; *Quæ non habent annexam conditionem*, which have not a condition annexed, as upon the sight of which our faith on those conditional promises should any way depend.

I join unto promises of salvation the absolute declarations in the word, because there are many such manifestations of God and Christ delivered in the word, as they are the objects of our faith, which yet we do not ordinarily term promises, though they are tantamount thereunto, as they are objected to our faith. And indeed all such truths and declarations may be taken for and turned into absolute promises, and absolute promises into such naked declarations ; such declarations, I mean, as these, that Christ ' came into the world to save sinners,' &c., which is delivered in way of a saying: ' This is a faithful saying,' or grand assertion of the gospel, rather than in a direct promissory way. And in terming these declarations rather, I conform to the language of the Holy Ghost, who, when he most setly proposed God and Christ as the objects of our faith, useth that expression to do it by, Rom. iii. 25, ' Whom (*i. e.*, Christ) God hath set forth to be a propitiation through faith in his blood, to declare his righteousness,' &c. Then again, ver. 26, ' To declare, I say, at this time his righteousness, that he might be just, and a justifier of him which believeth in Jesus.' It is used, you see, both of God and Christ as in relation to our faith. You have the like also 1 Tim. ii. 5, 6, ' For there is one God, and one Mediator between God and men, the man Christ Jesus, who gave himself a ransom for all, to be testified in due time.' And 2 Tim. i. 9, 10, the like, ' Who hath saved us, and called us with a holy calling, not according to our works, but according to his own purpose and grace, which was given us in Christ Jesus before the world began, but is now made manifest by the appearing of our Saviour Jesus Christ, who hath abolished death, and brought life and immortality to light through the gospel.' Where not only God and Christ as Saviour, &c., but the very eternal purposes and grace of God and Christ of saving, as they are properly and only to be limited to the elect, are said to be the matter of the gospel. And the manifestation and naked declaration of this, according to its plain intent and purpose, is the gospel in its height and eminency, and the seed and head of all the promises of salvation, from which they are all derived and flow, and into which they all do again run, as rivers into the sea. And therefore by absolute declarations I intend all in the word wherein those purposes of grace are indefinitely revealed ; I say *indefinitely*, because there is no naming the persons of the sons of men to whom they are intended, and yet they are in that manner revealed, and with that intent, to draw men in to believe for their particular salvation, as well as any other promises whatever. And this I hope will appear plainly in this discourse, but especially in that which follows it, unto which this is but introductory, the professed subject thereof being to shew how faith of adherence may make use of the absolute revelation of electing grace, though wanting assurance thereof; which I have long since in print promised to publish.*

Mr Bulkely, in that New-England controversy, seems to be an opposer of this opinion, that absolute promises are the means and primary object of full assurance of faith, through an immediate testimony of the Spirit, without conditional promises; by which only, says he,† in the ordinary course, if we will have any trial of our estates by the word, we must have it by the conditional promises; yet would I not, says he further, make the absolute promises useless. I acknowledge they are of singular use; 1st, In that they shew us the only cause of our salvation, even free grace, and no other; 2dly, They are a foundation for the faith of adherence or dependence to stay upon. There be two acts of faith, saith he, one of adherence or dependence, another of assurance. There be also two kinds of promises, absolute and conditional. Mark now how these do fit and answer one another, the absolute promises to the faith of adherence, the conditional to the faith of assurance. For example, God comes and says, For mine own sake will I do thus and thus unto you, in an absolute promise. Here is a ground for the faith of adherence to cleave unto; though I be most unworthy, yet will I hang upon this promise, because it is for his own sake that the Lord will perform this mercy, that he may be glorified. There be also conditional promises,—' He that believeth shall be saved,'—by means of which (we have the experience and feeling of such grace in ourselves) we grow to an assurance that we are of those that he will shew the free grace upon. And thus the absolute promises are laid before us as the foundation of our salvation, which is wrought in the adhering to the promise, and the conditional as the foundation of our assurance. And though I do not wholly fall in with this latter part of his conclusion, as if conditional promises served only for a foundation of assurance, yet with the former part, that absolute promises are suited and fitted unto faith of adherence, or of the act of justifying faith, properly and truly such, I fully close with, and do add, that it is they that are the most proper objects for such a faith, and not conditional promises. And I shall endeavour to demonstrate this, in the case of one who is now a-beginning first to believe; for as everything must have a beginning, so must a man's believing; and of that case it is I now specially treat, though I do withal judge that the true act of faith as justifying doth, throughout the whole of a man's life, even of him that hath assurance, lie not in an assurance I am justified, but in that of adherence only, as I have elsewhere ‡ shewn.

It is not unknown that besides those believers who have, through grace, attained unto a full assurance of faith, there are two ranks of other true believers whose faith doth fall short of assurance: 1, such as are now a-beginning to believe, as the jailor, Acts xvi. ; and, 2, such as have had for some long time true faith already wrought, and many fruits thereof in the course of their lives, and yet ' walk in darkness, and have no light,'

---

* In my preface unto Christ set forth, in 4to.
† Discourse of the Covenant, p. 149.
‡ Part II., Book II., Chap. I, of this discourse.

and are fain to betake themselves to live by a pure and bare faith of recumbency, or of mere casting themselves on God and Christ, renewed afresh (even as they did at first) for their salvation.   And so they do as good as continually begin to believe, as if they had never believed before ; and this they do, although they have some glimpses of good hope at times, which yet not rising up to overpower and silence doubts, they return to make that kind of faith their sole life.   And although there may be found some difference between these two, yet I put them both into one bag, as we say, and range them together in my ensuing discourse, which I shall prosecute in the person of one who is now but a-beginning to believe ; concerning whose case there is the most difficulty, how to instruct such an one to make use of such absolute promises and declarations, and how he should come to close with them, and with what faith.   And so, whilst I shall speak to this case of the one, I shall but speak to the case of the other.   That which we inquire after is, what object he that is first to believe may find to set his foot first upon, and which may become a ground to him of that special act of faith whereby he lays hold on Christ for his own salvation.

I suppose him humbled for sin, and convinced that unless he have a ground for his being saved, from something else than what is in or from himself, he must perish.   I suppose him looking about him into the world, and crying out thereupon, as they in Acts ii. and the jailor, ' What shall I do to be saved ?'   I suppose him, also, to see and apprehend his way to be to believe, and cast himself on God and Christ, looking about him for a ground or foundation in the word, unto that his faith.

Now then I shall proceed.

And here I shall proceed both negatively and positively.

1. Negatively, I shall shew, that no qualification in a man already wrought can be a ground and object for his first act of faith, so that in the sight of it he should be certainly and personally persuaded to act that faith on God and Christ.

1st, It is not his humiliation or sight of his sin, or of his being in a lost condition, wherein if he remains he must perish.   For the sight of that but leaves him where he was, and it is faith by which his condition must be altered.   The sight of sin and misery may and doth indeed put a necessity upon his soul to look out for salvation, and that is it which makes him cry out, ' What shall I do to be saved ?'   And it is such a work, as without it he would never seek out for Christ, nor go to him to save him.   But for him to build on that sight as that which he, having had wrought in him, he may with confidence believe in Christ, is all one as to say that a malefactor's being convicted, and cast, and condemned at the bar by a judge and his own conscience, should be a ground for his hopes of pardon and salvation ; whereas the procedure so far with him is clean contrary, though it be indeed a preparation to quicken him to seek for a pardon, yea, and makes him capable of it in this respect, that as by our law none is capable of a legal pardon, until he be legally condemned, so nor is such a man of a gospel-pardon till he is thus convicted.   The proper work or effect of such a humiliation, is wholly and altogether to possess the soul with the apprehensions of no other objects than what belonged to his unregenerate and unjustified estate, and which would argue him still to be in that estate ; and the prospect of this fills his mind, having nothing else in his eye ; and though there is and may be somewhat of what is spiritual in that sight of his, yet as Christ said to him, John xiii. 7, ' What I do (to thee) thou knowest not now, but thou shalt know hereafter ;' so we may say of the present work that is upon such a man, that after some light and dawn of faith is broken in upon his spirit, he may afterwards come to see what God was then a-doing with him, but not at that present when nothing but darkness is upon the face of that earth.

It is true also that those words of Christ's, ' Come unto me, all ye that are weary and heavy laden, and I will give you rest,' do contain a particular invitement to such, rather than any other sinners, who also doth invite all others; and it is a special condescension in Christ to speak thus particularly to those that are heavy laden, because of all others they are apt to be discouraged; yet still that wearisomeness is not a ground or foundation for that act of his first believing, to build itself upon it for his being saved. He that will rest in the sight of that, and not come to Christ, will sit down short of salvation, nor is this a ground of his faith, or of his coming to Christ. But when such do come to Christ out of a sight and sense of their burden, yet it is not upon the sight thereof as a spiritual qualification which should render them more acceptable, but it is the sight of their sins with which they are burdened, and the sense of the load thereof, and thereupon of their need of ease, that drives them to come upon Christ's so gracious invitation. They poor creatures look at nothing but themselves, and their sins and loads, and are taken up wholly therewith, and with desire of ease.

That great maxim of the apostle (Rom. iv. 5, ' But to him that worketh not, but believeth on him that justifieth the ungodly, his faith is counted for righteousness') doth confirm all this, and withal doth exclude the sight of any other work wrought, or qualification whatsoever that may put in to be a ground to any man's faith. Under these words, ' to him that worketh not,' I understand all qualifications, and holy dispositions, and actions, for they are included under the name of works, as in opposition to faith, and so in Scripture language inward works as well as outward. And the root or principle inherent in the soul of either, are accordingly here excluded from having to do either as ingredients into justification itself, or into a man's faith or believing for justification.

Also, 2dly, by 'him that worketh not' is there meant, not he that worketh not at all really, but who when he comes to be justified looks at no work of his, or anything in or from himself, but singly believes on him that justifies the ungodly.

And so, 3dly, instead of looking to any good in himself, he views nothing but the contrary, ungodliness, as in himself considered at that time, and the present business he is taken up about namely, to be justified, and to believe that he may be so. And although this is spoken of them that are in their state godly and holy, for this is a maxim fetched from Abraham's example after he was converted many years, even Abraham when he came to be justified in that point looked upon himself as ungodly, and viewed no works at all in himself, and was in his own eyes as if he had had none; yet this maxim doth much more punctually suit one that is now coming forth of his natural state, and hath nothing but ungodliness to view. And unto the sense of those things a man's humiliation brings such a man, and therein doth the proper work of it lie; and our supposition being of one that begins to believe, it cannot be otherwise with him.

2. We are now to consider what positive grounds, or *motiva fidei*, what motives of faith, or what drawings forth of faith are here; or wherein doth the hope concerning this thing, as the Scripture speaks, lie? My assertion is this, that it must be some absolute declaration or promise (which are tantamount) about what is simply in God and Christ as touching our

salvation, the light of which coming into the soul is and must be the *objectum motivum*, the moving object, the persuader (as Heb. xi. speaks) of a man's faith, to draw in his soul thus at first to cleave to God and Christ for a man's personal salvation in particular, and hereon his faith is built. And the reason is evident from what is foregone ; for if no present or precedent qualification in such a soul can prove an effectual persuasive or encourager in part or whole, as a condition or qualification in the person, then it must remain that what is absolutely declared to be in God and Christ, without respect to such conditions as first wrought, must be the ground and *objectum motivum* of his faith.

Obj. But some will here say, A promise that mentions the condition of faith itself is a sufficient and obvious ground to draw on faith at first, which is usually set forth in this syllogism : Whosoever believeth on him (meaning Christ), shall never perish ; but I believe, saith the soul, therefore I shall not perish. And is not this a conditional promise (will they say) which a man may at first close with ? and thus to close with such a promise in the former way of such a syllogism men usually are taught.

Ans. An answer unto this I return, first in general, that when I exclude conditional promises from having an influence into our first act of believing, my intention is not, nor can it so be understood as, to exclude our believing itself from being a necessary requisite qualification, condition (call it what you will), for I have already supposed it absolutely necessary to our being estated into the actual and personal possession of those good things in those promises or declarations which I call absolute. Yea, my very question, and the state thereof, as I have proposed it, presupposes so much, and takes it for granted, for it is queried with what faith a soul is to close with such a promise ? So as my inquisition runs after this, whether such absolute promises be not a proper object of faith, which indeed is required necessarily to our instating into salvation ? and whether those promises be not proposed with an intention in the Scriptures as such ? My search is after an object of faith, what it is, and on what inducement a man doth so believe, or what is the object of that faith. Every act must have an object, and so justifying faith must have so too ; and what that must be is my inquest. And my affirmation is, that absolute declarations of God and Christ (in the promises and otherwise), as Saviour and justifier, are the proper object of such a faith. And therefore when I exclude all conditional promises, my exclusion in this argument only is of a conditional promise that should be the object of that first faith, as that which the soul first viewing to be in itself already wrought, should thereby be heartened and persuaded to begin to believe on God and Christ for its personal salvation. The meaning of that promise, whoever believeth on him shall be saved, is but to shew that an act of believing is absolutely and necessarily required to be put forth by him that will come to be partaker of that salvation. But still this will remain firm and indubitate, that it is those absolute promises or declarations that are the objects or foundation and sole ground of that act of believing ; and so absolute promises are the objects of faith as the conditional act whereby we are to be estated into the possession of those promises ; so as this objection is no prejudice to my assertion, it touches it not. More summarily take my assertion, thus it is : not that those absolute promises (objectively such) require not faith in us ere we be partakers of the salvation in them, for that were to say that God saves his elect absolutely, without requiring anything to be wrought in them, which sense we have before abhorred ; but the meaning is, that they require not any intervening condition unto faith itself, upon the sight of which as a groundwork faith should come to lay hold upon them; but they are exposed barely and nakedly unto faith as objects to be laid hold upon (that is, God and Christ in them) for our salvation, so as though those promises (whoever believes, &c., and the like) in which faith is mentioned, are but conditionally in this sense, that they hold forth an act on our part to put forth as that without which no man shall obtain salvation, yea, by which he is instated into it ; yet let the whole Scripture be searched, and there is not, nor can there be, any instance brought of promises that do mention the condition of believing, wherein a preceding condition is first mentioned as that which must first be seen and viewed by the person who is to believe, to be in himself, and which he should build his first act of believing upon. And in the argument we have in hand, as hath been stated, that only can be called a condition which is a condition to believing itself, and which is supposed to be propounded to that end, that faith seeing such and such qualifications wrought in the soul, should thereupon be induced to believe, so as that condition should be an evidence to him to take or challenge that promise as his own, and thereby belonging to him as if he had been personally named. Such qualifications I find set out indeed in promises for the faith of assurance after a soul's first having believed, as being signs of a man's being in the faith, and of his being justified by his faith foregone. But no such qualifications can be or ought to be built upon by one that comes first to Christ, or ought to be ingredients to his first act of justifying faith, nor indeed to any act of true, pure justifying faith as such ; for that were to make what is in ourselves after faith to be the foundation of it, and to mingle with it, and to make the first act of faith to be assurance that I am in the state of grace already, and thereupon I do believe that I am saved and justified.

This assertion our later and more knowing divines have more generally declined, which yet the papists would impose upon us protestants, as an absurdity generally maintained by us, whenas it is the Lutherans only that do at this day affirm the act of justifying faith to be an assured persuasion that our sins are pardoned.

I have often, therefore, reflected upon the application of such like promises, ' Whosoever believes shall be saved,' as it is ordinarily formed up into this syllogism, Whoever believeth hath, &c. ; but I believe, therefore I have eternal life. I have often reflected upon it, as fearing lest that this assumption, ' but I believe,' out of which they fetch a conclusion of assurance, ' therefore I have eternal life,' be not so well understood, but mistaken by many to be the first act of justifying faith.

I would therefore, in the second place, examine into what act of faith or belief that application of faith in the assumption, in the syllogism, ' but I believe,' is to be resolved into.

1. First, The most judicious do take the meaning of that ' but I believe' to be only this : I seeing and finding by experience with myself, that I have a true faith wrought in me, and such a faith as the Scripture describes to be true and unfeigned, therefore I apply that promise, ' whoever believes,' &c., with an assurance to myself, which is the conclusion. And this indeed I take to be the most proper sense and mind hereof, as it comes in that syllogism, that can be given of it, and, so understood, it is not to be disallowed. And I find it in that sense to be interpreted by our greatest divines ; but then let me give this animadversion upon it, that so understood, it cannot be that first act of justifying which an humbled sinner doth put forth, which is the point we seek for ; nor can this be the genuine act whereby the sinner is justified, and so not the act of justifying faith itself ;

and the reason is undeniable, because this believing is indeed but the sight and experience of a former, foregone, or forepassed act of faith, which the soul must have first put forth. It is that which, in this sense given, is the object of his assumption, ' but I believe,' and so we are still to seek as much as at first, and put to a new inquiry what that first formal act of believing was, and what it should be ; for to be sure this ' but I believe' is, and must needs be, another act than that first was, yea, and of another kind. First, it is another act, for it is an act of faith after another, namely, a former ; nor is it a mere repeating or renewal of the first act, but a sight of that other which was the first act thereby expressed, yea, and is founded upon the intuition of the first, in the strength of which intuition the soul says, ' but I believe.' It is a secondary and after act arising upon a first. Secondly, it is another kind of act, for it is a reflex act of the mind upon its own act ; but justifying faith is a direct act on Christ. And again, it is an act of another kind, for my seeing I believe is an act of experience, which hath sight and sense in it of what is in a man's self ; whereas the first act of faith must be a mere pure act of faith, and not of sight. And so, thirdly, they differ in their objects ; for the object of my seeing I believe is my own believing, but the object of my faith at first, when I began to believe, was and must be God and Christ as the objects : John iii. 16, ' Whoever believes on him hath everlasting life.'

2. Others have apprehended the meaning of this ' I believe,' to be a present act of assurance that I am justified (as supposing that faith of assurance hath for its object, ' I am justified'), and so that very first act to be the condition of the covenant. This opinion differs from the former, for in the syllogism before, it is the act of assurance that I am saved, which made the conclusion; and the sense that I believe is seeing and finding I put forth such an act. But this second sense cannot stand.

For, 1st, in such a syllogism, Whoever believes shall be saved ; but I believe, therefore I shall be saved, this ' but I believe,' if it be understood of assurance, doth make the minor proposition all one with the conclusion itself.

2dly, That actual justification which a sinner hath on God's part, through justifying faith, is a consequence of that faith, or follows or ensues upon that special act of faith, which is properly styled justifying faith, put forth on our part. And that God endows a soul with his justification upon that act, and not after this, the Scriptures do expressly affirm : Acts x. 43, ' To him gave all the prophets witness, that through his name whosoever believeth in him shall receive remission of sins.' This receiving remission of sin is made the end or issue of our believing. Thus also, Acts xvi. 30, 31, ' What shall we do to be saved ?' or, put into a state of salvation ? ' Believe on the Lord Jesus,' says the apostle, ' and thou shalt be saved,' which at present thou art not, until thou dost believe, nor until thou believest shalt be ; but on the contrary, without believing, a man remains in a state of condemnation, according to what our Saviour had declared, ' He that believeth not is condemned already.' The like you have in John viii. 24. All which places, and many other, might be alleged to speak, that as an actual justification there is obtained and received, so to be bestowed upon believing with such a faith, which the Scripture therefore calls justifying ; and a man is therefore required thus to believe, to that end that he may obtain and receive it. This being an assured truth, it will then follow, that not only faith of assurance that my sins are forgiven, is not an essential specifical act of justifying faith as such, but that it is impossible it should be such ; yea, and that it is a contradiction, that that act of faith whereby we believe ourselves justified, should be one and the same individual act with that which is called justifying faith; but especially it is a contradiction that this should be one and the same faith with the first act of faith. And, first, the impossibility of it appears in this, that that faith whereby a man is really and actually justified is, in order of nature, first, and must be supposed first before a man be justified, because, thereupon or therewith, it is that God doth justify him, and endow him with that benefit, Rom. v. And this is our justification, which is according to the rule of the word which we have by faith, and which God will proceed by at the last day, and without which he will not own any man to be justified and saved. But that other act, of faith of assurance, whereby I believe or apprehend that I am justified, must necessarily first suppose this act of justification on God's part, according to the rules of his word, to have been first passed upon a man, and therefore, must suppose also that he hath believed already; and by a former act of faith hath obtained justification, which till then he had not, but remained in a state of condemnation. Which first act of believing must therefore be such a believing with an aim and end that I may be saved and justified, and that my sins may be remitted in such a manner as hitherto they have not been remitted, and without which faith I must die in my sins, perish eternally; for so the word of God, which God will proceed by, everywhere tells me. And therefore it is that a sinner that first believes, as ever after also, doth apprehend such a necessity of believing, as was said, and doth at first, therefore, necessarily look on, and hath in his eye, that justification that is according to the rules of his word, and which he aims at as upon a thing to be obtained, and which he is to receive, and so to be a thing to come upon his believing, which was evidently the case of the jailor, and upon those terms required of him by the apostle. Whereas in the other act, of faith of assurance, whereby a man believes and apprehends that his sins are forgiven, he within that act doth suppose and look upon his justification as a thing obtained, and therefore it is impossible that the first act of believing, whereby a man is justified, and whereof justification is a consequence, and that *I am justified*, should be one and the same individual act, but they are necessarily two, not only in order of nature, but in time, one before the other. Yea, it would be a vain confidence, nay, a falsehood, for any man to believe with his first act of faith that he puts forth, that he is justified; for he cannot truly and justly believe it until he be justified. A thing must first be and actually exist ere it can be apprehended, or else it is but fancy to him that believes it, unless by way of prophecy.

2. Upon the same or the like ground it is no less than an apparent contradiction, that I should, by my first act of faith, believe that I may be justified, and withal to be first justified thereby, and by the same individual act believe I am justified from the same sins, for that would make one and the same act, and one and the same object of that act, to be at once an antecedent and a consequent of itself, to go before itself, and to follow after itself, which to me are a contradiction.

(1.) The object, namely, justification, should according to this opinion be bestowed upon a man before he can believe he hath it, and must actually exist, when yet justifying faith is declared to be that act upon which, and by which, justification is bestowed upon us, and first comes to be existent, which is a contradiction in one and the same object.

(2.) The act of faith, if it should be exercised and have a tendency upon both these objects at once, must be before and also after itself; for all acts are diversified by their objects and their tendency thereunto. Now, then, to affirm the first (or indeed any) act of faith justifying, to be a belief that a man is justified, is to make justification the antecedent to such a faith, for a thing must be before we believe it to be. And then on the other hand, that the first act should be the act whereby a man is justified, necessarily makes justification the consequent of its faith, and therefore these two would be a contradiction, and cannot consist together.

Obj. But it may be objected, that there is a justification in God's heart and intention from all eternity, and in Christ representatively dying and rising as a common person before a man believes ; and so faith is but to believe that which is already extant, and a man's justification by faith is but a justification *in foro conscientiæ.*

Ans. It is sufficient to say, let that justification or salvation after a man believes be what it will, yet to be sure it benefits no man without that justification of application to his person, as I may call it : for that which brings a person into a state of justification, according to the rules of the word, is done by God upon believing, and until then a man remains under condemnation, and may truly say, God will not, nor cannot own him to be a justified person, no, not in his court, the open court which he will keep and proceed by at latter day, according to the rules of which he will then reckon a man to be under condemnation whilst he was an unbeliever ; and, if a man had died in that unbelief, he must have condemned him, as he doth all other unbelievers that shall then appear before him : For ' shall not the judge of all the world do right ?' Gen. xviii. God will not look upon him as justified from all eternity, but as one that remains under unbelief, as the apostle speaks. He will not allege of any that he had justified him from eternity, and therefore save him, for his own declared word, which is the rule he judges by, would interpose and cause him so to pronounce and condemn that person that is under unbelief. And Christ hath sufficiently informed us in what he says, John xii. 48, ' The word that I have spoken, the same shall judge you at latter day.' And he speaks it upon occasion of the very thing in hand : ver. 46, ' Whosoever believes in me, shall not abide in darkness.' Thus he speaks affirmatively : ' And he that believes not on me, there is one that judgeth him,' ver. 47, 48. Thus he speaks negatively. And who is that that will judge him ? God. And by what will he judge him ? Even by this very word that Christ had spoken, ver. 48. And indeed that justification, according to the rules of God's word, is that which is the aim and drift of a humbled sinner, which he makes after, for it is that which he hears and understands, God calling upon him in his word for to seek it : ' Believe, and thou shalt be saved.' In answer hereunto the soul says, Lord, I believe that I may be saved ; and it is God according to his word that he hath to deal withal herein.

It is in vain to say, I am justified by faith only in respect to the court of mine own conscience. It is in vain to say that a man's apprehension and faith that he was justified from eternity, is all that justification which the Scripture so constantly speaks of to be by and upon believing ; for, according to that opinion, a man was as much justified before he believed as after, and his faith would add nothing new to his state, but only his own apprehension of it ; whereas the Scripture speaks of a man's justification by faith as of a real thing, and as a thing done anew ; for being justified by faith first, we have then peace with God, and peace with God is that justification which is in a man's own conscience, which there is made a fruit of justification by faith first, and whereof faith is also first the instrument ; and we have ' access by faith into this grace wherein we stand,' so that we are actually put into the state of grace before God, considered as he is the judge of all men, and thereupon we come to ' rejoice in hope of the glory of God.' But yet how far a believer wanting assurance, or one that begins to believe, may make use of God's eternal purposes as they are declared in the word, that he will justify sinners of the sons of men ; and how far such a one may urge and plead this as a motive which God hath declared to have been in his own heart, upon which he is moved to justify us in time ; and how far a soul may plead, that therefore God would be pleased accordingly thereunto to exert and put forth this justification of application, or indeed now actually to give it, which such a soul seeks for as yet to come, and cometh unto God for to obtain it ; how far I say the consideration of these decrees or purposes indefinitely made will promote and help forward such a one's faith, this is matter of another discussion ; but, in the meanwhile, what hath been at the present said may serve for an answer to the aforesaid objection.

These things having been thus on the negative cleared, both in shewing that no prerequisite condition in us is the object or ground for the first act of faith, as also that that act is not, nor cannot be, an assurance of our being justified, it comes next to be treated of affirmatively, what that first act of faith justifying should then be, both as to the object of it, as also for the kind of the act, &c. ; and then, after that, I shall shew that this act of faith is, and may be suited to the first sort of promises of salvation, which I have termed absolute, and how it may and is to apply itself unto them, which is the designed issue I drive all unto.

I shall therefore propose and pursue the sense which may rightly be, and is the mind of one that doth now first set himself to believe ; but I must give this caution concerning it, that it is not to be understood as any part of that fore-mentioned syllogism, nor to be made the *minor* of it in those terms, ' but I believe,' and yet is a true application of those promises fore-mentioned, ' Whoever believes shall be saved' ; for there is this difference between this sense and the two former, and the drift of the fore-mentioned syllogism formed up by divines on the behalf of Christians that have already believed, which is made for, and serves to express their assurance in which it ends, for the soul thereupon infers, ' Therefore I shall be saved.' But this expression, ' I believe,' expresses what he doth, and what he attempts to do, and doth not at last terminate itself upon its own act of believing, as the other did, but spends its intention wholly upon God and Christ, who are to be the justifiers of him, to whom he therefore hath recourse for his justification. This first act of believing, then, is not a studying of, or reflection upon, its own act, as seeing that he believes ; but it is a doing the thing in a direct manner ; he believes he doth the thing* by a direct act, and carries the soul forth of itself unto those who are his judges, and to be the justifiers of him, and doth this in a correspondency and an immediate answer or obedience unto that faith the promises call for, which directs him to, and requires of him to believe. Now then, affirmatively to set forth this direct act of justifying faith as properly such, in order to clear how absolute declarations or promises about salvation do suit it, and it reciprocally suiteth them, let us fully examine and consider these three things about it.

1. What is the proper object of such an act.
2. What kind of act it is that he then may put forth.
3. What is the aim and drift of him in his faith's acting upon that or these objects.

Which three do comprehend, as I take it, all that belongs to the substance of that act of believing ; for, as to the adjuncts of it, that it be unfeigned faith, spiritual faith, and that all these are in a spiritual manner

* Qu. ' He believes : he doth, &c.' ?—ED.

to be put forth, all these are supposed in all true faith ; but it is the substantialness of the act which we now inquire into.

1. The object of such a faith is God and Christ, according to what they have declared themselves to be, considered as in relation to their saving and justifying of the sons of men ; God considered as declared to be a justifier of sinners, and Christ as a saviour ; these two, or either of them believed as such, come all to one as to our obtaining of salvation on either, which I observe, as from many other instances, so in that of the jailor, Acts xvi., which I have had and shall have occasion often to have recourse unto ; for here, as the apostle had at first propounded Jesus Christ to him as a Saviour—' Believe on the Lord Jesus and thou shalt be saved,' ver. 34, —yet when actual believing unto salvation comes to be spoken of, ver. 36, it is only mentioned that he believed in God ; for whilst we believe on the one in a more distinct manner, we know the interest that either have in our salvation, and it is interpreted that we believe in both ; and the believing on the one in so explicit a manner is so far from excluding the other implied by it, as *in concesso* it involves both, and the soul knowing the interest of both, his faith may be really resolved into a faith of both or either of them.

I shall therefore give instances of God and Christ apart being set forth in the promises to our faith.

(1.) Christ, under the simple and absolute consideration of being a Saviour, is represented to us in the promises as the object of our faith : Isa. xlv. 22, ' Look unto me, and be ye saved, all the ends of the earth ; for I am God, and there is none else.' Christ is there spoken of, as appears from what follows in ver. 23. He is set forth as the only Saviour. ' There is no God else besides me,' says he ; ' a just God and a Saviour.' And we see him as such nakedly proposed to our faith, as these words shew, ' Look unto me,' &c. We have a place parallel to this in the New Testament : John vi. 40, ' And this is the will of him that sent me, that every one which seeth the Son, and believeth on him, may have everlasting life : and I will raise him up at the last day.' He that seeth the Son, *i.e.*, with a spiritual light, so as to believe on him. These are acts purely acting upon him as he is the Christ and a Saviour ; and the believing on that object requires no conditions first to be looked at by him that is to believe. And Christ had proposed himself before in like manner, as lift up on the cross and crucified (and thereby being become a Saviour), as the naked object for faith to look at : John iii. 14, 15, ' And as Moses lifted up the serpent in the wilderness, even so must the Son of man be lifted up ; that whosoever believeth on him should not perish, but have eternal life.' We have another instance of his being declared and set forth as a Saviour : 1 Tim. i. 15, ' This is a faithful saying, and worthy of all acceptation, that Christ Jesus came into the world to save sinners ; of whom I am chief.' The words are a bare proposal of him, wherein he is set forth as the immediate object to a sinner's faith. His being a Saviour, and his intent to save sinners of this world (not devils), is nakedly declared, simply so considered. He terms the manifestation of Christ ὁ πιστός λόγος, ' a faithful saying,' speaking of that faithfulness upon which faith may build ; for unto faith doth faithfulness relate as an object fitted for it, holding on this Christ as a sure foundation for faith : 1 Peter ii. 6, ' Wherefore also it is contained in the Scriptures, Behold, I lay in Sion a chief corner stone, elect, precious ; and he that believeth on him shall not be confounded.' And the apostle Paul in that text, 1 Tim. i. 15, asserts this ' faithful saying ' to be ' worthy of all acceptation.' He means that it deserves hearty entertainment and receiving by faith.   And of this faith on Christ the apostle had proposed himself an example in the preceding ver. 14, so that this faithful saying had been the ground of his own faith.

(2.) God the Father, as a justifier of men ungodly, is declared and set forth as the object of a sinner's faith : Rom. iv. 5, 'But to him that worketh not, but believeth on him that justifieth the ungodly, his faith is counted for righteousness.'   It is a bare and absolute declaration of him, what a God he is in and of himself in justifying, and he is proposed as absolute as absolute can be, in opposition unto 'all or any prerequisite qualification which the person to be justified should view in himself, collaterally, to induce him to believe.

1st, The justified person, or the subject, is the ungodly ; and God is set forth by this attribution, that he is a God that justifies the ungodly.

2dly, Therefore the man is ungodly in the person's eye who justifies. God looks on him as ungodly, as one without any work, or disposition, or qualification which he respects in justifying.

3dly, The person who comes to be justified is ungodly in his own thoughts and apprehensions of himself, as the foregoing words, viz., ' He that worketh not, but believeth,' &c., do shew.   The meaning is, he is such an one who looks at no work in himself on the account of which he should be justified, or for which, and upon which, he might believe that he shall be justified.   Yea, he is one who views nothing but the contrary, viz., mere ungodliness in himself, for which he should be condemned.   It is true, indeed, that an act of believing is required of him ; but that is but now a-putting forth by him, and therefore he builds not upon any former act of faith, for all in himself is in view nothing but ungodliness, and so there is an utter want even of faith itself, as any way seen by him, to induce him to believe on God.   Hence then it is that he believes on God nakedly, as viewed to be a justifier of men ungodly ; and it is under that consideration he believes on him.   And this is the faith which is imputed for righteousness, that noble and heroic pure faith which gives glory to God.   And herein his heart in believing answers unto God's heart in saving.   For look, as God doth not choose him unto salvation upon faith foreseen, or good works foreseen, so nor doth the soul believe in God upon works foreseen, or faith foreseen.   Such a first choice of us by God upon the foresight of our faith and working, would derogate from the freeness of that grace which is in his heart: Rom. xi. 6, 'And if by grace, then it is no more of works ; otherwise grace is no more grace.   But if it be of works, then it is no more grace ; otherwise work is no more work.'   That it is spoken of election appears by ver. 5, 'Even so then at this present time also there is a remnant according to the election of grace.'   God then looks into his own heart only for that which should move him to do this. And yet withal, it must be said that he actually saves no man without faith. As God thus looks in election at no faith or works in us, so the soul's first act of believing knows not, nor looks at any in his own heart to move or induce him to believe on God ; but the soul only looks at what is in God's heart, as declared in the promises, and at his sole free grace in justifying ; and yet he knows withal that faith is requisite that he may be justified, and that without it all the grace which is in God's heart would never justify nor save him, whilst yet he had nothing in his eye viewed in himself either directly or collaterally to move him to believe.   He hath nothing which either with a direct or squint eye he should consider, but only and merely God as justifying.

We have in the Old Testament a parallel to this Rom. iv. 5, of God's being a justifier of the ungodly purely considered: Isa. xliii. 25, 26, 'I, even I, am he that blotteth out thy transgressions for mine own sake, and will not remember thy sins. Put me in remembrance; let us plead together: declare thou, that thou mayest be justified.' This promise Mr Bulkely acknowledgeth to be an absolute promise, as such are those wherein God says, I will do thus or thus 'for mine own sake.' And that it is parallel to this text, Rom. iv. 5, is evident,

[1.] Because it is spoken of God as a justifier both in ver. 25, where he says, 'I am he who blotteth out transgressions,' and in ver. 26, where justification is expressly mentioned.

[2.] He instructs the persons who are to be justified to apprehend their own utter ungodliness: ver. 22–24, 'But thou hast not called upon me, O Jacob; but thou hast been weary of me, O Israel. Thou hast not brought me the small cattle of thy burnt-offerings, neither hast thou honoured me with thy sacrifices: I have not caused thee to serve with an offering, nor wearied thee with incense. Thou hast brought me no sweet cane with money, neither hast thou filled me with the fat of thy sacrifices; but thou hast made me to serve with thy sins, thou hast wearied me with thine iniquities.'

[3.] Which, when God had said, he sets forth himself barely, nakedly, and absolutely, and as alone considered in what is in himself, as the justifier of them. For this is imported by those words, ver. 25, 'I, even I, am he that blotteth out thy transgressions;' whereby he emphatically calls in all the thoughts and intentions of their minds to be first on himself, as he is in himself and of himself a God pardoning sins and justifying their persons, as the apostle with the like emphasis expresseth it when he speaks of him as justifying the ungodly.

[4.] God tells us that he blots out transgressions for his own name's sake, and for that alone; and that he doth it upon no other motives or ground but only what is in his own heart. That he doth it only for the sake of that great name of his, uttered and proclaimed on purpose (Exod. xxxiv.) to shew what inwardly moves him to be a God pardoning iniquity, transgression, and sin. 'I, even I (says God), who am Jehovah, gracious, merciful, abundant in kindness and truth, pardoning iniquity, &c., do blot out your transgressions, for this mine own name's sake.'

I remember that Zanchy says that that text, Exod. xxxiv. 7, is also spoken of Christ, who is God with God, and the justifier of us also for his own sake, and righteousness' sake. However, according to my former rule given, that God in Christ is always to be understood, Christ must be taken in, as the person in whom and in whose righteousness God justifies. So that, when I say that God, and what is in God alone represented in the promises, is the object of faith, it is to be understood only in opposition unto what is in us, and not as opposed to Christ, who is co-partner with God in this his glory, and who also was his counsellor; and in like manner God is not excluded when we speak of faith in Christ alone.

[5.] Lastly, To fix their hearts on himself alone when they would seek to be justified, he adds in that Isaiah xliii. 26, 'Put me in remembrance; let us plead together: declare thou, that thou mayest be justified.' As if he should say, If you can think of any other way of being justified than only me, tell it of me; but indeed there is none.

And these and such I call, 1, declarations and promises; for these two in this matter come all to one as to our purpose. And we use that expression of God and Christ's being declared and set forth as the objects of faith, because it agrees with those phrases used by the apostle to the same purpose (as was observed): Rom. iii. 24, 'Being justified freely by his grace, through the redemption that is in Jesus Christ.' Here both God and Christ are mentioned as the causes of our justification. He first speaks of Christ: ver. 25, 'Whom God hath set forth,' says he, viz., as an object of our faith, as justifying, 'to be a propitiation through faith in his blood.' And then he speaks of God the Father in those words, 'To declare his righteousness for the remission of sins that are past, through the forbearance of God.' He means the righteousness of God justifying, which he again repeats: ver. 26, 'To declare, I say, at this time his righteousness; that he might be just, and the justifier of him which believeth in Jesus.'

(2.) I call them absolute declarations and promises, because as they are the propounded objects of faith in this matter of justification, so they are simply and absolutely to be viewed by us; and no conditions or qualifications are to be considered in us, as upon the intuition of which we should come to believe in them.

And now give me leave to cast in my thoughts concerning that great convert Saul; for which if you will not take what follows as proofs, yet admit them as conjectures.

[1.] His first saving faith on Christ was but a bare act of recumbency at his first conversion; so that though he saw Christ in heaven appearing to him, yet this sight at that instant wrought not a saving act of faith; but Christ left that for his Spirit to work. The vision stunned him indeed, and put a stop to his career, and convinced him, as great miracles did others, that he was the Messiah whom he had persecuted. But the true and thorough work was done within his own soul, when he was retired alone with God and Christ. And my reason why he had not by that vision a true saving faith is, because he makes his having known Christ visibly with his bodily eyes to be a not knowing him, if compared with the knowledge which is the effect of the new creature: 2 Cor. v. 16, 17, 'Wherefore, henceforth know we no man after the flesh; yea, though we have known Christ after the flesh, yet now henceforth know we him no more. Therefore if any man be in Christ, he is a new creature: old things are passed away; behold, all things are become new;' which scripture some interpreters have applied to this very thing. And the same is evident also by this chief reason, inasmuch as he had that conviction, which first astonished him, by the law, which was preparative to an act of saving faith wrought in him after; for so himself gives the account, Rom. vii. 7, where he says that he 'had not known sin but by the law.' The Pharisees' principle was that lust was no sin; and therefore he says, verse 9, 'I was alive without the law once,' viz., before my conversion, while a Pharisee; but 'when the commandment came,' in the true light of it, 'sin revived' in my conscience, says he, 'and I died.' He then saw himself in a state of death, which wrought a death in the apprehension of his soul: Rom. vii. 10, 'And the commandment, which was ordained to life, I found to be unto death.' His meaning is, that that law, which he verily thought he should live by, was found by him, unto his utter confusion, to be unto death. And this apostle then in the beginnings of his conversion, lying under such apprehensions, with that great account of sins coming in withal, may very well be thought to have no mind to eat or drink, but to spend his time in humbling himself under the mighty hand of God. And then if we bring it to that account which he gives of the work of faith in him, Gal. ii. 15, 16, he there including himself with the rest of the Christian Jews, yea, and with his fellow-apostles, it shews that they altogether with him had come in but with such a faith. And it is certain that those converts during John the Baptist's and our Saviour's time had but a faith of recumbence, for they received not the Holy Ghost as a Comforter and as an assurer till after the ascension. And it was they who were the poor, the meek, the captives, &c., to whom Christ at first preached, Mat. v. 1-4; and who were the weary and heavy laden, Mat. xi. 28, 29; and who were wrought upon by John the Baptist's ministry, ver. 12; and then they cleaved to Christ: ' Whither shall we go ? ' said they; ' with thee are the words of eternal life,' John vi. 68. They had assurance that he was the Messiah. And the faith that Paul and the other apostles were justified by, was their believing on Christ that they might be justified (the words in Gal. ii. 15, 16 are express), and not a believing that they were justified already, and therefore it was not an act of assurance.

[2.] My second reason is from the narrative of his conversion, Acts ix. It is first said that he did not eat nor drink for three days, ver. 9. Now, that he was fasting all that while, and neither ate nor drank, shews his humbled condition, and that his sins came in upon him all that time. And that conviction you read him mention of himself, Gal. ii., that by the works of the law he could not be justified; which conviction in him was, as it is in us now, preparatory to faith in Christ.

[3.] And yet that Christ should say of him, ' Behold, he prayeth,' verse 11, doth as clearly argue that he had true justifying faith begun, such, viz., as, Gal. ii. 16, he mentions. The first part exactly agrees with his relation, Rom. vii. And withal the proofs that he had saving faith then is, that he prayed, and so prayed, as Christ gives an eminent signal approbation, and so an acceptation of it, with a *behold* to it : ' Behold, he prayeth.' And ' how shall they call on him on whom they have not believed ? ' says himself afterward, Rom. x. 14; and yet both his faith and prayer in faith seems not to have been an assurance, for it had not risen up unto that yet. And my reasons for it are :

1st, That he had not received the Spirit as a comforter till Ananias was sent to him to put his hands upon him, and to tell him he was a chosen vessel unto Christ, ver. 15; and therefore Ananias, as it would seem, breaking in upon him, calls him brother at first dash, ver. 17.

2dly, Had he had assurance of faith before the coming of Ananias, he would not have continued without eating and drinking so long, but would have received food to strengthen him, as he did upon his receiving the Holy Ghost, ver. 19.

[4.] A distinction of this double work of faith of recumbency first, and of personal assurance after, you may observe in Gal. ii., and that both were in our apostle, that of recumbency first, and then that of assurance expressed afterward, will appear by comparing verses 16 and 20 together.

First, He had a faith that he might be justified, and a faith it was upon a work of conviction in the first place; for it was wrought first, and was common to them all.

Secondly, There was faith of assurance: ver. 20, ' I am crucified with Christ: nevertheless I live; yet not I, but Christ liveth in me: and the life which I now live in the flesh I live by faith of the Son of God, who loved me, and gave himself for me.'

The last observation is, that it was the indefinite declaration, that Jesus Christ came into the world to save sinners, and so was the Messiah, which was revealed to him as the ground of that his first faith of recumbency, that he might be justified, and it was that drew him in. And my conjecture for it is (if you will not allow it to be proof), that after he had proposed his example, 1 Tim. i. 15, he commends that faithful saying, that Christ came to save sinners, after the story of his conversion that went before, in which he at once propounds his own example or pattern of obtaining mercy, and also the very ground of that his faith, to all that should afterwards believe, as it follows, ver. 16.

Obj. But you may say that his expression, ' whereof I am chief,' argues his faith to have been assurance.

Ans. 1. I answer, it is true that he had now assurance, and so could add it, that Christ came actually and personally to save him.

Ans. 2. Yet his end in doing it was not so much to express his faith as his sinfulness, and thereby to prevent and remove a great discouragement that keeps souls off from believing. viz., the greatness of sins, which in my example you may see, says he, is taken away, and so is no hindrance at all to believing. For that the scope of that addition centres in that scripture, 1 Tim. i. 16, shews : ' Howbeit, for this cause I obtained mercy, that in me first Jesus Christ might shew forth all long-suffering, for a pattern to them which should hereafter believe on him to life everlasting.' And therefore still it may remain firm that the object of his and all believers' faith at first is this saying, or the substance of it, as ' worthy of all acceptation, that Christ came into the world to save sinners ;' which, say I, is clearly an absolute indefinite declaration in the very sound of it.

The corollaries from this instance of Paul are these :

(1.) That both the work of humiliation and of faith wrought in him, were for the acts and objects conformable to the work of faith in all other believers, though the outward means and other circumstances were extraordinary.

(2.) By a faith of bare recumbency that we might be justified, founded upon an indefinite promise or declaration, we may likewise pray in faith for pardon acceptably before assurance obtained. Our faith and prayer both may be grounded upon no other than an indefinite promise, declaration, and example ; yea, and we may from thence be able to plead for the pardon of the greatest sins.

CHAPTER IV.

What act of faith it is which those that want assurance may exercise upon such absolute declarations and promises, and of the suitableness between that act and such objects.

2. All acts do receive their specification or kind from their objects and their tendency thereunto, and so we must next discern the kind of the actings of these men's faith from that (with difference from that other personal assurance) by their suitableness unto those their objects, viz., these absolute promises. In such absolute declarations and promises for salvation there are eminently two things to be attended.

(1.) The matter of them, or things contained in them, and absolutely promised or declared, and that are exposed to be the object and aim of faith.

(2.) The tenor of them as they respect persons.

(1.) The matter of them promised is either salvation itself, which is expressed in those promises of God's pardoning a man's sins for his name's sake, and of God's being our God, and writing his law in our hearts, and his saying, I am a Saviour, and there is none besides me, and many the like; or there are the causes thereof which do express the motives moving God thereunto, such as are the declarations of the riches of his mercy and grace, his free love, the good pleasure of his will for his name's sake, &c. Although these in the matter of them are thus absolutely declared or promised, yet the tenor of them to persons is not universal, as if God intended all and every man in such promises, as was said; but they are indefinite only, and promiscuous, yet are to be promulged or made known to all. This may suffice as to the object. Again,

(2.) There being two faculties in the soul, the understanding and the will, each of these have a proper acting and exercise of faith towards God and Christ, as they have revealed themselves in these declarations and promises, that so a soul may obtain the things therein. And we must allow even in them that first believe, as well as in any other that want assurance, actings of faith both in the understanding and also in the will. For every man that believes must believe ' with his whole heart,' as the eunuch, Acts viii., and ' with the heart man believeth to salvation,' Rom. x., and that with respect towards these absolute promises.

And in the first place, it must be granted that there is both an assurance of faith in the understanding, and in the will a firm adhering to the things revealed in the promises. *First*, In the understanding there must be an act of assurance. But how? and of what? Namely, of and about that first thing we noted in the promises, viz., the matter or things contained in them. And as in respect thereunto, look as the promises and declarations are absolute, ' yea and amen;' so every believer must have as absolute an assurance of faith thereof. As, for instance, a soul must be assured concerning Christ that he is a Saviour, and that there is none besides him, and that he came into this world with a most absolute purpose to save sinners of mankind (for they are only the dwellers in this world to which he came), which elogy or saying the apostle doth therefore propose and commend to the faith of men as the most sure and faithful saying that ever was uttered: 1 Tim. i. 15, ' This is a faithful saying, and worthy of all acceptation, that Christ Jesus came into the world to save sinners; of whom I am chief.' I say, he proposeth it to be entertained with all acceptation of faith and assent by them, and to be absolutely believed by them without wavering or doubting. And Christ himself imposeth the faith thereof as essentially necessary to salvation: John viii. 24, ' If ye believe not that I am he,' the Messiah, or Saviour of the world, as I have often declared myself to be, ' you shall die in your sins.' Thus likewise, concerning God, we must absolutely believe that he is a God of mercies, pardoning iniquity, transgression, and sin, Exodus xxxiv. 6, a justifier of the ungodly, Rom. iv. 5, a God of pardons, Neh. ix. 17 (so it is in the Hebrew). These things must be as verily and indubitably believed with full assurance of understanding (as it is termed, Col. ii. 2) as that we believe there is a God; for by the same necessity that he that comes to God must believe that he is, by the same parallel of necessity, he that cometh to God or Christ to be saved and justified, must as absolutely believe that he is a justifier of the ungodly. There must be fixed likewise in every believing soul a firm persuasion of the full resolvedness of God's and Christ's will, purposes, and intentions to save some of the sons of men effectually, concerning which there are likewise so many testimonies and absolute declarations in the word.

Lastly, There is necessary a belief of the infinite riches of mercy that are in the divine nature, which are as the sea that feeds and maintains the springs of those his purposes and intentions, and the streams issuing from those springs in overflowing promises with abundant kindness and truth. And the more the soul comes to be persuaded and possessed of all these things in the assurance of understanding, the deeper foundation is laid, and the stronger hold and obligation there is upon his will to draw it to trust on God for a man's particular salvation.

Secondly, In the will there is to be in every believer a firm and fixed adherence or cleaving unto God and Christ, and unto the good things promised by them: Ps. lxiii. 8, ' My soul cleaveth unto thee ' (so the Hebrew word is, it being the same that is used Deut. x. 20, and chap. xiii. 4); it is further added, ' My soul cleaveth to thee *behind*.* The meaning is, that when God seemed to turn away from him, and to leave him, yet the soul will not part so with him, but takes hold of him, though behind, when yet it cannot see his face and favour. A soul that hath assurance, and sees the face and favour of God to stand towards him, may be said to cleave unto God before ; but when God turns away his face, that soul cleaves to him behind ; that is, it both will and doth lay hold on him through adherence of faith, as it resolves never to leave and forsake him, however he should seem to deal with it. Thus Ruth is said to cleave to Naomi, Ruth i. 14, which act of cleaving to her, when Naomi bade her return, Ruth thus expresseth, verse 16, ' Entreat me not to leave thee, or to return from following after thee, for whither thou goest I will go; and where thou lodgest I will lodge : thy people shall be my people, and thy God my God.' And verse 17, ' Where thou diest I will die, and there will I be buried : the Lord do so to me, and more also, if aught but death part thee and me.' Which cleaving, verse 18, is further termed a being ' stedfastly minded to go with her,' analogically unto which this cleaving of the soul by faith to God is termed a cleaving with purpose of heart; that is, a stedfast fixed resolution of heart not to part with him, Acts xi. 23. And thus doth the will of a believer cleave firmly and stedfastly unto God, when yet God makes as if he would shake it off, and to depart therefrom. And whereas Ruth said, ' Nought but death shall part thee and me,' Job, he says, ' Though thou kill me, I will trust in thee ; ' that is, death itself shall not part me from thee, will this soul say unto God in his ultimate resolves. Nay, the soul says to God, Hell shall not part thee and me ; for thou art there, and I will cleave to thee if thou throwest me thither. Thou shalt never be rid of me, for that is my resolution. The reason of this fixedness of the will is from that spiritual sight and assurance that (as we said) is in the understanding, of the things themselves contained in the promises, the understanding being thereby invincibly possessed of those riches of mercy and goodness which are in God, of that mercy and forgiveness that is with him, and that is there to be had, and of that abundance of grace and righteousness which is in Christ, and plenteous redemption for the salvation of sinners (Ps. cxxx.), and all these shining in those absolute declarations and promises, and through them into the soul. Faith in the understanding lets down into the will the absolute and complete goodness of the salvation promised, and that in the causes of it ; and the will is drawn thereby with as invincible a resolution to cleave unto God for the obtainment thereof. And then again, another reason of this its cleaving, is, that God, though he hide his particular favour and grace from this soul, and holds it yet in suspense as to that, yea, and turns away, as was said : yet, in the mean time, he secretly by his right hand upholds that soul, and draws it by that his efficacious power to cleave to him ; and that also

* For this reading of the words, see Piscator, Dutch Annotat., Genebrard, Muis.

follows in the next words of that verse, in that psalm fore-cited, 'Thy right hand,' that is, thy power, 'upholdeth me,' and causeth me thus to hang upon thee, though it be but behind; and if he seems to go away, yet then the soul is carried to follow hard after him the more; as our translators have rendered it, 'My soul follows hard after thee.' And hence it is that though God should defer him long, yet he continues to seek him. And thus you see, as to the matter of those absolute promises, there is both an assurance in the understanding, and a firmness of adherency in the will, even in him that at present wants sight and assurance of the face and favour of God, which was the case of the psalmist at that time, and therefore the same may be in any that wants that assurance.

And these two acts are (though in a greater or lesser degree) common unto all believers.

But, 2dly, there is further, the tenor of those absolute promises, which comes to be considered as they respect persons; and from thence it is that so great a difference is between the faith of him that hath a personal assurance of his interest therein, and the faith of these other believers that want it. As also from hence it is that difficulty ariseth, how such souls, wanting personal assurance, may yet come to lay hold on such absolute promises for their own persons, and with what kind of faith.

(1.) What is the difference between that act of faith, which the apostle to the Hebrews calls 'full assurance of faith,' Heb. x., as comprehending not only an assurance of the things and matter of the promises, as that God's absolute will is to save sinners, &c., but together therewith an assurance that I am the very individual person whom God means to save, &c. Between this faith, I say, and the faith of single and simple adherence, the difference lies herein, inasmuch as faith in the understanding of him that is an adherent only comes short in this, that he doth not as yet firmly and prevailingly over his doubts believe that himself is the individual person intended by God in the promises, concerning which the other is fully satisfied, and accordingly can and doth with assurance apply those promises to himself, that they are his, &c. So as indeed the former hath a whole or complete assurance, both of the matter and also of his own personal interest; but this other poor soul hath but an half assurance, namely, of the matter, &c., but not of the second, viz., his personal interest therein, touching which God is as yet pleased not to reveal that to him.

(2.) As to the difficulty mentioned, viz., how such souls may yet have recourse to such absolute promises, and with what kind, or rather degree, of faith; for answer hereto, I still take that rule along with me, that faith is to be some way or other answering and conformable to what is in the promise, or it is not faith; and that if it comes up to the tenor of it, as we see it hath done to the matter thereof, it must needs be true faith. And my grand assertion here about it is, that there is and may be place for actings of true faith both in the understanding and the will of such an one, answering and conformable unto the tenor of these promises, as we heard there was in each of those faculties towards the matter of them. And this correspondency must be distinguished by its tendency towards that tenor of them. Now, this suitableness and conformity between this faith wanting personal assurance, and the tenor of these promises (which I call absolute) lies thus.

1. On the part of the promises, the tenor of them is indefinite to persons, and not universal to all men. It is true those second sort of promises fore-mentioned, which express a condition whereunto salvation

is annexed, are universal, that is, to all and every one that hath the qualifications in them. And in that strain they run, ' Whosoever believeth shall be saved; ' and more emphatically, Rom. iii. 22, the apostle speaks of ' the righteousness of God, which is by faith of Jesus Christ unto all, and upon all them that believe,' where he ingeminates the universality to all, and upon all them that believe, but not to all men absolutely : *Promissiones evangelii universales sunt, non absolutè, sed respectu credentium*, says Paræus very well in his commentary on that text : the promises of the gospel are universal, not absolutely, but with respect to believers. But in absolute promises it is not so, for they mention no such qualifications already wrought.

[2.] In this very tenor of them which thus respecteth persons, we must consider that they have yet something of absoluteness, or of certainty, concerning persons, which is as certainly to be believed, and yet something that is but indefinite ; both which I shall specify, to the end that I may by and by shew the punctual conformity of faith wanting personal assurance unto the tenor of those promises.

1st. That which is absolutely or certainly declared in those promises concerning persons, for all faith as of a certainty to build on, is this :

(1.) It is most certain and absolutely declared in such promises concerning persons, that some shall have those promises fulfilled on them : Heb. iv. 6, ' It remaineth, therefore, that some must enter in.' Which declaration made thus under the gospel, speaks the true intent of all absolute promises as to persons, shewing they are understood, but only of some, and yet certainly and absolutely of some. The expression is, ' they must enter in ; ' for which also the apostle there allegeth an oath of God, than which nothing could make the promise more absolute. Likewise those passages of Christ's evidence the same thing : John x. 16, ' Other sheep I have which are not of this fold : them also I must bring, and they shall hear my voice,' &c.

(2.) It is absolutely certain also in those promises, that these persons are (1.) Of all sorts of sinners, and all manner of iniquity shall be forgiven, except that against the Holy Ghost, says Christ, to some or other. (2.) Of persons in all ages or successions of times. (3.) In all nations, and of all places : ' Look unto me, all the ends of the earth, and be saved ; ' and ' Thou hast redeemed us out of all nations, tongues, and kindreds,' &c., Rev. v. 9. (4.) Out of all ranks and conditions, bond and free, poor and rich, kings, and all in authority. By all men, all sorts of men are intended.

2dly, Yet these promises are withal still indefinitely uttered as to persons. For if some, and but some—' that I may win some,' says the greatest converter of souls—are saved, then still not all ; if out of all nations, then not all in or of a nation. And truly in their saying, ' Thou hast redeemed us out of all nations, tongues, and kindreds,' he makes the very redemption of Christ to be but of some in all, and they that speak this speak it not of themselves, as they had been justified, called, and sanctified. No; they say not, Thou hast called us out of all nations, &c., but plainly, Thou hast redeemed us with thy blood out of all nations, so limiting it to redemption. They speak of those namely on whom Christ, in shedding his blood for them (they speaking it to Christ), had his redeeming eye, which he had not in redeeming unto the rest of those nations, which are therefore distinguished from these even by a redemption of them, which is not of those other. And there is a vast difference between saying, Thou hast redeemed all nations, as the Universalists say, and, Thou hast redeemed us, a select company, out of all nations, as they speak here. There is no such univer-

sality the promises are made unto, though these promises are to be promulged to the universality of all mankind. And the promises are then
to be styled indefinite, whilst they absolutely and certainly declare that
some must and shall enter in, and that all shall not, and yet do no way
signify who they are, either by any discernible mark or character of difference, or by naming those persons (God reserving that to himself, and leaving it in suspense) until the qualification of faith and such other graces
are wrought in them. And those promises which are made unto such
qualifications we call conditional promises, which are in their tenor universal ; but not so these absolute of this sort which we speak of, for they
can bear no other title, as they respect persons, but of indefiniteness,
though they be otherwise never so absolute. If we will take an impartial
survey of all absolute declarations and promises of salvation, they will be
found thus indefinite, as in respect to persons, as they are proposed for
objects unto our faith. Thus it is in that grand proclamation which was
made on purpose as the foundation of Old Testament faith, wherein the
riches of the mercy in the divine nature are discovered and exposed, ' The
Lord, gracious, merciful,' &c., Deut. xxxiv. 6. This, as it respects persons,
to whom God means to be gracious, have this professed restriction premised thereto by God himself the promulger : ' I will be merciful to whom
I will be merciful ; ' chap. xxxiii. ver. 19, ' I will proclaim the name of
the Lord before thee, and will be gracious to whom I will be gracious, and
will shew mercy on whom I will shew mercy.' The import of which, what
is it other than that he will absolutely be merciful unto some, even those
whom he will, but not to all ? And who those are to whom he will be
merciful he reserves within himself, and yet professeth to proclaim this,
that all the people might know it, and accordingly Moses published it to
all. And this was of all other the first most solemn promulgation of mercy
publicly made that ever was made before, and so the tenor of it is *mensura
reliquorum*, the measure of the rest. That God also will blot out, or pardon
transgressions for his name's sake, Isa. xliii. 25, is an absolute promise,
fitted to the faith of any one that hath a will to believe. It speaks to no
condition or qualification, but the contrary : ver. 22–24, ' But thou hast
not called upon me, O Jacob ; but thou hast been weary of me, O Israel.
Thou hast not brought me the small cattle of thy burnt-offerings, neither
hast thou honoured me with thy sacrifices : I have not caused thee to
serve with an offering, nor wearied thee with incense. Thou hast bought
me no sweet cane with money, neither hast thou filled me with the fat of
thy sacrifices ; but thou hast made me to serve with thy sins, thou hast
wearied me with thine iniquities.' He names no person but Jacob ; that
is, his people elect, as elsewhere he calls them ; yea, and there also, ver. 21,
' The people he had formed for himself, to shew forth his praise,' who are
in other scriptures termed before their calling, ' children of God,' John
xi. 52 ; his people, Acts xv. 14, and Acts xviii. 10. But who these are,
till they believe, none knows. Yea, and he limits this pardon unto them :
Micah vii. 18, 19, ' Who is a God like unto thee, that pardoneth iniquity, and
passeth by the transgression of the remnant of his heritage ? he retaineth
not his anger for ever, because he delighteth in mercy. He will turn again,
he will have compassion upon us ; he will subdue our iniquities ; and thou
wilt cast all their sins into the depths of the sea.' The words are purely
what are in Exod. xxxiii. and xxxiv., and they whom they concern are but
the remnant whom he hath chosen for his heritage, which who knows but
he ? The like we have also in that declaration concerning Christ's intention of coming into the world to save sinners, commended for such a

faithful saying, for all our faith to receive and accept : 1 Tim. i. 15, 'This is a faithful saying, and worthy of all acceptation, that Christ Jesus came into the world to save sinners ; of whom I am chief.' It is sinners in the world indefinitely, he says not all, not all universally, which the very sound and tenor of the speech shews. And it is of great force to confirm it to be so, that he speaks of that redemption by Christ, and that sort of purpose therein to save these sinners, to be every way one and the same with that which he had of saving the apostle himself, which the apostle came then to find and discern, when Christ had by such an overflow of love and almighty power wrought faith in him: ver. 14, 'And the grace of our Lord was exceeding abundant with faith and love, which is in Christ Jesus.' And therefore he was now able with assurance to put in his own name, in saying, ' of whom I am chief.' And in saying so he puts himself (we evidently see) into the same rank and number, sort and heap, of all the sinners that were redeemed, and all of them redeemed with the same grace and intention that Paul himself had been redeemed with, and made the subject of in Christ's heart. He himself was redeemed with no other aim than they all were. That which did put the difference was, that he was the chief of that rank in sinning. And surely Christ's aim and eye at him in dying for him was out of a special grace and love, whereby he died not only to make him salvable, as some would dilute Christ's intention in dying for the non-elect, affirming that Christ died for all men thus far, barely to make this proposition true of all men, that if they would believe they should be saved. It is certain that he died for Paul with a further intention of love than so ; even efficaciously to give him faith, and invincibly save him. For that grace in converting him effectually it is he there so predicates, ver. 14, ' The grace of our Lord was exceeding abundant with faith and love,' &c., and magnifies Christ for having come into the world to bestow it on him. Christ did not die with one intention for Paul, and another intention for others, for he ranks the other sinners for whom Christ died in common with himself, together in one rank with his own person. He puts himself and them in the same rank. Now Christ died for him as a chosen vessel to himself, &c., as Christ himself that died for him from heaven speaks of him, Acts ix. 15, and in dying bore the same love to the rest of those sinners he died for that he did to Paul ; he dying for him and them considered in one body, Eph. ii., whereof Paul was but a member. And therefore Paul propounds himself as a pattern of this grace unto all that should by virtue of Christ's dying come to believe : ver. 16, ' For this cause I obtained mercy, that in me first Jesus Christ might shew forth all long-suffering, *for a pattern* to them that should hereafter believe on him to life everlasting.' And withal commends this faithful saying thus indefinitely uttered, ' that Christ came into the world to save sinners,' as the most accommodate object to their faith, upon which they should embrace and lay hold on Christ, as it had been so to him, when in his humiliation he had seen himself to be the chiefest of sinners. To conclude this, I will say, that after all the wringing, and writhing, and turning things this way and that, and when men have said all that they can, it will be found that the world, which is the adequate object of Christ's aim in dying (which he is elsewhere said to have come to save, and is thereupon proclaimed to be the Saviour of the world, John iv. 42) is no otherwise to be understood than of men in the world indefinitely taken. Yea, and that other phrase of ' all men,' of whom likewise he is said [to be] the Saviour, will after all agitations issue in and come to its being an indefinite expression (as we have explained it), noting out men in all nations, of all ranks, ages, conditions, and sorts of sinners over all the world.   And so it imports an indefinite-ness, and not an universality of persons to have been intended in it ; and so all these declarations and promises of salvation which are absolute are to be understood.

I come now to demonstrate the suitableness of the faith of one that knows not of a certainty of himself to be intended, unto the tenor of the promises as it respects persons.   Let us see then what actings of faith there may be in such an one for his own personal salvation, although he is not assured of his personal interest, and view withal (which I mainly intend) the correspondency which faith in such an one doth hold with the tenor of such promises, as it hath been opened; which will at once evince that such a faith is saving; for if faith answers the promise, it is certainly true saving faith ; as also make way to instruct us how in such a case we may apply ourselves unto absolute promises, which is the point I ultimately drive at.

I shall, as I have done before, when I shewed the correspondency of such a man's faith to the matter of the promises, go over the actings of the soul towards the tenor of them, and that as to both the understanding and will.

1. These absolute promises do in the tenor afford and lay before faith in the understanding of such an one, these great truths that follow, which are productive of faith in his will, and do draw on this will to close with God and Christ, with acts therein suitable to the tenor of the promises for his particular salvation.   They present to faith in his understanding : 1st, That there are some, and those not a few, persons whom God cer-tainly and undoubtedly intends to save, and whom he will effectually give faith unto.   And although the man may yet be suspensive whether his own person or no be included, yet in the mean while faith may and doth meet with and come up to this part of the promise, in that he fully believes that some shall be saved.   And he may and doth believe this piece of the tenor of it, notwithstanding his wavering as to his own person, even as absolutely as the promises themselves, viz., that God is absolutely (that is, certainly) resolved to save some with a free and efficacious grace.   ' There are that shall come to me,' says Christ, John vi. 37.   And again, there are those that are the children of God (in God's purpose) who shall hear my voice, John xi. 52 ; and the belief of this at once gives hope as concerning this thing ; for if the example of that one person, Paul, is proposed by himself, and the Holy Ghost speaking in him, as a pattern and flag of mercy held out to toll and invite others in, who were after to believe (as in that 1 Tim. i. we may read), then much more are we encouraged when we hear that there are a many for whom Christ came into the world with an absolute intention to save them.   Thus Christ speaks : ' My blood,' said he, ' that is shed for many for the remission of sins,' when now he was to die, Mat. xxvi. 28 ; and when they shall come together in that last great general assembly, it is said of them, Rev. vii. 9, ' Lo, a great multitude, which no man could number, of all nations, and kindreds, and people, and tongues, stood before the throne, and before the Lamb, clothed with white robes, and palms in their hands.'   And likewise the belief of thus much concerning persons in a matter of so near and great concernment as a man's salvation is, will, through the Spirit's drawing, quicken and stir up the will to put in for it for a man's self (although he knows not certainly that he is the person intended), and accordingly to endeavour after the obtaining of it.   This we manifestly may find in the coherence of the 6th and 11th verses of Heb. iv., ' Seeing therefore it remaineth that some must enter therein' (namely, that rest), ' and they to whom it was first preached entered not in, because of

unbelief,' the confirmation of which he prosecutes in the following verses. In the 11th verse, he draws forth this inference from that his former : ' Let us labour therefore to enter into that rest,' says he in ver. 11, ' lest any man fall after the same example of unbelief;' which punctually answers in the way of exhortation unto both parts of his foregoing doctrine in that ver. 6 ; and the true reason of such an inference may be seen in the ordinary practice of men : for if when men know aforehand that one, yea, but one shall, in running a race, obtain a crown, yet all that are habilitated for a race will venture their ability and skill to run for it, and this when it is but for a ' corruptible crown,' as the apostle enforceth his exhortation, 1 Cor. ix. 24, 25, then how much more when we know that not one only, but many, and so great a multitude shall obtain, and that the gage or price at stake is not a corruptible, but ' an incorruptible crown,' as the apostle (ver. 25) further heightens and raiseth his motive and argumentation to this our very purpose in hand.

2. These absolute promises and declarations do lay before the understanding of such an one, that these some or many are of all sorts (as was said), out of all nations, ages, both of succession of times, and ages of persons, and also of all sinners of all sorts, in all the degrees, and sizes, and proportions of sinnings, even the chiefest, as the apostle's vision shews, Acts ix. 12 ; all manner of beasts, wild and creeping things, from the basest worms to the most loathed and monstrous beasts, were involved in that sheet, which was the figure of the church catholic, represented unto Peter, as those that were to be called and converted out of all sorts of sinners, even the vilest. These declarations, in like manner, hold forth that it is God's very design to comprehend and take in of all these, whatever their sins, their ranks, their conditions be. He would have some of all kindreds, families, callings, that he might be said to extend his rich free grace unto an *all*, all in some respect. And this opens the door of hope to the soul we are speaking of, yet far wider. For he now looking upon himself round about in all circumstances whatsoever, and viewing himself all over, may see that whatever rank, condition, or sinfulness we can suppose him to be in, or he finds himself to be in, yet he finds that his own condition is not only not to be excluded, but taken in in that indefinite way mentioned in the promise. The very same condition and degree of sinfulness that he stands in, is to be found in the persons of some or other, whom in the promise God intends, and so comes to be comprehended in the promises ; and, further, he may thereby see, in such absolute declarations, all objections of all kinds that can any way be made by carnal reason (which is so jealous of God), or that can be alleged either from his sins, or circumstances, or conjectures, wholly to be removed and answered ; and all this these absolute promises do suggest and prompt him with. And though still he demurs whether his person, singly and particularly considered, be certainly the man whom God will own still further, yet, even as to that point, namely, his person singly considered, he hath this to say, that seeing God hath no where, nor by any fatal mark or brand, as upon Cain, set him out for destruction, why then (may he not well think thereupon) shall I exclude myself ? ' There is no difference,' saith the apostle, ' for all have sinned ;' being therefore all alike, whoever they be that have sinned, they are capable alike of being ' freely justified by his grace, through the redemption that is in Jesus Christ,' Rom. iii. 22–24. The meaning is, that there is no difference of sins, small or great (as to the point of God's free grace to justify a man), which is any bar that shuts any man out. He finds, likewise, that as there is nothing of good in him that should move God to be merciful to

him ; so, nor on the contrary, nothing of evil that will be of power to divert God from his declared resolution to pardon all manner of sin *de facto* (but that one against the Holy Ghost), as Christ that bore our sins, and paid the price for us, tells us.   So as his single individual person stands free of all incumbrances, of all *quare impedits*, of all that should prejudge him, and let him ; he stands as free for free grace as freely to accept and receive him, as ever any man did whom it hath accepted, anything in the whole word of God notwithstanding.   It is not that such or such sins, or manner of sinnings after illuminations, &c., shall be a cross-bar, or spoke, or hindrance against a man, no more than sins before ; for, whenever a man cometh to God to be justified, whether after calling or before, he comes and sues it *sub formâ impii*, as looking upon himself as an ungodly person, whilst he is a-suing for justification, and appears in that court.   He is not to consider his being already godly ; there is no difference, no, not in that respect neither.   He may see that it is pure free grace in God's heart he hath to deal withal, and to treat with God by, and to try what quarter it will give ; and it is the glory thereof that moves God to be merciful where he will be merciful ; and where he proves to be gracious, he is to an ὑπερ-πλεόνασμα, he is to an overflowing superabounding fulness gracious to them. Those that run in a race, or strive for masteries, have the confidence of their own skill, or strength, or use, and accustomed agility for their confidence, and do venture thereupon ; but this soul hath the absolute grace of God before him to rely upon, and so ventures upon what it shall be willing to do for him.

3. These absolute promises do, together with all these considerations, hint to him an *it may be ;* that is, that he may be one God will be merciful unto.*   If it must be somebody's lot (in that language the apostle speaks, Eph. i.), then, says he, why not mine ?   So prompts the Holy Ghost often such souls ; and this, though but a far-off apprehension, hath brought many a soul near, and drawn and encouraged them to come to God for their particular salvation.   The people of Nineveh believed God in his threatenings, Jonah iii. 5 ; and this thought withal fell into them by the suggestion of the Spirit : ver 6, 9, ' Who can tell if God will return and repent, and turn away from his fierce anger, that we perish not ? '   And, says the prophet, Joel ii. 14, 15, ' The Lord your God is gracious and merciful, slow to anger, and of great kindness, and repenteth him of the evil : who knows if he will return and repent, and leave a blessing behind him ? '   In the case of the child David sought the Lord : for, says he, ' I said ' (that is, I had this saying or apprehension of faith in my mind), ' Who can tell whether God will be gracious to me ? ' 2 Sam. xii. 22, in sparing his life ; and yet the prophet had told him it should die ; but David thought it might be but of the nature of a conditional threatening, which by prayer might have been diverted.   And, in other scriptures, promises are uttered in the slender style of an *it may be,* as Zeph. ii. 3, ' It may be ye shall be hid in the day of the Lord's anger.'   Some of these were promises and apprehensions in case of temporal deliverances, others of eternal salvation connexed with them.   However, my argument is strong from either, for these so indefinite expressions uttered in temporal promises with but an ' it may be,' and ' who can tell but that God ?' &c., did yet however draw them in to seek God with a true faith for the obtaining the things promised, the faith in them answering to the utterance and tenor of the promise from God ; then much more

---

* Interrogo nunc credisne, O peccator, Christo? Dicis, Credo. Quid credis? Gratis universa peccata tibi per ipsum *posse remitti*. Habes quod credidisti.—*Aug. Gerard, de Just.* p. 1050.

in the case of eternal salvation, if the promises thereof speak, or whisper rather, but an *it may be*, and *who knows?* should we be drawn to believe. And so much (for certain) these absolute promises do speak of hope to such a soul before us, yea, or any soul whatever that hears and observes them; and if they leave but such a hint or impression upon the soul as David had and spake of—' I said, who can tell but God will be gracious to me ?'—that so such a soul comes but once to say within itself, Who can tell but God will be gracious to me, in pardoning and saving of me ? This *it may be* in the soul's apprehension may and will have, through the Spirit's assisting, and God the Father's drawing (without which never so certain and direct promises made to all universally, or particularly to any one by name, would not have any drawing virtue in them to work faith), I say these *it may bes*, or *I may be the person*, may have as much power and force in them to win the heart to believe, and by faith to put in for them, and to pray to obtain them, as in temporal salvations they had. For the reason is the same in both, yea, and the weight far the more on this side of salvation eternal, by how much a man's salvation (the subject-matter of such spiritual promises) is infinitely nearer to such a man's soul, to move and stir him, than all or any temporal salvation is or can be supposed to be to any. This the apostle hath instructed us in, as touching the very point before us: ' They strive for a corruptible crown,' says he, ' we for an incorruptible;' it is an inference from the less to the infinitely greater. And a soul once made apprehensive to purpose, as we say, of the weight of salvation, the massy import and concernments thereof joining all their forces with these so weak *it may bes*, will yet, as smaller and more weak cords, twisted with greater and stronger, have together a mighty power in them to draw the soul, when withal God shall be at the end of these ropes, and draw with them. And how slender these hopes, and however contemptible some may and do account them, which these *it may bes* do afford, yet they are from God, who is pleased to speak in that style to us men; and ' the weakness of God,' when he comes to work upon souls by them, ' is stronger than the greatest power of men.' He can draw a mighty whale to shore with a twine thread. He can hold fast the greatest ship in the most tempestuous storm by the cable of a slight straw.

Now, behold the correspondency and conformity of such an apprehension of faith in such a soul unto the indefiniteness of these promises in the word; just as God speaks, so they believe. God is a gracious and merciful God (that is, absolute), and it may be God will be gracious to you, and who can tell ? So says the promise on God's part, as it is spoken unto us; that is, it is but indefinitely spoken. And then says the soul, Who can tell but he will be gracious to me (as David said, ' It may be God will bless me for Shimei's cursing to-day') ? So speaks the heart as it were in an echo to the other voice in the promise.

4. There is a fourth act of faith may be in the understanding of one that is not yet assured of his present personal salvation, and it may be an act of assurance too, as for the future, namely, that if that faith which in his will he is now a-putting forth (of which next) prove true spiritual faith, and that he hold fast the beginning of his confidence unto the end, then it is an absolute certainty that he shall be saved. And this is a great addition, that crowneth all the former considerations with a further hope; and who is there that is at the very brink of believing would not, upon this and the other considerations, cast himself in upon God's mercy ? ' He that plougheth should plough in hope; and he that thrasheth in hope should be partaker of his hope,' 1 Cor. ix. 10. The apostle speaks it to

another business; but I may thus far apply it to this in hand, that as it is
a comfortable encouragement to a ploughman to plough and to cast in his
seeds into the ground, because he is in an ordinary way hopefully assured
he shall, if his corn take root, have an expected and desired crop; and
with that hope he ploughs, and in the hope of it doth at the present throw
away his seed. Do men take pains to plough, and venture to sow their
corn in hope? Then how much more should we! We endeavour, as the
apostle's word is, and take pains to believe, knowing that if our seed that
is cast come to have a root, as Christ in opposition to the thorny ground
insinuates, it will bring forth fruit unto perfection, and 'in due time we
shall reap if we faint not.' And this is a sowing far more certain for the
hopes of it than that other, and yet we see men ordinarily venture both
their labour and seed corn. Yea, this venture to believe (for so I call it
as to the soul's own apprehension) upon these *it may bes* of salvation, are
far more sure and certain than our exercising faith and spending prayers
upon those *it may bes* of temporal promises for things outward. For faith,
although it be true faith, doth often prove uncertain and issueless as to the
obtaining of the particular thing we aimed at in such promises for outward
things (which was David's case in that instance mentioned), but this
adventure of faith and of our souls on these *it may bes* for salvation, if it
prove true faith in the end, though in the lowest degree, will never be unsuccessful as to that salvation we seek for. For Christ hath said, 'He
that seeks' (continues so to do) 'shall find, and to him that knocks it
shall be opened.'

2. I shall now consider these acts of faith in the will in such a believer,
and how conformable those also are to the indefinite tenor of absolute promises. Let us next consider what acts of faith in the will (that are true
acts of faith) such a soul may put forth, and which may stand with these
indefinite apprehensions, when very far short of an assurance that he is
the person; for which the pure, absolute promises afford him no further
ground.

(1.) There may be a coming unto God and Christ. The act of coming,
which is so often used to express believing both on God and Christ (as
Christ himself expresseth it in his sermons, and we read of coming unto
God through Christ, Heb. vii.), is an act of the will (as Rev. xxii. 17,
'Let him that is athirst come, and let him that will,' &c.). And the
saving act of faith is expressed by it: John vii. 37, 'If any man thirst,
let him come unto me and drink;' and it follows (as explaining what he
meant by coming), 'He that believeth on me,' &c. And the aim, end, or
errand of such a soul in its coming, and for which it comes, is said to be
that it may be saved; that is its business it comes unto God and Christ
for. Now, such an act may well stand with the fore-mentioned indefinite
apprehension as concerning his own person, and with that suspensive uncertainty (as I may term it), for in that respect he may yet come to have
it given and made good to him, although he knows not that he hath, or
certainly shall have, a share in it. And therefore undeniably the saving
act in the will may be put forth without such a personal assurance. That
phrase of coming is taken from what is ordinary with men, and is on purpose chosen out to express the aim of such a faith in such a condition.
For a man useth to come to another for a thing that is in that man's
power to bestow whom he comes to, when yet he utterly hath no assurance from him that he shall obtain it, and yet ventures to come. Nothing
is more ordinary in common practice than this, and therefore the act of
faith which is without assurance is most aptly set forth thereby. And

truly that speech of Christ's, 'Him that cometh unto me I will in no ways cast out,' John vi. 37, was spoken as on purpose to the heart of many an one that comes (especially at first), to hearten him against, and obviate this very fear of being rejected; and who therefore so comes, as in his own thoughts he may remain suspensive in himself, whether he shall be received as to salvation, which is his errand, yea or no, especially in the case of him who but now first comes, seeing that until he hath come and put forth such an act, he cannot come to know whether it will be a true and spiritual act of faith, or coming with a true heart, yea or no.   Yet however at his first coming the intent of his soul in coming is, that he may be received.   And come he must first in a direct line to Christ ere he can reflect upon his coming, whether it be with a true heart (as, Heb. x., it is explained), nor will he know his welcome unto Christ until he actually comes or hath come.

And that the aim of such an act of coming to God or Christ, or God in Christ, is purely that he may be justified, and that this is that genuine act whereupon a man is indeed justified, the example and instance of the apostles themselves, as it is alleged by one of the greatest of them in the name of himself and all the rest of them, doth manifestly declare: Gal. ii. 16, 'We, knowing that a man is not justified by the works of the law, but by the faith of Jesus Christ, even we have believed in Jesus Christ, that we might be justified by the faith of Christ, and not by the works of the law.'   In which words he tells us plainly, that by such a faith, having such an aim or tendency in it, that they might be justified, it was that they came to Christ.   And it is spoken of their having renounced works for justification (which the Jewish principles did lead unto), and their betaking themselves unto faith, that they might be justified, from the first of their conversion unto Christ.   Those words, 'even we,' do point unto the other apostles together with himself; even we that were the first-fruits of Christianity, and eminentest among believers, had yet but the same like faith at first which all believers else have, viz., that which was pitched upon the righteousness of God and our Saviour Jesus Christ (as Peter, 2 Peter i. 1, speaks), which he styles 'like precious faith,' which was then and is to be for ever common to all believers, both small and great, at first; which faith (as by comparing this in the Galatians appears) was not a believing at the first dash, that they *were* justified, but a believing that they *might* be justified, and so a coming unto Christ with this aim and errand, that I may be justified as to the future.   And if any would question whether it were spoken of all the apostles or no, yet however, to be sure, it was Paul speaks it of himself, and Peter of himself, who was the chief of the apostles ; and of Peter, who professed his faith in the name of all the apostles, Mat. xvi.   For, if you observe, it is the continuation of a speech he had begun to make unto Peter personally : ver. 14, 'I said unto Peter,' &c., and this is part of what he said to him, 'We who are Jews by nature, and not sinners of the Gentiles, knowing that a man is not justified by the works of the law, but by the faith of Jesus Christ, even we have believed in Jesus Christ, that we might be justified by the faith of Christ, and not by the works of the law ; for by the works of the law shall no flesh be justified ;' in which he proceeds to confute and reprove Peter, who by Judaism had exposed no less than the great point of justification by faith. But Paul appealeth to his own experience at and from his first conversion, and often after, by what a faith he had lived to be justified by it, and presseth it on him ' before all' that were present (as he relateth it in verse 14), as a commonly received principle amongst believers, yea, and even amongst us too, says he, that are Jews, and not Gentiles. And that the act of coming to Christ, whereby faith is expressed, includes this as the end and intent of that coming, and is indeed in the form of it, viz., ' that I may be saved,' or, ' that I might be justified,' that speech of Christ's shews (although spoken to Pharisees, and yet spoken of the contrary act of unbelief in them, and so as the contrary illustrates wherein the spirit of true faith lies), ' Ye will not come to me that ye might have life,' John v. 40 ; that is, you will not believe, which is a coming to me with that intention to have life from me ; which all those whom I save do put forth and exercise towards me, and do come unto me for ; but these proud justiciaries did scorn to do it, and would not thus come. That particle ἵνα, *that*, denotes out the end or aim which he is to take up, who would come to Christ, or believe on him savingly, and imports not only what is the event or consequent upon believing.* And as the sole aim of a soul in believing is, that he may be saved, so likewise God's will and intention in requiring faith is declared to be, that he that believes may have life, John vi., God's aim answering that of the believers. And again, that this is the aim and business of the soul in coming, Christ's invitation to come shews : Mat. xi. 28, &c., ' Come to me, ye that are heavy loaden, and I will give you rest ;' which promise in the last words doth at once speak to what their souls were burthened for the want of, and most of all desire, namely, rest ; and also guides and directs those souls with what they should intend and design in coming to obtain from him, even rest : ' And you shall find rest to your souls.' Now, as this act of coming with this intention, that I may have rest, doth and may well stand with a suspensive uncertainty, that I am the person, so it may and doth answer to the indefinite apprehension the understanding of such an one hath. The understanding tells him from the promise, that he may be the person whom God may justify ; then in correspondency, says the will, I do believe, or come to God and Christ, that I may be justified, and so he exactly comports with the indefiniteness of the promise as to his person ; for as *that* holds forth an *it may be God will*, &c., so the aim of his coming is, that he may be saved. And it is certain in experience, that with such a poor and slender *it may be* at the first, many a soul hath cast anchor within the veil blindfold (as seamen cast their anchors when yet they see not the earth at the bottom of the sea, or know that their anchor will take hold, nor yet know how to trail it or apply it certainly to that earth, so as to be able to say, it shall without peradventure fasten and take sure hold thereon, but a long time perhaps comes back to them again), and yet have in the end found a firm and sure holdfast in the heart of God and grace of Christ, to hang upon with the whole weight of their souls, the weight of their sins hanging upon them also, with all the *pondus* of them.

CHAPTER V.

That election-grace, and the immutability of God's counsel indefinitely proposed in the promises, is the object of faith.

For when God made promise to Abraham, because he could swear by no greater, he sware by himself, saying, Surely blessing I will bless thee, and multiplying I will multiply thee. And so, after he had patiently endured, he ob-

---

* ἵνα *ut* significat finem, non solum consequentiam.—*Brugensis in verba.*

tained the promise. For men verily swear by the greater ; and an oath for confirmation is to them an end of all strife. Wherein God, willing more abundantly to shew unto the heirs of promise the immutability of his counsel, confirmed it by an oath ; that by two immutable things, in which it was impossible for God to lie, we might have a strong consolation, who have fled for refuge to lay hold upon the hope set before us : which hope we have as an anchor of the soul, both sure and stedfast, and which entereth into that within the veil ; whither the forerunner is for us entered, even Jesus, made an high priest for ever, after the order of Melchisedec.—HEB. VI. 13–20.

The 11th verse begins an exhortation, whereof all that follows is the prosecution. The words of that verse are these : ' We desire that every one of you do shew the same diligence, to the full assurance of hope unto the end.' Here are two things distinct : 1st, An exercise, and diligence ; 2dly, This is directed towards the attainment of full assurance of hope unto the end ; which is somewhat parallel to that of Peter, 2d Epist. i. 10, ' Brethren, give diligence to make your calling and election sure.' To exhort them to all diligence, he lays before them the examples of the eminent saints that they had known in their times,—ver. 12, ' That ye be not slothful,'—and refers unto using that diligence he speaks of : ' Be followers of them who through faith and patience inherit the promises ;' that is, that have got possession, and obtained, and have arrived unto eternal glory. And by patience, he doth not only mean patience in suffering, but constancy in well-doing, especially waiting by faith for the attainment of the promise, as patience is taken in Rom. ii. 7, ' Who by patient continuance in well-doing, seek for glory and immortality.' As for that other part, ' the full assurance of hope unto the end, he begins at ver. 13, to propound the example of Abraham more particularly and eminently, and shews how God, to assure him in his hope, did give him a promise and an oath, both which you have in ver. 13 ; that is, he arrived at the end of his days at the enjoyment and fulfilling of the promises, as those other saints he spake of, ver. 12, are said to have ' inherited the promises.' Some refer his obtaining the promise to what was in this life, in having Isaac given him, &c., and by having the comfort of it ever after while he lived. But he had obtained the promise of Isaac before this oath was given, and therefore it is rather to be understood to mean it after that oath given, upon his offering up Isaac, he having patiently endured to the end of his days, as his exhortation (verse 11), had said, that then he attained the full possession of it.

The assurance which was given to Abraham was the greatest that heaven could afford, a promise and an oath. I say the greatest, as, 1st, the apostle himself argues, ver. 16, if amongst men an oath, when they swear by God, that is greater than themselves, is of such authority, as it ends all strife, though men be liars, and may be supposed even in swearing to lie, yet an oath taken by God, or by their gods, whoever they be, is accounted so sacred, and of such authority, as all men rest in it, and there is an end of strife ; much more when God shall take an oath. This you have, ver. 16, ' For men verily swear by the greater, and an oath for confirmation is to them an end of all strife.' For that God himself should swear, the apostle says, ver. 18, that ' it was impossible for God to lie therein.' It cannot be supposed of him, though of men it may, so ver. 18. But, 2dly, Whom did God swear by ? He sware by himself : ver. 13, ' Because he could swear by no greater, he sware by himself ;' he staked himself ; as if he had said, I will cease to be God if I do not perform this.

Tl e thing he sware to was to bless Abraham with all blessings, and that unto the end; ' Surely blessing I will bless thee.' And if he sware by himself to perform this, then all the power in God, and long-suffering of God towards Abraham, were engaged to the uttermost to work upon Abraham's soul, and to bear with him effectually to attain this. And whereas those that should read but hitherto what Paul said of the oath to Abraham, would expect of Paul he should declare how this oath did concern those whom he exhorted, or otherwise it had been in vain, and an example not applicable to his purpose, which was to exhort them to the ' full assurance of hope unto the end,' such as Abraham had. And whereas, because it was a voice from heaven, they might think that this was singular and proper to Abraham alone, he therefore proceeds in the 17th and 18th verses to apply it to them to whom he wrote, to all the heirs of promise and salvation, and together therewith expounds what was the matter intended in the oath and promise. Thus he applies it in these words: ver. 17, ' Wherein God, willing more abundantly to shew unto the heirs of promise the immutability of his counsel, confirmed it by an oath.' (1.) Observe that word, ver. 17, ' wherein God willing,' &c. ' Wherein,' or in which oath and promise he had spoken of before. (2.) It is made to the ' heirs of promise,' and therefore to all that are heirs with him, which all that are Christ's are said to be: Gal. iii. 29, ' And if ye be Christ's, then are you Abraham's seed, and heirs according to the promise.' (3.) In verse 18 he shews the intent of the oath to be, that we all do believe that have the faith of Abraham; which faith he doth describe by such acts and terms as might include the weakest of believers, unto that end that all such might have strong consolation. So as we are to look upon Abraham in this manner of dispensation (though it was so singular an example in him) to him personally, as that he therein was, Rom. iv. 16, ' the father of us all.' As in the case of imputation of righteousness by faith, it is said in the same Rom. iv. 22–24, ' It was imputed to him for righteousness. Now, it was not written for his sake alone, that it was imputed to him; but for us all, to whom it shall be imputed,' &c. And indeed this is held forth in the very promise which was then given him, and which the oath confirmed. The promise is in Heb. vi. 14, ' Surely blessing I will bless thee.' Now in Gal. iii. 14 the same blessing that was given to Abraham is said to ' come on the Gentiles that were after to believe;' and so, in blessing Abraham, he blessed us all that are heirs of promise; and we have the same promise with him and them. For in the latter part of the promise, ' In multiplying I will multiply thee,' all the spiritual seed are included. ' In multiplying I will multiply thy seed,' or all seed to thee, says God, Gen. xxii., which were the spiritual seed, heirs of promise of salvation with him, and children of the promise with his Isaac, Rom. ix. 7, 8.

Let us next consider what is the matter of that promise and oath. 1st, in the letter of it, it is to bless him and us with ' all spiritual blessings in heavenly things,' imported in this doubling the words, ' In blessing I will bless thee,' and so thy seed. I will bless thee with faith, with holiness, with perseverance to the end, and salvation at the end. But, 2dly, the apostle brings forth a deeper and higher matter that this oath and promise did intend, and that is, the immutability of his counsel confirming the promise by an oath. So, then, his own counsels about Abraham's salvation, and of us all, are the same kind of decrees for the salvation of us all that was for Abraham's.

1. If you ask what is meant by his counsel here, I answer, it is his everlasting decrees and purposes taken up within himself concerning Ab-

raham's salvation, and of us all; and it is the same kind of decrees for the salvation of us all that was for Abraham's.*

1st. I say God's decrees and resolute determinations concerning our salvation are imported by the word *counsel*. Concerning Jesus Christ to be crucified the apostle utters himself thus, Acts iv. 28, that the Jews did but ' whatsoever God's hand and counsel determined before to be done.' His counsels, then, are his determinations and purposes.

And, 2dly, they are his purposes within himself, and so differ from a promise. A promise made, is God's outward declaration to do so and so for us, but his counsel are his purposes within himself, decreeing so and so, as in Eph. i. 9, and v. 11, compared.

3dly. His counsel imports these his purposes which have been from everlasting: Acts iv. 28, ' What thy counsel determined to be done aforehand.' And so it imports the same that foreknowledge doth, which in matter of our salvation is said to have been before the world began. And what other is this counsel of his in matter of Abraham's and our salvation, but the very same we find Eph. i. 3, 4, 9, and ver. 11 ? ' Blessed be the God and Father of our Lord Jesus Christ, who hath blessed us with all spiritual blessings in heavenly places in Christ Jesus, according as he hath chosen us in him before the foundation of the world; in whom also we have obtained an inheritance, being predestinated according to the purpose of him who worketh all things after the counsel of his own will.' What is the counsel of God here, is election and predestination there.

2. As his counsel shews it to be his electing love and purposes, so the oath shews these to be immutably fixed and pitched, and that to shew forth the immutability of the promise the oath was given, as verse 17 of my text imports. God's oath shews an unchangeableness; not a peremptoriness only, but an irreversibleness, and that the matter sworn to shall never be recalled. Therefore, in Psalm lxxxix., when God mentions his oath to David, the type of Christ, and to his spiritual seed (the same that was here made to Abraham's seed), says God there, in the 35th and 36th verses, ' Once have I sworn by my holiness, that I will not lie unto David, his seed shall endure for ever.' Ver. 34, ' My covenant will I not break, nor alter the thing that is gone out of my lips;' it having been thus confirmed by an oath. Our divines have generally owned this notion, and from thence, in the case of our redemption by Christ, that he should suffer in our stead, have observed that all God's threatenings of the law (as the law itself also) was given without an oath added, and that so God might dispense with any commination or exchange of the persons threatened, and put Christ in their stead; for all those threatenings were without an oath. For if they had had an oath annexed to them, we had been everlastingly undone and lost, and Christ's redemption would not have saved us. But now the gospel coming, and promises thereof, because God intended them with an immutability, he hath therefore confirmed them by an oath, Heb. vii. 21. Those priests, viz., of the law, verse 19, were made without an oath, and therefore were changeable; as, verse 12, he says both law and priesthood were to be changed, because made and given without an oath; but this with an oath, and an oath irreversible, ' by him that said unto him,'—unto Christ, namely,—' The Lord sware, and will not repent, thou

---

* Jacobus Capellus doth analyse the matter of these 17th and 18th verses. Cujus duo sunt præcipua capita. 1. *Quænam electionis!* ostendere *hæredibus salutis*, ii sunt electi. *Immutabilitatem*, quam sit firmum et immutabile suum prædestinationis decretum, *Consilii sui* secundum electionem scilicet.—*Capellus in verba.*

art a priest for ever.' Where he gives an oath, he will never repent, nor make alteration of it, viz., of what he hath sworn unto.

3. I add, that such an oath is absolute ; and though there are qualifications that God will work, which are necessary to our salvation, and unto the complete performance of the oath, yet these conditions God supposes and includes in the oath, and by the oath undertakes to work them, and effect them in us. When, therefore, God took this oath concerning Abraham's blessing, ' I blessing will bless thee,' &c. (which also takes in the salvation of all the spiritual seed), God did absolutely swear and undertake to perform and accomplish it, and to that end, withal, to give all these qualifications requisite to the full performance. God doth not swear by halves in it, but to do the whole as to Abraham and our salvations. Why, now, I appeal unto all sober spirits that will consider things, whether they will or dare say that God should make an oath for Abraham's salvation, when yet, according to the principles of free-will grace, as they state it, the performance of this oath must depend upon Abraham's will, and to the end of his days, and his will must cast the issue of it, and God would only have been to give him such assistance as he should have a power to do so and so. It was Abraham's will that must have cast the event, which is so mutable and changeable as any of ours is, or can be supposed to be. Can we think that God, in swearing that he would save Abraham, and bring him to obtain the blessing, as the phrase is here, should depend upon the mutability of such a man's will? He was to live many days after this ; and if God in his oath had not undertaken to carry on his will effectually and invincibly, as well as to save him in the end, if he went on to will, there is a supposition and a possibility that his oath might have failed, and that God should have taken his own name in vain. I might say the like concerning Isaac, who was included in the oath, who was a young man at this time, he being the first of the seed, the pattern of the rest. He was included in the seed absolutely, and God's promise was absolute, as to give him Isaac, so to continue Isaac, that his covenant might continue with him for ever as it was. And do we think that God would betrust an oath, such an oath, as to cease to be God if it were not performed, upon any creature's will ? What though they suppose he should foreknow certainly their wills would hold out unto the end, yet, would God honour a creature's will, so mutable a thing as they say it is, as to venture and pawn an oath upon it, and swear for their salvation in this manner, so as to say, If Abraham be not faithful Abraham to the end, I will not be God ? Do you think that God would debase himself so much, if that the keeping Abraham and Isaac, and by consequence us all unto the end, had not depended upon his will, so as to overcome and carry on theirs and ours infallibly unto the end ? If God sware by himself, then certainly he sware by all himself, and will therefore put forth all in himself to the utmost whereby to make good his oath ; and therefore his will and power to the utmost whereby to make good his own word, nay, to make good himself. Their principles put God upon these straits, that though God will vouchsafe such means and helps as by the laws of free-will-grace they say he doth use, yet if the will of Abraham in the freedom of it, or of any or of all the saints, shall be deficient on its part, then God cannot save him, for he hath tied himself up unto the principles of the liberty in the will, to act or not to act, according to its innate liberty, and so according to this principle he should swear by his holy self to work what he is not able to work, nor can undertake to work. It may be objected, that something in Abraham was made the cause of that oath : ver. 16, ' By myself have I sworn, saith the Lord ; for

because thou hast done this thing, and hast not withheld thy son, thy only son ; that in blessing I will bless thee.' And therefore it was not an irre-spective or an absolute oath, but founded upon an act of Abraham's. 1st, I answer in general, the papists, as Pererius,* would draw this particle *because*, set before the promise and oath, ver. 17, and then again repeated, ver. 18, and put after the oath, to favour their merits. And truly the force of those particles will as soon, yea, rather make for their merits, than for God's having in his decrees had a simple fore-respect unto this famous act of Abraham's obedience as foreseen, and upon the fore-sight of which he should have thus immutably resolved and taken up such a purpose in his decrees; but it will serve the turn of neither.

1. Because the promise or matter sworn unto was given to Abraham long before this his high act of obedience, and therefore it cannot be the merit of this obedience, nor yet could the foresight of this obedience after to come any way be the ground of making that promise ; for it is the pro-mise that contains the matter of the oath sworn to. Now God long before this oath gave the same promise to Abraham without an oath, which here he confirms with an oath: Gen. xii. 2, 'I will bless thee, and thou shalt be a blessing; and in thee,' that is, in thy seed, as here, Gen. xxii., 'shall all the families of the earth be blessed;' as here in Heb. vi. it is said, 'all the nations,' &c.; and the same again is in Gen. xviii. 17, 18. And the apostle also, Heb. vi., affirms the same, by saying that the promise had testified the same thing that this oath did, and that the oath was but a confirmation thereof. If indeed the promise had been but now first given upon his obedience, there might have been some colour for merit, or a respective decree, but so it was not. And it is inconsistent to think a promise declared a long time before should be in respect unto an act that was to come after ; for it must be something that had at that present been performed by Abraham, upon which, as foreseen, if anything foreseen had been the ground of it, the promise should have been declared. For it being so that at the giving of the promise he was actually and indubitably estated thereinto, and possessed of it, it therefore must have been some present or former act of obedience, upon the respect of which, if any such respect had been, the promise should have begun to be uttered to him. Now in that Gen. xii., those promises are said to have been given him at, and together with, God's first command and invitement of him to go out of his own country, and as antecedent to any act of obedience first put forth by him. Thus we have the account in ver. 1–3, 'Now the Lord had said unto Abraham, Get thee out of thy country, and from thy kindred, and from thy father's house, unto a land that I will shew thee: and I will make of thee a great nation, and I will bless thee, and make thy name great; and thou shalt be a blessing: and I will bless them that bless thee, and curse him that curseth thee: and in thee shall all the families of the earth be blessed.' There you have the promises and the date of them; and then his obedience follows after as the effect of those promises uttered to him, and moving his heart thereunto. Thus expressly, ver. 4, it follows, 'So Abraham departed, as the Lord had spoken to him,' &c. So that of the two, it must be said that Abraham had rather an eye and respect unto the promises first given absolutely unto him, than that God had a respect unto Abraham's obe-dience foreseen, and that he did thereupon declare them. And it will remain that God's eternal counsels had first resolved to do such and such

* Cum sit causale, et denotat causam meritoriam, non obscurè significatur, Abrahamum egregio illo facto, meruisse ut sibi tales promissiones à Deo darentur. —*Pererius in verba.*

things for Abraham out of mere grace, and from thence put them into promises, and uttered them to Abraham without mention of respective conditions upon which he should give forth these promises, as foreseeing Abraham would do so or so, and those promises drew his heart to that obedience upon the manifestation of them.

But, 2, although we grant that these promises and this oath after them might have been given with a respect unto some former or present act of obedience, yet still the decree or counsel that determined to give those things promised, might still be, yea, and was, absolute ; that is, without respect to those acts. Even as a father may and doth often absolutely resolve within himself to give such and such good things to his child, and yet defers giving the promise of them to him until such or such an act or acts of obedience are performed by him; and then in giving the promise of them professeth an high approbation of that obedience, and as a gratification or remuneration of it to him, makes the promise, although the counsel and determination of it in his heart had been absolute. And so indeed in substance and effect the apostle speaks here, that both the promise and oath were but to shew or declare the immutability of his counsel and absolute determination taken up before, so as still the decree and the immutability of it was fixed first, and God did but by these utter and declare it. It was not his oath made his counsel for the future immutable, but his counsel being immutable, he did by his oath shew it, and gave demonstration thereof.

3. That singular obedience was the occasion of the oath, as Rivet speaks. ' By myself have I sworn it,' says God ; ' because thou hast done this, and hast not withheld,' &c. But it was the immutability of his counsel that was the supreme cause why Abraham did that thing. It was that which was the cause of that obedience in Abraham, and of the oath and all ; and if he had not been greatly strengthened by the promise before given, which had absolutely declared and shewn what his counsel was, Abraham had never arrived at so high an act of gracious obedience as this was.

Nor, 4, would God for one singular act of obedience have sworn then his perpetual perseverance, which was to consist in so many other acts of grace to succeed for so many years yet to come till after Abraham's death, had not his own grace immutably decreed it first, and therefore it was that he did not stick to make declaration of it by an oath irreversibly, which if it had been left to Abraham's will, only assisted with power to persevere or not to persevere (as it is said of all other believers by the Arminians, that so they are left), God would never have ventured an oath thus.

But, 5, what he sware to Abraham here therein did God in person swear to all Abraham's seed, the heirs of promise with him, whosoever they be, and therefore their salvation and perseverance is as sure as Abraham's, though they never do or did perform any such high act of self-denial as Abraham here did. And therefore this must wholly flow from the immutability of God's counsel both towards Abraham and them all alike, or else Abraham had this promised him upon more hard and higher, yea, unnatural terms than the rest have.

The corollary which I infer from hence is, that the promises of Abraham's salvation and ours are but extracts, transcripts of God's everlasting decrees concerning man's salvation. His counsels within himself are the original, and those are the types. The matter of the promises are the decrees of election. Promises are but God's inward counsels put into words and into writing ; as when a man makes his will which he had contrived within himself, he sets it down, and seals or swears to it before witnesses. Or promises are but the expressions of election, but concerning persons and things only. There is this differing case between the case of Abraham and Isaac in this particular, that the person of Abraham by name was expressed in the promise made of them. But the promises made of the rest of the seed are as to persons made indefinitely, concerning whom the persons are not named, but yet intending' them very persons, and them only, and therefore they are called children of promise as well and as much as Isaac was. And in that place Isaac is called a child of promise as he was an elect child of God, and declared by promise so to be, to prove election, which is the subject of that chapter; and first Isaac, then Jacob's instance brought for the proof of it.

It is next to be considered, how doth this oath, as to the matter of it, belong to us?

1st. It doth, *re ipsa*, in the nature of the thing, belong to us as well as to Abraham, and our salvation is sworn to as well as Abraham's, and therefore it is made sure, whether we have attained the assurance of it or no, if we be true believers. And indeed I desire my salvation to be no surer than Abraham's was, and it is as sure by this oath as his was.

2. Yet it tends to the same end that it was made for to Abraham, which was for the confirmation of him in his faith, and to us to give ' assurance of hope,' Heb. vi. 11, for that is the head of this discourse, and he carries it along in his eye, ver. 17, to give a strong consolation; even as it served to give Abraham assurance, so it serves to give us.

As for observations upon this oath as it relates to us, and Abraham's example therein in the tendency of it to give us assurance, I would consider this oath two ways.

(1.) In the matter of it, as it is to be made use of by all believers as a ground for them to attain assurance by.

(2.) In the circumstances of it, as by the story it appears it was personal and singly given to Abraham, and God's dealings with him in doing of it are to be considered, which are not common to all believers, but yet hold some parallel with God's dispensations to some eminent saints in the New Testament, as in relation to his giving assurance to them as he gave to Abraham.

My observation upon the oath in the matter of it, as it is common to all, is this, that the immutability of God's counsel in his electing grace doth in the whole of it lie as a fit object to all believers, even the weakest, so as it is not only warrantable for them to have recourse to it, and apply it to themselves, but it is their duty. I shall prove and explain this by parts.

1. That it belongs to all believers, we have shewed before from ver. 17 and 18. But,

2. That which I observe for this purpose is, that his scope was to relieve even the weakest. Do but observe how, ver. 18, when he describes believers, his description of them is such as includes the weakest, and such as have not attained a faith of assurance but of recumbency, although the faith of those that have assurance may be included in that description. Yea, in the general it may be observed in that verse, that he speaks of consolation, and ' strong consolation,' as of a thing which yet might be obtained, as distinct from the faith which he doth describe, for so the words run. He speaks of their consolation as of a thing which they might have for the future. But the faith which he describes is that which in the time past all those had already attained, and might now attain to this strong consolation, so that their strong consolation is a distinct thing from their first faith exercised at conversion; and he chooseth to decipher all believers by

the acts that were at first, though continued still, that so he might be sure
to include all the seed. But let us examine every word whereby he doth
describe their faith, and it will be found to be such as I have said, and
which the weakest, even they that want assurance, have.

1st. His first expression, ' We that have fled for refuge.' This speaks
the very heart and condition of one who at first begun to believe, and doth
not necessarily import assurance that he is saved, or that he shall certainly
be saved. For it speaks but his running and flying for refuge and shelter
to be saved. And, as I said, it speaks the very heart and condition of such
a man at that time, and in his first act of believing (though he exerciseth
it all his life, whether with assurance or without it), but his condition at
first is that which this holds forth. (1.) He hath a sense of present
danger, and that the extremest, as a man in danger of death by reason of
his own sins that come upon him, together with an apprehension that the
wrath of God abideth on him in the estate he hath thereunto continued in;
and so (2.) flies out of, and from that condition (and that word imports a
terminus à quo) or, if you will, he flies *à Deo irato*, from an angry God (or
from out of that dominion wherein there remains nothing but wrath to him,
if he continue therein), unto a God of grace, and his dominion of grace in
and through Christ, as the Scripture expresseth it, Rom. v. and vi. And
this his then condition, and this act of flying for refuge thereupon, doth not
necessarily contain in it assurance of being saved, &c., but only a hope
that he may be saved from the wrath to come, even as coming to Christ
imports a believing on Christ that we may be saved (as Christ speaks when
he says, ' Come unto me, that ye may have life '), as also a believing on
Christ that we may be justified, as the apostle's speech is, which imports
not a knowledge that we are justified or that we have life. And thus much
the metaphor here barely insinuates, whether it be taken for one that is in
danger of his life, and seeks to save it by flying to another dominion, or to
a privilege place, as the murderer fled to the city of refuge, Num. xxxv.,
not as then knowing he should be able to arrive thither, or whether the
gates would be set open to him; or whether it be taken for such a flight
as that of Joab to the horns of the altar. And all we believers may from
our experience well know that the first acts of faith at conversion, and perhaps for a long while after, were but such as these; and yet we can all say,
we, seeing our lost condition, have fled for refuge, all of us.

2dly. If we consider what it is to lay hold on the hope set before us, the
question here may be about the word *hope*, whether the thing hoped for
should be that intended, or the hope which out of the gospel offers itself
to, and riseth up in and to a man's own heart and apprehensions from
what is in and out of the revelation of grace made therein. And thus we
may take hope for the grounds thereof set before the soul in the gospel,
together with the hopes which they beget in men's hearts upon the revelation of them, that the salvation spoken of may be theirs, and he or they
may be the person that shall obtain it. This I find to be the sense of
Calvin,* and of the most considerative late interpreters; and my main
reason (as theirs also seems to be) is, that in the next verse he says,
' Which hope we have as an anchor,' &c. Now the hope there compared
to the anchor of the soul must be the hope which a man hath in his own
heart for himself to obtain it, and it cannot agree to the object of hope or
thing hoped for, since the things hoped for are such for which this anchor is

---

* Certè in vocabulo spei est metonymia, effectus pro causa accipitur: Ego promissionem intelligo cui spes innititur; neque enim iis assentior qui spem accipiunt
pro re sperata.—*Calvin in verba.* Thus also Cameron, Jacobus Capellus, Gomarus.

cast into within the veil. And I add not simply the act of hope in our hearts, but withal the grounds of that hope, as arising from out of the revelation of the gospel ; or as Calvin doth most aptly express it, *confidendi materiam*, the matter of hoping, there being in the word *hope*, as he says, a metonymy of the effect for the cause, and so the promise on which hope bears up itself and is grounded, is connotated in that word hope. So then I expound the words thus, that to a man truly a-working upon by the Spirit of God, the same Spirit (as he is a Spirit of faith to him) doth begin to raise up in his heart a hope, from some declarations or other in the gospel about the grace of God, and the intent of Christ coming into the world, and the tenor of such promises laying forth this before him, that there is an hope for him that he may be saved, notwithstanding his sinful condition ; as it is said, ' There is hope in Israel concerning this thing.' And he is said to ' lay hold on this hope,' which the Spirit of God hath thus raised up to him and in him, as a man is said to lay hold on the hopes of such a pre-ferment, which the intimations of the person in whose power it is set before him, and he resolves not to let slip the opportunity of it, but to put in and seek it with all his might. So here this believer lays hold fast upon the hopes that have been begotten in him, and the grounds thereof, and will not cast them away, but holds them fast, and that strongly too (as the word signifies) with all his might, and he will not at any hand forsake those mercies which he hopes may be his own. Hope is taken here, as Cameron would have it, in opposition to an utter despondency, whereby a man doth cast away all hope, and lets all go ; as they in the prophet, who said, ' there is no hope.' Now then this also does not necessarily speak full assurance, but a faith rather that wants it. For,

1. Because that is barely and simply called hope, with distinction from full ' assurance of hope,' in ver. 11. Here is the hope of the recumbent expressed, but there the hope of one fully ascertained and insured. And, again, this hope is distinct from ' consolation' in the same ver. 18 ; and hope thus singly taken in this distinction (ver. 11), speaks a lower matter than assurance, and we use, in ordinary phrase, to say of a matter we are not fully certain of, I hope well. Under the Old Testament, when assur-ance was so rare a thing, for they were generally under bondage, their faith was expressed by this, ' those that hope in his mercy.' I observe there is hope, as it is in us sometimes single and simply said, and there is a good hope, which is rising up to some degrees of assurance ; and in all languages, when we would express hopes that are exceeding promising, we call them good hopes when yet we are not sure ; and this word we have, 2 Thes. ii. 16, ' Now our Lord Jesus Christ, and God, even our Father, which hath loved, and given us everlasting consolation, and given us *good hopes* through grace, comfort your hearts ;' that is, more and more, with further degrees. And that consolation which is already vouchsafed, but under good hopes, is yet called ' everlasting,' because it is such as will not (finally) be taken from us, though suffering many interruptions at present. The consolation under such good hope is everlasting consolation, but it riseth not up to strong consolation, which the apostle says they may here attain, and which those that have an anchor that holds fast may yet want.

2. This hope is said to be set before them to lay hold on, because the groundwork and foundation is in the promises, and the things declared in the gospel, which give the heart this hope for its own salvation ; as, for example, the promise being indefinitely expressed concerning some, and that there is a seed shall be made partakers of it, and that Christ died for sinners ; by such promises as these indefinitely expressed doth the Spirit

of God work a hope in the heart of the weakest believer, and causes the heart to think with itself, why may not *I* be the man that shall obtain? And from such expressions set before us, the heart doth gather itself up into hope, and by the power of God lays hold on them in such gospel-manifestations that may give it hope. As to Benhadad's servants, a word, though afar off, did give them hope concerning the life of their master, and they laid hold upon it; and, says the soul, take away this hope and you take away my life. The devil comes and persuades a man to cast it away; but, says the soul, I have laid hold on it, and I will never let it go; I will hold it and keep it, and hold to it. And though neither of these words, either of ' laying hold,' or that it is said to be ' set before us,' do express that we have possession of it, or apprehensions that it is ours already, but that we view it before us; and likewise the word to lay hold, or to retain so fast as I will not let it go, is short from being a persuasion that it is already mine, but argues indeed that I would have it mine, and therefore lay hold upon it, and seek it that it may be mine, and that I would keep it for mine, yet with hopes it shall never be taken away.

3. That similitude of an anchor, though it would seem to express an assurance of hope, in that it is called ' sure and stedfast,' is more inclining to express the hope of a recumbent, than assurance of hope; for he that casts anchor, casts anchor in the dark, blindfold as it were, in the bottom of the sea. It expresses a pure act of faith, joined with hope, of what a man sees not, and it is usually cast in extremities, just as when a man fears he may be cast away, knows not but he may; and when he casts it, he knows not whether it will take hold of the ground or no; and sometimes it comes back again. And whereas it is said, it is an anchor sure and stedfast, it follows not that he speaks in respect of a man's own apprehension, but it is so *re ipsa*, in the nature of the thing itself, through God that secretly strengthens it. That weak hope which a poor believer hath doth stay it, and but stay it, as a ship in a storm, that it shall not split upon rocks of despair. God makes a mere *it may be*, and *who knows* but that God will be merciful to a man, which is as slender a hope as may be, and as a weak straw for holding the heart in a great extremity of temptation, and yet God makes it as strong to hold the heart that it shall not sink or be cast away, as the strongest cable that is. It is sure, because it breaks not, snaps not asunder, as the ropes of the anchor use to do; and it is stedfast, because where it hath took hold, there it sticks, and holds the will as firm to cleave to God that he will not let him go till he bless him and assure him, when the assurance in the understanding of the party, that God will certainly save him, may be fluctuating, and in that respect his soul cast up and down, and ready to sink, and that in the storms of doubtings to the contrary. Therefore it doth not necessarily imply fulness of assurance.

CHAPTER VI.

How absolute election and absolute promises are the ground of faith of recumbency.

The ground of all faith is an expression of God in his word, which is either a command or a promise. Now the grounds of justifying faith are accordingly the promises of justification and salvation by Christ contained in the word, and the command of God to rest on them for their salvation. Now that which I would establish is this, that indefinite promises may be, and are sufficient ground to draw the heart in to believe. By indefinite promises I understand such as are not made universally to all men, as some would have the promises run, as that God hath loved all, and Christ died for all ; nor such as particularly design out the persons that shall be saved, or are intended (as conditional promises do, and the promise first made to Abraham personally did design out himself as intended) ; but they are called indefinite, because they mention that only some of the sons of men are intended by God, not all, and that without mentioning particularly or personally who those persons are ; so as they are not indefinite as leaving the thing promised uncertain, for salvation is absolutely pronounced unto some of the sons of men, but only because they design not the persons who are certainly intended. Such are those promises, ' Christ came into the world to save sinners,' ' God was in Christ reconciling the world,' which is made the matter of the gospel's ministry ; and though the promulgation of this be made to all men—' Preach the gospel to every creature'—yet this is not the gospel to be preached, that God hath promised to save every creature, though, upon this promulgation of them, it becomes the duty of every one to come to Christ, and a command is laid on men to do it. Now a soul that is newly humbled looks out for a promise upon which he may come to Christ. He cannot rest on promises conditional, for he sees no qualifications of faith or any grace in himself. It is true, says that soul, ' he that believeth shall be saved,' but I am now to begin to believe, and have not faith yet ; and what ground will you give me of believing ? For this there is no answer, but to lay such promises before him : ' God so loved the world, that he gave his only Son,' ' Christ came into the world to save sinners,' &c. But how, will the soul say, should I know I am one ? That, I say, all the world cannot yet assure thee of ; no promise is so general as certainly to include thee, none so certain as to design thee. How then ? says the soul. Say I, they are all indefinite, and exclude thee not ; they leave thee with an *it may be thou mayest be the man ;* and it is certain some shall be saved, and there is nothing in thee shuts thee out, for God hath and will save such as thou art, and he may intend thee. As therefore there is in such promises a certainty of the thing promised, that it shall be made good to some, so there is an indefiniteness to whom, with a full liberty that it may be to thee. Now if the heart answer but the promise, two things are begotten in it.

1. An assurance of the thing promised, that the promise is as true as that God is, which is the assurance James requires, chap. i.

2. But then, concerning the party's own interest that is to believe, the soul is not assured, nor can be, that he is one intended, till he hath indeed believed ; but the indefiniteness of the promise begets only an hopefulness that he may be intended, and that is all that can be required of such a soul, and enough to draw forth (if his assent be spiritual) true acts of justifying faith, of trusting, waiting, coming to Christ, &c., which when the command shall also back and urge him in particular unto it, and make it a necessary duty to him, though yet he knows not certainly he shall be accepted, all this serves to draw him on to faith, through the power of the Spirit accompanying both.

Now that such indefinite promises, backed with the command, are grounds sufficient enough to draw on such acts of faith, there are these proofs :

1. We have the first in Heb. iv. 11, ' Let us labour therefore to enter into that rest, lest any man fall after the example of unbelief.' By entering into rest there, he means faith : ver. 3, ' We who have believed do

enter into rest.' It appears also from the opposition, when he says, ' Lest any fall after the example of unbelief;' so as he evidently exhorts unto faith. Now this exhortation, ' Let us therefore endeavour to enter in,' or truly to believe, and so take heed of a false faith, is an inference of something said before. Now what was it the apostle had mainly driven at in all his discourse before ? Even this, that there was a promise of rest, verse 1, and of a rest that remains for the people of God, ver. 9. More particularly, if you examine what promise this is upon which he exhorts to faith, it is expressed plainly in the 6th verse, ' Seeing it remains that some must enter into rest, let us therefore endeavour,' &c. This was not an universal promise, that all men might enter in and be saved ; nay, it is the contrary, for this promise was fetched by the apostle out of an oath God had made against some that they should not enter in, for so it is in the 5th verse, ' If they shall enter into my rest.' It is such a promise as shews that some are excluded with an oath ; it is a promise that, in the letter of it, hath swearing in it that some shall not enter, and is but by implication or illation a promise that some shall. It is indefinite, for he says, that only some must enter in, not naming who, but only speaks of some, and so leaves it, yet with a certainty of the thing promised unto some, in saying some must enter in. There is a *must* put upon it, that some shall and must. In the 9th verse he calls those for whom the rest remains, ' the people of God,' the elect, and yet upon this indefinite promise he exhorts every one. He says not only, ' Let us' (viz., all) ' endeavour to enter in,' but, verse 1, he says more expressly, ' Let us fear, lest, a promise being left' (or forsaken of us), ' any of you should come short of it.' So as though it is but an indefinite declaration of God's mind to save some, yet every one is bound to put in for it, and to take heed that not any one fall short.

2. I shall prove this by reason. 1st, If the indefiniteness of God's mind declared concerning his intent of saving but some be not sufficient ground to faith, then all those divines whose judgments having been for particular election and reprobation, and so they must needs understand the mind of God's promises not to be universal, could never have come to have believed savingly, which would be too hard a censure. Since therefore the indefiniteness of the promise was the ground of their believing, this also may be ground sufficient to any man's faith.

2dly, Faith in us is to be but answering unto, and conforming to the promise in the word ; and if it be, it may be true faith. Now there are promises in the word that speak but indefinitely, that speak but *it may bes*. Thus Moses propounds the promise to the people when they had sinned : ' I will go to the Lord,' says he, ' peradventure I shall make an atonement for you.' Thus the Ninevites reason too : Jonah iii. 9, 10, ' Who knows but the Lord may be merciful ?' And yet this wrought repentance, as Christ tells us. So likewise speaks Joel, chap. ii. 13, 14, ' Turn unto the Lord, for he is gracious and merciful, and repenteth him of the evil ; who knows if he will return and repent ?'

3dly, In temporal promises believers exercise true acts of faith, and it is required of them to believe about them ; and yet these promises are but indefinite, not absolute to their persons, though it is certain that God will perform them to some. Now, therefore, why may it not be as well thus in matter of salvation ?

4thly, Answerably the acts of faith themselves required of us, are suitable to such promises. Trusting, and waiting, and coming to Christ, and casting one's self upon him, are the acts of application in our faith. Now these are indefinite acts of the soul, *i. e.*, which are and may be performed when we know not certainly that a thing shall be ours, or that we shall obtain it.   They are often performed by men in other cases with the greatest venture that may be, as in Benhadad's servants, that put ropes about their necks, and sackcloth on their loins : ' Peradventure,' say they, ' he will save our lives.'   Thus men come to Christ, John vi. 37, when they know not but they may be cast out.   Yea, such a submission is an act of faith, and hath its chief exercise in case of not knowing that a man is certainly intended.

5thly, Where there is but a true hopefulness, there may be faith : 1 Peter i. 21, ' That your faith and hope might be in God.'   And to beget an hope, the indefinite promises do serve sufficiently.   This saying, that Christ died to save sinners, I not knowing but I may be one, may breed hope.   If you had no promise, then indeed you were without hope : Eph. ii. 12, ' Without hope, without promise.'   But where there is but a promise indefinitely revealed, there may hope be begotten ; and where hope is, there may and ought endeavours to be, and so an endeavouring to enter in and to believe ; when thou canst not say to the contrary, then ' there is hope concerning this thing,' Ezra x. 2.   And if there be so, then there may be faith of recumbency, or trusting on Christ to perform it to me.

6thly, Where love may be begotten, there may faith or trust also, for faith works by love ; but love may be begotten when there is not a certainty that we shall obtain.   How many fall in love that are taken with a person's excellency and beauty, and suitableness to them, though they have but little hope, no assurance they shall obtain the party's good will !   This we see daily in human experience, and why may it not be so in this case ? Yes, we see it to be in many that love God for his being good to sinners, &c., though they apprehend not certainly that he will be so to themselves. And if love to God is thus produced, why may not faith or trust be so begotten ?   Yea, is not the purest and greatest trust shewn in putting one's self into the hands of a spirit whom we know to be noble, though we certainly know not how he will deal with us ?

7thly, The main thing that is in faith, and which draws on the heart to cleave to the goodness of the promise, is the sight of the things promised in their reality.   Thus it appears through the whole 11th chapter of the Epistle to the Hebrews, that faith being the evidence of things not seen, they saw and were persuaded of them, and embraced the promises.   Now, therefore, if there be but a spiritual sight, and assurance, and persuasion of the existence, and worth, and excellency of the things promised (as Christ's righteousness, justification, &c.), though the assurance of the interest be wanting and be left but indefinite, this will cause the heart to venture all for them, and to rely on God, and come unto Christ, and this is enough.   On the other side, if it were a truth that God intended and had promised to save all, and this were preached and believed, yet if men saw not the excellency of things promised, the persuasion of their interest would not move them.

8thly, It is plain peevishness not to come in to Christ upon such indefinite promises.   It is such an obstinate temper as was in them who would not believe unless he would come off the cross.   Thus men will not come to him unless he will assure them by a general promise that all may be saved, and are intended, and so themselves particularly.   It is as if men should say, We will not go to church, for there is not room for all ; and unless a church be built into which all may come, we will not stir. You do not so in case of advantage or preferment.   Men use all endeavours

for a place or a living which many put in for, and but one can obtain it.
'Though all run,' says the apostle, 'yet but one obtains;' and yet the
worth and glory of the thing moves, because it is a crown, 1 Cor. ix. 25.
So why should it not be here? Yea, if you be affected with the things
themselves, you will be glad to venture.

9thly, Upon such indefinite promises, it becomes a duty to come to
Christ for life, and God may back such promises with a command justly,
and therefore faith may be wrought, and men are to come in upon
such promises. Many duties are commanded upon mere uncertainties.
Thus the believing wife is commanded to stay with her husband, 'For
what knowest thou' (says the apostle, 1 Cor. vii. 16), 'but thou mayest
save thy husband?' In like manner doth God command thee to go to
Christ for salvation, although his promise holds forth but a *what knowest
thou but thou mayest save thy soul?* and wilt thou not go to him? So then,
although the promise were but uncertain in respect of its performance to
thee, yet it is certain that God commands thee upon this to go to Christ
and trust on him, and give thy soul up to him; and this command is
not indefinite, but universal, and therefore a soul eyeing both hath full
ground to come in.

But yet let me add this, that together with the indefinite promise to
save, God, where he works faith, conveys a secret hint, to the soul whom
he draws to believe, of his mind, and good will, and inclination towards it.
Christ doth some way or other break his mind to it, and God gives the
heart a special ticket of favour from himself, over and above that indefinite
revelation in the word, ere the soul will come at him, which is part of that
teaching of the Father meant, John vi. 45, 46, 'He that hath heard and
learned of the Father, comes unto me.' God whispers in a man's ear that
which doth specially encourage him, and so Christ also doth by his Spirit.
Thus it is said, John x. 3, that Christ 'calleth his own sheep by name,
and they hear his voice.' The meaning is, that whereas there is a general
invitation goes to men's ears to come to Christ, and a general indefinite
proclamation, which all men living in the church do hear or may hear,—
and this is the voice of us ministers, and God's voice in and by us,—yet
there is conveyed with this a secret voice, and private ticket, and impress
on their hearts whom God means to save, of special mercy towards them;
which voice only his own sheep hear, whom also he is said to call by
name, to shew it is thus particular, it being a special intimation, as if a
man were called by name, as Cyrus was called by name; and as of
Moses God says that he knew him by name, *i. e.*, took special notice of
him, so doth Christ of those whom he calls by name, and that makes
them follow him. And the want of this is given as the reason, John x.
26, 27, why the Jews believed not, for Christ says they were 'not his
sheep;' and therefore, in the dispensing the promises, he did not thus
speak to their hearts as to believers he did, for he adds, 'My sheep hear
my voice' (the voice before mentioned), 'and I know them, and they
follow me.' He brings this as the reason why he dispensed not that voice
to them, and the want of that he assigns to be the cause why they believed
not. And if you consider verse 16, it will appear that the reason they are
not called his sheep, is not because they believe not already; for there he
calls those his sheep whom he had not yet brought in, 'whom yet I must
bring in,' says he; and how will he bring them in? 'They shall hear my
voice;' he will call them by name too, as he had done others. And therefore (says he) this is the reason why you, being not of my sheep, believe
not; for if you were, I would speak to your hearts, and cause you to hear

my voice, and to come in; which, because I vouchsafe not to you, therefore it is ye believe not.

Now, concerning this secret hint or ticket given, which I make to be in faith, let me add this to prevent mistakes. I do not mean that it is always so loud a voice as shall quell and prevail against doubts in a man's sense, so as to triumph with assurance that Christ is his. No, that is not the extent of it; for we should 'condemn a generation of righteous men,' if I or any other should teach so; but it is such a special intimation as really gains the heart, and encourageth it to come to Christ, and carries it on against discouragements, and it doth the deed so prevalently, as that they follow Christ wherever he goes, and will never leave him. To explain my meaning further, you must consider, that in the speaking of a Spirit in and to our spirit, though the voice be entertained, yet it is not always distinctly discerned to be from another. Satan, when he works effectually on the children of disobedience, 2 Thes. ii. 9, 10, so as he makes them believe the lie of popery, yet their souls perceive not a voice of Satan distinct from their own thoughts, for then they would not believe the error; but their hearts close with the suggestions of the devil, and as soon as cast in they are entertained as their own thoughts, yet upon Satan's effectual working. Thus when the Spirit of Christ from Christ speaks the mind of Christ to the soul, to cause it to believe in him that is true, it follows not it should discern that voice distinct from its own thoughts in its own sense, but his own thoughts from it effectually entertain such an apprehension so as to carry him on to Christ. And the reason is, because every thought in a spirit, such as a soul is, is a kind of speech; it is called λόγος, and therefore the very speeches of the Spirit cast in are often not discerned from the man's own. Thus if a man's ear did form sounds in itself, and voices in itself, then a secret whisper would not be discerned from its own noises, as a loud voice would be. There is a loud voice of the Holy Ghost coming as a witness to assure, and then he speaks so loud and so distinctly as a man discerns it to be distinct from his own spirit, and infallibly to be the voice of God; and it is as if a voice from heaven should say, 'Thy sins are forgiven'; but this first voice of Christ in the extent of it being to carry the heart on to Christ, and not to assure it, therefore it is not always discerned as distinct, yet so as the heart is taught effectually this lesson, to go to Christ; and that other voice is therefore called a witness, because it hath relation to this hint given to put it out of question. It is like the secret scent a bloodhound hath gotten of the hart that is struck, when the master hath bade it go seek, which though he see not the hart, yet it carries him on till he find him out. So this secret voice of the Spirit, though it prevails not against doubts in a man's sense, yet it carries him on against discouragements, there being an impression of Christ's special inclinableness to it, which cannot be worn out by any temptation.

Now, if this be in faith (as you see it is), then it is not an easy work; for, you see, Christ vouchsafes not this to all to whom the gospel is preached. He did not vouchsafe it to those Jews who heard the outward voice of his mouth as a minister of circumcision, and who believed not because they heard not his special voice, which he did not vouchsafe, because they were not of his own sheep. Can all the angels in heaven, or ministers on earth, procure this voice to you, or bring you news of it? No; and yet without it the heart makes not after Christ. And therefore Paul makes this to be the great difficulty to bring a natural man in to believe, because all his understanding cannot know God's mind in the

word, unless the Spirit reveal it: ' Who knows the mind of a man, but the
spirit that is in him ? so nor doth any know the deep things of God, but
his Spirit,' who is a privy counsellor, and is in his bosom.   And therefore
he concludes to shut nature out herein: ' Who hath known the mind of
the Lord ?   But we have the mind of Christ,' 1 Cor. ii. 16.

CHAPTER VII.

How the faith of a believer should depend on electing grace for salvation.

Though a believer views God's electing love, and depends on it for his
salvation, yet he doth not so commit his soul to that one single act of God's
choosing persons as so to rely on it that God having chosen men's persons
on his part, they themselves should care to do nothing as on their parts.
No; this is the highest degree of profaneness and contempt, and a per-
verting of our whole Christian religion, and to bring in that of Simon
Magus, and indeed the devil's divinity, for he was the most famous
sorcerer in the world, Acts viii. 9–11.   It was *depths*, as they themselves
termed their doctrine; but the Holy Ghost, who penned the Epistle,
animadverts upon it, and calls them *depths*, Rev. ii. 20, 24.   The Gnostics
took no other part of the Christian profession but that, ' By grace ye are
saved,' and so left men unto a licentious liberty, which Peter speaks of:
2 Peter ii. 19, ' Whilst they promise them ' (*i. e.*, their disciples) ' *liberty*,
they themselves are the servants of corruption.'   That was the latter part
of their doctrine; and Jude supplies the forepart in saying, verse 4, that
they ' turned the grace of God unto lasciviousness.'   And yet even this
hath been affixed as a calumny upon them that profess the doctrine of
irrespective election.   I will therefore explain in these following particulars
the true dependence of a believing soul upon electing love for salvation.

1. A soul who hath begun to be wrought upon by ' tasting how good the
Lord is ' in his electing grace, or (as the apostle speaks, Col. i. 6) ' since
the day he first heard of it, and knew the grace of God in truth,' hath
been affected with it, casts himself upon it to be saved.   And so quick,
and speedy, and operative was the power of God in the ministry of those
first times, and to such a height did their convert hearers ascend, as to
apply themselves unto a dependence on that grace for salvation.   Where
God hath thus begun it in us (and we cannot begin any good thing unless
God himself begins), we may look toward his electing love.   Nor is any
man fit to look toward the grace of God in election, till God awaken him
with the gracious knowledge of it, no more than a sinner not yet convinced
of his sin by nature, and his being under the wrath of God for sin, will
ever look after Christ as a Saviour.

2. It is not my design to consider whether all saints, from their first
conversion, know this grace of God in election, as that grace upon which
salvation doth depend; but whether sooner or later, as God pleaseth to dispense great discoveries of grace to him, and whenever his soul begins to
take in the sense and savour of this grace, he should follow on with might
and main in his inquest after it.   Let him ' follow on to know the Lord '
and his grace, and God will ' rain down righteousness upon him,' as the
prophet speaks in the psalmist's words.   Let him ' follow hard after him,'
where the words in the original are ' follow him behind;' *i. e.*, if thou
shouldst lose that sight of his face, and the taste that he is good begins to
grow less and less in thy heart—yea, and he to try thee turns away his

face from thee, yea, and turns his back on thee, as offering to go away—then down on thy knees, and like an importunate beggar follow him behind, and with the most vehement earnestness desire him to give thee his grace, and that manifestation of his face again, that overcame and took thy heart at the first, and then thou shalt be saved.

3. Let such a soul be sure to look at and take all along with him the whole complex of God's methods and holy purposes and decrees of grace belonging to the doctrine of election. Now there are two sorts of decrees: the first is an act of absolute election of the persons that are elected unto salvation; the other is of the means by which and through which God brings men unto salvation, who are in that manner elected. And both these are decreed with the same peremptoriness as to the decreeing of each, and with like absoluteness indispensably; so as no man ever was or will be saved without his diligent attendance to the decree of the means, as well as to that of his salvation, which is the decree of the end, as we call it. And the putting these two together doth pave the way of seeking God according to election complete. These two sorts of decrees we find distinguished and stated to our hands: 2 Thess. ii. 13, ' God hath from the beginning chosen you,' namely, your persons, ' to salvation.' With that he begins; and this is that election first mentioned, Eph. i. 4. And it is our foundation, that is, of our persons elected, and also of all things else (the means) decreed in order to our salvation; and these two decrees are alike fixed, and made absolutely necessary to be attended to; but the latter as subordinate, or rather subservient to the other, and ordained to accomplish and bring into effect that first original act, the election of our persons, by bringing us to that salvation which was ordained to us. And this decree of the means the apostle subjoins in those words, ' Through sanctification of the Spirit, and belief of the truth,' that is, of the gospel, which in New Testament speech has that title, the truth, by way of eminency. Which true means are indeed no other than a true, saving, justifying faith, and holiness of heart, and new obedience. And these two, as they are the decreed means to bring us to that end of salvation, so they are parts or pieces of that salvation itself which we were chosen unto by the first decree, and which God has ordained, not as conditions of that original act, of which he had said before, he had ' chosen us from the beginning unto salvation.' Conditions they are not, in any sense, either of the Arminians, who would have a man acknowledge when he has truly believed that then he is actually elected, and not before (now, according to our doctrine, God chooses no man *for* his faith, but *unto* faith, and *through* faith), or of those other divines that orthodoxly do hold election of persons, who do call them *quasi* conditions, but *as it were* conditions, no more than a pepper-corn, if it be required as an acknowledgment of a rent-farm, which is the lowest diminutive term. But I am afraid to give it, lest it should diminish from the praise of the glory of God's free grace, and lest he should not brook it.

There are two points which God is especially tender of: that of justification is the one, and his free grace in election is the other. But God is especially tender in point of election; for that act is wholly within himself, wherein he has no creature to look on, but the ideas of us which himself hath formed and represents us to himself by. In which first act also within himself, his grace, the highest principle in him, assumes to himself the most sovereign absolute freedom. If you come to that point with him (and it is of that point he speaks it), God in his sovereignty proclaims, Rom. xi. 35, ' Whoever hath first given him, he shall be recompensed,' be it but a pepper-corn. I am afraid to diminish an hair from God in speaking what will have the sound or preference of the least such appearance in the point of justification. It is not the proud notion of merit only (though the primitive fathers used the word in a good sense, but our protestants have generally avoided it), but of works too, must be exploded. God loves not faith as a work, though it saves his children whom he loves, much less will he admit it to be considered in election, which is a purely pure act of himself within himself. Besides, I cannot see that what is a part of salvation itself (at least the beginning of it) should have put upon it the nature of a condition. If a father should say, Marry my daughter, upon a condition that you marry her, I should think he at least speaks not so properly; for to marry her is to have the person herself, and not the condition of having her. And whereas the Scripture says, ' Look unto me, all the ends of the earth, and be ye saved.' Looking (there) unto him is not the condition of being saved, but that whereby we are saved, and so ' he that believes hath eternal life.' Marrying a man's daughter (in the case mentioned) is not a condition, but an essential ingredient into the constitutive nature of the thing, and the means of enjoying her person.

Both the decree of, and production of the means decreed, is in Scripture expression termed the fruits which flow from his original decree of the election of the person, in the virtue of which God bestows them; and God's choice of the person is the cause of our performing them, according to that of the Psalmist, Ps. lxv., ' Blessed is the man whom thou choosest' (there is the first decree, and then follows), ' and causest to approach unto thee.' So as the bestowing of these means which we are to observe and perform are seminally contained in the choice of the person, and in the love out of which he is chosen. Yea, the love that God bears to the person chosen is that which moveth God's heart to appoint the means, and then to work the means in the heart. Yea, further, this love moves God to the act of election itself, and is therefore the original grace of all grace, even as that we call original sin is the cause and matrix of all sin. Let no man therefore (this being the order of God's decrees) separate what God hath inseparably and unalterably joined.

5. Hence, and above all, the principal object which I propose to your eye and pursuance is this love and grace which was and is in God's heart, and is that love which is the cause of all, but especially of working faith, and quickening at the first, and ever after, according to Eph. ii. 4–6; yea, this love and grace is the cause of election itself, and of all the fruits of it: Eph. ii. 4–6, ' But God, who is rich in mercy, for his great love wherewith he loved us, even when we were dead in sins, hath quickened us together with Christ (by grace ye are saved); and hath raised us up together, and made us sit together in heavenly places in Christ Jesus.' It hath been even his love from everlasting which hath done it, according to that in Jeremiah, chap. xxxi., ' I have loved thee with an everlasting love.' Let the soul then infinitely admire that love, and possess his heart with all the royal and glorious properties of it, as that it is free, absolute, unchangeable, everlasting, &c., as follows in those royal titles in which the Scriptures do array and present it to the sons of men; and let him admire and adore that the great God should love so well his mere creatures, out of which love that absolute decree of election did then flow, and all those purposes concerning the means which that love all along continued unto a man's conversion, and doth then work, and put them into execution unto salvation itself (for this love is *actus continuus*, as the eternal generation of his Son is, and yet from everlasting both), so as at and before, yea, unto the very moment before a

man's conversion, it is one and the same love for the substance of it that
at any time was or shall be; and it is the same love which wrought conversion itself, and which works every good work in us that belongs unto
salvation, though, according to the general rules of his own word, he hath
obliged himself from discovering it any way, no, not to the men themselves,
until that fulness of time be come, appointed by his secret will, for every
elect man's first conversion and calling; and therefore this love is the principal principle and object, which is to be addressed unto and pleaded,
and God plied with the utmost intenseness of a man's soul and earnest
diligence, both for the manifestation of itself after conversion, and also to
convert a man who is as yet to be converted; and this I eminently propose
to be noted in this seeking of God in the way of election; and my proposal
of it is for two uses or improvements of it in the matter of election.

1st, That the soul may implore this love, and the grace of it, to manifest
and discover itself unto the soul of the person by an intuitive light of the
Spirit, joined with a word of promise, with an overpowering efficacy, as
when in prayer God sometimes answers, ' Thou art a person so beloved!'

2dly, That the soul may also wait with the most vehement expectations
and longings (with a ' neck stretched out,' as the apostle's word* is) how
the work of God goes on in him, and how the discoveries of God's grace
do rise and spring up in him unto a more perfect day.

3dly, That the soul may humbly beseech that pure free love both to
fulfil all and each of those designed graces and blessings decreed, together
with that act of election, to fetch and dig out every grace thou wantest, or
art deficient in, in the exercise thereof, and to draw it forth out of that full
and inexhaustible mine of glory which is in God's grace: Phil. iv. 19,
' God shall supply all your need according to the riches of his glory by
Jesus Christ.' And the soul is to regard all and each of these as con-
sequential fruits that spring from such a love, and were as peremptorily
decreed to be in a subordination, as fruits of that great act of the election
of persons.

For a conclusion, let me but lay open the heart of one scripture: Col. i.
5, 6, ' Whereof ye heard before in the word of the truth of the gospel,
which is come unto you, as it is in all the world, and bringeth forth fruit, as
it doth also in you, since the day ye heard of it, and knew the grace of God
in truth.' The grace of God principally meant, ver. 6, is the grace of
elective love, which is properly in God's heart toward us. But what
should be meant by the grace of God made known by preaching by their
faithful minister, and which, being known by them in truth, brought forth
faith and love in them from the day they heard it? The grace of God, as
it stands in this coherence, must be either the grace which was by the
gospel made known to be in God's heart toward sinners, to move them to
come in to God, and so to work faith in them, whereby to be reconciled to
God; or else it is the laying open what the grace of God required to be
wrought in them, and so to direct them how they should turn to God; or
else both of these, which is the truth. It is not what the grace of God
required to be wrought in them that only or chiefly should be intended by
grace, because that grace of God intended is that grace (if you observe the
series of the words) which, after it is known, brings forth that fruit spoken
of; ' fruit in you,' says the apostle. Now that cannot be understood
chiefly or only of inherent holiness or faith, for *that* grace itself is the
thing that is the very fruit itself, said to be brought forth, and that in them,
as the phrase there is. And therefore it is not the grace, or the knowing

* Apparently ἐπεκτεινόμενος, Phil. iii. 14.—Ed.

of that grace begun experimentally to be in them, that is wholly or chiefly meant. There must, therefore, be another grace of God, that was the cause of that grace or fruit in themselves, which could be no other than the grace in God's heart towards them, taught and discovered to those Colossians by the preaching of the truths of the gospel, ver. 5, which gospel itself is therefore styled ' the grace of God which bringeth salvation;' that is, the blessed news to sinful men of salvation by the sole grace that is in God's heart towards them, Tit. ii. 11 ; and this doth most properly and principally bear the name of grace, and of the grace of, God, and is in God himself, who is the ' God of all grace,' 1 Pet. v. 10, and is the cause of all grace in us, and that by its appearing, being made known to us in truth. This is *gratia gratians*, the grace that makes us gracious.

But now the inquisition will be, what grace of God borne to us men should be here meant, whether to all men alike in common, a love of God alike to all men; or the grace of election, exerted at election of some men chosen out by God out of the rest of mankind, designing particularly salvation to their persons, but promulged and proclaimed to all men, so as his love to mankind hath *appeared* to all men, but is not *intended* to all men. That this grace should be intended here, there are these reasons which prove it.

(1.) Because the truth and reality of God's grace, indeed, is but to a remnant: Rom. xi. 5, ' Even so then, at this present time,' when the apostle wrote, ' there is a remnant, according to the election of grace,' ver. 5 ; whose very persons (God's choice carries the sway in it) are styled ' the election:' ' The election hath obtained, and the rest,' that are not elected, ' were blinded,' ver. 7. And this election is but of a remnant whom God had reserved to himself, or they had all gone alike to the fire, and been as Sodom and Gomorrah, if they had been left to their own free wills.

(2.) I find election itself expressed by finding grace in God's sight, whilst others of the sons of men' are not vouchsafed it. Thus Moses his election is expressed, Exod. xxxiii. 16, ' Wherein,' pleads Moses. to God, ' shall it be known that I' (Moses myself) ' and this people have found grace in thy sight?' The phrase is used to express the being God's own chosen people. And as for Moses, God owns it, and expresseth it to himself: ver. 17, ' I will do as thou hast spoken, for thou hast found grace in my sight.' And he speaks more expressly for election yet, ' And I know thee by name.' And as for the people of the Jews, Jer. xxxi. 2, 3, the chosen elect among that people are said to have ' found grace in the wilderness,' the rest being cut off by the sword; and thereby their being an elect people is also expressed, for there it follows, ' I have loved thee with an everlasting love;' and that, I am sure you will say, imports their election. And as for Moses, whereas he grew bold upon that encouragement, ' I know thee by name,' to ask of God to see his face and his glory, God gave him this answer, ' I will make all my goodness to pass before thee,' and will proclaim the name of the Lord before thee, ' The Lord, the Lord God, gracious and merciful,' &c., viz., all the attributes of his gracious nature. But to whom should the attributes be applied for their salvation? ⟍ God there makes a reserve of the elect only to be the persons who should have the benefit of these attributes for their particular salvation; and therefore adds, ' I will be gracious to whom I will be gracious, and I will be merciful to whom I will shew mercy.' As if he had said, I have indeed proclaimed all the attributes of grace and mercy that are in my *nature*, in common to all the people, but with this reserve to myself, that as to my *will*, which governs the management of those attributes unto persons for their salvation, this I keep the

counsel of it unto myself, ' according to the counsel of my own will,' Eph.
i. 11. And so answerably it is in Exod. xxxiv., ' I will be merciful to whom
I will be merciful.' And the apostle Paul allegeth these very words, ' I
will,' &c., to prove the point of election to be by special grace, and the
good pleasure of his will, in the case of Moses his election, and in the case
of hardening Pharaoh. And that phrase, ' they found grace,' doth not
import a grace inherent or discovered *in them*, but a grace from God
without them, or dwelling in God's heart *towards them*, and coming from
without *upon them*, not in them. And it is to be observed that that is the
phrase God himself, in expressing his shewing mercy to the persons whom
he there chooseth (as hath been opened, Exod. xxxiii. 19), ' I will be merciful on whom I will be merciful.' And to bring this home yet nearer to
these Colossians, and what is spoken of their receiving the grace of God
without them, which was the cause of their so quick conversion, as I
observed, this was truly the grace of God *inventa et non quæsita*, in Isaiah's
words, ' I am found of them that sought me not,' as he promised. And of
whom and what sort of men did he prophesy it? Expressly of those heathen
Gentiles, that had been heathens to the time of their conversion: Isaiah
lxv. 1, it follows in that verse, ' And I said, Behold me, behold me, unto
a nation that was not called by my name;' which was punctually fulfilled
in this city of Colosse, who were heathens, till the day they heard the
gospel of the grace of God; but from that time brought forth fruit, and the
like was in all the world. We poor ministers in these times stand picking
the lock, which asketh often much time, but the apostles and primitive
ministers broke open the door of faith, as it is called.

OF THE OBJECT AND ACTS OF JUSTIFYING FAITH.

PART II.

Of the acts of Faith.

BOOK I.

The acts of faith in the understanding is a sight of Christ, a discerning and knowledge of his excellencies, and a hearty assent to the truths of the gospel concerning him.—That this mere assurance of the object, or a general assent to the truth of the promises, is not the act of faith justifying, but an application is necessary.—What the acts of the will are, which are exercised on Christ in believing.

CHAPTER I.

That faith in the understanding is a spiritual sight and knowledge of Christ.—That it is a sight distinct from bodily sense, and from reason, and other ways of knowledge.—That this sight hath the greatest certainty in it, and realiseth to the mind the things believed.—That the true believer sees the spiritual excellency and glory that is in Christ, so as to have his heart affected with it.—That he sees an all-sufficiency of righteousness in Christ.—That he is persuaded of Christ's readiness to save sinners, with some secret intimation that there is mercy for himself, though a sinner.

And this is the will of him that sent me, that every one that seeth the Son, and believeth on him, might have everlasting life.—JOHN VI. 40.

THE subject I intend to treat of is to set forth to you those special acts of justifying faith exercised upon and towards our Lord Jesus Christ. And (that I may be distinctly understood) when I say the acts of faith, I do limit myself simply and merely to those acts which are of faith as justifying. There are the offices of faith (as you call them), which are many and diverse, each whereof have several acts ; as for example, it is the office of faith to justify, it is the office of faith to sanctify, it is the office of faith to enable you to live in communion with God and with Christ in all your ways, &c., in all conditions. Now I single out one of those offices of faith, and that is, as it justifies, as it treats with Christ about justification ; and I shall consider the acts that it performs as such. There are likewise several degrees in faith, in which every one of those offices is performed. There is weak faith and strong faith, there is faith of assurance and faith of recumbency. Now in discoursing of the acts of faith, my scope is not to speak of the high degrees, but those that are more essential, and are ingredients in the lowest degrees of faith of recumbency, wherein a sinner treats with Christ about justification. There are also the effects of faith as it purifies, and sanctifies, and conformeth the soul to Christ, and bringeth joy and peace, and worketh love, and the like; my scope is to handle none of these now. And thus by shewing you what my scope is not, I do thereby open to you particularly what it is that I pitch upon. Now there is no one scripture that puts all the acts of faith, as it treateth with Christ about justification, together; neither shall I be able it may be to speak of all, but I purpose to follow the method that is here in this text; and I begin first with that of seeing: 'He that seeth the Son,' &c.

I purpose in a brief way to lay open those acts of faith (as it justifies a sinner) whereby the soul doth pitch upon Jesus Christ as the object thereof. There is no one scripture that mentions all, neither shall I be able to mention all to you; yet those that are more eminent, and may come under what is here in the text, I shall go over with as much brevity as I can.

In these words, compared likewise with the 37th verse of this chapter, you have three several sorts of acts of faith:

1. Seeing the Son: 'Every one that seeth the Son.'

2. A coming unto him; so verse 37 (for you may take that verse in likewise), 'He that cometh unto me.'

3. A believing on him: 'And believeth on him.'

Now it is to be remarked, that that faith by which we are saved, which the apostle calls 'believing to the saving of the soul, is seated in the whole heart, so you have it in Acts viii. 37, 'If thou believe with thy whole heart;' and indeed every faculty, and every power of the soul in believing doth put forth a several sprig, a several *fibra* into Jesus Christ; as you see in the roots that are in the earth, every root shoots a small string into that by which the tree and the root is united thereunto; thus are we rooted in Christ, and grounded in him, as the expression is in Col. ii. 7, which is then when the faculties do thus shoot forth several acts suitable to themselves, into our Lord Christ, and then the soul believeth on him.

I will begin first with the first act of faith here, and that is *seeing*, which notes out that act of faith which is in the understanding, which we call the act of knowledge. Hence we find that in Scripture our being justified by Christ is ascribed to the knowledge which we have of him; you have it in Isa. liii. 11, 'By his knowledge shall my righteous servant justify many;' when he saith *by his knowledge*, he doth not mean that we are justified by the knowledge that is in Christ (though perhaps in some sense that might be said), but it is by the knowledge we have of him. The word *his* there is taken objectively; it is called, you see here, a seeing the Son: here is the act, and here is the object; the act it is seeing, the object is the Son. In this sight of Christ there are four things which I would speak to:

(1.) It is a spiritual sight or knowledge of him.

(2.) It is a sight in distinction to bodily sight, and in distinction from reason, and other ways of knowledge.

(3.) It hath a certainty in it.

(4.) It hath a reality in it.

(1.) It is a spiritual sight, which doth distinguish it from all knowledge of Christ after the flesh; for there is indeed a sight of Christ, and a real sight of Christ, which is contradistinct to faith, a sight of the bodily presence of Christ, and this the apostle speaks of in 1 Peter i. 8, 'In whom, though ye see him not, yet ye believe;' and the truth is, our faith shall end in such a sight, for we shall one day see him as he is, and to be believing in the mean time, having not seen, is that blessedness which is pronounced, John xx. 29. When Paul was converted he saw Christ, his eyes were elevated to see Christ, whether as in heaven or in the air I will not dispute, as some do; but certain it is that he saw him, and yet that was not a sight of faith. Now in 2 Cor. v. 16, 17, he prefers that knowing of Christ after the new creature, by that spiritual sight the new creature hath of him, to all the knowledge of Christ after the flesh in any such visible manner; thus wicked men shall see him at the latter day, and be never the better for the sight of him; but it is a spiritual sight of Christ by the eye of faith that saveth a man. In 1 Cor. ii. 14, the apostle tells us, that spiritual things are not known by the natural man, because they are spiritually discerned, so that the knowledge of a spiritual man is a spiritual knowledge. The meaning is, it is such a knowledge and sight of Christ as is suitable to the spiritualness that is in him, it takes in a genuine notion of him. Spiritual things may be set out by words to the reason and to the fancies of men, so as to take with them; but we do not know them nor see them till we see them purely and nakedly, by an impressson the Holy Ghost makes upon us, that conveys the proper, and native, and natural image to us. As for example, go take a song in music, that is set or written, or pricked upon a book, a man may be taught the art of music, so that he may know the proportions and harmony according to the rules of art that are in this lesson as it is set or pricked upon the book; this artificial harmony of it he may know, but yet notwithstanding the real, natural harmony, the ear only taketh in when this lesson is sung. Why? Because the ear is that sense which is suited to take in the harmony and sound of music. Thus as God hath given us an understanding to know spiritual things thereby, the reason that is in them, the rational exercises of them, so far forth as they may be set out by words, all this the natural man takes in, but still there is that which is natural and proper to the things themselves, which he understands not.

(2.) It is, in the second place, called a sight, to distinguish it from reason and other knowledge. So faith is expressed, 'He that seeth the Son;' and in Heb. xi., 'They saw the promise afar off,' and Abraham 'saw Christ's day,' John viii. 56. And though Christ is now come, and exhibited, and is taken again out of our view, yet it is the sight of him that saveth us. It is not merely knowing him, but it is knowing him in a way of sight, for we may know him in a way of reason, we may gather one thing out of another, and so have the knowledge of him, and yet not have that which is faith about him, though whatsoever a man doth believe he hath reason for it; reason subserveth and comes in to confirm it, yet the act of faith lies in a sight, rather than in a knowledge that is made up out of reason.

The Holy Ghost still, when he speaks of faith, expresseth it to us by the knowledge of the senses, Philip. i. 9. Spiritual knowledge is there called sense; the word is so, if you read your margin, and it is so in the original, 'That your love may abound in knowledge and in all sense;' so the word is. It is true, indeed, that faith is said to be of things not seen, Heb. xi. 1, but yet itself is said to be a sight. The things themselves are not seen, that is, to reason, and to the bodily senses they are not seen: but the mind hath a new sense, as it were, put into it, by which it sees them otherwise than either reason or sense could present them to a man.

The Holy Ghost (to make this a little out to you), when he doth work faith in us, and reveal Christ and spiritual things to us, doth two things :

First, He doth first give us a new understanding, a new eye, as it were on purpose, that is as truly suited to behold spiritual things as the natural eye is to behold colours : 1 John v. 20, ' He hath given us an understanding to know him that is true ;' that is, a new eye to see Christ with ; he puts a spiritualness into the understanding ; he doth not create a new faculty, but endues this with a new activity, which is as much as if he gave us a new understanding.

Secondly, When he hath done so, himself comes with a light upon this new understanding, which light conveys the image of spiritual things in a spiritual way to the mind, such an image of the things as is taken off from the things themselves, such as no form of words, no reasoning, not all the wit and parts of a man, no discourses about Christ and spiritual things, would ever form in him. The angels, who have seen Jesus Christ in heaven in his glory, if they should all come down, and use all their art, all their rhetoric, come with all their pencils to paint and set out Jesus Christ to us in the most lively manner that can be ; yet all they could do, or could say, would not beget (without the power of the Holy Ghost, without his art joined with it) such a sight of Christ as faith gives us. If they should all set themselves to beget an image of Jesus Christ in our minds and understandings, it would be but a *parhelion,* as they call a false sun ; as we cannot see the sun but by his own light, so we cannot see Jesus Christ but by his own light, and by the light of the Holy Ghost.

There is a seeing of spiritual things merely by the effects, and there is a faith wrought thereby ; for the devils they have a sense, and they have a knowledge, and a real knowledge too (so far forth as effects go), that there is a God, for they feel the lashes of his wrath upon their spirits ; yet, notwithstanding, this is not faith, this is not that faith which is the spiritual faith, which is the faith of sight, which here this text and the Scripture speaks of ; so that now it is a spiritual sight of him which is in the nature of faith. And the truth is, it is such an image of Christ framed in the heart (and when I say an image, I mean not the image of Christ in holiness, but the image of knowledge of him ; for a man knoweth nothing, but there is an image of it framed in his mind) ; such a sight of him by which we know him, as all the creatures, and all the knowledge, and all the description of him in the world, would never work. As you have it in 1 Cor. ii. 9, ' Eye hath not seen, nor ear heard, nor hath it entered into the heart of man, the things that God hath prepared for them that love him.' He speaks there of the things of the gospel, and so of Jesus Christ eminently above the rest, and of the knowledge of them. There are such images of these things created there by a peculiar artifice of the Holy Ghost, as never entered into the heart of carnal men. It is his peculiar art (that is the truth of it), which is in no knowledge else, that is thus in faith. It is not that which we shall have in heaven, for that is seeing him face to face ; it is not such a knowledge only as we have of other things here below, which yet we believe really, though we never saw them ; but, I say, there is a peculiarity in it, which the Holy Ghost works in the hearts of the people of God, which is the sight of faith. It is therefore called in 1 Cor. ii. 4, ' The demonstration of the Spirit.' There are two principles in Scripture which all knowledge, even of spiritual things, is reduced unto. The one is called the ' revelation of flesh and blood,' Mat. xvi. 17 ; the other is called

the ' demonstration of the Spirit,' 1 Cor. ii. 4. ' Flesh and blood,' saith
Christ to Peter, ' hath not revealed these things to thee ;' implying that
there was a knowledge which flesh and blood works in us, which is the way
of man's nature : but then there is another knowledge which ariseth from
the demonstration of the Spirit. It is light (as the apostle tells us in Eph.
v. 13) that makes all things manifest. How comes your eye to see colours,
or to see anything else ? Why there is a light comes, and that light takes
of the image of the colours, and of the things you see, and brings them to
your eye. Now spiritual things are all nothing else but light ; now God
himself and Jesus Christ is nothing else but light ; and so is heaven, it is
called ' the inheritance of the saints in light.' Now the Holy Ghost comes
with the beams of this light, and every one of those beams doth bring the
image, the natural, native image of the thing to the eye, to the understanding ; and therefore the apprehension of it is called sight, and we are therefore said by the psalmist to ' see light in his light,' Ps. xxxvi. 9 ; the beams
of the sun, you know, convey every of them an image of the sun, and such
an image of the sun whereby you see the sun, so as nothing else can represent the sun to you ; and so the Holy Ghost he doth cause the beams of
God, and of Christ, who, as I said, is nothing else but light, for to shine
into our hearts, and all those beams which he letteth and bringeth in, they
convey the image of God and of Christ to us, and so we see him. In
1 Pet. ii. 9, we are said to be ' translated into his marvellous light.' It is
called ' marvellous ' because it is above reason, or the natural knowledge of
a man ; and it is called ' his light,' not only because Christ works it, as in
Eph. v. 14 it is said, ' Christ shall give thee light,' but because it is the
light of himself, it conveys the image of himself to the heart.

Yea, let me tell you this, the sight of faith is so genuine a knowledge,
that though it differ in degrees, yet the very same knowledge that Christ's
human nature hath of himself, the same knowledge in its degree doth the Holy
Ghost work of him in the heart of a Christian. This is a great speech, but
it is true the knowledge whereby Jesus Christ knows and sees himself, you
must needs say is a natural knowledge of himself : that is, he sees himself
as he is in himself, not by hearsay. Now look what spiritual representations Jesus Christ hath of God, and of himself, and of his own righteousness, in his mind, the Holy Ghost coming fresh from the heart of Christ,
stampeth the very same upon the heart of a Christian in his measure. You
will say, How prove you that ? the text is clear for it, in 1 Cor. ii. 16, ' We
have the mind of Christ.' He speaks there of spiritual knowledge ; that
whereas other men have the letter, the literal knowledge, yet they have not
these thoughts, have not that mind stamped upon their minds which is in
Christ himself ; but such we have (saith he), we have the mind of Christ,
we have those spiritual thoughts as it were from his heart, because we have
the Spirit which works in us, impresseth upon us the same thoughts of
him that are in his own heart of himself. All other enlightenings that
men have, they are from Christ indeed ; he is said, John i. 9, to be ' the
light that enlighteneth every man that comes into the world' with all sorts
of common knowledge. As now go take the light of the night, all the light
you see in the night by the moon, it is all the light of the sun, but yet it is
not that light whereby the sun conveys its beams to the eye when it riseth,
and when a man beholds it ; so men that are not regenerated, that have
but a temporary faith, they have a light from Christ, such as is the light of
the sun shining in the moon ; they have a light, as from the effects ; they
have a light also which the letter of the Scripture, and the Spirit shining
upon it, begets in them ; but still it is not a sight of the thing itself, it is

not seeing the Son, it is not such as when the image of the Son himself is conveyed into the mind and understanding by the Holy Ghost. We may know there is a sun by what light we see in the moon, but it is another thing to have a beam of the sun itself shine into a man's eye, whereby the very image of the sun is conveyed into his eye. And therefore this sight of faith it is called sight, because it is thus elevated above all rational knowledge of Christ whatsoever ; it is a further thing, though joined with it ; it is (I say) superadded to reason, let it be elevated and enlightened ever so much by the Holy Ghost in a rational way.

Go, take a temporary believer, it is true he sees those things, by the help of the light of the Spirit, which nature would never help him to see, and yet it is but by natural understanding, remaining natural, and reason elevated, and reason improved, and reason enlarged and convinced. But faith goes higher than all this, faith is more than a man's having an optic glass set before his eye, to see that which else he could not see, because it is so far off ; the eye of itself is capable of it, if it stood nigh it. There is more than all this in faith ; it is as it were a new eye, to see those things in such a manner as all the optic glasses in the world would never help a dim eye to see at a distance. Therefore, now faith (as I said afore), is called the ' demonstration of the Spirit ;' all other knowledge is but by derived images of the things of Christ, by hearsay, so much of Christ as may be conveyed to us by words and by rational discourses, the Holy Ghost enlightening them. In all this there are but secondary images conveyed to the hearts of carnal men, more or less, as they are more or less enlightened ; but to see the Son as he is in himself, as here the text holds it forth, this is proper to believers. So that, take any man that hath been never so much enlightened in the knowledge of spiritual things, and not savingly enlightened, when that man comes to turn to God, and to believe in earnest, he will say he never saw these things before, he will say he doth now see Christ so as he never saw him before, and that he sees God in that manner as he never saw him before. And though he knew never so much before, yet now after he is turned unto God, he sees that ' old things are passed away, and all things are become new ;' as the apostle says in 2 Cor. v. 17, and he speaks it in respect of knowledge. Let now a carnal man speak of Christ, and let a holy man who savingly believes speak of the same Christ, and of spiritual things, they shall both speak of the same things, yet the knowledge, that is, the sight which the believer hath of Christ, and of spiritual things, is clearly differing from that of the other.

I shall open but one scripture to you to express this ; it is in John iii. 12. Our Saviour Christ had been discoursing with Nicodemus, about the point of regeneration, which is a thing belonging to the kingdom of heaven. Now, saith he, ' if I have told you earthly things, and you believe not, how shall you believe if I tell you of heavenly things ?' What is his meaning there of having told him of earthly things ? He had spoken of heavenly things, and why doth he call them earthly ? Because he had expressed them under earthly words, and he had not given light, he had not gone forth with what he spake in a spirit of irradiation to Nicodemus his heart ; hence, therefore, Nicodemus clean mistakes Christ. But now when Jesus Christ doth enlighten a man, whilst he or the ministers of his word speak earthly things, he stamps the impress and image of the heavenly themselves upon the heart, and then a man believes ; he conveys them in their heavenly hue, conveys them in that notion and apprehension that his own heart hath of them, and therefore, John iii. 11 (saith he), ' We speak that we know,

and testify that we have seen.'   And ' we,' too, who are believers, ' have
the mind of Christ,' 1 Cor. ii. 16.   So that a believer hath such a kind of
knowledge of heavenly things as Jesus Christ himself hath, such a knowledge of the Son as Jesus Christ hath of himself, in his measure ; it differs
indeed in degrees, but it is of the same kind.

Hence it is that a believer is said, when he believeth, to witness to the
truth of God, ' to set to his seal that God is true,' John iii. 33.   What is
the reason ?   Because he knows the truths of God, the great truth especially about Christ, which is the thing eminently he witnesseth unto, and
he knows it not by reason, but by sense, by sight, and therefore he is a
witness.   For you know, if any man give a testimony merely by hearsay,
we account it as no witness in comparison ; but if a man speak by sense
and by sight, then he speaks like a witness.   Now, because a believer takes
in spiritual things by a spiritual sense, by a spiritual sight, therefore he is
said to witness when he doth believe.

And the sight of faith, though it is joined with reason, yet it is intuitive.
We do not gather the knowledge of Christ out of other things, but it is a
sight of himself.   In 1 Cor. xiii. 12, we are now said to ' see through a
glass darkly,' yet we are said to see.   Rational knowledge is to gather one
thing out of another, but the knowledge of faith, so far as it is a knowledge
of faith, is to see a thing in itself, to see Jesus Christ in himself.

That I may demonstrate this yet further, you shall find that the knowledge of faith in the souls of men, is not proportioned to the compass of
their natural understanding.   Why ?   Because it is a way of knowledge
above what the understanding naturally hath, or can be improved, or raised
up unto, remaining natural ; it is therefore a way beyond it, it is by way
of sight.   What is the reason that God hath chosen fools, rather than the
wise men of the world ?   ' You see your calling,' saith the apostle, ' how
that not many wise men after the flesh,' &c., 1 Cor. i. 26.   If God had
meant to convey the knowledge of spiritual things only to those that know
him here in a rational way, and by reason, elevated by the Holy Ghost,
certainly he would have chosen the wise men of the world, because they by
knowledge would have glorified him more in such a way of knowledge.
No ; but he chose the fools of the world, because he hath a way of conveying himself to their understandings beyond the way of reason, and that
is by way of sight.   Therefore you shall observe, men who are ignorant in
a rational way, that cannot make out a rational discourse of spiritual
things, that cannot lay before you a rational connection of one truth
with another, and when they speak of them, though they have otherwise
much grace and holiness, they will speak incoherently of them in their
expressions, and yet it is apparent that yet these men, as being godly, have
as strong and deep a knowledge of heavenly things as those who have
infinitely more strength of natural reason.   Why ?   Because faith goes by
way of sight, it goes in a way beyond and above reason, and the knowledge
of God and of Christ in a rational way.   When we come to heaven, will
God then proportion to you a knowledge of himself (and degrees of happiness depend upon greater degrees of knowledge of him), according to men's
parts and understandings which they had in this rational way here ?   No ;
but he lets in a light of himself, a light of vision, which he that hath the
lowest parts, if God let in no more* light to him, shall know more of him
than these of far greater parts, into whom he hath not let in so much light.
And so doth God here, because that faith is sight, and is the prelibation,
the beginning of heaven.

This is clearly (as to me), also the difference between that way of knowing God which believers have now, and that which Adam had in innocency; if Adam had stood, he amongst his children that had the most parts (those parts being all carried in a rational way), should have known more of God than he that, it may be, was more holy, and had lower parts. But it is not so in the second Adam, because he hath a way of letting things into the mind beyond the way of reason, by the way of sight and spiritual light, conveying beams of himself to us, which conveyeth those images of himself and of spiritual things to us, which neither eye hath seen, nor ear heard, nor ever entered into the heart of man remaining natural.

I will only give you a caution, that I may not be misunderstood; for as this is a great truth, so I would clear it from mistakes. The light of faith doth not destroy reason, but makes use of it, subordinates reason to itself, restoreth, rectifies it, and then useth it, even as reason makes use of sense; though the acts of reason, the thoughts of a man in a rational soul, are clean differing to what he hath in the sensitive soul, yet reason makes use of sense. And thus the Holy Ghost makes use of all the rational discourses and descriptions of Christ in the word, makes use of the letter of the word, but by them conveys those spiritual thoughts of Christ, which all that letter cannot hold forth to a man. And, as I said afore, if the angels from heaven should come and preach Jesus Christ to us, should with all their pencils go and paint out what knowledge they have of Jesus Christ, they could not beget one such sight of Christ in the heart as the Holy Ghost doth when he comes to work faith. And yet the apostle tells us it comes by hearing, and in hearing. The more rationally the preacher discourseth out of the word, and lays open the meaning thereof in a rational way, so much the better, because it is suited to the minds of men; yet where the Holy Ghost works faith, he conveys a light beyond all that reason, though he makes use of that reason too. This word of God hath an harmony of reason in it, and if a man would open a place of Scripture, he should do it rationally; he should go and consider the words before and the words after; but yet still, if the Holy Ghost comes not with a further light than all this rational opening of the word affords, a man will never believe, for faith is a sight beyond it. The Holy Ghost useth motives to move you to holy duties, but then he comes with a power joined with those motives beyond the moral force of them. He useth signs out of your own hearts to comfort you, but he comes with a light over and above those signs; for if you should stick there, you would never have comfort; so he useth reason; he destroyeth it not, but subordinateth it.

The apostle saith that the Scripture is not of any private interpretation, 2 Pet. i. 20. If the Scripture might be known by the light of reason (it is written rationally, and suiting to reason, I acknowledge), but if the Scriptures might alone be known, and the meaning of the Holy Ghost therein, by the light of reason, they were of private interpretation, for man's reason is but a private interpreter in comparison of the Holy Ghost the author; yet notwithstanding he useth reason to interpret it; but when he hath done, he himself comes and seals up to a man's spirit that this is the meaning of the Holy Ghost in it, or else a man never believes. So that it is the light of the Holy Ghost now that casteth the balance; and he doth this not only in the principles of religion, but in deductions of principles too; for though a man gather by reason one thing from another, yet if he have not the light of the Spirit to seal up those deductions, he doth not believe in a spiritual way; therefore it is called in Job xxxiii. 16, ' sealing of instruction.' If the Holy Ghost do not go, and by a supernatural light reveal the truth to a man, all the reason in the world will never work spiritual faith in his heart. Hence now you see why it is called sight.

The end why I have insisted so long upon this is, as to open it, so to take you off of yourselves, and all your own knowledge, that you may therefore seek out to the Holy Ghost to make spiritual things evident to you by their own light, in their own hue, that you may not rest in rational knowledge, and in notional knowledge of the things of the word, for you may go to hell with all that, unless you have a spiritual sight of the things themselves.

(3.) As faith is a spiritual knowledge, and as it is a sight beyond that of reason, though of spiritual things, which yet are suited to reason, so the knowledge of faith is a certain knowledge. So you have it in Heb. xi. 13, 'They saw the promises afar off, and were persuaded of them;' that is, they had a knowledge of assurance of the things they did believe. I say the knowledge of faith it is a certain knowledge. And why? Because it is a knowledge of sight. What a man sees, it is certain that he sees it when he sees it. What is the reason? Because *sensus non fallitur circa proprium objectum,*—Sense is never deceived about its proper object. Therefore if it be a spiritual sight and a spiritual sense, it hath a certainty joined with it. The knowledge of faith it is called assurance in Heb. x. 22, but in Col. ii. 2, as you do increase in it, you are said to ' increase in all riches of the full assurance of understanding, to the acknowledgment of the mystery of God, and of the Father, and of Christ.' It is very emphatical. He tells us in the following words, that there are 'hidden in Christ all the treasures of wisdom and knowledge;' and his scope is to prefer the knowledge of the gospel, and of Christ therein, to all other knowledge. Nay, saith he, it doth not only excel all other knowledge in regard of the object of it, but it is a knowledge that, when it is genuine, when it is saving, it excelleth as to the riches of assurance in the knowledge itself. It is such an assurance, and so rich, as you cannot have from your senses, or anything else. The apostle heaps up expressions; he calls it *assurance,* he calls it *full assurance,* he calls it *full assurance of understanding,* he calls it *riches of full assurance,* and he calls it an *acknowledgment;* words enough, one would think, to make knowledge sure.

But let me here add a caution too. My meaning is not that every saint that is a true believer hath an assurance that Jesus Christ is his, or that he hath the assurance of his own salvation. No; many believers have not that, neither is that essential to faith or to the act of application. This doth not lie in believing that Christ is mine, for if it did, God would give it unto every man; but the act of application is real application, giving myself up unto Christ, that he may be mine, and I his. But now, though there is not an act of assurance of my own interest, yet there is an act of assurance of the thing I believe on. I do never truly believe, unless there be an assured persuasion of the truth of the things on which I believe, and which I believe. Thus you must understand those scriptures where you have mention of the assurance of faith, as in Heb. x. 22, ' Let us draw near with a true heart, in full assurance of faith.' And so in James i. 6, ' If any man pray, let him ask in faith, without wavering, for he that wavereth is like a wave of the sea, driven with the wind and tossed.' Of which place many have mistook the meaning; for is the meaning this, that when a man comes to ask a promise at the hands of God, he must believe, without wavering, that he shall have it? No; if this were the faith that James here meant when he saith, ' If any man pray, let him ask in faith, without wavering,' who almost is there (unless in some special manifestations of God to him) that doth thus ask in prayer, or can ask temporal promises with such a faith, without wavering? But yet there is a faith which is without wavering; that is, there is an assured belief of the truth of those promises, that God made them, and that he is faithful to perform them according to the intention of them. Here now is a persuasion of the thing, and an asking in faith without wavering; and, saith the apostle, ' He that wavereth is as a wave of the sea, driven with the wind and tossed; a double-minded man is unstable,' saith he, ' in all his ways.' What is the reason that carnal men are unstable, and that they do not walk fully up in the ways of religion? It is because that their faith in the things do not rise up to a stableness; it hath a wavering in the belief of the principles themselves, so far forth as they are principles of practice. Whereas now, if these things were spiritually and prevailingly rooted in their hearts, above the natural darkness of unbelief, that there is a God, who is a rewarder of those that seek him, and that Jesus Christ is the Saviour of the world, and that he hath made these and these promises, and is thus gracious and willing to receive those that come unto him; if these things, I say, were believed in a real and spiritual manner, and that the hearts of men were, without wavering, persuaded of them, without question it would draw men's hearts, and cause them to walk answerably, and keep them from being driven with the wind and tossed.

So that this is the apostle's meaning (which is the thing I drive at), that in all faith there is a fixedness, an assuredness, a persuasion, namely, of the things that I do believe; but it doth not follow that it should be an assured persuasion of my own interest in the things themselves, for so who asketh in faith? Many poor souls that even ask salvation at the hands of God, they do not ask it as fully believing, and being assured that they shall be saved, and yet in the mean time they fully believe that salvation that God hath made known to them, and with which their hearts are taken, and that is the persuasion and assurance of faith. I shall give you some scriptures that this faith is a knowledge that riseth up to a persuasion, to an assurance, John vi. 69. Peter there, in the name of all the apostles, confesseth his faith, and the faith of all the apostles: ' We believe,' saith he, ' and are sure'—of what? that we shall be saved? no; but—' that thou art that Christ, the Son of the living God.' Of this a man must be sure, or it is not faith; and so likewise he must be sure of all other things that are fundamental unto faith; the things which he lays hold on, and which his soul pursues after, he must believe with a certainty that they are. When Jesus Christ was to go out of the world, what was it that he thanks his Father for, and why? I can (saith he) comfortably leave the world, and leave these disciples in the world; for ' I have given unto them the words which thou gavest me, and they have received them,' John xvii. 8. Wherein now lay their receiving them, and their believing them? for that is the meaning of receiving. ' They have received them,' saith he, ' and have known surely that I came out from thee.' He had begotten in them that faith which rises up to assurance, and he distinguisheth them thus from the world: ' I pray for them,' saith he in the very next verse, ' I pray not for the world;' for indeed the world do not surely know or are persuaded of the things that are in the word, for if they were, certainly that persuasion would alter the frame of their lives, and would make them walk answerably, and cause them to be holy. If a man be unstable in his ways, it is because he is unstable in the belief of the principles he professeth to walk by; and so indeed hereby Christ distinguisheth the faith of the world and the faith of those that were his disciples, whom he had wrought upon: ' They have surely known,' saith he, ' that I came out from thee;' and ' for these,' saith he, ' I pray, but I pray not for the world.' And the truth is, this full persuasion or assurance of the thing, it is an effect of the former property I mentioned, viz., of spiritual sight; for if I see a thing, and see it really (which is another property of the knowledge of faith, and which I shall speak to by and by), it always begets a certain persuasion in me that the thing is. Perhaps I may not reflect upon my own knowledge, yet notwithstanding an assurance and a full persuasion doth always and most necessarily follow a real sight of a thing. Take a man that is awake, he can and doth say with himself, and say it by way of difference and distinction from one being asleep, I know assuredly such a man is before me, I know assuredly that the sun shines. Why? Because he sees the man, and he sees the sun; whereas if a man be asleep, and in a dream, it may be he thinks he doth the same, but still there is no certainty in it. But now look where there is a reality of sight, there is also always accompanying it so far a full persuasion and assurance; and the man is able to say, that the knowledge he hath is different from all other knowledge. So that, I say, this is the third thing in this sight of Christ which a believer hath, he hath an assurance of the thing. This even the poorest and meanest believer hath, take him out of those temptations and doubts which the devil may suggest to him; take him when he is himself, he hath an assurance that is of the things themselves. And the reason is clearly this, because he sees spiritual things by their own light; and the ground of faith, the very *formalis ratio*, is the light and demonstration of the Spirit. Now, that is more infallible than all that a man knows by his outward senses, or by reason, by how much the witness of the Spirit is above the witness of nature, and the light of the Spirit above the light of nature; as an oath hath more certainty in it than a promise, so the light and demonstration of the Spirit hath more certainty in it than all the rational apprehension a man hath of Christ. In a word, the heart of a believer, by the light of the Spirit, sees more reason to believe that these things are so and so which the word saith, that there is such a Christ, so glorious and so good; he hath, I say, more reason to believe it than he could have by all the demonstrations that sense or reason can afford. As when a man sees the sun by its own light, it hath riches of evidence in it, hath it not? so when a man sees Christ by his own light, it produces riches of assurance, namely, that the thing is. I say not that it carries with it riches of assurance that Christ is mine, or that I shall be saved, for that is another thing; all the torches in the world cannot give that light which the sun itself gives, no more can all the rational apprehensions a man hath give him such a sight of Christ as a believer hath by the demonstration of the Spirit.

(4.) This knowledge of faith is a real knowledge, a real sight of Christ and of spiritual things. I do not speak of visions and revelations extraordinary, but it is such a knowledge as doth give a man a real possession of the things, and doth make the things themselves really subsisting to a man's spirit, and he feeleth really that there is such glory, and excellency, and sweetness in Jesus Christ as the word holds forth, and indeed as is in Jesus Christ himself; for now the Spirit of Christ is present, and joineth with his spirit, for always sight hath, as a certainty, so a reality joined with it. A man may have by way of reason a conviction that things are, he may know that things do exist, as now a man may know by the light of the moon and by the light of the stars that there is a sun, which shines upon them, and that this sun existeth; but when a man sees the sun itself, here is a knowledge *sub esse præsenti;* here is a presence of that sun to him, which makes it really existing to him. Such is the knowledge of faith; and therefore in Heb. xi. 1 faith is called ὑπόστασις, the evidence, that which gives a subsistence to the things not seen; that is, by the outward senses, or by the light and dictates of reason. Now, suppose that there were an artificial instrument made, by which things that we never saw, or never took in with our bodily eyes, might be really conveyed into our minds and fancies, such (if it were possible) as might stamp the image of them upon our fancies, we would say this were a very strange kind of instrument. Optic glasses they do not so much; they indeed will present a thing to you which you glimmeringly discern afar off, but you must first discern it with your bodily eye; but now if there were an engine as could present a thing afar off, which your bodily eye never beheld, and stamp it upon your fancy, this you would say were strange. Now, the Holy Ghost hath an art to do this, and he doth do it, though he useth the word, and the description of Christ in the word, and useth the promises, yet that image of Christ and of heavenly things which he works in the heart of a believer is by a peculiar art of his own which he useth, and it is far beyond, infinitely beyond, what we can take in by our fancies, or senses, or anything else; and therefore, because the knowledge of faith hath this reality in it, you shall find that there is almost no sense but in the Scripture faith is compared to it. And this is merely, I say, because it is such a knowledge as hath a reality of the things known conveyed to a man's soul, though they be absent. It is compared to hearing: John x. 16, 'My sheep hear my voice;' and they hear it so as to discern it from the voice of a stranger. It is compared to eating: John vi. 54, 'Whoso eateth my flesh,' &c. And elsewhere it is compared to tasting: Ps. xxxiv. 8, 'Taste how good the Lord is.' Hence in John vi. 55 Christ saith 'his flesh is meat indeed, and his blood is drink indeed;' that is, the soul finds a reality in it, and it is not as when a man dreams he eats, but Christ and the promises, and the things that the soul feeds upon, they have a reality in them, they are meat indeed and drink indeed, and the soul finds them so. They that are temporary believers have a show of this, both of a sight, and of a reality of sight, and they are said to taste of the powers of the world to come; but yet let me say this to distinguish it from this other.

1. They do not see spiritual things in their spiritual nature, as they are in themselves, though they may see an accidental goodness in them, and so be taken with them, and so may taste of the sauce of that flesh of Christ which it is sauced up in, as I may express it; that is, that accidental goodness which it is presented to us in, with those benefits that accompany it, as freedom from hell and the like; but the spiritual, the genuine, the native excellency that is in Jesus Christ himself, this they do not see, nor is it made real to them. Now, to see a thing, or to know a thing in the effects, or in the accidental goodness of it, is not to see or to know the thing properly and truly; but to see a thing in its own true, genuine notion, to see the spiritual excellency that is in Jesus Christ, and so to have the heart taken with him, considered in all his spiritual excellencies, this is spiritual sight; and indeed this is only to know the things themselves, which the other doth not.

2. And then again, though there be a seeming reality in the knowledge and impression that is made upon the heart of a temporary believer, yet it is but as the knowledge one hath that is asleep, and dreams that he sees and converseth with a man, which sight then seems to be exceeding real, and indeed is more real than the picture of a man is, because in his fancy

he seems to have the reality of the man presented to him with whom he converseth, and his image seems, as it were, to be stamped upon his fancy; but yet it is but a phantasmatical knowledge; it is not that knowledge and sight of a man which men have that are awake, that giveth a subsistence, as the knowledge and sight of faith doth, which is such a knowledge as is suited to the things themselves, a spiritual knowledge, and a real knowledge also. I told you before, that the knowledge of a believer is to have such thoughts, in his measure and degree, as are in the heart of Christ himself. Now those things which yet are not (as the day of judgment is not yet), yet are present to the heart of Christ; and therefore it is said, God 'calleth things that are not as if they were,' Rom. iv. 17. If now I have the mind of Christ, if I have that spiritual notion of things to come, of heaven that is to come, stamped upon my heart, that is in the heart of Christ, that I know them in that manner he knows them, in my degree and proportion, then it is present to my heart as it is to his. Jesus Christ doth not only know things, but they have a subsistence, they are present to him: 'All things are present and naked with him with whom we have to do,' Heb. iv. 13. So much faith then, so much openness and nakedness, and so much presence of the things we believe. You shall find in 1 Cor. ii. 9, that the things of God are said to 'enter into our hearts.' It is not only that we know the images and notions of things, but we have the presence of the things themselves; therefore, in Heb. xi. 13, believers are there said to 'embrace the promises.' What is the reason they are said to embrace them? Because they so saw them as having a reality in them; they did not embrace a cloud, but they felt a presence, a subsistence, in the things promised, in God, and in Christ, on whom they believed, though Christ was not then incarnate. And in John vi. 47, 51, and 54, when a man is said to believe, he is said to 'eat the flesh of Christ, and to drink his blood,' as truly as a man eats meat or drinks wine, and he feels a presence, even as a man feels the presence of the wine he drinks to strengthen his spirits. He doth not only know that there is wine, and sees it, but he feels a power and virtue joining with his body and with his spirits; so a man knows and feels the presence of Christ and of heavenly things in his spirit, while he believes, and finds a reality in them: 'My flesh is meat indeed,' saith he, to shew that faith feels as true a reality in the things believed, as a man doth in the meat he eats. And indeed, what is the reason that carnal men leave Christ for the pleasures of the world? Because the pleasures of the world are real things to them; therefore, unless God make the things of another world real too, a man will never leave realities for notions. All that reason or notions can represent of Christ, will never take a man's heart off from the real things he sees here below; and therefore God comes, and he weighs down the reality of the things of this world, by the reality of the things of the other world. And so much now for this first thing in faith, viz., that it is a sight: 'He that seeth the Son,' saith he; and so you have the act seeing, with the kind and properties thereof.

I come now to the acts of faith in the understanding, as terminated on the great object of faith. I shall confine myself to Christ, because he is the great object of our faith; and for that I shall say these few things to you.

First, The soul that God doth give faith to, sees the spiritual excellency and glory that is in Jesus Christ, and the heart is taken with it: in 2 Cor. iii. 18, saith the apostle, speaking of the beholding of Christ, 'We see as in a glass the glory of the Lord.' I mention it for this, that it is called a seeing of his glory; that is, that surpassing excellency, even to a glory, that is in Jesus Christ. Every one whom God draws in to believe, he doth sooner or later cause some glimpse of the glory of Christ in a spiritual and real way to pass before him, which takes the spirit, so that he is like one that is fallen in love with one at first sight, when the party is passed by; but there is a sight, a glimpse that has taken the heart; so though that glimpse of Jesus Christ seems to be gone, yet there is that impression upon the soul, and upon the heart, that other beauties and glories are but as shadows in comparison of that which is in Jesus Christ. And such a sight of the thing, though it be but *in transitu*, takes the heart for ever. The church in Cant. v. 9 had such a sight of Christ, for see how mightily she magnified him; and though that sight was vanished, yet she was so taken with it, as she seeks all the world over for him, insomuch as others stand wondering at her; ' What is thy beloved,' say they, ' more than another beloved?' They saw no such beauty in him: ' Oh,' saith she, ' my beloved is such a beloved as is thus and thus;' and so she falls a-setting out of his glories and excellencies. It is such a sight as doth put out a man's eyes to all things else for ever doting upon them as formerly he did; even as they that go on pilgrimage to Mahomet's tomb, after they have been there, they use to burn out their eyes, that, after that sacred sight, they may never behold creatures more. Such a thing now is really wrought in the heart of a Christian in some measure; as Christ saith, ' He that drinketh of this water shall never thirst any more,' John iv. 13. So he that hath thus seen Jesus Christ, he never sees anything more as he saw it before; he may have his heart taken with folly and vanity, yet not so as before, because he hath seen the Lord Jesus; there is that impression made by that sight of the glory and excellency which is in him. You have this in 2 Cor. v. 17, ' If I have known things after the flesh,' saith he, ' henceforth know I them no more'; that is, I can never value carnal things at that rate I have done; I see through them all, saith he; I do not value them now by a fleshly sight and consideration. If I have seen them so, I see them now so no more. Why? Because I have seen Jesus Christ by the knowledge of the new creature, and now old things are passed away, and all things are become new. Even as God has moulded fancies to faces, so he hath framed and moulded the knowledge of Christ to Christ; and even as the eye is framed to colours, so is the new understanding suited to Jesus Christ; it is a spiritual understanding, and so suited to a spiritual Christ; that having taken in the image of Jesus Christ in the real and spiritual notion of him, the heart is moulded into it, and that heart can never be taken with any other beauty or carnal thing of what kind soever that is here below: 1 John v. 20, ' He hath given us an understanding, that we may know him that is true.'

Secondly, When God draws the heart to believe, it sees also an all-sufficiency of righteousness in Jesus Christ, and in his satisfaction: Ps. cxxx. 7, ' With whom is plenteous redemption;' and in Rom. v. 17, it is said, ' They receive abundance of grace, and of the gift of grace;' you have the like in Philip. iii. 8, ' I count all things,' saith he, ' but loss and dung, for the excellency of the knowledge of Christ Jesus my Lord;' and next to the knowledge of Christ, what is most valued by him? The righteousness of Christ; and therefore saith he in the next verse, ' That I may be found in him, not having mine own righteousness, but that which is through the faith of Christ.' Now a man sees that satisfaction, and that worth and fulness in the righteousness of the Lord Jesus, that if he might have the righteousness of Adam, or the righteousness of the angels, or as great a righteousness made his, to be his, and be inherent in him, and he to be justified by it, he would throw it all away as dross and dung in comparison of the righteousness of the Lord Jesus, which he sees held forth to him.

The *third* thing that the soul sees, and is persuaded of when God draws the heart to him, it is the graciousness that is in the Lord Jesus Christ; and that in two things :

First, In the general; in his readiness to receive sinners. Whatsoever thoughts a man had before of Christ (as when a man is first humbled he is apt to have hard and sour thoughts of Christ), yet when he comes to know ' the mind of Christ,' as the apostle saith, 1 Cor. ii. 16, that is, to know his gracious inclination, God doth make an impression and stamp of the gracious heart and inclination that is in Jesus Christ to receive sinners, and sets it as it were upon the heart, and he persuades them better things of Christ than either what they naturally, or when they are first humbled, think of him.

Secondly, There is stamped upon the heart of a Christian some secret hint or whisper of mercy to him; I do not say it riseth to assurance, for then it would quell all doubtings ; but in every one that God takes to himself, as he lets him see the readiness that is in Christ to receive sinners indefinitely, so there is some secret kind of whisper of mercy and grace to him, a secret hint, as I use to call it. In John x. 3, it is said, that Christ calls his sheep by name, even as he called Moses by name, and Cyrus, which implies a special intimation; and Christ he doth distinguish, and saith, the reason why others that were not his sheep do not come, is because they do not hear his voice. Now that you may not mistake me, though it be a whisper, yet it is but a whisper and a hint, which the soul oftentimes in itself doth not so discern as to reflect upon it, but yet it is full enough to carry the heart after Christ, and never to leave him. I use to compare it to the scent of a bloodhound ; when he is sent to seek, though he finds not, yet having once had the scent he never leaves, but hunts up and down till he finds it, and though he knows not where it is, yet it is enough to carry him on. So the soul, when it hath wound Jesus Christ, as we may so speak, this hint, this whisper is enough to carry on to Christ, so as never to leave him, and that with some encouragement, though it doth not rise up to assurance, and prevail over doubtings. I distinguish it thus : assurance is when the Spirit of God so speaks to a man that he speaks as a witness, when he comes in and evidenceth to a man the truth of his estate, and that Jesus Christ is his ; and when he speaks as a witness he will speak so loud as to prevail over all temptations, and over all doubts, or else he will lose his end; for a witness must so speak as to put the thing out of doubt, or else he is no witness. But now in this secret whisper of faith he doth not so, he doth not come then to speak as a witness, but he comes to speak then as one that would work the heart into Jesus Christ, and carry on the heart to Jesus Christ, and in this case a secret whisper, which he himself doth really back, is enough to carry on the heart, though it is not enough to quell all doubts and temptations. Insomuch now as when a man is humbled, and sees his misery, and the like, and when he is walking alone, or is in prayer, he thinketh in himself, well, I may find mercy from God, Jesus Christ may pardon me, &c. This he may take for his own thoughts, because it doth not rise to that height as when the Holy Ghost speaks it as a witness, and in such a distinct manner from his own thoughts as that he should rest satisfied in it. Nay, a man is apt to take such thoughts, and to fling them away, and discerns them not from other thoughts put into his mind about other things ; yet for all that the Holy Ghost, that puts them in, leaves them not, but carries them on in a way of encouragement and hopefulness, and never leaveth him till they have boiled up either to the vision of Christ, or to the assurance of Jesus Christ as being his.

CHAPTER II.

That the mere assurance of the object, or a general assent to the truth of the promises, is not the act of faith justifying, but application is necessary.—This proved by several reasons.

As I have explained the nature of the act of faith in the understanding, so now I will shew that true justifying faith includes more in it, or that it is not a bare general assent to the truth of the promises, though never so spiritual; for still in Scripture the act of faith that justifies is called 'believing on him,' so Rom. iv. 5, and everywhere almost we find it thus: 'He that believes on him that justifies the ungodly;' it is not he that believes only that God will justify the ungodly. It is an ancient received maxim of divines, *aliud est credere Deum, et in Deum ;* for to believe *on him* implies a particular application. Those that are for general assent urge those scriptures most, Rom. x. 9, 'If thou believe with thine heart that God raised up Christ from the dead, thou shalt be saved ;' and that in 1 John v. 5, 'He overcometh the world that believeth that Jesus is the Son of God ;' and ver. 10, 'He that believeth not the record God hath given of his Son, makes God a liar.' But it is observable that, in both places, believing on him, which is an act of application, is added, as that which makes this general assent a complete act of faith. Thus Rom. x. 11, he confirms his saying by the Scripture, which withal interprets his meaning: 'For the Scripture saith, He that believeth on him shall not be ashamed ;' and so in 1 John v. 10, 'He that believeth on the Son of God.' He leaves it not, therefore, in a general assent. I shall now give the reasons of my assertion.

Reason 1. Faith doth not consist merely in assent, because a man, in believing, comes not in simply as a witness to a truth, for so the angels do believe, and testify the truth, and might be said to have faith justifying, Rev. xix. 10. They are said to 'have the testimony of Jesus ;' they testify that God is true in his promises. But when men believe, they come not in barely as witnesses to the New Testament, but as legatees for a portion in it; they therefore rest on it for themselves, and so their faith makes an application of it. When some have reasoned against general assent to be faith, in that the devils believe, as James says, it hath been answered that the devils' assent, though it is operative to cause terror, yet it is not a spiritual assent and sight of it, such as a believer in the general hath of the things he believes. And they say true, for there is a difference in a regenerate man's believing there is a God, and it is another sight than devils have. But yet still the argument will hold, if fetched from the good angels, for they do in as spiritual a manner as the saints believe the truth of the promises, and assent to their goodness, and see the excellencies of Christ, and adore them, and yet do not believe with a justifying faith. And why? Because these promises not concerning their salvation, they trust not in them; they come not in as legatees, but as witnesses and admirers. Now, then, if an act of general assent spiritual be common to them with believers, surely God hath not put the act of justifying upon what is common to both (whenas it is in them, it justifies them not), but rather upon such an act as is proper to man, and not in them; and that is trusting, relying on the promises, and on that Christ whom they believe to be the Son of God, for their salvation.

Reason 2. Justifying faith is seated in the whole heart, as he said in Acts viii. 37, ' If thou believest with thy whole heart,' thou shalt be saved.' Yea, and so it is in this Rom. x. 9, ' If thou shalt believe with thy heart that God hath raised up Jesus,' &c. Now, if only a general assent, though never so spiritual, in the understanding, which is but one faculty in the heart, were that act that justified, then the will should be excluded, which, if faith be with the whole heart, it is not. And now, if the will come in to put forth an act, then an act of application must be also added to that general assent, such as indeed is to trust in Christ, to cast myself on him, to wait upon him, which are all acts of the will. It is true indeed that in the understanding part, there is no other act of faith required absolutely unto justification, than a spiritual sight of, and assent to the truth and goodness of the things believed. This is all God exacts of the understanding, for an assent or assurance that these things are mine is not of the essence of faith, but there are acts of the will besides that go to make up faith ; therefore, Heb. xi. 13, there are three things attributed to faith : First, A real sight of the promises : ' They saw them.' Secondly, A persuasion or assurance of their truth and goodness : ' they were persuaded of them ;' and these two make up a spiritual general assent in the understanding. But then, thirdly, is added their embracing them : ' they embraced them,' which is an act of the will, or an act of application ; so, Rom. iv. 5, to believe that God justifies the ungodly, is the act of general assent, but to believe *on him* that justifies the ungodly, is an act of application ; it is an act of the will, resting on him for a man's own particular salvation.

Reason 3. Yea, by this act of the will is the union on our parts completed between Christ and us, and we are thereby made ultimately one with him. Now one main end of faith is to make an union with Christ on our parts, and that, as it is done without assurance that Christ is mine, so it is not chiefly made by a general assent ; and to the union made on Christ's part, it is not necessary I should then apprehend it when Christ first doth it, because it is a secret work done by his Spirit, who doth first apprehend us ere we apprehend him, as he first loves us ere we love him, Philip. iii. 12. But for the making a real union with him (so far as on our part it is made), it lies not primarily in believing Christ is mine, or that Christ is, but in joining myself to his person in the shooting in of my will into him, in taking him, and consenting to be his ; to believe he is mine is indeed to apprehend that union, and to believe spiritually he draws in the heart to it, but to have my will drawn to him, to rest in him, to cleave to him as the fountain of life, Deut. xxx. 20, it is that makes the real union. As in marriage, consent makes the match, so the consent of the will to have Christ as my Lord, king, head, husband, makes the union ; for the main subject by which we are united to Christ is the will, for by the will we cleave to those things we apprehend good, and shoot our souls into them. But if that which united on our parts were such apprehensions whereby we perceive we are made one with Christ, it should be in the understanding most, and so that which makes the union should be *assensus de Deo*, a believing something of God, not a cleaving to God, and that which I am united to should mainly be a proposition. Indeed, when I apprehend myself united unto Christ, then my will cleaves more to him, is drawn out more to him, as those that are new married, when a man can say, ' I am my beloved's, and he is mine ;' but he must be my beloved afore. As he that lusts after a woman commits adultery, and so is made before God one flesh with her, though not afore men, so he whose heart is taken with the beauty of Christ, and cleaves to him, hangs on him, is united to him, for a marriage-glance makes afore God a union with Christ. Such acts of faith make the union, and therefore upon such acts of recumbency Christ sheds grace and life into the soul, having recourse to him as the only fountain of life; but when assurance comes, then a man can plead this union, to fetch strength from Christ by virtue of it, and so then a man discerns the connection between Christ and his grace, how it flows from him; but it flowed before.

CHAPTER III.

What the nature is of this special faith of application.—That besides a spiritual faith or wisdom to know all other divine truths savingly, there is a special faith on Christ and God's free grace for justification; or, that God in Christ, as a saviour and justifier, is the object of that special faith which is justifying.

That from a child thou hast known the holy scriptures, which are able to make thee wise unto salvation, through faith which is in Christ Jesus.—2 TIM. III. 15.

It is of justifying or saving faith that I profess to discourse. It consisteth of two words : 1, *justifying*, or *saving*; 2, *faith*. And so it calls for two things to be handled by him that will handle it thoroughly, as distinct commonplace heads. The *first* is the doctrine of justification through faith, as it is an act of God upon us, upon or through our believing. And, *secondly*, there is the doctrine of the nature of that faith itself; and which of these two a man begins to handle first (we living under the sunshine of the gospel), it is not much material.

Under that head of the doctrine of justification itself by faith, there are these things :

1. Whether, upon a man's believing, there is an act of justification passeth from God, so as in a true sense a man may be said to be then justified, so as not before? And how that this may stand with God's justifying of us with Christ when he rose, and with God's justifying of us in Christ from everlasting? Or if you will, whether that faith be only for the manifestation of a man's justification to himself, or it be not also for the alteration of a man's condition before God?

2. That nothing but faith in man is that principle which God hath ordained to receive this blessing, and faith only, and faith without works.

3. Under this head of justification comes the treating also of this, how it is that faith is said to justify, or how God looks at it, whether as an habit, or an act, or an instrument, or a condition, or what.

4. There are the objects of this faith, both Jesus Christ as the matter of justification (which I have at large discoursed of in those treatises long since published to the world). And, secondly, there is God as justifying, for the soul ' believes on him that justifieth the ungodly.' So that as Jesus Christ is the author, and cause, and matter of justification in his death, and resurrection, and ascension, and intercession, &c., so God in his grace and mercy, and in all his acts therein, is also the object of faith; and a glorious justification it is, wherewith God justifies us. How great, how free, how unlimited is it, and such as no sins can hinder! A justification total at once, and eternal for ever. These things I have discoursed of before in the first part.

Now concerning faith itself, by which we are justified (I taking it at present for granted that we are justified through faith, which is the language of the Scripture), that which now we are to do, it is to make the inquiry, what this faith is.

The first thing in the general which I pitch upon towards the inquiry after the true nature and notion of faith, is this, that the faith by which we are saved and justified is a special faith, pitched upon God's free-grace, and Christ as matter of justification to us, as its special object; as you shall see out of this scripture, and many others also, in the proof of it.

The proof of this great truth I might have founded upon many scriptures, as you shall see anon; but I did choose out this, because it clearly distinguisheth a special faith from a general faith, and distinctly puts the business of salvation upon that special faith. If you mark it here, he tells us, verse 16, that 'all Scripture is given by inspiration, and is profitable for doctrine,' &c. And that all the things revealed in the Scripture, be they what they will, are all of them able to make a man wise unto salvation, and so to beget in him a 'wisdom,' which indeed is nothing else but 'faith.' Take it in the general notion of assent, what prudence is to all virtues, that faith is to all graces, it is 'wisdom to salvation.' But yet there is in it a special faith, without which all the knowledge a man hath, yea, all the knowledge that is unto salvation, would not be unto salvation, were it not for this; and that is (as the text hath it), 'faith in Jesus Christ,'—'which is able to make thee wise unto salvation,' saith he, 'through faith which is in Jesus Christ.' So that these words which I have now read, they hold forth to us a twofold faith or wisdom, as you may call it, for the Scripture calls faith wisdom sometimes, and wisdom faith.

There is *first* of all a general faith, respecting all divine objects, which is here called wisdom, and wisdom unto salvation (in that sense unto salvation as repentance is unto salvation, and as other graces are said to be unto salvation), which is a belief and knowledge of the Scriptures, and all things revealed in them, and a having a man's heart suitably affected with the things according to the nature of them; as to believe a God, and all the attributes of God, all the promises, and all the threatenings, or whatsoever else is contained in the book of God, which being taken by faith into the soul and heart of a believer, makes him wise unto salvation; this, I say, is properly called general faith. Faith (as I said before) is often called by the name of wisdom in the Scripture; as in Luke i. 17 it is said, that John Baptist should 'go before him in the spirit and power of Elias, to turn the hearts of the fathers to the children, and the disobedient to the wisdom of the just;' that is, he should bring them to the faith of their fathers, and to the same knowledge, joined with wisdom; to the same creed (for the materials of it) which the prophets and fathers held, and were saved by, and the doctrine of which the Jews in those times had generally corrupted. All these spiritual things are taken into the soul, and apprehended by such a principle of wisdom in heavenly affairs as human wisdom serves to in earthly affairs. Faith is therefore rightly called wisdom, because it superadds unto notional knowledge in things spiritual, as wisdom in men superadds unto knowledge notional in worldly businesses. That knowledge which constitutes a man a wise man, as such, in worldly matters, beyond a man simply knowing, is such a degree or kind of knowledge as over and above the notion affects and strikes the spirit of a man to act accordingly, and puts him on to practise; whereas the like knowledge in others, though it may be more clear and distinct for the notion, is overly, and affects not the man, nor is strong enough to overcome his affections to the contrary. Now, look what difference there is in this twofold knowledge about temporal things, the like there is as to spiritual; there is an enlightening of the Holy Ghost, which clears up the notion of all things spiritual to be known, unto which faith is a farther special gift superadded, to affect and strike the heart with them, as the gift of wisdom added to knowledge useth to affect in outward affairs. Take then faith as it hath thus all the Scriptures, and all in them, for its object, and as it thus strongly makes an impression on the heart to act accordingly, and it is a wisdom unto salvation.

But yet, *secondly*, there is a peculiar or a special faith, without which the other is not, nor would be, of itself alone effectual unto salvation, and that, you see, is faith in Jesus Christ,—a faith of the promise of grace and salvation in and through Jesus Christ, as it is several ways expressed in the New Testament.

Now, you see, the apostle doth not only hold forth this distinction, but he doth withal shew that all the faith, and knowledge, and wisdom we have, though never so spiritual (for even of such he speaks), will not make us wise unto salvation, but only through faith in Jesus Christ.

So that the observation to the scope in hand, which I raise out of these words, and purpose to discourse of, is this, that that faith which doth save —the other may be unto salvation, as all graces are—that which truly saveth and putteth me into the state of salvation, or upon which I am put into that state, is a special faith, which here is said to have Jesus Christ for its object, or (which is all one) that hath the grace of God in Christ to rely upon. Faith on the promises of salvation and justification through Christ, and through the free grace of God in him, is that special faith without which all the true wisdom, the spiritual wisdom, spiritual faith, believing all things else whatsoever, would not otherwise be unto salvation. This, I say, is clearly the scope of the words, that besides that faith whereby we believe, and believe spiritually (yea, and unto salvation too), all the things revealed in the word of God, there is a special faith by which we are saved, and by means of which all the rest of our faith in all other things is wisdom unto salvation: 'is able to make thee wise unto salvation,' saith he, 'through the faith which is in Jesus Christ.'

Now, in the opening and treating of this point, I shall do these things:

1. Give you some explication of it.

2. I shall deliver some concessions, some things that may and must be yielded unto and granted, concerning this general faith, and the difference between it and special faith.

3. I shall offer some proofs of Scripture for to make the point good.

4. I shall urge some reasons why that God hath not ordained to save any man by the most spiritual faith of all things in the world, if a man could be supposed to have it, without this other special faith of application. If a man, I say, did believe all the Scriptures, and all things in them, and that with an affection answerable and suitable to such objects themselves therein revealed, yet that man would never be saved without a special faith, which hath Jesus Christ and the grace of God in him for its object.

You shall find in your protestant writers a great deal of do about this faith; I would open to you that which I conceive to be the nature of it, and the sense wherein I would press it upon you. And,

1. To begin with the explication of it. I do not call it a special faith because it hath a special root and principle created on purpose in the hearts of men to be the root of it, so as that that general faith we speak of should have one root, and this special faith another. No; but the same faith, for the root and principle of it, in the spirits of men, whereby I

believe all things else in the word of God, the power of God, the justice of God, or whatever else, that wisdom whereby a man knows savingly all things in the Scripture, all truths whatsoever, and the goodness of them, that faith whereby I truly and spiritually believe that there is a God, is also the root of that faith whereby I am possessed of salvation, or whereby I am justified, with the same principle of faith whereby I believe all things else unto salvation, with the same principle also I believe on Jesus Christ, and on God as justifying. It is clearly the scope of Heb. xi.; I will not stand now to open it. You know the ordinary similitude that is given: it was the same eye by which the Israelites beheld all the things in the wilderness, and wherewith they did behold also the brazen serpent; and yet notwithstanding they were cured by beholding the brazen serpent, and by nothing else. I confess this similitude will not in all things hold, but yet it is that by which it is illustrated; I only speak now by way of clearing of this term, special faith, and not by way of confirmation. Abraham, by the same faith whereby he did believe in the promised Messias, in the seed in whom all the nations of the earth shall be blessed, Rom. iv. 21, by the same faith he is said to have believed the power of God, that he was able to give him a child.

Secondly, It is not called special in this sense, that only a faith on Christ, and on God's free grace, is proper to the elect, but that wicked men and devils, and men that shall be damned, may have a true general faith upon all objects else whatsoever; it is not, I say, meant in that sense neither, it is not meant subjectively special. There are they who say that as for the belief of all things in the general in the word of God, that is common to devils, because in James it is said, 'They believe there is a God, and tremble,' James ii. 19; but, say they, to have a special faith to believe in Jesus Christ, this is proper to the elect. But it is evident that in every man that shall be saved the faith whereby he believeth all things in the word of God is a new kind of faith, and all things become new to him. The spiritual man judgeth all things spiritually, knoweth them spiritually, and so believeth them spiritually, as you have it in 1 Cor. ii. 14, 15. And as the devils know there is a God, and believe that, so they know and believe that Jesus Christ is a Saviour: Mark i. 24, ' I know who thou art,' saith the devil, even ' the Holy One of God;' yet he did not know this spiritually as a true believer.

Thirdly, It is not called special in respect of any special act that is proper to it, and it alone; that is not the specialness neither which I intend. Some by special faith mean that special act of assurance of a man's salvation, and make that to justify. The truth is, there are many protestant writers, and holy and godly men, that have in all their oppositions against the papists urged a special faith in this sense. But not to insist on a long confutation, the faith of the apostles at first was not a faith of assurance; they ' believed, that they might be justified,' Gal. ii. 16. Others by special faith understand that other act of trust or confidence, and going out of a man's self, and they say that therein lies this same specialness of faith. Now, I grant indeed that an act of trust, and confidence, and reliance is required to faith, it is that which I would rather call the act of particular application, as hereafter may be shewn. And they contend for this as that special faith, in opposition to those which hold that the general faith, the belief of the things themselves, as that Christ is the Son of God, and the Saviour of the world, and that God justifies the ungodly, being spiritually believed, is that act upon which God justifies us. But I would not make the specialness of faith to lie in respect of any act which this faith hath proper to it, since there are none such but what we find common to our faith on other objects. For if it be said that the act of saving faith is a trusting upon this object, viz., the grace of God for salvation, why, this act of trusting is not proper and peculiar only to faith justifying, nor hath only the grace of God justifying for its object, but it is common to this faith to pitch upon other attributes of God. I rely upon God for all spiritual things else besides salvation and justification; I rely upon him for his Spirit; I go out unto Christ for holiness, and strength against sin, and for duty; I rely on him, and trust on him, and come unto him for temporal things; I trust him for to sanctify me; in a word, all the promises of good things are the object of that act of trust on God. The like may be said of assurance. I may have assurance from God of other things as well as of my justification; so as special faith, whereby we are saved or justified, which the apostle here speaks of, is not so called, because it hath a peculiar act appropriated to it.

Fourthly, and *lastly*, Therefore, that I call (and I think it ought to be called, and only ought to be called so) a special faith, whereby we are justified, which hath, 1, an eminent special object, proper and peculiar, appropriated to it; which hath, 2, a special aim; and, 3, which hath a special effect, or a special consequent rather, or, if you will, concomitant, or that which doth accompany it.

First, I say it is to be called special faith, in respect that God hath framed on purpose a peculiar and special object for it. Whether the act be believing the thing or object itself, in the truth and goodness of it, or relying upon it, or call it what you will for the act of it, now that is clear in the text to be *faith in Jesus Christ*. Look over all the Scriptures, and all the divine and spiritual truths in them, the belief of those things is not special faith, though they may sanctify the heart, though the heart may be answerably affected thereto, till it come to faith in Jesus Christ, or to trust in the special mercy and grace in God for pardon and justification. I will put both these together; it is either, I say, the free grace of God, who is our justifier (for God as justifying is as much the object of faith as Christ himself, and more), which is the object of this special faith, or else Jesus Christ and his righteousness, as the matter of our justification and salvation, and faith as it respects these two as they are objects, and that for justification, that I call, I say, special faith. I will not stand much to shew you, as I might do, that what in the Old Testament is called trusting in the mercy of God, and believing on the mercy of God, that in the New is called believing on Christ, and how that both come to one. If therefore you will have the language of the New Testament, the special act of justifying faith is to believe upon God as justifying: 'To believe on him that justifieth the ungodly,' so Rom. iv. 14, and to believe on the righteousness, or on the blood and sanctification of Christ, or on Jesus Christ as for righteousness; so the text speaks here, 'Through faith in Jesus Christ.' These two make up the special object of faith.

And, secondly, the believing these, and on these, *as for salvation*, and having that special aim and intent so considered also, is called, and ought to be called, special faith. It is not coming unto God or to Christ for anything else temporal and spiritual, but as coming for salvation and pardon of sin, believing that a man may be justified, as it is expressed, Gal. ii. 16. This, I say, is the peculiar aim of special faith, and in that respect it ought to be called special, as it comes to God for justification.

And therefore, thirdly, there is a special consequent or concomitant, which doth accompany and follow upon it, and that is, it doth in a special manner *justify and save* a man, which no faith else, though never so spiritual, upon any other object, is said to do.   In Rom. iii. and in Rom. iv. this is clearly made out ; the apostle speaks there, as you all know, of faith as it doth justify, and that faith alone justifies without works ; and as faith doth thus justify, what doth he make there to be the object of it ? First, Jesus ; so chap. iii. 22, ' The righteousness of God,' saith he, ' which is by the faith of Jesus unto all and upon all them that do believe,' namely, on Jesus ; and ver. 26, he is said to be ' the justifier of him which believeth in Jesus ;' and ver. 28, he concludeth, that by such a faith, and no other, a man is justified.   And as he makes Jesus thus to be the object of it, so God as justifying too ; so chap. iv. 5, ' To him that worketh not, but believeth on him that justifieth the ungodly ;' namely, on God, who is the justifier, whose righteousness it is, and so called, because he is the bestower, the imputer of that righteousness, as you may read in the 21st and 22d verses of the 3d chapter : ' The righteousness of God which is by the faith of Jesus,' saith he, ' whom God hath set forth (ver. 25) to be a propitiation through faith in his blood, to declare his righteousness,' &c.

And therefore this denomination of special faith (say I) it ought to have from these three things : 1, because it hath a special object made and appointed for it, viz., the grace of God justifying and saving, and our Lord and Saviour Jesus Christ, and his righteousness the matter of our salvation and justification ; and, 2, in respect of the aim the heart hath in believing, that it comes to these as for salvation and justification ; and, 3, that upon thus coming God is said to justify, as faith genuinely and spiritually pitcheth on these objects ; you have all these in that one place, Gal. ii. 16, ' Knowing this, that a man is not justified by the works of the law, but by the faith of Jesus Christ, even we have believed in Jesus Christ, that we might be justified by the faith of Christ, and not by the works of the law : for by the works of the law shall no flesh be justified.'   Here is, first, you see, faith described by a special object, and therefore called ' the faith of Jesus Christ,' the faith in Jesus Christ, and again, the faith of Christ ; it is three times so mentioned in relation to this special peculiar object, so that the faith which justifies us is a special faith in respect of the object ; secondly, it is a faith which hath a peculiar aim, which believeth in Jesus that the soul might be justified : ' We believed in Jesus, that we might be justified,' saith he.   To come to Jesus Christ for anything else than for salvation, and for justification, is not a special faith ; and then, thirdly, there is a special concomitant, or that which doth accompany it, a special effect, or call it what you will, and that is, that we are justified, though not by the act of believing, yet upon believing, which is evident by this, for how else did they believe ' that they might be justified' ?   And it follows after, ' By the works of the law shall no flesh be justified ;' but oppositely by and upon believing a man is.   And it is this special relation to its object which makes this faith (to speak in the Scripture language, and if you will you may call it by that name instead of special faith) to be called ' precious faith.'   What is it that makes it so more precious than the belief of all things else whatsoever ? either of the truth, or power, or faithfulness of God ; or be the thing what it will be, what is it that makes it excel all such faith of any kind ?   It is the object of it ; so you have it in 2 Peter i. 1 : he writes ' to them' (because none else are true Christians) ' that have obtained like precious faith with us ;' we translate it ' *through* the righteousness,' it is ἐν, *in*, or *on* the righteousness of God, and our Saviour Jesus Christ.   Faith, as it is pitched upon this as its special object, hath a special excellency, and is precious faith, and in this respect every man's faith is as precious as that of the apostles themselves was, though they might excel in degree, yet its preciousness is not from its own degree of acting, but from the object that it is pitched upon, even because it is faith in God, and in our Saviour Jesus Christ.

And let me add this too, it is not only special, as we say of remedies of a disease, that there are many remedies for such a disease, Oh, but this is a special one, not only a sovereign one above all the rest, but it is the only special remedy; for faith only as it is pitched upon the righteousness of Christ, and the free grace of God in him, so it only justifieth.

So now I have expressed to you by way of explication what I mean by special faith in that sense wherein it doth differ from some who would have it called special in other respects. Now the consideration of this point is of exceeding great moment, both to direct your hearts what faith especially continually to exercise, as will appear in the use of it, and also especially to clear the doctrine of saving justifying faith. The papists and popish spirits, what have they done? They say that there is a general faith; that is, that faith which a man hath of all the Scriptures, and the things revealed in them, which they call *fides catholica*, catholic faith, and this they affirm to be the faith that justifies. They say, that faith saveth and justifieth, or God doth save and justify me upon my believing that he is true, that he is omniscient, that he is all-powerful, as well as upon believing on his grace and mercy, and upon God as justifying. They say, that faith doth justify and save as well when it looks to the law, when it believes that God created the world, when it doth believe the first Adam, as well as when it believes the second Adam. They say, that to believe truly the justice of God condemning, is saving and justifying faith, as well as to believe the mercy and grace of God pardoning and saving. The truth is, according to their doctrine, to believe the devil to be an accuser, is a part of justifying faith, as truly as to believe that Christ is an intercessor and a Saviour; to believe that of Moses, that ' Cursed is every one that continueth not in all that is written in the book of the law to do it,' is part of justifying faith, as truly as to believe that Jesus Christ was made a curse; and indeed to hold this, is consonant to all their principles. For how do they assert that faith justifies? Say they, faith doth not justify us in relation to its object, but either as it is a disposition, and so to believe the threatenings of the law, disposeth, say they, to faith, or else it justifies as all other graces do. Now, love to man they say justifieth, as well as love to God. So the belief of all the stories in the Bible, they say, that justifies a man, as well as to believe in God that justifies, or in Jesus Christ that died. It agrees, I say, with the principles of their doctrine, they make all to be parts of righteousness alike; the whole wisdom whereby Timothy did know the scriptures (as they say) saved him, as well as faith in Jesus Christ; whereas here the text is clear, that all the other were made wisdom to him unto salvation, but through faith which is in Christ Jesus; that had he known all the rest never so much, or never so spiritually, they would not have saved him, had he not had special faith in Jesus Christ. In a word, that faith that sanctifies also justifies with them. Now the belief of all things in the Scripture is a means of sanctifying (as must be acknowledged), but that which doth justify us is a special faith, pitched upon the grace of God justifying. and upon our Lord Jesus Christ. So much now for the explication of this thing.

2. I come next, for the further explication of it, to some concessions, as I call them, or grants, some things that may and must be yielded to, as concerning faith upon these objects.

(1.) That all other spiritual faith pitched upon any other object besides God as justifying, and Christ as for righteousness and salvation, is a saving faith in a large sense.   I say that spiritual faith which hath all the Scriptures, and all things in the Scriptures for its object, may be called a saving faith in this sense, that it is unto salvation; so the text is clear, ' The Scriptures, they are able to make thee wise unto salvation.'   All things delivered in the Scriptures being believed, the faith and the belief of them is unto salvation, it tends unto salvation; but how?   As all things else are said to be unto salvation that are true graces in a man, so it is called ' repentance unto salvation,' ' repentance unto life.'   Unto life it is true, without which God saveth no man, and which are in order to it; but special faith pitched upon Jesus Christ, and upon the grace of God, is saving in a higher sense than so; for if you mark it, those other are said to be unto salvation only because and by reason of special faith; they would not be unto salvation, but only because joined with, or subservient to, or springing from faith in Jesus Christ : ' They are able to make thee wise unto salvation,' saith he, ' through faith which is in Jesus Christ.' It is called wisdom unto salvation, but yet in a more peculiar manner this special faith is the faith which saveth us; for the other is called only wisdom unto salvation, even through this faith.   Now if that the other be unto salvation, as through the faith in Jesus Christ, then the faith in Jesus Christ must be in a special manner saving.   Now how is that in a special manner saving, but because there is nothing else in man that doth receive salvation, and the right to salvation, as I have shewn elsewhere?*   All other general faith, that is, faith upon all other things else spiritually and truly apprehended, is a wisdom unto salvation; but it is not peculiarly said to be saving, or to be that which saveth us : we are only saved through faith on Christ and his righteousness.   To clear by the way likewise another thing, you shall find that the apostle doth apply that place, Hab ii. 4, ' The just shall live by faith,' both unto that special faith in man which lays hold on the righteousness of Christ for justification and salvation, and likewise to that general faith, whereby we believe all things else in the word of God.   He applies it first unto justifying faith clearly in Rom. i. 17, where, speaking of the gospel, he saith, ' It is the power of God unto salvation, to every one that believeth, for,' saith he, ' therein is the righteousness of God revealed from faith to faith : as it is written, The just shall live by faith.' Now, in Heb. x. 38, he likewise saith, ' The just shall live by faith ;' but the faith he there means is a general faith, as believing that there is a God, and all spiritual objects else, as he opens it throughout that chapter, which, in the general notion of it, he calls, ' the substance of things hoped for, and the evidence of things not seen,' in the following chapter, Heb. xi. 1. So that I say, in a large sense, it may be said that all graces as well as this are unto salvation.   In a large sense we may be said to live by that general faith (as I may so call it) to live by the belief of anything else in the word of God, with affections suited to that knowledge and that faith. It helps us to mortify lusts, it helps us to quicken many graces in us : whatsoever God sanctifies us by, that faith takes it in, and so in a sense it may be called a life of faith; in temporal temptations it upholds us by many temporal promises, a thousand considerations there are in the word which are not the objects of special faith; but now the faith by which we live the life of justification and of salvation, the faith by which we live in God's sight (as the Scripture's expression is), is only a special faith, which, in Rom. v. 18, is called, ' justification of life ;' and indeed this very dis-

* In Eph. ii. 8, in the 1st vol. of his Works. [Vol. II. of this edition.—ED.]

tinction and difference doth salve a great objection of the papists, and doth reconcile those two places, Rom. i. 17, and the whole eleventh chapter of the Hebrews.

(2.) The second concession, or grant, or caution (call it what you will), which also is a great truth, is this, that it is the same principle of faith by which we believe all things in the Scripture thus savingly and unto salvation, and by which we believe on Jesus Christ too; it is the same principle, or seed, or habit of faith by which we believe that Christ is the Son of God, and by which we believe on him for righteousness; it is the same principle of faith by which we believe that God is (as the apostle saith, Heb. xi. 6), and by which we believe on him for justification. You have an instance in Abraham; by the same faith whereby he believed, and looked at the promised Messiah, in whom all the nations of the earth should be blessed, whereby he was justified, and which was accounted unto him for righteousness, by the same faith he believed the power of God, ' that God was able,' as the expression is in Rom. iv. 21. And this answers another objection also, a great one, which is used to be made; for, say they, saving faith is commended to us in the Scripture by other acts than by the act of justifying; it is said to overcome kingdoms in Heb. xi. 33, and to have done all those great acts which were done in the Old Testament, which yet were not acts of justifying faith; and the apostle doth make justifying faith, and the faith that did all those great acts, to proceed from one and the same root. We answer, indeed it is true that justifying faith is commended to us by other acts which it hath done besides that of saving men; and the apostle's scope in Heb. xi. is to set out that faith whereby we are justified, by all things else which it doth, thereby to commend it the more as justifying us, as indeed it must needs do. Just as the Scripture doth, it sets out Jesus Christ not only as a Saviour, but it sets him out also in a world of excellencies else, as that in him and by him all things were created also, and that he is the judge of all the world and of all mankind, that he is the head of all principalities and powers, of all the angels, and by a thousand excellencies besides, and all these are to commend him so much the more to us as a Saviour; so the apostle sets out faith in this Heb xi. (and you shall find it likewise in other scriptures), that the faith that justifies us is said to do a world of exploits for us besides justifying. But yet it doth not justify us as doing any of those things; as Christ he doth not save us as he is a head of all principalities and powers, or as all things were created in him and by him, but he saves us as dying upon the cross; only it is the same Saviour that doth the one and the other, and therein lies his excellency. So it is here as to faith, and that answers what the apostle's scope is in that Heb. xi. It is not so much to treat of faith as justifying, as to shew forth the excellency of that faith which doth justify in other things, which it continually doth for them it justifies.

(3.) There is this also to be granted, that special faith it is not true in any man, and therefore saveth no man if joined with unbelief and denial of many other things besides believing on Christ for righteousness. There are, I say, many things which, if a man should deny and not believe, besides believing on Christ and on God that justifieth, he would not be saved, nor could he believe savingly with this special faith I now mention unless he believed them. In 2 Tim. ii. 18, the apostle saith that denying of the resurrection did ' overthrow the faith of some;' for, saith he in 1 Cor. xv. 13, 'If there be no resurrection, then is Christ not risen: and if Christ be not risen, then is our preaching vain, and your faith is also vain, and ye are yet in your sins,' and so you overturn the faith in Christ for the pardon of sin; so that now a man cannot have a right saving, justifying faith upon God as justifying, or upon the righteousness of Christ, if he deny many other things.   There are those that say they believe on Christ as a Saviour, believe on him as an intercessor and mediator, and yet, notwithstanding, deny him to be God.   Now, although we are not saved by believing that Jesus Christ is God, but by believing on his righteousness, and on his satisfaction and obedience, as the scripture expresseth it, yet, notwithstanding, we cannot savingly believe the one if we deny the other.   And the truth is, those that deny Jesus Christ to be God, they do clearly, be they who they will be, take away the gospel and the foundation thereof, and the satisfaction of the wrath of God for sin made by Jesus Christ, which the gospel holds forth, and which is the object of our faith. That place in 2 Peter i. 1, which I quoted before to another purpose, is a place that affordeth abundance in it to the present purpose: ' To them,' saith he, ' that have obtained like precious faith with us, in (or on) the righteousness of God and our Saviour Jesus Christ.'   Here you see he describeth the faith of the primitive Christians, that special peculiar faith, which yet was common to all them that were true believers ; it was upon the righteousness of our God and our Saviour Jesus Christ.   Now, here is the question, Whether that our God and our Saviour be two distinct persons, or whether it be meant only of Jesus Christ? for in the original it is, and so Beza reads it, our God, and our Saviour Jesus Christ.   To decide this, it is clearly meant one person, viz., Christ. For, *first*, the article τοῦ clearly carries it ; it is not said twice, as it would have been if two persons had been intended ; it is not said, ' of our God and of our Saviour Jesus Christ,' but ' of our God and our Saviour Jesus Christ.'   And then, *secondly*, you shall find that this is the style of the New Testament, that when it speaks of God the Father, he is called God and the Father, and when it speaks of Christ, he is called God and our Saviour ; as, for example, speaking of God the Father in Eph. i. 3, saith he, ' the God and Father;' God and Father there are one person, and he speaks not of two, but of one ; for (which also confirms the first reason) the article ὁ it is put before God, but not before Father, it is not the God and the Father, but the God and Father, speaking of one ; the like you have in 1 Cor. xv. 24, and in Col. ii. 2.   This, I say, is the proper style of the New Testament concerning God the Father.   Answerably, when the Scripture speaks of Jesus Christ, he is called God and our Saviour ; so you have it expressly in Titus ii. 13, ' Looking for the appearing of the great God and our Saviour Jesus Christ.'   As by God and the Father is meant God the Father, so by God and our Saviour is meant Jesus Christ.   Here now is the faith, the common faith of the primitive Christians ; it is faith on the righteousness of him who is our God and our Saviour, and men can never truly believe upon his righteousness unto salvation unless they believe that he is a God as well as a Saviour, for he had never else been a Saviour had he not been God, and his righteousness had never been the righteousness of a Saviour had it not been the righteousness of God ; and therefore to deny him to be God is to deny his satisfaction, and he that denies the one denies the other ; ' denying the Lord that bought them,' saith he in 2 Peter ii. 1.   Now then, though special faith hath for its object Jesus Christ as a Saviour, and his righteousness as that of a Saviour, yet a man must believe other things too concerning Jesus Christ, as here he must believe that he is God also.   There are many other things a man must believe, and believe them strongly too, which fall under the nature of general faith, which yet are necessary to special faith, so that he who denies them cannot have true special faith. Take away Christ as being God, and you even take away the Saviour too, for they go both together ; and accordingly it was the general faith of all those primitive Christians to believe in the righteousness of Jesus Christ as God and as our Saviour.

(4.) The fourth concession or grant which I shall mention, which, though it seems to be all one with the other before, yet hath a difference, is this, that to this special faith on Christ and on the grace of God, there is the faith of other things requisite, either implicitly or explicitly. It is not only that he who denies some things, which are believed with a general faith, cannot have a true special faith, since the denial of the one cannot stand with the truth of the other, which was the meaning of the foregoing concession ; but that unless a man believe many things, which yet are but the objects of a general faith, either implicitly or explicitly, he can never come to have true special faith. We may see this in the instance of the eunuch in the confession of his faith, Acts viii. 37. He says no more but that he believed 'Jesus to be the Son of God,' but yet withal, his faith was pitched upon Christ as a Saviour dying for sinners, for the occasion of his believing was Philip's interpreting to him the 53d chapter of Isaiah, which openly mentions Christ's being wounded for our sins ; and the eunuch adds in his confession, that he believed Jesus to be that person who was intended, and he believed too that this person was the Son of God, as that which alone made his death and offering himself for sinners satisfactory unto God, for he accordingly desires to be baptized for remission of sins as obtained by Christ. His believing him to be the Son of God is indeed only mentioned, because this was the great thing necessary in order to his believing on him as a Saviour, but yet this last is as strongly implied and intended. To the same purpose we have another scripture, Heb. xi. 6, ' He that cometh to God must believe that he is, and that he is a rewarder of them that diligently seek him.' He that cometh to God is he that cometh to believe on him, cometh to him for salvation, for faith is often so expressed, though special faith lies in coming to God for mercy, believing upon his grace, believing on him that justifieth the ungodly ; yet a man must believe first that God is, and that spiritually, and he must be wise in that point savingly too. A man must believe also that God is just, and the justifier of him that believeth in Jesus, that he is true and faithful in his promises ; therefore a man is said, when he believeth, to ' set to his seal that God is true.' Yet, to believe the truth of God, to believe the justice of God, to believe that God is, all these belong to general faith, to the same faith wherewith I believe a thousand things else in the Scripture. Only let me say this, it is not necessary that a man should believe all these explicitly, that is, in distinct propositions, especially not in a method and order, first this and then that ; as to say, First I came to believe that God was, and then I came to believe that God was true. But when God comes to reveal himself as a justifier, then, as when the sun in one beam sheweth the whole sun to the eye, so it is here, that often at once when God reveals himself as a justifier of the ungodly, to be believed on, he also with that beam enlightens the soul with the knowledge of what other perfections are in him, which may conduce to represent him to us as a justifier of the ungodly. To illustrate this by the instance of Adam's first sin ; as in that there were many sins concurred, but that one sin which the Scripture reckoneth, that one disobedience by which we all fell, was eating the forbidden fruit, so it is here : though there are many acts of believing, yet the one act which justifies is that which regards Christ, and his blood and righteousness. When Abraham was to believe in the promised Messiah, in the promised seed, ' in whom all the nations of the earth should be blessed,' he believed in the power of God too, as I said even now out of Rom. iv. 21 ; and it was absolutely necessary for him so to do, for he knew, according to the promise, that the Messiah could not come unless he had Isaac.   Now, though his faith looked at Christ especially, yet 'to support this faith that the Messiah should come, he believed in the power of God to give him Isaac ; his special faith was supported by his belief on the power of God ; and yet his belief on the power of God, that God was able to do thus and thus, was not that which justified him, for it was but a general faith, and yet I say it supported his special faith.   You have the like in Heb. xi. 19, when he thought to offer up Isaac : his eye was then upon Christ, whom God would raise from the dead, but yet he believed that God was able to raise up Isaac, without which he should never have Christ, nor Christ should never have come.   Abraham's faith was twice put to it, in believing on the power of God concerning Isaac : the one was for his being conceived and born, and the other was when he offered him up ; you have the one in Rom. iv. 19, and the other in Heb. xi. 18.

So that now faith in the general of these truths, that the word of God, or the promises of God, are true, that God is faithful, that he is just, that he is powerful, all these they are the supports of special faith ; but yet still that special faith which I am justified by, is only that whereby I believe upon the grace of Christ, and upon the grace of God as justifying.   Therefore that which divines do say to clear the point of faith justifying alone, may be applied here.   Faith, say they, doth not justify alone, as if it were unaccompanied with other graces ; as the eye though it sees alone, yet if it were alone, if it were out of the head, it would not see.   Now the same do I say of this special faith, it would never come to justify us, if it were not supported with acts of general faith.   A great many of such nerves meet in this eye of special faith upon the grace and mercy of God, and concur therewith ; and though they are before that act, yet are in order unto justification.   When men are humbled for sin, upon the sight of sin as sin, they could never be thus spiritually humbled for sin, if they did not know God spiritually, and the goodness of God : I mean, take goodness in the general sense, as God is good and sin is evil, they could not see sin to be the greatest evil, except they saw God to be the chiefest good ; for as God knows sin by knowing himself, as the schoolmen speak, so we know the evil of sin in that light whereby we know the goodness of that God against whom we have sinned, and from whom sin hath drawn us ; but now a thousand of these acts, if you could suppose so many to precede, are not those whereby we are justified, but they are in order to justification.   A man is never justified, till he be wrought upon to a special throwing of himself upon Christ and his righteousness, and upon God as justifying.

CHAPTER IV.

That a special act of faith on the free grace of God as justifying sinners, and on the blood and righteousness of Christ, is the only true justifying faith.— This proved by several arguments.—What are the reasons why God hath singled out this special faith to be that faith upon which he justifies.—The uses.

3. Having explained the nature of special justifying faith, and what acts conduce to it, I come now to demonstrate, that it is only by this special

faith that we obtain an interest in Christ and his righteousness unto salvation and justification.

(1.) You know that there is a special part of God's word, which is the gospel, even as Christ, the grand subject of it, is called eminently ὁ λόγος, 'the Word,' John i. 1. Now what is the gospel? Truly it is nothing else (take it strictly in the special sense and meaning of it) but that doctrine which holds forth the grace of God justifying, pardoning, and saving sinners, and which holds forth Jesus Christ made righteousness to us. Now then, this gospel it is called in a peculiar respect 'the word of faith;' and for what respect but this? because it is a special object of a special faith which God saveth us by. The apostle, in Rom. x. 8, speaking of the gospel in distinction from the law, and from all else in the Scripture, saith, 'This is the word of faith which we preach.' What is that same special word of faith? He tells us, ver. 9, 'That' (so we read it, but some translate it *nempe*, or), 'namely this, if thou shalt confess with thy mouth the Lord Jesus, and believe with thy heart, thou shalt be saved;' and the Scripture saith, ver. 11, 'Whosoever believeth on him shall not be ashamed.' This is called the word of faith, which holdeth forth this special object of the special faith of a believer. And then again, in Gal. iii. 1, 2, the gospel it is called the 'hearing of faith,' having spoken of Christ being crucified before their eyes in the words before; so also in 1 Tim. iii. 9, it is called 'the mystery of faith.' Now as the gospel is called in a special manner the word of faith, so in us that faith is called special faith which relateth to this word, and the rest is rather called 'wisdom to salvation,' whereby we know all things else in the Scripture; but this carries the name of faith, and is called 'faith in Jesus Christ,' and therefore it is is called 'faith of the truth,' 2 Thes. ii. 13, that is, of the gospel; it is not only faith of truth, take it in general any truth revealed in the word, but faith of *that* truth; 'God hath chosen you to salvation,' saith he, 'through faith of *the* truth.' As the gospel is called the word of faith, so on the other side faith is called the faith of the gospel, Phil. i. 27. Thus it is a special faith, because it has this special object.

(2.) Then again add this to it, that though the apostles were to preach all the word of God, yet they had a special ministry: 'The word of faith which we preach,' saith Paul in Rom. x. 8. Now the faith that is to be in Christians, it is to be suited to their ministry: 'So we preach, and ye believed,' 1 Cor. xv. 11. Now then, if that preaching of remission of sins in the name of Christ, if preaching the righteousness of God through faith, the righteousness of faith which is in the Son of God, if this were the special proper ministry of the apostles, then that is the special faith of a Christian which is suited to this ministry. Now it is evident that this was the special thing that they preached. In Acts xx. 24, thus saith the apostle, 'So that I might finish my course with joy, and the ministry which I have received of the Lord Jesus.' What was that? 'To testify the gospel of the grace of God.' Take the gospel as it holds forth the grace of God, that is, that special grace of God, his free grace in pardoning, saving, and justifying sinners, this is the special ministry (saith he) which I received of Jesus Christ. You have it likewise elsewhere often professed by the apostle.

When Jesus Christ began to preach, he began with this, Mark i. 15, 'Repent, and believe the gospel,' the gospel of grace, and the gospel that holds forth Christ; and as he began, so he ended with it: Mark xvi. 15, 'Go and preach the gospel, and he that believeth shall be saved.' And when he was in heaven, what was the commission he gave to Paul? Paul said, in the place I cited even now, that his ministry was to ' testify the gospel of the grace of God.' Now what was Paul's commission given him by Christ from heaven ? See Acts xxvi. 18, ' I send thee to the Gentiles, to open their eyes, and to turn them from darkness to light, and from the power of Satan unto God ; that they may receive forgiveness of sins, and an inheritance among them which are sanctified by faith that is in me.'

(3.) Consider this likewise, that when any of the people came to Christ, or came to the apostles, to know what to do to be saved, still they directed them to faith upon a special object for salvation. What saith Paul to the poor jailor in Acts xvi. 31, when he asked what he should do to be saved ? He gives him the most sovereign, special, only remedy, ' Believe on the Lord Jesus, and thou shalt be saved.' He doth not bid him believe on God simply, and believe that God is powerful, just, &c., but he points his faith to that which is the special object of it, ' Believe on the Lord Jesus,' saith he. You may have in the Scripture, and in the New Testament, descriptions of one that shall be saved, by faith on other things besides believing on Jesus Christ, but you shall never have a direction (when a man comes to ask what he shall do to be saved) unto any thing else. So in John vi. 29, Christ himself, when they asked him, what they should do, that they might work the works of God, he directs them to this, ' Believe on him whom he hath sent.'

(4.) Consider, that all the saints from the beginning of the world, especially under the New Testament, do profess their trusting upon the special grace and mercy of God, as the special object of their faith. You have them brought both together, both the saints in the Old and in the New Testament, in Acts xv. 11, and they both meet in this centre, in this special faith. The apostle there had in the very words before spoken of their fathers under the Old Testament, and he had said, that the law was a yoke, which neither we nor our fathers were able to bear ; how shall we be saved now ? and how were they saved then ? Mark what follows : ' But we believe that through the grace of our Lord Jesus Christ'—I take it, that by the grace of our Lord Jesus Christ is not meant the grace personally in Jesus Christ, but that grace which God beareth us through Jesus Christ— ' we shall be saved, even as they,' or (as the words is in the Greek), ' after the manner they were ;' and all by believing, and that for salvation, having that special aim, and acting our faith upon the grace of God in Jesus Christ. This (as I said before) was the special faith of all the primitive Christians : 2 Peter i. 1, ' To all them,' saith he (for none else are true Christians but those), ' that have obtained like faith' (even this special faith), ' on the righteousness of God and our Saviour Jesus Christ ;' and in 1 Peter i. 21, there you shall see what manner of Christians they were, and what their faith was upon : ' Who by him do believe in God that raised him from the dead, and gave him glory, that your faith and hope might be in God.' This is the description of the primitive believers, they believed in God through Jesus Christ, in God justifying through Jesus Christ ; and this was the faith of the apostles themselves : Gal. ii. 16, ' We,' saith he, speaking of the apostles, ' have believed in Jesus Christ, that we might be justified ;' and there, ' in him, and the faith of Jesus,' is three times mentioned, as being that which only we are justified by ; and in Rev. xiv. 12, you have all the saints described by this, that they keep the faith of Jesus ; they are described by this special faith.

(5.) Lastly, It appeareth that it is through this special faith that we are thus saved, having this special object, because it is not said only, that all that do believe shall be saved through him ; which you have in Acts xiii. 39,

'By him,' saith he, 'all that believe shall be justified, and receive forgiveness of sins.' But whereas some might say (and truly it might be objected), Suppose I believe, though it be on something else, yet I may be saved by Christ, and for Christ's sake meritoriously; therefore, to obviate this, there are two places more, which if you do but add, you will see that it is not only all that believe shall be saved *through* him, but, through him all shall be saved that believe *on* him also; that is, as none but believers, and such as have faith, are saved, and saved through faith, so their faith must be on him too by which they are saved; for so it is expressly said in Acts x. 43, 'Through his name whosoever believeth in him shall receive remission of sins.' The like you have in Acts xxvi. 18, 'By faith which is in me.' And therefore now here is the thing wherein the strength of the argument lies: the Scripture doth not only say, 'He that believeth shall be saved;' for so it saith too, He that repenteth shall be saved, and faith is not only said to be unto salvation, for so repentance is said to be unto salvation; but it is plainly expressed, He that believeth is saved by believing on him. *Qui credit et credendo quidem salvatur*, who believes, and is indeed saved by believing. And this is yet more express: Rom. iii. 22, 'This' (says he) 'is it that is witnessed by the law and all the prophets, even the righteousness of God, which is by faith of Jesus Christ, to all and upon all that believe.' He confesses not himself to have said, on them that believe, but more emphatically also adds, by faith; so as this righteousness is not only said to be on them that believe, for it is on them that repent too, but it is also expressed that it is by believing: 'It is the righteousness of God, which is by faith on them that believe;' and this faith is the faith of Christ. Add to this that place in Gal. iii. 22, where there is the like duplication, 'The Scripture hath concluded all under sin, that the promise by the faith of Jesus Christ might be given to them that believe.' It is given, and by believing on Christ. And all argues, that as salvation is by faith alone, so that it is by faith upon this special object, upon Jesus Christ.

4. But you will ask me, What is it in Christ that is the special object of this special faith?

I shall give you an answer out of the Scripture in a word or two. You shall find it to be faith in his blood, and faith in his righteousness, or in his obedience. Faith in his blood you have in Rom. iii. 15, and faith in his righteousness you have in that place I have so often quoted, 2 Pet. i. 1. These are the matter of our justification, which the soul hath recourse unto, to be accepted for, and to have them imputed to it.

If you ask, answerably to both these, for what it is that the soul comes to Christ, believeth on his blood, believeth on his righteousness, to obtain what?

I answer, It is to obtain two things, the one answering his blood, and the other answering his righteousness, viz., 'remission of sins, and an inheritance among them that are sanctified,' these being the two legacies which the soul comes for; and both 'by faith that is in me,' saith Christ, in Acts xxvi. 18; so that indeed there is the whole obedience of Christ, active and passive, blood and righteousness, for remission of sins, and for an inheritance, as thus you have them singly mentioned in several scriptures; and to give you them both in one scripture, Rom. v., first at the 9th verse, saith he, 'Being now justified by his blood;' and what doth his blood serve to justify us from more peculiarly? 'From wrath:' 'Being justified by his blood,' saith he, 'we shall be saved from wrath through him;' and elsewhere we are said to be justified from sin and from wrath; and then, in ver. 18, 19 of that chapter, 'As by the disobedience of one many were made sinners' (viz., that act of Adam's disobedience imputed to them), ' so by the obedience of one many are made righteous' (so the word is), they are constituted righteous by that righteousness and obedience. He had spoken of his blood before, ver. 9, he now speaks of his righteousness, for he opposeth it to that actual disobedience of the law which Adam committed, which consisted of one act; but this is abundance of grace, and of the gift of righteousness. My brethren, we are not made righteous by the act of believing; no, we are constituted and made righteous by that obedience of Christ on which we believe; the text is express for it. Now observe it, as *justified by his blood* takes away wrath, as you have it ver. 9, so our being made righteous by his obedience is for ' justification of life.' Read the very words of the 18th verse, where, speaking of justification of life, which is distinct from remission of sins, and freedom from wrath, he saith, it is by having the righteousness of Christ made ours, we being made righteous by his obedience. So that, I say, this is the special object of faith, and this was the faith of the primitive times.

4. I now come to shew the reasons (which have the greatest harmony in them with all other truths, and have as much conviction in them, being added unto Scripture, as any) to make this thing good, why that God should single out this act of faith, as having in a special manner his grace, and Christ's righteousness for salvation, in its eye. Why God, I say, should single out this act of faith, as that upon which he is said to justify; so that let a man have never so much faith concerning God himself, under all other consideration, be it a belief of the power, justice, truth, or whatsoever it be that doth glorify God never so much, if it be not (if we could suppose them severed) faith towards God as merciful, saving, justifying, &c., it is not justifying. Or, let a man believe never so much of Jesus Christ, and that spiritually too, if he do not believe in Christ as a Saviour, for righteousness and pardon, on his blood for justification, and on his righteousness to be saved by it, all the other faith will do him no good, neither is any other faith said to save or to justify. Now the reasons why God hath singled out this special act of faith in such a peculiar manner, as that which should be peculiarly saving, and upon which he saveth men, they are these :

(1.) Consider what is the end of faith. It must needs be this : to bring us to God, that we may come to him, and close with him, and so may fear him, obey him, or whatever else you will put upon it. Without this, all the world must yield that the end of faith is not attained ; therefore in the Scripture that faith that saveth us is everywhere expressed by a coming to God, and a coming to Jesus Christ. You have the expression frequently in John v. and John vi. ; as, on the contrary, unbelief in those that have the gospel preached to them is expressed by not coming to Jesus Christ, and by departing from the living God; so you have it in John v. 40, and Heb. iii. 12. Now none will come to God unless upon a special ground of confidence in God justifying and accepting. To believe all of God else, to believe that God is true in his word, in all his promises, and not to have the substance of that promise in the eye, viz., that God is a justifier and a Saviour, will be ineffectual; all other promises, and believing on God under all other notions, will never bring a man to God, or make him come unto him, Heb. xi. 6, ' None cometh to God but he that believeth that there is a God, and that he is a rewarder of them that seek him.' Special faith is here expressed by seeking of God. You have the like in Isa. xi. 10, the which if you compare with Rom. xv. 10, they both will open to you that in Heb. xi. 6. In Isa. xi. 10, saith the prophet, ' In that day' (speaking of Christ) ' there shall be a root of Jesse, which shall stand for an ensign to the people, and to him shall the Gentiles seek.' Mark the expression, *seek*; and now compare with this, Rom. xv. 10, and see there what the apostle renders and translates the prophet's seeking into. ' And again,' saith he, quoting this place in Isaiah, ' Esaias saith, there shall be a root of Jesse, and he shall rise to reign over the Gentiles, and in him shall the Gentiles trust.' Mark it, *seeking* and *trusting* they are put all for one ; I allege it for this, that the notion of seeking in that Heb. xi. 6, is believing on God, and expressed both by seeking and coming to him. Now, saith the apostle in Heb. xi. 6, there must be a twofold apprehension in a man for the ground of his coming to God : 1, an apprehension and a spiritual belief that God *is ;* 2, that he is the *rewarder* of them that seek him, or (if you will, in the apostle's language elsewhere) of them that trust in him, or believe in him. It is not therefore simply the belief of all things concerning God that will bring a man's soul to seek to him, or to come to him, unless God be considered as he promiseth himself a reward, as he did to Abraham. The blessing of Abraham in forgiving his sins, and giving him heaven, whereby was it expressed ? ' I will be thy reward,' saith God in Gen. xvii. 1, or it may have relation to that in Ps. ix. 10, ' They that know thy name will put their trust in thee, for thou hast not forgotten them that seek thee.' Thou art a God that dost regard, and hast a special regard to them that seek thee, and do trust in thee ; for seeking and trusting are put both for one in that psalm likewise. Now what was the name of God in the Old Testament, which did draw in the hearts of all his people to trust in him, and to seek him ? It was, ' The Lord God, gracious and merciful, pardoning iniquity, transgression, and sin,' Exod. xxxiv. 6. This was his name, and those that knew it and believed it spiritually, they trusted in him, and looked upon him as one that was a rewarder, and ' not forgetful ' (which is all one, for a diminutive expression implies more than it expresseth) ' of them that seek him.' So that now, if a man would come to God, and be brought to him, it is not all the general faith about God that the soul of man can take in, let him know never so much of it, that will do it, unless he withal know him in his special promise of favour, and of being a reward to them that trust in him ; otherwise men are driven away from God, men will never come to him, if it were not for a promise of special mercy, pardoning them, accepting them, and rewarding them : ' There is mercy with thee that thou mayest be feared,' saith the psalmist in Ps. cxxx. 4–7. No man would fear God, would come to him, would seek to him, or worship him, or meddle with him, let him have never so much faith in all things else, if it were not that there is ' mercy with him, and plenteous redemption,' as it follows there. Men would not seek God, nor come to God, but under the notion of a God promising reconciliation in Christ, promising to be a reward in Christ, and to be favourable in Christ.

The papists (that I may shew you the deceits and mistakes of men all along as I go in this great point) they tell us that it is general faith, faith to believe all things else of God, as well as to believe upon God giving of himself out to us in special promises, that is justifying faith ; and therefore they do find fault with Calvin, and blame him and others of our protestant writers, for saying that the schoolmen erred in making God (simply considered) the object of faith ; and for saying that God in Christ, God as justifying, God as rewarding and pardoning sin, as he is thus, is the special object of faith ; and they seem to argue strongly for their opinion. I shall mention their argument, and answer it in a word. Say they, the primary object of faith must needs be God himself, simply considered, in all his attributes, and not in any special manner, God in Christ, or God in respect of grace and mercy; because, take God as justifying, and God revealed in Christ, that is but a secondary thing to God himself, it is but *attributum secundarium*, an attribute at second hand, by reason of his own purpose taken up to shew mercy to sinners, therefore, say they, that which is not the primary thing in God cannot be the primary object of our faith. And then farther they argue thus too: vision in heaven succeedeth faith, but to know God in himself, or God to be all in all, to know God in all his excellencies, this, say they, is the perfection of heaven; therefore God so considered must needs be a more perfect object of faith than to consider God as justifying us, or God revealed in Christ; for, say they, faith and vision have the same object, only with this variation, that God is revealed obscurely to our faith here in this life, but clearly in the world to come.

For answer to this, and so to clear this first reason that I have mentioned before I go off of it, I say, God himself, simply considered in himself, is not the primary object of our faith; for faith cannot see God as in himself, none can see God and live; that is appointed indeed for vision in the world to come. We must therefore make that the primary object of our faith which is suited to us, and suited to the way of believing by God's ordination, and to a man's mind and spirit here in this life, as we are in our way to heaven; and therefore now to go and throw off Christ and faith in him, and make communion with God as God all in all, immediately in himself, to be justifying faith, though there is such a communion with him in the world to come, when God shall be all in all, yet this is not suited to what we see here in this life, therefore we must take that to be the primary object of faith which is ordained to be so unto us while we are here. Now, God is revealed to us here in this life two ways: either by such words or names which he hath given himself as do express his attributes, which are his back-parts, as that he is called just, and faithful, and true, and gracious, and merciful, and knowing all things, &c.; or else God is to be considered as he is revealed to us in Jesus Christ, in the word of the gospel which is preached to us, for what is Jesus Christ but God manifested in the flesh? Now, then, of the two, which do you think is the chief object of our faith, whether God revealed in his attributes, or God revealed in Christ? Certainly God revealed in Christ. I yield you that God known in himself is beyond both these, for both these are but means to know him by; but of the two, I say, God in Christ is the special object of our faith, the other is but a secondary thing in comparison of this. Why? Because it was the knowledge of God which they had in the Old Testament; and the truth is, that aboundeth with such a knowledge of God, in words expressing his attributes, and if that had been the more perfect, then all that addition that Jesus Christ hath brought by the revelation of himself had been in vain. Now, if our minds could arrive at God immediately, we needed neither the one nor the other.

So that the sum of the answer is this, that it is true that the knowledge of God simply considered in his nature, in his being, in all his excellencies, when he is known, is most excellent; but the question is of that way of knowing him which God hath appointed us in this life. And so, I say, the knowledge of God in Christ is the most excellent, and Jesus Christ is he that makes all the attributes of God (which is another way of knowing him in this life) more conspicuous than they were in the Old Testament; therefore Christ, and God revealed in Christ, pardoning, justifying, saving, and all that Jesus Christ hath done to that end, is to us the primary object of faith.

(2.) Another reason why God hath appointed such a special faith to be justifying, is, because men that are sinners (for in that consideration the strength of the reason lies, or at least there is thereby a further strength added to the former) can never come to close with God; they can never come to seek him, but under the representation of God in Christ, and of God pardoning, and God justifying. This is certain, that the more strongly a sinner believes all things that are in God, all his excellencies, his holiness, his power, his justice, take all the attributes that are in God; the more strongly, I say, he believes these, if he should not withal apprehend this God as one that not only hath mercy in his nature, but that holds forth mercy in his promises, and in Christ, for the pardon of sin and for salvation, the more it will drive a sinner off from God, unless the special grace or mercy of God, as it is held forth in the promise, be revealed to that man's soul; and then, indeed, the more strongly he believes all the excellencies that are in God, the more such a belief will strengthen his heart to come to God, and to believe in him, when once he hath closed with him under the notion of merciful, and justifying, and pardoning in and through Christ; otherwise, I say, it puts men off from God; so it did Cain, so it did Adam, who ran away from God. And what is the reason that the devils believe and tremble? It is, because all that they know and apprehend of God hath no special promise of mercy to them as sinners from that God. They know that God is merciful, but because there is not a declaration of God's will to be merciful to such as are in their condition, because they know that his mercy is limited to men, that good-will is to men on earth, as the angels sung, Luke ii. 14, and not unto devils in hell, that no name is given unto men by which they can be saved but only the name of Christ, and not to devils; therefore the more, I say, that they know of God, the more they tremble, and the more they go off from God; but it is God apprehended under that special notion, as one that hath a name of being merciful, put out in his promises to such sinners as we are, that draws sinners to him.

So that let papists and popish spirits, that would have a general faith to save us, dispute what they will, that God, considered in himself, is the chief object of faith, yet still clearly take us as sinners, God, as a justifier of sinners, out of his infinite mercy and grace, is the chief object of faith unto us. You have it plainly in Rom. iv. 5, ' To him that believeth on him that justifieth the ungodly, is faith accounted for righteousness.' Go, take a man that is ungodly, and how will this man ever come to believe in God, unless under this notion, that he is one that justifies the ungodly? And therefore that is the faith that is accounted for righteousness. It is not believing that God is true, or holy, or just, simply considered in himself, if a man believe these never so strongly, that will justify him; but to believe on God under this notion, that he is a justifier of the ungodly, this is a man's faith which is accounted to him for righteousness. Without this, it is certain sinners would have no heart to come unto God. You have an excellent expression to this purpose in Eph. iii. 12, where, speaking of Jesus Christ, and so of God, considered as in Christ revealed, he saith, ' In whom' (having spoken of Christ in the very words before) ' we have boldness and access with confidence by the faith of him.' Here is the special faith expressed, which is pitched either upon God as justifying in Christ, or upon Christ through whom God justifieth. Now go, take a sinner, he would never have any boldness, never have any confidence, so much as to come to God; he would have no heart to do it; he would be driven off from him, if he did not first look on God as in Christ; for, mark it, he mentions Christ twice, ' In whom we have boldness by the faith of him.' The meaning is this, that take the reality of the thing itself, the access, the leave that God giveth for sinners to come to him, it is in and by Christ. *In whom*, saith he ; God really admitteth men to him, or else would not do it. And as thus for the reality of the thing, it is in Christ, and without him there would be no access to God, so it is only that man who apprehendeth Christ, and cometh to God through Christ, that hath this access with confidence, and therefore that is added, *by the faith of him*. For this is a true rule, which will never deceive us, that look what it is that moveth God to accept us, the apprehension of that in God strengtheneth our hearts to come unto him to be accepted. Now if God did not look upon us in Jesus Christ, there were no acceptation of us on God's part; and if we, on the other side, did not by faith look upon God through Jesus Christ, there would be no confidence, no boldness, but the heart would go back; therefore he puts in both, ' In whom,' saith he, ' through the faith of whom, we have boldness, and confidence, and access to God.' If there were a glass (to make such a supposition) through and by which the sun did shine upon the world, and take that glass away, and the sun did not shine; and, on the other side, if that the eyes of men and other creatures were so weak that they could not behold the sun but through that glass; if both these were true, what a great necessity were there that the means of the sight of the sun should be still as through that glass. So is it here; God himself, out of Christ, shineth not upon sinners, neither can the sore, the weak eye of a sinner dare to behold that God, which is a consuming fire, but as looking through this glass; and therefore, I say, though man in his primitive innocent state had another way and means of coming to God, as Adam had, yet notwithstanding now, as sinners, we have not. And let me tell you this too, that, take Adam's condition, there was a special kind of faith even in him too. He must have believed and known (at least if not by faith, by some other ways,—whether it was by the law of natural righteousness in his heart, I dispute not) that this God did accept him to life, and that he was in his favour. It is true, indeed, he had this knowledge by the intervention of his own good works; otherwise, though Adam had known God to be omniscient, to be holy, to be just, to be true, and to be happy, and perfect, and blessed, if that he had not taken all these attributes of God in at this little hole, the beams shining in at this hole, that this God justifieth me, approveth me upon my obedience,—he had the sight of this through his works and holiness, because the law between Adam and God stood as between a creator and a creature,—all the other knowledge would not have comforted Adam's heart, had not he, I say, apprehended God to justify him; though then, indeed, the way of justification was on the account of Adam's holiness, and through his works. Hence now, therefore, God, as justifying and approving of Adam as a person in his favour, and God as his God was the primary notion under which Adam looked upon God, and to him all the other were but as secondary in comparison of this, much more is it so to a poor sinner. And therefore, now let us consider God justifying us out of grace (for otherwise, if we consider ourselves under the first covenant, all the attributes of God come in upon us with terror), and then all his attributes shining but through this one consideration, that God is a God that justifies sinners, come in sweetly upon us. And therefore, let popish spirits say what they will, yet still unto us as sinners it is God as gracious, God as justifying, it is God as in Christ revealed, which is the proper and special object of justifying faith. For, consider, when a sinner doth turn to God, and come to believe in good earnest, what is the chief thing he hath in his eye in the knowledge of himself? He hath the guilt of sin, poor soul! I am, saith he, obnoxious to the wrath of the great God; this is the chief, the first thing he hath then in his eye; therefore, now answerably in his seeking unto God, what hath his faith recourse unto? To that God who justifies the ungodly, and to that Christ through whom he doth it; and therefore he hath recourse to them for justification first, and sanctification afterwards. And why? Because the power of sin is not first in his eye, but the guilt of sin, therefore answerably justification (take him as he is a sinner), and God as justifying, and Christ as justifying, must needs be in his eye first, and then afterward Christ as sanctifying. Adam, he might have leave to study all the attributes of God, one after another, by pieces and parcels, and pick and choose which he would think of first, even as scholars do pieces of divinity; and God might draw out an act of faith and knowledge of or to himself, under this attribute or that attribute, as he pleased; but this poor soul that is a sinner, when it comes to God, he hath not the leisure to look over all things else in God, or, if he hath, he is terrified with them; but, saith he, I am lost. And what is the first question he asketh? 'What shall I do to be saved?' That is the first question in order of nature; therefore, now, if you will answer this poor soul's question, you must tell him of God in Christ, and of God's saving and justifying sinners in Christ.

(3.) A third reason why God hath appropriated our salvation to such a special faith on Christ is, because it is unto that faith, the object of which only pacifieth the heart against condemnation, that God only doth annex justification. If to any at all it must needs be that faith, the object of which alone pacifieth the heart against guilt and condemnation; but now only the faith that is in Jesus Christ and his righteousness, and upon God as justifying, hath that for its object which alone is able to quiet and pacify the heart against condemnation, therefore God hath annexed alone to this faith our being justified. Yea, it is this which first puts in the chief life into the soul: Rom. i. 17, 'The righteousness of God is revealed from faith to faith;' and it follows, 'The just shall live by faith.' The greatest death is in the guilt of sin, so that if we could suppose that a general faith could act against the power of sin, yet it could not raise the soul from death in the guilt of it, until the righteousness of God which acquits it be revealed, Col. ii. 12, 13; to this also accord those places which express, that 'he who seeth the Son hath life,' and that 'he who believeth on the Son hath life,' John iii. 26, 1 John v. 11, Gal. ii. 20. But will you first, before I proceed to prove this, mark how I express myself; I say, that faith, the object of which serveth to pacify; I do not say, that faith, the act of which always pacifieth, but whose object alone I must have peace from. Look what thing, what consideration, what apprehension alone must give that soul peace and quiet against condemnation, certainly faith upon that object is it which God hath annexed justification unto. Always the act of faith upon Christ and upon grace doth not bring peace, but there is that in the thing believed, or that will do it in the event. Now the reason of the consequence of this is clear, for justification you know is opposed to condemnation, therefore that object of faith, and that of faith which serveth to pacify the heart only against condemnation, the belief on that thing certainly only justifieth. Now there is nothing but God as justifying, and our Lord and Saviour Jesus Christ, and his righteousness, through whom God justifieth, that is able to pacify and quiet the heart of a sinner; nothing else will do it. We use the like argument against the papists, that therefore we are justified by faith alone.

I will give you clearly a scripture for this, and so pass from it. In Rom. iii. and Rom. iv., the apostle discourseth of faith as justifying, and he makes the object of that faith in chap. iii. to be Jesus Christ; he calleth it ' the faith of Jesus,' ver. 26, &c.; he also makes God as justifying the ungodly the object of faith in chap. iv. ver. 5, and he doth shew that we are justified alone by faith as acted upon those two objects, and not by the works of the law. Now how doth he conclude in chap. v. ver. 1? ' Being justified by faith,' saith he (that is, by this faith on God justifying, and on Jesus Christ, which is the faith only by which he had proved we are justified in the words before), ' we have peace with God through Jesus Christ;' that is, this the only faith that pacifieth the heart; faith only as pitched upon these objects nakedly, and barely, and singly will quiet the heart, and bring peace with God; nothing else will do it. Now I appeal to the experience of all believers, and in this case I may very well do it; I appeal to all your consciences, you that have been exercised in the conflicts of faith and believing, what hath ever quieted your hearts? All that you knew of God or of Jesus Christ would not do it, till you came to lay hold upon the grace of God as justifying ungodly wretches merely for his own name's sake, and till you laid hold on the Lord Jesus Christ, through whom you are justified; nothing else but God nakedly and simply considered, without anything in yourselves, hath ever quieted the heart of you sinners. As the apostle argues from experience in a like case, so do I argue from experience in this case too. The apostle in Gal. iii. 2, when he would prove that it is the gospel only that conveys the Spirit, saith he, ' This only would I learn of you,' you that are so much for the law, I pray tell me your experience, I appeal to your own experience (and experience in this case is a sure rule), ' Received you the Spirit by the works of the law, or by the hearing of faith?' What doth he mean by the Spirit? He means the Spirit of God sealing up salvation to them, as in Eph. i. 13, ' You were sealed by the Spirit of promise,' and ' we have received the Spirit, the anointing,' 1 Cor. ii. 12. Of this Spirit he speaks, for afterwards he speaks of the common gifts of the Spirit, ver. 5. Now I appeal to you, saith he, what was it that did bring this Spirit down into your hearts, thus sealing up salvation to you? Was it all the works of the law that ever you did? No; it was by the hearing of faith, saith he. Now the thing I cite this for, is to shew that in a case and argument of this nature the apostle appeals to the very experience of Christians. What is the reason that the experience of Christians must needs decide such a case as this is? Because that God's dispensations are alway suited to his own appointments or ordinances; that is, you will find that God will only bless his own way, and his own means. Now then (saith the apostle) if works of the law had been a way and a means through which God conveyed his Spirit, some of you would have had the Spirit conveyed to you by works of the law; I appeal to you if ever you had. But, on the contrary, you have found it, and generally found it, that the Spirit was conveyed to you by the hearing of faith. Certainly then this is the truth. Why? Because experience would not second this unless it were God's own appointment and ordination, that the hearing of faith conveyeth the Spirit, for that which God sanctifieth to be effectual hath always the substance of his own ordination in it. Now then in the like manner do I here argue, that faith whose object only quieteth the heart against condemnation is certainly that as pitched on that object alone upon which God doth justify us; now nothing can, or ever did, or will quiet the heart (I appeal to all experience), but this special faith pitched upon the grace of God justifying immediately and freely, and upon the Lord Jesus Christ made justification to us.

(4.) The soul can lay hold upon no promise that God hath made (it cannot only neither come to him, nor treat with him, but can lay hold upon no promise else), neither by way of assurance, nor by way of recumbency; it cannot with any heart cast itself upon God or Christ for the performance of any promise further than as it hath pitched, either by way of assurance or casting itself, upon the special mercy of God to pardon, or accept it in Jesus Christ; and therefore this must needs be the first and principal act of faith. I do not say, that no man can cast himself upon God for any other promise till he be assured that God doth justify him; but till he hath dealt with God for justification as a God that justifieth the ungodly, and as a God thus merciful, and till he hath dealt with Jesus Christ, and come to him for salvation, this soul can never come to him for any other promise with any cheerful heart. It is most certain, you cannot have recourse to God for other promises with any boldness and heartiness further than your hearts are in a proportion strengthened to rest upon, and to have recourse unto the grace of God to justify, and unto our Lord and Saviour Jesus Christ, through whom we are justified; it is a thing which you may make a use of now by the way.

Take this for a rule, that your way when you would deal with God for any temporal promise, it is to renew your faith for your justification and salvation. I will give you an instance or two for it; in John xi. 26, 27, &c., there was the sister of Lazarus, Martha, who was to deal with Jesus Christ, and he with her, concerning the raising of her brother; Christ he tells her that her brother shall rise again: ver. 23, 'Yea,' saith she, 'I know that he shall rise again in the resurrection at the last day.' Christ now he was to bring her heart off to this, that he should rise sooner, that he would raise him up now, which she was very backward to believe. What doth Jesus Christ do therefore? He puts her first upon this, to renew her faith upon him for salvation, so you have it clearly, ver. 25, Jesus said unto her, 'I am the resurrection and the life: he that believeth in me, though we were dead, yet shall he live: and whosoever liveth, and believeth in me, shall never die.' Here you see he draws her on to believe in him for salvation, and to renew that faith. There are a great many observations which may be made out of these words; as, first, this, you see the special faith of the gospel, which Christ would have us put into our creed. You know there is a creed which we call the apostles' creed, but here is one main article of a creed which Christ hath made: 'Believest thou this?' saith he. He doth catechetically instruct her in this main point, namely, that he is the resurrection and the life, and that whosoever liveth and believeth in him shall never die. To believe, therefore, with a special faith on Christ for salvation, and against condemnation, this is the great thing of the gospel; and Christ he doth urge it upon her, that he might bring her faith first off to this, and then it would be easy for her, more easy for her, having renewed that faith upon Christ for salvation, and not dying, to believe that he would raise her brother, which was a temporal mercy which she was then treating with him about, and which he was rather bringing her off to be persuaded of. Hence therefore I conclude, that if you would have any temporal mercy, or believe in any promise else, first believe in him for salvation and against condemnation, believe on him for pardon of sin, renew such acts of faith. Another thing I observe by the way, out of those words, is this, her answer is, ' Yea, Lord, I believe that thou art the Christ, the Son of God.' Hence some say, that to believe that Christ is the Son of God is true faith, and faith enough.   But you must join Christ's words and her answer together, for Christ doth nct call her to believe that he is the Son of God, but to believe on him that she might not die, and therefore I say, put her answer and Christ's words together, and the meaning is clearly this, she believed him to be the Son of God, and she believed in him also that she should not die ; and having brought her heart off to this, it was more easy for her now to believe that Christ would raise up Lazarus her brother, than which she desired nothing more of a temporal mercy.

You shall find, likewise, that when men and women came to be healed, as for instance the man sick of the palsy, Mat. ix. 2, when he was brought to Christ to be healed of his palsy, what doth Christ first say to the poor man when he came to him ?   He said unto him, ' Son, be of good cheer ; thy sins be forgiven thee.'   They brought him to be healed of his palsy ; you see Christ, afore ever he heals his palsy, speaks first to the man, ' Son, be of good comfort ; thy sins be forgiven thee.'   What do I argue out of these words ?   *First*, that Jesus Christ, the good Physician, he knew the sore of the man's heart ; poor man, he would fain be healed of his palsy, but the desire of forgiveness stuck in his spirit, and his faith stuck most at that ; for Christ here he speaks *ad cor*, to the heart, and therefore, afore he would heal his palsy, he first speaks to that which was most in his eye, and which the man most wanted, and which he came for : ' Be of good cheer ; thy sins be forgiven thee.'   The words argue that the man was exercised about this, how his sins should be pardoned through Jesus Christ that was the Saviour of the world ; therefore Christ first tells him, thy sins be forgiven ; for the man thought with himself, Alas, the curing of my sickness will do me no good, if that my sins remain !   What doth Christ therefore ? He answereth according to the man's thoughts ; Thy sins, saith he, are forgiven thee.   Again, thought the poor man, this temporal mercy will not be granted, unless he forgive my sins too ; my sins brought this disease upon me, and it will not be taken away unless my sins be forgiven.   Therefore Christ, speaking to the poor man's heart, tells him first that his sins are forgiven.   Hence, I say, I argue that the man's soul was more exercised about the forgiveness of his sins than about his palsy ; therefore, I say, any of you too cannot come with comfort to believe any other temporal promise, or anything else, unless you come first, either by assurance to believe your sins are forgiven, or to deal with God about forgiveness, as this poor soul did.

I might give you the like instances in many others that were healed, and I might exemplify this to you in the business of Abraham.   The Lord did make a promise to Abraham which seems to be but an outward promise, (and take the letter of it, and it was but an outward promise) concerning the multiplying of his seed.   And it is a thing that Bellarmine objecteth. You talk, saith he, that your faith that justifies is pitched only upon God as justifying, and upon Jesus Christ.   The faith that Abraham was justified by was believing the multiplying of his seed as the stars of heaven.   In Rom. iv. 3 it is said, ' The Scripture saith, Abraham believed God, and it was counted unto him for righteousness.'   Now, where is it said that Abraham's faith was counted unto him for righteousness ?   You have it in Gen. xv. 6.   And upon what occasion was it spoken, that his faith was counted to him for righteousness ?   It was believing of that promise, that God would make his seed like the stars of heaven.   Now, saith the great objector, here is your justifying faith ; it is merely faith upon a temporal promise.   But you shall see how this man is mistaken, for read but the first verse of that Gen. xv., and mark what God saith afore he makes him that temporal promise, if you will make it such, though, if I had time, I could shew you it is more ; but take it so. Saith God there first, ' Fear not, Abraham : I am thy shield, and thy exceeding great reward.' There God makes a special promise of mercy and blessednsss unto Abraham, and having made this, he makes him a promise of multiplying his seed, ver. 5 ; ' And he believed in the Lord' (ver. 6), ' and he counted it to him for right-eousness.' That is, his faith was exercised upon the special promise, by reason of which, and by virtue of which, God did bestow upon him this other promise, of making his seed as the stars of heaven. I could give you another answer to it, but I only allege it for this purpose, that temporal promises are believed in, but in the strength of having first closed with God and with Jesus Christ, under special promises of mercy, pardon, and forgiveness, and of receiving of happiness and of blessedness in and through Christ. There is no treating with God for any promise, till that faith hath thus pitched itself upon his free favour in Christ, either by way of assurance, or by way of casting a man's self upon him to be justified ; for a man treateth with God before as an enemy, and will a man come to an enemy for anything, whenas his heart is not with him ? Therefore further, when the soul doth come to God, having some promise out of God's heart, that he is a justifier of such as he is, and so resteth upon him to be justified by him, he will then have recourse to him for anything else too. And the truth is, a man hath no heart to treat with God till then about anything ; therefore, in 2 Pet. i., 3d and 4th verses compared, he saith that, ' through the knowledge of him' (that is, our Lord Jesus Christ, for he had spoken in the verse before of believing in the righteousness of God and our Saviour Jesus Christ) ' are given unto us exceeding great and precious promises.'

The last sort of reasons which I shall give you for the confirmation of this, viz., why that God hath singled out special faith thus to justify us upon ; and why he doth not justify us upon general faith, be it never so good ; and why, though we believe other things never so spiritually, and let them have never so spiritual effects upon our hearts, yet it is only be-lieving upon God as justifying and saving which is the right faith. I say, the last sort of reasons to evince it are these, because it suiteth every way, and agreeth with all the principles that are held forth in the doctrine of faith and justification ; and the contrary opinion doth disagree with all true orthodox, sound principles held forth about it.

1. In the first place (for this contains some two or three particulars in it), it was a meet thing, and well suited together, that God should bestow all benefits upon us (if he will bestow them through faith), through that faith that is suited peculiarly to, and is pitched upon, the benefits which he doth bestow. It is a rule which Christ hath, and he hath it twice : he hath it in Mat. viii. 13, and he hath it in Mat. ix. 29, 30. The rule is this : ' Be it unto thee according to thy faith,' saith he ; so it is in Mat. ix. 29, when the poor blind man did come unto him to be healed. He hath the very same expression in Mat. viii. 13 : ' Go thy way, and as thou hast believed so be it done unto thee.' That is, look what is the proper aim of your faith, that by God's ordination doth God upon believing be-stow upon you. Now if a man had the faith of working miracles, and if he would work a miracle, why according to his faith it would be unto him. If a man came to Jesus Christ to be healed, it was to him according to that faith. Therefore, now, according to this rule then doth God give forth justification, when a man's soul comes to him to be justified, believes on him as a justifier, when he comes to Jesus Christ for that righteousness

which should justify, when he believeth on Jesus that he may be justified, as it is in Gal. ii. 16. Saith the apostle in Rom. iv. 5, ' He that believeth on him that justifieth the ungodly, his faith is counted for righteousness ;' that faith, and no other, for that is his meaning. To believe on Christ, or upon God, under any other notion, though it may make a man holy, yet it will not justify a man. You may see the truth of this in the outward elements of the sacraments, as bread and wine in the Lord's supper, and water in baptism ; look what it is that they are ordained by God to signify, that they seal up to us : they signify the blood of Christ, and the death of the Lord Jesus, and our being one with him therein ; and as they signify these by God's ordination, so they do seal up these to us in a more eminent manner. So it is here ; look what it is that the heart comes to God for, that is it that God returns again to the spirit ; therefore he returns not justification to a man till he come to him to be justified ; therefore it is that special act upon which this great benefit is given forth. I do not say that every man that comes to Christ hath the exact notion of the word, justified by Christ. Alas, the ancient language of the fathers was, of being saved by Christ, for they were not acquainted with this word justified. Our divines of the Reformation speak more distinctly than they, but they meant the same thing. Only I should add this caution, that benefits of a kind, if a man come to God for any one, God gives him all the rest ; all benefits which are out of us, as adoption, sonship, pardon of sin, which are all acts without us, if a man come to God for one, suppose sonship, he gives him all the rest ; and according to the kind of faith is the benefit bestowed.

2. Again, That God justifies us by a special faith, it agrees with this principle also, viz., with the way of God's justifying us ; and what is that ? It is not that God doth justify us by faith, as it is an act put forth by us, an act of ours, or a quality in us, but he doth justify us by reason of the objects laid hold upon by faith, the free grace of God, and of Jesus Christ ; so that not so much faith as these are said to justify, being apprehended by faith. I might be exceeding large in manifestation of this ; it is a received principle amongst all our orthodox divines ; I will only mention that in Gal. iii. 8, ' The Scripture foreseeing that God would justify the heathen by faith, preached the gospel, saying, In thee' (speaking of Abraham personating Christ) ' shall all nations be blessed.' By blessing here he means justification clearly, for he speaks of taking away the curse in the following verses ; the thing I cite it for is this, to observe that this expression, ' In thee shall all nations be blessed,' serves wholly to take off all from a man's self, when you come to the business of justification. ' In thee' (saith he), that is, in Christ, in that seed, they shall be blessed, for sot he apostle explains it : verse 16, ' not seeds' (saith he), ' but seed,' namely, Christ. It is not therefore being blessed in believing, or blessed by faith, or through faith, as it is an act, but it is through faith as laying hold upon Christ ; it is in Christ, *in* in Christ, and *in* in only him. Now mark how this truth suiteth others ; if we are justified thus, by Jesus Christ as the object of our faith, and by God as he is the object of our faith (because he is the justifier, and Christ's righteousness is the matter whereby we are justified, and in that respect we are said to be justified by faith, because faith lays hold upon these objects), then assuredly it is only faith as pitched upon these objects, by which and upon which we are justified. This necessarily and clearly follows, if (I say), by God as justifying us (out of ourselves) and by his grace, and by Christ's righteousness (which is out of ourselves in him), and by faith, not as a quality or act, but only as apprehending these ; if in this

sense we are only said to be justified by faith, then it is evident that faith by apprehending these, and by no other act, is said to justify us.

Therefore, do but see the mystery of other opinions. What is the reason that the papists say, that faith alone in Christ doth not justify? This is the true mystery of it, they do not hold that the grace of God is the justifier of us, nor the righteousness of Christ the matter of our justification, therefore faith doth not justify in respect of its object with them, but it justifieth us only as a righteous quality in us, and a righteous act performed by us; and therefore with them the belief of any truth, whatsoever it be, justifies as well as the believing on Christ, or on God that justfies the ungodly; therefore they say, faith justifies as a disposition; that is, as any other grace or disposition in us, and not *per modum apprehensionis*, as laying hold on Christ and his righteousness; and their πρῶτον ψεῦδος consists in this, that they assert faith to be only an assent, (and so it may be pitched on any other truth as well as Christ dying), and not a fiducial apprehension of Christ; this agrees with their principles, and the other agrees with ours.

And what is the reason that others, who hold that faith justifies as an act, lean to this, and say, that general faith is that which justifies? Because if it justify us merely but as an act, pitch it upon any other object as well as this, it will be to us for righteousness, and indeed it may be as well.

But we are justified by Christ, and through faith, even as you would say an house is enlightened by the sun, and enlightened by opening the window. it comes all to one, for the house is enlightened by opening of the window, because opening of the window lets in the sun that enlighteneth it; so it is here, for therefore faith is said to justify, because it lays hold upon, and lets in Christ, and God as justifying, into the heart of a sinner.

3. Again, in the third place, if a man were justified upon any other act of believing of any divine truth, though believed never so spiritually and truly, and not on this special act of believing on Christ, and on God as justifying, he were plainly and clearly justified by sanctification; as, for instance, if I believe that God is holy (this I call part of a general faith), and believe it spiritually and rightly, it makes me holy as he is holy, in my affections. Here now the belief of God's holiness, if it be a true belief, with the whole heart, serveth only to frame the heart to holiness answerably: now then, if I should be justified by believing that God is holy, I should clearly be justified by being sanctified. To give you another instance, I believe that God is just, and therefore I fear him: Noah (the text saith), 'moved with fear, prepared an ark,' Heb. xi. 7. He believed that God was just and true in his threatenings, and so feared God; if Noah now had been justified by this faith of his, he had clearly been justified by faith sanctifying, or, if you will, by sanctification; for what is holiness and sanctification but a right knowledge of God in the mind, with suitable affections framed in the heart accordingly? If therefore a man were justified by any other faith than by faith throwing himself upon Christ for justification, he should be justified by sanctification. So again, I believe that God is thus and thus excellent in himself, thus and thus happy and blessed, that he hath all these perfections in him, here now is faith in my understanding; therefore I love God, here now is the work of that faith upon my heart, answerable to the faith I have of him in my understanding. If now I were justified by that faith which knows God to be thus excellent, I should be justified by sanctifying faith, by faith as it is sanctification; or, if you will, by sanctification itself: for, I say, sanctifi-

cation is nothing else but faith in the mind, having suitable affections thereunto in the whole heart. Therefore, though justifying faith sanctifies most of all faith else, and all other faith, though never so spiritual, would not sanctify without it, because it alone lets Christ and God into the heart, that doth sanctify me, and justify me too, yet still, I say, faith no way doth justify but as it lays hold upon God as justifying, and Jesus Christ, whose righteousness is justification to us. Add to this to confirm it, that in Adam acts of trust in God were required, as well as acts of love (which, whether they had a supernatural revelation for their rise or no is not material to this point), but yet Adam's faith had not justification by grace, and by imputation for its object. He indeed was justified by such acts of faith (as being acts of the image of God in him), as well as by acts of love, and è contra (as the papists speak); but to have such an act singled out, in respect and relation to such an object, this is proper and peculiar to, and is the very pith and marrow of the covenant of grace, namely, grace justifying us by imputation, and this was the way to make it a distinct covenant from that of Adam's; whereas, if by general faith on other objects, or upon any other grounds or promises, we were justified, it would have been the same way, and the same faith for act and object that Adam was justified by.

I should add one reason more, and that is this, it agrees with the nature of faith, which is a trusting; but I will not enlarge further upon this, but only give you a use or two.

Use 1. By this you may have a very great light to distinguish things. It is an excellent thing to consider the several ways of conversion, as popish spirits do lay it forth, and as the divines who are of the reformed churches, opposite to them, do lay it out. Read a popish divine, and see how he will describe conversion, and the work of God in saving a man; he will tell you that he saw his sinfulness, that he was contrite under it, humbled under the sight of it, that he feareth God, hateth sin, upon the sight of the evil of it, and begins to have good purposes. There are seven dispositions the papists have (the Council of Trent hath them), which they make conversion to consist in; and then what do they say when a man hath all these dispositions in him? Through their general faith, believing the threatenings of God, believing the goodness of God, and the evil of sin, &c., then a man hath holiness infused into him by the sacrament, when he goes to it, being thus prepared by his own dispositions, and so here is the man converted; thus they tell the story of it, but they leave clearly out special faith in Jesus Christ, and upon God for justification, and upon his free grace, and so all their justification is merely by what is wrought in themselves. And, my brethren, here is much of the ordinary conversion of protestants described in this: many men that profess the Lord Jesus Christ, if you go down into their hearts, you shall find no treating with God in the way of his free grace, or with the Lord Jesus Christ, as the matter of their righteousness, to be justified through his blood, and to apprehend it through special faith.

Use 2. It doth teach us what we should especially live by, by what faith and upon what object we should especially live; we should live upon that faith which is exercised upon the free grace of God, which is ordained to be the special object of our faith, and upon the Lord Jesus Christ, and upon his righteousness. Every man, you know, hath three lives in him: he hath the life of reason, which the reasonable soul liveth; and he hath the life of sense, which is the life that a beast liveth; and he hath the life of a plant. If I may make comparison, as the life of reason is the eminent life of a man, which a man as a man leadeth ; and if you exhort a man to live as a man, you would exhort him to live the life of reason in a more eminent manner, though he exercise other acts of life too ; so it is here, the eminent act of faith is to live upon the free grace of God in Christ, to live upon the righteousness of God revealed in the gospel, revealed from faith to faith, for by faith the just do live, Rom. i. 17. Now though to live upon all other truths else, and to act them and digest them, is also a living by faith ; so the apostle speaks in Heb. x. 39 ; yet notwithstanding comparatively this life is but as if a man should cease to live the life of reason, which is proper to a man as a man, and live only the life which is common to other creatures. The life of a Christian lieth especially in living by faith on Christ, by ' the faith which is on him,' as the Scripture calls it ; that is, the nobleness of his spirit as he is a Christian ; and if there were no more ends of it but only this, that it is the most precious life, it should draw up your hearts to live this life of special faith. In 2 Peter i. 1 saith the apostle, ' To them that have obtained like precious faith with us, in the righteousness of our Saviour Jesus Christ.' What is the reason that the faith of all believers is called alike precious ? Because it is pitched upon the righteousness of Jesus Christ, which righteousness being possessed by a weak believer, and made his own by believing, he hath the same precious faith the apostles had, the preciousness of it lying in this object. Hence, I say, all faith is alike precious ; but, if you come to other faith whereby you believe other truths, here indeed it is not alike precious faith. He that hath the strongest faith on the power of God, simply so considered, he hath a more precious faith than he that hath a weaker faith in that power. I allege it for this, that the preciousness of justifying faith lies as it is exercised upon this precious object Christ ; and therefore, if you would live that life of faith which is most precious, most so in God's esteem, most excellent in itself, live upon this Christ.

Use 3. I might enlarge upon that by way of use which I hinted before, namely this, that you cannot believe heartily and strongly on anything else, but as your faith on this Christ and his righteousness receiveth increase. You cannot believe on God for temporal things, no, not for spiritual things, not for sanctification and making of you holy, further than your faith receiveth increases, and attaineth to more degrees in this thing, that it is more and more exercised upon Jesus Christ and upon God as justifying. But you will say, Alas, I believed that long ago, I am already assured that God doth justify me, and shall I now go and live upon that faith, as the great faith by which I must especially live ? Yes, certainly, for Abraham did so ; you have that great place in Rom iv. 3 for an instance of it. ' Abraham,' saith he, ' believed God, and it was counted to him for righteousness.' The words are taken out of Gen. xv. 6, Abraham had been assured of his justification long before ; in Gen. xii. 1, 2, &c., you shall see there God had blessed him, and he upon the faith of it had left his country, and God had assured him of his justification, given him as much assurance of it (for he spake to him personally face to face) as Christ did to the man to whom he said, ' Thy sins are forgiven thee ;' and yet Abraham he hath the promise often renewed to him, and his faith often renewed in it ; and that place which the apostle citeth to prove that he was justified by faith was not the first act of faith he put forth, but a faith he had many years afore, and this is the faith Abraham lived upon. When he had Canaan promised him, he had recourse to that God that justifieth, and then laid hold upon the promise of Canaan ; when Isaac was promised, he had recourse to that promise in which it was said,

' In thy seed shall all the nations of the earth be blessed,' Gen. xii. 3. Still he renewed his faith upon the special mercy of God, and upon Jesus Christ; and he did this again and again, and it was his element, his orb, his sphere in which he moved; and when any temporal promise was propounded to him, he renewed his faith on this, and so believed that temporal promise. This should be that life of faith which we should live for our justification by God and by Christ; it is the eminent thing of the gospel, which of all other God will have glorified, and therefore would have us live upon it.

Use 4. And we may learn likewise from hence how to seek and obtain all other things: ' First seek the kingdom of God,' saith Christ. What doth the kingdom of God consist in ? ' In righteousness, and peace, and joy in the Holy Ghost,' saith the apostle, Rom. xiv. 17; that is, the righteousness of Jesus Christ, whence peace ariseth, and joy in the Holy Ghost; seek after this, saith he, exercise faith upon this, and then all other promises will come in upon you. Paul, though he had his belief for justification in Christ many years before, yet, saith he, ' I account all things but loss and dung.' He inured himself to cast away his own righteousness, and to wrap himself in Christ, he would still exercise a special faith; ' I have,' saith he in Phil. iii. 8, 9, ' accounted all things loss, and do account them so, that I may win Christ, and be found in him, not having mine own righteousness, but the righteousness which is of God by faith;' so that, I say, he still renewed a special faith upon Christ, and upon the righteousness of Christ. If a man would have any other promise made good to him, this is the way to have it. You see how Christ taught Martha to do it, to believe on him, that she should not die, and then she would easily believe that her brother should be raised from the dead. It is special faith, and therefore we should in a special manner exercise it. So much for this subject, which I have, with as much brevity and clearness as I could, opened; consider it now as a truth of very great moment, and which confuteth many errors that run abroad in the world, not only in the hearts of popish divines, but protestants also.

CHAPTER V.

The acts of faith in the will.—The believing soul trusts in Christ alone for help.—That this confiding in Christ is the act of faith which justifies.— The nature and properties of a true confidence in Christ.

Having displayed to you the knowledge of faith as it is expressed to us by sight in the understanding, and having proved that a bare assent to, or a mere belief of, the truths apprehended by us, is not saving and justifying faith, but that a special act of faith on the mercies and free grace of God, and on Christ as a Saviour, is necessary, I will proceed on to those other acts of faith which are in the will (which is the next faculty), and which the heart puts forth toward Jesus Christ therein.

1. As the soul sees the spiritual excellency and the glory that is in Jesus Christ, so the will doth set the highest value and esteem upon that excellency that is in him, a value and esteem far above what a man hath for all other things whatsoever; and this is to believe. This you shall find in 1 Peter ii., 4th and 6th verses compared: ' To whom coming, as unto a living stone, disallowed indeed of men, but chosen of God, and precious. Wherefore it is contained in the scripture, Behold, I lay in Sion a chief

corner stone, elect, and precious: and he that believeth on him shall not
be confounded. Unto you therefore which believe he is precious.' It is
clear that the apostle here speaks of faith, and he makes the foundation of
our believing on him to be seeing his preciousness; and therefore in Isaiah
xxviii. 16, which the apostle here quoteth, you have this stone's being a
precious stone and believing on him both joined together: 'To him
coming' (saith he, verse 4) 'as to a living stone, chosen of God, and precious;' that is, you believe on him under the notion of seeing his excellency and his preciousness. And therefore the closure of all in the 7th
verse is, 'Unto you which believe he is precious,' that is, you esteem him
precious; and it is spoken not as a consequent of faith, but as that which
goes before faith, or is joined with it, and is requisite to it, for therefore
the soul comes unto him because he is precious, as the 4th verse hath it,
even under that notion.   There are four things under the apprehension of
which a man comes to Christ, as these words hold him forth: 1, as he is
a stone that hath a foundation which the soul may build upon; 2, as he is
a living stone, and a fountain of life unto all that believe on him; 3, as he
is the only appointed means by the Father, 'chosen of God;' 4, as he is
precious, which is the thing I cite it for, both precious in himself and in
all that he brings with him. In Mat. xiii. 45, 46 you have a believer
compared to a merchantman seeking goodly pearls; his mind is set, as all
men's minds are, to find precious stones; that is, to attain to that which
he accounteth precious. Thus when the soul is first humbled for sin, it is
taken off from seeing anything in the world that can help it; and therefore
it seeks after somewhat else. And what will it seek after? After that
which is precious, after pearls, after graces (for such our graces are, which
our souls are said to seek after), that will beautify him, and make him
acceptable unto God, these indeed are pearls, and goodly pearls. Yea,
but saith the text, he found one pearl of great price, so verse 46, a pearl
that was more excellent than all, and he went and sold all that he had,
sold away all his graces (for that is the meaning), he accounted all, even
grace itself, to be loss and dung. He put no value or price upon these
pearls; but if his graces may serve to honour this one pearl, and that this
may be set so in them all, that they all may be obscured, he cares not, so
precious is Christ unto him. So you have it likewise in Paul, in Philip.
iii. 8: 'I have accounted all things loss for the excellency of the knowledge of Christ; yea,' saith he, 'I do account them dung.' I have done
so heretofore, when I was first turned to God, and I am of the very
same mind to this day; I do account them so to this very hour. This is
the first thing in believing on Christ, which is an act of the will. He that
believeth on him, unto him Christ is precious.

2. He that believeth on Christ, God stampeth upon that man's will, upon
his heart, an instinct after Jesus Christ, and after mystical union with him,
so as he can never be quiet without him. This you have in John vi. 44,
45: 'No man can come unto me, except the Father, which hath sent me,
draw him. It is written in the prophets, that they shall be all taught of
God: every man, therefore, that hath heard and hath learned of the Father,
cometh unto me;' that is, believeth on me. Now what is the teaching, the
effectual teaching, that the Father exerts upon the spirit of a man, when he
draws him to Christ Jesus, and sets him on work upon coming to him and
seeking of him? Why it is this, God doth plant in that man an impression,
an instinct (what shall I call it?) after Jesus Christ, so that nothing will
satisfy him but Christ. That which is here called teaching, is elsewhere
put for a natural instinct, such an instinct as a man hath after a thing which

he can never be quiet without, such as parents have to their children. This teaching that the Holy Ghost (I will not say only aims at, but) eminently aims at here, I interpret by that in 1 Thes. iv. 9, ' As touching brotherly love, ye need not that I write unto you.' It is not a teaching from words to love one another, ' for,' saith he, ' ye yourselves are taught of God to love one another.' It is an impression stamped upon one saint to love another saint ; there is, as it were, a natural instinct upon their spirits to do so. So saith Christ, ' All that come to me, they are taught of God ;' *i. e.*, their coming to Christ is from another thing than merely a teaching of them by way of knowledge : it is putting an impression and stamp upon their will, that they can never be quiet till they come to Christ, and this is called a drawing of the Father. It is such an instinct as God put into the beasts that came to the ark, for what guided these poor creatures to the ark, that they should come running by couples thither ? Why, the Lord made an impression upon their fancies, and upon that which is answerable to our affections, that they were never quiet till they came thither ; and thither the poor creatures must come for refuge. Such an instinct doth God put upon the heart of a believer, a marriage affection, call it what you will, an instinct of mystical union with Christ. The angels they know Christ, and they see his excellency, and they value him, but they have not this marriage affection to him that the soul of a believer hath ; they have an affection of love and of fear of him as a Lord, but they have not that affection to him as to a husband. Such an instinct as this doth the Holy Ghost put into the heart of all those whom he doth work upon. We see it in other creatures. That I may express it by way of similitude, take a dog : when he is sick, there is a grass he runs to, and he doth it by an instinct ; this is that which must cure me, saith he : not that he doth of himself make such inference, but there is an impression stamped upon the nature of that creature by God, whereby he is taught of God to do so. And so the hart, as some say, when it is struck, it presently runs to the herb called *dictamnus*, and is never quiet till it do so ; it is taught of God to do it. So is a man taught of God to go to Jesus Christ. Certainly it is the main meaning (I will not exclude others), and the most eminent, of that place, that he that believeth on Jesus Christ, he is thus taught of God. The angels they are taken with the glory of Christ, and are affected with it ; but a believer hath an affection after mystical union with him.

3. The soul that hath thus an instinct after Christ, and so cometh to him, looks up to him for help, with a confinement to him alone. I will have it from you, saith the soul, or from none else. This you have in Isa. xlv. 21, 22 : ' There is no God else besides me, a just God and a Saviour. Look unto me and be ye saved, all the ends of the earth ; for I am God, and there is none else.' Who is this God here ? What person ? It is clearly the Son of God, our Lord and Saviour Jesus Christ ; for if you look into Rom. xiv. 11 and Philip. ii. 10, you shall find there this place quoted, to prove that Jesus Christ is Lord both of quick and dead, and that he shall come to judgment. And it is evident too to be Jesus Christ by this, because he speaks of all the ends of the earth looking unto him ; for when Christ came, he brought salvation and the gospel to be preached to all the ends of the earth. The Jews they looked upon God the Father ; but when Christ came, he drew the eyes of all the ends of the earth unto him. Now, saith he, ' look unto me.' What is faith ? Faith is a casting up of the eye unto Jesus Christ for help, as they did upon the brazen serpent ; they saw other things besides, but with another eye, whenas they looked upon that as the only remedy. So when the soul hath seen Christ,

seen his excellency, and hath an instinct after him, and doth but open his eye, nay, his eyelids, towards Christ, the meaning of that look is, I will have help from you, and only from you ; and here is a glance or cast of faith.   And as it is a looking unto Christ, so it is a looking with a confinement to him alone.   This is clear out of the text : ' I am a Saviour,' saith he, ' and there is none besides me ;' therefore so look unto me, as to confine yourselves to me alone.   The soul of man would seek an hundred ways, when it is humbled for sin, to relieve itself; but now to have all these holes that a man would run unto stopped, and to be confined alone unto one, when God hath wrought this in the heart too, there is a great step and proceeding on in the work of faith.   As in taking of God to be a man's God, he takes him so to be his chiefest good, as he is divorced from all things else, with a confinement of all his expectations of happiness only from him—' Whom have I in heaven but thee ?' saith David, Ps. lxxiii. 25 ; —so in taking Jesus Christ to be our Saviour, as Paul resolved to know nothing else but Jesus Christ and him crucified, so the heart resolveth too, when it goes about to believe in earnest, and it is stopped up from all ways of relief else.   When Paul (that I may make the comparison) was surrounded with his lusts, in Rom. vii. 24 saith he, ' Oh wretched man that I am ! who shall deliver me ?'   When he spake that speech, he was as a man that looked round about him, and saw no help, and so he cries out, ' Who shall deliver me ?'   At last he spies out Jesus Christ : ' I thank God, through Jesus Christ my Lord,' saith he.   And so doth the soul ; as in sanctification, so in justification, it looks about it, sees help in nothing, and betakes itself alone unto the Lord Jesus.

Jesus Christ he is more, far more jealous of your faith than of your love. He will give you leave to love subordinately other things besides himself, and with himself, but he will not give you leave to believe on any, to look for help from any but from him.   This faith is reserved for him alone. The eye of a man that believeth is shut up to all things either in his own heart, or whatsoever else there is that may help him, and his eyes are only upon Christ, as the phrase is in 2 Chron. xx. 12.   When a man comes to be saved by Christ, he doth Christ this honour, that he resolves to have peace and quietness, and satisfaction and salvation, and all only in, and from, and by Christ.   As a man, when he would honour a physician whom he trusteth, saith he, I will take physic of none else but of you; I will die rather; so, saith the soul to honour Christ, you alone shall save me ; ' Asshur shall not save us,' as it is Hos. xiv. 3.   ' And truly in vain is salvation hoped for from the hills, and from the multitude of mountains,' Jer. iii. 23.   They used to worship upon their mountains, therefore now to look to the mountains for help was to look to their duties, to their worship, to their sacrifices for help; but now they renounced all this, and fixed on God alone, ' in whom the fatherless find mercy.'   The soul, when it is helpless, when it is graceless, when it is fatherless, then it resolves to look to none else but unto Jesus Christ for help.   This, I say, is a great proceeding in faith also, to resolve thus to have help from none else, and to confine itself only to Christ; for the soul to say, I will so throw myself upon him, and upon that free love in him, that, if he will not save me, I will be lost for ever.   Thus the heart of a believer doth look to him as the only Saviour, and as such an one that ' there is none else besides him.' And this is the third act of the will.

4. As a man thus looks to Jesus Christ for help, and confines himself unto him alone, so he then comes to him.   This you have here in this John vi. ver. 37, ' All that the Father giveth unto me shall come to me,

and him that cometh to me I will in no wise cast out.' The soul goes out of itself naked, a naked soul, to naked Christ, empty, and stripped of all things, and comes unto Christ, and deals and treats with him about everlasting salvation. You have faith also expressed under this notion in Heb. vii. 25, 'He is able to save to the uttermost them that come unto God by him.' And the like is in 1 Pet. ii. 3, 'Unto whom coming, as unto a living stone.' The Holy Ghost hath on purpose, in a gracious manner, variously expressed faith to us, because the apprehensions that souls have of their own way of believing is various. Some souls cannot say they have received Christ, but they can say they have looked up to him, and confined all their expectations to him, and they have come to him, &c. Now, when the soul comes to Christ, what is the business and errand that the soul hath? for one comes to none but he hath some business, some errand with him. See how Christ himself expresseth the errand and aim of the soul in coming to him, John v. 40, 'Ye will not come to me, that ye might have life.' This is the errand of the soul, it [comes to Christ, that it may have life from him. He doth not only express there what is the consequent of the soul's coming to him, namely, that it might have life as the consequent of its coming, as that which he will bestow, but that which is the aim, the errand, and business that faith hath with Jesus Christ; therefore, Heb. vi. 18, we are said to have fled unto him, fled to him as unto a city of refuge. Now what was the aim, and business, and errand that a poor murderer had that fled to the city of refuge? He came thither, with all might and main, to be let in there, that he might have succour and help, and that he might be safe; and when the high priest died, he was delivered. So the soul comes unto Christ for refuge, comes unto him that he may have life. We have it to the same purpose expressed Gal. ii. 16; speaking there of the faith of all the apostles, saith he, 'Even we who are Jews by nature, and not sinners of the Gentiles,' we apostles, 'knowing that a man is not justified by the works of the law, but by the faith of Jesus Christ; even we,' saith he, 'have believed in Jesus Christ, that we might be justified by the faith of Christ.' How doth he express faith? He expresseth it by this—a coming unto, or a believing in Jesus Christ, that we may be justified, that we might have life; this being the aim, and errand, and business the soul hath with Christ in its coming to him. Here, now, lies that act of faith (if it be a spiritual act, if it be joined with that spiritual sight I mentioned before), it is not that we believe that Jesus Christ did justify us, and had justified us, but we believe that he may justify us. When the apostles first believed, this was not the act of faith they put forth, that they were justified, but 'we have believed,' saith he, 'that we might be justified.' So that the aim and errand the soul hath with Christ in coming to him is, that it might have life, and accordingly it comes unto him.

5. The soul's coming unto Jesus Christ, and treating for salvation with him, doth grow up to a believing on him, to a resting on him, to a trusting in him for it. I shall not need to give you many scriptures to prove that this act of trust is the great and eminent act that is in faith, and that upon which God doth rather pronounce and pass the sentence of justification upon a man than any other. The text hath it here, and you shall find it almost everywhere, that it is called believing on him. Some would place that great act of faith whereby we are justified in believing the thing, in believing him to be the Son of God, and a Saviour. I confess it is a great act of faith, but that is only the act of the understanding whereby we see and know him, which I have opened before; but the

eminent and the principal act of the will of a man (and he must believe with his whole heart) is trust, is believing on him: 1 Pet. ii. 6, ' Behold, I lay in Sion a chief corner stone: he that believeth on him shall not be ashamed.' And you have the like again in Rom. ix. 33. You shall hardly have a place which, usually, men allege to prove that all the act of faith as justifying lies in believing the thing, but immediately after follows this phrase, ' believing on him,' on purpose to shew that the bare belief of the thing is not the only act of faith, as some would have it to be. As, for instance, in 1 John v. 4, this is made the great act of faith there, ' This is the victory that overcometh the world, even our faith.' And what is the faith? ' He that believeth that Jesus is the Son of God.' One would think now that the apostle would make all believing to lie in believing the thing, in believing that Jesus Christ is the Son of God, and accordingly is this place cited by some; but mark what he saith at the 10th verse, ' He that believeth on the Son of God, hath the witness in himself;' there is believing on him too mentioned. Another place that is cited is in Rom. x. 9, ' If thou believe in thy heart that God hath raised him from the dead, thou shalt be saved.' Here now the faith that saveth us is called believing the thing, namely, ' that God hath raised Christ from the dead;' but if you read a little on, you shall find that believing on him cometh in the 11th verse, ' The Scripture saith, whosoever believeth on him shall not be ashamed;' so that, indeed, the eminent act of faith in the will is this trusting, is this believing on him. It is called rolling of a man's self upon him, leaving, committing, or betaking a man's self to him, as Ps. x. 14. It is the Old Testament expression, but it rightly expresseth the nature of faith.

There have been some that would make the act of faith in the will to be a cleaving unto Christ for his excellencies. The truth is, that is nothing but love, it is not faith; but that act of the will, which is properly faith, answers unto Christ as a Saviour, and as a means of salvation appointed by God. Now go, take Jesus Christ as a Saviour, and as a means of salvation appointed by God, it is not love answereth to that in Christ, but it is a trust and believing on him. It is not a cleaving unto Jesus Christ for his excellencies, that is that proper act of faith which we call justifying, but it is that act of the will which hath relation unto him as a Saviour, and as the means of salvation; and the proper act that answereth to that, is trust and confidence. Assuredly, God hath singled out that to be the eminent act of justifying faith, which is proper to the elect of mankind, in whom he works faith in; now, to cleave unto Jesus Christ for the excellencies that are in him, to see him spiritually, and to love Christ upon the sight of him, and to value him, and to prize and esteem him (all these that I have named before), are all in the good angels, that yet have not faith; they believe that Jesus Christ is, for they see him every day, and they see the grace that is in him more than we do, and are taken with it more than we are, they likewise hear us preach, and attend our sermons, and pry into the things delivered, and they know all the truths about Christ as well as we. If God therefore should have made these to be those proper acts of faith, they would have been such acts as are common to the good angels, and therefore he hath singled out rather that to be the act of faith justifying, which is proper and peculiar to the elect sons of God; and what is that? It is believing on him. The angels they do not believe on him as a Saviour and Redeemer, they have not this act of trust and confidence, they do not come unto him, or rely on him for salvation, therefore, I say, God hath singled out this believing *on him* as the eminent act of faith justifying: ' He that seeth the

Son, and believeth on him,' saith Christ, John vi. 40, and in John xiv. 1, ' If you believe in God, believe also in me ;' and so in a multitude of places else. And there is a great deal of reason that this act of faith should be pitched upon, to be the eminent act upon which God justifies us. For,

(1.) It is an act that is competent to all estates of a Christian, while he is here below. When the soul is in temptation, when a man comes to die, when he first believes, let him be in what condition he will, this act of trusting in God is that act which is common to all believers in all estates. It is most reason and fit therefore, that this act of faith should be pitched upon as the eminent act in our justification. If assurance that Jesus Christ is mine had been to be it, though many of the saints have it, yet they have it not always ; when they first began to believe, even the apostles themselves came unto Christ that they might be justified, and so it was not believing that they were justified. But now, let the saints be in the heaviest desertion that can be, let them be in never so much darkness, in never so great temptation, either when they first believe, or when they come to die, or at any time in all their lives, still, whether they have assurance of the love of God, or not assurance, yet (as the psalmist saith, Ps. lxii. 8) they ' trust in God at all times ;' and the soul still comes to Christ and relies on him. Therefore, I say, there was the greatest reason in the world, that of all acts else this should be pitched upon. The first act of faith cannot be assurance, for the thing must be made mine, before I can believe it is mine ; and afterward temptation comes, and overthrows a man's assurance, but it never overthrows a man's believing on Christ ; since this is that anchor that tides it out all a man's life, that cable that bears the stress in all storms, as well as in the fair weather, it is reason that to it the act of justification should be attributed. Now let the ship be in what storm it will, it is this that holds it, this is the cable, this act of our believing *on him*. You shall find that you can bottom your heart on God, and on Christ, when you cannot believe that he is your God and your Saviour.

(2.) Of all acts of faith, this of pure trust doth honour God most, and hath indeed more of faith in it. The purer the trust is, the greater the trust is ; and the greater the trust is, the greater the faith is ; and the greater the faith, the greater honour comes unto God. The end why God hath ordained faith is, that his free grace might be glorified ; now his free grace is glorified by no act of faith more than by this of pure trusting in him. In Rom. iv. 20, where Abraham's faith is set out to us, it is set out by this, that ' he gave glory to God.' You do not honour God so much with your love, you do not honour him so much by being assured of his love, as you do by trusting in his love. It magnifies the sovereignty of God, which God aims at to magnify in our salvation, it leaves the soul at God's feet, for that is the posture of the soul, when it says, Here I am, and I will trust in thee alone ; it magnifies the faithfulness and fidelity of God, and faithfulness is that attribute which, in one that makes a promise, is the chief thing he aims at. Now faith takes hold of Christ through a promise, therefore it is a grace suited and fitted to magnify the faithfulness of God in making this promise ; and so there is nothing that doth glorify the faithfulness of God more than believing on him. If a man have assurance, he doth glorify God in a way of rejoicing, in a way of triumphing, in a way of thankfulness, but pure trust doth another way glorify God, it glorifies God in a way of obedience. I do shew as much admiration and esteem of a man, if I am sueing to him for his friendship, and depend upon him, and do all acts I do in such dependence, as I do by acts of requital and thankfulness when I am assured he is my friend ; and so it is here, and therefore now hath God chosen out this act of trust and confidence, believing on him, as John vi. 40, ' He that seeth the Son, and believeth on him.' I shall now assign a property or two of this trust and confidence, that I may the more fully explain it. And,

[1.] This confidence in God is to trust perfectly upon him; that is, wholly and entirely. I use the Scripture phrase, which you have in 1 Pet. i. 13, and I shall thereby open a scripture to you, which (as I take it) our translation hath not rightly rendered, and I find very learned interpreters of the same judgment ; he exhorts them there to trust perfectly in the grace that hath been brought to them, through the revelation of Jesus Christ. We read it, ' hope to the end ;' look in your margins, the Greek is, ' hope perfectly.' ' Hope perfectly,' saith he, ' on the grace that is brought;' for so it is in the original, φερομένην, and not, that is to be brought, as we translate it. Hope and trust in the Scripture are usually put for one and the same, as Job xiii. 15, ' Though he slay me, yet will I trust in him ;' it is, ' I will hope in him '; and many other places might be given. Now, saith the apostle Peter, ' trust perfectly, or entirely, on the grace that is brought in the revelation of Jesus Christ ;' it is not only said to be the revelation of Christ, which shall be at latter day, but it is a revelation of Christ which we have now under the gospel. The gospel is said to be the revelation of Jesus Christ, and in the revelation of the gospel and of Christ is the grace of God made known to us. I shall not need to heap up places to shew you that by the revelation of Jesus Christ is meant the gospel ; in Rom. xvi. 25, you have the word so used : ' The preaching of Jesus Christ, according to the revelation of the mystery,' &c. You have the like in Gal. i. 12, where Paul, speaking of his knowing the gospel, he useth the very same phrase : ' I was taught,' saith he, ' by the revelation of Jesus Christ ;' and ver. 16, ' It pleased God to reveal his Son in me ;' and so in other places. That which I cited the text in 1 Peter i. 13 for is, that he saith, ' Trust perfectly upon this grace, which is brought or tendered to us' (and to trust upon free grace and Christ is all one ; the gospel reveals nothing for matter of confidence to us, but the free grace of God, and Christ himself). Now when he saith, Trust perfectly upon it, what is his meaning ? It is this : he would have you to do it entirely, both for subject and object, as I may so express it ; he would have all in you to put this trust and confidence in him, to believe on him with the whole heart; and he urgeth this exhortation, because the soul hath a great deal within itself that doth not come forth to trust in Christ ; for though all in a man believes in this sense, that there is never a faculty but goes out to Jesus Christ, especially the will, yet there is a great deal of infidelity still remaining, and so a man cannot trust perfectly in this life. As for subject, take the subject of confidence, that is, all that is in a man doth not trust perfectly and entirely without doubting in the grace brought by Jesus Christ ; but take the object, and so even the meanest believer may trust, and doth trust perfectly, in that grace which is brought to light in the gospel by Jesus Christ ; that is, he relies upon nothing else, he entirely, and wholly, and fully, and with the whole will, doth lean upon our Lord and Saviour Christ, and upon nothing else ; upon nothing in himself, and upon nothing in the world else, but upon that which revealeth grace, and Jesus Christ unto him ; no, he relies not upon the promises further than they have the grace of God and Jesus Christ as the subject of them. And this is the property of all true faith, that it doth trust perfectly in that grace that is in God, and in our Lord and Saviour Jesus Christ. As now when the soul doth magnify and glorify God as the great God, it doth do it perfectly and entirely in this sense, that it sees how great a God he is, and that there is none besides him so to be honoured and glorified. It falls short indeed of honouring him perfectly; as for the subject, that is, all in a man cannot do it; but yet, saith he, I see that God requires all that is in me to glorify him, therefore I will glorify him alone, and thus entirely glorifies the object; and so in this sense doth the soul trust perfectly in the grace that is revealed in the gospel.

[2.] The soul doth trust Jesus Christ with all and for all. I will put them both together; with all it hath, or ever shall have, and for all it ever looks for. It doth trust Jesus Christ with all, even as in Gen. xxxix. 6 we read that Potiphar trusted Joseph;—I bring it but for an allusion, to shew what confidence he had in Joseph, and what ours should be in Christ —the text saith, that ' He left all that he had in Joseph's hand, and he knew not aught he had, save the bread which he did eat.' Now if you come to believe on Christ you must thus put your trust in him, thus believe on him, thus leave yourselves, and all you have and are, with him, and at his disposal, and at his service; even as if you should out yourselves of your estate, and put it all into another man's hands, and be at his finding for ever; so Paul in 2 Tim. i. 12: ' For the which cause,' saith he, ' I suffer these things: nevertheless I am not ashamed; for I know whom I have believed, that he is able to keep that which I have committed to him against that day.' What did Paul do when he came to believe? Saith he, I had a little righteousness, and I flung it all away, I resolved that I would never trust in it; I had learning, and knowledge, and parts, and I threw it all away, I gave it all up to Christ, to be at his dispose. He took Jesus Christ upon those terms, to give up all to him; and, saith he, For the which cause I suffer these things, I do trust him beforehand, I have committed to him all I am and have, I have not my reward yet, but I trust him, and he goes upon trust with him; he beforehand hath put me upon a great many sufferings, and for this cause I suffer all these things, because I know whom I have believed. If Christ now should fail, Paul he had been the most befooled man that ever was, he had missed of all the happiness he should have in this world; for usually they that believe in Christ, they are of all men most miserable in respect of the world; but mark it, ' Nevertheless,' saith he, ' I am not ashamed, for I know whom I have trusted.' When a man believes he puts off all to Christ, and betakes himself to him, and to what he shall do for him, and if Christ should fail this man of his trust, the poor creature would be the veriest fool that ever was; but I know I shall not be ashamed, saith Paul; and in relation to this doth the Scripture often use this word: ' He that believeth shall not be ashamed.' Isa. xxviii. 16. Oftentimes a man trusteth God for the salvation of his soul, and goes on so to do, and doth not of a long while know that God hath received him; he hath not received an earnest-penny a long while, not of what he trusted God for: for joy in the Holy Ghost is the reward of faith. Now to stand this out of purse for many years, before a man receives a penny, this is a great and mighty trust, yet thus oftentimes the soul doth; to be sure at first it doth so. A man parts with all, leaves all with Jesus Christ, betakes himself clearly and entirely to him, and whatsoever he is or can be in this world, he leaves it with him; and to be disposed of according to the directions that he shall give to his spirit and conscience for evermore. I expressed it before by that of Potiphar to Joseph, but there is a more lively expression of it, and that in a way of faith, though not upon Christ as justifying, yet it was drawn out of that faith which also doth justify; the instance is in that poor widow of Zarephath, in 1 Kings xvii. You know she had but so much meal in a barrel, and oil in a cruse, as would make a cake for herself and her child; and behold, saith she, ver. 12, ' I am gathering two sticks, that I may go in and dress it for me and my son, that we may eat it, and die.' What saith Elijah to her ? ' Fear not ; go and do as thou hast said : but make me thereof a little cake first, and bring it unto me.' Alas ! it would make but a little cake in all, for it was but a handful of meal, and a little oil in a cruse, even little enough all of it to serve Elijah himself ; yea, but, saith he, make me a cake first. This woman had need have a great deal of confidence in the prophet's words, that there should be meal and oil multiplied for her and her son, after Elijah had done ; she might have thought that the prophet, as a man half-starved, had come to put a trick upon her, to get away that little provision she had. Let me be served first, saith he ; she went and did according to the saying of Elijah, and made a cake for him first, and then you see the oil and meal increased, but first God would have her trust the prophet. Even thus doth God and Jesus Christ deal with us ; when we come to believe on him, he will have us to trust him first, and put over all to him ; and to do so is to trust perfectly.

God himself did betrust us all with Jesus Christ, and he was faithful to us, and Jesus Christ trusted all with God. How many millions of souls were to save after Christ died ! How many thousands are to come yet under the New Testament ! Christ died afore these are saved, he trusted his Father with them, and God the Father trusted him too, for he saved I know not how many thousand souls afore Christ died. The like he requires of us ; ' Make me the cake first,' saith he, and so the soul doth put over all nakedly and entirely unto Jesus Christ, when it comes to trust upon him ; it is to throw a man's self out of all possibilities of what he may be in this world. Indeed, a man must do so, if he take up Jesus Christ in earnest, for he knows not what Christ will call him unto, or what truth he will have him hold forth ; now for the soul to come nakedly thus, and to give itself up to Jesus Christ, and to do this beforehand oftentimes, when he doth not know whether Christ will save him or no ; to do this first, as the poor widow did to the prophet, this is a great matter. For a man to venture to sea, without either sail, or oar, or mast, or anything of his own, and to be wafted by free grace, and Jesus Christ, to commit himself to those winds that shall blow from him, and from that promise he makes, this is the great trust, and this the soul doth when it comes to Christ.

And as it trusts him with all, so it trusts him for all ; and all the happiness it looks for, is to be at Christ's finding for evermore ; nay, to be so at his finding, that not only its comfort shall be from him, but all its strength to perform any duty shall be all from him, so as not to do a duty without him, no, not to eternity, to receive all happiness from him, and all comfort from him. Nature, pure nature was never brought up to this, it did not know what it meant. Adam was not called in this way to trust on God, he had a stock of grace communicated to him, which lay in the use and exercise of his own free will. Now, saith nature, therefore I will see a stock before I trust, give me my portion of goods, as the prodigal said ; I will see something in myself, by which I may be able to do this, or to do that, I will see the money in my purse, before I set a-work upon this or that ; this naturally the soul doth. But now when the soul comes to trust on Christ, it doth not so, it trusts him for all, for all grace here, and glory hereafter ; it believes now upon him, and trusts him, and knows not whether it shall be able to do it the next hour ; ' The life which I now live,' saith the apostle, ' I live by the faith of the Son of God ; and it is not I that live, but Christ that liveth in me,' Gal. ii. 20.   And to do this quietly, too, is an act of entire trust; for when faith doth grow up a little, though it doth not grow up to assurance, yet it will grow up to the quieting of the heart thus, and that beforehand; and when a man is able to say, Whether I shall be saved by Christ I know not, yet I find abundance of ease and quietness by resting and trusting on him, this is a perfect confidence; thus faith is expressed in Ps. xxxvii. 7 : (now as it is a trust in promises, so it is much more in Jesus Christ), 'Rest in the Lord, and wait patiently for him,' and 'he that trusteth in me is at perfect peace.'   And as it is in Lam. iii. 29, 'Put our mouths in the dust, if so be there may be hope.' Yea, a great act of this trust is to believe against hope, as it is said that Abraham did, in Rom. iv. 18.   For the soul to cast away itself upon God, in such a pure trust as this is, that let God at any time throw it into any distress, so that he knows not what will become of himself, yet to be content, and to submit to it, and quietly to leave himself with God, and with Christ, this, though it is hard, yet when faith doth get a little heart and strength, it doth this, being enabled by the power of God to do it.

6. Sixthly, As the soul thus comes to Christ, and believeth on him, trusteth him with all and for all, so it abides by him, and will not stir away from him, in respect of waiting on him in his own way, both for the manifestation of his grace, and love, and salvation, with submission and quietness. I shall not say, that every soul that believes, finds distinctly all and every one of these things in him; I do not urge that, but I shall yet mention those that are in the hearts of believers, some one or other of them.   And as this is as main a thing as any other, I shall open all the particulars of it.

(1.) The soul abides by Christ, and there lies, as the man did at the pool of Bethesda, or as he did that did fly to the city of refuge, who durst not stir from thence for his life, for if he should be found out of that city of refuge, he was a dead man, and therefore he went thither to take up his dwelling there; and this (as I said before) the apostle alludes to in Heb. vi. 18, when he speaks of faith : 'Having,' saith he, 'fled for refuge to lay hold upon the hope set before us.'   In Acts xi. 23, it is said, that when 'Barnabas came to Antioch, and had seen the grace of God, he exhorted them all, that with purpose of heart they would προσμένειν, cleave unto the Lord;' that as they had come to him, and given up their souls to him, so they would abide by him, remain and continue with him, and not go away; therefore you shall find in the Epistle to the Hebrews, that the apostle opposeth to faith, departing from God.   You have it first in chap. iii. verses 12 and 14, where he alludeth to the Israelites departing in their hearts and spirits from the guidance of that angel in the wilderness (which angel was Christ, as he shews in 1 Cor. x.), 'Take heed,' saith he, verse 12, 'lest there be in any of you an evil heart of unbelief, in departing from the living God.'   Do not you err in your hearts through unbelief, as they did; that angel from whom they departed is the living God, is Jesus Christ himself.   And saith he, verse 14 (in which expression of his there is very much), 'we are made partakers of Christ, if we hold the beginning of our confidence stedfast unto the end.'   It is clear that he speaks of faith; the word ὑπόστασις, which we translate confidence, is the same word that is used in Heb. xi. 1, 'Faith is the evidence, or the subsistence, of things not seen.'   Now when he saith, we should 'hold the beginning of our confidence stedfast unto the end,' his meaning is, that as they came nakedly unto Christ for salvation, from him, and in him alone,—for when a man's soul first cometh to Christ, it is certain he doth so, for he is emptied of himself,—so they should continue waiting upon him, that they may be made partakers of him ; he mentions that, because the thing the soul aims at in believing, is to be made partaker of Christ ; seeing you did so at first, saith he, did you at first come nakedly unto him ?   Continue to do so still, and to wait nakedly upon him ; and he gives this reason why they should do it : ' For,' saith he, ' he is the living God.' If you wait upon men, and wait long upon them, you think with yourselves, they are but men, whose breath is in their nostrils, therefore I may lose all my labour, if I wait long before they answer me in what I desire ; but, saith the apostle, wait upon Jesus Christ, for he is the living God ; if you should wait never so long upon him, he liveth in the end to answer you ; and this indeed, in Heb. x. 38, is called living by faith, in which place also the apostle opposeth unto faith departing from God : ' If any man,' saith he there, ' draw back, my soul shall have no pleasure in him ; but we are of them that believe to the saving of the soul.'   Believing there, you see, is opposed to withdrawing from God.

(2.) I added likewise, that believing is waiting on him in his own way, even as at the first we came nakedly unto Jesus Christ, at the first looking to nothing in ourselves (for so we did if we believed) ; and when the soul hath begun thus to close with Christ, and with him alone, it finds that Jesus Christ long defers before he manifesteth himself ; and it is apt thereupon, if not to depart, yet to desert from him, and to ease and help itself some other way than by waiting and believing on him.   Now the apostle would have us still to exercise such acts of faith as we did at the beginning : ' Hold the beginning of your confidence stedfast,' saith he, and still continue to wait on him, and to cleave to him, and to believe on him.   The Galatians, you know, were soon diverted (as the apostle tells them, chap. i. ver. 6) from the gospel they had received unto another gospel ; they had begun to believe in Christ, and in him alone, but afterwards they were diverted to works, and to what was in themselves, as the soul is apt to do too much.   ' You did run well,' saith he, chap. v. ver. 7 ; 'who did hinder you ?'   ' This persuasion,' saith he, ver. 8, ' cometh not of him that calleth you.'   I desire you, saith he, to consider when you were called, how you were drawn to believe on the Lord Jesus ; remember but the first work of faith, how nakedly without works, or any thing in yourselves, you came unto Jesus Christ ; you are now diverted, and fallen away from the grace of Christ, that is, from seeking salvation in a way of free grace ; do but now remember (as he said in another case, ' Remember thy first love ') your first faith.   Certainly this your new persuasion is not of him that called you.   If this new way that you have taken up, which diverts you from Christ, had been the way, surely he that called you would have persuaded you so at first when he drew your hearts to him.   The apostle speaks clearly of the point of waiting ; for, saith he, speaking of himself and other believers that professed faith in Christ, and kept it up in the integrity of it, ' We through the Spirit wait for the hope of righteousness by faith,' Gal. v. 5 ; you began to do so too, saith he, but you would not wait as you began, but you would needs divert to ease yourselves to works, and to something in yourselves.   But, saith he, I have confidence in you through the Lord, that you did close with Christ at first ; you will be brought about again, for God will never let you rest in yourselves ; so he saith, ver. 10, ' I have confidence in you through the Lord, that ye will be no otherwise minded ' in the end.   So that now to continue to wait thus upon the Lord Jesus, to wait though a man's eyes fail (for so David saith he waited, Ps. lxix. 3), is a special act of faith ; it is a very great subjection of the creature for to wait nakedly upon God, and not to know, as oftentimes it falls out with many poor souls, what God will do with them. The business of salvation it is so great, and self-love is such a strong principle in a man, that a man had need have such a principle of faith to quiet him in the mean time; for self-love is impatient in matters of great moment, and would be put out of doubt presently, and so the heart is apt to turn to itself and to works; and it is apt also out of peevishness to say, as he did out of wickedness in 2 Kings vi. 33, 'What should I wait for the Lord any longer?' The prophet Habakkuk, speaking of faith (for though he speaks it in the case of the Babylonish captivity, yet the apostle, citing that saying, applies it to the matter of justification and salvation, whereof the deliverance from the Babylonish captivity was a type), saith, chap. ii. 3, 'The vision is yet for an appointed time, but at the end it shall speak,' and speak home to the heart, and be accomplished, and not lie, though it tarry, and therefore wait for it; 'Because it will surely come, it will not tarry. Behold, his soul which is lifted up is not upright in him: but the just shall live by his faith,' ver. 4. This text the apostle cites in Heb. x. 35: 'Cast not away your confidence,' saith he, 'for yet a little while, and he that shall come will come, and will not tarry. Now, the just shall live by faith.' It is an allusion to these very words of the prophet.

(3.) I mentioned also that the soul waits thus upon Jesus Christ with submission and quietness. A man doth not know how his soul may be put to it, and sometimes it is put to it with manifold temptations, and oftentimes those temptations are answered with nothing but submissions. Certainly submission unto God is the clearest answer of all other unto doubts or disquietness of spirit; and whensoever a man arriveth there, he is always upon ground, and will cease floating. Such acts of faith as these doth God enable his servants sometimes to put forth; for I do not mention only those that are simply and absolutely necessary to salvation, but those acts that the soul puts forth towards Christ in its treaty with him for salvation in some instance or other; in Lam. iii. 26, 29, the place I cited even now, where the prophet speaks of waiting, saith he, 'It is good that a man should both hope and quietly wait for the salvation of the Lord. He sitteth alone, and keepeth silence, because he hath borne it upon him. He putteth his mouth in the dust, if so there may be hope.' In those eastern countries, the manner of those that did profess an absolute subjection to another was to fall down at their feet and to kiss the dust, as amongst the Turks they do to their emperors at this day. Now, saith he, thus should the soul wait upon God, put his mouth in the dust, if so be there may be hope; not only wait when there is hope, but if there may be any hope, if there may be any supposition of hope, he is to wait upon God with putting his mouth in the dust. Faith it is ordained to glorify God his own way, and in glorifying of him to cause the heart to apply itself to him in the great business of salvation. It is said of Abraham in Rom. iv. 20, that 'he believed and gave glory to God.' Faith it is the great instrument of giving glory to God. Now, in the matter of salvation, what is most eminent in God? what is the flower of his glory in the way of justifying and saving a man? It is the freedom of his grace. If it be grace, then it will be free: 'I will have mercy because I will have mercy, and I will have mercy on whom I will have mercy,' Rom. ix. 15. Faith, then, it is also an instrument of glorifying even grace in all the ways of its freedom, according to all the advantages that free grace hath over us to glorify itself upon us, as it is free to accept us, or free to refuse us. For a man now to wait upon the Lord in the time of distress, and apply himself thus to the freedom of his grace by faith with submission, this, I say, is the highest way of faith's glorifying that which is highest in God in the point of salvation, for a man to cast away himself thus into the freedom of the grace of God. Absolute submission God requires of no man ; that is, that men should be content to be damned, or the like ; but hypothetical submission in supposed cases is what God enableth his servants to perform to him ; that is, submission with *ifs:* 'If the Lord,' saith David in 2 Sam. xv. 26, 'say thus, I have no delight in thee ; behold, here am I, let him do to me as seemeth good unto him.' He spake it indeed in the point of a temporal business, or a business which concerned the service of God ; had it been in the case of his own salvation, it had been the highest acting of faith in the world. What he saith in that case, the soul too saith with an *if;* 'Here I am, let the Lord do to me as seemeth good unto him.' You know that saying of Job, chap. xiii. 15, 'Though he slay me, yet will I trust in him.' In this case, this same venture for salvation thus with submission glorifies the freedom of the grace of God, and the freeness of the grace of Christ ; however, a man loseth not his end, for usually when a man begins to have such submissions appear in his spirit, God hath instantly done, and all doubts and temptations are by this answered, and so the heart is quieted, and indeed there is no objection beyond it.

7. Seventhly, True genuine faith, in its coming to Christ for justification and pardon, righteousness, or whatever else, applies and fashions the heart to ' the law of faith.' I use that phrase here, that Christ enableth the heart to apply itself in coming to Christ for all these, according to ' the law of faith,' for you have the same in Rom. iii. 26 in another case, but it is applicable to this. There you shall find that the apostle speaks of the law of faith, by which he saith works are excluded, and he argues thus : If a man believe in Christ for salvation at all, works must wholly be excluded, according to the law of faith, that is, according to the nature of faith ; if it be true faith, and genuine, it is impossible, saith he, that works should have any mixture with it. It is such a phrase, as we say, the laws of friendship, that is, which a man must keep to, and which are essential to him, if he will be a true friend, and not feigned ; so saith the apostle, if works be mingled with faith, it is against the law of faith, it overthrows the nature of faith. As a man saith, such a thing is against the law of arms, that is, when a man doth things contrary to the principle of arms, as when a man is treating, to use acts of hostility, so it is against the law of faith to mingle works with it. When he saith therefore works are excluded, he saith it is by the law of faith, by the law of the nature of faith, as I may express it ; even as elsewhere, Rom. xi. 6, he saith, ' If it be of works, it is no more of grace ;' for it is the law of grace to be grace only, and it will admit no works amongst it, and so it is the law of faith, or else it is no faith at all, if you come to Christ for salvation, to renounce works. Now, what the apostle saith of the law of faith, in that sense I shall make use of to the purpose that I have in hand, namely, this, that if it be true and genuine faith which a man comes with to Christ for salvation, then it will apply itself towards Christ, according to the necessary laws and nature of faith, and according to what by believing he seeks for at Christ's hands. Now, do but consider when the soul comes to Jesus Christ to believe, what is it that according to the law of nature in faith is necessary, that if you will believe, and believe in earnest, and believe honestly, the heart must do ? It is this, that whatsoever I would have from Christ, my heart doth apply itself suitably and answerably to Christ again, as a creature should do ; whatsoever I would have Christ be to me, in my proportion I desire answerably and suitably to be to Christ again.

As for example, if I come to a man and desire him to be my friend, and I come on purpose to him for friendship, why now the law of friendship requireth friendship from me again; it is necessary, according to the law of friendship, that that should be the purpose and frame of the spirit of a man in so coming. So saith Solomon: Prov. xviii. 24, ' A man that hath friends must shew himself friendly.' You read in Scripture (that I may yet explain this further) of a ' faith unfeigned;' as in 1 Tim. i. 5, unfeigned, without hypocrisy, without guile. You read likewise in Heb. x. 22 of drawing nigh unto God with assurance of faith; you read likewise there of a true heart: ' Let us draw nigh with a true heart, in full assurance of faith.' Now, it is not that truth of heart is itself that which God doth justify a man for, or that *that* hath any ingrediency (as not faith itself, not as a work) to justification; yet notwithstanding it is that which doth naturally flow from believing, if a man believe truly and in earnest, and is so conjunct with it as it is an essential ingredient, even to faith its being an unfeigned faith, faith without hypocrisy, without guile. I observe that when the Scripture speaks of believing for justification, it doth not only speak of an uprightness of sanctification, but of an honesty, and uprightness, and unfeignedness in the act of faith itself. You have it in Hab. ii. 4, where he speaks of living by faith, he speaks of an upright soul; another man, saith he, that doth not believe, ' his soul is not upright in him.' And so in Psalm xxxii. 1, 2, ' Blessed is he whose transgression is forgiven, whose sin is covered. Blessed is the man unto whom the Lord imputeth not iniquity, and in whose spirit there is not guile.' This very place of the psalmist the apostle quoteth in Rom. iv. 7, 8, to hold forth this great truth, that our justification before God doth lie and consist merely in God's not imputing sin to us, but the righteousness of the Lord Jesus, and so consists in nothing in us. And therefore, if you observe it, you shall find that he leaves out this sentence, ' and the man in whose spirit there is no guile.' Why? Because it is not uprightness, or anything in us, that is any ingredient in our justification, and yet the prophet David hath it of the man who believeth thus for justification; he is a man, saith he, in whose spirit there is no guile; that is, he is sincere in the very point of believing for justification and blessedness, of which he there speaks. And it answers to those other phrases of ' faith unfeigned,' or faith without guile, and of ' drawing nigh with a true heart, in full assurance of faith.'

CHAPTER VI.

That where there is true and unfeigned faith, the soul is prevailed on to consent to give itself to Christ in all services and obedience.—That yet this choosing of Christ to be our King and Lord, and submitting to him accordingly, is not that act of faith which justifies a man.

I will now explain what it is for a man to believe unfeignedly, or according to the very law and nature of faith: and I shall open it to you briefly.

Thou comest to believe in Jesus Christ; let me ask thee this question, What is it thou aimest at in thy coming to him? what wouldest thou have from him? what wouldest thou have with him? what is thy intent, thy business with him? The soul will say, I would have pardon of sin, and I believe on him for the forgiveness of my sins; for ' blessed is the man whose sin is forgiven;' and forgiveness lies only in him. Why now, according to the law of faith, according to that ingenuity* and unfeignedness of faith, what will be the issue of it? Thou wilt let fall all the weapons that are in thy hand against God presently. It floweth, I say, naturally, from the very law of believing. As, for example, if a traitor, having been a rebel against his prince, should come to him for his sovereign grace and favour, to pardon and forgive him, he comes to seek pardon of his prince, who may choose whether he will pardon him or no; and then certainly the very law of his coming to him for grace, requireth (and requireth it naturally, and it cannot be otherwise) that this man should come nakedly, and come upon his knees, and lay aside all his hostility, and his weapons which he hath used against him. So it is likewise with the soul that comes to Jesus Christ for the pardon of sin; it is against the law of faith to do otherwise, as truly as it is against the law of arms for a man in a treaty for peace to come and practise any act of hostility. This you shall find in the Scripture to be natural unto faith, and to flow from it as naturally as any thing can do, Hos. xiv. 2. There the prophet sets them a-work to seek by way of faith, mercy at the hands of God: ' Take with you words,' saith he, ' and turn to the Lord; say unto him' (this now is the voice of faith), ' Take away all iniquity, and receive us graciously'; and, ver. 3, they coming thus unto God, say, ' Asshur shall not save us,' *i. e.*, no creature shall help us, ' for in thee the fatherless findeth mercy.' We look for help from thee alone, and we come to thee for grace; take away all iniquity, and receive us graciously. What follows upon this? what follows as a natural and necessary consequent upon it? Read the 8th verse, ' Ephraim shall say, What have I to do any more with idols?' God doth not come in here, and say, Ephraim, you must leave your idols; but Ephraim saith it himself, and he saith it as finding it inconsistent with what he is seeking for: I am seeking for grace at the hands of God, and to have all iniquity taken away, what have I therefore to do any more with idols? This is the voice of faith, and the law of faith. So again, when you come to believe, let me ask you, What do you come for? do you come for pardon? what is it in God that should move him to give you pardon? Oh his free grace, his infinite love! What kind of love is it you seek for, as that which only must pardon you? A love unchangeable, such a love as is not bestowed upon the rest of the world, which millions of nobles, and great ones in the world, have no interest in; a love that continueth to everlasting, a love that freely accepts you for nothing in yourself. This indeed and in truth is the aim of your faith, for you can have pardon from no other principle in God, but from such a love as this. If that faith now aims to have from God such a love, out of which, and out of no other a man can be pardoned, and casteth himself upon God for this, and without this is never quiet; if faith come to God for this, if it be faith unfeigned, if it keep to the law of faith, if it be faith without guile, if there be a true heart in this faith, if there be an honest heart (for that is another expression that Luke hath, Luke viii. 15, and he means not only in respect to commands, and the like, but in relation to the word of the gospel, holding forth Christ to us, to believe on him), if, I say, a man have an honesty of faith, and an ingenuity* of faith, and cometh unto God for such a love, it must needs frame and fashion in a natural way the heart to a suitable disposition unto God. I find in Acts xi. 26, where Barnabas bids them by faith to abide by the Lord, it is said, he exhorted them ' with purpose of heart' to do it. There is a purpose of heart that is always the ingredient in the nature and being of faith, for faith you must know is seated in the whole man, hath its effect upon the

* That is, ' ingenuousness.'—ED.

whole heart, therefore it draws out all in a man, that as the will doth trust in Christ, so there is a cleaving to him with a genuine purpose of heart. Whatever now faith would have from God, and comes to God for, it comes to God upon the terms of the law and nature of the thing, to return in its proportion that to God again; the heart behaves itself accordingly, and must needs do so when it comes to believe. Abraham when he believed upon God for to have his Son Jesus Christ (for he saw his day, and knew that he was to be put to death, or at least that he was to be saved by him), would he have God's Son from God? doth he believe this in earnest? and doth he come to God for salvation through his Son to be given for him? This faith now being honest faith, faith unfeigned, genuine faith, saith he, God shall have my son again; and though Abraham had not that distinct thought when he first believed, yet there was seminally in his heart, when God called him to give up his son to God; and you have it there in James ii. 22. Further, when the soul comes to Jesus Christ for pardon, I ask thee again (and do but consider it), what is it that thou dost come to Christ to be pardoned through? I come to him to be pardoned through his blood, and through his sufferings, his having borne the wrath of God, which is the only all-sufficient sacrifice of himself, offered up to God when he bore our sins upon the cross. Dost thou so? The very law and nature of faith, if it be genuine, hath this seed and principle in it, which I say is naturally and essentially an ingredient in it, that it will make thee to say, as the apostle himself cries out in Rom. vi. 2, 3, &c. How shall I then live in that which Jesus Christ died for? Do I come for every part of Christ's obedience to be counted mine? Certainly then the very law of faith frames the heart to this, to conform myself to that obedience of his, to apply myself thereto. The law of faith seminally doth all this, and it is not only in the case of assurance of the love of God, but in the case of depending upon the love of God; not only in the case of assurance that Christ died for me, but in depending upon this, that Christ died for me. Thus faith hath a thousand ways whereby it sanctifies the heart, by going to Christ for virtue, by looking to the example of Christ, by looking to its oneness with Christ, and the like; but the truth is this, that that which we call sanctification (or call it what you will), is contained seminally in the very law of faith, when it is actually drawn out and exercised. You call it repentance, and sanctification, and the like, but seminally it lies in believing, and in the very law of believing, if it be faith unfeigned, if it be a true and genuine act of faith, which I take it is the reason why all is ascribed to believing. It is not as if the soul when it comes to believe, and sees itself lost without Christ, &c., concludes, I must repent to perform a condition of my justification: no; but the very nature of the thing doth it; for if a man come to God otherwise, he may be answered as Isaac answered Abimelech, Gen. xxvi. 27, 'Wherefore come ye to me, seeing you hate me, and have sent me away from you?' Or, as Jephthah said to the elders of Gilead, Judges xi. 7, 'Did not you hate me, and expel me from my father's house? and why are you come unto me now, when ye are in distress?' If any man comes thus to God, can he think he shall be accepted? So that, I say, repentance and sanctification, take the acts of it, they are all seminally included in faith, and flow from it, if it be faith unfeigned, and without guile, if it be faith that resteth upon Christ for the blessedness of having our sins covered. But let me add this for caution's sake, though this is what the law of faith, when the soul comes to treat with Christ for justification, requireth; yet it is not that upon which, and that act for which God doth justify us; but rather, I say, whatever God respecteth in faith, trusting on him is certainly that act which he hath singled out for the purpose of our justification.

The soul, in treating with Jesus Christ for justification, according to this law of faith mentioned, doth apply itself to all, and the whole that is in Christ, or of Christ, or belonging to Christ, and doth give up the whole soul to God and to Jesus Christ. If a man do believe with faith unfeigned, this is withal included in the very nature of it ; although indeed when I come to Jesus Christ as a justifier, for that is my particular business with him, I believe on him that justifieth the ungodly ; yet being come, faith corresponds or applies itself to all that is in Christ, or of Christ, or belonging to him any way. I shall endeavour to explain and prove this. You have often heard it, and I find it in some discourses urged that faith is not only a believing on Christ, but a taking and a receiving of Christ, and that therein also lies the act of justifying ; but I do not urge it so; for I take it, that the formal act of justification is when the soul resteth and believeth on the Lord Jesus, and the Scripture carries it so throughout. Yet withal notwithstanding this taking of Christ, this applying the whole soul to whole Christ, and all that is of him, or in him, or belonging to him, is essential to this faith, it is included in it, even in the very nature of the faith itself, if it be unfeigned faith, if it be honest faith, if it be faith that is faithful, as I may so express it. I shall endeavour to explain this by degrees.

(1.) I lay this down for a most certain truth and principle, that God hath ordained the spirit of faith to be that great principle in the soul till it come to heaven, whereby the soul shall immediately treat with Jesus Christ or God in Christ, all those ways whereby he is to be treated withal by the soul ; so that all sorts of transactions between God and Christ pass through the cognisance of faith, and are let first into the soul by faith. So that as Jesus Christ himself is a mediator between God and us, in bringing us to God, so the spirit of faith in the soul is that whereby the soul doth treat with Christ, is both the spirit of faith which the Holy Ghost who acts the soul in the ways of believing, and the principle of faith in the soul itself. When you come to deal with Jesus Christ, or with God through Christ, all things else are shut out of doors, and there is none that appears, or are seen together, but God and Christ, and the spirit of faith in the soul, and the soul acting faith towards God thereby ; so that whatever excellency is in Christ's person (besides his being a Saviour, or the object of justification), whatever relation besides God hath put upon him to bear towards the soul, and ordained him to be unto it (as there are multitudes of them, as an head, an husband, a prophet, lord, and king), all these that faith which doth justify is also ordained to take in, and unto these all doth the soul that comes to Christ for justification suitably apply and demean itself, it being, as was said, the only eminent principle that is ordained to treat with Christ ; so as although the consequent of believing may be love, and mourning for sin, &c., yet that which transacts all with Christ as he is a king, as he is a priest, as he is a prophet, as he is excellent and glorious in himself, is faith ; and it is faith that transacts all these first and primarily, nakedly and immediately, with Christ, and then love and all other things arise. Hence therefore faith that comes to Christ for justification is such as is fitted to take in and apply itself to all that is put upon Jesus Christ in his relation to us, and all that faith shall be instructed in, it apprehends it and closeth with it. For otherwise there should be something in Christ ordained by God to be to the soul, which the soul should not have a principle to take in or apprehend ; for whatsoever Christ is ordained to be to the soul, the soul apprehends it only by faith. Yet,

(2.) Although all such applications of the soul to Christ by faith, as of consenting to be Christ's, the taking the person of Christ to be mine, &c., are the proper peculiar acts of faith, yet are they not that formal act of faith as justifying; but the Scripture puts this upon what is here mentioned, seeing and believing on him; and although the soul is thereby married to Christ as an husband, as Rom. vii. 3, 'To bring forth fruit to God,' yet to take him under that notion as an husband, is a conjugal act, whereas justification is a forensical act in God, and believing upon him is answerable. And then again, to take him upon consideration of his excellencies as an husband, is an act of love, and so if this was the justifying act, love would go before faith, whereas love ariseth from the acts of faith. Yet,

(3.) Although thus to take Christ, and to receive Christ as a lord, and as a king, and a husband, and apply the soul accordingly to him, be not that formal act of faith as justifying, yet all such acts do flow from, and are contained in, the very nature of that act of faith that seeketh justification from Christ, and this according to the law of faith before mentioned, so as if it be faith unfeigned, faithful faith, that soul who comes to Christ for justification, if it comes truly to him as such, doth withal necessarily take him as a lord, as a king, as a husband, in all his relations, and accordingly applies the soul wholly to him. You shall find therefore in John i. 12 that which is elsewhere called believing on his name, is there called receiving of him: 'As many as received him, to them he gave power to be the sons of God, even to as many as believe on his name.' He that doth believe on the Son, he also receiveth him; and how receiveth him? He receives him as he is a Lord as well as he is a Saviour; that is clear and evident from what is the occasion of this speech in the verse before, for that which others are blamed for in that 11th verse is, because they received him not as such: 'He came unto his own;' that is, he came unto his own house, as a lord and master over his own house (for so indeed the phrase implies, the phrase εἰς τὰ ἴδια, to his own, as it is elsewhere translated; so in John xix. 27 John is said to have received Mary, Christ's mother, εἰς τὰ ἴδια, to his own home or house; the like you have Acts xxi. 6); 'and his own received him not.' They did not receive him as one that came as a Lord, and that was to be the 'Lord over his own house,' Heb. iii. 6, as we are said to receive a king when we acknowledge him, and are subject to him as such. Now then you see he explains the one by the other, believing on his name by receiving of him, and receiving of him by believing on his name; now from hence I infer that whosoever believes on the name of Jesus Christ for salvation, it is in the nature of that act to receive him also as a head, as a lord, as a husband, as a king, &c. And that which further explains this is Col. ii. 6, 'As you have received Christ Jesus the Lord' (mark the words), 'so walk ye in him.' All obedience is but walking in Christ, as faith is receiving of Christ, and that as Jesus the Lord; now what is said of receiving Jesus as a Lord, it is true of receiving him under any other relation he bears towards us, wherein the word doth manifest him, as a husband, as a head, as a prophet, as a king, &c.

(4.) The next thing I add to explain this, is, that yet it may be, that at the first when a man comes to believe on Christ for salvation, he hath not those distinct thoughts of taking Jesus Christ as a king, and as a husband, and the like, though still it is included in the very nature of that act of faith that comes to him for justification (if that faith be genuine), so as the heart doth virtually and implicitly do all this in the very coming to Christ for justification. And as to this *first*, Christ is pleased to deal with some men in their coming to him so distinctly, as haply to propound all of Christ at first, and to carry on the soul in that way and manner in the whole treaty with him. Thus it was with Paul from the first, who sought Christ's person first, and then his righteousness : ' Lord,' saith he, ' what wilt thou have me to do ?' Acts ix. 6 ; and Philip. iii. 8, ' I count all things but loss and dung, that I may win Christ :' I have, says he, and do so at present too. He had done so from the very first, and what was the order and design of his faith ? ' That I may win Christ' (says he) ; he mentions that first, that he may have his person first, and that being found in him he might have his righteousness, and not his own. And I myself have known some, that when they have seen their lost condition, have come unto Jesus Christ, and looking about for a warrant for them in particular for this, they have found this ground, that God hath commanded them to believe, and so authorised them to go to the Lord Jesus, of which being assured, and then going to Jesus Christ, he told them that he could not deny them his righteousness, because he is his Father's servant : and it is true they had his warrant, and so he must give it them ; as if I have a ticket from the king, to have so much money from the lord treasurer, he being but a servant, and I having the king's warrant, he cannot deny to pay it to me ; but withal, the soul thus coming to Christ, authorised by the command of God so to do, Christ hath yet dealt thus with that soul : It is true (saith he), I cannot deny you that righteousness which you come to me for, for I am appointed by my Father to give it unto all that come to me for it. But know withal, that my Father hath appointed me to be as a king to you, to be as a lord, to be as a head to you. I say, thus distinctly hath the thing been driven, and the treaty been made. But,

Secondly. All souls are not thus distinctly dealt withal, but they have this virtually and implicitly : for, first, many poor souls, when they first come to Jesus Christ, their minds are swallowed up so much about pardon of sin, that their present thoughts did then only in an explicit way look upon Christ as a Saviour, though that act of faith in coming to him only as a Saviour, being such a faith as is genuine, and true, and in earnest, and ingenuous (at the same time that the soul seeks salvation by him), it includes a disposition to be anything Christ would have it to be towards him, or a submission to Christ in anything which he is ordained by God to be unto the soul ; yet so as that they have not such explicit thoughts at that moment drawn forth, they do not make such an explicit consent of taking him to be their king, and their head, and the like, to make a marriage with him ; I say, they have not these distinct thoughts drawn out in their first coming to Christ, whether it be in respect to the taking and receiving him as a lord and husband, or whether in respect to the taking Christ himself the Saviour, many cannot say, that the revelation of Christ to them was under the consideration of God's offering, or giving Christ unto them, and that so they did receive Christ and take him ; but they can say, they have come to him, and yet in their very coming (as the truth of it is) they do take him ; but because taking of him implies a looking at him as given, yea, the phrase to take him, implies an apprehension in them, that he is given to them as theirs, for a man is to take only what is his own, and so in common understanding it would seem to imply that the faith of a believer hath for its ground a thought that God hath given Christ for him in particular, which many truly believing souls cannot find ; they must therefore come to him as given by God for sinners, &c.

Thirdly. Neither doth God so drive on this treaty about justification, that he should keep off and suspend to justify the soul coming to Christ for salvation, till the soul first doth distinctly apprehend that it must have his person before it can have his righteousness, and that he is to be to it a Lord and King, as well as a Saviour. We cannot conceive that God should forbear to justify the soul, till it comes to have such distinct thoughts, for such distinct apprehensions of Christ many poor souls cannot tell how to make out at the first, neither doth Christ drive on the treaty of the soul with him in such distinct terms. But as was said, this is in the very nature of the act; and though they come to Christ only for justification, yet if it be a coming unto him in good earnest, they do, by that very act, take whole Christ, and all that is in him, and all that he is ordained to be to the soul. For as it is in marriage, though a woman marries one that is rich that all her debts may be paid, yet she marries him, and takes him as an husband, to all other ends and purposes else. Or I may illustrate it by a comparison of the contrary, which your ears may well bear, for we use to illustrate one contrary by another. Those that are properly conjurors, they never make a distinct and explicit contract with the devil, but by going to him to do such and such things for them, they take the devil to be their head, and they give their souls up to him by an implicit covenant, even by their very going to him. So doth the soul by going to Jesus Christ in earnest, to be justified by him, and that according to the law of believing, though it comes to him at first for nothing but justification, yet because the law of believing doth require a man to take whole Christ, the soul doth it, and doth apply itself to that law, that whatsoever the word doth reveal concerning Christ, the soul corresponds with it. And if faith be genuine and ingenuous, it naturally includes this in it. If I seek salvation from him who, being all excellency and glory, became nothing, and emptied himself of all for those who are saved by him, who gave his whole self to purchase that salvation which I seek, the law of faith then requires that I should submit, and apply my whole self to him, and to all in him. But yet so it is, that the soul is drawn out to do all this, as upon coming to Christ, he is revealed to the soul, and it is instructed in him. In John i. 12, he having said, 'As many as received him,' then, as it were, thinking that this needed an explanation, he mentions by way of interpretation, 'even as many as believed on his name;' and this explication is on purpose to relieve many a poor soul, who thinks with itself, Alas, I cannot remember that I did thus distinctly receive him as my Lord and Head, or that I saw God the Father giving of him to me, to be such unto me. Ay, but hast thou believed on him? Then thou hast received him: 'As many as received him, even those that believe on his name.' The like you have in Luke xiv. 26, compared with Mat. x. 37: 'He that hateth not father and mother, is not worthy to be my disciple;' so it is in Luke. But in Mat. x. 37, 'He that loveth father and mother more than me, is not worthy of me.' Because whosoever comes unto Jesus Christ, and gives up himself to be a disciple to him, the very nature of the thing is to come to him for himself, and upon his so doing, he hath Christ himself. It is, you see, made all one. Now I say, it is all virtually contained in our coming to him for justification, because that the soul, when it comes to him in earnest, comes with that truth and with that unfeignedness that still, according as Christ is revealed, what he is ordained to be to the soul, so it doth and would apply itself to him; and this is evident also by this, that these poor souls that come thus to Christ distinctly for justification, though they cannot say, I remember when I was married to Jesus Christ, I cannot remember when I took him as my Lord, and King, and Head, &c., under such distinct ideas, or that the treaty was so driven on, yet they do all to him that a wife should do to a husband, they seek to please him and content him; they do all to him as servants should do to a master; and this by reason of coming to him for justification, and dependence upon him thereon, though it may be they had not, in their first closing with him, such distinct thoughts, that they came to him as a husband and as a master; and though they cannot say, that they have put forth an act of taking Christ as an husband or lord, under that distinct notion, and that such a formal contract hath passed, yet such a seminal, virtual disposition of their souls they express abundantly in supposition, and tendency of their desires towards him, wishing, Oh that he would be a husband to me, and how infinitely should I rejoice if I might be so happy in him! And though I cannot say that I have taken him under this thought, yet my soul renounceth all other lords, according to that in Isa. xxvi. 13.

Again, the truth is, that faith as to our perception is a confused thing at first; it is like the chaos, but yet like to that it hath the seeds of all things in it towards Jesus Christ; and even as in making the world God brought forth one thing after another out of that confused lump—first, he said, ' Let there be light,' and then light started up, &c., and he was six days in perfecting of the whole—so it is in faith; it is, I say, a confused lump at first, but there is the substance in it of all that ever the soul shall be to Christ, or that Christ shall be to the soul; and in drawing forth these, God doth not tie or keep himself to any constant method; he doth not make every soul to say distinctly, I will first take Christ, and then take his righteousness. No; but many a poor soul (it may be) comes to Jesus Christ first for his righteousness, and by coming to him for his righteousness, the truth is, he takes Jesus Christ himself; and yet in the natural way of method, and in the dependence of the things, a man hath first Christ, and then his righteousness. And besides, the order of these actings in the soul is as the ministry is under which a man liveth; for there is that obediential principle in faith, that whatsoever the word of God shall call for at your hands, faith is ready to apply itself to Christ accordingly. There is many a poor soul cannot say, I have taken Christ to be my husband, and yet it will shew conjugal dispositions; it will say, Oh that he were my husband! and if he were my husband, how infinitely should I rejoice! It cannot say, I have taken Christ for my Lord, when I began first to believe; but this it can say, Other lords besides him have ruled over me, but I have renounced them all; I will make mention only of his name. So that the truth is, this taking Christ as a Lord is virtually and seminally in every soul that comes to Jesus Christ for salvation, for it takes whole Christ; and as it relies only upon him, so it receives all that is in him, and all that belongs unto him; and God, who judgeth righteous judgment according to the real substance of the thing, and stands not upon formal thoughts and explicit contracts, or distinct apprehensions in the person believing, as if the want of them should make void what is substantial, justifies a man upon that faith which God sees and knows to have such a true genuine principle in it.

Having thus explained my meaning as clearly as I could, I shall now prove the substance of this truth from the Scripture. The covenant of grace under the law directed believers to look on God as their God, and to avouch him to be such; David calls him Lord, Ps. cx. 1. And in so doing, the very nature and law of faith requires and causeth the heart, according to this principle, to apply itself to Christ as to a father and as to a lord, which the prophet refers to, and interprets it, Mal. i. 6, ' If I be a father, where is my honour? and if I be a master, where is my fear? ' It is impossible the heart should come to God to be a Father (if it come to him in earnest), or come to Jesus Christ to be a Saviour, but it will turn to him, as it is in

Jer. iii. 19, ' Thou shalt call me Father, and not turn away from me.'   And
Jesus Christ, he expresseth this to be the believer's case all along in his
preaching, as in that place I quoted even now, Mat. x. 38, ' He that loveth
father and mother better than me, he is not worthy of me ; ' that phrase
doth necessarily imply that he that comes to Jesus Christ takes Christ,
and he hath Christ, whole Christ ; it is the very nature of the act to do so ;
for why else doth he speak of that man as possessing himself, for he doth
not say, He is not worthy of my righteousness, but, ' he is not worthy of
me ; ' so that it is there implied that the soul takes Christ himself under all
relations.   Why?   Because he parts with all other relations for him ; he
hates father and mother in comparison of Christ, and it is because he comes
to Jesus Christ to be all these to him ; and this Christ argues from the
nature of the thing itself, as is imported in that phrase, ' he is not worthy
of me ; ' i. e., he deals unworthily and unsuitably to what he came to me
for.   And hence it comes to be made inconsistent with faith, and against
the nature of the act, for a man believing to go on in any sin : John v. 44,
' How can ye believe, which receive honour one of another ? '   And when
Christ speaks of the soul's coming to him for rest, Mat. xi. 28, he mentions
his yoke, as elsewhere taking up his cross ; and in Luke xix. 14, he expresseth their unbelief by this, that they would not have him to reign over
them.   Our Lord and Saviour Christ, he was a mean man in view, and all
the world contemned him, and the gang of the world was against him, and
he that would keep his correspondency with the world, and hold in with
the world, and have honour from the world, he would never believe on him ;
for if he did believe on him in earnest, he would let go all his correspondency
with the world, and take Jesus Christ, ipso facto, as his Lord and as his
Master.
     And the apostles preached accordingly, as you shall find in Acts ii. 36 :
' Let all the house of Israel know assuredly, that God hath made that same
Jesus, whom ye have crucified, both Lord and Christ.'   He would have them
know this, and know this assuredly, that God had made him, as Christ the
Messiah to save them, so he had made him Lord ; and in Acts v. 31 you
have the like : ' Him hath God exalted with his right hand to be a Prince
and a Saviour.'   Whoever therefore comes unto him as to a Saviour, if he
come in earnest to him for salvation, if it be faithful faith, if it keep to the
law of faith, he doth also necessarily apply himself to Christ as to a prince ;
for, mark it, for what end doth the apostle quote this ?   They had said, ver.
29, ' We ought to obey God rather than men ;' and then they give this
reason for it, because he is exalted to be a prince (they say), therefore we
ought to obey him ; and upon those terms we and others also have believed
on him.   In like manner they add, verse 32, ' We are his witnesses of
these things ; and so is also the Holy Ghost, whom God hath given to
them that obey him ;' that is, that have received Jesus Christ as a Prince
as well as a Saviour, giving that as a true description of believers.   Hence
therefore faith is not only opposed to doubting, but it is opposed to disobedience.   You have an express place for it in 1 Peter ii. 7, ' Unto you
which believe he is precious : but unto them which be disobedient, a stone
of stumbling,' &c.   Unbelief, you see, and unbelievers, are expressed by
being disobedient.   Why ?   Because virtually and seminally taking Jesus
Christ as a Lord and a King, in all things to obey him, is contained in the
very nature of faith.   You have it in your very creed—' I believe in Jesus
Christ the Lord '—and the same is imported too in that text (though it be
not the whole meaning of it), Eph. iii. 17, ' That Christ may dwell in your
hearts by faith.'   This phrase imports an having received him into the

heart by faith, as a Lord into his own house; and so it answers to that in John i. 11, 'He came to his own,' &c.; εἰς τὰ ἴδια, to his own house, as Lord over it. There is in a believing soul a door of faith opened, Acts xiv. 27, to receive the King of glory; thus the heart sets open all its doors, as you have the expression, Ps. xxiv. 9, 'Lift up your heads, O ye gates; even lift them up, ye everlasting doors; and the King of glory shall come in;' and gives up all the keys unto Jesus Christ, and sets him up a throne, there to dwell and rule. And that is the reason why, though heaven is his throne, and earth his footstool, yet he delights to dwell in a broken and humble spirit, and in a believing heart, because he can rule there, and he may do what he will in that heart; and accordingly we are said to receive him when we do believe. Hence therefore you shall find in Scripture that all the profession of faith and of Christianity is expressed to us by this very thing, calling of Jesus Christ Lord. You have it in 1 Cor. xii. 3, 'No man can say that Jesus is the Lord, but by the Holy Ghost.' He was speaking of their being converted to the faith, and he expresseth it by calling Jesus the Lord. To the same purpose is the apostle's exhortation, Heb. iii. 1, 2, 'Let us look to Jesus, the Apostle of our profession,' to guide us, as well as to him our high priest to save us. And answerably he speaks, Heb. v. 9, that 'he becomes the author of eternal salvation to them that obey him;' and it is such salvation as is eternal in the issue. In 2 Cor. v. 15 you shall see it is made the very law of believing: 'The love of Christ constrains us; because we thus judge, that if one died for all, then were all dead: and,' saith he, 'he died for all, that they which live should not henceforth live to themselves, but unto him which died for them, and rose again.' You see it is included in the very nature of the thing. Do I believe that Jesus Christ died for me? or, do I come to Jesus Christ to be saved by his death and by his resurrection, I myself being a dead creature without him? Thy heart then cannot but judge that it is the very law of the thing, that therefore I should live to him that died for me and rose again. Compare this now with Rom. xiv. 7: 'None of us,' saith he, 'liveth to himself,' that is, none of us that are true believers; for 'to this end,' verse 9, 'Christ both died, and rose, and revived, that he might be Lord both of the dead and living.' Do I come to Jesus Christ now to be justified by his death, and by his resurrection? Why, he that died and rose again both died and rose again that he might be Lord both of the dead and living. Hence therefore, saith he, none of us liveth to himself; the natural and necessary law of the thing requires that we should live unto Christ. So that, I say, if it be faithful faith, if it be faith that is genuine, and that keeps to the law of believing, according to the nature of the object, when it comes to Jesus Christ, to be justified by his death and by his resurrection, by the like reason it gives itself up to Jesus Christ, as to a lord and king, and all the relations that God hath set forth in his word that Jesus Christ is; therefore in 2 Cor. viii. 5 you have an expression of the soul's resigning itself up perfectly unto Jesus Christ, that it giveth up itself and all that is in it unto the Lord, and applies itself to him as to a lord and king. 'This they did,' saith he; 'first, they gave their own selves to the Lord, and then unto us, by the will of God;' that is, unto us the apostles, to guide them and direct them, but they gave their own selves up first to him. For faith causeth the heart to apply itself to the law of believing, and to all that is revealed concerning Christ in the word. It takes whole Christ, and gives up the whole soul, and that is included in the very nature of faith; so that a man cannot believe in deed and in truth unless he doth thus. Therefore now, why should we make repentance, and sanctification, and such things conditions of the covenant of grace (as many do), whereas they are all seminally included in faith; and it is impossible for a man to believe but all these things must follow. God shall not need to stand treating with sinners in such a manner as this, You come to me for salvation, therefore thus and thus I expect you should do. God need not insist on such things as conditions; for if the soul doth come to him for salvation, all this is included in faith itself, and they are part of salvation itself; and when God bids me do all these things, he doth but bid me be saved. If a prince should say to one, I will give thee my daughter in marriage if thou wilt but marry her and take her for thy wife, will a man now say that this is a condition? No; it is that without which he cannot come to enjoy her, without which she cannot be his wife, or he have communion with her; the very law and nature of the thing requires it. So it is here, and therefore is faith made the sole condition (if I may call it a condition, for there is no need to call it so much), because it virtually includeth all these. He that believeth truly, according to the law of faith, he takes whole Jesus Christ, and gives up his whole soul to him, to be ruled and disposed by him for ever. As for instance,

1. Dost thou come to Jesus Christ to be justified? and dost thou do it in earnest? Thou dost take Jesus Christ to be the fountain of grace to thee for evermore, thou dost come to him with a resolution to be nothing in thy own account to eternity, and that Jesus Christ shall be all in all to thee, and do all in thee, and for thee, and thou reckonest thyself to be a cypher, and that for evermore.

2. Dost thou come to Jesus Christ to be saved and justified by him in earnest? Thou comest to take Jesus Christ, with all the life of Christ, and all that belongs unto him. As when one takes a husband, she casts her fortune with him, as we say, to live with him; so dost thou in receiving Christ. This is Paul's phrase in 2 Cor. iv. 10, ' That the life of Jesus may be made manifest in our body;' he speaks it when he was persecuted. And what life was that? It was a life of persecution to which he cheerfully submitted. Thus thou dost subject thyself unto a conformity to all that did accompany the life of Christ personally here upon earth; thou sayest as Ruth to Naomi, Ruth i. 16, ' Entreat me not to return from following of thee: for whither thou goest, I will go; and where thou lodgest, I will lodge: thy people shall be my people, and thy God my God.' Thou takest Jesus Christ to follow him all the world over, with all the disgrace that shall accompany him; thou takest Jesus Christ with losses, and with crosses, with all inconveniences, with his crown of thorns as well as with his crown of glory, as oftentimes hath been expressed; and Christ need not make a bargain with thee to do so, it is contained in the thing itself, if thou come to him in earnest. Thou takest Jesus Christ with all his graces, the meekness of Christ to subdue thy pride, &c. For there is nothing in thee naturally but is contrary to Christ; thou takest him to have every thought brought in subjection to him. Thou takest him with all his offices; thou takest him as thy prophet, that is, whatsoever truth Jesus Christ shall reveal to thee—and thou knowest not what truths he may reveal to thee in this world, afore thou goest out of it, for which thou mayest suffer, and be called even to lay down thy blood—thou receivest it, yea, and thou wilt watch and observe where truth is, and where the Spirit of God stirs abroad in the hearts of his people, so as a child may lead thee, as the prophet says, Isa. xi. 6; thou wilt take the least hint of light, the least beam, and neglectest nothing that riseth up in the church to consider

it ; and so thou takest him as a king also to rule thee, and to be under no sceptre but under his, and under no government but under his : Isa. xxvi. 13, ' Other lords have ruled over us, but we will make mention only of thy name.' Dost thou come to Jesus Christ in earnest for justification ? Thou art pleased with him in all things, with all the counsels of Jesus Christ, all his decrees and purposes, all the ways of his providence, all that is contained in this whole book, that is his will and mind. Thy soul, because it is well pleased with Jesus Christ, is well pleased with all that is his, and thy heart will say, I wish nothing wanting either in Christ or in what belongs to him ; and this is all included in the very nature of faith. If I believe in earnest, if that my faith be suited to the object that faith believes upon, though God may draw these things out of the lump, out of the matter or chaos of faith, by degrees, one thing after another, yet it is all there, even when the soul first comes to lay hold upon Christ ; therefore we are said to go on ' from faith to faith,' and that the ' righteousness of God is revealed from faith to faith,' Rom. i. 17.

CHAPTER VII.

What the errors are to which men are obnoxious in believing.—How the fatal mistakes are to be rectified.

They do always err in their hearts.—HEB. III. 10.

The apostle's scope in quoting this psalm, was to exhort them not to harden their hearts against Christ, or against the Messiah's voice ; and the psalmist's, even as the apostle's design here, was to press this exhortation by the example of their forefathers (who in this were types of them), that they should take heed of dealing with the Messiah as their forefathers had done with Moses, which he enforceth from the fearful issue and event that befell them in so hardening their hearts against Moses that God sware against them in his wrath, that they should not enter into his rest of Canaan, which was therein a type of heaven, into which Christ's ministry propounds an entrance by faith ; and this oath was a most binding one, for the form of it, ' If they shall enter in,' is an abrupt breaking off in a vehemency of spirit, and imports the highest resolution that they shall not enter in ; it is an usual form of oath elsewhere used by God, as Ps. lxxxix. 36, ' If I fail David ;' it expresseth with the greatest vehemency that God would not fail him : so Mark viii. 12, ' If a sign shall be given to this generation' (for so it is in the Greek) ; which is explained by another evangelist : Mat. xii. 39, ' A sign shall not be given them.' And it is such a kind of oath as wherein is expressed most peremptoriness and resolution, according to our usual way of speaking (which if I do !) ; and it is a most binding comprehensive oath, for it may have all things put in for to swear by ; it is as much as if he had said, If so, then I am not God, not true, not just, &c. What one will may be put in to bind it, so as it is swearing by all things in God. Now the sin for which he sware against the Jews in the wilderness was unbelief, which is expressed here by not knowing his ways or proceedings, and by erring in their hearts ; they are both but expressions of their unbelief ; for ver. 12 he explains it, bidding these ' Take heed that there be not an evil heart of unbelief ;' and so, ver. 18, he again explains it, ' To whom sware he, they should not enter into rest ?

those that believe not, so as they entered not in because of unbelief,' ver. 19, which we find to have been their sin : Ps. lxxviii. 19, ' Can God furnish a table ?' and ver. 22, ' God's anger waxed hot, because they believed not on God, nor trusted in his salvation.'   And so now under the gospel this is the sin for which God will swear against men.   There are three sins, of which this unbelief consists, mentioned here :

1. Ignorance of God's ways ; for the mercies of God in pardoning are called his ways : Isa. lv. 9, ' My ways are not as their ways ;' it is spoken of pardoning, which men not knowing depart from God.

2. An erring in heart, not going the right way, but taking wrong ways.

3. An hardness of heart, not receiving in, or entertaining the word with dispositions and impressions suitable to the word, and such as it requires, with a soft heart.

Now the thing I mean only to insist upon, is, concerning the erring in heart ; that is, in unbelief.

Obs. That men, by nature, are exceeding apt to err in the way of faith and believing on Christ.

The point is natural from the words, as also from Rom. x. and Rom. ix. 32, where he shews how the Jews could never be brought to this way of believing, but being ' ignorant of God's righteousness,' that is, this of the righteousness by faith, went still about to set up their own.   They turned the ceremonial law, which was gospel in the type, and taught them to go out of themselves unto the Messiah by faith, as their true high priest, offering himself a sacrifice and his own blood for them, into a way of works, and thought that for these sacrifices, as they came from them, they should be accepted, of which David saw the vanity, Ps. li. 16.   This I take to be the apostle's meaning in his expression, ' They sought it as it were by works,' and not by faith exercised on Christ, as shadowed out by those ceremonies.   If God would give them any other laws, ceremonial, judicial, or moral, they would receive them.   ' Whatever,' cry they out, ' the Lord says, we will do,' Deut. v. 27, and the grave and wise, religious and devout spirits among them would set themselves to live thereby ; but the way of faith they could never endure.   The reason of it is, because this way of faith, and of being saved by Christ, is a new way, whereof there are no footsteps in nature, neither corrupt nature nor pure nature ; therefore, Heb. x. 20, Christ is called the ' new way,' whereas the old way, to be saved by something in ourselves, nature hath gone in, and conscience, though blindly, puts us upon it (for some footsteps there are in corrupt nature left) ; but here is no tract, no footstep, no guide to lead us to Christ but the Holy Ghost, who alone must guide our feet into these ways of peace : thus the apostle speaks, Gal. v. 5, ' We through the Spirit wait for the righteousness of faith.'   This he spake to the Galatians, who, having once received Christ, and clearly committed themselves to him, did yet recede to works ; and as Abraham, after he had received the promise, turned unto Hagar, who was the type of the covenant of works, hoping to have Ishmael, the typical issue of that covenant, to live in God's sight, so did these Galatians turn to a covenant of works, hoping to live thereby. They turned from Christ to the law, because this is the way of nature, and nature will ever return to itself and its own ways : ' But we,' says the apostle, ' through the Spirit, wait for the righteousness of faith.'   This is above the way of nature, and therefore it is what the Spirit must teach us ; and he doth, saith Paul, teach us.   Faith also is called the way ' by which we have access unto God,' Eph. iii. 12 ; and, Acts xiv. 27, it is called ' the door of faith.'   Now, men are naturally blind, as the men of Sodom, and cannot find it, and, as shepherds do, come in at the wrong door, John x. 1, so sheep also; for, ver. 9, he speaks it of salvation, and believing on him, as well as of false teaching.

Let us then desire God, above all things, to guide our hearts aright in the way of believing, or (to transfer the apostle's speech, 2 Thes. iii. 5) to direct our hearts in believing on, and waiting for Christ, as his phrase there is, ' even to guide our hearts into the ways of peace;' for it is a secret hidden tract, and being a way clean out of a man's self, a path which even pure nature never trod, it must needs be hard to find. Many seek righteousness, but not in a way of faith at all, as the Pharisees and papists, and those who have no more than a principle of morality amongst us, Rom. ix. 32. And even those that pretend faith, and to go that way to heaven, do yet bewilder themselves, and go out of their way ere they are aware of it. And indeed this way of faith is a way that few find, Mat. vii. 14; and let us ministers give never so plain and express directions, which the natural man's head carries away with him, yet without a peculiar teaching and leading of the Spirit, his heart will go wrong. As our life is hid with God in Christ, so the way to come unto it is hid. The Holy Spirit must take us by the hand, and lead us in unto God and Christ. It is like going up to some high lantern or minster by a way and an ascent which a man never went before; he sees several stairs, and is apt to take this way and that way, if left alone, and to mistake dangerously too, for if a man sets but a step wrong, he may fall and ruin himself.

My purpose is not to go over the differences of false faith and true, but only the mistakes in the way of faith and of believing; and those not all, but a few by way of instance. Nor do I intend to speak of the hindrances, or impediments, and pull-backs in believing; of the stumbling-blocks that lie in the way, and do hinder poor souls (such as are the discouragements from the greatness of their sins, not being humbled enough, &c.), but only of the errors and mistakes in the way of believing. Nor shall I discourse of the errors about faith in the doctrine of it, or the opinions about it, but of the practical errors in men's hearts, for of these the text, Heb. iii. 10, speaks, ' They err in their hearts,' &c. And,

I shall consider the errors of common and ordinary professors of Christ, of common protestants, as you call them, who yet are sound in their opinions about the doctrine of faith. Now, their errors are,

1. When, knowing the things that Christ hath done and suffered, they rest in a general assent to these, as that Christ came into the world, and that what is said in the word of him is all true, and the promises true, and think this is to believe, and so rest in this, without any special application, as those professors did, James ii. 19, whom, therefore, James confutes, by telling them that the devils believe thus as well as they. If, indeed, a man were only to be a witness to the truth of the gospel, and to the legacies God hath given and bequeathed therein, and that faith were no more but to give in testimony, as I acknowledge that in part it is such an act, then this might be good faith; but, alas, there may be witnesses to a covenant, and who may assent to the truth of all the promises, who yet are nothing concerned in them. Witnesses give evidence in things wherein they have no title, and so the angels are said to ' have the testimony of Jesus,' Rev. xix. 10, and the devils also bare witness to him; but a man is to believe as a legatee, that is, as one that hath an estate bequeathed in God's will, and therefore appropriation is necessary for him. You shall nowhere almost in Scripture find, where the general assent to the gospel is made and acknowledged to be faith, but that in the same Scripture, not far off,

an act of application comes in, and is mentioned as that which makes up complete that act of general assent: so Rom. x. 9, 'If thou confess with thy mouth, and believe with thy heart, that God hath raised up Jesus from the dead, thou shalt be saved.' Here is all put upon an act of general assent; well, but, ver. 11, this act is expressed with an act of application joined to it, 'For the Scripture says, whosoever believeth on him shall not be ashamed:' so it follows; now to believe *on* Christ is more than an act of general assent; it is to give up my soul to him to save it, and thus to trust myself with him, to commit myself to him; and to renounce all things else is an act of the will, and not barely of the understanding in general assent, as you may observe 1 John v. 5, 10, compared together.

2. A second error of these common professors is, that when they endeavour to add application to faith, yet they take a not doubting for that application, and exercise not their souls at all unto positive acts of believing. Their faith is a mere want of doubts, not an application of Christ with comfort. As they never doubt but that Christ is theirs, so they never have many thoughts about him as theirs, but do take it for granted, as a thing they never call in question, and yet it was never proved to them; but Rom. iv. 20, it is not only said, that Abraham ' staggered not at the promise,' but also, that ' he gave glory to God by believing:' not only by not questioning God's power, by a careless kind of taking it for granted, but by exercising daily acts and thoughts of faith on the promise, he daily glorified God by acts of believing, which thoughts do glorify God more than any thoughts else.

A man possesseth not Christ by faith as he doth money in his cupboard, or evidences of land that lie by him, which he takes for granted he hath, and yet perhaps never looks on them once in a twelvemonth. No; Christ is as meat that a man feeds upon, chews, digests, and his stomach works upon continually, and the man lives upon him every day, and that is the application of faith, John vi. 53, and if other bread be our daily food, then surely Christ much more; and therefore answerably it is called the life of faith: ' The life I live is by the faith on the Son of God,' Gal. ii. 20. Now life is a continuation of action and motion; and as the heart is the principle of life, and always beats, and if it lies still a man dies, such is faith; it is not a sleeping thing, a not doubting simply that Christ is mine, but a continual active whetting my thoughts upon Christ as mine, or casting myself upon him to be mine, a living on him, and in him. But these men live in a good opinion of themselves, and of Christ's being theirs, and they are not sued nor troubled in it by Satan's tentations, and no doubts come to put them out of possession, and this they account faith, and take it for granted they shall never be cast out.

3. Many in their practice do make this application of faith to be a believing and a persuasion only, that their estates are good, and so make faith only a good persuasion and opinion of their present condition; so as the object, the *terminus* of their faith, is their own estate, and not Christ and his love; their faith is not a good opinion of him, or founded upon the daily thoughts they have of his merit, satisfaction, mercy, grace, righteousness, &c. But their faith is a good opinion of themselves, arising out of the self-flattery of their own hearts, so as they honour not Christ in their thoughts so much as themselves; this is a judgment of charity to themselves rather than faith on Christ. I call it that charitable opinion which one Christian is bound to have of others, that they are the children of God, and that their estates are good, and that they are in Christ; now such a charitable opinion of themselves, whereby, as the apostle says of the

Hebrews, they are persuaded good things of themselves, is the only faith of a great many persons; but this is not to believe on Christ, but on themselves. And that their own estate is indeed the object thus of their faith is evident by this, that if any man go about to discover their present natural condition, whilst they are without true faith, not to be good, they presently fly out, and say you would bring me to unbelief and despair, for an apprehension that their present estates is good is that, and all that, which they account faith, whenas indeed those that seek their good would but bring them from a false belief of their estates and of themselves to a good and a true belief in Christ, and upon God's free grace, which are the prime objects of faith.

4. Some men if they can but get daily into their hearts such kind of thoughts about Christ as they hear believers are said to have, then they think they apply Christ indeed, when yet indeed they bring in as true a formality in the matter of believing as they do in matters of duties, without real apprehensions of Christ, or without the power of them on their hearts, and without framing their affections suitably to the things which they believe. They do but mumble over a few set thoughts of faith as they do their prayers, without communion with God; if they think over such and such thoughts of faith towards Christ every day, as papists use to say over such and such prayers every day, and can but force their guilty hearts with quietness to entertain such thoughts, and to let them have passage through them, and if they can but keep down doubts, that they may not arise to interrupt them in such thoughts, then they verily think that they believe, whenas yet these thoughts pass through them but as drink doth through men in a dropsy, they digest it not into nourishment and substance, but it runs through them, and leaves no strength, no vigour behind. Whereas to apply Christ is not simply to take him into thy thoughts only, and think thus and thus barely of him, but to strike forth a sprig or fibre from every faculty into him, to be rooted in him, to draw nourishment from him, to digest him, to give up thy soul to him, and to be one with him, John vi. 56.

5. A fifth error in the faith of this kind of common protestants is, that though they put some trust and confidence in Christ, and in their opinions and sayings profess that they renounce all but Christ, yet still secretly their own righteousness is the ground even of that their very trust on Christ, and so they make themselves the rock of that their trusting upon that only truly rock Christ. Thus they use to think that Christ will rather save them for the smallness of their sins and good dispositions, and so that in that respect they are nearer to Christ than others. The young man that came to Christ, came indeed, but encouraged by his having kept the commandments from his youth. These men stand as it were on two boughs, whereof the one is a rotten one, and so must needs fall and perish. One foot they have on Christ, but another upon themselves, on their own good works, which, though they trust not in under the notion of merit (as the papists hold), yet in a lower way they trust in them, as those which their souls in their confidence put their weight most upon, and as those which commend them to God, and make them rather accepted by God; and so they trust not perfectly on the grace revealed by Christ, 1 Peter i. 13. These use Christ and his righteousness as many ministers that are in suit for livings do the king's title, they procure that also to strengthen their own title, which they have otherwise from their patrons, but rely not chiefly on the king's, but to make all sure do take it in. Such is the case of these men; their souls have secretly recourse to their own goodness natural more

than unto Christ, although in the mean time they are sound in their opinions about justification by faith and by Christ only. For look, as all men by nature are atheists in heart, saying therein that ' there is no God,' when yet their opinions about God are right and good, so these justiciaries are papists in their hearts, and therein they practise this popery, whilst they are protestants in judgment and opinion, in the point of justification by Christ alone.

All these have had all this application and thoughts of faith without being humbled and emptied of themselves, so as it is but the natural opinion of themselves, which out of self, which was never yet thrust out of them, men use to have of themselves ; so as the mind is full of itself, and Christ doth but swim upon the top of their thoughts, they build Christ upon sand, and digged not first into themselves to let him in as a foundation, as he that built upon a rock did, Luke vi. 48. He cast out all false earth, and did let in a foundation ; but men, though they build upon Christ, yet they lay him upon their own earth undigged up at all, and so the waves do easily come between their thoughts and Christ, and temptations part them in the issue, and overthrow all.

Secondly, I shall give some further instances of men something humbled for sin, and of the mistakes that such are apt to fall into in the way of be-lieving.

1. If men come to be a little humbled, then they are apt to apply Christ too soon. If the earth be scared and raised a little, they let in Christ as a foundation presently, when yet all the false earth is not cast out. Self-flattery helps them to receive the word with joy immediately, as the stony ground did ; or if they be pricked a little, they apply the plaster when the corrupt matter is not let out, nor the sore launched * to the bottom, and so a slight apprehension of Christ skins over the sore again, and the core in it, and in the end it breaks out worse than ever. The law is a school-master to drive to Christ, but some run away from school too soon, and so want the grounds of learning, and so come to nothing. When in the uni-versity, as I may allude, they never thoroughly parsed their former estate by nature, nor saw all the faults in it, and therefore all the duties and exercises they perform anew are false and improper ; therefore he, in Luke vi., is said not only to have digged, but to have ' digged deep.' Now by this digging deep, or being humbled, I do not mean deep terrors (for it is not necessary that all earth should be digged out with pickaxes, God useth such tools unto none but only hard earth, but small shovels and spades may empty some), but so as men must be thoroughly emptied by a spiritual insight into their former estates, and see to the bottom of the naughtiness of it, and their own inability to help themselves, ere the Rock Christ be laid.

2. A second error of such is, that the ground of their applying and taking Christ, is an encouragement from this, that they are not such great sinners ; and so though as they are sinners, they see that they have need of Christ, yet because they have not been so great sinners, they think they shall the sooner be received by him, and thus they are encouraged to believe. They think because they have fewer debts they shall the sooner be forgiven, whereas it is all one with God and Christ to justify a small sinner and a great; and as the greatness of any man's sins averts not God a whit the more from justifying that man, so the smallness of a man's sins moves him not a whit the more to pardon a man. Free grace, as it respects no good to allure it, nor it is free, so nor no evil to put it off from us, nor less evil to

* Qu. ' lanced ' ?—ED.

incline it towards us. In this matter of justification (it being freely by the grace of God, Rom. iii. 23, 24), 'All,' says he, ' come short and are alike, there is no difference' in this respect. As the distance between the heavens and the earth is such as hills are not considerably nearer to the heavens than mole-hills, and the distance is so vast above both as the difference of hills and mole-hills holds no proportion, but is nothing, so it is in this case; for any man therefore to think, that because he is a smaller sinner than others, he shall be the sooner accepted of God, is to derogate from free grace, and to build something on himself. But,

Thirdly, I shall give instances in men that have been more thoroughly humbled, and of the errors they are liable unto.

1. When men have been humbled and terrified for sin by God's wrath, and filled full of disquietment, which is counted by some the only deep humiliation, then they rest in this, because they have been thus humbled, and so build not upon Christ, but upon their own sight of sin and misery. If indeed man's heart had this rock in the womb of it, as the earth hath other rocks, so as it were but digging till you come at a rock that is buried in it; if men's hearts had Christ under that false earth, which were to be digged out, then indeed it were but digging, and so then afterwards building; but there is this difference, that as Christ must be laid into the heart, and this after a digging out the false earth, so the end of this emptying us by humiliation is but to make room for Christ, the heart being full afore of itself, so that, after all, this rock must be brought in, and laid, *de novo*, anew, 1 Cor. iii. 11. Christ as a foundation is said to be laid, not as growing there, and therefore after men have digged, if then they let all alone, and say they have been troubled for sin, and know the smart of it, and therefore Christ will save them, they build on emptiness. This is as if men should think the ground must needs be good, and seed must needs be sown in it, because it hath been broke up and ploughed, whenas many fallow grounds are ploughed. Because they have been under the school-master's hand, therefore they think they are come to Christ, and must needs have learning, whenas many come up to the highest form at school that are never sent to the university, or admitted into a college, and many are soundly lashed, and yet get no learning. Though none can be pardoned till they be condemned by the law, yet many are condemned, and put into stocks and irons, that are never pardoned; these have a promise, 'Come to me, ye that are weary and heavy laden,' and they make use of it as of a promise speaking ease to their very being weary, whereas it is but a promise of invitation unto such to come to Christ, so as without coming they shall never be eased. Ease lies not in being weary, but in coming to Christ; and yet many are heavy laden that come not to him, but would get ease and rest in and from this very thing, that they were once heavy laden.

2. If men escape this error, and do not rest in being humbled, but begin to build and fill up the hole they digged, yet they lay not in the first place Christ as their foundation, they lay not in Christ nor God's rich mercy in him as the first thing to fill up their own emptiness, but they fill up the hole they have digged with new earth of their own new obedience and reformation, duties and performances, and build upon them. What in humili-ation was discovered amiss, that they endeavour to reform, and do begin to turn over a new leaf; the sins which were set upon their consciences they turn from and mourn for, and then build their faith on these reformations, so leaving Christ out, and not laying the strong rock, the everlasting foundation of God's rich mercy in him alone, so as their humiliation hath set them a-work to get grace and reformation, but not to get Christ, and to

make him their aim, and him in the first and chief place, which yet was
Paul's aim, Phil. iii. 8 (which place I delight often to urge), ' That I may
win Christ,' where Christ is made the aim, as you see, and God's free
mercy in him the aim of faith.   And this is another error and outlet at
which men leave the way of faith quite, which error some that have faith
begun are apt to run into, and though at first they were set in the right
way, yet go out, and leave aiming at Christ, and exercising faith on him,
and fall a-resting in reforming.   These, as the Colossians,* are diverted
from Christ to the rudiments of their own hearts.   This is the way of
reason indeed, which thinks doing the contrary sufficient to make amends
for the former miscarriages; but this is not a way of faith, and this is as
rank popery (though finer) as any is at Rome, and yet secretly practised in
men's hearts.

3. When men hear of Christ as a mark set up, and that him they must
have ; and so now they have set Christ up as their aim, and look to the
having him alone, because they hear this is necessary to salvation; yet
then this error is apt to fall on them, and prevent them of true faith, if
Christ rectify it not, that they think to get him by their own endeavours ;
and that secret conceit carrying them on in all, undermines faith as well as
the former, for they think to make out Christ, and work out a faith out of
themselves, by their own endeavours for time to come.   The former were
diverted from Christ unto their own new acquired righteousness and obedience, and fell a doating upon that; but these have Christ in their eye, and
do pursue after him, but yet their hearts secretly make account to attain
him through their own endeavours.   But the soul must be emptied as well
of all conceits of its own ability for time to come, as of all opinion of its
own righteousness past or present, or Christ doth not become all in all.
As men do derogate from Christ, and free grace that bestows him as a gift,
if they have an eye to their own graces and obedience instead of him, so
also if they have an eye, or secret confidence of their own endeavours,
thereby to attain him, Christ is not set up as yet, so as he must be, in such
a heart.   It is true, men may and must endeavour after faith, as Heb.
iv. 11, ' Let us endeavour to enter into that rest ;' entering into rest being
there put for believing, as appears verse 3 ; yet we must use endeavours
but as means, wherein Christ gives the heart strength to believe, and so to
endeavour in a waiting wholly on Christ to have faith given.   So as men
must come to see their own utter inability to believe, and that as God finds
them Christ, so he must give them hands to take and receive him by.   In
Rom. x. 6, 7, we have a *caveat* against this error ; for speaking of the way
of believing, and that Christ is to be believed, and confessed to be the only
Saviour, yet since the heart will be apt to say, ' Who shall ascend up to
heaven,' to bring Christ down to me, therefore he there says, ' Say not in
thy heart, Who shall ascend ?' &c.   The heart is apt to be setting up
ladders of its own making, and to say in itself, I will go pray, and seek
Christ, and so get him ; but thou must to Christ as ' near thee,' to give
thee power.

4. When the heart is humbled, and emptied of all righteousness past,
of all reformations and righteousness, and endeavours to come, and knows
that Christ bestows himself for none of those, but is wholly and absolutely
free in it, yet when the soul is thus left stripped and naked, and no righteousness, no abilities of its own do encourage it, yet still the mere self-flattery
in one's spirit that springeth immediately from self-love, will be apt to step
in, and help one to think, that rather I than another shall have mercy;

* Qu. ' Galatians' ?—Ed.

that although God shews mercy freely without respect to anything within us, yet *I* (will the heart be apt to think), rather than another, shall find it, and God will have pity on *me* rather than another. This same *self* will flatter one too much, which thought, though not seconded by any respect to any righteousness, or anything of a man's own, you will find will arise from that very self-flattery in a man, from which it is natural to a man's spirit to think well, and hope well of a man's self; even as Peter in another case said, ' Though all others, yet not I.' There is a natural self-confidence arising out of that great love which we bear to ourselves, that will offer its help to form up our faith for us. As Haman thought, I am the man the king will honour; so the heart is apt to think, ' I am the man God will save'; and this not so much from any encouragement or drawing of the heart by God, but out of the natural forwardness to think well of ourselves. Labour therefore to find your encouragement to believe to come from the consideration of what is in Christ, from his all-sufficiency, free grace, and love alluring you, and not from your own heart's persuasions merely; listen not to what self-flattery will say, but what Christ will speak in a promise; and acknowledge in believing not only the freeness of grace (that it respects no qualification in any, and shews mercy for no righteousness, ability, &c.), but also the sovereignty of that grace shewn too towards those persons whom it accepteth; see how that when all persons are stripped of all quali- fications, and are presented naked before God, and as divested of all con- siderations of good or ill in them, that should move him for or against them, that besides this freedom in accepting without respect to such considerations, he sheweth a sovereignty in his gracious will, in accepting this man rather than that, and which he exerciseth in his accepting you. And the thoughts that this depends thus upon the mere sovereignty of God, will keep down and poise this same *self*, which else will be apt to encourage one's heart above what it should; the thought of that sovereignty will lay thee yet lower, and dash all self-flattering conceits that would strike in to make out a faith, and give a hope. It will make thee to see, that any one is as fair for it as thou, and that God out of a sovereignty accepteth or refuseth, and that so it falleth as his will pitcheth; only withal thou mayest think, that thou art as fair for it as any other, even in that respect, and so there is no cause of discouragement. Do but only make the scales even in thy apprehensions and hopes for mercy, and let no qualifications in thyself, nor no self-flattering conceits of thyself, cast the balance, but reduce thy faith to a pure absolute dependence upon God's will for thy acceptation, and so shalt thou find God from himself in the end secretly swaying thy heart to rest on his love, and to quiet thy heart in so doing, and then shall thy faith give him the whole, full, and entire honour, in accepting thee, and derogate nothing from him.

5. Many make a promise the sole ground of their faith, and look no further than the letter of it; and so as the Jews were deceived with the letter of the law, and saw not into the bottom of Moses's ministry, so some are deceived with the letter of the promises, and look not to Christ in them; they see not that he is the jewel in the casket, but rest upon the superscription without, and look not to what is within; they have got some promise or other, but they never regarded to believe on Christ in and by that promise, who is the great promise that is conveyed in every promise: ' In whom all the promises are yea and amen.' They stick in the letter, take the whole shell, but crack it not, whereas it is the kernel within that is the food of faith. A child hath more wit than these men; give him a nut, and he will desire you to crack it, for there is a kernel in it that he

desires, or else he will bid you take it again. So says faith when it comes to a promise, Give me Christ in it, or I will have nothing.

6. Men seeking Christ, and finding some sweetness, their faith rests in that, and looks not out still for Christ himself and union and communion with his person ; a present is sent, they rejoice in that, and they let the man that it came from go. Rom. v. 1, one fruit of faith is having peace with God : ' And not only so, but to joy in God through Christ,' ver. 11. Mark it, it is not only a joy *from* God, but *in* God through Christ. Take heed then of resting in joy infused, when God and Christ are not the immediate object of thy joy, and communion with them in believing the chief thing desired by thee.

7. Men hearing that it is Christ's righteousness imputed by faith must save us, they seek for the righteousness of Christ as it were severed from himself, and the aim of their faith is carried forth after his righteousness, without seeking him first or chiefly, but seeking his righteousness primarily to be theirs at God's hand ; as if the suing for the money which this surety of ours paid for us, and that God should accept it for us, were all. No ; the surety himself must be ours first, and that is the right way of faith, to seek Christ first, and then to apply his righteousness for pardon. That was Paul's method, first to be found in him, then his next thought was of not having his own righteousness, but his, Philip. iii. 8, 9.

Though this I must add, that it is not Christ simply or abstractly, but Christ concretely considered, with his righteousness as he is a Saviour and Mediator, and as given for the remission of sins, who is the object of faith, and which the believer hath in his eye ; for he is first egged forward on to lay hold on Christ by the sight of sin, and as seeing righteousness in Christ that will pardon, yet so as he is to believe on him to that end, that ' in his name he may receive remission of sins,' Acts x. 43, and so as to believe upon himself first, and in believing to close with his person first.

8. Many men take Christ with his benefits, but yet chiefly for his benefits, and that is as bad as the former; this is to marry him for his portion. As you are not to sever it from himself, so nor to desire him only for it, for you hear both must go together, first him, then his righteousness ; that is Paul's method, Philip. iii. 8, 9, ' That I may win Christ,' him first ; then follows, ' Not having mine own righteousness, but the righteousness of God by faith ; ' that is, Christ's righteousness imputed by God unto faith.

BOOK II.

Of faith of assurance.—That all justifying faith is not assurance of our personal interest in Christ.—That yet assurance of salvation may be obtained. —How assurance is caused by three witnesses in heaven, and three on earth, and of the difference of their testimony.—The discoveries and manifestations which Christ makes of himself to the soul.—Of joy in the Holy Ghost.— Directions unto the faith of such who want assurance how to take in, and to make use of God's eternal, electing love, in believing with comfort.

CHAPTER I.

That justifying faith is not assurance of our personal interest in Christ, though it be an assurance of the truth of the promise.

He that hath the Son hath life; and he that hath not the Son hath not life.— 1 JOHN. V. 12.

THE first conclusion we will begin with and premise as a foundation to what follows, is, that that act of faith which justifies a sinner, is distinct from knowing he hath eternal life, and may therefore be without it, because it doth not necessarily contain prevailing assurance in it. By prevailing assurance, I mean such an assurance as overpowereth doubts and sense to the contrary, so as, in the believer's knowledge, he is able to say, Christ is mine, and my sins are forgiven; such an assurance whereby a man is a conqueror, as Paul speaks, Rom. viii. 37, when he expresseth such strong assurance. And this I first lay down, not only for more clear and orderly proceeding in this point, but also thereby to allay the cavils and exceptions which men have against the doctrine of assurance. When it is affirmed that none are in the estate of grace, and true believers, but only those who are, or have been, undoubtedly assured, by an overpowering light of the Spirit in their own sense, that Christ is theirs, and that their sins are forgiven them; when it is asserted, that then, and not till then, they did begin to believe, by such an assertion the generation of many just ones is condemned, whose faith, either through weakness, never came to such a growth of persuasion, or through temptations and prevalence of fears and doubts are interrupted in it, who yet cleave to Christ with full purpose of heart, and walk obediently towards him in all their ways. And, indeed, if that were the meaning when assurance is spoken for, that it were made the essential act of faith whereby a believer is justified, there were just cause for many and great exceptions. And yet my scope further herein is, not to encourage any to rest in such a faith, without such assurance, and content themselves with it, as many do, making a bad use of such a doctrine, and so neglect seeking for a further work of assurance to be superadded. No, the next conclusions shall manifest the contrary; but the intent of this present conclusion is, to keep such as have their hearts drawn to Christ, and upheld to believe, though without such prevailing assurance, from such discouraging thoughts, as therefore to think their estates accursed, and that they cannot be in the estate of grace, because they want such a work; for if faith be without it, then such souls that do entertain such thoughts do entertain an untruth, and that against their own souls, and the work of God in them, and make him a liar. And also my end is to keep off those that have assurance superadded to faith, from censuring the present condition of many of their brethren, as if they were without grace, because they want such assurance.

First, I will therefore first prove, that true faith may be without such assurance.

1. Because justification and blessedness hath been pronounced to such a condition as hath wanted this assurance, and this by Christ himself, who is to judge at the latter day who are in the estate of grace and who are not. Thus, Mat. v. 3, in the first sermon, whereof we have the notes, of blessed persons recorded, he pronounceth a blessedness to the poor in spirit, to the meek, to those that mourn, to those that hunger and thirst after righteousness, all which estates want assurance. Now Christ's scope was not to draw those in which such dispositions were, to begin now to believe, for that were to found faith upon conditions; but his scope is to shew that such have true faith begun. Poverty of spirit is when they apprehend themselves poor and empty, it is not being spiritually poor, for then they could not be pronounced blessed, but an apprehension of their condition, as such (opposite to the apprehension the church of Laodicea had of themselves, who thought themselves rich, and that they had need of nothing), and so implies want of assurance. So mourning under the sense of their sin and misery implies wanting comfort, as the promise that they shall be comforted implies, which comfort assurance brings always with it, and is indeed the thing promised to these, afterwards to be given them. So hungering after righteousness implies emptiness, and the thing promised is fulness, so as all these want assurance, and all these Christ pronounceth blessed, and none are, or can be called blessed, but such whose sins are at the present forgiven; as Paul after him defines the blessedness the Scripture speaks of to consist in this: Rom. iv. 6, 7, ' David describeth the blessedness of the man unto whom God imputeth righteousness ;' he gives a description, a definition of it, that it lies in this, ' Blessed are those whose iniquities are forgiven, whose sins are covered.' If blessedness then lies herein, then surely the estate of those persons was such as their sins were forgiven, and yet they wanted assurance, and yet not faith, for a man is justified only thereby: Rom. iv. 5, ' To him that believeth on him that justifieth the ungodly, his faith is counted for righteousness.' Therefore, these that were poor [in] spirit, that mourned, that hungered and thirsted after righteousness, had faith lay at the bottom, as is necessarily to be supposed; for a man never comes to be truly poor in spirit, till he sees the riches that are in Christ and in free grace; for it is Christ's fulness, and the sight of it, that empties a man, more than all the legal sight of his insufficiency and misery, and yet the believer in the sight of all this fulness still thinks himself therefore deeply poor (wanting assurance), for though he admires that there should be such riches, yet he hath no share in them in his sense yet, and no power to lay hold on them. Faith in its first act discovers at once with one eye a man to be poor and ungodly, and with the other looks up to Christ's riches, and to him that justifies the ungodly, Rom. iv. 5. So hungering and thirsting after Christ's

righteousness (to instance in no more) doth imply faith as the bottom of it; for none can so hunger truly, but he that sees the true worth and preciousness of Christ. ' Unto them that believe only Christ is precious,' 1 Peter ii. 2; and Christ is precious not out of self-love only, but out of an apprehension of the suitableness and fitness of all that is in him for them, for true hunger also implies that. What makes the stomach hunger after things but suitableness? Thus the soul hath an instinct to Christ as its meat and nourishment, and that supposeth faith also, though assurance be the eating of him with comfort and filling contentment; and as hunger goes afore eating, so faith goes afore assurance. Now if such souls Christ pronounced blessed here, surely if they should die in this condition, at the latter day he would not go back from his word, but he would say, ' Come, ye blessed,' also. Neither is their blessedness pronounced to a future condition to come, which these dispositions made way for, for, besides what is before said, Christ in the very words tells us, he speaks it of their present condition, 'theirs is the kingdom of God.' This he spake to such as John's ministry had converted, and that truly, who (as it is in Acts xix. 4) did teach the people not humiliation only, but faith also, ' saying to the people, that they should believe on Jesus Christ.' And Christ he comes after to preach assurance to such, and to tell them that their sins were forgiven them. As a farther confirmation, I will add to this an instance or two.

(1.) Let us look on the poor publican, and let us consider his estate, which Christ there approves, and we shall find it to have faith in it, and yet not assurance, Luke xviii. The Pharisee he had an assurance that his estate was good, built upon himself; for, ver. 9, Christ's scope was to discover their presumption that trusted in themselves that they were righteous, and to this end tells them of a poor publican that indeed comes into God's presence, but it is at a distance: ' he stood afar off.' Had he had assurance, it would have encouraged him to have drawn near with boldness: Heb. x. 22, ' Let us draw near with full assurance of faith.' But, on the contrary, he was so much cast down with shame, that he could not lift up his eyes to heaven, and yet he lifts up an eye of faith: ' Lord, be merciful to me a sinner.' He flies out of himself, and hath recourse to God's mercy, which, by all his carriage, and the opposition made, he had no assurance of. The presumptuous Pharisee could do nothing but give thanks, his assurance was so great. This man in an humble prayer begs that mercy that he yet wanted in his own sense, and yet Christ pronounceth the state of this man justified: ver. 14, ' I tell you,' saith Christ (and I promise you I will believe him), ' that this man went to his house justified, rather than the other.' He was then certainly justified, and therefore out of his example he makes this promise to such as are truly in his condition, that ' they shall be exalted,' in the same verse.

(2.) That also of the woman of Canaan, to whom Christ would give no outward word of encouragement, who yet had true faith, which Christ extraordinarily commends, Mat. xv. 22–26.

Besides these instances, I will give you demonstrations of it, and then the reasons and grounds of it.

(1.) The first demonstration is drawn from the state of desertion, wherein a true believer may want assurance, when yet he continues to believe; ' for the just live by faith,' Hab. ii. 4. Therefore as when the heart ceaseth beating the man dies for it, so when faith ceaseth exercising itself the believer would die. And again, that which is a true act of faith to continue our union with Christ, may be a true act to begin that union.

Now, it is not assurance continues our union and being in the estate of grace, therefore it doth not necessarily begin it. And now then if in the course of a Christian's life he be brought to live by faith without assurance, then much more may he begin to live by it, for at the beginning it may be supposed weakest; as a man that hath had experience he hath lived may be brought into a swoon, when he doth not perceive himself to live, or into a frenzy, so as he doth think himself dead, and to live amongst ghosts, as some have done, so much more may a child that is in the womb live and not know it. Thus Heman likewise, as to his spiritual state thought himself (through a frenzy) a man dead, and to be 'free among the dead,' and to be one whom God had cut off, and remembered no more, Ps. lxxxviii. 5, and from whom God did not only hide his face in regard of the light of his countenance (which some have said is the only desertion can befall a Christian in which he retains his assurance, and doubts not but that God still is his God though he hides his face), but had cast him off, verse 14, he says he was one 'cut off by his hand.' And yet when Heman had such desperate thoughts prevailing over assurance, he had faith, and expresseth it in verse 1: 'O Lord God of my salvation, I have cried night and day afore thee.' Mark it, and you will find that it is just the voice of faith wanting assurance: he cannot call him his God; he says not, 'My God, my God,' as Christ could, when he wanted the light of God's countenance,—assurance of faith remaining in him when the comfort of faith was wanting,—but yet Heman doth look up to God as the God of his salvation; that is, as that God who must save him, and in whom his salvation, if ever he be saved, lies; from whom he looks for salvation, and to whom he hath recourse for it, though he could not say, God is my salvation. Yea, and thus it had been with him from his youth, verse 15, either he had once assurance, and now had lost it, or from his youth and first beginning had ever wanted it. And if it was either of the two, the argument holds good to prove faith not to be assurance, for still he hath recourse to God by faith in prayer, and so had faith in his heart, when yet he was under terrors and apprehensions of God's casting him off. Why should I instance in Job, David, Jonah, and many more? I will only give that direction in Isaiah l. 10. The prophet having in the verses immediately afore expressed that triumphing assurance, 'It is God that justifies me, who shall condemn?' now, saith he, if a soul that fears God wants such a light as comfortably enableth his soul to say so, yet 'let him trust in the name of the Lord.' You see then that he might exercise faith in that condition. And to say the case of this man the prophet speaks of was not a state of justification, is a gross absurdity, for the prophet calls God his God; though the dejected soul could not say so, yet the prophet says so for him.

As for those that will say, that faith is a triumphing, a prevailing assurance, I would refer them but to ten or twenty years' experience, which may (if they be not the more wary) lamentably confute them ; for they may fall into this darkness as well as Job did, and then if they do so, what is the faith they live by ? It is that of Heman's, a casting themselves upon the God of their salvation, a cleaving to him; it is that of the church in the like distress: Lam. iii. 24, 'The Lord is my portion, says my soul, therefore will I hope in him.' God did not aloud say to her soul that he was her God, but he enabled her soul to say that he was her portion; that is, to pitch on him, and choose him, and rest in him, and betake herself to him, as all the good and portion she ever looked for, which act of recumbency afforded hope as the consequent of it. Faith notes out a betaking a man's self to God, a choice of him as a man's portion, as one all the good I look for lies in, and therefore I will hope in him, for help is to be had only in him, and from him, and I will do anything that there may be hope for me. Now if sometimes those who have assurance are brought to this faith, then surely it is good faith ; and if it be good faith after assurance, then it may be so before ; and yet to this, one that hath had assurance may be brought.

(2.) That there may be true faith without assurance is evident from this, that if doubting be a corruption, as you will easily grant it is, then as all other corruptions may prevail against the spirit and other graces, so may doubting prevail against assurance of faith, and there is no more privilege of freedom promised from the one than the other. If David may fall into a gross sin, and murder and adultery may prevail, I know not but that doubting may prevail too. For believers are perfectly freed from the prevailing of no sin but that against the Holy Ghost ; and if the power of sin may prevail against grace in other faculties, I know not but the guilt of sin may prevail against assurance in the conscience also. And further, I am sure that though the Holy Ghost, the witness, be God, yet the light he witnesseth by is but a creature, a beam, a voice, a saying to a man's soul, ' Thy sins are forgiven ;' and therefore, as other prevailing workings may be interrupted, so may that also, and then what faith have men recourse unto, but such as is a casting a man's self on free grace, that faith which stood them in stead at first ? It is not the remembrance of his former assurance will uphold a man, for he may grow blind, and forget he was purged from his old sins, 2 Pet. i. 9. He speaks of assurance in that and the following verses. Assurance depends on strict and holy walking, and so may be interrupted by our remissness and negligence.

(3.) That true faith may be where prevailing assurance is not, appears by this, that the sense of belief of general principles and foundations of faith may be over-clouded and prevailed against by temptations to the contrary, and by the atheism of a man's heart, so that a poor believer shall say, I doubt whether there be a God or no, whether the Scriptures be true or no ; I cannot find I believe the truth of the promises. Thus the natural atheism of the heart may overflow, and seem to conquer this faith that there is a God, and yet then the soul believes strongly, at the same time, that there is a God ; and it appears in its actions, though not in its sense and light, for the soul fears this God in all its ways and walks, as believing this truth. Hence I argue, that if faith in the general may be overpowered in sense and inward light, when yet a man truly believes, then much more may the particular persuasion of a man's being in the estate of grace, which is but a deduction out of those general principles, be, in a man's sense, prevailed against by doubting, when yet secretly he doth most truly believe. The apostles, when Christ was dead and crucified, did almost begin to call in question the general principles of faith ; they were much staggered in them, as appears from that speech, Luke xxiv. 21, ' We trusted,' said they, ' it had been he should have redeemed Israel, and it is now the third day,' when he promised to rise, and yet we see him not. His sufferings staggered their faith, and therefore, ver. 25, he calls them ' slow of heart to believe what the prophets had written ;' and yet then they did secretly believe, and had recourse to the sepulchre, and an eye what should become of him. Thus Thomas also would not believe the resurrection of Christ, a main article, unless he saw him. Now if the faith in the principles may be in the heart, and yet be prevailed against by doubting, then much more the particular conclusions derived thence to ourselves, which are at no time so fully assented to as the other ; and yet faith must then be in the heart, for a man dies else. If the main root and stock may seem dead, much more the branches and the buds.

(4.) Wicked men are not immediately bound to have assurance, and therefore it is not the essential act wherein faith consists. They are condemned, you know, for not believing. Now if the first act of faith commanded were to believe that Christ is mine, and that my sins are forgiven, how could a man in the state of nature be bound to it ? For such an assurance of Christ being his, is not a truth in the state wherein he stands ; but yet he is every hour bound to come to Christ as the fountain of life, and to cast himself on him for his pardon, and to choose him as that means appointed by God for remission ; for Christ blames the Pharisees that they did not do so : John v. 40, ' Ye will not come to me, that ye might have life.' Therein, therefore, lies the act of faith which justifies.

CHAPTER II.

The reason why there may be true justifying faith in a man, and yet he want assurance.

As I have given arguments to prove that all true faith is not assurance, I shall now give the reasons why there may be true faith in a man who yet wants such assurance.

1. Those essential acts that are attributed to faith, and whereby it is expressed, fall short of expressing assurance in a believer's sense. Faith is expressed by seeing Christ, and his worth and excellency, John vi. 40, by looking on him as they in the wilderness did on the brazen serpent, not as that which had already healed them, but looking on it as the means appointed to cure them, and that only. So also faith is expressed by coming to him, which implies not so much a persuasion that a man's sins are forgiven by God, as a having recourse to him to forgive them, as a flying to him that is gracious, and chosen by God on purpose ; as a ' coming unto him as unto a lively stone, chosen of God,' 1 Pet. ii. 4 ; and so, John v. 40, they are blamed for not coming to him that they might have life ; and because such may truly come, who yet in their own sense may fear whether he will receive them and do them good ; therefore Christ assures such, John vi. 37, ' He that comes to me I will in no wise cast out.' Christ speaks it to assure such as do come, who, though they come, yet wanted this persuasion in their own sense. To go up to Christ for help is to trust or believe on him, as to go down to Egypt for help is called a trusting on that nation, Isa. xxxi. 1. This coming argues a choosing him, a betaking a man's self to him. Again, that act of trusting on him (as there, in Isa. l. 10, trusting on the name of the Lord is commanded, when light is wanting) doth not necessarily imply or require a prevailing assurance that God is my God, and that my sins are pardoned by him ; but there may appear a great trust in the want of the sense of this. As for example, then a traitor trusts a king, when, upon a proclamation of pardon indefinite, he comes in, and lays down his weapons, and refers himself to him ; when he leaves all his hopes among the rebels, and puts his life, his service, and all into his hands, ' if there may be any hope,' as the church in the Lamentations says, Lam. iii. 29. Such a trust was in Job : 'I will trust him, though he kill me,' Job xiii. 15, when yet God fought as an enemy against him. For trusting hath two several significations with it. The one intimates a

quiet security that the party that is trusted will do such or such a thing, as when a man says, I trust and am persuaded he will do such a thing for me; the other signification intimates that, upon an high esteem of a man's goodness, faithfulness, ingenuity, and indefinite expression of himself and carriage to others, a man puts over all to him, and commits himself, his cause, and all, upon his good will and grace, to obtain his suit; and this reliance is then accounted the greatest trust, when the man cannot say he hath a particular assurance from him in whom he confides. Thus says the psalmist, Ps. x., 'The poor leaves himself with thee,' Ps. x. 14; he rolls himself on God, Ps. xxxvii. 7, which, in ver. 3, is expressed by trusting.

Again, waiting is another act of faith, which implies a looking for help from Christ, a waiting for pardon from him, not an assurance of pardon already attained. Waiting is an act of faith, whereby a man renounceth all vain hopes and helps, and betakes himself wholly to Christ, and continues to look for help from him and none else; and this act doth not reach so far as to assurance in sense, for assurance is the thing waited for, and yet this waiting is faith. He that made the 130th Psalm was a believer, being a penman of holy writ, and it is likely to be David himself; but whosoever he was, he was then in a sense of the want of forgiveness; ver. 1, he says he was in 'depths.' And what depths? It appears by the third and fourth verses, that it was the want of forgiveness that troubled him; for he pleads, 'If thou markest iniquity, who shall stand?' and 'there is forgiveness with thee.' In this case he could not say his sins were forgiven him. Nay, he felt in sense that God retained them, and marked them, and set them on upon his conscience, and therefore that which, in this case, he builds his faith upon is this, 'Forgiveness is with thee.' It is there to be had; and answerably, an act of waiting suitable to that estate is put forth, a waiting for the Lord, ver. 5; and 'in his word' —that general promise of pardoning sinners—'do I hope.'

2. We have another reason why faith may be without assurance, if we consider the main object of faith, which first, and primarily, and adequately in the first act of it, is here in the name of Christ, John i. 12, that is, himself, his person. The object of faith is not so much this proposition, *that Christ is mine* (that is an axiom), but Christ himself, and therefore faith is still expressed by believing on him, and receiving him, John i. 12; and the reason is, because faith is that which completes the union betwixt Christ and me. Now the things united are his person and my soul, and that which makes the union is my cleaving to him as my chiefest good, and giving myself up to him, and joining myself to him, consenting to be his, and taking him to be mine, and not this proposition, that my sins are forgiven, though I acknowledge forgiveness of sins is that which my faith also aims at in him. But further consider,

First, That Christ, and Christ alone, is the first promise, and the great promise that faith looks at, and that justification and salvation, and the promises of all a man's privileges he hath, or is to have by Christ, are secondary, and therefore to be believed in the second place, and are made in Christ, and not to men till they are in Christ, for all promises are yea and amen in him, and is made all in all to us. So as ere any man can believe his sins are forgiven, or look upon any privilege which is to be had by Christ as his own, he must first be united to Christ, and Christ must be made his; there must be an act of faith closing with his person, consenting to be his, and receiving him as indefinitely offered, to be his (if he will take him), and then, and not before, can any man come to believe he hath the pardon of his sins, or that he shall have glory, and be saved. These secondary promises they are the object for assurance to work upon, but the person of Christ is the object of faith, which faith fixeth on, and the believer first comes unto Christ, and takes him, and therefore assurance of justification and salvation must necessarily come in after believing on the person of Christ. Now Christ, who is the great promise, is but indefinitely offered, though that offer indefinite is made known to all; therefore, answerably, it is not required that the act of faith should be assurance; but the promise of justification and glory, &c., are determined, and made definite to them that are believers, &c., and accordingly they still run in that strain; and therefore to believe them requires assurance. And then,

Secondly, The assurance that Christ's person is mine, is not the first object of the first act of faith, for he is not mine till I have taken him; then he becomes mine, according to the rules of the word. This indeed the heart may have, and hath, a secret hint of, of especial good will in God and Christ, in the offer of himself to a poor soul, conveyed through the indefinite promise. The believing soul doth think that God means Christ for him, and designs Christ to him; but this is not assurance, for he cannot say that Christ is his till he hath taken him; it is the taking a gift makes it the man's that takes it, and not the offer of it. So that till out of such a hint, conveyed through the indefinite promise, a man hath taken Christ, there is no room for triumphing assurance, for a man to say that Christ is his. Again,

Thirdly, If we consider in what faculty faith is said principally to reside, it will appear, that the main act of faith is not assurance. It principally is seated in the will, for the consent of that, and the knitting of that to Christ, makes the union, as consent in marriage doth; therefore believing is called receiving him, John i. 12, and coming to Christ, and being drawn to him, is the phrase by which it is expressed, and that principally is of the will. Now if the main act of faith were an assenting to an overpowering light that Christ is mine, and a setting it down that my sins are pardoned, then the main act that made the union were in the understanding; but now, that first work upon the understanding is expressed by seeing him, but not by seeing him at the first to be mine; so babes are said to know the Father, 1 John ii. 13, but not to know that he is their Father. When men assent not to the worth that is in Christ (though ignorance whereof is the ground of men's refusal of him), then it is that they make God a liar; but to close with Christ's person as tendered to me, that is the main act of faith. And it should be granted, that by drawing, John vi. 44, is meant a drawing my understanding to assent that Christ is mine, yet a drawing of the will is mainly intended.

Fourthly, Hence, therefore, I argue in the fourth place, that assurance comes in but to confirm and seal to what pure faith hath done, and therefore follows upon faith, and so all expressions that express assurance imply: as when it is called establishing or confirming, sealing and giving in earnest, and a witnessing, all these suppose an act of faith already passed, which estates us into Christ and salvation, to which assurance comes in as a confirmation. For an earnest supposeth first a bargain made, which that confirms, and a witness supposeth some act passed, a deed made, and then there is place for a witness, and so a seal comes in after the deed is drawn and concluded, to add a confirmation, so that the first act of faith doth not include prevailing assurance in it, but after men believe then comes in sealing: Eph. i. 13, ' After ye believed, ye were sealed with that Holy Spirit of promise.' And therefore the sacraments of the Lord's supper and baptism, which are seals and instruments of assurance, are to be administered after a man hath faith, or is supposed to be in a state of grace: ' Let a man examine himself, and so let him eat,' 1 Cor. xi. 28. They are not to begin grace, but to confirm it; whereas were faith assurance, they might begin it.

Add to this, *fifthly*, that assurance comes in as a reward of faith, as a light superadded to faith, that when a man hath trusted God upon his bare word, and a secret hint of a promise, and hereby hath set to his seal that God is true, and borne the stress of many overpowering doubts and temptations, and yet cleaves to Christ, though not fully knowing in his sense Christ is his, then God sets to his seal; therefore, says Christ, Rev. ii. 17, ' To him that overcomes I will give to eat of the hidden manna.' A man's faith must fight first, and have a conquest, and then assurance is the crown, the triumph of faith; but faith must be tried first; and what tries faith more than temptations, and fears, and doubts, and reasonings against a man's estate ? That triumphing assurance—Rom. viii. 37, 38, ' We are more than conquerors. And I am persuaded that nothing shall separate us from the love of God in Christ Jesus'—comes after a trial, as none are crowned till they have striven, and therefore establishment comes after suffering; so 1 Peter v. 10, ' After ye have suffered a while, establish, strengthen, settle you.' This putting into joint and rooting is after suffering; if they should have had it before, he would have prayed absolutely for it; and this the apostle also imports in 1 Peter i. 7, 8 in speaking of the joy of believing (' believing in Christ, ye rejoice with joy unspeakable and glorious : receiving the end of your faith, the salvation of your souls'), the context argues that this joy unspeakable and glorious, which thus accompanieth triumphing assurance, is called receiving salvation, and the end of faith, and the reward of faith, which is tried with manifold temptations, ver. 7, and therefore it is called the earnest of heaven, and God therefore dispenseth it voluntarily and freely.

Add to this, *sixthly*, that that light which causeth assurance of faith is a distinct thing, and superadded to faith; and the Scripture speaks of it as a thing distinct from faith (though it doth coalesce with it, and they both make one), and may be separately considered, and is called sense as so considered; for either it is by a reflex act upon grace in a man, and then it is experience (as the apostle calls it) which breeds this hope, or by an immediate discovery of the Spirit with joy unspeakable, which hath sense and sight in it; and therefore Job, though he believed afore, yet when this light broke in afresh, ' I heard of thee,' says he, ' by the hearing of the ear; but now mine eyes have seen thee,' Job xlii. 5; and therefore, too, Isa. l. 18, assurance (when it is spoken of in the distinction it hath from faith) is called light, and the want of it darkness; in which darkness yet the light of faith shines, but so as comparatively with that light which comes in with assurance, the soul is said to be in darkness, and to walk by faith, and not by sight; though I confess even the light of assurance is not sight compared with the sight in heaven, when we shall see Christ as he is, 1 Peter i. 8, compared with 1 John iii. 2, yet comparatively to naked faith, and the ordinary light that faith hath, it may be called sight and sense; so as I may say to one that believes, having strong sights and lights of God daily, as Christ said unto Thomas, ' Thou hast seen and believed,' John xx. 29, but the other believes though he sees not.

I will now shew how in such acts of faith as these all the main ends of faith are and may be attained and accomplished by indefinite acts of recumbency, and trusting on God, though wanting assurance; as, for instance,

First, The first main end of faith is to glorify God's free and rich grace and Christ, and to attribute all to them in point of justification and salvation, and to magnify and set them up alone in my heart; that is it for which Abraham's faith is commended: Rom. iv. 20, 'He was strong in faith, and gave glory to God.' Now I acknowledge that when assurance comes, it enableth the heart many ways to glorify God more than mere naked faith, or casting a man's self upon Christ doth, for it hath all the other hath, and more; and besides, it causeth the heart to be more thankful, and more fruitfully and cheerfully obedient; it perfects love, opens and gives vent to a new stream of godly sorrow, adds new motives, enlargeth and encourageth the heart in prayer, winds up all graces to a new and higher key and strain, causeth a spring tide of all; and yet so as God is, and may be as truly, and in as right a way, glorified by those acts of faith in a state of mere recumbency, as by the other, though I do not say so amply, and with so large a revenue as when assurance comes. Now a man doth rightly glorify God's rich grace and Christ by two things: first, when the heart attributes all that wholly and fully unto Christ and God's grace, which God in the Scripture ascribes to them in point of salvation; and, secondly, when the heart is bowed in all the carriages, and dealings, and practices of it, to demean itself accordingly—viz., in a word, to give unto God that which is God's, as Christ says in another case. Now both these a soul that is as yet but hung upon Christ doth and may do, for that soul in a spiritual manner sees the riches, the fulness of grace in Christ, adores, admires it, renounceth all vain hopes in all things else, resolves to have help no way else, robs and detracts nothing from Christ in the secret practices of the heart, for it deals with nothing else but Christ for salvation; the soul hath, for what it apprehends to be in him, left all its own righteousness, parts, abilities, comfort in all creatures, and accordingly walks every day. Only the soul wants this prevailing light, that this grace and Christ is his, which when it comes, though it adds to his comfort indeed, and so causeth him in a way of particular thankfulness to glorify this grace in relation to himself, yet the faith of recumbence attributes as much to the grace itself as the other of assurance doth, by way of praising, glorifying, and admiring it. And this faith of recumbence expresseth thus much by resting on Christ, parting with all for him, as well as the other glorifies him in other acts of rejoicing in him, &c. The grace of Christ is as truly glorified by the one as by the other, only in a several way; the one honours it by acts of dependence upon it to be obtained, the other by way of thankfulness for it as already enjoyed. As the saints under the Old Testament believed as truly on Christ, though yet to come, as we now on him though already come, and it was but a differing circumstance of Christ to come, and already come, made the difference (and yet such a difference as thereby we receive more grace and comfort than they had); so the saints that want assurance of Christ being yet theirs, or his benefits theirs, by depending on him that he may be theirs, and all his benefits theirs, they glorify him as truly as they that believe all his benefits are theirs, and in present possession (only I confess there is a new edition of many graces in a man by the coming in of assurance, there is much grace and comfort that follows); as a man may shew his true love in admiration of the worth, and parts, and faithfulness of one to whom he sues to be his friend, and honours him as much by acts of observance to gain his friendship, as he may do by acts of requital when he is assured of his love to him. It will, I confess, add much to the cheerfulness of all he doth go about for him, when he knows him to be his friend; but he honours him no less truly in the one than in the other, and these acts of recumbency do change and purify the heart as truly as acts of assurance, and carry it on to obedience, for not only the beholding Christ in his glorious excellencies do change the heart, 2 Cor. iii. 18, but the expectation and dependency the soul is put into, works an holy ingenuity. For God's love, and so great a favour out of free good will in God being the aim, the expectation of the soul, that God would pardon his sin out of as great a love as if Christ were yet to be given, how can he look for such love at God's hands (and without it the soul reckons itself undone), without answering God again with all the love in his heart? How can a man profess that he expects such kindness at God's hands, and be unkind to him?* How can the heart be able to look God in the face, if it be so disingenuous? Can the soul come to Christ to pardon sin through his death, and live in it? Why Christ may and will say, How would you have me to pardon these sins? Through thy death, Lord, thinks the soul, and so expecteth ; and how then canst thou find in thine heart to live in them? Now, though all these effects are in a more direct way wrought by faith of assurance, yet they are as truly all wrought by faith of recumbency or expectation, when it is in earnest. And let me add this, that in two respects the soul in such a state honours God's grace more.

1. It honours that property and attribute of grace, that it is free; for a man, in trusting God, when he knows not in his own sense that grace is his, yet refers himself to it, and devolves himself on it, and doth all in dependence upon it, as much as one that is assured doth; and herein he gives a real acknowledgment of, and magnifies the prerogative and freedom of this grace. And,

2. Though all the acts of grace (as they are of themselves) are less and weaker that accompany such an estate than those that flow from assurance, which, like the early and latter rain, make the heart more fruitful, yet if you put upon these acts of recumbent faith the relation of being trials, so they glorify God more, and are more acceptable; for it is not simply acts of faith, but the 'trial of faith,' which is 'found to honour and glory,' 1 Pet. i. 7; that is, to the honour both of that grace, and also of Christ who is the object of it. Faith, when it is tried, glorifieth God most in some regard. Now, therefore, to leave all hopes and comforts, and rest wholly on Christ for life and comfort, and to obey him, &c., when I know not that he is mine, though the acts of grace be fewer, yet the trial is greater. As mercies draw out love more, yet afflictions do try love more, and therefore make it exceeding acceptable; so assurance draws love out more, makes a spring-tide of it; but a state of recumbency tries it. A servant that is in health may do more work than one that is sick, and yet what a sick servant doth is as much accepted, because it is a trial of his faithfulness, though it be less.

Secondly, The second main end that faith serves for, is to put men into the estate of grace and justification before God. It is that act upon which God pronounceth a man justified, therefore we are said to be 'justified by faith,' and to 'have access into this grace wherein we stand,' Rom. v. 1, 2, for though God loves a man from all eternity, yet he cannot save a man, and pronounce his sins forgiven, according to his rules in his word, till an act of faith hath passed, so as by reason of that act I am before God, according to his revealed will, in that estate I was not in before ; and so according to the rules of his word (which is the rule he will judge by), he can after that act pronounce a man's sins forgiven, which before he could not, if he keeps to his rules, as all other estates are conveyed by some mutual act,

---

* See my sermons on friendship with God, out of James ii. 23, the first reason of the doctrine.—M. S.

so is the estate of grace. The main intent then of this act of faith being that God may justify me, and that I may be saved, it is not therefore absolutely necessary to such an act that I should know I certainly do perform it, but it may suffice to do the deed, that God knows it; for real justification, and to be in the state of grace, and so accounted by God, is the main end of it. And therefore the apostles, though they knew the Father, and believed on him, John xiv. 1, 7, yet they knew not that they did know the Father, ver. 8. It was necessary they should know the Father, and honour his free grace by believing on it, or they could not have been justified; but it was not necessary they should know this, for then they had not indeed been justified. That I should know I am justified is not necessary to God's justifying of me, but the intent of it is for my comfort, that I may have peace with God in my conscience; 'Therefore being justified by faith' (which is the prime act), 'we have peace with God,' as the fruit of it, Rom. v. 1; it tends to my joy in believing, and that I may have strong consolation. Now to the having a thing, it is not necessary that I know I have it, for a man may have a thing and think he hath lost it, and a man's hand may be so numbed with holding a thing that he may not know that he holds it. As to a being in the devil it is not necessary to know it, so nor to a being in Christ; God then hath chosen out such an act to justify a sinner as shall be common to all ages of Christians, that the least may not be excluded, such an act as is common to all times and all estates. This act is faith of recumbence; but faith of assurance, knowing myself to be in Christ, and to be justified, could not have been such a common and constant act that justifies, unless we will say it cannot be prevailed upon by doubts. Yea, I must be first justified by an act of faith, resting on Christ for justification, ere I can come to have assurance I am justified; for faith at first looks at my estate, not as in God's decree of election, but as it is laid down in the rules of the word; and according to the rules of the word I am not in a state of justification till I have believed on Christ for justification, and on him that justifies the ungodly; and therefore in Scripture men are said to believe 'that they may be justified,' Gal. ii. 16; in that text the apostles themselves are said to do so. So then the first act of faith is casting myself on Christ for justification, and not believing that I am justified.

I come now to answer the objections, the answers to which afford new reasons of the thing.

Obj. 1. If faith be not an apprehension that Christ is mine, wherein then lies that special application and appropriation of Christ, and the promise which is made to be in faith, and urged upon believers?

Ans. 1. I answer, First, We urge a special application as absolutely necessary in opposition to the papists' faith, who teach their followers that to believe only the general truths, that there is a God, and that Christ hath died, and to believe as the church believes, is true faith, which we say may be in devils, as James also affirms, James ii. 19. But we say, moreover, unless there be a further application, it is a vain faith; but then understand rightly what that particular application is, namely, when my heart is, by the belief of the generals, drawn in to Christ in particular, to rest on him for my own salvation; when I assent not only as a witness to a will, but come in as a party, as a legatee, put in for a share, that Christ and all his benefits may be mine, and so give myself up to him, when special mercy to me is the aim of my faith. Here now is a true application and appropriation, for I rest not in a general assent, but my faith joins my heart to Christ, consents to take him as mine, and to be his, and the scope of my cleaving to him is that he may be mine. And this, as it is more than papists' faith, and is indeed the life of faith, so also is it less than assurance, which is rather a verbal challenging him as mine than a real appropriation. I apply Christ, when I believe on him that I may be saved, as well as when I believe he is mine, and I shall be saved. In the instance of the man in the Gospel that sold all he had to buy the pearl, that bargain of his made the pearl his, and did appropriate it to him, for thereby he bought it, and it was not a persuasion of its being his made it first his, but a selling all that it might be his, though that persuasion came in afterwards.

Ans. 2. Secondly, For further clearing of this, I answer: You must know that there is a twofold application, the one is real, which makes a thing mine; the other is axiomatical, whereby I say it is mine; or, if you will, the one is an apprehension of the understanding, when I judge and discern, and can challenge this as mine; the other is in the will, when I choose it for my portion, cleave to it as mine, take it to be mine. Now the main and first act of application of faith lies in the will, for that is the faculty that is drawn to Christ, whereby I come in particular to Christ, and join myself to him; it is therefore called receiving Christ, John i. 12, and therefore Christ puts it upon their will, John v. 40, ' Ye will not come to me that ye might have life.' As, for example, there is a double appropriation of meat or apparel, the one a challenging a lawful right, when I can say this meat is mine, I have a right to it, but the other is eating it, digesting it, and making it one flesh with me, and that is the true, real application that appropriates it; and so for clothes, it may be insignificant to say they are mine, and belong to me, they may do so, and I never wear them; but the true appropriation of them is to put them on, and wear them. So in medicines, to apply them to the sore for cure, to bring the salves and the flesh together, that is the real proper application of them. Thus it is in faith also, the cleaving to Christ in my will, the hungering after him, and digesting him, the putting him on, the laying my soul to him, this is the proper real application of him, this is an act af the will; but to apprehend he is mine, and so to challenge a right in him, that is but an axiomatical application, an act of the understanding, though where it is in truth it increaseth that application, and draws the will more unto Christ. Now if the main application of faith lay in believing that Christ is mine, then it were mainly an act of the understanding, and a proposition were the chief object of it, and not Christ's person, and that drawing spoken of, John vi. 44, were specially drawing the understanding to assent, whereas it lies mainly in drawing my will to him, to choose him to be mine.

Obj. 2. But you will say, I must believe Christ is mine ere my will can thus apply him, as I must believe meat is mine ere I eat it, and that clothes are mine ere I put them on.

Ans. I answer, If the condition of making meat mine be to eat it, and if a father offers a child a suit, saying, it shall be his if he will wear it, then he must eat that meat first, and put those clothes on, that they may become his; and so it is here.

CHAPTER III.

That Assurance of Salvation may be obtained.

These things have I written unto you that believe on the name of the Son of God, that ye may know that ye have eternal life, and that ye may believe on the name of the Son of God.—1 John V. 13.

The doctrine of assurance is that which of all other civil men and popish spirits do gainsay and calumniate, which they do out of ignorance, as men are apt to ' speak evil of that they know not,' Jude 10. Now assurance of salvation such men never had experience of, as Christ (speaking of the Spirit as a Comforter, John xiv. 17) says, ' The world cannot receive him, for it knows him not.' Neither are such men solicitous about it, for assurance of earth here contents them, and makes them think themselves happy enough. They oppose this doctrine of assurance also out of envy, because they think much that so great a privilege should be bestowed upon any which themselves want, and therefore envying that others should exceed them in so great a happiness, as this must needs be acknowledged, which indeed is able to outvie all other, they deny it, and would make it a thing impossible, and a fancy in them that have it. And the devil bears a great part in it also, who, when he cannot hinder the salvation of Christians in the event, would hinder their comfort ; and as he knows how much this assurance-office increaseth spiritual traffic, and raiseth the customs of God's glory and revenues of grace double, by encouraging Christians to trade more in all manner of holiness, so his spite therefore is exceedingly at it to put it down ; and indeed if he could get the opinion to prevail, that no such thing is to be attained, Christians would give over looking after it. And then, too, all our hearts naturally being fruitful of doubtings and distrust, are apt to join in with our enemies, and to be glad to hear of a doctrine of doubtings ; and then also that presumptuous security which stills the hearts of many is at the best but blind careless hope, and that, too, counter-checked with a world of real guilt, so as in their own sense they cannot call it a certainty or infallibility ; and then such persons labouring after assurance (as in their opinions having thought it attainable), in the real pursuit of it find it so difficult that they are apt to give over, and to think it like that of the philosopher's stone, a devised invention, good indeed if it could be procured, but not to be had ; and then those also who have attained it cannot demonstrate it to others, especially not to those who have not experience of it, for it is ' hidden manna, a white stone which none knows but he that receives it,' Rev. ii. 17. ' A stranger doth not meddlle with his joy,' Prov. xiv. 10 ; that is, it is a business he is not skilled in, as the opposition shews, for the words afore are, ' the heart knows the bitterness of his soul,' that is, terrors of conscience are best known to him that hath them. Carnal people will not believe there are any such troubles for sin, and when men are troubled they ascribe it to any other cause; much less then will they believe their joys and assurance, which are more remote from their reason than the other. So as it is no wonder if that thing be denied which the most are ignorant of, and do envy at as the greatest happiness in others, and which the devil opposeth, and which is so hard to attain, and which is not demonstrable or obvious to sense.

Now my purpose is both to establish and vindicate this work and doctrine of assurance, it being both a work which furthers and advanceth the power of godliness in their hearts who enjoy it (as shall be shewn), and also it being a branch and appendix of faith, an addition or complement to faith, and therefore is called the assurance of faith, Heb. x. 22, it therefore lies next in my way. Now this text, 1 John v. 13, doth not only assure us that assurance of salvation may be obtained by believers, but further refers us to this whole epistle for the proof thereof: ' These things,' saith he, ' have I written unto you that believe on the name of the Son of God, that ye may know ye have eternal life.'

I shall speak something of the coherence of the words, though indeed the words are the close and argument of the whole. In the 7th and 8th verses he tells us of fixed witnesses to confirm believers' faith, for of faith he had spoken, ver. 5, 6, and in ver. 10, 11 he tells us of the record or testimony which these witnesses give in their evidence of, which contains the sum of the gospel, and the object that faith is exercised about. 1. That eternal life is to be had alone in Christ. 2. That this eternal life he hath given to all believers; ' that God hath given us'—that is, believers, for to them he writes and intends his Epistle—' eternal life.' Both these would God have to be believed and embraced, and for the confirmation of both serve those six witnesses. First, he would have men believe and rest in, and take his Son as the only fountain of life, which proposition the witnesses in heaven do especially confirm, which is called believing on him. And then, secondly, he would have these believers that have taken his Son, and believed in him, know and believe that they shall certainly be saved, because they have his Son, and life in him; for ' he that hath the Son hath life,' and he partakes of eternal life; and to that end God hath appointed the three witnesses on earth in a believer's own conscience, ver. 10. And to these two heads, especially the latter, is it that all this Epistle of John drives at; that whereas there are many souls that do entertain that first record, that Christ is the fountain of life, and so depend on him, and rest in him alone, but yet are backward to entertain the other, namely, that they have the Son, and that they belong to Christ, and that they believe on him aright, therefore for such did he intend this Epistle, that they may come to the assurance of faith concerning their own particular estates: ' These things have I written to you,' saith he, ' that have believed on the name of the Son of God, that ye may know that ye have the Son, and that ye have eternal life.' And yet not for these only doth he write, but also that they which have some knowledge of this begun may know it yet more, that so they may go from one degree of faith to another, and further believe on his name. And because this text refers us to what is written in this Epistle, I will content myself with what may thence be gathered as touching both (it being a point the text calls for), viz., that not only believers may know they have eternal life, but that these things were written to assure them of it.

First, Therefore let us argue from the scope of the whole Epistle; those arguments which the Holy Ghost spends whole books upon, are certainly both of necessary and of common use. As when Solomon writ a book on purpose to shew the vanity of the creatures, when Paul writes an whole epistle to prove justification by faith, as that to the Galatians; and another epistle to shew the natures and offices of Christ, as that to the Hebrews, these must be regarded as very considerable. Now John wrote his Gospel to prove Christ to be the Son of God, thereby to draw men to believe on him, that they might have eternal life: John xx. 31, ' These things are written that ye might believe that Jesus is the Christ, the Son of God;

and that believing ye might have life through his name;' and therefore he endeavours through the whole to give all the characters and demonstrations that he was God, as divines observe. So, likewise, he wrote this his Epistle to teach them who believe how they may know that they do believe, and that they have eternal life, and to that end gives all the evidences and means that may tend to this. He not only demonstrates that eternal life is given to believers, but gives evidence that they might particularly know their interest. The signs given in this Epistle tend to this purpose. And farther to assure you that this is his scope, the beginning of the Epistle doth answer to this his conclusion, for he puts in the argument of the whole, 1 John i. 4, ' These things we write unto you, that your joy may be full.' Joy ariseth only out of some good we know, and know, too, to be ours. Men, in a vulgar sense and phrase of speech, may be said to be happy, though they do not know it, as a king that is asleep, and a believer in a temptation, but rejoice in that their happiness they cannot, unless they know it; or at least it cannot be full joy else, not so full for parts as Christians are here capable of. Full joy ariseth only out of the possession of the chiefest good, and the knowledge of it, and that is eternal life, and Christ in whom it is. Let the happiness be never so great, if the persons know not that it is theirs, their joy is diminished and detracted, and can in no sense be said to be full joy; and therefore the apostle says not only that he wrote these things that they might have eternal life, the chiefest good, but that they might know it, that so their joy might be full. Moral philosophers, disputing against Plotinus, who said the happiest condition might be without knowledge, bring this very argument against him, and argues truly, that reflection or knowledge of a man's happiness is necessarily required to it, for otherwise it is lessened. Reflection is a part of the perfection of a perfect action, and a man should see but imperfectly, he should but half see, who did not observe he saw; but especially a reflection is essentially required to joy (which is the companion of happiness), and to full joy.

Secondly, He wrote these things that they might have fellowship and communion with God and Christ. A soul may have real union, and the marriage knot which can never be untied, that is knit by faith, and by casting a man's self on Christ, but yet mutual fellowship and communion, and a mutual expression of love, and walking as friends, may be wanting. But now the comfort of friendship lies in the mutual knowledge and sense of each other's dearness and love. A man can have no hearty fellowship with one he thinks, for all that he knows, to be his enemy. Such suspicions are the bane of friendship. These things, therefore, the apostle wrote that we might have fellowship with Christ, as he had. Now, the fellowship that he had with God, he says, was this, chap. iv. 16, ' We have known and believed the love of God to us.' This fellowship lies not in God's bearing us good-will simply, but in knowing and believing it, and that in such a manner as God hath it, that as he certainly doth bear love to us, so we certainly know it, and this fellowship he calls ' dwelling in love;' for the soul walks in the assurance of it, and works in it, and lies down in it, as a man doth in his house, and he possesseth God's love, and knows it is his own, as he knows his house is his own.

Therefore, *thirdly,* he calls upon believers to behold and consider God's love, as it is in a special manner set upon themselves in making them sons; ' Behold,' says he, ' what manner of love the Father hath bestowed upon us, that we should be called the sons of God,' 1 John iii. 1. Of all things in God or men, love desires to have itself considered and taken notice of, as much as wisdom, and power, or any other thing whatever, and therefore he calls on them to behold God's love; and, above all, love desires notice to be taken of the party beloved, whom it is in special directed unto, more than of any other, for the emphasis lies in the speciality of it; therefore he would not have them run out in general thoughts of admiring God's love to mankind, and his giving his Son, but as having bestowed him on us. For when this great benefit is thus specially apprehended, it doubles our admiration of it, and then it takes and affects us. And to this purpose he bids them view their present condition into which they were put, viz., the estate of grace, to look on this more than God's love in giving Christ to die, and offering heaven, &c.; they were to regard their being put into the present possession of it; 'That we are called,' says he, 'to be his sons;' and he bids them view it again and again what now at present they were: 'Beloved, now we are the sons of God,' says he, ver. 2. He exhorts not only to blind hopes of heaven, and indefinite considerations of God's love to some, but to a joyful persuasion of their present particular happiness in that now they were sons; and though the world knows us not to be such men, yet to our comfort we may know it, for to that end he brings in the world slighting us, as not knowing us, because it appears not what we are and shall be: 'But we know,' says he, 'that when he appears we shall be like him;' and let the world think of us what they will, we know what they are, and what ourselves are: chap. v. 19, 'We know we are of God, and that the whole world lies in wickedness;' so that his scope is evident. Now, would the Holy Ghost lose all this labour, as if none could attain this assurance he should? Hath he not said, his word shall not return empty?

And again, *fourthly*, he shews the blessed effects that would follow upon this assurance.

1. The more assurance a man hath of being now at present the son of God, the more true hope he hath of what is to come in heaven; and the more true hope a man hath, the more will he purify himself as Christ is pure, chap. iii. ver. 8. Carnal men calumniate this doctrine, as that which makes men secure, and more bold to sin, for if they were sure of heaven, then they might think to live as they please, as being sure to get thither: no; it works a clean contrary effect, it makes a man purify himself. This doctrine he goes on at large to prove in the following verses, shewing that assurance is so far from making men unrighteous, that he whom it works not thus with, to make him more holy, hath no true assurance in him, but is manifestly the child of the devil, so ver. 10; so chap. ii. ver. 6, 9. Nay, there is not a greater means to keep from sin than assurance; therefore (says he), as my end of writing is, that you may know you have eternal life, so also, 'that ye sin not,' chap. ii. ver. 1. Now if there were danger of looseness in assurance, he could never have made these two ends meet in one epistle together, had not the one been a means to the other. Yea, and says he, when a man hath sinned, there is no speedier way to recover that man again, and reclaim him from sin, than assurance; therefore, says he, in the same chapter, 'If any man sin, we have an advocate with the Father, Jesus Christ the righteous, who is the propitiation for our sins.' He bids them consider and believe this, and maintain the assurance of it, to raise them again. Then David's heart began to gush, and bleed, and break, when the prophet told him his sins were forgiven; and therefore the apostle he useth that as a motive to the confession of sins, viz., the assurance that God will pardon them, chap. i. ver. 9, when a man knows not but out of his own mouth he may be condemned, he is loath to

confess; but when a pardon comes, he cares not what he lays open.
And then,

2. Assurance perfects our love to God, chap. iv. 16, 17. 'Herein is
our love made perfect,' ver. 17. Herein, that is, hereby, 'that we know
and believe God's love to us,' ver. 16. As we cannot love one heartily,
whom we apprehend to be an irreconcileable enemy, so we cannot love one
perfectly whom we do not know to be a friend; therefore, as full joy ariseth
out of assurance of God's love, so perfect love ariseth only thence. Men
may love God afore as one who may be reconciled to them, but now their
love is perfected; men may believe afore, but now their faith is perfected,
and what is wanting supplied. And this perfect love, which ariseth out of
assurance of God's love, doth cast out fear and jealousies, and suspicions,
and a servile slavish temper; it throws out such fear as hath torment joined
with it, as apprehending God a judge, and ourselves under bondage. This
fear the assurance of God's love frees us from, and casts out; much of which
remains in many souls that have faith, and some love to God begun;
therefore, when assurance comes, their love is said to be made perfect,
there is that degree added which frees them from their fears, and which
completes their love begun. Now God would have all his children serve
him without this fear, he would have this child of bondage cast out (that I
may allude to the casting out of Hagar), yea, and that he would have us so
freed from such fears he hath took an oath, Luke i. 74, 'that we should
worship him without fear;' and we shall serve him the better, though men
[that] have nothing but self-love in them, think that fears and doubtings
are the only means to keep men in awe. And,

3. As this assurance will breed full joy, perfect love, and cast out fear,
so also confidence in God, and a certainty that our prayers are heard,
which the apostle brings in as another motive to get this assurance, chap. iii.
ver. 19, 21, 22, and so in the verse after my text, ver. 14, 'This is the
confidence that is in him, that if we ask anything according to his will, he
hears us.' He brings it in as an effect of knowing we have eternal life;
for doubting that our persons are accepted, makes us doubt whether our
prayers be; and until then we shoot at rovers, as it were, and know not
when our prayers will take or hit the white, whether they will come weeping home or granted. But when God hath given a man assurance of his
love unto salvation, he useth often to give him the like special assurance
for many special mercies, ver. 15, so as he knows he hath the petitions
that he desired of him, knows it even then when he asks them, as by the
context appears. This will encourage a man to pray, for then it is a man
hath access to God with boldness, freedom of speech and confidence, Eph.
iii. 12. And,

4. As love, so faith is made more perfect also; so as assurance helps
faith also, and till then there is something wanting in faith. And therefore in the text (if you mark it), says he, 'These things I write to you that
believe, that ye may know ye have eternal life, and may believe on the
name of the Son of God.' For when assurance comes in faith is increased,
for it receives a new degree, whereas before there is something lacking in
faith; as philosophers say, to see and not observe is but an imperfect
action, so to believe and not to know it is but half your faith; and therefore, Heb. x. 22, he exhorts to assurance of faith; and therefore, Mat. ix. 2,
the word translated, 'Be of good cheer, thy sins are forgiven thee,' is θάρσει,
that is, confide, believe, and be confident; and therefore, Eph. iii. 12, we
are said to 'have confidence in the faith of him;' and therefore he
urgeth it on them as their duty, as well to believe that God hath given

them eternal life, as to begin to believe that life is in Christ, and so to fly to him : and (says he) ye make God a liar in not believing the one as well as in not believing the other, ver. 10, for the believing not God in that 10th verse, whereby men make God a liar, is spoken to believers, and hath reference to this record, ' that God hath given us eternal life,' ver. 11 ; and therefore as they make God a liar that will not believe in Christ as the fountain of life, and as such a sufficient Saviour as God presents him to be (and the main ground men believe not, lies therein), for they thereby proclaim they believe not Christ to be as God says he is, so they that have believed (having that witness in themselves, ver. 10, which would assure them of the goodness of their estates, would they listen to it, and cherish it), if they give way and ear to the doubts of their own hearts, they give God the lie, and will not receive his testimony, which is greater than any man's, ver. 9.

CHAPTER IV.

The objections against assurance answered.

Now I proceed to answer cavils and objections which are most specious, and I shall answer them out of this Epistle, which is a sufficient abundary to establish this doctrine ; only I premise, that I will name no more of them but what may hence be confuted, nor add any further confirmation of those confutations than what the Epistle affords.

Obj. 1. The first evasion is this ; it is pretended that the persons to whom this great privilege is vouchsafed were men of extraordinary grace, as apostles, and some few such it may be attainable by, but every ordinary man cannot, nor must now look for this privilege.

Ans. I answer, As the scope of St John is to assure all believers, so he says in general that he writes it to them that believe; not to apostles only, but to you that believe, says St John, one of the apostles ; yea, he writes to all believers, for it was ever yet deemed a catholic general Epistle, as the title of it is. Yea, and if the apostle, and St John himself, had assurance (and if any of them had, I should think that this disciple, that Christ loved, and who lay in his bosom, and who knew his heart, and whom the disciples employed to get out Christ's secrets, had assurance), then other believers may have it too. He speaks to this purpose, 1 John iv. 14, 16, ' We who saw Christ do testify these things;' ' we know and have believed the love that God hath to us.' He tells them his scope was, that they believers might have fellowship with us ; you believers with us apostles ; that is, that they might have the same fellowship : ' And our fellowship,' saith he, ' is with God the Father, and God the Son,' 1 John i. 3. Yea, Christ told his apostles, John xv. 9–11, that ' as his Father loved him, so he loved them ;' and he had said as much afore in that sermon, and all this was to assure them that they should undoubtedly be saved, and greater assurance could not be given: ' These things have I spoken to you,' says he, ' that your joy might be full,' ver. 11, *i. e.,* ' that my joy might remain in you ;' Christ's meaning is, that his joy might be in them. Now Christ's joy arose out of assurance that the Father loved him, and he would have them enjoy the same joy, not for measure, for that is impossible, but for truth, to arise out of the same joy, and from the same grounds ; that so your joy might be full. Now the same joy that Christ wisheth to them, the same doth St John to all believers; and as Christ says that he spake those things that their joy might be full, so St John says that he wrote these things that their joy might be full also. So that (to wind up this) as Christ had assurance, and joy thence arising, so he here endeavoured to raise in his disciples the same, that they might have his joy, and full joy; and the apostles endeavoured too to beget the same joy in believers that was in themselves: 'That ye may have fellowship with us, and that your joy may be full,' 1 John i. 3, 4. Now wherein were the apostles to rejoice but in this, that their names were written in heaven; so Christ says, Luke x. 20, that as in matter of holiness Paul and the apostles propounded Christ as a pattern, and themselves as an example, as they followed Christ,—'Be ye followers of us, as we are of Christ,'—so in point of assurance Christ propounds his joy as the pattern for the apostles, and they theirs for believers; and therefore this privilege is not to be looked for only in them, but in believers.

Obj. 2. The second evasion is this; it is objected, that though assurance may be vouchsafed to some of lower rank than apostles, yet it is to such as are of long standing in Christianity, who after long experience have hope and assurance begotten in them.

Ans. I grant it, that many not till then have had it, yet it is attainable for others also; for all sorts of ages in Christ, for babes, young men, old men: 1 John ii. 14, 'I write to you babes';' ver. 12, 'for your sins are forgiven you.' He tells them so, because it is that thing he goes about to persuade them of; it is pardon which is the great thing they have in their eye when they are young, and that is the grand mercy they are in pursuit of, and which they most pray for, and are most solicitous about. And though they are but babes, and so have but little faith, yet he says, their sins are forgiven; to you, babes and infants, it is given to know this, which is hid from the wise and prudent. Christ therefore tells many new converts on the first day, that their sins were forgiven, and he tells this to those of ordinary rank, not disciples and apostles only: so he told that palsy man, Mat. ix. 2; so he said to Mary, who was lately a sinner, a known sinner, Luke vii. 37, 39 (and the Pharisees thought her so still), he tells her, ver. 48, 'Thy sins are forgiven thee;' and to another, saith he, 'Thy faith hath made thee whole.' And seeing your sins are forgiven you, though you be but of a day's standing, therefore you may take the comfort of it as well as others. And the apostle John gives this reason of his writing to them: 'Children, because,' says he, 'you have known the Father.' Aristotle observes it, and experience finds it true, that one of the first acts of reason in children is, to call upon their fathers and mothers, for they are apt to know them soonest of anything, and therefore the first words they speak are *Mam* and *Dad*, &c. So to babes in Christianity, one of the first fruits of the Spirit in them often is, to call upon God as a Father, to own God as a Father, to express child-like affection to him as to a father, and to seek his fatherly love; and though all babes cannot say he is their Father, yet they come to him as children to a father. Now this knowledge and instinct after God as a Father being in all babes, the apostle endeavours to raise it, and to teach them to know their Father more; but the Church of Rome teacheth her children to know their mother, but to doubt of their father, which is a sign they are bastards, and she a strumpet.

Obj. 3. The third evasion is, to object concerning the manner of assurance, though indeed they will grant that by an extraordinary revelation and certificate from heaven men may be assured, as Paul was, who was rapt up into the third heaven, and as those were by Christ when he was upon the earth; yet they deny that in the ordinary way of God's dealing with men such assurance is attained.

Ans. But St John here gives ordinary directions how men may come to be assured, for he writes an whole Epistle on purpose, which if men believe not, neither would they believe if one from the dead, or an angel from heaven, should assure them ; and he tells us, that there are not only witnesses in heaven, but also witnesses on earth, in a believer's own breast; a believer hath the witness in himself, and carries a work of faith and sanctification in him, to which if he give ear he may come to be assured, 1 John v. 8, 10 ; and to this end the apostle gives many signs of the work of grace in a man.

Obj. 4. Yea, but they object, fourthly, that let these signs be never so infallible in themselves, so as he that hath them in him shall surely be saved, yet the word names no man in particular ; it says not that thou, John or Thomas, hast these things in thee.

Ans. In answer to this, John tells us two things : *First*, That ' every one who believeth hath the witness in himself,' a work of the Spirit in him, whence this testimony may be fetched, chap. v. 10. And, *secondly*, that ' he hath given us his Spirit also,' chap. iii. 24, to witness and testify with the word, and with the work in a man's heart, and make application, chap. v. ver. 6. As therefore, when they ask how we know that the Scripture is the word of God ? for, say they, it is nowhere written that it is the word, we answer, that it is an authentical proof of itself, it carries its own testimony with it ; so is grace, and the word written in the heart of a believer : that word engrafted, and the law written in the heart, is an authentic evidence of itself ; and as God's Spirit accompanies his word with a divine light and authority, so he doth his own work in the heart ; there is but this difference, that the one is the word written with ink, the other delineated with the Spirit of the living God. And if the apostle says of the Corinthians, that they were so fair an epistle of Christ, that it might be known and read of all men, much more then is this true of themselves.

Obj. 5. Fifthly, they say, Yea, but our hearts are deceitful ; and who can know them ? and many are deceived.

Ans. I answer, that it is true that the natural frame of it is such ; and yet the apostle, in this Epistle, refers men to the judgment of their own hearts, as a witness in this point. 1. As for matter of condemnation, therein the testimony of a man's own heart may be right, and give in a right verdict, though it may be thus deceitful ; for in a man's own cause a deceitful person will take part with himself : therefore, if such an one condemns himself, his witness is so much the more authentic ; and therefore, says he, ver. 20 of the third chapter, ' If our hearts condemn us, God is greater than our hearts, and condemns us much more.' And, 2, as the testimony of our deceitful hearts, though deceitful, may be taken for condemnation, so the testimony of our renewed hearts may be admitted for the justification of a man's estate ; therefore he adds, ver. 21, ' If our hearts condemn us not, then we have confidence towards God.' 3. Though it be true that our hearts as natural are deceitful, yet, chap. v. ver. 20, he says, that ' the Son of God hath given us a mind that we may know him that is true, and we are in him that is true.' So that though our spirits are deceitful, yet that new understanding is given on purpose to know the truth, and to discern of it. And, 4, though our own hearts are deceitful, if left naked, yet he hath not left us without another witness to guide this new mind, and that is his Spirit : chap. ii. ver. 20, 27, ' You have received an unction, which teacheth you all things.' And that Spirit is one of the witnesses, chap. v. ver. 6, 8.

Obj. 6. Yea, but they object, sixthly, that there are many enthusiasms, and Satan joins with hypocrites' hearts, and deludes them, and so a man shall not be able to know the Spirit's witness from that of this great deceiver.

Ans. The apostle tells us, chap. v. ver. 6, ' It is the Spirit that beareth witness, because the Spirit is truth.' That is, did he not give an infallible testimony, he were not fit to be reckoned a witness; and if he is a witness, then he is so as to persuade men to whom he gives witness, for why else is he said to witness? And this record too is the record of God, which is greater than man's, and therefore infallible : chap. ii. ver. 27, ' This anointing,' says he, ' teacheth you all things, and is truth, and is no lie :' that is, doth not, cannot deceive you. A man may see a thing with false lights, and be deceived; but if I see a thing with the light of the sun, I see it with a true light, and am not deceived.

Obj. 7. They object yet seventhly, That it is true man may have such a knowledge, as is joined with some probable hope, and a good and a happy conjecture, which often doth not deceive in the end, but yet not such but there wants an infallibility, so as there may *falsum subesse*, be a mistake at the bottom.

Ans. I answer, How often doth John inculcate, ' By this we know,' and ' We know,' &c. ? and more expressly, chap. ii. ver. 3, ' Hereby we know we know him.' *We know him* was too little : he therefore adds, *But we know we know him ;* and chap. iii. ver. 19, ' We know we are of the truth' (how can this be without infallibility ?), ' and shall assure our hearts afore him.' If they themselves were to put words of assurance into any testimony or into any bond, they could not say more, or put in more expressions to put all out of doubt.

Obj. 8. True, say some in the eighth place, they may know at the present that they are the sons of God (' Now we are the sons of God,' 1 John iii. 2); but what will become of us hereafter? Whether we shall continue so, we know not.

Ans. The apostle answers them in that third chapter, ver. 2, 3, that indeed what the great glory of that estate hereafter will be, they knew not, nor the world knows not; and in outward appearance they are now (though for the present the sons of God) of all men most miserable; and therefore, in regard of their outward garb and splendour, it doth not appear what they shall be, as it doth not appear what wicked men shall be; but yet, for the certainty of our future condition, as now we are the sons of God, so ' we know that when he shall appear, we shall be like him.'

Obj. 9. Yea, but, ninthly, it will be said, there are many that seemed as good as yourselves, whom you thought good Christians, and they thought themselves such, and yet they have turned apostates; and will not their falling away dash a believer's assurance?

Ans. He answers, ver. 19 of the second chapter, that they were never true : ' They went out from us, because they were not of us ; if they had been of us they would no doubt have continued with us, but they went out that they might be made manifest that they were not all of us.'

Obj. 10. Yea, but yet, tenthly, in that there are such among professors, who are a great while not manifested to themselves or others, may not this however disparage and bring all to an uncertainty in the best, seeing they know not but they may prove such ?

Ans. No, says the apostle, ver. 20, ' but ye have an unction from the Holy One, and ye know all things.' He speaks by way of difference, and to answer the cavil ; and ver. 27, ' That same anointing teacheth you all things, and is truth, and is no lie,' and therefore by his teaching you are not deceived. And, among other things, he hath taught you the truth of your estates, even as it hath taught you that you shall abide in him ; and chap. iii. 19, ' Hereby we know we are of the truth.'

Obj. 11. But, eleventhly, it will be objected, will not this assurance make men licentious, and secure, and more careless ?

Ans. No, says the apostle ; however presumption in carnal hearts may work, yet in those who are truly godly it hath the contrary effect. For he that hath this particular hope for himself, hereafter to be like Christ, and to be at present the child of God, this hope conforms him to Christ here, to whom he must be conformed hereafter : ' He purifies himself as he is pure.' It works out corruption ; and, therefore, ver. 1 of the second chapter, he says, he wrote these things ' that they might not sin.'

Obj. 12. But poor believers they object, twelfthly, that they fall into sin, and then all their assurance is clean dashed and eclipsed.

Ans. As, in the third chapter, there is a seed mentioned which remains in them unshaken out, so they may if they sin go with a confidence to God through Christ, and recover themselves : ' If any man sin,' says he, 1 John ii. 1, ' we have an advocate with the Father,' &c.—an advocate that never pleaded bad cause, or was cast in his suit, and who pleads with a father and not with a judge, and who is ' Jesus Christ the righteous ;' whose righteousness is eternal, and which no sin can outvie, and which is made ours ; so as ' if we confess our sins,' chap. i. 9, 'he is a just God in nothing else but to forgive them, and to cleanse us also from all unrighteousness,' and hath bound himself to both by promise ; and hence, and hence only, ariseth full joy and perfect charity, ver. 4 of the first chapter, and ver. 17 of the fourth chapter. Love can never be perfect when a man is possessed with jealousies of enmity that may be for time to come ; therefore, ' true love casts out such fear,' ver. 18 of that fourth chapter. *Amare tanquam aliquando osurum, venenum est amicitiæ,* to love as one who afterwards will hate is the poison of friendship ; so that no joy can be full, though in the greatest good, the enjoyment of which for time to come is uncertain.

CHAPTER V.

How assurance is produced in the heart of a believer, by three witnesses in heaven, and three witnesses on earth.—The different nature of the testimony which they give.

For there are three that bear record in heaven, the Father, the Word, and the Holy Ghost : and these three are one. And there are three that bear witness in earth, the Spirit, and the water, and the blood : and these three agree in one.
—1 JOHN V. 7, 8.

As we have seen the apostle's scope, in this Epistle, to have been chiefly, first, to assure God's people ; and, secondly, to shew the fruits of such assurance as motives to it ; so, in the next place, let us consider what he hath written that may help a believer to this assurance ; what directions, what helps, what evidence he hath described, whereby he may come to be assured. This will both demonstrate that this is in the scope of this Epistle, as likewise shew that assurance may be had, by shewing from what grounds and proofs it is derived. He directs them to two trinity of witnesses, whereof three are in heaven, and three on earth ; for I take it that all these six witnesses have their evidence set to one and the same record, both that Christ is the fountain of life, and that God hath given to a believer eternal life. These witnesses do not part or divide their witness (as if the three in heaven should witness to the one part, and those on the earth to the other); but as each *classis* of these agree among themselves in one, so they both agree in the same testimony unto both; and, therefore, as the witnesses on earth do witness to a believer that he hath eternal life, so those in heaven do join singly in this very testimony also. And because, in all things we would have proof of, the greatest furtherance any one can do, is to produce and direct us to such as are the only true, faithful witnesses that can speak infallibly in the cause, therefore John, to help a poor believer in this great point of assurance, points out to him the sole infallible witnesses that can give in evidence, which, if he do attend unto, and examine, and seek unto for their witness, he may get evidence sufficient. And in this point he brings plenty out of both courts, both of heaven and on earth, three in either; that as none were condemned but under the mouth of two or three witnesses, so none are assured of salvation but by as many. These witnesses serve, as I said, to confirm two records: the one, that Jesus was that Christ, and the Son of God; the other, that we are sons in him, and heirs of life. We have the same, and as many as Jesus Christ hath. Now we are to consider them as they are witnesses to our title and adoption.

Of those three in heaven, and who are meant by them, there is no difficulty among interpreters. The being of the three persons, Father, Son, and Holy Ghost, and how they have given testimony to this part of the record, that Jesus is the Son of God, is evident in the story of the Gospel: the Father from heaven, saying, ' This is my well-beloved Son, in whom I am well pleased, hear him;' and Christ himself, who came from heaven, witnessed of himself, as often in the gospel of John is evident—for instance, John iv. 26; and the Holy Ghost witnessed this by descending upon him, Mat. iii. 16, 17; Acts v. 32.

But how these three witness salvation to a believer is a difficulty, and a thing not ordinarily observed. As also again, what should be meant by blood, water, and spirit, this hath puzzled interpreters. I accord with those who,

First, By blood understand the work of justification on a poor sinner, and, by a synecdoche and metonymy, all that which goes to his justification. By blood then here is to be understood both that which is the object of faith as justifying, which in Christ you know is chiefly his blood (which is called ' the blood of the New Testament, shed for the remission of sins;' that is, that blood which ratifies all the promises of the New Testament, his blood being put for all his obedience), as also that rich grace in God which sprinkles or applies this blood to poor sinners, and which faith in his blood looks unto: Rom. iii. 24, 25, ' Being justified by his grace, through the redemption that is in Christ: whom God hath set forth to be a propitiation, through faith in his blood.' All these synecdochically are comprehended in blood, in this place of John, even Christ's blood shed, and free grace sprinkling it, and the promises ratified by it, which are the object of faith. And by a metonymy the work of faith itself is also meant, which lays hold on this blood (the object connotating the act itself), that is, faith in his blood. In a word, the whole work of justification, and whatever goes to it, is meant by blood.

Secondly, By water I understand sanctification, both in the habits and fruits of it; for whom Christ's blood justifies, it also doth cleanse and sanctify, and washeth away the filth of sin; thus it is expressed John iii. 5, a man being regenerated, and ' born again of water and the Holy Ghost;' that is, of the Holy Ghost working as water, purifying and cleansing. So says the apostle too, Eph. v. 26, ' Christ gave himself for his church, that he might sanctify and cleanse it with the washing of water by the word.' And as habitual regeneration or sanctification, so actual cleansing a man's self daily is signified to us by water; thus in Isa. i. 16, ' Wash you, make you clean ; put away the evil of your doings ; cease to do evil, learn to do well.' Especially purifying the heart is denoted by it, which is done by faith, and follows upon believing; thus Jer. iv. 14, ' Wash thy heart from wickedness ; how long shall thy vain thoughts lodge within thee?' It makes the heart fruitful unto every good work, and every grace to grow up in a man, Ps. i.

And that these two witness that Christ is the Son of God may easily be conceived : as, first, that his blood is able to take away the guilt of sin (which nothing else could do), this argues it to be the blood of God, Acts xx. 26. The force of it lies in this, that it was ' offered by the eternal Spirit,' Heb. iii. 14, so likewise water witnesseth it, in that it should be able to subdue sin, wash away the power of it, change the heart, make a man a new creature ; all this argues him to be the Saviour of the world, Acts v. 31, and that these do also join to give in testimony to assurance, that God hath given a man eternal life, is also evident by that in Heb. x. 22, ' Let us draw near with full assurance of faith.' And what conduceth to effect that assurance, and to help it forward ? Both these here mentioned : first, ' having our hearts sprinkled from an evil conscience.' And by what is that done ? By this blood here meant; see Heb. ix. 14, ' How much more shall the blood of Christ, who through the eternal Spirit offered himself without spot to God, purge your consciences from dead works ? ' This blood, sprinkled on the conscience by faith, helps forward assurance of faith. The second is also mentioned, ' having our bodies washed with pure water ;' that is, our whole man sanctified and cleansed. He writing to the Hebrews, speaks in the language of the Levitical law, which he explains to them in all that Epistle, in which there was the sprinkling of the blood of goats by hyssop, which signified justification, or the sprinkling of Christ's blood upon the conscience, Heb. ix. 13, 14, and also they washed their bodies with water when they went to sacrifice and were unclean, which signified the sanctification of the whole man, body being put for the whole; as Rom. xii. 1, ' Offer up your bodies a reasonable sacrifice to God,' that is, your whole man ; which phrase he useth when he alludes to the sacrifices of the law, as there he doth.

Now then, the *third* witness, the Spirit, is the Holy Ghost, who comes down from heaven and dwells here on earth in the heart of a believer, and so takes part with him, and joins his witness to these other two, his testimony being the greatest, the clearest of all the rest. And his witness we may find Rom. viii. 16, ' The Spirit itself beareth witness with our spirits, that we are the sons of God.' He joins his testimony to the other two, and puts all out of question. Now, both these two testimonies of blood, that is, the work of justification and faith, and water, that is, sanctification, Paul shuts up in one, namely, ' our spirit ;' not our spirit as naked in itself, our natural spirit, which is full of deceit, but as framed and renewed to the obedience of faith and true holiness, and as enlightened and irradiated by the Spirit, and so fitted to witness the truth; and both those testimonies he calls the witness of our spirits, because our apprehending justification and believing, as also that of sanctification, are works seated in and of our spirits. The testimony of both those is fetched and produced out of the records that are written in our own bosoms, from those gracious acts and dispositions, and dealings of God with our spirits, in drawing us to faith, and justifying, and also sanctifying of us ; and they are called our spirits, to distinguish both those from that other testimony of the Spirit which is fetched out of the records in God's own breast, and quoteth not, nor referreth us not to any dealing of God with us, or work in us, but is an immediate voice of God's Spirit. And this John himself intimates unto us (to accord John and Paul), that by some of these witnesses he means the work of God in ourselves (which Paul calls our spirits), when he adds, ' He that believeth hath the witness in himself,' whereby he declares that some of those witnesses, both the work of faith and sanctification, are works of and in himself, and that they may give him some evidence. The meaning is, he carries in his own bosom written the matter of a good testimony, if produced, and viewed, and examined.

Having found out what the witnesses are John directs us unto, let us see how they witness.

First, The work of faith in Christ's blood, and the blood of Christ sprinkled by faith, have a testimony in them if examined; that is, when first a man sees he was brought in, and his heart won to believe, according to the true tenor and right course of the Spirit in the work of faith, and upon the right grounds, motives, and terms, and reasons the word chalks out, and according to the right aim, and intent, and purpose of God in the gospel, which is in justification to set up Christ's blood, and his rich grace; when he sees he came in at the right door of faith, as Acts iv. 27; when he sees that God's Spirit opened to him, and guided him in at the right door; in brief, when he hath seen the guilt of his sin as the greatest evil, an emptiness and insufficiency of help in himself, or anything in him for time past, present, or to come, and in all creatures and means whatever, and then hath had the fountain of Christ's blood opened to him, as Hagar had that well by the angel, which she saw not; when he spies Christ out, and his blood as the only means to help him, and sees the all-sufficiency of redemption in it to wash him, justify him, and prizeth it accordingly, and thirsts after a draught of it, and hungers after nothing but his righteousness, so as nothing can down with him else, and he eyes nothing but it, and resolves to have help from nothing but him; and when bethinking himself how to close with Christ, and to get an interest in that blood, he finds God graciously opening the riches, the freeness of his grace, that imputeth, sprinkleth it, and is enabled to see grace so free, so rich, that nothing in himself can hinder it, as nothing in himself can further it; and not only so, but when he finds God's Spirit secretly still dealing with him to take it, to take God at his offer of it, as being faithful, serious in it, as being also the richest purchase that ever the world had; when he finds God's Spirit reasoning with him in private, answering and taking away his scruples and objections that lie betwixt him and the taking of it, urging him, pressing him, laying afore him God's command to believe his threatenings, his invitations, his willingness, and he sees how welcome he shall be; when he finds God's Spirit drawing and winding in his heart to close with Christ and his blood, and, he knows not how, over-persuading him to rest in Christ, and to cast himself on him, causing him to trust in him, which else he should never have done, and so he takes Christ with all his offices, to give himself up to him, to rest in him, to go no further, no whither else for help; when he finds he can with some secret establishment of spirit implead the arguments of faith, wield faith's weapons, and find his spirit strengthened thereby against carnal reasons and guilt, so as he comes away from the bar and throne of grace with a kind of victory over the pleadings and condemnings of his heart, and is he not non-plussed, but sees in free grace and Christ's blood sufficient matter suggested to answer to all, and so he rests; when he finds that as out of self-flattery he is not encouraged to believe, but out of the importunity of God's Spirit that follows him with such thoughts, that God will have it so, so also that his heart is raised above self-love in it to God's aim and end in justifying, namely, to admire the riches of his grace, to adore the all-sufficiency of his blood, to ascribe all to it. And then, as the work of faith in Christ's blood, so the effect of his blood thus apprehended, impleaded, evidenceth it to him; for still when guilt ariseth he can oppose Christ's blood to it, and bathes his soul in thoughts of faith about it, and so finds the guilt quelled, allayed, his conscience pacified, stilled, and quieted by it, when no duties nor nothing else will give him ease. This, if a man observe these things, may be an evidence to him that Christ's blood is sprinkled on him. This is the testimony of blood— as, Heb. xii. 24, it is said, ' The blood of Christ speaks better things than the blood of Abel '—this same speaking comfortable things in the conscience of a man, and easing a man of his load, purging, pacifying, stilling, allaying the conscience when nothing but his blood doth it, not duties, not vain hopes; this is the witness of blood, though bloody iniquities cries loud, as the blood of Abel in Cain's conscience, yet this blood speaks better things ; and a man still in distress can have, with some support, recourse to this blood, when to nothing else, and finds the faith in it secretly supporting him. This is the first witness, when a man observes this ; for though faith is not assurance, yet upon believing a man may have some evidence from the work of it, and the effect of Christ's blood in his conscience apprehended by faith ; and therefore the Scripture points us to the work of faith, as that which may be known, and which gives in evidence. So in the first verse of this chapter he says, ' He that believes is born of God ; and therefore Christ said to that poor man, ' If thou canst believe ;' ' Lord,' says he, ' I believe ; help my unbelief,' Mark ix. 24. He could not have answered so unless he could have discerned the work of faith in himself. So that new convert, Acts viii. 37, ' If thou believest with thy whole heart, thou mayest be baptized.' Baptism was the ordinance to men newly converted, which conveyed the Spirit as sealing, baptism being the seal of righteousness ; and this man, before thus sealed by baptism, could tell he believed, for he answers, ' I do believe that Jesus is the Son of God.'

The second witness is the work and workings of sanctification, water. The believer finds that closing thus with Christ changeth him, renews him, washeth him from the power of sin, puts a new spirit and principle into him, clean opposite to sin, so as he cannot sin; he finds a new spring of gracious dispositions in him, still bubbling naturally up, and cleansing, and working out corruptions, John iv. 14; he finds many several streams of it, of love to God and Christ, and that for themselves, a stream of hatred of sin running against a stream of love to it; every grace is a stream in him, and all his graces do testify also, if they be observed. Read this Epistle of John ; you will find he cuts this water into many rills and signs, in every of which, as so many signs, believers may see and have some evidence of their estates. And he says not only that such dispositions are in God's children, but he presents them to them as signs whence they might know they have eternal life, it being his scope to help believers this way. One sign that he gives is a bent of heart to keep all God's commandments: chap. ii. ver. 3, ' Hereby we do know we know him, if we keep his commandments;' and verse 5, ' Hereby we know we are in him,' especially then, when ' the commandments are not grievous;' and chap. v. ver. 3,

'This,' says he, 'is the love of God, that we keep his commandments;' that is, this is the certain sign and fruit of it. So chap. ii. ver. 29, 'Ye know,' says he, 'that every one that doth righteousness is born of him.' So purging a man's self from sin upon the hope and assurance of heaven, is another sign described by him: chap. iii. ver. 3, 'Every one that hath this hope in him purifieth himself, even as he is pure.' So having a seed in a man contrary to sin, that he cannot sin, is another sign which he displays: ver. 9, 'Whosoever is born of God doth not commit sin; for his seed remaineth¦ in him: and he cannot sin, because he is born of God.' So love to the brethren is another distinguished character: ver. 14, 'We know we are passed from death to life, when we love the brethren,' when it is such love as we could lay down our lives, our estates, and goods for the church, ver. 16, 17; and this love is in deed and in truth hearty, real, ver. 18; then hereby we know we are of the truth, ver. 20; and then finding the Spirit dwelling in us, is another mark of our good state : verse 24, 'Hereby we know he abideth in us, by the Spirit he hath given us;' and then he gives signs suitable to those times, and to hinder their being mischiefed by the false teachers among them, chap. iv. And also he gives reasons still why such signs are infallible ; this you may observe if you read this Epistle, as when he shews that if we love God it is certain God loves us, chap. iv. verse 10, proving it by this strong reason, because his love is the cause of ours, verse 19 ; so he shews why love to the brethren is an infallible sign, chap. iv. verse 7, and chap. v. verse 1, because love is of God, and he is the fountain of it, and he that loves the begetter loves the begotten, and so on the contrary. And also he proves sometimes one sign by another : chap. v. verse 2, 'By this we know that we love the children of God, because we love God, and keep his commandments.' So that when one sign is not so evident, yet a man may have recourse to another : and then also, when a man's heart is raised by faith to overcome this world, to despise the good things of it, and endure all the evil, when he is tried in both, and overcomes both through faith, chap. v. verse 14, he makes it a sign of being born of God. And you shall observe withal, that he doth this by way of difference, giving the contrary as infallible signs of wicked men ; he that walks in any sin 'hates his brother,' such an one 'is in darkness,' chap. ii., 'knows not God,' chap. iii. verse 6, but 'is of the devil,' verse 8. 'And he that loves not the saints abides in death, and is a murderer, and hath not eternal life in him,' verse 14.

I shall name no more, but return to this testimony of water, and add this, that as that of blood is a testimony drawn from quelling the guilt of sin, and opposite thereto, so this of water is a testimony drawn from subduing the power of sin, and putting in contrary principles. Now as the power of sin, when it prevails, strengthens the guilt of sin against us, and raiseth doubts, so when the cleansing power of grace prevails, it helps to strengthen faith in Christ's blood. Faith having once rightly and alone closed with Christ's blood to justify the believer, and having ascribed all to it, then water may come in as a witness to justify that faith. Now the ordinary error is, that men neglect the blood of Christ, and the work of faith, and the sprinkling of it on their consciences for justification, and the evidence thereof, and betake themselves wholly to water, ere they have closed with this blood. They would see themselves sanctified ere they have closed with justification. But if a man hath been guided once aright in the work of faith, and his heart pitched right for justification, to seek it alone in blood, then water comes fitly in as a witness, and is to be listened unto ; but till then, the danger is, lest men should have that recourse to water which they should have to the blood of Christ, and rest therein for justification.

The third witness is that of the Spirit, whereby is meant an immediate testimony of the Holy Ghost, superadded to all these. The testimony of faith finding ease in Christ's blood, as rested in alone for salvation, is often prevailed against by the guilt of sin, and counter-checked; and that testimony of water is worn out and obliterated by the power of sin, which also strengthens that guilt; so as though the soul hath an assurance, depending on the prevalency of the fruits of grace in itself, which when the prevalency of that grace and faith is in the soul may give a certainty, yet it is such as even then the soul lingers after, and waits for a further discovery, and is taught to do so. There is therefore a third testimony, and that is of the Holy Ghost himself, which is immediate; that is, though it backs and confirms what the other two said, yet quotes them not, builds not his testimony on them, but raiseth the heart up to see its adoption and sonship, by an immediate discovery of God's mind to it, and what love he hath borne to it; which is not argued from what is wrought in itself, but God says unto a man's soul (as David desires), 'I am thy salvation,' Ps. xxxv. 3, and as Christ said upon earth to some few, 'Thy sins are forgiven thee,' so from heaven it is spoken by his Spirit (which yet dwells in the heart afore), that a man's sins are forgiven, and he is owned by the whole Trinity to be God's child. And this testimony was that which the apostles received, when they received the Holy Ghost after Christ's ascension as a Comforter, whom yet they had before already, and knew by the fruits and effects of him, both water and blood, faith and holiness, that he was in them, but yet not so as afterward, John xiv. 16–20, they now knew the Spirit, and he dwelt in them, verse 17, they knew before that they had grace, and that they believed; so Peter says, 'I believe that thou art the Son of God.' And after his death, afore the Holy Ghost was given, when Christ asked if he loved him? Peter says he did: 'Thou knowest I love thee,' John xxi. 16. They had the testimony of water and blood both, but they had not yet the Spirit as a Comforter immediately sealing up all: 'I will send you the comforter,' says Christ, John xiv. 16, 20, 'and at that day you shall know that I am in my Father, and you in me, and I in you.' Thus he promises that he would further manifest himself to them, that whereas they knew afore dimly, then they should know to purpose; and this likewise we find the Ephesians did receive after they believed, and had been sanctified: Eph. i. 13, 'In whom, after ye believed, ye were sealed with the Spirit of promise.' As seals are for confirmation, so they were sealed with grace and holiness, and the image of God before, for that follows upon faith; and they had trusted on Christ, had closed with Christ, and the word of truth, and gospel of salvation. But now when they by sheer faith had honoured God, by sealing to his word, then God comforts them by sealing them with his Spirit. And this witness is immediate, that is, it builds not his testimony on anything in us; it is not a testimony fetched out of a man's self, or the work of the Spirit in man, as the others were; for the Spirit speaks not by his effects, but speaks from himself, and confirms the other, and therefore is said to witness with the other, that is, comes in to strengthen their witness. And though the Holy Ghost joined with water and blood in their testimony (for grace without him cannot evidence, as it cannot work without him), yet so his testimony lay hid in theirs, as they are said to witness, and his testimony is concealed, though he allegeth them, and clears them up to a man, and therefore a man shall find the same signs sometimes evidence to him, and sometimes not, as the Spirit irradiates them ; and yet this testimony of his is over and above theirs, distinct from theirs, and severed from theirs, and therefore is said to make a third witness, which as witnessing in the other he could not be said to be.   But though this testimony of the Spirit be beyond the witness of faith or water, and above what the word in any sound or syllables carries with it, yet it is always in and with the word, and according to it, and therefore they are said to be ' sealed with the Spirit of promise,' Eph. i. 13.   It calls up some word that echoes to it, and goes with it. The Spirit opens God's mind in some words, and also, though it may come in from an evidence received and entertained from the former witnesses, blood and water, and therefore is said to witness with the other, as coming to back what they said, yet so as their testimony then comes to be considered but as the occasion upon which this of the Spirit is let in, and as the hint given; but it raiseth the soul up higher, and the other testimony as it were falls down, and God's immediate mind and acceptation out of the riches of his grace, entertains a man's soul and thoughts.   For as Christ received no testimony from man, though he says John gave testimony of him ; and as in some colleges when the college seal is put to, there needs no hands, no witnesses ; or as when the broad seal is put to by a king, he writes *teste meipso ;* so doth the Spirit speak in the language of a king, *teste meipso,* ' witness myself,'· and receives and borrows no witness from what is in us, but makes his own abundantly satisfy.   And this witness, though it is placed first (after the manner of the Hebrews and other Scriptures), yet comes in as the last of the three, as being the greatest, and that which puts all out of question, which the other did not so fully ; and therefore he is said to witness with our spirits, because their testimony is usually given in first ; this of the Spirit backs and confirms what they said, as seals come after a man's hand is set, as the greater witness ; or as an oath comes in after a promise to put all out of doubt, and to end the controversy, Heb. vi. 15–18, there it is said, that God makes a promise, and though that might assure, yet we have doubting hearts, and therefore he adds an oath to end all strife ; and ' that he might more abundantly shew to the heirs of promise the immutability of his counsels, he confirms them with an oath.'   So herein I may say, that though the witness of blood and water might assure, if men were watchful, and could observe their hearts, yet because that testimony ends not the strife so fully, therefore he being willing more abundantly to shew to the heirs of salvation their adoption, seals them with his Spirit, which is to them an end of strife, and for the present conquers all doubts.   And as when he swears, he useth no name but his own, for none is greater than himself, so when he thus witnesseth, he useth the help of no witnesses but his own, and upon this witness follows joy unspeakable and glorious, it being the earnest of heaven ; for it is a seeing my estate of grace and adoption, not in the effects or love-tokens, but in God's breast, as they in heaven do.   Now such joy follows not the other two witnesses, though peace and quiet may.

Having considered the witnesses on earth, let us consider the witnesses that are in heaven, since also these concur in giving assurance.   And besides what this place says, which to me is clear, let us see what evidence in other scriptures may be for this distinct witness.   In Rev. i. 4, 5, John, who had experience of this work, and had gone through these three forms, wisheth to all believers ' grace and peace,' not from the Trinity in common only, but from each apart : first, from the Father, ' from him who is, was, and is to come,' that is, from Jehovah, God the Father, the style of the whole being attributed to him who is *fons Deitatis,* the fountain of the

Godhead. It is meant of the Father, because the other two are afterward distinctly mentioned ; and then afterwards the apostle wisheth peace to them 'from the seven spirits which are before the throne.' By which he means the Holy Ghost, who is the author of all spiritual graces, and who in his gifts is various, and yet but ' one Spirit,' as the apostle says, 1 Cor. xii., the effect is by him put for the cause. And that he means the Holy Ghost is plain, because grace can be wished from none but God, and therefore he must mean the Holy Ghost, the third person of the Trinity. Then at last the apostle wisheth them peace ' from Christ Jesus, who is the faithful witness.' Grace is the original of that love and favour these three have in their hearts to a believer, and peace is the copy, the assurance of it in his own. He wisheth them peace from all these, from the Father, from the Son, and from the Holy Ghost ; you see he names them not only together, but as it were apart, from the Father, and from the Spirit, and from the Lord Jesus, that peace might be spoken from all these three witnesses. That promise made by Christ to his apostles, when he promiseth them to send the Comforter, John xiv., is a farther proof of this thing ; they then had an implicit knowledge of the three persons' love to them ; but he calls them to a more distinct bottoming, and pitching their thoughts on them all; ' Ye believe in God,' says he, ver. 1, ' believe also in me.' They could not have believed in the one but the other must be supposed, for none comes to the Father but by the Son, ver. 6. The thoughts of believers under the Old Testament ran much, and were drawn out more distinctly to God the Father : John v. 32, ' All men honoured the Father ;' and says he, ver. 9, ' He that knows me knows the Father ;' and ver. 17, he says, that they knew the Spirit. But all this was but implicitly, therefore he promiseth a more distinct manifestation of these, and their love to them with a witness after the Comforter should come, which he says he will send, ver. 16, and then they should know he was ' in the Father, and the Father in him, and they in him,' ver. 20. To clear this, consider,

First, That all three persons have each a peculiar proper hand in our salvation, God the Father in electing, Christ in redeeming, the Holy Ghost in sanctifying, as many places of Scripture shew. For God's intent in the gospel is as well to set up and magnify the three persons in a believer's heart, as his attributes, and the riches of his grace and mercy in common; therefore in Eph. iii. 3–5, Paul speaking of the knowledge he had in the mystery of the gospel, refers us to what he had writ afore in few words (not in another Epistle, but in this, namely the first chapter), wherein he presents to them, first, what in a more particular manner God the Father had done for them, from ver. 1 to ver. 6, that he had appointed and set out all the blessings they were to enjoy, elected Christ, and them in Christ, designed the persons who should enjoy them to the praise of the glory of his grace. Then, secondly, he presents them with what God the Son had done ; ver. 7–9, ' Redemption through his blood,' and the purchase of all the blessings God appointed to us, both remission of sins, and the making known the gospel, and the obtaining heaven by his blood. Then he shews them what the Holy Ghost hath done, how he had sealed them, and became the ' earnest of their inheritance,' ver. 13, 14. Now it being a principal scope of the gospel, as to draw men to salvation, and to magnify the riches of God's grace in common to all the three persons, so also to make known and have men take notice of, those three distinct hands these three persons have in our salvation. Therefore,

Secondly, Each of these three persons will have their love distinctly considered, and their several work, which manifests their love, distinctly viewed, and studied, and taken notice of by believers. And though, when one person is honoured, they are all jointly honoured in that one, and he that knows the one knows the other,—' He that hath seen me hath seen the Father,' John xiv. 9,—yet they will have their love considered so distinctly, that, as Christ says, John v. 23, ' They may honour the Son as they honour the Father,' and so the Holy Ghost also ; and take notice and acknowledge what they have done for them, and that they may believe on the Son as well as on the Father : John xiv. 1, ' Ye believe in God, believe also in me ;' he draws their thoughts to himself more distinctly than yet they were. And therefore,

Thirdly, As in point of believing we are to exercise faith on all three, so in point of assurance we may have an evidence from all three ; and therefore, as they are the object of an act of recumbency, so of assurance too, as witnesses. God draws out a believer's thoughts sometimes more distinctly and clearly, to consider and admire God the Father's love in electing him, in laying out all the blessings he should have in Christ, in choosing, appointing, and calling Christ to die for him ; in giving Christ to him, and him to Christ, in putting Christ to death himself, and becoming the executioner, in imputing that his death to him, &c. And then God carries the soul more clearly to consider Christ's love also in his work, in giving himself, and that so willingly, in having an eye to it when he hung on the cross, in bearing its name written in his heart, when he was crucified, and in taking all its sins on his back, which made his soul heavy unto the death ; and then God carries the soul on to a more especial taking notice of God the Holy Ghost's love, which is not considered ordinarily by believers. He brings souls to consider it is the Holy Ghost sanctifies them, who begat them, and formed the new creature in them, and who takes the pains to foster it, as a nurse its little one, day and night, and who endures with much grief their corruptions, which yet he cleanseth them from when they have defiled themselves, and who bears with them though they rebel and resist his motions, and who watcheth them, and attends them when they wake to suggest good thoughts to them, and when they shall go to the ordinances is ready to assist them. God makes them consider that all assistance in duties is from the supply of the Spirit, that all the comforts they have had is ' joy in the Holy Ghost ;' that he ' helps their infirmities,' indites their prayers, makes intercession in their hearts, leads them and guides them, and carries them in his arms as children ; that he keeps them for heaven, and hath took up their hearts as his temple, for ever to dwell there ; that he seals them up for heaven, and is the earnest of that inheritance, and he testifies that not only this is done, but that he doth it, and that it is his part, as you have them branched out, Rom. viii. and Eph. i., and by this distinct discovery of the love of all the three persons in their several workings, and contributing to the work of our salvation, they bear a several witness to a poor believer, so as he is carried on from witness to witness ; and as a man that is to have a testimonial goes to every man apart for his hand, so is the soul carried from one person to another.

I shall only answer an objection, and add a caution or two.

Obj. The objection is this, How the Holy Ghost is said to be a distinct witness on earth, and also in heaven, and to have also a distinct testimony as one of the three in heaven, from that of the three on earth ?

Ans. To answer this, consider that it is the Holy Ghost who is the reporter and recorder of all these six testimonies, and therefore is named in both, for blood could not testify without him, nor water; as grace cannot work, so nor comfort without him, unless he irradiates it, and opens the mouth of it to witness. This I think to be the most genuine intent of that place Rom. viii. 16, when he is said to 'witness with our spirits;' for grace in us could not witness if he joined not with it; yet he is said to have a distinct witness from theirs, because he hath a testimony beyond and without theirs; and so it is the Holy Ghost also that is the reporter of the Father's love, and of Christ's, and of his own, for as Christ says, John xvi. 14, 'He shall glorify me, and receive of mine, and shew it to you.' He it is that witnesseth Christ's love, and so the Father's also; they do all by him, and nothing immediately apart; and therefore, when Christ says he will manifest himself, in that place of John xiv. before quoted, he first promises the Comforter, as the manifester of him and of the Father. But yet they are said to be three, and their testimony apart several, because their love and work is distinctly revealed and witnessed by that Spirit, and his own also. And the soul is drawn to consider, that the person of the Father shews his love more especially in electing, the Son in redeeming, and he himself in comforting, &c. So that though he witnesseth all, yet it is in their name, and they are the persons concerning whom the witness is given; and his witness, as he is one of the three on earth, is distinct from that as he is one of the three in heaven. For as he is a witness on earth, the matter of his testimony is in general, the blessings themselves bestowed, justification, adoption, &c.; and the whole work of the three persons, as it is in common for salvation, is the thing witnessed, as it is also by water and blood. But now, as he is a witness in heaven, the persons that have done these come in to be more nighly considered; and his witness is of himself, and of what he hath done towards the believer's salvation. He opens the believer's heart to have fellowship with himself, and to see that he it is that hath sanctified, comforted him, &c.; so that he witnesseth his own part in this salvation. In the other testimony, he witnesseth that the person is sanctified, elected, &c.; but now he makes him take notice, in an especial manner, of the person sanctifying and sealing him, &c., and of the Father as electing, &c. And therefore, he influenceth the man to walk so as not to grieve him, to bear a respect to him that doth all this in that relation: upon which ground is that exhortation of the apostle founded, 'Grieve not the Holy Spirit, wherewith you are sealed,' Eph. iv. 30. For when a believer takes notice that the Spirit hath done all this for him, wrought all the grace he hath, and brought in all his comfort, he will have a respect to him, and have a distinct tenderness to him in that relation, as well as to Christ and to the Father. In the one, the Spirit is as the common broad seal of the whole Trinity, and of all the blessings bestowed upon us; in the other, he is a seal of himself in a more distinct manner, and so of the other two. As in seals of offices that a bishop or archdeacon give out, there is the seal of the office, and often they will set their own private seals on the back side also; so doth the Spirit, who, as he is reckoned among the witnesses on earth, is the seal of the office in common, the things sealed being the blessings and works of the whole Trinity in common; but in the other, their private seals are set to, and his among the other, which makes him a distinct witness.

Only now these cautions must be added:

First, That this distinct testimony of these witnesses in heaven is a thing many Christians have not observed in themselves, nor may happily never come to have a full experience of. God doth not deal with all in this manner. Many come not to have assurance at all, much less this. The people of

God under the Old Testament had it not, for the three persons were not so distinctly known in their several works in their salvation to them ; and therefore, when the apostle had discovered this mystery, Eph. v., how the Father elects, the Son redeems, and the Spirit seals, in the third chapter, ver. 4 and 5, he says, that in other ages this mystery, in this distinct manner, was not made known to the sons of men, not as it is now revealed. And the apostles also then had it not, John xiv. 1 : that is, not so distinctly, and in that manner I have spoken of it.   It is a thing many know not the meaning of, that yet have grace ; for their hearts are wholly drawn out to Christ, and they but implicitly apprehend, or seldom consider or think, what God the Father or the Spirit hath done.

And then, *secondly*, this caution must be put also in, that for the order of this distinct testimony in those that have it, or of taking notice of Christ's love, or the Father's, no rule can be set down.   Christ's love breaks in upon many first, and then the Father's.   What hath been said, is to shew such a work is in some, and may be had, and is to be aimed at, being now made known to you.

Neither, *thirdly*, is my meaning, as if believers could apprehend the Father's love thus apart from Christ's, or Christ's from the Father's ; or as if the one could be without the other, for the one is not to be severed from the other ; and if any thinks the Father loves him ere he hath had faith in Christ and rested on him, it is a Turkish, Jewish faith.   But yet things that are not in themselves, nor in our supposition, severed, may in our thoughts be more distinctly viewed, and apart sealed to us.

And, *fourthly*, though believers know and acknowledge what the three persons have done for them, yet that is not the work meant by the testimony of these witnesses.   As long as this knowledge is deduced but by way of consequence,—that is, when they consider that because they are sanctified, therefore they are justified ; and because they are justified, therefore they are elected, redeemed, &c.,—this is to know it by way of deduction. But it is an intuitive knowledge that I mean : to see it, and to have the heart affected, and the love of each distinctly brought home to them, and their hearts to dwell on the direct consideration of the work and love of each person, so as to come to have also fellowship with them all in prayer and walking from day to day.

The *fifth* caution is, that to direct poor souls humbled to faith, the way is not to direct them first to God the Father's love, but to cast themselves on Christ, who leads to the Father, Eph. ii. 18 and John xiv. 6.   For at first men apprehend God, according to the rules of the word, as an angry judge, and Christ as he that pacifies him, Col. i. 21 ; but when they are come to God, and cast themselves on him through Christ, then they are brought to see God the Father (whom before they looked on as a judge) to be pacified by Christ, and to have as willing an heart to save them as Christ himself hath.   It was suitably the speech of a godly person, ' As Christ makes intercession for me, so God loves to have it so.'

CHAPTER VI.

That since assurance is attainable, it is our duty earnestly to desire and endeavour the attainment of it.

Since then, as we have seen, assurance of our salvation may be attained, let us not rest and content ourselves in abiding in this wilderness of faith of reliance only, though it be that which brought us out of Egypt, and will lead us to Canaan, and is that by which God translateth us from death to life. Say of that state, This is not my rest, though I have much rest and quietness of heart in it and by it.

It is the duty of every one that doth believe to grow up to assurance, and it is his sin not to make out for it; it is his sin to sit down on this side of it. There is this difference between a believer and one in an unregenerate condition, that a man who doth not yet believe, and is not immediately (in that state) obliged to acts of assurance, yet is obliged immediately to believe on the name of the Son of God; but to be assured, cannot be the first act required of one that doth not yet believe. But now when once a man hath believed on the name of the Son of God, then the next and great duty that lies upon him, is to endeavour to know that he hath eternal life, and by all ways and means to seek after the knowledge of it. There are many duties which a man is bound to, but not bound to immediately. Every man in the world that hears of the gospel, is bound indeed to receive the sacraments, of baptism first, and then the Lord's supper, &c., but he is not bound to these immediately, but he is bound to be in the state of grace first, to be in Christ first; he is bound to repent, and to turn to God, and to believe on the name of the Son of God. But when once he is in the state of grace, all these things lie upon him then as duties. The apostle, 1 John v. 10, urgeth it as a duty, for a man that already believeth to seek after the knowledge that he hath eternal life; saith he, ver. 10, ' He that believeth on the Son of God' (if he have but that faith of reliance) ' hath the witness in himself;' the meaning whereof is not that he hath the prevailing act of witnessing, for then, if that were the meaning, every man that believes on the Son of God should have an act of assurance; but the meaning is, he hath the matter of it in himself; he hath the spirit of adoption within him, and he hath the blood of Christ sprinkled upon his conscience; and therefore, having the matter of assurance in himself, if he do not grow up unto it, it is through his own default; it is because he neglects or turns a deaf ear to the continual whisperings and secret suggests of the Holy Ghost concerning his condition, and rather willingly listens to Satan, and saith of all the Spirit's impressions, that they are but the voice and savings of his own heart, and doth not listen to the voice of the blood of Christ, which speaks, though with a still voice, better things than his conscience doth or can do, whenever he hath recourse to it by faith : for he never goes to Christ, and throws and bathes himself in his blood, but still there is a secret witness comes off with it, 1 John v. 8, more or less to the quieting of his heart. Now when men are as negligent in cherishing the dictates of the Spirit as they are in complying with his motions to good, when they regard not the voice behind them, but though God speaks once or twice, as Job says in another case, yet they never mind it; when they who have the matter of the witness in themselves thus go and throw it all off, and are in love with the contrary despairing and doubting thoughts, they are guilty of a great sin, which the apostle lays before them. He who doth this ' makes God a liar;' for as in that other part of God's record, wherein God hath set forth his Son Jesus Christ as a sufficient Saviour, and hath given that record of him, that he is his Son, and that in him is life, and that there is a propitiation in his blood, every man now that is in his natural estate that hears this, and comes not in and believeth, that receiveth not this record, he makes God a liar, he openly contradicts God's testimony, and proclaims that he believeth not that Christ is such a Christ as God hath testified he is, so on the other side, in a man that is in a state of grace, that hath faith, and so hath the Son and eternal life, all the fears and doubts that man hath to the contrary do in like manner make God a liar. The apostle John speaks that of not receiving God's record upon occasion of both; for as the six witnesses serve to shew us that Christ is the Son of God, so that we are the sons of God, and have eternal life when we do believe; and therefore that speech of his, 'He that believeth not the record God gave of his Son makes God a liar,' it holdeth as well of a believer's not believing he hath eternal life after he hath believed, as of his not believing on the Son of God. So that as it is the duty of every man to believe on Christ for salvation, and to believe this record that God hath given of his Son—and it is the great damning sin not to believe this, John iii. 18, and John xvi. 8, 9, and by not doing it men do make God a liar—so also it is the duty of every one that believeth, having the witness in himself, to grow up unto assurance; and if they encourage all fears and doubts to the contrary, so far they do in their measure and proportion make God a liar, in this respect, that they believe not the record that God hath given concerning believers, as well as his Son Jesus; for the not believing God, ver. 10, hath reference to this record, that God hath given us eternal life, ver. 11, so that the apostle, upon the very same ground, in the 10th and 11th verses of this chapter, urgeth those in whom God hath wrought faith, and to whom he hath given his Spirit, to grow up to assurance, and to know they have eternal life, that he urgeth those that are not believers to believe on the Son of God, he urgeth this common ground to both of them, of making God a liar.

Obj. But here will one thing be said, Are the meanest Christians obliged to this? and may the lowest Christians attain to this?

Ans. Yes, all sorts may; for you see John here writeth his epistle to all sorts: 1 John ii. 14, 'I write unto you babes,' as well as unto you 'young men' and 'fathers,' 'because your sins are forgiven you, for his name's sake, and because ye have known the Father.' And, saith he, your sins being forgiven you, I write these things even unto you, that you may grow up to the knowledge of this, and that you may know that you have eternal life; and though it be true, as I said, that the first act of faith which those that are newly converted do put forth cannot be assurance, yet it may be the very next act. Our Saviour Christ pronounceth to the poor palsy man even at the first that his sins were forgiven him, Mat. ix. 2, and so to Mary, Luke vii. 37, 48, when she was newly converted (yet she had believed first, which occasioned her coming to him), that her sins were forgiven; so that even babes in Christianity are capable of it. There are many things we attain not, because we do not set them up as our mark, but we rest below them, as in the case of perfection; as many, saith the apostle, as are thus minded, let them aim at that mark that I aim at. Men are [as] their endeavours, and as their mark and aims are. Now then, go home, and set this up for your mark and aim from this time forth; say with yourselves, I do see it is my duty to grow up to assurance that I have eternal life, it is my great sin to do otherwise; I see that it will improve all graces in me, it will help me to confidence in prayer, it will perfect my love unto God, it will make me serve him without fear, it will make me more holy, besides all the comfort it will bring in to me; this, therefore, I will set up as my mark, I will never pray but I will seek this in a more eminent manner; I will never receive the Lord's Supper but I will put this in, that the Lord would come in to bestow it on me; I will listen to all the witnesses I find whispering to my heart by the Spirit, or by the promises suggested to me, and that is this, of what it is that assurance be attained in this life, as far as this Epistle of John holds it forth. Let me first give this as a premiss to all that follows, that you may understand my meaning more distinctly, that though a man is assured of all implicitly at once, yet the Holy Ghost oftentimes doth distinctly set on first one thing and then another; you have experience of it in all your whole converse with God, that one truth is set on at one time, and another at another; so it is with the object matters of assurance.

First, He hath assurance of all those benefits which God hath bestowed, and of all the privileges which a man enjoys in Christ, as to know the pardon of his sins, and that I am justified, that I have right in eternal life, that I am a son; this you see the text holds forth: 'That you may know,' saith he, 'that you have eternal life;' so chap. iii. ver. 1, 2, 'Now are we the sons of God.' To see the privileges of a man's sonship, and to be assured of it, this is the first degree of assurance, or at least the lowest actings of it.

Now, to come to know that my sins are forgiven me, and that I have eternal life, &c., what is this? It is but implicitly the assurance of the privileges which I have in Christ, which, I say, is the lowest degree of assurance. Why? Because this is it which more suiteth self-love; all this while the soul may not have explicit sense so much of the love of God shed abroad in the heart, but explicitly or distinctly in his own consideration, his thoughts are taken up rather with view of the privileges which he hath in Christ, and he triumpheth therein. Now, as to love Christ for his benefits is the lowest degree of love, though there may be true love in it, so to have assurance of the benefits we have by Christ is the lowest degree of assurance.

Secondly, Besides assurance of my interest in all the benefits and privileges of a man who is in Christ, there is explicit assurance of the love of God in Christ; and this assurance John also holds forth in this Epistle, when he says, 'We have known and believed the love that God hath to us,' John iv. 16. It is not only a knowing and believing that I have eternal life, and that I am the son of God, &c., but withal explicitly to know also and believe the love that God hath to me, and to have my heart taken and swallowed up with that, which in the next words he calls dwelling in love, so as a man walks in it, works in it, lies down in it, shelters himself in it, as a man doth in his house. Now the love of God is brought home to the heart in and by two things (which also John here holds forth, for I confine myself to what he saith), 1, in those benefits which the Lord out of love hath bestowed upon me, and given me the assurance of, and over and above this, his love with them; and, 2, also in those works that God hath done to procure those benefits and privileges to me.

1. There is assurance of God's love in the benefits themselves: 'Behold,' saith he, 'what manner of love the Father hath bestowed upon us, that we should be called the sons of God,' 1 John iii. 1. He calls upon believers to behold, to consider it again and again, not to admire the love of God indefinitely. He calleth them not to an indefinite consideration of the love of God unto some, or what may be their lot, which, indeed, may draw in faith of recumbency, or reliance upon God for his love, but to a consideration of a determinate special love which God at the present bore to themselves in particular, and had settled on them, and had bestowed upon them, and is now at present estated on them: 'Now,' saith he, 'we are the sons of God.' And he calls them to consider the infinite greatness of this love: 'Behold what manner of love the Father hath bestowed upon us, that we should be called the sons of God.' Here is not only the

privilege of sonship, and the glory of it, set on upon the heart with assurance, but here is an admiration of that love set on more than the benefits themselves.

2. We ought especially to regard the works and actings of God for us, and to rejoice in the assurance of his love seen herein, and to have this love shed abroad in our hearts. This you have 1 John iv. 9, 10, where he speaks of the love both of the Father and the Son in what they have done for us: ' Herein is love,' saith he, on the Father's part in election, ' that he loved us first,' ver. 9, and also ' that he sent his only begotten Son into the world to die for us, and to be the propitiation for our sins,' ver. 9, 10; and herein is love on the Son's part, as in these common to him with the Father, in giving himself so willingly for us: ' Hereby we perceive the love of God, because he laid down his life for us.' It is the Son's love, whose life it was, he speaks of. Now for the heart to be taken with this love of God in what he hath done for us, and to have the heart steeped and dipped in that love, so as to taste and relish the love more than what is purchased by it, this is a further thing than the former; it is an higher degree of assurance; this is called, Rom. v. 5, ' the shedding of the love of God abroad in the heart by the Holy Ghost,' which is another thing than by way of consequence to apprehend this love, and the greatness of it, from the benefits bestowed, when we have them. This is when all the powers do taste that love as in itself diffused and brought home by the Holy Ghost, which all the arguments in the world and rational discourses can never do. When I have an assurance that my sins are forgiven, and that I am a son, &c., though if the Holy Ghost spake no more, yet I might, by way of argument, argue what a love this is; but to have the love itself brought home, and shed abroad in my heart, this is more, for the love is more than all the benefits, or than all that God hath done for us.

Thirdly, That which the apostle holds forth here, and intends in this Epistle, is not only an assurance of the benefits that they are ours, that we are sons, and have eternal life; it is not only the assurance of the love of God shewn in these benefits, and in what he hath done for us, and what love he hath borne to us, but it is a fellowship with God the Father and God the Son; so he tells you, 1 John i. 3, 4, ' These things we write unto you, that ye also may have fellowship with us; and truly our fellowship is with the Father, and with his Son Jesus Christ.' Now, to have fellowship with God, and with Jesus Christ, is more than simply to know and believe the love that God hath to us. It is when all the excellencies of God and of Christ are made known to us, and our interest therein, and all in an appearance of love. It is not only when God manifesteth his love in the benefits he hath bestowed on us, and in that which he hath done for us, but when all that is in God, and all the beauty and glory in him, appears to us clothed and apparelled with love, as he saith, 1 John iv. 6, ' God is love.' ' We know and believe,' saith he, ' the love that God hath to us;' in what he hath done, that is one thing; but then it follows, ' God is love;' himself, and all in himself, is thus manifested to us, this is another. There is, 1, the love that God hath to us; and then, 2, God himself is said to be love, and God is so to be apprehended by us, and so we ought to have fellowship with him, and to have an interest in all the excellencies and glory that are in him, and then the heart dwelleth in God (as it follows there), and God dwelleth in him. It is not a burning up of the flesh, as some speak, or that the creature ceaseth to be a creature, and is one with the Creator, God with God. No; that is an higher union than Jesus

Christ himself had in the flesh, by whom our redemption was purchased, and by virtue of which it was called the blood of God, and the righteousness of God (which can be said of no man in the world). But though the man Christ Jesus was one person with the Son of God, and so all his obedience was the obedience of God, yet he had a distinct being, and he had a distinct will from that of the Father, a will of his own: ' Not my will be done,' saith he, Mat. xxvi. 39, ' but thine.' Whereas now that other notion is of a higher union than the union that Christ had, and if men were raised up to such a union, then they might by their death redeem sinners, as Christ himself did. I therefore mean only that the glory of God objectively, and all that is in God in a way of love presented to the soul, filleth it, dwelleth in it; as if the sun should come down into a house, and dwell in it, instead of dwelling in heaven, and yet still the house remain what it was before; so it is here: God dwells in the heart, and the heart dwells in God, and yet still the heart remains what it was; that this is a further thing than that I spake of afore, and that it is more than for a man to know the love of God in what he hath bestowed on him, and done for him, is evident by that place in John xiv. 21, ' He that loveth me, shall be loved of my Father, and I will love him, and will manifest myself to him.' And the apostle speaks of this too, Eph. iii. 18, 19, where, besides ' knowing the love of Christ, which passeth knowledge,' there is a phrase of being ' filled with all the fulness of God;' that is, whenas all the fulness that is in God is presented to a man in a way of love; not that he is swallowed up into God, but God filleth him. He dwelleth in God, and God dwelleth in him, yet he remaining still what he was, and God remaining what he is too. It is not the fulness of God dwelling in us bodily, or personally, as it dwelt in the man Christ Jesus. No; that is proper to Christ by distinction, Col. ii. 9, from God's dwelling in us: ' In him,' saith he, ' dwelt the fulness of the Godhead bodily.' Now by body there is meant person, as they that understand the idiom of the Greek tongue know; as *soul* in the Hebrew is put for person, so many souls are said to come out of Jacob's loins, Exod. i. 5; so *bodily* in the Greek is taken [for] personally. There is, I say, a personal union between the fulness of the Godhead dwelling in Jesus Christ and himself, and therefore in the same place it is said to dwell in him, as the head of all principalities and powers; and all that is in God filleth him as our head, and dwelleth personally in him; which phrase, I say, is used by way of distinction from the creature. And yet all this while that the Godhead dwelt bodily or personally in him, he remained in the flesh, whereas the union that is now cried up is higher than this of Christ's, and while men seek to be spiritual, they detract from God, and run into blasphemy against God and Christ. But this communication of which I speak is objectively, when all that is in God is presented to the soul in a way of love; and when the soul hath fellowship and communion with him, all that is in God is his, and he sees himself an heir of God, Rom. viii. 16, 17, and he hath all that is in God to delight in ; and God manifesteth the beauty and glory that is in himself unto him in love, and so the soul dwells in God, and God in him, and all in love.

Fourthly, Add this to it, that there is communion and fellowship with all the persons, Father, Son, and Holy Ghost, and their love, severally and distinctly. This is that communion that John held forth, and which the Comforter, promised unto the apostles, brought them into, and which the apostle here would wind us up to, and put us upon the seeking after. Now there is an implicit communion with all these persons, so that if my heart be affected with the love of one, I may know the love of all the rest implicitly, as appears from John xiv. 7, 9, ' If ye had known me, you should have known my Father also;' but this is but implicitly, and therefore he saith afterwards, ' At that day ye shall know both me and my Father, and that I am in the Father, and you in me, and I in you.' ' Shew us the Father,' saith Philip, ' and it sufficeth us.' The poor man spake he knew not what, spake ignorantly, as oftentimes they did; but Christ here promiseth more, ' I will give you the Spirit,' saith he, ' and he shall be in you, and I will love you, and my Father shall love you, and we will make our abode with you.' Do not then stint yourselves here, that it sufficeth that you know the Father. No; Christ putteth you upon labouring after a distinct knowing of, and communion with all three persons; and the apostle John also speaks in the same strain : 1 John i. 3, ' That we may have fellowship with the Father, and with the Son ;' not only with the Father by having fellowship with the Son, and by having fellowship with the Son so to have fellowship with the Father, and so to have fellowship with the one in the other implicitly, but distinctly with the one and with the other, and distinctly with the one as with the other, and so to be acquainted with all, and to view the love of one as well as of the other; as Christ saith, John xiv. 1, ' Ye believe in God, believe also in me ;' so have communion with God, and have communion also with me. There is also an implicit knowledge of the Holy Ghost : ' You know him,' saith Christ to his disciples, John xiv. 17; that is, they knew him in his work, but they knew him not in his love distinctly, and they had not acquaintance with his person, and they had not the love of the Holy Ghost brought home to them. Now we are distinctly to have communion both with the Father, Son, and Holy Ghost, as he saith in that place : John xiv. 23, ' I will love him, and my Father will love him, and we will come unto him, and make our abode with him.' As the three angels that came to Abraham were all entertained by him, so for a man to converse with, and entertain into his heart, or rather be entertained by all three persons, and to have the love of them all distinctly brought home to his heart, and to view the love of them all apart, this is the communion that John here would raise up our hearts unto. And this John here in this chapter, ver. 7, 8, tells us, that there are three witnesses in heaven, who as they witness that Christ is the Son of God, so they witness to us that we are the sons of God, and that we have eternal life in his Son : ' There are three that bear record in heaven,' saith he, and these are three persons in the divine nature, and not three manifestations only ; for if so, then there would be as many persons as manifestations ; and when Christ saith, John xiv. 21, ' I will manifest myself unto you,' if Christ were but only the manifestation of God, then there would be a manifestation of a manifestation. No; he is a person : ' I will manifest *myself*,' saith he, ' and my Father he will manifest himself unto you ;' and so when it is said, 1 Cor. xii. 7, that ' the manifestation of the Spirit is given to every man to profit withal,' if the Spirit himself were but a manifestation, there were a manifestation of a manifestation. No; the Spirit is a person, and manifesteth himself, as Jesus Christ is a person, and therefore speaks of manifesting himself ; and as the Father is a person, and therefore saith he will manifest himself. They are three persons, and not manifestations only. Neither are they as the attributes in God, for if so there would be then more than Father, Son, and Holy Ghost ; there would be as many as attributes : wisdom is an attribute, and power is an attribute, and truth, and justice, and holiness ; and therefore if all in God were thus varied there were more than three. It holds forth therefore persons. Jesus Christ speaks as a person : John

xiv. 1, 'Ye believe in God, believe also in me;' and the Holy Ghost speaks as a person, speaks in the language of a person: Acts xiii. 2, 'Separate me Barnabas and Saul for the work whereunto I have called them;' you have the like in Acts x. 19, 20, 'The Spirit said unto Peter, Behold, three men seek thee. Arise therefore, and get thee down, and go with them, doubting nothing: for I have sent them.' Still, I say, the Holy Ghost speaks as a person. Now as these three are one in nature, so they become three distinct witnesses, and their very being three witnesses argue them three persons; let me also cast that in by the by. There is a notable place for it in John viii. 13, 14. The Jews there excepted against the testimony of Christ, and they said, that he bore record of himself, and therefore his record was not true. Why, saith he, I am not alone, but there is the Father that witnesseth with me, and it is written in your law, that the testimony of two men is true; and, saith he, I am one that bear witness of myself, and the Father that sent me beareth witness of me; so that in witnessing he joins himself with his Father, as equal with him therein, and makes himself and his Father two witnesses (you see how he stands upon it in that place), and himself as authentic a witness as his Father. Now as the Father and the Son thus witness, so saith the apostle in 1 John v. 7, the Holy Ghost also is a witness: 'There are three,' saith he, 'that bear record in heaven, the Father, the Word, and the Holy Ghost.' Now the witness that they bear is: 1, that Christ is the Son of God; and 2, that we are the sons of God, and that we have eternal life. When Christ was baptized, all three persons witnessed that he was the Son of God, and they all owned that nature that was baptized; the Father from heaven said, 'This is my beloved Son;' he speaks distinctly, the Holy Ghost he comes down from heaven, and with joy answerably, 'like a dove descended upon him;' and you heard even now of Christ his witnessing of himself: John viii. 13, 14, 'I bear witness of myself,' saith he; *teste meipso*; he speaks like God, like one that was as good a witness as the Father. Now what was done to Christ, the same is a believer capable of (for that is John's scope), capable to receive as distinct a witness, though not in a visible way, and by a voice from heaven, for God speaks not now so to the spirits of men, but yet in as distinct a manner. For the three persons, as they loved us distinctly (as might be shewn at large), so they bring home their love distinctly and apart to the soul, and the communion that John would raise us up unto is with all three persons distinctly, to view their love severally, and have it all severally brought home to our hearts, all of them manifesting their love unto the soul. Besides the three witnesses that are on earth, the water, and blood, and immediate testimony of the Spirit in common, there are these three witnesses of the persons in heaven, and therefore hast thou had the love of the Father brought home to thee? Rest not in that; get the love of the Son brought home to thee too, and then rest not until all three persons manifest their love to thee.

As in believing, sometimes a man's heart is drawn out to believe in God the Father; that is, look what is said of God the Father's love, and concerning his giving Christ, and choosing men to life, and in this his election regarding neither sin in them nor good (for free grace is properly the Father's), a man hath support from all such considerations, and he believeth in God, but whilst he doth so his heart it may be is not so distinctly drawn out to Jesus Christ at that time; so it is in assurance: sometimes a man's communion and converse is with the one, sometimes with the other; sometimes with the Father, then with the Son, and then with the Holy Ghost;

sometimes his heart is drawn out to consider the Father's love in choosing, and then the love of Christ in redeeming, and so the love of the Holy Ghost, that searcheth the deep things of God, and revealeth them to us, and taketh all the pains with us ; and so a man goes from one witness to another distinctly, which, I say, is the communion that John would have us to have.   And therefore ' grace and peace '—grace is that love that is in the nature of God, and peace is that joy that flows from the assurance of it— are wished ' from Father, Son, and Holy Ghost.'   Ordinarily you have it from the Father and the Son, but John (and he alone) pronounceth it from all three, Rev. i. 4, 5, witnessing, as the love of God, so the love of themselves distinctly ; as the grace of God the Father is brought home with peace, so the grace of God the Son, and of God the Holy Ghost, and therefore as our fellowship is with the Father and the Son, as he saith, 1 John i. 3, so also with the Holy Ghost, 1 John iv. 13 ; and this they in the Old Testament wanted.   And this assurance it is not a knowledge by way of argument or deduction, whereby we infer that if one loveth me then the other loveth me, but it is intuitively, as I may so express it, and we should never be satisfied till we have attained it, and till all three persons lie level in us, and all make their abode with us, and we sit as it were in the midst of them, while they all manifest their love unto us ; this is John's communion, and this is the highest that ever Christ promised in this life (in his last sermon, John xiv.), and you must know that this Epistle of John it answers to that sermon : ' At that day,' saith Christ, ver. 20, namely, when he would send the Comforter, ' you shall know that I am in the Father, and you in me, and I in you.'   That union and communion with the Father immediately, which is the whole of some men's religion, whilst it pretends to more spiritualness (for what more spiritual than for creatures to be swallowed up into God?), it runs into the highest derogation to God and to Christ that can be.   But that which Christ promiseth is, that they should know their union with the Father, but he leaves not out the Son. Poor Philip, he ignorantly said, ' Shew us the Father, and it sufficeth.' No, saith Christ ; the Comforter shall shew you your union with the Father, and with me too ; for you must never betake yourselves to the Father only, and leave me out.   Therefore now to talk of such a communion, wherein men betake themselves to the Father, and go to him immediately, this is not the communion which John had ; and he that denies the Son, and communion with him, denies the Father also.   The communion which the apostle exhorts to, is with all the three witnesses in heaven, which a man shall find when he comes there, and your communion for ever will lie in them ; the fulness of the Godhead dwelling then in you by vision, which now you take in by faith, and all three persons will be enjoyed and possessed by vision.   It is by a more high and elevated way, but it is of the same nature, and hath still the same object.

CHAPTER VII.

Christ's discovery of himself to the soul, instanced in the example of Christ's manifesting himself to Mary Magdalene, after his resurrection, as a pattern of his like dealings with believing souls, seeking him now after his ascension into heaven.

Jesus saith unto her, Mary.   She turned herself, and saith unto him, Rabboni ; which is to say, Master.   Jesus saith unto her, Touch me not ; for I

*am not yet ascended to my Father ; but go to my brethren, and say unto
them, I ascend unto uy Father, and your Father, and to my God, and your
God.*—JOHN XX. 16, 17.

We are married to an husband risen from the dead (as you have it in
express words, Rom. vii. 4) ; there is nothing can be supposed, therefore,
more welcome than to hear authentic stories of his deportment and converse, after his advancement, and so great an alteration, with any that were
his familiars before, and espoused to him, as we all are. And in this chapter, wherein you find his first flight after his being risen again, you have
two eminent such instances, the one in his demeanour towards a poor
mean woman, and the other towards his apostles, who were as mean creatures as herself.

It seems to me evident, that the most eminent scope of these stories left
to John, after all the rest, to record, is to hold forth this sweet and pleasant disposition of Christ our Lord to such souls as love him, and the
ground and intent of this relation is to shew how his spiritual dealings, and
all discoveries of himself to poor souls, now he is in heaven, do hold proportion and analogy with these bodily appearances and converses, accompanied with suitable spiritual impressions unto this woman.

And as a ground for this, I take in its coherence that promise, John
xiv. 21 ; he had promised to his apostles to comfort them personally ; not
by his Spirit only, but by his own personal seeing and conversing with
them again after his resurrection : ver. 18–20, ' Yet a little while,' says
he, ' and the world seeth me no more ;' for after his resurrection he
appeared not to one carnal man, but only to his own ; ' but you shall see
me,' and that alive, risen from the dead ; ' and because I live, you shall
live also ; and in that day' (as also by my Spirit after my ascension), ' you
shall know that I am in the Father, and you in me, and I in you.' Now,
lest others in after ages should think that they, being born out of time,
are therefore deprived of this privilege of Christ's appearings, such as he
made unto the apostles and others in that age upon his resurrection, he
adds that promise, ver. 21. So then these his bodily apparitions, with
spiritual impressions, as they were to these his disciples, were proofs and
pledges of like spiritual manifestations of himself to our faith unto the end
of the world.

Obs. 1. That Christ by a strong and strange providence singleth out some
special persons, to make them partakers of special privileges and discoveries
from himself. And it was a great privilege Christ vouchsafed to this
woman, in manifesting himself to her after his resurrection. It gladded
his Father's heart to see his Son risen again, as he utters it rejoicingly,
Ps. ii. 2, ' This day have I begotten thee,' speaking of the resurrection, as
appears from Acts xiii. 33. As Solomon's mother's heart rejoiced at the
day of his coronation, so God's heart is glad at the coronation of his Son,
of whom Solomon was a type. It must needs also proportionably rejoice
the heart of a poor soul, who so dearly loved Christ, to be the first that
should see him alive again, and in his new robes and dress ; and that
Mary had this first sight of him was not casual, nor fell out indifferently,
but electively, and as done out of choice by Christ, he had a set design to
take and find her alone, and so to honour her more eminently with this
discovery, and his providences were answerably strong to accomplish it (as
you may observe in the history), that it might appear he intended to put a
differing respect upon her from the rest. Mary Magdalene, and Joanna,
and Mary the mother of James, with other women, had visited his sepulchre,

and after them also Peter and John, Luke xxiv. But still our Lord withholds himself, and comes not out of his invisibility ; and Mary Magdalene herself, for whom this favour was designed, was deprived of the sight of her Lord at present, because they were in her company. But when they were gone home, and Mary stood without at the sepulchre (John xx. 10), and was now severed from the rest, Christ had her alone, and then breaks forth from out of his obscurity ; and that it was a designed favour to her, the Holy Ghost remarks, and puts a note upon it : Mark xvi. 9, that 'he appeared first to Mary Magdalene, out of whom he had cast seven devils.'

Are there not some of you here present, towards whom in eminent discoveries of himself, or in some other privileges, God hath held the like course, and hath made a manifest difference between you and others ? He hath shewn thee perhaps more mercy than all thy kindred, or than others of thine own rank, sex, society, and country, wherein thou hast lived. Hast thou not perceived how God hath revealed his secrets to thee a babe, when he hath industriously hid them from the wise and prudent ? Christ thanks God for this on his disciples' behalf, Mat. xi. 25, and wilt not thou thank him on thine own behalf ? Kings and prophets have desired to see and hear the things which you see and hear. We should learn to observe and study out such peculiarities of mercies, by considering what God hath done for us comparatively to others.

Another thing to be considered is, Who was this Mary to whom Christ vouchsafed this first discovery of himself ? I insist not on it that she was a woman, to whom Christ revealed himself, in his person, in such a manner as he vouchsafed not to the whole college of apostles ; however they excelled her in the discovery of the deep mysteries of the gospel, which was their glory, 1 Cor. ii. ; yet in the personal discovery or manifestation of the person of Christ himself, she is preferred before them. I therefore limit it to the revelation of his person, because there is a ' Spirit of revelation in the knowledge of him,' which consists in personal communion with him ; as well as there is a way of notional wisdom and prudence vouchsafed to ordinary Christians, Eph. i. 17, and many a poor soul is therein preferred to the holy, learned ones of the world, the reason of which is evident, because the promise of that manifestation is made to them who love him most, John xiv. 21, which weak ones, women and unnotional souls, often most do, and of this intuitive knowledge such souls are as immediately capable as the learnedest.

But there is another consideration beyond this, upon which the Scripture itself hath put the notoriety and greatest observation, and that is this, that she had been the greatest of sinners. We have this from the Holy Ghost himself, who would have us to observe it, and therefore upon this very occurrence he hath recorded it, there where he mentioneth this privilege, Mark xvi. 9. It is all one as if he had said, he appeared first to Mary, who had been of the highest rank of sinners ; so, then, as her sins hindered her not from being converted to Christ, but he shewed his power therein the more, so they hindered him not from vouchsafing to her the highest and choicest favour of manifesting himself. Take her fellow-parallel in this, the apostle Paul : ' Not only to me the greatest of sinners, he shewed mercy first in my conversion,' 1 Tim. i. 13 ; but, after conversion, he had that sight of Christ which exceeded this of Mary Magdalene's, and that of all other apostles. Fore-past sins then hinder not, but other predispositions concurring, invite Christ rather to the highest manifestations of himself. Neither doth this hold true only of great sins before conversion, but after it also, for who shall set the limits to the dispensations of free grace ? But what was it which was considered in this Mary Magdalene, which drew forth to her this peculiar favour of manifestation from Christ ? You read formerly of her love, Luke vii. 47 ;* but you find her heart here more full of it, even to a running over, than were the hearts of all the rest of the apostles. It was full sea with her when it was a low ebb with the rest, and it was that which took Christ's heart; do but compare the present springings and beatings of her heart and spirit with those of the apostles. ' But Mary,' says the text, John xx. 11, ' stood weeping without,' &c.; that *but* is a note of singular commendation put upon her for her affection, in comparison with the carriage of their spirits; they, after a little search, carelessly went home, ver. 10, but Mary yet was solicitous, and remained in a weeping posture at the sepulchre. Observe in her all sorts of characters of a prevailing passion of love in the midst of fears, despairs, and unbelief; *she stood,* she would not go away when they did, and, as she was not discouraged by their example, so all the halberts of the guards about her affrighted her not, she feared no colours, but love made perfect had cast out fear, and had fixed her with an unmoved courage at the grave, and a secret instinct of the Spirit arrested her, that she could not stir out of the circle; and then *she weeps,* which shewed that she could not bear the absence of him whom she loved, whereas the rest were gone away with dry eyes; and as she wept, she stooped down, looking into the sepulchre, though Peter and John had told her, and she herself had seen, that Christ was not there; yet, for all this, she looks, and looks again, and cannot content herself. It is the nature of vehement love and desire after what we want and value, to look, and search for it where we know it is not; so violent was her love and desire, that she would not trust her own eyes; yea, she was so overcome with these affections to her Lord, that though she saw two angels in white, who began to comfort her (ver. 12), yet love and desire after Christ had so transported her, that she minds them not, nor all their comforts; and out of restlessness and impatience of spirit, that suffered her not to continue in one place or posture long (as is the nature of violent affections), she turns herself back from them, as refusing to be comforted by them, and espied Christ, and thought him to be the gardener, and Christ discovers himself to her, and calls her familiarly by her name : ' Jesus saith unto her, Mary,' ver. 16. Now, I shall make some observations concerning Christ's thus discovering himself to her, and I shall make an analogy between this his bodily appearing in this case to Mary, and his spiritual manifestation unto such souls which seek him.

Obs. 1. That the persons unto whom Christ delights to manifest himself are such who are impetuously and passionately fond of him. They are such who can no way be satisfied but by seeing him, and enjoying communion with him; and when Christ stirs such a spirit unto an unconquerable desire after him, he answers it, and corresponds with it. As Jesus Christ knows what it is to love, so he doth love and value a soul's fondness of himself, and delights in nothing more. And as he knows that without manifestations of his love, the spirit which he hath made would fail before him, Isa. lvii. 16, so he answerably takes care that to be sure no soul shall die for love of him; it is his own promise, John xiv. 21, and this gives the full reason of this his dealing with Mary. Faith carries it in the point of justification from all other graces, but love carries from all other graces as to Christ's manifestation of himself to the soul; and Mary, you see, loved much, and there is no reward for such pure quintessential love as is fixed

---

* If the woman there mentioned was indeed Mary Magdalene.—ED.

on the person of Christ, but love again manifested, and the enjoyment of his person, nor else will, or indeed can recompense the loving soul.

Obs. 2. That Christ makes early discoveries of himself unto those believers who are vehement in affections and desires after him, when he defers the manifestations of his love to others, who though holy and having well settled affections, yet have them not so vehement and flaming. For let us but consider the different course which Christ held towards this Mary Magdalene and the other disciples, according to that different temper of spirit which was in her and them. We have two sorts of Christians exemplified in them and her. In the apostles we have an instance of judicious, wise, discreet professors, yet holy, that have true and solid affections to Christ, though not so flaming; who while they think to live by a solid and rational faith, and content themselves with it, are apt to think any extraordinary assurance, or special manifestation of Christ, to be idle tales, and will not hearken to them; or if they think there is anything in them, they come (as John and Peter did to the sepulchre) and see the grave-clothes of Christ, and rest in inferior discoveries of graces as signs in themselves which satisfy them, whereas these are but the grave-clothes of Christ, and severed from his person, afford but little hearty comfort; and they go again about their business, as Peter and John did, and think it a folly to look any further. But others are, as Mary, more affectionate, passionate Christians, that have great impressions made on their wills and affections, they know not how or why, that come to the throne of grace to seek Christ, and have his love from himself manifested, as Mary did, and find little, as she did not at her first coming to the sepulchre, the first time, that look, and look again, and see nothing appear, and yet will not go away. Now though the first sort are loved by Christ, yet he defers his appearing to them all day long, until night, until the evening of their days, as he did to his apostles; but the other sort of believers, being impatient after him, and lying down at his feet, and not stirring till they are blessed with a sight of him, are favoured with the appearance of him to them in the morning early, as Mary was, for it was early in the morning when this manifestation was made to her, and therefore, perhaps, it not being fully light, she took him for the gardener.

Obs. 3. That the time and season of Christ's discovery of himself to the soul is, when it hath run through the use of all means, and ventured difficulties for it. We see that Christ stayed from manifesting himself to Mary, who loved him so much, till she had been twice at the sepulchre, for she thought that he must be thereabouts, or nowhere, and would not go away, but stayed there, looked in, inquired for him of angels, ay, and of Christ himself too; but then, after the full use of means, though they in themselves were vain and ineffectual, Christ stays not a jot longer, but unexpectedly appeared, John xx. 14. She had said all her poor soul could say to express affection, and had done her due in the use of all means, and all in vain; and when Christ had left her to the extremity of mistakes and distresses about what she desired, then, at last he who had stood behind the curtain all that while, and under a disguise, steps out and manifests himself to her. And thus it often falls out (that the analogy may be observed), in the inquisition of poor souls after Christ in their own hearts, and in the manifestation of himself to them. He both useth gradual means in that discovery, and yet all along leaves them to doubts and distress, till himself breaks forth and appears. They would know whether Christ be risen in them, or to them, or not; they run to the ordinances, and first this angel, this minister, then another minister gives them encouragement, and sometimes reproves them for not believing; yea, they are bidden to remember the days of old, and God's dealings with them then, and they have promises brought home to their hearts in a seasonable manner, yea, and impressions and suggestions, sometimes in whispers, sometimes in loud testimonies to their hearts in prayer; but then they go abroad and talk with Christians stronger than themselves, and find them to have such a work upon them which they want, and find them to speak of such discoveries to which they are strangers, and then such and such corruptions break forth and over-power them, to think that Christ is stolen out of their hearts (as Mary says here, John xx. 13), and then all which they had received of Christ before seems as idle tales to them, and so they are possessed, as she was, with a fixed imagination, that either he was never in their hearts, but that in all hath been a counterfeit work, or that he hath been driven away by their lusts, or stolen away by Satan; and yet in the midst of this distress their love works, as Mary's did, and they inquire all over the city for him, as the church in the Canticles, Cant. iii. 1, 2. Then Christ sends angels, ministers, and good friends, one of a thousand, to comfort them; and they ask why the soul weeps, and tell it that it is in a mistake; but the soul is so far prepossessed with prejudice, that it turns away from all com-fort, as Mary did, and ' refuseth to be comforted,' Ps. lxxvii. 2; then Christ himself begins to appear, though *luce dubiá*, in some more doubtful light, as to Mary here, which yet is truly from himself, in impressions of ravish-ing joy, or the like; but they presently question this too, and discern not Christ in the business, but take him for another, as Mary mistook him for the gardener; they are ready to think, that Satan having stolen Christ from them, endeavours to delude them with false joys, and so they turn away from Christ, as Mary did, John xx. 14–16; but when Christ hath drawn out their affections towards himself to the utmost, in this dark way, wherein doubtings are mingled with their faith, which yet doth whet their love and desires after his presence, as it had such an effect on Mary, then at last he breaks forth in discovering himself to them, as Joseph did to his brethren; and his bowels turning within him, he can hold no longer, but appears as the sun out of a cloud, as Christ risen from the dead indeed, he appears like himself glorious to their souls. He appears to be such indeed as they looked not for. They, like Mary, sought for a dead Christ (as Christ is no other in our imaginations, till we see him to be what he really is, when he thus appears to us), but they find a living, quickening Christ, bringing heaven and glory into their hearts. The reason of this dispensa-tion of Christ is, that he may take their hearts the more when he doth appear, and that he may come to them with a greater evidence. *Nihil tam certum, quam quod ex dubio certum;* there is nothing more certain than that whose certainty is cleared out of doubts. And nothing proves more certain when made manifest, than what before was most doubted. And besides, he renders himself doubly welcome, when he comes not only unexpected, but at that time when we have had all our thoughts, desires, and hopes, seemingly baffled and frustrated with mistakes. Though Christ is now risen, and in heaven, yet he deals with us *more nostro*, in a way suited to our state, after an human way, and plays with us in *præludiums*, discovers himself, and withdraws. He appears first in such a dress as we shall not know him. Thus Moses contrived the discovery of himself, and of his love to his brethren, in such a taking way, and suffered their hearts to be pre-pared by all such circumstances, that when he should discover himself, a way might be opened to fill their hearts with a greater joy and astonish-ment, he laid a train for their affections, to blow them up at once. I need not tell you, that man hath such a principle in him, that is apt to be ever taken with such a story, when told, whether it be true or feigned, as relates the congress and meeting of two absent friends, or lovers, who ran through many difficulties and mistakes about each other ere they met. We all find the powerful influence of such relations. Who almost when a child hath not been moved to weep, in reading the story of old Jacob the father, and of Joseph and his brethren, and of his discovery to them? Christ our elder brother, though in heaven, yet plays with Christians, as those who are under age.* If you would frame a romance, it could not be more full of variety than is this manifestation of Christ to Mary; thus he dealt with his disciples going to Emmaus, he mingleth himself with their company, talks as a stranger, makes as if he would have gone farther, warms their hearts, breaks bread, and vanisheth. Have there been any such transactions between Christ and thee? They all have proceeded from the same love and pleasant kindness as these did towards Mary Magdalene, and are of the same kind, and shall be told as largely at the latter day, as this concerning her is recorded here.

Obs. 4. From the manner of Christ's discovering himself, observe, that nothing can give full joy, or thoroughly settle the heart in believing, and overpower all doubts, till Christ himself comes and manifests himself to the soul. If the vision of angels, and comfort spoken by them, could not have this effect on Mary, what then can do it? Though they sympathise with us in our distress, and in some cases suggest comforts to us, yet they cannot comfort us without Christ's appearance to our souls.

Obs. 5. When Christ himself comes on purpose to manifest himself, you then need no other witness. What cared Mary Magdalene for angels, or grave-clothes, &c., when she had Christ himself before her? As you need not light a candle by which to see the sun, so when Christ witnesseth immediately to our hearts it is enough; as when he swears by himself, there needs no other oath to confirm what he says.

Obs. 6. When Christ is pleased to direct one word, it sufficeth. 'Mary,' says he to this woman, and no more, John xx. 16. Thus when Joseph said to his brethren 'I am Joseph,' it was enough. She was before in the depths of distress, and ready to faint away; and one word from that mouth who speaks from heaven not only wipes away all tears, but fetcheth and revives her again. If a soul be never so far shot into despair, one glance of Christ's eye in prayer, and one beam from him, shoots it back again. Be not therefore discouraged in thy deepest desertions, since one word from Christ in a moment will revive thee.

Obs. 7. When he is pleased to appear, and speak to any soul, he doth it as punctually and effectually as if he called it by name. He is the good shepherd who knoweth his sheep by name, and they know his voice, John x. 3, 4. We are the stars in his right hand, Rev. i. 20; and he calleth all the stars by their names, Ps. cxlvii. 4. And well he may; for as hanging on the cross our names and the bills of our sins were brought to him, so now he is in heaven, as our high priest, he bears the names of the tribes on his breastplate, and hath our names to present to his Father; and when he speaks comfort, though he doth not vocally name us, as here he calls Mary, yet he speaks this comfort as punctually as if he named us. Thus in the manifestation of himself unto Moses, Exod. xxxiii. 17, says he, 'Thee have I known by name;' *i. e.*, I discover myself to thee as one that speaks to such an one by name. Doth he write any love-letters from

---

* Ludit in humanis divina potentia rebus.

heaven to thee? He punctually directs them to thy heart, as if he had wrote thy name.

Obs. 8. Christ must, when he appears, own us, before we can own him. He begins first, and calls *Mary;* then she answers, *Rabboni, Master.* As he loves us first before we love him, so he must manifest himself first before we know him, or rather are known of him.

Thus we have seen Christ's manifestation of himself to Mary Magdalene; let us now consider her carriage and behaviour.

Ver. 16, ' She turned herself, and saith unto him, Rabboni; which is to to say, Master.' She calleth him *Rabboni,* too low a word, and not full enough of reverence for Christ, considering that state he was now in. Thomas afterward riseth higher, and said, ' My Lord, and my God;' but she here plainly ' Rabboni,' which was the usual title given to those who were teachers among the Jews, and the old name which she used to give Christ before. Ver. 17, ' Jesus saith unto her, Touch me not; for I am not yet ascended to my Father.' It was a loving familiarity that she was entering into; she would fain have been touching of him, and embracing of his feet, as we read the woman did, Mat. xxviii. 9. The Greek word (here in John xx. 17 translated touch) ἅπτου signifies to hang about one, to cleave to one. It was a loving familiarity, such as she had used to Lazarus her brother* when risen; she thought to have enjoyed him as a friend, and as a friend on earth, with such a love answerable. It was this same woman that formerly fell at his feet, and washed them with her tears, and wiped them with her hair, and after that poured ointment upon his head; and she thought that she might use her wonted respect in such a familiarity, which became not that state wherein Christ was now. It is certain that she used no gesture uncomely for a woman to use to a man, her friend, supposed to be in an earthly state, for then she should have had some special reproof for it from Christ; neither indeed was her spirit at this time capable of any such thing ; but the unmeetness of it lay with respect to the present condition of Christ, which she considered not, and that was, that he being now risen, and so in that state wherein he was changed from an earthly to an heavenly man, 1 Cor. xv. 44, 45, that kind of converse which was once suitable was not so now ; as if a friend should be made a king, embracing or familiar speaking would not be so proper as bowing to him. It was then some familiar converse with him which she desired, such as she was wont to have, proceeding from her love unto him ; and therefore he only saith unto her, ' Touch me not, for I am not yet ascended to my Father.' The truth is (and you shall find it true in experience), when souls are admitted into near fellowship with Christ, there is an aptness in them to be too familiar, as here we see Mary was ; and therefore, it is a good lesson that is given to the church in Ps. xlv., who being advanced to be a queen, and to sit at the right hand of Christ her Lord, hath this counsel given her by God, ' He is thy Lord, worship thou him,' ver. 11. The King saith he shall greatly desire thy beauty, and so be familiar with thee ; but withal remember that ' he is thy Lord : therefore, worship thou him.' It is such a familiarity as still must be joined with the greatest observance. Or it may be, this poor woman, being in a kind of amazement, forgot herself, she knew not what she did, even as Peter when he was with Christ transfigured in the mount, the text saith, ' He knew not what he said :' no more did she now well know what she did. But why did Christ forbid her to touch him ? It is evident that he did suffer men to touch him after his resurrection. He suffered the disciples here in this

---

* Was Mary Magdalene the sister of Lazarus ?—ED.

chapter, ' he shewed them his hands and his feet,' and bids Thomas to
handle him ; and in Luke likewise, he bids the apostles feel whether a spirit
had flesh and bones ; and the women in Mat. xxviii., to whom he did appear,
they embraced his feet.   What should be the reason, then, that Christ would
not have this woman to touch him ?   Some say the reason was, because
Christ was now about to send her upon a message to his disciples, whom
he knew were in great need of comfort ; and therefore, though for her to
have communion with Christ had been exceeding sweet, yet, saith Christ,
do not you stand staying here with me, to shew your love to me as formerly
you have done ; do not hang about me, I have other work for you to do :
go and comfort those poor souls which are weeping at home ; go, tell my
brethren that I am risen again ; as for conversing with me, there will be
time enough hereafter for that : ' I am not yet ascended to my Father.'
This, indeed, is a very probable and good meaning, and shews that our
Lord and Saviour Christ took a great deal of care of his poor brethren, that
seeing now he was risen, and had begun to declare it, they likewise should
have the news of it, that they might be comforted.   But I rather think the
reason of the difference to be this, that he permitteth his disciples thus to
handle him and touch him, and forbiddeth her to do it, was because that
they might be witnesses that he was truly risen again with a true body, and
that so they might be fully satisfied of his resurrection ; but now this woman
she was already, by this appearance of his, fully satisfied in it, and therefore, as her aim was not to touch him for any such end, so there was no
need she should touch him for any such end for which the rest of the apostles
did indeed handle him, her aim only being to have some familiarity with
him.   Therefore, though Christ appeared to his disciples, and suffered himself to be touched by them, yet it was in order to beget faith, it was not in
a way of familiarity ; but now that faith that he was risen again being
begotten in Mary, he forbids her that familiarity with him that she was
entering into.   And observe the reason he himself gives : ' for,' saith he,
' I am not yet ascended to my Father ; ' the meaning whereof is this, that
he forbids her this familiarity in this earthly state wherein she was, and
forbids it also to all such.   But in that state of the world to come, when
he and she, both glorified, should meet, then she should have a full familiarity with him.   ' I am not yet ascended,' saith he, nor you with me ;
but one day we shall meet, though not in bodily embraces, for they profit
nothing, yet in bodily substance, and what is answerable and analogical
hereunto.   And it is as if he had said, When you and I shall be in heaven
together, with all my saints and children, you shall have familiarity enough
with me ; but now, saith he, this kind of familiarity is not ordained to you,
nor is it the time appointed.   I am not in a state to be familiar in that way
I was before ; but when I am ascended, and when you shall be risen again
and ascended, and shall have glorified bodies with me, then we shall be
familiar.   As one thing is forbidden to her, so to quiet her, another thing
is promised ; and it is implied that, when he is ascended, and his children
with him, when they shall have bodies taken up thither, and be where he
is, John xvii. 24, that then he will be familiar with them.   If you mark it,
he doth not say, Touch me not, for I am risen ; as if he had only intended
to shew that his present state allowed it not, or as if he meant to say,
Though you were familiar with me before my death, yet now you must not
be so, for I am risen.   No ; it is a higher reason : ' For,' saith he, ' I am
not yet ascended ; ' which clearly holds this forth, that indeed there is a
time after his ascension in which he and his people shall be familiar, when
he and they are in heaven together.   Stay but till then, saith he ; and in

the mean time, between me and you though there be a spiritual familiarity by faith now I am risen, and shall be when I am ascended, yet this kind of familiarity which you would now have with me, is reserved to the life to come ; and when I am ascended, and so you are with me, then we shall be familiar ; and therefore he addeth afterward, ' I ascend to my Father and your Father ;' we shall all be together one day, and then we shall be familiar.

This I take to be the meaning, and I know not how otherwise to resolve it ; other senses are put upon it, but to me this is most natural and genuine, and indeed most for our comfort. I will strengthen it with one instance, which I have often thought of, to this very purpose, and it is of our Saviour Christ's appearing in his transfiguration, when he carried up James, Peter, and John into the mount, and was transfigured before them. Now all the evangelists have this as a preface to that story, that Christ said, ' There are some standing here that shall not taste of death, till they see the Son of man in his kingdom.' So that that transfiguration was a glimpse or an entrance into that glory of his kingdom, which, with his saints and children, he is and shall be possessed of. Now in that kingdom, to shew that familiarity that shall be between his members and himself, you have Moses and Elias both (one having had his body in heaven afore, and the other, through the power of God, assuming his body, and being risen again) talking and familiarly conversing with him. Thus it will be in the kingdom of heaven ; and this, I say, Christ implies in this speech of his to Mary, ' Touch me not,' saith he, ' for I am not yet ascended ;' forbear this familiarity with me till we be in heaven together, for then we shall be familiar enough. He meaneth not that there shall be embracing of him, as here she would have done, but metaphorically, that there shall be an intercourse of familiarity between him and his children. It is a parallel phrase of speech with that in Mat. xxvi. 29 (and indeed the one interprets the other), ' I will not drink of this fruit of the vine, until that day that I drink it new with you in my Father's kingdom.' It is not that Christ will then drink wine, but he metaphorically expresseth the mutual joys which he in and with the saints, and they in and with him, shall have by the spiritual entertainment in heaven. Look, then, what familiarity there is amongst men at table, when they eat and drink together : such a kind of enjoyment, in a familiar way, shall the saints have with Jesus Christ in heaven, whereof there is some earnest here, Rev. iii. 20, as that there is but a metaphorical expression, so this of touching him here is : then in heaven they shall touch him, that is, they shall be familiar with him. He expresseth it in one place by that familiarity we have one with another at a supper, and in this place by her touching of him, or embracing him. It is certain that much of our happiness in heaven will lie in a blessed familiarity with Jesus Christ. Christ is a perfect husband, and all other husbands are but shadows of him, and there shall be the utmost familiarity then between us ; not that kind that is between man and wife here, but what transcends it, our bodies shall be made spiritual, 1 Cor. xv., as his also is ; and yet, as bodies earthly are suited each to other in converse earthly,—' they two are one flesh,'—so Christ's spiritual body and ours in an heavenly way ; yet I say that all such near converses here are but the shadows of it, because it will be transcendently more intimate, for we shall be one spirit with Christ ; therefore, in that 1 Cor. vi., where the apostle saith, that ' the body is not for fornication, but for the Lord, and the Lord for the body,' he addeth, ver. 14, ' God hath both raised up the Lord, and will also raise up us by his own power ;' that is, God hath appointed the very bodies of the saints (take them as glorified), for Christ to take pleasure in them, and for them to take pleasure in Christ ; and as he hath suited the eye to beauty here, so he hath suited those spiritual senses there to that glory which is in Christ.

Obs. 1. In the mean time, Christ being now risen and ascended, we may learn this, not to know him after the flesh. Mary here would have been familiar with him in a kind of human familiarity; our Saviour Christ refuseth this, to teach her that though he would one day be thus familiar with her, yet for the present that familiarity she was to have with him was by faith. ' Henceforth,' saith Paul, 2 Cor. v. 16, ' I know no man after the flesh; yea, though I have known Christ after the flesh, I know him no more.' Though the apostles had the earthly image of Christ in their fancies, yet, when they prayed to him, they did not set before them such a Christ as they had seen, but a spiritual Christ, as glorified, as ascended, as risen again; and under these considerations did they put forth their faith to him, and unto this doth he call Mary here, ' Touch me not, for I am not yet ascended.' If you will have any converse with me by faith, so it is; as for that familiarity to which we are ordained hereafter, that becometh not us now. So that, indeed, the least knowledge of our Lord and Saviour Christ in a spiritual way by faith, it is worth all the bodily knowledge we can have of him; though he should appear to us all a thousand times, and be never so much otherwise familiar with us, it were nothing in comparison of that we may have by faith. ' Though I have seen Christ after the flesh,' saith Paul, which expression of his, I think, may rise to this: though I was enabled, by the eye of my body, to behold him in heaven glorified (for so he did when he was converted, and so wicked men shall see him at latter day), yet that sight I have by the new creature, by faith, is worth more than all the other. That sight that the poorest believer hath of Jesus Christ by faith, is a higher one than that which Paul had of him by his bodily eyes. It was a means, indeed, of converting Paul, and it may be of the Jews; but else had not Christ wrought in him a touching of him by faith, a sight of him by faith, and by the new creature, that other would have done him no good, for it will do wicked men no good at latter day. Therefore now, if you will deal with Jesus Christ, you must deal with him by faith, you must touch him that way: there is no other, till such time as you come up to heaven, and be ascended with him; then, indeed, you shall see him face to face, and have familiarity enough with him. ' Touch me not, for I am not yet ascended to my Father; but go and tell my brethren,' &c.

Obs. 2. You see our Lord and Saviour Christ was not only careful to die for us, but to apply comfort to us. You shall read in the story of the evangelists that the disciples were got into a corner, and there they were weeping and mourning. Saith Christ unto Mary, What do you stand staying here with me? Go your ways, saith he, and tell my brethren; poor souls, they have need of comfort. Such are his dealings with poor souls now he is in heaven. He seeth such an one weeping and mourning after him. What doth he? Why, he doth in his providence order such a speech in a sermon : though he doth not tell the preacher so much, yet his Spirit doth secretly guide him. Go, saith he, and tell such a one such a truth as shall comfort his heart. Jesus Christ knows all your distresses, and as he sent Mary to his disciples, so he sendeth a word providentially, either publicly or privately, or he sendeth, indeed, his own Spirit—a better messenger than Mary was—down into your hearts, to be a messenger of comfort to you, when you go up and down mourning, and want comfort. Ye may see, I say, how careful our Lord and Saviour Jesus Christ is of those that are in distress, in want of him; how he takes care to have them comforted, therefore he despatcheth away this good woman to his disciples. That is one observation.

Obs. 3. Another observation is this, that for us to be means of performing of duty to others, to comfort them, and to bring others to faith and to believing, and to go about errands, and to do businesses that Christ sets us about, is much better in its season than enjoying communion with Christ. The thing is clear from this: Mary, though she had not been thus familiar with Christ, yet what a great deal of happiness would it have been to her soul, what comfort to have but stayed by him a while. No, saith Christ, I have better work for you to do than this, for certainly he did not send her to her loss. Go, saith he, as fast as you can, and tell my brethren; do that work and business, and refer the other till hereafter. And this was better for her, and she should have a greater reward than to have stayed there to behold him, and personally to have communion with him. To be employed in works for the glory of Christ and good of his churches, when he calleth us thereunto, is more acceptable than private communion with him in prayer, &c. Why? For we shall have familiarity enough with him in heaven. So he saith here, go and do that work I appoint you, and then fear not familiarity when you and I am ascended. Do you that I send you about, and believe me we will find a time for the other; we will meet in heaven. In the mean time, go and tell these poor souls that are mourning, and saddened for the want of me. This may hearten us in the work of our callings, to do what our hands find to do. Spiritual self must be sometimes denied to do carnal business. Christ denied glorious self when he left communion with his Father to come into the world, and to work out our salvation in it.

Obs. 4. Another observation from hence is this, that God doth oftentimes use means, very weak means, to reveal the greatest truths to his children, yea, to the greatest of his children. Here is the great point of the resurrection; yea, here is the great point of the ascension, which was higher than the resurrection. Whom doth he employ to break it first but a poor woman, and employs her to the greatest apostles. It is not ministers only that do always bring forth a truth; God oftentimes blesseth the meanest in a church to do it. Angels teach the women, they the apostles. He would honour, and he did honour Mary to bring the first news of the resurrection to the apostles; therefore we should not straiten truths only in respect of persons, but, as the Holy Ghost saith, 'a child should lead us,' Isaiah xi. 6; I mean in respect of truths.

Obs. 5. Again we may note this, that if we do know anything of God and of Christ, if any special thing be told us for the good of others, we ought to tell it, and not to keep it close. So soon as ever Christ had told Mary, 'Go tell my brethren,' saith he.

It is the first time he called them brethren. He called them disciples and apostles when he sent them forth to preach, and when he took his farewell of them to die, he called them friends; but now he is risen again, he calleth them brethren, not only to fulfil what was plainly foretold of him in Psalm xxii. 3 (which psalm, in the former part of it, is a prophecy of the crucifying of Christ), that as he made use when he was upon the cross of that saying, 'My God, my God, why hast thou forsaken me?' Nay, God had in his providence put into the Pharisees' mouths to speak the very words that he had foretold in this psalm; so now, being risen again, he useth that compilation which was prophesied that he should use, 'I will declare thy name unto my brethren;' therefore saith he here, 'Go tell my brethren.' Not only, I say, for this reason doth he call them brethren, but also hereby the more to break their hearts, for they were guilty of more sin against him now than they had been in all their converse with him. Some of them, namely, Peter, had denied him, and they had all forsaken him, yet when he riseth from the dead, the first word he speaks of them he calleth *brethren*, thereby to assure them how his heart and mind stood toward them, notwithstanding their sin and unbelief.

Obs. 6. Our Lord and Saviour Christ, in the manifestation of himself to souls, still riseth higher and higher. He had called them *servants* a long while, and they had called him Master; when he was to take his leave of them he called them *friends;* now he is risen he calleth them *brethren*, a relation that hath more sweetness, a higher style than any of the former. The longer you converse with Christ, the longer you live with him, the more sweetness you shall find in him, the more nearer and intimate passages of his love, and of the sweetness of his relations you shall find to increase and grow upon you. Hast thou found God sweet in one relation? Hast thou found sweetness in such a promise? He hath some further thing reserved to reveal of himself to thy soul. Hath Christ called thee friend? Wait but a while, and he will rise higher; he will call thee brother. You see here, after his resurrection, he speaks more kindly than he did before his death: ' Go, tell my brethren,' saith he; and now being ascended, and in heaven, his expressions are yet more sweet; he professeth himself to be a husband, and they to be his spouse. The longer thou knowest Christ, the more love thou shalt still find in him; he will still rise higher, and increasè in his expressions.

But what is the message he would have his brethren told ? ' Tell them,' saith he, ' that I ascend unto my Father, and your Father ; to my God, and your God.'

Here, you see, he doth not only satisfy this poor woman, that he was risen again, but he tells her a greater matter than his resurrection at the very first word, he breaks open to her the great article of his ascension. When Christ once begins to reveal himself to a soul, he goes still on to reveal greater and greater things. Mary here she would have contented herself with his dead body, she seems to desire no more: ' Tell me where thou hast laid him,' saith she, ' and I will take him away.' Poor woman, she had been unable to have borne away a dead body, but her affections goes beyond her strength, and now she hath not only Christ's body dead, but Christ's body risen ; and not only so, but she hath news of his ascension : ' I ascend,' saith he. Still our Lord and Saviour Jesus Christ will exceed our expectations in the manifestation of himself : you look for him risen, you shall find him ascending,—I speak in allusion to the text, —he will still be better than you can imagine, he hath still reserves beyond whatever your heart can think : ' I ascend,' saith he. As soon as he was risen, his heart was presently upon ascending into heaven. The truth is, it was his due to have ascended into heaven when he first rose, therefore he speaks in the present tense, ' I ascend,' I am going thither, though he was to stay a long while, forty days upon earth ; but, I say, as soon as he was risen, his heart was above, it was in heaven, all his mind was upon ascending ; he was held here indeed below, to do that service to his disciples and saints, to teach his apostles the mysteries of his kingdom, and of his resurrection, yet his heart was upon his ascension, so should every soul be. What saith the apostle ? ' Are ye risen with Christ ?' What is the next step ? Heaven. Ascend, saith he. Do we profess ourselves risen with Christ ? Let us not set our affection on things on the earth, let us ascend to heaven, ' let us seek those things which are above.' Christ was up in his affections sooner than in his body : ' I ascend,' saith he.

What is the reason that Christ would have Mary to tell his disciples at the first dash, that as he was risen, so he would ascend, and ascend presently, ascend soon ?

This is the reason, among others ; they did dream, and their thoughts ran upon nothing but a temporal kingdom, and such a kind of Messiah as should ' restore again the kingdom unto Israel.' Nay, the truth is, that even when he was ascending they could not be kept off, but still this ran in their minds, ' Wilt thou at this time,' say they, ' restore the kingdom unto Israel ?' For the apostles, you must know, were ignorant in many things, and though it was necessary that they should know infallibly, yet it was not necessary that they should know all things at all times. John did not know his Revelation a long time after he was an apostle. Now, to break off their thoughts from this carnal conceit, the first news he sends them word of, was, that he was to ascend ; he would not let them lie in an error so long ; how careful is our Lord and Saviour Christ, that as his people should not lie long uncomforted, so that they should not lie long in error ; the very first news, you see, that he sends his disciples, afore he speaks with them himself (to drive that error out of their hearts) is, ' I ascend,' saith he, ' I ascend to my Father, and your Father ; to my God, and your God.' You shall find that Christ, when he had spoken of his ascension before, he usually said, ' I go to my Father,' and ' I go to him that sent me,' &c. ; so John xv. 6, 10, 28, but now he puts their names in too : ' I ascend to my Father, and your Father :' for still (as I said) he reserves comforts for them. It became Christ, when he was risen from the dead, to speak higher things than he had done before. Now the scope and end principally of it is this, he had told Mary that he was not yet ascended, and that therefore she should forbear her familiarity with him ; ay, but, saith he, know, and tell my disciples too, that ' I ascend to my Father, and your Father,' and therefore where I am you shall be also ; I ascend to heaven, you shall ascend thither too ; for what is the reason that I go to heaven but because my Father is there ? I must go to my Father's house ; why, he is your Father too, and therefore you shall ascend too, and that by virtue of my ascension. We go to heaven by virtue of our sonship, or adoption ; therefore saith the apostle, Rom. viii. 17, ' If sons, then heirs, and heirs of God.'

Christ doth not say, I ascend to heaven ; no, he speaks higher : ' I ascend to my God, and to my Father.' For God considered as a Father is heaven, and therefore in that Rom. viii. we are said to be heirs of God ; not heirs of heaven, for indeed God is heaven.

' I ascend to my Father.' He shews here the reason why he was risen, and why he did ascend, and so why the saints shall rise and ascend ; because God is his Father, and God is their Father. What is the reason that Abraham shall rise one day ? Because he is the God of Abraham ; so Christ himself argues from that very thing in Mat. xxii. 32. So here he shews them the true ground why he was thus risen, and why he was to ascend ; because, saith he, God is my God, and my Father. And he plainly intimates that they shall go to heaven too, and rise again, as he had done ; for what God is to me, saith he, the same he is unto you. Is he my Father ? he is your Father too ; what the consequent was of his being my God and my Father shall be the consequent of his being your God and your Father. The consequent of his being my God and Father is, that I rose again, and am now going to heaven ; so the consequent of his being your God and your Father shall be, that you shall rise again, and go to heaven too. This is clearly the scope of Christ: 'Go, tell my brethren this,' saith he, 'that I ascend to my God,' &c.

I might shew here how he is the God of Christ and the Father of Christ, and that in him what he is to Christ he is likewise to us. But I will not stand upon that now.

Obs. 7. Only observe this, that the tenor of the covenant is altered,—it was the God of Abraham, of Isaac, and Jacob, and so the God of the Jews; but now it is the God of Christ, and so our God, because he that Abraham typified out is come. Abraham, with whom the covenant was made, was but a shadow, Christ is the substance. And so I proceed to the 18th verse.

Verse 18, 'Mary Magdalene came, and told the disciples that she had seen the Lord, and that he had spoken these things unto her.' There is little I shall observe out of these words, but only that which before I did. Mary she goes and doeth her duty, she leaves communion with Christ, and goes to perform that which Christ had enjoined her, as indeed we should. Though communion with Christ may be sweeter to us, as it is with a child to be with his mother all day, yet it is his duty to go to school all day, and then he shall come home to his mother at night; so it is our duty to be conversant in our callings, to be doing those things Christ sets us about, and it is more acceptable to God than to have communion with him all day long. You see Mary counts it so here; she leaves Christ, and goes and tells the disciples what he had spoken to her.

CHAPTER VIII.

Of joy in the Holy Ghost; that it springs from our communion with God the Father, Son, and Holy Ghost.

And these things write we unto you, that your joy may be full.—1 JOHN I. 4.

This apostle John was the love and delight of Christ when he lived upon the earth, nor had he less familiar converse with his Lord Jesus after his ascension and investiture with glory in heaven; hence the apostle makes this preface to his Epistle: 1 John i. 3, 'That which we have seen and heard declare we unto you, that you also may have fellowship with us: and truly our fellowship is with the Father, and with his Son Jesus Christ.'

The only begotten Son of God, coming out of the bosom of the Father, revealed the Father and his love; and, indeed, he only could do it, John i. 13. In like manner John, that bosom-apostle, who lay in the bosom of Christ, opens to us those breasts of consolation which himself had sucked; and as they were full breasts, so he writes these things that our joys may be full.

What therefore this Epistle aims at, we may guess by the frontispiece, to which also relates, and comes almost to the same thing, what he repeats at the end, and which is near the close of the Epistle: 1 John v. 13, 'These things have I written unto you that believe on the name of the Son of God, that ye may know that ye have eternal life, and that ye may believe on the name of the Son of God;' for however believers may be happy by having an interest in this life, yet then only they gladly rejoice when they know themselves to have it, and exult with a full joy when they know the life which they have to be eternal. Hence then there arises two things more distinctly to be treated of: 1. That it is the chief aim of the apostle to fortify the way for believers to attain communion with God, and to ascertain themselves concerning eternal life. 2. That thence only a fulness of joy doth redound : ' that your joy,' saith he, ' may be full.' The papists, who have made shipwreck of faith and a good conscience, to endanger others too would deprive the church of Christ of assurance of salvation, which is the trusty rudder to steer her in a storm, and so put her out to sea, not a calm sea, but unquiet and troubled (as Isaiah speaks, chap. lvii. 20), and there leave her to be driven about with the whirlpools of a fluctuating conscience, or to be tossed with the hurricanes of temptations, and at last to suffer shipwreck.

If in no other respect, in this at least, they are enemies of the Christian peace, of that which is the best peace, ' peace of conscience.' To overthrow them all I oppose this single apostle John alone against them.

But they will say that it is granted indeed that to the prophets, and apostles, and to Christians of the first magnitude, this extraordinary privilege of assurance is vouchsafed and manifested to them by extraordinary revelation, but that it is not discovered to the common sort of Christians by any revelation founded on the word. But, says the apostle, I have wrote these things (and indeed he wrote them on purpose) to that end, that they who believe may know that they have eternal life. What need is there of any heavenly messenger to tell them ? They have John, let them hear him. It is not only to the apostles that John, who was one of them, writes this, but to all who believe : 1 John i. 3, ' That which we have seen and heard declare we unto you, that ye also may have fellowship with us ; and truly our fellowship is with the Father and with his Son Jesus Christ.' His meaning is, that you believers may have communion with us apostles, in the same fellowship with Jesus Christ which we have. He directed this Epistle to all who believe on Christ, and to persons of all ages among them : 1 John ii. 12–14, ' I write unto you, little children, because your sins are forgiven you for his name's sake. I write unto you, fathers, because ye have known him that is from the beginning. I write unto you, young men, because ye have overcome the wicked one. I write unto you, little children, because ye have known the Father. I have written unto you, fathers, because ye have known him that is from the beginning. I have written unto you, young men, because ye are strong, and the word of God abideth in you, and ye have overcome the wicked one.' He doth not therefore speak of assurance and joy in the Holy Ghost as a privilege peculiar to grown believers, of the largest and strongest size, or to young men established in the faith, but to children themselves, to whom it is given (as our Saviour speaks, Mat. xiii. 11), more often given, to know this mystery of joy in the Holy Ghost.

If we read over the whole Epistle, we shall find that there are as many right and infallible marks, and certain signs given, whereby we may know our adoption, as there are verses in it ; such are, walking in the light, 1 John i. 6, 7 ; confession of our sins, ver. 9 ; observance of God's precepts, 1 John ii. 3, 5, observance especially of that precept of Christ which is the test of his disciples ; to love the brethren, ver. 10. Then he tells us (1 John iii. 3) that the greater our hope is, the more it will purify us ; and that whoever is born of God doth not commit sin, ver. 9 ; and that he hath given us the Spirit, ver. 24.

Obj. But the papists reply, that they freely grant that all these are certain signs of salvation in the general, but that the apostle John doth not name, or so much as intimate, any person to be assured of his salvation in particular. Whence therefore can any one promise himself that these signs are in him ?

Ans. The apostle himself furnisheth us with an answer to this : 1 John

v. 10, ' He that believeth on the Son of God hath the witness in himself:
he that believeth not God hath made him a liar; because he believeth not
the record that God gave of his Son.'   *In himself*, that is, in his heart,
assenting and agreeing to these signs; for as the word of God, which we
have in our hands, and which is divinely inspired, hath the inward testimony of the Spirit in itself, and is the evidence and judge of itself, by like
reason also λόγος *ille* ἔμφυτος, that word which you bear written in your
hearts, hath annexed to it a most credible and authentic evidence of itself;
' He who believes,' says the apostle, ' hath the witness in himself,' and
that witness is, that God hath given to us eternal life, ver. 11; and the
same apostle exhibits to us three witnesses (ver. 8) who use on earth to
confirm and seal to the consciences of believers their proper particular
salvation.   As there are three in heaven, who before had accomplished
their salvation established in the greatest reality (ver. 7), so ' there are
three that bear witness on earth, the Spirit, and the water, and the blood:
and these three agree in one,' ver. 8.   There is the spirit of adoption,
Rom. viii. 16, the water of sanctification, Heb. x. 22, and the blood of
Christ and justification, Heb. ix. 14.   Now in the mouth of two or three
witnesses every word shall be established, 2 Cor. xiii. 1.

Obj. But the papists again object that the heart of man itself is deceitful; who can know it ? Jer. xvii. 9.   And we experience daily many to
be deceived, and to be deluded with a false hope.

Ans. Be it so; yet to us who truly believe, Christ hath given us an
understanding that we may know him, 1 John v. 20, he hath put into us
that true new heart, that renewed understanding which judgeth all things,
1 Cor. ii. 15; and besides, he hath given us the Spirit, which is a Spirit
of truth, and knoweth all things, and teacheth us all things, 1 John
ii. 20, 21, 27; for all these signs of salvation which the Spirit hath inserted in the Scriptures he hath written in the hearts of believers, and
hath taught them to read them in themselves as well as in this Epistle, so
that there is no need that any man should teach us, ver. 27.

To which this also may be added, that since all knowledge chiefly owes
the certainty of its evidence, which is in itself, to the reality which is in
the object, faith, therefore, which is ἔλεγχος, an evident demonstration,
and ὑπόστασις, or real subsistence of the things which are believed, doth claim
to itself the highest certainty and infallibility.   For if the sense is not
deceived about its proper object, nor the understanding about its proper
object (which, since it is a sublimer and more abstracted power of the soul,
often corrects the sense), much less can faith, in which the image of God
chiefly shines forth, be deceived about its proper object, since it is more
noble than reason, and raised above it, and often convinceth reason of
errors and mistakes.   For it is the ὑπόστασις, the subsistence of things
believed, and the ἔλεγχος, the evident demonstration of them, and therefore challengeth to itself the highest certainty.   And indeed the certainty
and infallibility of knowledge chiefly ariseth from, and is owing to, both
the reality which is in the object, and to the evidence which is in the
knowledge itself.   Therefore, though hypocrites deceive themselves, and
being deluded with false appearances, dream that they believe, yet they
who are sincere believers, who are awake in the broad daylight of a clear
and bright faith, see and embrace the things themselves really subsisting.
But the papists, when they are so reduced that they cannot defend their
error in the grossest sense, in denial of all assurance of salvation, begin to
soften their opinion, and to smooth it with some little distinction, and
pretend to acknowledge that a man may have a conjectural and probable

opinion of his salvation, but not a certain and infallible knowledge, this they stiffly deny. But they shall not so evade the cogency of this apostle's reasoning, who not only often inculcates these and the like expressions, From this we know, and By this we know, but speaks more plainly, 1 John ii. 3, 'Hereby do we know that we know him;' and 1 John iii. 19, 'Hereby we know that we are of the truth, and shall assure our hearts before him.' Ay, say the cavilling papists, this doctrine doth render men secure indeed, too secure; this your assurance makes them careless, profligate, and loosed to all wickedness. The apostle, as foreseeing and aware of this cavil, meets with it, and prevents it at the first entrance of this second chapter: 1 John ii. 1, 'These things,' says he, 'write I unto you, that ye sin not.' To which also agrees what he says, 1 John iii. 3, 'And every man that hath this hope in him purifieth himself even as he is pure.' This assurance of faith, when it is genuine, begets an ingenuous spirit in the heart of the believer, Ps. li. 14, 15. There is not a stronger bridle to restrain sin, nor a quicker spur to holiness, than this hope, and assurance, and joy in the Holy Ghost.

But what though the believer falls into great sins, as the greatest lights have their eclipses, yet the certainty of faith is not utterly lost; for as the seed of faith remains in him, not as yet shaken out, 1 John iii. 9, so the firm establishment of faith abides also unshaken: 1 John ii. 1, 'My little children, these things write I unto you, that ye sin not. And if any man sin, we have an advocate with the Father, Jesus Christ the righteous.' We have assurance in this, that Christ being a righteous advocate, he will never be the patron of a bad cause, and therefore since he pleads ours, we may be sure to prosper in it. And he is not only a righteous advocate, but his own very righteousness pleads for us, and pleads not before a judge, but a Father, who in this shews himself just to us his children, that 'if we confess our sins, he is righteous to forgive,' 1 John i. 9.

Obj. But it is objected by others than the papists, Many fall by sinning so as wholly to fall away, though therefore it should be granted that believers may have assurance at present, yet how shall they be ascertained of the future?

Ans. But notwithstanding all, the foundation of God and faith stands sure; for what says the apostle of these who thus totally fall away? 1 John ii. 19, 'They went out from us, but they were not of us; for if they had been of us, they would no doubt have continued with us; but they went out, that they might be made manifest that they were not all of us.' But of those who are true brethren indeed, what says he? 1 John iii. 1, 'Behold what manner of love the Father hath bestowed upon us, that we should be called the sons of God! therefore the world knoweth us not, because it knew him not.' Ay, but they will object, that he says indeed rightly, that 'now we are the sons of God,' ver. 2, but leaves it uncertain whether we shall be so for the future. The apostle, to obviate this objection, goes on and says, that 'though it doth not yet appear what we shall be, yet we know that when he shall appear we shall be like him;' for, as he says 1 John v. 11, 12, 'And this is the record, that God hath given to us eternal life, and this life is in his Son. He that hath the Son hath life, and he that hath not the Son of God hath not life.' God hath now given us this eternal life, whose gifts are ἀμεταμέλητα, 'without repentance,' Rom. xi. 29, and the life which he gives is eternal, and so it is impossible that ever it should be cut off by any fate or death. And as it is given to us, and to be enjoyed by us, so it is deposited in Christ to be kept for us; and he is so powerful and so faithful as to preserve what is committed to his charge : 'And these things have I written to you,' says he, 1 John v. 13, 'that you may know that ye have eternal life.'

From this alone perfect love and full joy result ; for there cannot be perfect love in the heart of any believer which nourisheth a fear of any future hatred or enmity which God may have against him, nor can there be a full joy where the mind is obnoxious to the least suspicion of a change in its happy state. For any one so to love as that hereafter he will hate, is the poison and bane of friendship ; and thus for us to enjoy God the chiefest good, in so uncertain a manner as that afterwards we shall lose him, would afford more bitter than sweet reflections to our thoughts ; but the apostle wrote all in this his Epistle, 'that our joy may be full,' 1 John i. 4.

Having thus surmounted the chiefest rocks of those objections and doubts, with which the papists endeavour to obstruct the entrance (of which Peter speaks, 2 Peter i. 11) into the kingdom of God, let us now with full sails (that I may use Paul's word, πληροφορίαν, Heb. vi. 11) strive to enter into the harbour itself of joy in the Holy Ghost, a joy so great, a joy so full that we may rather be said to enter into it than that to enter into us. But we shall better understand how full and deep this joy is if we consider the fountain from which it springs. For as water will rise as high as its spring-head, so this joy doth too. Nor is there any need for us to search for the fountain afar off, for it is near to us (as that in Gen. xx. was to Hagar) since the verse preceding my text opens this spring to us : 1 John i. 3, 4, 'That which we have seen and heard declare we unto you, that ye also may have fellowship with us : and truly our fellowship is with the Father, and with his Son Jesus Christ. And these things write we unto you, that your joy may be full.' This communion with Father, Son, and Holy Ghost is the blessed spring from whence these clear, lively, and refreshing waters come, bubbling up unto eternal life, John iv. 14. All joy, which God as the most excellent and wise worker hath inserted into the actions of creatures to sharpen, excite, and animate them, doth either accompany or follow vital actions and operations, and a full, complete joy doth only attend such an action of our souls as is most vital, and most perfect ; and to such an operation there are these three things requisite :—

1. That it should have for its subject the most vivacious and lively power or faculty of our souls.

2. The object, about which it is exercised, must be the most noble of all other.

3. The power or faculty must be joined to this its object with the most intimate union. Even Aristotle's philosophical school teacheth us thus much ; but that great dictator of nature could never find out what this most perfect and vital operation was ; but the apostle John hath unlocked and opened this mystery out of Christ's school, and his most secret counsels. Communion with God and his Christ is this most vital and perfect operation of our souls above all other, and let us see how all the fore-mentioned particulars do exactly square with this communion, and are found in it alone.

(1.) For this operation, viz., communion with God and Christ, is most vital : John xvii. 3, 'And this is life eternal, that they might know thee the only true God, and Jesus Christ whom thou hast sent.' And indeed this communion is the only vital action ; for those who live in carnal pleasures 'are dead while they live,' 1 Tim. v. 6. And as the apostle denies that such live, so Austin denied that they had any joy, for as good is the sole object of the will, so of true joy likewise. Wicked men, as they only lust, not love, so they wanton, not rejoice.

(2.) This blessed communion hath for its seat both the understanding and will, which are called the quintessence, the very ' spirits of the mind,' Eph. iv. 22; these are the subjects and receptacles of this communion, and of this full joy, according to that song of Mary, Luke i. 47, ' And my spirit hath rejoiced in God my Saviour;' and this part of the mind, the spirit, is more sublime, pure, and more lively than any other, and formed for infinitely greater pleasures than all our external senses and appetites. These are vastly deep, and most capacious gulfs, which can at one draught take in and drink more of pleasures and joys than all the other lower powers of the soul (which are only subservient to these, as purveyors of pleasures for them), and they are able also to collect, to treasure, and heap up these joys unto eternity. But the gates of the senses are too narrow to admit an entrance of this full joy; therefore ' lift up your heads, you everlasting gates,' that I may speak in the psalmist's phrase; ' you gates of eternity,' viz., you higher powers of the rational soul, which only is immortal, ' that the King of glory may come in,' attended with this retinue, Ps. xxiv. 7, whom yet to receive even these passages of the soul are too narrow, though they are never so much enlarged. As the eye, too small and unequal to the light of the sun spread far and wide, cannot with one look behold and comprehend all its beams diffused through the whole compass of nature, ' the peace of God' doth not only surpass all our senses, but our understanding too, Philip. iv. 7.

2. This communion, as the most noble operation, hath the most perfect object. For our communion is with God, and with his Son Jesus Christ. Our communion is with God, who, as the Father of spirits, is the fountain and centre of our souls, and they cannot have any rest or complacent satisfaction but in the bosom of this their Father. Our communion is with that God who is ' the *Alpha* and *Omega*, the beginning and the end of all things,' who can do all things, who fills all things with himself, and who is ' all in all,' 1 Cor. xv. 20, in whom alone we feast upon that abundant heap of bliss and pleasure, which he hath but sparingly scattered in other things besides himself. All those delights which we, like bees, do but lightly touch in other things, we in a super-eminent manner do find and taste in God, who alone can fill and satisfy the various desires of our minds, and he doth indeed fill them; the enjoyment of him is the fullest and most satisfactory blessedness of our souls, for this enjoyment of himself is alone full, and sufficient to his own happiness from all eternity. It is full, for it fills all the Godhead, the possessor of it, and yet doth not empty itself; it is sufficient, for it hath a present and constant supply from him who is all in all, and therefore it must be full and most satisfying to us: ' I will be his God,' says God, Rev. xxi. 7, ' and he shall inherit and possess all things.'

Our communion is also with Christ, ' in whom all fulness dwells,' Col. i. 19, ii. 9, who, as he is ' full of grace and truth,' John i. 14, with grace he delights our wills, and with truth gratifies our understandings.

3. Then also the union, on which this our communion is founded, is of all other the closest, which by the help of 'faith in the understanding, and of love in the will, joins God and the soul into one spirit. For there are two arms of the soul wherewith we embrace God, the understanding and will; and there are also two hands in believers, adjoined to those arms, faith and love, by which we lay hold on God, and embrace him.

(1.) Faith, as it always unites us unto Christ, so sometimes it is strengthened and elevated by a light flowing from above, and makes us to rejoice with joy unspeakable: 1 Pet. i. 8, ' Whom having not seen, ye love; in whom, though now ye see him not, yet believing, ye rejoice with joy unspeakable, and full of glory.' David also speaks to the same purpose, Ps. iv. 6, 'There be many that say, Who will shew us any good? Lord, lift thou up the light of thy countenance upon us.' The greatness of this blessedness he illustrates, ver. 7, 'Thou hast put gladness in my heart, more than in the time that their corn and wine increased.' To this farther light is also added from that place in Ps. xxxvi. 9, 10, 'For with thee is the fountain of life, in thy light shall we see light : Oh continue thy loving-kindness unto them that know thee, and thy righteousness to the upright in heart !' This heavenly light, with which faith sometimes shines, is not a dry light, but drops with honey, and bedews the soul with the most delicious sweetness. What doth Philip pray for? John xiv. 8, 'Philip saith unto him, Lord, shew us the Father, and it sufficeth us ;' it was sufficient to satisfy him, what Christ promised, ver. 21, 'He that hath my commandments, and keepeth them, he it is that loveth me ; and he that loveth me shall be loved of my Father, and I will love him, and will manifest myself to him :' which he often performs, and sometimes illuminates the mind with light, which doth not only shew him conspicuous to be seen, but which doth exhibit him present to the soul in the most real and intimate presence, whence ariseth the most real and closest union and communion, and also the highest and most glorious joy. But if we consider the union which the senses and the understanding produce between themselves and other things, how superficial and merely outward is it ! and how weak and empty is that intercourse which they have with those things ! Now the joys which arise hence are of the same kind, they are not solid, but only plated or gilded over, for the substance of the things remain without, and only the shadowy and vanishing images of them enter in by the windows of the senses, and walk through the soul, and being deceived with a thin cloud, we do not embrace the things themselves. What thin and airy pleasures, therefore, doth the trifling enjoyment of all these things afford us ! The mind is only lightly touched with air, but doth not feed on true nourishing joy. These mere shadows of things leave the mind, which is formed to be sustained by firmer and more solid food, unquiet and hungering after the things themselves ; but faith, by an admirable art, which is peculiar to itself, and is unknown to reason, gives a reality to all things which it represents. Faith is the ὑπόστασις, 'the substance of things hoped for,' Heb. xi. 1, and affords to the things which it believes a real subsistence and presence of them before the mind, and doth not transmit its objects by the shadows of *species* only, which supply the place of the things themselves. And hence likewise the greatest and highest, the most real and solid, the truest and fullest, and most serene joy, is predominant in the satisfied mind.

(2.) I now come to consider the second bond of this communion, and the other cause of this 'joy in the Holy Ghost,' which is the conjugal union of the will to God in the bonds of love. For as soon as that threefold most blessed and kind aspect of the Trinity, of which we have spoken, hath shined on the soul, she kindles with an heavenly flame, and a reciprocal love to God ariseth in her ; for the love of God manifested to her, doth as with a fan make this flame of divine love to break forth. And hence the holy soul doth triumph, and is sweetly delighted, for that great conjunction of these two loves, both of that which flows from God to us, and that which is in us infused, never falls out, but it brings jointly with it an august and solemn jubilee in the heart.

Hence the apostle Peter hath joined these three most intimately together :

1 Pet. i. 8, ' Whom having not seen, ye love; in whom, though now ye
see him not, yet believing, ye rejoice with joy unspeakable, and full of
glory.'

[1.] ' You believing,' saith he, ' love.' The apostle John speaks answerably : 1 John iv. 16, 19, ' And we have known and believed the love that
God hath to us. God is love ; and he that dwelleth in love, dwelleth in
God, and God in him. We love him, because he first loved us.' His
meaning is, that whilst faith more clearly views all those infinite perfections, and all those infinite lovely things which are in God alone, the first
infinite and the first lovely being, and sees all these things mingled and
seasoned with love, whilst faith savours and discerns all God to be entirely
love, and whilst the soul sees God to be such an husband who looks for
no other dowry in his spouse than only a return of love for his love, and
whilst the soul also knows that all those are blessed with love who thus
place their love, the ingenuous soul, conquered and overpowered with love,
flows into this vast ocean with a reciprocal tide of love, and pours itself
wholly into it.

[2.] ' You loving,' says the apostle, ' rejoice with joy unspeakable.' It
is not easy to conceive, much less to speak, how much this intercourse and
sweet strife of love doth delight the soul. For,

First, A love that is yet single and divided, a probationary love, hath I
know not what self-sufficiency in it, and applauds itself in its own bosom,
is a price and reward to itself, and nourisheth itself ; and to love one who
yet loves not again, yields most abundant fruits, for love is the relish of
all things, and doth sweeten the most bitter circumstances of life. But
these considerations are very mean, and small, and only little gleanings in
comparison to that harvest of joy which springs from the mutual concourse
of two loves, and a fastened union of souls. It is sweet to love and
to be loved again : Prov. xxvii. 9, ' Ointment and perfume rejoice the
heart, so doth the sweetness of a man's friend by hearty counsel.' To
which answers that saying of David, mourning for the death of his Jonathan :
2 Sam. i. 26, ' I am distressed for thee, my brother Jonathan, very pleasant hast thou been unto me ; thy love to me was wonderful, passing the
love of women.'

Secondly, To all this we may moreover add, that the beginning of this
love is from him who loves without beginning, and without end ; without
measures, and without any preceding merit, and who receives nothing from
any other, but it is from himself only that he hath it, that he loves freely,
and therefore he loves the more vehemently, because he hath not love in
him so much as himself is love. As Bernard sweetly says, whose love we
taste not only to be stronger than death (Cant. viii. 6, since Christ laid
down his soul as a pledge of his love, John xv.), but better than life, as
David found it to be, Ps. lxiii. 3. As God rests satisfied in the love of
himself, so the soul rests satisfied in the love of God, and so in God himself,
whom therefore David calls his rest, Ps. cxvi. 7.

Thirdly, Nor is the joy of a Christian yet in its height and splendour,
for the soul doth not only perceive that she is loved again by her beloved,
but that she is most closely united with him, and that she enjoys her
beloved, which union Christ himself makes ; and as the enjoyment of him
is the blessed fruit of that union, so he is the efficient of it too.

First, The soul is united to Christ, for being allured by the sight of the
divine excellencies, and powerfully drawn by his love, as with a magnetic
force, she goes out of herself, and most earnestly desires union with God ;
this she breathes after with so great a vehemence, as she doth not only

desire to be united to Christ, but to be melted, to be transformed into him, as much as his being at present her absent bridegroom will admit; she reposeth and layeth close herself in the most inward bowels of his love, for whoever loves God is said to abide, and to dwell in God, 1 John iv. 15, 16.

Secondly, And behold now how good and pleasant it is, for God and the soul, as husband and wife, to dwell together in unity; and not only to cohabit, but to rejoice in one another: Isa. lxii. 5, 'For as a young man marrieth a virgin, so shall thy sons marry thee; and as the bridegroom rejoiceth over the bride, so shall thy God rejoice over thee.' Cant. i. 2, ' Let him kiss me with the kisses of his mouth, for thy love is better than wine.' And behold how Christ dismisseth his spouse filled with himself, and full of joy; for what virtue and efficacy must there be in the kisses of his mouth, whose lips breathe life, Gen. ii. 7. Souls, angels, and all the heavenly spirits, are the breath of God; and not only so, but he breathes the Holy Ghost himself, John xx. 22. These kisses of his mouth are better known by the impressions which they make upon us, than they can be by any of our expressions; we may experience the joy, but are not able to speak what it is; we may more easily obtain its possession, than learn perfectly the nature of it.* Nor doth Christ only give the kisses of his mouth, but the entire possession of himself, so that the soul takes hold on, and possesseth whole God, wholly as her own, so as it is free for her to enjoy all the sweetness of God (if it were possible to an infinity), and to draw out and taste all the pleasures which can be drawn from Christ, even to eternity.

But this joy, which is already so full, is yet more full and abundant, and flows to a greater exuberancy, so that I may use Job's words, Job xxvi. 14, ' How little a portion is heard of him;' and believers do more profusely and exuberantly rejoice that all these excellencies and perfections, which afford so much joy and delight to them, are in God, than if they were in themselves; for love, whose offspring is joy, a bright clear spark, and resembling its original, with a pure disinterested flame, loves God for himself, as God loves himself; and therefore loves all those perfections, which it sees to be infinite in God, and flowing from his essence, and with which his nature being crowned and adorned, shines with incomparable brightness. And besides, this sincere affection of the will doth wish and pray, that God may have all the revenues of his glory, arising from the present dispensation of things, and offers all these to him; and as this love is thus ingenuous, so this joy too is not less ingenuous and illustrious, for both of them are of the same nature and kind; therefore the believer doth congratulate and rejoice at all that beauty, glory, goodness, and sweetness, which he believes to abound most affluently in God, and he doth more sweetly rejoice (infinitely more), that God doth possess all these perfections in an infinite manner, and incommunicable (as to their essence), to other things, nay, to believers themselves, than he rejoiceth in his own felicity. So that this joy is a joy of friendship, as the fore-mentioned love is also a love of friendship, which our Lord Jesus, the fountain of love, taught us, when he reproved his disciples' ingratefully mourning for his departure from them: John xiv. 28, 'Ye have heard how I said unto you, I go away, and come again unto you; if ye loved me, ye would rejoice, because I said I go unto the Father, for my Father is greater than I.' Which glory and honour of his person his forerunner John the Baptist

* Quisquis itaque curiosius indagare voluit, non aurem, sed mentem paret; non audiendo, sed videndo gustatur manna hoc absconditum.—*Bernard.*

declared, when he lived upon earth, John i. 29, 30. The apostle Paul
boasts in 'the hope of glory,' Rom. v. 2, and the believer made an heir
with Christ may deservedly do so too; for he knows that joy (which
the apostle sometime enjoyed), though inexpressible, and he takes in some
little drops descending from that river, which waters and makes glad the
city of God; and the time will come that he shall be more thoroughly and
deeply plunged into the fountain of the Deity, where one flood of joy will
continually follow another without any interruption. We rejoice therefore
in hope of the thing, and we rejoice in the thing itself; we rejoice in the
possession, and also in the promise; in the present exhibition, and in the
future expectation; and as if all this joy were too little (which indeed is
exceeding great), and not noble enough, the apostle subjoins, Rom. v. 2, 3,
'And not only so' (he speaks in a rhetorical figure called *climax*), 'but
we also glory in tribulations,' &c., till at last we come to glory in God
himself, or in 'his love shed abroad in our hearts,' verse 5. The apostle
fixeth here the highest top of all, than which there is nothing more sublime
or more divine, that we do not only rejoice in those perfections of God,
with which he is blessed, but that the joy too is in some manner the same,
to which also that speech of Christ hath a reference: John xv. 11, 'These
things have I spoken unto you, that my joy might remain in you, and that
your joy might be full.' He doth not only say, that my joy may be concerning you, but that it may be and abide in you, viz., that very same joy
with which Christ doth rejoice, and therefore we are said to enter at last
into the joy of our Lord; not into that joy only with which saints and angels
do rejoice, but with which God himself rejoiceth. This is a wonderful
fastening of love, which is the cause that as one mind is in the persons
loving, so likewise one joy, not mutually only, but individually, and joining
into one flame, and this is the ἀχμή, the complete strength, and fullest
increase of joy; it is (as I may so speak) the *plenilunium*, the full moon
of it, than which nothing is fuller; for since the joy of Christ, the fountain of light, remains in us, that joy which we borrow from him must be
also full.

I will speak in a word what is the sum of all, and what is the highest
top of this joy; the joy of a believer is in God, and on the account of God,
their joy is God himself, and the joy of God himself, who himself is the
God of peace, and of joy, and of all consolation. What says God of all
the pleasures and imaginary joys of the wicked? Isa. lvii. 21, 'There is
no peace, saith my God, to the wicked.' But on the contrary, believers,
though sometimes they seem sorrowful, yet they are always rejoicing:
2 Cor. vi. 10, 'As sorrowful, yet alway rejoicing; as poor, yet making
many rich; as having nothing, yet possessing all things.' Though the
expression is 'as sorrowful,' yet of the joy it is not said 'as rejoicing,' but
'always rejoicing.' The happiness of the world may have an *as if* put to
it all, and as the world, so all its felicity passeth away (though an *as if*
cannot be said of the punishment of the ungodly, which is real, and endures for ever); but the joy of the godly is not with an *as if*, but is solid
and permanent; the very tears of praying believers are sweeter than the
songs and applauses of theatres. You may believe the apostle, who says,
Gal. v. 22, that true joy is 'the fruit of the Holy Ghost,' and that it grows
not on any other stock, whereas the joys of the wicked are the mere rinds
and shells of the fruits of paradise, and, as Tantalus his apples, deceive
any one who endeavours to taste them, and vanish into vapour and air;
they are nothing but the *spectrums* and apparitions of pleasures and joys;
they are like Jonah's gourd, which wither in a moment; they are like the

crackling of thorns under a pot, which is soon at an end, Eccles. vii. 6; it makes a loud noise, a great blaze, but as it ariseth and increaseth on a sudden, so the substance of it is thin and vanid ; it is a short-lived flame, and leaves nothing remaining; they are deceitful joys, which allure but do not satisfy us, which under a show of kindness hurt us, which emasculate our minds, and which in all respects have a greater mixture of troubles and misery than delight, Prov. xiv. 13. But, on the contrary, the joys of a believer are pure, without any mixture of a baser alloy: they are the drops and dews of heaven, and clear streams flowing from God the fountain of all pleasures; they are joys cleared from all filth and dregs: Isa. xxv. 6, ' And in this mountain shall the Lord of hosts make unto all people a feast of fat things, a feast of wines on the lees; of fat things full of marrow, of wines on the lees well refined.' They are joys co-natural to the mind, which both heal it and restore it to its right genuine taste of things; they are joys which when once the soul hath drunk and taken in, it will never thirst more to eternity, John iv. 14, for it will be abundantly satiated with them: Jer. xxxi. 14, ' And I will satiate the soul of the priests with fatness, and my people shall be satisfied with my goodness, saith the Lord.' They are joys which increase with their own growth, and in their agitation ferment to a greater quantity; they are joys which never fail, being full and sufficient to themselves; they are ' the breasts of consolation,' Isa. lxvi. 11; they are such joys which disarm all evils, and pulls the sting out of all sorrows, and sweetens the most bitter calamities, even death itself, the very remembrance of which how bitter is it to us! They are joys which infuse into us a true and invincible strength of mind, Neh. viii. 10, so that we glory and triumph in the midst of afflictions, Rom. v., and though storms and thunder-bolts may fall upon us, yet they are like hail falling on the house-top and shattered to pieces, and do not break us, but are themselves broken. The heavens and earth may fall into ruins, as Christ hath told us that they shall pass away, when not an *iota*, not a tittle, of this word and of this joy shall be diminished. And when the believer shall see this world declining to the extremest age, and long since condemned to the punishment of an old witch (2 Peter iii. 7, ' The heavens and earth which now are, are reserved unto fire '), at last all in flames, he will not only be in safety, but will stand erect and joyful upon the ashes and ruins of the world; and not having the least part of his happiness lessened by this universal desolation, he will cry with a great and cheerful voice, ' I have lost nothing.'

CHAPTER IX.

Directions unto the faith of such as want assurance: how to take in and make use of God's eternal, electing love in believing with comfort.

The applying acts of faith (as I have shewed) are two, the one of assurance, the other of recumbency, for in both I apply justification and Christ to myself; only the one is an application *axiomatical*, that he is mine, the other *real*. Now, to direct a soul that hath triumphing assurance added to his faith, and a right persuasion of his justification, overbalancing all doubts to the contrary, there is no great difficulty, for his thoughts may in the particular application of all these to himself follow God's ways in justifying him in particular, step by step, without any error (as Paul here doth), and take God's proceedings directly as they lie, to mould his thoughts of application thereby; his thoughts may climb up to eternity, and from thence with comfort view himself written in God's heart, and in the book of life, and then given unto and made one with Christ, and in him discharged from all his sins, justified by an eternal and unchangeable covenant made by Christ undertaking for him, and he may drink in all these with comfort, and utter this with triumph, ' Who shall condemn ? God hath justified;' and then he may come down from thence and see Christ's day, as Abraham did, and rejoice with Abraham, knowing as assuredly that Christ did represent his person, as that he took our nature. He may ' behold the Lamb of God,' as the Baptist says, carrying and bearing his sins all the while he was on the earth, and on his body upon the tree, and he may see himself then representatively in Christ fulfilling the law, undergoing the curse, dying on the cross, as truly as we all believe that we sinned in Adam, and were in the garden with him. And he may say, to the comforting of his own soul, I was justified in Christ when he arose, and discharged of all my sins, as truly as Christ was dead and is alive; and as Christ died unto sin once, and dieth now no more, so likewise he may reckon himself, as the apostle says, to live unto God for ever; he may look back upon himself when enwrapped in his blood, and in the pursuit of his bold and bloody transgressions in his former estate, that though his estate was then accursed, yet that his person in Christ considered, was really beloved of God; and, though he was not under the communication and dispensation of love and mercy, God being debarred by his rule from shewing it, yet he was under the affection of love and good will. But now, the partition wall being beaten down, and that which did let being removed, and his estate by faith altered, he finds God's favour flowing in amain upon him, and when he looks into the written revealed word, he may write his own name into every particular promise, and read in them all the sentence of his own justification pronounced.

But all the difficulty lies in directing the other sort of believers, or beginners to believe, how they should take in, or make use of a right application of Christ's dying for us, and of God's thus justifying us, as hath been spoken. The difficulty lies in this, that they must have recourse to Christ's dying, because from thence their faith must fetch justification for themselves; who, yet in dying, they believe, aimed but at some particular persons, who were then also justified by God, as also from all eternity, and they alone. Now, so to have recourse to this death of Christ, as with assurance to apply it, and so as to apprehend that their names then were in that bill, this is it they want, and such an act of application they cannot put forth; and what other act of application is there to be put forth towards Christ dying, or God justifying, to cast themselves upon Christ and God ? To what end should they do it ? What ! to trust to Christ to die for their sins ! that is done already. What occasion then is there, or what suitable object is there, for such an act towards Christ as dying, or God as justifying, for both is done already, or not at all, and therefore to what end should they cast themselves on either ? To assoil this difficulty, there have been many ways thought of by some of late.

Some make the sole and proper act of justifying faith to be an evidence and overpowering persuasion of our eternal justification, and of Christ's having borne all our sins, as one with us, and that this persuasion is wrought by an immediate revelation of the Spirit; and therefore seem to exclude all acts of bare recumbency, and casting a man's self on Christ, from the canon of faith as unuseful; yea, condemn the exercise of such acts, teaching men so to wait for such a revelation, as till then not to entertain a thought that they have faith : which is an error against the generation of many believers, against Scripture and experience.

Secondly, Others assert that men are not to look at all to God's ways of justification from eternity, but only to the indefinite promise, when they exercise an act of taking Christ, and casting themselves on him; even as when a sinner is yet to be humbled for sin, the promise is not to be considered by him till he be humbled by the law; and so they judge men are not to trouble themselves with the thoughts of the other, supposing them to be an hindrance and a discouragement; but when men, after believing, have also assurance given them, that they have now obtained that justification which the promise holds forth, then indeed the consideration of God's ancient justification from eternity, and of Christ's dying for particular men, will come comfortably and seasonably in; and only then, and until then, they are not to look to it at all; so as the indefinite promises are given to recumbents, and the revelation of the other is for them that have assurance only.

Thirdly, Others say, that though there be but a special intention for some, yet it is so as to make all salvable, if they would believe; which error makes a supposal of another justification promised than what is the fruit of an eternal love, and satisfies not souls, which will rest in nothing but eternal love, and effectual intention of God and Christ, and prize it more than his death.

A fourth opinion asserts, that seeing there is wrought a condition of humiliation particular to God's elect, they seeing it to be wrought, under it cast themselves upon a promise, which intimates something in us as the ground of faith; and of all the former this is the most false. That which I shall say will both confute these and open a

Fifth way. And for our proceeding herein we resolve this difficulty into these questions :

Quest. 1. The first is more general, viz., What should be the occasion and object of the aim of a believer's faith in an act of recumbency ? The answer is made by these several propositions.

Ans. 1. Let him consider, that howsoever those who shall be saved were justified from eternity in God's secret will (and therefore it were in vain to have that in their eye, so as to cast themselves upon God for the beginning of such a justification, as if it were now to be begun, which is already past), yet there is a true and real act of justification which is begun to be performed when a man first believes, and which is an act to be passed according to the rules of God's revealed will, and which, in relation to God's proceedings thereby, is an act now begun to be performed when a man shall believe, and not before. This is the justification which the promises of the gospel holds forth, as an act for time to come, that God is yet to do ; and the performance hereof may be the object and aim of such an act of faith. Thus (Gal. ii. 16) the apostles at first ' believed that they might be justified ;' and so (Rom. ix. 30) the believing Gentiles are said to have ' attained to righteousness, having sought it by faith'; so as justification may be, and is to be, looked upon and entertained not only by assurance that it is already past, but also, and that first, by seeking and believing for the attaining of it for time to come, and by having it in our eye as a thing to be actually given and bestowed. So as they are in a great mistake who would have faith to be a particular evidence and apprehension of God's having already justified us, both from eternity, and in Christ's bearing our sins. And the foundation of their error lies in this, that they imagine that there are no other acts of God's justifying us but those two, and that before God we were as actually justified afore faith as after. And also their error lies in imagining that all the use and end of faith is but to clear up this to us, and to cause us to apprehend it; whereas there is a true, real, new act of justification begun upon a sinner, which doth not only alter the apprehension of his estate, but also his estate itself, from a state of sin and wrath to a state of righteousness and favour, and this according to the rules of God's revealed will. So as faith serves not only to give men the knowledge of their eternal justification, but actually to possess them of that in themselves personally which they had before only representatively in another; and this by a further act of God upon the sinner; which act being to be performed, since it is for the future promised, a sinner that either begins to believe, or that cannot put forth an act of assurance, may and ought to exercise an act of casting himself upon Christ to be justified, and thereby seek to attain the righteousness that is of faith. And to this end,

2. Because all acts of God's justifying us depend upon union with Christ, we having him, and being in him first, and then thereby having right to his righteousness, therefore, as the aim of a soul casting itself on Christ is to have justification from him, so to have union with him also; and thus it may and ought to cast itself upon God and Christ, to be made one with him. And there is the like reason and occasion for such an act as for the former, it being a privilege now to be anew obtained as well as the other. For though we were one in Christ before God in representation from all eternity, and when he was upon the cross, and by a covenant secretly made between God and him, yet there is an actual implanting and engrafting us into Christ, upon believing to be obtained, and not till then, which the apostle calls baptizing, and planting into Christ, and being in Christ, Rom. vi., 2 Cor. v. 17, Gal. iii. 27, until which time even those who were elect afore are said to be 'without Christ in the world,' Eph. ii. 12. So as he may and ought at first to look at Christ as yet to be obtained, and so to seek after that union with him which is yet to be wrought, upon which this justification yet to be attained depends; so Paul, Phil. iii. 8, says, 'We accounted all loss, that we might win Christ,' and obtain an interest and a share in him; so as if there be both an union with Christ, and a justification depending thereupon yet to be obtained, there is a just ground and occasion given for the casting a man's self upon Christ to obtain this; yea, and this very casting a man's self upon Christ, out of spiritual apprehensions and affections, is the very act which both makes this union, and estates us into justification; and therefore the seeing of Christ, and coming to him, are made the acts of justifying faith, John vi. 35 and 40. And further, to this end,

3. Though those acts of justifying us from eternity in his secret will were distinctly fixed, and set upon such and such particular persons by name, and not left at random, as that thus he would justify some, yet God in his revealed will (out of which our faith is to expect that our justification now in time is to be applied, and according to which God proceeds to the last act of justification) hath folded and summed up those fore-passed ways and passages of justifying such and such particular distinct persons there named, in his secret will, and hath gathered and expressed them in indefinite promises to some sinners indefinitely, and believers generally; which promises are the abstract, contents, and argument, as I may so call them, of the book of life, and of his secret and distinct purpose concerning some particular persons. And thus he hath done, both to fit the faith of poor souls with objects proportional, and suitable to such an act of recum-

bency; as also that he might have these to come between their faith and his decrees, and that they might take in those his eternal transactions first, as represented through the indefiniteness of these promises, and so cast themselves upon such promises for that their particular justification, which is promised, now to be performed. Therefore one that would believe, is bound first to have in his eye that last way of justification, that is to be performed the last of the three, according as it is held forth and promised in the revealed will of God, and from thence to ascend up to the other. His faith is not to climb up to the top of the ladder at the first; he is not to make it his first business to be assured whether he in particular were intended, ere ever he will exercise any act of recumbency, or look after any promise, or seek out for the justification that is to come. This proves a real hindrance to many, for it is to inquire into God's secret will to me, as the sole ground of my faith, whereas I am to learn it out of his revealed will; and I am to begin at the last step, and from thence to ascend to the other. And in relation to that third act of justification, which the indefinite promises hold forth, and presents the person with, and which a believer sees is yet to be performed, it is that a believer doth exercise an act of recumbency, and comes to Christ, and trusts in Christ to be justified *de futuro*, for the future. And the promises of that justification which is upon faith to be performed upon the sinner being thus indefinite, they do suitably require, and are fitted to draw forth an act of recumbency, to cast myself upon God and Christ for justification, seeing those his promises run indefinitely, that he will save some sinners, and justify all believers. And accordingly, as the promises thus framed out of those his particular transactions are indefinite, so the first acts of faith which he requires are but such acts as are suitable to their indefiniteness; namely, to cast a man's self upon them, that Christ and justification may be his; not at first to believe they are his, or that Christ hath done this for him: thus David did, Ps. cxxx., and thus the apostle would draw in the Hebrews to such an act of faith, and endeavours by faith to enter into his rest (Heb. iv. 11) upon this ground, because the promise is, that 'some must enter in.' And again, as he hath fitted the promises of that justification which is upon believing to be performed, to such an act of faith, so also, he hath represented and offered Christ also, who is to be made one with us for our justification, as a Saviour for sinners indefinitely, as one that came into the world to save sinners indefinitely, that did bear the sins of the world indefinitely for all sorts of sinners, that so this representation of his Son might draw on the heart of a poor believer to take him, and come to him, and cast himself upon him, that he might be his, and one with him, by that union which is yet to be accomplished upon believing. Now the indefiniteness of the promise, which fits it thus for faith, and in which the secret transactions of God are included, consists but in three things, which make them to differ from the other, *i.e.*, there are three things in the promise which make it indefinite.

(1.) There is the concealing of the persons, that whereas in God's decree and transaction with Christ the persons are named, here in the promise they are concealed; and it is said indefinitely to be for some, to that end that none might say he is excluded, and that is one thing makes the promises indefinite.

(2.) Whereas men might notwithstanding think, that yet those some might be limited to some certain conditions of men, or but to some kind of sinners, as not to great sinners, &c.; and so men might think, that for their condition and sins they might be excluded; therefore secondly, the indefiniteness of the promise lies in this, that it speaks indefinitely of all kind of sinners and conditions, be the case what it will, and the sin what it will, for to some in those conditions, and guilty of those sins, the promise is made.

(3.) The indefiniteness of the promise lies in this, that it names a qualification of faith, and so makes it general, that whosoever believeth shall be saved, so as a sinner may further see, that there is but a want of a true act of faith between him and justification.

And these indefinite promises do yet fully agree with those particular intentions of God, and not cross them at all: for, *first*, although God's justifying from eternity was fixed only on particular persons whom he looked on in Christ, and also that Christ in his death represented only their persons, and did bear their particular sins, yet the promise of that justification to come, which is the fruit of those transactions, might thus indefinitely be propounded, and say it may, that salvation is for some, and name none; and God might so express his purpose, as might put all men that hear it in expectation and dependence, concealing the particulars; for there is an indefinite truth, which results out of those particulars put together, and is the abstract of them. For if God in his secret will hath justified such and such particulars, and there is yet a justification to be performed upon believers, the promise, which is the contents of those particulars, may be presented indefinitely, that there is a justification for some, and this may be declared and propounded to all.

Again, *secondly*, if Christ died for such and such particulars, whose particular sins he did bear; and it be true withal, that amongst their particular sins, all kind of sins but that against the Holy Ghost were to be found, and that all cases of sins imaginable, and all circumstances and aggravations of sinning whatsoever, are found in one or other, whose sins Christ bore; then it may be propounded to a man's faith, that Christ died for all such sins as he is guilty of; neither is there any circumstance or case he can instance in, but it may be said Christ did bear it.

And so, *thirdly*, if God hath purposed to bless all those particular men with faith, and a serious will to receive Christ, from eternity, and if Christ also did die that he [might purchase them faith, then God might further express this promise of Christ and justification freely and generally, that 'he gave his only begotten Son, that whosoever believeth should not perish;' for so it will prove in the event.

Only, in the *fourth* place, I will add to these three former propositions this caution, that believers, when they are exhorted to look to the promises thus indefinitely made and propounded, they must take heed of imagining Christ's death for sins and sinners, to have been performed by him indefinitely, or at random, as if it were not then intended for such and such particular persons, and for the expiation of their particular sins. The indefiniteness of the promise ought not to breed any such opinion, which yet is the conceit that usually is taken up as the meaning of the indefiniteness of the promise; men looking at Christ's death but as an *individuum vagum*, and the benefits of it as an office, into which some one must be chosen, but that it was not intended and particularly resolved who they are. They think it is like a jewel of value, sufficient to pay all men's debts that shall obtain it, but intended for none in particular when it was first purchased; and they look at faith as that which first determines whose it shall be, because the Scripture says, 'Whosoever believes,' &c. These conceits you ought not to entertain, and take up as the meaning of God in the indefinite promises, for this is to make God to elect upon faith foreseen, and to make Christ die for propositions only, and qualifications, and not for names and persons; whenas Christ says, before he laid down his life, John x. 14–16, that he ' knew his sheep,' and that by name, ver. 3, ' and laid down his life for them;' and these are those who were yet uncalled, sheep of another fold, not yet brought home. As the high priest went into the holiest, with the names of the tribes on his breast, so Christ to the cross, with our names in his heart, and also died that men might have faith. And as he died for particular persons, so he did bear particular sins, and it was just with God, who professed to deal with him in justice, that Christ should know what he paid for, as it is requisite we should know what God pardons, to magnify his grace. And if he had laid down his life thus at random, without such a reference to persons and sins, his love to one in dying had not been more than to another of those he died for, nor the greatest sinners more beholding to Christ dying than the lesser. And that Christ did not make his payment at adventures, as we say, and that God would not have the promise so understood, appears by this, that in his revealed will, in which he hath set forth these promises, he hath withal revealed that Christ did die for particular persons, and did justify particular persons; but because in that his revealed will he hath utterly concealed those particulars, therefore the promises are propounded indefinitely. And thus you have an answer to the first question, namely, what a believer should cast himself upon God and Christ for? The sum of which answer is this, that he may, and must do it, to obtain that justification held forth in the promise, and that union with Christ which are to come; which promise is therefore propounded indefinitely, that Christ died for some, and that God will justify some sinners, and all believers; which indefiniteness is not yet so to be understood as if who those particulars are were yet unresolved of, and that upon believing it were only determined.

Quest. 2. But these answers do solve the difficulty but in part, and do leave still occasion for further queries. For although there is a justification to be obtained indefinitely propounded in the promise, which may be the aim of faith of recumbency, yet it being withal revealed what act of justification fixed and determined upon particular persons have been passed already, the question is, whether a believer in casting himself, for the obtaining of what is to come, should at all as yet take into consideration those fore-passed acts and intentions of God and Christ, or wholly lay aside the thoughts of them till he hath attained to assurance of faith, and in the mean while wholly and only eye that justification through Christ's death which is to come, as it is indefinitely held forth in the promise? For it may seem one thing to imagine, by reason of the indefiniteness of the promise, that God and Christ were unresolved of particulars, which conceit we gave that last caution against, and another thing to forbear such thoughts for the present, and to confine our thoughts in believing merely to that justification yet to be performed, as it is indefinitely offered in the promise, which occasioneth this question.

Ans. To this question I answer, that a believer may not only take into his consideration the justification which is to come, as that God hath promised to justify some sinners through Christ, but likewise he may consider in the like indefinite manner that God hath justified those whom he means to perform this promise unto, from all eternity, for whom also Christ died as one with him. And the grounds which sway me unto this are,

1. Because I find that the apostle doth set forth these eternal transactions of God with Christ about the justifying of sinners as the main and sum of

our ministry, to be declared to the sons of men in an indefinite manner, to draw men on to faith : ' The ministry of reconciliation,' says Paul, is this 2 Cor. v. 19, 20, ' to wit, that God was in Christ reconciling the world' (he speaks of those eternal passages), ' not imputing their trespasses unto them.' God was, that is, from eternity, reconciling, and not imputing the sins of the world, *i.e.*, of the world of elect, unto them ; for none will say that any other were then justified but those that are predestinated ; and this he would have all men to consider, to draw them in to be reconciled to God, as it follows.

And the reason of it is, *first*, because those eternal transactions are revealed as well as promises, and whatsoever is revealed is for all' believers to make use of. And, *secondly*, they are so revealed as that if indefinitely considered, there is no difference between the declaration of God's eternal decrees, and Christ's special intention in dying, whilst indefinitely propounded, and the indefinite promises of that justification which is to come. They come all to one in a manner, the indefinite promises being but the abstract of the other, they being but the extracts and copies of the former transactions, made up, and expressed in a promise of that justification which is the fruit of them. And therefore, *thirdly*, though they speak expressly only of that justification yet to be performed, yet they do necessarily, virtually include and presuppose that which is past, as that which is the cause of what is promised, and is to come. Yea, and *fourthly*, that justification which is in the promise is no other than such as is the sole and proper fruit and effect of the former, and therefore is to be conceived and looked at by a believer, as that which hath an inseparable dependence and communion with that forepast by God and Christ. So that whilst the soul aims at that which is to come, as the effect, it may look at the other as that which is and must be the sole cause of it, if ever he attaineth it. For the justification in the promise is such as can be from no other cause than those former special transactions in God and Christ towards him. For as the justification promised is promised to be unchangeable, such a justification as is true, stedfast, unalterable, so the promise which is made to every one that thirsteth runs in these terms : ' I will make an everlasting covenant with you, and establish the sure mercies of David,' Isa. lv. 1–3. Such a justification as was performed to David was sure, that ' though his children sin, yet my mercy,' says God, ' I will not take from him.' And such a covenant promised to be made to everlasting cannot but be presupposed as the proper fruit of that justification which hath been from everlasting, and is no other, and therefore may be looked at as the ground of it. If indeed there were any other justification in any of the promises besides that, which is the proper effect of that as the cause, then all those former intentions of God to sinners might be laid aside, and needed not to be considered, but there is not any such. For the blessings held forth in the promise are but the former blessings bestowed upon particular persons in Christ, folded up and made up in an indefinite promise ; and therefore the one doth mutually argue the other. For if a soul can challenge an interest in the justification promised, he may comfort himself with his interest in the former, and that he was one with Christ, dying and rising. And again, when it is said that Christ died, it must be thought he had either an unresolved aim, or a resolved. An unresolved aim would be unbecoming of him, and if it was resolved, then he died designing the particular persons for whom his death was meant. And again, all the knowledge hereof a recumbent in the way of his faith may make use of, as well as one that hath assurance, it is but turning the key another way, as the same arguments are used in logic and rhetoric; so Eph. i. 9, 10, that which brought in the Ephesians to trust in Christ, ver. 12, was the opening of the mystery of God's will and purpose together in his elect in Christ, 'according to the good pleasure which he purposed in himself.'

Quest. 3. But still all this doth but in general shew that these fore-passed ways of election and Christ's death may be taken in. A third question therefore will be, How, and in what manner, and what order, and to what end and purpose, a recumbent believer is to take into his thoughts these fore-passed passages, so as to make it a help to such an act, when as yet his faith can perform no other? How he is to draw them in, and make them ingredients, and how they are to have an influence into his faith, to be helpful to him? For this, I say, take these directions out of the former grounds laid. But before I give them I premise a caution, which also makes way for a right understanding of what follows.

The caution is, that the believer is not to take into his thoughts these fore-passed fixed acts of justification, to that end as to make it his only and first work and business, to inquire whether he was thus justified or no, so as until he is resolved thereof, he will sit still, and exercise no act of faith at all, nor look after any promise; for it doth prove a real hindrance to many, when that is the fruit of this their knowledge. Though indeed we are not to rest or quiet ourselves in any acts of faith till such an assurance is obtained, but to wait for it in all, yet we are not to do it so as to cast off the exercise of this other act of faith, and seeking justification to come, till we have particular evidence of that which is past. This is a wrong use made of God's ways, so to inquire after his secret will, concerning our particular, as to neglect his revealed; whereas we are so to look to what is past, as to quicken us unto, and not to keep us from, seeking that justification to come. So as we say that the knowledge of this fixed and eternal justification is then a help to an act of recumbency, when the believing indefinitely and in general that thus God did towards some, doth quicken our faith of recumbency. Which that it may do, take these directions.

1. The believer may take in the consideration of these ways of God's justifying, and Christ's dying for certain men, who were one with him. This in the general he may do, to the end to pitch and point the aim and scope of his faith aright, so as to aim at his casting himself upon God in Christ for such a justification as only is the proper effect of the former, so as distinctly he may make it the desire and aim of his faith, that he may obtain such a justification as doth only proceed from an eternal love, and as is the sole fruit of a former eternal justification, and of Christ's particularly dying for his sins. And the reason why in this way he may take it in is, because though he looks upon that of God's love which is passed as not now anew to be obtained, yet as to that part of it which is to come and to be manifested now in the actual bestowing of all the blessings of it, he may cast himself upon God now to obtain it (it being yet to come), and to have it performed to him in the strength and virtue of the former; apprehending and knowing that no other but such a justification is meant in the promise by God, nor can be obtained by any, but so that still the aim of his faith and prayers may be to be justified with the justification of God's chosen, and to be justified out of that love with which he justifies those whose sins Christ bore upon the tree. Thus David often in many particular blessings frames his prayers, which are but the aims and meaning of faith expressed and folded up into desires: Ps. cvi. 4, 'Remember me with that favour thou bearest to thy people: and oh visit me with thy salvation;' that is, that salvation which proceeds from such a special favour; Ps.

cxix. 132, 'Look upon me, and be merciful to me, as thou usest to do to those that love thy name.' Thus he dealt also in matter of justification when he came to die and to express his faith at last: 'This is all my desire,' says he, ' and all the salvation I look for.' What kind of salvation was in his desire and expectation? That which proceeded from the sure covenant, ordered and sure. And thus God's Spirit doth point the aim of the poorest believer's faith, so that the meaning of his faith, if he could express it, is, that he might be justified with the justification of God's chosen; with that justification which is the sole fruit of Christ's having borne his sins in particular.

2. He may consider what is already done by God and Christ towards the justification of some sinners thus indefinitely, as the cause of that justification which is promised. He may consider this, to that end, to quicken him to seek such a justification, as that must needs be, which is the fruit and effect of such transactions and intentions in God justifying, and Christ dying thus for particular men and sins; and he will thereby both strengthen and quicken the act of his faith, of casting himself upon God for the obtaining of it. For as one that hath assurance by his faith receives and turns all such considerations into comforts, believing they are true concerning him, so the other that wants assurance may turn them all into motives to quicken and to strengthen his heart the more eagerly to seek it, and cast himself with the stronger and faster act of dependency and cleaving to God to obtain it; there is all the difference, and these considerations will further the one as well as the other. And the consideration thereof may serve and be turned into a double motive to quicken and set an edge upon their faith.

First, By considering these proceedings of God in justifying thus from everlasting, &c., to be the cause of the justification which is in the promise, and which he is seeking, his heart will be the more inflamed to seek such a justification as that must needs be, which is the effect and stream of such special love both in God and Christ. And the more spiritual insight into, and conviction of, those proceedings a soul hath, the more he will come to see the freeness, the fulness, the absoluteness, the unchangeableness, the greatness of that justification which he is putting in for, and so his heart will be fired with it. For when a man shall hear and consider that God hath, out of an infinite unchangeable love, been a-justifying some men from eternity, and hath done it so resolvedly, as though knowing and making account what their sins would be before, yet he resolved they should be no bar nor no hindrance, and that no estate, no condition, should alter or interrupt his purpose towards such;—and when he shall also consider that further, God hath took such special order concerning them, that he hath given them to his Son, and reckoned to him their sins, and looked at them as one in him;—and withal considers, that the justification which is offered in the promise, is such as is the fruit, and proceeds from these; why, thinks he, this is such a justification as, if I obtain, it will fully answer all my fears, and wants, and doubts, and scruples; and it is such as none can be like to it, such as my heart may securely rest in; such as, if a poor sinner would himself have drawn his own pardon, he could not have drawn it more fully, nor can desire a better. And by these considerations will his heart be taken with a longing after such a justification as this; O Lord, will the soul say, justify me with the justification of thy chosen ones! And oh that it may be, that I might be the subject of it! And it may prove so, thinks he; and if I were to choose, I had rather be one of a thousand of those who are in possibility of being justified out of

such a love, than any other. And why ? Because this is such as if I
obtain it, and it prove mine, a sea of eternal love will come with it and fill
my heart, and I shall be out of the gun-shot of all cases that can fall out,
it being such a justification as shall have all the unchangeable love of the
great God, and the efficacy of Christ's death to feed it, and maintain it,
and us in the state of it. And thus he may consider all those passages,
to inflame his heart toward this love, and to draw it in, and this ere he
can say it is his. The souls of believers are usually taken with this way
and proceedings of God and Christ in justifying, and it so likes them, and
takes hold of their hearts, that they can never let go seeking of it. Thus
God propounds the consideration of the unchangeableness and of the everlastingness of the covenant, to allure the hearts of believers, Isa. lv., for
the consideration hereof doth quicken the heart to come in: says God,
ver. 3, ' Incline your ear and come to me, and I will make an everlasting
covenant with you ; even the sure mercies of David ;' that is, I will justify
you out of the same love I justified David with, yea, the mercies of Christ,
who is that spiritual David, shall be yours.

Secondly, By the consideration thereof he may strengthen his faith in
the persuasion of the certainty that such a justification shall be settled and
estated assuredly upon some, and that therefore it is to be obtained ; which,
if believed, will exceedingly help a man's faith to cast himself with the
more boldness and confidence on Christ to obtain it. When men look
upon God as one that contents himself with this, that he hath done his
part to save them, and that however it falls out, yet he contents himself,
for he shall have glory out of them, this will and doth work a carelessness
in men ; but when men shall be possessed with this thought, that God is
resolved upon it, to save some, and that Christ hath took sure order for
them, and that therefore there is a certainty in the thing, so as it is to be
had and worn by some, and that God is most serious in it, for he hath
been a-justifying from eternity, and Christ hath died for particular sinners ;
when this persuasion of the certainty of the thing itself is fixed upon men's
hearts, so that together with the greatness of it, they are also persuaded
that such a thing there is resolved on in God's breast to bestow, it will
draw men's hearts into a dependence upon God for it. When men believe
that Christ shall undoubtedly justify many, because he hath borne their
sins, Isa. liii., and that there is a rest into which some must enter in,
Heb. iv. 6, this will quicken them to labour to obtain it, as knowing it
is to be had. For to that end those considerations are there brought in,
and the chief hindrance of faith lies in not believing the thing, and the
certainty of God's purpose in it, that there is mercy with him, and plenteous redemption. The assurance of this, though but towards an Israel,
yet the certainty that Israel should be redeemed, caused him to wait,
Ps. cxxx. If men have no heart to the thing, though God meant to
save never so many, they would never be saved ; and if they have, they
shall be saved, though never so few are intended. Now there is nothing more effectual to persuade the heart of the certainty of the thing,
than the consideration of God's eternal justification and Christ's special
intention.

Thirdly. In the third place, These eternal ways of justification may be
considered as the cause of that justification in the promise, to that end, to
quiet and settle most of all those carnal objections, fears, and scruples in
men's hearts, which are most dangerous, and the greatest hindrances of
faith. And indeed the consideration of it will serve to quell all of them,
but only one, which of all the rest is least dangerous. For when a man

shall consider that the justification which only is to be obtained, is such as is the fruit of an eternal, unchangeable love, &c., all the objections taken from the greatness of his sins will be scattered; for God's eternal thoughts in pardoning are beyond all imaginations; and that love also regarded neither sins nor goodness, but pitched upon persons freely, and that when he knew what their sins would be when he chose them; and also, all fears of being rejected for often backslidings will vanish, because the justification to be obtained is to be the fruit of a love that is unchangeable; and all his fears likewise of provoking God to cast him off, and of falling away, and that he may one day fall by the hand of Saul, will dissolve, when he considers the blessings of eternal love to be the sure mercies of David, out of which God justifies. And though he hears and reads, that after such a sin, God took advantage of Saul, Esau, &c., and swore in his wrath against those in the wilderness, yet the justification he is seeking of, and hath in his eye, is such as, if obtained, he may be assured of it never failing, as flowing out of an ancient, peculiar love, and therefore proceeds not in shewing mercy by rules, or examples of dealing of others, and which knows no bounds nor bottom; but God excepts, and says, 'Though I make a full end of them, yet not of thee;' and he says also, I will have mercy because I will, and where I will, though I harden others. Now the believer, knowing the justification, which he now seeks, by reason of these former transactions, to be thus full, it quiets all such fears, and resolves all into one, whether he shall obtain it [or] no? That is all his care, his heart is eased of all other; and this is a good care, unless in case of utter despair, for this quickens him the more to seek at God's hands to reveal himself to him, and it keeps him in dependence. And when once his spirit is truly won and taken with the way of salvation, he will never let go his dependence, but like a burr, the more he is shook off, the more he will cleave on. Yea, and against that one scruple, whether it be for him, he hath, in such a way of dependence, many things to uphold him, that his soul can quietly wait, and by reason of a hint given, doth secretly more incline in his constant thoughts towards hopes than otherwise. Now take all other ways of justification, which are not conceived to be backed thus with an eternal justification and an eternal love, but wherein God proceeds as he sees cause, and let a man be supposed, in his own apprehension, to be estated into it, and that cloud cleared, yet if he knows his own heart, he must needs be filled with sad, and dark, and dangerous fears. Sometimes the greatness of his sins past must needs amaze him, and his often backslidings and falls after enlightening, if none of these damp his hopes, or if none of these disquiet him, yet, having no security of his own heart, he fears for time to come; and the doubts which arise about the thing itself, and the way of salvation he depends upon, will be greater, and of worse consequence, and make his heart sit more loose towards God, than when, on the contrary, his heart is resolved that the justification itself, which he depends on, doth answer all fears and scruples about his whole estate and condition, and all the query is only about his person, and this is a doubt which, when all others are resolved into it, God can easily answer when he will; and if at any time the spirit be ready to fail, he breaks in, and resolves it. It is a doubt which the security his heart hath from the way itself, about all other things that can be objected, doth countervail.

Quest. 4. As there yet remains in his heart that one scruple unresolved, whether his person shall obtain that justification to come, he knowing that it depends upon what is past already, the question is, What acts of faith, and of the applications of faith, he should put forth towards both the justification that is to come, and likewise towards that which is past, for his own particular ?

Ans. 1. It is true there are two acts of faith which he cannot put forth : 1. He cannot exert an act of application with assurance : he cannot put that forth towards either ; and indeed, if he could do it towards either, he might towards both. If, then, the sole application of faith that justifies, lay in assurance, he would have no faith, and therefore it is well for him that it doth not. 2. To cast himself to obtain justification past, is a contradiction and absurdity ; therefore that is not the act of application in his faith neither, though it may well be exercised towards what is to come.

Ans. 2. This I must suppose as a foundation for all, that there is yet an impression and hint wrought in the heart of the poorest believer, of special mercy towards him, which is it that hangs his heart upon what is past, and causeth him to depend upon what is to come. This I mention first, because this is the principle of all those acts that I shall after mention, and this is like the first principles which are indemonstrable, but the conclusions from thence are and may be demonstrated. So about this I cannot give you any direction, for that Spirit that works the mind, and searcheth the deep things of God, must work it in you. It is the principle of faith, and is indemonstrable ; only what acts of faith this principle may be drawn forth into, as conclusions from that principle, this I will direct you unto.

This, therefore, being given by God to the heart, and supposed by us, such an one may be directed and enabled, before he hath assurance, to put forth these acts of application for his particular.

(1.) He may put forth an act of renunciation of salvation by all other ways of justification supposable, than such as is by Christ's special intention in dying, and justification from eternity. And this he is to do, not in his opinion only, when the query is about truth or falsehood, but he may and can, and is to be directed to do this for his own particular salvation, when he is consulting on what way to pitch as for his own salvation ; and that not of necessity only, because there is no other way, but out of choice. For when once in general he hath viewed the certainty, the stability of this way of salvation, in the whole progress of it, and how, when obtained and declared, it secures the heart ; and so his heart fully approves it, and sees also how it magnifies God's love and the riches of his grace, and Christ's love also ; and withal his heart hath had that undiscerned hint of intention towards him, he so approves it, not only as best and truest in itself, but as best for him also ; and doth constantly venture, and resolves constantly to venture, his particular interest upon this way of salvation alone ; and betakes himself to it, to deal and trade in his thoughts with it for his own salvation. He ventures not only his own interest upon the truth of it, but upon the performance of it to him, and all other ways that can be supposed or presented to him as possible, he utterly renounceth. He betakes himself to this rather, and chooseth to venture to be saved by virtue of these eternal past transactions of God and Christ, than any other. And though this hint is not boiled and raised up unto assurance, and he cannot yet say that he was justified from eternity, and that Christ had a special eye to him, yet he is content fully to hang expectation upon it, for his own particular ; and as David said of the law, ' I hate all false ways, but thy law do I love,' so says he of this way of the gospel, of these ways of God, which are yet past finding out, that this way of salvation he loves. And though, for aught he knows, there may prove a venture in it to him, yet he had rather venture to be saved this way, than saved the other way ; and had rather be one of a hundred that should have a draw for this, than one of two for another.

(2.) He may put forth an act of dependence upon God for the obtaining that justification to come, with submission to, and with reference, and by virtue of that which is past.

[1.] It is an error that men imagine that there can be no room for dependence, but only when all is yet to be resolved on by him on whom we depend. For though I suppose the foundation of all their salvation that shall be saved laid in God's heart, and in Christ's heart, and the thing resolved on, yet if the actual performance and execution be yet to be accomplished, as it is, there is room for a dependence. As if it were known that a prince had resolved to bestow an office on some particular man, but not declared who it is, every man capable might live in dependence for the actual bestowing it upon himself in particular, as well as if they knew he were not resolved, but might dispose of it this way or that way. Men therefore falsely conceive that if God and Christ were yet to make their will, then they would seek to them with dependence, because they hope that they might gain their hearts towards them, by obedience and dependence, to dispose of Christ's death and the riches of it towards them; but when their will is made and sealed up from eternity, they think there is no room for dependence, when yet there is the greatest of all other.

[2.] For there may be a dependence with submission, which Jeremiah calls waiting quietly, and putting the mouth in the dust, Lam. iii. 26, 29. The top and flower of God's glory in the ways of justification is his freedom therein; and therefore, as it is called grace, a being 'justified freely by his grace,' so free grace too; which freedom is shewn most in justifying some and condemning others, and in directing the course and progress of these his ways as he pleaseth. Now faith is appointed the instrument in us that should glorify God's grace in all the prerogatives of it, to glorify it as God glorifies it; and therefore, among other things, faith ought to glorify the freedom of it as well as the riches of it in pardoning; and this it cannot do more than by submitting its own salvation to this free, disposing, ordering grace of God, and to let God have his liberty in it. Faith frames the heart, and turns and applies it to the freedom of God, and glorifies him according to all the advantages his grace hath over men, whereof this is one of the greatest, viz., his freedom. It casts away itself in the glorifying of it, it ventures upon it with submission, because it is free; and if it falls out that the soul attains it, he glorifies that freedom, acknowledging that it was God's free mercy which saved him. If he thinks it may be otherwise (though in this case it cannot, however he may think so), yet withal he thinks that there is an instance of God's freedom that will be glorified, and he commits and submits himself, not to the sufficiency of God's and Christ's grace, but to the freedom of it, and launcheth himself into it without either oar or stern,* and commits himself to those vast waves, and the current and stream of God's mind towards him, to save or drown him. Thus David in a particular case exerciseth his faith, and if he had no other acts in matter of his salvation, this act of faith would have saved him. What says he? He submits himself to God's own thoughts towards them: 2 Sam. xv. 25, 26, 'If I shall find favour in the eyes of the Lord, he will bring me again, and shew me his habitation. But if he say, I have no delight in thee; behold, here I am, let him do to me as seemeth good to him.' He refers himself to God's thoughts wholly, with an holy dependence and submission. And thus faith may exercise acts of submission and dependence towards what is past, as well as for the obtaining of what is to

* That is, 'rudder.'—ED.

come; or rather faith may act for the obtaining of what is to come, by virtue of what is past already, and so it honours God in both.

[3.] And faith may act, not with a bare and naked submission only, but with a reference also to be justified by virtue of what was done then, which I may do, though I cannot tell whether I was then justified or no. This I know, that some men were justified then, and that what is to come hath an inseparable connection thereupon; therefore in casting myself upon what is to come, I may refer to what was done then, and I may have recourse to be justified now by virtue of that justification then performed by virtue of Christ's intention towards me. For as a man may refer to that he knows not the event and purpose of, so I may hang all my expectation upon what was done then, and I may refer to God's heart and Christ's heart towards me then, not only with a bare act of submission, but with hopeful expectation, which is the greatest trust in the world. For if the matter were now to be begun to be cast, the support of a man's dependence might be a confidence in himself, that he might do something which in the end might incline God, and then a man's trust were in his own heart; but when I refer to what was past before I was, I refer merely to God's heart towards me; I then refer with dependence on the bare free thoughts of God and Christ, which is the most naked, purest trust in the world. Now this is not only nakedly to submit, but it is to exercise faith in this manner; as if the soul should say, Lord, by virtue of what Christ did, and thou didst from all eternity towards me, now justify me. As a man may and ought to exercise the thoughts of faith which God works in him, though he thinks they are but his own thoughts; as a man is to pray, though when he prays he knows not whether he prays aright, so a believer is to refer to God's thoughts towards him, although he know them not, and to cast anchor in the dark; he ought to make trial what God's heart is to him, and to cast anchor upon it, though he cannot fathom it. And whilst his faith appeals thus to God's heart and Christ's heart towards him, God doth the thing, he hitting right. And again, men may and ought to take in thus by way of reference what is past, because they must be justified, if ever they be so, by virtue of what is past, and therefore their casting themselves upon God for justification may be with this reference, that it should now be performed to them by virtue of what is past. God and Christ did mutually trust each other about our salvation. God trusted Christ, ere he died, for saving many thousands, upon Christ's bare word, and Christ trusted God to see the fruit of his death in many thousands yet to come, and he sees his seed and is satisfied; and if they trust one another, shall not we?

(3.) A soul thus referring to what is past by God and Christ, for him to obtain justification by virtue thereof now, may yet be bolder in the exercise of his faith. For all these thoughts of what God and Christ hath done, he may turn into pleas to God, and plead before God the ancient passages of that his transaction with Christ about him, and try how they will take upon his heart, and see what God says to them. Thus Habakkuk, in the name and person of poor believers, puts God to it, to draw out his thoughts towards them in his prayer which he makes, Hab. i. 12: 'O Lord,' says he, 'art not thou from everlasting, my God, and mine Holy One?' He puts him to it, and reminds him of his ancient thoughts; and he puts the question to God, to see what he would say to it; and what doth God answer again? Ere he goes any further, he hath a gracious persuasion, an echo of God's heart towards them, 'we shall not die.' So do thou, go and turn all that thou knowest about God's eternal transactions with Christ towards sinners, and Christ's undertakings and undergoings for sinners, go and turn them all into holy pleas and queries with God daily in thy prayers, as touching thine own particular. Ask him, ' Art thou not mine, Holy One, from everlasting?' 'Lord, look on me again; dost thou not know me?' Desire him to look into his own heart, and view the *idea* he had of thee, and the thoughts he had towards thee from everlasting; boldly ask him, if he did not then commend thee to his Son, and write thy name in his heart himself? Mind him of all those secret passages, go over them all, and turn them into queries, which another soul which hath assurance would do into comfort and thanksgiving. Go down from thence, and spread all that Christ hath done before the face of God, tell over all the story of his being in the garden, on the cross, and say, Lord, did not Christ do all this for me, a vile wretch, by thine own appointment? Had not Christ me in his heart, when he hung on the cross? and hadst thou not me in thine eye, as one with him, when he suffered? and didst not thou then, unbeknown to me, charge these and these particular sins upon him? &c. I say, turn all into such queries about thyself, put God to it, see what he says to these things. How often is God so put to it that he cannot deny it, but plainly confesseth all this was true while the soul is a-speaking? However, whilst the soul is thus pleading, he finds thereby his load taken off, his mind eased; and why? Because he hits God's very mind, speaks the bottom of Christ's heart, and so finds the blood of Christ speaking better things than the blood of Abel. He shall find in these pleadings God's eternal love, and Christ's death, to be as a plank to a man a-sinking, to have a reality in them, to bear his heart aloft. He shall find, whilst he is pleading thus blindfold, as I may so say, and casting anchor in the dark, that his pleas take hold, and establisheth, and settleth his heart in the midst of all tossings. Thus as a bold man will by putting questions draw out another's secrets, so by such pleas and queries doth the heart often in a holy cunning draw out God's mind. However, thereby doth the soul find a support, and he shall find them to take with his heart, and to take with God; that as in preaching God's mind, if a son of peace be present, it takes with him, and his heart closeth with it, and is won; so in pleading over God's mind, and questioning thus with him, a man being a son of peace, and hitting right, God owns him, and all he says, to be true.

(4.) Under such an act of referring himself to God's heart and former proceedings, and in such a way of pleading, he may improve every promise, and all the fulness that is in Christ. Is there any benefit that God's love ever intended to bestow, or that the merits of Christ's death purchased, or can help a man unto? In the same way he refers to and pleads Christ's death for his justification, he may refer to it for all blessings else, for that way of salvation he depends upon will help him, and be improvable for all. If a man be sick, he can plead, Lord, did not Christ bear our sicknesses and infirmities? Was not his soul made a curse to redeem me from all miseries? Lord, I refer to his death for my recovery, as well as for my salvation, by virtue of it heal me! And he may have upon these pleadings of his, all things done for him, and by virtue of Christ's death; and his faith may make use of it, and have recourse to it for all, and receive all from it, as well as he that hath assurance. Indeed, happily he may want the discerning of seeing all done by virtue of Christ's death, as he that hath assurance hath, but it may be as truly done upon these acts of faith for him, as upon acts of assurance.

(5.) Since God, when he justifies now, doth it out of the same frame of heart and free love renewed, or rather continued, out of which he chose and elected, I may, without looking back to that love as electing, cast myself upon him, to bear such a love now to me as he did bear to his elect, and out of it to justify me, and so contract all that is said of eternal love in electing, down to a present love to be set on me, to justify me. For, as out of that love he elected, so out of such a love afresh taken up he justifies; and that is yet to come, and so I rest not on love or free grace as electing, but on such a grace or love as out of which he elected me, to justify me ; a love that shall have all the attributes of God freely, unchangeably exercised in it, all but* from eternity that electing love had, and is differing but in order to a different act of election, than of justification now,† and so free grace and electing love are for substance the same ; and in so doing I do draw but a model, map, or description of what a love I desire God may bear to me, alluding to the pattern of that love I hear he bare men, in electing them in the mount of eternity.

* Qu. ' that ' ?—ED.   † Qu. ' of election then, of justification now ' ?—ED.

BOOK III.

Of the actings of faith in prayer.—That we are not bound to pray with assurance of obtaining the very particular blessing which we ask.—That God, neither in the revelation of himself and of his attributes, nor in his promises, hath obliged himself to give us the very particular blessing which we ask.— That the essential acts of faith in praying do not necessarily require that we should have such a certain particular persuasion.—How we are in prayer to act faith upon temporal promises, and how upon spiritual.

CHAPTER I.

That God hath not, by any revelation of himself or attributes, engaged himself to give us the very particular blessing which we ask, and therefore we are not bound to pray with faith of assurance of obtaining it.

But let him ask in faith, nothing wavering: for he that wavereth is like a wave of the sea, driven of the wind and tossed. For let not that man think he shall receive anything of the Lord. A double-minded man is unstable in all his ways.—JAMES I. 6–8.

The absolute necessity of faith in prayer he doth vehemently and peremptorily express.

1. *Vehemently:* He doth not say he shall obtain no great or large gifts or favours, but nothing, not anything, without this.

2. *Peremptorily:* 'Let not that man think;' let him not entertain so much as a thought that God will hear him; 'let him not think that he shall receive anything of the Lord.'

The apostle binds up our faith in prayer strictly unto such a belief as hath a not doubting or not wavering accompanying it, and under that resolute manner presseth it, as that on which the stress of all asking in faith in prayer should lie. He instanceth in one particular of wisdom for all other, but thereupon gives the same common rule for praying for anything else which we may think or make account to obtain. Thus extensive is his caution, reaching to anything, as those words shew: ver. 7, 'Let not that man,' namely, that wavereth, 'think he shall receive anything of the Lord.' He cannot regularly, or according to God's ordinary course which is set about praying, receive anything. God may hear us afore we ask, but if we think to receive anything by prayer, it must be by praying in faith, 'without wavering.' So as this is proposed as a general rule holding in all prayers, that whatsoever we pray for, we 'pray in faith, nothing doubting.' But then here comes the difficulty, the last words immediately foregoing having been, 'Let him ask, and it shall be given him,' and these words coming next, 'But let him ask in faith, nothing doubting;' the coherence whereof would seem to carry it thus : let him ask in the faith and confidence of this, that he shall receive the thing itself he prays for when and whilst he prays, nothing doubting but that he shall receive it, and otherwise he shall not obtain it.

The text thus understood, hath been a mighty stound and plunge to many poor souls, that have lived in a lower region and way of believing. If this be the case, will some say, then I never yet have prayed one faithful prayer in all my life. Nay, I have not prevailing assurance, that is, a faith with a nothing doubting ; no, not for my own salvation, but am full of doubtings and sinkings of heart about that great point. I have not obtained so much in and by all the prayers I have hitherto made, and how much more may I say as to particular requests of what I stand in need of, that I never yet had this happiness to be able through faith to say I shall receive them afore I did receive them. Yea, those Christians that have assurance of their salvation, do find in experience very few of their petitions for particular mercies answered, wherein they have had a full forehand persuasion that they should receive the very particular.

It must therefore be looked upon as a case of very great moment and usefulness to resolve, and which requires a thorough discussion, to satisfy the many scruples about it.

The case I propound thus :

Whether it be a necessary requisite unto praying in faith for the obtaining any or every particular thing a Christian prays for, that he should pray in or with such a special faith and persuasion as amounts to a not doubting that he shall certainly receive it, so as if he fall short of this persuasion of faith in prayer, he must not think to receive it ?

First, I lay down this assertion :

That there is a true spiritual and effectual praying in faith, which doth obtain and prevail with the Lord, that yet is short of, and rises not up unto this special persuasion of faith without doubting, that I shall certainly receive the very particular I seek of the Lord.

Many pregnant instances and examples in Scripture might be alleged to prove this assertion, which I omit, because they may pertinently fall in, and will well mingle with several pieces of the discourse. I know also it is a commonplace head in our modern divines to handle, what it is to pray in faith, by the measure of which I might proceed to demonstrate this assertion; but this I decline now, for it will fall in with my following method. But I choose rather, for the clearer-demonstration of it (for I know no better or more conducing and fairer way), to take a survey of the most essential things unto faith in prayer, and chiefly because, in so doing, it will not only prove, but withal discover the very foundation and intrinsecal grounds how and whereupon it comes to pass that such a special persuasion of faith in prayer is not of absolute necessity to obtain the blessing desired. Now these essential things, &c., are two.

1. The principal object of faith, which faith in praying eyes, and acts upon, to move God to bestow what he asks.

2. The proper genuine acts of faith in praying, which yet fall short of being assured I shall receive the particular mercy prayed for.

And my demonstration for both these is founded on this great truth, common to them both, that they do admit of a latitude : First, unto our faith in praying ; and, secondly, unto God in answering ; so that it is not necessary either that faith in its acting upon these objects should rise up to that assured persuasion that you shall receive, or that God should grant you the very particular; but God and faith both have room and line enough left them ; God to answer the prayer in some other thing, and faith to ask the blessing without such an assurance.

1. I begin my demonstration with the primary objects of faith in prayer (as our divines call them), which are these things in God which our faith in prayer treats with God upon, which faith presents to God, and pleads with God, and urgeth upon God that it may obtain ; or which are the principal supports unto faith, that do strengthen it to continue to pray, and hearten it that it shall obtain.   And my diligent inquiry shall be, whether an acting on these in our prayers doth necessarily require and exact such a particular persuasion, &c.

Now the prime and principal objects of faith, by which it thus deals with God in prayer, are three.

(1.) Some special attributes of God, as his wisdom, power, mercy, which faith applies itself unto, and treats with God by.

(2.) The promises, general or particular, of such or such good things, which faith lays hold upon, and urgeth unto God to be fulfilled by virtue of those attributes.

(3.) The name of Christ, in which under the New Testament we are explicitly to put up all our prayers, as for which and whose sake God will bestow all he hath promised.

Now if there be a due application of the soul unto God in and through all these, according as the nature of these may require, then it is certain there is true faith, and a due acting of faith in prayer.   For what is or can faith be other than a suitableness in its acting upon its proper object, for the glorifying of God thereby ?   All acts do receive their distinguishing kind and genuineness from their tendency and conformity to their objects, and so must faith; and it is true, genuine, unfeigned faith, when it puts forth such and such acts as its true and proper object doth require.   And it is certain, that to pray in and with such a faith, so levelled towards these objects, must needs be a praying in faith, and so must obtain.

Now the most bottom ground why a faith duly acting in prayer upon these objects, and pleading these motives, may yet fall short of a certain persuasion, ' I shall receive the very particular,' &c., lies in this one proposition.

Prop. That God hath not in the revelation of himself, through these objects to our faith, so bound up himself in, or by virtue of, any or all of these, though duly implored in prayer, that he will certainly give the very particular we shall ask in true faith on these, the nature of these things not absolutely or necessarily requiring it, as they are to us revealed.

And the inferences from hence will be,

1. That if God be not certainly bound up by any one, nor all of these therefore mentioned, then by nothing else, for these are those, and such as for which he is pleased and moved to grant all that he doth grant to us by prayer.

2. And hence it will follow, that if God be not necessarily bound up by these to give the very particular, that then our faith in prayer is not bound up to a certain persuasion, I shall receive that very particular; for our receiving must be from God's giving, and his declared intention in giving some way answerable thereto.   And therefore, if God professeth not to be bound up to give, &c., our faith cannot be bound up absolutely to think we shall receive.   And again, that must needs be acknowledged right faith, that treats with God in all and each of these, according to God's own intention in his revelation of all and each of them ; for then God is truly sought to, when according to the tenor of his own will and revelation of himself.

And take notice, that the materials of the demonstration of this assertion proposed (which I shall carry through all these three places mentioned), will serve also to direct and instruct us how to form and level our prayers aright, and teach us how to apply our faith to God's attributes and promises.

1. I affirm, that the attributes of God, to which faith is to apply itself in prayer, have reserved to themselves a latitude, or a liberty left unto God in what particular to answer our prayers, as shall be most for the glory of any of those his attributes which we implore. That God as represented to us by his attributes, and so his attributes, are the grand object of faith in prayer, appears by the prefaces unto all the eminent prayers recorded in the Old and New Testament, the saints therein taking into their prayers such or such particular attributes as had nighest conjunction with, and affinity unto, the particular things they pray for, as being the next and immediate cause of them, and so strengthen their faith for the obtaining that particular.

Before I fall into the particular instances of attributes to demonstrate my foresaid assertion, I shall again renew the memory of this, that it is the nature and property of faith, and that which God ordained it for, to apply and turn itself every way, to each and every attribute, according to the kind and nature of each, and according to that way and manner of dispensing and giving forth things to us, which each attribute doth hold forth, and in doing so it honours and glorifies that or those attributes, according to the nature and kind of each attribute and way in their affecting* things for us. And hence it comes to pass that faith in prayer is such a latitudinarian, that it is not bound up to a certain persuasion or belief, that it shall receive this or that very particular which it asks, and is bound to ask, and which particular promises, according to a man's sense of need, direct faith unto. And the reason is clear, because the kind or nature of these attributes, and the way and the manner of the dispensation of them, doth admit of a latitude in God's intention, in his engagement of those attributes, for the performance of the promises prayed for; and God for the glory of them, as became him, necessarily reserved a liberty how and in what particular to answer our prayers as shall be most and best agreeable to the nature of the attributes, and for the manifestation of the glory of them. And hence if faith applies itself (as so it ought) to God in pleading his engagement of any of those attributes, according to their kind, it must be with a reserve on faith's part, leaving God's performance unto his own latitude reserved. I only except what may and doth fall out sometimes, that God is pleased to give a special persuasion and assurance (as sometimes especially in spiritual things he doth), otherwise in the ordinary way and course faith must leave all to God, with submission to want the mercy sought when it shall be most for the glory of that attribute it hath or had recourse unto in prayer; for God's will disposeth itself in giving unto us, according as he intended the glory of such and such his attributes; and this (which is a sure ground in itself) gives measure to our prayers, and faith therein, and is a main foundation to decide this case.

(1.) We ought to apply ourselves unto God's all-sufficiency and power, with a firm assurance in it. But though as to his power he requires that we should confide in it to obtain the thing prayed for, yet he exacts not as to his will for us to believe that he will certainly effect it, but left that part rather unto an humble submission, whether he would do it, yea or no, for he would have that left to him. Thus when the two blind men came to him, Mat. ix., who prayed vehemently to him—ver. 27, 'Two blind men followed him, crying, and saying, Thou Son of David, have mercy on us'—all the question that Christ asked them was this, 'Jesus

* Qu. 'effecting'?—Ed.

saith unto them, Believe ye that I am able to do this?' ver. 28. He says not, believe ye that I will do this, but only that I am able to do this; and doth your petition, that I would do this for you, proceed from a faith on my power, that I am able? 'They say unto him, Yea, Lord;' and they spake their heart as far as their faith went, and as far as Christ's question reached. And look, as Christ did not ask them, whether they did believe he would cure them, so neither did they express that they believed any such thing; he loaded their faith with no more but that of his power, and as to the belief of that, Christ was absolute to require it; but as to the belief of his particular will, for that particular thing, there is not a word spoken. And yet Christ in answer to their faith in praying, approved their faith by saying, 'Be it to you according to your faith,' ver. 29;* for it came up to his demand, and the performance testified thereunto, that it was such a faith as he required, for thereupon their eyes were opened. And these were all the transactions that passed betwixt Christ and the men in that particular, and yet they obtained what they prayed for thereupon. Now, that which was faith sufficient in them to obtain by prayer will also be in us. And further, suppose this faith had not been put forth in the way of prayer, that is, if we suppose they had not prayed, but only believed this, yet it must be acknowledged that the same faith put into a prayer must needs be good, be as good faith to obtain. For look, what is true faith out of prayer, that faith if it be formed up into a prayer, doth according to the measure of it make prayer in faith; and so it all comes to this sum, that it is as if these blind men had explicitly said, Lord, we come to thee to be cured, and believe thou art able, which makes us come; and though yet we know not whether thou wilt, yet we come, and we leave that to thee. Now, would not this have been praying in faith? And will not the circumstances of those transactions justify it to be so? Yes, without question; and yet I need not say how much it fell short of assurance that they should have the thing.

Another instance, more express than this, is in Mat. viii. 2: 'Behold, there came a leper, and worshipped him, saying, Lord, if thou wilt, thou canst make me clean.' This faith of his was put forth in praying, for it is said 'he worshipped;' the other evangelist says 'he fell on his face.' It was an adoration, with supplication to be cured. He acknowledges him to be Lord of all diseases, even as that centurion had, who said, *Si voles res acta est:* If thou wilt, the thing is done. Thus says the leper, 'Thou canst make me clean,' and in this latter he is positive, nothing wavering; but as to Christ's will, he puts an *if* to that, '*If* thou wilt,' &c. Where, *first*, he manifests his desire and request, that he would cure him; yet, *secondly*, speaks as one not assured that Christ would do it; and, *thirdly*, as one that resigned up himself to his will, and left it to him to do as he pleased, having 'made first his request known' with a faith on his power; and though he believes absolutely that he could heal him, yet he prays not absolutely that he would, but with a reference and submission to his will:† 'If thou wilt.' Now, observe how abundantly Jesus Christ approved this faith as thus put forth in praying. 'I will,' says he, 'be thou clean' (it is the imperative). He had asked, 'If thou wilt,' with an *if* to that; but Christ answers him positively and absolutely: 'I will,' says he. 'Thou canst,' says the poor man; he speaks that absolutely of his power, and

---

* Fides quam Christus laudat est de potentiâ ipsius, non de potentiæ ipsius exerci[tati]one.—*Brug. in verba.*

† Judîcio et voluntati Christi resignat quicquid sit magis utile, idque, scit Deus nescit homo.—*Alapid. in verba.*

Christ speaks as absolutely of his obtaining: The thing is done, says he, 'be thou clean.' And the reason of this difference of believing on his power and on his will (that the one must be absolute, the other needs be but indefinite) is, because if we do not believe his power absolutely, that he is able to do the thing, we do not believe he is God, nor do we come to him and glorify God as God; but to believe he will, or that he will not, do a thing, or may not, this detracts nothing at all from his being God, but, on the contrary, exalts him in the acknowledgment of the liberty, dominion, and sovereignty of his will. And it is evident that our Saviour Christ puts the great pillar of faith upon believing his power: Mark ix. 23, Jesus says unto the father of that child possessed with the devil, 'If thou canst believe, all things are possible to him that believeth;' and the father cried out, and said with tears, 'Lord, I believe; help thou my unbelief;' for even belief of his power is not so full, without all wavering, but it may have an imperfection accompanying it. But I cite it for this, that faith is said to be omnipotent, as God's power is; faith on his power can do all that God can do, and this even in the point of pardoning sin. Moses hath recourse to the power of God, Num. xiv.; so that to believe that he is able to pardon, lying at the feet of his will, is good faith.

Obj. But you will say, Power is but an attribute only, and will our believing on one attribute thus obtain?

Ans. A believer's dealing with and applying himself to any attributes of God, that is effective of the thing, with a spiritual faith exercised upon it, is a prevailing faith in praying; and the reason is, because it engages all the attributes while it applies itself to one, although I do not explicitly think of the rest, even as to touch Jesus Christ anywhere by faith, but the hem, conveys all Christ, and all of him. If I deal by spiritual faith with him to be justified, and no more, yet adoption, sanctification, and all follows; and as the apostle says, Rom. vi., 'If we be planted together in the likeness of his death, we shall be likewise in the likeness of his resurrection;' ver. 5, 'If we be dead with Christ, we believe that we shall also live with him.' If we have one benefit, then all.

(2.) We have to do with God's mercy in praying in faith. I need not enlarge upon that, for it is our constant plea: Rom. x. 12, 'He is rich in mercy to all that call upon him.' It is spoken especially to what he is to men, in or upon their prayers, for it is to 'them that call upon him.' Now directly mercy will be acknowledged mercy in the glory of it, and that is to be free; that attribute, therefore, deserves a greater latitude yet as to particulars, wherein he will shew mercy; and is in that respect more regulated by his will than any attribute whatsoever. Mercy will be exalted as mercy, Isa. xxx. 18, and therefore in its freedom, which is the top glory of it; and therefore in that place where he himself gives himself the most full, absolute declaration of mercy, and the characters of his nature, Exod. xxxiv.; yet in the 33d chapter he prefaces thereunto, 'I will be merciful to whom I will.' If he is free to be merciful as to the persons, then how much more in the things wherein to be merciful. For of anything he hath to bestow, mercy is most his own, it is his riches, and he hath enough of them, and 'shall he not do what he will with his own?' And having such abundance and variety of them, if he doth not gratify us in one thing, he hath to do it in another, and hereby mercy is exalted, as you heard the prophet speak. And if it be thus then that attribute which our hope is most in, yet it doth not require a certain belief that we shall receive the thing we ask, but God himself reserves a liberty to himself, and leaves thereby a latitude to our faith.

(3.) God's wisdom also reserves a liberty to itself, and gives line to faith: Isa. xxx. 18, ' The Lord will wait, that he may be gracious to you, and therefore will he be exalted that hath mercy on you : for the Lord is a God of righteousness : blessed are all they that wait for him.' The meaning is, he is a God of wisdom, a wise God, he knows what is every way best, and therefore waits to be gracious in the best way, that his mercy may be most exalted ; he waits not only the fittest season wherein to be merciful, but in what particular things most to gratify us, and will find out a time wherein it is best for us. Though a believer therefore coming to God, hath all the promises of God before him, and his own judgment is, that he hath more special need of such or such a promise, yet God's wisdom (who is a God of judgment, and also made all the promises), having much more all those promises afore itself, also considers for its own glory and its own good, in what, or by which promises to answer us ; and as it is for the glory of his wisdom to order the passages of his providence, so as to be past finding out, so also his dispensations to his people in answer to their prayers, have much of the like variety, that he should not always do it one way. It is true God hath promised that he will withhold no good thing, but what that good thing is that shall be good for us, that he only is judge of, who as he is a Father, is termed also to be a heavenly Father, whilst he sits in heaven, considering what to give us that is good for us : Luke xi. 13, ' If ye then being evil, know how to give good things to your children, how much more shall your heavenly Father,' &c. Thou askest of him some earthly thing, as thou thinkest it best for thy need, but he answers thee as a heavenly Father : Mat. vi. 32, ' Your heavenly Father knows that you have need of all these things.' Earthly fathers know but what are earthly good things, and of them they give to their children such things as they judge best ; but God judges as a heavenly Father, and so of what is best as in relation to heaven, and thy coming thither, and his thoughts are herein as far above earthly fathers as heaven is above earth. He hath also declared, that all things shall work together for thy good ; but what particular dispensation shall work for good to thee, and how, this he says not, nor dost thou know. It may be the contrary to what thou desirest shall work for good, and that lies in his wisdom only to judge and dispose of, upon the glorifying of which in his own way thou must wait. So that wisdom reserves to itself a latitude, and it is meet it should, for the glory of itself, for there the glory of it lies. Hence, therefore, if faith applies itself as it ought unto God's wisdom, according to the kind and way of dispensation of it, why then faith also must be left to a latitude too, and not be bound up to the particular that thou suest to him for, but must wait also on him for what his wisdom will judge best, and so indeed it is added, Isa. xxx. 18, that ' because he is a God of judgment, and waits thus to be gracious his own way, therefore blessed are those that wait on him,' *i. e.*, that wait on him as such a God ; a God of judgment ; for waiting is but an act of faith continued.

(4.) A fourth thing about which it hath to deal with God in prayer is, the glory of God, and so it is to frame its petitions, not only for what shall stand with the glory of God, but what shall be most for his glory. The apostle shews, that faith of all other eyes God's glory, and treats with it : Rom. iv. 21, ' Abraham was strong in faith, and gave glory to God.' And as it is the object of faith in common, so of faith in particular, as it is put forth in prayer, and which faith applies itself unto in praying. This we have in the Lord's prayer, in the close, ' For thine is the kingdom, power, and glory ;' and in the first petition, ' Hallowed be thy name,' which is the measure of all that follows; and we are hereby taught to enforce all our prayers with this, as with which God is principally moved to grant us our requests, and which the soul in praying, if it prays aright, maketh use of as pleas unto God to grant those requests; and it is the highest plea, and most effectual way to obtain that faith hath, or can have, in praying.

Now it is certain, that what that particular should be, which, as concerning my particular condition, should be most for the glory of God, that only is known to him, who as he knows our concernments and interests, so his own above all. We pray indeed for what we judge would be most for his glory, as concerning us, and make a great plea of it, and God highly accepts it from us, because it is what is best in our view and judgments; but he performs according to the riches of his own glory, according to his own destinies and vast purposes of glory to himself, so as a man may pray in the highest faith, and in the sublimest way, according to what he judges, and yet still not know certainly that he shall receive; for what is most for God's glory, God only himself knows. It is true, indeed, that all the promises, which are the declarations of his will, are for his glory: 2 Cor. i. 20, ' All the promises of God, in him,' namely, Christ, ' are in him yea, and in him amen, unto the glory of God by us;' there is none but doth tend to his glory, more or less, but the performance of which of them to my particular will be most for his glory, that still is reserved to himself. And this attribute of his glory hath a mighty compass and room to answer thee in, by some promise or other, though yet it doth not give thee the particular thou desirest, according to that one particular promise which thou hast singled out to urge. Yea, as this gives a greater latitude than any of the former attributes, singly considered, and so therefore an answerable allowance must be given unto faith, in respect unto this attribute above all other; for what is and will be most for his glory, he alone is the sovereign judge of. ' Therefore,' says the apostle, Rom. xi. 36, ' of him, and through him, and to him are all things; to whom be glory for ever.' That other royalty also of his kingdom, or of his being king, is appropriate and essential to him as he is God (Ps. xciii. 2, Ps. lxxiv. 12), which David's faith so often lays his foundation on in praying, and therefore is so arctly conjoined in the Lord's prayer with his glory; and therefore every son of his that comes to him as to his king (as David often did, when he says, ' My God and my King '), as he hath great encouragement, because he is his king, who can do anything, so he must consider that his kingdom is of a vast extent, and that he hath many dominions, and an infinity of designs and ends towards persons of all sorts in those dominions, that he hath many irons in the fire, many concernments and ends of a greater breadth than what thy narrow desires or concernments are, especially as they are comprehended in the shallowness of thy understanding, for they are of a greater breadth than any one particular promise can or doth contain. In the administration of a kingdom, a favourite very near to his prince comes with a request to be gratified; he has had many large promises of all sorts given him, and his particular request in his view is but a small one, as the life of a friend that hath run into treason, or the like, and he thinks the grant of it will not be a prejudice to any of his prince's affairs; but that king having a large dominion, and many persons, yea, perhaps parties and interests to deal with, this business and request of his may fall cross unto, and interfere with some very great interest of his own, which this favourite knows not of, and so he denies him his particular request, but yet takes care to gratify him in another, that shall be best for his particular. And as he hath a kingdom to administer, so he deals in politics, and hath more general ends than a subject can think of or imagine, and knows that which none of them can do ; he hath a vast extent of affairs in that kingdom, and his honour is interested to see all things, as they shall tend to his more general ends ; and thus it is much more with God, who is the King of kings, and the greatest that ever were are but as petty constables to him.   He hath designs upon particular times, wherein the saints do live, which are part of the administrations of his kingdom, and he hath such designs in those times, as according to his ordinary providence he cannot do that for his people that live in this age, at this time, which he can and doth in another for them.   General providences, or at least more general than thy particular, do cross often particular requests, whereof in the end we come to see a reason. This some understand (and I believe rightly) to have been Baruch's case, Jer. xlv.   Poor man, he was miserably discomposed for the common calamity which Jeremiah had threatened : ' Thou didst say, woe is me now' (says God to him, ver. 3), ' for the Lord hath added grief to my sorrow, I fainted in my sighing, and found no rest ;' and he had besought God much for the averting of that calamity, the thoughts of which lay so heavy upon him and pressed him down ; but especially, he had sought for a quiet condition for himself in these turbulent times to come, ver. 5, ' Seekest thou great things for thyself? Seek them not.'   What were the great things ? what preferment, or honour, or riches ?   He was a man too godly to be so ambitious and worldly.   No ; he only desired to live in the land quietly, that he might have such a particular privilege, and he sought it for himself ; it was a thing he sought for himself, as the text saith, he sought only *quietem in communi inquietudine*, quiet and ease amidst the common disturbance ; and great things these were to seek, in respect of God's common providence at the time he lived in, *ardua et difficilia*, things hard and difficult to be done.*   Therefore God tells him, ver. 4, ' That which I have built will I break down, and that which I have planted will I break up, even this whole land ; and seekest thou great things, and hard things for thyself ?'   It is contrary to the general design I have, and therefore too great or too hard for thee to obtain.   Yet thus far God gratifies him, as far as ordinary providence would reach and extend : ' I have given thee,' says God, ' thy life for a prey in all other countries,' but I cannot gratify thee in this ; although he had a promise sufficient to have asked this upon, viz., ' Honour thy father and thy mother, that thy days may be long in the land which the Lord thy God giveth thee.'

CHAPTER II.

That God hath not in his promises obliged himself to give us the very particular blessing which we pray for, and therefore we cannot pray with assurance of obtaining it.

I shall now carry on the same demonstration touching promises, the second object of faith, viz., that the manner of God's declaration of them is such as God hath not bound himself so up but that there is this liberty reserved, in what particular promise he thinks best for us to answer our prayers, and as shall be most for his own glory, especially considering how promises are taken in by us into our prayers.

I come then to promises, the second object of faith before mentioned, and therein to consider, whether the promulgation of them, as God hath

* Castellio *in locum.*

been pleased to make it, doth not reserve the like liberty to God, as hath been shewed of his attributes, and so by consequence the same latitude to faith in prayer, which is a putting of promises in suit; so as that notwithstanding that God hath engaged himself in promises, we may pray in faith, although short of such a persuasion, that we shall receive the very particulars we ask for. I shall discuss this point under a general consideration of promises; and, indeed, the general consideration had of them will much conduce further to discover and lay open the very bottom ground or root why a faith short of such a persuasion may be prevailing to obtain, and will withal stub up by the roots such objections as may be made against it.

The objection may be framed up of these particulars, that there being one attribute not hitherto mentioned, viz., God's will, which hath drawn in those other fore-mentioned attributes into a confederacy with itself, to assist and perform what that will determines; and this will being revealed in particular promises, his will hath thereby put out of its own hands all liberty to answer or not to answer our prayers. These promises also now serving wholly as directions and sea-marks to guide how to steer the course of our prayers; and God having moreover made superadded promises to hear our prayers, and further his purposes and contrivances about his church, being known to him from the beginning (as all his works are, Acts xv.), and that being the purest part of his providence, and therefore eminently called foreknowledge; and he having before ever he made any promise considered all, and cast and given forth his promises according to the idea of those his purposes, as his purpose is to grant upon their prayers, therefore there should and ought to be a special persuasion of faith in our prayers, that we shall receive the very particular.

Now for assoiling this objection, and for the better clearing the bottom reason of what I am pursuing, I have cast this general consideration of promises into these three heads :

First, As touching the matter of them, or things promised.

Secondly, The tenor they are delivered in, as in relation to persons. These two as they lie in the words abstractly considered. But,

Thirdly, A distinct consideration must be and apart had of them, as they are taken by us into our prayers, and therein urged unto God.

First, Touching the matter of them, there are these assertions.

1. God hath so framed and suited his declared promises to his secret purposes and designs, of what he means to bestow upon his children, that there is extant some either promise, or instance, or declaration (which always implies a promise in them), for all and every good thing he means to bestow. He hath so drawn out his purposes into promises, as the sea into rivulets, that, I may safely say, there is no particular good thing he hath purposed to bestow, but there is a declaration of his will, either by instance or promise for it. God's will is open and manifest in this, that we have the whole of his secret will, as it concerns us, touching good things to be bestowed, in his revealed will; and as his children are ' children of promise,' Heb. vi. 17, and ' heirs of blessing,' 1 Peter iii. 9, which are of equal extent, because promises and blessings are of like equal extent, so in like manner there is no blessing but is a blessing of promise some way or other; and like as God blessing us in Christ blesseth us in nothing out of him, so whatever he blesses his children withal, it is by, and not out of, a promise. Whatsoever is given is given by a word, and there is nothing we need or can desire but there is some promise or other for it, as the matter of it.

2. It is also further true, that whatsoever God actually performs there

is a word for it; this assertion is a consequence of the former. He rules the world by his word, or if judgments be on the world, or particular persons, they are shewn in some threatening, or some instance of the like in the word, and they are all but ' executing the judgments written,' Ps. cxlix. 9; and therefore God's dispensing judgments upon men is synonymously called his taking hold of them: Zech. i. 6, ' But my words and my statutes, which I commanded my servants the prophets, did they not take hold of your fathers? and they returned and said, Like as the Lord of hosts thought to do unto us, according to our ways, and according to our doings, so hath he dealt with us.' In which place you have, 1. God's thoughts, what he meant to do, which is his secret will. 2. You have God's thoughts put into words, suited unto his will. 3. You have the performance, they took hold of them, so that they are suited to both the threatenings and purposes, which are in this respect parallel. It is said not a word fell to the ground, 1 Sam. iii. 19, 1 Kings viii. Again, performances and promises are adequate.

Secondly, The tenor of promises is to be considered apart from the matter of them, and it lies in this, how the declaration of these promises doth intend and respect particular persons. And as to that there are these assertions:

1. Though there is no good thing but is in some promise or other, as hath been said, yet God's secret will was never to perform or bestow all and every good thing *in specie* (which he hath promised) to all and every one of his children personally; nor is it declared anywhere in the word that he will do so. This is apparent in temporal promises of temporal things. He hath not given riches to all saints, nor wisdom, nor honours. There are not many rich, wise, or noble, though some are so; and yet, because he will bestow of all these upon some, therefore there are promises that do particularise all these.* The like may be said of many promises in spiritual privileges, gifts, degrees of grace, &c. The sense of this assertion you may take up and conceive of thus, that our God, the God of all grace, and the God of all comforts, having the whole body of his elect before him, and all parcels of good things in prospect and intuition, his will was to give all and every good thing *in specie* among them, and in his secret purposes he dispersed and ordered them amongst them.

2. Every good thing that every one of them hath he hath it by promise, yea, and to that very end it was that God made such manifold promises, particularising every good thing in one of them or other, because he would bestow nothing without or besides a promise in his word.

3. Take the declaration of promises as they respect persons, and so when God made and gave forth all these promises of his revealed will, he had in his eye whom he meant to bestow these particularities of things promised, in their several kinds, upon, and so made these promises with a special intent unto them, and *de facto* bestows them upon them individually, although in his word he named not those particular persons, but keeps and reserveth that in his own breast, both what good things, and whom he would bestow them upon.

4. The declaration of God's will, and his intent in such promises, is for the most part not universal to all and every saint. Some promises indeed

---

* Gerard upon those words, John xiv., ' Whatsoever ye shall ask, I will do;' though he peremptorily determines there is no prayer but God answers, yet in his giving an account why so many prayers come short, one of them is, ' Deus nuspiam in verbo suo dedit ejusmodi promissionem, quod in temporalibus velit dare nobis omnia quæ desideramus.'

are universal, but then they run in the strain as that doth, ' Whoever believes shall not perish,' John iii. 16 ; but many other are but indefinite, and so to be understood by us. This indefinite tenor of promises is clear in the case of the promises to work miracles, which may illustrate what I mean about these other. These promises we have John xiv. 12, ' He that believes on me, the works that I do he shall do also ; and greater works ;' Mark xvi. 17, ' And these signs shall follow them that believe : in my name they shall cast out devils ; they shall speak with new tongues,' &c. These speeches are but indefinite, and yet run in this strain, ' He that believes on me,' &c., but are not made to whoever believes. No, not in those times : 1 Cor xii. 10, ' To another is given the gift of working miracles,' &c. But if you hear of such a promise, ' He who believes shall be saved' (as Mark xvi. 16, Christ had said), you must understand it universally of all that believe. For in that tenor of universality it runs, John iii. 16, ' Whoever believes,' &c. But there are absolute promises of salvation, which are the object of faith, which are not universal to all men ; the promulgation of them is, indeed, to be made to all, but the promises themselves are not intended to all, and we see it in the performance, which falls out accordingly, both which promises and performances are yet adequate as to God's secret intent ; he in his secret intent having those individual persons in his eye, whom he would bestow such and such particular things upon, and made those promises with an eye to them, but still not naming those particular persons in his word, there was a reserve in his breast on whom he would bestow them. And so because his will and intent was to perform them to some, therefore he hath given forth all sorts of particular promises in that tenor mentioned, ' He that,' &c. ; and yet because his will was to perform each but to some, therefore these promises run in an indefinite strain and tenor. I call them indefinite, because the declaration made in them respecteth not all persons, but some, and those not declared who they are.

Obj. But you will say, that all and every Christian hath a right to every promise.

Ans. What greater instance is there than that of Christ himself ? And yet although all things are Christ's, and the promises of all things are made in him to us, as the great founder of them—2 Cor. i. 20, ' In him all the promises are yea and amen'—he never had the performance of all and each of the good things of this world promised *in specie*, but less thereof, and more of the contrary, than any of his children. And what of them he hath in the other world is *per modum eminentiæ*, in a way of eminence, as the holy apostle (that was but a small draught of him) says of himself, that though he had all things, viz., in the right, yet he was ' possessing nothing.'

5. Promises being thus indefinite, it is sufficient for any to obtain them that their faith on them be but an indefinite act, and so a faith answering to the tenor of the promise. An indefinite act from us is rightly and duly suited to an object that is but indefinitely proposed by God to us, and to such an indefinite act is suited. I mean that, as the promises declare not individually whom the things promised are intended unto, so the faith, though in the understanding part not certainly knowing that I am the person, yet in the will, puts forth indefinite acts, answerably to that suspense in the understanding ; so that I cast myself upon God to obtain that thing promised, by virtue of that promise which must and shall be made good to some, and what do I know but unto me ? And these indefinite acts of faith are good faith, for they are answerable to the mind and tenor of many promises that run in the style of a bare *it may be*, which you meet with so

oft in Scripture, both concerning spiritual and temporal things ; and who knows but God may intend it to me, says the soul ; and therefore I do put in for it, and am bound so to do, both in respect of my own needs, and God's promulgation of it to me as well as to any other. From hence there ariseth these three corollaries :

(1.) As faith is good faith, because it answers the tenor of the promise, so it is a praying in faith when my prayers answer to such a faith, without a certain knowledge that I shall undoubtedly obtain.

(2.) Such promises as are declared by God being, in the respect before-mentioned, but indefinite, hence this attribute, the will of God, stands in great freedom, which he hath reserved within himself, how to perform these promises : notwithstanding they are the declarations of his will, and he hath on purpose (that he might retain this liberty within himself) in that manner uttered them. And by this it will appear that as great a latitude is left to his will, notwithstanding the promises given forth, as to any other attribute whatsoever before specified, which latitude lies in which and what promises he will be pleased, and is pleased, to gratify such and such persons, doing it to some in one thing, to others in another ; and it is according to his will in all, as it is said of bestowing his gifts, it is ' according to his will,' 1 Cor. x.

3. Again, on our part, hence it comes to pass that his ways and judgments, which are the performances of his promises and threatenings, are past finding out ; and accordingly, his will in dispensing this or that to particular persons, is past finding out, notwithstanding the declaration of all sorts of threatenings and promises particularly made in his word. If a man would go about to make a collection from the word, of all such threatenings or promises, together with all the variety of instances, which are interpreters of his mind in either, wherein either are set forth as performed (as that when men have lived to such a degree of sinnings, the threatening hath been executed, as several instances do set out), and will thereupon say, that upon such a sinner God will certainly bring such a judgment, because I find he did bring it upon such and such sinners, in such a case, which we have instances for, and those suited according to the threatenings ; in the end he will find a great latitude and variety of judgments, of several sizes and proportions, in those various instances which the word holds forth, and some instances of the same kind, in the highest measure, on whom God forbore to bring the execution of such punishments, whilst he hath brought upon the smallest sinners of that kind the same. If he shall, besides, also consider those many intermediate instances, of higher and lower sizes, between either of these two extremes of greatest and smallest, that have or have nct been punished *ad libitum*, as God thought meet, that man will conclude, from all such collections, that no man can make a certain judgment what God will do, from such instances of such judgments joined together. And thus it is in promises, and the instances belonging to them ; for God's faithfulness and truth are as well engaged in his threatenings as his promises, and there is so great a variety of degrees of qualifications of the persons that the promises are thereby made unto, as there will appear that God hath bestowed and fulfilled such and such a particular promise to one that had less of that qualification ; as in giving riches to some, when yet he hath passed by another that hath had more of that grace or qualification that the promise is made unto, and yet he leaves him in deep poverty, as he doth many of his precious ones, notwithstanding his promises and their prayers ; and therefore no absolute judgment can be made, which is the point in hand.

Thirdly. The third consideration of the promises is, as they come under our prayers, or are put into suit by us in prayer. The former considerations shewed what latitude is left to God for the performance, and to our faith in believing, as to the promises, considered in the matter of good things promised, and the tenor as to the persons. Next follows the consideration of them, as any of them are upon occasion singled out by us, and taken into our prayers ; for God hath not made promises, or doth bestow good things promised, altogether as they lie abstractly in his word, but hath made special promises besides unto our prayers about them, or when we ask them, or supplicate about them : ' Ask, and it shall be given ;' ' Ask wisdom of God, and it shall be given.' And this may seem such an obligation on God's part, that although the promises of the good things themselves, abstractly taken, and severed from our prayers, may not ascertain us of obtaining, yet when the addition is made of God's promise to bestow them when they shall be prayed for, that makes such double obligation on God's part as may afford a certainty to our faith, that we shall obtain the very particular we pray for. But concerning promises as thus considered and proposed, I offer these assertions or proposals.

1. The promises we do put in suit for good things we pray for, are but a few, in comparison of the many that God hath made in his word. The promises in our prayers are but like the gleanings, in comparison of a great harvest ; what through our negligence in prayer, straitness of comprehensions to glean and gather them, I may say of them as the apostle doth of the earth, that it stands in the water and out of the water, so do the promises stand out of our prayers, an ocean of them, as well as some are taken in. For what the psalmist says of the law, that it is ' exceeding broad,' and that there is no ' end of its perfection,' the like we may say of promises, if we take them in all particulars of them ; and for multitude, they are such as we cannot number them, for our understandings are narrow as they are broad. So as God hath, besides what we put in suit, a multitude of other promises that lie afore his understanding, and which he intends to his children ; and hence it comes to pass, that he hath a mighty compass and roomth, by reason of the breadth of the promises, to answer us in, besides what we pray for.

2. Consider those few promises that we single forth, and take down in our prayers, and then put up to God, or consider the good things promised, which you request in prayer, and you will find that they are but as they are first taken in by our apprehension, and according to what we judge of them to be best for us. For prayers are formed by us, and so put up to God, as they lie before our understandings ; and alas, poor creatures, as we are said to know nothing as we ought, in general, so nor particularly what to pray for as we ought. No, not as to the matter we are to pray for. The apostle hath told us so, and that in relation to our prayers, Rom. viii. And though there is so great a choice of promises that lie exposed before us, with so great a variety and multitude for us to pick and choose, yet we know not what is most expedient in our condition, and which to single forth and pitch upon. But as Calvin observes, we are blind and ignorant in seeking God ; yea, and although we know our own evils, the sores of our hearts, our needs and wants, yet our minds are more confused, and clouded, and tangled, than to know what rightly to pitch upon, or what is most meet and expedient as to our present need. So that there falls out a great variation of the compass by our steering aside, between what the needs of our prayers point to, and God's intentions are oftentimes towards us.

3. Hence we are attentively to consider the infinitely wide difference between promises, as they lie before God's understanding and intentions of his good will towards us (as in Jeremiah the prophet himself hath expressed it, ' I know the thoughts that I have towards you;' and yet even those thoughts lie in some promise or other in the word, as it is afore him), and what we are apt to pitch upon by reason of our clung understandings and confused apprehensions, when his promises lie afore us, and are chosen by us. The corollaries which arise from hence are these.

(1.) We may see the reason why God gives, and that by virtue of promises, so many and so great good things, besides, and without, and above our prayers. 1. He doth this besides and without our prayers : ' I am found,' says God, ' of those that sought me not;' and he gives things that enter not into our thoughts and heart. And, 2, he doth it above and beyond our prayers, ' more than all we are able to ask or to think,' as the apostle saith ; for why ? The reason hath been told us, even because promises are of infinite breadth, and the declarations of his will, as they lie before his understanding, and his word, which is in his eye, are exceeding large. And we may truly say, that for God to do according to what is let in, or comes into our minds, is not the main part of what he intends, he is so abundant in kindness and truth, above all we can sue for. God is greater than our hearts in this respect, and knows his thoughts and intentions towards us, infinitely beyond those short ideas we shape forth to ourselves, for ourselves, out of his promises. Miserable, at least imperfect, should we be, if God should answer us but according to those imperfect models, draughts, and proposals of our petitions. We should have been infinitely disadvantaged, if God should have bound himself up to our prayers, and have given nothing else.

(2.) We may also hence see how it comes to pass, that God's will may still retain that great freedom and latitude as to performance of promises, notwithstanding his promise is to hear our prayers, and that he may still be executing his will, according to some promise or other, as they lie before his divine understanding and will, therein performing as he judgeth most expedient; as Christ saith, ' It is expedient for you I go away ;' when yet at present that word brake all their hearts, to think of his departure. But by the taking in of those fore-mentioned things, we may with satisfaction discern how both these things may stand together, that God may still deal with us according to his declared will in promises, and yet deny us that individual we seek in prayers, notwithstanding his promises to hear our prayers.

CHAPTER III.

That the essential acts of faith in prayer are such as do not necessarily require a certain persuasion of obtaining the very particular blessing for which we pray.

I come to inquire into the principal and most essential acts of faith in praying, and shall still carry on the same demonstration founded on this, that the essential acts of faith do admit of the like former latitude, and are such as do not necessarily require that in praying we should have such a particular persuasion of obtaining the particular blessing which we ask.

1. The first and main act of faith in praying is, a firm belief and persuasion of the fore-mentioned grand and fundamental object of faith, as of

God and his attributes, and the truth and faithfulness of his promises ; and hereof our assertion is, that there must be an assurance of faith, or a certain firm and fixed persuasion, without wavering, of the fundamental objects of faith.   This assurance of faith, excepting in times of great tentations and overflowings of unbelief, we must always retain, and by virtue of a firm faith in these we must always pray, or we must not indeed think to obtain anything of the Lord.   And this, as it is a great truth, so it will prove to be the main intention of our apostle, when he says, ' But let him pray in faith, nothing wavering.'   The apostle in his Epistle to the Hebrews lays and makes this fundamental necessary unto both faith and prayer : ' He that cometh unto God,' says he, Heb. xi. 6, ' must believe that he is, and that he is a rewarder of them that diligently seek him.'   And thus to do, being of the substance of faith (verse 1), must be firmly believed, without wavering ; and as our apostle here (James i. 7), exhorts to pray in faith, so in verse 5 you may observe how he had first set forth God as a God that giveth liberally, &c., and thereupon his exhortation is, to pray in the faith of God, as such a God that giveth liberally ; and also our Saviour Christ doth, as an introduction to his exhortation unto faith in prayer (Mark xi. 23, 25), preface this, verse 22, ' Have faith in God,' says he, speaking of faith in praying to God in Christ's name, of the prevalency of whose name with God an assurance also is required under the New Testament : John xvi. 23, ' Whatsoever you ask the Father in my name, he will give it you.'

Obj.   You will here say to me, This is but a general faith, what profit is there in praying with a faith that is such ?

Ans.   I answer, That there is much advantage every way, if the general faith you pray be the same with that in Heb. xi., if it be a faith which is there said to be a ' sight of him that is invisible,' ver. 27 ; that is, a seeing God in himself and attributes by a spiritual light and sight of faith, which doth render and present God and Christ subsistent, and really present too, and with the soul in prayer.   This very sight and presence of him, when we come to pray, will in some good degree cause us to pray in faith.

If you ask how or wherein ?   I answer, By operating and working in the soul two eminent things in prayer, that have a great tendency to obtain the desired blessing.

(1.) This sight of God and Christ, with this foresaid assurance of faith, will humble the soul deeply in the presence of this great God.   And,

(2.) This sight of him presents us with that in God which will encourage us to pray, and to ask the things we would have ; and these are good steps unto praying in faith.

(1.) There is an humbling act of faith put forth in prayer.   Others style it praying in humility ; give me leave to style it praying in faith.   In faith, which sets the soul in the presence of that mighty God, and by the sight of him, which faith gives us, it is that we see our own vileness, sinfulness, and abhor ourselves, and profess ourselves unworthy of any, much less of those mercies we are to seek him for.   Thus the sight of God had wrought in the prophet : Isa. vi. 5, ' Then said I, Woe is me ! for I am undone ; because I am a man of unclean lips, and I dwell amongst a people of un-clean lips : for mine eyes have seen the King, the Lord of hosts.'   And holy Job speaks thus, Job xlii. 5, 6, ' Now mine eye seeth thee : wherefore I abhor myself, and repent in dust and ashes.'   This is as great a requisite to prayer as any other act ; I may say of it alone, as the apostle here, that without it we shall receive nothing from the hands of God.   God loves to fill empty vessels, he looks to broken hearts. In the Psalms how often do we read that God hears the prayers of the humble, which always involves and includes faith in it: Ps. ix. 12, 'He forgetteth not the cry of the humble,' and Ps. x. 17, 'Lord, thou hast heard the desire of the humble: thou wilt prepare their heart, thou wilt cause thine ear to hear.' To be deeply humbled is to have the heart prepared and fitted for God to hear the prayer; and therefore you find the psalmist pleading *sub formâ pauperis*, often repeating, 'I am poor and needy.' And this prevents our thinking much if God do not grant the particular thing we do desire. Thus also Christ himself in his great distress, Ps. xxii., doth treat God, ver. 2, 'O my God, I cry in the day-time, but thou hearest not; and in the night-season am not silent. Our fathers trusted in thee. They cried unto thee, and were delivered. But I am a worm, and no man; reproached of men, and despised of the people;' ver. 6, and he was 'heard' in the end 'in what he feared.' And these deep humblings of ourselves, being joined with vehement implorations upon the mercy of God to obtain, is reckoned into the account of praying by faith, both by God and Christ, Mat. viii. There comes to him a poor man to heal his servant, 'beseeching him,' says the text, which (the man believing that he was God, and the Son of God, as ver. 9) is to be interpreted to have been a supplication or prayer put up unto him. He came not to him as one friend useth to do to another, that entreats a favour from his friend as such, but as to one that was God: 'There came to him a centurion, beseeching him,' says the 5th verse. He beseecheth him for his servant that lay at home sick, and he tells him his case; saith Christ at the 7th verse, 'I will come and heal him.' Ver. 8, 'The centurion answered and said, Lord, I am not worthy that thou shouldst come under my roof.' This being joined with that faith the 9th verse speaks of, Jesus Christ thereupon pronounceth, 'I have not found so great a faith, no, not in Israel;' and his coming and praying in that deep humility is to be reckoned in unto his faith, which did obtain. Thus faith in prayer lays its foundation.

(2.) To come to God with such an assurance of faith, 'that he is,' &c., Heb. xi. 6 (as hath been fore-mentioned), doth many ways encourage the soul in prayer, and raiseth hopes to be heard, and so excites him further to pray, more than that general faith, as I may call it.

[1.] For when God doth *sistere se præsentem*, make himself thus present to faith, this will mightily encourage the heart with a hope that he hears the prayer. If the soul but knows it hath 'communed with God' (as it is said of Abraham, Gen. xviii. 33), and God with it, a man doth from thence carry away a secret persuasion, even this at least, that God hears him, and that his prayer is accepted; and will you say this is no great matter? If Christ but says, 'It is I,' Mark vi. 50, then, 'Be not afraid, or be of good courage,' *Bono animo sitis*, will follow thereupon. His real presence doth scatter fears and misgivings of heart, as the sun doth clouds, and works a persuasion of acceptation, both of a man's person and prayer. If the soul can but say, I have seen God to-day, as Job, or as an holy man once said, I am sure Christ is alive, I saw him—it was in prayer—this morning; if God presents himself as the living God, this will hearten the soul to believe on him, and pray to him for anything whatever.

[2.] If the soul believes with assurance of faith that God is a rewarder of them that seek him (as it is in the fore-cited Heb. xi. 6), this also leaves a persuasion that a man's prayers shall not return empty, that he 'doth not seek him in vain,' Isa. xlv. 19, but that he shall have a reward and return of his prayer one way or other. David makes this very attribute of his being a God hearing prayer as a foundation of his faith in prayer. Ps. lxv. 2, 'O thou which hearest prayer, unto thee all flesh (that is, man) shall come,' and therefore do I come among the rest; and this is in the substance of it a parallel speech unto that in Heb. xi., 'that he is a rewarder of them that diligently seek him;' as also of our apostle, 'that he giveth liberally to them that ask.' And Calvin's outcry and inference from thence is, that we do never seek God in vain; and *nunquam irritas fore preces* he hath up an hundred times in his Commentaries on the Psalms. Yea, this very faith on God, as hearing prayer, in the substance of it, helped David against the grandest objection which the heart can have to discourage it from believing that his prayer shall be heard, viz., prevailing iniquities in point of guilt, and the conscience of sins that have in a godly man's practice for a while prevailed. But here upon this, that God is a God hearing prayers, David's confidence riseth, that these should not hinder a man's hope of being heard (and these if anything would), but notwithstanding them, David is still resolved to pray, and would have others to do so too, because God is a God hearing prayers, which he will never be if he hears not sinners; and so it follows, ver. 3, 'Iniquities prevail against me; as for our transgressions, thou shalt purge them away.'

But though this faith in God, that he is a God hearing prayer, makes something towards an hopefulness that I may obtain the very thing, and towards a certain confidence that God will some way or other answer me, yet still whether certainly or no in the very thing I ask, this scripture speaks not; and so still it may fall out, I may pray in faith, when not necessarily with a confidence I shall have the thing. And yet this I may say hereof, that this faith hath obtained a good degree of praying in faith, when put up in Christ's name, which the gospel doth require.

The particulars of such like principles, fundamental unto our faith in prayer, are divers others besides this, of all which there must be a firm belief without wavering, as of and about several attributes of God, and also the truth and faithfulness of God in all his promises. Likewise, there must be a belief of the name and interest that Christ hath with his Father, in whose name I come; and the necessity of a stedfast faith of these is founded on the same reason that the faith that there is a God already instanced in is founded upon; and the same fruits and consequents to encourage the heart in prayer doth follow the faith of them as we have seen doth the faith of that other, that there is a God. There must be an *hypostasis*, a subsistence of all these fundamentals in a man's heart, and he must fixedly believe them, and that with spiritual faith, as that there is a God, and he a rewarder, so that he is able to help and succour me in any distress. Also, I must fixedly believe that he is a God merciful and gracious, and willing to help, and gives liberally, &c., there ought not to be a doubting here. Martha firmly believed the resurrection, and doubted not; she believed the thing when yet she wavered about the application of it to that particular, whether her brother should be raised up then or no before the general resurrection. And indeed you find the belief of these things, in Heb. xi., to be the *basis, fulcrum, substantia*, the foundation and support that bears up all; and therefore, to pray in the faith of such as these principles, without doubting, is required; and it is the belief of these doth make a man continue in prayer. Yea, and when all is said to the contrary, the faith of these is the main of faith, and the faith of these causes us to cleave to God, and to follow after him, and not to take any denial, because we believe those things are in him, and such promises made by him. Only it is a spiritual faith that doth this, a faith which makes God real, and all his attributes real, it is a faith in earnest. Now, when I say he believes these things, which are the foundations, without wavering or doubting, my meaning is not that a true and firm believer may not have many injections cast in to the contrary by Satan, and many reasonings of his own speculative understanding, and great degrees of unbelief mixed with the faith of them, as hath been the case of many poor souls that have been exercised long with this temptation, that there is no God, and reasonings to the contrary, yet so as still the belief of those things remaineth firm in his practical understanding, which carries him unto obedience and all duties; and in like manner, to cleave to God in prayer, such a one prays and behaves himself as verily believing there is a God, to purpose; and his cleaving to God, and following after God, clearly shews that he believes there is a God in earnest. My meaning also is not as if God did not grant many requests upon prayer when men are very weak in faith of those things.* There came a poor man to Christ about his child vexed with the devil, and says to him, ' But if thou canst do anything, have compassion upon us, and help us.' Christ discerned his faith was very weak in the great business of his power, that he should put an *if* to it; ' And Jesus saith unto him, If thou canst believe, all things are possible to him that believeth ; ' and the man cries out with tears, ' Lord, I believe ; help my unbelief.' He began to gather up a faith upon the power of Christ, he plucked up an heart to believe through the power of the Spirit, yet discerning a great deal of unbelief, and darkness, and deficiency, even to this very point; for it was the power of Christ therein which was the thing spoken about, as appears both by Christ's speech and his. As a cannon discharged makes a recoil until it comes to that which firmly holds it, so it is with many a poor soul his faith in prayer.

But my further design is to shew, that such a faith as this, which is without wavering, and a praying in such a faith, is that which well suiteth with the scope of the apostle here in this place.

1. The persons that he gives this caution to, about asking in faith, nothing doubting, were certainly temporary professors of religion, or as we usually call them, hypocrites, that in the end waver in their faith about religion itself, and the spiritual principles of it ; and when they come to a stress of persecution, which was the case of those times, the wavering that is in their hearts appears in their prayers, and in their irresolutions and readiness to fall off, and in making them to close with any shifts or pretensions that may colour their deserting those principles which the persecution is directed against. And my reason why he points to, and levels the dint of this caution against such, is, because, ver. 8, he doth expressly say, speaking of those men, ' A double-minded man is unstable in all his ways.' As he is wavering in his prayers, so in his mind, which makes him unstable in his whole course, which proceeds from his not having spiritual prevalent convictions of the principles of faith which he doth profess ; and this looseness or shockiness is seen in their prayers between God and them, but especially when they come to be in any stress. I have compared it thus : there are two pins in a wall, the one is loose, and yet hath a room in the wall, and seems firm, and there is another pin that is riveted, so that it is fixed indeed ; the difference of these two pins you will see when you hang any weight upon them, and put them to a stress. When you come to hang any thing upon that which is loose, and not fixed, itself and all will tumble

---

* Ames well distinguisheth, that ' Dubitatio minuens tantum assensum consistere potest cum fide infirmâ, sed non illa dubitatio quæ tollit assensum,' and for that he quoteth this very place, James i. 6–8.—*Medulla l.* 2 *c.* 5 *de fide, Thes.* 44.

down with it.   And thus it is in times of temptation, that the wavering of their faith is seen in such apostates.

2. The very word here used, διαϰρινόμενος, translated 'wavering,' or doubting, is used in Scripture elsewhere to express the opposite to that faith which is fixed, as to the principles to be believed, and unto them applied.

(1.) I find it used of Abraham's faith, whereby he believed the power of God, that God was able : Rom. iv. 20, 'He staggered not at the promise of God through unbelief ; but was strong in faith, giving glory to God ; and being fully persuaded that what he had promised, he was able to perform,' &c.   The word translated *he staggered not*, is the same that is used here, translated *not wavering*.   And this commendation of his faith is not that he staggered not in the belief of the will of God, for he had a personal promise from God, that God would do it, and therefore no wonder if it be not said, he doubted not of that ; but that which his faith is commended for, was that he staggered not at the power of God, but was fully persuaded God was able.

(2.) The same word is used in Mat. xxi. 21, when he speaks of faith in prayer, ' If you have faith, and doubt not, you shall say unto this mountain, Be thou removed ; ϰαὶ μὴ διαϰριθῆτε ; if you do not stand disputing or wavering, whether it is possible for God to do this, or not to do it.   If you think in respect of the power of God it be too hard or difficult a thing, this is to doubt* in Christ's intention, so as indeed it is the believing, or doubting about his power, that the word is there pitched upon, consonantly unto that of that too often confident apostle, Mat. xiv., who, walking upon the waters, and his faith sinking together with himself, Christ reproved him, and said unto him, ' O thou of little faith, wherefore didst thou doubt ?' His doubting was not of Jesus Christ's will, for Christ had resolved him of that in bidding him come to him ; but when he saw the wind boisterous, he began to doubt of his power.

(3.) The word διαϰρινόμενος signifies disputing, or a disceptation against a thing : Acts xi. 2, ' When Peter was come to Jerusalem, they of the circumcision contended with him ;' it is the same word that is used here.   So those men of whom the apostle speaks are διαϰρινόμενοι, disputing, wavering and reasoning against things in religion, principles in religion (which they had professed), upon occasion of persecution.   The hearts of such use to begin to cavil against religion, and call in question this or that which they professed, as willing to be rid of it.   Now prayer is to be put forth with a faith opposite to such a reasoning, or (as it is translated) such a wavering, and as being fully satisfied of the truth of those things, they should never have so much as a thought to desert them ; and therefore we find, 1 Tim. ii. 8, that as we should be without wrath, so χωρὶς διαλο· γισμοῦ, without reasoning, disputing against : we must pray with a heart fixed in the principles of faith.

(4.) Even here in the text it is an attribute of God that is proposed to the faith of a man that prays, and to believe the truth of it fixedly, which attribute is this, that God ' gives liberally, and upbraids not ;' and to doubt of this goodness and readiness of God to hear prayers, and return answer to them, is the principal thing which the apostle had in his eye, whilst he says, ' But let him ask in faith, nothing wavering.'   So then the faith he intends is about the reality of the truth of this, and other the like attributes given to God.

---

* Multi enim, quia putant id quod petunt esse arduum et difficile, hinc diffidunt se á Deo id impetraturos, ideoque non impetrant.

2. A second act of faith is of adherence, or cleaving unto God, for the good things promised, and of recumbency, coming to, and casting one's self on God to obtain it, with trusting on God, and waiting on him. And these may strongly be exercised and put forth in prayer, effectually to obtain, when yet a particular personal persuasion, that a man shall obtain the very thing he asketh, is wanting. The truth of this assertion, concerning such acts of faith as these, although deficient in special assurance, might be carried through the whole Bible in many particular instances, as of David for his child, Hezekiah for his life, &c. But I shall content myself with this only, and fix and centre upon this one argument for it : that there may be a true exercise of these kind of acts of faith, and effectually put forth in prayer, for the great and grand business of a man's own salvation, who yet may want personal assurance of his salvation, from whence ariseth an invincible demonstration that there may be a true faith, and praying in faith for all other things whatsoever, short of such an assurance. For the truth of the antecedent, I need not much insist upon it, it being so frequently true in experience, and now so generally entertained and acknowledged by our divines ; and few or none of protestant divines, holding that faith of assurance, or a particular persuasion of a man's own salvation, is that essential act of faith by which we are justified and saved. That the first act of justifying faith, in him that begins to believe, is not an act of assurance that he is justified is most clear, for that were to say, that a man should first believe he is justified, that he might be justified by that act, which is a contradiction. The aim of the first act, yea, of the true justifying act of faith, as justifying is always and all along a believing on God, that a man ' may be justified : ' Gal. ii. 16, ' Knowing that a man is not justified by the works of the law, but by the faith of Jesus Christ, even we have believed in Jesus Christ, that we might be justified by the faith of Christ, and not by the works of the law : for by the works of the law shall no flesh be justified.' It notes forth both the aim of the soul, when it puts forth faith for justification, as also that justification follows upon believing, unto which agrees that speech of Christ, though spoken to the contrary, and to unbelievers, and shewing what unbelief is : ' Ye will not come [to] me that ye might have life ; ' that is, ye will not believe (which elsewhere is expressed by a coming to Christ), with that intent to have life from me, which all those whom I save do come unto me for. That particle, ' *that* ye might have life,' denotes out the end or aim which he is to take up, who truly comes to Christ, or believes upon him, and it signifies not only what is the event or consequent* that would follow upon believing.

And yet a faith on some promises or declarations or other for salvation the man must have ; for faith and promises, &c., in the word are relatives, and on promises made unto conditions or qualifications, not wrought as yet in him (we speaking now of a first act of faith justifying put forth) he cannot then in the first act of his believing lay hold, both because he hath no such qualifications as are certain and proper characters of a person already in a state of justification ; nor would he discern any such in himself if we could suppose he had them ; for the true and genuine work of humiliation doth altogether divest a man of all, and presents him to himself as empty of all good, and lays him naked afore God as an ' ungodly ' person, Rom. iv. 5, and he sees and views nothing but sin in himself ; and faith being that which first puts him into a state of justification, Rom. v. 1, he therefore can neither lay hold on any promise made to believing itself, for he is supposed now to begin to believe, and never to have done it before ;

* . *Ut significat finem, non solum consequentiam.* —*Brugensis in verba.*

and therefore he is wholly left unto absolute promises and declarations, and to throw and cast himself upon God and Christ in them, as a man that is in a ship that is sinking under him doth cast himself upon a rock that is afore him, and that immediately with his whole weight, and without the help of plank or board, or anything to convey him to it; so here is the rock Christ, and the soul now flung upon it, it having nothing else to set his foot upon.

This condition is much the same with that of a person that, after long conflictings with various doubts and tentations about his spiritual estate, is ever and anon turned out of all within himself, as in his own apprehensions, that should give him so much as ease in his hold on Christ, and so he wanteth prevailing assurance, though perhaps his faith from some experiences, &c., is a-growing up towards it. In this case this man may and doth find it the safest, easiest, and shortest way for his faith to have an immediate recourse unto absolute promises, and to use such pleas in prayer as may be fetched from, and picked up out of them, and taken up from them; for they usually contain in them naked discoveries, and layings open of the causes and original of man's salvation, and those very things which move God and Christ to save us, as there is the motive in that promise: 'For my name's sake I will blot out thy transgressions.' The manner of such souls is to turn them into pleas from out of those promises, and to return them upon God as motives to him to save their souls in particular.

The corollary from this will prove to be an invincible demonstration for that grand assertion which is my general subject; for if justifying faith and praying with faith for justification doth not at first, nor oftentimes long after, rise up to assurance of faith, or a certain persuasion that I am justified, or that I shall be justified, and remains but an adherence or coming to Christ that I may be justified,—unto which faith yet the promise of being justified is made, and the prayers from out of that faith are heard, and shall be answered, though the soul as yet apprehend it not,—the corollary from thence is, that then certainly such a faith wherewith a believer comes to God to obtain such or such a particular mercy promised (which is far less than salvation), and prays in such a like faith, though far short of a certain persuasion of obtaining it, must needs be of prevalency with God to obtain, though he hath not assurance. The reason of the consequence is, à majori ad minus, from the greater to the lesser. Justification is the greater, if not the greatest spiritual blessing by far (however, to be sure salvation is), and is absolutely necessary, as without which a man cannot be saved; but many other spiritual blessings, as those promises about such degrees of grace, &c., the like also of such or such temporal mercies and promises, are infinitely of less necessity and moment to us, and in no respect absolutely necessary; and therefore if faith of recumbency prevails to obtain the greater, then much more the less. It would be strange that such a faith of recumbency and adherence, wanting personal assurance, and praying therewith, should obtain the greater, and that the same kind of faith for other mercies should not obtain the less, or that God should ordinarily part with the grand blessing, the blessing of blessings, upon so low and cheap a rate of believing, as this seems to be for the degree of it, in comparison with that of assurance, and yet hold all other mercies at a higher price and rate, and hold them harder and faster, so as none should obtain them unless they be first assured they shall have the very particular they ask. Who would not think that if faith of recumbency be good faith for salvation itself, it should not be for all things that are less than salvation itself, yea, that are comprehended in it, and go with it, and have all the promises annexed to it ?   I may say, as the apostle says of God's giving Christ, ' If he hath given his Son, how shall he not with him give us all things ?'   So here, if he hath committed the keys of life and salvation into the hands of faith of recumbency, to open this great mass of treasure, shall he shut up all his lesser cabinets from all capacity of opening them ?   I may boldly say, how shall he not give us all things, with the same faith, and give power unto it over all other blessings whatever ?

2. Neither can any account be given why that the same person should be obliged unto so hard and high a condition of believing, as faith of assurance is, and which is a further special gift of God superadded unto faith of recumbency, or else he shall not receive mercies of any inferior rank and kind, when yet if he prays for the transcendent mercy of the whole of his salvation, but with a faith of recumbency only without assurance, he shall receive it, when yet not the other without that highest degree of faith, as the contrary assertion doth and must suppose.

3. Let this consideration be added, that it is hard to suppose that this same believer should be obliged to pray for all other things with a faith of assurance, whilst yet he wants assurance of the main, viz., of his own salvation, which is as the grand lease upon which the promises of all other mercies, as lesser causes, do depend ; yea, and whilst he conflicts daily with, and is under, doubtings of his personal interest in salvation, his real interest in which must give him interest in all other promises.   And in this case, who will not readily see that assurance of his interest in the love and favour of God, that is the fountain of all other blessings, and of his interest in Christ, the purchaser and channel of all blessings, must be had first, as that which must in any ordinary way be the foundation of his assurance, that he hath or shall have any of the smaller rivulets or streams that flow therefrom ?   He must in reason be assured of the grand lease ere he can claim, or with assurance sue for particular demesnes belonging to it.   What more absured than to think that we must be bound to ask all other things else in the name of Christ as being our Christ, to be given us out of God's special grace and love, and all this with an assurace we shall receive from thence, whilst yet we are in doubt, or at least do not certainly know that Christ is ours, or that God certainly loves us.   This were to put men's faith upon contradictions.   I deny not, but in the case of the faith of miracles, those that wrought them were persuaded and assured God would work such a miracle by them ere they would declare that they would attempt it, or did attempt to work it.   And also I grant, that many of those that had such a faith were not yet believers with a saving faith.   But the case is far otherwise here, for in and unto them the working of miracles did not depend upon that special love of God which he beareth to his children, but in the fate* in hand.   All blessings given to any true believers, after justification, comes out of the same love that salvation itself doth ; and therefore, if this believer suppose faith of assurance that he shall receive them, it must withal be an assurance that God out of that special favour will bestow them on him, for otherwise his supposed faith of assurance terminates itself in God's bestowing the things without a persuasion of God's love to give them; and if so, then he prayeth but with such a faith of assurance as was common to men unregenerate, that did work miracles, who barely had a faith God would do the thing by them, but without a respect of a love borne to their persons therein.   And so it would be a contradiction to say the same person should

* That is, ' fact, or deed.'—ED.

want faith of assurance of God's special love for his salvation, and that yet he should pray for particular blessings out of a faith of assurance, that God out of such a love would give him them.   At least it would be a faith of miracles, to have such an assurance for particular blessings, when a man wants assurance of God's love.

4. Yea, and lastly, he should be obliged to this assurance (if such a tenet were true) about things which are not so certainly proposed, viz., the promises of degrees of grace, &c., as also temporal things, which are not with an absolute certainty proposed in the promises of them.

CHAPTER IV.

How we are in prayer to act faith upon temporal promises.

The next object of faith, on which it acts in praying, is the promises. Faith in prayer treats with God by his promises; and though it treats with God, and with God only through Christ, yet it deals with promises. Prayer is a putting promises into suit, as you do bonds and bills, which are your specialties.   I reckoned up five attributes before, which did not bind you up to believe you should have the particular thing which you ask.   I add two more, the will of God and the faithfulness of God; and when you come to promises, you have to do with these: 1, you have to do with the will of God for promises and declarations of his will; and, 2, with the faithfulness of God, that he will perform that which he hath promised.   Now, mark it, put but these five things together; in appearance they would seem to answer any distrust which you may have concerning receiving the particular mercy requested.

1. Promises are a declaration of God's will.

2. When I am in present need of anything, I find a promise, and then it is faith's duty to lay hold on that promise, and to put it in suit, and to urge it to God.

3. When I come to pray, I am moved hugely to urge that promise, and this by the Spirit of God.

4. God's faithfulness lies at stake to perform it; for you will say, he cannot deny himself.

5. I come and pray in Christ's name, which hath great efficacy with God.

Now, put these things together, and what should hinder but that I should obtain ?   But though you put other things together, and put all these things together, yet it will be found that faith may not rise up to an assurance, nor is it bound so to do.

To assoil this particular, the main thing to be done is to shew what latitude God's will in his promises do allow to faith, that it shall not bind it up, that I must be necessitated to believe that I shall have the particular thing.   If we will know the true meaning and intent of God in his promises, we must search into the nature, and kind, and tenure of the promises; and thereby we shall find that God, in making these promises, hath not bound us up to any particular persuasion, that I must believe I shall receive the very particular mercy which I ask.   This must be granted, that look what God promiseth, so faith ought to believe.   This we must stick to, and bide by.   Look what is the true intent and meaning of God in making promises, that faith must be persuaded of; but take any promises, and there is not such a declaration of the will of God in them, as shall bind me up to such a persuasion of assurance, that I shall receive the particular blessing.   The promises are of three sorts:

1. Personal promises, made to particular persons; as the promise of a son Isaac made to Abraham, which in itself was a temporal promise, but there was added Abraham's salvation in the seed of Isaac, of whom Christ should come. David likewise had the temporal promise of a kingdom, and he had the promise of salvation through his seed, namely, Christ. Now, this must be said, that they were bound up to a special faith, and to a persuasion that God would do this thing for them, for the promises were made to them personally, and to both of them with an oath. But these cannot be drawn to an example to us, to bind us to believe we shall have the like.

2. The second sort of promises are promiscuous promises, promises in common, as it is called ' the common salvation,' and therein is not put in *me*, or *thee*, or *you*, but they are made in common and at large. Now, take the promises that are in common and promiscuously, and they are distinguished according to the subject-matter of them, and also the tenure of them. The matter of them varies with the kind of them, and so will vary our case in hand to speak to it; and the tenure of them depends upon what is the matter of them.

(1.) Some promises are of temporal things, that is the matter of them.

(2.) Other promises are about things eternal. The apostle hath made this distinction to our hand: 1 Tim. iv. 8, ' Godliness hath the promise of the life that now is, and of that which is to come.' Now, you see, there are differing matters promised, either temporal things, or things belonging to salvation. This makes a very great variation in the promise; and accordingly they differ in their tenure, or manner of promulging. God hath framed the tenure and form of promulging them according to the matter of them; and as we say that he works contingently in contingent things, necessarily in necessary, so he hath delivered promises of temporal things one way, and promises of eternal things another way.

(1.) I begin with temporal promises to God's people, and concerning them I have this maxim or assertion.

[1.] For the tenure of them; they are but indefinite, not universal to all the people of God. The people of God have indeed all the promises before them; but take any temporal particular promise, and it is not universal to all the people of God, but is in God's intention indefinite, and designed but to some of them. God's intent in making them was never to perform them to all godly men in all things. There is no good thing temporal (be it deliverance, riches, honours, &c.) but God hath given a promise of it; for whatever good he doth any of his children, he doth it by a word, a promise, and there is no distress or want any of us are in but there is a promise suitable for it, if we could find it. But yet I affirm that God never intended to give all these outward things to all his saints; for not many of them are rich, not many noble, &c.: from this is clear that he did not mean such promises for them all. But the case stands thus : God had the whole body of the elect afore him, and he gives all among them, and disperseth all among them; and whatever good thing any man hath, he hath it by a promise, and through prayer on that promise. Hence it necessarily ariseth, that it is impossible that every man that prays should have every temporal promise for which he prays performed to him, for God never intended it. I seek such a mercy which God hath promised, and God takes liberty to answer my prayer another way, and yet still performs the design of his promise.

Obj. But have not I right to all the promises, as I am a Christian ? and therefore doth not God intend them all to me ?

Ans. Had Jesus Christ right to all the promises ?   You will say, Yes;
and you say rightly, for in him were ' all the promises,' both of this life
and that other, ' amen.'   Yet you know and find that our Lord and
Saviour Jesus Christ had but few of them fulfilled to him *in specie*, or in
kind; he that was the founder of all the promises, and for our sakes
became poor, had not the promise of riches fulfilled.   For our sakes he
was despised, and his face more marred than any man's, and so he had
not the honours of this world, though he had the right to all.   How then
were the promises fulfilled ?   Virtually he had all; and now he hath all
riches and honour, and all to dispose of, as the angels' song in the Revelation shews.   Now, it is said, Rom. viii. 32, if God gives Christ, ' how
shall he not with him give all things ?'   What saint in the world ever had
all things in kind ?   None.   How is it then he hath all things virtually ?
How is it that he hath as good as all things ?   I give you Paul's instance :
2 Cor. vi. 10, ' As sorrowful, yet always rejoicing; as poor, yet making
many rich; as having nothing, yet possessing all things.'   *In solido*,
virtually, eminently he had all, while he had God and Christ; as Christ
had all while he was in the world, when yet he had nothing, for he had
not a hole to hide his head in.   That the promises must needs be indefinite,
and not universal, is evident also by this, that in the Old Testament they
were not universal, for they were never performed universally (this very
point was the quarrel between Job and his friends; they insisted on it,
that all godly men had outward prosperity, and Job says the contrary);
yet in the Old Testament they were in their prime, in their auge,* in their
dominion, for there was a constellation of outward promises then, yet not
performed to all saints.   Why else doth Jeremiah complain, saying,
' Thou art an enemy to me ?'   And why doth David make such complaints, Ps. lxxiii. ?

When thou comest to pray for such a good particular temporal thing,
and hast it not, thou mayest as well say thou hast not Christ, as say that
God doth not answer thee.   Why ?   Because with Christ thou shouldst have
all things (as the apostle tells us), but not all things *in specie*, in the kind;
no, God never meant it.

Now then what kind of faith ought we to have about temporal promises ?
The promises are not made universal to all godly men, for they are but
indefinite ; hence your faith that applies to God must be suitable to the
promise, and so if the promise be indefinite, your faith must be indefinite.
And what is that ? the Scripture prompts it everywhere, and it is this
thought of thy heart, ' It may be God will be gracious to me in this thing ;'
and this, it may be, makes me pray, and urge this promise, being in need,
to put in for it ; but whether I shall receive it or no, I am not certain, but
I throw myself entirely upon God.

[2.] Temporal promises for the tenure of them are conditional, that is,
they are made to such and such qualifications in men, which if they do
fall short of, God is not obliged to bestow them, or to perform them,
though they pray for them ; though they are declarations of his will, yet
they are declarations of his will upon condition, viz., to them that fear
God and pray to God.   I make an argument from threatenings, which are
declarations of God's will as well as promises.   You shall have some
threatenings uttered, which seem very peremptory declarations of God's
will, yet there seems to be a condition of God's will, why God does not
perform them.   Such was that threatening denounced to Hezekiah, for
God came upon him by a prophet, with the same assurance by which God

* That is, αυγη, splendour, brightness.—ED.

inspired Scripture: Isa. xxxviii. 1–3, 'Hezekiah was sick unto death, and Isaiah the prophet said unto him, Thus saith the Lord, Set thy house in order: for thou shalt die, and not live. Then Hezekiah turned his face toward the wall, and prayed unto the Lord, and said, Remember now, O Lord, I beseech thee, how I have walked before thee in truth, and with a perfect heart, and have done that which is good in thy sight: and Hezekiah wept sore.' Here is no condition mentioned, but it is with the same light spoken by the prophet with which he wrote his prophecy; yet notwithstanding there was a tacit condition, it being but about a temporal thing, and Hezekiah understood this, and therefore he turned his face to the wall and prayed. Here he did set himself to perform that condition which might prevent this threatening, for the threatening was upon such a condition, if he did not pray and thus humble himself. On the other hand, that you may see God's liberty, we find, 2 Sam. xii., that the prophet expressly tells David, that the child which he had by his wife Bathsheba shall surely die. What doth David do? Thought he, This is but a conditional threatening, I may get it off if I humble myself: ver. 16, 'David therefore besought God for the child; and David fasted, and went in and lay all night upon the earth.' Here he performed that condition upon which threatenings used to be diverted, but God took his liberty for all that, and the child died; yet, says David, ver. 22, 'While the child was yet alive, I fasted and wept: for I said, Who can tell whether God will be gracious to me, that the child may live?' He had reason to do as he did, to fast and pray; for 'who could tell?' &c. Here are clear instances on both hands: David prayed against the prophet's words on the one hand, and Hezekiah prayed, and God reversed his threatening. Now promises are conditional as threatenings are, and being so, consider what an uncertainty (let me say it) there is in point of conditional promises, such as temporal promises are, and therefore ordinarily there is not required a certain persuasion that they shall be granted.

Obj. But I have, saith the believer, some evidence I am a godly man, and here is a promise to them that are righteous and fear God, I put this in suit, and shall not I have it?

Ans. 1. Let me first tell thee, that God doth not always perform the promise to him that hath the qualification, for God takes a great liberty, as by comparing these instances in David and Hezekiah plainly doth appear.

Ans. 2. I would say this to thee, the promises of temporal things to conditions, are made yet to particular conditions of righteousness and fearing God, and they are not made to every righteous man fearing God; for example, take Ps. xli. 1–3, 'Blessed is he that considers the poor: the Lord will deliver him in time of trouble. The Lord will preserve him, and keep him alive; and he shall be blessed upon the earth: and thou wilt not deliver him to the will of his enemies. The Lord will strengthen him upon the bed of languishing: thou wilt make all his beds in his sickness.' These promises are not made to all sorts of righteousness, but they are made to that part of righteousness which any man is eminent in, viz., the laying to heart the miseries of others, and considering the poor, which many a saint dear to God doth not do. Thus take also what David says: 'I have been young, and now am old; yet have I not seen the righteous forsaken, nor his seed begging bread,' Ps. xxxvii. 25. Is this made to righteous men in general? No; it is limited: ver. 26, 'He is ever merciful, and lendeth; and his seed is blessed.' A man that abounds in that kind of righteousness of doing good, and being liberal, says he, God will remember it, and his seed shall be blessed.

Ans. 3. I answer again concerning conditional promises, that the truth is, it is at the pleasure of God, upon what degree of that qualification he will be pleased to bestow and perform the thing promised. It is evident that promises temporal in every kind, nay, in any kind, are not performed to all that are righteous, or fear God; no, he does not do it to them that are qualified in the highest degree for the promise, not to them who in the highest degree have been merciful; lesser saints that truly fear God will have more of such promises, and saints that are more exactly holy shall be most afflicted; and truly the nature of communion with God calls for this. I will hold communion with that soul, says God, and that soul shall have much communion with me, and therefore I will afflict that soul for every little going aside; God will take that at the hand of a lesser saint, which he will not take at the hands of a higher saint.

Ans. 4. God takes advantage to put off or not perform a temporal promise, which a man hath prayed for. He takes a small occasion, according to his liberty, to put it off and not to perform it. It is a strange thing to consider the liberty God takes in performing promises. You shall have a man break the conditions over and over, and yet notwithstanding the Lord fulfils the thing to him. So in Hezekiah's case, fifteen years was granted him, and notwithstanding the pride of his heart, still God goes on to perform his promise, for he lived his fifteen years. Now that God takes occasion, on the other hand, for a small matter in comparison to put off a temporal promise, the instance of Moses and Aaron is a very great proof. When Moses and all the people of God came out of Egypt, truly the promise was without any clog, to carry him and the people into Canaan; and of all men Moses had the most reason to expect that he should carry them into Canaan, for he was their leader, and had brought them out of Egypt, and had endured that people in their murmurings, and suffered more than ever any man did in governing them. Moses understood this promise, and it was that which made him pray so hardly about it, and God did deny him upon the most small occasion that could be: Deut. iii. 22–25, 'I besought the Lord, saying, O Lord God, thou hast begun to shew thy servant thy greatness, and thy mighty hand: and I pray thee, let me go over and see the good land that is beyond Jordan, that goodly mountain, and Lebanon.' But in the 26th he says, 'The Lord was wroth with me for your sakes, and would not hear me: and said, Let it suffice thee; speak no more unto me of this matter.' Now consider with yourselves this instance: this poor man was the meekest man in the world, and had never been angry but in God's cause, unless in this business, and then he was rash with his mouth, and did not sanctify God afore them, as God challenged him for it, Num. xxvii. 14. Would not God pardon such a man as this, that had been humble, and sought God? Nay, there was more than all this, that made the denial of the going into Canaan the harder to him, because it was a privilege the patriarchs had, to be buried in Canaan, Deut. xxxiv. Therefore, you that think to have promises temporal upon conditions, you depend upon very great uncertainties, for God upon the least trip may take occasion to cut you short of them. It was the case of God's people, Num. xiv. 34; he had promised they should go into Canaan, but you fail first, and break your word with me, says God, I will justify myself that I did not perform the promise to you; 'But you shall know my breach of promise,' *i.e.*, you shall know that I do not fail in my word, but you are wanting in your performance.

Ans. 5. If you take temporal promises, they that live by free grace are heartless to urge the condition of the promises. They are loath to say, I have such a condition, Lord, therefore do such a thing for me.   The people of God that live upon free grace under the gospel, run rather out to self-humblings ; and if it be truly examined, it will be found that David's pleading his righteousness up and down, was his pleading against his enemies.   There is, indeed, one passage which appears otherwise, Ps. lxxxvi., where ' he desires God to be merciful to him ; for,' says he, ' I am holy.' In truth the meaning is, I am thy favourite, I am an ingratiated saint with thee (and you have it so in the margin), I am one whom thou favourest (as in the salutation of the angel it is, ' Hail, Mary, thou art full of grace :' so the papists make it, but it is, ' Whom God hath grace unto') ; and the frame of David's spirit was to plead free grace thereupon, ver. 5.

Obj. But would you have us to leave off eyeing all conditions, and make no use of them that way ?

Ans. 1. God often doth perform the promises according to the conditions performed.

Ans. 2. God made them to this end, that all that plead the promise should look to it, that they have performed the condition ; and though saints under the New Testament are heartless to plead such things, yet they should make sure to have the condition, not as that *for* which, nor as that *unto* which, but as that *without* which God will *not* fulfil such things, for he doth not fulfil them to his children without them.   Now suppose thou followest such a promise, and seest such a condition in it, and thou dealest with thine own heart, and the power of God, to have the thing promised, and God disappoints thee after all, what then ?   Thou art made more holy, there is the answer ; and if thou art made more holy by seeking the condition, there is no hurt done thee.

Ans. 3. Temporal promises, in the performances of them, are to be understood disjunctively ; that is, God will either give thee this blessing or a better, either the one or the other.   God promised Abraham, that he would give him the land of Canaan for a possession ; the promise was made personally to himself, Acts vii. 5, ' though he gave him no inheritance in it ; no, not so much as a spot of ground to set his foot on,' and yet God had promised that he would give it to him for a possession, and to his seed after him.   Here is a promise made, and truly the Lord comes off in it, Heb. xi. 14, 15, 16.   God gave him a better country ; and, indeed, all the patriarchs lived as strangers in the land God gave them, expecting a better country.   Abraham had no hurt done him, that he had not the land in possession which was promised to him, for he was taken to a better country. Thus God also dealt with Aaron, when he said to him, ' Go up that mountain and die ;' Aaron was shrewdly hurt, for he was carried to heaven.   God does commute promises (as the law word is), doth transfer them, interchange them one for another.   Moses looked for that promise of Canaan, and as you heard, he died and went to heaven so much the sooner.   Nay, you heard how his body must not go into Canaan, it went to heaven.   For who appeared in the transfiguration but Moses and Elias ?   Insomuch as Moses hath been in heaven so many thousand years before other saints shall have it.   Well, then, if thou dost ask riches, and repairs in thy estate, and God gives self-sufficiency, that is, content, here whilst thou seekest a temporal blessing, God recompenseth thee with a spiritual blessing.   As one said to another, What shall I give to take thee a box on the ear ?   Says he, Give me an helmet, and strike as hard as thou wilt ; so God brings thee into afflictions, and gives thee patience and consolations to bear them, and this is security and defence enough for thee.   James pronounceth it a blessed thing to endure, and that we should count it all joy to undergo trials, if they bring forth patience, James i. 2, 3. To the same purpose the psalmist speaks, Ps. cxxxviii. This psalm was made upon occas in of his having been in the midst of troubles (as ver. 7 shews), hazards, and dangers from enemies ; now what doth he say ? Ver. 3, ' In the day when I cried, thou answeredst me ;' and how did he answer him ? He was in distress, and God strengthened him with strength in his soul, in his inward man, and therein performed his promise much better.

Ans. 4. That which makes a further uncertainty yet to faith, and a greater latitude on God's part to perform these temporal promises, is the alteration made concerning them under the New Testament, in comparison of what was under the Old. The largeness of performance of temporal promises was predominant under the Old Testament, when that constellation reigned conspicuously ; for they were helps to their faith, as pledges of spiritual things ; nay, their degrees of holiness had signs from their prospering in outward things ; thus I understand that Ps. cxii. 1–3, ' Blessed is the man that feareth the Lord, that delighteth greatly in his commandments. His seed shall be mighty upon the earth : the generation of the upright shall be blessed. Wealth and riches shall be in his house ; and his righteousness endureth for ever.' It speaks not only of a man that fears God, and delights in him, but of one who doth so greatly, that man according to the dispensation of those times should be blessed, so as that his seed should be mighty upon earth, &c. But Jesus Christ being become an high priest of good things yet to come in the other world, Heb. ix. 11, ' And he having obtained a more excellent ministry, by how much also he is the mediator of a better covenant, which was established upon better promises,' (Heb. viii, 6), as his coming wrought alteration in the law (Heb. vii. 12); so it wrought an alteration in the dispensation of promises, and in the performance of them. Good things yet to come began to be the eminent promises, because Jesus Christ is now come, who is the heavenly man, 1 Cor. xv. Read the Old Testament, and there you find, ' Blessed shall you be in your basket and store, blessed in the field,' &c. ; but read Eph. i., you shall find, that when Christ is come, who hath ' blessed us with all spiritual blessings in heavenly things,' the blessing now is communion with God, increase of faith, larger measure of the Spirit. These are the blessings above board, and promises of temporal things are subservient to carry us through the world, and for our living in the world to get more grace. What did they serve Jesus Christ for, but to carry him through the world ? To this end do the promises of outward things serve, and it is enough if we have meat, and drink, and raiment ; let us be therewith content, saith the apostle. They are not now so much as pledges to our faith, as they were to believers under the Old Testament. No ; the best use of them is, that they are means to raise our hearts to serve God more cheerfully, 2 Cor. iv. Now, then, you see the dispensation is plainly altered, and therefore now temporal promises are mightily diminished, and impaired, and abated, and checked.

2. But yet, secondly, they are further checked by the promise of the cross and persecution. What is the meaning of that saying, Mark x. 29, 30, ' You shall have an hundredfold in this life' ? How ? ' With persecution.' Instead of promising temporal things, he proposeth leaving all, and instead of all you shall have persecution. You shall have an hundredfold, not of the things, for they are taken from them. How then is it ? In having spirituals, which God makes up to them.

3. Yet further, under the gospel it falls usually out, that to whom God means to do most good in a gospel way, he brings things clearly and per-

fectly contrary to temporal promises upon them; this you shall find in the apostle Paul, 1 Cor. iv. 8. The Corinthians had less grace: ' You are full,'says he; ' ye are rich, ye have reigned as kings without us:' ' we,' that are the leaders of you, the eminent Christians ' to this present hour, are both hungry and thirsty, and are naked, and buffeted, and have no certain dwelling-place; and labour, working with our own hands,' &c., ver. 11, 12. How many temporal promises was poor Paul's faith deprived of? Under the Old Testament, as a man was more righteous, God ordinarily prospered him; but now, according as a man is more holy, God ordinarily afflicts him. Therefore, now as to praying in faith about temporal things, and with a certainty, you see how many ways it is cut off.

I shall make two conclusions, from what hath been said about this alteration under the New Testament.

1. God on his part finds, and thinks himself in greater liberty, and takes greater latitude for performing temporal promises now, than he did under the law, and he indeed herein deals with us as he pleaseth. If he took such a liberty in the Old Testament (as Ps. xxxvii. expresseth he did), that when the wicked prospered, the godly went down the wind; if he took such a liberty in Jeremiah's time, that Jeremiah complains of it, much more may we think that he will do it under gospel-dispensations. Only a little to relieve you, consider that God seems more peremptory to undertake for necessaries in this life; it is a thing he hath declared, 1 Tim. vi. 8: ' Having food and raiment, let us be therewith content.' He propounds no other terms but so; and the reason is, because we cannot live without them, we cannot serve him without them, and so he does undertake for these things. That promise which is enforced by five affirmations, and indigitated by four negatives, Heb. xiii. 5, ' I will never leave thee, nor forsake thee,' that promise absolutely comes in about providing for families, for such as are married, and have children, as the coherence shews. Our Lord and Saviour Jesus Christ seems, Mat. vi., to put us off from any vehement seeking for these things. No, not by prayer; for he tells us, ' Your Father knows you need these things,' therefore do not spend thoughts on them, do not seek them vehemently, for you have one who takes care of you, and knows your needs (if one should say so to a child, it would make him careless); he knows you need all these things. *All these things;* that is a good word, but consider it is not all you wish for that you need, ver. 31. If we live, God will provide necessaries, and if we die, if we should die for him, for the Lord, that is a privilege and advantage beyond all temporal promises, beyond all advantages of living in the world, and enjoying all promised temporal blessings.

I might shew you how precious our lives are to him, and that he will not cast us away. The world lives upon meat and drink, but we live upon God's love and care. What saith the apostle, 2 Cor. iv. 11, 13, ' For we which live are always delivered unto death for Jesus' sake, that the life also of Jesus might be made manifest in our mortal flesh; we having the same spirit of faith, according as it is written, I believed, and therefore have I spoken; we also believe, and therefore speak.' What a long while did Peter and Paul live! A man would wonder that men that lived in continual jeopardy, should live forty years preaching, as they did (for they died within two years of the destruction of Jerusalem), and they lived by the power of the resurrection of Christ. ' Precious in the sight of the Lord is the death of his saints.' Who knows how he disposeth of their lives? Now, as on God's part he takes a liberty about performing temporal promises to us, yet with that caution to give necessaries, so our faith, touching outward things, should be answerable ; our faith should be at less certainty to obtain outward things than they had in the Old Testament, yet our prayers should be earnestly and vehemently for our lives, that we may live to serve God. The alteration of God's dispensation on God's part must needs alter our faith.

CHAPTER V.

Concerning praying, and faith in prayer, for performance of promises purely spiritual.—A division of spiritual promises into three sorts.—A discussion concerning absolute promises.—How this maxim is to be understood, that absolute promises are to be absolutely sought by us.—With what manner of faith in prayer any soul may deal with God for the performance of those promises.

Promises purely spiritual are such as purely concern our salvation.

There are three sorts of promises that concern salvation.

1. Such as are absolutely absolute, *absolutissimæ ;* that are absolute indeed, *primo primæ ;* such are all those immediate declarations of God's purposes to save, and all such promises as hold forth so much of the covenant of grace : Jer. xxxi. 33, ' I will write my law in their hearts.' Which promises God makes without respect had to any prerequisites at all in men, as unto which he should have respect in his making those promises ; which God is so far from, that in those promises he undertakes to perform the conditions.

2. A second sort of promises are absolute in this sense, that they express a certainty of performance of them, but yet do suppose prerequisite qualifications first wrought by God, and a continuation thereof ; and though not *for which,* yet as *upon which,* and *not without which* first wrought, they are ever performed to any. The qualifications are such as faith and repentance, &c., which do at first put a man into a state of grace, according to that of the apostle, speaking of faith, ' Whereby we have access into the grace wherein we stand,' Rom. v. 2. They are such promises as these :. ' Whosoever believeth hath eternal life, and shall never perish,' John iii. 16, and John xviii. 36 ; ' He that believeth shall never die,' John xi. ; ' They shall never enter into condemnation,' John v. 24. Unto this sort belong all promises of perseverance, and of giving the possession of salvation in the latter end of our lives ; and these, because of the certainty of the performance, though made unto such and such qualifications, I do call secondarily absolute.

3. There is a third sort of promises belonging to salvation, which I call aditional promises, as those that are made of giving more or less degrees of grace, and of preserving a man through his whole course from falling into gross sins, and of giving joy and peace in believing, 'joy unspeakable and full of glory,' and peace which passeth understanding. These I call additional to salvation, because they belong but to the *bene esse,* to the better being of a Christian, and yet have salvation in them, as the apostle's word is ; *i. e.,* they belong to salvation, but not absolutely to the *esse* or being of a believer, as such, or as without which he is not a believer, and shall not be saved ; whereas those two former are essential to salvation itself, without which none is or can be saved.

According to this division of promises, I shall first shape this general division of answers to the point in hand, viz., how we are to act faith about each of these promises, and to manage our prayers about any of them.

1. As to that third and last sort of additional things and promises of salvation, they are those that are the occasions and matters of the greatest complaints amongst Christians. We pray indeed for such and such graces, and holy dispositions, &c., but we find no more performance of them than we do in temporals ; and this causeth a great discouragement, scruple, and sadness, rising even unto this, that God therefore answereth not our prayers at all, and that therefore we pray not in faith.

2. As to the second sort of promises, which I call secondarily absolute, they being of the essence of salvation, and the final possession thereof being annexed unto the qualifications of faith, &c., first wrought ; a believer that sees, and spiritually perceives the qualifications wrought in himself, may further by a faith of certainty believe and pray for the performance thereof. He withal must diligently attend unto a continuing in that faith and mortification of lusts, &c., which are to be the consequents of the first faith wrought, to the end to obtain such promises. For even such promises are uttered with an *if;* thus it is said, that ' we are made partakers of Christ, *if* we hold the beginning of our confidence to the end,' Heb. iii. 14 ; and such is that promise of Christ, ' He that endures to the end shall be saved ;' and such is the contrary threatening of the apostle, ' If ye live after the flesh, ye shall die ; but if ye through the Spirit do mortify the deeds of the body, ye shall live,' Rom. viii. 13. So as hypothetically it may be said, that if those that have true faith once, should not continue and exercise to do those things throughout the future course of their lives, they would certainly perish. But yet because God hath absolutely undertaken, without *ifs* or *ands*, to keep and to preserve them out of his faithfulness, and to sanctify them ὁλοτελεῖς, which word imports finally and totally (as his promise is, 1 Thes. v. 23), therefore believers may pray absolutely, that is, with a belief of certainty, for the performance of those promises, and God's continuing to preserve them to the end.

3. But, thirdly, as to that first sort of absolute promises and declarations, which I call most absolute, there is in experience found (as well may be thought), some difficulty in the thing itself, how a man may apply his faith thereto, whether in an absolute way, or how ? and consequently, how he may make use even of such promises in praying, and wind them into his prayers, and pleas for his salvation, by virtue of them.

There is a trite and common maxim passeth up and down (but I fear is not so well understood by all), viz., that spiritual promises and things being absolute, therefore all men are bound to pray absolutely, or with a faith of certainty about them. And the supposed grounds for this are,

(1.) That faith in us being to be answerable to the matter and nature of the promise, and the things therein promised, therefore if the promise be absolute, then the faith ought to be absolute, and then as absolute a praying for them in such a faith ought to be also ; and that absoluteness of faith required of all in praying for them, is understood to be a faith of certainty, or assurance that they shall absolutely, that is, certainly, obtain them.

(2.) A second supposed ground is, that this is a commonly received difference between temporal promises and spiritual ; that the temporal are to be prayed for conditionally, &c., and so with an *it may be*, therefore oppositely all spiritual promises, and the performance of them, are to be prayed for absolutely, without any *if* or *it may be*. And hence men think, that every man is bound to seek for these with such an absolute faith as is certainly persuaded they shall obtain, although a man cannot assure himself the like of temporals. Here I judge it conducible to the point afore us, to consider how that common maxim is to be understood, as in relation unto our prayers about absolute promises.

1. Let no man deceive himself that these are called absolute promises, as if God would save men without those qualifications mentioned wrought in them. Let not any man imagine that he should seek for salvation absolutely, thinking that though he should want those qualifications, yet he should obtain it. No ; for some of those very promises instanced in, are to work the very conditions themselves, and are thereby differenced from the covenant of works. I may absolutely say, as the apostle doth in my text, without those qualifications, 'Let no man think to receive anything of salvation from the Lord ;' for without true faith and holiness, which are a part of writing the law in our hearts, no man shall see or be accepted of God, Heb. xii.

2. The matter in those absolute promises, which is salvation itself, and the qualifications promised to be wrought, are absolute indeed in this sense, that they are things of an absolute necessity, as to man on his part ; mark that. Both the things themselves are necessary, and that every man should seek after them for himself also is necessary.

(1.) The things are of absolute necessity. Christ calls them, as most interpret that speech, that 'one thing necessary;' and in this sense indeed, in respect of the kind of absolute necessity of them, these spiritual promises are rightly distinguished from temporals, which do not contain matters of absolute necessity. It is not necessary to have honours, riches, pleasures, which yet are the materials of many promises ; but to be saved is, for the man is destroyed else. So as the things are of absolute necessity to every man.

(2.) Thereupon it is of as absolute necessity, for every man to seek for the accomplishment of them to himself, for it is his own salvation : ' Work out your own salvation,' Philip. ii. 13 ; of which working, there spoken of in the general, this of a man's seeking to God by prayer is one great part. It is an argument of sufficient cogency that is couched in that clause, ' your own salvation.' And thus, and in this sense, in respect to man, these things, I confess, are absolutely necessary.

(3.) But then, thirdly, we must take in God's part too, whose mind in such promises is, that although the matter of these promises be most absolute every way, yet as to the tenor of them, that is, the declaration of them, as to the persons to whom he intends them, so they are utterly indefinite, that is, are intended but for some, and not to all men universally ; which is manifest in this, that God doth not write his law in the hearts of all men, as we see in common experience, and which the apostle would have us observe in saying, ' All men have not faith.' Hence, therefore, it comes to pass, that though all men ought, out of their own necessity, to put in for a share and interest in the things therein promised, yet as necessarily, I say, it doth fall out, that in the first puttings forth of faith towards such promises, none can or must think to set out with a full persuasion, or an absolute faith, as in this argument and upon this occasion I term it, that they shall obtain, as if they were infallibly certain that their individual persons were absolutely intended by God in those promises. No ; and the reason is, because evidently they are not universal promises, and therefore men cannot, nor must not, at first dash, or at their first entrance into faith, believe that they are elected, or be assured of their personal interest in such promises. No ; but all they are capacitated to do, in point of believing at first, is, to comply with the indefiniteness of the promise, by a faith that is suitably indefinite as to their persons, whereby, though not knowing of a certainty they are the persons, they yet cast themselves upon God and Christ, to be made partakers of the salvation promised therein. The promises being made to some (and who knows or can tell, but God may be gracious to me ? as I have elsewhere shewn), they wait on him to find the accomplishment.

And then indeed, after a soul hath exercised these indefinite acts of faith, turning therewith and thereupon unto God with its whole heart, then indeed believers may come to be assured, with a faith answering to, and corresponding with, that certainty which is found in that second sort of promises, which I have termed secondarily absolute. They endeavouring to believe, or to enter into that rest, as the apostle speaks, Heb. iv., if they find that in doing so, they arrive at true spiritual faith and sound repentance, and that in the event these actings of both prove to be such, then indeed they may be assured of their personal interest in, and God's intendments of their particular persons therein, because then they find that God hath wrought the qualifications in them, according to his promises and declarations in those first sort of promises made, unto which qualifications salvation is absolutely, that is, certainly, annexed ; and by those qualifications thus wrought, their persons are set forth and declared to be those whom God, in the first sort of promises, had indeed intended. But until these qualifications be wrought, or whilst they are but in the working, and a man's heart under the anvil, or but in hammering thereunto, or whilst they are not discerned by themselves to be in them, they can but apply themselves with a faith suitable to that tenor in which God hath on his part uttered (as in respect of persons) in those his most absolute promises, which, as to persons, are but indefinite. And to be sure, if we will deal with God, we must treat with him according to his own way and manner of revelation. For it is from him we are to have our salvation made over to us, and therefore this application of faith must be suited to the tenor of the promises ; it must be even an indefinite faith (as I may call it), in respect unto a man's own personal interest, yet with a firm cleaving unto God, and to the good things promised, to obtain them through a casting ourselves upon him, though we be not assured we are the persons who shall infallibly obtain (for the event must shew that), and yet we are, as in respect of our pursuance after the salvation promised, to seek for it, out of the same necessity that a man condemned to die doth seek for his life. And the parallel between the case of such a one and of this other holds very much alike. For if a king should declare his absolute purpose and intention to be to pardon some in such or such a rebellion, but says not whom, though he declares withal he will be sought unto in such an humble and submissive manner (as he himself will be the judge of) by them that shall obtain that pardon. In this case those that sue for it, not knowing whom he intends personally, nor whom he will judge to seek it in that manner he desires, they in their seeking cannot be absolutely, that is, certainly assured they shall find grace ; and yet they pursue it out of an absolute necessity as to themselves. And so the case falls out to be oftentimes in souls that seek for salvation,—I judge some difference may be found in these two cases, yet in this main they are alike,—for many believers, though true, yet do not, nor cannot a long while, judge or discern in themselves, whether they seek and apply themselves to God with such an unfeigned faith as the word describes and God requires, so as they are enforced, and yet enabled by God to seek him by such a faith, as the event must prove whether it be true or no ; and yet they make a venture of a believing, and of a turning unto God (as the consequent of that faith), submitting unto God, and leaving it for him to judge of, and to give them the Spirit whereby to discern the truth of it.

Lastly, To move and stir up all men to come to God with such an indefinite act of faith, God makes an universal promulgation of these promises, though they shall be accomplished but in some persons, that men may be assured that they shall be most certainly fulfilled unto some that thus lay hold on them, and so they are universally made known. He would have the promulgation of them to be universal, to the intent that every man that hears them, finding himself nowhere excluded, and withal not knowing but he may be one of those *some* who shall have those things promised fulfilled in him and upon him, may thereupon (and he ought to do so) apply himself to God by acts of believing, and to prayer for his particular attainment.

2. We shall now consider with what manner of faith, and level of such faith in prayer, any sort of soul may treat with God for the performance of those absolute promises. To the end I may assign to every one their right and due elevation of faith in prayer, about absolute promises, I must necessarily set out the several climates that all or any believers are brought into, or do live in ; and according to the elevation of their faith must their applications in prayer necessarily be supposed, and accordingly measured forth to be.

The several elevations of believers are these:—

(1.) The first elevation is of such as are *in ipso articulo, vel apice conversionis,* upon the point of believing in God and Christ for salvation, and who, through that faith, are turning to God, and have been humbled for sin, &c., without which no man will come to Christ. I plainly mean those that are now to put forth a first act of saving faith, having never done it before, which was the case of the jailor, Acts xvi. 30, 31, ' What shall I do to be saved ? ' said he ; ' Believe in the Lord Jesus,' said the apostle. And as everything must have a beginning, so every one that is saved must have a first beginning to believe.

(2.) The second sort are such as have had (and that perhaps for some time) a true faith already wrought in them, and some fruits thereof in the course of their lives. They are such as have truly come to God through Christ for salvation, and from the first putting forth of faith have also continued to pray, and to seek for salvation at the hands of God, and yet, through God's dispensations towards them, are kept under, without prevailing assurance that they are or shall be saved, although withal there be some lesser degrees of hopes growing up towards assurance, that are added to, and do accompany their faith more or less.

(3.) The third sort is of those that have triumphant assurance of salvation, whether obtained by experience of their own graces, and manifold gracious dealings of God with them, or further by a superadded immediate testimony of the Spirit, by whom the love of God is shed abroad in their hearts immediately, beyond all those experiences. You have both in Rom. v., where it is first said experience breeds hope, that is, an assurance (in which sense the word hope is there used in 1 John iii. 2, 8), and then further, that the love of God, which is shed over and above immediately into the heart by the Holy Ghost, breeds a hope or assurance beyond what experience gives, which he there calls a hope which maketh not ashamed ; no, not in respect of the continuance of that assurance in our hearts.

Now as touching this last sort, of such as have personal assurance of faith, there is not, nor can be, no difficulty how either their faith should come to close with such absolute promises mentioned, or how they may take such promises into their prayers. And as touching the first and second sort, there is often found small difference in the attainments of their faith, they being fain to live mostly upon a mere act of adherence and recumbency, without additional comfort. I shall therefore speak to both in a notion common to both, which is the consideration of men wanting prevailing assurance.

1. There is this general rule, that whatever degrees or actings of faith in any of these mentioned are to be allowed unto true faith, the prayers also that are put up in such a faith must be allowed to be a praying in faith to all intents and purposes, which therefore shall be accepted of God, and shall obtain and have power with God (as the phrase used of Jacob is) for what the man prays for. And, the reason is clear; for if the faith be such as wherewith God is well pleased, as the apostle's aphorism of it is, then certainly the prayer put up, though but according to the proportion and elevation of that faith, must be accepted as a praying in faith also. And the proof of this is from what the apostle says in treating of saving faith, Rom. x. 15, where he so nearly links faith and prayer together, and makes them of so like an extent in regard of obtaining salvation itself, as evidently shews the truth of this maxim; and to that end he brings together two things sometimes far remote in place one from the other: speaking of each singly, first, he speaks for faith, 'Whoever believes on him shall not be ashamed,' ver. 11; secondly, he speaks for prayer, 'Whosoever shall call upon the name of the Lord shall be saved;' and this conjunction of each one with the other, and his prescribing the same influence for salvation unto each, doth plainly hold forth there three things :—

(1.) That true faith from the first sets a man upon prayer for what his faith aims at, which was his own case during the first three days of his conversion : 'Behold he prays,' says Christ, Acts ix. 11, for now he had begun to believe.

(2.) Such prayers out of that faith do obtain salvation, which is the matter there spoken, and is the great aim of faith at first.

(3.) He speaking this of faith in prayer in general, and so of all the degrees thereof, and accordingly of all praying out of all, or any such degrees of faith as a man hath attained, therefore all such praying out of that faith which he hath, is accepted to obtain. And my ground for this is, that the apostle utters those speeches of faith and prayer in the general, 'Whoever believes,' ver. 10, and 'Whoever shall call on the name of the Lord,' &c., and therefore means that all and any of them that do believe, and do call upon the name of the Lord, with whatever degree of true faith, shall be accepted according to the degree of faith in prayer. And in verse 11 (which is the middle between them two sayings), you have this reason of it given, 'For the same Lord over all is rich unto all that call upon him,' whether out of a strong or weak faith, whether out of a faith of recumbency to obtain, or assurance that they shall obtain, which accords with what our apostle says, 'He giveth liberally to every one that prayeth in faith,' I add by way of explanation to both, be the faith of what degree and elevation whatever.

2. A second maxim or rule is this, Upon these, and such like general dictates of the Holy Ghost, I may warrantably conclude, that so as a man's faith in all these three several conditions fore-mentioned doth rise, so far a man's praying in those degrees of his faith, or his putting forth faith in prayer, will rise also. The stream never riseth higher than the fountain, but so far it will. A man can but pray with that faith which he hath, and his prayer shall be accepted according to what he hath, agreeable to that assertion of the apostle, 2 Cor. viii. 12, 'It shall be accepted

according to what a man hath, and not according to what a man hath not.' So that as the apostle speaks of God's judging men at latter day, that those that are without law shall be judged by what light and power they had without the law, and those that have sinned living under the law shall be judged by the law, and the light and power they had there-from (and in like manner they by the gospel that had the light of it, and all in their due proportions), so I may say of praying in faith, he that prays in faith of bare recumbency without assurance, shall by that faith obtain what he prays for without assurance; and he that prays with some hope-ful trust of obtaining, though not rising up to full assurance, which is some-times the case of the second condition, he shall obtain according to the measure of his faith, although short of full assurance. In short, I may say of them all, as Christ did, ' Be it unto you according to your faith.'

OF THE OBJECT AND ACTS OF JUSTIFYING FAITH.

PART III.

Of the properties of Faith.

BOOK I.

Of the excellence and use of faith.—That good works are not slighted by exalting faith.—Of the excellence of faith, in that it gives all honour to God and Christ; and that for this reason, God hath appointed it to be the grace by which we are saved.—Of the excellency of faith, as it hath a general influence on all our graces.

CHAPTER I.

The excellency of faith displayed in several particulars.

In discoursing of the properties of faith, first, I will begin to shew the excellency that is in faith above all obedience else. But before I come to demonstrate the excellency of faith, I will first premise these few considerations to all, that I shall speak of faith's excellency, because men think faith too much magnified and works slighted.

1. Faith, in itself, is of all graces the meanest and the lowest, a poorer and a more beggarly grace than to love, by far: for in loving God, we return something to him, love for his love, we give as well as we take; but in believing we receive all from God; so Gal. iii. 22, 'the promise' is said to be 'given to them that believe,' and ver. 14, to be 'received by faith.' We lay but hold upon what he offers, Christ and the grace that is revealed through him. Now as *præstantius est dare quam accipere*, so to love and obey is, in itself, better than to believe, it is more honourable for us. Believing is passion rather than action, for indeed God puts Christ upon us and into our hands, or we would not take him. We do but sit still, as it were, when we believe, and see what God will do in us and for us; and therefore God the rather chose to advance this grace, which is the weakling, to all the rest. God chose to shew his power in this grace; and that which is the most foolish in the eyes of reason, hath God chosen to be his agent.

2. Therefore it is not faith, as it is a quality or an act simply in itself,

that we shall or do commend it to you; it is not for any worth in itself, but as it is an instrument singled out by God to do all by in us. As Peter said of himself, having healed the cripple, Acts iii. 12, ' Why marvel ye, or look ye so earnestly on us, as if by our own power or holiness we had done thus?' No; be it known to you, that we are but the instruments. So may faith say, It is not any excellency or holiness in me above other graces, that doth anything more than they; I am but an instrument of conveyance. Thus a seal of wax is of itself of far less worth than a pearl or piece of gold, and yet it may ratify a covenant, which a piece of gold doth not do. ' Now he that believes hath set to his seal that God is true,' John iii. 33; and so the covenant is struck up betwixt God and him, and therefore it is more precious than any grace else, yet but as an instrument, not in itself.

3. It is such an instrument as, in all that is attributed to it, Christ who is the object of it, and God who is the worker by it, are magnified and glorified when it is commended. So that in commending faith, and desiring you so earnestly and above all to believe, we do desire you but to set up Christ in your hearts above works, and above obedience, and to let him be all in all. We desire you but to magnify God's free grace above your own merits, and what you can earn, and to magnify God's power above your own. If God had used any other grace, some honour would have reflected upon it, and so much have been taken away from God; but ' by grace ye are saved, and through faith' (as the instrument), Eph. ii. 8. And why is it of faith, and not of any works or disposition in us else? ' Lest any man should boast,' ver. 9; for, Rom. iii. 27, ' boasting is clean excluded by the law of faith;' that is, an ascribing anything to a man's self, or to anything in a man, is excluded, for that is meant by boasting. Did not faith do all? Or if works did anything, a man would boast; for whatever faith is said to do, Christ is still as fully said to do, as if he did it without the help of faith; for faith is but the bare fetching it from Christ, or receiving it from him, or suffering Christ to do all in me. And therefore, what is said to be done by faith, is all one in Scripture phrase, and in God's account, and in the believer's esteem, as to say, that Christ doth it; so that Christ is no whit afraid you should attribute too much to faith.

1st, In Scripture phrase, therefore, to be justified by faith, and to be justified by Christ, is all one; to be in Christ, and to be in the faith, is all one and the same; for faith doth all by going to Christ. Memorable is that place, Acts iii. 16, when Peter speaks of healing the cripple, he says, ' Christ's name, through faith in his name, had made the man whole.' What he attributes to faith is wholly attributed to his name, and to faith but as in his name, and his name manifested through it; and so his blood, through faith in his blood, justifies: and therefore it is promiscuously called ' the righteousness of faith, and ' the righteousness of Christ;' for it is all one. Faith robs not Christ a whit; and so to live by faith, and to have Christ live in me, is all one, Gal. ii. 20.

2dly, And thus it is in a believer's account also, for it is the very instinct of faith, the form of it, to attribute all to Christ; it is not faith else; it is the property of it to do so; ' I live by faith,' says Paul, Gal. ii. 20, ' yet not I, but Christ lives in me:' faith still comes in with *yet not I.*

And, 3dly, Thus it is in God's account; and therefore Christ cares not how much he attributes to faith, for he doth but closely herein attribute all to himself: when he says, ' All things are possible to faith,' Mark ix. 23, he derogates nothing from himself, he doth not put faith into commission with himself, but it is all one as to say, all things are possible to my power, which faith makes use of.　Christ, when he had done a miracle, or pardoned a man, would seem to put off all from himself, in saying, ' Thy faith hath saved thee,' and ' thy faith hath made thee whole :' which was enough to have made any man proud of his faith ; and had it been any other grace, it would have done so ; but he knew that that faith which was in their hearts whom he saved and healed, said within them, Lord, thou alone hast made me whole.　Thus faith doth trust Christ, and Christ doth trust faith. So as when we attribute so much to faith, we do but attribute it to Christ, and desire you but to honour him.

Secondly, We will shew you the prerogatives and excellencies of faith, which (as the apostle says in another case) are ' much every way.'

1. You will see what it doth, that works do not.

2. You shall see that all which works do, it doth, and much more also ; and therefore we commend it to you above all, and more than all.

1st, It is in a primary sense the sole instrument in the covenant of grace, and works and obedience are but subservient, and as a consequence annexed to it, though as necessarily annexed as the other.　Our great business in the covenant of grace is faith, as the form of the covenant of works lay in doing.　Therefore still the two covenants, and the righteousness conveyed by both, are differenced by doing and believing only : Rom. x. 5, 6, and Gal. iii. 11–13, &c., Acts xvi. 30, 31, and the reason is couched in three words, in Rom. iv. 16, ' Therefore it is of faith, that it might be of grace, and that the promise might be sure.'

1. That it might be of *grace*, given freely, requiring nothing, but receiving.　If God had required giving again any thing from us as the condition, then it had not been of grace, that is, not every way of grace, Rom. xi. 6, if it had been by any works as the condition, then grace had been no grace.

2. Therefore it is of faith, because this covenant is a *promise*.　So it is called, as in that place, so in Gal. iii. 14, 17–20.　Thus he calls the covenant of the gospel throughout in that chapter, and therefore mentions faith only as the instrument to lay hold of it, as answering thereunto ; for what is there should answer to it but faith ?　For though it contains commands, yet power to do what is commanded is also promised, to give a new heart, &c. ; and therefore faith is that which alone answers to it, to lay hold on those promises.

3. Therefore it is of faith, that it might be *sure;* therefore it was both necessary to be by way of promise from God to give all and do all, and to require nothing but receiving and believing the promise from him, that the covenant might not depend on us, but on God and his promise, and upon nothing in us but receiving and believing the promise.　God, in the covenant of works, had to do with pure nature ; betwixt which and God, till there came a breach, there could be no cause of suspicion of God's love to man ; and therefore love was required, and not faith primarily ; but, in the covenant of grace, God hath to do with terrified consciences ; which, if anything else than faith should have been required, could not have been raised up to any persuasion of God's love and favour.　But now, a poor soul, though humbled, and seeing no worth in himself, and a soul in desertion that sees no righteousness of its own, yet may come to the promise to have salvation sure to itself by faith, though for the present it hath nothing to bring to the covenant.　God requires humiliation indeed afore, because men will not believe else; and he requires obedience after, as that which necessarily follows upon faith, so as a man cannot truly believe but it will follow, as heat follows light.　Yet, upon believing, the bargain is struck up ;

and though faith be the great instrument, yet we say withal, that works are necessary to be in the person justified, yet not to justify. Thus heat is as necessarily in the sun as light; yet it makes not day by its heat, but by its light. Works of new obedience are required as necessary to the possession of salvation, but faith is that alone which puts us into a condition of having the title and right to it, by the blood and righteousness of Christ. Obedience is necessarily required in all that are made sons, and so cry, ' Abba, Father ;' for if he be a father, where is his honour ? But it is faith alone that makes us sons, Gal. iii. 26. And though we are as necessarily ordained to sanctification, as to faith and to salvation through both, 2 Thes. ii. 13, by which, as the necessary way, we come and are brought to salvation as the goal, yet it is by faith alone that we are put into that estate : Eph. ii. 8, 9, ' By grace ye are saved through faith, and that not of works,' &c. Then might some say, works are not required ; yes, says the apostle, as a necessary means you are ordained to come to salvation by, which is the end of your faith, and which are a necessary condition of that estate, though faith alone puts us into it ; for he adds, ver. 10, ' We are his workmanship, created to good works, which God hath ordained we should walk in.' They are the condition of the subject that shall be saved, who must be made meet, not the condition of the promise of salvation itself. They are the condition of faith, or of the person believing ; but as sight is that which saves us in heaven, by which we have all our happiness communicated to us, so is it faith that saves us here.

2dly. Accordingly faith doth all in us, till it hath brought us to salvation. It carries along this great venture of a man's soul safe to heaven, and leaves it not till it hath put it into Christ's hands in heaven, till itself ends in sight. It begins and it ends with us, and stands by us, when else all would fail.

(1.) It begins, for it gives us the first ken of Christ and happiness. When the soul is bartered and tossed in the waves of humiliation at first, it is faith climbs up to the top of the mast, and spies Christ out to get on board him, when all was in despair, and thought to be cast away : ' By faith we have access into this grace,' Rom. v. 2. And,

(2.) When we are in the state of salvation, faith doth all; for whenas all graces else would soon be overcome and cast out again by lusts, and would soon be tripped up from off their standing, faith is able to keep its legs and standing, Rom. v. 2. Therefore, 1 Peter i. 5, we are said to be ' kept through faith unto salvation.' If we were in any other grace's keeping, we were undone ; for how soon would all our love be non-plussed if that were the condition of the covenant ! How soon did all graces fail in Adam ! But faith is never non-plussed, it still trusts in God; and therefore above all armour else faith is commended, Eph. vi. 16, as that which stands us in stead when all else fail : ' above all, take the shield of faith.' When a man's head-piece is cracked, his shield will hold, and he will safely lie under it when all weapons else are taken from him. Let lusts, devil, hell do what they will, the believer is secure, if lusts rage ; whereas other graces left to themselves would say, ' Who shall deliver us ?' Faith raiseth up itself : ' I thank' (saith the apostle, Rom. vii. 25) 'my God through Jesus Christ,' &c. Let Satan roar and cast in fiery darts, faith quencheth them, Eph. vi. 16; we 'resist him, being stedfast in faith,' 1 Peter v. 9. Let God frown and terrify us, and do what he will, faith can look upon him and trust him, Job xiii. 15. Thus faith fights it out against all opposition. When a man comes to die, it is faith that resigns and delivers a man's soul into Christ's hands : ' These all died in faith,'

Heb. xi. 13; and salvation is therefore called 'the end of our faith,' 1 Peter i. 9.

2. All the works in the world cannot unite you to Christ, and enable you to lay hold on him and justification by him; this is faith's work alone. That ties the marriage-knot betwixt Christ and you, as nothing makes man and wife but consent; though there be love and kindness, yet that makes the match. So doth faith: Hosea ii. 20, 'I will betroth thee to me in faithfulness; and thou shalt know the Lord,' that is, believe in him; as Isa. liii. 11, 'By his knowledge he shall justify many.' Faith on our parts makes the match; therefore (John vi. 47 compared with all the following verses) Christ calls believing ' eating his flesh, and drinking his blood,' whereby we are as nearly joined to Christ as to the meat we eat. Now, though all the members in you serve to many good purposes, yet you can make meat only yours by eating it, and you have but one mouth to do it with, and no member else can let it down into your body to nourish it, so is there no grace can receive Christ but faith; no duty, no performance can help thee to him. It is true indeed the union on Christ's part is in order of nature first made by the Spirit; therefore, Philip. iii. 12, he is said first to ' comprehend us ere we can comprehend him;' yet that which makes the union on our part is faith, whereby we embrace and cleave to him, and come to have any communion with him; and it is faith alone that doth it. Love indeed makes us cleave to him also, but yet faith first, for faith works love; and we cannot love him till we believe he loves us, 1 John iv. 10, 16. And though love may cleave to him as to a lovely object in general, yet our union to him, as to a head and husband, offered to be ours, faith makes. Faith brings Christ into the heart, and then love clings to him, which else it could not do. We are united not on to Christ as good for us, but as given to us; now faith makes that union of receiving him as given, though love makes the other. All communion, too, that is between Christ and us is by faith; by it we draw near to him, Heb. x. 22, by it he reveals himself to us. All our fellowship with him is transacted by it; it is as the priest between Christ and us, that deals between us and him for us.

3. Faith makes things it believes real and present, and to subsist to the heart, and therefore it is called ' the subsistence of things hoped for,' Heb. xi. 1; and so causeth us to have a real communion and fellowship with the person of Christ daily, insomuch as Christ is said to ' dwell in our hearts by faith,' Eph. iii. 17; whereas, though a man loves many that are absent, let love cannot make them present to talk with them when he would, though it may make pictures of them, and so please itself in them, but faith makes Christ present.

4. Faith is that mother-grace which begets children on all graces, and stirs them up, and sets a-work. I will not say that the first act of faith begets the habits of all graces first; for ' he that believeth is born of God,' 1 John v. 1, and itself is a part of that image in righteousness begun. The opinion that the first habits of all graces should arise from faith, hath risen out of the experience godly men have had, that faith did first open the sluice, and set the wheel a-going, and stirred up their graces, which we attribute to faith most gladly. It is that grace that begins all the acts that are begotten on other graces, therefore it is said to ' work by love,' Gal. v. 6. I am sure it causeth the first love to God and Christ, for we cannot love him till he loves us; and as to all that obedience to God which love works in us, it is not love so much as faith that works by it; and in this sense it is said, James ii. 22, that ' faith worketh with works.' (1.) Faith lets in

all the strength we do all with : ' The life I lead,' says the apostle, Gal. ii. 20, ' it is by faith in the Son of God.' (2.) All the motives which influence us to work, faith sets on : ' That I should live to him,' says the apostle, ' who gave himself for me,' 2 Cor. v. 15, Gal. ii. 20. And 2 Cor. v. 14, 15, says he, ' The love of Christ constrains us :' but how ? ' because we thus judge' (by faith namely) ' that Christ died for us.' (3.) All acceptation of our works, when we have done them, are through faith, that stamps Christ's acceptation on them, mints them, and makes them current : Heb. xi. 6, ' Without faith it is impossible to please God ;' as faith justifies our person, so our works. (4.) When love, which is the fulfilling of the law, falls short, then faith hath recourse to a righteousness, which makes it up ; therefore, Rom. viii. 3, ' the righteousness of the law' is said to be ' fulfilled in us.' How ? Rom. x. 4, ' Christ is the end of the law to every one that believeth.'

5. Whatever works doth or can do, faith doth it much more. It may say as Paul said, in regard of the rest of the apostles, ' Are they apostles ? so am I, in labours more abundant ;' and yet says faith, ' I am nothing,' though I do all. Doth a man in working obey God ? In believing he doth much more, Rom. i. 5, Acts vi. 7. Doth works please him ? Faith much more, for it makes all accepted ; therefore in the Gospel Christ is taken with nothing but their faith still ; he still speaks of that, and in one place wonders and cries, ' Great is thy faith !' Do works increase sanctification ? Rom. vi. 22, ' Having your fruit in holiness,' &c. Faith doth it much more, it is the instrument by which the heart is purified, and faith doth it in a more nimble way, by going to Christ, Acts xv. Therefore, when the apostle would exhort them to grow in all grace, he exhorts them to grow in faith. Do works glorify God ? ' Let your works so shine before men, that they may glorify your heavenly father.' Faith doth it much more, Rom. iv. 20. Abraham ' was strong in faith, giving glory to God.' It sets up all his attributes, but especially free grace (for that faith only doth), which God ordained most to be admired, Eph. i. And as only faith glorifies that attribute, so faith only honours and magnifies Christ, and is created on purpose to do it. A few thoughts of faith glorify God more than a thousand acts of obedience. Yea, the greatest glory our obedience doth reflect upon God ariseth from this, that it proceeds out of faith, that we should trust God so far as to venture all our obedience beforehand : 1 Tim. iv. 10, ' Therefore we both labour and suffer reproach, because we trust in the living God.'

CHAPTER II.

The excellency of faith shewed in farther instances.—That it is ordained to give all the glory to God, and therefore God puts the greatest honour upon that above any other grace.

*That the trial of your faith, being much more precious than of gold that perisheth, though it be tried with fire, might be found unto praise, and honour, and glory, at the appearing of Jesus Christ.—*1 PET. I. 7.

The scope of the apostle (from the third verse) lies especially in three things. The 1st is to comfort them against afflictions, which is the general, which runs through all. And, 2dly, he doth that by setting out the greatness of salvation, which God hath appointed as the end of their faith, ver. 11.

3dly, His design is to commend and set out to them, that they might live by it, the excellency of that grace of faith, both as that which should keep them, as he saith, ver. 5, they are ' kept by the power of God through faith unto salvation ;' unto that salvation he had spoken of before, as likewise being that grace which bears the shock of all the trials and tentations which they run through in this world, and overcomes them all ; which grace, therefore, eminently above all else, shall be ' found unto praise, and honour, and glory, at the appearing of Jesus Christ.'

It is faith here he means that shall be ' found unto praise, and honour, and glory, at the appearing of Jesus Christ ;' for although he saith, ' The trial of your faith might be found unto praise,' &c., yet either first it is an Hebraism, trial of faith, that is, faith tried : or otherwise if you take it (as some), for the afflictions themselves that do try our faith, if they be so precious, much more precious than gold, then faith itself that is tried must needs be much more. If the fining pot and the furnace, as Solomon saith in the Proverbs, which doth try the gold and silver, and which is cast away when the gold is tried, be of such worth and excellency, then the gold and silver itself much more. But it is not afflictions or tentations that shall be found unto praise, and honour, and glory, at the latter day ; but it is faith being tried by all those, that shall then be found unto praise, and honour, and glory, and that shall be crowned by God, as of all graces the most glorious and the most eminent also. And because that this grace is a hidden grace, and the glory of its transactions are not seen (as an anchor under water), therefore he saith, ' It shall be found unto praise, and honour, and glory, at the appearing of Jesus Christ.'

Jesus Christ is the chief object of faith, and faith honoured him when he was not seen, as the text hath it here : ver. 8, ' Whom having not seen, ye love ; in whom, though now ye see him not, yet ye believe.' Because that faith honoured and trusted him thus when it saw him not, therefore will Jesus Christ, when he shall appear, honour this grace ; that is, he will acknowledge an honour to be in it, and give the crown of all that is in us, unto faith : ' It shall be found,' saith he, ' unto praise, and honour, and glory, at the appearing of Jesus Christ.' And although that faith shall cease then (as the apostle elsewhere tells us), as the pillar of the cloud, and the pillar of fire ceased when the people came out of the wilderness into Canaan, yet notwithstanding the glory of faith, and the fruit of faith, and the end of faith, and the crown that shall be given to faith, begins but then. It shall be found, viz., for its past service, ' unto praise, and honour, and glory, at the appearing of Jesus Christ.' Now then, having to myself and to you also proposed the handling of the doctrine of faith in all those particulars which are useful,—I have shewn you some of the acts of faith, and also the author of it, and what is done for you when you believe,—I shall in the next place come to shew you the excellency of this grace, and what a great deal of honour and glory there is in it, and shall be put upon it at the latter day. To manifest this unto you, let me lay this for a foundation, before I speak of that honour that God hath put upon it ; that of all graces else faith is the meanest and lowest, it is the poorest and the most nothing ; but God always takes things that are not, and he filleth the hungry, and sends the rich empty away ; he hath respect unto the low estate of this grace. It is in itself, I say, the poorest and the most beggarly grace of all other, if you compare it but with love, or with any else. It was love, whereby Adam was united unto God, and not faith, which was answerable to that covenant ; and love had something whereof to boast, but faith hath not ; for in loving we return something unto God, for we return love to him, we give him love for his love, although he loveth us first; we, I say, do return something unto him again; we give as well as take; but in believing we do nothing but receive from God. The promises are said to be 'given unto them that believe,' Gal. iii. 23, and ver. 14, to be 'received by faith.' Now you know what Christ himself said (it is a speech of his recorded in Acts xx. 35), 'It is more blessed to give than to receive.' So it is more honourable in itself to love God and to obey him, than merely to believe and to receive from him. But because God will not be beholden to the creature, and it shall never be said that any creature gave first to him, and was not recompensed again, hence therefore he hath taken faith, which of all graces else is the most empty (it is indeed nothing else but an open mouth for God to fill), and hath chosen to put glory upon it : ' Go ye,' says Christ, Mat. ix. 13, ' and learn what that meaneth, I will have mercy and not sacrifice.' I find by Christ's own alleging it, that this saying is used in a double sense, or a double meaning, as indeed many scriptures are so intended by the Holy Ghost ; either that God doth prefer mercy shewn by a man to himself, or by one man to another, before sacrifice to himself (and so it is urged, Mat. xii. 7, upon an occasion of the Pharisees murmuring at the disciples plucking the ears of corn on the Sabbath day), or else Christ meant (which indeed is the scope of Mat. ix. 13, comparing it with Hosea vi. 6, out of which Christ quotes it) to shew that God delights in his own shewing mercy more than in all our sacrifices, and that he delights more in our knowing him to be merciful and to be gracious, which indeed is seen in our believing on him, than in all our obedience which we perform to him. And that this is Christ's meaning is plain, for he speaks in the verse before of his own saving that which is lost, and of being a physician to them that are sick : ' They that be whole,' saith he, ver. 12, ' need not a physician, but they that are sick.' And then he presently adds, ' But go ye and learn what that meaneth, I will have mercy and not sacrifice ;' that is, I that am the Son of the great God, that am the Messiah, delight rather in being a physician, in healing, in shewing mercy to poor souls, than in all obedience as from you. And in Hosea vi. 6 this is also added : ' I desire the knowledge of God more than burnt-offerings.' What is it in us that in us answers to mercy and grace in God? It is faith, it is the knowledge of him. You must know that the Old Testament useth much the phrase of knowing for believing: as in Isa. liii., ' By his knowledge shall he justify many;' and Jer. ix. 23, ' Let him glory in this, that he knoweth me which exercise loving-kindness in the earth.' Now then here is the sum of this text, that God is more pleased, infinitely more pleased, thus in giving, in pouring forth his grace upon us, in shewing mercy to us, than he is with all our sacrifices, or whatever else we offer to him ; and therefore answerably he is more pleased with our knowing of him to be gracious and merciful, and so in believing on him (for this knowledge doth in the law of it always contain suitable affections to God, and is the principle of all in us), than with all burnt-offerings. The least thing that God could have required of you, the meanest act upon his being merciful to you is this : do but know that I am merciful, do but believe it, do but rely upon it. The apostle, in 1 Cor. i. 30, saith, that God ' made Jesus Christ unto us to be wisdom, and righteousness, and sanctification, and redemption.' To what end ? ' That according as it is written,' saith he, ' he that glorieth, let him glory in the Lord.' Now where is this written ? It is in Jer. ix. 24, ' Let him that glorieth, glory in this, that he understandeth and knoweth me, that I am the Lord which exercise loving-kindness in the earth ;' which brings us to the point in hand ; and it is as if he had said, I will give you leave to glory in your faith if you will. Why? Because your faith it is merely knowing how good I am; so that when you glory in your faith, in your knowing of me, which exercise loving-kindness in the earth, the truth is, you glory in the Lord, for so you see the apostle interprets it. It is but as if God should say this, I am thus great and glorious, a God that exercise loving-kindness, and delight more in shewing mercy than in all I receive from you, only I desire to have this mercy apprehended and believed by you. And when the creature comes to apprehend God to be thus merciful, it excludes all boasting, the very law of this knowledge doth, because it is suited to its object; it gives all honour to that God whom it knows to be thus gracious, it admires and adores him for it. Faith, my brethren, it is a passion, it is not an action, therefore it is compared to seeing the Son; now take the sense of seeing, and *fit intramittendo, non extramittendo*, it is done by receiving something in, not by sending anything out. The eye sees by receiving, by taking in the beams of the light, or by taking in the image of the colours from the object, irradiated by the light, and not by sending forth a light of itself; and so indeed is faith. Therefore it is that God hath chosen faith, because it is, if I may so express it, a mere passive grace. We shall know God by vision hereafter, and we know God by faith here; and both are parallel in this, that as heaven is but knowing God as we are known, it is but seeing his glory, and so being glorified thereby, as it is in John xvii. 24; so faith is but a knowing of God, and a giving glory to him, according to that knowledge of him, drawing on the whole heart answerably to live unto him. Saith Paul in Gal. iv. 9, 'You have known God, or rather, are known of God.' Mark how he diminisheth and draws down even faith itself as low as possible. He seemed as if he would have put something upon our knowledge of God when he had said, 'You have known God,' but he takes away what he gives: 'You are rather known of God,' saith he. So that our knowing God hath nothing to commend itself at all, for it is a mere receiving, it hath nothing to glory in itself, no, not as it is knowledge, but from its object; for the thing it labours to apprehend, it is to be 'known of God.' The honour and glory of this grace I shall shew you by demonstrating two things.

1. The honour which this grace is ordained to give to God.

2. The use and hand it hath in our salvation. God honours it for both; for God hath a respect to both these.

1. To demonstrate the honour which this grace is ordained to give to God, I shall premise, that whatsoever honours God most, certainly God will honour that most. It is the rule that God himself gives in 1 Sam. ii. 30. Therefore if that this grace shall be 'found unto honour and glory at the appearing of Christ,' it must be upon this ground, because it hath given most honour and glory unto God; for, saith he, 'Them that honour me, I will honour.'

(1.) Take faith in the general nature of it. God hath appointed this grace to be the universal receiver, as I may so express it, of all the revelation of his glory which he dispenseth unto mankind in this world. Look what the eye and light is to this whole creation, this visible frame of heaven and earth, and all the glories that God hath stamped upon it, that is the light of the Spirit and faith in the heart of a believer to all those glorious things in the new creation, in that new world which God hath revealed in the gospel, which the gospel is the map of. All those things which are there revealed, they are all taken in universally, and apprehended by this grace of faith. God having made this glorious frame of heaven and earth, if he had not made also an eye to have seen all this, all that he had done

had been in a manner lost, in respect of his end in it. So is it in this
new world, which Ps. viii. speaks of; saith the psalmist there (speaking
indeed of the gospel, and of the things of the gospel, and of Christ, as the
apostle interprets it in Heb. ii.), in allusion unto man's contemplating the
heavens, the moon, and the stars, and the like, ' When I consider thy
heavens, the work of thy fingers, the moon and the stars which thou hast
ordained.' How comes he to consider all these? Because he hath an eye
to see all these, which doth let in the knowledge of all these into his mind.
If a man's body had not had this small member, the eye, he could not take
into his consideration at all the heavens, or the moon and stars, &c. So
it is here; God hath made a new world, whereof Jesus Christ is the sun,
and he hath made a whole new creation, ' a new creature,' and revealed a
world of glorious truths, which have infinitely more harmony in them
than there is in the old creation, and the law thereof. Now this
little eye of faith, which God creates in the soul, and the light thereof, is
that which takes in all these, without which the glory of all these would be
lost. Therefore we are said to ' behold the glory of the Lord,' in 2 Cor.
iii. 18. And as the eye is a mighty large sense, of a most large comprehension,—you see it can run up to heaven presently, it can go from east to
west, and take in half the heavens at once,—so is faith in the soul; it doth
draw in God and all his beams, draws in Christ and all his glory through
a narrow cranny. Faith is a strange grace, for it doth in this partake of
divinity itself. For wherein lies the excellency of God's knowledge? His
omniscience lies in this, that all things past, present, and to come, are
present to him. Faith doth this too; it doth not only take them all in,
but makes them all present. ' Abraham saw my day, and rejoiced,' saith
Christ in John viii. 56. And Heb. ii. 9, ' We see Jesus crowned with
glory and honour.' Faith makes all God's decrees from everlasting, and
the day of judgment, and life to come, present to the soul; it makes Christ
hanging upon the cross present. This is that grace which hath therefore a
kind of a participation of divinity and omnisciency in it. It is the universal
receiver of all that glory which God himself revealeth unto mankind.

(2.) I might shew you, that God hath made this grace an adequate
instrument to honour and glorify his free grace by all the ways he would
have it glorified; and to honour and glorify Jesus Christ in all ways that
he would be glorified. Free grace in God himself, and in Jesus Christ,
who is God's servant, and faith in us, these three are a measure adequate
one to another, and in God's ordination ordained to glorify each other.
As Jesus Christ did fully glorify free grace, and all the attibutes of God
besides, and served free grace in its own way, so hath God appointed
faith such a principle in the soul, as to apply itself to glorify free grace and
Christ, to their full satisfaction, and to detract nothing from them.

(3.) Hence it is that God is not regardful, is not shy to put this grace
in commission with Christ and with himself, and with all his own attributes.
He glorifies it so much, because indeed it glorifieth him. It sets all the
attributes of God on work, and it is said to do all that those attributes do,
and all that God himself doth. It sets the power of God on work, and
then it glorifies his power. It is said of Abraham, Rom. iv. 20, 21, that
he ' being strong in faith, gave glory to God.' And what was it he gave
God the glory of? ' He was fully persuaded that what he had promised,
he was able also to perform.' It was a persuasion which gave this glory to
him, and it was a persuasion of the power of God in God for the raising up
of Isaac. Hereby now he gave glory to God; yea, hence, because without
faith God should lose his glory, therefore the want of it puts a stop to his

attributes in their working. As faith sets all the attributes of God on work, so it doth give them scope, vent, and time, as we say, that without it they will not work, they will do nothing. It is said, Mat. xiii. 58, that when Christ came to Nazareth, ' he did not many mighty works there, because of their unbelief.' Faith holds the arm of God's wrath, and of his justice, and it lets loose the arm of his power, and wieldeth and manageth all that is in God ; and God he is not shy to attribute all to faith that he himself doth. You shall find this in many instances in Scripture. Take that memorable place in Acts iii. 16, see how strangely he speaks there ; ' Know,' saith he, ' that his name, through faith in his name, hath made this man strong, whom you see and know.' You see here that he putteth his name, and faith in his name, both into commission together for the making this man strong ; and his name is all his attributes, his mercy, and his goodness, and his power, and whatsoever else was employed in doing that great miracle to this poor man. And here now is the reason also couched why that God is not jealous to put faith into commission with his own name, because that faith gives all to his name again, it gives all to God. Faith, if it be genuine, will not rob Christ a whit ; therefore in the Scripture you shall find, that what faith is said to do, Christ is said to do, to save, and to justify, and to sanctify, &c.

The Scripture calls the righteousness of Christ the righteousness of faith, and the reason is this, because it is all one in respect of the soul's account, which truly believeth, and it is all one in God's account. It is all one in the soul's account to say that God doth it, and Christ doth it, and faith doth it, because the law of faith, the genius of faith, the form of faith, lies in this, in attributing all to God, and all to Christ, and nothing to itself. While God doth all upon believing, faith attributes all to him ; it is not faith else, for it is the genuine property of faith so to do : Gal. ii. 20, ' The life which I now live in the flesh, I live by the faith of the Son of God.' But mark 'how he diminisheth it : ' Nevertheless I live ; yet not I, but Christ liveth in me.' Faith still comes in with, ' It is not I,' even then when all is attributed unto it. It is its essential property so to do, and to give all unto God. Thus it doth in the soul's account. And thereupon in God's account it is all one too. You shall find that Christ seems careless what he attributes to faith. The truth is, this grace trusteth Christ, and Christ trusts this grace with all ; for he knew that when he attributed anything to faith, he closely attributed it altogether to himself. It were a strange thing to hear that faith should be made omnipotent, that you should make another God of it as it were (as I told you even now it was made omniscient, because it maketh all things present to it), which is only attributed to God, Matt. xix. 26, that ' with him all things are possible ;' and Christ (Mark xiv. 36) makes it a property of God only, ' Father,' saith he, ' all things are possible unto thee.' Were it not blasphemy now to say of any creature, or of any man, that all things are possible to him ? When Christ, in like manner, took on him to forgive sins, in Matt. ix. 3, they quarrelled with him, ' This man blasphemeth,' say they ; ' who can forgive sins but God only ? ' But now you shall find in plain words in Scripture (even of Christ himself, who hath said it, Mark ix. 23), that ' all things are possible to him that believeth ;' it is, you see, the very same phrase that is used concerning God himself. I need not to tell you that you are saved by faith, and that you live by faith, and are justified by faith : no, what is said of God is said also of faith. And when Christ saith that all things are possible to him that believeth, it is as if he had said, All things are possible to me ; because the grace he ascribes all this to gives all unto God again, it only apprehends the power of God, is but persuaded that God is able, and so resteth upon it; this is faith. Christ, when he had done a miracle, when he had saved a man's soul, when he himself was present in it, yet he would seem to put it off from himself, and to put it upon the man's faith: 'Thy faith hath saved thee,' and 'Thy faith hath made thee whole,' and the like. Had these speeches been spoken to any other grace, had he said it to humility itself, it would have made it proud; but because he speaks it to faith, which still comes in with '*It is not I*,' and that God doth all, and though I live by faith, yet it is the Son of God that liveth in me, and doth but merely know God, and take in what is in God, and what is in Christ, and sets all these a-work, so long faith is still nothing. Though as Paul said of himself, that he did more than all the apostles, so though this grace doth more than all graces else, more than the angels in heaven, yet notwithstanding 'I am nothing,' saith the poor soul, 'I have done nothing,' 'It is not I, but the grace of God that is in me,' And because that faith doth thus glorify God in this high and transcendent manner, by giving all to him, hence it is that God puts so much honour and glory upon it; and it will be found even thus high 'unto praise, and honour, and glory, at the appearing of Jesus Christ.' And therefore when we exhort you to believe, what do we exhort you to? To set up Jesus Christ in your hearts, to set him up a throne there, to ascribe all to him, and to go out to him for all, and to set up God in your hearts, and to attribute all to him, to make him and Jesus Christ all in all. This is that is done when we exhort you to believe. So that there is no danger in commending this thing to you, for the very nature, the very law of the grace itself, if right and true faith, is to empty the creature of all, and to give all unto God.

CHAPTER III.

The excellence of faith, in that it is most active, and hath the greatest influence in the whole course of our salvation from first to last.

2. This grace will be found of all other unto honour and glory at the appearing of Christ, if we respect man's salvation. This I shall make forth to you by running over some particulars. I will not stand to shew you the excellency of faith in this respect, that if there be any condition of the covenant of grace, faith alone is it (as our divines speak), and it is that alone that God requires, but I say I will not stand upon that; only this is it that I will hold forth to you, that this grace is that which carries the soul on from first to last, and never ceaseth till it hath brought it to salvation. In this little poor brittle vessel God hath ventured the blood of Christ, ventured in it the souls of his redeemed, the dwelling of his Holy Spirit, and all the works of the Spirit; they are all in this brittle vessel through the power of the Holy Ghost acting the soul by it, to set the soul safe on shore in the other world; and it ceaseth not, I say, till it hath carried the soul to Christ, and put it immediately into his hands. It begins all, and it endeth all, manageth all till the soul comes to heaven. I say in this life, my brethren, there are two principles of life to mankind, as there is of life and nourishment to the sons of men: the one is in the womb by the navel-string, by which it takes in all its nourishment then. But no sooner is it out of the womb, and cometh into the world, but it hath another principle to take in nourishment by, and then the other is cut off, and is of no use. So it is here; there are two principles we are to live by for evermore; there is faith, which is a seeing of Christ absent, and there is vision, which is seeing of

him present in heaven. We are here in this world as children in the womb, in comparison of the other; and the glory of the other differs from that we have here, as much as the glory of the king upon his throne, from what he was in the womb. Now all the while we are here, it is this principle of faith that we live by, which is as the navel-string to convey nourishment to us; but when faith hath performed all its offices, and we are grown up ' unto a perfect man, unto the measure of the stature of the fulness of Christ,' which is for heaven, then the soul is carried into the other eternal world, and then indeed faith ceaseth, and the soul lives by vision. Faith is both nurse, and midwife, and all, to the soul, both for the beginning and carrying on, and doing all, till you come to the other world. I shall run over some particulars to manifest this to you.

(1.) It is faith that prepares the soul for Christ. A man's conscience may be first set a-work in the sight of sin, set upon by all, and they may humble him, and bring him down very low; but that which strikes the great stroke in preparing you for Christ is the taking you off for ever from all abilities, and from whatsoever is in yourselves, and out of that emptiness to go to Jesus Christ. Now it is faith only that doth this; that only is the emptying grace which is the filling grace of Christ. Though the Spirit begins upon a man's conscience first, yet it is faith that perfects that work of making you nothing, and then it comes and raiseth you up to all things in Christ. Now as it is a rule, both in the law of nature and of common-wealths, that it is the same power must make void a law that makes a law, the same power that creates must annihilate and bring to nothing, so it is the same faith that brings the soul to nothing, and empties it of itself, and of all things else, and that brings it unto Jesus Christ, and fills it with the fulness that is in him. It is all but faith digging downward, and working upward. In John xvi. 8, it is said, ' The Spirit shall convince the world of sin, and of righteousness.' The thing I quote it for is this, the word there that is translated ' convince,' is the same that is used in the definition of faith in Heb. xi. 2. You know faith there is called ' the evidence of things not seen;' the word is ἔλεγχος, *conviction*, the same that Christ useth here when he saith, ' The Spirit shall *convince* the world of sin;' that is, he shall work faith in them to see their lost condition ultimately. The same spirit of faith and conviction that convinceth me of righteousness, convinceth me of my lost condition; and therefore he adds, if you mark it, ' Because ye believe not on me;' for that is the ultimate conviction that prepares a man for Christ. To take a man off of his own bottom, to make him see that he hath no ability to believe in Christ of himself, this faith doth; and having done thus, convinces a man of his lost condition ultimately. What is the reason the first promise is made to poverty of spirit by Christ, in Mat. v. 3 ? Certainly in poverty of spirit there he includes faith, and Christ would not have pronounced a blessed-ness but upon forgiveness of sins, and that is upon believing; yet it is eminently denominated poverty, because it is a work of faith, as making the soul poor. It is faith only that makes a man fling away his own right-eousness, and to count it dross and dung, as you have it in Phil. iii., and to lay hold upon the righteousness of the Lord Jesus. It is faith that ultimately strikes that great stroke in preparation so much spoken of ; and truly other preparation will not drive a man to Christ.

(2.) And then when the soul is thus ultimately emptied by faith, and is lost, it is faith that first spies out Christ, as that all-sufficient satisfaction received by God the Father. When the soul is in a storm, and is even cast away in his own apprehension, when it hath thrown overboard all his own goods, all his own righteousness, all his own hopes, all his own abilities, or whatever it be, and if God should leave the soul in that condition, the wrath of God, like mighty waves, would break in upon it, and swallow it up. What doth faith now? It climbs up to the top of the mast. Oh there is Christ, I have spied out the Lord Jesus, and it makes out to him instantly, gets aboard of him presently. Therefore now the entrance into the state of grace is attributed unto faith, in Rom. v. 1, ' We have access by faith into this grace wherein we stand.'

(3.) Then again, though there is a radical union that we have with Jesus Christ, without all preparation, for he takes us before we take him, yet notwithstanding, all the communion we have with Jesus Christ is transacted by faith. The union, on our part, is mainly and primarily by faith : it is that which, on our part, ties the marriage knot; it is not love, but consent, that makes man and wife. It is the heart's coming off to be Christ's, and going unto Christ to be his, and to be righteousness for him, and to be a head and a Saviour to him ; this is it which makes a union, and this is done by faith. There are but two things that do marry us unto Christ, as Hos. ii. 19 clearly holds forth : ' I will betroth thee unto me in faithfulness and in loving-kindness ;' that is now on God's part. But what is on our part? It follows : ' and thou shalt know the Lord.' There are but these two things make the match. Here is the faithfulness and loving-kindness of God on his part ; and then here is on our part, ' You shall know the Lord.' I opened that before out of Jer. ix. I need not stand to repeat it, for in the Old Testament you shall find that faith is expressed, as there, by our knowing of God, who exerciseth loving-kindness in the earth. Now though that love doth unite too, for the soul is united to what it loves by love, yet it is faith that brings Jesus Christ into the heart, and reveals him to the soul in all his excellencies and his glory. We apprehend his love first, or his excellencies first, how lovely he is, even before love unites the soul to him. So that faith is first, and though that love may unite us to him, as for the excellencies in his person, yet take him as he is a mystical head, and as a husband, and a husband given, so it is faith that goes out to him as such, and goes out to him with an instinct after mystical union with him.

(4.) And then, all fellowship and communion with him, to be sure, is by faith. Unto all communion and fellowship with another, there are two things required. The first is, to make that person real and present ; and the second is, to have a familiar bold access. Now it is faith only that doth both these things to us, and therefore it is faith that lays the foundation for all the fellowship and communion that we have with the Father and with the Son, the which the apostle John so much commendeth. First, it is faith only that makes God and Christ present, that so we may have fellowship with them, for we only have fellowship with those that are some way or other present to our spirits. It is not love that makes another present ; it may set the fancy on work to make pictures of the party absent, but it is divine faith alone that hath the art to make God and Jesus Christ present. It ' sees God that is invisible,' &c., causeth God to dwell in the heart, and bringeth Christ down from heaven, and causeth him to dwell in the heart. There is no more of God to my soul than that which by faith it takes in of him ; therefore wicked men are said to be without God and without Christ in the world, for so far is God and Christ got into a man's soul, as he by faith sees him, and takes in the knowledge of him, and takes him in so really, as love could not make that reality ; it may set the fancy on work, as I said, to make pictures in the fancy and to talk of him, but the party is not there present, so as faith makes God and Christ to be to the soul. And then again, it is faith that makes us familiar with God: all our ' access with boldness' it is ' by the faith of him,' as Eph. iii. 12 hath it ; ' beholding him with open face,' we come to him with open face, with confidence and boldness. The communion we have by faith with Christ, is often compared unto eating and drinking, as in John vi. 46. It is so for the reality of it : ' My flesh is meat indeed,' saith he. Now a man hath many members in his body, but he hath communion with his meat no way but by his mouth and stomach, and indeed he can have it no way else : the hand takes it, the eye sees it, and the like, but unless the mouth and stomach receive it, the man starves still. Faith alone is that which takes Jesus Christ to fetch nourishment from him, makes a man find the sweetness that is in him, and draws virtue from him, makes my soul in this respect one with him, and he with me.

(5.) And then all the joy we have in Jesus Christ, it is through believing : Rom. xv. 13, that you may be ' filled with all joy and peace through believing.' In John iv. 14, unto him that believeth there is promised a fountain of living water, springing up in his own heart, which faith is indeed the fountain of, for you see it is to him that believeth. He that believeth hath the witness in himself, hath the fountain of all joy in himself ; so the next words to the text, ' In whom believing, ye rejoice with joy unspeakable and full of glory.'

And thus, as it brings us into communion with Christ, so it brings the Spirit also down into the heart. I acknowledge that the Holy Ghost comes down without all preparation upon a man's heart, for how else is a man prepared but by the Holy Ghost, when he comes to convert a man ? Yet there is a coming of the Holy Ghost down upon a man's soul upon believing. The great promise of the Holy Ghost, which the New Testament so much speaks of, to seal a man up to salvation, to give a man fellowship with the Father and with the Son, which was the great coming down of the Holy Ghost you read of in the primitive times in respect of grace,—he came upon men in respect of gifts, but that is nothing to salvation,—but that great promise of sending down the Holy Ghost to seal up a man's salvation, and to give him communion with God the Father, and with Jesus Christ, and to fill him with the fulness of God, the coming of the Holy Ghost to this purpose we receive by faith. The text is express for it, Gal. iii. 14, ' That we might receive the promise of the Spirit through faith.' And that is the reason, I take it, that in John xiv. 17, Christ speaking of that coming of the Holy Ghost upon the apostles, he tells them that they had him already, they had him so far as to enable them to believe : ' He dwelleth with you,' saith he ; but there was a farther having of him as a Comforter. Now he tells them there, that the world cannot receive that Spirit, because it seeth him not, neither knoweth him. I take it the meaning may be this, that the world cannot receive the Holy Ghost to come thus as a comforter, as a sealer, which is the thing promised there to the disciples, till such time as a man knows and sees, that is, believes. For otherwise, if this were true, that no man could receive the Holy Ghost till he knoweth him and seeth him, I would ask, How comes a man unconverted (as all once are) to know him and see him, and to see Christ ? By faith, that must be acknowledged. And who works this faith ? The Holy Ghost certainly. Therefore there is a receiving of the Holy Ghost, as a comforter and as a sealer, upon believing.

And then I might likewise shew you, that all our standing in grace is by faith. Rom. v. 2, ' By whom we have access by faith into the grace wherein we stand;' and stand by faith, for as we have access into the grace by faith, so we stand by it too. And in the words a little before the text, we are said to be 'kept by the power of God through faith unto salvation.' Mark it, faith is joined there in commission with the power of God. Doth the power of God keep you? Faith keepeth you too. And as I said before, God is not shy of attributing that to faith which is proper only to himself, because faith attributes all to the power of God, and gives that the honour. But I say, we are kept through faith; for, my brethren, if the way of our being kept were by other graces, we were in a miserable case, we should be at a loss ever and anon; but faith is never nonplussed. Adam did not live by faith, and what then? He had no access into the grace in which he stood, no, in which he fell rather; but 'by faith we have access into the grace wherein we stand.' Faith it stands, and stands out all storms, as I may express it to you. Whenas waves are ready to overwhelm the soul, what doth faith? It leads a man to the Rock that is higher than he, as the psalmist hath it, Ps. lxi. 2. All a man's other graces are but like quicksands: if he stand upon them, he is soon swallowed up. It is faith that carries the soul to Christ, who is the rock, and upon whom, when the soul hath set its footing, it standeth sure. If the soul be in any disquietness, what recovers it? It is faith. 'Why art thou cast down, O my soul? and why art thou disquieted within me? Trust thou in God,' Ps. xlii. 5. There is the remedy. Be you in any great tentation, if you can but get to believe, and to see God and Christ, so as that by faith he become but present to your spirits, and that you can see that in him that draws your hearts to rest upon him, your tentation is gone presently; it is impossible that any man can be miserable if he believe. 'Thou wilt keep him in perfect peace whose mind is stayed on thee.' It is a famous place that in Isa. xxvi. 3. And how is the mind stayed on God? By faith. If a man be fallen, what reduceth him again? It is faith. If you let go your faith when you fall into sin, you will fall down to the bottom; as when a man is going up a ladder, if his foot slip, and he let go his hands, what can hinder him from falling to the ground? When Christ foresaw that Peter would sin against him, what said he? 'I have prayed that thy faith fail not.' If thy faith fail not, that will recover all again. 'If any man sin,' saith the apostle, 'we have an advocate with the Father.' Let him go to Jesus Christ, and begin to recover himself by faith, and then let him mourn for sin, &c. Renew thy faith, and thou renewest all. It is faith that bears the brunt of all tentations. When all other graces are under hatches, and dare not look out, faith will be above board, and steer the ship still. 'Above all, take the shield of faith,' saith the apostle. A shield, you know, stands a man in stead when his sword is gone, and when his helmet is cracked; and when all his other armour is gone, he may lie safely under his shield, for that used to cover the whole man. It is faith that can deal with the wrath and anger of God, and with all the fiery darts of Satan, and makes a man, when he hath done all, to stand; so the expression is in Eph. vi. Other graces in such a case, poor things, they will all stand trembling, and cry out, 'Who shall deliver us?' But faith says, 'I thank my God, through Jesus Christ,' he is he that will deliver me. And it quencheth all the fiery darts of Satan too. We may in this case speak of faith, as the Scripture speaks of God in Isa. lix. 16, 'He saw that there was no man, and wondered that there was no intercessor; therefore his arm brought salvation.' Indeed faith is the arm of the Lord, and that brings salvation to us, when all other graces are at a loss. It is faith which can bear out conflicts with God himself. This was it that bore Christ

upon the cross, and enabled him to say, ' My God, my God,' when God
had forsaken him.   And when God seems to be a man's enemy, and to
fight against him, he secretly upholds faith within him to stand it out :
' Though he kill me,' saith Job, ' yet will I trust in him,' Job xiii. 15.
And when God, who is greater than our heart, and is able to condemn us,
and when conscience, that hath so much guilt laid up in it, is against us,
then can faith have access with boldness unto the throne of grace ; or at
leastwise the soul thereby is enabled to trust in God.

I should shew you here likewise, that faith is the mother of all graces ;
and when I say so, my meaning is not, as some have said, that all habits
of sanctification, and of all graces, they are wrought upon us after faith,
and after the act of believing.   No ; ' he that believeth, he is born of God,'
John v. 3 ;* and faith itself is a part of the new creature, which God
works in us.   But though it be not the mother of all the habits of grace in us,
which are all wrought in the whole lump at first ; and though God draws faith
out first, yet it is that grace that sets all other graces a-work, that sets all
wheels a-going.   When God hath drawn out faith to lay hold upon Christ,
then it works by love, it is faith that then goes out for strength in Christ,
that manageth all motives to move to obedience, and to live to him that
died for me.   It is faith that fetcheth all acceptation for every work we
do ; ' without faith it is impossible to please God.'   As faith justifies the
person, so it justifieth, and (as Luther was wont to say) it fulfils the whole
law in Christ.   Why ?   Because I have recourse to Christ, which hath a
righteousness beyond mine, and it throws away its own righteousness :
therefore it is called ' the end of the law to him who believeth,' Rom. x.,
that is, the perfection of the law.

I might shew you also, that it overcomes the world, it overcomes all
the good of the world, and all the evil of the world ; and likewise how it
sweeteneth all crosses.   It overcomes all the good things of the world.   So
Heb. xi. 13, Moses, by faith, ' seeing him that was invisible,' forsook
Egypt, and ' refused to be called the son of Pharaoh's daughter.'   It brings
in objects so strong, so vigorous, so transcendently glorious into the soul,
that it mastereth reason, and sense, and lusts, and all.   It overcomes the
evil of the world : Heb. xi. 33, ' Through faith they subdued kingdoms,
stopped the mouths of lions, quenched the violence of fire, escaped the
edge of the sword,' &c. ; 2 Tim. i. 12, ' Therefore I also suffer these things :
for I know whom I have believed, and am persuaded he is able to keep
that I have committed to him.'

And when you come to die (let me but add that), it must be by faith ;
faith, as it begins all, so it ends all.   It is that which must stand you in stead
when that king of terrors environs you.   It is not your own graces that
will help you ; but if thy soul hath been familiar with God by faith (for
there is a familiarity grows upon God by exercising acts of faith towards God),
faith will resign up the soul immediately into the hands of God and Christ
with boldness.   ' Lord,' saith he, ' into thy hands I commend my spirit.'
That very speech was the voice of faith, and it was the greatest trust that
ever was.   ' These all died in faith,' saith he in Heb. xi., and therefore
salvation is called ' the end of our faith,' in this Epistle, chap. i. ver. 9.

I shall in a word make a use of it, and so conclude.   And the use is but
plainly this, to pitch your hearts upon seeking that at the hands of God
and of Jesus Christ, and upon exercising that especially which will most be
found unto the glory of God in you, and most to honour and glory unto

* This is a mis-quotation.   In 1 John iv. 7, we read, ' Every one that loveth is
born of God.'—Ed.

you also, at the appearing of Jesus Christ, and that is this grace of faith. There is no grace glorifies God so much as this ; a few thoughts of believing glorify him much more than a great deal of obedience. This will be found at the latter day. If you find that this grace hath not sprung up in you, or abounded in you, seek unto God that this grace of all graces else may abound ; and to that end I have set out the excellency of faith to you. It is the great work of God ; so Christ said when they asked him, what they should do that they might work the works of God ? ' This,' saith he, ' is the work of God, that ye believe on him whom he hath sent.' Our Saviour Christ, when the apostles said unto him, ' Lord, increase our faith,' Luke xvii. 5, he did presently on purpose fall on the commending it yet more to them, and setting out the excellency of faith, and told them what great things it could and would do, to the end he might make them inflamed yet more after believing, and that their hearts might be set yet more upon endeavouring after it. You say well, saith he, to say, ' Lord, increase our faith ;' for of all graces else it is good to seek the increase of that, because it is such a grace as can do all things, that can set on work all that is in God, and set a-work likewise all other graces.

CHAPTER IV.

How good works are not slighted by exalting faith alone to have an interest in our justification.

The second thing which I propounded, was to invalidate a false corollary, that corrupt minds are apt to deduce from our putting so much of the power of godliness to faith, and attributing so much to it, as that it should be the sole instrument of justification, of union on our parts, and communion with Christ, and more to be looked out for than all works else. Hence men take occasion to think, that inherent holiness and obedience issuing thence, are hereby slighted, and that this tends to have works of holiness neglected. But for answer,

1. As for slighting of works and inward holiness, we are bold to profess, that take faith when it beholds with open face the glory of Christ, who is the desire and delight of faith's eye, and when it is a-viewing over the beauty of Christ from top to toe, and every part of his righteousness wrought for it and imputed to it ; and then when it casts its eye upon its own inherent holiness wrought in itself, and all the good works of holiness wrought by itself, which to eternity it shall be enabled to do, it will think meanly of them all. Yea, if the rich and glorious righteousness of all the angels in heaven should offer to present itself to a believer's thoughts with a supposed imagined offer of exchange, it will and doth slight them all in comparison of this of Christ's, which faith hath in its eye. As the sun puts out the lesser stars, so doth the righteousness of this Sun put out the glory of the obedience of all the morning stars, saints and angels. What says Paul, Phil. iii. 8, 9, when faith is broad awake, and the Sun of righteousness arisen on him ? Then he accounts all the righteousness and conformity to the law but as dung and dross, which our divines interpret rightly of his righteousness and works done after conversion as well as before. ' But what' (says Bellarmine) ' doth he account the fruits of the Spirit, which are for God's relish, and pleasing to him ? doth he call these dog's meat ? It is a blasphemy to do so, if that be his meaning.' But take these two things with you, and you will not say so : 1st, That it is

but a comparative contempt, not simply ; he slights indeed his own righteousness, but how ? For the super-excellent knowledge of Christ Jesus my
Lord, and in comparison of winning Christ, and being found in him, which
faith can only help you to.   And he not only slights but also renounceth
his own righteousness for the righteousness of faith, that is, the righteousness that faith hath in its eye and keeping, not his own.   And in this
manner (comparatively, namely), we find Paul seeming to slight the law.
It would stumble a man to hear how he speaks of it, as when he calls it
' a schoolmaster' and ' a prison,' Gal. iii. 23, 24 ; and ' beggarly weak elements,' Gal. iv. 9 ; ' the ministry of death,' 2 Cor. iii. 7 ; and ' engendering
to bondage,' Gal. iv. 34.   But these were spoken but comparatively to the
glorious things that are revealed in the gospel, not simply, for otherwise
he commends the law as ' holy and good,' Rom. vii. 12, as ' ordained for
life,' ver. 10. ' The law is good,' says he, ' if a man use it lawfully,'
1 Tim. i. 8.   But if they would set it in competition with the gospel, then
it is Paul slights it ; and though he says that in itself it is glorious, 2 Cor.
iii. 7, yet says he, in comparison with the gospel, the ministration of
righteousness, it loseth its lustre, and hath no glory in this respect, by
reason of this glory that excelleth, ver. 10.   And, 2dly, this is only in the
point of justification, and in relation thereunto.   If the statute law offers to
be brought into that court, or works be impleaded there, then faith casts
them out with indignation.   If they will stand at the bar and give in witness, they may be heard, and their witness is not slighted ; but if they
would have a hand in the sentence of justification, then they are cried
down, and bidden to stand by, and hear faith alone to plead a man's case.
    2. Then a thing is slighted, when the respect that is due to it is not
given it ; but when more than is due is denied, it is not slighted.   A man
slights not an inferior magistrate if he gives him not the honour due unto
a king, nor a king if he gives him not the spiritual honour due to a minister.
As the priests slighted not the king when they drove him out of the temple,
and denied him to offer sacrifice, so we slight not works nor inward holiness, if we attribute not that to them which God is pleased to attribute to
faith, or to Christ rather (for faith is but Christ's instrument to glorify
himself by), if we say they cannot help to justify or unite to Christ ; nay,
if when they will presume to do faith's office, we slight them not if we drive
them out of the court, for all honour that is due to these in their places we
give to them.   Indeed, because love had once the honour to unite us to
God as the primary and immediate tie of union, and works had the prerogative of justifying,—' Do this, and thou shalt live,'—therefore, they are apt
to look for the same respect still ; but sin broke the covenant of works,
and made void that covenant, and then God put these out of commission,
and out of these great offices, and substituted faith ; and if they will be
content with their places, and give Christ and free grace the throne, they
shall have honour enough under him.   We will acknowledge the new creature to be worth all the creatures else ; and though the soul be more worth
than a world, yet inward holiness in the soul is worth all men's souls
devoid of it, though but an accident ; and so, though a logician would
reckon it less worth than the meanest substance, yet a poor soul and a
believer esteems it more worth than millions of worlds, and thinks a dram
of grace, a shred of this, in value above all rubies, as Solomon speaks.
Yea, and if they could be severed (as yet in imagination and supposition
they may), grace is more worth than superadded glory, and a Christian
prizeth it, values it more than simply happiness.   Glory is the embroidery
of grace, and the stuff is of more worth than this embroidery, if they could

be severed ; yea, indeed, grace itself is glory, 2 Cor. iii. 18. It is the image of Christ, and called glory, and makes the church all glorious within. As sin is worse than hell, so grace is more worth than heaven, take heaven only for our joy and happiness there. Paul was content to part with heaven for ever (if you take heaven for a comfortable communion with Christ), but no offer could have been so great as to have bought of him one dram of grace and inward holiness, and of the love which he had to Christ in his heart, or of one good work that he had done for him. It was the saying of an holy man, that he would willingly of the two rather have more grace here, and exchange it for and abate of degrees of glory hereafter. ' But yet hereby,' says Paul, ' I am not justified.' Yea, though God justifies us not for inward holiness, yet he prizeth us the more for it, and every degree of holiness added makes us more lovely in the sight of God, and more amiable, 1 Peter iii. 4. ' A meek and quiet spirit is before God of great price ;' it is that which makes our persons beautiful in his eyes, and makes him greatly desire us, and to have communion with us, and to delight in us : ' So shall the king greatly desire thy beauty,' Ps. xlv. 11. That God delights in one more than another, is because he hath bestowed more holiness, more beauty on them. It is not indeed that which caused him to set his love on us, but it is that which draws it out : Cant. iv. 9, ' Thou hast ravished my heart, my sister, my spouse,' says Christ of the graces in his church. It is true, we are ' accepted in the beloved,' in Christ through free grace, Ephes. i. 6, and it is faith makes the match ; yet inward holiness doth cause him to delight in us, and to take more pleasure in us. And so as to every act of obedience we acknowledge a great deal of worth in it, as that it is a fruit of the Spirit, a child begotten by Christ, Rom. vii. 4, 5, and therefore if the soul prizeth Christ, it must needs prize the begotten by him (as John says, 1 John v. 1, in case of loving our brother), and the soul will desire still to have more children by him. And likewise as it is fruit by Christ to the glory of God, it glorifies him though it justifies not us ; and what is grace but making God's glory our end ? and if so, then a man desires to be filled with works ; and that being his end, his desire of holiness is infinite, as the desires of a man's end are to be. And likewise he prizeth it as a rich treasure for himself laid up in store against that day, 1 Tim. vi. 19, when he shall receive bills of exchange in heaven ; therefore a man is said to be rich in good works there, as well as rich in faith elsewhere, James ii. 5.

3. Neither may anything we attribute to faith cause a neglect of holiness and obedience. 1st, Indeed it is true, if we attributed all this to an idle faith, to a faith that had no efficacy to change a man's heart and life, and thought true faith might be without cther graces, as the papists do, and that it might stand with a reigning sin, and then made such a faith the instrument of our union with Christ, &c., then this calumny might justly be laid upon our doctrine, and that which we profess. But on the contrary, we profess that so much faith as there is, so much holiness and obedience too, and that it doth as necessarily follow upon it as light doth from the sun. When we say (as the apostle doth), that in Christ nothing availeth anything but faith, we add withal, ' which worketh by love,' Gal. v. 6, and that that faith which is without holiness is dead (as James says), as you say, that is a dead drug that works not. If we made faith an idle hand to receive pardon only, then it were something ; but we make faith a labouring and a working hand also : ' Remembering,' says the apostle, ' your work of faith,' 1 Thes. i. 3, John vi. 28, 29. It is full of works, as Chrysostom says, it hath all good works in the belly of it ; and therefore Col. ii. 7, the

being ' established in faith' hath ' abounding in thanksgiving' joined with it, for fulness of faith makes the heart full of thanks, and therefore full of obedience. We profess that he that lies in any known sin, or neglect of any duty, doth deny the faith, 1 Tim. v. 8, that is, denies really what in words he affirms, and he shews he wants faith, and grace, and all. Yea, we say that the way to increase in holiness, is to increase in faith : 2 Peter iii. 18, ' Grow in grace, and in the knowledge of Jesus Christ.' This is the root ; water that, and you will be fruitful. The more faith there is, the more love there is too ; and the more love, the more a man is constrained to love God again, and that love is laborious and desirous to please him, so as works do necessarily follow faith, not *necessitate infallibilitatis* only, as fruit doth from a good tree, and these are fruits of the Spirit, but in a sweet manner, *necessitate coactionis*, for ' love constrains.' And as the grace revealed teacheth the understanding by a logical illation to deny ungodliness, Titus ii. 12, so it teacheth the heart by a physical instinct to love God when believed, and to mortify sin, and to put off corruption. ' If you have learned and been taught the truth as it is in Jesus,' you will put off the old man; for if you know Christ as in truth he is to be known, that will follow, Eph. iv. 21, 22. And indeed not Christ only, but Christ apprehended by faith, doth it, and must needs do it when he is beheld by faith. As the sun heats through a burning-glass, so doth Christ, when he is let into the heart by faith, change it ; and therefore, 2 Cor. iii. 18, we are said to be changed into his image by beholding his glory, by the Spirit that is in him. And that is one reason among others why we make faith to be the primary grace, because it virtually contains all the other in it. As love is said to be ' the fulfilling of the law,' Rom. xiii. 8, and so contains all the commandments,—' Thou shalt not kill, thou shalt not steal, &c., and if there be any other commandment, it is comprehended in this word, Thou shalt love thy neighbour' (as the apostle says), it is recapitulated, reduced to those as to the head, the sum of all, that virtually contains all,— so I say of believing, that it alone is the fulfilling of the gospel, and it virtually contains love and all works else. For the object of faith is Christ as he is presented to us in the gospel. Now he is presented not as justification only, but as sanctification also ; therefore he that takes Christ as he is given, takes Christ for both, and Christ is made both, and he doth turn to him as well as believe in him in that very taking him. Therefore faith is receiving Christ as a Lord, and repentance is walking in him, Col. ii. 6, and therefore repentance is called ' a turning to Christ,' 1 Peter ii. 25. As when a man takes a place on him, it is supposed he subjects himself to the conditions and work required in it. As when a man marries a wife, it is supposed he will love her ; so when a man receives Christ as the truth is in him, it is supposed he is to obey him ; therefore it is called ' the obedience of faith,' for all obedience is spoken in that one word, John vi. 38 ; when they asked what they should do to work the works of God, Christ tells them, ' This is the work of God, to believe ;' they meant all works ; and he answers the question by pointing to this one work, as containing all works else in it.

BOOK II.

The difficulty of faith.—That it is above all the powers and faculties in man.
—That all which is in man is so far from enabling him to believe, that it
doth withstand his believing.—That faith is the work of the alone mighty
power of God.

CHAPTER I.

Of the difficulty of faith ; how hard it is to attain to believe.

Now that I have shewn you the use and excellency of this grace of faith, I
will discover to you the difficulty to attain it ; and this is useful to be done,
both to make men the more to seek out for it, as also to get out of themselves to God to work it.   And it is indeed necessary, because else men
will rest in an easy, slight faith, which is always a false faith ; for naturally
men do imagine it the easiest of all things else required in us to salvation,
that it is the easiest thing of all the rest to believe, and they wonder that
any should make any difficulty in it.   Men think if they could but do other
things as well as believe, they should do well enough.   To pray, and to
keep the Sabbath, and to part with lusts and beloved sins, these things
indeed are hard and difficult, and to a man impossible ; but to believe in
Christ for salvation, this they make nothing of ; and whatever they do,
they will surely believe and never despair ; and if they come to a poor soul
that is any whit troubled, they rate him, and use to say, Thou art a fool
indeed, canst not believe ?   And hence of all works else men mind this of
faith the least.   They make a business of it to be humbled, and to have
strength to perform duties ; but to believe, they think that would easily
follow if they could but do other things that God requires.   And hence
also men do wonder so at such poor souls as are humbled and cut off from
carnal hopes, that they should keep such ado and such a toil to get Christ,
who is the object of faith, and to lay hold upon Christ, which is the main
act of faith ; that they should run up and down from this ordinance to that
in such a restless manner, turmoil themselves about obtaining him, as if
there were any question to be made of having him at any time, or any
difficulty in it.   What need then is there, say they, of so many complaints
of the want of Christ ? of so many heart-breakings and pantings after him ?
of such troubling of ministers how to obtain him ?   Men wonder at this,
because they know not, and assent not to the power and greatness of the
work of faith.   Now this difficulty of the work of faith might in the general,
by many ways, be made good.   As,

1. From setting forth to you the excellency, and preciousness, and glory
of this grace, which are two epithets Peter gives it, 1 Peter i. 7, and
difficilia pulchra, the most excellent things are difficult to compass.

2. From the wonderful effects of it, and privileges we obtain by it.   It

is that grace which God alone hath put in trust to give livery, and seisin, and possession of Christ, and heaven, and all things else. It is that elixir, the least dram whereof turns the heart of stone into a heart of flesh, brings Christ down from heaven into the heart, makes use of all the grace, power, virtue, that is in him; which only can command it, and doth do it; which can do all that God's attributes can do, having all God's attributes, wisdom, power, mercy, &c., to use, and manage, and set a-work for its own and the church's good. Faith of miracles did cast out devils, removed mountains, brought down fire from heaven, healed diseases; but justifying faith doth more. It is the greatest wonder-worker in the world; it resists Satan, quencheth all his darts, bears the stress of all temptations, overcomes the world, and therefore itself must needs be difficult.

3. I might demonstrate this to you by comparing faith with all other works to be wrought as necessary to salvation. We will only set it by that which of all other is the easiest, and that is to humble men, and pull down their plumes and proud thoughts. When men think themselves to be rich, and to have need of nothing, then to see themselves poor, and blind, and miserable, and naked, how hard is it! What towers doth self-righteousness erect! What high thoughts are elevated by self-flattery! and how strongly doth carnal reason fortify all these! How many weapons of warfare hath God prepared, and doth he use to batter down these! And how many shifts, and shelters, and burrows hath the heart to fly unto! Until all these be stopped, the heart is not taken, and to stop all these is out of the power, wisdom, and foresight of any man, and it must be the Spirit must do it. Now, if this be so difficult, then to bring men to believe must be much more; for besides, all this fore-mentioned is but to prepare for believing. And if all this must be done to prepare the way for Christ, what difficulty is it to bring Christ into the heart! And indeed, if then it were easy, and Christ would come alone, yet inasmuch as the work that makes way for it is so difficult, in that respect if no other, faith might be said to be difficult also. Yet besides, all this is but destroying and pulling down; and we see in the works of art which men are able to do, it is easier to destroy than to build up, to wound than to heal, to cut and break off from the old stock than to engraft into the new, to slay than to make alive and bring a new soul in; and yet such is the work of faith in comparison of the other. And moreover, thus to humble men, there is much assistance in a man's own heart to further it. There is a conscience in him, not capable only, but ready to convince him, if he would but hear it speak. There is matter enough might be picked and alleged out of his heart and life to condemn him, and persuade him that his estate is miserable and damnable, if but produced; and therefore at the day of death it is so easy to persuade men to such thoughts, and at the day of judgment they will be easily convinced. And this state of sin and wrath is the common condition of all men, and was surely every man's once, so as it is a wonder it should be so hard to convince men of it; for to pull down this house should seem to be a matter of no great difficulty, for it is ruinous, and apt to fall of itself; nay, would fall but for false supports put under it to hold it up. But to bring men to believe, there is no principle in men that hath any power to give assistance to it, but it must be wrought anew; there is nothing to be raised out of what is in a man's self that can give any ground for it, for it is founded upon nothing in a man's self. And it is the condition but of a few to obtain Christ and this precious faith; for ' all men have not faith,' nor never had, nor never shall, because it is the faith of God's elect.

4. To empty out of a man's heart his false faith, and to convince him he is an unbeliever, how hard is it! The Spirit must 'convince the world of unbelief,' John xvi. 9. The law, as it required not faith, so it discovers not unbelief; as it is a sin against the gospel, so the gospel discovers it; and it is a still sin, that lurks and makes no noise, for it shews not itself in positive acts, as envy, uncleanness, &c., but in a privative way, and so goes stilly on, steals the heart away from God and Christ; and by a bare doing nothing doth all, and gives way to the reign and stirring of all lusts, which therefore are perceived, but not it. If therefore to convince the heart of unbelief be so difficult, which yet is in the heart already, then to bring in faith, to make faith anew in the heart, must be much more difficult; and if to cause the heart to see faith when it is wrought cost so many years' search in many poor souls, what is it to work it?

But to let such as these and many other demonstrations go, we will reduce the main grounds that may demonstrate this difficulty of effecting faith in the heart to these two heads:

1. Let us consider what is done by God for a man in heaven without him, when faith is wrought.

2. What unability, yea, and obstacles, there are to the work of faith within a man.

1. If the difficulty lay only in regard of what was to be wrought in us, it were enough, as the second head will abundantly discover; but, besides this, at the bestowing faith, and at the celebration of this great union by faith between Christ and us, there must be a special consent and concurrence, and joint-meeting of all three persons in the Trinity, when this match is made. As God called a council when he made man,—' Let us make man,' says he, Gen. i.,—so there is as solemn a council called of all the three persons when this new man is made; and especially at the work of faith, for then Christ is bestowed. Conjunctions of sun and moon are not every day, especially not in one climate, especially not great conjunctions of the planets. Now, it is at a great conjunction of the whole Trinity; and when their special consent is that Christ shall be bestowed upon such a soul, it is then only and at such a time that faith is wrought, and in such a soul only. Though Christ be offered at other times by us ministers with warrant from God, yet at that time when faith is wrought he must be actually given *to* thee, and not *for* thee only. He was given for thee from the beginning of the world, and upon the cross; but now he is actually given to thee, and thou to him. The Father as a Father stands by, and says in heaven, Son, I give this soul to thee, to wed and betroth to thyself for ever; take him and own him as thy own from everlasting. And therefore says Christ, John vi. 37, ' All that the Father giveth me shall come to me.' A deed of gift, and a delivery, is passed, by God the Father, of the soul into Christ's hands, and of Christ to the soul by him also. Take (says God) this Christ my Son for thine, with all that he and I am worth. There is a giving of Christ before the soul receives him, and a giving *de præsenti*, in the present time, as distinguishing it from that which was from everlasting. And Jesus Christ, as a loving husband, bestows himself, and embraceth the poor soul as his, which he had formerly redeemed by his blood, but hitherto had lived without him. He apprehends or embraceth the soul first ere we apprehend him, Philip. iii. 12. As he loved us first ere we loved him, so he must apprehend us first ere we can apprehend him, and therefore our apprehension of him by faith is to ' apprehend that for which we are apprehended;' we give up ourselves to Christ, because he gives himself first to us. And then furthermore, Christ puts forth his

arm from heaven, vᵢ.., the Holy Ghost, as the joiner together of both, and who is called 'the arm of God' in working faith, Isa. liii. 1. He is sent into the heart, Gal. iv. 6; and he creates hands in us to comprehend Christ again, who apprehends us, and to embrace him in the promise who hath now embraced us, Heb. xi. 13; and gladly to embrace him, and not to let him go. And having him now hand in hand, we have manuduction, we are led by the hand by Christ to the Father through the Spirit, Eph. ii. 18, who therefore joined our hands together. Now, to get all the three persons thus joined at once effectually and actually to bestow Christ and the Spirit of faith upon a man, is not within any man's command. God indeed stands ready to do it at all times when the word is preached and Christ offered; but actually thus to do it, this is rare. It is not accomplished to the elect at all times, not till the fulness of time of calling comes, nor to any other but them. Faith is a receiving Christ; and until the time comes that the Father actually bestows Christ on thee, thou canst not receive him; yea, and he must put his hand into thy hands too: John iii. 27, 'A man can receive nothing unless it be given him from heaven.' And that thou dost receive him, and hast a heart to do it, that must be given thee. And however men may think the least obstacle of faith to lie in this, because God is ready to do all this to every man when the gospel is preached; yet when Christ gives the reason why some believed not and others did, he resolves it into this, John vi. 36, 37, 'I said to you, that you have seen me, and believed not.' Why? 'All that the Father giveth me shall come to me;' and verse 64, giving the reason why Judas believed not, therefore it was, saith he, I spake to you of this giving of the Father, both of you to me, and me to you, and of faith to you to come unto me. And this is the reason why the elect have not faith at all times wrought. There is a fulness of time for drawing and knitting a soul to Christ, as there was for Christ to take flesh. And canst thou appoint the time of this their meeting? Canst thou send forth, and hast thou power of calling this great general council together when thou wilt? Canst thou move God to give his Son at this time to thee, or Christ now to take possession of thee? No; all is a gift, and actually then bestowed, though given afore, when faith is wrought. This match must be concluded in heaven ere in thy heart, and the Father must say Amen to it, the Son Amen to it, and the Holy Ghost Amen to it, ere thy heart can say Amen to it; and therefore think not that it is an easy matter to believe.

2. If you consider what inability, yea, what obstacles, are in the heart itself savingly to believe, you will grant it is difficult.

(1.) There is nothing in the heart to help towards it.

(2.) There is all in the heart, and without the heart, against it.

(1.) There is nothing in the heart that induceth it to believe. There is no principle to promote it and help it forwards.

1st, To clear this, consider that it is true (as all grant) that we have a *posse remotum*, a remote capability; we have faculties wherein this faith may be engrafted, so that God shall not need to add a new faculty into the soul; but this will and understanding of ours, which was apprehensive of and comformable to the law, is the same which is to apprehend Christ, and to be made conformable to the obedience of faith; and the same natural faculties are the subjects of both. There need not a new finger to be added to the hand to apprehend Christ withal; and there are no more faculties in the soul when it is regenerated than when it was in unbelief, only they are endued with new powers and abilities.

2dly, But yet some affirm, and those such as are godly and judicious, great divines, that though new faculties are not added, yet the understanding and will of Adam, in the state even of pure nature, wanted that habit or principle whereby believers are enabled to believe in Christ.   To believe and put trust in God as a faithful Creator he had power to do, but not in Christ as a Mediator.   So that as the way of salvation by Christ is new, and contrary to that whereby Adam was to attain to life; so there must be a new principle to attain it, a new spring which might turn the stream of all the faculties from looking to be saved by doing, to which they naturally tend, and which might direct a man to glorify God by believing.   It is a new instinct to carry the soul of itself to Christ, as before it was carried out to works.   As the law of faith and the law of works are different, Rom. iii. 27, and this law of faith is a new law, so it was not written in Adam's heart.   This assertion, I confess, if it could be clearly proved, would argue faith to be exceeding difficult indeed, as being not only out of the reach and power of corrupt nature, but of pure nature also.   But this I list not now to dispute.

3dly.   However, whether it was in Adam's power to believe or not, yet sure I am, that the objects propounded to be believed are of a higher difficulty, infinitely higher than any which that state was capable of.   Adam in innocency could not have been set so hard and sublime a task and exercise as to believe in Christ is, and all his other lessons given him to learn were easy in comparison of this.   So that suppose we have no other principles than what we had afore in Adam, yet this faith is a difficulter piece of service than he was set about; for example, for Adam to believe that God made him and the world (which was a point of faith to him as well as to us, though the world was not six days' standing, for the making of it was not a thing to him seen, and therefore it is reckoned as an act of faith, Heb. xi. 3), this was easy in comparison of our believing God himself to be made man, and to come down into the world clothed with our frailties. This would have put all the faith in him to a stand, and made him stretch his eye-strings, for the angels themselves put out their necks to behold it. So to believe that the soul that sins shall die, and that on that day he did eat of the forbidden fruit he must die the death, was easy for him; for if by doing he lived, he might well believe that by transgressing he should die; and yet his faith was easily overturned in this, he believed it not long, and therefore fell.   But to believe that God would give, or hath given his Son to death, and that God would ' make him sin who knew no sin,' this would have staggered and amazed his faith.   So for him to believe that whilst he pleased God in all things he should continue in his favour, and live by doing so, and be justified by it, was easy; for his own sense of God's love, brought into his heart and maintained by obedience, might persuade him to it, and he had a sacrament of the tree of life to confirm him in it, and God's remunerative justice might assure it to him.   But to believe that God will and doth justify an ungodly person, and account him as righteous as the angels, would well nigh have posed, if not non-plussed his faith.   And further, to believe that when that ungodly person to be justified hath not one dram of power to please God with, yet he ought to live in another, and to have a principle of life and grace out of himself, and to have his life and abilities hid in another, fetched from another who lives in him, and all to be fetched by believing, this would have been a paradox in Adam's divinity, and would well nigh have overthrown it, for it crossed and contradicted the faith which he had in that his estate, which was maintained by a stock of grace in himself committed to his own hands to dispose of.   As the psalmist said, ' I thought to understand this, and it was too high for me;' so may I say, when he should have attempted to believe this, he would have found load enough to charge his faith with, if it had not been too high for him.   When our Saviour Christ, John iii., conferred with Nicodemus about the easy and most familiar things which concerned salvation, the truth of which even earthly light might convince him of, as that ' what is born of the flesh is flesh,' and therefore corrupt man's nature is so ; nature and sense might have instructed him in all this, and in a farther truth also, viz., that therefore if ever this nature enters heaven, it must be changed and born again, and that image which at first was lost must be restored.   He that heard of the state of innocency would have easily assented unto this, that the same image must be renewed ere God accepts us, and yet this sets Nicodemus his mind in an uproar, John iii. 12, and yet these things Christ tells him were but earthly in comparison, ' and if ye believe not these,' saith he, ' how shall ye believe if I tell you of heavenly things ?'   Now what were those heavenly things but the truths of the gospel which are necessary to be believed, which Christ brought down from heaven, because they had never grown in Adam's garden, who was a man of the earth, earthly ?   And he instanceth in some of them in the following verses ; he instanceth in the human and divine nature of Christ, and their union, and the doctrine of faith, and in being cured by believing on him, as they in the wilderness were by the brazen serpent ; he instanceth in that amazing thing also, that God should so love the world as to give his only begotten Son, that whoever believeth on him should not perish.   Now to believe these and the like things, must be by a power derived from heaven.

4thly. But sure I am, that whether Adam had such a power, yea or no then, yet now in corrupt nature it is utterly lost and gone ; for besides the general reason that the whole image of God is lost, there was a special reason why he should lose this of faith above any other part, for he fell by unbelief, and therefore all the ruins fell upon that arm, and broke it all to pieces.   The special guilt of that sin shattered that part of God's image all to shivers.   We are ' shut up under unbelief,' Rom. xi. 32, and faith is the way out of that miserable condition we are in, when the door is locked and barred by unbelief, and we cannot open it, nor shoot nor break open the lock.   To believe but the law of Moses, how hard is it !   And though men have a conscience, in which the law is written by nature, yet Christ tells the Pharisees, John v. 47, that they did not truly believe Moses.   How hardly are men brought to believe the threatenings, especially with application, when yet they are thundered out against all, and there is a guilt tells us that we deserve death who do such things, Rom. i. 32, much more hardly are men brought to believe the promises, which belong but to a few : ' If ye believe not Moses's writings,' says Christ, ' how shall ye believe my words ?' John v. 47.   He argues à minori ad majus, from the less to the greater.   Did I say to believe the law ?   I may say that to do the whole law exactly is as easy as to believe savingly in Christ.   This is a received maxim among all divines, and despairing Spira set his seal to it out of woeful experience, when he spoke these words, You command me to believe.   I say I cannot ; your command is as impossible to me as to keep the moral law.

5thly. All the principles left in man will help nothing towards the attaining of it.

1. All the parts of wit and wisdom in the world will not help us to believe : 1 Cor. ii. 5, ' Faith stands not in the wisdom of men, but in the power of God ;' the wisdom of other men cannot beget it, nor the wisdom

of a man's own heart cannot attain it, or give the least inclination to it, but the alone power of God, for of that likewise he speaks, and therefore says he, ver. 6–8, ' The wisdom of the princes of this world,' that are the wisest, ' came to nought, and could not reach it. Eye hath not seen, nor ear heard, neither have entered into the heart of man, the things which God hath prepared for them that love him.'

2. Natural conscience cannot arrive to faith, it will set you a-doing indeed, but not a-believing ; it will discover other sins to you, but not this ; for the Spirit must convince of unbelief. The law of works is written in conscience, but not the law of faith ; and therefore men that make conscience of private prayer, and of keeping the Sabbath, and of avoiding uncleanness and adultery, and dare not omit or commit any of these, yet make no conscience of believing, nor are struck with a sense of unbelief. Nay, therefore believers themselves, that take thought about other things, are often careless of believing, look not at this as the main duty, the great command, the highest obedience.

3. All the duties thou canst perform cannot beget one jot of faith : Rom. ix. 16, ' It is not in him that wills nor runs, but in God that sheweth mercy.' Though Paul was as exact in keeping the law as ever man was, yet, 1 Tim. i. 13, he was an unbeliever. If a man should go and make money (as I may so say) of all he is or hath, and put all into one stock, if he should call in all his strength which is put out, and is in the hands of learning, riches, honours, &c., and convert and turn every thought for every moment's time he is to live upon nothing but believing, and trade with all that he can make for nothing but for faith, he could not compass one dram. Let him take his flinty heart in one hand, and all the promises in the word of God in another, and strike his heart and them together to eternity, he would not strike out so much as one spark of saving faith.

4. All external means cannot work faith. Christ preached, and preached as powerfully as ever man did, he ' spake as never no man spake,'—John vi. 63, ' The words I speak to you are spirit and life,'—yet the Jews remained unbelievers ; and Judas, that heard all his sermons, and missed not one, yet remained an unbeliever ; for it follows, ver. 64, 65, ' There are some of you believe not. For Jesus knew who should betray him. And therefore I said to you, that no man can come to me except it be given him of my Father.' And though he preached plainly as well as powerfully, John x. 24, 25, yet still they doubt, as they themselves say there ; nay, says Christ, ' My works bear witness of me,' ver. 25, ' but yet ye believe not ;' there is something else in it ; it is because ' ye are not of my sheep,' ver. 26 ; and ver. 37, ' If I do not the works of my Father, believe me not ;' yea, John xv. 24, ' he did works which none other did ;' and ' if ye believe not me, yet believe the works.' But though such works as were never done before were added to such words as were never spoken by any but him, yet these admirable works and words did not effect faith in their hearts : John xii. 37, ' Though he had done so many miracles, yet they believed not on him.'

5. As there is nothing to help to work faith within or without a man, so all in him is against it. As,

(1.) All thy sins, both the power of thy sins, and the guilt of thy sins, oppose thy believing.

1st. The power of thy sins is opposite to faith ; for till the heart be divorced from every lust, thou canst not give Christ and faith entertainment. It will forbid the banns of matrimony between Christ and thee. Thou canst no more take Christ for thy salvation and portion, and set him up in thy heart, than thou canst at once look up to heaven, and down upon the earth : ' How can ye believe,' says Christ, ' whilst ye receive honour one from another ?' John v. 44.

2dly. The guilt of thy sins causes thee to depart from God, and bids Christ to depart from thee: ' Depart from me,' says Peter, ' for I am a sinful man,' Luke v. 8. Guilt of wrong and enmity is always suspicious, and makes a man look upon God as an enemy, and therefore he dares not trust him. Men will rarely trust a reconciled enemy, nor will men be brought to venture themselves upon a God reconciling himself through Christ. Judas runs to the Pharisees when he had betrayed Christ, but he durst not come at Christ, his guilt would not suffer him. Sins will tell thee, and defiled conscience will tell thee, that thou must look for no mercy, and that ' there is no hope,' Jer. ii. 25, and when we would look for salvation, yet it is far off ; for because our sins testify against us, and we know them, therefore the guilt of them ariseth and puts off such thoughts of mercy, and discourageth the heart. As presumptuous men think they shall be saved because their sins are so small, so poor humbled souls, when they see their sins once, surmise that they shall never have mercy, because they are so great. What! I! a blasphemer, a contemner of mercy, shall I obtain mercy? The soul cannot believe this. Though sin when slighted furthers presumption, yet when discovered it hinders faith.

(2.) All the righteousness that is in a man for time past, and endeavours for time to come, also hinder the work of faith.

1. Righteousness for time past is a hindrance to it, for men cannot have any righteousness in and of themselves but self will be conceited of it ; and a conceit of their own merit hinders them from seeing their need of, and looking out for Christ's. The Pharisees, that thought themselves righteous, were so far from faith or coming to Christ, that Christ says he came not to call such. The Jews ' going about to establish their own righteousness, submitted not to the righteousness of God by faith,' Rom. ix. 31, 32, and Rom. x. 3. As the law was not given for a righteous man, that is truly such, so nor the gospel is not given for him that hath any conceited righteousness of his own. Faith is that whereby we ' believe in him that justifies the ungodly.' As Laodicea, that thought herself rich, was thereby kept off from coming to Christ by faith, to buy gold of him, so the more goods have been increased, and the richer a man hath thought himself, the loather he is to break and become a bankrupt, and to suffer so much loss, and to stand at the courtesy of free grace, and put off his robes and come as a beggar, and lie naked at Christ's door. And,

2. Endeavours for the time to come also hinder and spoil faith. A man, when he sees his former sinfulness and want of faith, and hath suffered the wreck of all his former estate, is apt to begin of his own cost to build a new ship to set to sea in, and lades it upon a new stock with new wares of duties he never did afore, and launcheth it into profession, and thinks by his own rowing, and tugging, and hauling, in the end to arrive at Christ, who goes as fast from him as he makes after him, whilst he thus goes out in his own strength. But if he would tie his cockboat to the ship of God's free grace, and commit himself to sea with it, and suffer the stream of it, and the gales of the Spirit, to carry him on in the use of means, he might attain to faith, and to the righteousness of God. Rom. ix. 32, the Jews sought it but as a by-faith, but as it were by the works of the law ; and I may in this case allude to it, a man must seek Christ and faith, but it must be in a way of faith, else though the duties be evangelical which they endeavour to perform, yet they are, as it were, the works of the law, as the

apostle's phrase is, and will be accounted as legal.   A man may seek the righteousness of faith, and yet not by faith, or in a way of faith and sense of a man's own inability, and so seek after the faith itself, 'as if it were a work of the law;' and then, as Paul says, as a man condemns himself in what he allows, so he undoes himself in what he endeavours, and goes to hell by striving to go to heaven.   The people of Israel, if they would have gone into Canaan by the way of faith in God alone, who offered to cast out their enemies before them, they might have done it, but that way they rejected through unbelief, and then set to it by their own strength; but they were beaten back by their enemies, and God commanded them to go back again even to the brink of the Red Sea; so doth God deal with souls that have gone far into the wilderness, and are nigh believing and laying hold, yet subject not their souls to God's way of working faith, but attempt it by their own strength, and this casts them behind-hand, and they are to begin the work anew, and so they are brought thereby as far off as at first, and have need to be humbled of those their new endeavours, and then they are fit to enter.   God hath said that no man shall prevail with his own strength, 1 Sam. ii. 6.   And thus to endeavour after faith with our own strength is like the scrabbling and striving of one that cannot swim, which sinks him the sooner and the more, and is opposite to the way of faith; for faith fetcheth all strength from another, since that is essential to that grace, and is one rule in the law of faith, as the apostle calls it, and therefore strivings for faith out of our own strength are most opposite to the law of faith.   A man's own strength prevents and supplants supply by faith, which is passive, and a receiving borrowing grace.   And therefore Christ tells us plainly, that 'many shall strive to enter, and shall not be able,' like a man that would open the flood-gate of a sluice; one who attempts to break open the door of unbelief, which is shut against all the world, is like to a man who would open the flood-gate of a sluice, the more he pulls to open it, the more he keeps it shut, whilst he doth it out of his own strength, whereas, if he would go on the other side of the stream, and commit himself to it, the stream would do it alone, and carry him through it.

3. All parts of natural wisdom and reason are against faith also.

1st, For besides that some rest in knowledge, Rom. ii. 17–20, knowledge and gifts also puff up, 1 Cor. viii. 1, but he whose heart is lift up believes not, Hab. ii. 4.   They are opposed; nothing opposeth faith more than pride, nothing makes proud more than knowledge; and therefore, to confound the pride of the world, he chose out this grace of faith, which by making a man become a fool, saves him, 1 Cor. i. 19–21, and confounds all men's admired wisdom by 'saving them that believe.'

2dly, And again, carnal reason keeps men from faith, because that is the form of a man as a man, and will be listened to.   The philosophers defined a man to be *animal rationale*, a rational animal; now faith hath a reach beyond all this, and therefore when a man ties himself to reason, and consults with it, he is kept from believing; and when he would believe, he must not consider what reason says to the contrary.   So Abraham, Rom. iv. 19, being not weak in faith, considered not his own body, that whereas reason and consideration, out of wisdom and reason, would have raised many an objection up, he consults not with it.   And therefore God hath chose this grace of faith as that which fools are as capable of as wise men; yea, and more, for they are apt to be credulous, and out of a sense of their want of wisdom to resolve their judgment into another's.   Yea, and therefore God hath 'chosen the poor and foolish things of the world,' because faith in them is more easily wrought.   'Have any of the rulers believed in him?' John vii. 48, 49. 'But this people that know not the law are accursed.'

3dly, The more reason a man hath, the stronger objections he will raise up against believing; therefore, in temptations, the more knowledge a man hath, the stronger he pleads against himself, and his wit serves to make his indictment the more full, and to dispute against his own salvation the more shrewdly, as Spira did, to the amazement of the standers by, invent such objections as another would not have dreamt of. And thus it hinders afore and in the working of faith. Afore, what is it keeps men from being humbled? Their carnal reasonings, their strongholds. Now all that reason, which, before a man was humbled, shewed its strength in maintaining the goodness of his estate, when he is humbled, turns head, and pleads against a man's estate, and against his having any interest in mercy; and indeed, whilst a man will go in a way of reasoning, and consider his dead soul, he will never believe. A man must believe above and against all reason; as Abraham considered not his dead body, so nor must he consider his dead soul. And hence it is that we have more ado with carnal reason after men are humbled than before. Self-flattery, when that was general, used and commanded all the reason in a man to fight for a good opinion of his estate; and when self-flattery is slain, and that good opinion of a man's self with it, then unbelief turns all the same force and weapons another way, and all the reason in a man is employed to fight to keep a man in it.

4thly, Self in a man is against it also, and the greatest enemy to it; and therefore in faith there is the greatest self-denial that is in any other grace. To deny a man's reason, and subject all his thoughts to the authority and wisdom of another, and to give God leave to take away all reason and wisdom from me, and to resolve my thoughts into his words, and to think as he thinks, whatever my own thoughts are, all this is hard. And so to be content to be nothing of myself for ever, and to do nothing of myself, to throw myself away, to lose, to forget myself, to be lost to myself, dead to myself (as Paul was, Gal. ii. 20 and 2 Cor. xii. 11, who, though he did more than all, yet says he was nothing, in those words, 'Not I, but Christ,' &c.), and to take Christ into my heart not only to rule all, but to do all, to have the glory of all, both the grace and the glory I have, to have no reason, no will, no power, no life of my own in myself, but Christ to be all, this is to believe, and this is a farther self-denial than was in pure nature in Adam. This self is brought to by losing and forfeiting itself, and this only in point of faith. Adam, though he had grace from God, yet he had it in himself, and of himself could work, and could say, This have I done, and this is my righteousness of my own weaving, and this is my happiness of my own keeping; and it was allowed him to say so. But now cut off *that same I*, away with that self, make it a cypher to eternity; though it be something as a creature, and have a name in the catalogue of beings, and is advanced to the highest state of happiness, yet let it be nothing in doing, nothing in righteousness, nothing in glorifying or making itself happy, and let Christ be all. Adam was as much in his aims and designs to deny himself, as we now, in point of sanctification, he was herein to aim at God as much as we, and to respect himself as little ; but in point of believing we fall lower, for that empties us, annihilates self, fetcheth righteousness, power, life, all from another, as well as it works to another. And this is therefore difficult, because it is a higher strain of glorifying God than Adam knew, or than the heart is either in pure or corrupt nature acquainted with. Self rests in itself, and would not go out of itself; this is natural to it, and it was used to do so when it was at the best, and therefore this way of believing is a way which self would never take, but it will fall a-doing and performing duties, and keeping the law, and mourning for sin ; and if you have any work for it to do in itself within doors, it will fit to it, but to go abroad and beg all of Christ, to live upon alms, to stand to the courtesy of Christ and grace, and to do this for eternity, self was never brought up to it.   It would live of itself, of its own lands and revenues, though lesser and meaner, rather than be in dependence, though to enjoy a kingdom.   And though going to Christ be a short cut, yet it had rather go about, make a new way of works, than go to Christ, and by Christ, who is the Way and the Life : ' Ye will not come to me,' says Christ, John v. 40, ' that ye might have life ;' no, they will undertake to fulfil the law rather. The Pharisees and the Jews did so ; they would rather appeal to it that was their condemner, to Moses who accused them (as Christ says, ver. 45), than come to Christ who offered to save them.   They would rather go to the law, that was ' the ministry of condemnation.'   The Galatians, that they might be eased a little in point of believing, would be in bondage to the ceremonial law, which they nor their fathers were able to bear.   And papists will rather give over kingdoms, and put themselves into monasteries, lie in hair, live upon the alms of others, whip and rend their bodies, keep strictly to their canonical hours, than go to Christ, than cast off works, and betake themselves to faith.   And the same you may see in poor humbled souls ; they run to every duty, but never dream of faith, that that must ease them.   Thus Christ's sheep will hang upon every briar ere they come to him.

4. If there were nothing in us against it, yet the devil opposeth it more than any thing.   He opposed not the moral virtues of the heathen, nor doth he oppose a deluded Christian in performance of duties ; but when he comes to lay hands on Christ, when he will go that way, then he musters up all the forces he can.   ' The god of this world blinds the eyes of them that believe not, lest the light of the glorious gospel should shine to them,' 2 Cor. iv. 4.   This is the point he would keep them blind in, viz., the knowledge of Christ by faith ; and hither tend all his delusions and oppositions, that our faith might fail.

CHAPTER II.

That all the faculties and powers in man do not afford him abilities to believe. —That all human wisdom is so far from promoting faith, that it sets itself against it.

By grace ye are saved through faith ; and that not of yourselves: it is the gift of God.—EPH. II. 8.

I shall proceed on still in opening of that faith which saveth us, of that faith which justifieth us, and ceaseth not till it hath put us into the hands of Christ.   I shall now proceed farther to shew you the greatness of it in respect of the working of it in our hearts, and the disproportion that is between our hearts in which it is wrought, and this grace itself.   I will shew how hardly it is attained unto, that it is fetched out of the rocks (as I may so speak), by an almighty power.   And to that end I have chosen this text, and especially this particle here, ' and that not of yourselves, it is the gift of God ;' which I intend not so much to discourse of by way of exposition, for that I have done before,* as to lay open the thing to you in a common-place way; only in general take the scope of the apostle before in this chapter. His scope is to magnify the free grace of God, as the sole author of our salvation, which he magnifies in two respects :

1. By shewing the misery that a man lay in when God first set his heart upon him, 'dead in trespasses and sins,' deserving a thousand deaths, 'children of wrath,' &c., vers. 1, 2, 3.

2. By laying open the way of God's bringing us unto salvation ; and he tells us this, that seeing free grace was the contriver of our salvation, and its end was to magnify itself, therefore, it having the making of its own laws, it would be sure to order our salvation so, that though of necessity something was to be wrought in us, or we could not be saved, yet it would pitch upon such things as should have as little an ingredient into our salvation as possibly the thing itself would bear : ' For by grace ye are saved,' saith he, ' through faith : and that not of yourselves ; it is the gift of God ; not of works,' &c.

There are but two things required of us, faith and works. The apostle puts a difference betwixt these two clearly ; and he tells us, that faith is taken up into commission, as it were, when works are not : ' By grace ye are saved through faith, not of works ;' no, by no means. Though works are as much required as faith, yet God doth by no means own them, doth not so much as look upon them in the matter of salvation. For indeed faith is that grace that doth so glorify God and his free grace, that he is not jealous, as it were, to put it into commission even with himself and with Jesus Christ. But now, when God had therefore required of us as little as could be in the matter of salvation, when he had required only that we should know this grace of his, and lay hold upon it (without doing of which, his grace would be lost), and that in laying hold upon it, faith should give all the glory unto free grace, here man might step in and say, I have faith in myself, or I contribute something to the getting of faith, and to the attaining thereof. No, saith the apostle ; we will cut you short there, that still free grace may be magnified. It is true ye are saved through faith, but that faith ' is not of yourselves, it is the gift of God.'

This now is enough for the opening of the words, and shewing you the apostle's scope. The thing then that at this time I intend to discourse of is this, to manifest unto you that saving faith is not of yourselves. That is my theme, put what title you will upon it : to shew you, I say, that there is nothing in yourselves that contributeth to the working of faith in you ; and in doing of this I have this aim, namely, that when you see that all in yourselves, or all that you can do, can no way help you to the attainment of faith, you may come to understand both the several false ways that men do take in the matter of believing, and also may the more clearly see, in the negative, what the right way of believing is, and what the nature of justifying faith is ; and likewise, that by seeing your inability to attain it, you may come to prize it the more, and that you may be emptied of yourselves, not only in respect of the grace you believe on (for you believe only on free grace), but in respect of this also, that you must come to free grace itself even to work this faith, to believe upon it. For what can lay a man more low in himself than this, that when he sees himself lost, and that God hath provided a remedy, and requires nothing but faith, honest faith, faithful faith, as I use to call it, that yet the man of himself is unable to attain to this faith ? And further, I have also this end in it, that you that have

* In his exposition on Eph. ii. in Vol. I. of his works. [Vol. II. of this edition.— Ed.]

your hearts taken off by God, and have been taught and led in the right way of believing, and enabled to do it, may be thankful to God, and go on in a way of dependence upon him for the perfecting of the work of faith in you, for every storey, every garnish in this building, as well as the foundation, is not of yourselves. And likewise further, that those that think that faith is so easy to be had, may indeed be convinced that they have no faith: faith, saith he, ' it is not of yourselves, it is the gift of God.' I shall not go about to shew you, in the general, the greatness of the work of conversion, and that that is not of a man's self, and how that to change the heart, and to create new faculties, to turn a man from darkness to light, and from Satan to God, and the like, is a great work, and requires an almighty power. No ; I shall keep strictly to the point of believing, and in that not speak so much of the habit of faith, as of bringing the soul to the acts of faith, clearly and plainly to close with Jesus Christ, and to trust upon free grace, and in nothing in a man's self. I shall particularly demonstrate these two things:

1st. That all that is in man, or all that is from man, can no way help him unto this faith. Yea,

2d. That all that is in man, and all that is from man, is against it. And therefore, certainly faith is not of ourselves, it is the gift of God.

(1.) I shall only premise this in the general, which I will but briefly touch upon, that if we take pure nature, that is, nature in innocency, in Adam afore he fell, it was far above it to believe those things which we do now believe. I will not stand to dispute that point, whether Adam, yea or nay, had that principle of faith we have. Only this is what I say, that if Adam had the same principle of faith that we have, yet to believe those things which, when we believe to salvation, we do believe, was infinitely, if not above the proportion of his faith, yet above what it was put to believe. If the wheels be the same, yet there is a new spring put in, which doth turn all the wheels, and the stream and course of them, another way. And that is, whereas Adam sought salvation from God by doing, and by obedience of the faith he had, which indeed sets all the wheels in him a-going, here comes a new spring into the heart, which turns all the wheels quite another way, and sets the heart a-work to seek salvation out of itself, in another. There is a new instinct, a new genius therefore, carrying the heart unto another, unto Christ, to be saved, differing from what the genius, and spring, and instinct of Adam's faith carried him unto. The truth is, the law of faith (as the expression is in Rom. iii. 23) which is written in our hearts, is differing from that law of works that was in his heart, and was written there. So that I say, suppose that he had a principle of faith such as we have, yet he was never put to believe that which we are ; yea, certainly it was far above the proportion of it so to do. I shall but give you an instance or two.

1. He believed that God made him, and that God made the world (I will not dispute whether his faith might be resolved into sanctified reason or no). It was an easy thing for him to believe also this, that God, when he made him, had a consultation, expressed in Gen. i. 26, ' Let us make man,' and let us make a world. But was he put unto it to believe that that God who made the world would himself be made man ? If he had the same principle of faith we have, yet I believe it was so dim as it could hardly have seen so far without new spectacles, but it would have stretched his eye-strings, have put his eyes to it, to have discerned this, even as it puts the angels' necks to it, as Peter speaks, 1 Pet. i. 12, to stoop down to behold this.

2. Adam believed that the soul that sinned should die, and that on that

day he did eat of the forbidden fruit he should begin to die.   There was reason for him to believe this, because he found that by doing the will of God he lived ; therefore he might very well on the contrary believe, that if he transgressed the will of God, he must die ; and yet you see how easy his faith in this thing was overthrown.   The devil came with a suggestion of a doubt, Gen. iii. 2 : ' Yea, hath God said that you shall die the death that day you eat ? ' And how easily did the tempter hereby prevail against his faith ! But what if God had said to Adam, that God himself shall die, and that God himself should be made sin that knew no sin, and be made a curse ! If such a thing as this should have been propounded to his faith, and if the devil had come with such a suggestion, ' Yea, hath God said ? ' he would have put his faith to it.

3. For Adam to believe that whilst he pleased God in all things, he should continue in his favour, and should be justified in so doing, it was easy ; why ? Because he had a principle of conscience in him, which was still to give him peace by doing, and to give a testimony of the favour of God towards him.   He had a principle adequate to this in his own bosom, and it was natural unto him, for he had the notion of the remunerative justice of God, whereof he had the image also in his own bosom, that might assure him of it.   But to come to believe that God will justify the ungodly, and to apprehend myself to be ungodly, and then to believe that God will justify me, and to believe that God will and doth account an ungodly person as righteous in his sight, as all the angels in heaven are, in point of justification, this would have posed, have non-plussed Adam's faith.   And further, when that ungodly person, though justified perfectly, should continue still imperfectly holy, and not have a dram of power and ability in himself to please God, but he must turn himself out of doors, go and live in another, must fetch a principle of life and grace from Christ,—as Christ tells us that we must do: John xv. 5, ' Without me ye can do nothing ;' and as the apostle's faith was, Gal. ii. 20, ' I now live ; I live by the faith of the Son of God ; and it is not I, but Christ that liveth in me,'—all these would have been parables, solecisms in Adam's opinion.   Faith, therefore, by which we are saved, may well be said not to be of ourselves, for it is indeed above this pure nature, this pure self.

(2.) But besides, a second consideration in the general about it, may be this.   If Adam had power to believe all these things, which I will not dispute nor utterly deny, yet now it is above self, for he utterly lost it, and we all have lost it, and so lost it, that of all things else which we are able to do, we are weakened in the point of believing.   Besides the general reason which is common to the loss of all grace else (viz., if that faith had been a part of the image of God, the whole being lost, it had also been lost with the rest), I say, besides that general reason, there is this special one to evince this, that in losing that faith he had, we are utterly disenabled of ourselves to believe.   For, do but consider, where was it that the temptation entered in ?   Certainly it was in a way of unbelief.   We will not dispute whether that faith he had might be resolved into spiritual reason or no.   Yet a faith it might be called, and so answerably his first sin may be called unbelief. ' Yea, hath God said ?' saith the devil to Eve ; and at that she staggered, became dizzy, reeled and fell, and fell upon that arm, and broke it all to pieces.   If a man be killed with a shot in his eye, we know that shot piercing the eye, and carrying that away with it, kills the whole man ; and the man being killed, it must be an almighty power that must go to the raising of that man presently again ; but now it were a farther thing to raise that eye, beyond and besides raising the whole man, because the whole body remains, but this eye must be made anew; so it is here. In Rom. xi. 32, we are said (and it is an emphatical expression), both Jew and Gentile, to be ' shut all up together in unbelief' (so you have it in your margins), ' that God might have mercy upon all.' Do but mark what he compares unbelief unto (that I may fit it to that thing we have in hand, namely, that in the matter of believing we are of all the rest most disenabled), he compares it to a prison or bonds. Suppose now that a man had life in him, yet if he be shut up, if he be manacled in fetters, as likewise the word signifies, he is utterly disenabled. And it imports first, that God in a special manner hath shut up all unbelief. Other sins (if I may so speak) are they for which God imprisons men ; but to the end they may be surely imprisoned, he makes unbelief the jailor, and we are all as it were shut up in a dungeon, with a door of unbelief fast locked upon us. Therefore now the apostle makes the greatness of the mercy of God to lie in giving faith, as appears by the context ; God, saith he, ' hath shut them up altogether in unbelief,' over and above their other sins, that when they were all thus cock-sure the prisoners of death, ' he might have mercy upon them.' In Gal. iii. 22, you have the like phrase : ' The scripture,' saith he there, ' hath concluded all under sin' (the word is a compound, συνέκλεισεν, of the same root κλείω), hath shut up all under sin. There are, as I may so speak, outward prisons of all a man's sins else in which he is shut ; but in Rom. xi. he makes unbelief to be, as it were, the inner prison. So that God now shews a farther mercy in giving of faith. And notwithstanding all a man's sins, the promises which are by faith in Jesus Christ given to them that believe (as it follows there in Gal. iii. 22), may come and knock at the prison-door, and tell this poor man, We have broke up all your other prison-doors, and have passed through all those prisons, and if now you will but believe, do but come out of this dungeon you are in, and you shall be delivered. Alas ! saith the poor soul, though all the other prison-doors be set open, and there be a free access unto grace, notwithstanding all my sinfulness, yet I cannot believe. No more indeed he cannot, for he is shut up under unbelief. Therefore, now what saith the text in Gal. iii. 22 ? ' The promise is given to them that believe ;' and as the promise is given to them that believe, so Eph. ii. 8 tells us, that ' faith is the gift of God :' for a man being shut up under unbelief, locked up in that inner prison, the promises may come and knock a thousand years at the prison-doors, and all to no purpose, unless God, as the expression is, Acts xiv. 27, ' open a door of faith' unto him. So that we are in a special manner in this corrupt estate shut up under unbelief, over and above all the loss we sustained by Adam. But these are yet but general demonstrations. I shall now come to the particulars, and by the grace of Christ manifest this to you.

1. That there is nothing in a man (in the condition we lie in by nature) that can help forward, or is any way conducing to the work of saving faith in the heart ; and that unless God come by an almighty power to work it, he can never believe. And,

2. That all that is in a man, and all that comes from him, duties or endeavours, or what else you will, are all against it. To make manifest the first of these, I shall go over all that is in you, take you all in pieces, your understanding, your will, your affections, your conscience, and shew you in all these particulars that faith is not of yourselves, it is the gift of God.

1st. I will begin with the understanding. All the parts of wit and of wisdom that all the wise men of the world have had since the creation, or shall have to the end of the world, if they had met in any one man's heart or head, could not help him in the least to believe on Christ in a saving manner. The thing is demonstrable abundantly. What says the apostle ? 1 Cor. ii. 5, ' That your faith should not stand in the wisdom of men, but in the power of God.' It cuts the throat of a man's free will directly. Therefore he tells us in ver. 6–8, that the wisdom of the princes of this world came to nothing as to the matter of believing. Nay, in 1 Cor. i. 18, 19, he tells us, and he prosecuteth the same all along almost to the end of the third chapter, that God had a design by setting up faith in the hearts of his people to save them, thereby to confound the wisdom of all the wise men in the world : ' The preaching of the cross,' saith he, ' is to them that perish foolishness; but unto us which are saved it is the power of God. For it is written, I will destroy the wisdom of the wise, and bring to nothing the understanding of the prudent.' And ver. 21, ' After that the world by wisdom knew not God, it pleased God by the foolishness of preaching to save them that believe.' This poor thing faith, to save men by, he sets up as a principle in the hearts of his people who are saved, to confound the proud principle of wisdom, parts, wit, and understanding, that the wise men of the world boast themselves so much of. And as God in man's redemption had an eye to confound the devil, as appears by the curse in Genesis, so he chooseth out that which is the most excellent thing in man, as that which in the way of saving man he would most confound. I will do it, saith he, by the foolishest object, Christ crucified ; by the foolishest instrument, preaching ; and by the foolishest means within a man, mere faith ; and by this I will accomplish that good and salvation which all the wise men in the world by their wisdom shall never attain. He doth not say, he will confound the wise men, for he saved many wise men—not many wise men indeed, so ver. 26, in comparison of the other, but some wise men—therefore he says not that he will confound the wise men of the world, but ' the wisdom,' in the abstract ; for they must lay their wisdom aside when they come to believe, and become fools. The apostle there useth two or three words very observable. In the 19th verse he saith, that God reprobateth, maketh no use of the wisdom of the world in point of salvation. And ver. 20, he saith that God hath made it foolish, he hath put a scorn, an affront upon it ; and he shews that wise men are the greatest fools in the world, whilst poor souls scramble up to heaven by believing.

And then again, if you will know the reason why God doth it, and the reason likewise why wisdom in a man cannot attain to it ; the reason why God doth it is, that he may confound that which is in man his chiefest excellency, as wisdom is, and that it may be in his power (mark it) to save whom he will, and that it might be in his power only to raise men up to what degrees of grace and faith, and so of glory to come, he pleaseth. And this he doth whilst he makes no use at all of wisdom in this point, but makes use of faith. Why ? Because he can make the foolishest people that are, believe, as much as the wisest men in the world. Nay, he can raise up a principle of faith unto an higher degree in a simple man, if he pleaseth, than the wisest and learnedst man in the world can attain to by all notional learning. He therefore pitched upon this grace of faith to confound the wisdom that is in man, so that all his parts and wisdom cannot help him one whit. This might be insisted upon largely, but it needs not.

And not only doth the natural wisdom in man fall short in it, but it is in itself a hindrance to it.

1. For reason, which is also joined with wisdom, is utterly against the way of faith. ' I thought,' saith he in Ps. lxxiii. 16, ' to comprehend this ;' he thought to do it by his own wisdom, and that thought spoiled him.

So saith wisdom, for it is a puffed up principle, I think by my own brains and wit to attain this ; which a foolish soul cannot do. Pride, of all things else, is most opposite unto faith : ' The just shall live ·by faith' (saith he in Hab. ii. 4), and he opposeth living by faith to him whose heart is lifted up in him ; and wisdom and knowledge puffeth up, as the apostle saith in 1 Cor. viii. 1. It is therefore in itself the greatest enemy unto faith. When the wisest man in the world comes to see his natural condition, and comes to believe, it lays that man as low as the poorest and simplest creature in the world : I would not care (says he) if I were a fool, if of a king I were a beggar, so I had but one dram of faith to interest me in Jesus Christ. So that now he that is a rich man, when he comes to believe, he rejoiceth, as James saith, that he is brought low, &c.

2. And then again, reason, which is the form that constituteth man as he is man, and is the highest thing in man till faith comes, is utterly against it. For when faith comes, it deposeth reason, which before ruled as king, it subdueth it, even as reason itself subdueth sense. Reason therefore riseth up against it ; for when reason comes to be put from its kingly power and regency, which it hath retained in a man all his days, when a stranger shall come, and tell reason of strange things in another world, which it never heard of, never took in before, and upon the news of this, though it sees not one jot of reason in it, yet it must lay itself down at the foot of this stranger faith, and receive the law at his mouth ;—reason, that hath been the supreme principle, and the king and dominator in the heart of man, will never do this, but it will stir and raise up all the force it can against it to resist it. When faith shall come and say, I will have all these counsellors of yours, all your carnal reasonings, put away from you, reason flies upon the height still, still consults with flesh and blood, and will never yield of itself. In Rom. iv., when Abraham came to believe, reason would have been putting in many objections. Do but consider your body, being now dead (saith reason), and consider the deadness of Sarah's womb. But what saith the text ? ' Abraham being not weak in faith, he considered not his own body being now dead, when he was about an hundred years old, neither yet the deadness of Sarah's womb : he staggered not at the promise of God through unbelief ; but was strong in faith, giving glory to God,' Rom. iv. 19, 20. He gave himself up unto faith.

3. And, thirdly, the more and stronger reason a man hath in him, when he comes to believe, he will find the harder pull of it, and have the stronger objections. In men that are in distress of conscience, the larger their knowledge is, the deeper is their distress ; because the more knowledge a man hath, the more arguments he finds out against himself ; and all the reason a man hath will but serve to make his indictment the fuller against himself, and enable him the better to dispute, and the more shrewdly to argue against himself. As Spira, being a man of a strong reason, you know how he reasoned against himself, to the amazement of all men.

4. Carnal reason (if you would know how it is a hindrance) hinders both before faith and after. Before faith it is an hindrance, for you will never believe till you see your natural condition. Now what is it that hinders men from seeing that ? All men are ready to acknowledge themselves sinners, but they will not acknowledge themselves to be lost and undone. Why, carnal reason useth all the strength it hath to build up high towers, and plausible shifts and pretences to make a man think he is in a good condition. All the reason a man hath is mainly exercised in maintaining the dispute of this against his conscience, or the grumbling in his heart about the goodness of his estate. Again, on the other side, when

once a man comes to be humbled, and then should come to believe, all this reason turns head again, and useth as much strength of objection against himself, why he should not have mercy, and tells him he must have this and this qualification before he comes to Jesus Christ. I say it useth as much strength in this case too, and turns the weapons it used afore quite another way. And let me tell you this, never any man comes to believe, if he will go the way of reason, while he stands considering his dead soul; as Abraham, if he had considered his own dead body, had never believed. The self-flattery that is in every man, while he is in his natural estate, is the general of all the forces of reason in him, it leads on an army of reasons to fight for this, that he is in a good estate; and though his conscience and the word of God tell him the contrary, yet he will maintain this stiffly; for he must lose such an opinion of himself if ever self-flattery should yield to the contrary. Now when God hath killed this general self-flattery, and then faith comes to lead up all the forces in a man too, then doth unbelief, then doth despair come and turn all the same forces another way. So that there is as much to do, and more, yea, infinitely more, to raise men up to bottom their hearts in a way of faith, and rightly to rest upon Christ and free grace, and to have peace with God, being justified by faith, than to shew them their natural condition. You see now that wisdom and reason in man conduceth nothing to believing, but that it is all against it.

CHAPTER III.

That all the workings of a natural conscience will not help a man to believe; but that, on the contrary, they withstand faith.

You have another principle in you (and there is a great deal of hope from that, for it is a good principle), and that is your conscience; which is indeed the best principle in a man, for it doth instigate a man to good, and hath a moral goodness in it. But let me tell you this, that take natural conscience, for we speak now of what is in nature, though never so much enlightened, and let it remain still in that state which by nature a man was in at first, and it conduceth nothing to believing; nay, it is the greatest enemy to it that the heart of man hath. Therefore still, ' Faith is not of yourselves, it is the gift of God.'

1. I confess it is a good principle in a man; it tells him of his sinfulness, but, alas! it will never help him a whit in believing. Come to conscience, and consult with that; it sets you a-doing indeed, but it will not direct you one whit in the way of faith, but rather setteth you out of the way clean contrary. It is capable of what the law saith, for itself is but the law written in the heart naturally; and it hath an ear to hear what the law saith to a man under the law, but it is deaf to what the gospel saith, and understandeth not a word of it. If you speak to natural conscience concerning a Saviour, and urge it to believe on him, its answer will be like to that of the Jews (and it was this principle of conscience which made them so speak), John ix. 29, ' As for Moses, we know that God spake unto him; but this fellow, we know not whence he is.' Just so saith conscience; Moses I know, and if you talk to me of the law, and what I ought to do, I can hear it; but as for the gospel, the truth is, I know not the thing, it is a stranger to me.

2. Nay, which is more, conscience enlightened will help to discover all sort of sins, and tell a man roundly of them; but conscience alone will never discover unbelief to you, in the bottom of it, and will never tell you

of that ; but it must be a spiritual light in the mind and judgment that doth it. In John xvi. 8, Christ saith that it is the Spirit,—and he speaks of the Holy Ghost's coming as a comforter,—that must convince of the great sin of unbelief. There are two sins which are out of the jurisdiction of conscience to set them home upon the heart ordinarily. One is the guilt of Adam's first sin,—a man's conscience may help him through spiritual discerning to see the corruption of nature, but not the guilt of Adam's sin ordinarily,—and the other is, want of faith in Christ ; for a man to see that to be the great sin, and to have it set home upon the heart, it is the Spirit of the gospel that must do this. What comes within the compass of the law written in the heart, that conscience will tell a man of; but this is the law of faith. Come to men troubled in conscience, that make conscience of all sort of things, the truth is, they make no conscience of the matter of believing, as if there were no such command ; nay, they think they do well to argue against themselves, and that they do well to refuse the promises, and they please themselves in so doing. Men will wrangle and cavil against the command of faith, and against themselves ; whereas yet all other sins stare them in the face. Now to have the heart discern unbelief as the great sin, and to have it set home upon the soul, and to look upon faith as the great work of God, and that this I must attain to, or else I am undone, conscience will never help a man to this ; it is the Holy Ghost in your hearts, and the gospel, that must do it.

3. Let me tell you also, that conscience not subordinated unto faith, as in natural men it is not, is the greatest hindrance to believing that can be.

(1.) It is the greatest hindrance of it, first, in respect of the guilt of sin. For what is the great hindrance in believing ? The greatness of your sins, your hearts clearly misgiving you in that. Now it is conscience that is the subject of them ; and it is the conscience raiseth and conjures them up, as I may so express it, against thee ; for all the sins that lie in that dark cell thy heart, are made by conscience to appear and stare in thy face, therefore it is called an evil conscience ; for though to represent a man's sins is good, yet it is called an evil conscience, because the state of a man is evil, and it is his conscience is the representation of the man's state, and tells him so, it being the subject, the drain, the sink of all a man's sins, where they lie till such time as God stir that sink. Now what is it that keeps men from believing ? The greatness of their sins, when their conscience is awakened, it continually presents to them their sins ; and all the discouragements they have, as from their sinfulness, are from a conscience unsprinkled with the blood of Christ, unsubdued unto faith. Conscience hath not learned its lesson from faith, it hath not gone and dipped itself in the blood of Christ by faith ; for if it had, it would be quiet, and not always suggesting to a man what his sins are, so as to discourage and hinder him from believing. This the Scripture tells us : Heb. x. 22, ' Let us draw near with a true heart, in full assurance of faith, having our hearts sprinkled from an evil conscience.' What is it that sprinkles the conscience ? It is the Holy Ghost in the soul, that by faith takes the blood of Christ and sprinkles it upon the conscience ; so you have it in Heb. ix. 14, ' How much more shall the blood of Christ, who through the eternal Spirit offered himself without spot to God, purge your conscience from dead works, to serve the living God ? ' There is nothing then that can satisfy the conscience in respect of the guilt of sin, but the blood, and death, and resurrection of Jesus Christ. When a poor soul looks upon itself as thus sinful, and upon Christ as so holy, he saith as Peter did unto Christ, ' Depart from me, for I am a sinful man, O Lord,' Luke v. 8. And there-

fore your consciences, by stirring up the guilt of sin, do hinder you from believing; and whilst that conscience shall be suffered to speak louder than faith,
it will cry faith down, till that faith comes and brings in the blood of Christ;
and then that cries louder, as the apostle's comparison is in Heb. xii. 24.
Otherwise, I say, unless the conscience be sprinkled by the blood of Christ
through the Spirit of faith, the guilt of sin in the conscience will cry down
faith in a man's heart, and the voice of sin there will be louder than the
voice of the blood of Christ. In Isa. lix. 11, 12, they say, ' Salvation is
far off from us ;' they thought there was no hope. Why? Their sins did
fly in their faces, and discouraged their hearts ; for, say they, ' our transgressions are multiplied before thee, and our sins testify against us ; for our
transgressions are with us ; and as for our iniquities, we know them.' Slight
thoughts of sin further presumption, but sin discovered as it is in itself,
hinders faith. That I who am a blasphemer, injurious, &c., that I should
have mercy, is this possible ? saith the soul. I need not insist upon this,
for you all feel it.

4. Conscience hinders faith if it be not subordinated to it, for conscience
is a secret enemy, and the closest enemy that can be of any other thing
that is in man unto the way of believing, and hinders the work of faith
more closely and secretly than anything else, till Jesus Christ and his
Spirit hath subdued and subordinated it to be a servant unto faith. To
express my meaning, and to convince you of this, you will all yield that
know anything of God, that there is nothing so opposite to the gospel as
the law is, unless it be subordinated to the gospel. It must have, in a
manner, all the formality of it destroyed, though the materiality remain.
If any man seek for salvation in a legal way, he must needs acknowledge
he crosses the way of the gospel and the law of faith, as Paul expresses it
in Rom. iii. and ix. 32, 33, and the whole Epistle to the Galatians is
evident for it. Now if that the law be thus in itself, as it is a covenant of
works opposite unto the gospel, then likewise is natural conscience (though
never so much enlightened, if it remain still a natural conscience, as it doth
till faith hath got the victory of it) also an enemy unto faith, and must
needs be so. And the reason of it is this, because that natural conscience,
and the light it takes in by the Spirit, or however otherwise, is the vicegerent for the law; for it is that principle in a man which God hath set up
for to make a man apprehensive of all that the law shall say. It doth keep,
as I may so express it, the law's court in a man's heart. Now, on the
other side, this great principle of faith, and the Holy Ghost acting of it,
and acting the soul in a way of faith, is that which keeps the gospel's court;
that is, all its proceedings concerning a man's condemnation, justification,
salvation, absolution, they are all despatched by faith, and that in the way
of an evangelical covenant.

Now, my brethren, this is a certain truth, likewise, that all men in their
natural condition, they are under the law. Let them be never so much
enlightened with the knowledge of the gospel, yet, notwithstanding, for
certain the law is the predominate principle in them ; as, on the contrary,
he that is brought into the state of salvation, he is under grace ; it is the
apostle's distinction in Rom. vi. 14. And being under grace, under the
free grace of God in Christ, under the gospel, he is under faith as the
supreme principle in his heart. As the strength of sin is the law, so the
strength of conscience is the law; but the strength of faith it is the gospel,
and the grace of God in Christ. The apostle, in that Rom. vi., compares
the law and grace to two sovereigns, two kings, which do sway the heart
and spirit in their several ways ; that is, if the person of the man be still

under the law, then the law sways the heart in a legal way; if he be under grace, then doth the free grace of God in Christ sway the heart in a gospel way; and the one doth this by reason and the means of conscience, and the other by means of the Spirit of faith. Now then, go take a man in whom hitherto the highest and supremest principle in him hath been the conscience remaining in its natural defilement, though never so much enlightened, it will be true to its master, true to the law, and will never subject to this new stranger faith, that will bring the free grace of God in Christ as a supreme sovereign over the other. It will stand for it to the death, it will (I say) be faithful to him whose vicegerent it is; it will strive, and especially in the point of justification. If it have not the face to do it plainly and directly, it will do it secretly, and it will turn the very gospel into a legal way. If it will comply with the knowledge of the gospel, and the knowledge of faith exceeding far, yet still it will seek to undermine it; it will carry on the heart in a way of works, yea it will turn the duties of the gospel themselves into works, and underhand seek to be justified by faith.

5. Conscience, if it did proceed aright, so as to help faith, yet it should do no more than what the law is to do. And what is the law's office? To shew a man his sinfulness, and his inability to help himself to do anything; to discover corrupt nature to a man, and send him with a new petition to the court of free grace, and, as I may so express it, to follow the allusion taken, Gal. iii. 24, to whip the soul thither, and to be a schoolmaster hereby to faith. This, I say, is that which conscience should do if it proceed aright; it should lay open all a man's sinfulness to him, send him with a petition to the throne of grace (as in Heb. iv. you have it), where grace sits as king, and thereto own grace as a sovereign, and to take the law from its mouth, conscience itself professing that it finds the heart so corrupt, and such an utter inability in it, that it can never attain to God's favour by itself, or any course which conscience can prosecute. Thus conscience should accompany faith to Christ, and deal with Christ nakedly and immediately, both for justification, and likewise for sanctification and glory, and whatever he is to receive. Now conscience should wait to receive a new commission from the throne of grace, and from faith, for to subserve faith in this, to direct the soul merely in what is to be done, but lets faith take its course for to supply strength to the soul to do all that it doth, for to live out of itself in another, and still to have recourse for acceptation and justification alone on that Redeemer. And when the soul hath been dealing with Christ, conscience will sometimes come in to confirm as a witness that a man lives as a justified person should do, when he hath thus acted faith upon Christ; then conscience still is subordinate unto faith, and receiveth its commission and power from it. But this you shall find by eternal experience, and it shall be found at latter day in the hearts of all men that have not saving faith, that let there be never so much enlightening, their consciences will still work in a legal way, and will in the tenor of their proceedings take a clean contrary course; and whilst conscience holds its commission from the law, it will direct and sway the heart legally, and undermine faith in the power of it. It will still set the heart a-work to seek the favour of God by doing, though it be by doing things that the gospel itself commandeth. It will still, I say, proceed according to that legal tenor, though it will diminish it much. And therefore you shall find this to be true, that whenas conscience hath subdued the heart in a way of humiliation to see a man's own sinfulness, and hath brought the heart under, and then conscience is upon the throne again, then it hath the sway of the heart; then it will listen (natural conscience

will do so, though thus enlightened), to hear all that the heart ought to do ; and look what sinfulness it sees in itself, it will set itself to practise the contrary, and put the heart upon doing of it, and will whip the heart as a runaway home to his master. But how ? To serve out his years, and to make up the time that is lost, and by such ways to get and obtain the favour of God, yea, to get faith itself ; and then, upon conforming to what it hears the word say, whether out of the law or out of the gospel, it will take upon it to pronounce a peace, and a justification, and an absolution ; for the natural office of conscience in the old covenant is to accuse, and so to excuse, and to give peace when a man doth well. And thus, instead of being a witness, it will become a judge ; it will take upon it to pronounce upon the heart the sentence of absolution. Yea, and if that a man is enlightened thus far as to be convinced that by the works of the law no flesh shall be justified, what will conscience do ? It will go and turn all the duties of the gospel, faith, and repentance, and mourning for sin, and all things else, into duties of the law ; that is, the heart shall have that resting upon them which natural conscience had upon the duties of the law. In Rom. ix. 32, there is an excellent exposition of the apostle's ; speaking of the Jews that had the ceremonial law (so much light of the gospel they had), he saith, 'They sought not righteousness by faith, but as it were by the works of the law.' Mark his phrase, ' *as it were* by the works of the law.' Some of them that were more enlightened, and saw their own sinfulness, knew that their own righteousness alone would not stand them in stead, and they sought after evangelical graces, as love unto God, and the like. You may read of one of them, a scribe, that came unto Christ, in Mark xii. 34. I know, saith he to Christ, that though the rest of the Jews and pharisees trust in all these sacrifices as mere works of the law, yet a man must have an inward work, he must love God with all the heart, and with all the understanding, and with all the soul, and with all the strength ; and this, saith he, is more than all whole burnt-offerings and sacrifices. And our Saviour Christ tells him upon this, that he was not far from the kingdom of God. But what doth he do now ? Though that which he pitched upon was that which is required by virtue of the evangelical covenant, yet his legal spirit turned this as it were into a work of the law ; he sought salvation as it were by the works of the law, and so did the Jews, though they were very much enlightened many of them. And in Rom. x. 2, saith the apostle, ' I bear them record, that they have a zeal of God, but not according to knowledge.' That zeal there which he speaks of is a zeal arising from conscience ; a conscientious zeal, as we use to call it, whereby they set themselves to aim at the glory of God, yet it was still as it were a work of the law. I do not say that any man doth attain to true love of God, or truly to aim at the glory of God above a man's self ; I do not say that any man attains to that who is not in the state of salvation, I believe the contrary plainly. But this some of them pitched upon, and did think thereby to obtain salvation, even as well as by outward works of the law. Therefore, saith the apostle, they are utterly mistaken, their conscientious zeal utterly misleads them, for it is not according to that knowledge of faith which the apostle clearly meaneth, which teacheth us to fling away all in ourselves, and to submit unto the righteousness of God, as it follows there, ver. 3.

6. And therefore, now when conscience hath once gone and got up into the throne—that is, when it hath subdued the heart to legal humblings,— the soul is then in most danger of being misled in the way of believing, when it comes just to the point. Why ? Because that conscience having

got the dominion, so as it never had so before fully till now, it will seek to hold it, and to sway the heart its own way; and if gospel-light comes in, conscience still will turn it, as it were, into the light, and tenor, and way of the law, to seek salvation still by works. But when faith, and when the Holy Ghost comes, he sets up, as I said afore, grace upon the throne, and natural conscience must then take its commission from faith, to direct a man in serving the living God, as it is Heb. ix. 14. For the truth is this, and I ought to say it, that still there is a use, and a great use of conscience; and therefore you find that obedience is made to spring from 'love and a good conscience, and faith unfeigned,' 1 Tim. i. 5, and those are the principles that Paul reckons up; and he saith of some, ver. 19, that they had 'made shipwreck of faith and a good conscience.' For still conscience remains in a man as a guide, when it is sanctified and purged by faith, that he may serve the living God; but then I say it must be indoctrinated by faith, and purified by faith; for it is faith itself that fetcheth out this legal strain that is natural to the conscience, and subdues, as all the rest of the whole heart unto faith, so conscience also. Now, in all natural men, the truth is, conscience runs into a *præmunire*, goes beyond its commission, takes upon it to absolve, to justify, to give peace, and to do it in a predominate way to faith; it does it from doing, and from what a man sees in himself, and not from the law of believing.

You may by this see the true and clear reason why that in all natural men by nature, though never so much enlightened, their spirits are acted in a legal way. The reason is clear, because that conscience is the highest principle in nature. Conscience is a principle in a man that believes, and it ought to be so when it is purified and made more quick, and enlightened with a more spiritual light to guide him in the way of serving God, but it is not the supreme principle; no, it is but an under principle unto faith; for if the matter of the law be an under thing to the gospel, certainly conscience is so to faith. Now, therefore, whilst that conscience remains the supremest principle of all things else, it must be a deadly enemy unto faith, and still sway the heart its own way, and it must needs do so till the Holy Ghost hath subdued the whole heart to a way of believing in the Lord Jesus. By what I have now said, you may see then and understand, from the proper principle that is in all men's hearts, what is the reason why they are thus misled in a way of doing, and that they 'seek righteousness not by faith, but as it were by the works of the law.' And so I pass from this principle of conscience, and from shewing how that that is an enemy unto faith, and I come to the will.

CHAPTER IV.

That all the powers of a man's will cannot enable him to believe.—That faith therefore is an effect of the infinite power of God alone.

I now come to demonstrate that the power and faculty of will in a man doth not help him to believe, but is against faith.

1. Take the will of a man in his natural condition, let that will remain but still natural, and let it be excited and stirred up never so much by light, or by conscience, or anyhow otherwise, yet till that almighty power comes that puts a new life into it, there is both first an inability in it to help a man in believing; yea, there are principles in it that are all contrary unto faith and to believing. First, to make it out to you that a man's will

is thus disenabled to believe, yea, that nothing is more unable than the will is to give up the whole man unto free grace and to God's own way of salvation by Jesus Christ. Consider how this truth is sadly confirmed to us by manifold experiences, and by the Scripture also.

If we come to many men that are upon their death-beds, or in distress, and under the fears of hell and of the wrath of God, having their consciences enlightened, and God having struck sparks of hell-fire into them, which have taken hold of all the gunpowder there, we shall find that the will in such distress, when it comes to the point of believing, sinks into a discouragement under thoughts of an impossibility. For ask them then if they will be saved? Yea, they would give ten thousand worlds to be saved. Will you but then throw yourselves upon Jesus Christ and upon free grace, and let your hearts be quieted in so doing? for to have the will brought to a quietness, this is the proper effect of faith there, to have this storm allayed, and the winds still, by rolling a man's self, and committing this little cock-boat to those waves of free grace to save him; it comes to this point, you shall find that the will sticks at nothing more, and these poor souls will then tell you that of all things else they cannot do it, and they will profess they cannot, and you shall see they cannot do it. Now, if there were any ability in the will of a man to close with the Lord Jesus Christ entirely and wholly, certainly a man would then do it, whenas he himself professeth he desires salvation more than millions of worlds. I remember in the story of Spira, who yet I believe was a believer and is in heaven, that he being left to the nakedness of his own spirit, and divested of the Holy Ghost to strengthen his heart in believing, to join with his will—for so the Holy Ghost doth when a man is enabled to believe and to rest himself quietly upon God—when all objections were answered, and all the promises of the gospel laid before him, as they were abundantly by many that came to him, and that pitied him with the greatest tenderness that can be, he still complained of this, I have a wound in my will, and I cannot do it, I cannot believe; as once one said, being exhorted to lay hold upon Jesus Christ, Bid me, saith he, pointing up to heaven, lay hold upon yonder star!

Besides the manifold experience that we have of the truth of this point, I shall give you a scripture or two for it. In John i. 13 the evangelist, speaking, at the latter end of the 12th verse, of them that believe, he adds, verse 13, 'which were born not of blood'—for say not you have Abraham to your father—'nor of the will of the flesh.' Take the natural will that every man hath, and it will not help him to believe. No; he that believeth truly he is 'born of God;' so saith the text in 1 John v. 1. 'He that believeth on the Son of God' (as verse 10 hath it, for you must take both together), and doth do this truly, 'he is born of God;' and his being born of God, so as to believe, is not of the will of the flesh. Compare these two places together, and they clear this point fully. And in this Eph. ii. what is the eminent thing that the apostle in the series of his discourse doth hold forth as the reason why faith is not of a man's self? He had said afore, verse 1 and verse 4, that we were 'dead in sins and trespasses;' and that faith is a new life, ver. 5. And where lies the death most? Truly you will find in verse 3 that it is in the will: 'fulfilling,' saith he, 'the wills of the flesh;' so it is in the original. As the chief subject of death is the heart, so the chief subject of this spiritual death is the will of a man. And (saith he) know this, that you being dead in sins and trespasses, and dead in your wills especially, ye are saved by grace through faith; and that not of yourselves, it is the gift of God. It is the will, *i. e.*, the heart especially, that is the seat of faith ; 'with the heart a man believeth to salvation,' Rom. x. 10. To embrace mercy and grace offered according to the word, to close with it upon God's own terms, to bring the will off to this, this is a great point indeed ; for he must be born of God that believes truly, because it is not through the will of the flesh, for that is a dead will, utterly unable to believe. And because I have fallen upon that place in Rom. x., give me leave to speak a little out of it. The apostle there doth shew you (that you may see what a hard thing it is for the soul to believe thus) what plunges the hearts of men are put to when they are emptied of themselves and of their own righteousness. He had shewn in the former part of that chapter, and in the latter end of the 9th chapter, that it was the great error and fault of the Jews that they sought righteousness ' as it were by the works of the law,' as I said even now. Now whenas a Jew, in whose case the apostle puts it, for he had discoursed of the Jews all along, should come to be convinced that he could have no righteousness by doing, see but what plunges that man's heart will be put to : ' The righteousness which is of faith,' saith he, ver. 6, ' speaks on this wise : Say not in thine heart, Who shall ascend into heaven ? (that is, to bring Christ down from above) ; or, Who shall descend into the deep ? (that is, to bring up Christ again from the dead).' Here you see the law of faith, when it comes to direct a man, doth begin to empty out of him abundance of sayings that the heart is apt to run into. Say not in thy heart, saith he ; the Holy Ghost goes to the bottom of the heart, and fetcheth up those despairing thoughts that arise out of the fainting, and succumbency, and despondency of the will ; and he pitcheth upon those sayings that the heart in that case is apt to form up against itself when a man is emptied of his own righteousness.

I will open this place of the apostle a little, ' Say not in thine heart,' &c. The heart, when once it hath lost a bottom in itself, and is cast off from that legal way, is apt amongst other things to run into all sort of thoughts of impossibilities of ever attaining unto life. He expresseth the case as in the instance of a Jew living under the old law, that had heard in the abstract that there should be a Messiah, and that God must be satisfied by that Messiah. Now how would that Jew reason with himself in this case ? He would say, Who shall climb up into heaven, to bring down a Messiah from thence ? for he that must be my Messiah, and must save me, must come down from thence. *Quis, quis,* saith he, Who, who can go up to heaven and climb up thither ? No man hath a ladder to do this ; and though the angels go thither, can all the angels in heaven persuade the Messiah to come down from heaven and die for me, and do thus and thus for me, that I may be saved ? He speaks, I say, in the case of a Jew that is put off from the law, and lies under terrors of conscience, and hath heard of a Messiah, and that God for his part is willing to save men if the Messiah will do thus and thus. Such sayings as these, and such thoughts of impossibilities, will rise up in the man's heart ; ' Who shall ascend into heaven to bring Christ down from above ?' or when he is brought down from heaven here upon earth in the nature of a man, who shall persuade him to undergo the wrath of God for my sins, and to satisfy for them, or they must never be satisfied for ? or if he be willing to do it, who shall support him in undergoing this ? Or ' who shall go down into the deep, into the abyss, to bring up this Christ again from the dead ?' for he must rise again, or else he can never satisfy for my sins, and so I shall never be saved. Oh who can do all this ? A Jew now would have all these thoughts, and have tired himself in these impossibilities concerning his salvation, if once he see he cannot have it by the law, which hitherto he hath gone by. And these words which the apostle here useth, he quoteth out of Deut. xxx. 11. Now you must know this, that though Moses had most of all preached the law, and given it at mount Sinai, and had hid the gospel under the types and shadows of legal ceremonies ; yet now when he was to die, he doth, through the Holy Ghost coming upon him, preach the gospel and deliver the covenant thereof clearly and plainly to the Jews ; for you may read in Deut. xxix 1, that he calls it ' the words of the cove-nant which the Lord commanded Moses to make with the children of Israel in the land of Moab, beside the covenant which he made with them in Horeb.' It is another covenant ; and therefore the apostle pertinently quotes the words of this last great sermon of Moses, to distinguish the covenant of works and the covenant of grace. Now then he propounds this covenant unto them ; and when the soul comes to enter into that cove-nant, being left naked by the law, Moses sheweth the averseness that is in the heart thereunto, and how apt the spirits of men are to turn aside into all sort of thoughts of impossibilities in the way of that covenant. When the law was given in Horeb, Exod. xix. 8, when that other covenant was given, oh then they were very forward, as if they would have undertaken to have fulfilled the whole law : ' All that the Lord hath spoken,' say they, ' that will we do.' But when Moses comes to preach this other covenant, besides that which he had taught them before, he knew well enough, as the 11th verse of that Deut. xxx. hath it, that they would say in their hearts, ' Oh this is hid from us.' ' But this commandment,' saith he, ' which I command thee this day, it is not hidden from thee, neither is it far off : it is not in heaven, that thou shouldst say, Who shall go up for us to heaven, and bring it unto us, that we may hear it and do it ? ' (you may see that they made a greater difficulty of this covenant, than they did of fulfilling the law delivered in Horeb) ; 'neither is it beyond the sea, that thou shouldst say, Who shall go over the sea for us, and bring it unto us, that we may hear it and do it ? ' They were apt to say that this covenant was hidden from them ; and the word there used for *hidden* is used by Moses also for what is too hard, for what is impossible, as in Gen. xviii. 11, the angel tells Sarah, when the promise was made of Isaac, ' Is any thing too hard for the Lord ?' Now if you look into Luke i. 37, you shall find, that unto Mary the mother of our Lord Christ, that unto her, being in the same unbelief in some degree of it, the angel useth the same expression, only changeth the word *too hard* into *impossible :* ' Is any thing impossible for the Lord ? ' That which is here *hidden,* is all one with *hard,* and that is all one with *impossible.* So that this is his meaning, when he saith, ' Say not this com-mandment is hidden from thee '; that is, ' Say not that it is impossible for thee to attain it.'

And, by the way, let me give you this note upon those two places last quoted. Isaac, you know, was the type of Christ, eminently made so in Rom. iv., and also in Heb. xi. Now it is observable that the angel used the same word to Sarah the mother of Isaac, when his birth was promised, that the angel useth to Mary, whenas the incarnation of Christ, typified out by Isaac, was promised also. Now the instances which Moses gives of climbing up to heaven, and going over the sea, were to the Jews the lan-guage of impossibilities. They were ready to say, You may as well bid me go climb up to heaven ; and where shall we have ladders to do that ? You may as well bid us go over the world, and fathom the great gulf, the great sea, and fetch things from far, which in those days, because they wanted the loadstone, and therefore could not launch out into the vast ocean, but were fain to creep along by the coasts, was thought a thing impossible ; you may as well bid us do these things as bid us believe in this word, and join with this covenant you now give us. This their hearts were apt to say. Now the apostle, alluding to this place, and giving the interpretation of it, speaks in the language of a Jew that is to believe on Christ as to come, and as coming to die for him ; which Jew, when he shall hear that he is a sinner, and that the law cannot help him, nor all his sacrifices and oblations, but that there must be a mediator that must satisfy God for his sins, and this mediator must come from heaven to do it, and he must go to hell too, and be fetched up again from thence, will presently say within himself, ' Who shall go up to heaven' to persuade the Messiah to come down and die for me ?   Alas, it is impossible I should be saved if this be the way of salvation.   And when the Messiah is here, and is to undergo the wrath of God, and to die upon the cross, who shall support him ?   This the soul of a Jew would be apt to speak, as sinking under the desperate impossibilities of this way of salvation.   Now these impossibilities which the heart of a Jew would forge, and did forge unto themselves, the same under the gospel do the spirits of men, if the Holy Ghost leaves them but a little unto themselves. Though they hear what God hath done, that he hath gone and sent Jesus Christ from heaven for them, and hath fetched him again from the deep (for what Moses calleth the sea, the gulf, that the apostle interprets hell, at least by way of allusion), and that God requires nothing in the world of them but to believe this ; so saith ver. 9 of Rom. x., ' If thou shalt believe in thine heart that God hath raised him from the dead, thou shalt be saved.' Yet notwithstanding, though a Christian knows all this, and though the gospel and the way of believing is most clearly and nakedly preached, the soul, when it forecasteth with itself all his own sinfulness, and unworthiness, and discouragements, will sink under the same thoughts of the impossibility of his salvation that the Jew had : he will still be saying, Who shall climb up to heaven, to bring Christ down to this heart of mine ? or where shall I have a ladder to reach up to close with Jesus Christ ? or if I be sinking down to hell, who can go and get Christ to put forth his arm to pull me out again ?   This, I say, is the manner of the spirits of men, even under the gospel.   The scope of the apostle there, is to hold forth two contradictions, namely, that of all things else, it is the most easy to believe, and that of all things else, it is the most impossible ; so taking in all that the sinful heart of man is apt to say of itself.   It is easy, a man will say, for it is no more but this : there is Christ, and there is the word, God hath done all for you ; he hath sent Christ down from heaven to die for you, and all is ready, and God requires nothing of you, when the news is brought to your hearts, but closing with it.   So that take the act in itself, and it is the easiest thing in the world that God requires, the smallest matter that could be required of the sons of men.   But yet, when a man is divested of his own righteousness, he will have thoughts of a thousand impossibilities, as this despairing Jew had, and he will still have such sayings in his heart, Who shall bring this Christ down hither ? and who shall move this Christ to pull me up from the deep when I am sinking thither ?   Is it possible that God should ever do thus for me ?   Is there any hope that he should regard my soul so from everlasting, as to persuade his Son to come and die for me that am thus and thus a sinner ?   Is it possible that ever salvation and I should meet ?   That though God hath sent Christ down from heaven, and he is come up again from the deep, is it likely that Christ should do this for me ?   I may as well think to climb up to heaven, and take hold of Christ there, and go down into the deep, and come up with Christ there

in my heart, as to believe·this.   The heart, I say, is apt to fall into these
thoughts of impossibilities.

I have been the longer upon this, because it gives light to that scripture, which is exceeding difficult to understand.   I know there is another
meaning of the words, namely, that when the soul is emptied of itself, and
hears that there is a Christ, it thinks to get him by endeavours.   What
though I have nothing in myself, yet I hope to climb up to heaven, &c.
But the text clearly holds forth likewise, these despairing sinful thoughts
which the soul is apt to have when it comes to believe ; therefore what
saith the apostle in the following verses of that chapter ?   Though God requires no more of men but that they believe that God hath raised Christ
from the dead, and that all these impossibilities which the Jew might
plead are taken away, and that God looks for nothing more than that the
heart and the word meet, yet how doth the apostle complain, that although
they have heard, yet ' who hath believed our report ? ' verse 16.   For a
man so to believe it as to give up his soul unto it, who hath done it ?   Few
do it ; so that, though Jesus Christ be thus nakedly and plainly taught,
and men need not frame the Jew's impossibilities of moving Christ to come
down from heaven and die, and of supporting him under his Father's
wrath, and bringing him up again from the grave, yet to persuade them to
rest quietly in this Christ, and to have their hearts and wills quiet in so
doing, how hard a business is it ?   When the soul is humbled for sin, and
stripped of itself, it is the greatest impossibility, as to his own power, to
believe ; ' Who hath believed our report ? ' and why ?   Because the arm of
the Lord is not revealed.   It must be the arm of the Lord, an almighty
power, that must do it.

I shall end this thing only with giving you the reason of it, why it is
thus hard, and why the heart fancies all these impossibilities in faith, that
though God hath done so much, yet to believe that God should have done
this so for me as that I may come and rest upon it, and to have my heart
quieted in so doing, is of all things in the world the hardest and the most
impossible.

This is a rule which I believe will be found true, that look what power
God puts forth in doing anything, the same power is required to draw the
heart in to believe that God is able, or that God hath done that thing ; I
mean to believe the thing in earnest, so as to venture all my soul for ever
upon it.   This is partly the scope of that place in Eph. i. 18, 19, where
the apostle saith, that ' the same power that went to raise up Christ from
the dead, goes to the working of faith in them that believe.'   The Jew
now in his despair (because Christ was not as yet come) must needs conclude that it must be an almighty power and engagement that must draw
Christ from heaven, and support him under the wrath of God, and bring
him from hell to be a Saviour unto him.   But now, after all this is done,
there must yet go as great a power to cause a man to believe that Christ
hath done all this for him, as there did to make Christ do this.   The
place is express in that Eph. i. 19, where the apostle plainly saith that
the same greatness of power which wrought in Christ when he was raised
from the dead, works in those that believe, in causing the soul to rest
quietly upon this Christ for justification and salvation.   So that, although
God now requires nothing of us under the gospel but to believe the thing
is done (in the manner I have spoken), yet there must be as much power
go to work that faith in the soul, as to bring Christ from heaven, and to
raise him up again, which was the thing the Jew in his despairings stuck
at.   This is a great truth (and I shall give you a further ground for it),

that it is all one for God to do a thing, and to make a man believe it, and that the same power is required to the one as much as the other. In Mark ix. 22, 23, the father of the possessed child comes to our Lord and Saviour Jesus Christ; and what saith the poor man in the doubtings of his spirit, and misgivings of his heart? 'Lord,' saith he, 'if thou canst do anything, have compassion on us and help us.' There he questions Christ and his power. What answer doth Christ give him again, who had more reason to question him than he had to question Christ? 'Jesus said unto him, If thou canst believe, all things are possible to him that believeth.' Here Christ and the man do, as it were, stand looking one at another; 'If thou canst help me,' saith the man, 'If thou canst believe,' saith Christ, all things are possible. I observe this from it, that Jesus Christ makes it the greatest matter to believe; when the poor man asked him if he could do that which required an omnipotent power, saith he, Canst thou believe? And he gives the reason of the hardness of it, because he that believes aright, that man's faith doth invest itself, as it were, and doth join issue with the omnipotent power of God; and he that believeth the one, viz., that an infinite power that can do thus and thus, his faith is stretched to a kind of infiniteness; therefore saith Christ in the next words, 'all things are possible unto him that believeth.' Now, for a man when he is convinced of his sinfulness, to believe that God is able to pardon him, or to believe anything else in the matter of salvation, there must be as great a power come from God to make a man do this in earnest, to work this in a man's heart that this is possible to be done, as there is power in God to do it; God can as easily do it as he can do the thing itself, and he can as easily do the thing itself, as make the man believe it. As there is a hand of omnipotency stretched out to do things of omnipotency, so there must be an eye created by the omnipotent power of God to elevate the soul of a man to see it, and the will quietly to rest upon it, and to leave all else, and to betake itself to this power of God, to this will of God, this grace of God, and mercy of God. I say, comparing these two places together, Christ speaks as if the working of a man to believe were a matter of as great power as to do the thing. So far as anything is impossible to any one's thoughts, so far it is incredible; so far as it is possible, so far it is credible; and therefore, if a man believes that this thing is possible to be done which requires an infinite power to do it, he must believe in that infinite power, and it must be infinite power that must stretch the soul to believe this, and to rest quietly in it. Therefore to draw the heart to believe is all one as to bring the Messiah down from heaven, and up from the grave again, though the thing itself, on our parts, seem a poor matter to it; yet take the act itself, the same power goes to the one as to the other, and the heart of a man under the gospel will be as apt to object impossibilities, and doth object, as the Jew himself did before the Messiah came.

CHAPTER V.

That all in man's will is opposite to faith, and withstands his believing.

As there is thus an inability in the will to the way of believing, so there is an adverseness. Not only is there nothing in the will which can help a man, but there is a resistance in the will to the work of faith, and to believing. I shall give you one scripture for it, which is John v. 40. Saith Christ there, 'You will not come to me that ye might have life.' The

place is full to the point in hand.   Our Saviour Christ speaks complain-
ingly, and wondering at it, as you shall see by his discourse.   I and my
Father, saith he, I profess to you, require nothing of you but that you
would have a will to come unto me, that your wills be but brought off to
close with me according to my worth ; that you would be but a willing
people, as it is in Ps cx., and as he saith in Rev. xxii. 17, ' He that is a
willing man ' (so the word is in the original) ' let him take of the water of
life freely.'   Thus speaks he here, I require nothing else but that you have
a will to come unto me ; and as he said at the 6th verse of John v. to the
man that had an infirmity thirty-eight years, ' Wilt thou be made whole ?'—
that is, hast thou a will to be made whole by me, by leaving all things else,
and giving thyself up unto me and my power ?   I require nothing else of
thee,—so saith he to these Jews, I require no more of men to be saved, but
that they will come unto me ; yet, saith he, and he speaks wondering at it,
' you will not come to me that ye might have life.'   It is certain of the
Pharisees, whom he spake to, and so of all men else, that their wills pitch
upon this, that they would be saved.   It is clear these Pharisees did so.
You think, saith he, to have eternal life in Moses's writings.   I know there
is one Moses in whom ye trust, ver. 45.   But mark it, and see the infinite
stubbornness and averseness of the will of man in his natural condition by
this instance.   You would fain have eternal life, saith he, and you think to
have it by the Scriptures and Moses's law, and so you choose rather to venture
your salvations upon doing all that Moses hath said, and you will rather
go and trust in Moses as a lawgiver, as one that hath presented God as a
judge to you, who hath cursed you if you continue not in everything the
law requires to do, and so venture upon that curse, rather than you will be
brought off to come to me for everlasting life.   This is clearly his scope.
In reading the Scriptures, saith he, you will make such interpretations of
them as shall fit your cursed opinions of attaining salvation in a legal way,
rather than you will go search the Scriptures a little more to see how Moses
prophesied of me.   ' Search the Scriptures,' saith he, ' for they are they
which testify of me ;' but you will not come to me that ye might have life,
you will trust in Moses rather, yea, in Moses that accuseth you, for in your
consciences you cannot but find that Moses doth accuse you.   I come as a
Saviour, and require nothing of you but a will to come unto me, and you
will not do it : you will go venture yourselves upon a killing letter, upon a
ministry of condemnation, and not upon the law of free grace.   Nay, Christ
aggravates the sin of man's will by this, ver. 43, ' If a man come in his
own name, him you will receive.'   These cursed Jews (give me leave to
call them so, for the wrath of God came on them to the uttermost) did and
would trust upon I know not how many false Christs, that in those days,
and after Christ's ascension, told them they were Messiahs.   They came
in their own names, merely in their own power, without any miracles ; but,
saith Christ, I am come in my Father's name, and not in my own name,
and I am come with all power and miracles, and yet you do not receive me,
you will not believe me, no, not for my work's sake.   What can be clearer
than this, that in the wills of men there is that inbred in them, that of all
things they will take any course rather than clearly, and nakedly, and entirely
give up themselves to Jesus Christ, to have eternal life in his way ?

The reasons of this averseness in the will of man to the way of believing
are chiefly these :—

1. The will of man is set, if it will be saved, to be saved in its own way.
It is natural to men, if they be not saved that way, that they themselves
would, for the will to grow sturdy.   If God will save them in their own

way, then, indeed, they are willing to be saved, but they will not be saved in God's way. Look what way the heart of a man naturally fancieth to itself to be saved in (as it doth the way of doing and the like), that way the will sticks to; and you may move the earth off of its centre as soon as move the heart off of that way it is set upon. A man is apt to be in a chafe if he cannot have a thing his own way. As in that instance of Naaman, in 2 Kings v. 11, 12, ' I thought,' saith he, in a pet, and in a chafe, ' that he would surely have come out to me, and do so and so. Doth he bid me go and wash in Jordan? I could have washed at home in better waters than all the waters of Israel.' So that because the way for his cure, which was designed by the prophet, was so contrary to the way that his fancy and mind pitched upon, hence therefore he would have none of it. So is it with the sturdy spirits of men to this day. The way that pure nature went was a way of doing, and the will of man sticks to that way still, and never will be brought over but by an almighty power; for you may as soon throw the earth off the hinges of it as stir and remove the will from its obstinate posture. If you have any work for me to do, saith the will or conscience, I will be doing, but to believe, I am resolved against it.

I will give you an instance of it in the Galatians. It is evident the apostle thought they had true grace many of them; it is clear in Gal. v. 8, ' This persuasion cometh not of him that calleth you;' and I am confident, saith he, that God will bring you off again. But yet, notwithstanding, see the madness of it, as he himself calls it; and truly it is a strange thing, but that nature will have its course in the hearts of men, otherwise I say it is the strangest thing in the world, that these Galatians, so that they might ease themselves a little of waiting through the Spirit for the righteousness of faith, would choose to be in bondage to the whole ceremonial law. Nay, which makes the wonder yet more, the Gentiles (such as these Galatians were) never had the ceremonial law given them, and therefore though the apostle did permit the Jews to continue in the ceremonial law after the ascension, though they were believers, yet Paul flies in the face of the Gentiles if they offered it; for, saith he, you were never under it; yet, I say, these Galatians would rather put themselves under a yoke which they were free of, which God never at any time put upon them, than through the Spirit wait for the hope of righteousness by faith. So prevalent is this strain of spirit which is in the consciences and wills of men, and such an averseness to the matter of believing, not an averseness to salvation, for all men desire that, but to the way of salvation, which is by faith in Jesus Christ, that men would rather do anything than believe. The great contest between God and the hearts of men is practically, though men know and discern that God will have them saved in his way, yet they will be saved in their own way and upon their own terms; and rather than they will believe in Christ, which is God's way of salvation, they will put themselves under the hardest bondage that can be. You may see it verified in the papists, and truly there is a world of this popery in the hearts of all men; they would rather go and give over their kingdoms, put themselves into monasteries, lie in hair, live upon the alms of others, tire out themselves by saying the whole book of Psalms over once every twenty-four hours, and to that end rise twice or thrice in the night, break their sleeps, whip and rend their bodies, do all this rather than betake themselves to faith; for indeed there is nothing they jeer more and contemn, than the way of justification by faith. And many of Christ's sheep themselves hang in these briars, and do not come home clearly and fully to this way of God; they will sit down in humiliation I know not how many years before they will stir a foot to Jesus Christ, and the free grace of God ; they will go and spend all their time and thoughts in proving the old work (which hath, it may be, been true and sound in itself), rather than stir immediately unto Jesus Christ and free grace, to begin a new or a farther work upon them. Experience shews how true this is in the souls of men ; and the reason is this, because man sticks in this, to be saved in his own way, and will not be saved in God's way ; even just as Naaman the Syrian acted in the instance before mentioned.

2. The second reason, or rather the second and chief thing in the will of man that makes it thus averse, is that self, as I may so call it, that is in every man.   That which we call self, or sticking to a man's self, and pleasing of a man's self, this same self is strongest in the will above all other powers in a man.   The will is the throne and seat of self, even as the heart is the seat of spirits ; and self will always rest in itself, as the earth doth upon its centre, and will never be removed till that Jesus Christ flings it off of its own hinges.   Now as the will is the chief seat of self, so the chiefest of self-denial lies in the will in the way of believing ; as when a man comes to believe, there is a great deal of self-denial in the understanding, but the great self-denial lies in the will.   There is a great deal of self-denial in the understanding: Prov. iii. 5, ' Trust in the Lord with all thine heart, and lean not unto thine own understanding.'   There are no things more opposite than faith, and leaning unto a man's own understanding ; therefore I say there is a great self-denial there, to give up all my thoughts for ever to the wisdom and authority of another, to give God leave to take out both my eyes, and only to take me by the hand, and lead me and guide me whither he will, and to strengthen me and teach me the way whither I should go, to bring every thought into the obedience of Christ ; this is great self-denial.   But the will is more put to it.   You shall find in Rom. x., that Paul doth resolve the reason of men's not believing into the wills of men, and into the want of self-denial there.   He begins to tell them a strange thing at the latter end of the 9th chapter : ' What shall we say ? ' saith he, ver. 30.   I will tell you a strange thing, which you will all wonder at, and know not what to say to ; yet I must say it.   And what is that ?   It is this, saith he : ' The Gentiles, which followed not after righteousness, have attained to righteousness.'   This is a contradiction, that those that did not follow nor pursue after righteousness at all should attain it, especially you will think so when you hear the rest : ' But Israel, which followed after the law of righteousness, hath not attained to the law of righteousness,' or, ' the righteousness of the law.'   There must be some great reason of this. He tells you the reason of it.   First, he saith that the righteousness which the Gentiles attained was ' the righteousness which is of faith ; ' so ver. 30, ' But Israel,' saith he,' ' hath not attained to the law of righteousness.' Why ?   ' Because they sought it not by faith, but as it were by the works of the law,' so ver. 32.   And God, saith he, hath made these two so contradictory one to another, that he that doth seek righteousness as it were by works, though he may mince the matter much, yet he shall never attain to it ; for the Holy Ghost hath pronounced it in Gal. v. 4, that ' Christ is of no effect' to him that goes that way.   So that these two being incompatible, hence it was that the Jew could not attain to the righteousness he sought for.   But what was it that hindered him ?   The apostle satisfies us : Rom. x. 3, ' They being ignorant of God's righteousness, and going about to establish their own righteousness, have not submitted themselves unto the righteousness of God.'   He ascribes it first to an ignorance in them ; there now comes in the understanding, ' they being ignorant,'

saith he, ' of God's righteousness.' But then the other two hindrances lie in the will, and they do lie in the will where self hath its principal seat and throne. For, he saith, ' they sought to establish their own righteousness ;' mark that word, ' their own righteousness.' When we are said to be saved, it is according to God's own purpose and grace (as I remember the expression is in 2 Thes. i. 12). Here now doth self come in, and will needs set up its own righteousness. He brings it in like to a design that a company of men have in a state ; as they would set such a one up king, and all their courses bend that way, or as a stepmother would set up her son to be king against the true heir, so they sought to establish their own righteousness ; there lies the reason, you see self is in it, they sought to establish it because it is their own. And they were zealous in this ; for they being ignorant of God's righteousness were zealous of their own. And this word *establish* is exceeding emphatical ; it is making a thing that is tottering to stand ; like setting up a dead man or a sick man, if you set him up again and again, he falls : but yet their design was, that though all their works of righteousness did fall before their own consciences, and their own hearts misgave them, yet self was so strong in them as it would needs be still making their own righteousness to stand ; they sought to establish it, as the apostle saith. As man is said to seek out many inventions, so all the endeavour and sway of their heart went that way, which notes out the natural design, and project, and drift of their hearts, that they sought to establish their own righteousness.

2. But then a second thing in the will is, a pride which would not be subject to the righteousness of God ; so the next words are, but ' have not submitted themselves,' saith he, ' to the righteousness of God.' They had some glimmerings of it certainly, both in the ministry of the prophets and holy men amongst them, who did teach in their synagogues, but still they would not submit, and all that could be done could never bring them to it. It is the same word that is used in Rom. viii. 7, where, speaking of the corruption that is in us, of flesh, he saith it is ' enmity against God, for it is not subject to the law of God, neither indeed can be.' There is a great deal of enmity naturally in men against the law of God, against the duties and commands of it ; but there is ten thousand times more enmity in the wills of men against the way of the gospel. Here the word likewise is a passive word ; they would not be subjected, all that could be done would not bring them under. So that clearly and plainly you see, it is not only an ignorance in the understanding, and carnal reasonings there ; it is not only a sinking of the will out of apprehensions of impossibilities, and fostering all such apprehensions (as it is ver. 6 of Rom. x.) ; but it is also a going about to establish their own righteousness, and a not submitting, out of pride of heart, a secret pride of spirit of self in a man, unto the righteousness of God ; that is, that righteousness which God out of ourselves in Christ hath provided for us.

Now let us consider what of self there is in the will, and how far the principle of self is against believing, and how far self is denied in it, and that not in the consequence of believing, but in the acts and concomitants of it.

And before I shall say what I have to say thereof in the particulars, let me say this to you first, that of all corruptions in your hearts, the working of self in the will of a man is the most still, the most secret. It is not drawn forth into propositions ; a man doth not say distinctly within himself, I will have none of God's righteousness, but mine own. No ; the workings of self-love in a man do seldom come forth into such distinct thoughts, but it is inlaid, and it works naturally, slily, slowly, and strongly; yet when a man shall resolve his actions into principles, he shall find that *that* is at bottom. So that I say it may be you will not find what I shall now say of this self, to arise in distinct thoughts within you, but yet the principle of self being in the will sways it that way, that it will not submit to the righteousness of God. It is inlaid, I say, in it, and connatural. The thoughts of unbelief are seldom drawn forth into propositions. Who almost in his heart doth distinctly and deliberately think there is no God? Yet the thought that there is no God sways all the life of a wicked man: 'The fool hath said in his heart, there is no God,' and that is the reason of all his sinfulness. Who is there that saith within himself, I will thus and thus love myself, I am resolved and purposed so to do? It needeth not, it is inlaid in a man's heart, and there needs no new purpose or resolution so to do.

Now let us consider what self-denial God requires in the will when a man comes to believe. I will not urge that which some have urged, as that in believing the soul must so come to God as to aim more at glorifying God in it, than the saving of himself, and have such a distinct thought within himself. That this should be the aim of a man's faith when first he comes to God and to Christ, or that this should be the self-denial that God requires, distinctly so to do, is too hard to put the truth of faith upon. You shall observe the Scripture speaks unto men coming out of their natural estates, and when they come to believe, and inviteth them upon principles of self-love. 'What shall I do to be saved?' saith the poor heart. 'Believe, and thou shalt be saved,' saith the Scripture. Only the law of faith is to do so and so for him that died for thee. The truth is, to say that the glory of God should be the aim of a man's heart in his first believing, or else his heart is not right, is to make the love of God to be before faith in a man. Neither will I urge the point of self-denial, which is higher than the former, that a man must be content to be disposed by God as he pleaseth, be willing to be saved, or to go to hell, to be disposed in any way, so God may be glorified. I wonder that any should make this at least a part of preparation to faith, which is the highest act that can be supposed to flow from believing at any time, and than which nothing is greater. That any should make that to go before faith, which God seldom or never puts men to when he hath given them assurance, and hath given them communion with himself, for then they are out of the supposition of it. I say this is hard to me, and certainly it is not this self-denial that is thus the concomitant of faith. And I shall say of it, through the grace that is given me, only this, that as in the sin against the Holy Ghost, for so I use to call it, there is such an enmity in the heart of a wicked man that sins that great sin, as to desire above all things to be revenged upon God, for that is the property of that sin; as that, I say, is the highest degree of sin, so this is the highest disposition of grace. Now millions of wicked men have never that spirit of enmity against God drawn out, as they that sin that sin have. So, on the contrary, there is many a soul that has abundance of grace and holiness, and goes to heaven with it, that never had this disposition of self-denial drawn forth out of it. It is indeed a duty, but upon occasion, when the heart is put to it, either in desperate temptations, or else sometimes in a way of supposition hypothetically, when the soul enjoys most communion with God. It is when God begins with his sovereignty to contend with the will of man, and resolves to break it. I will not say but there is that in grace which will do it, for there is no attribute in God but the image of God in us hath somewhat to answer and comply withal; therefore if God will shew his sovereignty in the salvation of men, if his sovereignty will put the heart to it, where the image of God is there is a principle to comply with that sovereignty. But this I say, God doth not do it, or but seldom, and but to a few: and therefore this is not that self-denial (which I am now to speak to) which is a hindrance in the way of believing. God doth not insist on the denial of mere self, but of sinful self. Now to put a man upon a being contented to go to hell that God may be glorified is the denial of mere self, and God doth not always put this upon men. I confess it is a forfeit, which, because we are sinners, God may take of us and make us vail to; but God doth not ordinarily put men to it. Christ indeed in the gospel puts men upon the denial of sinful self, 'How can you believe,' saith he, John v. 44, 'if you love yourselves?' but not upon the other. And though Paul did it, and Moses did it, yet it was not in pursuit of their own salvations, and as a condition of being saved, but in zeal to God for the salvation of others. The truth is, God leads men on in the way of believing rather by glorifying his free grace in saving men, not only in saving them at last, but in letting them see that his glory and their good are joined together, and that this should strengthen their faith, that in their salvation God will be infinitely glorified. And God loves us so well, as he would have us in seeking salvation from him, and in seeking his glory, therein to love ourselves also. But now to come to those self-denials which are in the will, and which are opposite to the way of believing in a more ordinary way. There are two objects of faith, the one is Christ and the righteousness God placed in him, and of God's appointment; and there is the free grace of God towards us, which is in the heart of God himself, and which is delivered to us in all those indefinite promises which are in the Scripture. Now the will of a man is to deal with both these, and is put upon a self-denial in both these.

1. Indeed though God did not take that forfeiture, namely, to make the condition of salvation this, that a man should be content for the glory of God to go to hell, seeing he deserved it, I say, though he doth not urge that forfeiture, yet he will have you saved in and through another person than yourselves, or you shall never be saved; and he will have your wills come off to it, and this is a just and a necessary forfeiture for God to urge upon the wills of men. 'The life that I now live,' saith Paul, 'it is by faith in the Son of God,' Gal. ii. 20. And I say that this forfeiture hath God taken of men by reason of the fall. Saith God now, It is true I did trust your own wills once with power and ability to save yourselves, and you had all in your own hands, but you have forfeited yourselves to destruction, and you have forfeited your own power for ever, forfeited the having of it in you as you had it before; therefore now I will betrust it in the hands of another, whom you shall live in, whom you shall have recourse unto for every penny you receive, and you shall have recourse continually unto him as beggars, even unto my Son the Lord Jesus Christ. This forfeiture I say God takes of us as we are sinners, and it is well he did so, and indeed salvation must come that way, or we could never else be saved. Now then if I must go thus out of myself, and continually live upon another, then self in me must for ever be laid aside, as it necessarily follows: and God therefore hath made the way of salvation the most contradictory unto self, and to the way of self, that can be; he hath set up not our own, but his righteousness, and that righteousness too in another. Now this self-denial is the hardest self-denial in the world. To make this forth to you: Is it not a great matter, think you, for the soul to be content to be nothing in itself, and Christ to be all for ever, to throw away and to forget itself, to be lost to itself, and

dead to itself, as Paul said he was, Gal. ii. 19, 20. And ' I have nothing,' (saith he, 2 Cor. xii. 1) ' though I have done more than all the apostles.' Is it not a great self-denial, not only to take Christ into the heart to rule all a man's passions and desires, but that he must not only rule all, but do all there; and that he must have the glory of all that is done? And so to have the glory, as that all boasting, no not a thought of it, must rise or lift up itself? I say not that faith doth actually keep down all such thoughts in a man, but this is the way of believing which the spirit of a man must subject to. Faith excludeth boasting, boasting even in works, and in works of righteousness, that is clear in Ephes. ii. 9. For a man to say, I have nothing but the grace of God in me, this, I say, is the greatest self-denial the creature can be put to, and it is certain that the natural sway and bent of the heart is most opposite to this of anything. Now this self hath gotten by forfeiting itself through sin, that it must be lost thus forever; but it is well lost, for it is lost in him that saves it with a greater salvation. And this forfeiture doth God take of self in everything, so that self, as it were, loseth the right of the creation, that is, that law which passed between the creature and the creator about it, which was this, that according to the law of creation it had his righteousness in his own keeping; it could say, This have I done, this is my own righteousness, of my own getting, though you gave me the stock to set up withal; this is the happiness of my own keeping: and it was allowed him to say so. You have it clearly, Rom. iv. 2–5, in the apostle's distinguishing the two covenants, ' He that is saved by works, he hath whereof to glory,' saith he, as Adam had, and the reward came of debt, of a natural due: but now self must fall lower. A man must not only have all this boasting of self for ever excluded, but he must reckon himself for ever ungodly, as it follows there in that Rom. iv. 5, I must believe on him that ' justifies the ungodly.' Now that a man should be in himself ungodly, cuts off that same *I*, that same *self*, makes it a cypher to eternity; that though a man is a creature still, yet the truth is, he is rased out of the catalogue of creatures, ' Of him ye are in Christ Jesus,' 1 Cor. i. 30. It is a mighty expression of the apostle's. You were something once, but now you are what you are in Christ Jesus. To have self, I say, thus to be a cipher in being, nothing in doing, nothing in righteousness, nothing in making a man's self happy, yea, to be an ungodly self in a man's own account, worse than nothing (as that place in the Romans shews), and Christ to be all here, is a self-denial that the heart is brought to and brought off to, and gladly brought off to, when it comes to believe. Adam was to aim at God, and to make God his end in all things, as we do, and to respect himself as little, but in the point of believing we fall lower, for that emptieth and annihilateth us. How should this be done, think you? How shall a man be brought to this? You may as soon fling the earth off its centre, and hang the huge hills in the air. If you should see the earth remove and hang in the air by virtue of a load-stone, what a miracle would this be to us! as hard a thing is it to throw self off of itself. For the truth is, the other having been the way of nature, even in pure nature, self will never, especially now when corrupted, go out of itself. If you have any work for it to do within doors, it will do it; yea, and work itself to death, even for salvation, as many have done; but to go abroad, to live upon alms, to stand to the courtesy of another, this is what self was never brought up to; and therefore like one that had a great estate in his own hands, will think much to come down and live upon mere courtesy and upon alms, he will rather be content to scrabble up anything, though it be much less than what he might have upon courtesy and upon the alms of others, to get a living, nay, if he can get but husks, he would rather do it than enjoy the fairest life in coming under another. So it is here. This is therefore, I say, the highest self-denial, and yet this is the self-denial of faith, and that in the will of a man, in relation unto Jesus Christ, whom God hath appointed us to live by.

2. Faith is likewise to deal with the free grace of God. What is the eminent principle of God's free grace? It is his will; 'I will be merciful,' says God, Exod. xxxiii. 19, Rom. ix. 15, 'to whom I will be merciful;' and 'he hath made known to us the mystery of his will,' so the gospel is called, and the promise of salvation, Ephes. i. 9. Our wills now must come and deal with this will of God, and to be sure that is cross to self. Now to mention the self-denials in that respect, I do not say these things are always drawn into distinct thoughts, but the heart doth this by a new inlaid principle, which God puts into the spirit of a man.

1st. The first thing herein is this, that though God doth not urge this, that a man shall so take Christ, that is, that a man shall be contented to be damned so as God be glorified, if he save him. No; the poor soul doth seek for, and God treats with it for salvation; therefore why should that be urged as a condition, or a qualification, or preparation before a man comes to believe; yet, if you believe, and believe in earnest, you submit to God to be disposed of in this world, not according to your wills, but according to his own will. The law of believing carries this with it: 'When thou wast young thou wentest whither thou wouldest,' saith Christ to Peter, John xxi. 18; that is, when he was first converted; 'but when thou shalt be old, another shall carry thee whither thou wouldest not.' It was Christ in his will that carried him whither his fleshly will would not. Now this also is a forfeiture we have brought upon ourselves by sinning. The truth is, we brought it upon Jesus Christ himself, for he thus resigned his whole self to God: 'Not my will, but thy will be done;' yea, it was to the undergoing of his Father's wrath, though he knew it was not for eternity. But to be in this world as Christ was, to be content to be poor and to be despised, let a man be never so great, to have all his high thoughts brought down when the glory of God in believing is manifested unto him; and for him that is of high degree to 'rejoice that he is made low,' James i. 10; for a man so to value the favour of God and free grace which he seeks, as to be contented to be disposed of thus, or else he is not worthy of it, as Christ saith, Mat. x. 37, 38. O 'let me be as an hired servant,' saith the prodigal, Luke xv. 19, so I may be in thy house; for a man to say, though I am a dog, yet let me have some crumbs, some mercy, let me have salvation—saith Paul, 'If by any means God would save me' —here is a self-denial now that faith bringeth, and here is a great deal of load upon the will; even in this, if there were no more. But then again,

2dly. We are brought to this self-denial likewise, being sinners, to make a venture of our souls (if I may so express it) upon him that is free to save us or to destroy us, to throw away ourselves in a dependency upon such a God as shews mercy freely, and to venture entirely upon this free grace and rich love of his. Faith is the greatest venture that ever was made in the world; it is more than to commit a little cockboat without oars to the mercy of waves and winds, to be carried to such a shore. This God hath fairly obtained by our sins. He carries it freely, as we must all know, he commands us to believe, to venture ourselves thus upon him. All believers, when they come first in, make this venture more or less: 'We believe that we may be justified,' Gal. ii. 16. They did not know that they should be justified certainly, the apostles themselves did not. Now to venture a man's self upon a *who can tell?* as I may so express it, and as the Scripture expresseth it in Joel ii. 14, ' Who can tell if he will return and repent, and leave a blessing behind him ?' And for the will in this case to deal with one, that if he be of one mind, ' who can turn him ?' as it is in Job xxiii. : this is a great self-denial ; for mark it, when self in a man is awakened, and awakened with apprehensions of so great a matter as salvation and damnation is to a man's soul, when the soul is awakened to purpose, and a man comes to God with whom he deals upon terms of free grace, all in self must needs be infinitely solicitous accordingly. Look how high a man's value of salvation is, look of what moment he apprehends damnation to be of, so far is self up in arms, all up in arms about it ; and what saith self ? O let me be assured presently. As in all points of moment you know what infinite fears a man will have if he have not assurance, because of the greatness of the thing, for the greatness of the thing hinders quiet trusting ; and, when self is thus awakened, especially corrupt self, for we have nothing else in ourselves by nature, what a bustle must this needs make in the soul of a man to make this great venture ! How solicitous is he ! And how hard to be quieted by a pure trust in God ! In this case, for the soul to be called so from itself, and from its own standing, to be persuaded to leave its own footing, and all the carnal support and the confidence it once had, in the way that is natural to it, by which it gets peace, to be persuaded, I say, to go and throw itself off of this standing ; self is in this case the most wary principle that can be. Therefore now to go and venture upon this God, and upon the freedom of his grace, upon the promises of God, upon the commands of God, to stand at God's arbitrement thus, and to refer a man's will to his will, and to cast a man's self into those everlasting arms (as they are called in Deut. xxxiii.), to leave a man's own standing ; it is as if a man should leave his own standing and cast himself into the arms of a mighty giant that stands upon another pinnacle, one whom he hath also wronged and abused often, and he himself hath no hands to lay hold upon him neither, but he must depend upon his catching of him. Here is the greatest venture, the greatest trust, the greatest self-denial that can be ; thus the heart throws itself out of all possibilities, and submits to the free grace of God in Christ, and this is done in believing. And then,

3dly. In the way of believing self is yet often-times more put to it ; for God makes a man wait, and makes him wait long ; so that though God doth not put a man to that submission that he should be content for his person to be damned so God may be glorified ; yet he puts him to this submission oftentimes, that he shall wait his time for revealing of his grace and love to him. And therein God shews the freeness of his grace exceedingly, that although it is certain that whoever doth venture himself thus, that doth thus throw himself upon the Lord Jesus Christ and God's free grace, shall certainly obtain in the issue ; yet for the manifestation of this I will be free, saith God, I will take my own time. Now, in this case, for the soul still to submit to this free grace of God, to wait upon the manifestation of it, and this when God hides his face, as in Isa. viii. 17, ' I will wait upon the Lord that hideth his face from the house of Jacob, and I will look for him ;' for the soul I say to do this, and to do this with any quietness, in a matter of so great moment, is the greatest self-denial that can be. The eyes of men are apt to ' fail with looking for the salvation of God,' as David expresseth it in Ps. cxix. 123 ; but to be brought to wait, and for a man to be glad that he may do so, for it is for his soul, there is that pride in the will that opposeth this, and opposeth nothing more. There is a pride, there is an impatiency in the will, when the soul doth find itself lost, and taken off from itself, and hang in the air, as it were, and hang by a thread; self in this apprehending the danger, must needs be impatient. If God will come and assure it presently, it would be quiet; but to be brought to wait, and still not to be assured, I say this is the hardest thing in the world to do. In this case the quarrel is not in men's understandings; no, there is a foundation laid enough to draw the understanding in; a man sees the riches of grace that is in God, he sees the promise to be indefinite, he hath the universal command upon that promise to draw him in, *i. e.*, that it is God's will that he should do so, and so he hath a warrant to come to God. But I say in this case the quarrel lies in the wills of men, that they can wait no longer: and what doth the will do? It sends to the understanding, and saith, Oh look out, Is there any tidings yet? Do you see any better ground yet of hope? Oh I am lost and undone, I can wait no longer! The wills of men are apt in this case to say so, in a world of sinking discouragement. And this I say is the pride that is in the will: 'His soul which is lifted up' (saith he in Hab. ii. 4), which is haughty, that is, which hath that reigning in him, 'is not upright, but the just shall live by his faith.' For a man to see other poor souls to have comfort, and that he should not have it, to see how God had dandled others, as it were, even from their first turning to him, and shined upon them, and yet still hides his face from him, this causeth self to swell, and the bigger a man's will is, the more it swells in such a case as this. You have two principles in your wills, the one opposite to the other, that is, self-flattery and impatiency. If a man will go and believe in a carnal way, self-flattery will help him to believe, that is, a man loves to have a good opinion of himself; and while he hath but slight thoughts of his sinfulness, if God should say, I will but have one man saved, he would be apt to say as Haman, when the king asked him, 'What shall be done to this man whom the king delights to honour?' Haman thought in his heart, 'To whom would the king delight to do honour more than to myself?' So will a man be apt to say, I am the man whom God intends to save. But when that this self-flattery is killed, then despairing impatient pride riseth up, especially when a man is not assured for the present; and therefore then to be quiet and still, and quietly to wait upon God, this I say is the greatest self-denial that can be, and this self-denial is and lies in the wills of men.

4thly, If God comes in with his wrath upon a man's soul, as sometimes he doth when the soul goes on thus in a way of waiting on him: if God hide his face from him, and not only so, but comes in with terror and wrath upon him,—though still God in all such cases doth not put his heart to this, to be contented to be damned so God may be glorified; yet this he puts the heart upon, and requires of self, in such cases, that a man should take part with God, and this is a just thing laid upon a sinner that waits upon God for salvation, namely, that he should acknowledge himself worthy to be destroyed, that he is in the hand of God as the clay is in the hand of the potter,—the soul is to have no repining and grudging thoughts allowed for that present wrath that is upon him, but to judge himself full of his own fruits, and to say as they in Micah vii. 9, 'I will bear the indignation of the Lord, because I have sinned:' and the like expression you have in Isa. xxxix. 8. Such a kind of submission it is that God requires of a man in a way of believing. And take this from the word of God, there is nothing will quell murmurings in such cases; heart-risings against God, which do arise from the pride of the will, and self in the will, which is the proper seat of them (for the will is the chief seat of self), nothing I say allays and quiets them but only faith. And the quarrel lies not in want of understanding, so much as not having a will to submit, and it is nothing but faith, waiting quietly upon the Lord, and submitting a man's self to God, that will quiet the heart in such cases. Now I say not that every man hath this when he first cometh to believe, but God draws it forth in the course of a man, and in his way of believing, as he hath strength, and there is occasion for it. And unto this the will must needs be opposite and averse, and therefore still faith is not of yourselves, for this self that is in the will is in itself most opposite unto faith: ' By grace ye are saved, through faith, and that not of yourselves ; it is the gift of God.' I shall not need to make uses, for the things themselves are practical and experimental ; and if the Spirit of God go home with them into your hearts and spirits, he will make uses of them for me.

BOOK III.

*Though faith be a difficult work, yet we ought to use our endeavours to believe.
—What those endeavours are.—Cautions about using them.*

CHAPTER I.

*Though faith be a difficult work, yet we are to use endeavours to believe.—
What those endeavours are.*

THAT we are to endeavour to believe, is generally granted. The only
question will be, what kind of endeavours we mean? We will take the
most of them out of the 4th chapter of James, where he directs sinners
what to do. As,

1. To cleanse their hands and hearts, taking heed of hindrances and
impediments which may hinder God's working of it, or provoke him to
leave off the work; to refrain all ill company, which quencheth all good
motions; as all sins also of what kind soever, which grieve the Spirit.
Thus the apostle, Heb. xii. 1, bids us 'lay aside every weight that presseth
down, and the sin that so easily besets us;' those sins our natures are
most prone unto. And, Heb. iii. 12, when he had bidden them in the
12th verse 'take heed lest there were in them a heart of unbelief,' he subjoins in the 13th verse, 'lest any of you be hardened through the deceitfulness of sin;' for as unbelief keeps off from God, so nourishing any sin
keeps in unbelief. So Heb. xii. 16, 17, when he exhorts men to 'take
heed they fail not of the grace of God,' he adds, 'lest any lust of uncleanness, as in Esau, causeth you to sell your birthright and part in heaven.'
The patient, though he cannot give himself physic, and make it work, yet
he can abstain from drink ere he takes it; he can bring an empty stomach.
A woman cannot of herself conceive nor quicken the fruit of her body, but
yet she can take heed of what may destroy it, and hinder quickening and
conception. She may beware of journeys, dancings, violent motions which
may cause it to miscarry; and so much the more careful are they that are
to bring forth a prince, an heir of a kingdom. Now, such an one is the
new creature which is a-forming in the heart. And though abstinence
from sin, and fearfulness to offend, can no way further the work, yet
because the contrary may hinder it, we are to endeavour it. And to this
hath that text a reference, Phil. ii. 13, when he speaks of 'working out
salvation with fear.' He means not a doubting fear (as the papists would
have it), but a fearfulness of displeasing and offending God, upon whom
the work depends; as the apostle speaks, 1 Cor. ii. 3, 'I was with you,'
says Paul, 'in much fear,' &c. Now this, in consideration of their dependence upon God, men are able to do; for in respect of men whom they
depend upon, they can and do forbear their dearest pleasures, and why not
much more for God and the work of grace?

2. Men may endeavour to be humbled for their sins, and take such considerations into their hearts as may serve to humble them; which, though it is not faith, nor works faith, yet it leads to it: James iv. 9, 'Be afflicted, and mourn, and weep,' says he, giving counsel to sinners what to do: 'let your laughter be turned into mourning.' Men can give over their carnal mirth, and go alone and consider their sins, and set themselves to mourn for them, and humble themselves in the sight of God; and 'God,' says he, 'shall lift you up,' raise up your hearts to believe. Though men cannot cast in the seed, yet they can go about to plough the ground that fits for it, and breaks the clods, Hosea x. 12. And because this is preparatory to faith, therefore endeavouring after this is endeavouring for faith, because it is an endeavouring for that which fits for faith, and is necessarily pre-required. Only this, it is not all the humiliation in the world can give them power to believe; as many think, Oh, if I were thus humbled I could believe! But, on the contrary, when they are humbled it is a new work to create faith; as though the seed in the womb be prepared for the soul, and made fit to receive it, yet it is the almighty power of God must send and put a soul in. But because God never gives faith to unbroken hearts, therefore men are to endeavour after this work.

3. There are duties and ordinances God hath appointed, in which to bring our hearts before him; which I think James means when he says, 'Draw nigh to God, and he will draw nigh to you,' James iv. 8. He means coming to these duties wherein God's presence is seen; as Korah, Dathan, and Abiram, being priests, and conversant in ordinances, are said to draw nigh to God, Num. xvi. 9, 10. And this also men may do; they may come unto God, and present their souls before him by prayer, by hearing the word, by good conference, by reading, &c., and look up to him, and say, 'Lord, now do thou work,' Luke xi. 14. He promiseth the Spirit himself, who is the beginner of all grace, to them that ask him. When therefore a man comes to these means, wherein God dispenseth faith, and lies at the pool still, he may be said to endeavour after faith.

4. There are special opportunities wherein God draws nigh in his ordinances. When God stirs a man's spirit, and strengtheneth it to ask and endeavour, then a man should bestir himself, and hoist up sail while the wind blows; as when the pool was stirred, the diseased stepped in. There are times when God's bellows blows the coals, as the prophet speaks; and then if we be not purged, we are not purged. And 'working out our salvation with trembling,' I think hath reference to it, Philip. ii. 12. He means trembling to foreflow* any opportunity. But now this is the error of men, that when God doth draw nigh to encourage their hearts still to seek and wait on him for faith, they rest in these as the work of faith.

5. But lastly, I conceive that these are not all the endeavours are to be used after faith; but further, souls humbled are to attempt the exercise of the very act of believing; that is, they are to take promises into their thoughts, and to bring their hearts to them, to look up to Christ, and consider his fulness, and attempt to lay hold upon him, to exercise thoughts of taking him, and treating the marriage with him, and consider what is in him, may move them to take him; and what is in the promise may be a ground for their faith, and to encourage them; and so far as God strengthens a man's heart, so far go and try, and try again, and see when and what thoughts of faith will take thee. We have an express place for this, Heb. iv. 11, 'Let us labour to enter into that rest, lest any man fall after the same example of unbelief.' In the former part of the chapter, he shews

* That is, to forego, or let slip.—Ed.

that men entered not in because of unbelief, so as faith is the means of entrance; now, therefore, he exhorts men to labour to believe; not to knock and ask only, but to put forth thoughts of faith, to set their feet in, to endeavour this daily. And therefore, ver. 16, he bids men 'come to the throne of grace, that they may obtain mercy;' those that had not yet obtained it, must come that they may obtain it. But you will say, we cannot come. Why come, says he, to obtain help itself, in the next words. So Heb. xii. 2, he exhorts them to 'look to Jesus, the beginner and finisher of faith;' to look to him as the beginner as well as the finisher. And my reasons why men are to endeavour and attempt the immediate acts of believing, are,

(1.) Because God commands men to believe and to come to Christ, 1 John iii. 23. And therefore Christ, when any came to him, would still urge faith on them: 'Canst thou believe?' says he, Mark ix. 23. And so the apostle Paul, when the jailor came trembling, 'Believe,' says he, Acts xvi. 31, 'on the Lord Jesus, and thou shalt be saved.' Now, if we are to endeavour to practise other commandments to shew our duty, as I said before, then to believe also; and my inability to do it right hinders not, nor frees me not from attempting to do it, and reaching as far as I can.

(2.) If ministers are to present promises and motives unto men, then those considerations, and motives, and promises which the ministers of the word are to present to hearers and humbled souls, to beget faith in them, humbled souls may and ought with application to consider alone, and digest and exercise thoughts of faith about. 'The word was preached,' says the apostle, Heb. iv. 12, to the Israelites, promises preached, but 'they profited them not, because they mingled them not with faith;' therefore, says he, 'let us take heed, lest a promise being left us, any of us should seem to come short of it,' for want of applying those promises. And though it be true that but some shall enter in, yet the promise is indefinitely made to all, ver. 6, and upon that ground, ver. 11, he exhorts all to labour after faith, to look up to Jesus as the author of faith.

(3.) Men are to inure their hearts to the same thoughts of faith believers have, so far as recumbency or casting a man's self upon Christ, and bringing their hearts to promises goes, because God works on us as upon creatures reasonable; and the same considerations, and thoughts, and objects of faith which believers have in their minds, a man that is yet to believe may think over and over. They differ only in the manner, in the *formale*, not the *materiale;* and as fruits, they have the same form and shape, they differ but in relish and taste. And God doth often engraft true thoughts of faith upon the notions we had being unbelievers, and changeth them into true thoughts of faith whilst we are a-thinking them; as the loaves were increased in the breaking them, and as the water was changed into wine in the pouring of it out. So that men believe often truly ere they are aware of it, by exercising their hearts to thoughts of faith; and whilst they attempt it, God helps them, as to pray, so to believe. And therefore it is their error that would have souls humbled to lie still, and see if God will begin to draw their hearts to believe, and not to attempt till then. It is indeed a man's strength to sit still, but there is a twofold sitting still: the one is a doing nothing at all, not setting a foot forward, not a thought towards believing, and that is naught; but the other is a quelling all conceits of abilities in myself to believe, and not to suffer a thought to stir upon that ground, yet so as to think thoughts of faith, with a quiet dependence upon God. Sitting still is not opposed to using means, but to trusting in means. Again, sitting still is opposed to turbulency of thoughts, that a man's 'thoughts should be quiet and sedate for the event, and yet use the means. Only I add this caution : first, that though a man attempts to believe, yet he should not expect power from himself to believe ; but in attempting and thinking thoughts of faith, expect power from God, and do it in subordination to God's power. A man is to bring his heart to the promise, and then expect power from the promise to close with it. Secondly, that a man's soul do not rest in his own endeavours, but still wait for a farther work.

CHAPTER II.

That the resting in our holy duties and endeavours is an hindrance unto faith ; but a right performance of them is very well consistent with it, and needful.

When we shew that in the working of faith, and in men's coming on to believe, duties, and good performances, and new endeavours, become to many the greatest hindrances to believing on Christ alone, and do interpose themselves and come betwixt Christ and the soul ; men taking up a rest, and putting confidence in them ere they come to Christ. When, therefore, we cry out against this resting in duties, and shew the vanity and emptiness of all you can do to save you, or obtain Christ and God's favour, and bid men, as Luther, take heed not of their sins only, but of their good works also ; then men are apt to say and think that we do cry down all good performances, and speak downright against good duties, and do drive men wholly off from the performance of them ; and not only carnal men are apt to think so, but this is the case of poor broken souls, that when this their error, and the emptiness of all their performances to this end is discovered to them, their hearts flag, and they sit down discouraged, and their hands grow feeble in the performance of them. And we find Luther complaining of nothing more than this mistake and cavil which accompanied his doctrine, the chiefest of whose thoughts and breath was spent in this very point, to beat men off from carnal confidence in works (as the deepest and most bottom corruption in man's nature), and to bottom their faith immediately upon Christ, wherein he makes the power and the truth of faith to consist ; which, whilst he endeavoured, this calumny was still raised, that he spake against good works and holy duties. And still this shadow follows this truth ; and to this purpose he still professeth,[*] that as it was the hardest thing in the private exercise of men's spirits not to consult with duties, to lay works aside, and to cast a man's soul out of duties, and to lay all upon Christ, so it is the difficultest matter in all the circle of theology, to give both their limits ; for, whilst duties are only taught, faith is lost, and whilst faith is urged, carnal people dream (says he) that good works are spoken against. And thus, whilst Paul taught justification by faith without the works of the law (Rom. iii. 28), this objection was started up, that he made void the law, which cavil is therefore there met withal by him : ver. 31, ' Do we make void the law ? No ; we establish it.' So whilst Christ taught that publicans and sinners went into heaven before Scribes and Pharisees, they cast this aspersion, falsely deduced from that his doctrine, that therefore he was a friend to publicans and sinners.

1. To clear this therefore, first, it might be alleged, and that truly, that our scope, when we speak thus against their good works, is chiefly to dis-

* Luther in Gal. v.

cover that works performed in a state of unbelief by carnal men, are wholly sinful and abominable; and though, if we take them in the abstract, they are to be pressed upon them as their duties, though they spoil them in the performance of them, yet that, in the concrete as performed by them, we cannot but declaim against them, and discover their sinfulness to them. Now for wicked men to argue from the concrete to the abstract, and to infer that, because we speak against wicked men's best performances, and discover them to be sinful, that therefore we speak against the duties themselves commanded, or that they are not their duties, this is an argument fetched out of the devil's topics.   We profess that wicked men's best works occasionally prove their greatest sins; as Luther says of the evil world, *Tunc est pessimus cum est optimus,* they are then worst when they seem best; and the more holy in appearance they are, and the more good works they do, *eò purius diabolo serviunt,* they serve the devil more purely. But it follows not that therefore we speak against the duties themselves.

2. But, secondly, I shall propose more pertinent and proper considerations to the thing in hand: first, by way of explication, I will premise two or three general considerations; and then, secondly, draw up formal and direct answers to this cavil and mistake.

(1.) The first thing that I premise by way of explication is, that when we speak against trusting and resting in duties, as opposing the work of faith, we mean not only resting in them with an opinion of merit, and satisfying God in the most gross and popish sense,—for that opinion may be renounced, when yet the heart practiseth a more refined, fine-spun popery secretly,—and that is, that though men expect that it is Christ alone must pardon them, and think that their performances are not able to satisfy God for their sins, but Christ's satisfaction is it which must stand them in stead, yet they look upon their own performances as those which may compass Christ and an interest in him, and they look at them as motives that may prevail with God to give them Christ; which secret opinion is not much less derogatory from God's grace and Christ than the other, for Christ is more than justification, because he brings justification and all with him.   If he hath given us his Son, 'how shall he not with him give us all things?' Rom. viii. 32. All are less than Christ; and therefore to think, though not to merit, yet to obtain Christ for our own performances, and so to rest in them, is as bad as the former.   It is indeed a new shift, beyond what gross popery dreamt of; yet as it is in laws, though never so direct and express cautions be made to prevent all evasions, yet cunning heads will invent new to defraud and go beyond the statute; so though our divines have expressed themselves never so fully against works, yet men renouncing merits, their hearts have yet farther inventions of resting in works and duties, as motives to move God, they think, to give them Christ, which yet are as opposite to faith as the other, and therefore are excluded by the apostle, Rom. x. 6, ' The righteousness of faith,' saith he, ' speaks on this wise, Say not in thy heart,' &c.   For let us preach Christ never so fully, and let men's opinions be never so much convinced, yet their hearts are apt, in their secret consultations about their own salvation, to think of a course of doing : ' Who shall ascend up to heaven, to fetch Christ thence ? '   Though the way be by Christ, yet they think, by doing, to get him and procure him.   No, says the apostle ; it is by a sheer way of faith, closing with him as freely given, and put into your mouths and hearts.

(2.) The second thing I premise is, that as God, in giving Christ, and in justifying us by Christ, looks at no performances either as meriting or as moving him to do either, so faith, that apprehends and lays hold on Christ as given, and upon justification in him, whether by an act of casting a man's self on Christ for justification or otherwise, looks not at duties, or all that ever a man hath done, either as meriting or moving causes, that do further him any way in either, or prevail with God to bestow either. So that look as there is an exact opposition between grace and works in God (Rom. xi. 6, that if it be of mere grace, then all duties are excluded ; and if of works, then grace is excluded, so as these two cannot mingle), so there is as exact an opposition between faith and duties, in point of apprehending Christ and justification by him ; for faith is a grace chosen on purpose to suit with God's free grace, to cause our thoughts to answer to his in this great business, to take Christ as given, upon the same considerations that God bestows him, and so his righteousness too. Therefore, to be justified by grace and by faith, is all one ; and therefore, ' it is of faith, that it might be by grace.' And when we are said to be justified by faith without works, what is the meaning of it, and why is it attributed to faith, but because faith is the sole instrument of apprehending God's giving me Christ, and justifying of me ? As also because in that its apprehension, as God in justifying looks not to works, nor any thing in me, as the moving cause, or any way conducing to it, so faith apprehends it, having no eye to works, why it apprehends it, and so is said to justify without works, that is, to apprehend it, having no eye to works as moving causes. Yea, as God looks not to faith itself, as a work, but only as an instrument apprehending, so faith looks not on itself as a work, any way having any influence into obtaining Christ and his righteousness, but only as a hand receiving it. And therefore, God chose this grace of faith, knowing that though, when the believer believes, he performs a work, yet he would not look to that act as a work, but look to Christ and his free grace : as Luther expresseth himself, ' When I believe, I use to imagine, as if there were no such quality in me as faith,' &c. ' So as,' says he in another place, ' I do not know whether there be any righteousness else, or unrighteousness in the world.' Hence then it comes to pass that faith, when it goes about its proper business of laying hold upon Christ and justification through him, is careful to shut out and exclude works ; it beats all duties and graces off with poles, as it were, from putting their hands to this ark, which it alone is appointed to touch and possess ; and it is exceeding jealous of duties, lest they should step in and spoil her virginity, as Luther calls it, which she reserves for Christ, which is tainted and polluted, if works mingle their help with faith in this business. For, as I said before, if it were any way of works, grace should be no grace ; so if the soul thought it any way of duties, it were no faith. And therefore Paul, though he had never so many performances to boast of, and elsewhere to men he doth boast of them, yet in point of justification he thinks not of them : ' Though I know nothing by myself, yet hereby I am not justified,' but it is the Lord that freely of himself doth, without relation to any thing in me. And therefore, 1 Pet. i. 13, we are exhorted to trust perfectly, to trust and lean, fully and wholly, on grace ; not so as to stand mainly upon it, and lean to works, but wholly and upright upon it.

(3.) The third thing I premise is this, that man's nature is exceedingly prone to rest and trust in his own performances, and not to look out wholly to God's free grace and to Christ ; *Malum hoc est communissimum* (as Luther calls it), the most common evil, and deepliest rooted. Some of our divines, as Chemnitius, &c., have gone about to shew that, from Cain and Abel to this very day, this hath been the great and standing controversy in the world, and difference between the world and believers, whether we are accepted before God by works or by faith. Cain thought by sacrifice to do it, and neglected faith; but Abel, though he brought sacrifice also, yet, Heb. xi., he offered it by faith, not resting in it, and so ' by faith offered a more excellent sacrifice than Cain, by which he obtained witness he was righteous,' which the other did not, thinking alone by sacrifice to do it; the apostle puts the difference on purpose, Heb. xi. 4. Thus, in Asaph's time, God by Asaph corrects it as the common error of that age, and shews it was not by works, not by sacrifice, that they are accepted, Ps. l. 7, 8. Thus it was in Isaiah's time also, ' Have we not fasted, and thou seest not?" Isa. lviii. 2. And thus in Christ's time too, ' What shall we do to work the works of God ?' John vi. 28. They thought to obtain righteousness by doing, and therefore Christ, as correcting their error, points them to believing. Thus the Pharisees ' trusted in themselves,' says the text, ' that they were righteous,' Luke xviii. 9, that is, the righteousness they trusted unto, it was that only in themselves, and out of themselves. In a word, Paul says of them all, Rom. ix. 32, 33, that they ' sought not righteousness by faith, but as it were by the works of the law.' The promise of salvation they hoped for as well as believers, but, as some expound that place, in Acts xxvi. 7, of the unregenerate Jews, they hoped to come to the promise by works; which promise, though Paul also looked for by faith, yet they thought by serving God day and night only to attain it; that was their way to attain; but Paul, though he aimed at the same promise, yet sought it by faith. And this was the general error of all the twelve tribes, as he says there. And this was the reigning error in popish times, that they still trusted in their works, and though they knew Christ as a redeemer, yet they left him, and faith in him, and sought justification by the works of the law. Now, that a corruption should be so general in all ages from time to time, and so universal and so irreclaimable, that all Christ and his apostles did could not work men off from it, this argues that it is most natural, and that nature sticks here. As why have Pelagian controversies been still in the church started, though still more refinedly, but because there are *Pelagianæ fibræ*, Pelagian fibres in every man's heart, as he said, roots, and a spring of it within ? Now the other error about works hath been more ancient than this, and more lasting, because more natural. Yea, so natural is it, that even believers, that have faith begun, are apt to rest in, and trust too much in duties. The apostles could not get rid of all the grudgings of it, Mat. xix. 27. ' We have forsaken all, what shall we have therefore ? ' And though he tells them what they should have, yet elsewhere he beats down that. Therefore Luke xvii. 7, 8, 9, Christ there endeavours to beat down all swelling conceits of their performances in them, tells them that when they had done all they could, they must confess themselves unprofitable servants. And upon what occasion comes it in ? Look the 5th and 6th verses, and you will find that it is upon occasion of a conference about faith, they desiring the increase of it, and Christ commending it, and telling them, that a grain of it was more worth than all their works, and then he comes in with this assertion, as removing the main hindrance of it. And therefore the Galatians, a whole church that had received Christ, yet how soon, says the apostle, were they removed to another gospel from the grace of Christ, Gal. i. 6. That other gospel was looking partly to works and partly to Christ, and joining Christ with the law. And this we all find by experience to be true more or less; and the reason is, because reason hath the law for its object, and to be justified by the works of the law, and accepted for them; and so when men hear of grace and Christ, they think that yet they should go that way too. This most agrees with reason and the dictates of a natural conscience, for it was that way which in innocency was the way, and so some sparks of light that men should be saved by works are in every man's heart, as well as of the duties of the law, the legal way of salvation; and though a man be brought to acknowledge that Christ pardons, yet he will have as much of his own way as he can, so that natural reason hath some knowledge of justification by the law; but of justification merely by grace, now man is fallen, this reason is ignorant of, and there is no such spark of light sown in man's heart by nature; therefore the apostle, Rom. x. 3, gives this as the reason they were ignorant of God's righteousness, that is, of God's way of justifying. And therefore it must be revealed, Rom. i. 17, and when it is revealed, it is entertained only by faith; and that not to faith at first, but from one degree of faith to another, for faith only is apprehensive of it; so as if God would make a man more and more to cast himself upon Christ's righteousness, and add a farther insight into it, he must add to a man's faith; and look how much carnal reason there is, and want of faith, so much relying upon duties there will be even in the best. And though men's opinions may be set right, yet this being an innate spark and principle in the heart, which is rooted out of it only by faith, therefore the heart under-hand will have recourse and rest in performances more or less; for we, in the working of our hearts, are not guided by our notions, but by the rooted principles of nature; therefore though men's judgments are convinced that there is a God, and that fully and clearly, yet atheism is rooted, and a settled principle in the heart, and therefore sways in the workings of a man's spirit; and accordingly, as 'the fool says in his heart, There is no God,' so naturally a man says in his heart, Duties must help me to Christ. And therefore the righteousness of faith is brought in as checking and contradicting such sayings that are apt to arise in a man's heart, which are not wrought out by opinion, but by a principle of faith, and a divine light accompanying: ' The righteousness of faith says, Say not in thy heart, Who shall ascend into heaven, to bring Christ down from above,' Rom. x. 6. And therefore, in another place, God carefully meets with those thoughts of their own righteousness, Deut. ix. 4, ' Speak not in thine heart, that for my righteousness the Lord hath brought me in to possess this land,' &c., either as the moving cause, or the meriting cause. And ver. 6, he comes over it again with a more special instruction in this point when he says, ' Understand, therefore, that the Lord thy God giveth thee not this good land for thy righteousness;' for of all else the heart is most uncapable of this lesson, to discern the way of faith and works. And as ignorance and opposite reason, so also pride (which is the other reason there, Rom. x. 2, used by the apostle) makes men to trust in their duties, ' they being ignorant of God's righteousness, and going about to establish their own righteousness.' He brings both in as reasons why they submitted not to God's righteousness of faith, for they would set up their own. Nature desires to do so, because as self-love hath set up itself for a man's God and end, so for a man's Christ also; there is the same reason of the one that is of the other, and pride is seen in both; for we would have wherewithal to boast. Therefore, Deut viii. 14, 17, he bids them take heed of the lifting up of their hearts, in saying, ' My might, and the power of mine hand, hath got me this wealth.' As it is thus in matters of wealth, so pride makes men think that through their prayer and their fasting, they should get Christ. And this corruption was so rooted, that the main end of the forty years' troubles in the wilderness was to work out this conceit, and that by humbling them, ver. 16, which shews that pride was the original of this corruption.

These things premised, the answers to that fore-mentioned cavil and mistake are easily framed. As,

1. In drawing men on to a right way of believing, we speak not at all against duties, but only discover, and bid men beware of this corruption which so naturally accompanies the performance of them in men's hearts, which because it is so natural, and so prevalent, and so dangerous, therefore it is as much to be spoken against.   Now this corruption is but accidental to the duties; and therefore the duties, however, ought to be performed, and are holy and good.   We speak not against the things, but the ground of performing them, with an eye to them, as anything that might move God to give you Christ, which you are apt unto.   And thus as when we speak against merits of works in our controversy with the papists, we speak not against works, but their performing them upon that ground; or, as when we speak against things lawful, and say, that more are damned for things lawful than unlawful, and that they condemn themselves in what they allow; and, that more are cast away upon sands than upon rocks, viz. gross sins; we in this speak not against the lawfulness of the things, or forbid men to use them, but against their corruption that place so much their happiness and rest in them, that they are kept from God their chiefest good.   Now as things lawful step in betwixt God and men, so duties step in betwixt Christ and them, but both through their corruption; and in this sense Luther said, *Cavendum est a peccatis, imo a bonis operibus,* we are to beware of sins, ay, and of good works too.

2. When we tell you that the performing of duties in many does hinder faith, the meaning is not that of themselves they do so, for one command of God doth not hinder another; but it is so by reason of your corruption, that is apt to rest in them, so they do hinder men.   As the law stirred up concupiscence, and was the occasion of evil, so are works the occasion of opposition to faith; and therefore the apostle says, Rom. ix. 29, 30, many that are profane attain to the righteousness of faith sooner than others that follow the righteousness of the law; not that the righteousness of the law is in itself contrary, no, this is not Paul's meaning, for, verse 32, he makes the question how it came so to pass: 'Wherefore? Because they sought it not by faith;' had they sought righteousness in a right way, duties would not have hindered them.   For this you must consider, that grace and works, faith and works, are opposed.   But how? Only in point of justification, and attaining of Christ; so that we should not look to them, or use them with an eye to them as causes to move God to bestow Christ on us. Herein they only clash; and it is man's corrupt opinion too that sets them at odds.   It is the pride of nature that will bring duties in to justle out faith, else they would not hinder but further each other.   Not so much works as boasting are 'excluded by the law of faith,' Rom. iii. 27.   Let the heart lay boasting aside, and resting in them and faith, and they will do well otherwise, and both glorify God; or, as Luther says, when faith goes to believe and to deal with Christ, then she shuts works out, and will be with her spouse alone; naked Christ with naked faith, and works stand at the door as servants, that when faith will walk abroad, they may attend her.

3. We speak not against duties, but would reduce you to a right method and order in attaining to the right performance of them; and that is, to get faith first as the cause of all obedience, and which makes all accepted, without which God is not well pleased with all you do, and not to look at duties as the cause of faith. *Bona opera non pariunt fidem, sed fides parit bona opera.* Good works do not bring forth faith, but faith brings forth good

works : Titus iii. 8, ' These things affirm constantly that those which have believed may be careful to maintain good works.' That is the right method, first to exhort men to believe, then to fall a-doing. A physician bids his patient first take physic, and then drink broth ; he forbids him not to drink, but to take physic first : so we exhort you to take Christ, and then fall a-working.

4. Whereas you may ask, Are duties no helps afore faith ? I answer, fourthly, Holy duties may be considered both as duties commanded to be performed by God, and so we say all ought to perform them. And secondly, also as means appointed by God to convey Christ, as conduit pipes convey water ; or to bring us to Christ as boats convey us over the water, and so they are back-doors to let us in to Christ : and so we exhort you to them. But the thing we speak against is, that either men rest in the performance of them as duties only, and look not at them further as means ; or, if they do, yet regard them rather as motives to move God to bestow Christ than simply as means, in the use of which God bestows salvation. Now if the heart rests in them, or looks at them in this manner, then we speak against them.

5. When we go about to shew you the vanity and emptiness of them, we do it not that simply they are vain in themselves, but vain to that end you use them for, and that is to get Christ for them, or to be justified by them. For though they serve not to that end, yet they may serve for another, the other ends above mentioned. If a man that is troubled in conscience would go and take physic, his taking physic may be useful to him, and not in vain, for he may other ways have need of it ; but yet to the end to cure the wound of his conscience, we may say it is in vain, to make him look to a higher means. And so when we say, the labours of chemists going by their art to get gold is vain and ridiculous, we do not mean that it is simply so ; for it is many ways useful, yet not to make gold. So we say of duties, they are useful, but not to justify you, not as you think by your art to get and work Christ out of them. No.

6. When we speak against resting in duties, what is our scope ? To bring Christ and you together, naked Christ and the naked soul ; that you may not embrace clouds, but Christ in all ; that you may not rest till you have Christ in your eye beyond all duties ; that you may have the work of faith in your eye above all works. This is all our scope, as it was Christ's, who directed them above works to believing, as that great work of God ; and as it was Paul's scope, who directed them to seek it by faith, Rom. ix. 32. We speak not against duties as servants to attend faith, but we would marry you to Christ, and have him to be your husband, and not duties your paramours.

CHAPTER III.

Cautions about using our endeavours to believe.—We must act in subordination to God's power, as working in us both the will and the deed.—We must also renounce all ability in ourselves.

*Wherefore, my beloved, as ye have always obeyed, not as in my presence only, but now much more in my absence, work out your own salvation with fear and trembling : for it is God that worketh in you, both to will and to do of his good pleasure.—*Philip. II. 12, 13.

Having proved that we are to use endeavours to believe, and that a right and due performance of duties is not incompatible with faith, my next business is to add some cautions to be observed in using our endeavours, and in attempting to believe, and going forth to believe, and continuing so to do. There are cautions which it becomes those to have who are in dependence upon God, and his free grace, and his power to work faith in them at pleasure, as the text hath it: 'He works,' saith the text, 'the will and the deed according to his good pleasure.' Now, although the apostle shews here how the soul is to manage and behave itself, not only in the point of believing, but in working out our salvation in all the particular duties of it, yet what the apostle saith here is in a more special manner applicable to believing, because that is what we are saved by: 'Believe on the Lord Jesus, and thou shalt be saved.' It is the great work of God.

In the text you have,

1. A duty, which is that I am exhorting you to, to work out your own salvation, which is eminently by believing; for it is faith unto salvation: 'Believe, and thou shalt be saved;' and work it out (saith he) to perfection, as the word signifies.

2. You have here the manner in which this is to be done (which is the thing I chose the text for), it is 'with fear and trembling.'

3. Here is that which should cause this fear and trembling in working out our own salvation, and that is the point in hand, 'for it is God that worketh in you both to will and to do;' therefore, saith he, 'work it out with fear and trembling.' And this now, the words being rightly opened and interpreted, doth hold forth how the soul in all its endeavours, in a subordination and dependence upon the power of God to make the faith I put forth true faith, and to help me both in the will and the deed; it shews how the soul, I say, ought to demean itself to God therein as in dependence upon that power.

I will first open the words a little, and then proceed. The papists say, that by fear and trembling here, is meant doubting, opposing it to all certainty and assurance of salvation, a doubting whether that God will save you or no, which, say they, keeps the heart awful. For they go only a legal way, and a way to work upon self-love only; and I confess if that were the way of God's working grace and faith upon a man's heart, if it were to work merely upon self-love and in a legal way, their interpretation would be the best; for it is with a fear and trembling whether ever God will work it in me, yea or no; and therefore to have that awfulness continually upon a man's spirit would be best to rouse self-love, and to provoke that, and work upon that. But this sense cannot stand, for the text hath respect to that place in the Old Testament which these words are taken out of; and, as Austin observed long ago, these words are taken out of Ps. ii. 11. And the Septuagint there useth the very words in the Greek which are used here by the apostle, and therefore surely the Holy Ghost had an eye to it. Now, saith the psalmist there, ver. 11, 'Serve the Lord with fear' (speaking of Christ), 'and rejoice with trembling, kiss the Son,' &c., which is indeed especially believing on him, closing with him. Now if it were meant of that popish doubting, it had been the greatest contradiction in the world to say, 'Rejoice with trembling;' because for me to rejoice in that salvation which Christ bringeth to me, and to be doubtful of it, is a contradiction. Yea, the word here *rejoice* signifies the highest rejoicing, to rejoice so as to leap for joy; as high a rejoicing as rejoicing 'with joy unspeakable and glorious,' for it is a rejoicing with glory. So then he commands at once the highest assurance, the highest rejoicing, and yet withal to tremble; he speaks therefore of such a fear and trembling not as hath doubting, but such as may stand with the highest joy that is; and therefore he doth not mean a diffidence, a continual hesitation and dubitation, or a consternation of mind, as they would carry it; for then, I say, it had been the greatest contradiction in the world to bid them rejoice with trembling, if by trembling had been meant a consternation and diffidence of mind.

But besides this, you shall find if you search the New Testament, that this phrase of trembling, as it is used there, hath plainly another meaning and sense than this which the papists put upon it.

It is opposed first to high-mindedness or confidence in one's self: Rom. xi. 20, 'Be not high-minded, but fear.' Fear therefore is opposed to self-conceitedness, and to trusting in a man's self, and therefore it notes out a working out of our salvation with the highest submission and dependence upon God, who is the worker of it. And that this should be the meaning of the word here in the text, is clear from what follows: 'For it is God,' saith he, 'that worketh in you both the will and deed;' and therefore fear and trembling is opposed to conceitedness, and high-mindedness, and confidence in a man's self, and it is an exhortation to submission, as I might shew you out of James iv. 7, where he saith, 'Submit yourselves to God,' speaking how they should behave themselves for God to give them grace, as in opening that place would appear; I say then, it is opposed in the New Testament to high-mindedness and conceitedness, and is put for a submission to God, to be low and empty in a man's self, in respect of any strength in a man's self.

And then again it is put for a fear of offending or displeasing one; so the phrase of fear and trembling is used again and again in the New Testament. You received Titus (saith he, 2 Cor. vii. 15) 'with fear and trembling.' With fear and trembling they received that holy messenger of God, that was an holy evangelist. What! were they in a fear, in a hesitation and dubitation that Titus would do them hurt? No; surely that popish interpretation of fear and trembling cannot be applied to their receiving of Titus; but it hath this meaning, they were afraid of doing anything which might offend or displease, or be distasteful to a man so eminently holy; and he being an evangelist, they received him with all submission to his doctrine; and therefore the word *obedience* is annexed to it: 'Remembering the obedience of you all, how with fear and trembling you received him.' Even as if Christ himself were upon the earth, and a man should converse with him, how would a man fear in all his ways lest he should do anything that should not be suitable to so holy and so heavenly a spirit as he hath in whom God dwelleth. So that indeed the meaning of the words, 'Work out your salvation with fear and trembling,' is this: it is as if the apostle had said, Seeing you have a work begun in you by God,—for so he tells them they had, and gives them as much assurance of it as the testimony of an apostle could do: chap. i. verse 6, 'Being confident of this very thing (saith he), that God, who hath begun a good work in you, will perfect it until the day of Jesus Christ.'—As he therefore by his power hath begun to work in you all at the first, so you must depend upon the same power to continue to work in you the will and the deed, and yet you are to co-work with him, in a continual subordination to that power which hath begun to work in you; you are so to work out your salvation as to fear to offend that God upon whom your salvation dependeth, to tremble lest you omit any opportunity wherein this God begins to work upon you; for you must be beholden to him for salvation, if ever you have it, and it is he that worketh in you the will and the deed. Work out therefore your salvation with your own endeavours, but with the highest fear and trembling, that is, with the greatest humility and submission of mind, and dependency upon the power of God, who must do all, without all self-confidence, or self-conceitedness, or trusting in your own power, and with the greatest fearfulness to displease that God upon whose good pleasure the will and the deed in perfecting of it dependeth. In a word, this exhortation of the apostle is a caution against security, and the giving over of the use of all means and ways further to work out our salvation. It is a caution against pride and self-conceitedness, and going on out of high-mindedness in our own strength. It teacheth us how to manage our hearts in the use of our own endeavours, namely, so as to fear to offend that God upon whose power we depend for so great a work, and also to tremble to omit any opportunity wherein this God doth work upon us. This is the general scope of the words. And so you have the meaning of the phrase. I shall now come to such particulars as, added to all the former I have delivered, will perfect and complete this particular subject which I have spoken of concerning faith, which you may remember was this, namely, to shew you how to manage and guide our souls for the manner of our endeavouring after believing, and in believing ; how to manage our souls, I say, and our endeavours, after such a manner as that we may co-work with God in a way of subordination to his power.

1. Therefore (and I shall keep myself exceeding much to the sense of these words, ' with fear and trembling'), we do work with God in a subordination to his power, when we go forth in a renunciation of all our own abilities, in a continued distrust of all our own abilities. And this is to work it out with fear and trembling, because God works in us the will and the deed ; ' Be not high-minded,' saith he, ' but fear ;' be not self-conceited, do not stand to go forth upon your own legs. There is no danger at all for men to attempt believing, and to attempt it again and again, whilst still they go forth in doing of it, with a perpetual renunciation of their own strength. We use to tell you (and we tell you truth in it), that there is nothing hinders faith more than a man's own endeavours to believe. But how ? Endeavouring in his own strength. And when we say that self, and all in self, and from self, is against faith, the meaning is this, that confidence in a man's self, and in his own endeavours, is that which undoeth men. The great mischief lies in the rising up of such thoughts as these, I will go pray, and I will believe, and I will work out a faith in Christ, which the heart is exceeding apt unto ; and you that have experience of the spiritual conflicts and spiritual attempts and exercises of spirit in the way of believing, cannot but find it. The heart, I say, is apt still to be saying, as he in Ps. lxxiii. 16, ' I thought to know this,' and this is it which we speak against ; as the apostle James, chap. iv. 13, 15, teacheth men to check themselves : ' Go to now,' saith he, ' ye that say, To-day or to-morrow, we will go into such a city, and continue there a year, and buy and sell, and get gain, &c., whereas you ought to say, If the Lord will, we will do this or that ; but now,' saith he, ' you rejoice in your boasting.' What he saith of civil actions, and of our dependence upon God therein, holdeth much more, infinitely more, of spiritual actions. Why ? Because that an ordinary providence accompanieth us in civil actions ; the same providence that accompanieth beasts in all their actions, doth accompany men in an ordinary way, and so men may better say of such things, We will go to such a city, and do this, and do that ; yet you see the apostle checks their hearts in the midst of such thoughts ; much more then are we to suppress all such thoughts in things that are spiritual, in which we depend upon God only, and upon him alone, and upon a good pleasure of his in a more

immediate manner. We should take our hearts at it, and do but watch your hearts, and you will take them at it again and again. It may be that such thoughts will not come into distinct propositions in your hearts and spirits, but they will lie there taken for granted. We should take our hearts at it, I say ; and when you find your hearts will go out to attempt any spiritual thing, or to attempt believing, and to say, I will do this, or I will do that, and so go forth upon that ground, and in your own strength, assisted by such a conceit, you should, when your hearts are so doing, check yourselves. Even as they said in Jer. ii. 18, ' What hast thou to do in the way of Egypt ?' so you should say to your hearts when you find them so doing, What hast thou to do to go out in thy own strength, in any con-fidence in thyself ? Men may say, and it is ordinary for them to do so, that it is God that doth all, and we can do nothing, and yet in the mean time trust in themselves, and in their own strength. The Pharisee him-self, as the text saith, Luke xviii. 9, trusted in himself, yet if you read on, you shall find him thanking God for all that he had, and that he was not like other men, as if that God had done all, and he had done nothing ; whereas the very scope of that parable is to speak against those that trusted in themselves. Let this point, continual acting self-renunciation (that is, continually to act a renouncing of yourselves in your going forth in all things that you do, especially in the point of believing), be settled on your hearts. You are as frequently to exercise these acts negatively, as to exercise acts affirmative or positive ; that is, as frequently to renounce your own strength in the doing of a thing, as to do it. I will not insist upon such places where when the saints have done thus and thus, still they cry, ' Not unto us, Lord, not unto us,' as Ps. cxv. 1, though there is the like reason in the doing of a thing, that there is after the doing of it. And so in Isa. xxvi. 12, ' Lord, thou hast wrought all our works in us and for us ;' they are not content only to say so, to acknowledge that God doth all, but as it follows there, verses 17, 18, they add, ' We have been with child and in pain, and we have as it were brought forth wind.' Thy soul, it may be, hath been humbled and terrified ; thou hast had a world of conceptions within thee, but still thou hast brought forth nothing ; say thou then, Lord, thou hast wrought all my works in me and for me. What, I say, they do when God had wrought all in them, that do thou still whilst thou art a co-working with God. So in Hosea xiv. 3, when they were to seek salvation, because such thoughts of self-confidence will arise, they do pre-vent and forestall them, they do renounce beforehand all carnal confidence : ' Asshur shall not save us.' Why do they speak this, but because they knew their hearts would be apt to run to Asshur, for he speaks there not of temporal deliverance but of spiritual, and alludeth to what they were wont to have recourse unto for temporal deliverance, to express what the Spirits of men are apt to have recourse unto for spiritual. ' Asshur,' say they, ' shall not save us.' They lay that for a conclusion before they begin, We will dam up that door, there shall not a thought come in of having recourse unto anything, or of having any confidence in ourselves, or in any-thing in us, or in anything we can do, ' but in thee the fatherless find mercy.' The Scripture delights much to run upon these negatives. It is not content only to express positively that we are to believe, and that we are thus to believe, and upon this to believe, but that we are in the doing of it to renounce whatsoever is in us. To give you some instances for it.

(1.) See how the apostles speak, Gal. ii. 16, for they speak of their own faith there : ' Knowing that a man is not justified by the works of the law, but by the faith of Jesus Christ, even we have believed in Jesus Christ,

that we may be justified by the faith of Christ.' Here now were two principles laid in their hearts; here was first a negative one, and that principle
was riveted in them, they knew they could never be justified by any works
of their own; 'Knowing,' saith he, 'that a man is not justified by the works
of the law.' And he comes in with a negative again, 'That we might be
justified by the faith of Christ, and not,' saith he, 'by the works of the
law.' This was the first principle that was inlaid in their hearts; and then
the second is a positive one, 'But by the faith of Jesus Christ.' And as
this was the opinion and judgment of the apostles, so their practice was
answerable, for mark the practice of their hearts upon this: 'We therefore,'
saith he, 'have believed in Jesus Christ, that we might be justified by the
faith of Christ, and not by the works of the law.' While they believed, they
excluded the works of the law in their own hearts, and renounced them.
There was an act, I say, of renunciation, even in the work of believing.
'Not by the works of the law,' saith he, 'but by the faith of Jesus Christ.'

(2.) Where the apostle expresseth the doctrine of faith, Ephes. ii. 8,
(and men's hearts should answer the doctrine) he comes in with two negatives there also, 'Not of ourselves,' saith he, and 'not of works.' He hath
two negatives to all the affirmatives that are there. Why? To teach the
hearts of men, that still in the way of believing they should shut the back-
door, as I may so express it, that no thoughts of self-confidence may come
in and mingle themselves with the rest of their souls when they go to believe. As Abraham, when he sacrificed, had a double work, one was to
kill the sacrifice, and to lay it on the fire, and to offer it up; and the other
was to drive away the fowls that came down upon the carcasses; so you have
a double work when you go to believe, if you will go forth in the power of
God. As you are to attempt to believe in a subordination to the power of
God, so you are to beat off and drive away all thoughts of self-confidence
and self-conceitedness, to be ever a renouncing of yourselves, as you would
be of lusts that rise up.

(3.) You have the like expressions in Rom. ix. 16, that so you may see
how the Scripture runs still upon negatives, to teach men's hearts what
to do: 'It is not, saith he,' 'of him that willeth, nor of him that
runneth.' And the apostle there brings it in by the by, as a conclusion of
what he had spoke concerning the doctrine of election. 'So then,' saith
he, 'it is not of him that willeth, nor of him that runneth, but of God that
sheweth mercy.' One would have thought it had been enough to have
said, 'It is of God that sheweth mercy.' No; but he would bring in the
negative, he would have men renounce their own willing, and their own
running, and to depend upon that God that shews mercy.

Now, if thou hast had abundant experience, and liest under a deep sense
of thine own unability to believe, the many experiences thou hast found of
attempting in vain, as thou thinkest, to believe, are apt to discourage thee.
But do thou now mind what the Spirit of God shall direct thee to, and that
is this: do not go turn all the experiences of the vanity of thine own
attempts into discouragements, that because thou hast found it to be in
vain, therefore it shall be so for time to come; no, but go turn them all
into self-renunciation; let all this confirm thy heart, that faith is therefore
not of ourselves; let it, I say, confirm thee in that more, and inlay that
principle into thy heart more, so as that thou shouldst maintain that against
the next time in all the attempts thou settest upon believing. And if thou
dost so, thou dost work with fear and trembling, thou dost go forth and
co-work with God in a subordination to his power, to glorify that alone.
Discharge all thine own strength continually, discharge it of any help at all

that thou expectest from it.   If it would rise up and attempt, disclaim it; yea, because it will rise even whilst thou art setting upon the work, let it be the first thing thou dost to say, 'Asshur shall not save us;' Lord, not of myself, not anything in me, but through thy power, I throw myself upon thee.   Suppose that the act thou aimest at be to go out of thyself only to Christ, yet if thou hast but this thought, I will go out of myself to Christ out of my own power, or without renouncing of thyself, thou art still in thyself.   Such thoughts hinder God from working: even as Jesus Christ did not work miracles in his own country because of their unbelief, so, whilst self thus riseth up and mingleth itself with that strength which God giveth, God withdraws his assistance.   The words in Heb. x., quoted out of Hab. ii. 4, 'His soul which is lifted up,' signify, as Pareus well observeth, *ponens seipsum*, &c., that is, that soul that doth make a bulwark of itself, and trusteth in itself; for when the heart betakes itself to its own strength, and goes out in that, it leaves to trust in God; and it is not endeavours, but it is endeavours without renouncing of what is in a man's self endeavouring, which frustrateth faith, for God hath said, 'In his own strength shall no man prevail,' 1 Sam. ii. 9.   Men that are convinced of the necessity of Christ, and that they must get Christ, what do they say within themselves?   I will pray, and I will fast, and I will go to Christ: that same *I will* spoils all.   They are like to swimmers that are beginning to swim, their very scrabbling and pawing in the water of themselves at first, their very eagerness is it which makes them sink, whereas if they lay but still and committed themselves to the stream, even that would carry them. To act out of a man's own strength is opposite to the very fundamental law of God, it doth prevent and supplant the power of God in working with us. That I may express it to you by a similitude which is more familiar, you know that the apostle expresseth faith by the opening of a door, in Acts xiv. Now a man's endeavours to this are like as if a man in the water should be to pass through a great sluice, and he should go on the back-side of it, and pull and pull, the more that he pulls, and the more he would open it by pulling, the worse he is, whereas now if he would commit himself to the stream, it would open it, and he might pass through it.   So that now that is the first thing, fear and trembling imports a renouncing of all confidence in a man's self.   And let a man attempt still with a renunciation of a man's self, and all in a man's self, and act and practise this, and then attempting to believe will never hurt him, or put him off from faith, but he will find that God will co-work with him in the doing of it.

CHAPTER IV.

We must use our endeavours to believe, being fearful of doing anything to offend that God upon whose power we depend to work faith and all other things in us.

2. Fear and trembling here, in relation to God's working the will and the deed in us, is extended also to fearfulness of offending, of sinning against that God that must work.   So that now that soul that depends upon the power and good pleasure of God for working faith in him, and would work in a subordination to this power of God, the law of this dependence lays this obligation upon him, that in relation hereunto he should be fearful even in this respect, of offending or provoking God, upon whom he doth depend to work in him both the will and the deed.   There are, I

say, many motives to keep us off from offending God, but especially when
the soul hath this consideration in his eye, his being in a continual dependence upon God for working of faith, or for working out his own salvation.
The apostle, James iv. 5, doth give such sinners direction as indeed were
fallen back, or had strong lusts to which they were subjected, how they
should demean their souls towards God for the giving of them more grace
to overcome their corruptions. 'Do ye think that the scripture saith in
vain, the spirit that dwelleth in us lusteth to envy?' The words are taken
out of Gen. vi., for we have them nowhere else in all the Old Testament.
'The imagination of the thoughts of man's heart are evil, and only evil
continually.' The apostle here puts in for evil, envy, by a metonymy for
all the rest, for that sin these Jews were most guilty of. He therefore
instanceth in that peculiarly, as being peculiar to that nation, and he had
spoken of envyings and strifes which they had amongst themselves in the
words before. Now, saith he, it is true, this is your nature, and you have
it from the womb, but there is a God that giveth more grace, and it is his
gift : 'But he giveth more grace,' saith he, verse 6, that is, he hath grace
and power enough to overcome this spirit of envy in you, and he hath promised to do it. But then let me tell you this, you must depend upon this
God, and you must walk as those that do depend upon God to give more
grace to overcome this corruption. Now, what he saith in the general to
such, is applicable to the point in hand. Now, what doth he prescribe
them ? He prescribes them submission to God, and emptiness in a man's
self of all confidence in himself: 'He resisteth the proud,' saith he, 'and
giveth grace to the humble : submit yourselves therefore to God ; resist
the devil, and he will flee from you,' verse 7. He bids them first submit
unto God, as he that was the giver of all this grace, whereby their corruptions must be overcome ; that is, give your souls up to him to be
wrought upon in his own way, and, although you are to use endeavours,
as afterwards he directs them to humble themselves, &c., yet in all, saith
he, submit to God, and go to him, and tell him, that he is as free to work
or not to work as he pleaseth. Lord, say to him, I urge not anything in
myself, I put my mouth in the dust, I present my soul before thee, and
submit unto thee. For that is certainly the meaning of it, for he speaks
not here in respect of afflictions, but in respect of a dependence upon God
for to give more grace, if you mark the coherence. A man should not say,
I have prayed and fasted these many years, and yet God doth not come.
'Submit yourselves to God,' saith he ; acknowledge thine own unworthiness, and thine own vileness, that such is the cursed nature of thine, as it
is pure grace to give thee anything, and if it be grace it is free. Why dost
thou complain as if God were bound to give it thee ? No, saith he, submit
to God. That is one thing, but that which is proper to the second particular I mentioned, is what followeth : 'Resist the devil, and he will flee from
you.' Although the lust of envy rise, saith he, yet it never comes to any
act of consent, never breaks forth into any act of consent, never produceth
any gross effect, but the devil is in it. Now, then, 'resist thou the devil.'
What is the meaning of that ? That thou dependest upon God to subdue
this spirit of envy in thee that is still arising, resist the devil. He means
this, that the lusts in a man put him not upon a gross act without the
devil ; the devil is in it then, therefore resist, keep thy will stedfast against
this Satan, 'resist the devil, and he will flee from thee.' There is a com-
pact, as it were, between God and Satan in such cases ; he doth say to
Satan, If that soul doth resist thee, thou shalt flee. Even as when Christ
was tempted, there was this law of the temptation, that if Christ did resist,

if he stood out from consent, the devil was to leave him. So that in deed and in truth, the effect of this exhortation, ' Resist the devil,' it is this, that though these lusts rise again and again, yet they should, in dependence upon God who gives more grace, not give up their will to the consent, for the devil can never hurt us without the consent of our own wills. It is, I say, to take heed of giving consent to a gross sin, when we are in dependence upon the power of God to give grace or faith, or anything else we would have of his Spirit. And he mentioneth this, to what end and purpose ? Not as if these moved God to work, for a man's fear to offend God doth not move him to work, but because it is uncomely, it is against the law of dependence, against the obligation of it, to do otherwise. When a man depends upon the power of God to work more grace, to work the will and the deed, for a man then to commit gross sins, is against the law of dependence. So you have it in Heb. iii. 13, ' Take heed lest your hearts be hardened through the deceitfulness of sin.' As he bids them take heed of unbelief, so of being hardened with the deceitfulness of sin, it is all one with resisting the devil in the interpretation I have given ; for as unbelief makes a man depart from God, so consent to sin keeps men in unbelief, and so casteth the work behind-hand again and again. Now, though a going on in a dependence upon God, with a fearfulness to offend God, upon whom a man dependeth, doth not move God to do anything, for what he doth is of grace, yet, notwithstanding, by way of removing an impediment, it hath its place, for there would be a hindrance otherwise. As a patient that takes physic can do nothing to make the physic work, yet he can abstain from what shall hinder the working of it, he can abstain from drinking, or from eating before it, or whatever else is required ; and as a woman, though she cannot conceive, yet she may take heed of what is any hindrance of conception, of journeys, and violent motions, and the like ; so it is here, though a man cannot further his own salvation by working anything at all, simply considered, as what himself doth, and though a fearfulness to offend move not God simply, yet the contrary would put God off, that is certain ; and it is against the law of dependence between God and us. Therefore saith the apostle here, while Christ is forming in your hearts, take heed of doing anything that will provoke the great God ; and if you will have more grace, resist the devil, and you will find this to be true, ' he will flee from you.' So that, though this fearing and trembling doth not help forward our salvation, *propriè et per se*, as they say, that is, in itself properly, or as if it did reach the effect itself, yet it doth it *per accidens*, it removeth that which would be destructive, and would hinder. Though it doth not move God, yet not to do it may provoke God.

If you ask what sins a man should forbear in dependence upon God, and upon the power of God in working faith ?

(1.) I may instance even in this of envying, because James instanceth in it. There are some sins that are more contrary to a dependence upon the power of God to work in us ; as now to think with one's self, I have waited thus long upon God, and he doth not answer ; I have attempted to believe, and I know not whether I have true faith in me or no, but others have ; such a soul was wrought upon but the other day, and he is full of assurance. Envying at this, and thinking much of this, is contrary to dependence upon God. Take heed therefore, lest the devil go and get thy consent to such envyings ; take heed lest thou nourish and cherish them in thy heart ; resist the devil in these, that he may flee from thee ; for these, I say, are contrary to that dependence thou hast upon the power of God, for is not his power free ? ' You lust and have not,' saith he, James iv. 2, ' because you ask amiss;' and you envy and lust, and have it not while that disposition is in you. For remember it is grace which is the thing you ask; and if it be grace, shall not God do with his own grace what he will? Therefore if he will give it to another sooner than unto thee, shalt thou envy him? What art thou depending upon? Art not thou depending upon the power of God? And is not that free? Submit thyself to God, and put thy mouth in the dust. It was Cain's sin, that when he was to deal with God for acceptation, and his brother's sacrifice was accepted and not his, he was wroth and full of envy against his brother; and that spoiled him, and undid him. It was Esau his sin that he envied, because Jacob was accepted and not he. When thou seest others that have attained to much assurance and to much faith, and still thy spirit is kept under hatches, under temptation, and under much inability to believe, this example of other younger Christians than thou, that have attained sooner than thyself to much assurance, because God flows in upon them, the example of this, I say, should rather encourage thee than cause thee to repine. As beggars at a door, though they are not served first, yet when they see others served they do not repine at this, but they are encouraged to see that still others as they come are served; so, suppose others are served first, yet God will lift thee up in his due time, as the apostle saith: 'Submit unto God,' saith he, James iv. 7, 'and he will lift thee up in his due time.' So Peter also hath it, 1 Peter v. 6. God hath a time to lift thee up if thou wilt submit unto him. You know the example of the woman of Canaan, when Christ saith to her, First let the children be served, she answers, 'Yea, but dogs may have crumbs when the children are served;' let me but have crumbs while they are eating, or crumbs after they have done, it will serve my turn. She was so far from repining that Christ had children, that he would first give to this and then to that before her, that she says, Lord, I confess I am a dog, give me but the crumbs when they have done. Such a spirit as this, that thus goes forth in a dependence upon God, without repining, and thus submits unto God, with such a spirit will God co-work. Let it be so far, I say, from causing thee to repine, as let it strike thy heart with a sense of thy own unworthiness, and encourage thee to continue in thy dependence.

(2.) So likewise impatience is another sin. When thou hast waited long, Oh, thou criest out, I can wait no longer, as the psalmist said. He spake it in respect of evil doers and their prosperity in temporal things: 'Fret not thyself because of evil doers,' as being a thing opposite to quietness and trusting in the Lord. For a soul to be thus turbulent, and to be up in arms if God come not presently, this is contrary to dependence. Remember that God 'giveth grace to the humble,' grace to those that put their mouths in the dust: Isa. xxx. 7, 'Your strength is to sit still;' and, as Lam. iii. 28 hath it, to 'sit alone.' There is a double sitting alone, or sitting still: the one is to do nothing at all, and not to stir to lay hold upon God and upon Christ at all. This is not the sitting still or sitting alone the prophet means; but there is a sitting still in respect of impatiency, of quelling all impatient thoughts, in opposition to turbulency of spirit which ariseth from a man's self, that if God must not give him what he would have now he can stay no longer. I say the heart must be quiet, it must be sedate, it must submit to God, wait upon God, and he will do it in his due time. And so much for the second direction imported by this fear and trembling.

CHAPTER V.

We ought to use our endeavours to believe, being very watchful not to neglect any gracious opportunities which God affordeth us.

3. We should also tremble for fear of omitting any opportunity that God giveth. That you have also James iv.; it follows there, verse 8, 'Draw nigh to God, and he will draw nigh to you.' And when God doth draw nigh to you to give more grace, then especially draw near to him. Now, drawing nigh to God is coming to such duties, or using such means, wherein God doth draw nigh to a man. Mark the apostle's phrase; he doth not only say, Go, pray, or go, humble yourselves, or fast, and the like, although he exhorts to these afterwards in the case of relapsing, but he prefaceth all here with this: first, 'Draw nigh to God;' that is, point the aim of your souls to be to draw nigh to the presence of God, and let nothing satisfy you in all you do but God's drawing nigh to you, which if you do you will never rest in any duties you perform. He exhorts you so to draw nigh unto God. I will not insist upon that, but as I take it these words, and so likewise the trembling to omit any opportunity, do import that there are special times wherein one hath a more special dependence upon the power of God for the working of faith. There are special times, I say, in which God doth draw nigh; and a man should tremble to omit any such opportunity. It is intimated in the text here likewise, Phil. ii. 12, 13, for 'it is God,' saith he, 'that worketh in you the will and the deed, according to his good pleasure.' Mark that expression; there is a good pleasure of God, saith he, which exalteth and sheweth itself in this, in helping men, and working with men when he will, and how he will, and at such a time as he himself best thinks meet. Now then, as the diseased men (you know it is the ordinary comparison) that lay at the pool, when the pool was stirred, presently stepped in, so do you join with God, and work out with God, when you find that he begins to work, as sometimes he doth, in a more especial manner. You shall find in Jer. xxxi. 18, that when Ephraim found that God began with him, having been formerly wild and unaccustomed to the yoke, when God began to chastise him, and so to work upon his heart afresh, Ephraim says, 'Thou hast chastised me, and I was chastised: turn thou me, and I shall be turned,' that follows; I take the meaning to be this, it is as if he had said, Lord, I have gone on like an unruly heifer unaccustomed to the yoke; thou hast begun so far as to lay a great chastisement upon me, and thou hast awakened my heart; O Lord, take this time to turn me! Now, turn me, and I shall be turned. Alas! I cannot do it of myself; I shall be an heifer again if thou lettest me alone, but thou begunnest to chasten me, and to open my heart, and it is in order to turning to thee. Lord, now turn me, and I shall be turned. When you find God doth draw near to you, use all that strength that God doth give you in drawing nigh to you; convert the whole stock of it to attempts on believing. If a man have but a little stock to trade withal, he will employ it in what is absolutely necessary, he will not go and lay it out in everything which soon it may be spent upon, but what is absolutely necessary and best for him. When God doth draw near to thee, and begins to enlighten thee, do not go and pray after knowledge, and gifts, and the like; no, turn thy strength to faith to believe, that is the one thing necessary, and God will be as willing to help thee that way as another, for this is the great work of God. And let me say this to you likewise, when God doth

draw near to your hearts by promises or by exhortations, attend to them. You read the word, and you attend upon the word, and you have exhortations and promises delivered to you in the word. Now thou art a poor soul, and liest at the pit's brink of believing, thou comest and hearest a promise that doth nearly concern thy condition, for it speaks to the very thing, to that which thy soul hath long desired and sought for, and is a promise fitted and suited to thy present condition; or there is an exhortation made to thee in what thou readest or hearest, that is as fully directed to thee as thou canst desire, to stir thee up to do that which thy soul saith, this is the thing which thou must do next. Now I say, when God comes thus nigh you, either by suggesting promises thus, or by what means or ways soever it be (and the more occasional the better), whether by exhortation or the like, be not coy now, for God draws near to thee, do thou close in and clap in with that promise, or with that exhortation, and say, Lord, now set this exhortation upon my heart, this promise upon my heart, this is the thing thou hast spoken of so long, now set it upon my heart. ' Be not faithless, but believing,' saith Christ to Thomas, John xx. 27. There is a coyness and an averseness in the soul to put it off, saying, I see not enough to persuade me; but be not faithless, saith Christ, but believe. Christ had answered Thomas to his own desire, had fitted him just, for, saith Thomas, ' Unless I see the prints in his hands and in his side, I will not believe.' Why, saith Christ, now have I used a means and a way fitted to thy own desire, here are my hands, and here is the hole in my side, feel them, and be not faithless, but believe; strike in now with this to believe. So I say to thee, God comes with promises and exhortations that do fully suit thy condition, now do thou look up to God, be not faithless, but believe.

I shall give you some suitable instances, first in promises, and then in exhortations.

(1.) When any promise comes that is fitly spread for thy sore (as I may so express it), a plaster fit as can be, a promise that is suited to the wants and indigencies of thy own estate, Lord, say thou, do but set this seal upon my spirit. Still as he offers and brings thee a promise, do thou go and speak to him again; as he speaks to thee in a promise, do thou urge him to fulfil it. Thus, I say, when God doth thus draw near to you, do you draw near to him. I shall give you but an instance or two of the soul's thus drawing near to God.

1st, The first is the instance of the apostle Paul in Rom. xv. 9–13, he had there, in ver. 9–11, begun and heaped up four promises together—I do not know the like in all the Scripture—of the Old Testament, that did assure him that God did intend mercy to the Gentiles: 'That the Gentiles,' saith he, ' might glorify God for his mercy; as it is written, I will confess to thee among the Gentiles. And again, he saith, Rejoice, ye Gentiles, with his people; and again, Praise the Lord, all ye Gentiles. And again, Isaiah saith, There shall be a root of Jesse, and he that shall rise to reign over the Gentiles, in him shall the Gentiles trust.' Here were promises now fully fitted to the Romans who were Gentiles, speaking to their very condition, to help and to strengthen their faith. When he had delivered these promises that thus nearly did concern them (and the last of all the promises he mentioned was, ' in him shall the Gentiles trust '), instantly what doth the apostle do? He claps in with a prayer to God for them, teaching them what they should do upon the like occasion, a prayer that God would make good these promises to them. ' Now the God of hope,' saith he, those are the very next words, the God of faith (for faith and hope are oftentimes taken for one in the Scripture) 'fill you with all joy and peace in believing.' The promise before was, 'In him shall the Gentiles trust;' here comes a prayer now, O Lord, wilt thou make good these promises to these Gentiles, teaching them by this what they themselves should do upon all such occasions. 'The God of hope,' says he, 'fill you with all peace and joy in believing, that ye may abound in hope through the power of the Holy Ghost.' The thing exhorted to being above their power, and lying in God alone to work, to shew this dependence, and what way they were to take upon all such occasions, he prays thus for them. And this was the usual manner of the apostle, for you shall find him praying in all his Epistles for those to whom he wrote, and he tells them the words he used for them in his prayer, and his end was to teach them to pray for the same thing. When he would exhort the Ephesians to pray that God would give them eyes enlightened to know the great things of the gospel, how doth he do it? 'I also,' saith he, Eph. i. 15, 16, 'after I heard of your faith in the Lord Jesus, cease not to give thanks for you, making mention of you in my prayers.' Therefore you yourselves are much more bound to do it. It was but a more artificial way of the apostle's to set them on work by his example, that if he did thus for them, much more they should do it for themselves. The text is extreme pertinent to the thing in hand, that when God comes thus to us in a promise, we should presently clap in with God. When the apostle had spoken of trust in God, or hope in God, to which the Gentiles should come, and there was a promise and prophecy to that purpose, he knew that God was only to work it, therefore he goes to him, and goes to him as the God of hope. And why is he called the God of hope? Because he alone is the God that works hope in the heart. His prayer then is, Thou hast said, that the Gentiles shall hope in thee; thou that art the God of hope, work it in these Gentiles. He calls him 'the God of hope' in the same sense that he had called him 'the God of patience and consolation,' in ver. 5, after having spoken, ver. 4, that the Scriptures were written to give us comfort and patience: for a man must have all his comfort from the Scriptures, for comfort from them is the true comfort, and a man must keep to them. 'Thou art the author of all comfort,' says the apostle, 'therefore comfort them;' for that is the meaning of it. So here he calls him 'the God of hope,' because the thing he desires is hope in God, and he was the only God to work it. Now as the promise was that the Gentiles should trust in him, so the thing he prays for is, that they may be filled with all joy and peace in believing. And when you hear a promise, do not pray barely and scantily for the thing promised. He had mentioned no more but trusting in Christ, but he prays, you see, for joy and peace, and for abounding in it too, and that through believing: and (let me tell you) all joy and comfort that is not in the way of believing is no true joy and comfort. And then, thirdly, he adds, 'through the power of the Holy Ghost.' It is the power of God must work it. He goes forth in the sense that it is the power of God that must do it for them, yet because God had promised to do thus and thus, he doth therefore strike in to move God that was the God of working faith, to do it by the power of the Holy Ghost. You see the place is every way pertinent to the thing in hand, for he had spoken of a promise, and of a promise to the Gentiles at large, which promise depends for the fulfilling of it upon the power of God and of the Holy Ghost; he therefore presently prays that God would make it good to these Gentiles, and thereby he teacheth them that when they hear such promises they should go to God, who is the God of that promise and of that work, to work it in them, and that in a dependence upon the power of God. God indeed is not much taken or moved of himself by this, for he is moved only by what is in himself, but he takes an occasion to do it when we thus go to him with his own promise; and therefore let us strike in still, as a promise is brought to us by his providence, either in the preaching or reading, or hearing of the word, or any other way, or occasionally, that suiteth our condition.

2dly, There is another instance of the woman of Canaan, Mark vii. 27. Our Saviour Christ did seem to put her off, but the truth is, he did intimate a promise to her (and therefore I quote the story of it as it is in the evangelist Mark): ' Let the children first be filled,' saith he; ' for it is not meet to take the children's bread and cast it unto dogs.' He doth not deny the dogs wholly, mark it, but he was ' a minister of the circumcision to confirm the promises made unto the fathers,' as you have it, Rom. xv. 8. He was to serve the circumcision first: now he doth not say that the dogs should not have the leavings; no, but saith he, but let the children *first* be filled. This poor woman catcheth hold of that word presently, for that word had a hint in it; therefore, thought she, surely the dogs may have the leavings, they may have the crumbs that fall while the children are eating; and therefore she retorts this upon Christ, that though the Jews were children, and she a Gentile being a dog, yet according to the analogy of that very similitude and metaphor he useth, she might have crumbs, and when the children were filled she might have what was the refuse and overplus. Thus Christ, you see, gives this secret hint, and there was indeed a great hint in it. Now, saith the text,—this is it I quote it for,—Christ said unto her, ' For this saying go thy way.' One evangelist hath it, ' Be it as thou wilt,' thy will be done as it were, and not mine; thou shalt carry it: but here the text saith, ' For this saying, go thy way; the devil is gone out of thy daughter.' Christ in appearance speaks half popery, that he should thus respect her faith and her saying; therefore Bellarmine urgeth it for the point of faith to justify a man in a formal and in a meritorious way. No; but the meaning is this, that upon the occasion of her expression of her faith thus taking hold of the promise, and catching hold upon what Christ had said, and retorting it upon him again thus, he spoke thus graciously to her. As she upon occasion of his words said, ' The dogs may have the crumbs,' he upon occasion of her saying is overcome, and yieldeth to her. So, say I, when thou takest occasion upon a promise to strike in, as this poor woman did, upon occasion of thy striking in, God cometh in to thee; he is taken oftentimes with the retorting of a man's spirit to him again with his own words. You will say when you hear promises, Oh, if I knew they belonged to me in particular, I should be encouraged to lay hold on them. Alas! do but think with yourselves how remote the instances of promises I have given you, both as to the Romans and this woman, were from determinately pointing at them. The promises the apostle reckons up were made to the Gentiles, and there were millions of Gentiles besides these Romans; yet the promises being indefinite to the Gentiles, the apostle prays, that God would fulfil them to the Romans. How remote was the poor woman of Canaan from the promise. She was a dog, and there were ten thousand thousand dogs such as she, yet she takes hold of the hint that Christ gave her, and her need makes her clap in and strike in with it. Therefore do not stand and say, Till God fit the promise to me, that I shall have a full and absolute assurance that this promise is mine, I will not believe. No; strike in afore: Paul did here for the Romans, and you see the poor woman did so.

(2.) The like I may say for exhortations. When God doth come with exhortations to you to believe, the promise is laid before you, and you are pressed and urged to lay hold upon them. Consider now that excellent saying of Luther, 'Faith doth but suffer God to do good to it.' When God, I say, comes and pins promises to you, puts them into your heart, when he doth come with exhortations in the ministry of the word to lay hold, then lay hold and strike in, for God draws near to you ; say, Lord, set this exhortation upon my heart ; let that which thou exhortest me to, work it in me. You shall find this, that in the Scripture there are exhortations to such things as you cannot do, as to make you a new heart. You have such an exhortation in Ezek. xviii. 31, where the prophet exhorteth us to make us new hearts. Saith the poor soul, Alas, how can I make myself a new heart ? Lord, thou knowest I cannot do it. What doth God besides ? As he makes this exhortation in Ezek. xviii. 31, so in the same Ezekiel, chap. xi. 19, he makes promises of giving a new heart : ' I will put a new spirit within you,' saith he, ' and I will take away the stony heart, and give you an heart of flesh.' Here now as in one place he exhorts them, so in another place he makes a promise to give it. The apostle James giveth them this exhortation, James iv. 8, 'Cleanse your hands, ye sinners.' And the same you have in Jer. iv. 14, 'Wash thine heart from wickedness.' Now look in Ezek. xxxvi. 25–27, and you shall find a promise that God will pour his Spirit upon them, and wash them from all their filthiness.' And so in Deut. x. 16, he exhorts them to circumcise their hearts : you shall find in the same book, chap. xxx. 6, this promise, ' I will circumcise thy heart, and the heart of thy seed.' Well then, when you hear exhortations to anything, consider that God's promises are as large as his exhortations, as to the matter of them ; that is, there is nothing he exhorteth unto, but there is some promise or other for to work it. Now then I say, that when God comes and exhorts thee to that which thou art next to do, do thou go and urge God with his promise, and say to him, Lord, this is that thou now exhortest me to, and it is that which I have waited for long, and now thou puttest me upon it afresh ; thou hast made a promise to work it : Lord, work it in me, according to thy promise. Thus I say, when God comes upon thee with an exhortation, strike thou in with him ; when he draws near to thee, draw thou near to him. And this is another way of working out our salvation with fear and trembling, fearing to omit any opportunity wherein God comes near us, either by promises that concern our condition, or by exhortations ; and where exhortations come near thee, there promises are made answerable in some place or other, and do thou urge the promise together with the exhortation ; and not only tell him of his promise, that he hath promised to give what he exhorts thee to, submitting thyself to him, laying thyself at his foot, but also tell him this, that it is as easy for him to speak the word in thy heart to do it, as it is for him to speak to thy outward ear, for he may do the one as well as the other. You shall find that God wisheth that there were such an heart in his people, that they would do thus and thus. Tell him it is as easy for him to do it, as it is for him to wish it. What saith the poor man in Mat. viii. 2 ? ' Lord, if thou wilt, thou canst make me clean.' The truth is, he had not a promise, he had nothing to have recourse to but the power of God, which now we are dealing with in the point of faith, speaking to a soul that is in dependence upon it. This I am sure of, saith he, it must lie in thy will if thou dost not do it for me, for it is in thy power to do it. What saith Christ in answer ? Shall any soul come to me and say at latter day, that he told me I was able to do that for him which in faith he asked, and would not, or shall challenge me that I did not ? No ; ' I will,' saith he : ' be thou clean.' Christ will not have a soul to be frustrated that comes thus, and acknowledgeth his power, and submitteth unto it, for so this poor man did : Lord, saith he, I am unworthy to be healed ; for it is a modest way of expression ; it lies only upon thy will, and I subject myself unto it. And so the ruler whose daughter was sick, deals just so with his power, Mat. ix. 18 : ' Speak the word,' saith he, ' and she shall live.' He submitteth himself to him. When poor souls, I say, do thus, as it were, lie at the catch, and wait for a word or for an encouragement from God, and upon occasion of a word of exhortation from God, do go to him and tell him of his power, that if he will, he is able ; and when he hath made an exhortation and a promise, do urge this upon him, the Lord will hear such a soul in the end, and he will, in the end, satisfy his desire. Nay, suppose thou beest guilty of a great deal of unbelief and impatience, and envying of others, and what is said in the word by way of reproof, comes near thee and strikes thy very soul, go thou and take an occasion upon those very reproofs to go to God, to work the contrary of that in thee which he reproveth thee for. In Luke xvii. 5, ' the apostles said unto the Lord, Increase our faith.' The truth is, it does not cohere with the words before, and so all interpreters do generally acknowledge. Now then, the comparing of one scripture with another will help us out. What is Christ's expression in the words afterward ?   ' If you had faith as a grain of mustard seed, ye might say unto this sycamine tree, Be thou plucked up by the root, and be thou planted in the sea ; and it should obey you.' Now if you look in Mat. xvii. 20, there you shall find it thus : ' Jesus said unto his disciples, Because of your unbelief you could not cast him out : for verily I say unto you, if ye had faith as a grain of mustard-seed, ye shall say unto this mountain, Remove hence to yonder place, and it shall remove ; and nothing shall be impossible unto you.' Now clearly, by comparing one place with another (Christ using the same expression, ' If ye have faith as a grain of mustard-seed,' and speaking in one place of removing a sycamine tree, for he used both certainly, and in another of removing a mountain), it is evident that the occasion of the apostles' saying, ' Lord, increase our faith,' was, that Christ chid them for their unbelief, and told them that the reason why they could not cast the devil out of the child was, because they were a faithless generation. And now upon Christ's chiding them thus for their unbelief, what do they do ? ' Lord,' say they, ' increase our faith.' Poor men ! So that now, when God meets by a reproof with what the heart is in this way guilty of, let that be an occasion to thee, as it was to the apostles here, for to go to God, and thus to pray to him, Lord, do thou take this away from me ; do thou work in me the contrary to that thou reprovest me for. And as that prayer had an effect upon Christ, to give more faith to his apostles, so thou wilt find a suitable effect of thy prayer too.

Lastly, Acknowledge still all that God doth do for thee in the way of believing. I told you, in one of the premises I made, that God doth give power to one thing when he doth not to another, and that you are to act so far as he gives power. This text, in Philip. ii. 12, 13, hath it, that he works the will, and he works the deed, first the will, and then the deed itself, and he goes on thus by degrees, and this of his good pleasure. He will work the will first one day, and the deed another ; he will produce a desire after the thing, and then the thing itself afterwards. Now, still as God doth work, acknowledge his good pleasure in it ; and so far still as God enables thee to do, to act in the way of believing, so far do thou acknowledge his grace and good pleasure in it : ' Lord,' saith the poor man, Mark ix. 24, ' I believe, help thou my unbelief.' Christ asked him, if he

could believe ? how far he could go in believing ?   Lord (saith he), I can
believe a little, help thou out with the rest.   He acknowledgeth God in the
one, and hath recourse to him for the other.   In Rom. ix. 17, saith the
apostle, ' It is not of him that willeth, nor of him that runneth, but of God
that sheweth mercy.'   His scope is, that they should be thankful to God,
and not ascribe anything to their own willing, or to their own running,
when they had done ; and withal, to remember that, in depending upon the
power of God, the greatest dependence of all was upon his mercy.   The
thing, I say, is to that purpose wo: th your observation, and you may make
a distinct thing of it if you will.   When thou art in a dependence upon
God, and practisest these fore-mentioned rules, though weakly, yet thou
sinnest against him again and again, and art put off by it ; and whereas
thou art to work out thy salvation with fear and trembling, thou provokest
him oftentimes, and sinnest again and again against him, yea, against the
very obligation of that dependence thou hast in thy eye for power from
God to work and help forward faith in thee.   To comfort thee in this,
observe how these words come in.   They come in as a corollary from the
testimony of Moses in the verse before : for ' he saith to Moses, I will have
mercy on whom I will have mercy, and I will have compassion on whom I
will have compassion.   So then,' saith he, ' it is not in him that willeth,
nor in him that runneth, but in God that sheweth mercy.'   Why doth he
use the word *mercy* here ?   Because that soul that is in dependence upon
God to work the will and the deed in salvation, hath as much to do, if not
more, with the mercy of God as with the power of God, for it is mercy sets
that power on work.   Suppose thou sinnest against him, and provokest
him, yet be not discouraged, remember that in willing and in doing thou
hast to deal with God that sheweth mercy.   In waiting on his power thou
wilt sin against him again and again, therefore, still remember, ' it is not of
him that willeth, nor of him that runneth, but of God that sheweth mercy.'
So here in the text it is intimated too, ' It is God that works according to
his good pleasure ;' that is, the good pleasure of his everlasting will, as it
is in Eph. i. 5.   Now the apostle doth not use this speech to take men off
from running, but to put them in mind, that if in running they do backslide,
and do contrary to God's pleasure, and provoke that God upon whose
power they depend, they should yet remember that he hath mercy as well
as power.   His mercy then should encourage thee still to depend upon that
power though thou sinnest against that power, and still thou shouldst have
mercy and power in thine eye.   The psalmist puts them both together in Ps.
lxii. 11, 12, ' God hath spoken once ; twice have I heard this ; that power
belongeth unto God ; also unto thee, O Lord, belongeth mercy.'   Therefore, now, if you will go to work out faith with God, and to work out your
own salvation in a way of believing, as you are to have recourse to the
power of God, so you must have recourse to his mercy ; and, though you
fail in these directions, yet remember that ' it is not in him that willeth,
nor in him that runneth, but in God that sheweth mercy,' ' out of the good
pleasure of his will.'

BOOK IV.

Though faith be a difficult work above our power, yet God commands us to use our utmost endeavours to believe.—The reason why God commands us so to do, and how the infinite power of God in working faith, and our own endeavours, are very well consistent together.—Discouragements removed, which may arise either from our own unability to believe, or from the sense of our great sinfulness, or from the thoughts of an absolute decree of election, resolving to save only some particular persons.—Directions to guide us in our endeavours to believe.

CHAPTER I.

Though faith be a difficult work above all our abilities, yet God commands us to use our utmost endeavours to believe, and it is our duty so to do.—The reasons of it assigned.

Let us labour therefore to enter into that rest, lest any man fall after the same example of unbelief.—HEB. IV. 11.

WHEN I proved before* that all our natural powers are so far from helping us to believe, that in this matter they disable us, I might likewise have come to the affections, and it were easy to shew how that they are all against the work of faith, and opposite to it, and in this I might be very large. For take all those affections which we call good, and are raised up in the hearts and spirits of men, while in their natural condition, as 'zeal for God' (which men are capable of), as the apostle calls it in Rom. x. 2. Zeal, you know, is the intending of all the affections. Now one would think that in the heart of those men where we see a zeal of God, or a zeal for God, this zeal should not be an enemy unto faith; yet the apostle tells us plainly it is in that Rom. x., I do my countrymen (saith he) no wrong: ver. 2, 'For I bear them record they have a zeal for God, but it is not according to knowledge,' *i. e.*, it is not according to faith, for by knowledge he means faith there; for, ver. 3, says he, 'they have not submitted themselves unto the righteousness of God.' I might instance, I say, in all other affections whatsoever that are good. And as for evil affections, you will easily believe that they are enemies to faith, as all the lusts of men are. You need take but one scripture for it, John v. 44. Christ speaks there in the language of impossibility, of inconsistency, that faith should ever be wrought in the heart while lusts remain, that they and faith should stand together: 'How can ye believe,' saith he, 'if ye receive honour one of another, and do not seek that honour that is of God only?'

I might likewise shew you that all that comes from us, either take righteousness that is past or all endeavours for time to come, as they cannot

* In Book II. of this third part.

help us to the attainment of faith, so they are enemies to the way of believing. If we consider all the righteousness that comes from us, let corrupt nature be never so much advanced, it is an enemy, it strengtheneth the enmity that is in the heart against the way of believing. Men cannot have a righteousness of their own, as they count it, but they are conceited of it. If men have any appearance of righteousness, oh it must needs be grace, it must needs presently be accepted. And the conceit of our own righteousness is that which hinders us from seeing need of, and looking after, Christ and faith. The Pharisees thought themselves righteous, and they were so far from faith and coming unto Christ, that Christ professeth he came not to call such, Mat. ix. 13. As the law was not given for a righteous man (the law in the legal tenor of it), so nor the gospel neither. Faith, in the fundamental law of it, as I have formerly expressed it, is directly opposite to that conceit of a man's own righteousness, which is in every one's heart by nature. Herein lies the pith of faith, to ' believe on him that justifies the ungodly,' and that in opposition to all in a man's self ; so you have it, Rom. iv. 5. You know Laodicea, that thought herself rich, was kept off from going to Christ to buy gold of him ; and the richer a man's heart and life is of appearing goodness, the loather he is to break (as he must do), and become a bankrupt, that he may have Christ ; the loather he is to suffer so much loss, and to count all things else but as dung and dross, as the apostle saith. As a man's own righteousness for time past, so some kind of endeavours for time to come, are a hindrance to faith. I do not only mean endeavours of changes, and reformations of heart and life, and the like, that these undermine faith, but oftentimes endeavours after faith itself, when they are put forth in a man's own strength, do hinder and undermine faith. Endeavours for the time to come, if they be not guided aright, do secretly undermine faith, and the work of it. A man when he sees his former sinfulness and want of Christ, and the necessity of faith, and hath suffered a shipwreck of all his own righteousness, yet he begins to build a ship anew of his own cost, and he thinks by hauling, and tugging, and rowing, in the end to arrive at Christ ; and whilst a man doth so, Jesus Christ goes as fast from him as he makes after Christ, whilst he doth it out of his own strength. Whereas if a man would give up and lay his naked soul, that little cock-boat which hath so great a venture in it, if he would put it into the ship of God's free grace, as I may so express it, and commit itself unto it and unto Christ, and suffer the streams and gales of the Spirit in the use of means (using of them but as means), to carry him along, the soul would attain unto faith, But men seek after faith itself, not in a way of faith, but as a work of the law, in their own strength, which strength man, under the legal covenant, once had. To beat down this presumption is the apostle's design, Rom. ix. 16, ' So then it is not of him that willeth, nor of him that runneth, but of God that sheweth mercy.' In such a presumption a man ' condemns himself in what he allows,' as the same apostle says in another case ; a man undoes himself in what he endeavoureth, and if God be not the more merciful, a man goes to hell, endeavouring and striving to go to heaven. This the apostle clears in this chapter, out of which I have now chosen my text, which refers unto the example of the Israelites ; for he had propounded the example of the Israelites and their unbelief, and their falling short of Canaan, as types of us under the gospel. Now it was not only their lusts, the flesh-pots of Egypt, that hindered them from coming into Canaan, but it was because they sought to go into it, and yet not by a way of faith. You know God offered to carry them thither, to cast out their enemies before them, if they would have gone in his way—even those that perished they might have entered—but that way they rejected through unbelief. And then you shall find in Numb. xiv. 40, that they would enter upon the work in their own strength, and rose up early in the morning to do it; but what doth God do for this? He brings them back again to the very brink of the Red Sea, where they were afore. So it is even with poor souls that have gone far in the wilderness, and are nigh heaven, nigh as it were to believing; and yet not subjecting their souls and endeavours unto God's way of working faith, but attempting it in their own strength, they are cast behind-hand again, and in their own sense are as far off as at first; and when God hath humbled them for endeavouring in their own strength, they are fit to enter. For God hath said in 1 Sam. ii. 9, 'By his own strength shall no man prevail;' but men seeing no strength in themselves to save themselves, and being convinced of that, yet think they may go out in their own strength to get this Christ that shall save them, and so being still in themselves, they never prevail, for by a man's own strength he shall never prevail; so doth the Holy Ghost speak, he speaks it of all things else, but especially it holds true in the matter of believing.

You see in this text, Heb. iv. 11, that the Holy Ghost makes an exhortation to us, by faith to labour to enter into that rest: and this text I shall make no other use of, nor of anything about it, but merely so far forth as it may become a subject to this common-place we have in hand. And there are two ends or purposes which this text will serve for. The one is to shew you, that notwithstanding what you have heard, that faith is not of ourselves, it is the gift of God; yet we are to labour to enter into that rest, and labour to believe. And the second thing it serves for is this (and it is a great point), that an indefinite promise, that is, a promise that God will save some, not naming who, is a sufficient ground to draw in any man's heart to believe, take whatever ground of faith is held forth in the word. And this is natural to the text, and to the coherence of it; for he had said, ver. 6, 'It remains that some must enter into rest:' and his inference from that is this, which we have here in the 11th verse, 'Let us labour, therefore, to enter into that rest.' When men hear that faith is not of ourselves, but that it is the gift of God, there are these three things do usually arise in the spirits of men.

1. Either men do cavil at this doctrine, as lying as a stumbling-block in their way, that if all that we can do cannot produce faith, but it is the gift of God, and that God must do all, then say they, men were as good sit still, and not labour and endeavour at all after it, for God must do all; and these are cavillers.

2. On the other side, such poor souls as desire to attain to faith, and to labour for it under the use of means; yet hearing that faith is not of ourselves, yea, that a man's own endeavours, if they be out of a man's own strength, as I have said, cannot obtain faith, yea, they are hindrances unto believing; they are discouraged and disheartened from all endeavours; they think it cuts the sinews of all endeavours, strikes at the root, and causeth all to wither.

3. There are those that do expressly teach, and have taught this doctrine, that a man having seen his lost condition, is to do nothing else but to stand and wait, whenas God, without any puttings forth, or actings towards faith, will by an almighty power overpower his soul to believe.

Now then, that there may be an answer and satisfaction given to all these three, I have taken this text as the bottom for that discourse, that shall be an answer to them all.

After I have opened the text very briefly, and shewn you how it is a bottom to what I shall deliver, then I will come to do these three things more especially. I shall answer first the objection made, as it is a cavil. I shall, secondly, answer it as it is a discouragement to good souls. And, thirdly, shew you what kind of endeavours they are, and how they are to be managed, which God hath appointed to attain unto faith.

But first I must open the text, and I shall do that exceeding briefly. You see it is an exhortation that we should endeavour to enter into that rest.

1. Let us consider what is meant by entering into rest, which is to be the object of our endeavour. There are two things intended by it.

The *first* is more general, viz., the possession of heaven, that we are to make sure of that, that we be not as the foolish virgins, upon whom the door was shut, whenas others entered in, Matt. xxv. 10. Thus entering into rest is often taken in Scripture for the full possession of heaven. So in the 10th verse of this very chapter, our Saviour Christ's ascending into heaven is called his entering into rest after his work was ended, as God entered into rest after his work was ended. And (Matt. xxv. 23) when men come to possess heaven, it is called ' entering into their master's joy :' as when a man is said to have a full possession of an office given him, he is said to enter upon it. An heir that was under age had a right and title to his inheritance, yet he enters upon his land and estate when he comes to years : so that now if you take it in this sense, then this is the meaning of it, that we should endeavour to be found in the number of those that shall enter into that rest.

But, *secondly*, by entering into rest is meant more particularly the attainment of true saving faith, whereby we come to have a sure title to that rest in heaven, and to make at present thereby such an entrance upon it as gives a right before possession, which comes afterwards. And this I make plain to you by these two reasons.

First, By what is said at the third verse of this very chapter, ' We which have believed do enter into rest :' so that faith is clearly and plainly an entering into rest, in the apostle's sense, in this chapter. In having an estate of land passed, besides the writings there are two ceremonies used ; there is entering upon some part of it, and there is a giving of some piece of the ground, as a tuft of earth, and the like. So is it here ; we by faith do enter upon this rest, and we receive then an earnest of joy, the seal of the Spirit, the first-fruits of heaven. It is evident also that by entering into rest is meant believing, by the very words that follow my text, for the very next words are, ' Lest any man fall through the same example of unbelief.' He sets before their eyes the example of the Israelites, and of those Israelites that went far towards Canaan ; and yet, saith he, through unbelief they never entered into it. Now let us, saith he, take heed of falling through unbelief as they did ; let us therefore labour to attain to true faith, by which we enter into rest, and have such a right to it as we shall never be dispossessed. And so now you see that by entering into rest is meant believing.

Secondly, The word here translated *labour* signifies to study to enter into that rest, to have all the powers and faculties in us intended in attaining to true faith. He expresseth it by a word that signifies the labour of the mind, which is proper to scholars and students, whose minds are taken up with the greatest intention and the greatest labour. Now, saith he, there was never any scholar studied more to find out what is truth, giving up his understanding unto God, who is the great enlightener, never any philosopher ever gave his mind more to find out natural truths, than a believer doth to attain unto true faith ; we are to 'search for it as for silver :' when he therefore saith, 'Let us labour to enter into that rest,' his meaning is, that we should use the utmost of our endeavours to attain to it, and to attain, as to the rest, so to the entering into that rest.

And so I have done with the exposition of the words, and you see how they are a bottom to that discourse which I mean to proceed in. I shall come now to those particulars which I have laid down to discourse of.

1. I am to answer this great cavil, made either by secure profane persons, or by those that are opposite to the doctrine of free grace, viz., that if faith be not of ourselves, and all that is within us be against it, and that God must do all, then we are not to endeavour. The apostle, you see, speaks point blank against it ; and notwithstanding the Israelites (who were types of temporary believers under the gospel, and of such as attain not to true faith) endeavoured to enter into Canaan, and yet fell short, he makes this use of it, that we should therefore labour for to enter into that rest. But for the answering of this, as it is a cavil, more particularly : (1.) I say this, that this doctrine, that it is God which works faith, and that doth all in us in the matter of believing, is attended upon and clogged in this, with a like cavil that all other mysteries of the gospel are. The mystery of the gospel lies in this, it is a reconciling of contradictions ; and all your cavillers take part with one part of the contradiction to overthrow the other. As now, that God should peremptorily elect men to salvation, and yet man's will should be free ; how can these two stand together, say the cavillers against free grace and God's everlasting love ? So likewise when they hear that God works conversion in men unresistibly, say they, how can this be if God work upon the free will of man ? So now here, when we say that it is God only worketh faith, and that it is his gift, and that all our endeavours are not able to produce it, what do they presently conclude and retort upon us ? Then we were as good lay all endeavours aside. But really this is all one with that deceit which hath damned many a soul, viz., if I be elected, whatever I do I shall be saved. It is all one with that kind of cavil of the papists, that hath accompanied the doctrine of justification by Christ alone, and by faith in him, and that without works ; for, say they, we were then as good do no good works at all. So now is it here, if that faith be not of ourselves, but it is the gift of God ; then say they, we were as good sit still and endeavour nothing at all. This is the first thing in the general that I premise ; that it is, I say, but a like cavil to all those that carnal men have made against all the truths of God, the mystery of which lies in reconciling these contradictions. But,

(2.) Secondly, To speak more directly to those that cavil thus, and that say it is therefore in vain to use endeavours. Let that man appear or stand out from all the rest at the day of judgment, or now in this world, that is able to say, I used my utmost endeavours to attain salvation, and could not attain it, God would not give it me. If he did not use his utmost endeavours, then God is clear. I will not stand now to dispute, whether *de jure*, as we say, if a man should use his utmost endeavours, God infallibly would work grace in that man's heart ; but, *de facto*, we may challenge all the sons of men. And let me tell you this, that at the latter day, when men shall come to be condemned—I speak this to clear God— God will not go and say, I therefore condemn you because you did not put forth an act of saving, justifying faith. No ; but he will condemn men because they did not put forth that uttermost, which, through that assistance corrupt nature had from him, they might have put forth. When God comes to judge all mankind, it is said, that he will 'judge them that lived under the law by the law; and them that lived without the law, he will judge without the law,' Rom. ii. 12. Now, it is true, in rigour, whether men know the law or not, God might condemn them upon it as if they knew it, for they knew it once in Adam, and are bound to know it; but he will not go that way to the work; but if men have lived without the law, he will consider them but so far forth as the light of nature went, and so far judge them; and if they have lived under the law, then he will proceed in judgment so far as the law went, and that spirit and strength that accompanies the law; and so if they lived under the gospel, he will condemn them for not using that assistance, that spirit and strength, that accompanies the hearts of men that live under the gospel, and leads them on to faith. He will not condemn men for negatives, but rather for what is positive; because they loved darkness rather than light, and because they would not believe, but cleave to their lusts.

For if any man attempted and fell short, the impediment did lie in his own will. That point will never come to be disputed, whether he could or no. God will cut off all with this, he would not. *Impii non posse est ejus non velle*, the impotency of a wicked man is his not willing; and yet this inability to will is not merely a moral, but a natural impotence. That they cannot is resolved by Christ into their lusts as the reason: John v. 40, 44, 'Ye will not come to me that ye might have life;' and 'how can ye believe' (and why, where lies the difficulty?) 'that receive,' says he, verse 44, 'honour one from another?' The impediment lies in themselves, in their willing the contrary, in their 'loving darkness more than light.' If indeed the impediment were extrinsecal wholly, a door.locked on thee, or that God held it so fast in his hand that thou couldst not wring it out, then there were room for complaint; but it being intrinsecal, in thy will, thou hast no cause to complain.

(3.) For answer to this cavil, I say, that there is no man would make this cavil, or would complain, that endeavoureth in a right way; and if he endeavoureth not in a right way, there is reason God should complain rather of him. For I ask, Upon what ground is it that thou thinkest to attain unto faith? If thou thinkest to obtain it for thy own endeavours, and by them to compass it, I say this plainly to thee, it is pity thou shouldst ever attain it that way: 1 Sam. ii. 9, 'He will keep the feet of his saints, and the wicked shall be silent in darkness; for by strength shall no man prevail.' And my reason is this, because it would be dishonourable unto God, for God never gave it upon those terms. If he should, he then should lose the glory of his grace, and grace should be no grace; it would be then of debt, as the apostle saith in Rom. iv. 1–3. Now, then, if ever God give it he will give it of free grace, or he will not give it at all: 'Not of works,' saith he, Eph. ii. 9, 'lest any man should boast.' On the other side, if any one doth endeavour, in a subordination unto grace, in a dependence upon grace as it is free, that he is content to venture his endeavours upon the free grace of God towards him in Christ, as thinking that nothing he doth moveth or swayeth God anything at all, but that God is as free after twenty years' endeavours of his as the first day; I say, if any one doth endeavour thus, that man shall be sure to attain it, and he shall have no cause to complain. And if he should miss he would not complain, because he sought it upon such terms that God was still free, and he depended upon free grace, and he endeavoured still in a subordination thereunto; and so howsoever he had his end, and he would never complain. In a word, either a man seeks salvation in subordination to free grace or not; if not, it is justice to deny him, because his endeavours, if they speed, would derogate from God's grace. If he seeks salvation subordinately to free grace, then, however it falls out, he will have his end ; for if he obtains, he says, not unto my endeavours, but to thy grace, be the glory ; and so he magnifies free grace. If he obtains it not, yet, Lord, says he, thy grace is magnified, and the freeness of it demonstrated in this, that so many endeavours missed, because thou wert free whether thou wouldst save me or not.

(4.) Let all such cavillers consider that the Scriptures do speak the clean contrary, and those very places that hold forth that God doth all according to his good pleasure, do infer from thence that we should therefore endeavour in our proportion. You have it in Philip. ii. 13, 'Beloved brethren,' saith he, 'work out your own salvation with fear and trembling : for it is God that worketh in you, both to will and to do of his good pleasure.' Here the apostle lays down this position as strongly as any caviller upon earth can, for he tells us that it is God that not only works the deed but the very will in us ; and that he doth not only give power to the will, and then the will puts forth the act, but that he works the very act of will : 'It is God,' saith he, 'that works both the will and the deed.' And this he saith he doth of his good pleasure. He so works it as he will not be obliged to do it to this man or that man, or upon this man's endeavours or that man's endeavours, but out of his good pleasure, when, and where, and how he will. Here, I say, the objection is made as strong as any man can make it to raise this cavil upon it, therefore let us do nothing. But see how the apostle urgeth it to the quite contrary : 'Let us *therefore*,' saith he, 'work out our own salvation with fear and trembling : for it is God that works in us, both to will and to do of his good pleasure.' And again, whereas men are apt to cavil and say, Many have endeavoured, and they have missed, therefore we had as good sit still. What doth Christ say ? He infers likewise the clean contrary from it in Luke xiii. 24 : 'Strive to enter in at the strait gate ; for many will seek to enter, and shall not be able ;' not be able through their own lusts, and through their their own wills, that undermine their endeavours. Observe it, he draws the very clean contrary inference, that because many do seek to enter, and shall not be able, therefore, saith he, do you do more. He bids them take more pains : Do you strive, saith he, wrestle it out, even as wrestlers and contenders for masteries use to do, as the apostle saith in 1 Cor. ix. 24, endeavouring to put nothing to the venture, or to an uncertainty, as far as possibly you can : 'Thus strive,' saith he ; 'for many have sought to enter, and have not been able.' So that now these that make this cavil must needs run point-blank against the Scripture, which, you see, makes an inference quite contrary to it. I might add also that of our Saviour Christ in John vi. 27, where when they had taken a great deal of pains to follow him for the loaves, he diverts their labour to something else, and he bids them labour or work for the meat that endures to eternal life. But they might say, Why, but it is a thing that is not of ourselves, it is the gift of Christ, and why should we labour after it ? Yes, saith Christ ; 'Labour you for the meat which endureth to everlasting life, which the Son of man shall give you ;' and notwithstanding he is to give it you, yet do you labour for it. But I shall make use of this place when I come to shew you what acts we are to put forth, and truly one plainly in a word is this, to believe ; for so it is there, ver. 28, 29, 'Upon this say they unto him, What shall we do to work the works of God ?' or, what do you mean by this labouring ? Saith Christ, 'This is the work of God, that ye believe on him whom he hath sent.' He puts them upon believing itself, and the exercising thereof.

2. Now to prosecute those three heads mentioned, I shall shew you, and give a reason or two why, though faith is not of ourselves, but is the gift of God, yet notwithstanding he requires endeavours at our hands as means to attain it; and though he works both the will and the deed of his good pleasure, yet his good pleasure is that we should co-work with him. How to manage and guide your endeavours herein I must speak to in the last head. In the mean time there are these reasons why God hath joined both the one and the other.

(1.) That by our labouring and endeavouring we may shew and acknowledge what our duty is. It is God's command that we should believe and lay hold upon Jesus Christ, and cast ourselves upon him for salvation, therefore it is our duty, and we are to labour to attain this, and to labour after it in truth and in the spiritualness of it; not so much to shew what we are able to do, but what we ought to do, and what our duty is to do. It is not required to shew our ability, but our readiness. Our weakness and our inability doth not cut the bond of our duty. We set young children to school with their hornbook at their girdles oftentimes, long before they have skill, or are capable of skill, to read them; we teach them to take up a book, to look upon the letters, to shew them thereby what it is we would have them do, and what it is we intend to bring them up to. So doth God himself with us. And we do like and approve it in little children, that they will sit at school with a book thus in their hand, rather than be still at home careless, playing with babies and rattles, and the like.

(2.) God requires men's endeavours to this very purpose, that men may see their inability, which is a great lesson that furthers faith. Nature will and doth think it can believe and repent, till it makes trial; and as we use to put conceited persons upon services to shew them their folly and their weakness upon trial, so God deals with us. Men, if they saw not their own inability, would be apt to say in their hearts as they Deut. viii. 7, 'My power, and the might of my hand hath done this:' and they would not see their disability but by attempting to do something. Thus Christ suffered the woman that had the bloody issue to use all means else ere he cured her, to shew her the inability and insufficiency of all means; and she spent all upon physicians that could do her no good, that so she might fly to him. And thus God left nature to use all her shifts and inventions to attain to happiness, and to use all her wit and strength ere he sent his Son into the world: 1 Cor. i. 21, 'After that in wisdom men knew not God,' that is, after trial made of the strength of natural wisdom, but not till then, 'it pleased God to save by the foolishness of preaching them that believe.'

(3.) God hath appointed our endeavours and means to be used, not as duties only, but as testimonies and evidences that we do wholly depend upon God for to work all our works in us and for us, seeing in the use of means and endeavours of ours God useth to come. Carelessness giveth over the use of means; but when a man dependeth upon God for a thing, that dependence will make him to use those means whereby to attain it, as a testimony he doth depend upon God, and so God requires it. In Luke v. 4, when Peter had fished all night and caught nothing, saith Christ unto him, 'Launch out into the deep, and let out your nets for a draught;' Simon answering, ' said unto him, Master, we have toiled,' toiled to weariness (so the word signifies), and 'toiled all the night,' which is the opportune season for fishing, ' and have caught nothing; nevertheless,'—this is it I quote it for,—' at thy word I will let down the net.' His meaning is, as if he should have said, although all the endeavours we have used hitherto have been frustrate, notwithstanding the fair opportunities we have had, having had all the night before us to fish in, and we have took abundance of toil, cast in the net again and again, and all to no purpose, ' yet at thy word,'— that phrase implies that he did it merely in a dependence upon Jesus Christ, and upon his word,'—' at thy word,' saith he, ' I will let down the net,' as an evidence that he depended upon the word of Christ, and subjected himself unto it, when he himself had little hope, as those words imply, ' We have fished all night, and have caught nothing.' When they used rams' horns seven days in compassing the city of Jericho, they did not use them as a means that would be effectual in itself to the blowing down of the walls, but they used them as signs that they believed his word, and that they did depend upon him to effect that which they desired, because God had said and appointed that in that means he would do it. So doth God command and require endeavours, not so much as means, though they have likewise the nature of means, but as signs that we depend upon him who worketh all in all, and hath appointed to work them by those means.

(4.) God hath appointed to us to use endeavours, and that we should strive to enter into that rest, that salvation may be prized, that the gift of faith may be valued. It is not that those endeavours promote our salvation so much, but it is that it may cost us somewhat, to the end that we may value it. The salvation of men cost God much ; it cost him his Son, it cost his Son his blood, it hath cost the Holy Ghost abundance of attendance upon us. Now we are the men to be saved, it is our own salvation : therefore there is a great deal of reason that it should cost us somewhat too. Those things that come to us very lightly, we do as lightly regard them ; it is in the nature of man so to do, and God deals with us as with men. Things, I say, that are easily gotten are lightly esteemed ; we may see it by experience in those that think they have had faith ever since they can remember, how slightly do they speak of it, and how lightly do such kind of souls esteem of it. If we had salvation and faith dropped into our mouths, we would the more lightly regard it ; therefore God would not have us slothful for the attaining of faith, not slothful for the discovering of faith, not slothful in holding fast the profession of faith unto the end : so you have it in Heb. vi. 12. ' We desire,' saith he, ' that every one of you do shew the same diligence' (that is, after conversion) which you have shewn before, ' to the full assurance of hope unto the end, that ye be not slothful,' &c.

(5.) Even for this very reason doth God require us to endeavour, though he himself works all, that when our endeavours without him have proved unsuccessful, his power in working faith at last might appear the more. When a man hath endeavoured and used the means long, and to no purpose, as he thinks, if in the end God comes in, it magnifies his free grace and his power towards us. As in that instance before quoted in Luke v. 5, when they had toiled all night, and took nothing, that then there should be so great a draught of fishes taken by casting down the net once more, this made Peter fall down amazed, this made him acknowledge Jesus to be the Lord, and to say to Christ, ' Depart from me, for I am a sinful man ;' so struck was he with the greatness of that power that appeared in that work. God doth sometimes hide his power under means, and lets men endeavour that they may see even by experience their own inability, which lesson is hardly otherwise learned. We had scarce ever learned this great lesson, that it is God that works faith in us, but by the experience of our own inability, and that experience of our own inability is taught us from attempting endeavours according to God's command. Nature is apt, and will be apt, to try if it can work faith out of itself; it is apt to think I will take the promises and this heart of mine, and strike the one against the other till sparks come out; and till a man see by his own experience that nothing comes out, he will never believe himself to be so unable to attain it as he is. We use to put conceited persons upon hard services and businesses, to the end they may even by their own experience see their folly and weakness. It is experience that must teach us the truth of this doctrine, or else we are apt to say as they in Deut. viii. 17, ' My power, and my might, and my hand hath done it.' And therefore Christ suffered the poor woman that had the issue, first to use all means, to spend all that she had upon physicians, that when the inability of all means else should appear, the cure he was to work on her might the more be magnified.

(6.) In the last place, I add this as an answer unto this cavil, that in using those means God hath appointed, and such endeavours as God requires of us, there is nothing derogated from the power of God in working when he works faith, neither doth the power of God exclude such endeavours, but both may well stand together. First, I say, the use of them doth nothing derogate from the power of God in working, no more than the clay and the spittle which Christ used to restore the blind man to his sight. They of themselves could conduce nothing to the effecting of it, but in seeming appearance would rather put one's eyes out more; yet Christ, who might have restored him otherwise, would have this used, and his power did no less appear in the working of it thus, than if he had wrought it immediately without it: so God may and doth shew as much power in our using the means, as in working without them. Did not God, think you, shew as much power in taking of a rib from the man to make the woman of, and in taking red earth to make the body of the man out of it, as he shewed in the first day's creation, when he made all things out of mere nothing? God, even in some miracles, seemed to use means, which might have some show and colour of working the effect wrought, as in healing Naaman's leprosy, the washing in Jordan might seem to have likelihood of a remedy for a disease, and God did it to hide his power. Thus too, in such works as are standing works (as the conversion of souls is, which is the standing miracle of the world), God loves to hide and clothe his power under our endeavours, and in using means, as well as in working it immediately; and as he is found of those that sought him not, so he is found also of those that seek him; and alike power, and alike free grace appears in both. And then again, on the other side, the power of God doth not exclude men's endeavours, for though God doth not work faith in men for their endeavours, as the moving cause, neither doth he work by them as adjuvant causes, that reach the effect; yet, as concomitant instruments, he doth. You have that clear in that expression of the apostle in 1 Cor. iii. 8; at the 7th verse he had said, that ' neither is he that planteth anything, nor he that watereth, but God that giveth the increase:' yet, notwithstanding, at the 8th verse, he saith, that ' we are co-workers with God, and labourers together with him.' So that I say, although man doth nothing, and it is God that doth all, and faith is not of ourselves, but is the gift of God, yet there are endeavours and means that God hath appointed for the attaining of faith, and both these may stand together. And so let this be enough, if not too much, for the answering of that objection as it is a cavil; namely, that if God work all, and we do nothing in the producing of faith in us, then men were as good sit still, and not labour and endeavour at all after it.

CHAPTER II.

Discouragements against using our endeavours to believe, which arise from the thoughts of the difficulty of faith, as being above our own power, considered and answered.

I come now to answer the discouragements of poor souls that even lie at the brink of believing, as I may so express it, who yet being sensible of their own inability to believe, and that they are not able to attain Christ without Christ and faith, are therefore apt to sink into discouragements, and to think it is in vain to attempt it, to practise or to go about believing, or to put forth any act of faith at all, especially if they have done it, and felt no comfort in their own sense, nor felt any power coming in beyond what in an ordinary way doth assist men. I say, in that case, they are apt to be discouraged, and to give it over as in vain, and not to set upon it. Now, for their sakes, I shall do two things :—

1. I shall remove their discouragements.

2. I shall give what directions are suitable unto such souls, which indeed, in the close, will be this (as you shall see afterwards), to put them upon believing, and upon exercising the acts of faith continually, for so Christ did, and so did the apostles.

1. I will first remove their discouragements; and to such souls as are sensible of their own inability, the first thing I shall say, as in relation to their discouragement, is this, that to be cast down in the sense of thine own inability and insufficiency to believe, or to act any spiritual good as of thyself, is a great part of faith. It is the negative part, it is the emptying part, as I may so call it, as the other is the filling part; it is part of that poverty of Spirit which Christ makes the promise to in Mat. v. 3. Now, if the sense of thy own inability be kept within its own bounds, and thou carriest this principle continually along with thee in thy heart, the more thou hast of it the better it is, for still, as God digs deeper in discovering this unto thee, the higher he builds in the work of faith and believing, and he will certainly do it; and so far it is but a foundation of giving all unto God. And let me say this to you, God's end in bringing men to salvation that way, viz., to take all power from them of what is in themselves, it was not that any should be discouraged, but that they might go out of themselves unto him for help ; and, therefore, now to maintain a constant sense thereof is one direction which I shall afterwards give you. But I will now speak to the discouragement itself. When your souls are brought to this emptiness as in yourselves, for you upon this to be discouraged, and to give over the work, do but consider the ground of this, and consider the sinfulness of this. For a man to be discouraged, and to give over the work, either because he cannot do it, or because he thinks it will never be done, and therefore he will do nothing, no not that which he finds his heart strengthened to do, because he knows not whether it be the power of God in it, yea or no ; for a man, I say, thus to be discouraged, is to despair of the power of God ; it is to add to the sense of thine own inability, a despair of the power of God too. You must know it is a peevishness if a man doth not wait upon the power of God in its way, as it is, on the contrary, a meek and humble temper to wait upon the free grace of God in the freedom of it. Yea, the truth is, the ground of this discouragement is the highest pride ; for when a man hears that he can do nothing of himself, though withal he hears that God is able to work faith, and to work it

instantly, if therefore he will sit still and do nothing, the ground, I say, of this is the highest pride. For the true reason of this discouragement, if you resolve it into its causes, is indeed this, that men would have their own endeavours to be means to compass grace. This is the way of nature. Now, although thou seest thine own inability, yet thy nature riseth up with another corruption; and because thou canst not have it by thyself, and because thou canst not prevail by thy own strength, when it is once discovered, therefore thou wilt do nothing at all. This, I say, is the working of pride one way, even as to be conceited of a man's own strength, till he is sensible of his own inability, is the working of it another way. It is all but pride working two several ways, that because a man findeth that it is not in his own power to attain unto faith, to attain the Lord Jesus Christ, and that he cannot compass it to himself in his own way, even as men do wealth, therefore he will sit down in a pet discouraged, and fling off all. It is not therefore the doctrine that we can do nothing, and that God must do all, that discourageth, but it is the pride and the corruption that is in the spirits of men. For would flesh reject and renounce using endeavours as in its own way, and use them in a way of subordination unto God and to his power, a man would be so far, if he come once to this, from being discouraged, as there is nothing more will quicken. As when a man comes to submit unto God, when his heart is brought to lie down at the feet of free grace, instantly he hath peace; so when the heart is once brought to renounce seeking salvation in a man's own strength, and not only so, but to set upon the business in a subordination to the strength and power of God, the strength and power of God falls upon that man.

2dly. Let me speak to this discouragement by way of removal or taking of it away. In the way of believing there are two eminent discouragements: the one is concerning the will of God, whether he will accept me into grace and favour; and this ariseth from the doctrine of election, that seeing salvation and the free grace of God is pitched but upon a few, how there can be an object of faith propounded to the sons of men, and a ground for them to believe, that do not know whether they be elected, yea or no; or how do I know whether this Christ is mine or no, whom you bid me to believe upon? And unless I be elected, all that I do will be in vain, and all will be frustrate. But, besides this, there is another discouragement, and that is concerning the power of God, that is requisite to the working of faith; because we are unable of ourselves to believe, will some say, and it is God that worketh faith in us, therefore I will not put forth any act of faith until I feel the power of God in my own sense coming upon me, overpowering me, and drawing my heart to believe. The truth is, that both these objections or discouragements do in a manner come to one, at leastwise there is a great deal of parallel betwixt them, and the same thing that answers the one will answer the other. I will afterward answer the first objection, by shewing, that election is so far from being a discouragement, that it is the greatest encouragement to any soul in the way of believing that can be. But now I shall only make a parallel of this objection with the other, and so shew you how the discouragement may be taken away by the same reason or consideration in the one, that it is removed and taken away in the other. I say, both these discouragements are alike, and they come all to one; for a soul that doth not know whether it is elected or no, whether God will accept it, doth but venture its faith, and its going to God, and to Christ, in a subordination to his free grace, upon God's good pleasure, and the freedom of his will; and one that is sensible of his own insufficiency, doth but venture his believing, and endeavoureth in a subordination to the power of God, so as the thing comes all to one ; yea, so far as any man may have hope and ground to think that God may accept of him (which may be the ground for faith notwithstanding election), so far may that man have a hopefulness that the power of God will accompany him in the exercising of faith. And the reason of it is clearly this, because the power of God is set a-work by his will, and both these are commensurable and proportionable ; and so far as the will of God goes, so far his power goes ; and so far as I have hope, and have ground to hope that God may accept me, so far I have ground also to wait upon him, to put forth that power to accompany me, and to strengthen me, and enable me in believing, and in all the acts of it. As therefore men do make a venture upon the will of God in casting themselves upon it to save them, and accept them (and it is the best venture that ever was made), so far men ought to attempt the exercise of faith without discouragement, in a way of subordination unto the power of God, and to put themselves into the stream of it. The truth is, when all is done, God will be trusted in both.

3. Join but these two following things together, and do but consider what a great encouragement this doctrine is, that it is God only that must work in us, rather than a discouragement. I say, join but these two things together, which are both true : first, that God doth all, which is the objection ; but, secondly, take this in too, that this God who doth all, useth graciously to come and join with men while they are acting and exercising of faith, and his power raiseth them to believing savingly and spiritually ; if you consider these two things together, that instead of a discouragement, it is the greatest encouragement that ever was or could be supposed to be. Now thus it is, only God will be free, he will take his own time, he will shew his liberty in the time as well as in the person. But when we take the pen in our hand, and often attempt to write after the copy, though of ourselves we know not how to write a letter, yet in obedience to him, going about to do our duty, he takes us by the hand, and strengthens and enables us to do it. The poor impotent man at the pool of Bethesda, that attempted to go in, and cried out to go in, and could not for thirty years, yet at last the poor man having continued thus long lying there, Jesus Christ came and healed him ; not because he lay there, but to shew that he blessed his waiting on him. In that James iv., what says the apostle ? James iv. 8, ' Draw nigh unto God, and he will draw nigh unto you.' To draw nigh unto God is to draw nigh unto him, as in putting one's self under ordinances and means (as of Korah, Dathan, and Abiram, it is said they did draw nigh unto God), so by believing. ' Let us draw nigh,' saith he, ' with full assurance of faith,' Heb. x. 2. And when men put themselves under such means where God's presence useth to be, then doth God use to draw nigh unto them, ' Draw nigh unto God,' saith he, ' and he will draw nigh unto you.' I could give you a multitude of places, as Prov. i. 23, ' I will pour out my Spirit upon you ;' and Mat. vii. 7, ' Seek, and you shall find ;' and Luke xi. 13, ' He will give the Spirit unto them that ask.' Thus God, though he doth all, yet he is graciously pleased to join with us (and how, I shall shew you by and by), and to act us through his strength acting of us, and to come in and work that for us which we aim at. And if so, then it is the greatest encouragement to us which can be, that God doth all. If that God should have said to you that are the sons of men, I will give you assisting grace, which yet I leave to the liberty of your wills to join withal, or not to join withal ; in this case all the sons of men, when it had been thus of themselves and their own power, would have fallen off from God, and would have turned this grace into wantonness. But if God shall say,

I will not deal with you according to the way or the will of the creature, but whilst I assist your will to do thus and thus, I will come in with a farther power, and I will do all for you and all in you, and so draw the creature to wait upon an higher power, and to act in a subordination there-unto, this way of salvation is the greatest encouragement that can be; and why is it so? Because that in this case God undertakes to do all, and it is better to wait in a way of uncertainty (if I may so express it, though it is not so), in a dependence upon the power of God this way, than to have gone the other way as Adam did, and as all legal Christians do; for what saith the heart? Here is my comfort, that that God, in depend-ence upon whose power I act, still so far as he assisteth, and depend upon his power to work all in me, he is able, and nothing is too hard for him. I have an hard heart, a base unbelieving heart, apt to depart from the living God; but I depend upon the power of God to overcome this hard heart, to draw me in to the Lord Jesus, and there is nothing too hard for his engagement. I say, to depend upon such a power, whenas you have that power also that doth engage itself, that when he doth give a will to use such and such means, he often and ordinarily comes in; to depend, I say, upon such a power is the greatest encouragement that can be.

I shall make a parallel of it now, with the throwing of a man's self upon the free grace of God to save him in the way of election. Men usually say, that election is the most discouraging doctrine in the world; but really whosoever throws himself upon the riches of the free grace of God, and depends upon such a love as God manifesteth to the elect to save him, will find all objections are answered, whether they be taken from unworthiness, or any other reason, they do all vanish before it, only this one remaineth, whether thou art the person or no. And for that I say, there is an easy answer, that the indefinite promise, as I shall in the sequel shew you, is the ground of faith. So now when you come to depend upon the power of God, faith doth as it were make but one venture, and that is at first; for if once you find that power of God to be engaged, it is so engaged as that it will for ever do all in you, and carry it on for ever afterward, and that you may be sure of. So that indeed all the venture you make is at first to get this faith wrought in you; but if this power be once engaged, it will go on, it will everlastingly save you; and therefore Christ still makes an encouragement of it. When he had said, Mat. xix. 24, how hard it is for a rich man to enter into heaven, as hard as for a camel to go in at the eye of a needle, the disciples, the text saith, were discouraged; 'What man then shall be saved?' say they. It was merely because they did dream of being saved by something in a man's self. How doth Christ answer? 'With man this is impossible,' saith he, 'but with God all things are possible.' He tells them this to raise up their hearts again; therefore, saith he, do but you venture upon the power of God, though the work be thus difficult, and *that* will overcome your lusts, and *that* will subdue the hardest heart, and strongest earthly mind. Christ, I say, in that place, makes it an encouragement, and indeed it is the greatest.

4. The next thing that I would say for the encouragement of such, is this, that if God do give thee an heart to labour and to endeavour still to renew thy faith, and thou dost renew thy faith continually upon it, God will bestow and doth bestow usually the thing in the end. In Luke xi. there is a parable exceeding clear to this purpose. Christ there exhorts them to pray, and to continue to pray, and he doth it upon this ground, by the parable of a man's friend coming to him, whom in the end he heareth, because of his importunity, ver. 8. Now though God doth not hear for

thy importunity, yet when he gives thee a heart that doth in a way of importunity and constancy exercise acts of faith, never stand disputing whether they be true acts of faith. Suppose thou hast not true faith at present, suppose thou shouldst not have it, suppose thou be but a temporary believer, if he enable thee to continue thus, he doth usually join with the believer in the end. And so Christ concludeth that parable, and bids them seek and they shall find; for, saith he, he giveth the Spirit unto them that ask him, ver. 13.

5. Though God doth all, yet he doth it usually in the use of means, and in them useth to come. When we have the pen in our hands, and offer to write, though we make never a true letter, yet he often takes a man by the hands, and guides and strengthens it. The man that lay at the pool, when, though impotent, he still attempted to go in, though he could not, John v. 7, yet he still lying at the pool, Christ comes and heals him. Yea, though the principle out of which they use the means be not spiritual but natural, yet God takes the advantage of it to work. It was not a right ground moved Naaman to wash in the waters of Jordan, and yet God healed him, using the means, which else he would not have done.

6. Though some should have failed that have used the means (as believers themselves sometimes), yet this should not discourage men to neglect them. It discourages not in other things. Men forbear not procreating, because it is God puts in a soul, and the dependence is well nigh as great in the first as in the second birth. Men forbear not to sow because some years have proved barren. We forbear not to preach, because every sermon takes not effect; we are not discouraged, because God hath bidden us wait if at any time he will give men repentance, 2 Tim. ii. 25. If preachers wait for the salvation of others, then men ought to do so for their own; and so much more should they, whose salvation it is, be content to venture endeavours, because, says the apostle, Philip. ii. 13, it is 'their own salvation.' Men will venture journeys for their own preferment.

7. That some have missed, should quicken us the more to the more heed-taking; for they failed because they put not more strength to the work, but grew slothful and negligent. Upon this ground our Saviour Christ provoked his disciples: Luke xiii. 24, 'Strive,' saith he, 'to enter into the strait gate: for many shall seek to enter in, and shall not be able.' That which these men would use as a discouragement, Christ turns into a reason, therefore do you strive or wrestle, or put to your utmost strength, for many have striven, and faintly endeavoured, that came short, therefore lose it not for a little more pains. So the apostle in 1 Cor. ix. 24, because many run that miss, therefore he exhorts them to endeavour 'so to run that they may obtain,' to endeavour to make all sure; so do I, says he; 'I therefore so run, not as uncertainly,' that is to say, this consideration quickens me to use my utmost care and endeavour.

8. That God doth all, should so much the more quicken us also; so the apostle argues: Philip. ii. 13, 'Work you out your salvation with fear and trembling, for it is God works in you the will and the deed,' i. e., seeing this great work depends upon God, to work how and when he will of his good pleasure, let not us think therefore to be idle, but set ourselves to the use of those means with the more fear and trembling, which God hath declared his pleasure is that we should use, as those that wholly depend upon his working all in all, and therefore fear to provoke him and put him off, tremble to neglect any means or opportunity he hath appointed.

9. If God give men a heart to continue endeavouring, though he gives it not *therefore*, yet it is a sign he means to bestow grace on them. It is his

bounty and mercy to set thy heart a-work about salvation, and it is a mercy which he affords to few; be thankful for what thou hast received, and not discouraged, and God may give thee more. There are but a few in the world that do seek him, and if he should turn away any that do, he would have fewer.

10. The ground why men are discouraged is, because they would have their endeavours a means to compass grace, and think by their own strength to prevail, which when it is discovered to them that it is bootless to endeavour, then they sit down discouraged, and sit down in a pet, and fling all away, because they cannot have grace in their way. But if that be the root of the discouragement, it is pride and corruption, and not the doctrine that God doth all, which discourageth. For would flesh renounce the opinion of its own strength, and its using endeavours its own way, and use them in subordination to God as means appointed by him only, then this doctrine would discourage no man, but quicken him. So that endeavours are not spoken against, but this way and ground of endeavouring, as thinking by what we do to obtain mercy; and it is not this doctrine that God doth all which discourageth, but pride and corruption, which because it hears it can do nothing, therefore it will do nothing; for there are other motives enough to persuade a man to endeavour, as that it is a man's duty, &c.

Obj. But you will say, If I should act faith upon God and Christ, I should do it all in a natural way, it would be a natural act, and not a spiritual act; and doth God in such cases come and join with men by his almighty power, working faith in them? To that I answer, that sometimes God doth do so. I will give you but an instance of it, parallel thereunto; it is of Naaman the Syrian. He came not out of his own country in a way of faith, but he had a providential hint given him by a maid that lived with him, that was a Jew, that if he went into the land of Israel, he should be cured by a prophet that was there. And when he came into Judea, and had spoken with the prophet, he had a reproof from one of his servants, that told him it was but a very small matter he was bid to do, and it was no great business for him to try. Upon this he went and tried, and upon no other ground but this, yet you see God cured him, and cured both his body and soul at once. When the woman of Samaria came to the Samaritans, she brought abundance of them unto Christ, and her speech did beget a kind of faith in them; but when they came to Christ himself, then say they, ' Now we believe, not because of thy saying, but for his own word.' So that in deed and in truth, though God begins to act a man's spirit, suppose in a natural way first, yet he doth turn it into a spiritual way in the very act. When thou takest a pen in thy hand to write, then God takes thee by the hand, and writes for thee. It is in this as it is in prayer; a man goes to prayer, puts himself into the presence of God, and the Holy Ghost falls upon him, and he not knowing how nor what to ask, he teacheth him what to ask with groans that are unutterable, as the apostle speaks.

11. Let me say this to you, it is encouragement enough to you to act and exercise the way of believing (as I shall shew you afterwards); it is, I say, encouragement enough that God may thus join with you, although neither I nor all the world can give thee any certain evidence that he will. I dare not say (not for all this world, as some do), that if a man useth such abilities as God giveth him well, then God will certainly give him faith if he go on so to do. To make a certainty of it, I say I cannot. But it is encouragement enough, though there cannot be a certainty made

out, that God oftentimes doth so, and it may be the ground of a thousand duties. Thou art a poor soul, and knowest not whether thou hast faith or no, yet thy soul desires to receive the Lord's supper, and art in question whether thou shouldst or no. Why, if there be that work which thou hast reason to judge may be grace, it is a ground for thee to perform that duty, for otherwise none can go to the Lord's supper but those that have assurance. And answerably to this, ' What knowest thou,' saith the apostle Paul, ' but that thou who art a believing wife,' staying with thy husband that is otherwise troublesome to thee, ' mayest convert him ? ' and upon this *What knowest thou?* though thou art not at a certainty God will, there is a ground of staying with thy husband, and of using all means to bring him unto God, and it is encouragement enough. Though, then, you have acted faith, and still you find not the power of God come upon you in your sense, drawing you to believe so as you aim at, this, I say, ought not to discourage you. Why? Because you ought to do as much for your own salvation as you would do for another's, or as ministers, or as a godly people are to do for the salvation of another. We forbear not to preach because every sermon taketh not effect ; because in 2 Tim. ii. 25, God hath bid us wait if at any time God will give such an one repentance. Now, if that be a motive and an encouragement strong enough, that God *may* do it, then it may be encouragement and motive strong enough to thee, that God may at last strike in and give thee power to believe. It is the apostle's own words (I quote it as comparing it with what a man may do for his own salvation, upon the like ground he is to do for the salvation of another) in Phil. ii. 12, ' Work out your own salvation with fear and trembling, for it is God that worketh in you both to will and to do.' I put the emphasis upon the words *your own.* If men are to wait thus for the salvation of others, because God may peradventure give them repentance, much more, then, though God doth all, art thou to wait, and in the mean time to act faith, and to work out *thy own.* Why? Because it is *thy own* salvation. And that others have missed who have endeavoured, is not a discouragement neither, so much as an encouragement, for there are thousands that have obtained. I have known some souls that have gone to God, and have taken Jesus Christ tremblingly, and the word hath stuck in their teeth whilst they were giving thanks unto God for giving them Jesus Christ, and God hath fallen upon them, and given them full assurance of his love before they had done. I say thousands of souls have gained this way, as well as some have missed. ' We, of his fulness,' saith the apostle in John i. 13, have received grace for grace.' Therefore, as men coming from a dole, who have gone there and have obtained, are examples of encouragement unto others, so should the example of all such who have obtained faith and salvation encourage thee. Let me say this to you, faith is the greatest venture in the world, so I use to express it ; and when all is done, you must make a venture upon it. You make a venture upon God's will when you throw yourselves upon it to accept you ; and you make a venture upon his power when you act faith with a subordination thereunto to work faith upon you. You must resolve to cast away your own endeavours for the glorifying of his power, as you must cast away your own righteousness for the glorifying of his free grace, and to be glad to put your mouths in the dust; and yet if there may be any hope, and if there may be faith, you ought to work out your salvation, because he worketh in you both the will and the deed. In all things else men do so. Husbandmen cast the seed into the ground, and wait for the increase, because it is God that giveth it, and men do the like for preferment. In all such natural things,

I say, men do act upon a dependence and in a subordination to the power of God, and should they not do so in matters of salvation?

CHAPTER III.

That the sense of heinous sins is another great hindrance of faith, which disheartens men from endeavouring to believe.—These discouragements answered and removed.

Though God commands and encourageth us to believe, yet there are certain discouragements lie in men's way. As, therefore, when the children of Israel were to return from the captivity, God bids his ministers take away the stumbling-blocks,—Isa. lvii. 14, 'Cast up, cast up, take away the stumbling-blocks out of the way of my people,' that they might not be hindered in their journey, saith the Lord,—so when we do exhort you to be reconciled to God, there are certain stumbling-blocks to be removed, there are certain discouragements which we must therefore remove, the chiefest whereof is the boundlessness and heinousness of men's sins; and when their eyes are opened to behold them, they are apt to be discouraged with the sight of them, and to think that reconciliation belongs not unto them. Now then, I shall display the riches of God's mercies in pardoning the greatest sins, to take away this discouragement, as it hinders you from coming in to Christ. And if sin be the greatest of them, that ought not to discourage you from coming in for mercy: for do but consider the sins of Manasseh, as they are set down 2 Kings xxi., 2 Chron. xxxiii. It is said, verse 6, that 'he did much wickedness in the sight of the Lord, and provoked him to anger.'

1. His sinning was much for continuance, for it is said he was king over Israel fifty-five years, being twelve years old when he began to reign, and it was towards the latter end of his days when he humbled himself.

2. His guilt was much in regard of the sins themselves, for he made a covenant with the devil, gave away his soul to him; verse 6, he dealt with familiar spirits. Add to this, murder, and that of the innocent; for it is said, 'he filled the streets of Jerusalem with blood, from one end to the other,' 2 Kings xxi. 16. So to this, idolatry, a sin greater than all the other, and it was the worst sort of idolatry: 2 Chron. xxxiii. 9, 'He made them to do worse than the heathen whom the Lord had destroyed before them.' Add to this, that it was a relapse, though not of himself, yet of the whole kingdom; for though his father had destroyed the images, broken down the altars, yet he did build them up again, and set up idolatry in the house of God, and he there set up a carved image, the idol which he had made—all this he was guilty of, 2 Chron. xxxiii. 3–10. And those sins were not confined only to his own person, but he made Israel also to sin; and for these sins were the children of Israel carried into captivity, Jer. xv. 14. He would not pardon them in regard of a temporal punishment. And Manasseh did all this against admonition, 2 Chron. xxxiii. 10. He sinned also against education, for he had a good father, and he lived twelve years under his government, in which time, no doubt but he instructed him; and he sinned also against the greatest mercy that could be, for he was made king of God's own people. Thus, you see, his sins were very great, and yet, for all this, the Lord had mercy on him: 2 Chron. xxxiii. 12, 13, 'And when he was in affliction, he besought the Lord, and humbled himself greatly before the God of his fathers, and prayed unto

him, and he was entreated of him, and God heard his supplication, and brought him again to Jerusalem into his kingdom.' He humbled himself greatly because he had sinned greatly; for when one hath sinned greatly, without great humiliation the Lord will not give mercy; but when he did so, the Lord did hear him, and brought him to his own kingdom. A greater sinner than he could not be, and yet see how gracious and merciful the Lord was to him.

Obj. But this was but the example of one man, it is not like the Lord will deal thus with me or any other,

Ans. Look but to that nation which was co-partner with him, the people of the Jews; see how they combined with him in the same sin: Jer. ii. 2 (for Jeremiah lived in those days, and he made his prophecy to this people), ' Go and cry in the streets, I remember the espousals, and the kindness of thy youth,' &c. There he shews how they sinned against their education, when they were brought up in the wilderness under the hands of Moses and Aaron, for then Israel was holiness unto the Lord: verse 21, ' Yet I had planted thee a noble vine, holy and righteous seed; how then art thou turned a degenerate plant of a strange vine unto me?' They sinned also against deliverances, against promises of amendment: verse 20, ' Of old time I have broken thy yoke, and burst thy bonds, and thou saidst, I will not transgress,' &c. They sinned also against much mercy: verse 5, ' What iniquity have your fathers found in me? Have I been a barren wilderness unto you?' The Lord was not a wilderness, but a paradise, abounding in infinite mercies towards them. They sinned also against many prayers: Jer. iii. 4, ' Didst thou not cry unto me, Thou art my father, and the guide of my youth?' God doth, as it were, by way of mockery, lay open their hypocrisy, and reproacheth them, that when they had sinned, then they cried out, ' Thou art my God, and the guide of my youth.' They sinned also against example; yet now, what doth God say unto them? Jer. iii. 6, 7, 8, ' Behold what Israel hath done! She is gone up to every high mountain, and hath played the harlot. And I said, after all this, Turn you to me: but yet she turned not,' &c. Yet see what the Lord saith, verse 12, ' Go and proclaim those words in the north, Return, O backsliding Israel, saith the Lord, and I will not cause my anger to fall on you.' And whereas they had a proverb amongst them, ' If a man put away his wife, and she go from him, and becomes another man's wife, shall he return unto her?' No; yet says God, ' Though thou hast played the harlot with many lovers, return unto me;' only acknowledge thy fault, that thou hast transgressed against me, and I will graciously receive thee. Jer. iii. 1, 19, the Lord makes an objection (in that verse 19), saying, ' How shall I put thee amongst the children, and give thee a pleasant land, a goodly host of the heritage of nations?' They were such a polluted people, that he could not tell how to take them to himself; yet if they would but come and say, ' Thou art my father,' and submit themselves, the Lord would receive them. Thus, we see, the Lord was not merciful to one man only, but to a whole nation. See this instance farther: Ezek. xx. 7, ' Cast ye away every one your evil works, but they rebelled against me.' But saith God, verse 9, ' I wrought for my name's sake,' &c. After he had brought them out of Egypt, and gave them his judgments and Sabbaths, yet there also they rebelled as much as in Egypt: verse 13, ' But the house of Israel rebelled against me in the wilderness,' &c. What doth follow? verse 14, ' Yet I wrought again for my name's sake, that it should not be polluted,' &c. And again, verse 15, ' I also lifted up my hand that I should not bring them into the land that I promised them,' &c., ' yet,' says God, verse 17, ' nevertheless, I spared them,' &c. Notwithstanding, for all this (verse 21), the children of Israel rebelled yet again, they walked not in God's statutes, but provoked his fury against them; and yet (says God, verse 22), ' I withdrew my hand, and wrought for my name's sake,' &c. But (verse 28) when they came into the land which God had given them, when they saw every green tree, and every high hill, they committed worse abominations there, they offered their sacrifices, &c. ' Yet,' saith God, verse 41, ' I will sanctify you, and accept you, when I bring you out from the people, and I will be sanctified in you before them.' Thus, also, in Neh. ix., there are brought in I know not how many *yets* of sinnings, and *yets* of mercies, one after another, as striving which should overcome. Mercy enters first, and begins, verses 8, 9, 10, and then comes in their rebellion, ver. 16, 17, and an aggravation of that their sinfulness, ver. 16; but a *yet* of mercy follows, verse 19, ' *Yet* in thy manifold mercies thou forsookest them not.' Though he had spent manifold mercies, yet he goes on, nevertheless, in acts of mercy, and though they persisted in acts of sinnings six or seven times, yet God hath the last word in mercy, verse 31. And this God hath not done to one man, but to a whole nation, therefore sin should not be a bar to hinder you from coming in to believe on Christ, and to be reconciled to God.

1st, Because God is merciful. If men were not sinners, God would not have had an opportunity to shew mercy, for mercy is a helping of those that are in misery. And if we were not enemies, there was no need of reconciliation. All the saints in heaven had not had need of reconciliation, if they had not been enemies.

2dly, He delights in mercy. If he had not delighted in it, would he have bruised his only Son for it, and have made him an offering, Isa. liii., that so a way might be opened for a display of mercy by satisfaction made unto justice ? And if he had not had pleasure in mercy, he would not have delighted to have put his son to grief.

3dly, There is very abundant mercy in God: 1 Pet. i. 3, ' Who according to his abundant mercy,' &c. And Ephes. ii. 7, it is called ' the exceeding riches of his mercy,' not only riches, but exceeding riches, that will never be drawn dry.

4thly, He may pardon the greatest sins, because his mercy is free; and as he doth not look to any good in the creature to move him to shew mercy, so he doth not look at any sin to dissuade him, and therefore sin cannot hinder thee from reconciliation; and thus herein consists the freeness of grace. Now this is the difference between love, mercy, and grace, that a man may love one that never offended him, and mercy is towards those that are in misery, but grace doth what it doth freely, and doth not look at anything in the creature. In Ezek. xxxvi. 22, it is said, ' God wrought for his name's sake,' and therefore because God works for his own name's sake, no evil can hinder him from shewing mercy. See then how easy a thing it is for God to shew mercy. A stomachful man will say that he can do anything but pardon. But God is the father of mercies, and so he doth beget mercies. And as it is natural for the ear to hear, the eye to see, so it is natural to God to shew mercy.

5thly, God will pardon the greatest sins, because of the end he aimed at in setting up this way of grace and mercy. It was ' for the praise and glory of his grace,' Ephes. i. 6, that sin should not hinder; nay, the more sin there is, the more is his grace glorified. As it is with a physician that professeth to come merely to shew his skill, the greater the disease is the gladder he is, for he shall shew the greater skill if he cure it. When to shew mercy is the plot of grace, sinfulness and misery is the subject of that plot for it to be shewn in. What contrivances will mercy have to shew itself in this case? ' Where sin doth abound, there doth grace abound much more;' and therefore it is that God doth let his people many times run on so far in sin, because grace may abound so much the more.

To help you in this, do but lay to heart the examples of such whom God hath pardoned. ' He hath shewn mercy to me first,' saith Paul, 1 Tim. i. 16; and do you think that he did begin and end with him? No; he shewed mercy to me first, says the apostle, ' that I might be a pattern to them that should believe to eternal life.' Think of that which Christ says, Mat. xii. 31, ' All blasphemies shall be forgiven but that against the Holy Ghost.' Here you see all manner of blasphemy, which is the highest kind of sin, and that against the Son of man, and the means of grace, which is a higher degree, pardoned. Christ, who hath been at the sealing of so many pardons, saith that he hath seen all sin pardoned, except the sin against the Holy Ghost.

Obj. Well, but you will object, that your sins have been of long continuance.

Ans. I answer, The mercies of God have been from everlasting. God hath laid up thoughts of peace from the beginning; and therefore, though thy sin hath been for many years, yet it hath been but as yesterday with God; and as long as thou hast not been sinning longer than he hath been thinking of mercy, cast not off all hope of mercy. God's mercy is like a mighty river that hath run from everlasting. Do but think how long men did lie in their sins before the flood, and yet he forgave them.

Obj. But you will argue the reiteration of your sins.

Ans. I answer, That God doth reiterate his mercy, Isa. lv. 7. He ' multiplies mercies to pardon,' and heaps up mercy, &c. And we do not only read of the greatness of his mercy, but also of ' the multitude of his loving-kindnesses;' and it is said that he doth heal backslidings (and what is a backsliding but the falling into the same sin again?), and what is the reason of this? Because he loves freely; and therefore, though he fall into the same sin again, yet do but remember the sure covenant of mercy and grace that he hath made.

Obj. But you will say, I have sinned stubbornly.

Ans. I answer, God doth pardon that also, Isa. lvii. 17, 18, ' He did go on stubbornly, but yet,' saith God, ' I have seen his ways, and I will heal him; I create the fruit of the lips, peace, peace to them that are afar off.' The Lord can help though we be never so far off from him.

Use. The use of all this is, not to encourage any to sin against God, though the world be ready to practise it, and to say, Because grace abounds, therefore sin may abound much more. But it should not embolden any to sin against him, for his anger shall smoke against such an one. But if any soul is cast down in the sight of his sins, let him look upon the infinite riches of mercy and grace in God, and they will take away that bar that hinders him from reconciliation; and though his sins be never so great, yet if they be not against the Holy Ghost they may be pardoned; yea, all blasphemy else. Christ, under whose hands all pardon goes, doth say it. Therefore believe against the time of distress, take hold of the mercy of God in Christ: but cursed be that heart that doth make himself by this presumptuous. You may trust in God as much as you will, only your hearts must be conformable; and if you walk worthy of reconciliation, you cannot trust too much.

CHAPTER IV.

That men should not be discouraged from believing by the doctrine of election. —That the consideration of God's having, by his electing decree, appointed only some few, chosen by him unto salvation and eternal life, ought to be no discouragement to obstruct our endeavours to believe.

Though, by the foregoing considerations, men may be brought to acknowledge that the greatness of their sins ought to be no bar to their believing, yet many will stumble at the doctrine of particular election, as importing that God designs salvatiou only to a few. Therefore, say they, though we should come in, and seek it never so earnestly, yet we might miss of it. If indeed we could be certainly assured of obtaining it, this would give life and hope to stir for it.

But for satisfaction of this scruple, we shall not need to fetch an answer from the universality of God's love to all, or of Christ's death extended to all on condition they will; I shall, therefore, rather propound such considerations as may persuade men, notwithstanding the true doctrine of absolute election, to come in and believe, and which may convince them of their neglect, and of their just damnation if they do not; and to this end I propound these ensuing considerations.

1. Unless thou didst undoubtedly know that thou shouldst certainly miss of salvation, and unless God had declared that thou art none of the number, there is hope concerning thy being saved. There is an *it may be*, which is as much as we find many promises expressed in. Thus, as in Zeph. ii. 3, so in Joel ii. 12–14, God exhorts them to turn unto him with their whole heart, ' for he is gracious,' &c., 'and who knoweth if he will turn and repent, and leave a blessing behind him?' If it be no more, yet God expects that you should have upon this a hope which may quicken you, and stir you to cast yourselves upon his free grace, and since all is in him, to refer yourselves to his mercy, depending upon him in the use of all means. ' Let us turn,' say the poor Ninevites (who therefore will rise up in judgment against thee), ' for who can tell but the Lord may repent of the evil?' &c.; and God did repent, Jonah iii. 9, 10. They saw there might be a door of escaping, and they were, though ' prisoners, yet of hope,' Zech. ix. 12 ; and venture they would for a pardon, though they did not know certainly they should obtain it.

2. But further, suppose it more unlikely than likely, that thou shouldst speed in this suit, that considering it is a case of absolute necessity, to seek out for reconciliation and peace, there is a strong ground to move thee to seek out for it, and to spend the utmost of thy endeavours to attain it, and to think it an infinite mercy, that it is not declared to be absolutely impossible for thee. In case of absolute necessity, we see men weigh not improbabilities, but do put themselves and all their endeavours upon a venture, though the business be very uncertain. As for example, men being pressed to the wars, though it be certain that some shall die, and those in all probability who fight in the fore-front, or venture upon some desperate piece of service, yet it being necessary for them to undertake that service as commanded them upon pain of life, and there being some possibility that they may escape, and that it may fall out so, in this case they are content to hazard and venture themselves. Therefore also, why not much more in this case shouldst not thou venture, though there were more unlikelihoods that thou shouldst not obtain, than that thou shouldst?

But I will give you another example, of the two* lepers, 2 Kings vii. 3, 4. They reasoned with themselves, 'If we enter into the city, then the famine being in the city, we die there : if we sit here, we die also. Come, let us fall into the camp of the Aramites: if they save our lives, we shall live; and if they kill us, we are but dead.' Thus in a case of necessity they chose that which, though it had many improbabilities in it, yet might fall out otherwise than they feared. There was an *if it may be* made of saving their lives, and yet a most unlikely one, for they did not know but that the Aramites might be resolved to cut off all the Jews, and spare not a man alive ; and if they meant to spare any Jews, yet of all others, they might well think they would cut off them, because being lepers, they were unfit for service or employment, and might infect the camp. And now then, suppose that this were thy case, that of all others, thou wert most likely not to obtain mercy, that, being a persecutor, a contemner of grace, &c., shouldst in all probability be cut off, yet there being some possibility, in a case of such necessity, come in and venture thyself. And the necessity is greater in thy case ; for as to these lepers, there might have been supposed some miraculous way of preserving them, but for thee, there is no other way than of faith : God hath no other. And then the death which the lepers should die, both in one way and the other, would be alike ; but if thou seekest not, thou wilt die a worse death.

3. But in this case of reconciliation, there is, supposing the doctrine of particular election, both a certainty that God intends it for many, and it is of equal and indifferent likelihood in view, that it is intended for thee as for any other, which, besides that great necessity to enforce thee, may add much encouragement and hopes to thee. For thou heardest before that none of thy sins are any bar at all (and if anything, they must hinder), no sin but that against the Holy Ghost. Though there be many signs of election, yet none of absolute reprobation. But on the contrary, no former dealings of God with thee, nor no dealings of thine with him, though never so base and injurious, no circumstance of any sin, either that it hath been so often and so long lain in, and committed after such mercies, conviction, deliberation, can exclude thee from hopes of mercy; nay, none of these do argue thee further off from mercy, than another that is in the estate of nature with thee. There is nothing can be said concerning thee, but it might have been said of some who have reconciliation with God for their portion. As no temptation hath befallen you but what is common to man, says Paul, 1 Cor. x. 13, so nothing can be objected against thee, but hath been and is common to those who have obtained mercy. No leprosy makes thee unfitter or unlikelier to be saved than another. So that lay but these two together,—first, that some in all ages shall find mercy, and that thou art as fairly capable of it and as nigh as another, since there is no qualification in the statute to exclude thee, no exception against thy country, sex, age, parts, &c., for God did look to none of all these when he chose men : Acts x. 34, 'He is no respecter of persons,'—so as thou mayest say, as they did, Acts xv. 11, 'I believe that through the grace of Christ I may be saved as well as they ;' for grace is free, and requires nothing in the person, not in one way nor another, to whom it intendeth favour ; and therefore, I seeing nothing against my hope of having salvation, as well as nothing why I should deserve it, I am as near it as another, and therefore will stand for it. In 1 Kings xx. 31, when they heard the kings of Israel were merciful kings, and that they had spared others in the like case that they and Benhadad were in, and when they saw nothing in their condition which had not been pardoned in others, they upon this say, 'Let us put

* ' Four.'—ED.

ropes about our neck : peradventure the king of Israel may save thy life.' It was but a *peradventure*, and a greater one than can be supposed in thy case, for they had heard only in the general of the kings of Israel ; but whether this king Ahab were of such a disposition, they knew not, and yet they ventured upon it to seek to him ; but thou hearest that this great God is a God gracious, merciful, &c., and that he hath pardoned thousands in the like condition.

4. Thou art not only thus equally capable of it as well as another, but there is a probability and a likelihood that God doth intend thee, because thou hast heard that he is a merciful God, and willing to be reconciled by his own appointment. The news of it is directed to thee by himself, and he hath bidden thee to stand for it, and to come in for it ; for the word of reconciliation which we preach is made known but to a few, and those too to whom it comes, it comes as an act of mercy ; and by God's direction, it comes rather to one place than another, rather to one man than another ; as, why was Paul forbidden to go into Bithynia, Acts xvi. 7, and called to go into Macedonia, and bidden, Acts xviii. 10, to stay at Corinth and preach ? but because, as God says there, 'I have much people in this city.' When the plague comes to a place wherein any man lives, whenas other places are free, he fears lest God might intend to take him away by it rather than the others in other places, and still looks on himself if he hath no token on him ; so when the gospel comes to the place wherein thou livest, and thou hast not the sound of it confusedly, but the knowledge distinctly of it to thy ears, thou hast cause to think it exceedingly probable that God doth intend thee for salvation, and that the kingdom of God is come nigh thee. It is a great probability of election that the gospel is come to thee, 1 Thes. i. 5, and it is a sign that God means to save thee, and hath chosen those to whom he makes known this mystery of his will of reconciling and gathering souls to himself, Eph. i. 9. Those servants of Benhadad had no intimation of mercy from Ahab himself, or by his direction, but thou hast from God ; for the mystery hid from all ages, and now from most of the world, is revealed unto thee, and he hath directed the gospel to thee in an especial providence, and since he hath not proclaimed this pardon to all persons, but to a few ; therefore thou being among them to whom this proclamation of mercy is sent, hast cause to put in for it, and much encouragement also to do so.

5. Especially this gospel offering great salvation, as an addition to this peace and reconciliation made with God, ought to excite and encourage thee to seek it. The lepers thought only to save their lives, and so did Benhadad, for he was perhaps out of hope of having his kingdom again ; but thou hast not only hope of saving thy life, but of having eternal life ; and this, added to the capableness of thy attaining it, and the probability annexed to it, should exceedingly quicken thee to seek out for it. For in case of preferment, when a great office is void, a living or a fellowship in a college, which will certainly be bestowed on some, as soon as a man shall hear of such a thing, and have a hint of it from the party that bestows it, and be told from him that he is as fair for it as any other, that he is as capable, that there is no clause in the statute to exclude him and shut him out, and that he hath as good means to make for it as any other, how would he be quickened to use his utmost endeavours, to lay out his money, and to put in for it, when yet he knows that there are many suitors, and that the place can be bestowed but upon one ? Now this is the case in hand ; the gospel offereth great salvation, so great, as the apostle can no otherwise express it, Heb. ii. 3, but in this phrase, ' How shall we escape if we neglect *so great*

salvation?' And this thou art as fair for, and canst make as good means for it, if thou comest to Jesus Christ, as another. This the apostle intimates, 1 Cor. ix. 14, speaking of his endeavour to be partaker of the gospel and the salvation in it: ' Know ye not,' saith he, ' that they which run in a race run all, though but one receives the prize?' Yes; all will venture, and therefore why not thou? Will not this practice of men in case of a ' corruptible crown,' as he calls it, though there be an uncertain tie* in it, condemn the neglect of seeking an incorruptible crown (as ver. 25), and stop men's mouths from pleading that few can attain, and some may miss it?

6. Consider God's manner of revealing and making known this reconciliation to be had (suppose but by a few), yet it is indifferently to be propounded unto all, as importing that all should be stirred up at the hearsay of it, with the hope of it, to endeavour after it. Christ bade them say to every house to which they came, Luke x. 5, ' Peace be to this house;' and God expects that every one to whom this news comes should look out for peace as a thing belonging to him, Luke xix. 42. Yea, he commands all to whom it comes to stand for it, and to use all means to attain it, 1 John iii. 23, Acts xvii. 30, and he will condemn men if they neglect to do so, Heb. ii. 3, and not only doth so, but beseecheth you to be reconciled, to come in and seek it at his hands; and if one that had a great preferment in his gift should do so, would it not mightily encourage you with hopes to attain it, if he should send to thee to stand for it?

7. With this news which thou hast heard of willingness in God to be reconciled, &c., thou either art affected and moved to come in or not affected; for one of these two things must fall out. If thou beest not affected at all to listen after it, thou hast no cause to complain that thou shalt not obtain it; for can any complain he cannot obtain that which he hath no heart to nor mind to obtain? But if thou beest affected with it, and hast a heart desirous to obtain it, if thou art set a-work to seek out for it, if God hath enamoured thee with his Son, and given thee an high esteem of reconciliation with him, and given thee a heart to seek after it, this may give thee a rational presumption of success, for there is more than a probability that it is intended for thee, and that thou art a son of peace: Luke x. 6, for if it be hid, ' it is hid to them who are lost: in whom the God of this world hath blinded the minds of them which believe not,' 2 Cor. iv. 4.

Professors who have a work of the Spirit upon them have usually spent their chiefest thoughts in poring upon that work, to discern the truth of it from a temporary work, and so by way of signs to apply conditional promises unto themselves, thereby both diverting from faith in Christ and from looking up to him (and so dishonouring him), and also putting too much upon their own graces. Now I would have them rather to make this use of all such workings, that though they doubt of the truth of them, yet they should however look on them as encouragements in a way of believing, to facilitate the work of faith the more, that though no such works can be made a ground of faith, yet they may help to remove stumbling-blocks which lie in the way of it, even in as full a manner as encouragements from the promises of the covenant, as made to believers and their seed, may help the children of believers more than others when they come to believe. For there are but a few in the world whose hearts God enlighteneth and affecteth with the powers of the world to come; and half of them whom he doth so stir are usually such as are elected and savingly wrought upon; thus there were as many wise virgins as foolish among professors. Now, therefore, though thou canst not tell what to make of thy work in itself,

---

* Qu. ' uncertainty'?—ED.

nor art able to say whether it be grace or no, and so canst not fetch assurance from it, yet thou mayest from it be encouraged to hope that possibly thou belongest to the election of grace, and so it may help thee to go to Christ with more probability of success.   For now thou art not within an hundred to one of salvation, but at least within two to one; so that it is but half odds that thou art one to whom God may shew mercy.   And thus encouraged (using it no farther), thou mayest go to Christ lightened of many fears at which others stick, thou having so fair a lot for heaven. But because such are in this respect in the like probability of salvation, as the children of believing parents, I refer them unto that consideration, that what encouragement their being under their parents' covenant may give them, the same may these strong workings and stirrings of the Spirit of God give these.

8. If thou wilt seek salvation, and dost continue to seek it, there is a certainty that thou shalt obtain it; and it is a false slander to say, that there being few elected, therefore my salvation may prove uncertain though I seek it.   Now, that there is a certainty promised to seeking, is plain from what Paul says, 1 Cor. ix. 26, 'I therefore so run, not as uncertainly;' that is, I so run that I shall be sure to speed.   He had said in ver. 24, as I shewed before, that in the Olympian games many run, but yet but one receives and wins the crown, and yet many will run, though it be so uncertain; but, says he, in endeavouring after salvation in the gospel, of which he there speaks, if you will but endeavour to run as you ought, with your utmost might, you shall be sure to obtain; as many as will take pains to do it, and use all means, as he speaks there, shall be successful.   Some indeed fall short through lazy running; but, says he, 'so run, that you may obtain;' that is, there is a running and a seeking which will certainly obtain; 'I therefore,' says he, 'so run,' and so running, shall obtain, not as uncertainly, but so as I shall be sure to enjoy the prize.   And so Christ also hath said, 'Seek, and you shall find; knock, and it shall be opened to you.   And he backs this by a strange convincing demonstration to assure them of it: Luke xi. 4, 5, if one comes to a friend at midnight, and desires some necessary thing of him, though he be one who hath no list to rise, ver. 7, nor regardeth the relation of friendship at all in it, ver. 8, but saith he hath all his children already in bed with him, ver. 7, yet for his importunity's sake he would rise in the night: 'Now then, I say unto you,' says Christ, 'knock, and it shall be opened.'   Though the door seem shut against thee, though thou shouldst think God intended not friendship to thee, and had, as it were, all his friends about him already, yet he will open to and let thee in, ver. 10.   He confirms it by experience, that there was never yet any turned away, but every one that asketh receiveth, and that seeketh findeth; and there was never any yet that did so that was sent away empty.

CHAPTER V.

Some general considerations premised to open a way for the following directions to guide us in our endeavours to believe.

Having thus removed the discouragements of faith, I now come to some directions to guide us in our endeavouring to believe.

I shall first in general explain to you what I intend, by way of premise, that so my scope and meaning may be apprehended.   My scope is not to give directions about all ways, and means, and helps, outward and inward, to attain faith, such as you would give to mere carnal men; that is, to men that do lie still in the profaneness of their hearts, and in the looseness of their estates, insensible of anything; I will not, I say, go about to shew what such men should do, and what endeavours they are to use; no, I speak to such as are under discouragement, and lie under the sense of their own inability to believe, for it is that objection which occasioneth what I shall speak. I do not mean neither to shew you what preparative works there are to faith, or to insist upon them; but I speak to a soul that is brought to the brink of believing, that is convinced of its poor ruined state, which indeed is the first part of faith, for so self-emptiness is; one that lies at the pool, as the cripple at Bethesda, that is, made sensible of his own disability, and lies under that discouragement. I am only, I say, now to deal with such an one; and therefore all that I shall speak shall be pertinent as to the condition of such a soul, and I shall not meddle with anything else.

Now, the question is this, what such a soul is to do? Whether, as some have said, to lie still, and only to wait (as they in Acts i. 8) for the power of the Holy Ghost to come upon them? Whether he is not to stir till such time as God comes, and to his feeling and sense overpowers his heart to believe? Whether, I say, till God comes with such a power as is infinitely beyond his own, and enables him to believe, and draws his heart unto it, he is not at all to attempt it till then, not only because it is in vain, but because otherwise it will be an attempt in his own strength? or whether, yea, or no, the soul ought not, as the text here hath it, to labour for to enter, and to set his feet into that rest by believing?

I have two things to say to this. First, some generals are to be premised. Secondly, some directions are more particularly to be delivered. The generals which I premise shall be these four:

1. That God in working faith in the hearts of his elect, although he always shews an almighty power, the same that wrought in Jesus Christ when he was raised from death to life, yet notwithstanding he doth not always so affect the spirits of those in whom he works faith, as to make it appear to their sense, that it is a power of that almighty proportion. I say, God doth not always, in the sense of the party himself, come with a predominant overpowering power when he draws the soul to believe. He doth not always come as he did upon the prophets, with a strong hand, in a man's own sense, but he oftentimes sweetly insinuateth himself, and gently slideth into a man's heart, and mingleth himself and his Spirit, and power with their spirits, in a way of a compliance to the pace (if I may so express it) even of the natural motions in their hearts, and in a sweet and still way, yet omnipotently carries them on so to act. God is exceeding free in the working of faith and grace in the spirits of men, and he doth deal variously. In Job xxxiii. 29, having described a work upon one that lies on his sick bed, how he is troubled for his sins, and then sends for a messenger, one among a thousand, to shew unto him his uprightness, &c.: 'These things,' saith he, 'worketh God oftentimes' (mark that word *oftentimes*, not *always*) 'with man.' God is found of some that sought him not, and others he puts them upon seeking long before they find him. The power of the Holy Ghost comes upon a man as wind, but it doth not come always as a rushing mighty wind, in that predominant overpowering sense, as that he shall feel it to be a wind externally that doth thus and thus move him, as it came upon the apostles, Acts ii.; but oftentimes comes like a still wind, in a still small voice, as you know it did unto Elijah, 1 Kings xix. 12. When the Spirit of God came upon the prophets, sometimes he carried them by a

' strong hand,' as the word is ; but how doth he deal with Ephraim and the ten tribes, Hosea xi. 3 ?—and his dealing with them that were his people then, is a type of his dealing with his people under the gospel —he dealt with Ephraim as a nurse dealeth with her child when she teacheth him to go. ' When Ephraim was a child,' saith he, ' I loved him, I taught him also to go, taking him by the arms.' This comparison of a nurse teaching of a child to go, and so joining her strength with the strength of the child, would be a full comparison, if that the nurse did put the inward strength into the child, as God doth ; but yet allowing that disparity, it holds forth thus much however, and serves thus far to illustrate the thing in hand, viz., that God in working upon a man doth apply himself as it were to his natural pace, and yet works strongly. He doth not say that God dealt with Ephraim as Christ did with the lame man, make him go and leap and dance as it were presently ; no, he doth not let him feel always such an omnipotent power coming upon him as shall enable him so to do ; but he deals with him as a nurse deals with her child when she teacheth him to go. Now a nurse, you know, doth not take and hurry the child, doth not come with a power that shall be sensible to it beyond and above its own, and remove it from one place to another, as she is easily able to do ; but first she sets the child gently down, and then lets it try if it can feel his legs, as you use to say, and then if it can stand upon the ground, and then lets it try to set one foot before another. Just thus as the nurse deals with a child, and applies herself to its weak state and condition in teaching it to go, so doth God unto his children in teaching them to enter into this rest, and to believe, and in guiding all their steps therein. He first letteth a man see he cannot stand, letteth him see there is not a power in himself, then sets his heart upon Christ, and lets him try if he can stay and rest upon him, when yet he cannot walk in Christ, as he thinketh ; and then he taketh him by the arms, when yet it may be he cannot set one foot before another, and so gives him now a little strength, and then a little strength, insinuating and sliding in his power, his supporting and assisting power, according to the pace of the motions of a man's heart : and although in the working of faith he gives all power, and faith is not of ourselves, but is the gift of God ; yet he doth not always come with such an almighty and over-ruling power, when a man is sensible of his own emptiness, as to the man's sense shall hold proportion with the power that raised Christ from the dead. That same drawing that is spoken of, John vi. 44, ' No man cometh unto me except the Father draw him,' you may interpret by Hosea xi. 4, ' I drew them with cords of a man,' that is, I did not overhaul them ; but as one man would per-suade another, so I insinuated my love and my power to them, *humano more*, though there was an almighty power went with it. And it is inter-preted also by what follows in John vi. 44, ' They shall be all taught of God.' He by his almighty power puts an instinct into the heart (for that is his teaching) after Christ and after free grace, and causeth the man to renounce himself, and so sets the heart earnestly intent upon these things. The heart would have Christ, and, says he, why may not I have Christ ? and what is between me and Christ ? A thousand such thoughts God casteth in, and yet it is but like an instinct, though God himself be at the bottom of it. As we are said to be taught of God to love one another, it is not by a sudden shedding, in an instant, into the heart, abundance of love unto the saints ; but it is, as I may so express it, by a still and secret touch of the heart, whereby it is drawn on to love them, such as when the iron is touched with the loadstone. And observe, whom doth Christ speak this of when he saith, John vi. 44, ' No man can come unto me except the Father draw him ' ? It appears evidently by what follows at verse 64 of that chapter, that he speaks of his disciples : ' There are some of you,' saith he, ' which believe not. Therefore said I unto you, that no man can come unto me, except it were given unto him of my Father.' Now had all these apostles when faith was wrought in them, think you, seeing themselves first unable to believe, had they the sense of an omnipotent power, that with a strong hand carried on their souls to believe in a sensible and discernible way ? Clearly no ; for see what is said, John xiv. 6–8, of these very men of whom Christ saith, they had not come unto him unless the Father had drawn them, and unless the Father had taught them. See what is there said of these very men, I say, whom God hath shewn so much power in drawing them unto Christ : ' Whither I go you know,' saith Christ, ' and the way you know.' Thomas saith unto him, ' Lord, we know not whither thou goest, and how can we know the way ?' Either Christ here must speak what is false, or Thomas must speak what is false, one would think in appearance. The truth is, Thomas he did know, and he did not know ; and whereas, John vi. 45, he saith, ' They shall be all taught of God' to know him, here, John xiv. 7, he saith, ' If you had known me, you had known my Father also : and from henceforth ye know him, and have seen him. Philip saith unto him, Lord, shew us the Father, and it sufficeth us. Jesus saith unto him, Have I been so long time with you, and yet hast thou not known me, Philip ? he that hath seen me, hath seen the Father.' Yet Philip was drawn unto God, and drawn unto Christ, and was drawn too by being taught of God, and taught of Christ. There is no way then to solve it but this, that God, when he works faith, doth not always come with such a power upon the soul, that he shall be sensible that there is such an omnipotent power upon him working faith in him. No ; oftentimes though a man doth the thing, and truly believeth, and doth it by the power of God working on him, yet he scarce can discern it from his own power, and from his own thoughts. This truth is evident—and whoever he be that denies it, his own experience shall confute him before he die—by the light that God puts into the soul concerning the manifestation of himself unto us. There is a constant light that a Christian carries about him, that he walks by, such as is in the day, whether the sun shine or not shine, which yet notwithstanding keeps to the pace of a man's own understanding ; and there is a light which sometimes comes in upon a man, and is like the sun breaking through a cloud, that a man can look up and see the sun, and can confidently say, now I do see the sun ; and yet both these lights are supernatural, and both from the almighty power of God ; and he that hath that ordinary light of faith, which keeps pace with his own understanding, he believes, and he believes truly and strongly too ; and when those extra-ordinary lights cease, the ordinary one remains, and carries on the soul to Jesus Christ, and to faith in him. Job all his life had enjoyed an ordinary light of faith. ' I have heard of thee,' saith he, Job xlii. 5, ' by the hear-ing of the ear, but now mine eyes have seen thee.' There came another light in then. So I take it, Paul, when he was under that great temptation, 2 Cor. xii., he prayed, and he would fain have had his request, fain have had his corruption subdued, fain have had such a power manifested in his weakness as he might have seen Satan trampled under his feet presently. No, saith God ; ' my grace is sufficient for thee.' God insinuated himself strongly to support him, though Paul felt not such a sensible power as might presently overcome the temptation. The truth is, it is in the matter of working faith in the heart, as it is in the temptations of Satan. There are temptations of Satan which a man cannot discern from his own thoughts; and yet the devil is strong in such temptations. And again, there are temptations in which a man apparently feels the devil, and can distinguish them from his own thoughts, as in all those hellish blasphemies that are injected and cast into the soul. So it is in the workings of God, he doth sometimes insinuate himself into the soul so stilly and secretly, that a man cannot discern those insinuations from his own thoughts, but takes them indeed to be his own, and yet there is the mighty power of God that acts the spirit all that while. And then again, there are mighty workings of God that come with a noise, with a stupendousness. I shall only add one confirmation of it from Eph. i. 19, where the apostle prayeth that their 'eyes may be opened to see the power of God that wrought in them that believe,' and in their own hearts.

2. The second general premise that I shall add is this, that God in carrying on the heart to believe, gives power to one act and not to another, and he hath appointed that one act to be a step and a degree unto another. In 2 Thes. i. 11, the apostle prays that God would 'fulfil all the good pleasure of his goodness, and the work of faith with power.' The word *fulfil* signifies to perfect and accomplish a thing by degrees, to be doing of it I know not how long, as a man is about perfecting some masterpiece of work, or as a painter is perfecting of a picture, which he is fain to go over again and again before he hath fulfilled that idea he hath in his head. So is the very work of faith in the heart, which is what God hath in the idea of his own good pleasure and will, and he is a long while in perfecting it. You read in 1 Thes. iii. 10, that there was something 'lacking in their faith,' and a great deal lacking too; and here he prays that God would 'fulfil that work of faith;' and you see he saith it is the work of faith with power; that he would fulfil one part after another, and so as to make one a step unto another. 'After you believed, you were sealed,' says he, Eph. i. 13. 'After they had suffered a while, they were established,' 1 Pet. v. 10. Hence now—

3. (Which comes to the point in hand) A soul that is sensible of his own inability to do anything of itself, and is cast down in the apprehension thereof, may and ought to act in and towards believing, so far as it finds its spirit strengthened by God, not examining or staying till it knows certainly that this is such a power and such a strength as is so from God, as will now, at this instant, enable it truly and throughly to believe. Why? Because, as I said before, God doth not always carry on the work of faith by such an overpowering light, especially at first, but applies himself to the pace of a man's understanding and will; yet notwithstanding, because God doth give power to one act and not to another, still so far as a man finds his spirit strengthened by God, so far let him join with God, and all in a subordination to the power of God to work further, for still there is somewhat lacking to your faith; and in such a way as this, you will still find that God will come in and shew you greater things than these. In 2 Cor. xii., Paul would have had a power instantly to overcome that temptation. No, saith God; 'my grace shall be sufficient for thee;' *i. e.*, that power that I proportion out to thee shall be sufficient to uphold thee. Improve that, and join with that which I ordinarily give thee, and it shall be sufficient to carry thee through, though thou dost not attain what thou prayest for; for the truth is, Paul prayed for more, and all the answer from God was, 'My grace is sufficient for thee.' In James iv. 8 saith he, 'Draw nigh unto God, and he will draw nigh unto you.' Do but mark what that place holds out: when he saith, 'and he will draw nigh unto you,' he doth evidently mean a sensible drawing nigh of God to a man's spirit, that the

soul shall be able to say, This is God, and I feel my heart filled with his presence. Now in order to this, he bids us draw nigh first unto God. If now we should exhort a man that is cast down thus in the sense of his own inability, and should say unto him, 'Draw nigh unto God, and he will draw nigh unto you,' what would he say ? He would say, God must draw nigh unto me first, before I can draw nigh unto him, for I have no ability to do it ; why then do you say, Draw nigh unto God ? he must first draw nigh unto me, even as he must love me first, before I can love him. Of necessity, therefore, the apostle must suppose an insensible drawing nigh of God unto a man's spirit, to enable him to draw nigh unto God, that so God may draw nigh unto him sensibly, and apparently, and evidently. So far forth, therefore, as thou findest, by an insensible power in thee, that thy heart is strengthened to draw nigh unto God, do thou draw nigh unto him, still maintaining a sense of thy own inability to do anything of thyself ; and if thou wilt draw nigh unto him while he doth thus insensibly draw nigh unto thee, he will draw nigh unto thee manifestatively, so as thou shalt be sensible of his presence. I quote that place for this, that God doth give us strength to do one thing which is in order to some farther thing ; he doth give an insensible strength to draw nigh to him, so that the heart finds itself enabled to go into the presence of God, and cast down itself before him. In this case, saith the apostle, go and draw nigh unto him, join with this strength you find, and you shall find a farther strength, for the promise is there of an apparent drawing nigh, which the other was not. The like is certainly the meaning of Luke xi. 13, where Christ saith, ' He will give the Spirit unto them that ask him.' Will not a man be apt to say now, How shall I ask the Spirit if I have not the Spirit ? Therefore without all question this is his meaning, that when a man doth find that he doth want the Spirit, as he thinketh, yet, saith he, so far forth as thou findest thy heart strengthened to ask (which is yet the Spirit's working), go and ask. Here is the Spirit working insensibly to ask, as in order to obtaining the Spirit in a sensible way. The like is certainly the meaning of all those places, ' Seek, and ye shall find ; ask, and it shall be given you,' &c. So that this is the thing I drive at, let every one of you in the way of believing and acting of faith (seeing God goes thus stilly and yet strongly, seeing likewise that God doth do one thing that is in order to another, step after step perfects the work of faith with power), so far forth still as you find that your hearts are strengthened to do anything that is spiritually good, though it may be you cannot discern that it is spiritually good in the doing, yet strive to do it. Though James himself had said, ' Every perfect gift is from above,' and that no man can have wisdom (if he will have a perfect gift of it) but he must have it from the Father of lights ; yet, saith he, ' If any man lack wisdom, let him ask it of God,' James i. Let every man say that he will go so far as he finds strength to carry him, for God perfecteth the work of faith with power. When that poor man came to Christ, Mark ix., and asked him if he could do anything ? saith Christ, ver. 23, Yes, ' if thou canst believe.' Do but observe that phrase, ' if thou canst believe ;' it implies, indeed, that he could not do it without a strength and assistance, therefore the poor man afterwards saith, ' Help thou mine unbelief ;' yet Christ puts him upon this, so far as thou findest thy heart heartened, as I may so express it, so far as thou findest thy heart any ways strengthened, that thou canst say, I can thus far believe, try, and put it forth ; and so the poor man did : ' Lord,' saith he, ' I do believe ; help thou mine unbelief.' So now, there is many a poor soul that is not able to say, I have a heart to take Jesus Christ ; no, on the contrary, I have not the boldness to do it ; yea, when

I go about to do it, my thoughts fail me, and my heart misgiveth me in doing of it ; I have no strength at all to lay hold upon Jesus Christ. But canst thou go unto him ? Yes ; I find that, the soul will say, I have that strength put into me, that though indeed I cannot lay hold of his person, yet I can go unto him, and I can lay myself down at his feet. Still say I, so far forth as thou findest thy heart strengthened, so far forth still join with that strength, and act under God's activity upon thee. Say within thyself, Though I cannot go to him to lay hold upon his person, yet I can go to him to have power to lay hold upon him ; go so far with it, put forth so far as thou findest thou canst put forth. The truth is, God takes you as little children by the arms, though his power go along with you. Now if the child had but knowledge when the nurse first teacheth him to go, what would it say ? I cannot set one foot before another ; it is no matter, will she say, therefore set your feet upon the ground, and try whether you feel them or no ; and still so far forth as the child findeth strength, still so far it should act and go, being still held by the arms by the nurse. So do thou in a subordination to the power of God that is working faith in thee, and fulfilling the work of it with power. So far as thou findest thy heart heartened or strengthened to put forth acts of faith, or anything towards believing, so far still enter.

Those men that would have a soul that is sensible of his own inability lie and wait till God come with a sensible power to enable it to believe, and not to stir till then, what do these men do ? They exhort that soul to wait for a power from above, do they not ? Yes ; this is all one with what I say, for where hath the soul that sense ? Certainly from God. And where hath it that power to wait ? Certainly from God. ' No man can say Jesus is the Lord, without the Holy Ghost,' much more to be sensible of his own unbelief. Then the meaning must needs be this, that so far forth as God strengtheneth the soul to act, so far forth it should act ; or imagine it is in an ordinary way strengthened to wait, say I, if thou findest thy heart strengthened by God to go further, go further ; set one foot before another, for God doth apply his power to the pace of a man's will and understanding, and that not always in a discernible way as it is a power, but as a nurse doth to a child. Even to wait for the righteousness of faith and the power of God, is a work of the Spirit, and an almighty work too ; so saith the apostle, Gal. v. 5, ' We through the Spirit wait for the righteousness of faith.' And therefore, as the apostle saith in another case, ' So far as any man hath attained,' so far still let him join with that power ; that is, so far forth as he finds his heart strengthened (and the Holy Ghost still strengtheneth men when they act anything), so far let him still put forth. You shall find that Paul took the same course : Philip. iii. 12, 13, ' I do reach forth,' saith he, ' to those things which are before, and I press towards the mark,' &c. I do reach forward, I stretch all my sinews. The word there is a metaphor taken from a man in a race, or that is running towards the goal ; he doth not only use his feet, but he runs with his hands stretched out, that where his feet may not come, his hands, if possible, may come ; so saith he, I do reach forth, I do follow after it, as much as ever I did after persecuting the church (for the word is the same), so that still he applied himself to what he had attained, and still so far as he could, so far he reached ; and yet all this was the grace of God in him. So, I say, let the soul of every man that is thus made sensible of its own inability, act so far forth as he findeth the Spirit of God strengthening him. Do what thou hast to do with all that might thou findest thy spirit assisted withal.

4. The fourth and last general premise which I shall mention, and which indeed doth follow from all the former, is this, that such souls are not to stay from exercising acts of faith till they feel and discern that they are clothed with such a power as will and doth enable them truly to believe. They are not, I say, to stay until they discern this, that now I have such a power fall upon me, now I will believe, and this I have waited for, and I must lie waiting for it till I find this power. I yield this indeed, that you may seek and wait for the assurance of such a power that shall overpower your spirits over and above the ordinary pace of the natural motion of your own hearts to believe in Christ. Such a thing God vouchsafeth, such a thing the apostle prays for towards the Ephesians, chap. i. 19, such a thing the apostles themselves waited for (Acts i. 4), till power from on high came upon them, and the promise is made unto us for believing and sealing us as well as unto them, Acts ii. 41. We may therefore wait for such a power to persuade our hearts to believe beyond the pace, I say, of the motions of our own spirits. But yet, that which I add withal is this, that you are not to stay from attempting to believe till you feel such a power come upon you, not to stay till you can say, I feel a divine power now clothing me, which will enable my soul to believe. For,

1st, To stay from attempting to believe till you feel such a power, is perhaps ever to stay. Not only because that God oftentimes doth not give it even to those whom he doth give faith unto truly, but how dost thou know but that there is such a power now upon thee as, if thou dost join with it, thou shalt truly believe, which before thou didst not? For that must needs be seen when the thing is done, it is not seen in the cause, it is not seen in the feeling the power and the proportion of that first, but it is seen in the effect, it is seen in the acting of it, it is seen in the thing a-doing. If a mariner that is to set a ship over sea would say, I will stay till I feel such a wind blow as I shall be sure will carry me over, and last till I come thither; or a wind that should take the ship out of the port, and go and throw it on the other side, before I'll stir or hoist up sail, or give up my vessel to the wind, for this that now blows is not high enough, it is too still; this man might stay for ever, and never go over sea. But what do wise mariners do? Why when they see a gale, though it be but a still gale, yea, though it be but a side wind, if there be a necessity to go, they will hale and tow out with it; and though when they are at sea it begins to turn, yet still they wait, and make use of a side wind, and oftentimes meet with that wind that doth directly carry them over indeed.

2dly, To stay for such a power first, and wait for it, till thou mayest be able to discern that it will enable thee and overpower thee to believe before thou attemptest it, is to expect from God (ere thou puttest forth an act of faith) a greater assurance than of election. And would you stay till God persuade you that you are elected before you believe? Will you have that to be the first thing God persuades you of, and to be the bottom of your faith? In thy desiring such a power to come upon thee as to thy sense shall be such, thou desirest a harder matter, a greater thing than for God to come upon thee with his love, and to testify unto thee that thou art elected, and that he hath loved thee from everlasting, because such a power as shall be such in thy sense, is the immediate fruit of that love and of that will in him, I mean not the fruit in thee, but from himself. Nay, it is more than to stay believing till God assure thee and persuade thee that thou art elected, it is to ask a thing yet more hard. And what is the reason? Because election is a standing, permanent thing, a foundation always remaining, and is at all times, and if we could apprehend it, might be demonstrated to the soul ; but such a power as shall rise to that proportion as to thine own sense, thou shalt think I am now clothed with it, and shall be enabled to believe, that comes when God pleaseth, and is a fleeting thing, and so thou puttest thy believing upon the evidence of that which is not permanent, but is arbitrary and fleeting, and very difficult to be.

3dly, Wilt thou consider this, that though indeed it is the power of God that gives ability to believe, yet it is not the sense of the power of God in my heart that gives me my warrant to believe, therefore I am not to forbear till I feel such a power. It is, I say, indeed the power of God that gives thee ability, but it is not that which gives the warrant or the ground. It is the command of God to believe on the name of his Son, and it is the indefinite promise that Christ came into the world to save sinners, indefinitely thus expressed, and the like, that is the ground of believing. Therefore now upon the command thou art to attempt the duty, and to look up unto God for power to accompany thee in that duty, and thou art not to stay and wait first to be clothed with such a power as a warrant or ground for thy believing, as if else thou shouldst believe in vain. Yea, when thou hast pitched upon the right ground of believing, and attempted to believe, this power usually comes in and accompanies it. Thou art to do thy duty according to the command, that is the warrant, to begin and to leave it unto God to enable thee, to assist thee to do it truly, as well as perform any command else. It is true, indeed, no man doth believe in the event unless God doth draw him, yet no man doth first believe upon this ground, because he feels that God doth draw him. I acknowledge that God may apply himself to such an error in the souls of some, as I have found he hath done ; for God doth apply himself sometimes even to our errors rather than he will lose an elect child of his, which is the freedom of his grace, and so he may do in this case. One whose spirit is possessed with such an apprehension of such an objection and such a mistake, God may come upon him, and draw him to believe by a sensible mighty power ; but herein God doth in his infinite grace and mercy apply himself to this error rather than lose his child. Even as in the first age of reformation, when they taught that all faith was assurance that a man's sins were forgiven (which is as great an error as can be, it condemns the generation of many of the righteous), and yet God did apply himself unto this error in the experience of the most of that age, and came upon them accordingly.

Lastly, To end this fourth general premise. For thee to stay believing till thou feelest thyself clothed with such a power, it is indeed all one, and in a manner like to those other bars which are cried down so much, and many of them justly, and which do keep thousands from believing. Men think, I must have this, or I must have that first ere I believe, and so they are detained from believing ; and if it were not for the infinite goodness of God to them, they would be ' ever learning, and never come to the knowledge of the truth,' as the apostle saith in another case, 2 Tim. iii. 7 ; they would ever be in the way of believing, and yet never believe. One hears that there is such a course of humiliation to be run through, and as men that are to be cured must run through such a course of physic, or such things must be taken by way of preparation for such a medicine, so they are told that first this disposition must be wrought in them, and then that (many of which, the truth is, must have faith preceding them, or they cannot be wrought, as it may be easily demonstrated), and a man must go through each of those, in their several degrees, before he must attempt to close with Christ. Whereas, now go and take such a soul that hath run through all those several methods and courses, when it comes to believe in the Lord

Jesus, it is so far from being helped in his own apprehension by having had such things wrought in him, that it is possessed with the clean contrary thoughts. In souls that are most humbled, this is, as it were, the last thing in their being so humbled, that they see nothing in themselves; and this very sight of themselves, when they are sufficiently humbled, would be a hindrance of coming and closing with Christ nakedly; for whenas a man should close with Christ nakedly, and with Christ immediately, to come unto him under the sight and sense of such a thing wrought before, would be a hindrance unto faith. So, as the work of preparation is never a warrant or a ground unto any to believe, though it may really be a preparation without which a man would not believe, but it is not so apprehensively to the party; so it is here. Indeed, it is the power of God really that doth enable to believe, but it is not the power of God apprehensively, viz., that I see I am clothed with such a power, and I wait till I am clothed with such a power, and so I believe. There are a great many of such diversions from Jesus Christ. One saith, I must have Christ before I can have faith; another saith, I cannot take Christ till I find I have faith; whereas God giveth faith and Christ and all at once; and thy taking Christ is thy faith and thy believing; and upon thy attempting to believe, God gives all these at once. In thy going to him he gives thee power to come; as Christ saith, in doing of his will a man shall know him, so in falling to believe a man believeth. As in that question, whether the soul be first created, and then infused into the child, we usually answer that it is created and infused, and knit and united to the body, and all at once; so we may say here. But I say by those things before mentioned and answered, Satan diverts men from that which the apostle calls them to labour for, and that is to believe, and to enter this rest, Heb. iv. 11. And so much now for those generals which I have mentioned by way of premise.

CHAPTER VI.

Directions given to guide us in our endeavouring to believe.—That we ought to furnish our thoughts with all such considerations as are motives and encouragements of faith, and lay them up in our hearts, and meditate often upon them.—That we should attempt to exercise the very act of believing itself.—Objections answered.

What remains is to give some directions to guide us in our endeavours to believe.

Direct. 1. The first that I shall give is this, to provide and lay up in thy heart all considerations that are matter for faith and believing, that although the true act of faith be from the working of God alone, yet do thou cast in the seed (they are the materials of believing), and retain them in thy soul. As for example now, to go over some instances, it is true thou canst not see the excellency of Christ spiritually without an almighty power, which thou must wait till God be pleased to enable thee with. Suppose this, yet all those excellencies materially thou canst lay together, and thou canst furnish thy heart with the consideration of them, which are the materials that are to draw and win thy heart to Christ. So if we consider all those promises of free grace, that Christ ' came into the world to save sinners;' and ' Look to me, all ye ends of the earth, and be saved;' and ' I am thy Saviour, and there is none besides me,' &c.; and also if we consider all sorts of answers to all objections made of thy unworthiness and thy sinfulness, &c., all such things thou mayest collect together and furnish thy heart continually withal, these thou mayest study and chew upon, and revolve them in thy mind, as they of old that sacrificed, who though it is true could not bring fire from heaven to burn their sacrifice, yet they could, in dependence upon God, lay their sticks together, and fetch the bullock out from the stall, and bring it to the altar, and lay it thereon, and bind the sacrifice to the horns of the altar, and wait till fire came from heaven and set all on a flame. Suppose thou wert thus to wait till the power of God come sensibly upon thee, yet in the mean time thou mayest go thus far. The word which the apostle here useth, Heb. iv. 11, which we translate 'let us labour,' is 'let us study;' and it signifies the study of the mind. Let us study (saith he) as a man whose head ploddeth upon a thing, and gathers together many notions and materials for such a head, so let us study to believe and to enter into that rest. Saith Solomon, Prov. ii. 1, 'If thou wilt receive my words, and hide my commandments with thee' (it is Wisdom that speaks it, and by *commandments* there is not meant only the ten commandments, but it is a gospel precept, and they are the promises, the revelations of God that he means). If thou wilt do so, saith he, 'if thou seekest for wisdom as for silver, and searchest for her as for hid treasure; then shalt thou understand the fear of the Lord.' And yet, ver. 6, he saith, 'The Lord giveth wisdom; and out of his mouth cometh knowledge and understanding;' which in the language of the Old Testament is as much as to say, he giveth faith. But yet, saith he, do thou hide all the promises and all the commands within thee; do but thou search for them, and take them out of the veins where they lie in the Scriptures, and treasure them up in thine heart, and then God will come and he will mint faith for thee before thou art aware of it. Thus saith the prophet, Lam. iii. 19, 20, 'Remembering I remembered' (as it is in the original) 'my afflictions;' he chewed upon them. So likewise remembering he remembered what might comfort him, viz., all the materials of it: 'This I call to mind,' saith he, verse 22, 'therefore have I hope.' In Isaiah lxvi. 11, the promises are called 'the breasts of consolation,' which he saith they shall suck and milk out. Now, if thou findest thou canst not suck, or if thou suckest and none cometh, yet do as children do, who oftentimes lie with the breast and the teat in their mouths, so do thou; lie with such thoughts and promises as are the materials of faith in thy heart. And whilst thou endeavourest to suck, or perhaps canst not, yet lying so, thou shalt, it may be, find it flowing in upon thee before thou art aware of it; and whilst thou takest something of this into thy mouth, somewhat will go down.

I might likewise instance in all such motives as the Scripture useth to be urged unto God, to move him to be merciful and favourable to a poor soul. All such thoughts also thou mayest live in the midst of, and dwell in, and gather together a bundle of them, and lay them up in thy heart, and meditate on them continually. This is a certain rule; look what motives the Scripture holds forth as those which move God; they, whilst the heart thinks of them, move it to believe, rather than they move God to be merciful: and the intention of all the motives the Scripture useth to move God to be merciful to us by, is rather to strengthen and to beget faith in us, to move and raise up faith in our hearts, that God will be thus merciful to us, and to stir up hopeful thoughts thereof, rather than to move God himself. Multitudes of these instances might be given, as Ps. cxix. 12, when David would desire God to teach him his statutes, who only was able to do it, what saith he? 'Blessed art thou, O Lord; teach me thy

statutes.'   Here now is a motive, and a mighty one ; it is as if he had
said, Lord, thou art full of happiness, and thou art blessed in thyself, and
livest in the midst of happiness, and knowest no sorrow, knowest not what
the misery of a poor sinner is (*i.e.*, not in experience) that is ready to
perish ; thou art blessed, but I am a poor lost thing ; without thy help I
perish for ever.   Oh communicate some of that blessedness unto me, enjoy
it not alone ; let a soul ready to perish be blessed by thee.   Such things as
these move God ; why do they move him ?   Because they are the thoughts
of his own heart, which moved him to communicate himself to sinners,
moved him to choose men to eternal life.   Now look what doth and hath
moved God in his own nature and in his own will from everlasting, do
thou take such things into thy thoughts, and urge them unto God, and
they will beget faith in thee before thou art aware.   So likewise (Ps. cxliii.
9–12) saith the psalmist, ' Teach me, and quicken me,' &c.   Why ?   ' For
thy Spirit is good.'   What moveth God to save a poor sinner, and to amend
a naughty heart ?   Because his Spirit is good, and full of goodness : ' Thou
art good, and doest good,' saith he.   The psalmist likewise useth the same
motive, Ps. cxix. 68.   And Christ himself puts such motives as these into
our thoughts, and these beget faith when the soul liveth in them : ' You
fathers ' (saith he, Mat. vii. 11) ' know how to give good things to your
children, how much more shall your heavenly Father give the Spirit to
them that ask ? '   He speaks to a soul that thinks he wants the Spirit, yet
because this soul hears indefinitely that God is a father to some sinners,
and that he is an heavenly Father, who exceeds in bowels all earthly fathers,
therefore, saith Christ, ' How much more shall not he give good things,
yea give his Spirit to them that ask ? '   Now I say, whilst we take all such
motives,—and when I say motives, I mean not motives to believe, drawn
from our own good, but such motives as move God, for they are the greatest support of faith, and do rather serve to move us and stir our hearts to
believe than to move God, although they did move God once, for they were
the cause why he did from everlasting purpose good to us—whilst we take
these, I say, into our souls, and there let them lie, and think of them, and
revolve them again and again, there is a strength, a hopefulness begotten
in the soul from them, even as the stomach, by having meat put into it, is
strengthened by the food's being concocted, and digested, and assimilated
to it.

Now the reason why such souls may thus far labour and study to enter
into this rest, why they may take all such things into consideration as are
materials of believing, is clearly and plainly this : because if those that
are ministers of the word, and the preachers of it, are to present promises
and such motives to beget faith in men, if they may present them to their
judgments, and understandings, and thoughts, then those considerations
and promises, and the like, such souls ought to digest, to revolve, to think
upon, and still to say, Why is not my portion herein ?   In this Heb.
iv. 1, 2, ' The word,' saith he, namely the gospel, for so the word signifies
in the original, ' it was preached unto them, but it profited not, because it
was not mingled with faith in those that heard it.'   He compares faith
there to that digestive faculty, as the word implies, in the stomach, which
works upon the meat, and so by degrees doth assimilate the meat into the
body, and into the likeness thereof.   Now, saith he, that was the reason
the word profited them not, because they did not mind those promises, they
did not take them into their thoughts, they did not study them (as the
word here in the text also signifies), and it is answerable to what he had
said : verse 1, ' Let us therefore fear, lest a promise being left us of entering

into his rest, any of you should come short of it,' come short of it by not revolving those promises, and exercising your thoughts upon them.

Direct. 2. But then, secondly, we are to attempt the exercise of the act of believing. Let me urge that upon you also, for I shall speak to the thing itself fully and punctually. Let men exercise themselves, I say, to the act of believing, in the consideration of such promises, and of all such motives as are in Scripture held forth as moving God. And when I say they are to exercise the act of believing, my meaning is concerning going to Christ, and relying on him, and resting on him, and casting themselves upon him. They are not simply to seek to be humbled, or to abstain from sin, or to practise holy duties in expectation of mercy, though all these are to be done, but to inure the heart to familiar and constant acts of believing. This is what I direct and exhort unto, and shall give you grounds for it. Take the very words of this text: Heb. iv. 11, ' Let us labour (or study), to enter into that rest,' which I told you is believing. And why is it called entering into that rest ? Men think, when they come to believe, that they have a great long journey to go, as the people of Israel had in the wilderness, and that they must go through this and through that first, see this and see that first in themselves, and so perhaps stay in the wilderness forty years ; whereas the apostle tells us plainly, it is but going over the threshold, it is but entering into that rest. Therefore, saith he, do you attempt to do it, do you labour or study to do it, it is but a step, saith he ; you are even at the door, and what is the door ? It is the door of faith : ' We that believe have entered into rest,' saith he, ver. 3. Such souls should make this their daily task and study, and indeed all souls should do so. ' All a man's labour,' saith Solomon, Eccles. vi. 7, ' it is for his mouth.' You heard before that faith was compared to the digestive faculty in the stomach, it being that which works upon the promises as the stomach doth upon the meat. ' All a man's labour,' saith he, ' it is for his mouth.' Indeed, of the most men it is the great labour that they may eat, and by eating live. Now all a man's labour it should be for this mouth of faith, and to furnish it that he may live, and live by faith ; and as Christ compares it to the eating of his flesh, and the drinking of his blood, therefore above all else labour for this, and for all other in order unto this. And that I may put such souls upon this in an immediate manner, do but consider all these scriptures which I shall now give : First, that Christ says (John vi. 27–29), ' Labour not (or work not) for the meat that perisheth, but for that meat that endureth to everlasting life, which the Son of God shall give you : for him hath God the Father sealed. Then say they unto him, What shall we do that we may work the works of God ? Jesus answered and said unto them, This is the work of God, that ye believe on him whom he hath sent.' I told you even now, that all the labour of man it was for his mouth ; now here Christ makes use of that similitude, and though I cannot say he alludeth to it, yet he speaks in that allusion, and it is a place that may have an allusion thereto. ' Labour not,' saith he, or work not, ' for the meat which perisheth,' for outward meat, which is obtained by outward labour, but labour for that bread which the Son of God shall give you, that is, himself ; for a man goes to Christ for Christ, and Christ doth give himself to a sinner coming to believe on him : ver. 35, ' I am that bread of life,' namely, which the Son of God giveth. Now as he alone is that bread, so it is believing alone that doth make us partakers of that bread (as that 35th verse sheweth), ' I am that bread of life : he that cometh unto me shall never hunger ; and he that believeth on me shall never thirst.' Mark now the coherence of these words one with another to that which now I aim at : Before our Saviour Christ had said, ' Labour or work not for the meat which perisheth, but for that which endureth to everlasting life.' These Jews they plainly, and nakedly, and simply, and honestly ask Christ, without cavilling, what peculiar thing they should do ? (and in that case Jesus Christ always answers plainly) : ' What shall we do,' say they, ' that we may work the works of God ?' by works of God they mean works acceptable to God. You would have us labour, what works will you put us upon ? They thought now that there was not one special work only, but many works, therefore they express it in the plural ; and yet they thought there might be some other thing he would teach them than what Moses's law did. Christ, you see, both answers at once their question, and explains what he meant by labouring for that meat which endures for ever, and the thing he puts them upon is this, to ' believe on him whom God hath sent;' and this, saith he, is ' the work of God.' It is as if he had said, You speak of *works*, I put you upon this as *the work*. It is called ' the work of God,' as a broken heart, Ps. li., is called ' the sacrifice of God ;' that is, that which is acceptable unto God, which God delighteth in eminently. And as he puts them upon believing alone eminently, so he puts them upon it immediately. These Jews whose hearts, according to their question, and Christ's speech before, were so taken off from the consideration of earthly bread, come unto Christ thus with a naked, simple, plain question, to be instructed by him, as they in the Acts did when they asked the apostles ' what they should do to be saved ? ' You see how Christ answers them, he puts them upon believing, and thereby explains what he meant by labouring or working for that meat, in his own exhortation in the words before. And as he did here, so upon all occasions else he did likewise : saith he to the poor man (Mark ix. 23), ' If thou canst believe,' &c. Come try, let me see, saith he, whether thou canst. The poor man had said unto Christ, ' If thou canst do anything;' and Christ saith unto him, Do not doubt of power in me, for there is power enough in me, but canst thou believe ? Come let me see. He puts him, you see, upon believing. And so likewise, in another place, says Christ, ' Strive to enter in at the strait gate.' The words in the text here do clearly interpret his meaning to be to put them upon believing. You know, it is called ' the door of faith ' in the Acts, which Christ calleth 'the strait gate,' and bids them ' strive to enter in.' ' Labour,' saith the apostle, ' to enter into that rest;' and ' we that believe have entered into it,' saith he, Heb. iv. 3. As Christ did thus, so did the apostles also ; they did still put men upon believing as well as upon repenting. When the jailor in the Acts did, in a plain and blunt manner, ask them what he should do to be saved ? ' Believe in the Lord Jesus,' say they, 'and thou shalt be saved, and thy household.' Was the jailor, think you, to wait and expect till he received a power to enable him to believe ? No ; but so far as he found his heart strengthened, so far he was to attempt it. And, as this was the command, so they always held it forth clearly and nakedly to them. And to clear it more to you that souls are thus to make experiment of believing continually, consider but this farther. What course will you take ? Will you seek to God by prayer, as you are to do, and by the performance of all other duties ? Or will any man direct you to prayer because it is your duty, and because the Spirit of God may fall upon you in prayer, as oftentimes he doth upon men ? The same say I also, and there is just the same reason ; do thou fall upon believing, and though thou beginnest and attemptest to do it with a quivering heart, and layest hold upon Christ with a trembling hand, yet the power of God may fall upon thee in the doing of it. You use to stir up yourselves to other duties, and that because they are commanded ; for I suppose now that such a soul as I speak to resolveth not to do nothing ; if you mean to be idle, there is an end of it now ; if you mean to do anything, attempt to believe ; you have no more power to do any duty than you have for believing, or, at least, it must be the almighty power of God that must help you to perform any duty spiritually as well as to believe ; therefore, so far forth as you make conscience of performing any other duty, make conscience˳of this. In Isa. lxiv. 7, these two are joined together, 'None calleth upon thy name, and stirreth up himself to take hold of thee.' Here is prayer, calling upon God, and believing, both joined together, and stirring up themselves to do it ; for what is it to take hold of the Lord ? It is the same in Isa. xxvii. 5, 'Let him take hold of my strength ;' that is, let him believe (it is taking hold of the arm of the Lord), and let him stir up himself to do it, let him reach as far as he can to take hold of it.

I shall now, in the next place, answer such objections as oppose my preceding assertions.

Obj. 1. One objection will be this : If I have not God's power to concur, I shall not have true faith, I shall not put forth a true act of believing, and therefore I were as good forbear to exercise or attempt to do it.

Ans. 1. I answer first : This holds against the use of all duties else as well as against believing ; for unless the power of God doth enable thee, thou canst not think a good thought, and according to this, thy argument, thou shouldst forbear all thoughts that are materially good, as well as the act of believing. If you are not, nor ought to be deterred from any other duty, why should you be from this ?

Ans. 2. Secondly, I answer, Do you still try and renew thoughts and acts of faith howsoever. For if, in thy attempting to believe, God doth accompany thee, and evidence to thee that he doth come in, and fall upon thee, and perhaps manifest his love unto thee, thou shalt have cause for ever to bless God. If that thou dost attempt and thou fallest short, yet notwithstanding thou wilt then see thy defect, and thou wilt be humbled in thy own sight, as thou art in the defective performance of all other duties, and so wilt be put upon going to God for power with more eagerness. But, however, do not therefore forbear.

Ans. 3. Thirdly, Suppose that thy attempt to believe be in itself for the kind of it but a natural act, that is not yet spiritual ; yet though thou sow it a natural act, as I may so express it, it may rise up a spiritual one in the very doing ; and though thou sowest it in weakness, God may make it rise in power. God oftentimes ingrafts true acts of faith upon those literal notions we have of God and of Christ. It is evident by this, that after a man believeth savingly, who had much knowledge of the gospel before (and materially his thoughts now are but the same thoughts he had before, only they formally differ), God comes now in with a new light, and grace hath altered all into spirituals. And in the exercising such thoughts of faith doth God come in, and changeth them in the very doing. When Christ intended to do that miracle of turning water into wine, he doth not first change the water into wine, but he bids them pour it out, and in the pouring of it out the water was turned into wine ; so is it here, even as the loaves multiplied in the breaking and dividing of them. God doth change thy attempts to believe, they being done in subordination to his power, into genuine true thoughts of faith, whilst thou art a-thinking ; and thou believest thyself into true believing through the power of God before thou art aware of it ; and by plunging thyself, and by exercising thy heart and thoughts, and by wallowing up and down (how shall I express it?) in that sea of blood, thou wilt feel thy conscience eased, and grow up to a steadier familiarity in believing, and that in a way thou knowest not how. You find this in other duties, that when you go to prayer deadly and coldly, you meet with life and quickness from God even in the duty. Why may it not be so here?

Ans. 4. Lastly, To such souls as stick at this objection, I answer: Would any man exhort you unto any means in order unto faith, as to pray, or to hear, or to think of your sins, and the like? Why not to believing, why not to the acts of faith together with all these, and above all these? For mark it, if you be put upon prayer, what is prayer? This is certain, if thou thinkest with thyself, I shall now make but a natural prayer, and it will not be a spiritual prayer, let me tell thee this, let the prayer thou makest be what it will be, so far forth as thou prayest in any reality, so far thou hast faith proportionally to thy prayer. Consider what I say; if it be a spiritual prayer thou makest, and God turns it to be so, then he gives thee spiritual faith; therefore thou mayest as well concurrently believe as pray, for prayer is but the venting of faith. Therefore if thou wilt say, I will forbear the act of believing because it may prove a natural act, an act of mine own, and not genuine and true, thou mayest upon the same grounds as well forbear praying, for so far forth as thou hast an ability to pray aright in faith thou hast to believe, for prayer is the acting of faith, take it in its proportion, that is, whether you consider it naturally or spiritually. Men may exhort you to means of faith, but this you will still find, that all those means are as difficult things as faith itself: and therefore the apostle (Rom. x.), you see, directs unto faith as the most easy and short cut of all the rest; you may forecast, saith he, this and that, but 'the word is nigh thee, even in thy mouth and in thy heart, that is, the word of faith which we preach,' ver. 8. The apostle speaks just thus, as if one should be brought to a table full of meat, and he that is brought should say, What is it I should do that I may eat of this meat, and be partaker of it? Certainly any one would answer, The meat is here on the table, do thou fall a-eating: so doth the apostle say, 'The word,' saith he, 'is nigh thee;' it is next door to thy mouth, and to thy heart, and thy lips, do but digest it, which is the mingling it with faith, as he speaks in Heb. iv.; do but take it in thy thoughts and apprehension, and then it is in thy heart. Thou standest now at the threshold, do but step in: 'Enter in,' saith he. But will the man say, I must have a stomach to it? Mark what I say, if eating and tasting will be the way to beget a stomach, were it not best to fall to? So it is here; 'Taste and see how good the Lord is.' If there were meat that would get a man a stomach by eating it, assuredly then a man would first fall to and eat: now this meat, which is Jesus Christ, doth do so. If coming into the sun would give eyes to a man, and cause the films to fall off, as well as give a man light to see himself with, a man that is blind would not stand complaining of his blindness, and say, I will not go abroad, for I cannot see this sun, I will rather stay here in this dark dungeon, in this prison, till the sun force itself through the walls, or come in at some cranny, and so cause the scales to fall off my eyes. No; certainly he would go abroad into the air, that so the sun might cure him of his blindness. Jesus Christ is the Sun of righteousness, and he hath 'healing in his wings,' viz., in his beams, Mal. iv. 2. It is an elegant metaphor, comparing these diffusive beams to the spreading of the eagle's wings over her young ones.

How doth the iron come to have virtue to cleave to the loadstone? It is by being brought to the loadstone; so doth the soul get power to cleave unto Christ by coming unto Christ ; and the longer the soul is kept off from exercising thoughts of faith upon Christ, it is like the iron kept from the loadstone, it grows weaker and weaker.

Obj. 2. A second objection is this : you will say, I may build myself up in a temporary faith by this course, whereas it were better for me to go and search into the falseness of that if it be false.

Ans. 1. If you take the way of the Scripture, I do not know how any man shall be fully able to answer all those temptations about a man's being a temporary believer, but only by believing; I have known many souls beaten into that way at last, and never could have peace till then.   And I find this likewise, that take the Epistle to the Hebrews,—and there is no book in the New Testament, nor no passages in the New Testament, that hint more about temporary believers than that book doth, for he speaks of men that fall away through unbelief after enlightening, and he speaks extreme suspiciously of the Jews, for certainly many of them were such,— what course doth the apostle take in this Epistle to keep them from falling away ? He doth not go about so much to discover to them that their faith was a temporary faith; no, but all the course of that Epistle to such kind of men, supposing such among them, still runs upon this, to renew faith, and to ' take heed of departing from the living God through an evil heart of unbelief;' and ' let us,' saith he, ' hold the hope of our confidence unto the end,' Heb. iii. 6, 14. I say, the whole Epistle doth not lie so much in discovering this to be genuine, and that to be false faith, as in exhorting them to believe, for God indeed often converts such into true faith whilst they exercise it. And certainly, let men go on in a way of believing, and either their sins will make them leave off believing, or their believing will make them sound. And this you will find, that there is no way to cut the knot of all these temptations ; nay, there is no way for a man, of a temporary believer to become a true believer, but by exercising faith continually, so far forth as God strengtheneth his heart. And then as he said of prayer, that it will either make a man leave sinning, or his sinning will make him leave praying, so believing will either make him leave his unsoundness, or his unsoundness will make him leave his believing. If a a man be a true believer, and be troubled with that temptation, it is the only way to end it ; and if he be a temporary believer, and in that state, it is the only way to make him sound. It is that you see which the apostle directs to.

Ans. 2. Thou mayest, for aught thou knowest, be but in a temptation that thou art, or that thou mayest prove a temporary believer. That power which hath hitherto assisted thee, may be the same power which accompanies workings unto salvation, and then thou losest time to try it out that way ; and to try it out, it is the difficultest controversy in the world that ever any soul entered upon ; and thou wilt never bring it to a conclusion or determination but by believing. That must still end that controversy ; thou mayest sooner get a new title by believing afresh, than try out thy old title ; and after that thou hast renewed acts of faith, then thou wilt see the truth of all the work formerly wrought in thee, and not before.

Ans. 3. On the other side, if thou shouldst be a temporary believer at the present, which yet thou knowest not, then consider that the way to make thee sound is to put thee upon believing and renewing thy faith. Mark what I say, it is the way to make thee sound. If indeed that faith were nothing else but a secure taking for granted that a man is in the state of salvation, that might endanger thee. But that is not it that I put thee upon when I put thee upon believing, but it is to have a constant recourse, in a sense of thy wants, unto Jesus Christ, both for justification and for sanctification, and to act and exercise faith upon him, and to whet thy soul upon him, and to do this continually. Now, take this course, and let all thy imperfections and hypocrisies thou seest or suspectest to be in thee drive thee unto Christ to make thee sincere; let them drive thee unto Christ for justification, make that improvement and use of them, still to put thee upon believing; if anything will make thy heart sound, this will do it. Thus having recourse unto Christ, thou wilt see farther light to discern thine own emptiness and hypocrisy ten thousand times more than by poring upon and studying out thy own condition, by comparing that act and this act together, and this by-end and that by-end, and the like; for if thou goest thus by faith unto Jesus Christ, thou dealest with the fountain of grace; and by exercising thyself to faith in him, and so acquainting thyself with him, thy heart will be changed before thou art aware of it. As Solomon saith, 'He that walketh with wise men shall be wise;' so he that acquaints himself thus with the Lord Jesus, constantly renewing acts of faith upon him, he shall learn wisdom, he shall learn holiness, he shall learn how to go out of himself; he will shed light into him for to see his emptiness more, and he will shed Spirit into him for to fill him more.

The observation which I make upon the Epistle to the Hebrews is to this purpose and effect: the apostle there writes to all the Jews, whether temporary believers or other; but suppose they were such that did profess the name of Christ in the strictness of it, yet he speaks exceeding suspiciously of many of them. The Holy Ghost in no book holds forth so much the state of a temporary believer, and the issue and terror of it, than in that Epistle, both in the 6th, 10th, and 12th chapters; and therefore he speaks more distinctly of the sin against the Holy Ghost, which a temporary believer is nearer to fall into, and he threateneth and aweth them with that; yet notwithstanding, you shall find that there is no Epistle that doth by way of exhortation (though the apostle in other Epistles may commend the doctrine of faith, as he doth in the Epistle to the Romans, and in other places) so much exhort men continually to believing, all and every man: 'Lest any man,' saith he, 'fail and come short of the grace of God;' and, 'lest there be found in any man an evil heart of unbelief.' Read the 3d chapter; it is the whole scope of it, and it is the whole scope, in a manner, of this 4th chapter. He lays before them the example of those that fell in the wilderness, and tells them it was unbelief was the cause of it; therefore he bids them labour or study to enter into that rest, and to take heed lest they fall after the same example of unbelief. You are now, saith he, of the house of God, if you continue to be so; ye are partakers of Christ if you hold fast your confidence. So that I say, we are not so much to trouble ourselves with that great controversy, whether we be temporary believers or no, when we find the Holy Ghost stirring in us, but to improve that strength we have from the Holy Ghost in direct acts of faith towards Jesus Christ, going out to him for a supply of all imperfections and defects; and thus having recourse unto him, it will make a man sound; and as he said of praying, that praying would either make a man leave his sinning, or his sinning would make him leave praying; so certainly it is in the matter of believing.

Ans. 4. The last answer I shall give to the objection is this: thou canst not say thou art a temporary believer, thou mayest fear it. A true believer may fear it, but he cannot say he is such; and a temporary believer, though there is that in the word, which, if it were opened, might convince him, and shall do so at latter day, yet usually he cannot say it of himself that he is such an one. Therefore now, thou that wilt abstain from putting forth acts of faith for fear lest thou mayest build thyself up in a way of temporary believing, consider this, that though thou mayest build up a temporary faith, yet thou mayest not forbear putting forth true acts of faith, for thou mayest be a true believer for aught thou knowest, therefore thou art to go and cast thyself upon Christ, to follow on the motions of the Holy Ghost, and that assistance he gives thee. For wouldst thou quench the motions of the new creature? If thou knewest them to be so, I am assured thou wouldst not ; but if thou knowest them not, yet thou oughtest not to do it. I remember what a poor child about ten years of age once said : I am oftentimes, said he, tempted to take Jesus Christ, I see so much beauty in him, but I fear I shall be a hypocrite in doing of it. What a pitiful thing was this, that such a temptation should keep such a soul when he is again and again provoked by the Holy Ghost, from laying hold upon Jesus Christ, from taking of him.

Direct. 3. The third direction is only a farther exhortation to continue to renew acts of faith, and not to cease or faint, or to give over. The very scope of this 3d chapter of the Hebrews is to put them upon renewing acts of faith, and holding out to do so continually. He doth both bid them continue to do it, and also he bids them daily to renew acts of faith, and expresseth it under both kinds of expressions. First, he exhorts them to a constancy of holding out: ver. 6, to ' hold fast their confidence and the glory of their hope,' or ' the rejoicing of their hope,' or their faith ' unto the end.' And ver. 14, to ' hold fast the beginning of their confidence stedfast unto the end,' opposing it there to ' departing from the living God ; ' and therefore by faith to abide and stay by God. But that is not all : he exhorts them likewise to renewed acts of faith ; you shall see his expressions in the 7th verse, and so in other verses : ' Wherefore, as the Holy Ghost saith, To-day, if ye will hear his voice,' ver 7. Hearing his voice there is believing ; so he interprets it himself in the end of the chapter. So likewise, ver. 13, he bids Christians to ' exhort one another daily, while it is called to-day,' and therefore answerably, to renew their faith daily : for that is his scope, and the thing he calls upon them to do in answer to those exhortations. So ver. 15 : ' Whilst it is said, To-day, if ye will hear his voice, harden not your hearts ;' and unbelief will harden your hearts, saith he. I observe this, that he doth speak to these Jews converted ; suppose whether some were temporaries or no, however he speaketh to them all, even as we use to speak to any soul that is a-coming on to Christ, whom we would move to turn to God at a sermon, telling him that now is the day of grace, now is an acceptable time, and therefore cleave to him, and turn to him. Even such kind of motives as we would use to such an one, doth the apostle use to them that are already converted, or enlightened at least, and had long professed the name of Christ : ' Whilst it is called To-day,' saith he ; and ' take heed lest at any time' (so the word is in the original, ver. 12), ' that you do cease from believing,' or ' lest there be in any of you an evil heart of unbelief, in departing,' or neglecting it : but ' to-day,' saith he, ' hear his voice.' So that in deed and in truth, what we would say, or any man would say, unto one that is now to be converted, the same he saith to them ; for a Christian's life it is, and ought to be, a continual renewing of faith, and so a renewal of his conversion, as you have them put together: Luke xxii. 32, ' I have prayed thy faith fail not ; when thou art converted, strengthen thy brethren.' And the apostle contents not himself only to speak in the language of words of constancy, and to bid

them to do it daily, ' To-day,' &c., in a positive way; but he useth negatives too : ' Take heed, lest at any time there be in any of you an evil heart
of unbelief,' ver. 12.   Take heed, lest you let go your hold, lest you cease
to believe; for if you do not renew acts of faith, certainly corrupt nature
will renew acts of unbelief; and if one be not acted, or if it be intermitted,
the other will steal up.   And ' the house of God are we,' saith he, if we do
thus daily hear and obey his voice; and ' we are made partakers of Christ,
if we hold fast thus the beginning of our confidence.'   I take it his meaning is this : the doctrine, saith he, which we teach, it is the right way to
heaven; and you need not doubt of that, saith he, for it is that which will
build up the house of God, and will make men partakers of Christ.   Now,
saith he, if ye continue thus to act faith, and do but practise according to
that doctrine that is taught in the house of God, in the church, you will
become his house in deed and in truth, according to the doctrine taught in
the church.

Obj. Now there is an objection will also attend this direction, which I
would meet withal, and that is this : Yea, but will the soul say, I have
renewed faith often, and done it long, and I find not yet that power accompanying my faith, which doth evidence it to be true; and notwithstanding
all I have done, I do not yet know whether all the acts of faith I have put
forth be not in vain; and as they have been, so they may still be, and
therefore I had as good give over.

Ans. I will answer thee, speaking to this objection, so far as it relateth
to the point in hand, viz., the power of God co-working with us.

1. First of all, consider what Christ said to Peter when he came to wash
his feet, John xiii., and Peter reluctated : ' What I do now,' saith Christ,
' thou knowest not, but thou shalt know hereafter;' and if thou knewest,
thou wouldst not reluctate.   Christ requires obedience to that, the meaning
whereof he knew not at the present, but should know afterward; and when
the Holy Ghost came upon him after Christ's ascension, he found that
Christ thereby had sealed up to him the washing away of his sins, for God
made that unto them a temporary sacrament, though Peter knew not the
meaning of this at the present; and thus Christ doth many things unto us,
which we know not the meaning of till afterwards.   So say I to thee that
sayest, thou hast exercised acts of faith a long time, and knowest not whether
it be true.   Thou mayest know hereafter, though thou knowest not now,
when the Spirit comes on thee, and brings all things that are past to thy
remembrance, and lets thee see the truth of all that God hath wrought in
thee; when he comes to seal up to thee thy redemption unto the day of
redemption, there will a light come, that will shew thee that thou hast all
this while been a-believing, and a-believing truly and acceptably unto God;
and therefore, however, continue still doing so.

2. Though thou hast put forth acts of faith never so long, or never so often,
and hitherto in vain (' if in vain,' as the apostle speaks), yet continue still
to do it; and that because God works it of his good pleasure, you know
that is the encouragement.   Philip. ii. 14, ' Work out your salvation, for
it is God that worketh in you of his good pleasure.'   And in 2 Tim. ii. 25,
he bids them preach to men, and to continue in so doing, to see ' if God
at any time will give them repentance.'   Though a man hath preached
multitude of sermons, and men have heard multitude of sermons, yet
preach still, and go to sermons still; for though all the former have been in
vain, there may come a time in which God may give repentance unto men.
And the apostle, Heb. iii. 12, useth the very same word (though I confess
it is not in our translation), ' Take heed lest at any time there be in you an

heart of unbelief.' In this case, I say, as Paul saith in Heb. x. 35, he speaks it indeed in regard of afflictions or temptations outward, but all that is there said is applicable to this temptation, and to temptations inward: ' Cast not away your confidence,' saith he, ver. 35; and ver. 36, ' Ye have need of patience, that after you have done the will of God ye might receive the promise ; for yet a little while, and he that shall come will come, and will not tarry.' Suppose now thou hast acted faith, and findest as thou thinkest nothing come, yet do not throw away that confidence, that faith, that acting upon Christ, begotten in thee; cast it not away, as men are apt to do when they cannot attain the thing they seek for presently. I say in this case to thee, as the apostle said there, ' You have need of patience ; ' and what was the reason he thus spake, you have need of patience ? Because the truth is, God will try every soul that doth believe, he will try their patience, if not with outward afflictions, yet with inward ; and if not with inward, then with outward. Now I apply this to thee in this case, for if any soul needeth patience, then such a soul as this that makes this objection needs patience ; he needs it because God puts him to it, and patience there is put for a patient continuance, as in Rom. ii. it is called and interpreted, and so the meaning is, you need a patient continuance in renewing still your confidence and believing, that when you have done the will of God herein over and over, merely in submission to him, you may inherit the promise. He puts that in to quiet them in the mean time. And so say I to thee that art ready to faint, and to give up all, quiet thyself with this, that it is the will of God thou hast done all this while, and that it is his will thou shouldst rather act faith upon him, and have recourse unto him than to have forborne it; and though thou knowest not whether it be true faith or no, yet it is the will of God thou shouldst do it. ' You have need of patience,' saith he, ' that after you have done the will of God, you may receive the promise: for yet a little while, and he that shall come will come, and will not tarry.' Thou wilt find that God in the end will come, and will give thee, to thy own sense, spiritually and truly to believe. In the mean time, I say, quiet thyself with this, that that which thou art a-doing is the work of God: ' This is the work of God,' saith Christ, ' that ye believe on him whom he hath sent.' And this is the waiting and sitting still that the Scripture speaks of. It is not to sit still and to do nothing toward believing, but it is doing the will of God in continuing still to believe. And then the apostle adds, ' The just shall live by faith.' Will a man deliberate whether he shall put forth acts of life or no, whether he shall breathe or no ? Why, there is a necessity for him to breathe, it is that whereby he liveth ; and therefore though thou fetch thy breath hardly, yet fetch it still, for thou diest else. So he saith here, that faith is our life, therefore continue to put forth the acts of faith, or else thou diest. In Rom. v., speaking of the effects of faith, for that is the scope of that chapter from the beginning towards the middle, he saith there, that trials and afflictions, whereof this is the greatest, breed patience ; and what doth patience breed ? It breedeth experience. When a man hath patiently continued to wait, to exercise faith, in the end he cometh to experience that he hath true faith; you may apply it unto this as well as unto any other temptation whatsoever. And what is the issue of experience in the end ? It breedeth hope, that is, assurance ; for it is clear it is so meant, because he adds, ' Because the love of God is shed abroad in our hearts.' It produceth, I say, that effect in the end. So that still I say to such souls, they had need of patient continuance in renewing their confidence, and in living by faith, and in the end he that shall come will come. And as the

apostle there in Heb. x. adds, ' The just shall live by faith,' so he adds likewise, ' If any man draw back, my soul shall have no pleasure in him.' The
word is a word used amongst soldiers, not to recoil, not to give over, being
weary of waiting, or the like.   Now as the general hath no pleasure in such
a soldier, so saith he, in such an one ' my soul shall have no pleasure.'
And he adds the greatest motive in the world why men should continue
still thus to act faith, though their patience be thus tried ; for, saith he, it
is ' believing to the saving of the soul' (ver. 39), but this drawing back,
this recoiling, and seeking to do it, tendeth to perdition.   ' We are not of
them who draw back unto perdition,' saith he, ' but of them that believe
to the saving of the soul,' that is, that continue thus to believe ; for his
meaning and his argument lies thus : you must hold out, saith he, and
continue to believe, for you cannot be saved else ; and if you will forbear
to act faith thus, what will be the issue of it ?   You will draw back, and
then God will come to have no pleasure in you ; and this, saith he, tendeth
to perdition ; you hazard perdition by it, therefore it is necessary to continue
so believing.   Now I say to such a soul as is wearied out with such a temptation as this is, Whether dost thou mean to be saved, yea or no ?   Thou
wilt say to me, Yes.   Very good.   Whether dost thou mean ever to renew
faith upon Christ again or no ?   If thou sayest never, I have nothing to
say to thee, but only this, thou drawest back to the certain perdition of
thy soul.   If ever thou meanest to renew faith again, or else thou canst not
be saved, then, say I, though thou hast been discouraged a thousand and a
thousand times, yet continue to do it still, for if ever thou comest to salvation,
it must be by having fresh recourse to Christ, and exercising acts of faith
upon him.   Now by discontinuing to do it, thou dost not get more
power to believe ; if it were so, there were something in it ; but thou
drawest back, and puttest thy perdition upon a hazard, thou puttest
thy utter hardening upon a hazard, therefore cease not, no, not for a
moment.   And let me say this to thee likewise, Thou art discouraged,
because what thou hast done hitherto is in vain, and, therefore, thou fearest
that what thou shalt do will be in vain also.   When thou comest to thy
deathbed, or to lie under any great affliction or temptation, thy discouragement will be greater than now, for then Satan will tell thee, thou hast often
renewed acts of faith, and thou hast found it to be in vain, and thereupon
hast drawn back from God, and discontinued the exercising of such acts,
and therefore thou hast cause now to fear that God will have no pleasure in thee.
There is no way, therefore, say I, but for thee to hold fast thy confidence,
and to live by faith (thou hast need of patience, I confess that), and let the
necessity of the thing put thee upon it, for it is as necessary as the living
of thy soul is.   It is ' believing to the saving of the soul.'

Obj. But you will say, I am weary, I have so long time exercised faith, and
cannot find whether my faith be true or no, I find no strength by it, little
or no support by it.   What saith the apostle, Heb. xii. 12, for there is no
Epistle where he speaks to this point in hand more than this to the Hebrews ?
' Lift up the hands which hang down, and the feeble knees.'   Though even
all your strength be gone through weariness, yet use the strength you have ;
though these hands hang down through weariness, yet with that strength
you have lift them up once more, yea, again and again.   It is not in this
as in other weariness.   In other weariness a man gets more strength by
discontinuing to labour ; but where this kind of weariness is through long
waiting, by discontinuing thou shalt not have more power against the next
time.   No ; but if thou wilt lift up the hands that hang down, thou wilt
find that God will help to lift them up too.   In Isa. xl. 28, the prophet

there speaks to those that are ready to faint for waiting upon the Lord, and he bids them consider : ' Hast thou not known,' saith he, ' hast thou not heard, that the everlasting God, the Lord, the Creator of the ends of the earth, fainteth not, neither is weary ?' Consider, saith he, that God hath created the ends of the earth, and he upholds them every moment ; he hath done so from the beginning of the world ; and though the earth is continually changing, and the world a-moving, yet he fainteth not to hold up all this, as he did not faint at first when he created it ; and ' he giveth power to the faint, and to them that have no might he increaseth strength.' When thou thinkest I am even weary, I can believe no longer, yet lift up those hands that hang down, and strengthen those feeble knees, what strength thou hast put forth ; and that God who is the Creator of the ends of the earth, that fainteth not, neither is weary, will give power to the faint, and increase strength to them that have no might. Take a poor soul now that finds a defect of spiritual strength, Oh, saith he, I have no strength at all. If thou wert a young man, and wert put to do acts of activity, thou wouldst think thou hast natural strength enough to do such things withal. Now the prophet tells thee, that thou who hast the sense of no spiritual strength in thyself, thy case is more sure to have strength continued to thee, waiting upon the Lord, than a young man that hath never so much strength for youthful feats : ' Even the youths,' saith he, ' shall faint, and be weary, and the young men shall utterly fall ; but they that wait upon the Lord,' though they have no strength, ' they shall renew their strength, they shall mount up with wings as eagles, they shall run and not be weary, and they shall walk and not faint.' Therefore continue ; he that shall come will come in the end ; and in the mean time, he that upholds the ends of the earth upon nothing, he upholds thy heart to believe upon nothing. I mean, faith is a thing depending upon nothing in a man's self. The prophet, I say, compares the promised supply of spiritual strength with a present stock of natural strength, which a young man having, he thinks himself able to do any natural action. Yea (saith he), ' they shall mount up with wings as eagles.' An eagle when he grows old grows callow, as you call it, that is, all the feathers come off ; but washing himself in fountains, his wings and feathers come again, and he mounts up anew ; so, saith he, ' thou shalt renew thy strength :' though thou art even faint and grown weary, and though thou thinkest thy old stock of strength is gone, and thou hast believed all that strength out, and that thy soul is naked, and that there is nothing left, ' yet wait upon the Lord,' ' look again to his holy temple,' as Jonah saith, and ' he will renew thy strength, and bear thee up as with eagles' wings.'